United States of America
## Each State's Electoral Votes for the Presidency

A city employee, Marie, claims that her male supervisor, Richard, has been sexually harassing her. According to her, Richard has asked her out on a date on three different occasions and Marie has refused each time.  In addition, Marie claims that Richard has engaged her in inappropriate sexual conversations about pornographic movies. However, Marie also admits that Richard has never touched her in an inappropriate or sexual manner.

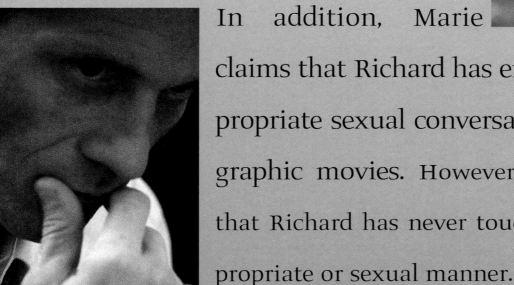

# YOU ARE THE MAYOR— WHAT WILL YOU DO?

To find out more about Marie and Richard's situation, and to see your choices as the city mayor responsible for deciding a course of action, log onto

## www.longmanparticipate.com

# Are you up for the challenge?

For every major topic in American government, **LongmanParticipate.com** offers five exciting, highly interactive exercises that will get you living what you only read about in your text...

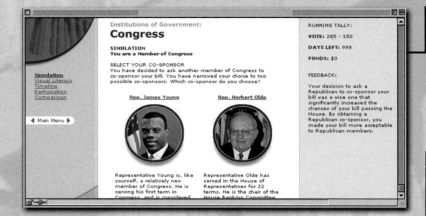

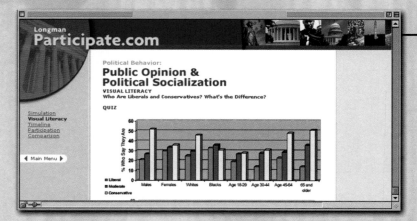

**SIMULATIONS.** You're given a role to play, an objective to reach, and the "rules of the game." How well you score depends on the decisions you make and your knowledge of American government! Some of your roles: *big city mayor, police officer, member of Congress, hotshot lawyer,* and *campaign consultant.*

**VISUAL LITERACY.** What is the relationship between race and the death penalty? Why do some states have strict gun control laws and others don't? *Visual Literacy* activities help you answer these questions by asking you to interpret data and interact with tables, charts, and graphs.

**INTERACTIVE TIMELINES.** Ever wondered which presidents were the most popular and why? Need to understand the evolution of social welfare policy for your next exam? *Interactive Timelines* make sometimes complex historical issues clear with photos, videos, and audio clips, that bring political history to life!

**PARTICIPATION.** You'll be asked to campaign on the Internet, correspond with your congressional representative, and assess how liberal or conservative you are. These activities get you involved in politics, or have you explore the impact of government on your life.

**COMPARATIVE.** Find out whether Britain has a bill of rights and whether Israeli citizens are allowed to marry people outside their religion in these thought-provoking activities. Each one asks you to compare and contrast aspects of the U.S. political system to those of countries around the world.

# Want to get a better grade?

**LongmanParticipate.com** was developed by over ten American government faculty from across the country, each with years of teaching know-how and experience using the Internet in their class. They designed **LongmanParticipate.com** to ensure it is not only fun, but that it does everything possible to help you get a better grade!

**Interactivity.** LongmanParticipate.com helps you learn by DOING. By experiencing American government, you gain a better understanding of it.

**Quizzes.** Beginner and expert level *Political Knowledge* Quizzes in each section allow you to test your knowledge of that topic, assess your level of understanding, see your progress, and prepare *for tests.*

**Feedback.** Each quiz and activity comes with feedback, so you know how you did, and why you answered wrong or right. Quizzes refer you to the appropriate chapter of your textbook for extra help.

**Instructor Help.** All of your work is saved to a separate web page which your instructor can access to offer help and feedback where you need it!

**Tied to your textbook.** "LongmanParticipate.com" icons in the margins of your text direct you to an activity on the site that will help increase your understanding of that particular topic. To make sure you get the most out your course, we're giving you two terrific resources —the book and the website— that work together to help you get a better grade!

## The Changing Constitution, Democracy, and American Politics

The Constitution is the basic rule book for the game of American politics. Constitutional rules apportion power and responsibility among governmental branches, define the fundamental nature of the relationships among governmental institutions, specify how individuals are to be selected for office, and tell how the rules themselves may be changed. Every aspiring politician who wants to attain office, every citizen who wants to influence what government does, and every group that wants to advance its interests in the political arena must know the rules and how to use them to best advantage. Because the Constitution has this character, we understand it to be a fundamental structural factor influencing all of American political life.

Constitutional rules, however, like all rules, can and do change over time. Their tendency to change with the times is why we sometimes speak of the "living Constitution." Constitutional changes come about in three specific ways: formal amendment, judicial interpretation, and political practices.

The Constitution may be formally amended by use of the procedures outlined in Article V of the Constitution (again, refer to Figure 2.3). This method has resulted in the addition of 27 amendments since the founding, the first ten of which (the Bill of Rights) were added within three years of ratification. That only 17 have been added in the roughly 200 years since then suggests that this method of changing the Constitution is extremely difficult. Nevertheless, formal amendments have played an important role in expanding democracy in the United States by ending slavery; extending voting rights to African-Americans,

timeline
**The History of Constitutional Amendments**

The Constitution has evolved over the years in three ways: through the amendment process, through evolving political practices, and through the Supreme Court's changing interpretation of the Constitution's meaning. Here antiabortion protesters demonstrate in front of the Supreme court building on the anniversary of the Court's *Roe v. Wade* decision to demand a reversal of that landmark decision.

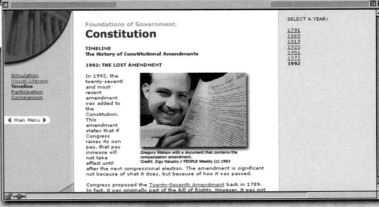

Foundations of Government:
## Constitution

SELECT A YEAR:
1791
1865
1919
1920
1951
1972
1992

**TIMELINE**
**The History of Constitutional Amendments**

**1992: THE LOST AMENDMENT**

Simulation
Visual Literacy
**Timeline**
Participation
Comparison

◀ Main Menu ▶

In 1992, the twenty-seventh and most recent amendment was added to the Constitution. This amendment states that if Congress raises its own pay, that pay increase will not take effect until after the next congressional election. The amendment is significant not because of what it does, but because of how it was passed.

Gregory Watson with a document that contains the compensation amendment.
Credit: Zigy Kaluzny / PEOPLE Weekly (c) 1993

Congress proposed the Twenty-Seventh Amendment back in 1789. In fact, it was originally part of the Bill of Rights. However, it was not

# MORE RESOURCES
## TO HELP YOU LEARN.

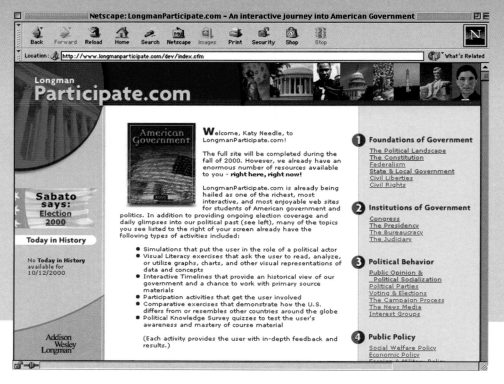

**Topic List.** Lists the 19 major topics in American government—click on one to call up activity sets and quizzes.

**The Newsstand.** A comprehensive list of links to news organizations, polling organizations, and general political and current events sites.

**Interactive Research and Writing Guide.**
A "how-to" interactive tutorial that includes: using the Web for research, preparing term papers and essays, avoiding plagiarism, and how to cite sources.

**Today In History.** A quick tidbit about an interesting political event that occurred on today's date.

**"Sabato Says" Election 2000.** Larry Sabato—the "most quoted college professor" according to the Wall Street Journal—offers insights about the 2000 presidential campaigns, the election, and the first 100 days of the new administration.

## *Facts about the subscription card that came packaged with this book—*

- It gives you access to **LongmanParticipate.com** for 6 months from the date of activation.

- The pincode on your Access Card can only be used once, by one person.

- Once you've chosen a user name and password, you will be able to get access to **LongmanParticipate.com** from any computer.

FOR TECHNICAL SUPPORT OR HELP WITH REGISTERING
please contact our Product Support Center at 1-800-677-6337

# The
# New
# American
# Democracy

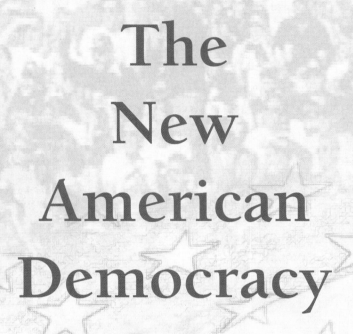

# The New American Democracy

## SECOND EDITION

**Morris P. Fiorina**
Stanford University

**Paul E. Peterson**
Harvard University

Longman

New York • San Francisco • Boston
London • Toronto • Sydney • Tokyo • Singapore • Madrid
Mexico City • Munich • Paris • Cape Town • Hong Kong • Montreal

## Dedication

*To George Cole, John Kessel, Wayne Merrick, and other members of
the Allegheny College Political Science Department, circa 1966*

*As well as to Harding C. Noblitt, Concordia College*

*All of whom introduced the authors to the wonders of American government*

*In appreciation for their teaching excellence*

Publisher: Priscilla McGeehon

Senior Acquisitions Editor: Eric Stano

Development Director: Lisa Pinto

Development Editors: Marjorie Anderson, Marion Castellucci

Marketing Manager: Megan Galvin-Fak

Supplements Editor: Jennifer Ackerman

Media Supplements Editor: Mark Toews

Production Manager: Joseph Vella

Project Coordination, Text Design, and Electronic Page Makeup: Thompson Steele, Inc.

Cover Design Manager: John Callahan

Cover Designer: Kay Petronio

Cover Photos: Copyright © PhotoDisc, Inc.

Senior Manufacturing Buyer: Dennis J. Para

Printer and Binder: Quebecor/World Color—Taunton

Cover Printer: Phoenix Color Corp.

For permission to use copyrighted material, grateful acknowledgment is made to the copyright holders on pp. 746–747, which are hereby made part of this copyright page.

**Library of Congress Cataloging-in-Publication Data**

Fiorina, Morris P.
    The new American democracy / Morris P. Fiorina, Paul E. Peterson.--2nd ed.,
      p. cm.
    First ed. published by Allyn & Bacon in Boston.
    Includes bibliographical references and index.
    ISBN 0-321-07058-5 (alk. paper)
      1. Democracy--United States. 2. United States--Politics and government. I. Peterson,
Paul E. II. Title.

JK1726 .F56 2000
320.473--dc21

00-061421

Please visit our website at http://www.ablongman.com/fiorina

ISBN 0-321-07058-5 (The New American Democracy, Second Edition)

ISBN 0-321-07059-3 (The New American Democracy, Alternate Second Edition)

1 2 3 4 5 6 7 8 9 10—RNT—03 02 01 00

# Brief Contents

## PART 1

## The Foundations of a New American Democracy

## PART 2

## The Ingredients of the New American Democracy

## PART 3

## Campaigns and Elections

# PART 4
# The Government

# PART 5
# Civil Liberties and Civil Rights

# PART 6
# Public Policy

# Appendices

# Detailed Contents

## PART 1
## The Foundations of a New American Democracy

### CHAPTER 1
### Democracy in the United States    2

CHAPTER **2**

# Establishing a Constitutional Democracy    30

## CHAPTER 3

## Federalism: Division of Power Among National, State, and Local Governments    64

## CHAPTER 4

## America: Unity Amidst Diversity    94

# PART 2
# The Ingredients of the New American Democracy

## CHAPTER 5
# Public Opinion    126

## CHAPTER 8
# Political Parties    218

# PART 3
# Campaigns and Elections

# PART 4
# The Government

## CHAPTER 12
## The Congress and Its Work    346

## CHAPTER 15
# The Courts    440

# PART 5
# Civil Liberties and Civil Rights

## CHAPTER 16
## Civil Liberties    472

# Chapter 17
# Civil Rights    506

# PART 6
# Public Policy

## CHAPTER 18
## Domestic Policy    540

# Contents of Boxes

## Chapter 16
## Civil Liberties

## Chapter 17
## Civil Rights

## Chapter 18
## Domestic Policy

## Chapter 19
## Economic Policy

## Chapter 20
## Foreign and Defense Policy

# Preface for Students

This text grew out of a decade of teaching the introductory course together. As we listened to each other's lectures each year we noticed that our course was evolving into one whose underlying theme was both more specific than and different from the themes that could be found in other American government textbooks. Specifically, elections and their repercussions gradually became the primary connecting thread that tied together our lectures and discussions. In part, this emphasis reflected our own backgrounds and interests. Fiorina has devoted his professional career to the study of elections—both narrowly, in the sense of why people vote the way they do, and more broadly, in the sense of how elections affect politicians, political institutions, and the policies they produce. Peterson began his career with a focus on citizen participation in the War on Poverty and later studied the way the federal system limited what local officials could do. In recent years, he has examined the ways elections shape government response to budget deficits, welfare needs, race relations, educational issues, and the changing foreign policy environment. But it was not just our own research interests that brought election issues to the fore. Both of us attempt to keep our lectures connected to present-day government and politics, and as a reflection of a changing reality, we found our lectures increasingly infused with the connections between elections and the work of government.

We have learned that students are keenly aware of the way elections affect the decisions and strategies of political leaders, as well as a great many other things that happen in government. As a result, we have written a different kind of American government textbook, one that gives a central place to elections and their consequences.

## Level and Tone of This Textbook

It is all too common today to criticize the preparation and motivation of American undergraduate students: the belief that students are less well prepared for college work and less motivated to undertake it than in the "good old days" is widespread. This viewpoint has led some instructors to oversimplify their courses and the readings they assign. This, in turn, has led some publishers to urge textbook writers to oversimplify their books to make them more suitable for this contemporary world.

Our view is that you may be different from students of a generation ago, but that does not necessarily mean that you are any less capable. Some think students are less proficient in skills such as writing. Perhaps so, but you also have skills that were nonexistent years ago. (We bet that on average you are better at surfing the Internet than your professors!) As for motivation, that is something not purely your responsibility. It is our job as teachers to make the material as stimulating to you and as relevant to your lives as possible. Our premise is that undergraduate students are fully capable of understanding information and analyses that are clearly expressed. For this reason, this book emphasizes meaning and significance. It contains considerable interpretation in addition to the essential facts.

We do not shy away from controversy. Some individuals in American higher education would protect students from intellectual discomfort. The consequences of such beliefs include well-intentioned efforts to place some subjects and arguments outside the boundaries of classroom discussion. We do not agree with this approach. Our view is that politics is fundamentally about conflict. People have conflicting interests and, even more seriously, conflicting values. Politics is the nonviolent resolution of such conflicts. People can settle their disagreements and rise above their dislikes through political deliberation, or they can choose weapons, as so many have over the course of human history.

We believe that you need to learn to engage in such political deliberation. Within the bounds of civil discourse, you should be challenged, even at times provoked. Education proceeds by defending one's viewpoints and by learning to understand those of others. Thus, in the chapters that follow, we consider arguments that some of you may find uncomfortable. In the realm of education, a better, clearer understanding supersedes all other values.

Although the study of American politics is far more than the study of current events, a book that emphasizes the importance of elections can make its points come to life by placing them in the context of contemporary politics. This second edition is a complete revision of the first edition, updated and enhanced to include information about important recent events such as the impeachment of President Clinton, the arrival of a new era of budgetary surplus, the latest Supreme Court decisions, the impact of Welfare Reform, and the 2000 campaigns and elections. Of course, these stories—like politics generally—continue to evolve, and we hope this text provides you with the information you need to understand future developments.

## *Specific Features*

This book has a number of specific features, many related to our elections theme. We call your attention to the following:

- Each chapter introduces you to the subject matter with an **opening vignette** on a high-interest issue or incident. Some are classics from American history, while others are current events. Examples include the debate over whether carrying a gun on school grounds should be a federal crime (Chapter 3—Federalism); a comparison of differing media and public responses to Vietnam War–era events (Chapter 9—The Media); President Clinton's stand on gays in the military (Chapter 13—The Presidency: Powers and Practice); and the recent uproar over affirmative action in California (Chapter 17—Civil Rights). Following each vignette is a list of the questions and topics that the chapter covers.
- To illustrate the book's focus on electoral forces, each chapter includes a box entitled **Election Connection,** describing the relationship between elections and institutions or policies, often by describing how a particular election shaped a feature of American government. For instance, Chapter 4's describes California's Proposition 187; Chapter 9's details the media's role in the election of 1960; Chapter 10's reports on the campaign finance scandals of 1996; and Chapter 19's discusses how the economy shaped the election of 1980.
- Each chapter contains a special box that compares a feature of American government with a similar feature in other countries. This **International Comparison** will give you a better understanding of the strengths and limitations of American democracy by letting you think about real alternatives, not just unattainable ideals. Chapter 1's looks at the timing of elections in other democracies; Chapter 2's looks at the making of a constitution in Russia; and Chapter 10's explains why campaign financing isn't such a big issue in other countries. Chapter 16's surveys what other countries are doing to protect privacy in the Internet age; and Chapter 17's outlines controversies over the civil rights of minorities in Great Britain.
- You are given an opportunity to exercise your own critical thinking by considering a **Democratic Dilemma** in each chapter. Are there instances in which democratic values are in conflict? Will policy changes or institutional reforms actually achieve the goals their proponents claim? This special box presents arguments pro and con, poses questions, and invites students to grapple with them. Examples include Chapter 1's consideration of the conflict between responsive and efficient government, Chapter 4's listing of multicultural issues, Chapter 14's reflection on whether or not bureaucrats should be partisans, and Chapter 18's discussion of the advantages and disadvantages of regulation.
- Each chapter includes full **marginal definitions** for key terms that are boldfaced in the text and included in the end-of-book Glossary.

## New to This Edition

This book has been extensively revised since its first edition. This second edition includes substantive rewrites and reorganization, the addition of new features, and the inclusion of the latest information on key topics. For example:

- Extended explanations of historical practices or terms appear in a new feature called **Window on the Past.** Chapter 4's explains the origin of the "melting pot" metaphor; Chapter 6's discusses the important Voting Rights Act of 1965, Chapter 15's explains the Supreme Court's pivotal decision in *Marbury* v. *Madison,* and Chapter 20's reviews the history of U.S. involvement in the Philippines.
- Because we are emphasizing what is new in American democracy, we provide the most up-to-date information and examples possible, including discussion of the following:
  - The 2000 elections
  - The politics of gun control
  - The projected federal budget surplus
  - Recent developments in state and local politics, including the history and implications of redistricting
  - The latest Supreme Court decisions concerning federalism, civil liberties, and other issues, including the reaffirmation of the Miranda decision
  - The impeachment and trial of President Clinton and resulting implications for future presidents
  - The emerging conflicts over U.S. trade policy
  - The civil rights of Latinos, Asian Americans, and gays and lesbians
- We have added new **critical thinking questions** to most figures, photographs, and boxes to provoke discussion and thought about the issues at hand.
- At the end of each chapter we include a new **On the Web** feature to direct readers to Web sites where they can find more information on the topics discussed.
- Throughout the text, icons can be found in the margins referring readers to *LongmanParticipate.com,* Longman's new interactive Web site for American Government. Each icon appears next to a particular topic and indicates that a simulation, visual literacy exercise, interactive timeline, participation activity, or comparative government exercise related to that topic exists on the site. Each activity provides feedback, helps the reader better understand the concepts presented in the text, and makes learning fun. See the insert at the front of this text for more information.
- Also included are new **Section Summaries** throughout each chapter, while a **Chapter Summary, Key Terms** (alphabetized at the end of the chapter, with page references), and annotated **Suggested Readings** appear in revised form at the end of each chapter.

## Supplements

- **LongmanParticipate.com (www.longmanparticipate.com).** More interactive, more comprehensive, and more engaging than any American Government Web site currently available, LongParticipate.com offers instructors and students an exciting new resource for teaching and learning about our political system that's easy to integrate into any course. For each major topic in American government, there are five highly interactive, in-depth exercises (simulation, visual literacy, interactive timeline, participation activity, and comparative government) and much more! Every new copy of the text comes with a *free* six-month subscription to this revolutionary new site. LongmanParticipate.com icons in the margins of this text direct students to relevant activities on the site.
- **Companion Web Site (www.ablongman.com/fiorina).** This companion Web site provides a wealth of resources for students and instructors using *The New American Democracy,* Second Edition. Students will find chapter summaries, practice tests, Web links, simulations, a guide to researching online, and a variety of other learning tools. Instructors will have access to portions of the instructor's manual, PowerPoint® slides, downloadable figures from the text, and teaching links.

- **Interactive Edition CD-ROM.** The Interactive Edition CD-ROM is a dynamic learning tool that combines your textbook with the latest in multimedia. The CD contains the full text of the book with contextually placed media icons—audio, video, Web links, practice tests, primary sources, and more—that link students to additional content directly related to key concepts in the text. It is free when ordered packaged with this text.

- **American Government Tutor Center.** This free tutoring service is offered only by Longman. When instructors order *The New American Democracy* packaged with the Tutor Center registration card, their students can contact our tutor—a qualified American government instructor—for help on material in the book. The tutor can be contacted in three toll-free ways: phone, fax, or e-mail.

- *Student Wizard* **CD-ROM.** Prepared by Michael Meager of the University of Missouri, this exciting new interactive program helps students learn the major facts and concepts through drill and practice exercises and diagnostic feedback. *Study Wizard,* which provides immediate correct answers, explanations of answers, and the text page number on which the matierial is discussed, maintains a running score of the student's performance on the screen throughout the session. *Student Wizard* also provides a link to the text-specific Web sites in the textbook to offer students additional pedagogical support. It is available in Windows and Macintosh formats.

- **Study Guide.** Prepared by Larry Elowitz of Georgia College and State University, this study guide contains a chapter outline, significant themes and highlights, learning goals, key terms, sample test questions, and essays.

- *Getting Involved: A Guide to Student Citizenship.* This unique and practical handbook guides students through political participation with concrete advice and extensive sample material—letters, telephone scripts, student interviews, and real-life anecdotes—for getting involved and making a difference in their lives and communities. This is free when ordered packaged with the text.

- *A Guide to the Internet for American Government,* **Second Edition.** Written by Carol Hays of Southern Illinois University, this guide demonstrates uses of the World Wide Web in the American government course. In addition to explaining links to important sites, the guide includes critical thinking exercises to get students to apply their knowledge of American goverment to the Web and use it as a resource for research.

- *Writing in Political Science,* **Second Edition.** Political science writing requires a distinct set of skills, vocabulary, sources, and methods of inquiry. This guide, by Diane E. Schmidt, takes students step-by-step through all the aspects of writing for political science courses. With an abundance of samples from actual students, the guide also features a section on how to address writing problems and a new section on how to evaluate and cite Internet sources. It is available at a significant discount when packaged with the text.

- **Discounted Penguin-Putnam Inc. Titles.** Longman is offering 22 Penguin titles, including De Tocqueville's *Democracy in America,* Riordan's *Plunkitt of Tammany Hall,* and Iron's *The Courage of Their Convictions,* at more than a 60 percent discount when ordered packaged with *The New American Democracy.*

- **California State Supplement.** This 64-page supplement is a brief primer on state and local issues in California for use in the American government course. It is available free when shrink-wrapped with the text.

- **Texas State Supplement.** This 70-page supplement is a brief primer on state and local issues in Texas for use in the American government course. It is available free when shrink-wrapped with the text.

- *Newsweek* **Discount Subscription.** Students can receive 12 issues of *Newsweek* magazine at an 80 percent savings off the regular subscription price! Contact your Longman representative for more information.

# To Our Colleagues

The chapters that follow speak directly to students in down-to-earth language. In this preface we address their teachers, our colleagues, in more professional terms, about the reasons we decided to write this text.

A generation ago, one of the leading political scientists of the century, Robert Dahl, published a textbook entitled *Pluralist Democracy in the United States.*[1] Dahl was the acknowledged leader of the pluralist school of American political science, which viewed American politics as a collection of arenas in which leaders of organized interest groups bargained over the substance of public policies, with public officials involved both as brokers and as representatives of broader societal interests. Political institutions, in turn, were viewed as regularized bargaining arenas in which leaders were constrained by formal rules. *Groups, bargaining, leaders,* and *representation* were the operative terms for understanding American politics.

American politics has changed a good deal since Dahl wrote. Indeed, Dahl himself recently noted a number of these changes:

> Without intending to do so, over the past thirty years or so Americans have created a new political order. Although it retains a seamless continuity with the order it has displaced, in its present form it constitutes something so new that journalists, commentators, scholars, and ordinary citizens are still struggling to understand it.[2]

Dahl argues that this new political order is more fragmented and more plebiscitary than the old one. The proliferation of interest groups combined with the deterioration of traditional party organizations has strengthened divisive forces and weakened unifying ones. Such political developments, along with social and technological changes, have left public officials more exposed to popular pressures than in the past. As a consequence, Dahl contends, representation and deliberation have suffered. He worries that these changes might create "a pseudo democratic facade on a process manipulated by political leaders to achieve their own agendas."[3]

Another leading political scientist of Dahl's generation, Gabriel Almond, weighs in with similar sentiments:

> Television and radio have largely preempted the print media and the primary opinion leaders. . . . Domestic and international events are brought into the living room with powerful visual and emotional impact—a telepopulism that constrains and distorts public policy. The deliberative processes of politics are diluted and heated by this populism, and by "instant" public opinion polls based on telephone samples.[4]

Although we do not agree with every particular of these indictments, they serve to emphasize that something has happened to American government since the days when an earlier generation of scholars characterized it as a pluralist democracy. For better or for worse, it has become something closer to a popular democracy. In the pages that follow we describe the forces that have brought about these changes as well as their impact on contemporary politics, institutions, and policies. But, we are getting ahead of ourselves here.

Each year as we considered the range of texts available for the introductory American government course, we decided that available books, however worthy, did not match our views. In the first place, many gave less emphasis than we would like to topics that are essential parts of contemporary American politics—elections, most obviously, but also closely related topics such as public opinion, political participation, and the media. Second, in many texts the role of prime mover implicitly is assigned to the courts, whereas we see electoral context as an important influence on judicial activity and judicial outcomes. Third, contemporary textbooks typically separate the study of elections from other major headings: constitutional fundamentals, bureaucratic politics, the courts, and the formation of public policies. As James Stimson comments:

> *In our texts public opinion is a chapter or two. The various branches of government are usually a chapter each. And the connection between what the public wants and what the government does is on the page fold between them. Public opinion is conceptualized as a set of measures and processes that do not speak to government. Governing institutions are studied in a manner which doesn't deny public opinion influence, but doesn't permit its active study. When citizens of Washington, D.C., could not vote the analogy was complete; all opinion was outside the beltway, all government was inside.*[5]

This book breaks down the artificial and unfortunate separation identified by Stimson. Rather than discuss public opinion in one self-contained chapter, political participation in a second, and elections in a third, then move on to a series of institutional and policy chapters, we give public opinion and electioneering their due in individual chapters devoted to those topics, but we continue to trace their effects on other political and institutional processes, culminating in discussions of why American public policies have the shape they do. Thus, the chapters of this text bear the familiar titles, but they are linked by an extended discussion of the pervasiveness of electoral influences in the new American democracy.

When we began writing the first edition of this book in 1993, we knew that our argument for the contemporary dominance of electoral forces would meet with some resistance. Most of the developments we described were fairly recent and we understood that some colleagues might not see as sharp a break with the pre-1960s era as we did. But the passing of seven years has lessened the novelty of our argument. Under Bill Clinton's "horse race presidency" the line between electioneering and governing all but disappeared, as the techniques of the campaign moved to the very pinnacle of government.[6] Our view that contemporary American politics is a "permanent campaign" is now common. In fact, the Pew Charitable Trusts recently organized a consortium of public policy think tanks to study the permanent campaign—how it has affected the range of American institutions and the policy process, with what consequences, and how (whether?) a line between electioneering and governing might once again be drawn.[7] This second edition now lies squarely in the mainstream of thinking about American politics.

We emphasize that to say that public opinion, political campaigns, and elections are of great import is to offer neither a celebrationist nor a cynical interpretation of American politics. On the one hand the shift to a more popular democracy is associated with a greater role for previously disadvantaged voices in the population. No longer are they supplicants—wards of the courts, so to speak; they now exercise electoral power. On the other hand the shift to a more popular democracy grants greater access to special interests and limits opportunities for reflective consideration of the long-range consequences of policy choices. But there is no reason to rush to a critical judgment. Future generations of scholars can judge whether the new order does more or less to advance the welfare of the American people than the old one.

Nor should our emphasis on elections suggest a focus on anything so narrow as what happens on election day or in the campaigns that precede it. When we say that elections play a dominant role, we are thinking not only of their direct effects but also of the indirect ways in which they affect the thinking of interest groups, parties, and public officials, both elected and appointed. It is not so much elections themselves as their anticipation that provides so much of the motive power in contemporary political life in the United States.

Finally, we understand that our colleagues will be understandably skeptical of any attempt to squeeze the study of American government into any single thematic frame—even one defined as broadly as our understanding and interpretation of electoral influence. The subject matter of American government is voluminous, and an introductory course must touch on its many aspects. We do not believe that elections explain all that needs to be known about all aspects of American government and politics. Our general approach is to consider the incentives at work in any situation. If electoral incentives are often a major force, they certainly are not the only one. Some leaders risk their reputations with the public for the good of the country. Some act out of ideological commitments, regardless of their electoral consequences. Some realize that foreign policies must take into account the interests of nations throughout the world. Where these and other nonelectoral factors are important, we recognize that fact and proceed accordingly. The result is a book that is more focused than most American government texts, but not one that forces the whole subject into a single theme.

In sum, we do not believe this book could or should have been written even as recently as a generation ago. For, although elections have always been central to American politics, we believe, with Dahl, that American politics became significantly more plebiscitary in the late twentieth century. The contributing factors are widely recognized. Transformations in the process of nominating and electing candidates produced an individualistic politics in which each candidate forms his or her own organization rather than relying on a common party organization. Transformations in communications technology—survey research, phone, fax, and the Internet—made it possible for politicians to learn the political impacts of their decisions almost instantaneously. Transformations in the media generated a seemingly insatiable demand for news material—a demand often satisfied by stories about political conflict. In this context, interest groups mushroomed, polls and primaries proliferated, and the permanent campaign arrived on the scene. Older concepts used to characterize pluralist politics—groups, bargaining, leaders, and representation—are still important, but a full and accurate account of American politics today must also include careful consideration of the roles played by the media, polls, and campaigns and elections.

## Approach and Organization

This book cuts across the old categories that characterize existing American government texts: historical development, political "inputs," institutions, and policy "outputs." Although we discuss all these aspects of American politics, we approach them in a more integrated manner. Following are a few illustrations of our approach:

- Contemporary practices are compared and contrasted with those existing in earlier periods, making the historical material more relevant to today's readers.
- Chapters on so-called political inputs focus on the choices of individuals, groups, parties, and the media as a response to the incentives they face.
- Analyses of Congress, the presidency, the bureaucracy, and the judiciary do not just describe the main institutions of government; they also show how elections shape the behavior of officeholders within these institutions.
- Civil liberties and civil rights are treated not simply as the result of judicial decisions but also as the product of electoral forces. These chapters are placed in the policy section of the book, instead of at the beginning as part of the historical foundations of American government, in order to highlight the extent to which basic constitutional rights are themselves shaped by public opinion and electoral outcomes.
- Discussions of public policies do not just list policy problems or classify types of policies, but show how elections in particular and politics in general shape the way policies are addressed and adopted.

Finally, the book offers a critical but fair picture of American government and politics. Any objective observer must recognize that American government and politics have numerous shortcomings. We point out many of them and explain why they exist. But throughout the text we show that, judged against realistic standards, American politics and government are not nearly as blameworthy as the evening news and tabloid shows often suggest.

*Supplements*

- **Companion Web Site (www.ablongman.com/fiorina).** This companion Web site provides a wealth of resources for students and instructors using *The New American Democracy, Second Edition.* Students will find chapter summaries, practice tests, Web links, simulations, a guide to researching online, and a variety of other learning tools. Instructors will have access to portions of the instructor's manual, PowerPoint® slides, downloadable figures from the text, and teaching links.

- *American Government Presentation Library* **CD-ROM.** This complete multimedia presentation tool provides a built-in presentation maker, 20 video clips, 200 photographs, 200 figures and graphs from Longman texts, 20 minutes of audio clips, and links to more than 200 Web sites. Media items can be imported into PowerPoint® and Persuasion® presentation programs.

- **Instructor's Manual.** Written by Linda Faye Williams of the University of Maryland, each chapter of this resource manual contains a Chapter Overview, Key Concepts and Objectives, Chapter Outline, Terms for Review, and Teaching Suggestions.

- **Test Bank with Practice Tests.** This test bank, prepared by Nancy Bond of Ranger College, contains hundreds of multiple-choice, true/false, short answer, and essay questions, all accompanied by an answer key.

- **TestGen EQ Computerized Testing System.** Prepared by Nancy Bond of Ranger College, this flexible, easy-to-use computer test bank includes all the test items in the printed test bank. The software allows you to edit existing questions and add your own items. Tests can be printed in several formats and can include figures such as graphs and tables.

- **Text-specific Transparency Acetates**. Full-color transparencies drawn from *The New American Democracy* are available.

- **Interactive American Government Video.** Contains 27 video segments on topics ranging from the term-limit debate, to Internet porn, to women in the Citadel. Critical thinking questions accompany each clip, encouraging students to "interact" with the videos.

- *Politics in Action* **Video.** Eleven "lecture launchers," covering broad subjects such as social movements, conducting a campaign, and the passage of a bill, are examined through narrated videos, interviews, edited documentaries, original footage, and political ads. *Politics in Action* is accompanied by an extensive user's manual, which provides background on the segments, links topics to textbooks, and discussion questions.

- **Longman American Government Video Archive.** These videos from a broad range of sources include famous debates, speeches, political commercials, and congressional hearings. The archive also includes series such as "Eyes on the Prize" and "The Power Game." Ask your Longman sales representative for more information.

- **Active Learning Guide.** This guide is designed to get students actively involved in course material and encourage them to evaluate and defend viewpoints. Included in this guide are role-playing exercises, debates, and Web-based group projects.

- *Choices: An American Government Reader.* This exciting new customizable reader allows instructors to choose from an archive of more than 300 readings to create a reader that exactly matches their course needs. Contact your Longman representative for more information.

# Acknowledgments

We want to thank the many people who helped us with the preparation of this book. Our deepest gratitude goes to the many undergraduate students whose expectations forced us to refine our thinking about American government over the past ten years. We also thank numerous cohorts of teaching fellows for their perceptive questions, comments, and criticisms. We are also especially grateful to Bruce Nichols, who first argued the need with us for a new-century approach to the introductory text on American government. The Center for Advanced Study in the Behavioral and Social Sciences provided generous support for Paul E. Peterson's work on the first edition of the text during his academic year there.

Harding Noblitt of Concordia College read the entire first edition manuscript in search of errors of fact and interpretation, saving the authors much embarrassment. In addition, portions were read by Danny Adkison, Sue Davis, Richard Fenno, Gary Jacobson, Barry Rabe, and Chris Stamm, whose comments helped with fact checking. We especially appreciate John Ferejohn and the undergraduate students at Stanford University who took his course and tested an early draft of the entire manuscript, and Jay Greene and his students at the University of Texas at Austin who used subsequent page proofs. Larry Carlton supplied important factual material. Research assistance was provided by Ted Brader, Jay Girotto, Donald Lee, Jerome Maddox, Kenneth Scheve, Sean Theriault, and Robert Van Houeling—as well as William Howell who, in addition to making many other contributions, helped write the regulatory policy section in Chapter 18. Rebecca Contreras, Alison Kommer, Shelley Weiner, and Sarah Peterson provided staff assistance.

We would like to extend our special thanks to Bert Johnson and Martin West of Harvard Univesity and Jeremy Pope at Stanford Univesity for the multitude of tasks they undertook to see this second edition into publication, and improved upon the first.

In the course of writing this book, we benefited from the advice of many instructors across the country. We deeply thank all the following, but we are especially grateful for the expert advice of Stephen Ansolabehere, Richard Fenno, John Ferejohn, Bonnie Honig, William Mayer, and Diana Owen.

The following are reviewers of the manuscript for our first edition: Joseph A. Aistrup, Fort Hays State University; Peri E. Arnold, University of Notre Dame; Bruce Berg, Fordham University; Stephen A. Borrelli, University of Alabama; Jeffrey Cohen, University of Kansas; W. Douglas Costain, University of Colorado, Boulder; Claude Dufour, University of Illinois, Chicago; Evelyn C. Fink, University of Nebraska; Richard Fox, Albuquerque TV-I Community College; James Gimpel, University of Maryland; Kenneth L. Grasso, Southwest Texas State University; Roger W. Green, University of North Dakota; Edmund Herod, Houston Community College; Christopher Howard, College of William & Mary; Jon Hurwitz, University of Pittsburgh; Joseph Ignagni, University of Texas, Arlington; Michael Johnston, Colgate University; William R. Keech, University of North Carolina; Kenneth D. Kennedy, College of San Mateo; Fred A. Kramer, University of Massachusetts, Amherst; Silvo Lenart, Purdue University; Brad Lockerbie, University of Georgia; Laurel Mayer. Sinclair Community College; David Mayhew, Yale University; Leonard Meizlish, Mott Community College; Richard Murray, University of Houston; Charles Noble, California State University, Long Beach; Colleen O'Connor, San Diego Mesa College;

Rex C. Peebles, Austin Community College; Richard Pious, Barnard College; David Robinson, University of Houston—Downtown; Francis E. Rourke, Johns Hopkins University; Daniel M. Shea, University of Akron; James R. Simmons, University of Wisconsin, Oshkosh; Dennis Simon, Southern Methodist University; Paul Sracic, Youngstown State University; Eric Uslander, University of Maryland; Shirley Anne Warshaw, Gettysburg College; William Weissert, University of Michigan; Christine Williams, Bentley College; Martin Wiseman, Mississippi State University; Thomas Yantek, Kent State University.

The following are reviewers who also assisted in the preparation of this second edition: Danny M. Adkison, Oklahoma State University; Donald P. Aiesi, Furman Univesity; Michael Bailey, Georgetown University; William Bianco, Penn State University; Nancy Bond, Ranger College; Michael Caldwell, University of Illinois, Urbana–Champaign; Thomas A. Chambers, Golden West College; Louis DeSipio, University of Illinois, Urbana–Champaign; Christine Fastnow, University of Michigan; Jon Hurwitz, University of Pittsburgh; Robert Jacobs, Central Washington University; Brad Lockerbie, University of Georgia; William Lyons, University of Tennessee; Cecilia Manrique, University of Wisconsin, La Crosse; Michael E. Meagher, University of Missouri, Rolla; Charles Menifield, Murray State University; David S. Meyer, City College of New York; Timothy Nokken, University of Houston; John H. Parham, Minnesota State Unversity, Mankato; James A. Rhodes, Luther College; Todd M. Schaefer, Central Washington University; Shirley Anne Warshaw, Gettysburg College; Linda Faye Williams, University of Maryland; Jeremy Zilber, College of William and Mary.

*M. P. F.*
*P. E. P*

# About the Authors

## *Morris P. Fiorina*

Morris P. Fiorina is Professor of Political Science and Senior Fellow of the Hoover Institution at Stanford University. He received a B.A. from Allegheny College in Meadville, Pennsylvania, and a Ph.D. from the University of Rochester. Before moving to Stanford, he taught at the California Institute of Technology and Harvard University.

Fiorina has written widely on American government and politics, with special emphasis on representation and elections. He has published numerous articles, and five books: *Representatives, Roll Calls, and Constituencies; Congress—Keystone of the Washington Establishment; Retrospective Voting in American National Elections; The Personal Vote: Constituency Service and Electoral Independence* (coauthored with Bruce Cain and John Ferejohn); and *Divided Government.* He has served on the editorial boards of a dozen journals in the fields of political science, economics, law, and public policy, and from 1986 to 1990 he served as chairman of the Board of Overseers of the American National Election Studies. He is a member of the National Academy of Sciences.

In his leisure time, Fiorina favors physical activities, including hiking, fishing, and sports. Although his own athletic career never amounted to much, he has been a successful youth baseball coach for fifteen years. Among his most cherished honors is a plaque given by happy parents on the occasion of an undefeated Babe Ruth season.

## *Paul E. Peterson*

Paul E. Peterson is the Henry Lee Shattuck Professor of Government and Director of the Center for American Political Studies at Harvard University. He received his B.A. from Concordia College in Moorhead, Minnesota, and his Ph.D. from the University of Chicago.

Peterson is the author of numerous books and articles on federalism, urban politics, race relations, and public policy, including studies of education, welfare, and fiscal and foreign policy. He received the Woodrow Wilson Award from the American Political Science Association for his book *City Limits* (Chicago, 1981). In 1996 his book *The Price of Federalism* (Brookings, 1995) was given the Aaron Wildavsky Award for the best book on public policy. He is a member of the American Academy of Arts and Sciences.

It is not only when writing a textbook that Peterson makes every effort to be as accurate as possible. On the tennis courts, he always makes correct line calls and has seldom been heard to hit a wrong note when tickling the ivories.

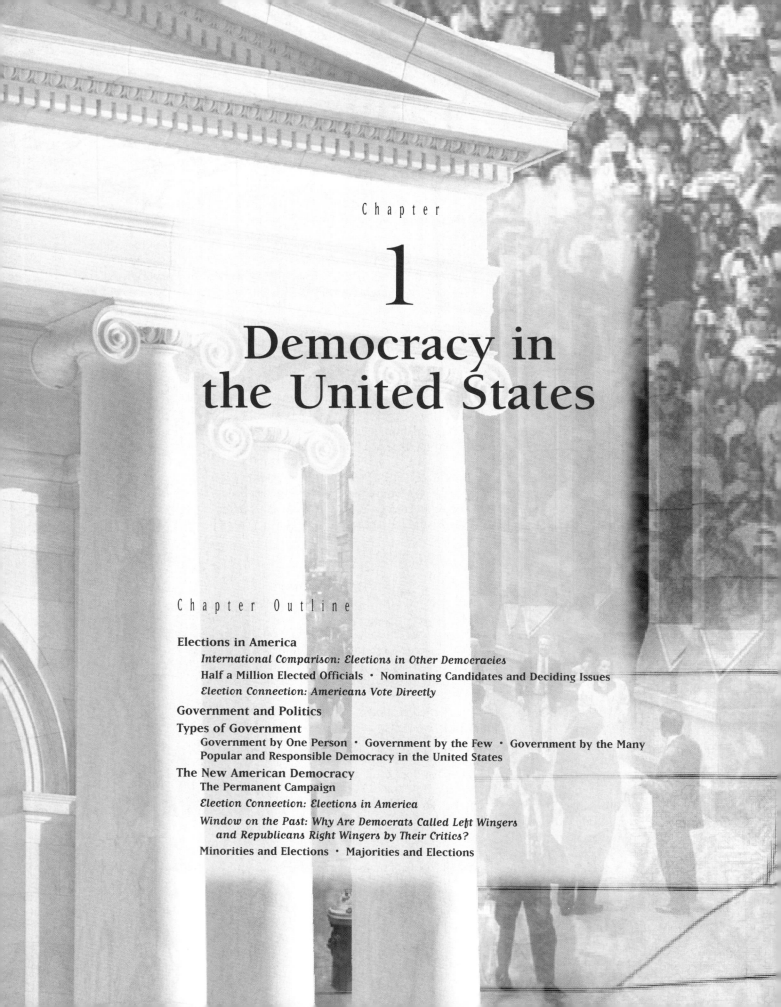

Chapter

# 1
# Democracy in the United States

On the night of November 3, 1992, at 10:30 P.M. Eastern time, the networks declared that Bill Clinton had picked the Republican "lock" on the presidency. Before Clinton, Republicans had won five of the previous six presidential elections, three of them by landslides. How had Clinton succeeded where his predecessors had failed? Clinton ran as a "new Democrat"—a faction of the party that in the mid-1980s began to argue that a majority of the electorate no longer supported the party's traditional positions. Polls indicated that many people resented taxes and had grown skeptical of ambitious government programs; moreover, they believed the Democratic party did not share their values. The new Democrats set out to move the party closer to the mainstream of American politics.

Seizing the opportunity created by an economic recession, Clinton addressed the hopes and fears of Americans. And significantly, only one of his main campaign issues appealed directly to old Democrats: a promise to provide universal health care coverage. New Democrat Clinton promised a tax cut, a pledge usually made by Republicans. He kept his distance from the civil rights leader Jesse Jackson, and he criticized black singer Sister Souljah for the racial hostility in the lyrics of her songs. Clinton appealed to middle-class values by praying in public, attending church on Sundays, emphasizing the importance of individual responsibility, and vowing to "end welfare as we know it," a phrase that would have sounded natural coming from the mouth of former Republican President Ronald Reagan.

Americans never have been enthusiastic about welfare; although they recognize an obligation to help the unfortunate, giving money to able-bodied people clashes with the traditional values of hard work and individual responsibility.[1] Criticism of the welfare system grew during the 1970s and 1980s, as the percentage of babies born to unmarried women soared, as working mothers and their husbands asked why they should pay nonworking mothers to stay home, and as conservative intellectuals charged that welfare had created a "culture of poverty."[2] The reality was that government spending on welfare was small compared to spending on many other government programs, and accounts of welfare abuses often were exaggerated. In particular, the media presented a biased picture, suggesting that the welfare population included more able-bodied people and more racial minorities than actually was the case.[3] But welfare critics won the policy debate, and by the early 1990s a majority of Americans were receptive to calls for radical reform.

During the campaign, Clinton promised to get people off the welfare rolls and into jobs within two years of receiving benefits. Following the election, however, plans for welfare reform disappeared, as the president chose to emphasize more traditional Democratic policies.[4] His economic plan called for tax increases, and he threw the full weight of his presidency behind a major overhaul of the health care system. Meanwhile, controversial social issues such as allowing gays in the military, handgun control, and a ban on assault weapons mobilized political opponents. The administration struggled through its first two years, and by the 1994 elections it was under concentrated attack. Republicans charged that new Democrat Clinton was just an old Democrat in disguise: he favored gays and opposed guns; he had raised taxes and proposed a massive government takeover of health care; and he had broken his campaign promise by doing absolutely nothing about welfare. Republicans swept to victory in the elections, capturing control of Congress for the first time in 40 years.

Welfare reform was high on the Republican agenda, and in December 1995 the Republican Congress challenged the president to approve a bill to "end welfare as we know it." Clinton twice vetoed the bill, arguing that its provisions went too far.[5] In the summer of 1996, the Republicans passed a weaker version of the welfare reform bill and sent it to Clinton for his signature.

Many Democrats denounced the bill. New York Senator Daniel P. Moynihan, the Democratic party's leading expert on social policy, charged that in turning welfare over to the states, the bill reversed 60 years of federal policy. Critics warned that the states would not fund programs adequately and that the training, jobs, and day care required to move welfare recipients into the workforce simply did not exist. Moynihan bitterly charged that the legislation was based on the belief that "the behavior of certain adults can be changed by making the lives of their children as wretched as possible."[6]

President Clinton stood in a commanding position in his bid for reelection, and many of his supporters felt that he could easily afford to veto the bill again. Republicans disagreed, believing they had Clinton on the horns of a dilemma. Then-Speaker of the House Newt Gingrich predicted that Clinton would accept the bill "because he can't avoid it and get reelected. That is the only reason."[7]

Despite Clinton's comfortable lead in the polls, his principal campaign adviser, Dick Morris, agreed with the Republicans. He urged the president to sign the bill, to avoid any risk that welfare would flare up as a campaign issue. To the dismay of many Democrats, Clinton agreed with Morris that the political risks of vetoing the bill were too great. He signed the bill, promising to seek changes in the next Congress. Other Democrats shared Clinton's fear of the dangers of not signing. Of the 16 Democratic senators who stood for reelection in 1996, only Paul Wellstone of Minnesota voted against the bill.

Fortunately, Senator Moynihan's worst fears appear to have been unfounded: Today welfare reform generally is viewed as a success. The number of recipients has declined significantly in most states, although some critics, who contend that a booming economy deserves much of the credit, fear what may happen if the economy turns sour. Whatever the ultimate judgment, however, the philosophy of American social welfare policy clearly has shifted from one of protecting the dependent to one of promoting individual responsibility.

THE STORY OF WELFARE REFORM IS TYPICAL OF POLICY MAKING in democracies, particularly in modern American democracy. Ambitious politicians offer proposals that are crafted to help get them elected. Their proposals are shaped by polls indicating the state of public opinion. Public opinion may shift, however, because, although it is rooted in stable, underlying values, opinion responds to social change, political debate, and the way the media portray social problems. When elected officials deliver on popular promises to the public, they take issues away from potential challengers. When they fail to deliver on such promises, they give their opponents ammunition. Ambitious politicians, electoral pressures, public opinion, and the media are all key elements of modern American democracy.

The elections of the 1990s underlie many of the most important developments in American government at the turn of the millennium. Indeed, the central theme of this book is that elections are the key to understanding contemporary American democracy. Not only are elections more important in the United States than in other democracies, but they are more important today than they were in most earlier periods of our history. In this chapter we address the following questions:

- Why are elections more important in the United States than in other democracies?
- How do elections enable citizens to control government?
- What are the characteristics of different types of government?
- Why has American politics become a "permanent campaign" in recent decades?
- How can minorities exert influence in a system based on majority rule?
- How do elections produce a reasonably good government?

## Elections in America

More than the politics of any other democracy, politics in the United States is driven by electoral influences. To avoid any misunderstanding, we emphasize three points at the outset. First, our notion of electoral influence is very broad. We are referring not just to what happens on election day nor even just to what goes on during the campaigns. Rather, when we write about the importance of elections, we include the anticipation of and the preparation for future elections. Looking ahead to the next election affects what presidents propose, what they sign, and what they veto; what Congress passes and what it kills; whom groups support and whom they oppose; whom and what the media cover; and whom and what they ignore. Just as the winner of an Olympic event may have been determined on the training fields years earlier, so the outcomes of elections may be determined by the actions of candidates, groups, contributors, the media, and other political actors far in advance of the actual campaigns.

A second important clarification is that when we emphasize the importance of elections, we are *not* making a naïve claim that "the people" rule. On the contrary, elections are not always free and accurate expressions of popular sentiments. Elections give more power to some groups than to others. Sometimes elections allow powerful special interests to block actions desired by the majority. And even if every election reflected the sentiments of a majority, leaders elected by different majorities at different times might deadlock. Whether elections are truly representative and whether they generally work to produce good government are questions that spark debate and disagreement. In fact, we repeatedly challenge you to think about these questions as we survey modern American politics and government.

Finally, to say that elections are a key ingredient in American democracy—even *the* key ingredient—is not to deny that other elements are important as well. Elections are part of a complex political system. They are closely bound up with the historical evolution of American government, the political behavior of Americans, the workings of the country's basic institutions, and the policies that the governmental process produces. All of these topics receive thorough treatment in the chapters that follow.

## International Comparison — Elections in Other Democracies

In contrast to Americans, many of whom can vote more than a dozen times for scores of candidates and issues in any given four-year period, citizens of other democracies vote for fewer offices and vote less frequently. Consider Great Britain, which elected John Major prime minister in 1992 and replaced him with Tony Blair five years later. In each of these elections, Britons voted for only one person—a candidate for parliament. Between these two elections, Britons voted on only two other occasions, for only two offices—their local councillor and their representative to the European Community.

Between Bill Clinton's two election victories, the French voted four times: for Parliament in 1993, for president in April and May of 1994 (they have a two-round system), and for local mayors in 1995. Similarly, between 1992 and 1996 the Japanese voted five times, twice each for the upper and lower houses of the Diet (their parliament) and once for local officials.

Even to our North American neighbors the United States looks peculiar. In Mexico a presidential election is held every six years. Congressional elections are held every three years. Some Mexican states hold state and municipal elections at the same time as congressional elections, while others hold them at a different time. But at most a Mexican citizen votes four times in a four-year period: in presidential, congressional, state, and municipal elections.

In Canada, too, provincial and municipal elections may or may not be coordinated with national elections. If the elections are not so coordinated, a Canadian votes at most three times (national, provincial, and municipal) in a four-year period, except for an occasional referendum, such as Quebec's vote on secession in 1995. Canadian officials are well aware of the contrast between the two systems. Prime Minister Jean Chrétien recently commented that "In your system, you guys campaign for 24 hours [a day] every [day for] two years. You know, politics is one thing, but we have to run a government."[a]

_____

[a]David Shribman, "In Canada, the Lean Season," *Boston Globe*, May 23, 1997, A3.

---

Because Americans take elections so much for granted, we begin by calling attention to the sheer amount of electioneering that occurs in the United States.

### Half a Million Elected Officials

The United States has more elections that select more officials for public offices than any other country on Earth. Unbelievable as it may seem, more than half a million people in the United States are elected officials, about 1 for every 500 Americans. If all elected officials lived in one place, the population would exceed that of Cleveland.[8]

*National elections*, in which voters choose the officials of the federal government, are held every two years. These important elections determine the president, the vice-president, 100 senators and 435 members of the House of Representatives. But although national elections get most of the media's attention, they are only the tip of the iceberg. Hundreds of thousands of elections occur at other levels of government.

In *state elections* the citizens of the 50 states choose their state public officials. In every state, voters elect the governor and the state legislature, and in nearly all states they also elect the lieutenant governor, the treasurer, the state's attorney, the auditor, and perhaps state railroad and public utility commissioners.

The number of elections explodes when we move to *local elections,* in which officials for all governments below the level of the state are chosen. Voters in cities elect mayors and city councils. Voters in the more than 3000 counties elect sheriffs, county treasurers, and county boards, among other officials. Voters elect the members of 90 percent of the nation's 16,000 school boards, as well as numerous officials responsible for the governance of towns, villages, and special districts.

Even the judicial system—often viewed as insulated from political pressure—is permeated by elections. In 37 states, voters elect at least some judges. Altogether, Americans elect more than 1000 state judges and about 15,000 county, municipal, and other local judges and officers of the court.[9] Moreover, in recent years judges have been increasingly subject to **recall elections,** in which dissatisfied citizens try to remove incumbents from office during their terms.

### Nominating Candidates and Deciding Issues

Although half a million elected officials sounds like a lot, there are far more elections than there are elected officials. First, many officials must win two elections before they can take office. In the **primary election**, each party chooses a nominee who then

**recall election**
Attempt to remove an official from office before the completion of the term.

**primary election**
Preliminary election that narrows the number of candidates by determining who will be the nominees in the general election.

## Election Connection

# Americans Vote Directly

More than people in any country other than Switzerland, Americans vote directly on laws. Every election finds state electorates deciding on an array of ballot measures, many of them interesting and unusual. For example, in 1998 and 2000 state electorates were invited to decide the following issues:

**Medical Marijuana, 1998**
Voters in Alaska, Colorado, Nevada, Oregon, Washington, DC and Washington State decided the issue of medicinal *cannabis*. Additionally, voters in Oregon voted on a referendum to block the recriminalization of marijuana. Voters in Arizona will decide on a referendum to block the gutting of Proposition 200, the Drug Medicalization, Prevention, and Control Act.

**Term Limits, 1998**
Three states tried to get around a U.S. Supreme Court ruling that the only way to impose term limits on members of Congress is by amending the U.S. Constitution. Alaska, Colorado, and Idaho all had measures that would allow candidates running for Congress to sign voluntary term-limit pledges. If they signed the pledge, then their ballot entries would include their name and the fact that they signed the pledge.

**Assisted Suicide, 1998**
Voters in Michigan decided whether to legalize physician-assisted suicide. If approved, "Proposal B" would "legalize the prescription of a lethal dose of medication to terminally ill, competent, informed adults in order to commit suicide."

**Abortion, 1998**
Two states, Colorado and Washington, considered amendments to ban the so-called partial-birth abortion.

**California's Propositions**
No state carries on as much direct democracy as California: here students protest a measure that would lengthen prison terms for juveniles convicted of gang-related offenses, and shift their trials to adult courts.

**Marriage, 2000**
In March of 2000, California voters approved the "Definition of Marriage Initiative," an initiative that identified marriage between one man and one woman as the only legally recognized form of marriage in the state.

**Taxes, 2000**
Twenty-one states will have referenda on whether to require voter approval of some new taxes.

**Education, 2000**
Six states will decide whether to adopt further school choice measures and implement voucher programs.

**Gambling, 2000**
Twelve states will have referenda on whether to legalize, expand, or restrict gambling.

Supporters of the initiative process argue that it allows voters to decide important questions themselves rather than have legislative lobbyists and professional legislators make the decisions. Critics argue that uninformed voters will make foolish decisions about complicated issues, and that special interest groups manipulate the initiative process.

*What do you think?*
- *Do legislatures make better decisions than electorates?*
- *Are special interests more powerful in legislatures or in initiative campaigns?*
- *On balance do initiatives improve democracy or undermine it?*

SOURCES: "Medical marijuana on 7 U.S. ballots" CNN/ALLPolitics 10/3/98; CNN/ALLPolitics-1998 Initiatives 10/30/98; "Debate Tonight on Definition of Marriage Initiative; Traditional values activist versus gay rights backers." *The San Francisco Chronicle* September 8, 1999; and Ballot Watch (**www.ballotwatch.org**)

**general election**
Final election that selects the office holder.

**initiative**
Proposed laws or state constitutional amendments placed on the ballot via citizen petition.

**referendum**
A law or state constitutional amendment that is proposed by a legislature or city council but does not go into effect unless the required majority of voters approve it.

**proposition**
A shorthand reference to an initiative or a referendum.

squares off against the other parties' nominees in the **general election.** In *nonpartisan elections,* where candidates do not run with party labels, primaries are sometimes used to narrow the field of candidates. Access to the primary ballot is open to any willing candidate who has the supporters to gather the required number of signatures and the money to pay the filing fees.

Second, to the extensive list of elections that choose office holders we must add those elections in which the people directly decide on public issues. In 27 states and the District of Columbia, citizens vote on issues by voting on initiatives, referenda, or both (see the accompanying Election Connection). An **initiative** is a proposed law or amendment to a state constitution placed on the ballot by a citizen petition. A **referendum** is a law or state constitutional amendment that is proposed by a legislature or city council but goes into effect only if approved by a specified majority of voters. Often lumped together as **propositions,** initiatives and referenda enable citizens to bypass elected officials and decide budgets, taxes, laws, and amendments to state constitutions directly.[10] Some states, such as California, frequently have more propositions on the ballot than elected offices to be filled.

Americans have become accustomed to the frequency and variety of elections, but observers from other countries are struck by the seemingly constant presence of Americans at the polling booths (see the accompanying International Comparison). Noted British analyst Anthony King argues that "American exceptionalism"—the distinctive shape of American democracy when seen from an international perspective—arises not from our individualistic political culture or from the fragmented nature of our institutions, as many have argued, but rather from the multitude and frequency of elections. King observes that

> Americans take the existence of their elections industry for granted. Some like it; some dislike it; most are simply bored by it. But they are all conscious of it, in the same way that they are conscious of Mobil, McDonald's, *Larry King Live,* Oprah Winfrey, the Dallas Cowboys, the Ford Motor Company, and all the other symbols and institutions that go to make up the rich tapestry of American life. In a meaningful sense, America is about the holding of elections.[11]

timeline
**The Initiative
and the
Referendum**

## Government and Politics

Ironically, although Americans choose hundreds of thousands of their public officials in elections, and although they use initiatives and referenda to make specific policy decisions, many Americans are frustrated by government. As recorded in Figure 1.1, Americans do not trust government as much as they did a generation ago. Citizens believe that government costs too much, delivers too little, and wastes their tax dollars. They think politics is needlessly contentious and often corrupt. Many are unenthusiastic about major-party presidential candidates like Al Gore and George Bush and yearn for new leaders like former POW John McCain. Many are suspicious about the established TV networks and major newspapers and turn to alternative information providers such as talk-show hosts and cable channels. Many are frustrated with existing political processes and support radical reforms such as constitutional amendments to limit the number of terms elected officials may serve.[12]

To some extent, suspicion of government is healthy. By their very nature, governments threaten human liberty. The great German sociologist Max Weber wrote that **government** is that institution in society that has a "monopoly of the legitimate use of physical force."[13] Government is the only institution that *legally* can take people's property (by taxing them), restrict their movements (by imprisoning them), and even kill them (by executing them). As George Washington put it a century before Weber: "Government is not reason, it is not eloquence—it is force."[14]

Because government has the power to coerce people, people have good reasons to distrust and fear it. Those who participate in politics generally do so because they

**government**
The institution in society that has a "monopoly of the legitimate use of physical force."

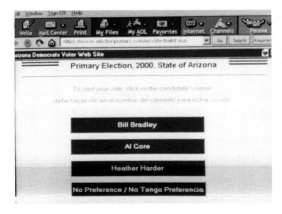

Online voting experiments are already taking place in states like Arizona. *How might online voting change the way the electorate looks, and therefore votes?*

**Polling Places**
Elections are so widespread and continuous in the United States that unusual locations are often pressed into service as polling places. This grocery store in rural Texas gives a busy parent the opportunity to cast her vote in a local election.

**Figure 1.1**

**Americans Have Grown Increasingly Skeptical of the National Government**

SOURCE: The American National Election Studies. *Note*: Data on the 1986 responses to the second question do not exist.

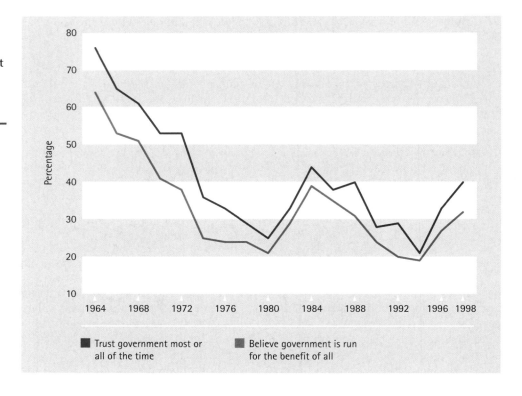

■ Trust government most or all of the time    ■ Believe government is run for the benefit of all

want to see the powers of government used for some particular purpose. At times the purposes are high-minded, as when Abraham Lincoln drafted soldiers to fight to save the Union. At times the purposes are less honorable, as when Richard Nixon tried to use the Internal Revenue Service to punish his political critics. Most of the time, the purposes are mixed. The country's recent president, Bill Clinton, offers a good example. No one would deny that he entered politics partly to satisfy his personal ambitions, which had been on display since high school.[15] But despite his obvious personal flaws, only a few of his most bitter enemies would deny that he also hoped to create a better country for future generations.

Because governmental power is fearsome and the motives of those who use it are mixed, citizens understandably are suspicious of it. Why then do we have governments at all? If former President Jimmy Carter were correct, government would be unnecessary. When campaigning for president, Carter professed that "All I want is . . . to have a nation with a government that is as good and honest and decent and competent and compassionate and as filled with love as are the American people."[16] These are noble sentiments, but with all due respect to the former president, government is necessary precisely because such qualities are often missing from human behavior. As another former president, James Madison, put it earlier, "If men were angels, no government would be necessary."[17]

If people were always good and honest and decent and competent and compassionate and filled with love, there would be little need for government. Governments are designed less for the times when people agree than for the times when they disagree. No matter who you are, what you believe, what you want, or how you behave, the unfortunate fact of life is that some of your fellow citizens dislike you for exactly that reason. People can settle their disagreements and rise above their dislikes through peaceful political means, or they can kill each other, as Americans did in the Civil War and as so many peoples of the world have done before and since.

Thomas Hobbes, a great English political theorist, made the most basic case for government and politics. A world without government would be nothing less than "a war of all against all." Life would be "nasty, brutish and short."[18] Government is not a perfect solution to human conflicts, so citizens *should* be suspicious of its powers. But

**One Man's Good Government**
When campaigning for president, Jimmy Carter said, "All I want is . . . to have a nation with a government that is as good . . . as are the American people." *How good would such a government be?*

government is the best solution for human conflicts that human beings have yet contrived, and civilized life is unimaginable without it. Of course, that still leaves an important question: What *kind* of government?

## Types of Government

British Author Samuel Johnson once commented that "I would not give half a guinea to live under one form of government than another. It is of no moment to the happiness of an individual."[19] Johnson's comment is silly—at best. Lives can be terribly damaged or greatly improved, depending on the type of government under which people live. Twenty-three centuries ago, Aristotle classified governments into three general types: government by one person, government by the few, and government by the many. Although others have proposed more complex classifications, Aristotle's simple scheme remains a useful place to begin our study of government.

### Government by One Person

Historically, pharaohs, emperors, kings, tsars, and other monarchs ruled by hereditary right or religious appointment, although, like modern dictators, they usually needed the support of an army or police force as well. The quality of government by a single ruler depends on who is in charge. The ruler can put the welfare of the people first, last, or anywhere in between. But placing the coercive power of government in the hands of one person requires unlimited trust in that person, and no one is so deserving. As another English political theorist, Lord Acton, observed, "power tends to corrupt and absolute power corrupts absolutely." In the twentieth century alone, millions of people died at the hands of rulers who gained near-absolute power—tyrants such as Germany's Hitler, the Soviet Union's Stalin, China's Mao, and Cambodia's Pol Pot.

### Government by the Few

Government by the few is called **aristocracy** if leaders are chosen by birth, and **oligarchy** if leaders are chosen on the basis of wealth, military power, or membership in a political party. Aristocracies ruled many countries in the past, but in the modern world, birthright no longer seems an acceptable justification for ruling over others. Oligarchies still exist, however. The most important one governs China, where a small group of Communist party leaders has remained in power since 1946. Oligarchies have some advantages over dictatorships; to a limited extent, members of the oligarchy can check and balance each other. But here, too, power tends to corrupt, as the few take advantage of their position to acquire wealth at the expense of the rest of society.

### Government by the Many

Government in which all citizens share power is called **democracy.** The word derives from the Greek word *demos,* which means "people." In its purest form, **direct democracy,** all citizens participate directly in making government decisions. In Aristotle's time, direct democracy was practical because citizenship was limited to free adult men with property, who in many Greek cities numbered no more than a few thousand. Direct democracy still exists in a few small New England towns where decisions are made at town meetings.

Direct democracy in large countries such as the United States is not practical. Even with such modern communications as cable television, fax, e-mail, and the Internet, every citizen cannot participate in every governmental decision. People would have to spend their entire lives attending meetings, deliberating, and voting in order to decide all the questions that come up.

Because direct democracy is impractical in the modern world, government by the many generally takes the form of **representative democracy,** an *indirect* form of

**Government by One Person**
Pol Pot murdered millions of his fellow Cambodians—all in the name of progress.

**aristocracy**
Government by a few leaders made eligible by birthright.

**oligarchy**
Government by a few who gain office by means of wealth, military power, or membership in a single political party.

**democracy**
System in which governmental power is widely shared among the citizens, usually through free and open elections.

**direct democracy**
Type of democracy in which ordinary people are the government, making all the laws themselves.

**representative democracy**
An indirect form of democracy in which the people choose representatives who determine what government does.

democracy in which citizens choose representatives who decide what government does. Free elections are the key feature of representative democracy, as its opponents well recognize. Soviet dictator Joseph Stalin once observed, "The disadvantage of free elections is that you can never be sure who is going to win them."[20]

Although they generally agree on the importance of free elections, political theorists disagree about many other aspects of representative democracy.[21] As shown in Table 1.1, most of the arguments can be summarized by distinguishing between two general types or models of representative democracy, a popular model and a responsible model.

**popular model of democracy**
Type of representative democracy in which ordinary people participate actively and closely constrain the actions of public officials.

In the **popular model of democracy,** citizens take an active role in government decisions. In its purest form, popular democracy strives to be as close to a direct democracy as a representative democracy can be. Elections are opportunities for the popular will to express itself. Elections provide *popular mandates*—instructions from the voters for public officials to adopt specific policies. In order for elections to work this way, citizens must be well informed about public issues and vote prospectively—that is, look to the future when they vote. As a result, each election is an occasion to decide the direction of public policies.

Those who favor the popular model say that democracy is more than a mechanical process for producing outcomes; it is also an educational forum in which individuals become better citizens by participating in democratic deliberation. Through participation the public can reach consensus and make better decisions. Thus popular democracy is expected to produce both better citizens and better policies. The process of participation transforms "private into public," "conflict into cooperation."[22]

**responsible model of democracy**
Type of representative democracy in which public officials have considerable freedom of action but are held accountable by the people for the decisions they make.

Critics say that popular democracies are inefficient systems in which everyone talks but no one acts. These critics favor instead a **responsible model of democracy,** in which citizens take a more passive role. Citizens choose public officials but do not tell them what to do. Elected officials have the responsibility to govern and must answer to the people for the decisions they make. In this model, elections are occasions on which citizens grant or deny *popular consent* rather than granting or denying popular mandates. Citizens need not be particularly well informed because they vote retrospectively, looking more to the past than to the future. In other words, they decide whether incumbents have done a good or a bad job. If the voters approve, they reelect incumbents; if the voters disapprove, they vote in a new group of leaders.

Critics of the responsible model say that it is hardly democracy at all.[23] In fact, critics sometimes refer to the responsible model as "elitist democracy" because elites—those who hold office, manage the parties, and lead the interest groups—dominate the political process. Those who favor the responsible model do not deny that it gives ordinary citizens a modest role relative to elites (whom they prefer to call leaders), but they claim that direct popular participation in government is unnecessary, or even harmful, because people often are poorly informed. Defenders of the responsible model believe that as long as the public can periodically judge the performance of elected officials, a responsible democracy usually will produce better government than does a popular democracy, because public officials are better informed than citizens as a whole.

### Popular and Responsible Democracy in the United States

In the real world, of course, pure types do not exist; every real-world democracy has both popular and responsible features. Yet democracies differ in the degree to which they tend toward one or the other form. Britain, for example, more closely resembles the responsible model. British voters elect members of Parliament, but in the normal five-year period between elections, the governing party has great freedom to undertake independent action—including fairly radical actions such as nationalizing and denationalizing entire industries.

The United States has always been a more popular democracy than its European counterparts. When the French scholar Alexis de Tocqueville visited the United States during the 1830s, he was astounded by the extent of popular participation. "It must

**Table 1.1**

**Two Models of Democracy**

| The Popular Model | The Responsible Model |
|---|---|
| Elections determine policies. | Elections determine leaders. |
| Citizens vote prospectively. | Citizens vote retrospectively. |
| Direct democracy is preferred. | Representative democracy is preferred. |
| Popular participation is necessary for effective democracy. | Clear accountability of leaders is necessary for effective democracy. |
| Democratic politics should advance the civic education of citizens. | Democratic politics should produce effective governance. |

be seen to be believed," he exclaimed to his fellow French citizens. "No sooner do you set foot on American ground than you are stunned by a kind of tumult. . . . Almost the only pleasure an American knows is to take part in the government and discuss its measures."[24]

From the earliest days of the republic, the principles of popular democracy were an important part of American politics. "Where annual elections end, there slavery begins," said the second president, John Adams, arguing that citizens must have frequent opportunities to instruct and judge their representatives.[25] The third president, Thomas Jefferson, wanted to "divide the country into wards." Jefferson thought that in these "small autonomous constituencies ["little republics," he called them] free men could control their own political destinies."[26]

The framers believed that words on paper—which they called "parchment barriers"—were no guarantee of good government. Words alone would not prevent majorities from violating the rights of minorities. The framers thought the rights of individuals could best be protected by "buttressing" the "parchment barriers" in the Constitution with something firmer: a system of checks and balances, which divided power among different representatives chosen in different elections. Each national office was assigned a separate **constituency**—a set of people entitled to vote for the holder of that office—and office holders were to be chosen by these different constituencies at different times. Thus senators were to be chosen by state legislatures for six-year terms; presidents and vice-presidents were to be chosen by electors (themselves chosen by the state legislatures) for four-year terms; and members of the House of Representatives were to be elected directly by the voters for two-year terms. Consequently, each public official was responsible to different constituencies at different times.

In this way, the framers constructed a responsible democracy, even while including many popular features. With power divided among many elected officials, each with her or his own constituency, leaders have the interest and capacity to resist both popular passions and attempts by would-be tyrants to seize power. According to Madison, "Ambition must be made to counteract ambition. The interest of the man must be connected with the constitutional rights of the place."[27] Two hundred years of nontyrannical government confirm the validity of his argument.

**constituency**
Those legally entitled to vote for a public official.

## Section Summary

Governments come in many varieties. Government by one person was common historically but is rare today. Government by a few people drawn from an aristocracy or oligarchy also was common, and it still exists. But democracy—government by the many, which generally means a majority—became the most common form of government late in the twentieth century. Democracies are not all alike, of course. Democratic theorists argue about whether democracies should be more popular (open and participatory at all times) or responsible (dominated by leaders accountable in periodic elections). Real-world democracies are mixtures of both ideas.

**The Permanent Campaign**
Candidates begin campaigning far in advance of the actual presidential election. As vice-president, Al Gore was rumored never to have missed an opportunity to campaign for the 2000 Democratic presidential nomination. *Is it feasible, or a good idea to limit the time candidates can campaign?*

## *The New American Democracy*

When the Constitution was adopted, few Americans had the right to participate in politics, but American politics has evolved in the direction of greater popular participation. Over the course of two centuries, more and more of the population has gained full rights of citizenship, the connection between representatives and the public has become increasingly direct, national institutions have become less insulated from popular influence, and the number and frequency of elections, coupled with the more extensive campaigning that accompanies them, have increased. These trends have accelerated dramatically in recent decades—to the extent that we believe it is no exaggeration to title this book *The New American Democracy*.

### *The Permanent Campaign*

**permanent campaign**
Condition that prevails when the next election campaign begins as soon as the last has ended and the line between electioneering and governing has disappeared.

The new American democracy is marked by the **permanent campaign**.[28] The term literally means that campaigning never ends: The next election campaign begins as soon as the last one has finished, if not before. The dust from the 1998 elections had barely settled before discussion turned to which party would win control of the House in 2000. Every action undertaken—or not undertaken—by the 106th Congress (1999–2000) was viewed as a potential issue in the upcoming presidential campaign. And before the 2000 presidential election even was settled, pundits began to speculate about the implications of the split verdict for the 2004 elections.

The deeper meaning of the term *permanent campaign* is that the line between campaigning and governing has disappeared. To some extent governing becomes a part of the campaign; in effect, it is a campaign strategy. According to Professor Hugh Heclo, the rise of the permanent campaign injects campaign values into the governmental process—a willingness to sacrifice long-term good for short-term advantage, the adoption of adversarial rather than collaborative mindsets, and a shift away from deliberation and education to persuasion and selling.[29] Not everyone takes such a critical view of the rise of the permanent campaign, but many observers are considering its significance, as we do in this book.

At least seven developments have contributed to the permanent campaign: the separation of election days, the decay of party organizations, the spread of primary elections, advances in mass communications, the explosion of interest groups, the pro-

## Election Connection — Elections in America

Americans are called on to vote far more often than the citizens of other democracies. Professor L. Sandy Maisel has compiled the following list of election days in various American towns and cities in just the two year period between the 1998 and 2000 elections.[a]

### Montgomery, Alabama

| | |
|---|---|
| October 1999 | Municipal elections (mayor, council) |
| June 2000 | Statewide and presidential primaries with runoffs later in the month |
| November 2000 | Federal and state elections Judicial elections |

### Bangor, Maine

| | |
|---|---|
| November 1999 | Municipal elections and referenda (state and/or candidate) |
| February 2000 | Presidential preference primary |
| June 2000 | Primary elections for federal, state, and county offices |
| November 2000 | General election for federal, state, and county offices |

### Athens, Ohio

| | |
|---|---|
| November 1999 | County, township, and municipal elections Elections to school board |
| March 2000 | Presidential primary |
| May 2000 | Congressional primary |
| November 2000 | Election of federal and state officials |

### Seattle, Washington

| | |
|---|---|
| February-May 1999 | Special elections (if necessary) |
| September 1999 | Primary elections for municipal offices (mayor, council, school board) |
| November 1999 | Municipal elections Statewide and local initiatives |
| February-May 2000 | Special elections (if necessary) |
| September 2000 | Primary elections for federal, state, and county offices |
| November 2000 | Election of federal and state officials Statewide and local initiatives |

There are so many elections and so many elected officials in so many jurisdictions in the United States that it is difficult to compile accurate data on the subject. For example, we had heard that residents of Houston, Texas, voted for more elected officials than Americans in any other jurisdiction. How many? A call to the County Clerk's office was met with a "we have no idea" response. Conversations with University of Houston professors elicited the estimate that a resident of Houston was represented by 126 elected officials, judges included, at all levels of government.[b] We challenge our readers to find jurisdictions in which citizens can vote for even more officials! Contact us at **www.awl.com/Fiorina**.

[a] L. Sandy Maisel, *Parties and Elections in America*, 3rd ed. (Lanham, MD: Rowman and Littlefield, 1999): 5.
[b] Professor Richard Murray, as reported by Professor Jay Greene, personal communication, April 10, 1997.

liferation of polling, and the increasing need for money. Together these factors have moved American democracy in a significantly more popular direction.

**Separation of Elections** In principle, all public officials could be elected on the same day and serve, say, the same four-year term of office. Everyone would stand for reelection simultaneously. Such an arrangement—one gigantic election day every four years—would greatly reduce the time taken up by campaigning and voting.

A century ago, most officials *were* elected on the same day. In 1885 a graduate student named Woodrow Wilson wrote that "This is preeminently a country of frequent elections, and few states care to increase the frequency by separating elections of state from elections of national functionaries."[30] In Wilson's time citizens of most states cast votes simultaneously for president, senator, representative, governor, mayor, state representative and state senator, city council, and so forth. Today voters still fill most offices on the same day in a few states, but the trend in the past half-century has been to separate election days.[31] Most Americans now turn out to vote for president at one general election, for governor at another, and for mayor at yet another. Primary elections, as well as those for local offices, are held earlier in the election year. Initiatives and referenda may be held on still other occasions. As a result, Americans are repeatedly called to the polls (see the accompanying Election Connection). For example, a conscientious citizen in California generally has to go to the polls on eight separate occasions in each two-year election cycle. And as election dates have proliferated, electioneering has become a pervasive feature of American politics. There is very little "quiet time" during which there are no campaigns.

**Decay of Party Organizations** Many political scientists think political parties are essential to the workings of representative democracies. Parties make it easier for voters to choose, and parties organize political power so that governments can govern. Since just before the Civil War, the two major parties in the United States have been the Republicans and the Democrats.

Although we cannot always detect clear differences between Republicans and Democrats, the two parties give voters a choice by advocating different political philosophies. The Republican party leans in a conservative direction, generally favoring smaller government, lower taxes, less regulation of business activity, and traditional family values. The Democratic party leans in a liberal direction, usually favoring a strong federal government, more extensive social programs, more regulation, and toleration of alternative lifestyles. Conservatives are called the "right" or the "right wing," liberals the "left" or the "left wing." (See the accompanying Window on the Past.) Because the philosophies of the two parties generally differ, voters have choices. And because party positions on issues shift only gradually, parties provide continuity and familiarity to political life, making it easier for voters to make choices.

A century ago many of the state and local party organizations were called machines, because they were strong, disciplined organizations that could mobilize large numbers of voters on election day. Public officials relied on the parties when elections rolled around. But governmental reforms and various social changes killed off the machines. As a consequence, today's politicians cannot depend on party workers

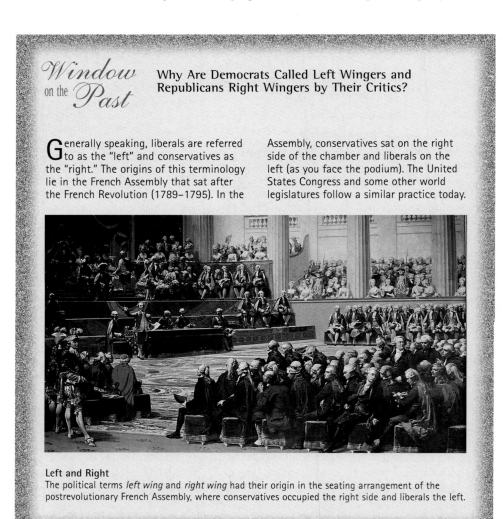

*Window on the Past*

**Why Are Democrats Called Left Wingers and Republicans Right Wingers by Their Critics?**

Generally speaking, liberals are referred to as the "left" and conservatives as the "right." The origins of this terminology lie in the French Assembly that sat after the French Revolution (1789–1795). In the Assembly, conservatives sat on the right side of the chamber and liberals on the left (as you face the podium). The United States Congress and some other world legislatures follow a similar practice today.

**Left and Right**
The political terms *left wing* and *right wing* had their origin in the seating arrangement of the postrevolutionary French Assembly, where conservatives occupied the right side and liberals the left.

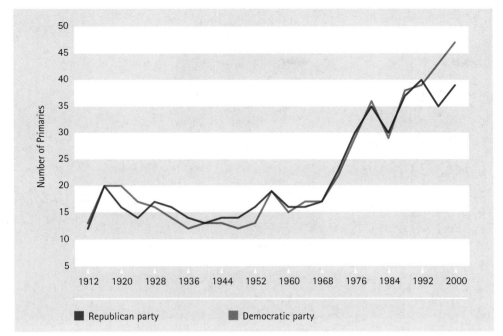

**Figure 1.2**

**The Number of Presidential Primaries Has Increased Greatly in the Past Three Decades**

SOURCE: Harold Stanley and Richard Niemi, *Vital Statistics on American Politics*, 2000 ed. (Washington, DC: CQ Press), p. 62 and data compiled by Sam Abrams.

to deliver the vote for all the candidates of the party. Instead, elected officials must build their own organizations and develop *personal* constituencies to achieve election and reelection.[32] Such personalized support is less reliable than the partisan support shared by numerous candidates in earlier eras.[33] Incumbents today must constantly invest their own time and resources to maintain their base of electoral support.

**Spread of Primaries** In most countries, small groups of party leaders select candidates for office. A century ago this was the standard procedure in the United States as well. According to reformers, candidates were picked in "smoke-filled rooms" by party "bosses." To eliminate the corruption that often accompanied such deal making, reformers passed laws giving voters the right to select party nominees in primary elections.

Although they came into use about a century ago, primaries did not become a significant part of the presidential nominating process until after World War II (see Figure 1.2). The first presidential candidate who owed his nomination in any significant degree to winning primaries was Dwight D. Eisenhower, elected in 1952. As late as 1968, the Democratic nominee, Hubert Humphrey, did not enter a single primary.

Today primaries contribute substantially to the permanent campaign. They greatly increase the number of elections, and because primaries often are held months in advance of the general election, they shorten the time between one election and the next. Behind-the-scenes planning for the presidential election of 2000 began in early 1997. The campaign was under way by mid-1999, more than six months before the primaries began in the spring of the year 2000, and only two and a half years into Clinton's second term. Nor is the permanent campaign limited to the campaign for the White House. Some members of the House of Representatives face primaries more than six months before their two-year terms end. On April 9, 1996, for example, a Texas Republican was defeated in a primary, scarcely 15 months after he had taken the oath of office.

**Mass Communications** Technological progress also has helped to make campaigns continuous. Fifty years ago, party workers passed out flyers and posted signs when the formal campaign began. Today's candidates make every effort to get their names in the papers and their pictures on television any time they can. Moreover, interactive mass

**What Gets Covered**
One of President Clinton's most scrutinized moments came while he was
denying an illicit affair in early 1997.
The dramatic value of his (false) denial
led the mass media—particularly the
cable channels—to replay this moment
again and again, following the story
for months. *Should the media have
covered this story as much as it did?
What was the news value of the story
to the public?*

timeline

**Major Events that
Changed the Political
Landscape**

communications provide citizens with more opportunities to talk back to politicians
as well as be talked to. Long-distance telephone rates are so low that many people are
willing to call or receive calls from anywhere in the United States. Dozens of cable
television channels enable candidates to communicate with small, well-defined
audiences. C-SPAN provides continuous coverage of congressional debates, giving
people outside Washington a chance to observe public officials directly. Radio talk
shows have increased in popularity. Candidate and interest-group Web sites on the
Internet have proliferated, and conversation on the Internet (often error-ridden and
conspiratorial) is perhaps the fastest-growing mode of political communication.

The effects of technological change have been intensified by changes in the culture of the mass media. The demand for content has been greatly increased by 24-hour
news services. Any move a politician makes might end up on television, and virtually
every move a prominent politician makes is now evaluated for its political motivations
and implications. Partly as a consequence of the media's insatiable appetite for news,
the distinction between public and private life has eroded. The financial and medical
histories of elected officials are treated as public knowledge, and reporters ask candidates almost any question imaginable, no matter how tasteless or unrelated to politics
and government.

**Profusion of Interest Groups**  The personal organizations that today's candidates
put together are based in large part on the numerous interest groups that have formed
during the past generation. At mid-century when political scientists wrote about
interest groups they referred mostly to a few large business, labor, and agricultural
organizations. Now there are thousands of generally smaller, more narrowly focused
organizations.

Many of the newer groups are outgrowths of the social movements of the 1960s
(the antiwar, civil rights, women's, and environmental movements) that cut across and
compete with traditional economic interests. Technology has played a role as well. In
the pre-computer, snail-mail era, it was far more difficult for small economic interests
even to locate each other, let alone to organize. Today, interest groups can monitor the
actions of elected officials electronically and then post information about political
developments on their Web sites or send blanket e-mails to their members. The technology provides the means to put the actions of public officials under a microscope,
and the existence of the groups ensures that some people have the motive to do so.

**Proliferation of Polls** The permanent campaign owes much to the profusion of polling. It is a statistical fact that one can obtain a reasonable snapshot of the state of public opinion by interviewing about 1000 randomly selected people. More than ever before, polls provide public officials with a fairly good approximation of the public's thinking about an issue.

Leaders always have been concerned about public opinion, of course. In the closing days of the Constitutional Convention in 1787, George Washington proposed a major change in the representational scheme for the House of Representatives so that the new Constitution would stand a better chance of being ratified by the states. Abraham Lincoln waited for a military victory before issuing the Emancipation Proclamation, abolishing slavery in the Confederate states, so that a happy northern public would be more inclined to support it. Politicians traditionally are portrayed as having their "ear to the ground" and their "finger to the wind." But until the introduction of modern polling, beliefs about the state of public opinion were only guesses. Modern polling techniques are much more precise and provide everyone the same information.

Polling has become a major industry, in part because elected officials hunger for information about the state of the public mind. Of course, it is not just the politicians who want to know about the state of public opinion; the media have become increasingly focused on it as well. As Figures 1.3 and 1.4 show, the media have made public opinion a much more important part of their coverage both by sponsoring polls and by incessant reporting of polling results. Some critics charge that the media find it easier to "manufacture" news by taking a poll and writing about it than to write about real news.

Polling contributes to the permanent campaign by making electoral implications immediately known. When a new issue arises, politicians no longer wonder about the state of public opinion—they find out within days or sometimes hours. Even if elected officials wanted to make decisions without thinking about their political implications, it would be difficult to do so: They are bombarded with information about political implications at every turn.

**Money** The permanent campaign is expensive. Polls, political consultants, and TV ads cost a great deal of money, and because candidates now have personal organizations, what economists call economies of scale are not so common as in earlier

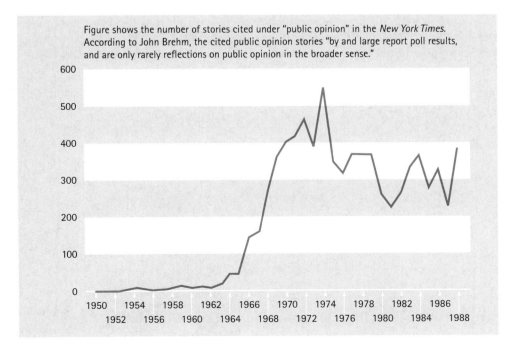

Figure shows the number of stories cited under "public opinion" in the *New York Times*. According to John Brehm, the cited public opinion stories "by and large report poll results, and are only rarely reflections on public opinion in the broader sense."

**Figure 1.3**

**Poll Coverage Exploded Between the Mid–1960s and Mid–1970s**

SOURCE: John Brehm, *The Phantom Respondents* (Ann Arbor, MI: University of Michigan Press, 1993), p. 4.

Figure 1.4

Today's Media
Conduct Their Own Polls

SOURCE: Data taken from Everett Carl Ladd
and John Benson, "The Growth of News Polls
in American Politics," in *Media Polls in
American Politics*, edited by Thomas E. Mann
and Gary R. Orren (Washington, DC:
Brookings, 1992), p. 23.

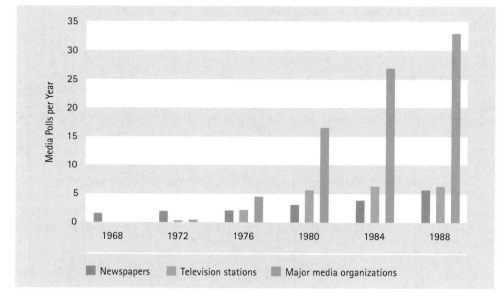

times. Thus the permanent campaign has greatly increased politicians' need for money. As Figure 1.5 shows, the total costs of election campaigns have increased dramatically in the past three decades. Campaigns for the House of Representatives, for example, were more than five times more expensive in 1996 than in 1976.[34]

Elections may occur every two or four or six years, but the quest for money is continuous. Nearly all governors serve four-year terms, but current estimates are that incumbents in large states must raise an average of $50,000 *every week of their term* to fund their campaign for reelection.[35] Similarly, U.S. senators serve six-year terms. The framers thought that such long terms would help to insulate senators from popular pressures and allow them to act more deliberately and independently than the members of the House, who serve two-year terms. But most contemporary observers believe that the Senate today is just as electorally sensitive as the House.[36] One reason is that Senate races are expensive; on average, senators must raise over $15,000 every week of their six-year term to run for reelection. Thus the effect of the six-year term has been partially offset by the constant search for money.

In recent years the scramble for money has led to a series of fund-raising scandals that have involved even public officials with long-standing reputations for honesty and integrity. In consequence, public interest groups have placed the issue of campaign

Figure 1.5

The Total Costs of
American Elections Have Increased
Dramatically in the Last Five Decades

SOURCE: Common Cause and respective volumes of Herbert E. Alexander, *Financing the 1951–1952* [and 1955–2000 vols.] *Election* (Washington, DC: CQ Press). *Note:* All figures have been adjusted for inflation in terms of 1999 CPI constant dollars.

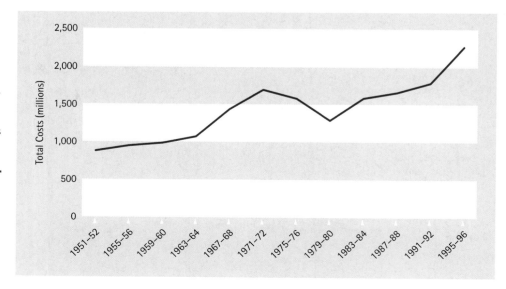

finance on the public agenda, but little has been done in recent years. We discuss the complicated issues associated with campaign finance in Chapters 10 and 11.

## Minorities and Elections

Once again we emphasize that to say that American democracy has moved in a popular direction *does not mean* that a majority of the people always govern. Elections by themselves do not guarantee that all citizens exert equal influence on the government. On the contrary, it is easy to show how special-interest groups and other numerical minorities influence elections and what their winners do. Factors that give minorities advantages include unequal participation, the nominating process, unequal campaign resources, and misinformed citizens.

**Voter Participation**  In nearly all elections, most people do *not* vote. Even in the 2000 presidential election, only 51 percent of the adult population voted. Turnout rates in other elections are much lower—in the single digits(!) in some local elections.

A single vote does not count for much, but collectively, the vote is an important political resource. Groups of people who vote at higher rates have more influence. For example, older people vote more frequently than the young or the poor.[37] Not surprisingly, programs for the elderly are much better funded than programs that serve the young and the needy. Turnout is not the only explanation, of course, but elected officials naturally tend to pay greater heed to the demands of frequent voters than to those of people who don't vote.

**Nominating Candidates**  Although primary elections were intended to enhance popular control, only party members can vote in many states, and turnout everywhere is much lower than in general elections. Those who vote in primaries are usually more involved and more committed than citizens who don't vote. Republican primary voters tend to be more conservative than the typical American, and Democratic primary voters tend to be more liberal. To win primary elections, candidates are tempted to appeal to the more extreme elements of their parties. As a result, elections

simulation

**How to Satisfy Aunt Martha**

**Turnout**
In 2000, despite massive get-out-the-vote efforts, barely more than half the electorate showed up at the polls. Political parties are always trying to activate more of their supporters to turn out and shift the balance of power in the election. *Why don't people vote?*

may give middle-of-the-road Americans a choice between two candidates neither of whom they may find very appealing.

**Campaign Resources** As we have noted, modern campaigns increasingly rely on expensive hired help: consultants, pollsters, and other campaign professionals. Higher-level campaigns that rely on TV advertising are especially expensive. Consequently, the first job nearly every candidate faces is raising money.

About a quarter of the adult population has ever given to a campaign, and a much smaller percentage regularly gives substantial amounts. Most fund raising is done by groups who typically have special political interests they wish to promote. Liberal and conservative groups, economic and environmental groups, women's groups, minority groups, or whatever—all have a perfectly legitimate right to participate in politics. But all have a point of view, usually one that is narrower than the point of view of the typical nonmember.

Moreover, even in today's technologically advanced world, campaigns require workers as well as money; this is particularly true of lower-level campaigns. Volunteers circulate petitions, stuff envelopes, knock on doors, make phone calls, stage rallies and other photo ops, and drive voters to the polls. To get volunteers, candidates may appeal to **single-issue voters,** people who care so deeply about some particular issue that a candidate's position on this one issue determines their vote. For example, many members of the National Rifle Association (NRA) are prepared to work against any candidate who supports gun control (Chapter 5). As a result, it has been difficult to pass laws regulating the sale of guns, despite support for the idea among a majority of voters. Pro-life and pro-choice activists are other familiar examples of single-issue voters. Candidates naturally give greater weight to the intense views of single-issue voters, from whom they recruit campaign workers.

**Uninformed or Misinformed Citizens** As we discuss in Chapter 5, most Americans are not highly attentive to politics. Politics often seems remote from people's everyday interests and concerns, and political controversies often are complicated and

**single-issue voter**
Voter who cares so deeply about some particular issue that a candidate's position on this one issue determines his or her vote.

**Local Politics**
Local races can rarely afford expensive television advertising rates. Here the father of candidate English volunteers his time. *Does a lack of media attention (and money to buy attention) mean that such races are unimportant?*

confusing. Moreover, nearly all of the players in politics present information and arguments that are biased; they are like opposing lawyers trying to win a lawsuit. Even the media exhibit well-known biases. Thus there are often opportunities to manipulate public opinion and elections.

## Majorities and Elections

Although single-issue voters and other kinds of special interests at times wield unequal influence, such groups lose much of their clout when a clear majority of the voters take a strong interest in a highly visible subject. In 1994 Congress approved a ban on assault weapons—despite the opposition of the NRA—once it became clear that most Americans opposed their unrestricted availability. And by the same token, acting in accordance with the moderate views of the American people, the Democratic Congresses of 1990–1994 did not pass the "Freedom of Choice Act," supported by pro-choice forces, nor did the Republican Congress of 1995–1996 adopt an amendment to outlaw abortion, as pro-life forces wished.

Moreover, majorities remain potentially powerful even when the public is uninformed about or unaware of an issue. Elected officials realize that the media spotlight might suddenly shine into what seemed to be a dark corner. Additionally, challengers pore over the incumbent's record, searching for unpopular votes cast, positions taken, or statements made. If found, such matters become campaign issues. Most of the time, incumbents think twice before taking actions in back rooms if those actions cannot be defended once the doors are opened.[38] And as we have noted, Bill Clinton signed an historic welfare reform bill about which he had serious doubts, because he knew a veto would have made welfare reform a major campaign issue.

Thus elected officials can take unpopular positions and still survive, because most voters are not single-issue voters. But elected officials cannot routinely take positions contrary to those of their constituents and expect to escape the wrath of the electorate indefinitely. Because leaders are never sure which potential issue will explode, they tend to be cautious in handling all of them. Hence the power of minorities is limited by the potential threat that the majority will become aroused. Ordinarily, majorities rule not so much by actively articulating their views as through the calculations of public officials who anticipate majority opinion long before it asserts itself.

### Section Summary

American politics and government are now well into the era of the permanent campaign. More than at any time in our past, the line between governing and electioneering has been erased. The permanent campaign arises from the huge number of elective offices and election days, the decay of traditional party organizations, the spread of primaries, technological advances in communications, the explosion of interest groups, the proliferation of polling, and the rising importance of money.

American politics is more open today than in the past, but that does not guarantee that it represents popular sentiments better. Political participation requires time, energy, and other resources, so some people have more opportunities to influence government than others. Still, majority sentiments always constrain the political process because of the possibility that an inactive majority may be aroused by some issue or condition.

## Reform?

The United States pays a price for the pervasiveness of its elections. Continuous electioneering creates a governmental system that is unattractive in many respects. Scandals—real and trumped up—are common; inefficiency and stalemate are widespread; important policy problems fester; and effective actions are delayed or compromised into ineffectiveness.[39]

Even though many citizens understandably are frustrated by American government, we should view proposals for radical reform cautiously. In particular, reforms often call for further movement toward popular democracy—more opportunities for constituencies to influence government, such as more elections (primaries, initiatives and referenda, recalls), more opportunities to exert popular pressure (open public meetings, electronic town halls), or more power for elected officials (oversight of independent boards and commissions). Americans apparently believe, with John Dewey, that "The cure for the ailments of democracy is more democracy."[40]

Such reforms overlook the tremendous popular pressure that political leaders are already under. Indeed, some scholars argue that popular influence on government may be part of the problem, not the solution.[41] Each public official answers to a somewhat different constituency. If all constituencies were similar, representatives would find it easier to reach agreement. But America is a diverse country, and the constituencies of elected officials reflect that diversity. People have conflicting interests and (even more important) conflicting values. Even if hundreds of officials were personally in agreement, which is unlikely, their views of governmental programs and policies often would conflict because they have an **electoral incentive**—the desire to be elected and reelected—to represent the views of the different constituencies that elect them.

**electoral incentive**
Desire to obtain or retain elected office.

Governmental decisions require agreement among many different public officials representing diverse constituencies. It is impossible to reach decisions without resolving differences generated by these constituencies. Unlike chief executives in the business world, presidents cannot fire members of Congress, governors cannot remove members of their state legislatures, and mayors cannot dismiss members of their city councils. Political leaders must either persuade their opponents or bargain for their support. Democratic politics resolves conflicts by negotiation, bargaining, and compromise.

With different constituencies, the electoral incentives of individual officials hinder their ability to work together. This being the case, reforms that shift American politics in a still more popular direction may worsen problems rather than improve them. If reforms are to be effective, they must take incentives into account. All too often, reformers forget that premise and substitute good intentions and rosy scenarios for realistic analyses. Accurate appraisals of reform require the kind of realistic, incentive-based institutional analysis that the framers of the Constitution provided us. Heeding their example, we try to provide this kind of analysis in the chapters that follow, and it is this kind of analysis that we ask from our readers (see the accompanying Democratic Dilemma).

## Benefits of an Electoral Democracy: A Pretty Good Government

As we mentioned earlier, an irony of the new American democracy is that although citizens have more opportunities than ever before to influence their government, Americans have been growing increasingly unhappy with it. In our view, a significant part of the sour national mood is difficult to justify on the basis of objective conditions. There is no denying that serious problems and unresolved conflicts exist, but there is more that is right with the United States than political commentary often suggests. Too often, critics apply unrealistic standards of evaluation.

An old maxim—frequently quoted by former President Clinton—states that "the best is the enemy of the good." Any policy or institution falls short when judged against some abstract standard of perfection. Perfection does not exist in the real world, but the wish for perfection in government and politics makes people unhappy

*Democratic Dilemma*

## Elections and Good Government

Popular political commentary often implies that democracy in the form of free elections leads automatically to efficient, effective government. If so, the trend toward more and more elections in the United States should lead to better and better government. But those assumptions are questionable. Robert Samuelson, a perceptive journalist, recently wrote this in a best-selling book:

> What aggravates popular frustration with politics—the sense of powerlessness to affect government—is the appearance that elected officials have become more, not less, important . . . Our political leaders have never been more exposed than now. The president is on national TV news almost daily. Live sessions of Congress, committee hearings, and important speeches are broadcast on C-Span. News coverage runs around the clock on CNN. Technology has made politics more visible and vocal; political leaders routinely pronounce themselves on a vast array of issues. And new technologies (constant opinion polls, focus groups, and call-in shows) provide more ways to gauge public opinion, or what passes for public opinion. Thus, technology creates the impression that our elected leaders have gained in power and can better represent the "people's views," when the opposite is true. Politicians' power has been diluted, and the explosion of various public opinions (often inconsistent) makes representing them more difficult.[a]

Samuelson's last sentence is a modern statement of a classic argument. Many thinkers about democracy have argued that there is a trade-off between responsive government and efficient government. A government that gives its citizens every opportunity to make their views known, and then carefully considers those views, is a government not likely to do anything very fast; indeed, it may experience gridlock when public opinion is divided. Conversely, they argue, a government that moves quickly and efficiently is likely to be a government that runs roughshod over the views of citizens who oppose its policies.

*What do you think?*
- *Is there a trade-off between responsive government and effective government?*
- *If so, what factors affect how much a government's responsiveness and effectiveness will conflict?*
- *Some critics believe that the gridlock of recent decades shows that the United States has gone too far in the direction of responsive government at the cost of effective government. Do you agree?*

[a]*The Good Life and Its Discontents* (New York: Random House, 1997), p. 194.

with their government and their leaders. The search for perfection causes harm when people abandon the "pretty good" for something worse. As the great American judge Learned Hand once commented, "even though counting heads is not an ideal way to govern, it is at least better than breaking them."[42]

If American politics and government are so blameworthy, why are the governments of so many new democracies adopting institutions similar to those found in the United States? And why, throughout history and continuing today, have so many people left family and country behind to start over in the United States? Historically, most countries have posted border guards to keep people in; the United States has them to keep people out!

Across the entire sweep of human history, most governments have been controlled by one or a few. Many were tyrannical: A government that did not murder and rob its subjects was about as good a government as people could hope for. Tragically, tyrannical governments are not just a matter of ancient history. Only a bare majority of the world's population today lives under governments that can reasonably be considered democratic, and in the twentieth century, governments have caused the deaths of 170 million people, *not including wars*.[43] In recent years Americans have watched in horror as civil war or genocide has erupted in Northern Ireland, Cambodia, Iraq, Azerbaijan, Bosnia, Rwanda, Burundi, Chechnya, Albania, Zaire, Kosovo, East Timor, and Sierra Leone. Official tyranny—and worse—remains a contemporary reality.

To be sure, Americans should not set too low a standard for their political life. No one would seriously argue that Americans should be satisfied just because their country has not dissolved into warring factions, as in the former Yugoslavia. But Americans should have realistic standards for evaluating their political system. Critics selectively cite statistics showing that the United States is worse than Germany in one respect, worse than Japan in another respect, worse than Sweden in some other respect, and

**Standing Firm**
This famous picture from the 1989 Tiananmen Square demonstrations high-lights the risks of opposing tyranny.

so on. But can one conclude with confidence that any other government of a large country works better? We think the answer is no. This judgment should not discourage us from continuing to strive for a better government, but it should remind us that we are striving for levels of achievement never yet attained by real governments responsible for large populations. Only when comparing the United States with other countries do we see that American democracy, for all its faults, has extraordinary capacities as well.

Defenders of democracy often cite Winston Churchill's remark that "democracy is the worst form of government except all those other forms that have been tried."[44] Churchill's observation applies with special force to the new American democracy, which carries this form of government toward its popular extreme. Citizens in the United States enjoy rights and privileges that citizens in other lands only dream of. Not only can American citizens vote more often, but Americans also can speak their minds more freely, find out more easily what their government is doing, and deal with a government less likely to discriminate against them on the basis of race, religion, gender, social status, sexual preference, or anything else.

Citizens of the United States have had a government that has a better record than most at protecting them against foreign aggression while usually avoiding unwise involvement in foreign conflicts. On average, citizens of the United States are wealthier than citizens of any other comparably large country. They are better housed, better fed, and better clothed. When compared with residents of most other countries, they enjoy better communications, a superior national transportation system, better medical services, and safer working conditions. Their physical environment is more protected against degradation. Even the large fiscal deficits that were such a political concern in the 1980s and 1990s compared favorably to the deficits of most other industrial countries.

Of course, the United States is not the best at everything. Economic inequality and poverty rates are higher in the United States than in countries with comparable living standards. More homeless people are visible on our city streets than in other industrialized countries—a sign that the safety net has gaping holes, although it may also be a sign that poor people in the United States move about more freely than the poor of other nations.[45] More people lack access to adequate medical care than in other devel-

comparative

**Comparing
Political Landscapes**

oped democracies. More people are murdered and more are imprisoned in the United States than in almost any other industrialized country. The distribution of income in the United States is more unequal than in other developed democracies. Just why the United States does poorly at some things and well at others will be considered in the pages that follow.

But although there is much to be learned from other countries, comparative analyses suggest that not much would be gained by substituting the institutions of any other country for the ones that the United States now has. Such comparisons reveal that the United States, for all its problems, has as good a government as exists anywhere, and a better one than most. Despite the dissatisfaction of many Americans with their government, they would be hard pressed to find a superior alternative.

In the chapters that follow, we trace the electoral theme of this chapter through the institutions and processes that make up American government, finishing with the policies that government produces. In the remainder of Part 1 we discuss the Constitution, the federal system, and the underlying cultural predispositions that provide the foundations for the country's political life. In Part 2 we discuss the people, groups, parties, and news media that constitute the elements of electoral politics. Part 3 looks closely at contemporary campaigns and elections. In Part 4 we turn to the central political institutions, Congress, the presidency, the bureaucracy, and the courts. In Part 5 we discuss civil liberties and civil rights, not solely as the foundations of democratic politics, but as rights and privileges that democratic politics regularly change. Finally, in Part 6 we discuss a broad range of important public policies, domestic and foreign.

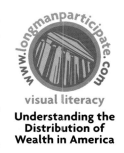

www.longmanparticipate.com

**visual literacy**

**Understanding the Distribution of Wealth in America**

## *Chapter Summary*

Elections are a more prominent part of democracy in America than in other countries because there are so many elective offices in the United States, because terms of office generally are shorter, and because Americans select candidates in primaries and vote directly on propositions as well. If free elections are the essence of democracy—government by the people—as democratic theorists believe, then politics in the United States is indisputably democratic.

Aristotle's classification of government types is still useful: government by the one, by the few (oligarchy), or by the many (democracy). In the latter half of the twentieth century the final type grew tremendously in importance. Some countries, such as the United Kingdom, favor a *responsible model* where citizens elect a government and then remain passive until the next round of elections. Some countries have a more *popular model* of government where elites are more responsive to public desires. The United States tends to fall in the latter category (although all governments are a mixture of the two models). Indeed, American democracy is more open to popular influence today than ever before. It is characterized by a permanent campaign. Changing technologies helped bring this situation about, especially developments in mass communications and public opinion polling. Institutional changes also contributed, especially the weakening of political parties, the proliferation of primary elections, and the separation of election days. Social changes, such as the explosion of organized interests, also played a role. And the increased need for money has contributed to the permanent campaign. Electoral considerations are never far from the minds of elected officials.

When balancing the costs and benefits of this movement toward a more popular democracy, it is not easy to decide which way the balance tips. Pervasive elections and electioneering change the way the government does business: It is more difficult to plan for the long run, and it seems harder to find acceptable compromises. Yet the advantages of more widespread participation are clear as well. The needs of once-excluded groups now are given at least some consideration. Citizens' concerns quickly become public issues. Imperfect as they are, American political institutions are still the envy of much of the world.

**On the Web**

The Democracy Network
www.dnet.org
An online voter guide with state-specific information. A project of the Center for Governmental Studies and the League of Women Voters.

The Federal Election Commission
www.fec.gov
This online portal of the FEC provides easy-to-use information regarding all aspects of elections—from electoral histories to campaign finance contributions.

Project Vote Smart
www.vote-smart.org
This richly informative site is supported by a nonpartisan group. It contains biographical histories, voting records, campaign finances and promises, and performance evaluations of elected officials and candidates.

## Key Terms

aristocracy, p. 11
constituency, p. 13
democracy, p. 11
direct democracy, p. 11
electoral incentive, p. 24
general election, p. 8
government, p. 9

initiative, p. 8
oligarchy, p. 11
permanent campaign, p. 14
popular model of democracy, p. 12
primary election, p. 7
proposition, p. 8
recall election, p. 7

referendum, p. 8
representative democracy, p. 11
responsible model of democracy, p. 12
single-issue voter, p. 22

## Suggested Readings

Blumenthal, Sidney. *The Permanent Campaign.* New York: Simon & Schuster, 1982. Describes the electioneering side of the new American democracy.

Chubb, John, and Paul Peterson, eds. *Can the Government Govern?* Washington, DC: Brookings, 1989. Collection of essays on problems of governing a democracy that is moving in the popular direction.

Cronin, Thomas. *Direct Democracy: The Politics of Initiative, Referendum, and Recall.* Cambridge, MA: Harvard University Press, 1989. The most up-to-date study of direct democracy in the United States. Takes a generally positive view.

Dahl, Robert. *Who Governs?* New Haven, CT: Yale University Press, 1961. Although it is a study of politics in New Haven, Connecticut, the book shows more generally how elections shape power and influence.

Downs, Anthony. *An Economic Theory of Democracy.* New York: Harper, 1957. Seminal theoretical discussion of how elections shape the activities of voters, candidates, parties, and interest groups.

Key, V. O., Jr. *Politics, Parties and Pressure Groups,* 5th ed. New York: Thomas Crowell, 1964. Dated but still useful text on parties and interest groups.

King, Anthony. *Running Scared: Why Politicians Spend More Time Campaigning Than Governing.* New York: Free Press, 1996. Provocative study by a British political scientist who shows how elections shape contemporary American politics.

Lowi, Theodore. *The End of Liberalism.* New York: Norton, 1969. Classic study of the way in which groups have gained power over government.

Mansbridge, Jane. *Beyond Adversary Democracy.* New York: Basic Books, 1980. Compares alternative understandings of democracy.

Marone, James A. *The Democratic Wish.* New York: Basic Books, 1990. Brilliant historical analysis that shows how Americans have long tried to cure the ills of democracy by extending citizen participation.

Schattschneider, E. E. *The Semi-Sovereign People.* New York: Holt, 1960. Classic analysis that explains why elections do not ensure equal political influence.

Stanley, Harold, and Richard Niemi. *Vital Statistics on American Politics,* 7th ed. Washington, DC: CQ Press, 1999. Indispensable source of facts and figures about American government and politics.

Tocqueville, Alexis de. *Democracy in America*, Vols. I and II, Philips Bradley, ed. New York: Knopf, 1945. Nineteenth-century French observer's insightful interpretation of the democratic experiment in the United States.

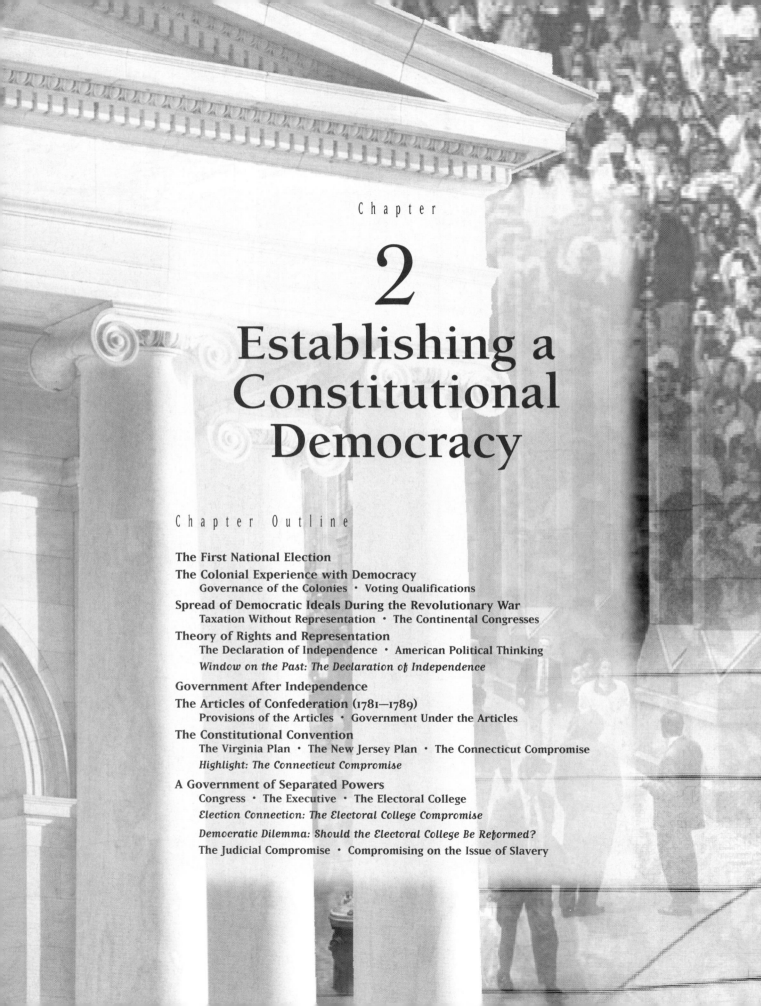

Chapter

# 2
# Establishing a Constitutional Democracy

Chapter Outline

Though the United States Constitution is revered today, it was subject to intense debate when presented to the voters for their approval in 1787. Proponents wanted a stronger national government that could resolve economic conflicts among states and negotiate more effectively with foreign countries. Opponents feared that a strong national government would lead to tyranny.

The debate over approval (ratification) of the document was particularly intense in the state of Virginia. Cried Patrick Henry, the eminent American patriot, "Before the meeting of the late Federal Convention at Philadelphia [where the Constitution was written] a general peace, and a universal tranquility prevailed in this country—but since that [meeting, people have become] exceedingly uneasy and disquieted." Escalating the rhetoric, Henry shouted: "I conceive the republic to be in extreme danger. Here is a revolution as radical as that which separated us from Great Britain. Our rights and privileges are endangered, and the sovereignty of the States relinquished. The rights of conscience, trial by jury, liberty of the press—all pretensions to human rights and privileges are rendered insecure, if not lost."[1]

When fellow Virginian James Madison heard these words, he privately questioned Henry's motives. Madison was the one person who, more than any other, had designed the Constitution, and he was concerned that Henry's opposition could doom its ratification. Writing to a friend, he suggested that Henry favored the creation of a separate southern nation: "I have for some time considered him as driving at a Southern Confederacy."[2]

Publicly, Madison argued that the proposed government, far from endangering the people's freedom, would protect them from a tyranny imposed by narrow, organized groups opposed to the general welfare of the people, groups that in Madison's day were called factions. "Among the numerous advantages promised by a well-constructed Union," Madison argued, "none deserves to be more accurately developed than its tendency to break and control the violence of faction." A majority faction—a group big enough to encompass a majority of the people but one with objectives harmful to the people as a whole—was especially dangerous, Madison believed. Such a faction was treacherous because it could easily suppress the opinions of minority groups.

Today, people in the United States and in other countries express much the same concern when they worry that a majority ethnic or religious group may suppress the rights of minorities. Madison argued that the Constitution would help solve this problem. It would prevent majority factions by dividing power between the state and national governments. It would also divide national power among Congress, the president, and the courts, making it extremely difficult for any branch of government to overpower the rest. Madison thought that the very size of the country was a "most palpable advantage" in keeping dangerous factions from getting too much power: "The influence of factious leaders may kindle a flame within their particular states, but will be unable to spread a general conflagration through the other states." Swayed by the arguments of Madison and his allies, the delegates to the Virginia convention rejected Henry's argument and ratified the Constitution.[3]

⭐ THE CONVENTION DELEGATES DESIGNED THE CONSTITUTION to appeal to the voters asked to select representatives who ratified it. This meant that the document had to be based on well-known political theories and on the colonial experience. In this chapter we review the circumstances that led to the Constitution's writing and ratification, answering the following questions:

- What experiences did colonists have with democracy prior to independence?
- What kinds of democratic ideals were spread during the Revolution?
- What was government like under the Articles of Confederation?
- How did the Constitutional Convention come about, and what happened there?
- What kind of government did the Constitution create, and how well has it withstood the test of time?

## The First National Election

The very foundation of the U.S. government is the result of elections held at about the same time in the 13 original states. The nation's basic governing document, the **Constitution,** was drafted in the summer of 1787 at a convention held in Philadelphia. The Constitution took effect only after state ratifying conventions in 9 of the original 13 states approved it.

Voters in 1787 were receptive to constitutional reform because the country's mood had lost much of the idealism that had unified it during the Revolutionary War. Persistent economic and political difficulties had also eroded the new nation's confidence. Many blamed the situation on the **Articles of Confederation,** the first basic governing document of the United States (1781–1789) and forerunner to the Constitution.

But even though the Articles of Confederation were unpopular, ratification of the Constitution was hardly inevitable. Victory was achieved only because the **Federalists,** those who wrote and campaigned for ratification of the Constitution, provided strong leadership, mobilized voters, sidestepped obstacles, and crafted powerful arguments in favor of ratification.

The Federalists offered an anxious public not only a new constitution but also the return of its revolutionary leader, General George Washington. Washington presided over the Constitutional Convention and was expected to become the first president. Other prominent Revolutionary War figures also attended the convention. Benjamin Franklin, the diplomat who had secured France as an ally and was now 81 years old, took part as a quiet-spoken senior citizen. James Madison, a key member of the Continental Congress, provided intellectual leadership. Alexander Hamilton, a hero at the decisive battle of Yorktown, emerged as a rising star during the New York ratification campaign.

The **Anti-Federalists,** those who opposed ratification of the Constitution, lacked a national leader. The one man who could have galvanized the opposition, Thomas Jefferson, author of the Declaration of Independence, was now serving in Paris as Minister to France. Though Jefferson was suspicious of centralized power and expressed doubts about the absence of a Bill of Rights, he admitted to his friend Madison that the document deserved ratification.

The Anti-Federalists thought the Constitution would be defeated if it was voted down in any of the 13 state legislatures. However, they were taken by surprise. The convention delegates, instead of following the rules for constitutional change set forth in the Articles of Confederation, made up new ones. Whereas the Articles said that any constitutional change required approval of the existing Congress as well as the consent of all 13 state legislatures, the new Constitution contained a provision saying it

**Constitution**
Basic governing document of the United States.

**Articles of Confederation**
The first (1781–1789) basic governing document of the United States and forerunner to the Constitution.

**Federalists**
Those who wrote and campaigned on behalf of ratification of the Constitution.

**Anti-Federalists**
Those who opposed ratification of the Constitution.

**Table 2.1**

**Voting of Delegates at Constitutional Ratifying Conventions**
Article VII of the Constitution provided that "The Ratifications of the Conventions of nine States, shall be sufficient for the Establishment of this Constitution."

| State | Date | "Yes" Votes | "No" Votes |
|---|---|---|---|
| Delaware | Dec. 7, 1787 | 30 | 0 |
| Pennsylvania | Dec. 11, 1787 | 46 | 23 |
| New Jersey | Dec. 18, 1787 | 38 | 0 |
| Georgia | Jan. 2, 1788 | 26 | 0 |
| Connecticut | Jan. 9, 1788 | 128 | 40 |
| Massachusetts | Feb. 6, 1788 | 187 | 168 |
| Maryland | Apr. 26, 1788 | 63 | 11 |
| South Carolina | May 23, 1788 | 149 | 73 |
| New Hampshire | June 21, 1788 | 57 | 47 |
| Virginia | June 25, 1788 | 89 | 79 |
| New York | July 26, 1788 | 30 | 27 |
| North Carolina | Nov. 21, 1789 | 194 | 77 |
| Rhode Island | May 29, 1790 | 34 | 32 |

SOURCE: Lauren Bahr and Bernard Johnson, ed., *Collier's Encyclopedia*, Vol. 7 (New York: P. F. Collier, 1992), p. 239.

would take effect as soon as 9 states ratified the document. Ratification was to be decided not by state legislatures but by specially elected delegates attending state ratifying conventions.

With energy and organization on their side, the Federalists won the first rounds in the ratification struggle easily. Conventions in 4 of the smaller states—Delaware, New Jersey, Georgia, and Connecticut—ratified the document by an overwhelming vote within four months of its signing in September 1787.[4] With Ben Franklin's prestige and some strong-arm tactics, Pennsylvania also quickly approved. Massachusetts signed on as well, after getting Federalists to promise to add a Bill of Rights. By the end of 1788, Federalists had persuaded 11 of the 13 states to ratify the Constitution, and George Washington was elected president in February 1789. North Carolina ratified later that year. Rhode Island, which had refused even to send delegates to the Constitutional Convention, finally gave its grudging approval on May 29, 1790 (see Table 2.1).

At the time the Constitution was adopted, the United States was not a modern democracy. For example, only male property owners ("freeholders") could vote in the election of delegates to the ratifying convention. Yet the provisions in the Constitution had to win the approval of a wide variety of these voters. Those who wrote the Constitution had to be sensitive to regional differences, immediate governmental needs, and inherited political traditions. In the next section we discuss the inherited political traditions—those ideas and institutions that had shaped politics during the colonial and Revolutionary War periods. Later in this chapter, we shall show how the Constitution is grounded in these traditions.

## The Colonial Experience with Democracy

Though the United States would become the world's first large, stable democracy, no sign of democracy is to be found in the first British plans for government in America. (See Figure 2.1 for the dates of important steps toward democratization.) At the time when Queen Elizabeth encouraged Sir Walter Raleigh to explore America in 1584,

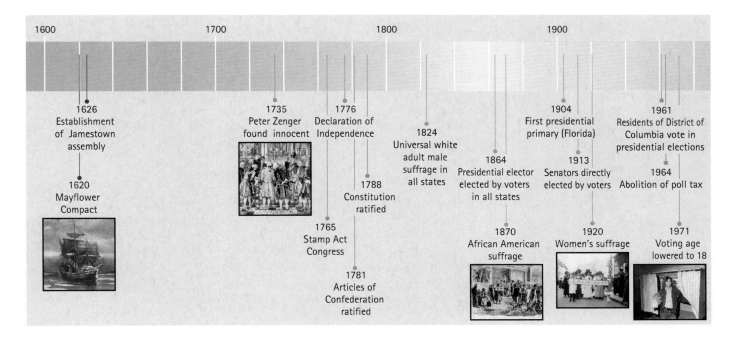

**Figure 2.1**

**Key Points in the Democratization of the United States**
*Which three points do you think are especially key?*

British rulers claimed to govern by **divine right,** a doctrine stating that God selects the sovereign for the people. Queen Elizabeth delegated her authority over the Colony of Virginia to Raleigh. But just a few years after the first permanent settlement in Jamestown, Virginia, the colonists forced the formation of a representative assembly. Relations between the settlers and the company that owned Raleigh's charter grew so strained that King James, who had succeeded Elizabeth in 1603, withdrew the charter. Virginia became a **royal colony,** one governed by the king's representative with the assembly's advice.

A small group of religious dissenters, now remembered as the Pilgrims, intended to sail to Virginia in 1620. After their ship, the *Mayflower*, was blown off course and arrived in what is now Provincetown, Massachusetts, the Pilgrims found that they lacked a clear governmental framework. The Pilgrims, rejecting the divine right of kings, believed that individuals should decide both religious and political matters for themselves. Their first political decision is still revered as the very beginning of the democratic experiment in America. Before leaving the ship the Pilgrims signed the **Mayflower Compact,** the first document in colonial America in which the people gave their expressed consent to be governed. The Pilgrims promised to "covenant and combine ourselves together into a civil Body Politick, for our better Ordering and Preservation." The principle that government resulted from the people's consent was thus established from the very beginning of colonial settlement.[5]

**divine right**
Doctrine that says God selects the sovereign for the people.

**royal colony**
Colony governed by the king's representative with the advice of an elected assembly. See *proprietary colony.*

**Mayflower Compact**
First document in colonial America in which the people gave their expressed consent to be governed.

## Governance of the Colonies

As European settlement spread across the eastern shores of the North American continent, so did issues of politics and governance. Many colonies were initially organized as **proprietary colonies,** governed either by a prominent English noble or by a company. Settlements organized by companies, such as the Jamestown colony, were founded almost exclusively for economic gain, including the search for gold. But several of the most successful colonies were, like the Pilgrims' settlement in Massachusetts and the Maryland colony established for Catholics by Lord Baltimore, founded as places for the practice of religious beliefs. The more economically motivated of the proprietary colonies often ran into political difficulties and were eventually reorganized as royal colonies. On the eve of the Revolution, 9 of the 13 had become royal colonies.

In both proprietary and royal colonies, power was divided between the governor and a two-chamber legislature. The **colonial assembly** was the lower legislative

**proprietary colony**
Colony governed either by a prominent English noble or by a company. See *royal colony.*

**colonial assembly**
Lower legislative chamber elected by male property owners in a colony.

Many European monarchs claimed that the very fact that they were the rulers was evidence that God wanted it that way.

**colonial council**
Upper legislative chamber whose members were appointed by British officials upon the recommendation of the governor.

**patronage**
Appointing individuals to public office in exchange for their political support. Widely practiced in the eighteenth and nineteenth centuries and continues to present day.

www.longmanparticipate.com

**participation**

**Democracy and the Internet**

chamber elected by male property owners in the colony. The **colonial council** was the upper legislative chamber appointed by British officials, upon the recommendation of the governor. Governors were appointed by either the proprietor or the king.

Governors could veto any legislation passed by the legislature, but usually, instead of vetoing legislation, they maintained support in the assembly by means of their **patronage** power—the power to hand out jobs and benefits. Governors appointed their political supporters as sheriffs, judges, justices of the peace, militia officers, magistrates, and clerks. In Massachusetts, for example, 71 percent of the members of the 1763 assembly were simultaneously justices of the peace, giving "the Governors vast Influence."[6]

Though the governors' patronage influenced colonial assemblies, the assemblies had the power to levy taxes, and they used this authority to achieve broader influence, often obtaining financial control of the salaries of the governor and his appointed officials.[7] In most cases, members elected to assemblies were substantial community members. For example, Thomas Jefferson won both public respect and election to the Virginia assembly after persuading the farmers of his community to work together and clear the Rivanna River, making it navigable for their common benefit.[8] As the power of the elected colonial assemblies grew, the colonial councils appointed by the governors lost position and prestige, gradually becoming little more than advisory bodies.

## Voting Qualifications

If the assemblies were gaining control over colonial affairs, this did not mean they were democratic in the modern sense of the word. From the very beginning, women, slaves, and indentured servants were excluded from the voting rolls, as Table 2.2 illustrates. Even male white voters usually had to meet certain property qualifications: In Virginia they had to own 25 acres and a house. In Maryland and Pennsylvania, voters needed to be worth 50 acres or 40 pounds. By 1750 these qualifications disenfranchised as much as one-quarter to one-half of the male population.[9]

**Table 2.2**

**Voting Qualifications by Colony at the Time of the Revolution**
*Despite the restrictions on who was eligible to vote, can elections held in the colonies be said to have been democratic in any way? In your opinion, who must be eligible to vote if a country is to qualify as a democracy?*

| Colony | Qualifications |
|---|---|
| Massachusetts | Male, 21 years old, property owner |
| New Hampshire | Male, 21, except paupers |
| Rhode Island | Male, 21, debt-free |
| Connecticut | Male, 21, property owner, civil in conversation |
| New York | Male, 21, property owner or renter, six months residence |
| New Jersey | Male, 21, one year residence |
| Pennsylvania | Male, 21, taxpayer, two years residence |
| Virginia | Male, 21, property owner |
| Maryland | Male, 21, property owner, one year residence |
| North Carolina | Male, 21, property owner, one year residence |
| South Carolina | Male, 21, white, taxpayer, property owner, two years residence |
| Georgia | Male, 21, taxpayer, six months residence |

SOURCES: Robert J. Dinkin, *Voting in Revolutionary America: A Study of Elections in the Original Thirteen States, 1776–1789* (Westport, CT: Greenwood Press, 1982); Robert J. Dinkin, *Voting in Provincial America: A Study of Elections in the Thirteen Colonies, 1689–1776* (Westport, CT: Greenwood Press, 1977).

## Section Summary

The foundations for the American democratic experiment were established during the colonial era. Signed in 1620, the Mayflower Compact was the first document to apply the principle that government ruled by the consent of the governed. Although in many colonies suffrage was restricted to male property owners, elections made a difference. Elected colonial assemblies acquired the power to tax and spend. Further, colonial leaders developed the skills necessary to bargain with one another and build public support for common objectives.

## Spread of Democratic Ideals During the Revolutionary War

The democratic practices that began during the colonial period were reinforced by the struggle for independence.[10] Liberties that the colonists had taken for granted suddenly had to be fearlessly defended against the power of the king. The revolutionary struggle began with opposition to a tax, swelled into a question of rights and representation, and finally led to a Declaration of Independence cast in language that would shape American politics for centuries to come.

### Taxation Without Representation

Though the revolutionary movement would eventually become a struggle for citizen rights and liberties, it began as a tax revolt. Because British military costs were rising, the British government decided to ask the colonists to pay the cost of keeping troops in the colonies; these troops were to defend against potential attacks by both Indian tribes and French and Spanish soldiers. In 1765, the British government announced it intended to impose a **stamp tax,** which required that people purchase a small stamp to be affixed to pamphlets, playing cards, dice, newspapers, marriage licenses, and other legal documents. To the British, the stamp tax seemed perfectly reasonable, especially in that colonial taxes were lower than those the British themselves paid. But to the colonists, who had never before paid a direct tax, it was an outrageous imposition by King George III on a free people.

Colonial leaders opposed what they viewed as **taxation without representation,** the levying of taxes by a government in which the people are not represented by their own elected officials. To organize their protest, 9 colonies sent delegates to a **Stamp Act Congress,** which became the first political organization that brought together leaders from throughout the colonies.

The Stamp Act Congress gave clear expression to the American demand for representative government. One of its resolutions boldly proclaimed "that the only Representatives of the People of these Colonies are Persons chosen therein by themselves, and that no Taxes . . . can be Constitutionally imposed on them, but by their respective Legislature."[11] In Boston a group of citizens calling themselves the "Sons of Liberty" decided to enforce the resolutions of the Stamp Act Congress. They hung in effigy the city's proposed tax collector and then looted his home—and that of the lieutenant governor for good measure. As violence spread throughout the colonies, tax collectors resigned their positions, others refused to take their places, and colonial assemblies banned the importation of English goods, making homespun clothes fashionable. Patrick Henry, who was one of the more outspoken members of the Virginia assembly (and who later became an Anti-Federalist), shouted, "Caesar had his Brutus; Charles the First his Cromwell; and George the Third ['Treason!' cried the speaker of the assembly]—*may profit by their example. If this be treason, make the most of it.*" In the face of a tax revolt inspired by rhetoric that compared King George with rulers who were overthrown and killed, the Stamp Act became unenforceable, and within a year Parliament repealed the legislation.[12]

The British ignored the American demands for representation. They also unwisely replaced the stamp tax with a tax on tea, arousing passions even further. Colonists were urged on by antitax groups and such leaders as John Hancock and Samuel

One of the infamous revenue stamps that fired colonists' opposition to the tax imposed on the American people by the Stamp Act of 1765. This particular two-pence stamp appeared on an almanac. *Why were many Patriots so opposed to this tax? Were they correct in saying it was unfair?*

**stamp tax**
Passed by Parliament in 1765, it required people in the colonies to purchase a small stamp to be affixed to legal and other documents.

**taxation without representation**
Levying of taxes by a government in which the people are not represented by their own elected officials.

**Stamp Act Congress**
A meeting in 1765 of delegates from 9 colonies to oppose the Stamp Act; the first political organization that brought leaders from several colonies together for a common purpose.

**Patriots**
Political group defending colonial American liberties against British infringements.

Adams, who began calling themselves **Patriots,** a political group defending American liberties against British infringements. In 1773 many Patriots organized the Boston Tea Party, a nighttime foray in which protesters disguised as American Indians dumped chests of tea into the city's harbor. Outraged at such law-breaking, Parliament punished the Bostonians by shutting down democratic institutions in the Massachusetts colony. It withdrew the colony's charter, closed its colonial assembly, banned town meetings, blockaded the Boston harbor, and strengthened the armed garrison stationed in the city.

### The Continental Congresses

**First Continental Congress**
The first quasi-governmental institution that spoke for nearly all the colonies (1774).

The Patriots responded by calling, in 1774, the **First Continental Congress,** the first quasi-governmental institution that spoke for nearly all the colonies. Attended by delegates from 12 of the colonies, the Continental Congress issued a statement of rights and called for a boycott of British goods, a measure the Patriots hoped would hurt the British economy. In Massachusetts, Patriots assembled guns and trained volunteers in military exercises.

To put down the rising insurrection, British soldiers marched out of Boston harbor on April 19, 1775, in search of weapons hidden in the nearby countryside. Warned by Paul Revere that the British redcoats were approaching, 600 Patriots at Concord fired shots that Ralph Waldo Emerson would later claim were "heard round the world." Certainly, word of the shots spread throughout the colonies, even to the Virginia assembly, where Patrick Henry cried, "Give me liberty, or give me death." Delegates from all 13 colonies soon journeyed to Philadelphia to participate in the **Second Continental Congress,** the political authority that, beginning in 1775, directed the struggle for independence. On July 4, 1776, the Continental Congress proclaimed a **Declaration of Independence,** the document asserting the political independence of the United States of America from Great Britain. For seven long years the Patriots valiantly fought the British soldiers. The **Tories,** colonists who opposed independence, lost their property and were imprisoned or chased from the colonies— some 80,000 fled to London, Nova Scotia, or the West Indies. In 1783 the British recognized American independence in the Treaty of Paris.

**Second Continental Congress**
Political authority that directed the struggle for independence beginning in 1775.

**Declaration of Independence**
Document signed in 1776 declaring the United States to be a country independent of Great Britain.

**Tories**
Those colonists who opposed independence from Great Britain.

## Theory of Rights and Representation

The democratic experiment had officially begun, with the new nation committing itself to government by the people. Americans transformed colonial practice into a political doctrine stating that if governments are to be legitimate, they must be headed by leaders who have been chosen in elections.

### The Declaration of Independence

No single document better expresses the democratic spirit that animates American politics than the Declaration of Independence. Written mainly by Thomas Jefferson, the document both denounced King George III and expressed the country's commitment to certain democratic truths. The Declaration asserts that God gave people the rights to "life, liberty, and the pursuit of happiness." To preserve those rights, the people form a government. But the people's consent is given on the condition that the ruler safeguard these inalienable rights. If a ruler violates these rights, the people may and should form a new government.

### American Political Thinking

The Declaration of Independence "epitomizes and summarizes" a train of political thought that originated in England.[13] By the time of the revolution, political thinkers who influenced the Patriots had long discarded the notion that kings had a God-given right to rule. In place of divine right stood three principles:

**The Declaration of Independence**

*The following selection comes from the Declaration of Independence. Although the document later criticized King George in specific terms, it began with a summary of what the colonists believed were democratic truths.*

We hold these truths to be self evident, that all men are created equal, that they are endowed by their Creator with certain unalienable Rights, that among these are Life, Liberty, and the Pursuit of Happiness. That to secure these rights, Governments are instituted among Men, deriving their just powers from the consent of the governed. That whenever any form of government becomes destructive of these ends, it is the Right of the people to alter or abolish it, and to institute new Government, laying its foundation on such principles and organizing its powers in such form as to them shall seem most likely to effect their Safety and Happiness. . . .

[W]hen a long train of abuses and usurpations, pursuing invariably the same Object evinces a design to reduce them under absolute Despotism, it is their right, it is their duty, to throw off such Government and to provide new Guards for their future security. . . .

*What do you think?*

- *Why did the writers of the Declaration of Independence include these "truths"?*
- *Why did they not just criticize the king?*

SOURCE: Declaration of Independence.

1. Government arises from the consent of the governed.
2. Power should be divided among separate institutions.
3. Citizen rights must be protected.

Each of these principles would shape the writing of the Constitution.

**Consent of the Governed** As early as 1651, Thomas Hobbes, England's greatest political theorist, said that kings governed not by divine right but by the consent of the governed. People form a government because, without a government, they live in a state of nature in which there is a "war of all against all." Without a government, everyone must resort to violence simply to avoid being a victim. Life becomes "nasty, brutish and short." Hobbes argued that only a sovereign king with absolute power can prevent the war of all against all. If power is divided among more than one person, conflict among them becomes inevitable.[14] As a result, people consent to be governed by one all-powerful ruler.

**Separated Power** Hobbes was ruthlessly coherent. Accept his premise that individuals are selfish and shortsighted, and his conclusion that the people readily consent to be ruled by an absolute sovereign seems almost inevitable. But the English, more pragmatic than consistent, shunned Hobbes's ruthless defense of absolute kingly power. Instead, John Locke's ideas became popular. Locke agreed with Hobbes that government arises from the consent of the people, but Locke did not think it was necessary for this power to be unified in the hands of one absolute and all-powerful king.[15] Instead, Locke argued that governmental power took several different forms, each requiring a different institution. A country's founders should create a **separation of powers,** a system of government in which different institutions exercise the various components of governmental power. Locke thought each institution should be constituted as follows:

1. *Legislative power*, the making of law, to be exercised by an assembly with two chambers, the upper chamber consisting of the aristocracy and the lower chamber chosen by the people.
2. *Executive power*, the enforcement of law, to be exercised by a single person, often a king.

**separation of powers**
A system of government in which different institutions exercise different components of governmental power.

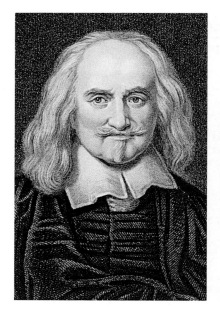

Thomas Hobbes (1588–1679) thought that humans are by nature warlike and selfish. His treatise *Leviathan* held that the only way to maintain human society was for individuals to consent to rule by a single, all-powerful leader or government. *How did Locke modify Hobbes's theory?*

Nearly 60 years after Locke's writings, the French philosopher Charles de Secondat, Baron de Montesquieu, added a third institution:

3. *Judicial power*, the application of law to particular situations, exercised by independent judges.

Great political theorists often come to conclusions that differ but little from existing governmental practice. So it was with Locke, who set forth a theory that closely resembled English government. England had a legislature or parliament consisting of two chambers: the House of Lords (representing the aristocracy) and the House of Commons (representing the people). Executive power was exercised by the king. The House of Lords appointed the judges.

Cynics have said that the English discovered Locke's wisdom before he set it down on paper. More accurately, Locke's genius consisted of making theoretical sense of English practice, giving the English a way of thinking about a government that had evolved haphazardly over many centuries.

**A More Participatory Democracy** Not long after Locke wrote, British practice changed. Power, instead of being separated among the three branches, was concentrated in a small group of ministers drawn from Parliament but appointed by the king. The system was held together more by patronage and corruption than by a balance of power among separated institutions.[16]

This patronage-based system provoked intense opposition from a group known as **Whigs,** who developed a counter-theory of citizen rights and representation. The most important political thinker among the Whigs was James Harrington. In place of parliamentary control over a large nation, Harrington favored small self-governing republics (small cities governed by virtuous citizen-leaders), each of which would pro-

**Whigs**
Political opposition in eighteenth-century England that developed a theory of rights and representation.

tect the freedoms of its own citizens. In place of patronage and connections, he called for the election of virtuous citizens for short periods of time. In place of an aristocracy of birth, he said ordinary citizens should choose leaders from the most noble among them.[17]

Still, Harrington and other Whigs were not modern-day democrats. Although they advanced a more participatory doctrine of rights and representation than previous theorists, they were of the opinion that only male property owners had the necessary virtues to be good citizens. Few philosophers took the time to explain why women could not also serve as good citizens. Not everyone was as frank as the philosopher and poet Alexander Pope, who blithely observed that "Most women have no characters at all." But such views were so widespread that English author Mary Wollstonecraft, writing in the same year the Constitution was drafted, was moved to lament, "It would be an endless task to trace the variety of meannesses, cares, and sorrows into which women are plunged by the prevailing opinion that they were created rather to feel than reason."[18]

Only many years later would the theory of rights and representation come to include women, the propertyless, former slaves, and other minorities.

**Colonial Interpretation of Whig Theory** Whig criticism of the British government made sense to many American colonists. The rough equality of colonial America stood in sharp contrast to the court intrigues in London. The rising colonial leaders thought of themselves as a natural aristocracy distinct from the inherited nobility in Britain. The more Parliament imposed taxes and interfered in colonial affairs, the more apparent became English corruption. The more the English government insisted on the ultimate sovereignty of the king, the more obvious it became to Americans that taxation without representation was illegitimate.

The Whig theory of rights and representation was explicated forcefully in *Common Sense,* written by Thomas Paine.[19] The book, which was widely read by colonial Americans in the months before the Declaration of Independence, declared kingship to be "the most bare-faced falsity ever imposed on mankind." Instead of contributing to peace, as Hobbes had said, a hereditary monarchy "makes against it." Peaceful government is better achieved by representatives "who . . . have the same concerns at stake" as the people. If elections were frequent, representatives would establish a "common interest with every part of the community."

SECTION SUMMARY

The American war for independence generated intense discussion of many philosophical ideas by the colonists. Concern about taxation without representation and other issues led the Continental Congress to incorporate into its Declaration of Independence the political theories of John Locke and the British Whigs. These concepts, including the principles that government arises from the consent of the governed, that governmental power should be divided, and that the rights of the people should be protected, later shaped the writing of the Constitution.

## Government After Independence

The Patriots in America gave voice to these participatory ideals during the 7 years they fought for independence from England. During the war, the colonies, now calling themselves "states," constructed governments of their own. For the most part, the 13 new states kept their colonial institutions much as they were, except "with Parliament and the King left out."[20] But the pace of democratization began to accelerate. Eight of the 13 states eased the property qualifications for voters, and 5 lowered them for candidates for the lower house of the state legislature.[21] The percentage of state legislators who had great wealth declined, giving new political opportunities to those from more

**Figure 2.2**

**The Wealthy in State Legislatures**
The percentage of wealthy legislators in state legislatures declined during and after the Revolution. *Do you think people are better represented by those of similar wealth? Why or why not?*

SOURCE: Calculated from Willi Paul Adams, *The First American Constitutions: Republican Ideology and the Making of the State Constitutions in the Revolutionary Era* (Chapel Hill: University of North Carolina Press, 1980), pp. 295–311.

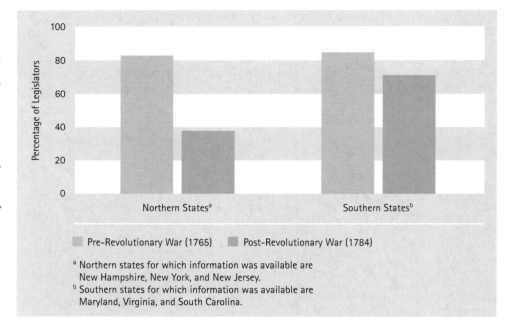

a Northern states for which information was available are New Hampshire, New York, and New Jersey.
b Southern states for which information was available are Maryland, Virginia, and South Carolina.

modest backgrounds (see Figure 2.2). Ten states required that governors be elected annually, and 6 limited the number of terms they could serve.[22]

Some believed that the Whig theory of the rights of man should apply to women. In a letter to her Patriot husband, Abigail Adams proposed giving women their rights and liberties as well: "In the new code of laws . . . I desire you would remember the ladies, and be more generous and favorable to them than your ancestors. . . . If . . . attention is not paid to the ladies we are determined to foment a rebellion, and will not hold ourselves bound by any laws in which we have no voice, or representation." But many of those who espoused Whig theory were unwilling to come to terms with all of its implications. Even Abigail Adams's husband, John, who later became the nation's second president, argued against making any changes in voting qualifications. If changes are made, "there will be no end of it," he said. "Women will demand a vote; lads from twelve to twenty-one will think their rights not enough attended to; and every man, who has not a farthing, will demand an equal voice."[23]

Some women did vote in eighteenth-century America. The New Jersey constitution failed to specify the sex of eligible voters, so female property holders in this state actually had the right to vote between 1776 and 1807, after which the state constitution was amended. New Jersey women did not vote again for over a hundred years. *How did the Constitution facilitate the gradual extension of the right to vote?*

# The Articles of Confederation (1781–1789)

The new country needed, above all, a sense of national unity. In one of its more inspired decisions, the Second Continental Congress helped bring the nation together by appointing George Washington, a Virginia plantation owner, as commander of a continental army—even though most soldiers initially came from northern colonies. But although the Continental Congress was prompt to take the needed military steps, reaching constitutional decisions took much longer. The idea of creating a national government was so foreign to the colonial experience that it took the Continental Congress nearly five years after declaring independence to write and win ratification for the country's first constitution, the Articles of Confederation. In the meantime, the Continental Congress did its best to govern by means of its own cumbersome procedures.

## Provisions of the Articles

Ratified in 1781, the Articles of Confederation amounted, in its own words, to little more than a "firm league of friendship" in which "each state retains its sovereignty, freedom and independence." The Articles granted the Continental Congress only limited powers. Although it could declare war, it could raise an army only by requesting states to muster their forces. Congress could not tax citizens directly; instead, it had to rely on voluntary contributions from the states. The Continental Congress could coin money, but it could not prevent states from also doing so. As a result, the country was flooded with many different currencies. Congress could negotiate tariffs with other countries, but so could each state. Most significant, Congress could not prevent states from interfering with interstate commerce. In fact, states imposed trade barriers on one another. New York, for example, taxed New Jersey cabbage and Connecticut firewood.[24]

Members of the Continental Congress were elected annually by state legislatures. Each state, no matter how large or small, was equally represented. On all important issues, a super-majority of 9 states (out of 13) had to agree before action could be taken.

The Articles of Confederation did not create a system of divided powers along the lines Locke had envisioned. Instead, the Continental Congress wielded all national powers, such as they were. There was no independent executive. A congressional Committee of the States headed by the president of the committee could make decisions between meetings of the Continental Congress, but this was an unwieldy committee because each state had representation. Nine of the 13 delegates had to agree before the committee could take action. Judicial functions were left to the states, except that disputes between states were settled by ad hoc committees of judges selected by Congress. The Articles could be amended by Congress only with the approval of all the state legislatures.

## Government Under the Articles

The unsatisfactory quality of the Articles became evident almost immediately. Virginia delegate James Madison came to see the need for a new constitution when he found it impossible, as a member of the Continental Congress, to keep states from issuing their own money. Trade among the states was impeded by constant quarrels over the relative worth of the coins of New York, Pennsylvania, and Virginia.

In addition to these trade difficulties, events were making it clear that the Articles had difficulty even keeping the peace. **Shays's Rebellion,** an uprising in western Massachusetts in 1786 led by revolutionary war captain Daniel Shays, was especially disruptive. A group of impoverished, back-country farmers, unable to pay their taxes or mortgages, tried to intimidate the courts into forgiving their debts. Because it took months to suppress the rebellion, many prominent leaders felt that state governments were too weak. Most embarrassing, a group of ex-soldiers from the continental army descended on Congress in 1783, demanding their rightful back pay. Members of the

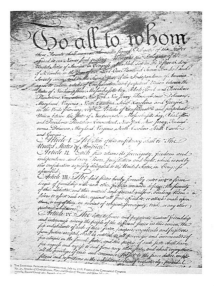

The Articles of Confederation, proposed in 1775, were finally ratified in 1781— eight years before the Constitution. Those eight years were marked by government instability. *How does the Constitution differ from the Articles of Confederation?*

**Shays's Rebellion**
Uprising in western Massachusetts in 1786 led by Revolutionary War captain Daniel Shays.

Scuffles broke out in western Massachusetts during Shays's Rebellion, when poor farmers and Revolutionary War veterans joined in an uprising. *How did this rebellion influence the writing of the Constitution?*

## Figure 2.3

**Map of Competing Claims**
This map shows only some of the competing claims being made in North America in 1787. Because the British had a superior navy, the United States was, in a sense, surrounded by foreign powers. *How did this threat influence the debates over the Constitution?*

SOURCE: Edgar B. Wesley, *Our United States: Its History in Maps* (Chicago: Denoyer-Geppert Co., 1965), p. 37.

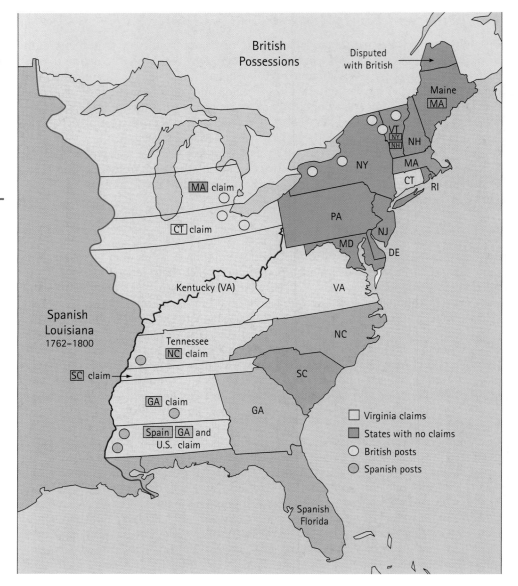

Congress appealed to the State of Pennsylvania for help, but when none was forthcoming, they fled to Princeton College.

Domestic unrest raised serious questions about political stability, but threats from foreign countries were even more disturbing. The British disputed the boundary between its Canadian colonies and the United States. Also, the British navy routinely intercepted American ships and dragooned U.S. sailors into service, claiming that anyone who spoke English must be British unless they could prove otherwise. Spain, in possession of Florida and the lands west of the Mississippi, claimed large segments of what is today Mississippi and Alabama (see Figure 2.3). Even France, a revolutionary ally, blocked U.S. trade with its islands in the West Indies and demanded repayment of money advanced during the revolution. The Continental Congress found it difficult to resolve these disputes, because it could not prevent states from engaging in their own negotiations with foreign countries.

## The Constitutional Convention

None felt the deficiencies in the Articles more keenly than George Washington and James Madison. An avid speculator in land west of the Appalachian mountains, Washington was frustrated by the inability of the states to work together to build canals and roads that would help develop the country's interior. Madison despaired at Congress's inability to raise money.

Madison and other reformers met to discuss needed constitutional reforms in 1786 at what became known as the **Annapolis Convention,** but, inasmuch as they represented only five states, they were unable to propose major constitutional changes. Later that year, however, in the aftermath of Shays's Rebellion, Madison persuaded Congress to ask each state legislature to elect delegates to a convention in Philadelphia to consider possible amendments to the Articles of Confederation. Every state legislature but Rhode Island's agreed to do so. Rhode Islanders were fearful that any revisions in the Articles would reduce the powers of their small state.

For the most part, states sent political leaders who favored major constitutional change; most of those opposed to changing the Articles stayed away. Patrick Henry, when asked to be a delegate, refused, saying he "smelt a rat." True, ten delegates abandoned the convention before the Constitution was completed, and another three refused to sign the document, but the great majority of those in Philadelphia agreed that the national government needed to be strengthened.

The delegates to the Constitutional Convention did not constitute a cross section of the population. The people who met in Philadelphia were bankers, merchants, plantation owners, and speculators in land west of the Appalachians.[25] Yet the delegates had not gone to Philadelphia just to protect the interests of their social class. They felt the country as a whole needed a stronger government that could provide political stability, effectively mediate conflicts among the states, and defend the nation from foreign threats.[26]

Nor were the delegates in agreement on all issues. Chosen by state legislatures, they had strong political connections within their home states. Coming from all parts of the United States, they represented different regions with conflicting interests. Two divisions were paramount. Delegates from big states often found themselves disagreeing with delegates from small states. And delegates from the southern slave states opposed those from northern states, whose economies did not depend on slavery.

These differences were submerged during the opening weeks of the convention, when a spirit of unity and reform filled the Philadelphia hall. But as the four-month convention progressed, the delegates pulled back from some of the more far-reaching reforms and searched for compromises that would produce a document that could be ratified.[27]

## The Virginia Plan

Three general decisions were made at the very beginning of the convention:

- Hold discussions behind closed doors. If debates were held in public, disagreements could be exploited by Anti-Federalists.
- Write an entirely new constitution instead of simply amending the Articles of Confederation.
- Use the **Virginia Plan** as the basis for initial discussions.

The Virginia Plan, which would win the support of most delegates from the larger states, had been prepared by Madison (with Washington's active involvement) prior to the gathering in Philadelphia. It proposed massive changes in the design and powers of the national government, creating a separation of powers along the lines that Locke had recommended. To win popular support for the new constitution, the Virginia Plan called for ratification by state convention delegates "expressly chosen by the people."[28]

Instead of a single Congress like that of the Articles, Madison proposed two chambers. The lower chamber—the future House of Representatives—would be elected by the voters. The upper chamber—the future Senate—would be elected by state legislatures.

The Virginia Plan changed representation in Congress dramatically from the pattern existing under the Articles of Confederation. Instead of each state having one vote, the number of both representatives and senators would depend on the size of a state's population. In short, under this plan, Virginia, Pennsylvania, and other more populous states would have much more power than under the Articles.

The Virginia Plan also gave the national government vast powers far beyond those enjoyed by the old Congress. The new Congress could legislate on all matters that affect "the harmony of the United States" and could negate "all laws passed by the several states."[29] It could also use force to ensure that states fulfilled their duties.

According to the Virginia Plan, the weak executive power under the Articles was to be replaced by a president to be chosen by Congress. The Supreme Court would have the authority to resolve disputes among individuals from different states, some thing that could not be done under the Articles of Confederation. The Virginia Plan received strong support from two of the most populous states—Virginia and Pennsylvania—as well as from states that expected to grow rapidly in population in the next few years—North Carolina, South Carolina, and Georgia.

### The New Jersey Plan

Delegates from smaller states, especially New Jersey and Delaware, were uneasy about the Virginia Plan. Two weeks or so into the convention, these states offered an alternative design prepared by William Patterson that became known as the **New Jersey Plan,** the small-state proposal for constitutional reform. (See Table 2.3.)

The New Jersey Plan also separated powers into three branches, but instead of creating a House and Senate, it kept a one-chamber Congress in which each state had a single vote. It also envisioned a more limited national government. Unlike the Virginia Plan, it did not grant Congress general legislative power. Instead it gave Congress specific powers, including the power to levy taxes on imported goods, the power to compel states to pay their share of taxes, and the power to regulate "trade & commerce with foreign nations" and among the states. The judicial branch could hear only specific types of cases, such as those involving treaties or foreigners.[30]

Despite these limitations, the New Jersey Plan still strengthened the national government well beyond what existed under the Articles. The supporters of the New Jersey Plan were not so much opposed to a stronger government as afraid that the big states would control it. As one delegate observed at the time, "Give New Jersey an equal vote, and she will dismiss her scruples, and concur in a National system."[31]

**New Jersey Plan**

Small-state proposal for constitutional reform.

---

**Table 2.3**

**The Virginia and New Jersey Plans**
The differences between the Virginia Plan and the New Jersey Plan illustrate the disagreements between large and small states at the time of the convention.

| Virginia Plan (favored by larger states) | New Jersey Plan (favored by smaller states) |
|---|---|
| **Key Difference** | |
| Each state represented in proportion to its size. | Every state has the same number of representatives in Congress. |
| **Other Differences** | |
| Congress has general power. | Congress has only limited, defined powers. |
| Supreme Court settles disputes among individuals. | Judiciary settles only certain disputes (for example, those involving foreigners). |

# The Connecticut Compromise

Vital to the success of the Constitutional Convention, the Connecticut Compromise allowed both large and small states to have a voice in Congress. *Are the differences between large and small states still important enough today to justify this representation scheme?*

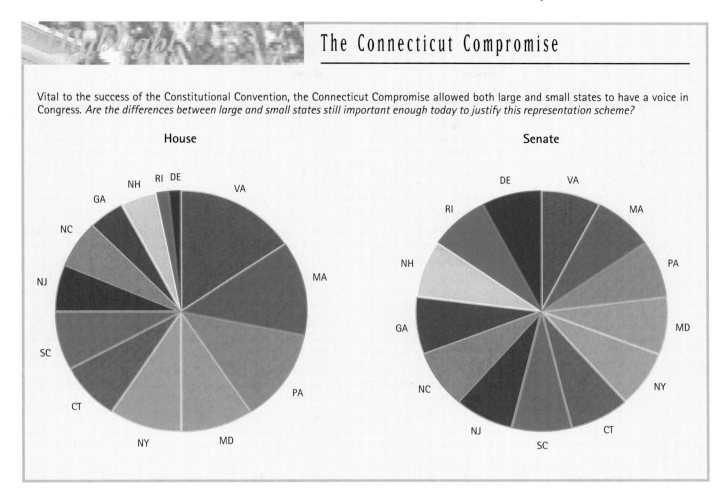

## House

## Senate

### The Connecticut Compromise

The convention nearly collapsed when a majority of the delegates rejected the New Jersey Plan. Delegates from the small states considered leaving Philadelphia, which would have killed all hope of successful ratification. The large states flirted with the idea of forming their own union and then using economic pressure to force small states to join. To calm these unsettled waters, Benjamin Franklin proposed beginning each session with prayer, though the idea was rejected on the grounds that no money was available to pay a chaplain.

To cool the debate, the most divisive issues were turned over to a committee controlled by moderates. The committee reported back a split-the-difference compromise offered by delegates from the middle-sized state of Connecticut. Proposing a Congress along the lines we know today, the **Connecticut Compromise** created a House proportionate to population and a Senate in which all states were represented equally. Small states were placated by their strong representation in the Senate. The large states were mollified by the requirement that representation in the House of Representatives be proportionate to a state's size.

**Connecticut Compromise**
Constitutional convention proposal that created a House proportionate to population and a Senate in which all states were represented equally.

## A Government of Separated Powers

Once the delegates accepted the Connecticut Compromise, they found it relatively easy to broker other differences between the Virginia and New Jersey Plans. Following the Virginia Plan, they created a government with three branches, legislative, executive, and judicial, dividing powers among them. But in a provision consistent with the New Jersey Plan, they limited the powers of all three branches.

## Congress

As called for in the New Jersey Plan, the convention delegates gave Congress a number of specific powers, including the powers to tax, coin money, regulate commerce, declare war, and maintain an army (see Table 2.4). But to address the concerns of the proponents of the Virginia Plan, they included the **necessary and proper clause,** which says that Congress has the power to "make all laws which shall be necessary and proper for carrying into Execution" its other powers. What is the definition of necessary and proper? Some thought it meant only what was absolutely essential. Other delegates thought it meant anything convenient and useful. The phrasing was ambiguous enough that all delegates could interpret the language to their own liking.

The delegates were also influenced by the Whig theory on rights and representation that had proved so powerful during the Revolutionary War. Following Whig theory, the Constitution said that members of the House of Representatives were to be chosen by the voters and were to be subject to reelection every two years. Still, the democracy that was created was more of a responsible than a popular type (see Chapter 1). It departed from the Whig theory by not establishing a limit on the number of terms that could be served. The delegates modified Whig theory even further when it came to the Senate. Senators were to be elected not by voters but by state legislatures, and they were given six-year terms of office.

The delegates settled on a delicate political solution to the question of voter qualifications. They said states could establish their own requirements, except that anyone eligible to vote for the lower chamber of the state legislature must also be allowed to vote in elections for the House of Representatives. By wording the Constitution in this way, the delegates avoided changing state voting requirements but still guaranteed the vote to everyone already eligible. This open-ended language also permitted the gradual, state-by-state extension of the right to vote to many excluded from the electorate in 1787.

---

**necessary and proper clause**
Says Congress has the power to "make all laws which shall be necessary and proper for carrying into Execution" its other powers.

---

### Table 2.4

**The Constitution and the Articles of Confederation Compared**
Many provisions of the Constitution directly address the failures of the Articles of Confederation.

| Weaknesses of the Articles of Confederation | How Addressed in Constitution |
| --- | --- |
| Congress could not levy taxes. | Congress has power to levy taxes (Article I, Section 8). |
| States could restrict commerce among states. | States cannot regulate commerce without the consent of Congress (Article I, Section 10). |
| States could issue their own currency. | States are prohibited from coining money (Article I, Section 10). |
| Executive was not independent of Congress. | An independently elected president holds the executive power (Article II). |
| There was no national judicial system. | The Supreme Court was created, and Congress was granted the power to establish lower federal courts (Article III, Section 1). |
| Amendments to Articles had to have unanimous approval of states. | Large majorities are necessary to amend the Constitution, but there are several different ways to do so (Article V). |

SOURCE: Articles of Confederation; U.S. Constitution, articles listed. See Appendix.

## The Executive

Some analysts have claimed that many convention delegates secretly harbored a desire to create an executive who had powers comparable to those of a British king.[32] But except for Alexander Hamilton, who actually made a proposal along these lines, the delegates were too practical to treat such an idea seriously. They knew that voters would reject out of hand a Constitution that threatened the return of anyone comparable to King George.

Instead, the Constitution keeps presidential power under tight congressional control. Presidents are made commander-in-chief of the armed forces, but only Congress can declare war. Presidents can call Congress into session and speak to Congress, but they cannot dismiss Congress or prevent it from meeting. Presidents are given the power to veto congressional legislation, but Congress can override a presidential veto with a two-thirds vote. (See Chapter 13 for a full discussion of how the constitutional system shapes the relationship between Congress and the president.)

Other presidential powers can be exercised only with senatorial **advice and consent,** support for a presidential action by a designated number of senators. For example, the president can sign treaties with foreign countries, but treaties can take effect only if two-thirds of the Senate gives its consent. Also, the president can appoint both judges and executive branch officers, but appointees must be confirmed by a majority of the Senate.

The impeachment clause makes clear the president's ultimate dependence on political support from Congress. The House of Representatives can impeach the president for "Treason, Bribery, or other high Crimes and Misdemeanors." If impeached, the president is tried in the Senate. If convicted by a two-thirds vote, the president is removed from office. Although no president has ever been removed in this way, Bill Clinton was tried but not convicted, Andrew Johnson avoided conviction by only one vote, and Richard Nixon chose to resign in the face of almost certain impeachment and conviction.

> **advice and consent**
> Support for a presidential action by a designated number of senators.

## The Electoral College

Although the Constitution sharply checked presidential power, delegates to the Constitutional Convention still expected the president to be a powerful political figure. As a consequence, they debated at great length on the method for presidential selection. Once again, the dispute divided the big states from the small ones. If the president were chosen by popular vote, big states would prevail because most people lived in big states. If the choice were made by the House of Representatives, big states would once again dominate. If the choice resided in the Senate, the small states would have extra clout.

The delegates finally agreed on a compromise that created the **electoral college,** those chosen to cast a direct vote for president by a process determined by each state. The electoral college is part of a complicated two-stage procedure that remains in effect today (see the accompanying Election Connection). The first stage involves selection of the electoral college. Each state chooses the same number of electors as it has senators and representatives in Congress. For example, Texas now has 32 electoral votes, because it elects 2 senators and 30 representatives. (In addition, as a result of the passage of the Twenty-Third Amendment, the District of Columbia casts three votes.) If a candidate receives a **majority** (50 percent plus 1) of the electoral vote, that person is elected president. In the 1996 election Bill Clinton received 379 out of 538 electoral votes, a clear majority, electing him as president. But if no candidate receives a majority in the electoral college, the action moves to the House of Representatives. If, for example, the vote of the electoral college in 1996 had been split three ways among Bill Clinton, Robert Dole, and Ross Perot, and none had received more than 50 percent of the electoral vote, then the election would have been decided in the House of Representatives. The last time this happened was in 1824.

> **electoral college**
> Those chosen to cast a direct vote for president by a process determined by each state.

> **majority**
> 50 percent plus one.

## Election Connection

# The Electoral College Compromise

Delegates to the Constitutional Convention found it difficult to agree on the best way of selecting the president of the United States. Large states wanted presidents chosen by a popular vote or by the House of Representatives. Small states wanted the president chosen by the Senate or by some process that would give every state the same vote. To win ratification by voters in both large and small states, some kind of compromise was needed.

The compromise the delegates reached was a two-stage procedure sufficiently complicated that both sides could claim victory. But the procedure can result in the election of presidents who have not received a majority of the popular vote.

### Election Procedure

*First stage* (gives the advantage to big states): Voters in each state choose as many electors as they have representatives and senators; the president is picked by a majority of electors; if no candidate has a majority, the three top vote getters go to the second stage.

*Second stage* (gives the advantage to small states): Members of the House of Representatives vote by state delegation; each delegation has one vote and must choose from the top three candidates. The winner must receive a majority.

### Problems

Second-stage presidents may not have received the most popular votes, and because they may be picked as the result of bargaining, many may believe that the president was chosen in a corrupt manner. The elections of Presidents Thomas Jefferson and John Quincy Adams, both selected at the second stage, were marked by extreme conflict.

Even a president selected by the electoral college may have fewer popular votes than another candidate. Presidents Rutherford Hayes and Benjamin Harrison did not have a popular majority. President John Kennedy had only 100,000 more votes than Richard Nixon but won the electoral college by a large majority.

SOURCES: U.S. Constitution, Article II, sec 1. *See* Appendix. Arthur M. Schlesinger, Jr., ed., *History of American Presidential Elections, 1789–1968*, Vol. 2 (New York: McGraw-Hill, 1971).

---

The Constitution does not require that the members of the electoral college be chosen by the voters. Instead, the manner of selecting electors was left up to the states. Constitutional silence on this key matter was not an accident. Some delegates thought the president should be elected by the people; others felt this could lead to mob rule. The Constitutional Convention compromised on the question, as it did on so many, by leaving the issue up to the states. Not until 1864 did the last state, South Carolina, give voters the power to vote directly for its electors (though by the 1820s, electors were chosen by the voters in the great majority of states).[33]

Some think the electoral college compromise has proved to be less of a success than the Connecticut Compromise. For example, in three elections (1824, 1876, and 1888), the candidate who won the most popular votes was not selected president. Some scholars favor eliminating the Electoral college altogether, on the theory that the candidate receiving the most popular votes should win the election. Others think that the electoral college, for all its faults, helps to maintain the two-party system and provides representation for both the states and the people (see the accompanying Democratic Dilemma).

### The Judicial Compromise

Most convention delegates thought the country needed a Supreme Court to adjudicate conflicts between the states. They also found it fairly easy to agree that justices should be nominated for lifetime positions by the president and confirmed by a majority of the Senate.

The delegates differed over whether the Supreme Court needed lower federal courts to assist it. Advocates of the Virginia Plan thought lower federal courts were needed because state courts "cannot be trusted with the administration of the National Laws."[34] Advocates of the New Jersey Plan said the state courts were sufficient. They also thought "the people will not bear such innovations."[35] The delegates compromised on the issue by leaving it to Congress to decide whether lower federal courts were needed. The first congress created a system of lower federal courts, whose essentials remain intact today. The Court system is described in Chapter 15.

*Democratic Dilemma*

# Should the Electoral College Be Reformed?

The presidential election of 2000, in which Albert Gore apparently won the national popular vote but the winner of the presidency depended on a few votes in Florida, set off intense new criticisms of the electoral college. Alarmed that the new president might not be seen as legitimate, academics and commentators called for constitutional changes that would make the winner of the national popular vote the president.

Yale's Jonathan G. S. Koppell pointed out that the electoral college was a byproduct of the outdated large state-small state controversy that had also led to the Connecticut Compromise. "It is time to rethink a system that is designed to satisfy the political exigencies of the late 18th century," he argued. Political scientist Benjamin Barber of Rutgers University went further, criticizing the electoral college as a "dormant sore on the body politic which has now gone cancerous." Richard Nathan of the State University of New York at Albany agreed that there was cause for concern. "This is a delicate time for our political system. It is broke, and we need to do something."

Some even speculated that in future close elections, candidates would seek out "rogue electors" who would switch their votes in the December balloting. Such efforts, said electoral college expert Walter Burns, could set off "a constitutional crisis that will put this country in a third-world category where elections are decided in the streets."

But others argued that the electoral college had served its purpose for hundreds of years, and that the controversy over the 2000 election was unlikely to be repeated. What was more, the electoral college may have prevented the 2000 election from becoming a larger crisis. Said Kenneth Janda, "if anything, this has really established the utility of the electoral vote system. If we were deciding by popular vote, there would be calls for a nationwide recount, and we would find disputed ballots in every nook and cranny of the country. Now, at least the issue is confined to one state." Political scientist Nelson Polsby warned that moving to a popular vote system "would encourage splinter parties, spoilers, and nuisance candidacies–hence more, not less, of Ralph Nader and Pat Buchanan."

*What do you think?*
- *Is the electoral college outdated and possibly dangerous?*
- *To eliminate the potential for future crises, should presidents be chosen directly by a plurality of voters, no matter where they live?*
- *Would this reform make it easier for third party candidates to win elections? Would the reform undermine the two-party system? Would it endanger the role of states in the federal system?*

SOURCES: Jonathan G. S. Koppell, "Some States Are More Equal Than Others," Los Angeles Times, November 9, 2000, p. B11; David Broder, "Bizarre Twists Raise Fairness Issue," Washington Post, November 9, 2000, p. A01; Mary Leonard, "How Popular Mandate Can Mean Defeat," Boston Globe, November 9, 2000 (Third edition), p. D1; Nelson Polsby, "Election 2000: What Does it All Mean? No Reason to Fix a System That Works," Boston "Globe, November 9, 2000 (Third edition), p. A19.

---

The delegates also seem to have disagreed on whether the Supreme Court should be given the power of **judicial review,** court authority to declare laws null and void on the grounds that they violate the Constitution. Although Madison's account of the debate over judicial review is sketchy, many delegates, it seems, favored judicial review as a check on the power of state legislatures. Yet when two delegates opposed judicial review, there is no record of anyone rising to its defense. Though scholars have puzzled over the lack of debate at the convention on an issue that would loom large in later years, the lack of debate is probably best explained by political expediency. Judicial review had provoked controversy in North Carolina and Rhode Island, and convention delegates avoided the issue because it might have endangered ratification.

Instead of calling for judicial review, convention delegates inserted into the Constitution an ambiguous phrase that has become known as the **supremacy clause,** which says the Constitution is the "supreme Law of the Land," to which all judges are bound. To some, this phrase simply told state judges to be mindful of the Constitution when interpreting state laws. To others, it gave the Supreme Court the power to declare both state and federal laws unconstitutional. The issue was not settled until 20 years later, when, as discussed in Chapter 15, the Supreme Court interpreted the supremacy clause as giving the Court the power of judicial review over both federal and state laws.

> **judicial review**
> Court authority to declare laws null and void on the grounds that they violate the Constitution.

> **supremacy clause**
> Part of the Constitution that says the Constitution is the "supreme Law of the Land," to which all judges are bound.

## Compromising on the Issue of Slavery

The delegates never seriously contemplated eliminating slavery under the Constitution, though one delegate said it was their moral duty to do so. The delegates knew that southern states would not ratify the Constitution if it abolished slavery. The

At the time of this cartoon's publication, only 11 states had ratified the Constitution. The cartoonist eagerly awaited North Carolina ("Rise it will") and Rhode Island ("The foundation good—it may yet be saved") joining the new Union. *Why was Rhode Island the last state to ratify the Constitution?*

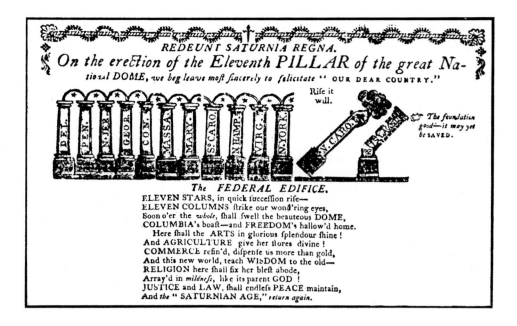

debate over the question of slavery took other forms. Northerners wanted to end the international slave trade. Most southerners argued that the slave trade, however despicable, was necessary to fuel economic growth in the unsettled parts of the South. The two sides compromised by agreeing not to abolish the slave trade for 20 years. Abiding by this provision, Congress waited until 1808 before taking that step.

Northern delegates did not want to count slaves when figuring state representation in the House of Representatives. Southerners thought they should be counted. The two sides came up with the expedient, if disreputable, **three-fifths compromise,** which counted each slave as "three-fifths" of a person. The clause identified slaves not as such but as "other persons." Failing to talk about slavery in explicit terms was yet another way of reaching compromise. Not until after the Civil War did the Fourteenth Amendment repeal the three-fifths clause.

North and South also split over tariffs. Northerners wanted to give Congress the right to impose tariffs on imports; southerners were afraid this provision would be used to protect northern manufacturing at southern expense. In exchange for the three-fifths compromise, southerners agreed to let Congress impose tariffs on foreign goods.

**three-fifths compromise**

Constitutional provision that counted each slave as three-fifths of a person when calculating representation in the House of Representatives; repealed by the Fourteenth Amendment.

## Section Summary

After the failure of the Articles of Confederation, delegates to the Constitutional Convention agreed, for the most part, that a stronger central government was needed. They made numerous compromises to hammer out the details of the new system, however. Chief among them was the Connecticut Compromise, which allocated Senate seats by state but House seats by population. Delegates also chose to allow Congress to check presidential power, developed the electoral college method of presidential selection, and set only vague generalities concerning the role of the Supreme Court. The founders addressed the issue of slavery only indirectly, through agreements such as the three-fifths compromise.

## *The Bill of Rights*

The delegates to the Constitutional Convention made one mistake so serious that it nearly ruined their chances of securing ratification: They failed to include within the Constitution clauses that clearly protected the liberties of the people. It is surprising that the delegates to the Philadelphia Convention, who in other respects showed excellent political judgment, made such a serious political miscalculation. Ever since the Revolutionary War, the Whig concept of rights and representation had been part and parcel of American constitutional thinking. Quite apart from the Declaration of Independence, with its ringing endorsement of the "right to life, liberty, and the pursuit of happiness," the Virginia assembly—also in 1776—had passed a Bill of Rights protecting free speech, the right of the propertied to vote, the right to a trial by jury, the right not to be compelled to testify against oneself, and other civil liberties.[36] Similar provisions were approved by statute or incorporated into the first constitutions adopted by most of the other states. Yet when South Carolina's Charles Pinckney offered a motion to guarantee freedom of the press at the Constitutional Convention, a majority voted the motion down—on the grounds that regulation of speech and press was a state responsibility.[37]

The convention majority may have been technically correct, but they failed to appreciate how powerfully the demand for the protection of civil liberties would resonate with the voters. To win popular acceptance, the Constitution needed to contain an explicit expression of the Whig theory of rights and representation that the country had taken to heart during the Revolutionary War. When it failed to do so, Thomas Jefferson wrote to Madison from Paris, saying that he thought a Bill of Rights needed to be added.

Eventually, the Federalists recognized their mistake. To win ratification in Massachusetts, Virginia, and New York, they promised to enact, as a series of amendments to the Constitution, a **Bill of Rights** that would guarantee civil liberties. Two states, North Carolina and Rhode Island, wanted to make sure the Federalists made good on their promise. Though they probably would have ratified the Constitution at some point simply to avoid becoming isolated states, they withheld their approval until after the first Congress fulfilled the Federalist promise to add a Bill of Rights. The Bill of Rights, which comprises the first ten amendments to the Constitution, has played such a central role in the country's constitutional development that all of Chapter 16, on civil liberties, is devoted to it.

**Bill of Rights**
The first ten amendments to the Constitution, which protect individual and state rights.

## The Anti-Federalist–Federalist Debate

Although the absence of a Bill of Rights gave Anti-Federalists powerful ammunition for their assault on the Constitution during the ratification campaign, their critique of the document was more broadly based. Drawing on the Whig theory of rights and

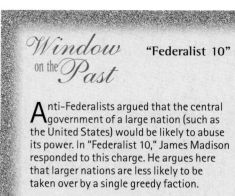

*Window on the Past*    "Federalist 10"

Anti-Federalists argued that the central government of a large nation (such as the United States) would be likely to abuse its power. In "Federalist 10," James Madison responded to this charge. He argues here that larger nations are less likely to be taken over by a single greedy faction.

The smaller the society, the fewer probably will be the distinct parties and interests composing it; the fewer the distinct parties and interests, the more frequently will a majority be found of the same party; and . . . the more easily will they concert and execute their plans of oppression. Extend the sphere and you take in a greater variety of parties and interests; you make it less probable that a majority of the whole will have a common motive to invade the rights of other citizens.

*What do you think?*
- *Do you agree with Madison's argument?*
- *If you were an Anti-Federalist, how would you respond?*

SOURCE: James Madison, "Federalist 10," in John Jay, Alexander Hamilton, and James Madison, writing under the pseudonym Publius, *The Federalist Papers* (New York: New American Library, 1961).

participation
**Democracy and the Internet**

*Federalist Papers*
Essays that were written in support of the Constitution's ratification and have become a classic argument for the American constitutional system.

**checks and balances**
Constitutional division of power into separate institutions, giving each institution the power to block the actions of the others.

visual literacy
**The American System of Checks and Balances**

representation, they attacked the Constitution for laying the groundwork for a national tyranny. They said the shift in power from the states to the national government took power from the people. The number of representatives in Congress was too small to include a wide variety of citizens from all parts of the United States. Presidents could become virtual kings, because they could be reelected again and again for the rest of their lives. The reelection of senators and representatives would create a political aristocracy.[38]

To answer these Anti-Federalist arguments, three Federalists, Alexander Hamilton, James Madison, and John Jay, wrote a series of newspaper essays, now known as the **Federalist Papers,** which are generally regarded as the finest essays on American political theory ever written.[39] The authors argued that tyranny could come from either without or within the country. The external danger came from European countries, who were eager to divide the new nation into several parts so that each could be controlled. The Constitution would help prevent such divisions by creating a stronger national government that could defend the country.

Threats to liberty could also come from groups and factions within the country seeking to impose their will on others. The greatest threat to liberty came from a majority faction, because it could so easily impose its will on minorities. The authors of the *Federalist Papers* said the Constitution would prevent majority tyranny by creating a system of **checks and balances,** a division of governmental power among separate institutions, giving each institution the power to block the actions of the others. In the first place, power was split between the states and a national government. Then, at the national level, power was divided among three branches: legislative, executive, and judicial. Finally, the legislative branch was divided into two chambers, a Senate and a House of Representatives. Each was elected in a different way, making it more difficult for any momentary majority to seize total power.

In retrospect, the Federalists seem to have had the better argument. The Federalists had a plan for the future; the Anti-Federalists had nothing to offer but the unsatisfactory status quo. When the Anti-Federalists claimed that the Constitution stripped the people of their rights and liberties, they relied on the not very convincing argument that the government of any large nation was likely to trample the liberties of the people. The writers of the *Federalist Papers* analyzed the situation more accurately; by creating a system of checks and balances that divided power into different branches and different levels, and by grounding each level in separate elections, they hoped to ensure that the ambitions of one group of politicians would restrain those of others.

James Madison (1751–1836), Alexander Hamilton (1755–1804), and John Jay (1745–1829), the authors of the *Federalist Papers. Why did Madison want a new constitution?*

## Amendments to the Constitution

The delegates to the Constitutional Convention, realizing that the document they were writing was not perfect and that unforeseen circumstances could arise, discussed ways in which the Constitution might be amended. Small states wanted unanimous consent of state legislatures. Big states felt that a unanimity rule would lead to stagnation and protracted conflict. Southern states were afraid that slavery would be endangered if amendments could be made easily.

To obtain agreement, a complicated formula was put together that allowed amendment by any one of four different procedures, as shown in Figure 2.4. The simplest, and the most frequently used, way to amend the Constitution requires a two-thirds vote in both Houses of Congress and then ratification by three-quarters of the state legislatures. Of the 27 amendments to the Constitution, 26 have been enacted by this procedure. On one occasion, the amendment that repealed prohibition, the state legislatures were bypassed in favor of state ratifying conventions attended by delegates chosen by the voters (the same procedure used to ratify the Constitution itself).

Amending the Constitution requires such overwhelming majorities that only 17 amendments have been enacted since ratification of the Bill of Rights, less than one amendment every 12 years. Thousands of amendments have been proposed over the

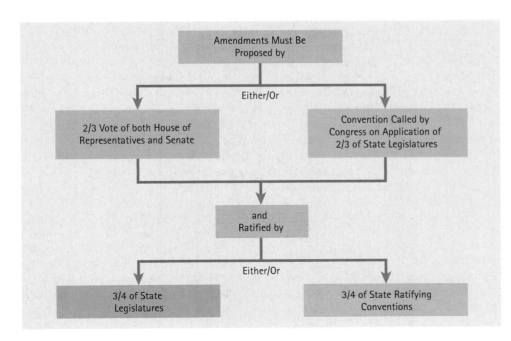

**Figure 2.4**

**Amending the Constitution: A Two-Stage Process**
*Why did the founders make the amendment process so complicated?*

SOURCE: U.S. Constitution, Article V. See Appendix.

### Election Connection

## Amendments to the Constitution Have Extended Liberties and Tightened the Election Connection

| Amendment | Year Ratified | Provision |
|---|---|---|
| XII | 1804 | Distinguishes electoral vote for president and vice-president. |
| XIII | 1865 | Abolishes slavery. |
| XIV | 1868 | Guarantees citizens the right of due process and equal protection before state law. Removes the three-fifths compromise from the Constitution. |
| XV | 1870 | Extends suffrage to African Americans. |
| XVII | 1913 | Direct election of senators. |
| XIX | 1920 | Extends suffrage to women. |
| XX | 1933 | Shortens time between election and the day Congress and the president assume office. |
| XXII | 1951 | Imposes two-term limit on presidents. |
| XXIII | 1961 | Extends presidential suffrage to residents of the District of Columbia. |
| XXIV | 1964 | Abolishes taxes on voting. |
| XXV | 1967 | Determines procedure for filling the office of the vice-president if it becomes vacant. |
| XXVI | 1971 | Extends suffrage to 18-year-olds. |
| XXVII | 1992 | Postpones congressional pay raises until after next election. |

SOURCE: U.S. Constitution, amendments listed. See Appendix.

comparative

**Comparing Constitutions**

decades, but nearly all have failed to win approval. The hurdles a proposed amendment must jump are so high that even popular amendments that have the endorsement of both political parties are not approved. For example, many people thought that the Equal Rights Amendment, which said that men and women had "equality of rights under the law," would win approval in the 1970s. The amendment received overwhelming support in both Houses of Congress in 1971–1972 and was quickly ratified by 34 states. But when the proposed amendment became intertwined with abortion and other disputed issues, it failed to win ratification by the final 3 state legislatures necessary to provide the required three-quarters approval.[40]

The one kind of amendment that seems capable of jumping the several high hurdles needed to achieve adoption is one that extends democratic electoral practices. Despite the complicated procedures that are in place, 13 amendments since the Bill of Rights have tightened the electoral connection well beyond what was originally envisioned by the Constitution—by broadening the electorate, by extending civil liberties, or by making more direct the connections between leaders and voters. Five amendments specifically extended the suffrage to citizens previously excluded from voting: African Americans, women, young people (ages eighteen to twenty-one), residents of the District of Columbia, and those unwilling or unable to pay a poll tax. Eight other amendments also have corrected procedural deficiencies thought to be inconsistent with democratic practice (see the accompanying Election Connection).

### SECTION SUMMARY

Originally, the Constitution was ratified by a small electorate of white male property owners. Amendments to this Constitution have broadened and extended popular participation, both enhancing and complicating the practice of American government. The Constitution laid the foundation, but the edifice erected on its pillars has proved more adaptable than even the delegates to the convention could have imagined.

## The Constitution: An Assessment

The debate over the Constitution did not end with its ratification in 1788. The influential historian Charles Beard wrote in 1913 that the Constitution represented a victory for the propertied classes against the masses of the people.[41] Beard pointed out that wealthy people wrote the document and that only people with property were allowed to vote in the ratification campaign. But modern-day historians Bernard Bailyn and Gordon Wood see it as moving the country toward the ideals of citizen rights and representation that motivated the revolutionary patriots.[42] In their view, the Whig ideals that spurred the war of independence were given practical expression in the Constitution.

### A Step Backward?

Both sides of this debate probably overstate their case. The adoption of the Constitution consolidated changes in citizen participation and representation that had already taken place in many states. The adoption of the Constitution did not extend the right to vote, but neither did it further restrict it. The Constitution divided powers that had been lodged in a single representative body under the Articles of Confederation, but each of the new entities—House, Senate, Congress, the courts—was ultimately grounded in the people. Senators were elected by the legislatures of each state, but the members of each state legislature were chosen in popular elections. Presidents were chosen by electors, but the electors were chosen according to state rules, which since the 1830s have generally called for direct elections by the voters. The judges were appointed for life, but they were selected by the president and confirmed by the Senate. If the U.S. government under the Constitution was a limited, responsible democracy in 1789, a more popular democracy evolved within the framework the Constitution set forth, though it took a Civil War to incorporate all races into the democratic process.

There remains much in the Constitution to criticize. The powers of the Supreme Court are poorly defined. The electoral college, though praised by some for representing both states and people, is thought by others to be a haphazard contraption that has more than once failed to work well. Many issues are papered over with vague, ambiguous wording.

Certain clauses in the Constitution are especially disturbing to the modern eye. Written by 55 prosperous gentlemen, the document falls far short of expressing contemporary democratic ideals. The Constitution explicitly permitted the slave trade to continue until 1808, even though many delegates thought it an evil practice. Nothing was done to extend voting rights to women, indentured servants, slaves, youths, or those without property. Until the Bill of Rights was added, nothing was said about basic freedoms of speech, religion, and assembly, which are now taken for granted.

But we cannot judge eighteenth-century decisions by twenty-first century principles. Most flaws were written into the Constitution not to frustrate voters but to achieve ratification. Compromises were made on issues related to slavery because that was the only way to get the support of voters in both northern and southern states. The Constitution says nothing about the right to vote, because every state had its own voting rules. Had the Constitution proposed changing them, the states would have seen the provisions as violations of their sovereignty. The procedures for electing the president were designed to reduce conflicts between large and small states. The one big mistake the convention could most certainly have avoided—neglecting to include a Bill of Rights—was corrected by the first Congress.

If we want to censure the Constitution for its undemocratic features, we must first criticize the limits on suffrage imposed by state voting laws inherited from the colonial period. Historians estimate that only 20 percent of the electorate and 5 percent of the adult population voted.[43] The country was no longer ruled by King George III, but it was hardly a full-fledged democracy. The Constitution was written to win the support of the white, male, property-owning population. That it could do so—and still leave open the possibility for greater democratization in the centuries to come—is to the honor, not the discredit, of those who met in Philadelphia.

### Achievements

Though it is easy to disparage the Constitutional Convention for what it failed to achieve, the delegates wrote a document that contributed to the solution of two of the most immediate and pressing problems facing the United States. First, it created a unified nation capable of defending American sovereignty from foreign threats. True, the United States would fight an unsuccessful war against Britain in 1812. But the Constitution kept the country from splitting into pieces at a time when Britain, France, and Spain were all looking for a piece of the action in the New World. Instead of falling prey to European ambitions, the United States profited from European divisions by seizing the opportunity to make the Louisiana Purchase, in 1803, which doubled the size of the country. The new lands were eventually incorporated into the Union as new member states.

Second, the new Constitution facilitated the country's economic development by outlawing state currencies and eliminating state tariffs. As a result, trade among states flourished, and the United States grew into an economic powerhouse faster than any had expected.

The Constitution also created a presidency that was first filled by George Washington, the country's most beloved political leader. His great prestige gave the national government the additional strength needed to overcome the many difficulties the new nation encountered (see the accompanying Election Connection).

### The Constitution Today

In addition to solving immediate problems, the Constitution created a framework that facilitated an ever more popular democratic experiment. In contrast to Thomas Hobbes, who said that a country could avoid chaos only by vesting power in a sovereign king, those who wrote the Constitution developed an alternative theory of checks and balances. If a constitution separates powers into many parts and each part represents a different set of interests, then liberty can be protected by giving minorities the opportunity to protect themselves from tyrannical majorities. The many compromises at the Constitutional Convention produced this kind of separation of power that set competing interests against one another. The interests of big states, small states, northerners, southerners, commercial entrepreneurs, farmers, property owners, and debtors were all woven into the constitutional fabric.

In the two centuries that followed, the main lines of conflict have changed. People no longer worry much about divisions between big and small states or differences between commerce and agriculture. The country today has quite different ethnic, gender, cultural, income, and generational differences to resolve. But the Constitution still gives the many different groups and interests clear opportunities to voice their concern.

**Constitutional Ambiguity: A Virtue**  The very ambiguities embedded in the Constitution have also been a plus. Written as compromises among conflicting interests, such vague phrases as "necessary and proper" and "Supreme Law of the Land" have had the elasticity necessary to accommodate powerful social and political

## Election Connection

# George Washington Is Elected as First President

The first presidential election was extremely dull. No issues arose and no campaign allegations were made; the vote was unanimous. Yet the votes cast by the electoral college on February 4, 1789, may have been as important as any ever cast. The election of George Washington as the nation's first president got the country off to a good start.

Unanimity was certainly an advantage, because the election process itself created many questions. In only five states did the voters choose the electors. Electors in two states—Rhode Island and North Carolina—did not vote because the states had yet to ratify the Constitution. The New York legislature, still opposed to the Constitution, refused to pick any electors. In New Jersey the electors were designated by the governor and his council. In four other states the electors were chosen by the legislature.

Yet virtually everyone was pleased with the new president. Though a great war hero, he had always deferred to the Continental Congress. As a former member of the Virginia colonial legislature, he did not disdain politics. Because he was both a speculator in western lands as well as a slave owner (known for his generous treatment of those who worked for him), he was acceptable to both northern and southern states.

*What do you think?*
• *Are war heroes as politically popular today?*

SOURCE: Stanley Elkins and Eric McKitrick, *The Age of Federalism* (New York: Oxford University Press, 1993); Thomas A. Lewis, *For King and Country: The Maturing of George Washington, 1748–1760* (New York: HarperCollins, 1993.)

---

forces the founders could not have anticipated. Over the centuries, the Supreme Court has interpreted ambiguous constitutional phrases in ways that have allowed the Constitution to remain a living document. In subsequent chapters we shall discuss ways in which the compromises of 1787 have been redefined and given new meaning in response to changing political circumstances.

The Constitution's extraordinary adaptability over a prolonged period of time constitutes no small accomplishment. Although the United States is often thought of as a relatively new country, its governing arrangements have remained intact for much longer than those in most other countries. Of all the great industrial democracies, only the British system comes close to enjoying basic governing arrangements that date back as far as those of the United States. And even the democratic features of British government are newer than those of the United States. Not until 1867 did most British men get the right to vote.

Most other countries have much newer constitutions. The latest Russian constitution was adopted in 1993 (see the accompanying International Comparison). The current Spanish constitution was promulgated in 1978, the French constitution dates back only to 1958, the Danish to 1953, and the German, Italian, and Japanese constitutions to the late 1940s.

comparative
**Comparing Constitutions**

## International Comparison

# Constitution Making in Russia

With the disintegration of the old Soviet Union in 1991, the new Russian Republic needed a constitution. In 1993, voters ratified one, creating a government not unlike that of the United States: three branches, including a president, a judiciary, and a two-chamber national assembly. In one chamber, all of Russia's 89 regions are represented equally. In the other, seats are allocated on the basis of population. A federal system divides power between national and local governments, and the constitution includes a bill of rights. Despite these similarities between the U.S. and Russian constitutions, major legal and political differences remain.

### Legal Differences

1. The Russian president can issue emergency decrees without legislative approval. Some wonder whether a future president will use this power to transform the country into a dictatorship.

2. Local governments in Russia depend almost entirely on the national government for financial resources, and many of their leaders are appointed by the president, which makes regional governments less independent than state governments in the United States.

### Differences in Political Circumstances

1. The U.S. Constitution was written by revolutionary leaders who had won the country's independence. The Russian constitution was written after the Soviet Union had lost the Cold War.

2. George Washington was revered as a military hero. The first Russian president, Boris Yeltsin, was a dissident political leader. Though initially popular, Yeltsin was so unpopular by the end of his second term that only 1 percent of Russians believed he could effectively bring order to the country.

3. The first U.S. Congress was controlled by the Federalists, strong supporters of the new Constitution. The most powerful force in the first years of the Russian assembly was the Communist party, which criticized the new government and evoked nostalgia for the Soviet past.

4. The Russian bill of rights was ignored when a local government, Chechnya, declared independence and a bitter war ensued.

Russia is still finding its way after the disintegration of the Soviet Union in 1991, and some are nostalgic for the old days of Communist rule. Here, a demolition worker shields the eyes of a statue of Lenin, founder of the Soviet Union, before authorities remove it from a place of honor in Bucharest, Romania.

SOURCES: Antii Korkeakivi, "The Reach of Rights in the New Russian Constitution," *Cardozo Journal of International and Comparative Law,* Vol. 3 (Summer 1995), pp. 229–250; Amy J. Weisman, "Separation of Powers in Post-Communist Government: A Constitutional Case Study of the Russian Federation," *American University Journal of International Law and Policy,* Vol. 10 (Summer 1995), pp. 1365–1398; "Russia's Election: A Grubby Spectacle," *The Economist,* December 18, 1999, pp. 19–21.

**The Stain of Slavery** Despite everything positive that can be said for the Constitution, the stain of slavery remains indelible. The Constitution validated the slave trade and stated that each slave could be counted as three-fifths of a person. The Constitution also explicitly required free states to return escaped slaves to the place from which they had fled.

Dividing and checking concentrations of power prevented the tyranny of the majority. But it also prevented a majority from undoing the tyranny of slavery. By denying the national government the capacity to bring slavery peacefully to an end, separation of powers helped perpetuate the slave system at a time when the practice was disappearing throughout the rest of the world. Perhaps it is too much to ask of any constitution that it provide the tools for resolving what had become an intractable problem. Perhaps it was, as Abraham Lincoln once said, only providential that "every drop of blood drawn with the lash shall be paid by another drawn with the sword."[44] It is not easy to think how the delegates to the Constitutional Convention could have designed a constitution that would have both freed slaves and won ratification by the voters of 1788.

## Chapter Summary

The colonists who settled the eastern coast of North America established incomplete but meaningful rules of democracy through such institutions as the Mayflower Compact and elected colonial assemblies. These democratic institutions were reinforced by the spread of philosophical ideals during the Revolutionary War. Of critical importance was the concept that legitimate governments get their power from the consent of the governed. This principle formed the basis for the U.S. Constitution.

The Constitution was written to rectify difficulties the country experienced under the Articles of Confederation. The national government could not raise its own army, levy its own taxes, or regulate commerce among the states. Many leaders believed the country was too weak to fend off potential threats from Britain, Spain, and France.

When drafting a new Constitution designed to address needs unmet by the Articles of Confederation, the delegates to the Constitutional Convention designed a new basic law acceptable to the voters who were asked to ratify it. As a result, they prepared a document built both on their own colonial experience and on political theories popular at the time. They also incorporated many of the ideals expressed during the revolutionary struggle against King George III.

The Constitution curbed the powers of state governments, gave Congress additional authority, created a presidency of limited powers, and established a Supreme Court as the head of the judicial system. By dividing power between the states and the national government and by further dividing the power of the national government among the legislative, executive, and judicial branches, the Constitution provided an enduring system of limited government well designed to protect the liberties of the citizens.

To win ratification of the Constitution by voters in all parts of the country, the delegates to the Constitutional Convention had to reach many compromises. Congress was given not a general power but a set of specific powers, along with the capacity to do anything "necessary and proper" to carry out these specific powers. Differences of opinion between delegates from big and small states were resolved by creating a Senate that gave equal representation to all states and a House of Representatives that represented states in proportion to their population. Presidents were selected via a complicated two-stage system, which included a cumbersome electoral college arrangement. The Supreme Court was neither given nor denied the power of judicial review. Differences between the North and South were settled via a compromise: preserving the slave trade for 20 years and counting each slave as three-fifths of a person.

The convention delegates erred in not including a Bill of Rights in the Constitution. But during the ratification campaign, Anti-Federalists insisted on, and the Federalists finally agreed to, ten amendments to the Constitution that became known as the Bill of Rights. Though the procedures for amending the Constitution are complicated, 17 amendments have been approved since the Bill of Rights was drafted, and 13 of these have shifted American democracy in a popular direction.

## On the Web

www.nara.gov/exhall/charters/constitution/conmain.html
The National Archives and Records Administration provides the full text of the Constitution, biographies of each of its signers, and high-resolution images of the document itself.

www.utm.edu/research/iep/l/locke.htm
The Internet Encyclopedia of Philosophy provides a biography of John Locke, as well as a review of his important works.

www.pbs.org/ktca/liberty/
This site, the companion to a PBS series on the American Revolution, provides a comprehensive account of the Revolutionary War, including timelines, accounts of battles, and biographies of key figures.

www.yale.edu/lawweb/avalon/federal/fed.htm
The Avalon Project at Yale Law School presents online all 85 *Federalist Papers,* which can be searched by keyword.

## Key Terms

advice and consent, p. 49
Annapolis Convention, p. 45
Anti-Federalists, p. 33
Articles of Confederation, p. 33
Bill of Rights, p. 53
checks and balances, p. 54
colonial assembly, p. 35
colonial council, p. 36
Connecticut Compromise, p. 47
Constitution, p. 33
Declaration of Independence, p. 38
divine right, p. 35

electoral college, p. 49
*Federalist Papers,* p. 54
Federalists, p. 33
First Continental Congress, p. 38
judicial review, p. 51
majority, p. 49
Mayflower Compact, p. 35
necessary and proper clause, p. 48
New Jersey Plan, p. 46
Patriots, p. 38
patronage, p. 36
proprietary colony, p. 35

royal colony, p. 35
Second Continental Congress, p. 38
separation of powers, p. 39
Shays's Rebellion, p. 43
Stamp Act Congress, p. 37
stamp tax, p. 37
supremacy clause, p. 51
taxation without representation, p. 37
three-fifths compromise, p. 52
Tories, p. 38
Virginia Plan, p. 45
Whigs, p. 40

## Suggested Readings

Adams, Willi Paul. *The First American Constitutions: Republican Ideology and the Making of the State Constitutions in the Revolutionary Era.* Chapel Hill: University of North Carolina Press, 1980. Reveals that much of what seems original in the Constitution was already in place in many states.

Bailyn, Bernard. *The Origins of American Politics.* New York: Knopf, 1968. Identifies the sources of the American Revolution in colonial thought and practice.

Beard, Charles A. *An Economic Interpretation of the Constitution of the United States.* New York: Free Press, 1913. Interprets the writing of the Constitution as an effort by the wealthy to protect their property rights.

Commager, Henry Steele, ed. *Documents of American History.* 6th ed. New York: Appleton-Century-Crofts, 1958. Collection of key primary documents in American history.

Elkins, Stanley, and Eric McKitrick. *The Age of Federalism.* New York:

Oxford University Press, 1993. Authoritative account of political life during the first decade after the adoption of the Constitution.

*The Federalist Papers.* New York: New American Library, 1961. Powerful defense of the proposed Constitution by Alexander Hamilton, James Madison, and John Jay under the pseudonym Publius.

Hartz, Louis. *The Liberal Tradition in America.* New York: Harcourt, 1955. A difficult but rewarding book that describes the distinctive quality of the American political tradition.

Morgan, Edmund S., and Helen M. Morgan. *The Stamp Act Crisis: Prologue to Revolution.* Chapel Hill: University of North Carolina Press, 1953. Readable account of key events leading to the revolution.

Roche, John P. "The Founding Fathers: A Reform Caucus in Action." *American Political Science Review* 55 (December 1961): 799–816. Identifies the election connection at the Constitutional Convention.

Storing, Herbert J., ed. *The Anti-Federalist.* Chicago: University of Chicago Press, 1986. Selection of Anti-Federalist writings.

Tuchman, Barbara W. *The First Salute: A View of the American Revolution.* New York: Ballantine, 1988. Shows how the struggle for power among European countries affected the outcome of the Revolutionary War.

Wood, Gordon S. *The Radicalism of the American Revolution.* New York: Knopf, 1992. Portrays the unleashing of a democratic ideology during the struggle for independence.

# Federalism: Division of Power Among National, State, and Local Governments

## Chapter Outline

In April 1999 two students at Columbine High School in Littleton, Colorado, killed 12 classmates, one teacher, and then themselves, in a tragedy that shook the nation. But few commentators noted that when the students lugged guns to school, they committed no *federal* crime—despite the fact that Congress in 1990 had passed the Gun-Free School Zones Act. This law had made it a federal crime to carry unauthorized weapons near a public school, but it was declared unconstitutional by the Supreme Court in 1995. The Court said Congress did not have the right to enact this law. Was Congress wrong to pass such a law? Or did the Supreme Court make a mistake?

Answers to these questions go to the heart of the current debate over the proper division of powers between national and state governments in the U.S. federal system. On one side, supporters of the gun-free school law said Congress had clear authority to prohibit dangerous weapons on school grounds. On the other side, defenders of the powers and rights of the states emphasized that gun toting in school was already against state law; by passing a law on a subject that was a state responsibility, Congress was intruding where it did not belong. It was doing so only in response to public pressure to "do something" to stop school violence.

The issue eventually came to the attention of the Supreme Court. After Congress passed the gun-free school law, Alphonso Lopez, a teenager with neither a criminal record nor a history of trouble making in class, foolishly carried a .38-caliber handgun to school. Instead of leaving the matter to be decided under Texas state law by the local police, a U.S. district attorney, acting on a complaint filed by a federal agency, prosecuted the youth under the new federal law. When Lopez was convicted and given a six-month term in a federal prison, he appealed on the grounds that the gun-free school law violated Texas sovereignty. The Supreme Court agreed, saying that the power to regulate guns on school grounds is a matter to be handled by state and local governments, not by Congress. Instead of landing in jail, Lopez joined the marines.

THE LOPEZ DECISION RAISES MANY QUESTIONS. What did the court mean when it said that the State of Texas and all other states are sovereign? How is power divided among the national, state, and local governments? What does this division of power—called federalism—mean in practice? In this chapter we consider what federalism means and how its meaning has changed over the course of American history. In doing so, we answer the following questions.

- How does the contemporary debate over federalism relate to debates on the topic at the time the Constitution was ratified?
- What did federalism mean prior to the Civil War?
- How did Supreme Court interpretations of federalism change following the Civil War?
- How has Congress influenced the nature of federalism through its power to spend money?
- What roles do state and local governments play in the United States?

## *The Federalism Debate: It's New but It's Old*

Federalism is defined in terms of **sovereignty**—that is, fundamental governmental authority. **Federalism** divides sovereignty between at least two different levels. In the United States, the fundamental units are the *national government* and the *state governments,* and each has the power to act independently of the other. For a democratic government to be called a federal system, each fundamental level of government must have

1. its own set of elected officials
2. its own capacity to raise revenues by means of taxation
3. independent authority to pass laws regulating the lives of its citizens

Local governments, such as cities, counties, towns, and school districts, are also important parts of government in the United States, but *they are not fundamental units in the U.S. federal system* in the same way that the national and state governments are. According to a long-standing legal doctrine known as **Dillon's rule** (after the Iowa state judge John Dillon), local governments are, in legal terms, mere "creatures of the state." A state legislature can, at any time, alter the boundaries of any local government, expand or narrow its power, or abolish it altogether. As a result, local governments are not considered part of the federal system, as defined by the Constitution. However, they play a major role in the day-to-day practice of federalism.

As a principle of government, federalism has had a dubious history. The great fighter for Venezuelan independence, Simón Bolívar, once observed, "Among the popular and representative systems of government, I do not approve of the federal system: It is too perfect; and it requires virtues and political talents much superior to our own."[1] Even today, the vast majority of countries in the world have **unitary governments,** in which all authority is held by a single, national government. In unitary arrangements, local governments are simply administrative outposts of the national government. In Britain, for example, Parliament has the power to abolish all local governments, a power it has often used to redesign the country's municipal and county governments. Even though Britain has granted some powers to local Scottish and Northern Irish parliaments, it could abolish or override these parliaments at any time (see the accompanying International Comparison).

Although most countries have unitary forms of government, federalism has long been thought to be ideally suited to U.S. conditions. Federalism was an essential part of the Constitution because the document could not have been ratified had the identity of the existing states not been retained. Federalism also facilitated the admission of new territory to the union, helped government adapt to ethnic and cultural diversity, and helped promote the nation's extraordinary economic development. As early as the 1830s, the keen French observer of American politics Alexis de Tocqueville noted, "One can hardly imagine how much [the] division of sovereignty contributes to the well-being of each of the states that compose the Union. In these small communities . . . all public authority [is] turned toward internal improvements. . . . The ambition of power yields to the less refined and less dangerous desire for well-being."[2]

### *The Contemporary Debate*

Long before federalism had gained international respectability, Americans had reached almost universal agreement on its worth. But the exact distribution of powers between the national and state governments has been a subject of great conflict over the nation's history. In fact, the debate over federalism continues today, and the two major political parties hold very different views about how power ought to be distributed.

Today's partisan debate goes well beyond the pluses and minuses of specific government programs: Each political party tends to have a distinctive conception of the best way to organize American government. Although differences between the parties are not always sharp and clear, Republicans tend to think that as many government responsibilities as feasible should be left in the hands of state and local governments.

**sovereignty**
Fundamental governmental authority.

**federalism**
Division of sovereignty between at least two different levels of government.

**Dillon's rule**
Legal doctrine that local governments are mere creatures of the state.

**unitary government**
System under which all authority is held by a single, national government.

comparative
**Comparing Federal and Unitary Systems**

comparative
**Comparing State and Local Governments**

## International Comparison

# Great Britain and the United States: Unitary and Federal Governments

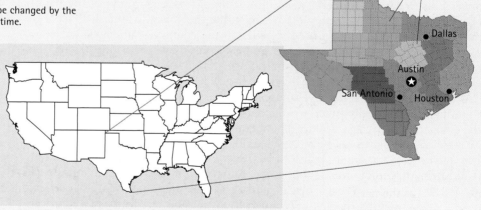

In Great Britain, which has a unitary government, the national government (Parliament) can reorganize regional and local governments whenever it wishes. In November 1998, Parliament created a new Scottish government, giving it authority over such areas as health, education, local government, and economic development policy. That same year, to put into effect a peace agreement reached between warring factions within the Catholic and Protestant communities in Northern Ireland, the British Parliament reorganized the government of Northern Ireland. But Parliament, if it so desires, can at any time eliminate the regional governments of Scotland and Northern Ireland, and it can pass legislation to override their policies.

In the United States, which has a federal system of government, Congress cannot change the constitutional powers of states, reorganize state government, or change state boundaries without the state's consent.

*In your view, what are the advantages and disadvantages of a federal system with regard to (1) political accountability, (2) efficient administration, and (3) cultural independence?*

**Britain: A Unitary Government**
Regional and local boundaries can be changed by the British national government at any time.

**The United States: A Federal Government**
States' boundaries cannot be changed without their consent, but city and county boundaries can be changed by states at any time.

They believe that much that is now paid for by the national government should be delegated to state and local governments. These Republicans reason that state and local governments are closer to the people, more in touch with their needs, and less likely to waste taxpayer dollars. Conversely, many Democrats think that such policy areas as pollution control, providing educational opportunity, and care for the sick and the poor are too big and affect the population too broadly to be settled at state and local levels. They think the national government must also play a role. However, some Democrats favor delegation of some federal programs to state and local governments.

In the early 1990s, the debate focused on the issue of **unfunded mandates,** the imposition of federal regulations on state and local governments without the appropriation of enough money to cover their cost. By 1993, countless mandates had reached the statute books.[3] For example, state and local governments had to ensure equal access to public facilities by disabled persons but were given little money to cover the new construction costs. Clean-air legislation asked state and local governments to reduce air pollution but skimped on the funding necessary to do the job.[4]

**unfunded mandates**
Federal regulations that impose burdens on state and local governments without appropriating enough money to cover costs.

Medicaid required expanded services for low-income recipients, but for many states, the law funded only half the cost of the program.[5]

On October 27, 1993, a number of state and local officials held "National Unfunded Mandates Day" to protest such policies. In a rally held on the steps of the City Hall in Columbus, Ohio, they called for a halt to the imposing of more rules and regulations on state and local governments unless the national government paid the cost. Complaining that cities were suffering "spending without representation," Columbus Mayor Gregory Lashutka said cities would have to spend $54 billion to comply with ten major federal mandates over the next five years.[6]

Members of Congress have strong incentives to impose mandates on state and local governments but to leave them unfunded. When a mandate is imposed, members of Congress get the credit for helping constituents. When it is left unfunded, Congress, safe at a distance, avoids the taxpayers' wrath.

Despite the long-standing popularity of unfunded mandates on Capitol Hill, the 1994 election slowed their growth, at least for the time being. Republican candidates campaigned in favor of governmental **devolution**, the return of governmental responsibilities to state and local governments. When Republicans won a majority in Congress, they passed a statute banning any new law that was not adequately funded. However, if Congress wishes it can—and sometimes does—ignore the law and pass new unfunded mandates anyway.

### Federalism and the Ratification of the Constitution

THE CONSTITUTION, TENTH AMENDMENT: *"The powers not delegated to the United States by the Constitution, nor prohibited by it to the States, are reserved to the States respectively, or to the people."*

The contemporary debate over federalism resembles a much older one that divided Federalists and the Anti-Federalists at the time the Constitution was being ratified. The Federalists (some say they should have been called Nationalists) took a position in favor of a strong national government. They felt that national strength was needed to overcome the rivalries among the states. The Anti-Federalists (some say they should have been called Federalists) wanted to keep the national government as limited as possible, fearing that a powerful national government could trample the liberties of the people.

The Constitution itself represents a compromise between these competing views. To appease those who wanted a weak national government, the Constitution denied Congress a general legislative power, instead giving it only specific, delegated powers, such as the powers to levy taxes and regulate interstate commerce. It also gave states independent authority, such as the responsibility for appointing officers in the militia (today known as the national guard). In addition, it guaranteed existing state boundaries, saying that no state can be stripped of its territory or divided into parts without its consent (see the accompanying Window on the Past). The Anti-Federalists also won (as part of the Bill of Rights) the Tenth Amendment, which reserved to the states all power not delegated to the federal government.

To satisfy the Federalists, the Constitution gave Congress, in addition to its delegated powers, the authority to undertake all activities "necessary and proper" to carry out its enumerated powers. It also enacted a **supremacy clause** stating that national laws "shall be the supreme Law of the Land . . . any Thing in the . . . Laws of any State to the Contrary notwithstanding," a statement that comes close to saying (yet does not quite say) that only the national government is truly sovereign. Table 3.1 summarizes the allocation of powers between the national and state governments.

## The Evolution of Federal Theory

Because the authors of the Constitution compromised on many of the differences between Federalists and Anti-Federalists, the issues raised at the time of the ratification campaign have never disappeared from American politics. Instead, the shape of

**visual literacy**
**Federalism and Regulations**

**devolution**
Return of governmental responsibilities to state and local governments.

**supremacy clause**
Constitutional provision that says the laws of the national government "shall be the supreme Law of the Land."

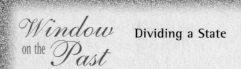

### Window on the Past     Dividing a State

States are clearly sovereign in at least one respect: Their boundaries cannot be altered under the Constitution without the consent of both the state and the federal government, except that Congress conceded to Texas at the time of its admission to the Union the right to divide itself into five states. Though Texans have never seemed much interested in this option, in 1819 Massachusetts (and Congress) did agree to let part of Massachusetts become the separate state of Maine.

Many such changes in state boundaries have since been proposed. Some people have said that California should be divided into northern and southern halves. Others have proposed separating New York City from the rest of the state. Some Floridians have proposed separating the panhandle region of that state from the peninsula. But only one state, Virginia, has ever lost a portion of its territory against its will. When the Civil War broke out in 1861, the counties in western Virginia formed their own government, which they called West Virginia. Despite the dubious constitutional standing of this rump government, Congress passed and Abraham Lincoln signed a law recognizing the new state.

American federalism has fluctuated over the course of American history, as the events in Figure 3.1 illustrate and the following discussion amplifies. Both Supreme Court decisions and the outcome of key elections have defined and redefined the nature of American federalism.

Supreme Court decisions have had a fundamental impact, because the Supreme Court has the power of **judicial review,** the authority to declare laws null and void on the grounds that they violate the Constitution (see Chapter 15). When the Supreme Court declares a law of Congress unconstitutional, as it did in the Lopez case, it not only limits congressional power but often expands the arena in which states are considered sovereign. The Supreme Court may also declare state laws unconstitutional, a power necessary for preserving national unity.

**judicial review**

Court authority to declare laws null and void on the grounds that they violate the Constitution.

---

**Table 3.1**

**Constitutional Division of Power Between National and State Governments**

| Powers Granted to the National Government | Powers Granted to the State Governments |
| --- | --- |
| Conduct foreign affairs | |
| Raise armies and declare war | Maintain state militias (the National Guard) |
| Regulate imports and exports | |
| Regulate interstate commerce | Regulate commerce within the state |
| Regulate immigration and naturalization | |
| Establish and operate federal court system | Establish and operate state court systems |
| Levy taxes | Levy taxes |
| Borrow money | Borrow money |
| Coin money | |
| Provide for the general welfare | |
| Make laws "necessary and proper" to accomplish the above tasks | Exercise powers not granted to national government |

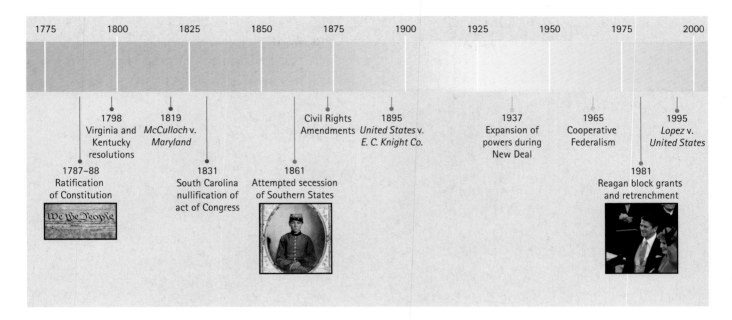

1775    1800    1825    1850    1875    1900    1925    1950    1975    2000

1798
Virginia and
Kentucky
resolutions

1819
*McCulloch* v.
*Maryland*

Civil Rights
Amendments

1895
*United States* v.
*E. C. Knight Co.*

1937
Expansion of
powers during
New Deal

1965
Cooperative
Federalism

1995
*Lopez* v.
*United States*

1787–88
Ratification
of Constitution

1831
South Carolina
nullification of
act of Congress

1861
Attempted secession
of Southern States

1981
Reagan block grants
and retrenchment

**Figure 3.1**

**Development of American Federalism**
Nationally elected leaders, state legislators, and courts have all shaped the evolution of American federalism.

Elections have been no less important for defining American federalism. Quite apart from the indirect effect that elections have on the makeup of the Supreme Court, they can have direct and immediate effects on the federal system. As the unfunded-mandates law reveals, changes in the control of Congress can have broad repercussions. In the pages that follow, we shall see how key national elections have often altered the shape of federalism.

## Dual Sovereignty

Much of the legal debate over federalism, both historical and contemporary, concerns the doctrine of **dual sovereignty,** which says that both the national and state governments have final authority over their own policy domains. As a legal and political doctrine, dual sovereignty is an American invention that challenges Thomas Hobbes's powerful argument stating there could be only one sovereign (see Chapter 2). If governmental power is divided, Hobbes said, the competing sovereigns will inevitably come into conflict with one another, driving the country into a state of civil war.

The *Federalist Papers* defended dual sovereignty by turning Hobbes's argument on its head. Whereas Hobbes said that anything less than a single sovereign would lead to war, the writers of the *Federalist Papers* argued that ensuring the division of power was the *best* way of preserving liberty. If power is concentrated in any one place, it can be used to crush individual liberty. Even in a democracy a tyranny of the majority may arise—and that is the worst kind of tyranny because it is stifling, complete, and seemingly legitimate. Dividing power between the national and state governments reduces the possibility that any single majority will be able to control all centers of governmental power.

**dual sovereignty**
A theory of federalism saying that both the national and state governments have final authority over their own policy domains.

## The Doctrine of Nullification

Dual-sovereignty theory was an entrenched part of constitutional understanding during the first decades following the adoption of the Constitution. Some thought state sovereignty so complete that they propounded the doctrine of **nullification,** which says that state legislatures can invalidate acts of Congress that threaten state or individual liberties. States first used this doctrine in 1798 in response to the passage of the Alien and Sedition Acts, which outlawed criticism of government officials (see the accompanying Election Connection). A Federalist-controlled Congress enacted the legislation to suppress the growing power of the Democratic–Republican party, led by

**nullification**
A doctrine that says that states have the authority to declare acts of Congress unconstitutional.

## Election Connection

# Federalism and the Election of 1800

Federalism was central to the events surrounding the election of 1800, one of the first major turning points in American democracy. The autonomy of state governments helped the country survive a crisis by facilitating the peaceful transition of power from one political party to another. But it also helped set precedents that would divide the country in the years to come.

Thomas Jefferson (1743–1826)

Aaron Burr (1756–1836). An artist's conception of his arrest for treason.

In 1798, with Congress under the control of the Federalist political party, president John Adams, also a Federalist, found himself embroiled in a foreign policy crisis with France. Upset by criticisms of the president and his party at this time of national emergency, Congress passed the Alien and Sedition Acts, which made it a crime to "write, print, utter, or publish . . . any false, scandalous and malicious writing . . . against . . . the Congress of the United States, or the President."[a] Opposition newspaper editors were soon imprisoned, and even Congressman Matthew Lyon was sentenced to four months in jail for insulting Adams.

Members of the opposition party, the Democratic-Republicans, were infuriated by the censorship laws. But because they could not expect the Federalist-controlled national government to help them, they went instead to the states. Thomas Jefferson of Virginia and his protégé James Madison drafted resolutions, which were passed by the Virginia and Kentucky legislatures, that nullified, or invalidated, the offending laws. They argued that the Alien and Sedition Acts were unconstitutional and that in claiming such broad powers of censorship, the federal government was tending toward "an absolute, or at best a mixed monarchy."

Conflicts between the two parties continued, reaching their height during the bitter presidential election race of 1800. Jefferson ran against Adams, choosing Aaron Burr of New York as his running mate. The Democratic-Republicans won the electoral college vote (see Chapter 2 for a discussion of the electoral college), but because of an oversight in the Constitution, Jefferson found himself tied with Burr—his own running mate—in the presidential balloting. (In 1804 the Constitution was amended to pre-

vent this from happening again. Rather than casting two votes each for president, electors now cast one vote for president and a second vote for vice-president.)

In such a situation, the House of Representatives decides who becomes president. But the House was controlled by Federalists, many of whom wanted nothing more than to frustrate Jefferson's ambitions, so the House went through 35 rounds of voting over 6 days without resolving the issue.

Again the Democratic-Republicans relied on their power in the states to give them leverage at the national level. If the Federalists connived to elect their own man president, Jefferson warned, Democratic-Republican-controlled states such as Virginia and Pennsylvania would take up arms. Finally several Federalist representatives lost heart, and Jefferson won the election. With Democratic-Republicans firmly in control of the national government, Congress repealed the Alien and Sedition acts. Later, Aaron Burr considered forming a separate western nation, and was arrested for treason. He was eventually acquitted.

*If the national government passed unconstitutional legislation today, or if it blocked the inauguration of a democratically elected president, should state governments resist? What is the role of federalism today in guaranteeing rights and liberties?*

SOURCE: Stanley Elkins and Eric McKitrick, *The Age of Federalism* (New York: Oxford University Press, 1993).

---

[a]Henry Steele Commager, *Documents of American History,* 6th ed. (New York: Appleton-Century-Crofts, 1958).

Thomas Jefferson. Invoking the doctrine of nullification, outraged Jeffersonians in Virginia and Kentucky passed state resolutions voiding the laws. Their defense of the right of free speech was praiseworthy, yet by using the doctrine of nullification to defend free speech, Virginia and Kentucky laid down a legal doctrine that would eventually help tear the country apart.

At first, the doctrine of nullification had no serious consequences. On the contrary, it was firmly rejected in **McCulloch v. Maryland,** a sweeping Supreme Court decision handed down in 1819 that is among the most important the Court has ever made.[7] The issue involved the Bank of the United States, an entity that commercial interests thought was vital to economic prosperity but that many farmers and debtors resented. Responding to popular opinion, the State of Maryland levied a tax on the

*McCulloch v. Maryland*
Decision of 1819 in which the Supreme Court declared unconstitutional the state's power to tax a federal government entity.

bank. McCulloch, an officer of the Maryland branch of the bank, had refused to pay the tax. Deciding in favor of McCulloch, Chief Justice John Marshall said that Maryland could not tax a federal bank, because the "power to tax involves the power to destroy."[8] If a state government could tax a federal agency, then states could undermine the sovereignty of the federal government. In declaring this state law unconstitutional, Marshall cast profound doubt on the power of the states to nullify acts of Congress.

Despite the *McCulloch* decision, the doctrine of nullification was not dead. The issue next arose shortly after the tumultuous election of 1828 that elected Andrew Jackson president. His vice-president, John Calhoun, formerly a senator from South Carolina, claimed that states had the power to nullify federal laws. A controversy developed over a tariff, a tax on imports, that was favored by northern manufacturers as a way of protecting local industry from foreign competition. Southerners opposed the tariff, because they wanted to sell their cotton to Europe and buy cheap manufactured products in return.

Calhoun's supporters in South Carolina called a state convention, which declared the tariff null and void in the state. The state even threatened to secede from the union if the federal government tried to collect the tariff by force. President Jackson prepared to use armed force to crush the dissidents, but cooler heads prevailed. Congress passed a lower tariff less objectionable to southern interests, and South Carolina agreed to pay the tax.

Though the overt issue was tariffs, the underlying, long-term question involved African Americans. Afraid that northerners would abolish slavery, southern leaders continued to espouse the doctrine of nullification as well as the right to secede peacefully from the Union. The issue was brought to a head with the election of Abraham Lincoln in 1860. Lincoln was the candidate of the new Republican party, which opposed the extension of slavery into the western territories and favored its eventual abolition. Seeing the Republicans as a direct challenge to slavery, white southerners invoked what they saw as their right of secession, and the United States experienced what Hobbes had most feared: a war between competing sovereigns. Only after half a million soldiers had died and a countryside had been laid to waste was the doctrine of nullification finally repudiated. After the Civil War, it was clear that whatever dual sovereignty meant, it did *not* mean that state legislatures could declare null and void the decisions of the federal government.

## *Court Interpretations of the Meaning of Dual Sovereignty*

Once the doctrine of nullification had been laid to rest, it was up to the federal courts, not state legislatures, to decide the meaning of dual sovereignty. Three clauses in the Constitution have provided much of the basis for the expansion of federal power: (1) the necessary and proper clause, (2) the commerce clause, and (3) the spending clause.

**simulation**
**You are
a Federal Judge**

### *Necessary and Proper Clause*

> CONSTITUTION, ARTICLE I: *"Congress shall have power . . . to make all laws which shall be necessary and proper for carrying into Execution the . . . Powers vested by this Constitution in the government of the United States."*

The delegated powers of Congress include those items specifically mentioned in the Constitution, such as the power to tax, borrow money, and establish a currency. The **necessary and proper clause** gives Congress the authority to "make all laws which shall be necessary and proper for carrying to execution" its delegated powers. The words *necessary and proper* were first analyzed by Justice Marshall in the same decision that challenged the doctrine of nullification, *McCulloch* v. *Maryland.* Maryland argued that Congress had no authority to establish a national bank, because a bank was not

**necessary and proper clause**
Constitutional clause that gives Congress the power to take all actions that are "necessary and proper" to the carrying out of its delegated powers. Also known as the *elastic clause.*

*necessary* for Congress to carry out its delegated power to coin money; it was only a *convenient* way of doing so. But Justice Marshall rejected such an interpretation as annihilating Congress's ability to select an appropriate means to carry out a task. "Let the end be legitimate," he said. "Let it be within the scope of the Constitution, and all means which are appropriate, which are plainly adapted to that end, which are not prohibited, but consistent with the letter and spirit of the Constitution, are constitutional."[9] Since this decision, the courts have generally found that almost any means selected by Congress are usually "necessary and proper." As a result, the necessary and proper clause has come to be known as the *elastic clause:* Over the centuries it has been stretched to fit almost any circumstance.

Even though an elastic interpretation of the necessary and proper clause has given Congress broad powers, the Supreme Court has said, as recently as 1992, that these powers are not without limit. Adding its voice to the rising political concern in Congress over increasing federal power, the Supreme Court, in *New York v. U.S.* (1992), declared that Congress cannot give direct orders to states. Though discussed in the arcane language of dual sovereignty, the case involved one of the most modern of political issues: the disposal of radioactive waste.

Disposal of radioactive waste has become a particularly annoying political problem. Millions of cubic feet of such waste needs to be buried someplace where it cannot be disturbed for thousands of years.[10] The problem has become an elected official's nightmare: Something needs to be done, and there is no way of doing it without making some people angry—really angry. Easily alarmed at the very word *radioactive,* citizens organize protests and demonstrations whenever a town is mentioned as a potential radioactive dump. Everyone knows the stuff has to go somewhere, but everyone also says, "Not In My Back Yard." This is generally known as the **NIMBY problem.**

After stewing fitfully over the NIMBY problem for several years, Congress discovered a politically painless solution: It required each state either to find an adequate burial site for its waste or to become legally responsible for any damages the waste might cause. Rather than making tough decisions themselves, Congress decided to place an unfunded mandate on governors and state legislatures.

As a result, the debate over domestic radioactive waste shifted to the states. In no state was the issue more hotly debated than in New York. Often, when state officials identified a potential dump, they were run off the site and burned in effigy.[11] Under the pressure of the federal law, New York officials decided to ignore the opposition and

**participation**

**Federal Regulations and Mandates**

**NIMBY problem**

Everyone wants the problem solved, but "Not In My Back Yard."

**Congress Dumps a Problem on the States, But the Supreme Court Says No**
Citizens organized protests and demonstrations whenever a town was named as a potential site for a waste dump. *Why did the Supreme Court reject Congress's response to this "Not in My Back Yard" (NIMBY) problem?*

dump the waste in Cortland and Allegany counties. But the elected boards for the two counties, to keep faith with county voters, filed a suit claiming that the federal law was unconstitutional. Justice Sandra Day O'Connor, writing for the majority, said Congress could not force states or local governments to bury their nuclear waste; such direct orders to a state violated its sovereignty.[12] It remains to be seen how widely the Court will apply this principle, but the old doctrine of dual sovereignty has clearly been revived.

## Commerce Clause

> CONSTITUTION, ARTICLE I: *"Congress shall have power . . . to regulate commerce . . . among the several states."*

The meaning of the **commerce clause,** which gives Congress the power to regulate commerce among the states, has been the subject of heated dispute. The courts have generally distinguished *interstate* (between-state) commerce, which Congress may regulate, from *intrastate* (within-state) commerce, which can be regulated only by the states. In the nineteenth century, intrastate commerce was defined as including all commerce that did not overtly cross state lines. Thus, for example, the Supreme Court in 1895 said, in *United States* v. *E. C. Knight Co.,* that Congress could not break up a monopoly that had a nationwide impact on the price of sugar, because the company that enjoyed the monopoly refined its sugar within the state of Pennsylvania.[13] The fact that the sugar was to be sold nationwide was said to be only "incidental" to its production.

The *Knight* case, which denied the federal government sovereignty over a large portion of economic activity, remained the reigning legal doctrine until the 1930s. In 1932, however, Democrat Franklin D. Roosevelt defeated Republican incumbent Herbert Hoover in a bitter presidential election that foreshadowed a period of expansion of federal power. Campaigning in the midst of the Great Depression, Roosevelt promised to use the power of the federal government to get the country going again. He and his Democratic party allies in Congress enacted a series of governmental policies known as the **New Deal,** a wide array of programs that expanded the power of the federal government for the purposes of stimulating economic recovery and creating a national safety net for those in need. Many Republicans opposed these New Deal policies, in part because they violated long-standing principles of federalism. At first the Supreme Court ruled against any expansion in federal power. But after Roosevelt's landslide reelection in 1936, the Court's position began to change.

A key decision involved the Wagner Act, a New Deal law that protected union organizers. Although the new law regulated activities within a state, Chief Justice Charles Evans Hughes declared it constitutional: "When industries organize themselves on a national scale, . . . how can it be maintained that their industrial labor relations constitute a forbidden field into which Congress may not enter?"[14] Relations between employers and their workers, once declared local, were now said to be part of interstate commerce.

With new appointments to the Court by President Roosevelt, the definition of interstate commerce continued to expand. In 1942 a farmer violated crop quotas imposed under New Deal legislation by sowing 23 acres of wheat. The Court ruled the law a constitutional regulation of interstate commerce, even though the farmer was feeding all the wheat to his own livestock. The Court reasoned that the farmer, by not buying the wheat, was depressing the worldwide price of grain.[15] With such an expansive definition of interstate commerce, hardly anything could be characterized as simply local or beyond the scope of Congress to regulate.

This broad interpretation of the commerce clause remained unquestioned until the 1995 case, *U.S.* v. *Lopez,* discussed at the beginning of this chapter. The Lopez decision has opened up an opportunity for the Supreme Court to place new limits on Congress's ability to intervene in state and local affairs. In 1997 the Court expanded the thrust of the Lopez decision by declaring unconstitutional a federal law that required state and local law enforcement officials to check the backgrounds of those seeking to buy handguns. The Court said that the federal government could not issue orders to state

**commerce clause**
Constitutional provision that gives Congress power to regulate commerce "among the states."

**New Deal**
Programs created by the Franklin Roosevelt administration that expanded the power of the federal government for the purpose of stimulating economic recovery and establishing a national safety net.

officials without violating state sovereignty, as protected by the Tenth Amendment. It remains to be seen whether the current move toward devolution taking place within the Supreme Court will further change the meaning of the commerce clause.

## Spending Clause

CONSTITUTION, ARTICLE I: *"Congress shall have power . . . to lay and collect taxes, duties, imposts and excises, to pay the debts and provide for the . . . general welfare of the United States."*

---

**spending clause**

Constitutional provision that gives Congress the power to collect taxes to provide for the general welfare.

---

The **spending clause** grants Congress the power to collect taxes to provide for the general welfare. The New Deal Supreme Court considered the meaning of this clause when it ruled on the constitutionality of the social security program for senior citizens that was enacted in 1935. A taxpayer challenged the program on the grounds that tax dollars were being spent for the specific welfare of the elderly, not for the general welfare. But the Supreme Court, now in tune with Roosevelt's enlarged conception of federal power, said it was up to Congress, not the Court, to decide whether any particular program was for the general welfare. "[T]he discretion belongs to Congress," said the Court, "unless the choice is clearly wrong."[16] So far, the Court has never found Congress "clearly wrong."

Not only did the Supreme Court refuse to restrict the purposes for which Congress could spend money, but it also conceded to Congress the right to attach any reasonable regulation to the money it spends. In 1984 Congress provided a grant to state governments for highway maintenance but withheld some of the funding unless states raised the drinking age from eighteen to twenty-one. South Dakota challenged the constitutionality of this mandate on the grounds that teenage drunkenness had only a remote connection to road repair. The Supreme Court rejected this argument.[17] State sovereignty was not violated, the Court concluded, because any state could choose not to accept the money. The regulation proved effective, inasmuch as every state has now raised its drinking age to twenty-one.

The congressional power to tax and spend has remained one of the broadest federal powers, because it allows Congress to attach whatever regulations it deems appropriate to the grants it gives to states. Upon this power has been founded the theory and practice of cooperative federalism.

### SECTION SUMMARY

The writers of the U.S. Constitution invented modern federalism and the associated doctrine of dual sovereignty between states and the federal government. Because the Supreme Court has the power of judicial review, the historical development of federalism has been greatly affected by what the Court says the Constitution means. Three constitutional clauses have provided much of the legal basis for the expansion of federal power: the necessary and proper clause, which gives Congress the authority to legislate where appropriate to carry out its powers; the commerce clause, which gives Congress the power to regulate commerce among the states; and the spending clause, which allows Congress to collect taxes.

**timeline**

**Federalism over Time**

## Cooperative Federalism

---

**marble-cake federalism**

The theory that all levels of government can work together to solve common problems. Also known as *cooperative federalism*.

---

Political scientist Morton Grodzins first propounded the theory of **cooperative federalism,** or **marble-cake federalism.** According to this theory, all levels of government should—and in fact do—perform all governmental functions together. Grodzins criticized proponents of dual sovereignty for viewing government as a layer cake, each level independent of and separate from the other.[18] He pointed out that in practice, agencies from different levels of government work together, combining and intertwining their functions to such an extent that the intergovernmental system resembles a marble cake.

In all policy realms, Grodzins said, one finds many levels of government working together on similar tasks. For example, law enforcement requires cooperation among the Federal Bureau of Investigation, state highway traffic control, the county sheriff's office, and local police departments. According to Grodzins, all levels of government should work together for three reasons:

1. Cooperative federalism is democratic. The involvement of all levels of government ensures that many different interests in society are represented.
2. Compromises are reached among officials elected by different constituencies. Federal officials listen to state and local officials, because the latter have influence with members of Congress. Similarly, state officials listen to community leaders, because to stay in office, state legislators must pay attention to local needs.
3. Professional administrators usually share many values, no matter what level of government they work for. Law enforcement officials have many things in common, whether they work for the FBI or the local police. Most educational administrators, whether federal, state, or local, were once schoolteachers.

The 1964 election of Lyndon Johnson, together with an overwhelming Democratic majority in Congress, provided an opportunity to test more fully Grodzins's theory of cooperative federalism. Over the next few years, Congress passed a broad range of legislation that greatly enlarged the number, size, and complexity of **intergovernmental grants,** programs funded in part by the federal government but administered by state and local governments. State and local governments are often required to provide matching funds for a program in order to receive the grant. The typical "match" is 50 percent of total costs, but it can be as much as 90 percent or as little as 10 percent. Intergovernmental grants have become a key feature of the federal system. In 1930 only $85.8 million was spent on intergovernmental grants to local governments.[19] As Figure 3.2 on page 81 indicates, grants to state and local governments had grown to $43.6 billion by 1962, and by 1982 they had more than tripled to $147.5 billion. (Unless otherwise indicated, all amounts in this chapter are calculated in 1998 dollars.)

> **intergovernmental grant**
> Grant from the national government to a state or local government.

Growth in the number and size of intergovernmental grants was facilitated by their popularity with most members of Congress. Many found they could profit handsomely from new projects begun in their home districts. As Senator Barry Goldwater said, "I don't care what the piece of equipment is—or how bad it is—if it's done in his state, the senator has to stand up and scream for it."[20] Though grants are often criticized as mere "pork barrel" projects that have little or no value beyond helping members of Congress get reelected, most grants are well received by the city or town lucky enough to get the money. Speaker of the House Thomas Foley once pointed out that "One person's pork barrel project is another person's wise investment in the local infrastructure."[21] For example, an embankment protecting West Fargo from floods, constructed at the behest of a North Dakota senator, was originally condemned as sheer pork. But in the great 1997 flood of the Red River, the embankment saved the town from disaster.

Representative Joe McDade of Pennsylvania proved to be one of the grand masters of grant making. From his position as ranking Republican on the House Appropriations Committee, McDade secured federal monies to help build a center for the performing arts, fund a microbiology institute for cancer research at the University of Scranton, restore an antique aqueduct, construct McDade Park in Lackawanna County (including a tourist-friendly museum on the history of coal mining), turn the home of minor novelist Zane Grey in Lackawaxen into a national historic site, finance a flood-control project, and convert a railroad station into a fancy hotel and restaurant. Needless to say, McDade was extraordinarily popular with his constituents. Though he was under indictment on charges of "racketeering, conspiracy and accepting about $100,000 in illegal gratuities," McDade's success in winning federal grants for his district enabled him to win reelection to Congress in 1994.[22]

## *Categorical Grants*

Though Republicans like Representative McDade benefited from federal grants, the theory of cooperative federalism was particularly well suited to Democratic party philosophy. Many Democrats saw federal grants as vehicles that could help the country address needs that state and local governments had long ignored. To ensure that grants are properly used, Democrats have generally favored **categorical grants.** These are grants that include regulations that specify how the money is to be spent. Although some of these categorical grants fund basic government services, such as the construction of transportation and sanitation systems, most have had social welfare purposes. Categorical grants provide compensatory education for those coming from disadvantaged backgrounds, fund special educational programs for the disabled, and train the unemployed. They have also been used to construct housing for low- and moderate-income groups. Food stamps are available for the poor. Rapid-transit operations are subsidized to help reduce commuting costs.

The **War on Poverty,** a wide-ranging set of programs designed to enhance the economic opportunity of low-income citizens, became the most famous and controversial of all categorical grant programs. Enacted in 1964 at the height of the civil rights movement, this poverty initiative required involvement of the poor in program implementation to the maximum extent feasible.

Several accomplishments of the War on Poverty remain evident three decades later. The popular Head Start program for preschoolers anticipated and paved the way for a nationwide system of child care and nursery school programs. Job Corps, a residential education and training program, paid off in better wages and employment prospects. Most notably, these antipoverty programs incorporated many minority leaders into the political process. From the ranks of the poverty warriors emerged many minority mayors, state legislators, and members of Congress elected in the 1980s and 1990s.

Despite these achievements, the War on Poverty is better remembered for the warring factions that it generated than for its substantive results. An annual budget of just $23 billion was simply not capable of financing a "war" against poverty. In addition, efforts to coordinate local social services suffered from repeated dismal failures. Finally, most of the job search, worker readiness, summer job, and other short-term training programs had only limited long-term benefits.

The main political objection to the War on Poverty was its emphasis on community mobilization. In many cities, poverty warriors antagonized local agencies and

**categorical grant**
Federal grants to a state and/or local government that impose programmatic restrictions on the use of funds.

**War on Poverty**
One of the most controversial of the Great Society programs. Designed to enhance the economic opportunity of low-income citizens.

**Food Stamps**
The federal government funds the food stamp program through categorical grants to state and local governments. These governments then distribute food coupons to eligible recipients, who buy the food they need.

elected officials by encouraging protests, demonstrations, legal action, and minority electoral involvement. Local officials questioned why federal monies should fund political opposition. Some blamed the program for the wave of civil violence that swept through American cities in the two years following its adoption. In 1974 President Richard Nixon, who had campaigned against the poverty war, persuaded Congress to transfer its most popular components to other agencies and to shut down the remainder.

## Problems of Implementation

The War on Poverty was only one of many categorical grant programs that came under tough scrutiny from those who studied their **implementation**—the way in which grant programs are actually administered at the local level. Aaron Wildavsky, Martha Derthick, and other implementation scholars gave three reasons for doubting that many intergovernmental grants were as effective as Grodzins had said:[23]

1. National and local officials, serving different constituencies, often block and check one another, making it impossible to get much done. For example, when Lyndon Johnson tried to build "new towns" for the poor on vacant federal land, he encountered the opposition of local officials who objected to the program's adverse effects on local property values.[24] Virtually no new towns were built.
2. When many participants are involved, delays and confusion are almost inevitable. It took over 4 years to get a job creation program in Oakland, California, under way. Jeffrey Pressman and Wildavsky pointed out that the long delay was caused at least in part by the sheer number of agencies involved in the decision. The program required 70 separate clearances. Even if each took an average of only 3 weeks (not an unreasonable length of time), the total delay would be 210 weeks—or over 4 years.[25]
3. Federal policy makers often raise unrealistic expectations by using exaggerated rhetoric, thereby guaranteeing disappointment. It was a mistake to equate the poverty programs with a "war" when only limited resources were available.

**Head Start**
Three decades after the War on Poverty launched a variety of such initiatives, Head Start remains one of the most visible and successful early-intervention programs for disadvantaged preschoolers like those shown above.

**implementation**
The way in which grant programs are administered at the local level.

**Unnecessary Complexity?**
Some think that the intergovernmental grant system is as convoluted as the pencil sharpener shown here. *Does it have to be this complicated?*

# Pencil Sharpener

Professor Butts gets his think-tank working and evolves the simplified pencil sharpener.

Open window (**A**) and fly kite (**B**). String (**C**) lifts small door (**D**), allowing moths (**E**) to escape and eat red flannel shirt (**F**). As weight of shirt becomes less, shoe (**G**) steps on switch (**H**) which heats electric iron (**I**) and burns hole in pants (**J**).

Smoke (**K**) enters hole in tree (**L**), smoking out opossum (**M**) which jumps into basket (**N**), pulling rope (**O**) and lifting cage (**P**), allowing woodpecker (**Q**) to chew wood from pencil (**R**), exposing lead. Emergency knife (**S**) is always handy in case opossum or the woodpecker gets sick and can't work.

The difficulty of achieving intergovernmental cooperation may have been exaggerated by these implementation theorists. Most implementation studies focused on problems that federal grant programs had during their first two or three years. More recent work has shown that many administrative problems were reduced with the passage of time. For example, the federal compensatory education program initially stigmatized disadvantaged students by separating them from their classmates in order to make sure that federal funds were concentrated on the most needy. But once this requirement was found to be counterproductive to education, federal administrators eliminated it.[26]

### Block Grants

Despite these more positive findings from recent research, the criticism of categorical grants by implementation theorists proved quite influential. To simplify federal policy, Congress replaced many categorical grants with **block grants**, intergovernmental grants with a broad set of objectives, a minimum of federal restrictions, and maximum discretion for local officials. Table 3.2 illustrates the difference between categorical and block grants and gives some examples of each.

The surge toward block grants has had three distinct waves, each influenced by the political circumstances prevailing at the time. The first wave of block grants began under President Nixon. The most comprehensive, **general revenue sharing**, gave state and local governments a share of federal tax revenues to be used for any purpose whatsoever. During this first wave, block grants did not replace categorical grants so much as supplement them. To win support for general revenue sharing and other block grants, Nixon was forced to agree to continue many of the categorical programs that Democrats in Congress favored. As a consequence, the total size of the intergovernmental grant program continued to grow throughout the administrations of Nixon and Gerald Ford, and by the late 1970s, as the top line in Figure 3.2 shows, they cost more than $155 billion.

The second wave of block grants came at the beginning of Ronald Reagan's administration, which, unlike the Nixon administration, enjoyed a Republican majority in the Senate. Reagan succeeded in converting a broad range of categorical grants in education, social services, health services, and community development to block grants. During this second wave, the new block grants not only had fewer restrictions than the older categoricals,[27] but their funding levels were also reduced to comply with the administration's overall policy of "shrinking government." The amount spent on block grants fell from $93.5 billion in 1977 to $64.1 billion in 1998, and most of this reduc-

**block grant**
Federal grants to a state and/or local government that impose minimal restrictions on the use of funds.

**general revenue sharing**
The most comprehensive of block grants, which gives money to state and local governments to be used for any purpose whatsoever.

### Table 3.2

**Categorical Grants and Block Grants: Some Examples**

| Type of Grant | Restrictions on Use of Funds? | Examples |
|---|---|---|
| Categorical grant | Significant | Food stamps (Created 1971): Provides funds to states and localities to supply food to eligible low-income residents. |
| | | Medicaid (created 1965): Provides health insurance to low-income and disadvantaged citizens. |
| Block Grant | Minimal | Housing and Community Development Block Grant (created 1974): Provides funds to states and localities for general development purposes. |
| | | Temporary Assistance to Needy Families (created 1996): Provides funds to states to design and implement their own welfare programs. |

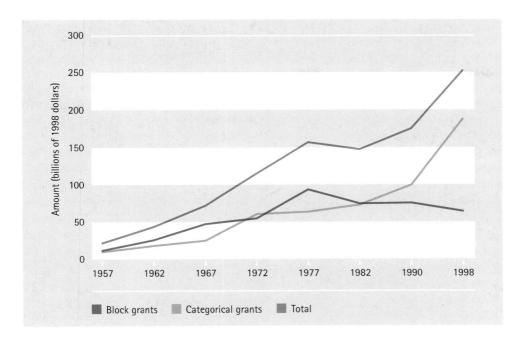

**Figure 3.2**

**Growth and Decline in Federal Grants to States and Localities**
Expenditures for categorical grants continue to rise, whereas expenditures for block grants have declined in recent years.

SOURCE: Paul E. Peterson, *The Price of Federalism* (Washington, DC: Brookings, 1995), Ch. 5; U.S. Bureau of the Census, *Federal Aid to the States for Fiscal Year 1998.* (Note: Totals exclude defense expenditures. Deriving precise estimates of block and categorical grants is a difficult undertaking. Here we have employed grants used mainly for developmental purposes as a proxy for block grants, and grants used mainly for redistributive purposes as a proxy for categorical grants.)

tion occurred in the early 1980s. General revenue sharing was eliminated in 1985, and the community development block grant, a major grant program for cities across the country, was cut from $7.7 billion in 1980 to $4.6 billion in 1998.[28]

The third wave of block grants took place after the congressional election of 1994, when Republicans captured control of Congress. Earlier block grant initiatives had not touched large social programs, such as Medicaid and Aid to Families with Dependent Children (AFDC). But in 1996 Congress transformed the AFDC program into a block grant that gave states almost complete discretion over the way monies could be used (see Chapter 18). Congress also tried to transform the Medicaid program into a block grant, but this was forestalled by a presidential veto. As a result, expenditures on categorical grants have continued to rise (see Figure 3.2).

Since the 1994 election, the debate over categorical and block grants has become a matter of intense political conflict. Each side can make a compelling case for its point of view (see Democratic Dilemma on page 83). Perhaps the best argument against both categorical and block grants is that even though they are often defended as a way of equalizing resources across the country,[29] federal grants in fact do not have this effect. Instead, federal grants are handed out to all states on a more or less equal basis, with wealthier states receiving as much or more federal dollars as poorer states. Figure 3.3 shows that on average, the ten richest states in the country get much more money from block grants, per resident, than other states.

Election pressures make it difficult for Congress to direct federal dollars to needy parts of the country. Members of Congress fight to get as much money as possible for their home states and districts. If they do not, their election opponents can make it a campaign issue. The experience of Massachusetts Senator Edward Kennedy, a Democrat, provides an illuminating example. In 1988 Kennedy had run on the campaign slogan "He can do more for Massachusetts," a reference to his many Washington connections dating to the time when his brother had been president. When Kennedy ran for reelection in 1994, a study showed that Massachusetts was receiving only 97 cents back for every dollar paid in taxes (instead of the $1.01 it had received in 1988). The finding fetched the following headline in a local newspaper: "State's Share of Federal Dollars Drops: Kennedy's Record in Last Decade, a Campaign Issue." Kennedy's Republican opponent accused him of not having "done the hard work to do very much [for Massachusetts] at all."[30] Though Kennedy still won reelection, the vote was surprisingly close.

**Figure 3.3**

**Block Grants for Traditional Governmental Services**
Richer states get as much money as or more money than poorer states. Is this unfair, or do rich states deserve more because they pay more to the federal government in taxes?

SOURCE: U.S. Bureau of the Census, *Federal Aid to the States for Fiscal Year 1998,* April 1999, Table 1.

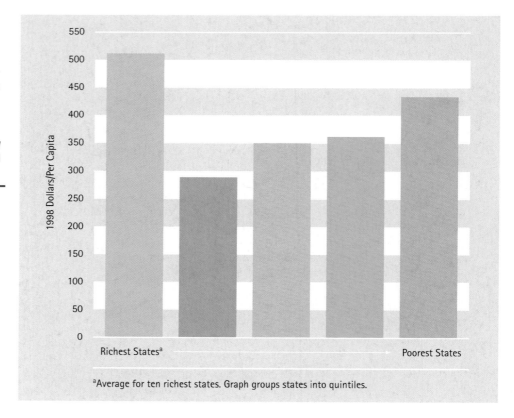

<sup>a</sup>Average for ten richest states. Graph groups states into quintiles.

Perhaps the best argument in favor of federal grants is that they are necessary to maintain properly funded social programs. Federal categorical grants, such as Medicaid, food stamps, and other social welfare programs, are especially important, because states, when not subject to federal regulation, try to shift the burden of serving the needy, the sick, and the poor to other states. In Minnesota, a state with generous programs for the poor, the proportion of new welfare recipients coming from out of state increased from 19 to 28 percent between 1994 and 1995, a time when other states were placing limits on welfare benefits. "We're really concerned," a county official said.[31] Fearful of migration from other places, many states feel pressured to offer fewer benefits than their sister states, creating a vicious cycle of cuts that President Clinton called a "race to the bottom." Between 1970 and 1993, welfare benefits in the average state fell by 42 percent.[32] In the two years following the reform of welfare that allowed states more flexibility, average state expenditures dropped 22 percent from 1996 levels. It is not yet clear, however, whether this decline is due to a race to the bottom or to continuing economic prosperity that has created job opportunities for the previously unemployed.[33]

Though the debate over grants has polarized between those in favor of a wide variety of intergovernmental grants and those opposed to all of them, the most sensible solutions may lie somewhere in the middle. In areas where state and local governments have traditionally concentrated their efforts, including transportation, sanitation, and education, it may be appropriate to keep the federal role to a minimum, because states and localities can be expected to provide these services whether they receive federal aid or not. But in other areas, such as Medicaid and food stamps, it may be important to establish federal standards so that states do not "race to the bottom." In 1996 Congress and the president in fact found it possible to reach compromises at this middle position. They made the biggest cuts in traditional programs. They also changed the AFDC program into a block grant welfare program. But the largest social programs, Medicaid and food stamps, remained federally funded categorical programs.[34]

## *Democratic Dilemma*

## Categorical or Block Grant: Which Is Better?

The debate over categorical and block grants has been intense and strikes at the heart of how broad we understand federalism to be. Because of the restrictions Congress places on their use, categorical grants reserve more power for the national government. Block grants, on the other hand, relinquish more authority to the states.

A supporter of block grants might make the following arguments against categorical grants:

1. Categoricals are *inefficient.* Federal regulations tie the hands of state and local governments, who have a better understanding of local conditions. Categorical grants for public housing—designed with urban areas in mind—may be tied to inflexible regulations that are impractical for rural states, such as Montana and Idaho.
2. Categoricals create *powerful interest groups.* Categorical grants typically contain restrictions that focus services on specific groups. These groups support powerful lobbies that perpetuate unnecessary policies.
3. Categoricals impose *unfunded mandates.* Federal funds do not cover the full cost of the rules that accompany them. In effect, this forces states to raise the extra money through taxes. By forcing states to raise and spend this money, categorical grants sap their independence.

A supporter of categorical grants might make the following arguments:

1. Categoricals are *necessary to achieve national purposes.* For example, many environmental problems are national in scope. If a state does not clean up its radioactive waste or allows its factories to spew smoke into the air, the resulting pollution can spread far beyond its own boundaries. The federal government needs to attach regulations to its grants to ensure that all states comply with the effort to achieve national policy goals.
2. If grants are not categoricals that include regulations, states will "*race to the bottom.*" Federal supervision of Medicaid, food stamps, and other welfare programs is especially important, because states, when not subject to federal regulation, often try to lower the benefits they make available, hoping that the needy and sick will move to other states.
3. Block grants are *wasteful.* If the federal government provides the money, it has every right and responsibility to make sure the funds are used for federal purposes. Block grants are a dream for local politicians—"free" money to be spent however they want without being held accountable to local taxpayers. When money is "free," it is likely to be wasted.
4. Block grants are simply the first step toward *eliminating needed federal programs.* After a program has been converted from a categorical to a block grant, its constituency is less well defined and it becomes harder to sustain the program's political base of support. Once the states are in charge of making policy decisions, it is easier for the federal government to abandon responsibility for the program altogether.

*Which of these points makes the most sense to you? Why? Which position do you find more persuasive?*

## SECTION SUMMARY

The federal government has greatly increased its use of intergovernmental grants since the early 1960s, giving rise to the cooperative federalism perspective, which says that different levels of government work together to solve problems. The two major types of grants are categorical grants, which come with specific rules about how funds should be spent, and block grants, which allow states more discretion. Despite problems with the implementation of categorical grants, and despite continuing criticisms of each type of grant by proponents of the other, the federal government still uses both types to achieve its purposes.

## *Local Government*

Because of the recent devolution of responsibilities to state and local governments, these governments play a more prominent role in the federal system than they have for several decades. Even before the most recent devolution, nearly half of all domestic government expenditure was paid for by taxes raised by state and local governments. This pattern, shown in Figure 3.4, is in keeping with long-standing American traditions. Nearly a century ago, the British scholar James Bryce identified the key role played by local governments in the American federal system:

> It is the business of a local authority to mend the roads, to clean out the village well or to provide a new pump, to see that there is a place where straying beasts may be kept till the owner reclaims them, to fix the number of cattle each villager may turn out on the common pasture, [and] to give each his share of timber cut in the common woodland.[35]

## Figure 3.4

**Domestic Expenditure of Governments**
State and local governments spend almost as much as the national government does.

SOURCE: Paul E. Peterson, *The Price of Federalism* (Washington, DC: Brookings, 1995), U.S. Bureau of the Census, *Statistical Abstract of the United States, 1998.*

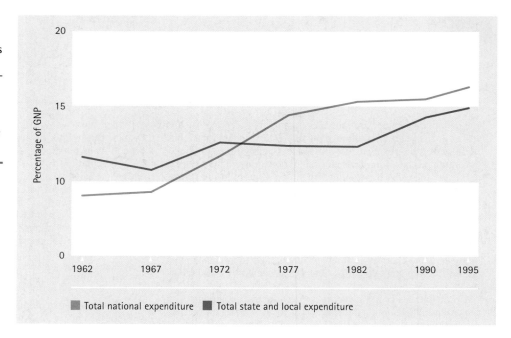

Though the nature of the work has been modernized since Bryce observed it, the basic functions remain much the same. Local governments maintain roads; take care of the parks; provide police, fire, and sanitation services; run the schools; and perform many other functions that affect the everyday lives of citizens.

### The Number and Types of Local Governments

In sheer numbers, local governments constitute an overwhelming and growing presence—there were over 73,000 in 1997, up from about 46,000 in 1942 (see Figure 3.5). There are several different major types of local governments, each of which has responsibilities that vary from state to state. Though the basic unit in most states is the

**A Local Task**
The basic functions of local government can range from garbage collection to, well, traffic control. As this photograph demonstrates, much of the time even the police in Washington, DC, have tasks less glamorous than providing security for the president.

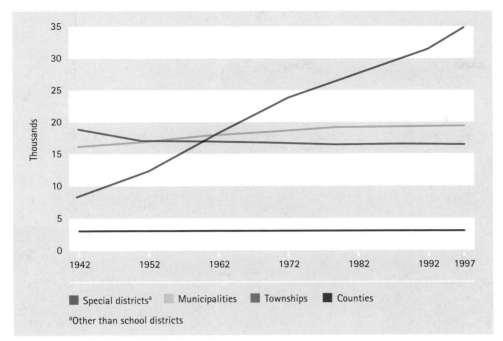

**Figure 3.5**

**Number of Local Governments, 1942–1997**
*Why do you think the number of special districts has increased so much over the last 50 years?*

SOURCE: U.S. Bureau of the Census, *Statistical Abstract of the United States,* 1998.

county, not all counties are alike. In some states they manage school systems, welfare programs, local roads, sanitation systems, a sheriff's office, and an array of other governmental activities. In other states they have hardly any duties. Many counties are divided into townships—there are nearly 17,000 of them nationwide—whose duties generally include local road maintenance and other small-scale activities.

As the population has become concentrated in urban areas, the total number of municipalities—cities, suburbs, and towns—has increased to nearly 20,000. In most states, these municipal governments have assumed many of the responsibilities once performed by counties.

States, counties, and municipalities have also created an extraordinary array of special districts—nearly 30,000 in all. Each special district has responsibility for only one or a few specific governmental functions. Such governments are unique in that they overlap the boundaries of other local governments, sometimes spanning many different municipal jurisdictions. As Figure 3.5 shows, special districts account for most of the increase in the number of local governments over the last 50 years. Some special districts run schools, others manage parks, and still others administer transportation systems or garbage collection. Even as specific a task as mosquito abatement can be the responsibility of a special district.

## Local Elections

Most local governments are run by elected officials, though special-district heads are sometimes appointed by other local governments. In the United States as a whole, the total number of elected local officials approaches half a million people. But despite the large number of local elections, actual rates of citizen participation in them are surprisingly low. If a particularly colorful candidate runs for mayor, or if ethnic or racial issues are raised, large numbers of voters can show up at the polls. But much of the time, the local electorate is about half the size of the presidential electorate.[36]

The near invisibility of local elections helps to reduce local participation rates.[37] The sheer number of elected officeholders often makes local government elections confusing to many voters. Newspaper coverage is haphazard. Local governments often

**A Local Election Campaign**
*Why do Americans vote at lower rates in local elections?*

hold their elections at times that coincide with neither state nor national elections, which further reduces turnout rates.[38] Surprisingly, local governments also oversee the administration of national elections. This local responsibility became a key issue in the close 2000 presidential election, when some voters in Palm Beach County, Florida, claimed that the county's confusing ballot design had led them to vote for the wrong candidate.

### Popularity of Local Government

One might think that this diverse, complicated, only half-democratic, seemingly irrational system could not possibly succeed. Yet local government remains very popular. According to the survey results shown in Figure 3.6, 37 percent of the population trust their local government more than other levels of government, compared to the only 19 percent who trust the federal government the most. Only 8 percent feel their local government is most wasteful of their tax dollars, as compared to 66 percent who feel this way about the federal government.

One explanation for the apparent popularity of local government, despite the low profile of its elections, is the ability of people to "vote with their feet"—that is, to move from one community to another—if they are unhappy with their local government. Americans are a mobile people: Over 17 percent move each year.[39] Every local government has to remember that if it is inefficient or unresponsive, its city or town will suffer a drop in population and property values. As a result, most local governments have good reason to be mindful of their constituents' needs, despite low voting rates.

**laboratories of democracy**
Doctrine that state and local governments contribute to democracy by providing places where experiments are tried and new theories tested.

Local governments also serve as **laboratories of democracy**, places where experiments are tried and new theories about government tested. If successful, an experiment may be copied by other town governments. If it fails, the experiment is soon abandoned.

Finally, the wide variety of local governments gives people a choice. Some people favor sex education programs and condom distribution in school; others do not. Some people think refuse collection should be publicly provided; others prefer to recycle

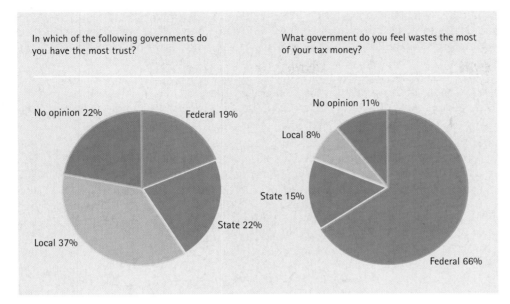

In which of the following governments do you have the most trust?

No opinion 22%
Federal 19%
Local 37%
State 22%

What government do you feel wastes the most of your tax money?

No opinion 11%
Local 8%
State 15%
Federal 66%

**Figure 3.6**

**Evaluations of Federal, State, and Local Governments**
*Why do you think more people trust local government than other governments?*

SOURCE: Thomas R. Dye, "Federalism: A Return to the Future," *Madison Review* 1 (Fall 1995): 3.

their own garbage. Some people think police protection should be intensive; others think an intrusive police presence violates the civil liberties of citizens. By giving people a choice, the diversity of local governments reduces conflict and enhances citizen satisfaction.

## Limits on Local Government

For all the strengths of local governments, they often do not have the resources to meet the needs of the poor, the sick, and the disabled. If a local government tries to provide substantial services to the needy, it runs the risk of attracting more poor people and driving away those who are better off. For example, in the early 1990s, Framingham, Massachusetts, provided a broad range of social services to disadvantaged residents, including group homes for recovering drug and alcohol abusers, halfway houses for juvenile offenders, counseling centers, and other programs for the poor. Though the programs were well administered, the growing number of clients provoked complaints from town leaders that the community was becoming "a magnet for everyone else's problems." Complaining that taxpayers were being asked to foot the bill for the education, security, and fire protection of low-income non-taxpayers, one candidate appealed effectively to local voters by insisting, "We can't afford this anymore."[40] Most local governments agree; from their own tax dollars, they spend less than 1 percent of the gross national product (GNP) on social programs. (But such is the variety of local government that one can find exceptions to this as to any other rule: San Francisco and New York City, for example, provide a broad range of social services for needy groups.)

Local governments also compete with one another to attract businesses. Although such competition usually has positive benefits in that it keeps local governments sensitive to the community's economic needs, sometimes the competition can get out of hand. With state help, one county in Kentucky outbid its neighbors for a Canadian steel mill employing 400 people. It ended up costing the state $350,000 for every job created. Such bidding wars have spread across the country. As one Michigan official put it, "Right now, all we are doing is eating each other's lunch. At some stage we have to start thinking about dinner."[41]

In other cases, cities compete to secure or retain professional sports teams. In 1995 Cleveland Browns owner Art Modell abruptly decided to move the football team to

www.longmanparticipate.com

simulation

**You are a Restaurant Owner**

Baltimore, which had promised him a new stadium, permanent seat licenses, and other financial incentives. Baltimore's mayor and Maryland's governor participated in the negotiations for the team and helped announce the move. Meanwhile, Cleveland officials were incensed. Mayor Michael White likened the move to "a kick in the teeth."[42] Undaunted, the city of Cleveland worked with major financial backers to bring professional football back to the city, this time as an expansion team. In 1999 the expansion Cleveland Browns played their first season in a brand new $283 million stadium.

### SECTION SUMMARY

The tens of thousands of local governments in the United States take various forms and perform many functions. Citizens do not turn out in large numbers for local elections, but they express greater approval for these governments than for governments at higher levels. Local governments may serve as laboratories of democracy, trying out new and innovative policies, but they are constrained by their desire to attract businesses and by their reluctance to enact generous social programs.

**participation**

**Explore Your State Constitution**

**governor**

State chief executive whose responsibilities roughly parallel those of the president.

## State Government

When the Constitution was written, the design of the federal government was adapted from that which existed in many states. Thus it is not surprising that the basic organization of most state governments bears a strong resemblance to that of the national government. Just as Congress has a Senate and a House of Representatives, the legislatures in all states have an upper and a lower chamber, except for Nebraska, which has only one. All states have multi-tiered court systems roughly comparable to that of the federal system. And every state has an independently elected **governor**, the state chief executive whose responsibilities roughly parallel those of the president.

State governments vary in many important ways, however. State legislatures vary greatly in size. Most lower houses have around 100 representatives, but in Alaska, Delaware, and Nevada they have as few as 40 members each, while in New Hampshire the lower house comprises 398 legislators. Some state governments hold their elections in even-numbered years, in conjunction with federal races; others do not. In some states, state administrative officers from the secretary of state to the attorney general are elected, whereas in other states, the governor appoints these officials.

State policies vary as well. For example, there is significant variation in the legality of assisted suicide, the rules governing a woman's access to an abortion, and social welfare policies. In South Dakota most consumer fireworks are permitted, but in Georgia even sparklers are against the law. In Nevada gambling is legal, yet in Idaho it is a misdemeanor.

**visual literacy**

**Explaining the Differences in State Laws**

Some scholars believe the reason for many of these differences lies in variation in state political cultures. Citizens from different backgrounds and historical traditions form governments and elect officials that reflect these traditions. Massachusetts voters, for example, hold more positive views toward active government than voters in Texas or Florida.[43]

### State Elections

Despite differences among states, state elections bear a strong resemblance to national elections. The same two political parties—Republican and Democratic—are the dominant competitors in nearly all state elections. For many decades following the Civil War, the party of Lincoln, the Republicans, dominated the North, whereas the South was solidly Democratic. These regional distinctions have broken down in recent years as a result of the civil rights movement and regional population shifts. Republicans now often win as many southern elections as Democrats do. A new trend

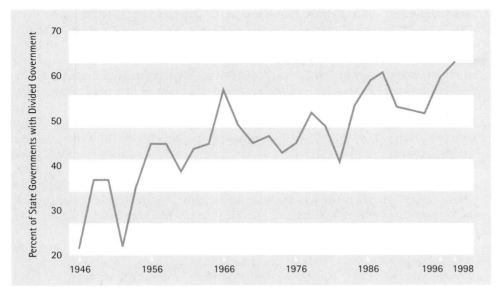

**Figure 3.7**

**States with Divided Government**
Increasingly, the governor is a member of a different party from the party that controls one or both houses of the state legislature. *Is this an accident or the result of conscious decisions by voters?*

SOURCE: Morris Fiorina, *Divided Government* (Needham Heights, MA: Allyn and Bacon, 1996); *The Book of the States*, Vol. 32: 1998-1999 (Lexington, KY: The Council of State Governments, 1998).

toward competitive politics and divided government has developed in most states, as the rising line in Figure 3.7 shows. Democrats have had the advantage in state legislative races; Republicans have more often elected governors. The voters may like it this way: Each party can act as a check on the other, and government does not drift to either political extreme.[44]

## Variation in State Government Responsibilities

The size and range of state responsibilities have grown dramatically in recent decades. As a percentage as GNP, state expenditures increased by over 60 percent between 1962 and 1995. States bear heavy responsibilities for financing elementary and secondary education, as well as for funding state colleges and universities. They maintain state parks, highway systems, and prisons. They manage welfare and Medicaid programs that serve low-income populations. They give grants to local governments to help pay for police, fire, and other basic governmental services.

The amount spent on government services varies from state to state. For one thing, wealthier states spend much more on public services. In 1995 the state and local governments in the ten richest states spent an average of $6600 per person on public services, whereas in the ten poorest states they spent, on average, less than $4500.[45] Many liberals say these differences in spending for education, health, and other public services are inequitable and should be rectified by federal grants. Many conservatives say that it is only to be expected that wealthier people will spend more on public services, just as they spend more for clothes, houses, and cars. In any case, federal grants have done very little, if anything, to reduce interstate fiscal inequalities.

Expenditures are also affected by elections. Each party has its favorite type of public service. The more often Democrats are elected to the legislature, the higher the expenditure for social services. The more Republicans who win, the higher the expenditure for traditional government services.[46]

## Recent Developments at the State Level

In recent years, state governments have evolved in several important ways. State political institutions have become more modern, the role of governors has grown, and states have begun to develop their own economic policies.

**Reapportionment and Professionalization** When the state constitutions were written, many of them included provisions freezing the boundaries of their legislative districts. In many other states, legislatures did not bother to change district boundaries to reflect shifts in population. Because the country became more urbanized in the first half of the twentieth century, by the early 1960s these rigid district boundaries meant that rural areas were grossly over-represented in state legislatures. Soon legal challenges brought these issues before the Supreme Court. In 1962 and 1964, the Court ruled that states must regularly redraw their districts to keep pace with population changes,[47] a process known as **reapportionment.** In the wake of these decisions, turnover in state legislatures rose significantly as they became more representative. In the longer term, the reapportionment requirements have caused regular partisan battles in many states, as Democrats and Republicans compete to draw district boundaries in the way most favorable to their party. The 2000 census will prompt another round of redistricting, so elections held from 1998 to 2002 will determine which party has the advantage in each state's reapportionment efforts.[48]

> **reapportionment**
> Redrawing of electoral district lines to reflect population changes.

As state government has become more complicated, state legislatures have also become more professional. Scholars associate higher legislative "professionalization" with lower turnover rates, higher salaries, more staff, and longer sessions. In 1995 California's legislature was among the most modern. Its members remained in session throughout the year, receiving $72,000 in salary, retirement benefits, and handsome per diem expense pay as well as the services of a full-time staff. Turnover rates were only about 18 percent. By contrast, Wyoming paid its legislators $125 dollars a day, had a turnover rate twice that of California, and limited its legislative sessions to a maximum of 40 working days in odd-numbered years, 20 days in even years.[49] During the 1990s, voters reacted against the professionalization of state government, as many states limited the terms of legislators, cut their staffs, and reduced their salaries and benefits.

**The Resurgent Governors** Being governor of a medium-to-large sized state has historically been one of the best ways to position oneself for a presidential run. Three of the last four U.S. presidents have been governors, and former governors have been major candidates in every presidential election campaign since 1976. George W. Bush's popularity as governor of Texas, coupled with the advantages of a well-known family name, quickly catapulted him into the presidential limelight.

Since 1950 many states have strengthened the office of governor, lengthening terms of office, reducing term limitations, and enhancing the governor's veto power over legislation. Most governors now have a **line item veto,** a power that allows them to reject specific parts of bills; ten governors have a particularly strong form of the line item veto, which allows them to eliminate or cut particular spending items.[50]

> **line item veto**
> Power of most governors to reject specific components of legislation rather than rejecting entire bills.

In the 1980s and 1990s the governors became influential players in several national policy debates. In the case of welfare reform, the National Governor's Association was active in giving states more authority over the design of programs serving low-income residents.

**State Economic Action** In the nineteenth century, state governments played an active role in their economies, granting charters to private corporations and investing their resources to assist in the development of key industries. After the New Deal, the federal government became predominant, and states relaxed their economic roles. Then, in the 1980s and 1990s, many states again became more active players in their economic development. States especially hard-hit by a decline in manufacturing jobs and the economic recession of the early 1980s sought to reinvigorate their business climate through tax incentives and active recruitment of firms from out of state.

States with large economies and significant international exports, such as California and Texas, arranged trade missions to countries such as Mexico, Japan, and Canada. Some of these missions met with greater success than most thought possible. In 1987, California governor George Deukmejian traveled to Japan to promote the sale of California rice. Most experts scoffed at his efforts, arguing that native Japanese rice was central to the country's national pride, culture, and self-sufficiency. "Negotiating for rice is like negotiating for Mt. Fuji," said one trade consultant. Nevertheless, the governor's efforts did not go unrewarded: By the late 1990s, Japan imported $100 million worth of rice from California, accounting for 20 percent of the state's rice crop. The skeptics had to admit that they had been wrong.[51]

## Section Summary

Though constitutionally separated from the national government, state governments have a lot in common with their federal counterpart. Each state's electorate is somewhat different in nature, so each state approaches its problems in a different way. But the state and federal arenas have enough in common that the states frequently serve as proving grounds for policies, and politicians, that may soon become prominent at the national level. In recent years reapportionment has played an important role in state politics, state government has become more professional, governors have gained political stature, and states have acted to promote their economies.

## *Chapter Summary*

Federalism divides sovereignty between the states and the national government. Its existence in the United States is the result of a compromise between Constitutional Convention delegates who believed that a strong national government was necessary to preserve stability, and those who feared that centralized power would lead to tyranny. Because the federal structure was a compromise, the Constitution does not clearly define the powers of the federal and state governments. As a result, the nature of American federalism has changed in response to electoral forces and Supreme Court decisions. Much of the debate over federalism has revolved around the meaning of dual sovereignty. The most extreme interpretation of dual sovereignty, the doctrine of nullification, was rejected with the end of the Civil War.

The power of the states was further eroded with the election of Franklin Roosevelt and the enactment of New Deal legislation that greatly enhanced the power of the federal government. Three provisions in the Constitution facilitated the expansion of federal power: the necessary and proper clause, the commerce clause, and the spending clause.

With the election of strong Democratic majorities in the 1960s, there emerged a new theory of federalism known as cooperative or marble-cake federalism, which holds that all levels of government can and should work together. In accordance with this theory, many new federal grants were given to state and local governments. Many of these grants were categorical in nature; they contained restrictions that specified how the money should be spent. In response to criticism of the implementation of categorical grants, Republican leaders called for their replacement with block grants that have few federal mandates or restrictions. The two parties remain divided over the merits of categorical and block grants.

Despite the expansion of federal power, state and local governments remain vital components of the federal system. Nearly half the domestic expenditures of the government are paid for with state and local tax dollars. Though few citizens participate in local elections, local governments are the most popular of all governmental levels, in part because people can "vote with their feet"—that is, they can choose to live in the local community they like best.

State governments can play key roles in economic development, and their governors are often well positioned to seek the presidency. Despite legal and structural variation, partisan battles on the state level can resemble those on the national level, as legislatures become more professional and voters increasingly often choose "divided government" wherein neither party dominates all policy making.

## On the Web

www.nlc.org
www.ncsl.org
www.nga.org
The National League of Cities, the National Conference of State Legislatures, and the National Governor's Association provide information and policy priorities for state and local governments.

www.newfederalism.urban.org/
On this Web site, the Urban Institute presents information about its ongoing assessment of new programs whereby responsibility devolves to the states.
www.min.net/~kala/fed/
Created by a doctoral student at George Washington University, this Web site covers nearly every aspect of federalism, from philosophy to economics to history.

## Key Terms

block grant, p. 80
categorical grant, p. 78
commerce clause, p. 75
cooperative federalism, p. 76
devolution, p. 69
Dillon's rule, p. 67
dual sovereignty, p. 71
federalism, p. 67
general revenue sharing,
    p. 80

governor, p. 88
implementation, p. 79
intergovernmental grant, p. 77
judicial review, p. 70
laboratories of democracy, p. 86
line item veto, p. 90
marble-cake federalism, p. 76
*McCulloch* v. *Maryland,* p. 72
necessary and proper clause,
    p. 73

New Deal, p. 75
NIMBY problem, p. 74
nullification, p. 71
reapportionment, p. 90
sovereignty, p. 67
spending clause, p. 76
supremacy clause, p. 69
unfunded mandates, p. 68
unitary government, p. 67
War on Poverty, p. 78

## Suggested Readings

Conlan, Timothy. *From New Federalism to Devolution: Twenty-Five Years of Intergovernmental Reform.* Washington, DC: Brookings, 1998. Excellent analysis of changing federal policy.

Dahl, Robert. *Who Governs?* New Haven, CT: Yale University Press,

1961. Classic study of local politics in New Haven.

Dye, Thomas R. *American Federalism: Competition Among Governments.* Lexington, MA: D.C. Heath, 1990. Comprehensive account of the way state and local governmental systems work.

Elazar, Daniel. *American Federalism: A View From the States.* New York: Harper & Row, 1984. Discussion of various regional political cultures in the U.S.

Elkins, Stanley, and Eric McKitrick. *The Age of Federalism.* New York: Oxford University Press, 1993. Account of the first decades of the federal system under the Constitution.

Fiorina, Morris, *Divided Government*. New York: Macmillan, 1992. Explains why control of many state governments is divided between the Democratic and Republican parties.

Grodzins, Morton. *The American System: A New View of Government in the United States*. Chicago: Rand McNally, 1966. Classic study of cooperative federalism.

Peterson, Paul E. *The Price of Federalism*. Washington, DC: Brookings, 1995. Contrasts the responsibilities of national, state, and local governments.

Pressman, Jeffrey L., and Aaron Wildavsky. *Implementation*. 3rd ed. Berkeley: University of California Press, 1973. Readable, fascinating account of the implementation of a federal program in Oakland, California.

Riker, William H. *Federalism: Origin, Operation, Significance*. Boston:

Little, Brown, 1964. Theoretical treatise on federalism.

Rivlin, Alice. *Rethinking the American Dream*. Washington, DC: Brookings, 1992. Calls for reorganization of the American federal system.

Smith, Jean E. *John Marshall: Definer of a Nation*. New York: Henry Holt, 1996. Excellent biography of the chief justice who helped define American federalism.

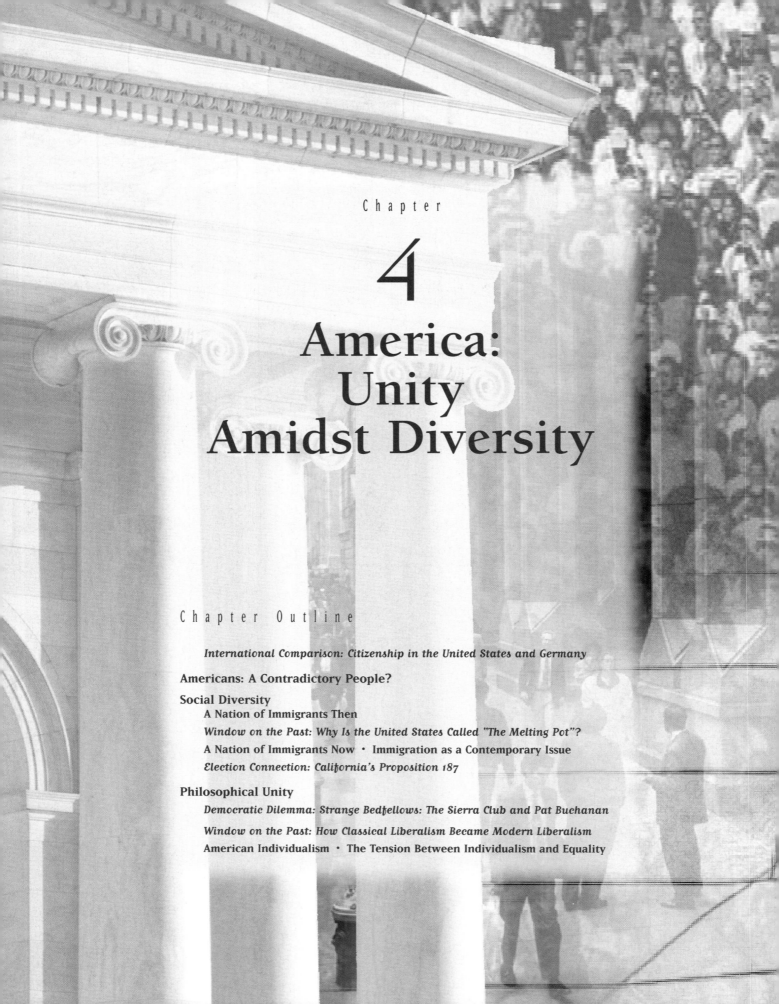

Chapter

4

# America:
# Unity
# Amidst Diversity

Chapter Outline

More than six years of war filled the interval between the Minutemen's stand at Concord that began the American Revolution and the British surrender at Yorktown that ended it. At times the military position of the colonies was desperate, but in the end the newly formed Continental Army and the colonial militias defeated the finest standing army in the world.

Well, not exactly. The Americans had a little help from their friends. The French Marquis de Lafayette and the German Baron Johann de Kalb were among Washington's top generals (although de Kalb died after suffering 11 wounds in hand-to-hand combat).[1] When Washington's army was suffering at Valley Forge and the American cause looked as though it might be lost, another German, Baron Friedrich Wilhelm von Steuben, arrived on the scene. An expert in military drill, von Steuben transformed the untrained Americans into a disciplined force that could stand against the British regulars. A Polish general, Casimir Pulaski, known as the father of the American cavalry,[2] was mortally wounded leading an international unit (Americans, Poles, Irish, French, and Germans) against British fortifications at Savannah. Another Pole, Thaddeus Kosciuszko, designed the defenses at Saratoga, where Americans stopped the British from separating New England from the other colonies. Kosciuszko also designed the fortifications at West Point that Benedict Arnold tried to betray to the British. A Spanish commander in New Orleans, Don Bernardo de Galvez, organized a force of 1200 men, including 80 free blacks and 160 Indians, and sailed up the Mississippi, taking British forts as far as Natchez. Then he captured Mobile and Pensacola. In all, de Galvez's racially diverse unit took about 3000 British soldiers out of the fight.[3] Without all of this "foreign aid," Americans might be singing "God Save the Queen" at the start of baseball and football games.

The international character of the "American" Revolution is not sufficiently appreciated. At the time, it was not unusual for soldiers to fight under a foreign flag. Generally they were mercenaries—professional soldiers who fought for pay. For example, the Hessians, whom Washington defeated on his midnight raid across the Delaware River, were employees of the British. In contrast, many of the foreigners who fought on the American side were volunteers (high-ranking army officers were not even paid until after the war). Their motives were mixed, of course. Some, like de Galvez, had the tacit support of their governments, and some had hopes of obtaining land or positions after the war. But many were sympathetic to the republican struggle; Kosciuszko, for example, donated his military compensation to the emancipation of the slaves. They fought for the American side, at least in part, because of their attraction to the kind of country that was being created.

On a less grand scale, millions of people have made choices like those made by these eighteenth-century foreign soldiers, and millions more continue to do so today. Carl Friedrich, a professor who immigrated to the United States from Germany, wrote in 1935 that "To be an American is an ideal, while to be a Frenchman is a fact."[4] In the second part of this comment, Friedrich was pointing

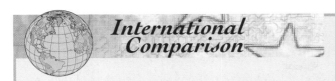

## Citizenship in the United States and Germany

Any child born in the United States is a citizen. A child born outside the United States is a citizen if either parent is a citizen and has lived in the United States for 10 years, 2 after age 14. Legal immigrants can become "naturalized" citizens after 5 years of residence: They must learn English, demonstrate knowledge of American history and government, renounce their previous citizenship, and swear allegiance to the Constitution and laws of the United States.

Practices in other countries differ considerably. In Germany, citizenship historically has been based on ethnicity. The constitution of the new German republic created after World War II carried over a 1913 law defining a German as "a refugee or expellee of German stock or as the spouse or descendant of such a person." As a consequence, Eastern European and Russian residents whose ancestors left Germany centuries ago can migrate to Germany today and quickly assume the rights and privileges of citizenship (as can Americans of German descent if they can make a case for hardship). But the children of Turkish "guest workers," born in Germany and speaking German as their first language, typically face enormous bureaucratic obstacles to becoming citizens because they are not Germans by blood. This situation has been a matter of considerable controversy in recent years. In 1999 the new government of Social Democrat Gerhard Schroder attempted to liberalize the law, but the proposals met strong resistance. A compromise reduced the residency requirement before an immi-

grant was eligible for citizenship from 15 years to 8 years and granted citizenship to any child born in Germany whose parents had resided there for 8 years or longer. Although Germany has been an extreme case of ethnically defined citizenship, most democracies follow practices closer to Germany's than to those of the United States. This international contrast raises a number of questions.

- *Why has the United States historically determined citizenship by beliefs rather than by ethnicity or nationality?*
- *Could countries like Germany define citizenship more as we do in the United States? Or is there something about other countries that naturally leads them to define citizenship in terms of ethnicity or nationality?*

More generally, some people argue that citizenship is an outmoded concept in today's globally integrated world where many people live for significant periods in other countries.

*What do you think?*

- *Should citizens have any more privileges than any other person who is a legal resident of a country? Should legal noncitizens subject to taxes and other national obligations be permitted to vote?*

SOURCE: *The Economist,* April 5, 1997: pp. 45–46; January 9, 1999: p. 17.

out that in most of the world, citizenship is defined by race or ethnicity: Members of a dominant racial or ethnic group *automatically* enjoy the rights and privileges of **citizenship.** Conversely, those not of the appropriate racial or ethnic group may not be able to become citizens even if they were born and lived their whole lives in the country.

**citizenship**
Status held by someone entitled to all the rights and privileges of a full-fledged member of a political community.

What of the first part of Friedrich's assertion—that to be an American is an ideal? Here Friedrich was observing that in most countries, one is born into a nationality—one is French, Japanese, Malay, or whatever as a simple fact that cannot be changed. In contrast, there is no American ethnicity. "American" is a status that can be achieved by members of any ethnic group. "American" refers not to a nationality but to a set of beliefs and values that can be embraced by people of any ethnic heritage.

UNDERSTANDING THE FUNDAMENTAL BELIEFS AND VALUES OF THE AMERICAN PEOPLE is essential to understanding American government and politics. The reason is that how institutional processes work depends on their interaction with the beliefs and values of the citizenry. Imagine, for example, that troubled countries such as Yugoslavia and Burundi were to adopt the United States Constitution and the body of law that has evolved from it. Would their politics look just like ours after they had had a few years to become familiar with the new arrangements? Most people intuitively would answer no. The histories, cultures, and economies of countries differ; consequently, the beliefs and values of their citizens differ, and it is the interaction of institutions with the society and culture that produces a country's politics. Moreover, because human beings

comparative
**Comparing Civil Rights**

create, maintain, and transform political institutions, when institutions conflict with social realities, they will be replaced, modified, or ignored. For these reasons, it is important to take a close look at the American people. The questions we seek to answer in this chapter are

- Who are the American people?
- What do they believe?

The focus of the second question is not on what Americans believe about the specific personalities and issues of the day; that is called public opinion, and we examine it in Chapter 5. In this chapter we are interested in the deeper beliefs and values of Americans:

- What do Americans consider to be the purpose of government?
- How do Americans believe their institutions should work?
- What authority do they consider legitimate?
- How do they view their rights and responsibilities as well as their duties and obligations?

**political culture**
Collection of beliefs and values about the justification and operation of a country's government.

These beliefs and values are the context in which American electoral democracy operates. Some scholars refer to such deep, shared beliefs and values as the **political culture** of a country.

## Americans: A Contradictory People?

Many international observers note an apparent contradiction in American society. On the one hand, Americans are more ethnically and religiously diverse than the citizens of other democracies. Most of the world's multi-ethnic democracies have been short-lived, Yugoslavia being the latest, tragic example. Conversely, most long-lived multi-ethnic societies have not been democratic; rather, they have been authoritarian states like the Austro-Hungarian and Soviet empires, in which central authority repressed ethnic and religious conflicts. The few multi-ethnic democracies that have survived often have done so by decentralizing—giving autonomy to ethnic, religious, or linguistic subgroups. Belgium, for example, is divided into three zones: the city of Brussels, a Dutch-speaking Flemish zone, and a French-speaking Waloon zone. Within the respective zones, each language group controls education and other important policy areas. War-torn Yugoslavia and decentralized Belgium are the rule; the United States is the exception, an unusual example of diverse people peacefully coexisting under the same democratic government.[5]

**socialism**
A philosophy that supports government ownership and operation of the means of production as well as government determination of the level of social and economic benefits that people receive.

**clericalism**
The exercise of political power by religious leaders and organizations, such as established religions.

**fascism**
Rule by a dictator supported by a strong party that permeates society; generally supports capital against labor and is associated with extreme nationalism.

**communism**
An extreme type of socialism based on the work of Karl Marx, who taught that history is a product of the struggle between those who exploit and those who are exploited.

On the other hand, many foreign observers have emphasized the homogeneity of American political beliefs, noting that more than in other democracies, Americans agree on fundamentals and share basic assumptions about the nature of a good society. On first hearing, this strikes many Americans as exaggerated, if not wrong: Certainly there is political controversy and disagreement in the United States. But consider that European democracies have major elements of **socialism** and **clericalism** as shown by their socialist and religious parties—the social democrats and Christian democrats, for example. In some European nations there are also elements of **fascism** and (until recently) **communism** as well. Efforts to establish socialism, an official church, or a workers' paradise are platforms that simply have been outside the mainstream of legitimate political discourse in the United States.

How might such a contradiction arise? That is, how does a society more ethnically and religiously heterogeneous than most develop a political culture more homogeneous than most? To answer this question, we must know more about the diverse makeup of the American population and the core beliefs that Americans share. In the next two sections, we describe the diversity arising from new immigrants continuously entering the United States, and we discuss the philosophy that has contributed to unity of beliefs and values.

## Social Diversity

In "Federalist 2," John Jay wrote,

> . . . Providence has been pleased to give this one connected country, to one united people; a people descended from the same ancestors, speaking the same language, professing the same religion, attached to the same principles of government, very similar in their manners and customs and who, by their joint counsels, arms and efforts, fighting side by side throughout a long and bloody war, have nobly established their general Liberty and Independence.

Such statements remind us that the *Federalist* was first and foremost a campaign document, for Americans were not nearly so similar—in ethnicity, customs, religious beliefs, or behavior—as Jay alleged. His exaggeration of American cultural and historical unity was a political tactic, an appeal for Americans to rise above serious divisions that threatened the ratification of the Constitution.

Contrary to Jay's campaign claim, the so-called New World was not settled by "one united people." Although the British were most numerous, the Dutch settled New York, and the Swedes established settlements in what is now Delaware and eastern Pennsylvania. The French were present on the northern and western borders, and the Spanish in the South, although the latter never were very numerous. As for the British, they were not all of a kind. New England was settled by Puritans (dissenters from the Church of England), whereas Virginia settlers were loyal to the Church. Maryland was a grant to a Catholic noble, Lord Baltimore, who welcomed his fellow Catholics, and Pennsylvania welcomed Quakers, who were unwelcome almost everywhere else. Moreover, after 1700, British immigration came increasingly from Scotland, Wales, and Ireland, and the indentured servants (who made up half the population of Pennsylvania, New York, and New Jersey) included thousands of Germans, Scandinavians, Belgians, French, and Swiss. And these were only the voluntary immigrants; the involuntary immigrants—slaves—were from Africa. (Native Americans, whose numbers had been decimated by wars and disease, were viewed as separate nations altogether.) All in all, historians estimate that in 1763, only 50 percent of the population of the colonies was English, and nearly 20 percent was African American.[6]

You may react skeptically to this description of colonial diversity. After all, a population consisting of groups of Europeans who worship at different Christian churches does not correspond to our modern-day view of diversity. But keep in mind that notions of diversity are relative to time and place. During the Thirty Years' War

(1618–1648), those northern European Christians (Catholics, Calvinists, and Lutherans) pillaged, raped, and murdered each other on a monumental scale; one-third of the population of what is now Germany died during the conflict. Near the end of that period, Puritan dissenters from the Church of England fought against Royalist defenders of Church and Crown in the English Civil War (1642–1653). Ultimately, the king and the archbishop both lost their heads. (This conflict had a faint echo in Maryland, incidentally, as Catholics, Puritans, and Anglicans for a time engaged in a "minor civil war."[7]) For perhaps the most appalling contradiction of the notion that northern European Christians were all alike, consider the St. Bartholomew's Day Massacre that began on August 24, 1572. In a forerunner of Hitler's "final solution," French Catholics killed 30,000 French Calvinists, moving door-to-door and farm-to-farm using swords, axes, and crude firearms.

**diversity**
A concept relative to time and place; currently refers primarily to ethnic and racial distinctions among people (as opposed to, say, class or occupational differences).

In the contemporary United States, **diversity** refers to people of color living among the white majority, to people with non-Western religious beliefs coexisting with those who follow Western traditions, and to people with nontraditional lifestyles enjoying the same rights and privileges as those who are more traditionally oriented. But as we have noted, diversity is relative to time and place. In 1640 Catholics looked upon Protestants with no more understanding (and possibly with less) than that with which a Muslim looks upon a Jew today. In 1844 Illinois Protestants murdered Mormon leader Joseph Smith, because, among other things, the Mormons practiced polygamy, an intolerable violation of "family values" as understood in that era. And to white Americans in 1900, Greeks and Italians were people of color who threatened the racial purity of America. *Relative to other countries, and to the times, America has always been diverse.* The national motto, imprinted on the United States Seal and on several coins, *E Pluribus Unum*—"out of many, one"—explicitly recognizes our diversity.

**multiculturalism**
The idea that ethnic and cultural groups should maintain their identity within the larger society and respect one another's differences.

**Multiculturalism,** the notion that the distinctive cultures of ethnic groups should be preserved and should be respected by each other and by the larger society is a matter of considerable political controversy today. But the debate is sadly lacking in historical awareness. For different reasons, both defenders and critics exaggerate both the homogeneity of the American past and the distinctiveness of the American present. The simple truth is that earlier generations of Americans found the immigrants of their eras just as "different" as do contemporary generations. Moreover, both defenders and critics of multiculturalism exaggerate the ease with which earlier waves of immigrants were assimilated into American society. In fact, the existence of distinct ethnic and religious groups and their desire to preserve some part of their distinctiveness underlie much of the history of political conflict in America.

Today's debates about multiculturalism, diversity, immigration, bilingualism, and related topics are not new; rather, they are the reemergence of debates that occurred in earlier eras. We review the history of immigration to America to show that, far from

**Miami's Little Havana and San Francisco's Chinatown**
Many urban neighborhoods are object lessons in American multiculturalism.

being new, many of today's controversies occurred as far back as the early nineteenth century. Past generations of Americans viewed Germans, Irish, Italians, and Jews every bit as negatively as some Americans today view Latinos and Asians.

## A Nation of Immigrants Then

After the successful campaign for ratification of the Constitution, the new federal government maintained the states' policies of unrestricted immigration, although not everyone was happy about it. One of the most cosmopolitan Americans of the time, Benjamin Franklin, expressed his resentment of Germans in various letters:

> Why should *Pennsylvania*, founded by the *English*, become a colony of Aliens, who will shortly be so numerous as to Germanize us instead of our Anglifying them, and will never adopt our Language or Customs any more than they can acquire our Complexion? [emphasis in original].[8]

Despite such misgivings, land was plentiful and labor scarce. The more rapidly the territory could be populated, the more rapidly economic development would follow. Immigration gradually increased, until by mid-century, immigrants from England, Ireland, and Germany were arriving in numbers as high as 400,000 per year. Irish immigration became a major political issue. To Protestant America the influx of Irish Catholics was threatening. Some Protestants feared that Catholics would put their allegiance to the Pope above their loyalty to the United States and might even plot to overthrow the government. Cartoonists of the period depicted the Irish as dark, hairy, ape-like people. In the 1854 elections, the anti-Catholic "Know-Nothing" party won 43 seats in the House of Representatives—comparable to 80 seats in today's House. (The party's name came from its secret password, "I know nothing about it.")

Immigration increased considerably in the 1860s and continued at a high rate until World War I. In the 1860s and 1870s, the first of an eventual half-million French Canadians crossed the northeastern border of the United States, and several million Scandinavians joined a continuing stream of English, Irish, and Germans (see Figure 4.1). Again, by today's standards such groups may seem alike because they are all of European origin, but many historians argue that a principal cause of state and local political conflict in the late nineteenth century was "ethno-cultural."[9] In the Midwest and much of the East, the Republican base lay in the native Protestant

**A Religious Martyr**
An Illinois mob murders Mormon prophet Joseph Smith in 1844. The diversity represented by his religion's polygamist practices was intolerable to Illinois Protestants—who feared a growing population of Mormons voting as a bloc in county elections. *Are there examples (hopefully less extreme) of conflict over diversity in your community today? Are there limits to diversity? Is there something society simply ought not tolerate?*

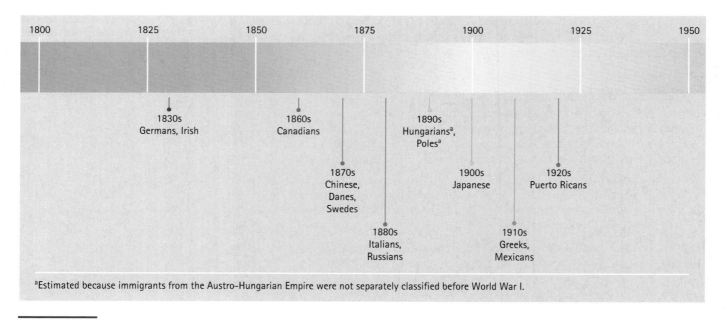

**Figure 4.1**

**Timeline: The Old Immigration to the United States**
During these decades, immigration by the indicated nationality group first reached 100,000.

SOURCE: Stephanie Bernado, *The Ethnic Almanac* (Garden City, NY: Doubleday, 1981): 22–140.

communities, whereas the Democrats sank roots in the immigrant Catholic communities. Politics revolved around such issues as the prohibition or regulation of alcohol, public funding of parochial schools, bilingual schools (mostly German, but French in New England), and Sunday "Blue Laws"—laws that restricted commercial and recreational activities on Sundays. The German Lutherans were an important "swing" group in some Midwestern states; they generally voted Republican but swung to the Democrats when conservative Protestants within the Republican party attempted to legislate on cultural issues of great sensitivity to immigrants. In Wisconsin, for example, the Republicans lost only two statewide elections between 1858 and 1890. One came after the party raised liquor license fees, the second after it passed a measure requiring English language instruction in the schools. According to Richard Wayman, "Throughout much of Eastern Wisconsin, German immigrants jealously guarded what they regarded as their right to preserve many of the customs they brought with them from Europe."[10]

Meanwhile, the adoption of the Fourteenth Amendment gave citizenship to African Americans, who constituted about the same proportion of the population in 1865 (one-eighth) as today. Because they did not choose to emigrate, but were forcibly abducted from their homelands, the African American experience differs from that of other immigrants. Nevertheless, it is important to point out that until the "Jim Crow" repression deprived them of fundamental political rights in the 1890s (Chapter 17), African Americans played an active role in the electoral politics of the post–Civil War South.[11]

African Americans were not the only non-Europeans to assume a place in the United States. The Chinese were the first Asians to immigrate on a significant scale. More than 20,000 Chinese participated in the California Gold Rush, which began in 1849. (Only two-thirds of the "forty-niners" were Americans, and only two-thirds of the Americans were white; large numbers of Cherokee Indians and African Americans panned for gold.[12]) More than 100,000 Chinese laborers helped build the western links of the transcontinental railroads. At first these newcomers were viewed positively as peaceful, hard-working (and cheap) labor. Soon, however, a virulent backlash set in. During the congressional debate on the Chinese Exclusion Act of 1882, California Senator John Miller characterized the Chinese as

machine-like . . . of obtuse nerve, but little affected by heat or cold, wiry, sinewy, with muscles of iron; . . . automatic engines of flesh and blood; . . . patient, stolid, unemotional, and persistent, with such a marvelous frame and digestive apparatus that they can dispense with the comforts of shelter and . . . grow fat on less than half the food necessary to sustain life in the Anglo Saxon.

Now, how could white Californians (even in the nineteenth century!) compete with such immigrants? In the eyes of Senator Miller, they couldn't:

> The experiment now being tried in California is to subject American free labor to competition with Chinese servile labor, and so far as it has gone, it has put in progress the displacement of American laborers, and the substitution of Chinese for white men. The process will continue if permitted until the white laborer is driven out into other fields, or until those who remain in the contest come down to the Chinese level.[13]

Such charges were as common then as now: Cheap foreign labor will undercut the standard of living of "real" Americans—a charge repeatedly leveled at immigrants through the decades.

Beginning in the 1880s the character of immigration changed, as millions of people from southern and eastern Europe followed their northern and western European predecessors. The new immigrants again were threatening to many "real" Americans, who by now believed that pre-1880 immigrants "were drawn from the superior stocks of northern and western Europe, while those who came later were drawn from the inferior breeds of southern and eastern Europe."[14] The following account was published in 1916, in a best-selling book by Madison Grant of the American Museum of Natural History.

> The transportation lines advertised America as a land flowing with milk and honey, and the European governments took the opportunity to unload upon careless, wealthy, and hospitable America the sweepings of their jails and asylums. . . . [T]he new immigration . . . contained a large and increasing number of the weak, the broken, and the mentally crippled of all races drawn from the lowest stratum of the Mediterranean basin and the Balkans, together with hordes of the wretched, submerged populations of the Polish ghettoes. . . . [T]hese newcomers were welcomed and given a share in our land and prosperity. The American taxed himself to sanitate and educate these poor helots . . . . The result is showing plainly in the rapid decline in the birth rate of native Americans because the poorer classes of Colonial stock . . . will not bring children into the world to compete in the labor market with the Slovak, the Italian, the Syrian, and the Jew.[15]

Again, the charges have a contemporary ring: Generous Americans of northern European Protestant stock soon would be a minority in their "own" country, overwhelmed by waves of Catholics, Eastern Orthodox, and Jews from southern and eastern Europe. Such sentiments were by no means limited to a small fringe of the population. Reflecting widespread popular concern, a government commission was established in 1907 to study the immigration situation. It issued an immense report in 1910. Here are some of the observations contained in the official report of the U.S. Immigration Commission:

> [Greeks]: *"There is no doubt of their nimble intelligence. They compete with the Hebrew race as the best traders of the Orient."*

> [Southern Italian]: *"excitable, impulsive, highly imaginative, impracticable . . . an individualist having little adaptability to high organized society."*

> [Persian]: *"is rather brilliant and poetical than solid in temperament. Like the Hindu he is more eager to secure the semblance than the substance of modern civilization."*

> [Poles]: *"are more high strung than are the most of their neighbors. In this respect they resemble the Hungarians farther south."*

> [Romanians]: *"more emotional than the Slav, less stolid and heavy than the Bulgarian."*

> [White Russians]: *"are said by travelers to be a distinctly weaker stock than the Great Russians and less prepossessing in appearance."*

> [Serbo-Croatians]: *19th century "savage manners" persist, "illiteracy is prevalent and civilization at a low stage. . . ."*[16]

Such ethnic stereotyping displays official insensitivity on a scale undreamed of today! No one should ever think that the American "melting pot" in any way resembled "Mr. Rogers' neighborhood," a community of harmony and love.

**Racism for Wages**
Immigrants like this Chinese railroad worker have often met with a hostile reception from "native-born citizens." *What, if anything, should government do to ease tension between new immigrant workers and the existing labor force?*

www.longmanparticipate.com

timeline
**The Fourteenth Amendment**

**Why Is the United States Called "The Melting Pot"?**

*This famous metaphor was popularized by a 1908 play of that name written by a Jewish immigrant, Israel Zangwill. In the play, David and Vera fall in love but learn that there is a seemingly unbridgeable gulf between them. David, a talented young violinist, is a Jew; Vera, a social worker, is the daughter of a Russian officer who supervised the pogrom in which David's family was killed. The final scene takes place on a New York rooftop, where David decides that he will live for the American future, not the European past. Here is the ending:*

VERA: Look! How beautiful the sunset is after the storm!

DAVID: *[Prophetically exalted by the spectacle]*
   It is the fires of God round His Crucible. *[He drops her hand and points downward.]*
   There she lies, the great Melting Pot—Listen! Can't you hear the roaring and the bubbling? There gapes her mouth *[He points east]*—the harbour where a thousand mammoth feeders came from the ends of the world to pour in their human freight. Ah, what a stirring and a seething! Celt and Latin, Slav and Teuton, Greek and Syrian,—black and yellow—

VERA: *[Softly, nestling to him]* Jew and Gentile—

DAVID: Yes, East and West, and North and South, the palm and the pine, the pole and the equator, the crescent and the cross—how the great Alchemist melts and fuses them with his purging flame! Here shall they all unite to build the Republic of Man and the Kingdom of God. Ah, Vera, what is the glory of Rome and Jerusalem where all nations and races come to worship and look back, compared with the glory of America, where all races and nations come to labour and look forward! *[He raises his hands in benediction over the shining city.]* Peace, peace, to all ye unborn millions, fated to fill this giant continent—the God of our *children* give you Peace.

SOURCE: Israel Zangwill, *The Melting Pot* (New York: Macmillan, 1912, ©1909).

Not all opposition to immigration reflected ethnic or religious bigotry. Some opposed further immigration for economic or political reasons. Although immigrants joined the industrial unions, union leaders believed that continued immigration undercut the bargaining power of workers. And indeed, American business encouraged immigration as a source of cheap labor. The Progressives, a reformist political movement (Chapter 8), opposed further immigration because immigrants were viewed as the foundation of the corrupt urban political machines. The Progressives believed that shutting off immigration would shut off the supply of uninformed, ignorant voters whom the machines could manipulate.

For many reasons, then, anti-immigration sentiment grew. After two decades of advocacy, a national literacy test was adopted in 1917 (as we shall see in Chapter 17, such a device had earlier been used to disfranchise African Americans and poor whites in the South). Supporters of the test did not disguise their motives. The noted Massachusetts senator Henry Cabot Lodge observed that the ". . . test will bear most heavily on the Italians, Russians, Poles, Hungarians, Greeks, and Asiatics, and very lightly, or not at all upon English-speaking emigrants or Germans, Scandinavians, and French."[17]

Contrary to what Senator Lodge believed, many would-be immigrants knew how to read or quickly learned, so stronger legislation was needed to close the door. A series of laws passed in the 1920s restricted immigration both quantitatively (the total was limited) and qualitatively (quotas gave northern and western Europeans preference over people from other areas).[18] The Japanese and other Asians were added to the Chinese as groups excluded altogether. By 1930 the era of the open door had ended, although Mexicans continued to enter the southwestern states to work in

American agriculture (joining those who had been incorporated when the United States took the territory from Mexico), and after World War II, Puerto Ricans in significant numbers emigrated to New York City. But before the United States closed its doors to immigrants, more than 35 million people had left hearth and home to come to America. These immigrants and their children were a large component of the growth of the United States from a country of about 10 million inhabitants in 1820 to one of more than 100 million in 1920.

Restrictions on immigration were part of a general reactionary movement that broke out after World War I. In the "Red Scare," immigrants were persecuted as carriers of Bolshevik, anarchist, and other subversive foreign ideologies. And Anti-Catholicism surged: Anti-Catholic and Anti-Jewish sentiments spawned a second Ku Klux Klan in the 1920s that counted 25–30 percent of the adult male Protestant population in its membership.[19] Not surprisingly, the 1928 Democratic presidential nomination of Catholic Al Smith caused a virulent reaction.[20]

Gradually, however, ethnocultural tensions died down. Several bigoted radio demagogues were popular in the 1930s, and social, occupational, and educational discrimination against Catholics and Jews was widespread into the 1930s. Indeed, not until 1950 did Ivy League universities eliminate informal quotas on admissions of Jewish students. But all in all, the cumulative effects of economic depression, World War II, revulsion against the Holocaust, and the Cold War led to a general reduction in ethnic and racial tensions that lasted approximately a generation. However, this short period from the early 1930s to the mid-1960s, during which ethnic and religious issues were relatively dormant, was the exception, not the norm. From the founding to the 1930s, the kinds of issues now discussed under the headings of multiculturalism and diversity were an important part of American politics.

**The Red Scare**
Americans have always worried about the threat immigrants pose to American values. The "Red Scare" of the 1920s was a particularly virulent reaction to immigrants who were thought to have Bolshevik, anarchist, or other subversive sympathies. The term red came from the color used by the Bolsheviks as their emblem in the Russian revolution of 1917. For six or seven decades after the Russian revolution, "red" was a common epithet for communist. *Now that communism is no longer perceived as much of a threat, what groups are vilified in the press today?*

## A Nation of Immigrants Now

The Immigration Act of 1965 opened the door to the largest surge of immigration since the 1890s. This has given rise to the contemporary debates about such issues as bilingual education and the provision of social services to immigrants.

In the 1965 legislation, Congress abandoned the national-quotas system favoring northern Europeans, with the result that immigration from Latin America and the West Indies increased rapidly. In addition, hundreds of thousands of new immigrants from Vietnam, Korea, Cambodia, India, Iran, the Philippines, and other countries became the first numerically significant Asian groups since the Japanese in the early years of the twentieth century (see Figure 4.2). In the 1980s the absolute number of immigrants—about 9 million—was higher than in any previous decade, although lower as a proportion of the population than it had been at the turn of the century. Three million came from Mexico, Central America, and the Caribbean, and nearly as many from Asia. Nearly half a million came from South America and almost 200,000 from Africa. These figures include only legal immigrants; an estimated 5 million people now live in the United States illegally.[21] As a result of this newest wave of immigration, by 1995 the proportion of the population of European origin had dropped to about three-quarters, and, as shown in Figure 4.3, it is projected to fall to less than two-thirds in the next two decades. In some large cities such as Los Angeles, whites of European origin are already a minority.

## Immigration as a Contemporary Issue

Today, immigration once again is a political issue. In 1994 California voters overwhelmingly passed Proposition 187, an initiative that denied state services to illegal immigrants and their children. And in 1995–1996, the question of eligibility for governmental services such as welfare was a matter of intense controversy at the national level. Much of this contemporary debate over immigration would sound very familiar

**Who Benefits?**
The Republican Congress passed, and President Clinton signed, the 1996 Welfare Reform Act. Some groups pressured the president not to sign because the act included a provision to keep *legal* immigrants from receiving welfare aid. *What level of government benefits should legal immigrants receive? What about illegal immigrants?*

to Americans of the early 1900s. Does providing services to immigrants impose a burden on native citizens? Do immigrants take jobs from native workers? Do hard-working immigrant entrepreneurs drive "native" shopkeepers out of business? As we have seen, such fears are not new, but that does not mean they are totally groundless. There are four problems associated with immigration today that are somewhat different from those of the past.

First, in contrast to earlier periods in American history, immigrants are not entering an economy hungry for unskilled labor. There is no exploding railroad industry to absorb today's immigrants as it absorbed the Irish and the Chinese. There is no expanding steel industry sending representatives to southern and eastern Europe to recruit laborers. The American economy is in transition between the old manufacturing economy that absorbed previous generations of immigrants and a new, globally integrated service and information economy, and many Americans, especially those lacking skills, are experiencing difficulties in the transition. Research indicates that competition from immigrants lowers the wages of low-skilled Americans who already are struggling to make ends meet.[22]

Second, even though studies show that immigrants make a net positive contribution to the national economy and pay nearly as much in taxes as they consume in government services, states do not share the burdens and benefits equally.[23] During the 1980s, for example, more than 75 percent of new immigrants (those who have the

**Figure 4.2**

Timeline: The New Immigration to the United States

SOURCE: The U.S. Immigration and Naturalization Service (http://www.ins.gov)

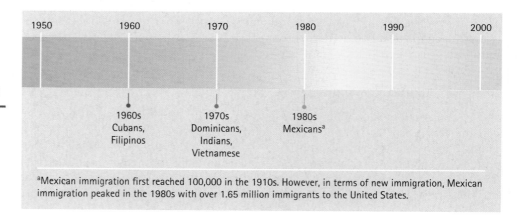

| 1950 | 1960 | 1970 | 1980 | 1990 | 2000 |
|------|------|------|------|------|------|
|      | 1960s Cubans, Filipinos | 1970s Dominicans, Indians, Vietnamese | 1980s Mexicans[a] |      |      |

[a]Mexican immigration first reached 100,000 in the 1910s. However, in terms of new immigration, Mexican immigration peaked in the 1980s with over 1.65 million immigrants to the United States.

## Election Connection        California's Proposition 187

California is on the cutting edge of American social and economic trends. Perhaps for that reason political controversies often surface there first. Such was the case with the immigration issue in 1994. Almost half of the nation's 4–5 million illegal immigrants live in California. Taxpayer resentment of the burden of providing services (education, Medicaid, welfare, police) interacted with ethnic antagonisms and an economic slowdown to create a backlash in the form of Proposition 187. This initiative would have denied state and local services to illegal immigrants and their children and would have instructed all government employees, including teachers, to report suspected illegals to immigration authorities. Although opponents of the measure charged that it was unconstitutional, and many proponents agreed, both sides felt that it would send an important signal.

During the summer, incumbent Republican Governor Pete Wilson was trailing Democratic challenger Kathleen Brown by 20 points in the polls, but Wilson was an experienced politician with a good instinct for important issues. He embraced Prop 187 and led the campaign for its adoption. Brown opposed it. Immigration was not the only issue in the campaign, and Brown was widely viewed as a poor campaigner, but by mid-October Wilson had transformed his double-digit deficit in the polls into a double-digit lead. In the Republican sweep a few weeks later, he thrashed Brown 55 percent to 40 percent.

Wilson's attempt to parlay his big victory into the Republican presidential nomination failed, and as expected, the courts eventually overturned Prop 187's provisions. But the campaign demonstrated the political importance of the immigration issue. In 1995 the new Republican Congress proposed legislation to discourage illegal immigration and restrict the benefits that legal immigrants could receive. Just before the 1996 elections, President Clinton signed a weaker version of the legislation that eliminated most of the provisions dealing with legal immigrants.[a] A few weeks earlier, however, he had signed a far-reaching welfare reform bill that reduced various benefits for legal immigrants. Ultimately, some of the cuts were restored in the 1997 budget deal.[b]

The questions raised by illegal immigration are difficult ones:

- *Should government actively check the citizenship status of people, which raises privacy concerns?*
- *Should people not legally in the country automatically be deported?*
- *If we invoke laws against illegal immigrants, how do we treat their children, who are citizens if they are born here?*

[a] Dan Carney, "As White House Calls Shots, Illegal Alien Bill Clears," *Congressional Quarterly Weekly Report,* October 5, 1996: 2864–2866.
[b] George Hager, "Clinton, GOP Congress Strike Historic Budget Agreement," *Congressional Quarterly Weekly Report,* May 3, 1997: 996.

greatest need for government assistance) went to six states: California, New York, Texas, Florida, New Jersey, and Illinois. Studies examining state and local economic benefits are inconclusive. But, the *states* that carry more than their share of the fiscal burden of immigration naturally take little consolation in the knowledge that immigrants provide a net gain for the *national* economy.

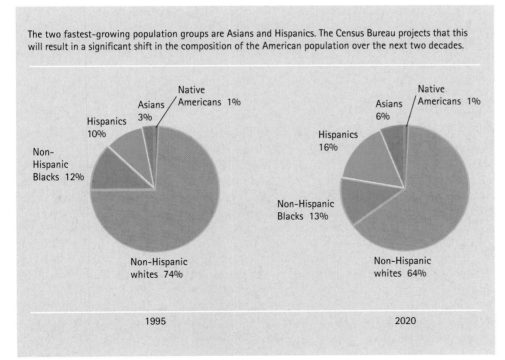

The two fastest-growing population groups are Asians and Hispanics. The Census Bureau projects that this will result in a significant shift in the composition of the American population over the next two decades.

**1995**

Native Americans 1%
Asians 3%
Hispanics 10%
Non-Hispanic Blacks 12%
Non-Hispanic whites 74%

**2020**

Native Americans 1%
Asians 6%
Hispanics 16%
Non-Hispanic Blacks 13%
Non-Hispanic whites 64%

**Figure 4.3**

**U.S. Population by Race and Ethnicity, 1995 and 2020**

The population of the United States is becoming less European in its origins.

SOURCE: Carole DeVita, "The United States at Mid-Decade," *Population Bulletin* 50 (1996): 19.

Even if unskilled labor were in greater demand and new immigrants were not concentrated so heavily in some states, immigration would still probably be a political issue for a third reason: The benefits and costs of immigration fall on different levels of government. Taxing and spending are more differentiated today than in the nineteenth century. Most of the taxes paid by immigrants are federal income and social security taxes; this revenue does not go to the governors and state legislators responsible for welfare and Medicaid bills. And within states, most of the taxes that immigrants pay are state income taxes, but it is the mayors and city councilors who hire and pay additional teachers, social workers, and police officers—and take the blame for the costs of those services. Immigration forces local and state governments to cut services, raise taxes, and beg for money from higher levels of government, options that elected officials naturally view as unpleasant. Many of them have responded by making immigration an electoral issue, trying to shift the blame to federal officials who collect the lion's share of the taxes but decline to compensate states and localities for their services.

Finally, while late-nineteenth-century law barred persons "likely to become a public charge," the immigration law adopted in 1965 gives preference to those with relatives already in the country: Two-thirds of all immigrants today are relatives of those already here. In consequence, a higher proportion of dependent persons—especially older people—have been admitted in recent years than in previous eras.[24] Thus, current U.S. immigration policy admits fewer taxpayers and more people in need of services than a law that gave first preference to productive workers. Even if immigrants as a group pay as much in taxes as they consume in services, many American taxpayers ask why *any* immigrants likely to be dependent on government services should be admitted.

In sum, a fairer geographic and political sharing of the costs of immigration, combined with changes in who receives preference for entry, would undermine the economic basis for opposition to immigration. But economics is not the only reason for opposition to immigration. Over and above economic costs, many opponents of immigration regard it as a threat to the American political culture. They believe that immigrants who speak different languages, believe in different religions, and practice different customs threaten American unity. They fear that the multicultural society created by the new immigrants will be a balkanized society, in which groups retain their own narrow identities and decline to become part of the larger American whole. They urge the United States to close the door before too much *pluribus* destroys the *unum*.[25] As we have seen, such fears were expressed as far back as the 1840s, if not earlier. Well, then, what does history say about the effects of the earlier immigrations on American unity? To answer that question, we need to know what unity some Americans seek to defend.

## *Philosophical Unity*

Given that ethnic and religious diversity are greater in the United States than in other countries, it is surprising that observers from abroad claim that Americans show less diversity in their beliefs and values than people in other countries. From the French visitor Alexis de Tocqueville in the 1830s to the Swede Gunnar Myrdal in the 1940s, visitors have claimed that Americans agree on a common core of beliefs and values that defines what it is to be American. These beliefs and values usually are described as "individualist," and the political culture they produce is generally referred to as a "liberal" political culture.[26]

The term *liberal* as used here is not the same as the "L word" used in contemporary political campaigns. The pejorative campaign usage implies that liberal candidates and office holders support big government and lack respect for traditional values. No wonder liberal candidates avoid the term, preferring to call themselves progressives, populists, or pragmatists instead! The classical meanings of the term *liberal* are more

## Strange Bedfellows: The Sierra Club and Pat Buchanan

There is an old expression that politics makes strange bedfellows. A recent example was provided by an internal struggle in the Sierra Club.[a] A highly visible and influential actor in environmental politics, the Club generally endorses Democratic candidates and proposals. In recent years, however, some of the members, including former Democratic Cabinet secretary Brock Adams and former Democratic Senator Gaylord Nelson (the founder of Earth Day), have allied with some Republican politicians in opposition to continued immigration. Their reasoning? Immigrants and their children account for more than half the growth in population today. Given that population growth is associated with increased consumption of resources, the anti-immigration faction of the Sierra Club argued that the Club should take a formal stance against the current liberal immigration laws. As one proponent put it, "It's a question of being environmentally correct versus being politically correct." Such a stance would have aligned the Sierra Club with Pat Buchanan and other supporters of restrictive policies. Given the Club's allies in the Democratic party, the situation was, to say the least, embarrassing.

The Club's board of directors argued that population growth is a global problem requiring global policies and that immigration simply moves populations around without worsening fundamental environmental problems. In a 1998 referendum, a majority of the Club's members endorsed the board's recommendation that the Sierra Club take no position.

*What do you think?*

- *How firm are political alliances?*

- *In the 2000 election some environmental groups considered endorsing Ralph Nader (Green Party) over Al Gore, the Democratic standard-bearer, who wasn't perceived as quite strong enough on environmental issues. When is making a political point worth offending a long-time ally?*

[a]William Branigin, "Sierra Club Debates Immigration Stand," *The Boston Globe*, March 8, 1998: A23. "Sierra Club in Turmoil," *The Boston Globe*, April 8, 1998: A18.

akin to those of the contemporary term *libertarian*, which signifies skepticism of government interference in all spheres of life. These different meanings naturally create confusion; for example, the Nobel Prize–winning "conservative" economist Milton Friedman considers himself a classical liberal.

Classical **liberalism** is a philosophy that emerged in Europe as medieval thought disintegrated in the religious wars of the seventeenth century. In contrast to earlier philosophies that viewed human nature as sinful and in need of tight control by religious and political authority, liberalism empowered the individual. Liberalism asserted the rights of the individual against the hereditary privilege of the nobility and the religious privilege of the clergy, and it affirmed the autonomy of the individual, first in the religious sphere, then in the political. Having liberated the individual in these ways, liberalism made the individual rather than the community the basis for society and government. Instead of viewing individuals as the product of political society—a view that goes back to the Greeks—liberalism makes society the product of individuals. Theorists such as Hobbes, Locke, and Rousseau formulated "social contract" theories that viewed political society as a contract between rulers and ruled that specified the rights of each as well as the duties and obligations of one to the other.

It was necessary to spell out rights and duties in some detail, because liberalism viewed human beings as primarily self-interested. Hobbes was the most pessimistic in this respect, but in general, liberal thinkers viewed altruistic sentiments as too weak to provide a reliable basis for government.

What kind of political principles follow from such a philosophy? First, individuals have basic rights—of religion, thought and expression, and property—that are not to be violated by government. Second, individuals are equal under the law; there are no distinctions based on heredity or religion. Third, to safeguard rights, government must be limited; despite Hobbes's initial defense of an absolutist state, liberal thinkers generally advanced theories of limited government. Fourth, governments are instrumental; the state exists to serve individuals, not as an end or value in itself. In this sense, liberalism stands President John F. Kennedy's famous exhortation on its head.

**liberalism**
A philosophy that elevates and empowers the individual as opposed to religious, hereditary, governmental, or other forms of authority.

## Window on the Past

### How Classical Liberalism Became Modern Liberalism

Why does conservative economist Milton Friedman consider himself a classical liberal? How could the same term, *liberal,* have stood for laissez-faire (free market) economics in the nineteenth century but for government regulation of the economy in the twentieth century (at least after Franklin Roosevelt and the New Deal)? The answer lies in the philosophical foundations of liberalism.

Liberalism emphasizes the rights of the individual. When the philosophy took shape, religion and government were the principal threats to individual rights. Individuals could be free to develop their capacities to the fullest only if they were free from religious or political persecution and free of burdensome laws and regulations. This concern of liberalism emphasized freedom *from*—from the interference of larger institutions. This type of freedom has been called "negative freedom" by philosophers.* Over time, howev-

er, as personal and political rights became firmly established, one strand of liberalism became concerned about other obstacles to the development of individual capacities. In particular, adverse circumstances such as poverty and discrimination could burden individuals. Some liberal thinkers argued that by alleviating adverse circumstances, government could help individuals develop to the fullest. They emphasized the freedom *to*—to develop one's full capabilities. This type of freedom has been called "positive freedom." Over time, this line of thought became sufficiently widespread that it appropriated the term *liberal,* leaving believers in laissez-faire economics to lead the "conservative" assault on big government.

\* Isiah Berlin, *Two Concepts of Liberty* (Oxford, England: Oxford University Press, 1958).

---

Kennedy urged Americans to "Ask not what your country can do for you, ask what you can do for your country." Classical liberalism suggests the opposite: "Ask not what you can do for government, but what government can do for you."

The preceding paragraph should have a familiar ring, for liberalism provides the philosophical foundation for the American constitutional order. In the *Declaration of Independence* Jefferson wrote,

> We hold these truths to be self-evident: That all men are created equal, that they are endowed by their Creator with certain inalienable Rights, that among these are Life, Liberty, and the Pursuit of Happiness.
>
> That to secure these rights Governments are instituted among Men, deriving their just powers from the consent of the governed;
>
> That whenever any Form of Government becomes destructive of these ends, it is the Right of the People to alter or to abolish it, and to institute new Government, laying its foundation on such principles and organizing its powers in such form, as to them shall seem most likely to effect their Safety and Happiness.

These eloquent sentences capture the four tenets of liberal philosophy: political equality, rights, instrumental government, and limited government. Moreover, what are the Constitution and its Bill of Rights, after all, if not an elaborate statement of the rights of citizens, the purposes of government, and the limits under which it must operate? Such statements and limits are necessary precisely because neither citizens nor their governors can be trusted—they are self-interested individualists.[27] For this reason the American constitutional tradition often is called a liberal tradition.

To some degree, philosophers and historians have exaggerated the philosophical consensus described in writings about the liberal tradition. Many of them refer to the

American "Creed" and the American "Ethos." Terms like these suggest a more unified and well-defined set of beliefs than actually exists. There is also an obvious tendency to romanticize or idealize the liberal tradition by incorporating into it all qualities that people consider desirable, regardless of their philosophical or logical consistency. Both kinds of exaggeration may occur together:

> There has been, in a doctrinal sense, only one America. We have debated fiercely, but as men who agreed on fundamentals. . . . The American political tradition is basically a liberal tradition . . . its articles of faith, a sort of American Holy Writ, are perfectability, progress, liberty, equality, democracy, and individualism.[28]

Unfortunately, these optimistic sentiments notwithstanding, progress often comes at a cost and inevitably leaves some people behind. Excessive individualism can disrupt society. And as we discuss below, liberty and equality are often in tension.

Additionally, some historians argue that writers in the liberal tradition have downplayed the importance of a **civic republican** tradition that coexisted with liberalism at the time of the Revolution.[29] According to Gordon Wood, civic republicanism placed more emphasis on the welfare of the community relative to the rights of the individual, but it lost ground to liberalism shortly after the Revolution.[30] Often called communitarian, this tradition certainly has not disappeared, and appeals like President Kennedy's to sacrifice for the general good periodically enjoy a positive reception.

| civic republicanism |
| --- |
| A political philosophy that emphasizes the obligation of citizens to act virtuously in pursuit of the common good. |

Other critics point out that the rights and privileges exalted in the liberal tradition extended only so far. In particular, they did not extend to the Native American tribes that were destroyed by the American settlers, and they did not extend to African Americans until a century after the Civil War forcibly removed the great contradiction of slavery. Full rights and privileges did not extend to women until even later.[31] And the rights of other minority groups such as homosexuals remain matters of political disagreement today.

We agree that there has been a tendency to exaggerate the scope, the homogeneity, and the inclusiveness of the "American consensus." But even granting these reservations about the notion of an all-encompassing "liberal tradition," there is plenty of evidence consistent with the more limited assertion that Americans are in widespread agreement on certain basic "liberal" principles, as well as for the assertion that Americans differ in systematic ways from the citizens of other democracies.

## American Individualism

Perhaps the most striking way in which Americans differ from people elsewhere lies in the balance they strike between individual responsibility on the one hand, and collective—especially governmental—responsibility on the other. Figure 4.4 compares the responses of citizens of 14 old and new democracies to a question about the responsibility of the state. Note that less than a quarter of the American respondents completely agreed that "It is the responsibility of the state ('government' in the United States) to take care of very poor people who can't take care of themselves." The wording of the question is demanding (do you *completely* agree?), but the proportion of Americans opting for governmental responsibility is only half as large as that in the next closest country (Germany) and barely a third as large as the average of the other 13 democracies.

Another survey of six long-established Western democracies found Americans to be similarly one-sided in their belief that individuals are responsible for their own welfare. As shown in Figure 4.5, barely a quarter of Americans supported a government-guaranteed income, whereas majorities of Germans, British, Italians, and Dutch supported it; a majority of Americans even rejected the mild egalitarian notion that the government should reduce income inequality. Little more than one-third of Americans felt that the government should provide a decent standard of living for the unemployed, compared to an average of two-thirds in the four European democracies.

**Figure 4.4**

**Americans Emphasize Individual Responsibility Much More Than People Elsewhere**

SOURCE: Everett Carll Ladd, *The American Ideology* (Storrs, CT: The Roper Center, 1994), p. 79.

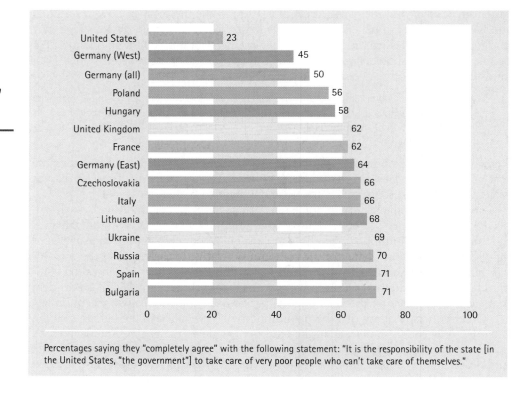

Percentages saying they "completely agree" with the following statement: "It is the responsibility of the state [in the United States, "the government"] to take care of very poor people who can't take care of themselves."

**Figure 4.5**

**Americans Are Far Less Supportive of Government Actions to Reduce Economic Inequality Than People Elsewhere**

SOURCE: Ladd, *The American Ideology*, p. 75.

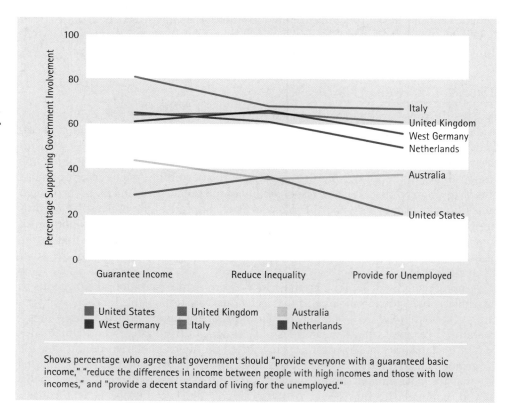

Shows percentage who agree that government should "provide everyone with a guaranteed basic income," "reduce the differences in income between people with high incomes and those with low incomes," and "provide a decent standard of living for the unemployed."

Interestingly, Australia seems to occupy a middle position between the individual responsibility favored by Americans and the governmental responsibility favored by Europeans. Australia, too, is a society of immigrants, and its citizens seem to share some of the beliefs and values of Americans.

Two general sentiments reinforce the American emphasis on individual responsibility. First, Americans are suspicious of governmental power and skeptical about governmental competence. In Samuel Huntington's view, "the distinctive aspect of the American creed is its antigovernment character. Opposition to power and suspicion of government as the most dangerous embodiment of power are the central themes of American political thought."[32] If people doubt the motives and abilities of government, they can hardly be expected to grant it expansive powers and responsibilities.

A second source of reinforcement for the emphasis on individual responsibility is simple: Americans believe that it works. Americans believe that hard work and perseverance pay off. More than people in other countries, Americans believe that hard work is the key to success; people elsewhere are less likely to see personal effort as a sure means to better one's life. As a consequence, an overwhelming majority of Americans are optimistic about getting ahead (see Figure 4.6). Once again, Australians are more similar to Americans than are Europeans.

One of the most striking features of the American belief in individual achievement and responsibility is that it is not closely tied to the actual social and economic circumstances in which Americans find themselves. One would think that those at the bottom of the economic ladder would be far less individualistic and optimistic than those at the top, but that expectation has been contradicted repeatedly. As shown in Figure 4.7, even the very poorest Americans reject a government-guaranteed income, and only the very poorest feel that the government should reduce income differences. There is little or no relationship between income and belief in the benefits of hard work: Two-thirds of the poorest Americans subscribe to this belief, just as do two-thirds of the most affluent.

Other studies reveal that poor Americans are as likely as the nonpoor to embrace the "work ethic" and as likely as the nonpoor to take personal responsibility for their condition.[33] The poor dislike the progressive income tax almost as much as the

**Figure 4.6**

Americans Are Much More
Optimistic About Their Chances of
Getting Ahead Than People Elsewhere

SOURCE: Ladd, *The American Ideology*, p. 76.

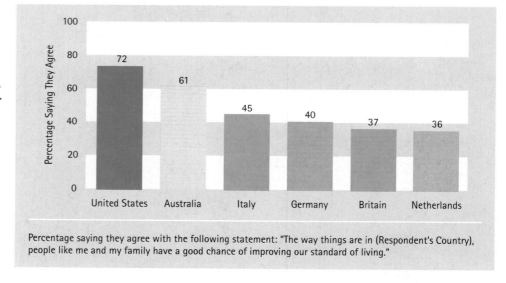

Percentage saying they agree with the following statement: "The way things are in (Respondent's Country), people like me and my family have a good chance of improving our standard of living."

rich.[34] And perhaps the most powerful illustration of American individualism lies in the attitudes of minorities. African Americans and Latinos clearly share less in the American dream than do whites. On average they earn less, work in less prestigious occupations, and suffer discrimination in many forms. It comes as no surprise, then, that they are a bit less likely than whites to embrace the individualist ethic, but it does come as a surprise that they embrace as much of it as they do. In terms of their belief in hard work and individual responsibility, black and Latino Americans are more like white Americans than like Europeans (see Figure 4.8). In sum, even those Americans who are faring poorly in an individualist social order still support its basic premises.[35]

**Figure 4.7**

Even Less Affluent Americans
Share the Individualistic Values
of the Larger Society

SOURCE: Ladd, *The American Ideology*, p. 68.

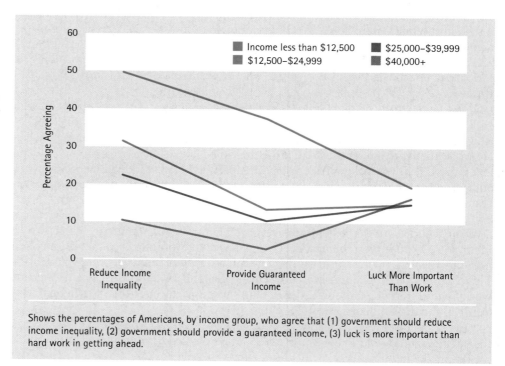

Shows the percentages of Americans, by income group, who agree that (1) government should reduce income inequality, (2) government should provide a guaranteed income, (3) luck is more important than hard work in getting ahead.

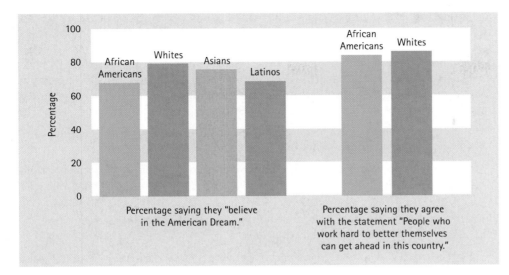

**Figure 4.8**

**Even Racial and Ethnic Minorities Share the Individualistic Values of the Larger Society**

SOURCE: Adapted from data reported in "People, Opinions and Polls: An American Dilemma (Part II)," *The Public Perspective* (February/March 1996): 19–35.

## The Tension Between Individualism and Equality

The findings on American individualism raise an important question: What about equality? Liberal philosophy attaches great importance to equality, and writers in the liberal tradition typically mention it just after liberty. Yet great inequalities exist in the United States. For example, not only has the income distribution changed little during the past six decades, it has actually become slightly less egalitarian since the early 1970s.[36] Nevertheless, Americans do not demand that such inequalities be eliminated or even lessened. Most Americans do not regard economic and social inequality as justification for government action.

At one time there was no great disparity between liberty and equality. Indeed, Tocqueville and other early nineteenth-century visitors were struck by the extent of social and economic equality in the United States. Liberty and equality were thought to be reinforcing in that free, hard-working people would achieve economic success, and an independent, economically secure middle class would safeguard society from radical threats to liberty. But economic development weakened the association between liberty and equality. For much of its first century the United States was a country of small ("yeoman") farmers, manufacturers, and merchants. But after the Civil War, the Industrial Revolution produced great concentrations of private wealth on the one hand and masses of low-wage workers on the other. Under such conditions, liberty and equality became detached; indeed, some Americans became disillusioned with a political system that could tolerate such massive social and economic inequalities. But reform movements typically focused on curbing the worst abuses of corporate power without attacking the foundations of an economic system that generated such great inequality.

The explanation of this apparent inconsistency is that the American political culture supports only a limited kind of equality. Liberalism emphasized equality before the law; one person had the same rights as another, regardless of heredity, religious faith, or relationship to some government official. As is consistent with this philosophical heritage, Americans display a strong commitment to legal, social, and political equality. But Americans are not committed to economic equality; rather, they agree with Madison, who writes of "the diversity in the faculties of men, from which the rights of property originate."[37] Americans regard economic inequality as not only inevitable but also fair (the rich deserve to be rich) and reject government action to do much about it.

**equality of opportunity**
The notion that individuals should have an equal chance to advance economically through individual talent and hard work.

**equality of condition**
The notion that all individuals have a right to a more or less equal part of the material goods that society produces.

Today it is customary to talk about this distinction in terms of the difference between **equality of opportunity** and **equality of condition**. Americans strongly support equality of opportunity: Everyone should have a fair chance, but may the best people—the smartest and hardest-working—win. Americans just as strongly reject attempts to bring about equality of condition, because that may involve rewarding people who are undeserving. Thus Americans favor affirmative action for women and minorities when the survey questions are clear that equal opportunity is the goal:

> Ninety-four percent agree that "Our society should do what is necessary to make sure that everyone has an equal opportunity to succeed."

> Seventy-nine percent agree that "After years of discrimination, it is only fair to set up special programs to make sure that women and minorities are given every chance to have equal opportunities in employment and education."

But Americans just as strongly oppose affirmative action when the survey questions indicate that equality of outcome is the goal:

> Eighty-six percent don't think "blacks and other minorities should receive preference in college admissions to make up for past inequalities."

> Eighty percent don't think "blacks and other minorities should receive preference in hiring to make up for past inequalities".[38]

simulation
**You are
the Mayor**

As far as most Americans are concerned, equality of opportunity should be sufficient. The rest is up to the individual. This belief also shows up in government policy. As social critics have pointed out, the United States spends a smaller proportion of its national income on social welfare than most other democracies. But the United States historically has spent a larger proportion of its national income on education than other democracies. Education is a means by which individuals improve their skills and make themselves fitter competitors. That idea resonates with Americans.[39] Direct government assistance, in contrast, looks like "welfare." Americans are uncomfortable with that idea.

### Section Summary

Americans are more diverse than people in most other countries when we think of diversity in terms of ethnicity, race, and religion. But Americans are less diverse when we think of diversity in terms of the general beliefs and values that constitute the political culture of a country. Americans share individualistic values that differentiate them from the citizens of other countries.

## *Religion and American Individualism: Contradiction or Complement?*

There is a further aspect of American beliefs and values that some observers find difficult to square with the notion of a dominant liberal political culture: Americans are more religious than people in other developed democracies. Americans are more likely to believe in God, to attend religious services, and to report that religion plays an important role in their lives. These beliefs may seem surprising when you consider that some other democracies have an "established" church—an official religion that is often government-subsidized. The Anglican Church is the established church in Great Britain, the Catholic Church in Italy, the Lutheran Church in Norway, and the Eastern Orthodox Church in Greece. Yet as Figure 4.9 shows, even in countries with established churches, citizens are not so involved with religion as Americans are.

Much of the original settlement of the United States was carried out by people seeking the freedom to practice their religion. These deeply religious people were trying to escape oppression and even persecution by the established churches of Europe. Of course, they had no problem with established religion in principle, as long as it was *theirs*: The Congregational Church was the established church of Connecticut until

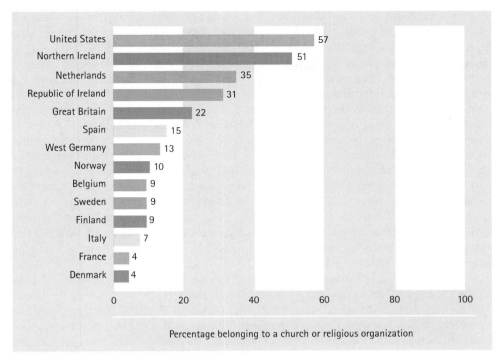

**Figure 4.9**

**Americans Are Far More Involved with Religion Than People Elsewhere**

SOURCE: Ladd, *The American Ideology*, p. 71.

1818 and of Massachusetts until 1833. (The constitutional prohibition of the establishment of religion originally applied only to the federal government, and even today, archaic provisions in some state constitutions require public officials to believe in a deity.[40]) Although the *institutions* of church and state are constitutionally separated in the United States, there never has been a political wall between religion and politics, as shown by American history in general and by the activities of contemporary religious groups in particular. On the contrary, a majority of Americans report that they will not vote for an otherwise qualified candidate who happens to be an atheist.[41]

The religious roots of the United States are often cited as an explanation for the "moralistic" nature of American politics. Throughout history, religiously motivated Americans have attempted to use government to change society—"to legislate morality," in the words of their opponents. More than people in other democracies, Americans have tried to use government to promote "moral behavior." Thus, at various times and places, laws restrict recreational activities on Sundays, prohibit people from drinking, and censor what people can read or watch. And Americans tend to evaluate their politicians, with the notable exception of Bill Clinton, in relatively more moralistic terms than do the citizens of other countries.[42]

Thus the importance of religion in the United States is indisputable, but how can one explain the coexistence of a high degree of religious commitment with the liberal tradition? Given its origins in a reaction against religious privilege, its emphasis on individual freedom, and its reflection in a capitalist society that celebrates individual achievement, one might think the liberal tradition would inevitably evolve in a secular direction, but there is little indication that it has. Are the religious roots of the original settlers sufficient to explain the persistence of religious sentiment in the United States? Is the influence of the Puritans, Quakers, and others who landed on American shores more than 300 years ago still present in the religious habits of contemporary Americans?

Many observers doubt that historical origins alone can explain the flourishing of religion in America, especially given all the developments since the early colonial period: westward expansion, the Industrial Revolution, immigration, and great wars, to name a few. These skeptics offer other explanations for the strength and persistence of religion in America. One explanation points to the diversity of religion—America's incredible number of mainstream religions, branches, and sects. If a person doesn't like one religion, there are numerous others to choose from, and exceptionally hard-to-please worshippers can always start their own. This range of options may make it easier to find a comfortable match with some religion in America than in other countries, where citizens typically have a much smaller range of choices.

A second explanation for the strength of religion in America is related to the first but focuses on the choices of the clergy rather than on those of the congregations. A religious institution that is supported by a government subsidy does not need to cater to its members to nearly the same extent as one dependent on their voluntary contributions. Because there is no established religion in America, and because there are so many religions and sects for worshippers to choose among, American religious groups must compete for members. Thus the clergy are motivated to adapt their "product" to the changing interests and values of their members and to provide services and auxiliary activities (youth clubs, sports clubs, even singles clubs) that members value. Just as the free market in economics encourages economic enterprise, a free market in religion may encourage religious enterprise: The clergy act as entrepreneurs and actively "sell" their respective religions. Thus Americans may be more involved with religion than people in other countries because, stimulated by competition, American religion offers them more reasons to be.

Perhaps the most intriguing explanation of the persistence of religiosity in the United States has been proposed by Robert Booth Fowler, who argues that the liberal tradition and religiosity do not conflict. He maintains, in fact, that just the opposite is true—the liberal tradition creates a deep need for religion. People steeped in the liberal tradition jealously guard their rights and hold themselves personally responsible for their successes and failures. They create a society characterized by social and geographic mobility and rapid social and economic change. Fowler suggests that many people find life in such a society precarious, or at least somewhat lonely:

> Religion has aided liberalism by being a *refuge* from liberalism. . . . [I]t provides an escape from liberal culture, a place of comfort where individualism, competition, this-worldly pragmatism, and relentless rationalism do not hold sway. In a liberal country with liberal citizens, religion is a place where one can come home . . . and *then* emerge refreshed for the battles of life in the liberal world.[43]

Thus Fowler sees religion as filling a gap in American lives. In contrast, citizens of democracies in which individualistic values are relatively weaker than communitarian ones do not feel so detached from each other and hence have less need for a religious dimension in their lives. Fowler's theory may help to explain the great religious "awakenings" that periodically wash over the United States. According to historians, the first such awakening occurred in the colonies in the 1730s and 1740s. The second started around 1800 and continued into Jackson's presidency (1828–1836). The third began in the 1890s and lasted about two decades. Some believe that the United States is now in a fourth awakening that began in the late 1950s. These religious awakenings precede periods of reform in political and economic life, and one theory is that they reflect a growing gap between the ideals Americans hold dear and the political and economic conditions that individualism creates.[44] Such arguments are plausible enough: Unconstrained individualism creates material prosperity, but some people eventually begin to wonder whether there is something more to life than money and success, and others are appalled by the self-serving behavior of individualists. Thus people may turn to religion for different reasons: as an avenue to personal satisfaction or as a means of constraining the behavior of others. For example, some people have suggested that the resurgence of evangelical Protestantism in the 1980s was in part a reaction to the excesses of the 1960s, a reaction that occurred when the baby boomers—the "me generation"—came of age.

## Section Summary

It is not possible to prove broad theories about the role of religion in any scientific sense. However, when they are considered together, the theories help us to understand the otherwise puzzling persistence of religion alongside a social philosophy that emphasizes individual freedom and autonomy. Religion continues to play a major role in American life, in part because Americans find it easier than people in many other democracies to find a comfortable set of beliefs, because the clergy compete more vigorously for their attention, and because the individualistic society creates a need for something larger than individual success.

## Why a Liberal Political Culture?

The time has now come to answer the question posed at the start of the chapter: How can we explain the apparent contradiction between a population that is strikingly heterogeneous in its ethnic, racial, and religious makeup but surprisingly homogeneous in the beliefs and values that constitute its political culture? Historically, opponents of immigration have feared that influxes of new, diverse peoples would alter or destroy the American political culture. Why have the opponents of multiculturalism been wrong in the past? Both traditional and newer explanations of the American commitment to individualism help to answer that question.

### Traditional Explanations of American Individualism

Traditional explanations assume an interaction between ideas and social conditions. As suggested by writers like Alexis de Tocqueville and Louis Hartz, the early settlers brought with them liberal ideas, and in contrast to the established social structure of Europe, they found nothing in the United States to offer resistance to such ideas. Hartz, especially, emphasizes the lack of a feudal tradition in the United States. There was no hereditary aristocracy or established church to provide the basis for the kind of conservative and clerical viewpoints that persist even today in Europe. Nor was there an oppressed peasant class that might form the basis for radical agrarian parties.

Perhaps as important as what the United States lacked, however, is what it had. In particular, it had a great deal of land. North America was a sparsely populated continent over which the United States steadily expanded.[45] Some historians suggest that the frontier operated like a social safety valve: Rather than revolt against intolerable conditions (the only option in the settled countries of Europe), struggling citizens found it easier to pack up their belongings, move west, steal some land from Mexico or the Native American tribes, and start again.

A plentiful supply of land and a scarcity of labor meant that ambitious individuals could and did succeed. The individualistic values the early settlers brought with them were reinforced by conditions in the new country. And with little in the way of an historical basis for any competing set of values, a liberal political order and a market economy thrived. As Hartz comments,

> where the aristocracies, peasantries, and proletariats of Europe are missing, where virtually everyone . . . has the mentality of an independent entrepreneur, two national impulses are bound to make themselves felt: the impulse toward democracy and the impulse toward capitalism.[46]

Generations of radical critics of American society have plaintively asked, "Why no socialism in America?"[47] Many complex philosophical and historical answers have been offered, but the simplest answer is that Americans never saw much need for socialism. Under the conditions that prevailed, individual effort usually was enough to provide an acceptable life for most people.

Still, questions remain. The frontier was officially closed more than a century ago, and labor shortages have not been of much concern for more than half a century. So even if social conditions in the nineteenth century reinforced the beliefs and values of the early settlers, of what relevance is that today? Moreover, the millions of immigrants who arrived after the Civil War were not from liberal societies. Most of them came from authoritarian states with established churches and had lived their lives in communal peasant societies that *did* have feudal traditions. What is the basis for *their* adherence to the individualist values of the liberal tradition?

**How Are We Socialized?**
Boys (age two and five) mimic their mother as she votes in the municipal elections. *What are the most influential forces that politically socialize young Americans? What influenced your beliefs?*

**political socialization**
The set of psychological and sociological processes by which families, schools, religious organizations, communities, and other societal units inculcate beliefs and values in their members.

Perhaps the answer lies in a process of **political socialization** that continues to instill liberal values long after the objective support for those values—social equality, an unsettled land, a frontier—has eroded. Certainly, material conditions are not the only factor that determines how people think and view the world; different cultures socialize their children in different ways of thinking and different ways of viewing the world, even under similar material circumstances. Beginning in the family and continuing in schools, churches, and other organizations, societies instill certain values and patterns of thinking in their members. Thus the explanation for the persistence of the liberal tradition may be a simple one: Socialization perpetuates a consensus established in the eighteenth century, a consensus so dominant that it was able to integrate tens of millions of immigrants who arrived a century and more later.

Many find such an explanation insufficient. For one thing, one of the principal means by which immigrants were integrated into American society was through the efforts of political parties, particularly the urban machines that we discuss in Chapter 8. The machines were interested in controlling government; to do that they had to win elections, and immigrant votes counted just as much as those of the native-born. Thus the machines organized each arriving group: In some Eastern cities the Democrats gained an edge by organizing the Irish, so the Republicans countered by organizing the Italians, and so on. But the urban machines were not the embodiment of liberal, individualist values. On the contrary, the machines were something of an anomaly in the larger American political culture; they were collectivist and clannish—with an emphasis on obedience and loyalty, not independence. Because machine politics and immigration are closely associated in American history, we might expect that political socialization would have pushed immigrants in a direction different from the liberal tradition.

## Newer Explanations

More recent explanations suggest other factors that might have preserved the liberal tradition over a long period and despite the influx of millions of diverse people from nonliberal traditions. Sven Steinmo argues that scholars have misunderstood the liberal tradition. Rather than liberal ideas shaping American government and politics, Steinmo argues the opposite—that the government and politics of the United States create and recreate the ideas.[48] Specifically, he argues that American government is so fragmented and decentralized that it can rarely act in a positive way to improve society. Often it is "gridlocked" or unable to act, and when it does act, it often does so via the exchanging of political favors among special interests. In consequence, successive generations of Americans learn the same basic lesson: Look to yourself because you cannot look to government, and best keep government limited because it will usually act against the public interest. Given their institutions, Americans would have learned this lesson whether they were originally liberal individualists or not, and new waves of immigrants learn what the natives already know.

Although it is somewhat one-sided, Steinmo's argument reminds us that, once established, institutions that originally *reflected* particular beliefs and values may come to *reinforce* those beliefs and values. Material conditions in the United States today may be far different from those of the nineteenth century, but political institutions are similar and work to preserve the ideas that gave rise to them.

Finally, just as Fowler suggests that there may be no conflict between religion and the liberal tradition, there may never have been any conflict between social diversity and the liberal tradition. In fact, the opposite may be true: Rather than posing a threat to American traditions, as many feared, the flow of diverse peoples to America may have reinforced and strengthened American traditions. How could that be the case?

The answer lies in what statisticians refer to as *self-selection*. With the tragic exception of African Americans, immigrants came to the United States voluntarily. True, many came when they were pushed off their land, or when crops failed, or when work was nowhere to be found. Emigration under such circumstances might not seem to have occurred by choice, *but not everyone chose to emigrate*. Only a small fraction of the potential immigrants—less than 1 percent—actually left their own countries. Many more chose to remain and endure the miserable conditions in which they found themselves.

What kind of person would have been most likely to leave family, friends, and village behind? Remember that immigration through most of history was not a matter of taking a train to Dublin, Frankfurt, or Rome and catching a flight to New York. Before the Civil War the journey usually took months, as immigrants walked to a port, then suffered through a long journey below deck on a sailing ship. Even after the Civil War, when the steamship shortened the ocean voyage and the railroad shortened the land journey, it still took weeks. Many (if not most) of the people who booked passage knew that they would never see their relatives or their homes again.[49] What kind of people made such a decision?

In all probability the people who immigrated already were—relative to their own societies—unusually individualistic. They were more willing to leave the communal order of Europe, more ambitious, more willing to run risks in the hope of bettering themselves—in Hartz's words, more likely to possess "the spirit which repudiated peasantry and tenantry."[50] Bigoted as it was, even the Immigration Commission in 1911 recognized that "emigrating to a strange and distant country, although less of an undertaking than formerly, is still a serious and relatively difficult matter, requiring a degree of courage and resourcefulness not possessed by weaklings of any class."[51] In short, although they had never heard of the liberal tradition, through temperament and experience, immigrants already possessed much of its spirit.

If so, immigration and the resulting diversity never were a threat to American values. On the contrary, successive waves of immigrants rejuvenated those values. People who were willing to endure hardships, eager to work hard, and convinced that they could have a better life were scarcely the kind who would support an oppressive government or religion. Rather, whatever their skills or education, the immigrants included many of the kind of ambitious individuals who already resided in the United States. Those who felt least at home in the United States probably were disproportionately represented among the third of all immigrants who eventually returned to their home countries.

We believe that this earlier pattern continues to hold. Today's immigrants too have left their homes and families in Asia, Africa, and South America. They have endured hardships to come to a new land with a different culture and language. In some extreme cases they have risked life and limb to emigrate, as with the "boat people" of southeast Asia who braved pirates, sharks, and storms, and the Cubans who swam from rafts to the Florida coast. Such people display a kind of individual initiative that can fairly be considered "American," regardless of their nationality!

During the 1994 battle over California's Prop 187, which denied government services to illegal immigrants and their children, prominent Republicans William Bennett and Jack Kemp raised eyebrows by publicly opposing the initiative.[52] Similarly, in 1996 Rudolph Giuliani, the Republican mayor of New York, made news by denouncing congressional attempts to limit immigrant eligibility for welfare and other governmental services.[53] In the 2000 presidential campaign, George W. Bush appealed directly for support in immigrant communities. The positions of these Republicans conflicted with the popular image that Republicans were unsympathetic to the poor and disadvan-

**Figure 4.10**

**Contrary to Popular Impressions, Immigrants' Beliefs About American Culture Are Strikingly Similar to Those of the Native-Born**

SOURCE: Gallup Survey Reported in *The Public Perspective* (August/September 1995): 15.

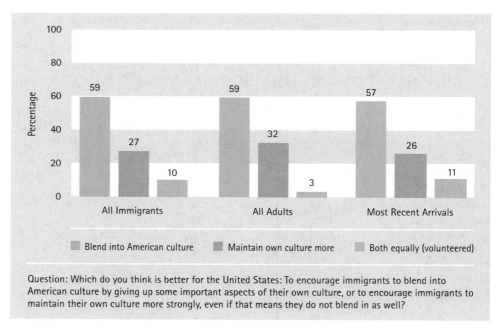

Question: Which do you think is better for the United States: To encourage immigrants to blend into American culture by giving up some important aspects of their own culture, or to encourage immigrants to maintain their own culture more strongly, even if that means they do not blend in as well?

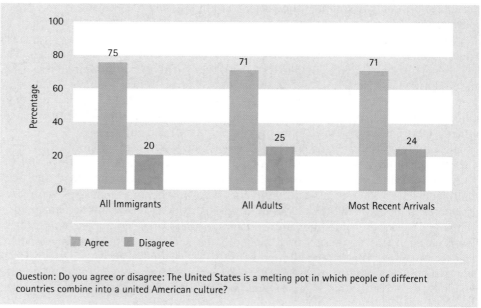

Question: Do you agree or disagree: The United States is a melting pot in which people of different countries combine into a united American culture?

## Democratic Dilemma

# Public Policy and Multiculturalism

The most extreme proponents and opponents of multiculturalism get most of the attention, but even moderate Americans struggle with many of the practical problems created by a diverse population. For example, although most Americans would reject any notion that government policy should discriminate against any minority group, many also are troubled by arguments that government policy should explicitly favor minority groups. Heavy majorities reject the strong form of affirmative action quotas. However well-meaning, attempts to guarantee jobs, college placements, and other outcomes to minorities clash with deeply held beliefs about individual achievement.

Similarly, although many Americans would reject the notion that government policy should actively discourage multiculturalism, they also are uncomfortable with the notion that government should encourage it. The best example is probably bilingual education. Education researchers are divided on its effectiveness, so the debate is heavily political. Opponents argue that it is ineffective and perpetuates group differences that might otherwise erode, whereas proponents claim that it is effective and is the only way to give linguistic minorities a fair chance in school. In 1998 California's proposition 227, which would mandate English–only instruction after one year, illustrated how deeply the divisions ran. After a

fierce campaign the proposition passed by a ratio of about 60 to 40. Latinos themselves—the principal consumers of bilingual education—were divided almost 50-50, according to the polls.

When we turn to the practices of social and economic institutions, the issues become even more complex. Some of the issues that Americans have struggled with in recent years are listed below.

*What do you think?*

- *Should colleges and universities create special programs of study for different ethnic groups? Should they require students to take multicultural courses?*

- *If members of an ethnic minority wish to live together, should a university make a separate dorm or house available to them? What effect does such housing have on the university community?*

- *Should a firm have to advertise widely for new employees, or should it be allowed to hire the friends and relatives of its existing workers, which may result in an ethnically homogeneous labor force? What are the pros and cons of each approach?*

- *Under what circumstances, if any, should bilingual employees be permitted to use their group's language at work, thereby excluding from communication those who speak only English?*

taged and also seemed to run counter to their partisan self-interest; after all, the media typically portray minority group members as Democrats.

These Republicans appeared to be betting that the earlier pattern of American history will continue in the future. They are betting that the Mexican laborers, Korean grocers, and Middle-Eastern service station operators are today's successors to the Irish laborers, Italian grocers, and Jewish shopkeepers of generations past. They are betting that although ethnic group activists often are allied with the Democratic party, most members of those ethnic groups are focused more on economics than on politics. Over time, such people will become middle-class Americans most concerned about their tax rates, their schools, and their property values—and willing to consider Republican appeals.

Whatever their motivations, there is support for Bennett's, Kemp's, Giuliani's, and Bush's belief that in the long term, today's immigrants, like yesterday's, will only reinforce the distinctly "American" political culture. For example, on the basis of extensive surveys, Professor Rodolfo de la Garza reports that

> . . . Anglos and Puerto Ricans who are native born and English dominant and have comparable education and income, are equally patriotic, trusting of government, supportive of economic individualism and willing to allow members of groups they dislike to hold rallies and teach in public schools. Puerto Ricans who express lower support for these values tend to be those who are foreign born and Spanish dominant. As they and their mainland-born children learn English, their support for these values becomes indistinguishable from that of Anglos who find themselves in similar socioeconomic conditions.[54]

De la Garza's studies of Mexican immigrants reach very similar conclusions.[55] As shown in Figure 4.10, a 1995 Gallup survey found that immigrants—even those who have been in the country ten years or less—are virtually indistinguishable from native-born Americans, both in their beliefs about economic opportunity and in their general attitudes toward assimilation.[56] Demographic data suggest similar conclusions. One widely noted study reports that, judging on the basis of standard measures of assimilation (citizenship, home ownership, English acquisition, and intermarriage), today's immigrants "overwhelmingly do what immigrants have always done: slowly, often painfully, but quite assuredly, embrace the language, cultural norms and loyalties of America."[57] Other studies suggest that the use of English as a principal language is occurring *more* rapidly among the children of today's immigrants than in the past.[58]

In sum, the evidence is mounting that American society is evolving along a path that does not support either the fears of the opponents of diversity or the claims of novelty and uniqueness made by its proponents. Ethnic, racial, and religious diversity can coexist with agreement on basic values. Although the process is not easy, Americans seem to be working their way through today's conflicts as they worked through them in the past (see the accompanying Democratic Dilemma). On balance, today's diversity is more likely to reinforce than to undermine the American political culture.

## Chapter Summary

For more than two centuries the United States has been a study in contrasts. On the one hand, this country always has been socially heterogeneous, containing a wider array of ethnic and religious groups than most other lands. On the other hand, the diverse citizenry of the United States has long shown a higher level of agreement on fundamental political principles than is found in other democracies—royalist, clerical, and socialist parties have never flourished here. The fundamental political principles that are so widespread in the United States grew out of a classical liberal political philosophy that stresses the rights and liberties of individuals, while giving much less emphasis to their duties and obligations to the community. Today that philosophy is reflected in a greater emphasis on individual responsibility and hard work and a greater suspicion of government than in other countries. Interestingly, this individualistic emphasis coexists with a greater degree of religious commitment than exists in other countries whose citizens are far less individualistic.

Throughout American history, many native-born citizens have feared that immigration was a threat to the distinctly American political culture. Much of today's multiculturalism debate is strikingly similar to debates that have taken place throughout American history. Recent immigrants want to maintain some part of their cultural distinctiveness. So did previous waves of immigrants. Those already here worry that the new immigrants are too different to fit easily into American society. So did native-born Americans a century ago. Such fears have proved unfounded in the past, and they probably will prove unfounded in the future. In all likelihood, immigrants reinforce rather than weaken the spirit of individualism in the United States. The very fact of their immigrating suggests that they possess the ambitious, individualistic outlook that is such a prominent part of the American political culture.

### On the Web

Immigration and Naturalization Service
www.ins.usdoj.gov
This comprehensive site, maintained by the U.S. Department of Justice, covers all facets of immigration in the United States. It provides statistical reports on the history of immigration to the United States, as well as information on the current guidelines for becoming an American citizen.

Academic Information: Religion Gateway
www.academicinfo.net/religindex.html
An annotated directory of Internet resources for the academic study of religion, this site is supported and maintained by a graduate of the University of Washington's Comparative Religion program.

## Key Terms

citizenship, p. 97
civic republicanism, p. 111
clericalism, p. 98
communism, p. 98
diversity, p. 100

equality of condition, p. 116
equality of opportunity, p. 116
fascism, p. 98
liberalism, p. 109
multiculturalism, p. 100

political culture, p. 98
political socialization, p. 120
socialism, p. 98

## Suggested Readings

Borjas, George. *Heaven's Door: Immigration Policy and the American Economy*. Princeton, NJ: Princeton University Press, 1999. Argues that immigration has hurt the poorest native-born workers, especially African Americans. Calls for restricting immigration and limiting it to better educated and more highly skilled people.

Erie, Steven. *Rainbow's End: Irish-Americans and the Dilemma of Urban Machine Politics, 1849–1985*. Berkeley, CA: University of California Press, 1988. Interesting account of the Irish urban machines that played such an important role in American political history.

Fowler, Robert Booth. *Religion and Politics in America*. Metuchen, NJ: American Theological Library Association, 1985. Stimulating discussion of the relationship between religion and political life.

Fuchs, Lawrence. *The American Kaleidoscope: Race, Ethnicity, and the Civic Culture*. Hanover, NH: University Press of New England, 1990. Dispassionate discussion of the problems and prospects of contemporary immigrants and African Americans. Prefers "kaleidoscope" to "melting pot" as a metaphor for the history of ethnicity in America.

Handlin, Oscar. *The Uprooted*. 2nd ed. Boston: Little, Brown, 1973. Sympathetic description of the ordeals experienced by late-nineteenth-century immigrants.

Hartz, Louis. *The Liberal Tradition in America*. New York: Harcourt, 1955. A classic, if impenetrable, discussion of the liberal tradition. Argues that the absence of feudalism allowed liberal ideas to spread without resistance in the United States.

Kleppner, Paul. *The Cross of Culture*. New York: Free Press, 1970. This example of the "ethnocultural" school of political history provides a detailed account of political conflict in the Midwest from the rise of the Republican party to the end of the nineteenth century.

Ladd, Everett Carll. *The American Ideology*. Storrs, CT: The Roper Center, 1994. A readable, data-based discussion of the core beliefs of Americans.

Lind, Michael. *Alien Nation*. A popular, unsympathetic, historically uninformed account of the post-1965 wave of immigration. Like much contemporary writing, it exaggerates the differences between immigration today and that of a century ago.

Lipset, Seymour Martin. *American Exceptionalism*. New York:

Norton, 1996. The latest work on the American political culture by an eminent senior scholar who has spent much of his career studying it.

Menendez, Albert. *Religion at the Polls*. Philadelphia: Westminster Press, 1977. Survey of the association between religion and voting since the founding of the country.

Mills, Nicolaus, ed. *Arguing Immigration: Are New Immigrants a Wealth of Diversity . . . Or a Crushing Burden?* New York: Simon & Schuster, 1994. This collection of essays provides a good overview of the contemporary immigration debate.

Portes, Alejandro, and Ruben G. Rumbaut. *Immigrant America: A Portrait*. Berkeley, CA: University of California Press. A sympathetic account of the post-1965 wave of immigration. Like much contemporary writing, it exaggerates the differences between immigration today and that of a century ago.

Schlesinger, Arthur, Jr. *The Disuniting of America*. Knoxville, TN: Whittle, 1991. An eminent senior historian complains about the contemporary influence of multiculturalism.

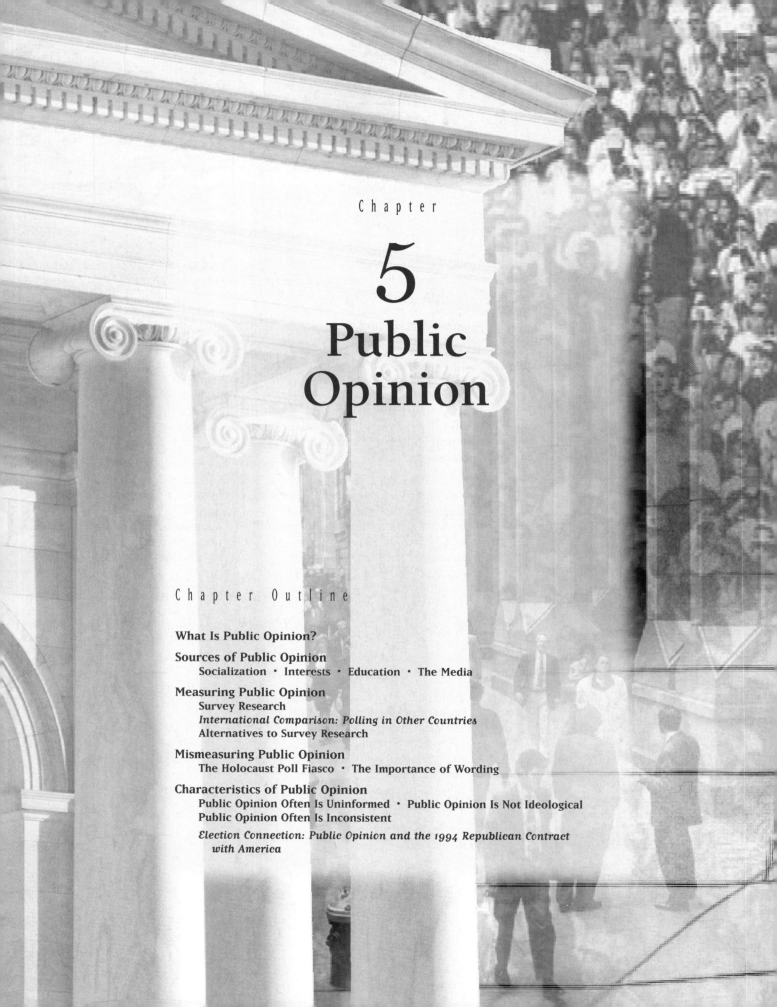

Chapter

# 5
# Public
# Opinion

On August 2, 1990, after months of wrangling about oil, territorial boundaries, and war debts, Iraqi troops surged across the Kuwait border and, in a single day, subjugated that small state.[1] In addition to the direct economic damage to countries whose economies depended on imported oil, the Iraqi offensive heightened world uncertainty about what would happen next. Would Iraq's President, Saddam Hussein, now order a move on Saudi Arabia? If that country, with one-quarter of the world's known oil reserves, were to fall under Iraqi domination, the economies of the West would be at the mercy of an unpredictable and unfriendly dictator. Moreover, a powerful Iraq heightened the danger to America's ally, Israel, and threatened the stability of the entire Middle East, if not that of the world.

President George Bush reacted without hesitation. He warned Iraq in the strongest possible terms, secured a United Nations (UN) resolution condemning the invasion, and sent 200,000 American troops to Saudi Arabia to bolster the Saudi defensive forces. For the next several months the administration engaged in diplomatic efforts to construct a multinational coalition against Hussein. On November 29 the UN adopted a resolution authorizing member states to use "all necessary means" to expel Iraqi forces from Kuwait if they had not withdrawn by January 15, 1991. This was the first time since the Korean war, four decades earlier, that the UN had authorized member states to go to war. By early 1991 a million UN troops lined the Kuwait border facing the Iraqi defenders.

The Bush administration found it a bit tougher to convince the Democratic Congress. Although the administration denied that it needed congressional approval to participate in the UN-sponsored war, many in the Congress thought otherwise. In any event, the administration understood that congressional approval would help build domestic support. The Congress began deliberating shortly after the New Year, and on January 12, after an impressive televised debate in the Senate, adopted a resolution authorizing the use of force against Iraq. The vote in the House was 250 to 183, and in the Senate a closer 52 to 47. Democrats accounted for virtually all of the opposition, raising the specter of Vietnam, charging that a war would really be about oil rather than Iraqi aggression, and asking that economic sanctions be given additional time to work. But in the end, enough Democrats (86 in the House and 10 in the Senate) supported the president to give him the victory.

On January 16, the air war began. CNN broadcast from downtown Baghdad during the bombardment, and in the days that followed, Americans were shown impressive military footage of technologically advanced weaponry. On February 24, the ground offensive began. Allied forces outflanked the entrenched Iraqis and in four days drove them from Kuwait, with great loss of life—50,000 or more Iraqi dead. The evening news telecasts showed throngs of jubilant Kuwaitis parading through the streets chanting "Bush! Bush! Bush!" On February 27, President Bush declared a cease-fire. On March 6, the president told Congress, "The war is over."

The United States had achieved a stunning military victory, with far fewer casualties than most had feared and expected: 89 dead and 38 missing in action

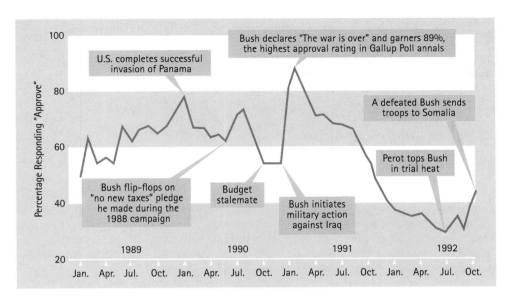

Figure 5.1

The Rise and Decline of
President Bush's Approval Ratings

SOURCE: The Gallup Poll. (www.Gallup.com)

(not until a decade later was it clear that physical illnesses called the Gulf War syndrome resulted from exposure to burning nerve gases and toxins). In the aftermath of the war, President Bush's approval ratings soared, reaching unprecedented heights of as much as 90 percent in some polls (see Figure 5.1). Most people conceded his reelection, only a year and a half away. Apparently Bush had been right and the Democrats wrong. Prominent Democrats who had been mentioned as likely opponents—Majority Leader Richard Gephardt, Senators Sam Nunn and Bill Bradley, Governor Mario Cuomo—all thought better of taking on the seemingly unbeatable Bush. With the Democratic "first team" on the bench, the field of play was left to "minor leaguers" like Jerry Brown, Paul Tsongas, and Bill Clinton.

But Bush's fortunes were slipping even as his strongest opponents were conceding him the election. As Figure 5.1 shows, within a year of his great success in the Persian Gulf, Bush's approval ratings dropped by 50 percent. He went into the election as one of the least popular presidents of the past 50 years and lost to Bill Clinton in a three-way race. The explanation for this startling reversal of fortune lies in shifting public opinion: During the 18 months between the war and Bush's defeat, the American public forgot about the war and turned its attention to the struggling economy.[2]

GEORGE BUSH WAS NOT THE FIRST PRESIDENT to find out that public opinion is a powerful but fickle force. On the one hand, American politicians and institutions seldom can obstruct an aroused public, but on the other hand, public opinion can shift rapidly from concern about one subject to concern about another, and political fortunes can shift accordingly. Some people believe that public opinion is more important in American democracy today than it has ever been.[3] Certainly, modern politicians have more information about it than ever before. But despite such developments, the role that public opinion plays in determining what government does continues to be variable and complex. In this chapter we investigate public opinion by focusing on these questions:

timeline

**Public Opinion
and Presidential
Approval**

- What is public opinion and how is it formed?
- How do we measure—and mismeasure—public opinion?
- What are some important characteristics of public opinion?
- Does public opinion determine public policy?

## *What Is Public Opinion?*

**public opinion**
The aggregation of people's views about issues, situations, and public figures.

**Public opinion** is the aggregation of people's views about issues, situations, and public figures. Although conceptions of democracy differ, public opinion is an essential element of all of them. As we explained in Chapter 1, in the popular model of democracy that emphasizes active participation in government, public opinion drives the democratic process and determines the outcomes. In the responsible model of democracy, in which citizens play a passive role of holding elected officials accountable, public opinion constrains the democratic process and the outcomes it produces by setting bounds within which public officials must operate.

Whichever model of democracy you favor, the reason for the importance of public opinion is captured nicely by V. O. Key's definition of public opinion as "those opinions held by private persons which governments find it prudent to heed."[4] Democratic governments find it "prudent" to heed the opinions of private persons, of course, because of elections. Note that in Key's conception, public opinion can be, but need not be, actively expressed. Even if public opinion is silent, or "latent," public officials may act or fail to act because they fear arousing it. This is the so-called law of anticipated reactions, whereby public opinion influences government even though it does so indirectly and passively.[5] When we say, "Public opinion wouldn't stand for that," we are referring to this latent, constraining function of public opinion. Thus Key's definition accommodates both the more active role of public opinion in participatory democratic theories and the more passive role in responsible theories.

## *Sources of Public Opinion*

The opinions that people hold reflect numerous influences, but most of these fall into several broad categories. These categories are not mutually exclusive, of course; often opinions reflect a number of different influences.

### *Socialization*

**socialization**
The end result of all the processes by which individuals form their beliefs and values in the home, schools, churches, communities, and work-places.

In Chapter 4 we noted that Americans are socialized to value individual responsibility, economic advancement, and other aspects of the liberal tradition. **Socialization** is an imprecise term that encompasses all the ways in which people learn beliefs and values in their families, schools, communities, religious institutions, and workplaces. Sometimes learning is the result of explicit teaching, as when schools teach citizenship and patriotism, but often it results from less conscious observation or imitation of others. For example, studies have found that many children will identify themselves as Democrats or Republicans well before they have any idea what the parties stand for.[6] And older children are very likely to share the party affiliation of their parents.[7] Thus a party affiliation formed long ago in a traumatic time such as the Great Depression may be passed down through generations of families.

Children begin to form political attitudes at an early age. Research carried out in the 1950s and 1960s generally concluded that the single most important socializing agent was the family and that within the family the mother was more important—she spent far more time with the children in that era. A few scholars concluded, however, that schools were more important.[8] In recent decades the increases in single parenthood and in the divorce rate have left many children in one-parent families. Moreover,

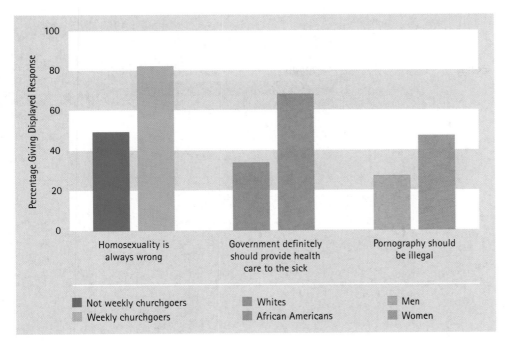

**Figure 5.2**

**Examples of Group Differences in Public Opinion**

SOURCE: General Social Survey, 1994.

the proportion of mothers who work outside the home has doubled since the 1960s. It is plausible, then, to suppose that the relative importance of the family as a socialization agent has declined, but there is little recent research to test such a supposition.

Socialization often works indirectly, by forming the beliefs and values that individuals act on later in life, but sometimes socializing agents consciously try to activate attitudes and influence public opinion. The Catholic Church officially opposes abortion, and rank-and-file Catholics are indeed less accepting of abortion than are mainline Protestants and Jews.[9] Most Fundamentalist Protestant churches officially condemn homosexuality, and rank-and-file members are indeed less tolerant of homosexuality than are mainline Protestants.[10] From the 1930s to the 1980s, labor unions typically supported the Democratic party, and union members were indeed typically more Democratic in their voting than other blue-collar workers.[11] Whether the influence lies in the distant past or in the present, differences among people with different socialization experiences emerge regularly on all kinds of issues. Figure 5.2 offers some examples of differences of opinion that are related to group affiliation.

## Interests

Although people form many of their attitudes in childhood, their political views continue to develop over the course of their lifetimes. Childhood socialization can be modified or even reversed by adult experiences. Some of the opinions people hold are based on their personal interests or the interests of others like them.[12] For example, blue-collar workers are more sensitive to a rise in unemployment that throws them out of work, while professionals and managers are more sensitive to a rise in inflation that drives up interest rates and depresses the overall business climate.[13] Homeowners were significantly more likely than renters and public employees to support Proposition 13, the famous 1978 initiative that rolled back property taxes in California.[14] Working women, who must balance the conflicting demands of home and work, are more supportive of gender equality than stay-at-home mothers.[15] The ill-fated war in Vietnam made many people skeptical in later years about committing U.S. troops unless critical national interests were at stake. Different life experiences give rise to different views on issues that become matters of public policy debate. Some examples appear in Figure 5.3.

**Figure 5.3**

**People with Different Life Experiences Hold Different Views About Politics and Government**

SOURCE: American National Election Study, 1994. The Gallup Poll, October 19–22, 1995; December 17–19, 1993; and April 16–18, 1994.

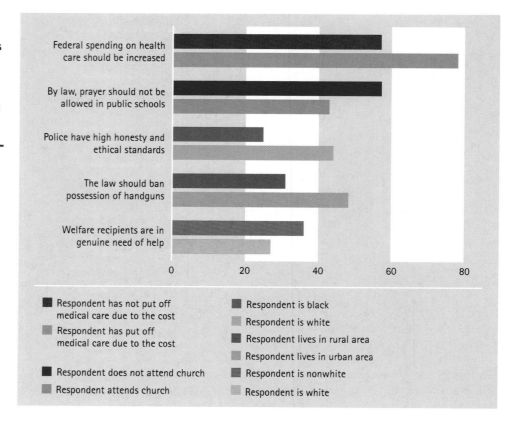

## Education

Although schools are socializing agents, and education certainly affects interests, education belongs in something of a separate category—especially higher education. In general, higher education is associated with a somewhat more tolerant outlook. More highly educated people are more tolerant of minority groups and practices.[16] Apparently, values emphasized in higher education—logical argument, open-mindedness, unemotional analysis—predispose the educated, liberals and conservatives alike, to a somewhat greater acceptance of people and practices different from them and theirs (see Figure 5.4). Higher education also is associated with a greater sense of

**Figure 5.4**

**Higher Education Is Associated with Greater Tolerance of Diversity**

SOURCE: American National Election Study, 1994.

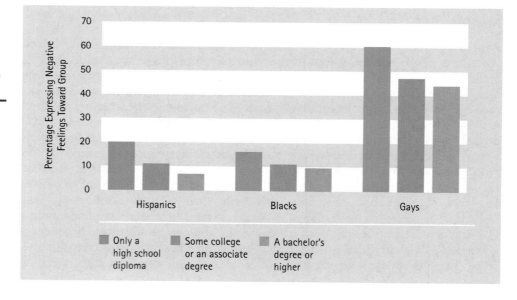

political efficacy—the belief that the citizen can make a difference by acting politically, and a greater sense of **citizen duty**—the belief that citizens have a duty to participate in politics.

### The Media

In recent years many people have expressed the fear that public opinion increasingly is being shaped by the mass media. This substantial issue is steeped in controversy, and we will treat it at length in Chapter 9. Suffice it here to say that under some circumstances the media can move public opinion, while under other circumstances the media are surprisingly ineffectual. Overall, little evidence to date supports the worst fears of media critics. For example, an extensive study of opinion change during the 1980 presidential campaign found that in the aggregate, TV and newspaper exposure had only marginal effects on preexisting views.[17] And more recently, despite the overwhelmingly negative coverage President Clinton received during the Lewinsky scandal, his job performance ratings scarcely budged. To repeat, we will consider this subject at length in Chapter 9.

#### Section Summary

The sources of public opinion are many and varied. People are socialized in families, schools, churches, and community organizations. Their occupational and material interests affect their views. Education affects people's views, especially by making them more tolerant. And although the effects of the media often are exaggerated, the media matter in complex ways that we will discuss later.

## Measuring Public Opinion

In the nineteenth century measuring public opinion was more an art than a science. Politicians may have looked at informal straw polls, consulted important local officials, or scanned the newspaper editorial pages to understand the public mood. But with the advent of modern survey research in the 1930s (especially by George Gallup) public opinion became a much more powerful political force. The key to this change was the development of scientific methods for the study of public opinion.

### Survey Research

Most often we measure public opinion via surveys, which commonly are called polls. Various firms and academic organizations contact individuals, ask them questions, and report the responses. Of these, Gallup is the most widely recognized name. Newspapers, magazines, and TV networks also sponsor regular polls—NBC News/*Wall Street Journal*, CBS News/*New York Times*, ABC News/*Washington Post*, *USA Today*/CNN—and base major stories on them. Indeed, some critics complain that there are too many polls and that the media become obsessed with polls as the election draws near. **Exit polls** of people taken as they leave the voting locations even enable the networks to "call" elections before the votes are counted! However, before we criticize polls and consider how they are used, we should know something about how they are conducted.

   **Survey research** is the technical term for the scientific design and administration of public opinion polls. The enterprise rests on work by statisticians demonstrating that relatively small samples from large populations can provide accurate pictures of those large populations. Surprising though it may seem, a sample of 1500 people can do a pretty good job of representing the opinions of the 200 million adults in the entire United States. The key is that samples must be "representative" and not biased in some way. In a **simple random sample,** for instance, every individual in the population has an equal chance of being part of the sample. If we drew 1500 social security numbers out of a hat, we would have a simple random sample of the population with social security numbers. Simple random samples generally are not practical

**political efficacy**
The belief that one can make a difference in politics by expressing an opinion or acting politically.

**citizen duty**
The belief that it is a citizen's duty to be informed and to participate in politics.

**participation**

**Which are You:
Liberal or
Conservative?**

**exit poll**
Survey of actual voters taken as they leave the polling stations.

**survey research**
The scientific design and administration of public opinion polls.

**simple random sample**
A sample in which every individual in the population has an equal probability of being included.

**Nervous Election Night**
Al Gore looks on as election returns come in. In recent years exit polls (surveys of voters taken as they leave the polls) have eliminated much of the suspense about election results. *What survey biases or sample problems (discussed in the text) might occur in an exit poll?*

**sampling error**
The error that arises in public opinion surveys as a result of relying on a representative but small sample of the larger population.

simulation
**You are a Polling Consultant**

**selection bias**
The error that occurs when a sample systematically includes or excludes people with certain attitudes.

because complete lists of the population to be sampled do not exist. Most surveys today are telephone surveys, so it might seem that random samples could be drawn from telephone directories. But many people have unlisted numbers, so a sample drawn from a directory would miss those who shared a desire for privacy. For this reason, survey researchers often use random-digit dialing: A computer randomly selects from all logically possible numbers within a given exchange. People with unlisted numbers may be surprised and irritated when they answer their phone and hear a pollster, but no one has given out their number—the computer has found them!

When you hear that a polling figure is accurate to ±3 percent with 95 percent confidence, those figures refer to **sampling error,** the error that results from using a representative but small sample to estimate the characteristics of a larger population. Statistical theory tells us how to calculate the expected accuracy of a sample. For example, if every reader of this book flips a fair coin 1500 times, 95 percent of you will get between 47 and 53 percent heads. That is a statistical fact, the same fact that allows a sample of 1500 Americans to represent the views of the entire nation to ±3 percent, with 95 percent confidence.

Even with a representative sample, however, the calculated sampling error may exaggerate the accuracy of the survey. Typically, more than half the original sample either never answer the phone or refuse to be interviewed.[18] Thus the people interviewed may be a biased subset of the original representative sample. Research shows that surveys tend to underrepresent men, young people, whites, and the wealthy.[19] In 1996, for example, pre-election polls overestimated Bill Clinton's margin over Robert Dole. Some commentators claimed that this was because pro-Democratic groups were more likely to respond to the polls than pro-Republican groups.[20]

The key to getting a representative sample is to make sure that individuals have no opportunity to affect whether they are in or out of the sample. For example, if we were to poll attendees at a hockey game, an opera, or even a political science lecture, our sample would be suspect, because the members of these groups share a common interest—in hockey, opera, or political science—that brought them together. This common interest differentiates them from other Americans. Thus survey researchers must continually be on guard for **selection bias,** the error that occurs when their sample systematically includes or excludes people with certain types of attitudes.

## International Comparison — Polling in Other Countries

In the United States, public opinion polling is part of everyday life. The media regularly report the latest polls on the president's standing; the standing of potential challengers, who would win "if the election were held today"; and how people feel about the issues of the day. During campaigns, polling reaches a fever pitch as people are deluged with poll results and stories about poll results. As we will discuss in Chapter 9, many critics believe the American media place too heavy an emphasis on polls, concentrating on who's ahead while giving short shrift to the implications of the election for government and public policy.

Although polling is common in other democracies, many have chosen to limit it to some degree.* For example, Canada allows no polls to be published in the last two days of a campaign. Spain bans publication of polls for the last five days of a campaign, France and Italy for the last seven days. Portugal allows no polls to be published for two weeks prior to election day! In the United States, any attempt to impose restrictions like these would be struck down on First Amendment grounds.

*What do you think?*
- *Should political polling be restricted in the United States? Why might polling be an example of giving people more information than is good for them?*
- *Are Americans—or their courts—obsessed with free speech and expression? What other values, if any, justify "reasonable" restrictions on speech and expression?*

*David Butler, "Polls and Elections," in Lawrence LeDuc, Richard Niemi, and Pippa Norris, eds., *Comparing Democracies* (Thousand Oaks, CA: Sage, 1996), p. 239.

### Alternatives to Survey Research

Recent years have seen the increasing use of **focus groups,** small groups of people brought together to talk about issues or candidates at length and in depth. These groups are too small to provide good estimates of public opinion. They are more useful for *influencing* public opinion than for measuring it. Interest groups and candidates use focus groups to test the appeal of ads, campaign slogans, symbols, and so forth. President Clinton's 1996 campaign slogan, "a bridge to the twenty-first century," was selected after it tested well in focus groups.

> **focus groups**
> Small groups used to explore how ordinary people think about issues and how they react to the language of political appeals.

Various other ways of measuring public opinion exist, but they are much less reliable than survey research. Mail surveys typically have low response rates, and generally we expect those who bother to fill them out and send them in to be a biased sample of the population—people who care more about the subject of the poll. The same is true for call-in surveys conducted by radio and TV stations. These may be good ways of generating listener or viewer interest, but they have little or no scientific value. Letters to the editor and letters or phone calls to elected officials also are unreliable. People who take the time and trouble to call or write are those who care about an issue or question. They are not representative of the much larger population who don't call or write because they don't care.

The latest rage in polling is Internet polls. The problem with Internet polling was highlighted by a mildly embarrassing experience suffered by the Democratic National Committee (DNC) in January 2000. The DNC Web site includes a weekly opinion poll. The poll in question noted that the United States was enjoying a large budget surplus and asked people to vote for one of two ways to use the surplus:

> "saving Social Security, strengthening Medicare, and paying down the debt," or "implementing George W. Bush's $1.7 trillion risky tax scheme that overwhelmingly benefits the wealthy."

Surprisingly, when the results were tabulated, 72.2 percent of the respondents favored tax cuts for the rich—mischievous Republicans monitoring the opposition had arranged for Republicans to vote in the Democrats' poll![21] This amusing episode graphically illustrates the problem with allowing the sample to determine itself. In a scientific poll, the investigator must control who is included in the sample and who is not.

## Mismeasuring Public Opinion

Poll stories routinely report sampling error, but despite the attention it gets, sampling is a relatively unimportant source of error in most professionally done surveys. Various

**measurement error**
The error that arises from attempting to measure something as subjective as opinion.

kinds of **measurement error** are much more troublesome. The reason is that someone's opinion is not an objective fact like the length of a stick. We can all measure the stick, and if we are careful,-our measurements will be quite similar. But opinions are different. They are not physical facts, like sticks; rather, they consist of subjective beliefs and judgments. Such beliefs and judgments, moreover, often are expressed as casual answers to questions the respondent has never really thought about. For that reason, how people answer a poll depends very much on the wording of the questions. Here is a striking example that embarrassed a reputable polling firm.

### The Holocaust Poll Fiasco

In the spring of 1993 the Holocaust Memorial Museum opened in Washington, DC. Coincident with the dedication of the museum, the American Jewish Committee released startling data from a survey conducted a few months earlier by Roper Starch Worldwide, a respected commercial polling organization. The poll indicated that 22 percent of the American public believed it "possible the Nazi extermination of the Jews never happened" and that another 12 percent were unsure. In total, one-third of all Americans apparently had doubts about whether the Nazis murdered 6 million Jews in World War II.

The news media jumped on the story, which fit the preconceptions of editorialists and columnists eager to find shortcomings in their fellow citizens. What was wrong with the American people? Had the educational system failed so miserably that in the short span of 50 years the greatest genocide in history had become a matter of mere opinion, to be believed or not, as one wished? Was anti-Semitism so widespread and deeply ingrained in the population that Holocaust denials by the lunatic fringe were making headway? What did the Holocaust Poll say about the American people?

Very little, it turned out. Social scientists knowledgeable about prejudice and public opinion were immediately suspicious of the poll findings, which seemed far out of line with what other contemporary surveys showed about both anti-Semitism and the historical awareness of the American people. The Gallup organization—a Roper business competitor—soon demonstrated that the Roper poll was gravely mis-

**Embarrassed by a Poll**
The 1993 opening of the Holocaust Memorial Museum was accompanied by a polling embarrassment that underscored the necessity of keeping public opinion poll questions clear and simple. *Why might a person have answered yes to the following: "Does it seem possible, or does it seem impossible to you that the Nazi extermination of the Jews never happened?"*

taken, because Roper had asked a confusing question. The exact wording of Roper's question was

> Does it seem possible, or does it seem impossible to you that the Nazi extermination of the Jews never happened?

One of the first rules of survey research is to keep questions clear and simple. The Roper question fails that test because it contains a double negative (impossible . . . never happened)—a grammatical construction long known to confuse people.

Gallup conducted a new poll in which half of the sample was asked the Roper question with the double negative and the other half was asked an alternative question:

> Does it seem possible to you that the Nazi extermination of the Jews never happened, or do you feel certain that it happened?

The difference in question wording may seem minor, but it made a great deal of difference. In the half of the sample that was asked the Roper question, one-third of the respondents again replied that it was possible the Holocaust never happened or that they were unsure, but in the half that was asked the alternative question, less than 10 percent of the sample were Holocaust doubters. Roper eventually retracted its initial poll results after doing its own follow-up studies. The whole episode had been the product of a simple mistake.[22] Of course, many will find it disturbing that almost 10 percent of the population doubt the occurrence of the Holocaust, but to put that figure in perspective, consider that in a 1995 survey, 10 percent of the American people did not know that President Clinton was a Democrat![23]

## The Importance of Wording

The point of the Holocaust poll example is that no one accused the Roper organization of choosing a bad sample. Roper is a reputable professional organization that probably selected a sample accurate to within ±3 percent of the American population, just as claimed. But they asked a poorly constructed question that resulted in a bad measurement.

What look like minor variations in question wording can produce significant differences in measured opinion. This is especially likely when the variations involve the substitution of emotionally or politically "loaded" terms for more neutral terms. A classic example comes from the policy area of government spending on the poor. Consider the following survey question:

> We are faced with many problems in this country, none of which can be solved easily or inexpensively. I'm going to name some of these problems and for each one I'd like you to tell me whether you think we're spending too much money, too little money, or about the right amount.[24]

When the public was asked about "welfare" in the spring of 1994, the responses showed that a large majority of Americans believed that too much was being spent:

Too little: 13%

About right: 25%

Too much: 62%

Conservatives would take heart from such a poll and use it to argue that welfare spending should be slashed. But when the *same people* in the *same poll* were asked about "assistance to the poor," a similarly large majority responded that too little was being spent:

Too little: 59%

About right: 25%

Too much: 16%

Liberals would take heart from such a poll and use it to argue that public assistance for the poor should be increased.

**Welfare Mother or Poor Mother?**
Americans are willing to help the "deserving" poor but not so willing to help welfare recipients. *Why do many Americans see some of the poor as more deserving than others? How will public officials respond to this attitude of limiting welfare benefits?*

Although *welfare* and *assistance to the poor* may appear to mean the same thing, many Americans evidently disagree. *Welfare* carries negative connotations; it seems to prompt people to think of lazy and undeserving recipients—the stereotypical welfare cheats. But *assistance to the poor* does not seem to be associated with these negative stereotypes. If anything, people seem unconsciously to add the modifier *deserving* to *poor.* Here is clearly a case where the careless (or clever) choice of question wording can produce contradictory findings on a major public issue.

Such examples are common, though reputable survey organizations work constantly to identify and eliminate examples like the preceding one concerning public assistance. Moreover, loaded questions are far from the only problem. Responses to opinion polls also vary with question *format.*[25] People tend to give more consistent answers to questions that allow graduated responses (agree strongly, agree somewhat, neither agree nor disagree, disagree somewhat, disagree strongly) than to either/or questions (agree/disagree). More people will choose a "don't know" or "not sure" answer if it is offered to them than if they have to volunteer it. People respond differently if given supporting arguments than if simply asked to choose between two sides of a question. People respond differently if earlier questions in the survey prompt them to think along certain lines. And people respond differently when surveyed after significant social, economic, or political developments than when surveyed before such events.[26]

SECTION SUMMARY

Scientific polling makes it possible to know a bit about what a country of hundreds of millions thinks on any given issue, simply by sampling a few thousand people. But this system is not without errors or problems. Hard numbers about public opinion that Americans receive often are much softer than they seem—and not just because pollsters resort to unscientific focus groups. Survey research is the only means of measuring opinion that rests on solid statistical grounds. But even there, the design of questions is a difficult and complicated process. Even the best-designed and -administered survey will still have some margin for error.

## Characteristics of Public Opinion

Why should the measurement of public opinion be so sensitive to how it is measured? As we have said, this is because public opinion is not an objective quantity like length or weight that can be measured with a simple physical instrument. On the contrary, the characteristics of public opinion often make it very hard to obtain reliable measurements.

### Public Opinion Often Is Uninformed

Americans are an accommodating people. If a pollster asks us a question, many of us will cooperate by giving an answer, even if we have not thought about the question or have no basis on which to arrive at an answer. A 1989 survey provides an extreme example. People were asked to rate 58 ethnic and nationality groups. Although one group included in the list ("Wisnians") was fictitious, 29 percent of the sample ranked them anyway.[27]

On many issues, people have little or no information. The extent of popular ignorance is most obvious when surveys pose "factual" questions. As shown in Figure 5.5, in 1995 only a third of the voting-age population could name their representative in Congress. Less than half could name either senator from their state. Barely half could name the Speaker of the House (Newt Gingrich, who had been on the cover of *Time* magazine), and only 60 percent could recall the name of the vice-president (Al Gore).

Elections are not SAT tests, of course; it is not necessary to know the answers to all sorts of factual questions in order to vote intelligently. But widespread ignorance extends beyond such factual questions to important matters of government and public policy. During the 1995 federal government shutdown, 40 percent of Americans

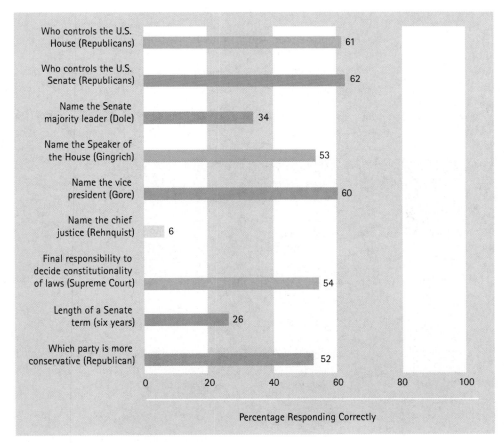

Percentage Responding Correctly

**Figure 5.5**

**Americans Are Not Very Knowledgeable About the Specifics of American Government**
This survey was conducted by Princeton Survey Research Associates in late November 1995 and early December 1995, after the Republicans took control of Congress for the first time in 40 years, and during the federal budget impasse of 1995.

SOURCE: "Why Don't Americans Trust the Government?" (Menlo Park, CA: The Kaiser Foundation, 1996).

## Figure 5.6

Interest in Politics
Is Much Lower Than Interest in
Popular Culture and Entertainment

SOURCES: *The World Almanac and Book of Facts, 2000,* Nielsen Media Research, and the Web sites of the magazines and programs. *Note:* The television ratings for prime time shows are for the period between September 1, 1998, and May 26, 1999. The magazine circulation figures are for the period between July 1, 1998, and December 31, 1998.

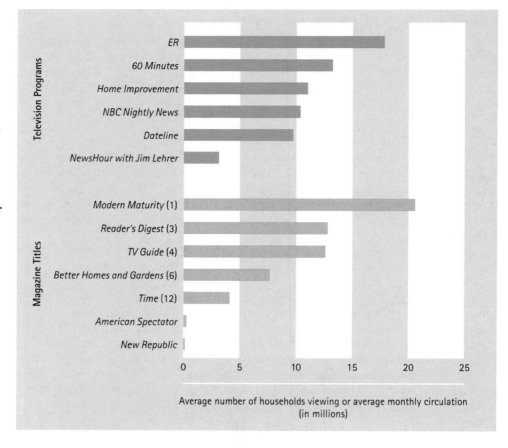

Average number of households viewing or average monthly circulation
(in millions)

were unaware that the Republicans controlled both houses of Congress (and 10 percent did not know that the president was a Democrat). And by more than a 2:1 margin, Americans believed—absolutely wrongly—that the federal government spent more on foreign aid than on Medicare. In fact, the United States spends four times as much on Medicare as on foreign aid, and the ratio is growing.[28]

Why do people have so little knowledge of basic facts and issues? The answer is that most people, most of the time, pay little attention to politics. Newsmagazines sell

**Entertainment Trumps Hard News**
The game show *Who Wants to Be a Millionaire* became one of the most popular television shows in 2000. Far more people watch each episode than ever watch the evening newscasts.

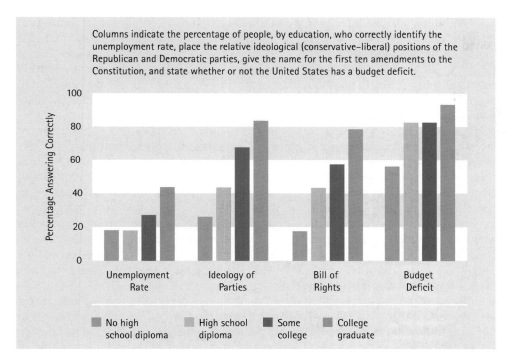

Columns indicate the percentage of people, by education, who correctly identify the unemployment rate, place the relative ideological (conservative–liberal) positions of the Republican and Democratic parties, give the name for the first ten amendments to the Constitution, and state whether or not the United States has a budget deficit.

**Figure 5.7**

**Higher Education Is Strongly Associated with Greater Knowledge of Politics and Government**

SOURCE: Data are taken from Michael Delli Carini and Scott Keeter, *What Americans Know About Politics and Why It Matters*, p. 189.

far fewer copies than entertainment and lifestyle magazines. Far more Americans watch sitcoms like "*Ally McBeal*" than watch Jim Lehrer's *NewsHour*. Figure 5.6 presents various contrasts in the entertainment habits of the American public.

Upon learning the full extent of popular ignorance, some politically involved students react critically, jumping to the conclusion that ordinary Americans are apathetic and irresponsible people who fall far short of the democratic ideal. Such reactions are understandable, but we think they are unjustified because they overlook the reasons why people pay so little attention to public affairs.

The simple fact is that most people have little time for politics; it is something of a luxury interest. They work long and hard to take care of the "necessities"—paying the bills, caring for families, and developing or nurturing personal relationships. Despite the importance of national and international politics, after dropping off and picking up children, commuting, working, and housekeeping, many Americans do not have the time and energy for the *New York Times* and *Nightline*. The effort required to stay informed competes with recreation and relaxation, for which many citizens have precious little time.

Those who criticize ordinary citizens for their lack of attention to public affairs often have jobs that enable them to stay informed with little effort. For example, in a university environment, political conversation is a common diversion, and for many professors and students it is relevant to academic pursuits. In such a context, professors and students find it easy to stay informed. Likewise, the jobs of many journalists involve following politics: If they are not informed, they are not doing their job. If everyone worked in a university or for the news media, no doubt we would all be much better informed. But most people do not, a fact that critics in academia and the media tend to forget.

The general point is that gathering, processing, and storing information is neither effortless nor free; it is costly. For most Americans, bearing such **information costs** brings them little in the way of corresponding benefits.[29] Few citizens feel that the resolution of conflicts in Kosovo, Rwanda, or the next crisis spot will be affected in any way by their state of knowledge. And when faced with a costly activity that has no obvious benefit, many of them quite rationally decide to minimize their costs. Thus, from a logical standpoint, the puzzle is not why so many Americans are ill informed; the puzzle is why so many are as well informed as they are.[30]

**information cost**
The time and mental effort required to absorb and store information, whether from conversations, personal experiences, or the media.

**Knowledge and Self-Interest**
People who provide or receive a service such as family day care represent an "issue public" that tends to know more about policies affecting that service. *What are some important issue publics in your community? Do you belong to an issue public?*

**issue public**
Group of people particularly affected by or concerned with a specific issue.

**ideology**
System of beliefs in which one or more organizing principles connect the individual's views on a wide range of issues.

**political elite**
Activists and office holders who are deeply interested in and knowledgeable about politics.

Of course, information costs do not fall equally heavily on all people. Education makes it easier to absorb and organize information; thus it comes as no surprise that more-educated Americans are better informed than less-educated ones (see Figure 5.7). And, as already noted, being engaged in certain occupations makes it relatively easy to stay informed. In addition, the benefits of information are not the same for all people on all issues. Most people will be better informed on issues that directly affect their lives or livelihoods. Parents and teachers are more knowledgeable than other citizens about school operations and budgets. Human services providers are more knowledgeable about welfare and other public assistance policies and budgets. Steel workers know about and have strong views on foreign imports, as do farmers about cotton and wheat subsidies. Such **issue publics** are different from the large mass of citizens in that their members' occupations or roles make information cheaper to obtain as well as more interesting and valuable.[31]

In addition to varying across people and issues, the costs and benefits of being well informed may vary over time as well. When a tax revolt erupts or a debate over condom distribution in the schools flares up, information levels surge as people get caught up in the controversy. But after the burning issues are resolved and the controversy subsides, information levels also return to normal.[32]

Of course, some people will bear information costs even when they get little direct benefit from doing so. They may consider it their duty as citizens to be informed, so they stay attuned to public affairs simply because they believe it is the "right thing" to do. Other people follow public affairs because they find it intrinsically interesting in the same way that some follow sports or the arts. For such people, following public affairs is a recreational activity; what others view as information costs they view as benefits. Probably most citizens know as much as they do because of considerations like these rather than because they derive any tangible benefit from being informed.[33]

Finally, we note that Americans are not unique in paying little attention to public affairs. Citizens in other countries are similarly inattentive and similarly lacking in knowledge. A 1998 British Gallup Poll, for example, found that only 40 percent of Britons today know that the United States once was part of the British empire![34] One interesting difference is that citizens in other democracies are more knowledgeable about foreign affairs than are Americans. This is presumably a reflection of the fact that geographic isolation and economic strength have made foreign affairs relatively less important in the United States.[35]

### Public Opinion Is Not Ideological

Another characteristic of public opinion that makes it easy to misinterpret is that even when people have reasonably firm views on issues, those views often are surprisingly unconnected to each other. It is common to note that the American people are not very ideological.

An **ideology** is a system of beliefs in which one or more general organizing principles connect your views on a wide range of particular issues. For example, if you are told that Smith is a liberal Democratic congressman, you will infer a great deal about Smith: that he is pro-choice on abortion, favors gun control, and supports a strong government role in health care. Conversely, if you are told that Jones is a conservative Republican congresswoman, you will infer opposite things about her—that she is pro-life, opposes gun control, and thinks that health care should be left to the private sector as much as possible. Of course, your inferences will not always be correct, but more often than not they will. The reason is that people who are deeply interested in and involved in politics, whether as activists or as office holders (traditionally called **political elites**), tend to have well-structured ideologies that bind together their positions on different policy issues. To know that such a person is a "liberal" or a "conservative" is to know a good bit about him or her.

Ordinary citizens are another matter. Professor Philip Converse showed long ago that ordinary citizens who are not deeply interested in or involved in politics (tradi-

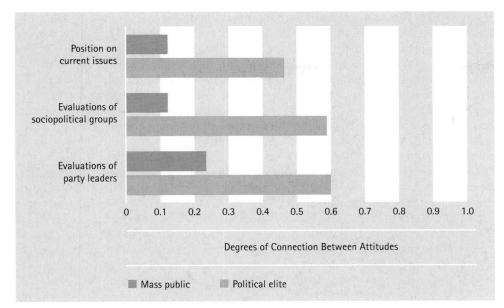

**Figure 5.8**

**Ordinary People Are Much Less Ideological Than Political Elites**

SOURCE: Data are taken from M. Kent Jennings, "Ideological Thinking Among Mass Publics and Political Elites," *Public Opinion Quarterly* (1992): 419–441.

tionally called the **mass public**) are nonideological.[36] Ordinary citizens' views on specific issues do not cluster together like those of elites. Rather than believe consistently in either activist or minimal government, citizens favor federal spending in some areas but oppose it in others. They favor regulation in some areas but oppose it in others. They favor toleration for some groups in some situations, but not for other groups in other situations. Figure 5.8 compares the consistency of the thinking of the mass public and of political elites.

Most survey questions are **closed-ended**; they ask people to choose from a set of prespecified alternatives. Sometimes, however, analysts ask **open-ended** questions that allow people to answer in their own words. When responses to such open-ended survey questions were analyzed in depth, Converse and his assistants found that by a strict scoring, only 3 percent of the 1950s electorate thought ideologically—the number could be expanded to a maximum of 16 percent by relaxing the criteria. The most common frame of reference was group allegiances: What kinds of people were the parties and their candidates sympathetic to? The second most common frame of reference was "the nature of the times": How had the parties and their candidates performed recently when given the chance to govern? Even when generously classified, ideologues were no more numerous than citizens who could articulate virtually nothing of political relevance. In the 1960s there was some increase in ideological thinking, as educational levels rose and the parties became more polarized, but the thought patterns of ordinary Americans remain far less ideologically coherent than elites often presume.[37]

Of course, it is possible that people may find ideological labels useful even if their personal views are not ideologically consistent or they do not show evidence of an ideological frame of reference when responding to survey questions. But even when the standard for ideological thinking is much weaker, the evidence for widespread ideology is absent. For example, *when given the option*, one-quarter to one-third of the population will not even classify themselves on a liberal–conservative scale, and another one-quarter put themselves exactly in the middle: "moderate, middle of the road."[38] Given these figures, perhaps it is no surprise that in 1995, only 52 percent of Americans considered the Republicans the more conservative of the two parties, while 17 percent thought the Democrats were, and 30 percent didn't know![39]

Once again, there is a common tendency to interpret the nonideological thinking of ordinary Americans in a negative light, and here again, we disagree with such judgments. Maybe it is political elites who should be viewed critically. Because they are ideological, they take that to be the norm and view nonideological thinking as the

**mass public**
Ordinary people for whom politics is a peripheral concern.

**closed-ended question**
Survey question that asks people to choose their answer from a set of prespecified alternatives.

**open-ended question**
Survey question that allows people to answer in their own words.

exception that requires explanation. In our view, ideologies are as much *social* as logical constructions. Personal views aside, can anyone explain the logical connection among supporting low capital gains tax rates, being pro-life, opposing gun control, and favoring high defense spending? Positions on such issues may go together for liberal and conservative elites, but *why* do they?

That ideologies are matters of social construction and convention is shown by the way they change over time.[40] From the 1930s through the 1950s, *liberal* implied a belief in government intervention in the economy in order to control powerful corporations, to provide a safety net for ordinary citizens, and to supply collective goods (such as electricity to rural areas) that could not be profitably supplied by the private sector. In the 1960s the terms of political debate shifted. Although present earlier, racial attitudes and opinions about civil rights became much more important components of liberalism than previously. By the time *liberal* became a dirty word in the campaigns of the 1980s and 1990s, the term had become synonymous with support for a hodgepodge of social issues that included tolerance of personal irresponsibility and contempt for traditional values. The economic content of liberalism had declined in importance, and as for government intervention, sometimes it was liberal (affirmative action), while at other times it was "conservative" (restricting abortion).

**visual literacy**

**Who Are Liberals and Conservatives? What's the Difference?**

The American people have a strong pragmatic strain that has often been noted by international observers accustomed to a more ideological style of political discourse. Perhaps the nonideological views of most Americans should be taken as evidence for common-sense pragmatic thinking, while the ideological views of elites should be viewed as evidence that they are neurotic. Whether you regard ideological thinking as good or bad, however, you should bear one point in mind. Because they presume that ideological thinking is the norm, party and issue activists, media commentators, and many public officials will conclude too much on the basis of opinion polls and voting returns. Support for one variety of government action may indicate nothing about support for another seemingly similar government action. Support for a candidate's position on one issue may suggest little or nothing about that candidate's "mandate" to act on seemingly related issues. The nonideological nature of public opinion means that elites often hear more than the voters are saying.

The most recent example of this common elite mistake was the federal government shutdown in the winter of 1995–1996. Although the new Republican majority in the House had paid considerable attention to public opinion a year earlier, once in office they greatly overestimated the degree of popular support for their program, inferring that their 1994 election victory was a blanket endorsement of balancing the budget, cutting entitlements, and cutting taxes—the things the new majority believed in (see the accompanying Election Connection). When President Clinton refused to accept the Republican plan and gridlock ensued, public opinion blamed the Republicans more than it did the president.[41]

## Public Opinion Often Is Inconsistent

Given that people often have not thought about issues, and given that most of them do not think ideologically, it should come as no surprise that public opinion often seems inconsistent. For example, in 1980, when Ronald Reagan defeated Jimmy Carter and the Republicans made striking gains in Congress, many in the media interpreted the election results as a "resurgence of conservatism" or a "turn to the right" in American politics. Republican elites were more than happy to accept such interpretations, and Democratic elites feared that such interpretations were correct. The evidence, however, was confusing.[42]

A poll taken in 1978 reported that an overwhelming 84 percent of the citizenry felt that the federal government was spending too much money. A smaller majority thought that the federal government had gone too far in regulating business. Popular sentiments like these appeared to be foretelling the Reagan victory in the next election.

## Election Connection

# Public Opinion and the 1994 Republican Contract with America

The 1994 congressional elections have been described as an "electoral meteorite that slammed into the American political landscape."[a] Although many observers thought that the Republicans had a chance to win the Senate, few gave them a serious chance to capture the House. When the dust thrown up by the "electoral meteorite" cleared, however, the Republicans had captured both chambers for the first time in 40 years, and the pundits were speculating that a new electoral era had dawned.

The architect of the Republican victory was soon-to-be Speaker of the House Newt Gingrich, and his

Newt Gingrich, backed by dozens of GOP candidates, announces the Contract with America, calling for tax cuts, term limits, and a balanced budget among other things.

vehicle was the "Contract with America." In late September, Gingrich had more than 350 Republican candidates attend a Washington rally where they signed a contract promising voters that within 100 days of taking control of Congress, the new House majority would adopt a package of congressional reforms and vote on ten planks dealing with the following issues: balanced budget, crime, welfare, families, a middle-class tax cut, national security, senior citizens' benefits, capital gains taxes, legal reforms, and congressional term limits.[b] Democrats as well as many nonpartisan commentators scoffed at this Republican media event. Not only did they think that many of the Republican proposals were electoral losers, but conventional wisdom holds that the out-party should simply attack the in-party, not promise anything specific.

Gingrich and the Republicans stood firm. Criticism of the Contract did not make them back away from it; indeed, they reemphasized it, even publishing it in *TV Guide*, a popular magazine with a huge circulation. The Republicans were confident in their strategy for a simple reason: The contract had been carefully put together with the aid of modern public opinion research methods. On average, the proposals in the contract were supported by comfortable majorities in national surveys, and the language that was used—the "frames"— had been carefully tested in focus groups (small groups of citizens brought together to talk about the proposals).[c] The Republicans believed that the more widely publicized the Contract, the better for them it would be. Of course, the Contract was not the only factor in the election, but the

Republicans' beliefs proved to be more accurate than the Democrats'. In mocking the contract, Democrats were swimming against the current of public opinion. In many cases they were swept away.

If imitation is the sincerest form of flattery, then the 1996 Democrats flattered the 1994 Republicans. In the summer of 1996, Minority Leader Richard Gephardt unveiled a new "Families First" agenda for the Democrats. It provided for tax breaks for child care and health costs and promised to get tough on crime and balance the budget. This time, the Republicans did the mocking, dismissing "Families First" as "nothing more than a product designed by their pollsters and their elite leadership in Washington."[d]

Some critics argue that the use of public opinion research methods to craft campaign appeals is troubling. Others argue that candidates have always tried to advocate what voters want and that modern methods simply give them a more accurate way to do so.

*What do you think?*
- *Do polls give good, needed information to elected officials, or do they allow politicians to avoid the hard work of considering public policy?*
- *Is the use of public opinion research methods to craft campaign appeals a negative development or a positive development? Why?*
- *How could this development be reversed?*

---

[a] Robert W. Merry, "Voters' Demand for Change Puts Clinton on the Defensive," *Congressional Quarterly Weekly Report*, November 12, 1994: 3207.
[b] Clyde Wilcox, *The Latest American Revolution* (New York: St. Martin's Press, 1995), pp. 48–56, Appendix A.
[c] On public support for the Contract proposals, see "The Direction Specified in Most of the 'Contract's' Planks Finds High Public Backing," *Public Perspective*, February/March 1995: 29.
[d] John Yang, "'Contract with America,' Meet 'Families First,'" *The Washington Post National Weekly Edition*, July 1–7, 1996: 13.

---

But then again, the same poll asked the *same people* which domestic programs they favored cutting and which areas of business activity they favored deregulating. Surprisingly, pluralities, often majorities, felt that most domestic activities deserved *higher* funding or *more* regulation.

Findings like these are common. After the Republican congressional victories in 1994, polls reported that large majorities wanted to balance the budget but not to cut specific programs, especially the large entitlement programs that underlay the budget deficits.[43] Such contradictory views recall the old maxim that "everybody wants to go to heaven but nobody wants to die." Everyone wants less government spending, but not in any particular policy area except welfare and foreign aid.

Obviously, such contradictory views confuse political debate. After his election, President Reagan claimed—with some justification—that he had been elected to cut government spending and deregulate the economy. Democratic leaders in Congress claimed—with some justification—that their party had been returned to power so that they could protect existing spending and regulatory programs. Both claims were plausible given the public opinion data. In 1994 Republican congressional leaders believed they had a mandate to balance the budget. But when they attempted to slow the growth of Medicare spending, they discovered that the mandate did not extend that far. In recent decades, the American people have never delivered a clear mandate either for the Republicans to cut and retrench or for the Democrats to tax and expand.[44] One consequence was the gridlock and deficits of the 1980s and 1990s. Although gridlock and deficits often were laid at the feet of divided government— Republican presidents and Democratic Congresses—divided government is as much a symptom of the conflicting views of the American citizenry as a cause of deadlock and deficits.[45]

Why is public opinion so inconsistent? There are many reasons. In the preceding example, most analysts think that the inconsistency arises from two sources. First, people have very inaccurate views of how much is being spent on programs such as "welfare" and foreign aid. Thus they believe, erroneously, that cutting such unpopular programs will free up sufficient funds to maintain or increase funding for more popular programs. Second, some voters believe that waste and inefficiency are so pervasive that spending could be increased in some policy areas if only government were more efficient. Anyone who looks closely at the budget figures realizes that such beliefs are mistaken. We hasten to add, however, that such mistaken impressions are partly the fault of elected officials, who, rather than trying to educate citizens, reinforce popular misconceptions for short-term electoral gain.

Not all examples of inconsistency reflect insufficient and inaccurate information, however. Citizens are so consistently inconsistent in their judgments about general principles versus specific applications of those principles that other explanations must be at work. We have seen that people favor cutting spending in general but not specific programs. They also oppose amending the Constitution but favor balanced-budget, term limitation, and flag-burning amendments. And perhaps most interesting of all, they support fundamental rights but regularly make numerous exceptions.[46] As Figure 5.9 shows, citizens favor free speech—but not for everyone, and not all the time. They favor freedom of the press and freedom of assembly—with "reasonable" exceptions. And they believe in the separation of church and state—but favor prayer in schools.

It is easy to label such inconsistencies hypocrisy, and some do. Or such inconsistencies may indicate that ordinary people do not have a clear understanding of rights, and perhaps they do not. But there are other, more positive interpretations as well. To the law professor, the newspaper editor, or the committed political activist, rights may be viewed as absolutes. As a matter of simple logic, to restrict them at all is to destroy them. But despite their commitment to individual rights, few Americans accept such an unconditional perspective. Americans tend to be pragmatists. The constrained thinking of ideology and the absolutist language of rights are foreign to the pragmatic, problem-solving American way of thinking. To the American people, rights are good things, but at times they conflict and must be balanced against other rights and other values.[47] Most citizens are prepared to make such trade-offs on a case-by-case basis.[48] Yes, free speech is a good thing, but should Nazis wearing swastikas be allowed to march down the streets of a neighborhood of Holocaust survivors? Many Americans believe free speech doesn't go that far. Yes, the accused have rights against unreasonable searches, but should the courts release murderers on the basis of legal technicalities? Many Americans believe that legal arguments often lose sight of the purpose of the legal system—justice. To adults familiar with life's conflicts and trade-offs, the legalistic language of rights belongs in the realm of theoretical argument, not the realm of real-world politics. They may feel no contradiction in advocating a right while simultaneously endorsing significant exceptions.[49]

**Just What Is Permitted?**
Americans are supportive of free speech in general, but many are willing to restrict hate groups. *If rights are considered as part of a trade-off, rather than as an absolute right, what will the consequences be for the substance of those rights? What sort of limits on extreme groups are permissible? For instance, is it fair to allow them to march, but not in a town filled with Holocaust survivors?*

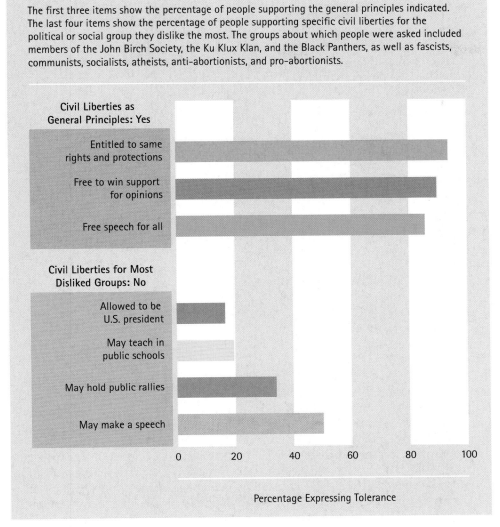

The first three items show the percentage of people supporting the general principles indicated. The last four items show the percentage of people supporting specific civil liberties for the political or social group they dislike the most. The groups about which people were asked included members of the John Birch Society, the Ku Klux Klan, and the Black Panthers, as well as fascists, communists, socialists, atheists, anti-abortionists, and pro-abortionists.

**Civil Liberties as General Principles: Yes**

Entitled to same rights and protections

Free to win support for opinions

Free speech for all

**Civil Liberties for Most Disliked Groups: No**

Allowed to be U.S. president

May teach in public schools

May hold public rallies

May make a speech

0    20    40    60    80    100

Percentage Expressing Tolerance

**Figure 5.9**

**Americans Tend to Endorse General Principles But Make Numerous Exceptions to Them**

SOURCE: Data are taken from John Sullivan, James Piereson, and George Marcus, *Political Tolerance and American Democracy* (Chicago: University of Chicago Press, 1982).

## The Perils of Polling: Public Opinion on Abortion

The abortion issue provides striking illustrations of a number of the features of public opinion discussed in the preceding pages, especially the seeming inconsistency of public opinion and its nonideological nature. In 1973 the Supreme Court handed down its *Roe* v. *Wade* decision, striking down any restrictions on a woman's right to terminate a pregnancy in the first trimester and limiting restrictions on that right in the second trimester. The issue has never left the national agenda since then, and there is reason to believe that most Americans long ago decided where they stood on the issue. When the *same* survey question is repeated over time, public opinion is strikingly constant. For example, a National Opinion Research Center (NORC) item reads as follows:

> Please tell me whether or not you think it should be possible for a pregnant woman to obtain a legal abortion if
> 1. the woman's health is seriously endangered?
> 2. she became pregnant as a result of rape?
> 3. there is a strong chance of serious defect in the baby?
> 4. the family has low income and cannot afford any more children?
> 5. she is not married and does not want to marry the man?
> 6. she is married and does not want any more children?

**Figure 5.10**

**Popular Attitudes Toward Abortion Have Been Remarkably Stable Since <u>Roe</u> v. <u>Wade</u> (1973)**

SOURCE: Calculated by the authors from the General Social Survey 1972–1998 Cumulative Data File. Note: Respondents who answered "don't know" are included in the calculation.

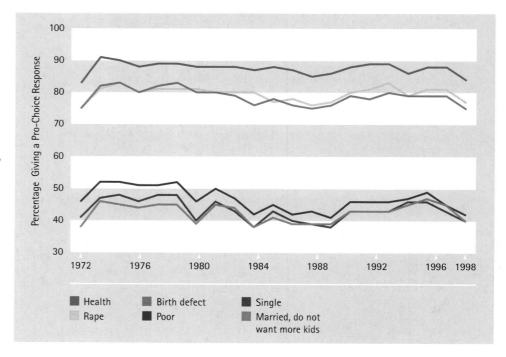

As Figure 5.10 shows, after moving in a liberal direction in the late 1960s, opinion stabilized at the time of the Roe decision, stayed remarkably constant for two decades, and then moved a bit in a conservative direction in the late 1990s. On average, Americans favor legal abortion in four of six circumstances, with large majorities supporting abortion in the first three ("traumatic") circumstances, but pluralities opposing abortion in the second three ("elective") circumstances.[50] Opinion changed little after the 1989 *Webster* decision, which opened the way for some state regulation of abortion, or after the 1992 *Casey* decision, which upheld some of the specific restrictions imposed by Pennsylvania. Thus the complicated picture that follows is not the result of uninformed, unconcerned citizens giving haphazard responses to polls. The complications run deeper.

Both pro-choice and pro-life spokespersons typically proclaim that a majority of Americans support their position. Unless the laws of arithmetic fail to hold in the case of this issue, one side or both must be wrong. But neither side makes up its figures.

First, consider the effects of question wording shown in two surveys that bracketed the 1989 *Webster* decision.[51] A *Los Angeles Times* poll asked

> Do you think a pregnant woman should or should not be able to get a legal abortion, no matter what the reason?

By close to a 2:1 margin (57 percent to 34 percent), Americans said no. As pro-life spokespersons claimed, Americans were pro-life. Should Democratic campaign consultants have advised their clients to flip-flop to the pro-life side? Well, probably not. A few months later, a CBS News/*New York Times* survey asked

> If a woman wants to have an abortion, and her doctor agrees to it, should she be allowed to have an abortion or not?

By more than a 2:1 margin (58 percent to 26 percent), Americans said yes. As the pro-choice spokespersons claimed, America had a pro-choice majority. Should Republican campaign consultants have advised their clients to flip-flop to the pro-choice side?

Which poll was right? Probably neither. Upon close examination, both survey questions are suspect. Each contains words and phrases that predispose people to answer in one direction. The first question uses the phrase "no matter what the rea-

**No Shades of Gray Here**
Demonstrators protest abortions. While pictures like this are common in the media, Americans generally hold a nuanced view of abortion rights. *Is it inconsistent to believe that a woman has a right to choose, but only under a limited set of circumstances.*

son." As shown by the NORC data in Figure 5.10, most Americans are not *unconditionally* pro-choice. If forced to choose yes or no, some generally pro-choice people will say no, believing that some circumstances are just not sufficiently serious to justify abortion. The CBS/NYT question leans in the opposite direction. A doctor's approval suggests a reasoned decision based on medically justifiable grounds. Some generally pro-life people might agree to abortion in such a case. Thus, even on an issue where many people have stable, considered opinions, variations in question wording can make a big difference in the answers they give.

A more general question of wording effect is called framing. We discuss this concept at length in Chapter 9, but briefly, **framing** means that the survey poses the question in a way that encourages the respondent to answer it from one point of view rather than another. For example, a CBS/NYT poll asked the following question:

> Even in cases where I might think abortion is the wrong thing to do, I don't think the government has any business preventing a woman from having an abortion.[52]

By close to a 3:1 margin (69 percent to 24 percent), Americans agreed with that sentiment. Apparently, the country stands firmly in support of abortion rights. On the other hand, when another CBS News/*New York Times* poll asked people whether they agreed or disagreed with the stark claim that "abortion is the same thing as murdering a child," Americans were deeply split (46 percent agreed, 41 percent disagreed). Similarly, a plurality or majority of Americans regularly agrees that "abortion is morally wrong" (51 percent agreed, 34 percent disagreed in the aforementioned CBS News/*New York Times* poll).[53]

The first question uses a "choice" frame. Individualistic Americans favor freedom of choice, especially when it involves freedom from governmental interference. The second and third questions use an "act" frame. Many Americans who favor choice nevertheless are troubled by the act of abortion. It is no surprise that the pro-choice side of the debate consistently employs one frame, the pro-life side employs the other. Nor is it any surprise that an accomplished politician like President Clinton, recognizing the conflict felt by many Americans, announced that he was pro-choice and against abortion.

Consistently inconsistent, Americans are pragmatic, not ideological when it comes to abortion. They favor the right to choose, but not an unconditional right to choose in every conceivable circumstance. Surveys show that rape, birth defects, and threats

**framing**
Stating an argument in such a way as to emphasize one set of considerations and deemphasize others.

**Figure 5.11**

**Americans Tend to Favor Abortion Rights, But with Restrictions**

SOURCE: Gallup, July 6–7, 1989.

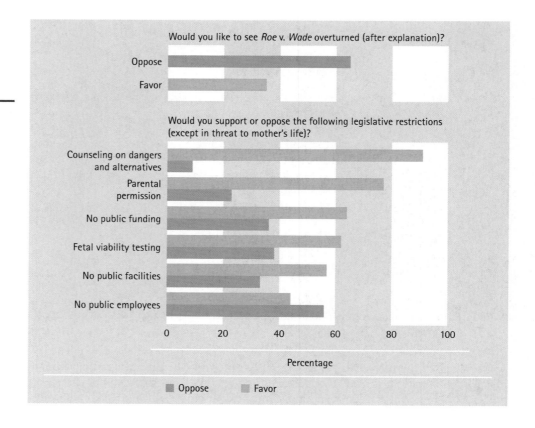

to the mother's health and life are overwhelmingly viewed as justifiable circumstances, but personal convenience and gender selection are not. The mother's age, financial condition, and marital status divide the population deeply. For this reason Americans oppose overturning *Roe*, but as Figure 5.11 shows, they approve of state laws that make abortion more difficult, and they oppose public funding. About 60 percent of the public approved of the Supreme Court's *Casey* decision, and Democrats were just as likely to approve as Republicans. Political folklore claims that the Supreme Court follows the election returns, but in the recent abortion decisions, it might well be said that the Supreme Court followed the opinion polls.

As in Figure 5.10, numerous polls have registered a slight downturn in support for legal abortion in the late 1990s. To those familiar with public opinion on abortion, this drop came as no surprise. In recent years some pro-life groups have focused their attention on an abortion procedure called "intact dilation and extraction" or "partial birth abortion," in which the fetus is destroyed after it has been partially delivered. Pictures and verbal descriptions offered by pro-life groups are quite gruesome, and majorities of Americans have consistently registered opposition to this particular procedure. Thus the debate probably sensitized some generally pro-choice Americans to the fact that they have conflicting views on the issue, leading to a slight drop in unqualified support.

In sum, public opinion on abortion is unlikely to please militants on either side of the issue, because they think in terms of unconditional rights. Pro-choice activists who play an important role in the Democratic party argue that any infringement on a woman's right to choose is unacceptable, even if that means the occasional abortion of a healthy, viable fetus. Pro-life activists who play an important role in the Republican party argue that any abortion is unacceptable, even if that means the occasional death of a woman. The great majority of the American people reject both extreme positions. Ordinary Americans are pragmatic and nonideological. They make tough decisions on a case-by-case basis, an endeavor that often leads to public opinion that looks inconsistent when viewed from a more ideological standpoint.

## SECTION SUMMARY

Inconsistency on abortion is the best example of the pragmatic, non-ideological public. Measuring the public's beliefs is a difficult science because an objective measure simply is not available. The costs of obtaining information are relatively high for some segments of the population. For good or ill, they will never seek out political knowledge. When the public becomes aware of an issue they treat it seriously, but in a way that does not conform to the elite ideologies. We believe this is not a weakness, though it is often described as such. Evidence that the public is "inconsistent" should always be carefully evaluated, because a closer look at the data may reveal what we normally see: a public more concerned with solving problems than adhering to a liberal or conservative position.

## *Governing by Public Opinion?*

Never before have American politicians had so much data about public opinion. Critics regularly complain that politics and government today are "poll-driven." As we have seen, however, given the characteristics of public opinion, trying to measure and interpret it is far from an exact science. Indeed, at times it is more like reading tea leaves! But even when public opinion is fairly clear, there is no guarantee that it will be reflected in public policy. The reason is that although individual politicians may be highly responsive to public opinion, the system as a whole may not be. Recent tragic events provide an illustration.

### *A Disconnect Between Public Opinion and Public Policy: Gun Control*

On April 20, 1999, two deranged students at Columbine High School in Colorado killed 12 of their fellow students and a teacher and wounded more than 20 other students. The killers used two shotguns, a semi-automatic pistol, and a semi-automatic

**Tragic Focus**
The Columbine shooting riveted media attention for months, spurring attempts at stricter gun control legislation in the U.S. Congress. *How much pressure does a tragedy like this put on elected officials? Does the public change its mind, forcing legislation, based on events like this one?*

rifle in their murderous spree. This was the fourth school shooting in little more than a year. Other crazed young males had shot teachers or students in West Paducah, Kentucky, in Jonesboro, Arkansas, and in Springfield, Oregon. Whether because of the cumulative impact or the sheer scale of the rampage, the Columbine shootings energized elected officials into action. In Congress, a juvenile crime bill had been going nowhere fast. The bill dealt mostly with the prosecution of young offenders for federal crimes and with federal grants to states to fight youth crime, but anti-gun members of Congress decided to use this bill as a vehicle for passing new gun control measures.

In the Senate a proposal to require nonlicensed dealers at gun shows to conduct background checks on potential customers narrowly failed, but some Republicans had second thoughts, and after still another school shooting (in Conyers, Georgia), the Senate reversed its earlier decision. In a highly publicized climax to the debate, Vice-President Al Gore cast the tie-breaking vote (under the Constitution the vice-president votes when the Senate is tied), and the Senate adopted an amendment tightening restrictions on sales at gun shows. By much wider margins the Senate adopted other provisions mandating trigger locks or lock boxes with every handgun sale, outlawing imports of high-capacity ammunition clips, and raising the age at which juveniles could buy handguns and assault weapons. The amended bill passed the Senate by a comfortable margin and then went to the House of Representatives.

House Republican leaders felt that the aroused state of public opinion required some response. Speaker Denny Hastert (R-IL) commented that "This is one of those rare times when the national consensus demands that we act" and promised that the House would pass a gun control measure.[54] But the issue was now thoroughly entangled in partisan politics. Vice-President Gore obviously believed that his highly visible gun control stance would aid his presidential bid, and congressional Democrats hoped to use the issue to help regain control of the Congress in 2000. The key target group was suburban voters—especially women, whom polls showed to be more pro–gun control than men.[55] To appeal to them, Democrats framed the issue as one of protecting children by restricting access to guns.

The Democrats were not united, however. A senior Democrat, John Dingell of Michigan, was an avid hunter and a former National Rifle Association board member. Dingell worked with Republican leaders to develop an amendment to weaken the Senate's gun show restrictions. Forty-five Democrats followed Dingell and joined Republicans to pass the weaker provision. However, angry liberal Democrats who believed the legislation did not go far enough then joined with angry conservative Republicans who felt it still went too far and rejected the bill! The House adjourned without taking up gun control again.

At first glance this story seems to be one of irresponsible or even corrupt behavior by the Congress. Certainly, that is the way the media portrayed it. The story line offered by the media was simple: Public opinion counted less than the campaign contributions and arm twisting of the NRA. But this account is too simple-minded—even for the media, who characteristically oversimplify politics (Chapter 9). Members of Congress do not get reelected by opposing an aroused majority of their constituents in exchange for an interest-group endorsement or a $5000 PAC contribution. Rather, the failure of the House to pass gun control measures shows the imperfect connection between aggregate public opinion and national public policy.

Consider public opinion. As Figure 5.12 shows, a clear majority of Americans favors tighter controls on guns in general, and even larger majorities favor the specific provisions—background checks, trigger locks, restrictions on magazine size—that were part of the rejected bill. Different polls showed a high degree of agreement on these questions. How then, could representatives of the people fail to pass gun control? The answer has two parts, one institutional, the second behavioral.

The institutional part reflects the often overlooked fact that only the president has the entire country as a constituency. Members of Congress represent congressional dis-

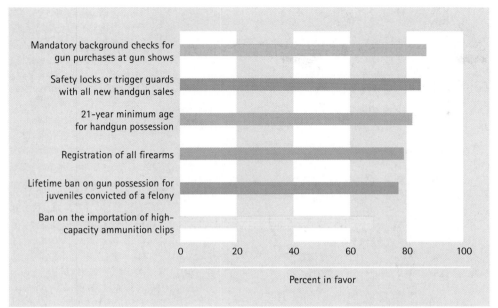

Figure 5.12

Most Americans Support
Gun Control Proposals

SOURCE: "Bear Arms—But More Regulation,"
*Public Perspective*, June/July 1999: 34.

tricts of 630,000 or so people, which may be very different from the country as a whole. The national distribution of opinion is of little importance to members of Congress; the distribution of opinion in their districts is what counts. And what counts even more is the distribution of opinion among the voters who elected them. Because polls show that more than 80 percent of self-identified Democrats favor gun control while only about half of self-identified Republicans do, we should naturally expect Republican members of Congress to be much less supportive of gun control, even if there were no NRA.[56] Furthermore, opinion differs by urban versus rural residence, with urban residents much more supportive of gun control than rural residents. In an outcome consistent with these facts, as Figure 5.13 shows, 81 percent of the representatives from rural districts voted for the Dingell amendment, and 87 percent of representatives from urban districts voted against it, with suburban and mixed districts in between. In sum, given that Democratic representatives tend to come from urbanized districts with lots of Democratic voters, and Republicans from less urbanized districts

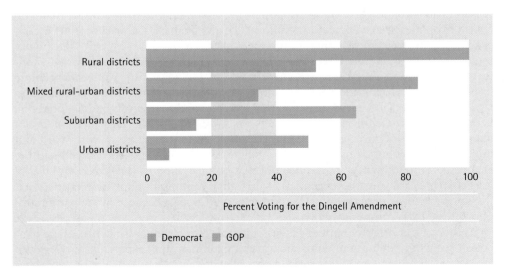

Figure 5.13

Rural Members Are Far More Opposed
to Gun Control Than Urban Members

SOURCE: Don Carney, "Beyond Guns and
Violence: A Battle of House Control," CQ
Weekly, June 19, 1999; and Roll Call Votes,
pp. 1496–1497.

**A Way of Life**
In some rural areas guns are simply a part of the way of life. *Why might rural Americans consider gun control legislation as an assault upon their values and lifestyles?*

with lots of Republican voters, House Democrats who followed *their* constituents' wishes *should* have been much more supportive of gun control than House Republicans who followed *their* constituents' wishes. The minority of Democrats who followed Dingell's lead came mainly from rural and mixed districts. Although no detailed study is available, we think it likely that a large majority of representatives who voted against gun control voted in accordance with the sentiments of majorities *in their districts*.

Still, given the high level of support for the gun control provisions, it is likely that some representatives did vote against district majorities. Was this the NRA at work? To some extent, probably yes, but remember that interest-group endorsements and campaign contributions don't vote. There have to be voters in the district who will act on the group's support. That is the second part of the explanation for the failure of gun control. Behaviorally, gun control supporters are less intense in their attitude than gun control opponents. As Democratic Minority Leader Richard Gephardt (D-MO) conceded, "The 80 percent that are for gun safety just aren't for it very much. They're not intense."[57] Indeed, although most polls registered a high level of support for gun control, the same polls indicated that the public did not regard it as one of the more important issues facing the country. Gun control ranked relatively low compared to issues such as social security, health care, Medicare, and education; one national poll had gun control twelfth in importance as a voting issue in the next election.[58] Not many supporters of gun control are intense, single-issue voters (if they vote at all), but the opponents of gun control are classic single-issue voters. Indeed, Dingell and the Democrats who followed him pointed out that popular support for gun control was at least as high earlier in the decade as it was after Columbine, but despite that fact, Democrats lost their congressional majority in 1994 in part because of the party's support for the ban on assault weapons.

Why are gun control supporters less intense than opponents? Part of the explanation seems to be cultural. Guns are a part of rural culture, especially in the South and West.[59] For rural voters guns are a part of everyday life, and urban problems are

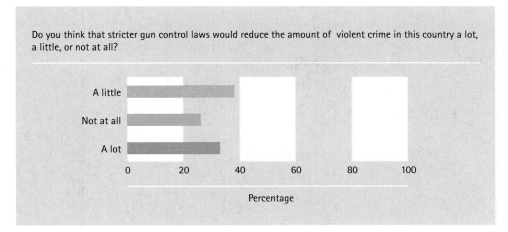

Do you think that stricter gun control laws would reduce the amount of violent crime in this country a lot, a little, or not at all?

**Figure 5.14**

**But Americans Do Not Believe Gun Control Would Do a Lot to Stop Violence**

SOURCE: "Increased Gun Control Not Necessarily a Cure-All," *Public Perspective,* June/July 1999:35.

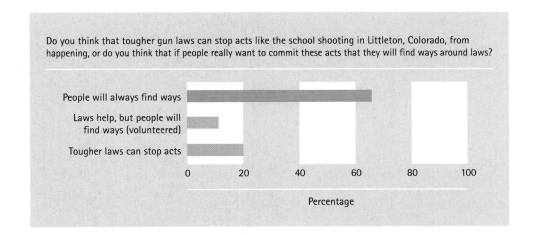

Do you think that tougher gun laws can stop acts like the school shooting in Littleton, Colorado, from happening, or do you think that if people really want to commit these acts that they will find ways around laws?

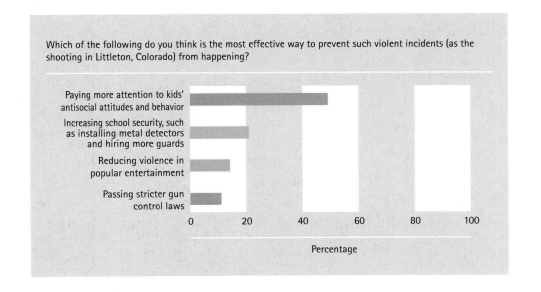

Which of the following do you think is the most effective way to prevent such violent incidents (as the shooting in Littleton, Colorado) from happening?

## Democratic Dilemma

## The "Intensity Problem"

Gun control illustrates what political scientists call the **intensity problem** in democratic theory.[a] The situation arises when people on one side of an issue feel much more strongly about it than people on the other side. Majority rule counts votes; it does not weigh them. But some believe that in a democracy, the intensity with which citizens hold their views should somehow be factored into the decision. They ask, "What if 51 percent of the people barely supports a proposal, while 49 percent bitterly opposes it?" Pure majoritarians reply that we cannot look into people's heads and measure how strongly they feel about an issue—how can we know who is more intense? Moreover, taking intensity into account would violate political equality, which demands that one vote count the same as another. Thus the number of votes is all that should matter. Others are uncomfortable with that answer, arguing that at times majorities should restrain themselves or that institutions should somehow work to measure intensity of preferences. Less philosophically inclined political scientists argue that whichever theoretical answer one prefers, the procedural and institutional complications of real-world democracies help to "weight" votes, as critics of pure majority rule would like: If citi-

zens on one side feel so strongly that they are prepared to donate money, work in campaigns, and vote in primaries, then their views are weighted more heavily by candidates than the views of apathetic citizens on the other side who do not participate.

*What do you think?*
- *Should pure majority rule determine the outcomes in a democracy? Explain your position.[a]*
- *Does political equality demand that every person's preferences be given exactly the same weight as every other person's?*
- *Can majorities be trusted to exercise restraint and not trample on the intensely held views of minorities? Why or why not?*
- *Does contributing time and money to campaigns and other political activities signify intensity, or does it just signify that one side has resources to contribute?*

[a]Robert Dahl, *A Preface to Democratic Theory* (Chicago: University of Chicago Press, 1956), Ch. 4. Willmoore Kendall and George Carey, "'The Intensity Problem' and Democratic Theory," *American Political Science Review* 62 (1968): 5–24.

far away. As Senator Alan Simpson of Wyoming once commented, "Where I come from, people think gun control means how steady can you hold your rifle."[60] Such voters view gun control laws as an attack on their personal freedom and lifestyle—an attack on their values. In contrast, gun control supporters see restricting guns less as a value and more as a means to the end of reducing violence. But as Figure 5.14 shows, they have relatively low expectations for gun control. Majorities do not believe that gun control would do much to reduce violence, and majorities believe that people will always find ways around laws. Other policies are viewed as more effective ways of reducing violence. Thus, although many voters believe that tougher gun restrictions are a good idea, they are sufficiently doubtful about the effectiveness of restrictions that they will not retaliate against an elected official who opposes such restrictions.

In sum, even when a clear majority opinion exists, there is no guarantee that it will translate directly into public policy. Public opinion is filtered through political institutions such as the electoral system through which representatives are elected, and the way in which campaigns and elections are conducted within the electoral system. Such filtering takes account of the fact that some people in the population feel much more passionately about some issues than other people do.

## *Does Public Opinion Matter?*

We have noted that individual members of the public are nonideological. But as James Stimson has observed, the public at large certainly understands that the Democrats are to the left of the Republicans on most issues.[61] Moreover, the public knew that Ronald Reagan was farther to the right than Richard Nixon and that George McGovern was farther to the left than Jimmy Carter. It may not be possible to separate the nuances of public opinion from the noise, but the general direction or "mood" of the public may be easier to gauge. Stimson shows, for example, that if hundreds of survey questions are analyzed together, they indeed yield a portrait of an electorate that was turning to the right in the years leading up to Reagan's election.[62]

In the same vein, Benjamin Page and Robert Shapiro have argued that, viewed *collectively,* the public is reasonably "rational." Analysis of thousands of poll questions asked between 1935 and 1980 shows that, in the aggregate, public opinion is more stable than the opinions of individual members of the public, that public opinion generally moves in accordance with events and conditions, and that public opinion reacts to new developments in natural ways. Moreover, taking such a broad, long-term view, Page and Shapiro find that American public policy follows public opinion. When trends in opinion are clearly moving in one direction, public policy follows, and the more pronounced the trend, the more likely policy is to follow it.[63] Similarly, recent research shows that when federal spending goes up, public preferences for continued increases go down, an effect that indicates some broad public recognition of the direction in which government policy has moved.[64]

The newer findings of Stimson, Page and Shapiro, and others provide an important corrective to much earlier work on public opinion. Given the characteristics of public opinion, it is clear that polling data should be treated cautiously. But that is not to say that public opinion polls give us no important information or that public opinion has no effect on public policy. Although the opinions of the individuals who make up the public are often poorly informed, unconnected, inconsistent, and changeable, the process of aggregation may cancel out individual error and enable the central tendency to emerge. Think of a grade school orchestra. Individually, the young musicians are so unsteady that it is difficult to identify the tune each is playing, but put them all together and the audience can make out "Twinkle, Twinkle Little Star." So it is with public opinion. On some issues and at some times, public opinion and public policy may not be closely aligned, but looking at the general direction of public policy over the long run reveals that public policy tends to follow public opinion.

That is, in fact, about all that the framers of the Constitution wanted. A Constitution that provides for federalism, the separation of powers, a bicameral legislature, a Bill of Rights, six-year Senate terms, and an electoral college certainly was not designed to translate public opinion directly into public policy. On the contrary, the Constitution sought to insulate senators and presidents from public opinion and to allow them to exercise leadership.

As we have noted, differing theories of democracy embody different ideas about the elements of democratic government. The popular model requires ordinary citizens to play a more active, directive role than the responsible model. But Americans are not well informed and, as we will see in the next chapter, often fail to participate even in such a minimal way as voting. Thus proponents of the popular model are disappointed by the ordinary citizen's modest interest in politics. Too often they forget that the structure and philosophical underpinnings of the American Constitution reflect the responsible model at least as much as the popular model. Many of the framers feared and distrusted public opinion and deliberately chose institutions that would constrain it.

## *Chapter Summary*

Public opinion is a basic element of democratic politics. If you believe that the people "rule," it is their opinions that democratic processes must translate into public laws and policies. Even if you believe that the people only "consent," it is their opinions that render public policies legitimate and allow them to take effect. According to either view, public opinion is a basic force that shapes what a democratic government does.

Measuring public opinion is an inexact science at best. The question wording, the sample, and the complexity of the issues make designing good public opinion polls very tricky. But other means of measuring public opinion—such as focus groups— are even less scientific and reliable than survey research. On many issues, among them abortion, the public truly does not have an answer that is easily quantified in a bar graph for an American government textbook. Public opinion exerts its influence largely through the calculations of public officials who understand that they can and will be challenged in free elections. Clearly, an elected official will hesitate to defy the will of an aroused public, but even if public opinion is not expressed, it may influence the actions of politicians who fear arousing it.

Despite the importance of public opinion, governing by opinion poll is difficult and not to be recommended. Citizens tend not to be well informed; their views are not firmly held, can change quickly, and often are not connected to other, seemingly related views. For these reasons, poll results often are misleading and often are misinterpreted by politicians and journalists. In the long run, American democracy follows public opinion, but in the short term, public policy does not always respond to public opinion.

---

### On the Web

American Association for Public Opinion Research (www.aapor.org)
An academic association interested in the methods, applications, and analysis of public opinion and survey research. This site includes access to the *Public Opinion Quarterly* index and its contents.

The Roper Center for Public Opinion Research (www.ropercenter.uconn.edu)
An academic, nonprofit center for the study of public opinion maintaining the world's largest archive of public opinion data.

The National Opinion Research Center (www.norc.uchicago.edu)
Based at the University of Chicago, the social science data site provides access to survey history, a library of publications, links, and information on general social survey methodology.

---

## Key Terms

citizen duty, p. 133
closed-ended question, p. 143
exit poll, p. 133
focus groups, p. 135
framing, p. 149
ideology, p. 142
information cost, p. 141

issue public, p. 142
mass public, p. 143
measurement error, p. 136
open-ended question, p. 143
political efficacy, p. 133
political elite, p. 142
public opinion, p. 130

sampling error, p. 134
selection bias, p. 134
simple random sample, p. 133
socialization, p. 130
survey research, p. 133

# Suggested Readings

Asher, Herbert. *Polling and the Public,* 3rd ed. Washington, DC: CQ Press, 1995. A readable introduction to survey research.

Cook, Elizabeth, Ted Jelen, and Clyde Wilcox. *Between Two Absolutes: Public Opinion and the Politics of Abortion.* Boulder, CO: Westview, 1992. Careful, disinterested description and explanation of American attitudes toward abortion.

Geer, John. *From Tea Leaves to Opinion Polls.* New York: Columbia University Press, 1996. Thoughtful consideration of a democratic dilemma: Do politicians lead public opinion or follow it? Concludes that rational leaders always follow on salient issues but often lead on less salient ones.

Herbst, Susan. *Numbered Voices: How Opinion Polling Has Shaped American Politics.* Chicago: University of Chicago Press, 1993. An informative historical survey of the growth of opinion polling, with a critical examination of its impact on contemporary politics.

Jacobs, Lawrence and Robert Shapiro. *Politicians Don't Pander: Political Manipulation and the Loss of Democratic Responsiveness.* Chicago: University of Chicago Press: 2000, Provocative argument that today's politicians follow their own strongly held preferences and that polls are only a tool used to determine how best to frame the positions that the politicians personally favor.

Ladd, Everett, ed. *The Public Perspective.* Storrs, CT: The Roper Center. This bimonthly periodical is indispensable for any student of public opinion.

Mayer, William. *The Changing American Mind: How and Why American Public Opinion Changed Between 1960 and 1988.* Ann Arbor: University of Michigan Press, 1992. Masterful survey of the changing contours of public opinion over the past generation, with careful dissection of the sources of opinion change.

Page, Benjamin, and Robert Shapiro. *The Rational Public.* Chicago: University of Chicago Press, 1992. Monumental study of public opinion from the 1930s to the 1990s. The authors argue that, viewed as a collectivity, the public is rational, however imperfect the individual opinions that members of the public hold.

Schuman, Howard, and Stanley Presser. *Questions and Answers in Attitude Surveys.* New York: Harcourt, Academic Press, 1981. A comprehensive study of the effects of question wording, form, and context on survey results.

Schuman, Howard, Charlotte Steeh, and Lawrence Bobo. *Racial Attitudes in America: Trends and Interpretations.* Cambridge, MA: Harvard University Press, 1985. Thoughtful examination of contemporary racial attitudes. The authors find that Americans have come to accept principles of equal treatment but remain quite divided on government policies designed to bring about racial equality.

Stimson, James. *Public Opinion in America: Moods, Cycles, and Swings.* Boulder, CO: Westview Press, 1991. Statistically sophisticated examination of American public opinion from the 1960s to the 1990s. The author finds that public opinion was moving in a conservative direction in the 1970s but reversed direction around the time of Reagan's election.

Zaller, John. *The Nature and Origins of Mass Opinion.* New York: Cambridge University Press, 1992. An influential reinterpretation of public opinion findings that argues that people do not have fixed opinions on many subjects. Rather, their responses reflect variable considerations stimulated by the question and the context.

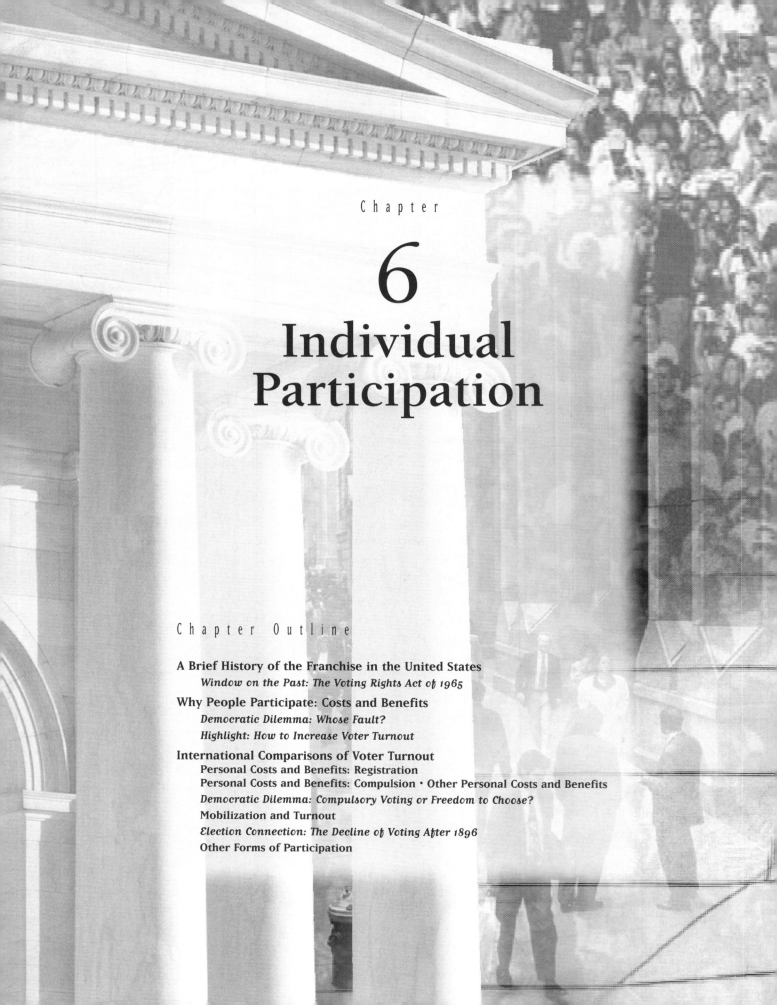

Chapter

# 6
# Individual
# Participation

Chapter Outline

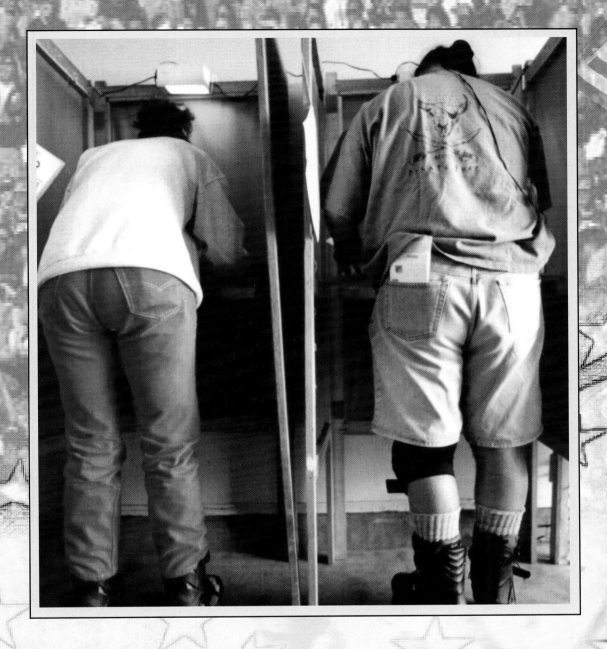

On the morning after the 1992 national elections, the lead headlines summed up the presidential outcome: Clinton Beats Bush! But farther down the front page, many papers carried another story: Turnout Rises! On November 3, 1992, 55 percent of the voting-age population cast a presidential vote, a 5 percent increase over 1988. Even more important than the amount by which voter turnout increased was the simple fact that it *did* increase, for between 1960 and 1992, turnout had dropped almost continuously from one presidential election to the next.

In 1994 the big story was the Republican capture of Congress for the first time since 1952. But the 3 percent increase in turnout over the 1990 level received some attention, too: In congressional elections as well, turnout had been declining for a generation, although not as steadily as in presidential elections. Alas, however, in 1996 the story was the opposite. Less than 50 percent of Americans voted for president, the lowest figure since 1924. Indeed, if we set aside the 1920 and 1924 elections because women had just gained the right to vote in 1920, and many (especially poor immigrant women) did not immediately exercise their right to vote, the 1996 turnout figure was the lowest for a presidential year since the United States became a mass democracy in 1828. The news was not much better in 2000 as barely more than half the eligible electorate voted.

International observers of American politics probably were surprised by the attention given to the 1992 and 1994 surges in turnout. After all, more than three-quarters of the British voted when they defeated Prime Minister John Major in 1997. Turnout was an almost unimaginable (to Americans) 96 percent in the 1996 Australian parliamentary elections. In 1999 the turnout rate was 91 percent in the Belgian parliamentary elections, 89 percent in the South African parliamentary elections, and 93 percent in the Indonesian parliamentary elections.

By the standards of other democracies, turnout in American national elections is exceptionally low. Moreover, in primaries and in local elections, turnout ordinarily is even lower. Ironically, here in the United States, where elections occur continually and have a greater impact on the calculations of politicians than in other countries, voter participation is significantly lower than in most other democracies. Only the Swiss vote as infrequently as Americans, a point to which we will return later.

Many Americans are concerned about turnout levels in the United States, because voting is widely regarded as the fundamental form of democratic participation. Indeed, in modern populous democracies, voting is the *only* form of participation for the great bulk of the population. About one-third of Americans report having signed a petition, and a similar number claim to have contacted a government official at one time or another, but substantially fewer make financial contributions to a party or candidate, attend a political meeting or rally, or work in a campaign. Two-thirds of Americans do nothing beyond voting.[1]

For most people, then, failure to vote means failure to participate at all. And if a bare majority—or even fewer people—vote, how representative are the public officials they elect, and how legitimate are the actions these officials take? Not very, in the view of some. Benjamin Barber charges that "In a country where voting is the primary expression of citizenship, the refusal to vote signals the bankruptcy of democracy."[2]

AMERICAN NONPARTICIPATION IS AN IMPORTANT QUESTION that we consider at length later in this chapter. We will begin, however, by considering a history of the **franchise**—the right to vote—in the United States, and what factors affect whether people vote or abstain. Then we answer in some detail the comparative and historical questions just introduced:

**franchise**
The right to vote.

- Why is turnout lower in the United States than in other democracies?
- Why has turnout declined in the United States?

With that background, we then turn to the larger question of whether low participation levels threaten the legitimacy of American government.

## A Brief History of the Franchise in the United States

By the 1820s the political system in the young American republic had grown stagnant. After the election of 1800, the Federalists were no longer a serious threat to capture the presidency or the Congress, and the party effectively disappeared after 1816. But the so-called era of good feeling was not the happy time the expression suggests. Economic depression, political instability, and popular discontent formed the backdrop for politics during much of the period. National politics was in the hands of a congressional elite elected by a minority of white male property owners. A congressional caucus, consisting of all the Democratic–Republican members of Congress, nominated the presidential and vice-presidential candidates, who, after 1800, were elected as a matter of course.

But in 1824 the caucus could not unite behind a single candidate for president. Four candidates vied for the office, including Secretary of State John Quincy Adams (son of the second president) and General Andrew Jackson, hero of the War of 1812. Although Jackson got the largest share of the popular vote for presidential electors (50 percent more than Adams, his closest competitor), no one got a majority in the electoral college, so the election went to the House of Representatives, as specified by the Constitution. There, Speaker Henry Clay delivered the victory to Adams, who in turn appointed Clay secretary of state, a position then considered a "stepping stone" to the presidency. The losers condemned this sequence of events as evidence of a "corrupt bargain" between Adams and Clay.

Outraged, Jackson's supporters redoubled their efforts. Determined to break the grip of the old Democratic–Republican elite on national politics, they spread their campaign outward to the newly settled West and downward to the grass roots of the country. In 1824, 6 of the 24 states had not provided for popular election of presidential electors (the state legislatures selected them), but that number fell to 2 states by 1828. Turnout increased in all the other states. In total, more than three times as many men voted for presidential electors as had voted in 1824, and Jackson easily defeated Adams.[3]

Despite the tripling of voter turnout between 1824 and 1828, only about 56 percent of the adult male population voted in 1828. The constitutional compromise had left voter qualifications up to the states. Although property qualifications for voting

**suffrage**
Another term for the right to vote.

**timeline**

**Patterns of
Presidential Elections:
Realignment
and Dealignment**

varied from state to state and were very unevenly enforced, in various forms they continued into the 1830s, and most states restricted the franchise to taxpayers until the 1850s.[4] Not until the eve of the Civil War could it be said that the United States had universal white male **suffrage** (another term for franchise). And not all voter qualifications were economic; until the 1830s, a few states even limited voting to those who professed belief in a Christian god. Jews were not permitted to vote in Rhode Island as late as 1830.

By 1860 all adult white male citizens had the franchise. In fact, white aliens often were permitted to vote, but free black citizens usually were not.[5] The Fifteenth Amendment to the Constitution, adopted in 1870, extended the franchise to black males, who at the time were heavily concentrated in the South. With the Republican Congress providing some protection for the party's newly enfranchised supporters, African American males were able to exercise their voting rights for almost two decades in some areas.[6] As described in Chapter 17, however, by the mid-1890s a reactionary movement disenfranchised black males by means of poll taxes, literacy tests, white primaries, and other procedures that could be used in a discriminatory fashion by white election authorities (backed up by violence and intimidation when necessary). Black Americans were effectively denied their voting rights in many parts of the South until the 1960s. Then, as we discuss in "Window on the Past: The Voting Rights Act of 1965" and Chapter 17, the Voting Rights Act reestablished the federal oversight of Southern elections that had been allowed to lapse in the 1890s. The result has been a steady increase in voting among African Americans.

Aside from the New Jersey exception (page 42) women had to wait even longer than African Americans for the franchise.[7] Wyoming in 1869 granted women the right to vote in territorial elections and in 1890 became the first state to extend the franchise to women in national elections. Eleven other states, mostly in the West, had followed by 1916. Finally, in 1920 the Suffrage Movement won its crowning victory when the Nineteenth Amendment was ratified. In theory, if not in practice, the electorate now was the voting-age population, not just the male voting-age population.

A smaller extension of the franchise occurred in 1961 when the Twenty-third Amendment to the Constitution was ratified. This amendment granted the right to vote for presidential electors to residents of the District of Columbia. (The District has no representatives or senators, although it elects a delegate to the House of Representatives.)

**After the Fifteenth Amendment**
In 1870 the Fifteenth Amendment guaranteed African American males the right to vote—at least for 20 years, until discriminatory practices and intimidation began effectively disenfranchising them. There were obvious reasons of bigotry for keeping the recently freed slaves from voting. *What were the more political reasons? What can we learn from the experience of African Americans about the expansions of the franchise?*

## *Window* on the *Past*

### The Voting Rights Act of 1965

*Daniel H. Lowenstein*
*UCLA School of Law*

The Fifteenth Amendment, added to the Constitution in 1870, prohibits denial or abridgement of the right to vote "on account of race, color, or previous condition of servitude." During the Reconstruction period blacks, most of whom lived in the southern states, voted fairly freely and effectively. The right to vote did not end overnight with the end of Reconstruction in 1877. However, over a period of about 30 years, violence, fraud, administrative bias, and legal changes were used to impair greatly the ability of blacks to vote, especially in the deep South.

During the 1930s, there were legal challenges to some of the devices used to deny the franchise to blacks, especially the Democratic party's "white primary" in states in which winning the Democratic nomination was tantamount to winning the election. Perhaps more important, blacks who fought for America in World War II began actively demanding the right to vote when they returned home after the war.

Considerable progress was made, especially in the "outer" South and in big southern cities, but voting rates by blacks remained low in much of the South and were almost nonexistent in deep South states like Alabama and Mississippi. By the 1960s strong voting rights legislation became one of the highest priorities of Martin Luther King and other leaders of the civil rights movement.

Incidents of violence against peaceful demonstrators, especially in Selma, Alabama, created a political climate in which such legislation was politically feasible. After the Selma incident, President Lyndon Johnson made a dramatic demand to Congress for a strong law guaranteeing the franchise, and Congress enacted the Voting Rights Act of 1965.

The Voting Rights Act originally "covered" Alabama, Georgia, Louisiana, Mississippi, South Carolina, Virginia, and large parts of North Carolina. The covered states were prohibited from employing literacy tests as a qualification for voting. At that time, literacy tests could be used to deny the franchise to blacks, partly because most blacks had been poorly educated in southern schools and partly because the tests were administered unfairly. Other provisions allowed federal officers to register voters in recalcitrant areas. Section 5 of the Act required the covered states to get "preclearance" from the federal Department of Justice before they could make any changes in their electoral procedures or systems. Some have criticized Section 5 as an unprecedented intrusion on state authority, but supporters insisted that it was necessary to prevent the South from repeatedly inventing new devices for denying the franchise.

The Voting Rights Act of 1965 was one of the most successful laws Congress has ever passed. Within two or three years, virtually all impediments to voting by blacks had been eliminated. After allowing for socioeconomic factors that influence the rate of voting, blacks in the South were voting at nearly as high a rate as whites, and sometimes higher.

Subsequent amendments extended coverage of the Act to the remaining southern states and many areas outside the South. In addition, the ban on literacy tests was extended to the entire nation and protection of the Act was extended from racial groups to language minorities, such as Hispanics and Asians.

The next and, to date, the last extension of the franchise came in 1971 with the adoption of the Twenty-sixth Amendment to the Constitution, which extended the right to vote to those between 18 and 21 years of age.[8] In most states, 21 had been the age at which eligibility began. During the Vietnam War the argument that Americans old enough to be sent to fight in our wars were old enough to vote gained support, and a Republican president, Richard Nixon, announced his backing for the amendment, even though many Republicans feared it would help the Democrats.

The uneven expansion of the franchise reflects the compromise adopted by the Constitutional Convention: Voting rights were left up to the separate states, which expanded the franchise in different ways at different times. Once the franchise was extended in one state, however, electoral pressures often led to similar extensions in

**Demonstrating for Women's Suffrage**
The suffragists put considerable pressure on President Woodrow Wilson to support the Nineteenth Amendment. Women initially received the franchise in only a few western states. *How did that increase the pressure on politicians to support a constitutional amendment?*

other states. In trying to appeal to newly enfranchised voters in one state, national candidates had an incentive to go on record as supporting similar expansions in other states. This dynamic operated in the case of youth suffrage and black suffrage but was most apparent in the case of women's suffrage.

The most important organization active in the women's rights movement was the National American Women's Rights Association (NAWRA). NAWRA followed a political strategy that in many ways anticipated the strategy used a half-century later by African Americans to win their civil rights. After a few states had granted women the right to vote, the suffragists could increase the pressure on the political parties and presidential candidates to support universal suffrage. With the victory of women's suffrage in California in 1910 and Illinois in 1913, the stage was set for the final push. Woodrow Wilson had won the 1912 election in a three-way race in which he received only 42 percent of the popular vote. He had not taken a clear position on women's suffrage; indeed, he once dodged the issue by saying that the question had never come to his attention. Many Democratic politicians were opposed to women's suffrage. They believed that women were more conservative than men and would vote against labor unions, against liquor interests, and against machine politicians—all key Democratic constituencies. Southern Democrats worried, moreover, that granting voting rights to women would raise the aspirations of African Americans for similar rights. Nevertheless, by 1916 Wilson was moving to a position in support of women's suffrage, promising to vote in favor in a referendum in New Jersey, his home state.

Wilson's change of heart reflected the fact that by 1916, the electoral votes cast by states in which women had the franchise amounted to one-sixth of the total, which to presidential candidates translates as one-third of an electoral college majority. When Republican candidate Charles Evans Hughes announced his support of a constitutional amendment, he put Wilson on the horns of a dilemma. Should Wilson move in a similar direction against the wishes of local Democrats, or should he risk giving to his opponent one-third of the electoral college votes needed to defeat him? Wilson's political position was precarious, and he could not hope to win if he did not hold the West. Partly on the strength of his new, moderate pro-suffrage position, he was able to carry 10 of the 12 women's suffrage states and was narrowly reelected.

Although World War I took center stage for a time, the war experience probably contributed to a willingness to consider political change. Seeing victory on the horizon, suffragists pressed hard for congressional passage of the proposed constitutional amendment, setting 1922 as their target date. NAWRA encouraged women to write letters, make campaign contributions, and use other conventional political tactics, but more militant suffragists engaged in more confrontational tactics such as protests and demonstrations. Women's suffrage soon looked to be inevitable, and politicians, fear-

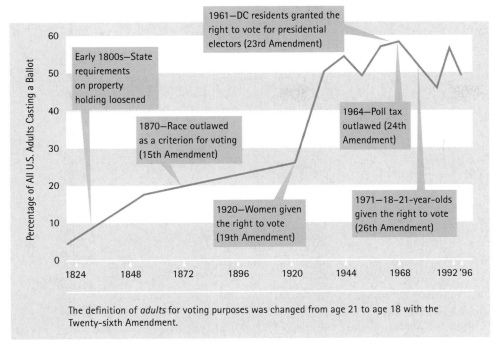

Figure 6.1

**The Right to Vote in the United States Has Been Steadily Expanded**
Note, however, that extending the franchise to new groups does not always result in better turnout.

SOURCE: Adapted from Harold W. Stanley and Richard G. Niemi, *Vital Statistics on American Politics 1999–2000* (Washington, DC: CQ Press, 2000), p. 12.

ful of being left behind, jumped on the bandwagon. Within three years a constitutional amendment had been passed by Congress and ratified by the states, in time for women in all 48 states to vote in the 1920 presidential election, two years ahead of the suffragists' original schedule. Interestingly, the United States was far ahead of most of the world in granting full rights of citizenship to women. France did not allow women to vote until 1945, and the last Swiss canton did not enfranchise women until 1990![9]

Today every mentally competent, law-abiding citizen over the age of 18 has the right to vote in the United States. (Convicted felons are not eligible in many states, a restriction that falls especially heavily on African Americans. About one-eighth of black males are ineligible to vote, a proportion that rises to one-third in such states as Alabama and Florida.[10]) Some have argued, probably tongue-in-cheek, that the right to vote should be further extended to children, perhaps by giving extra votes to their parents. But such proposals are not taken seriously—at least at present.[11]

### Section Summary

Figure 6.1 summarizes the expansion of the franchise and the corresponding rise in the percentage of the adult population that voted in presidential elections. Note that expanding the franchise does not necessarily increase voting proportionately. Sometimes it does, as when women were enfranchised in 1920. But sometimes it does not, as when turnout fell during the 1970s and 1980s, when young people were enfranchised and the courts were striking down restrictions on voting. This disparity between the right to vote and actual turnout reminds us that people decide whether to exercise their rights.

## Why People Participate: Costs and Benefits

In the weeks leading up to elections, the newspapers, the parties and candidates, and all manner of organizations urge Americans to get out and vote. Nonetheless, even in presidential elections, half the potential electorate stays home. After the election, some editorialists criticize the nonvoters for being lazy and uninvolved, while others criticize the candidates for being uninspiring and unworthy (see the accompanying Democratic Dilemma). No doubt there is some truth in both charges, but the question of why some people vote while others abstain is more complicated than newspaper

## Democratic Dilemma

# Whose Fault?

Who is responsible for the low voter turnout in the United States? Here are two views on the subject.

### It's the (Non)Voters' Fault

No one is disenfranchised in this country. Unlike days of old, there are no poll taxes, literacy tests, gender barriers, or property requirements to come between any citizen and the voting booth. If U.S. elections are marked by chronically low turnout, it is not because voters are kept away. They *stay* away. Some are apathetic, some are ignorant, some are simply self-centered. Why badger such people to register? What would they bring to an election?[a]

### No, It's the System

Can we expect people to turn out when nonresponsible political consultants, not only on the presidential level but also in cam-

paigns for all other major offices, can think of no tactic too low or too trivial to use to besmirch the character of, and reduce the turnout for, potential public servants—and when candidates for some of the highest offices in the land lack the character or courage to tell those consultants to shut up and go home.[b]

*What do you think?*
• *Is simply not voting a valid political choice? Why or why not?*
• *What is the most important reason people do not go to the polls?*

_____

[a] Jeff Jacoby, "Making It Too Easy to Vote," *Boston Globe*, July 18, 1996, A15.
[b] Curtis Gans, "No Wonder Turnout Was Low," *Washington Post*, November 11, 1988, A23.

editorials sometimes imply. Numerous factors influence whether a citizen gets to the polling booth. Steven Rosenstone and Mark Hansen divide the reasons for voting into two general categories: individual motivations and outside mobilization.[12]

**Individual motivations for voting** reflect the personal costs and benefits associated with voting. If you are paid by the hour and you take time off in order to vote, you lose a portion of your wages. If you are a parent who cares for small children, you must pay the cost of a sitter in order to vote. Even if you are a professional who can leave work early or arrive late, you do less work on election day if you take the time to vote. Moreover, not all costs are tangible. When you spend time on political activity, you have less time to spend on other, perhaps more attractive or fulfilling activities. For some people with little education or information, the entire voting situation is confusing and uncomfortable. Staying home enables them to avoid such psychological discomfort. If you are surprised that such seemingly small considerations could lower turnout, consider that turnout generally falls when the weather is rainy or very hot.[13]

There also are benefits to voting, of course. One reason, though not the only one, why late-nineteenth-century turnout levels were so high (usually over 75 percent outside the South) is that many people were paid to vote. For example, historians estimate that the going price of a vote in New York City elections in the 1880s was $2 to $5 (expressed in 1990s dollars) and that prices soared as high as $25 in particularly competitive circumstances.[14] Material rewards are a much rarer benefit of voting today, but direct payments for voting (sometimes called "walking around money") still exist

**individual motivations for voting**
The tangible and intangible benefits and costs of exercising one's right to vote.

**Potato Politics**
Becky Cain, Chair of the League of Women Voters, uses Mr. and Mrs. Potato Head to help persuade people to go vote. *What sorts of things must the League of Women Voters, and other groups, say to convince citizens to go to the polls? When do these messages have an ideological component?*

*Excerpted from Dave Barry, "Direct Deposit," *The Boston Globe Magazine*, November 30, 1997: 12–13.

## Highlight                                How to Increase Voter Turnout*

Humorist Dave Barry has written,

So, let's analyze the cash flow: Sleazeballs who want government favors give money to politicians, who give it to consultants, pollsters, advertising agencies, and television stations, who get you to elect the politicians, who thus get more money from sleazeballs. Do you see what's morally wrong with this, voters? That's correct: Your government, the government that your Founding Fathers fought and died for, is being sold over and over like a used mobile home, and *you're not getting a cut.*

I say this stinks. I say we should have a fair, honest, and democratic system whereby the money would go directly from the sleazeballs to the voters. That's right: I say we eliminate the politi-cians altogether and put the donors directly into office. The way it would work is, you'd go into the voting booth, and there would be a list of donors competing for each office, and next to each donor there would be a number indicating how many dollars the donor was willing to pay for your vote. When you pulled that donor's lever, the dollars would immediately come out of a slot in the voting machine.

If we had a system like this, voter turnout would be *way* higher.

---

here and there. And for some citizens, elections still directly affect material interests. For example, local government employees vote in low-turnout local elections at higher rates than do people employed in the private sector, and government employees in general vote at higher rates, other things equal.[15] Today, however, most of the benefits of voting are not material but psychological (although a humorous proposal to increase turnout is in the Highlight Box). Some people take civic norms to heart and feel a duty to vote; they avoid guilt by voting. Others take satisfaction in expressing their preference for a candidate or a position on an issue much as they might enjoy cheering for an athletic team. Such psychological sources of satisfaction are called **psychic benefits of voting.**

Psychic benefits are important, because in their absence, the personal benefits of voting almost never exceed the costs. The reason is that if you vote, you bear the costs of voting no matter what the outcome, but your vote makes no difference unless it affects the outcome. And your vote affects the outcome only if it creates or breaks a tie between the alternatives being voted on.[16] In all other cases you could stay home, and the election would come out the same way. In a small local committee or board, every member has the potential to be the voter who tips the scale, but in a state or national election, any single voter is insignificant. In the 1996 presidential election, for example, almost 100 million Americans voted. In the 1998 elections for the U.S. House of Representatives, an average of 141,000 citizens voted in each congressional race. Given numbers like these, in most elections the potential voter has every reason to believe that the outcome will be the same whether or not he or she votes.

Thus psychic benefits are critical. Unless the voter has a strong sense of duty or takes considerable satisfaction in expressing a preference, the personal benefits of voting generally do not exceed the costs: An individualistic perspective that treats voting as an instrumental act does not support high levels of turnout.[17] As we discussed in Chapter 4, Americans are an individualistic people. Moreover, they are not especially

> **psychic benefits of voting**
> Intangible rewards of voting, such as satisfaction with doing one's duty and feelings of solidarity with the community.

prone to put great weight on their civic duties. The combination of this individualistic outlook and the infinitesimal probability that voting will affect the outcome of a large-scale election has dismal implications for turnout. From a purely individualistic standpoint, the puzzle is not that turnout is so low in the United States but, rather, that turnout is as high as it is.

Why do so many people vote when personal benefits probably do not exceed the costs? Psychic benefits are an important part of the answer, because they do not depend on whether you affect the outcome; you get them just by casting your vote. Another important part of the answer is that people are encouraged or mobilized by others who have personal incentives to turn out the vote. **Mobilization** consists of the efforts of parties, groups, and activists to turn out their potential supporters. Campaign workers provide baby sitters and rides to the polls, thus reducing the individual costs of voting. They apply social pressure by contacting citizens who haven't voted and reminding them to vote. Various groups and social networks to which individuals belong also exert social pressures, encouraging the feeling that one has a responsibility to vote. Although pressures and benefits like these may seem small, remember that the costs of voting are relatively small as well. But however small the costs, unless they are balanced by some benefits, many citizens opt to stay home.

With some understanding of the general reasons why people vote or fail to vote, we can now address the questions raised in the introduction to this chapter. First, why do Americans vote at lower levels than citizens in other countries?

**mobilization**
The efforts of parties, groups, and activists to encourage their supporters to participate in politics.

## *International Comparisons of Voter Turnout*

More than voters in other countries, Americans are proud of their political institutions and constitutional traditions. But as Table 6.1 shows, Americans vote at much lower levels than people in most other countries, even those like Italy whose citizens are exceedingly cynical about politics. However, even though American turnout levels clearly trail those in many other countries, the statistical comparisons often published in newspapers are misleading in various respects. Procedures for calculating turnout differ from country to country, and the differences systematically lower American turnout figures relative to those in other democracies.

Turnout would seem to be simple enough to measure. The United States Bureau of the Census calculates **official turnout** in presidential elections as

No. of people voting for president / no. of people in the voting-age population

This definition seems straightforward, but it lowers American turnout as much as 5 percent relative to other countries. Consider the numerator. If, believing that all the candidates are bums, you either don't vote for president or don't vote for a recognizable candidate, you are not counted as having voted. Other countries are more flexible. In France, for example, there is a long tradition wherein disaffected voters scribble an offensive suggestion across their ballots (the English translation has initials "F.Y."). French election officials count such ballots, whereas most American officials would not.[18] Or if you cast a "frivolous" write-in vote (actual examples from U.S. elections: Rambo, ZZ Top, Batman), election officials in many jurisdictions ignore your vote rather than tabulating it as "other." Such decisions about what votes to count lower U.S. turnout figures by 1 to 2 percent per election.[19]

Factors that affect the denominator are more important. The **voting-age population** refers to the number of people over the age of 18, a number that includes some groups legally ineligible to vote: felons, people confined to mental or correctional institutions, and (most important) noncitizens. Counting the entire voting-age population rather than only the **eligible voting-age population** lowers U.S. turnout figures by another 3 percent.[20]

**official turnout**
Defined by the Census Bureau as the number of people voting for president divided by the size of the voting-age population.

**voting-age population**
All people in the United States over the age of 18.

**eligible voting-age population**
All people in the United States over the age of 18 minus those not eligible to vote because of mental illness, criminal conviction, or noncitizenship.

## Table 6.1

**Americans Are Less Likely to Vote Than the Citizens of Other Democracies**
The figures represent the average turnout (in percentages) in elections to the lower house of the legislature or parliament in 37 countries, 1960–1995.

| Country | Turnout | Country | Turnout |
|---|---|---|---|
| Australia (14)* | 95 | Costa Rica (8) | 81 |
| Malta (6) | 94 | Norway (9) | 81 |
| Austria (9) | 92 | Israel (9) | 80 |
| Belgium (12) | 91 | Portugal (9) | 79 |
| Italy (9) | 90 | Finland (10) | 78 |
| Luxembourg (7) | 90 | Canada (11) | 76 |
| Iceland (10) | 89 | France (9) | 76 |
| New Zealand (12) | 88 | United Kingdom (9) | 75 |
| Denmark (14) | 87 | Ireland (11) | 74 |
| Venezuela (7) | 85 | Spain (6) | 73 |
| Bulgaria (2) | 80 | Japan (12) | 71 |
| Germany (9) | 86 | Estonia (2) | 69 |
| Sweden (14) | 86 | Hungary (2) | 66 |
| Greece (10) | 86 | Russia (2) | 61 |
| Lithuania (1) | 86 | India (6) | 58 |
| Latvia (1) | 85 | United States (9) | 54 |
| Czech Republic (2) | 85 | Switzerland (8) | 54 |
| Brazil (3) | 83 | Poland (2) | 51 |
| Netherlands (7) | 83 | | |

\* Number of elections.
SOURCE: Adapted from Mark Franklin, "Electoral Participation," in Lawrence Le Duc, Richard Niemi, and Pippa Norris, eds., *Comparing Democracies* (Thousand Oaks, CA: Sage, 1996), p. 218.

## *Personal Costs and Benefits: Registration*

Far more important than our inclusion of noncitizens in the "voting-age population," however, is that other countries use a different denominator in their turnout calculations: Their denominator is the registered population. More than 30 percent of the American voting-age population is unregistered. When turnout is measured as the number voting among **registered voters**, U.S. figures jump to the mid-range of turnout in industrial democracies.

Before getting too complacent, however, note that registration is automatic in most of the world; it is a function performed by the central government, like maintaining social security records in the United States. Virtually everyone eligible is registered, so turnout rates are essentially the same whether they are measured as a percentage of the voting-age population or as a percentage of those registered. American practice differs in making registration entirely the responsibility of the individual, and scarcely more than two-thirds of the eligible population is registered. The United States is the only country whose figures differ greatly depending on how turnout is measured.

Thus, in theory, one way to raise U.S. turnout closer to world levels would be to institute an automatic registration system and relieve the individual citizen of the personal responsibility of registering. One proposal to move in this direction—the

**registered voters**
Those legally eligible to vote who have registered in accordance with the requirements prevailing in their state and locality.

**Rock the Vote**
MTV hopes its younger demographic group will be influenced by their more hip appeal to register and vote. *Is this likely to be true?*

"motor voter" law—was enacted in 1993. Preliminary research suggests that such reforms had little impact in 1996.[21] This is not terribly surprising. A few states have no registration or have election day registration at the polling stations. In these states everyone can be considered registered, and although turnout is higher than the national norm, it still falls well below the levels in many European countries.[22] Statistical simulations suggest that if every state used the most liberal registration procedures employed in any state, national turnout would be about 9 percent higher than it is at present.[23]

In sum, registration systems make a big difference; they raise the individual costs of participating for Americans relative to Europeans. But registration is not the only reason for lower U.S. turnout levels.

## Personal Costs and Benefits: Compulsion

The personal registration system makes voting more costly in the United States. In some other countries, public policy makes *nonvoting* more costly than in the United States. Would you believe that voting is compulsory in many countries? In Australia and Belgium, for example, nonvoters are subject to fines; not only the fine itself but also the clear understanding that everyone is legally required to vote helps generate 90+ percent turnout rates. In Italy, nonvoters are not fined, but "Did Not Vote" is stamped on their identification papers, threatening nonvoters with the prospect of unsympathetic treatment at the hands of public officials should they get into trouble or need help with a problem. Turnout in democracies with compulsory voting is almost 15 percent higher than in democracies without it.[24] Turnout in American elections would undoubtedly increase greatly if people were compelled to vote! (See the accompanying Democratic Dilemma).

## Other Personal Costs and Benefits

Several additional institutional variations raise the costs of voting for Americans. Elections in America traditionally are held on Tuesdays, an ordinary workday. In most of the rest of the world, either elections are held on Sundays or election days are proclaimed official holidays. In Italy, workers receive free train fare back to their place of registration, usually their hometown; in effect, the government subsidizes family reunions.

Some observers argue that U.S. turnout is low because Americans are called on to vote so often.[25] In most European countries, citizens vote only two or three times in a four- or five-year period—once for a member of Parliament, once for a representative to the European Union, and perhaps once for a small number of local officials. In contrast, Americans vote in even years for numerous national and state officials and in odd years (in many states) for numerous local officials. Primaries are held in the spring or summer. Referenda may be held simultaneously with these other elections or decided in special elections of their own. Some have suggested, not completely tongue-in-cheek, that turnout in the United States should be calculated as the percentage who vote at least once during a four-year period, a figure that would be more comparable to turnout figures for other countries. Interestingly, the only other country where voters are called upon to vote with anything close to the frequency that they are in the United States is Switzerland, which has a turnout rate comparable to that in the United States.

Finally, a smaller but interesting disincentive to vote in some areas has recently been identified. Some states use lists of registered voters to select people for jury duty. One study concluded that in such jurisdictions, turnout is 5 to 10 percent lower than it otherwise would be, but that estimate may be too high.[26] At any rate, the fear of losing a day's work or more if a trial is extended (think about the O.J. criminal trial!) probably is sufficient to motivate some citizens to forfeit their right to vote.

## Democratic Dilemma

# Compulsory Voting or Freedom to Choose?

After the 1988 elections, some disgruntled Democrats grumbled about the legitimacy of the election results. Although George Bush won a comfortable victory over Michael Dukakis (54 to 46 percent), turnout was only 50.1 percent of the voting-age population. To the losers this meant that only 27 percent of the eligible electorate (0.54 × 0.50) had actually supported Bush. If democracy at a minimum means popular consent, how could such an election be democratic? Can a bare quarter of the electorate consent for a majority?

After the 1992 elections the shoe was on the other foot. Disgruntled Republicans grumbled that Clinton had received only 43 percent of the popular vote. Thus, even though turnout had risen to 55 percent, less than a quarter of the eligible electorate (0.43 × 0.55) had supported Clinton. Was this "popular consent"? The 1996 elections underlined that question when less than 50 percent of the voting-age population went to the polls.

By ignoring the preferences of nonvoters, the United States treats them as though they had consented to the election outcome, certainly a dubious assumption to make as a general matter. Although some people are content whatever happens, and some are alienated whatever happens, surely many nonvoters would have voted for the loser had they bothered to vote. Hence, to treat the 20 to 25 percent—or less in elections other than presidential ones—of those who voted as consenting on behalf of the majority is at least questionable.

As noted in the text, some democracies make voting compulsory.[a] Greek electoral law provides for imprisonment of nonvoters for up to 12 months. That penalty is never applied, but other democracies do penalize nonvoters, at least sometimes. Australian law allows for fines of up to $50 for not voting (without a valid excuse), and estimates are that 4 percent of nonvoters pay fines. In addition to having their identification papers stamped "Did Not Vote," Italian nonvoters have their names posted on community bulletin boards.

In countries with compulsory voting, questions of majority consent do not arise. If nearly everyone votes, then by definition the winning party or coalition of parties receives a majority of the vote. Compulsory voting has been proposed for the United States. The author of one congressional bill in the 1920s argued that "we

**Compulsory Voting**
Filipino guards watch the polling place on election day. *How much should a government "watch" the polls? Can an election with guards or officials closely watching who votes be as free as one without those motivations?*

conscript the citizenry for duty in time of war, . . . why not conscript them to the duty of citizenship, in time of peace?"[b]

*What do you think?*
- *Should the United States have compulsory voting, as do Austria, Belgium, Australia, Italy, and numerous other democracies? Why or why not?*
- *Why shouldn't everyone who enjoys the privilege of citizenship be required to vote?*

[a] For an informative discussion of compulsory voting, see Richard Hasen, "Voting Without Law," *University of Pennsylvania Law Review* 144 (1996): 2135–2179.
[b] Quoted in Michael McGerr, *The Decline of Popular Politics* (New York: Oxford University Press, 1986), p. 193.

All in all, both intentionally and accidentally, American practices raise the costs of voting relative to those in other countries. When some citizens understandably react to those costs by failing to vote, editorialists criticize them for their lack of public spirit.

## Mobilization and Turnout

Not only do Americans face higher costs of voting and lower costs of nonvoting, but they also have less help in overcoming the costs of voting. The chief mobilizing agent in modern democracies is the political party. Parties have incentives to mobilize their supporters; indeed, they have often undertaken that task with excessive enthusiasm, as when urban machines voted the dead or reported more votes for their candidates than there were residents in their cities. It certainly is no accident that American

## Election Connection

## The Decline of Voting After 1896

In the late nineteenth century, American turnout levels reached all-time highs: in the five elections leading up to 1896, turnout averaged 80 percent of the male voting-age population. In the five elections following 1896, however, turnout averaged just 65 percent, and it has never since reached the late-nineteenth-century highs.[a]

What happened in 1896? As we will explain in Chapter 8, many political historians consider 1896 to be the central election in a "critical era," a period in which voting alignments changed in significant and lasting ways. The decades from the end of the Civil War to the mid-1890s were the most electorally competitive in American history. The parties of this period were stronger than before or since; historians liken them to military organizations.[b] Supported by the patronage system, the parties had ample *resources* to mobilize the electorate. And given the intense electoral competition, the parties had the *incentive* to mobilize the electorate—defeat would throw tens of thousands of party workers out of their jobs. But political developments were undercutting both the resources and the incentives that buoyed up the parties.[c]

Civil service and other reforms were beginning to eat away at the patronage system. And between 1888 and 1896, 90 percent of the states instituted some kind of personal registration system, raising the citizens' costs of voting, and restricting the parties' ability to vote the dead, vote people twice (or more!), vote the ineligible, and engage in other corrupt practices that raised turnout.[d]

Meanwhile, the Populists, a radical third party representing the agricultural West, merged with the Democrats and nominated William Jennings Bryan, who thundered that the Republicans would not be allowed to "crucify mankind on a cross of gold." After taking a look at Bryan, a majority of voters decided to take their chances with the Republican candidate, William McKinley, who won handily. Soon it became apparent that the Republican win had been more than a temporary victory. In large areas of the North and Midwest, the Democrats were no longer competitive. Their national majority now secure, the Republicans abandoned

the South to the Democrats, who completed their disfranchisement of black Americans. With party competition greatly reduced in much of the country, the parties no longer had the incentive to mobilize their supporters, and supporters no longer felt it important to vote. Meanwhile, reforms continued to sap the material resources the parties had relied on, and party organizations went into long-term decline. Although political historians continue to argue about the relative importance of the institutional and political factors that led turnout to decline, 1896 clearly was a watershed between a high-turnout, highly competitive electoral era and a low-turnout era of Republican dominance.[e]

*What do you think?*
- *If many Americans of earlier generations voted because they were paid to do so, in effect, should we be as concerned about low turnout levels today as many are? Why or why not?*
- *If compulsory voting (the "stick") is unacceptable, why not pay people (the "carrot") to vote? For example, your ballot stub could be a ticket in a lottery with large cash prizes. (This would have the additional effect of helping close the gap between turnout of the poor and that of the wealthy.)*

---

[a] Walter Dean Burnham, "The Turnout Problem," in A. James Reichley, ed., *Elections American Style* (Washington DC: Brookings, 1987), Table 5.3.
[b] Richard Jensen, "American Election Campaigns: A Theoretical and Historical Typology," presented at the 1968 Meetings of the Midwest Political Science Association.
[c] Walter Dean Burnham, *Critical Elections and the Mainsprings of American Politics* (New York: Norton, 1970), Ch. 4.
[d] Philip Converse, "Change in the American Electorate," in *The Human Meaning of Social Change,* Angus Campbell and Philip Converse, eds. (New York: Russell Sage, 1972), pp. 263–337.
[e] See the articles, comments, and rejoinders by Walter Dean Burnham, Philip Converse, and Jerrold Rusk in the September 1974 *American Political Science Review.*

turnout levels peaked in the late nineteenth century, when the efficiency of American parties was at a maximum and the ethics of American parties at a minimum. During this period the patronage system was at its strongest. With hundreds of thousands of government jobs at stake in elections, the parties had little trouble motivating their workers, not to mention their relatives and friends. And, unconstrained by conflict-of-interest or sunshine (open-government) laws, the parties were quite willing to do whatever it took to gain or keep control of government.

As we will see in later chapters, American parties have declined, at least as mobilizing agents. Voters are less attached to them than at any time in the past, and the parties have less in the way of inducements to turn out the dwindling numbers of faithful than they did in the past.[27] Indeed, as we discuss in the accompanying Election Connection and in Chapter 8, the lower levels of turnout in this century are associated with the Progressive reforms at the turn of the century, reforms that instituted the personal registration system and weakened the parties' control of nominations for office. A significant part of the reason why turnout is lower in the United States than in other democracies is that parties are (on average) much stronger and more active elsewhere than they are here.

Political parties are not the only mobilizing agent in democracies. As we will see in Chapter 7, interest groups and associations are alternative mobilizing agents. But

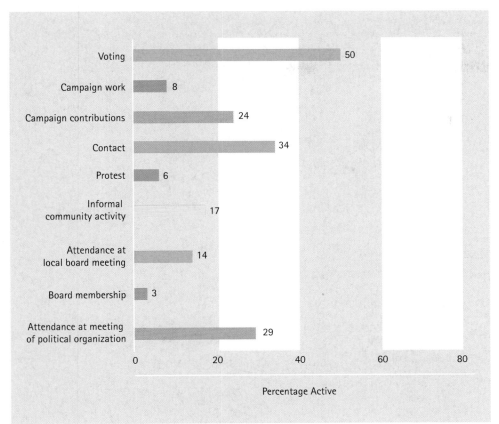

**Figure 6.2**

**Americans Are Even Less Likely to Participate in More Demanding Ways Than Voting**

SOURCE: Adapted from Sidney Verba, Kay Lehman Schlozman, and Henry Brady, *Voice and Equality* (Cambridge, MA: Harvard University Press, 1995), p. 50.

even though more organizations exist in the United States than in other countries, and even though many of them participate regularly in politics, they are not so deeply rooted in society as their counterparts elsewhere—particularly in the unions and in the churches, which are the very foundations of some political parties in Europe. Thus, here too, Americans receive less support from collective political actors than in other democracies.

Several analysts have dissected statistically the difference in turnout levels between the United States and other countries.[28] All other things being equal, American turnout should actually be somewhat higher than in Europe because of higher educational levels and American civic attitudes that encourage popular participation. But other things are far from equal. Powell estimates that differences in electoral institutions, chiefly registration systems, depress American turnout between 10 and 15 percent relative to Europe and that weaker party and group mobilization depress turnout by about 10 percent. In sum, it costs Americans more to vote, and they receive less support for voting than citizens in most other countries.

## Other Forms of Participation

Americans turn out at lower levels than citizens in other democracies. Moreover, they are significantly less likely to participate in other ways than they are to vote. As Figure 6.2 shows, Americans are significantly less likely to work in campaigns, to give money, and to attend meetings than they are to vote. It is a bit surprising, then, to learn that Americans are *more* likely to engage in these less common forms of participation than are the citizens of some countries where turnout is much higher. Figure 6.3 shows that even though only minorities of Americans work in campaigns or contact public officials, more of them do so than citizens in other democracies. The explanation lies in several of the factors just discussed.

**Figure 6.3**

Americans Are More Likely Than Citizens in Other Democracies to Participate in Ways More Demanding than Voting

SOURCE: Adapted from Sidney Verba, Kay Lehman Schlozman, and Henry Brady, *Voice and Equality* (Cambridge, MA: Harvard University Press, 1995), p. 70.

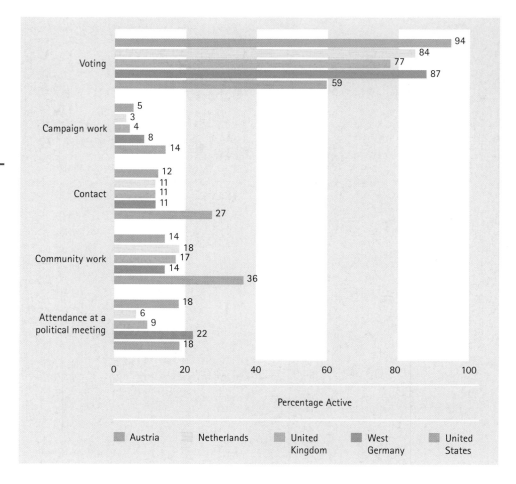

- Because there are so many elections to fill so many offices, not to mention primaries, initiatives, and referenda, there are far more *opportunities* for electoral participation in the United States than elsewhere. And because there are far more offices and government bodies in the United States, there are far more opportunities to contact an official, attend a meeting of a government board, and so forth. Even if Americans are less likely to take advantage of any particular participatory opportunity, the sheer number of opportunities would give them a higher level of political participation than in other countries where opportunities are more limited. As American elections have increased in frequency, and governmental bodies have increased in number, some studies have found increases in some kinds of campaign participation. For example, one study found that in the late 1980s, more people claimed that they gave money to candidates and tried to persuade others how to vote, as compared to the late 1960s.[29]
- Our individualistic political culture, with its emphasis on rights and liberties, encourages Americans to contact public officials and to protest government actions. In contrast, the political cultures of most other democracies are more deferential to authority and discourage ordinary citizens from taking as active a role in politics as in the United States. Citizens elsewhere are less likely to protest government decisions, and when they do, their governments are more likely to ignore them.
- Because American political parties are weaker today than in earlier eras, candidates construct numerous personal organizations, many of whose members are temporary. In other countries a small cadre of committed party workers shoulders most of the burden of campaigning year in and year out, but in the United States campaigns are fought by much larger groups of "occasional activists." These are

**Volunteer Work**
Volunteers stuff envelopes for a community food bank.

enthusiastic amateurs who drift in and out of political campaigns, depending on whether particular candidates or issues arouse their enthusiasm.[30]

- Finally, many Americans participate in politics indirectly by joining or supporting interest groups that take a more direct role by soliciting their members for signatures or contributions, encouraging them to go to meetings, and so forth. There are far more groups and associations active in politics in the United States than in other countries and hence far more opportunities for participation through groups. Groups are particularly likely to be the source of what is often referred to as unconventional participation: protests, demonstrations, and civil disobedience. We treat group participation in this and other ways at length in Chapter 7.

## *Why Has American Turnout Declined?*

For many people the problem is not only that turnout levels in the United States are lower than in other advanced democracies but also that turnout has fallen during the past generation. Figure 6.4 shows that in presidential elections turnout fell steadily between 1960 and 1988, before hitting a half-century low in 1996. In off-year elections, turnout declined more erratically, but it is significantly lower now than a generation ago. Rosenstone and Hansen report that the minorities of people who work in campaigns or attend political or governmental meetings also declined in number, although other studies reach slightly different conclusions. Even those who participate in such minimal ways as signing a petition are slightly fewer in number now than a generation ago.[31]

To many observers these declines in popular participation suggest that something is terribly wrong with American politics. This fear was reinforced in the late 1970s when analysts noted that participation was declining at the same time that trust in government was declining—recall Figure 1.1. Research soon showed, however, that the two trends were largely unrelated. That is, turnout declined among the trusting and the cynical alike, and the former were no more likely to vote than the latter.[32]

What makes the decline in turnout all the more puzzling is that two other developments in the past three decades led to an expectation of *rising* turnout. First, court

**Figure 6.4**

**Turnout in the United States Has Declined Since 1960**

SOURCE: Norman Ornstein, Thomas Mann, and Michael Malbin, *Vital Statistics on Congress, 1999–2000* (Washington, DC: American Enterprise Institute, 2000), p. 48.

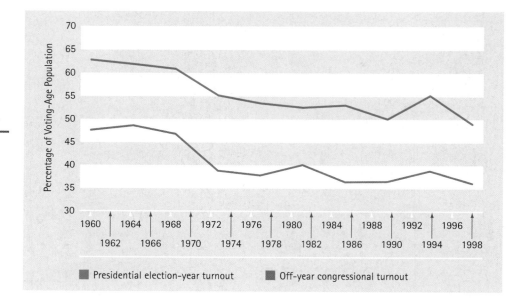

■ Presidential election-year turnout    ■ Off-year congressional turnout

decisions, federal legislation such as the Voting Rights Act and its amendments, and the Twenty-fourth Amendment to the Constitution have removed numerous institutional and procedural impediments to voting and thus reduced the personal costs. For example, poll taxes and literacy tests were abolished, state and local residency requirements were shortened, registration was made simpler and more convenient, bilingual ballots were permitted, and absentee voting was made easier. Such reforms were especially effective in the South, where they helped to overcome the terrible legacy of racial discrimination. Figure 6.5 shows how turnout among African Americans in the South increased sharply between 1960 and 1968.

Second, socioeconomic change should have raised turnout in the post-1964 period. That the potential electorate was getting younger as the baby boom generation came of age should have lowered turnout, because young people traditionally vote at

**Political Protest**
Americans may not turn out to vote quite as much as other nations, but protests are very common in Washington, DC. Here, Kosovar Albanians march in front of the White House in support of the NATO bombings. *Protest is an often controversial form of participation. When should it be? Why or why not?*

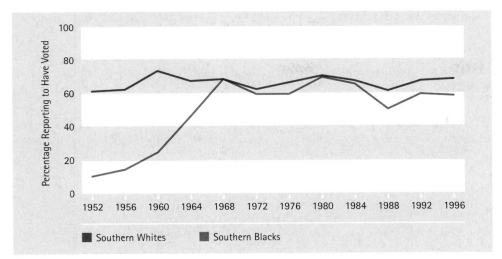

**Figure 6.5**

**The Civil Rights Revolution Opened Southern Politics to African Americans**
The turnout gap between African American and white voters narrowed as a result of the civil rights movement of the 1950s and 1960s.

SOURCE: American National Election Studies.

lower levels than older people. But that effect should have been more than offset by rising educational levels. Education is the single strongest predictor of turnout. Higher educational levels produce a keener sense of civic duty and help people deal with the complexities of registering and voting. Ruy Teixeira estimates that, other things being equal, the net effect of socioeconomic changes, chiefly education, should have been to raise national turnout by about 4 percent.[33]

What, then, explains the decline in turnout? There is not so much agreement here as there is on the explanation of turnout differences between the United States and other democracies, where, as we have seen, two factors—registration and political parties—dominate the answer. Several factors clearly have contributed to the decline in American turnout, but their precise importance is a matter of debate.

## Lower Personal Benefits

One reason why the decline in voting costs did not increase voting is that the benefits of voting may have declined at an even faster rate. Studies show that Americans today are not so interested in politics, don't care so much about who wins the election, and don't believe that government is as responsive as in times past.[34] Thus they do not see as much riding on their decisions as in years past, and they probably get less intrinsic satisfaction from supporting an admired candidate or party. One must be extremely careful in interpreting such findings, however. On the one hand, lack of interest in and concern about elections and government might be a *cause* of nonvoting; but on the other hand, such psychological detachment might also simply be a *part of the same syndrome* of disengagement as nonvoting.

Another political factor that has lowered the benefits of voting is that elections have become less competitive. As we discuss in Chapter 11, between the mid-1960s and the mid-1990s, the advantage of incumbency in congressional elections increased greatly, and a similar process occurred more slowly in state legislative elections. Many presidential elections in the 1970s and 1980s were landslides, and gubernatorial elections had become less competitive as well. When candidates win by large margins, the notion that one's vote actually makes a difference must seem more outlandish than ever. Probably more important, however, is that when elections are closely contested, campaigns have more incentive to get out the vote. Rosenstone and Hansen find that in states with competitive gubernatorial campaigns in presidential election years, turnout is 5 percent higher, other things being equal.[35] In a result consistent with such arguments, turnout dropped 5 percent in 1996 when Bill Clinton led Bob Dole by a comfortable margin from start to finish.

## Declining Mobilization

Statistical studies reveal that personal costs and benefits account for less than half of the decline in turnout. The larger part of the decline reflects the decreased mobilization efforts of parties, campaigns, and social movements such as the civil rights, anti-war, and other movements that were more active during the turbulent 1960s. Rosenstone and Hansen observe that

> . . . party mobilization underwrites the costs of political participation. Party workers inform people about upcoming elections, tell them where and when they can register and vote, supply them with applications for absentee ballots, show them the locations of campaign headquarters, and remind them of imminent rallies and meetings. Campaigns drop by to pick up donations, telephone reminders on the day of the election, and drive the lazy, the harried, the immobile, and the infirm to the polls.[36]

Parties still are active, of course, and candidate organizations are more active than ever. But polling and media advertising are probably not good substitutes for the kind of pound-the-pavement, doorbell-ringing workers who used to dominate campaigns. Voters may be motivated by the coaxing of a campaign worker standing at the front door or telephoning late in the afternoon of election day, but those same voters may not be motivated by an impersonal TV spot urging them to vote.[37] Thus a change in style from labor-intensive to high-tech campaigning may have indirectly contributed to declining turnout. And the fact that elections have become less competitive would further lower the motivation of campaigns to engage in difficult, time-consuming activity. When the result of an election is a foregone conclusion, the winning side grows complacent, and the losing side sees little reason to make a serious effort.

## Declining Social Connectedness

You might interpret a turnout line trending downward to mean that any given citizen is less likely to vote than a generation ago. Warren Miller has shown that such a view is incorrect.[38] The decline in voter turnout is what social scientists call a **compositional effect**: a behavioral change that reflects a change in the makeup or composition of a group rather than a change in the behavior of individuals in the group. Miller found that the pre–New Deal generation voted at very high levels. Turnout rates of older Americans (the New Deal generation) were never as high as those of their elders, but they were relatively high and remain so today. In contrast, the turnout rates of middle-aged Americans (the baby boomers) were low when they entered the electorate and remain low today. Turnout is declining because of the simple fact that older Americans accustomed to voting at high rates are dying and being replaced by younger Americans who vote at lower rates. Miller makes a persuasive case that the causes of the decline in turnout must lie in differences among the generations. Robert Putnam argues that the younger generation is less likely to participate in other ways as well.[39]

One interesting possibility that has received attention is a decline in what sociologists refer to as social connectedness. Stephen Knack raises the possibility that common thinking about voting is misconceived. Rather than voting being the fundamental political act, voting may not be a political act as much as a social act. Voting is related to giving blood, donating to charities, doing volunteer work, and other forms of altruistic behavior.[40] Thus, rather than looking for *political* causes of nonvoting, perhaps researchers should look for *social* causes. Interestingly, as Figure 6.6. indicates, although turnout is not related to trust in *government*, it is significantly related to trust in *people*.[41]

**Social connectedness** is the extent to which people are integrated into society—their families, neighborhoods, communities, churches, and other social units. Older Americans who grew up in a simpler time, when Americans were less mobile, more religious, and more trusting of their fellow citizens, may be more connected than younger Americans, who have grown up in a highly mobile, secular society where cyn-

---

**compositional effect**
A change in the behavior of a group that arises from a change in the group's composition, not from a change in the behavior of individuals in the group.

---

**social connectedness**
The degree to which individuals are integrated into society—families, churches, neighborhoods, groups, and so forth.

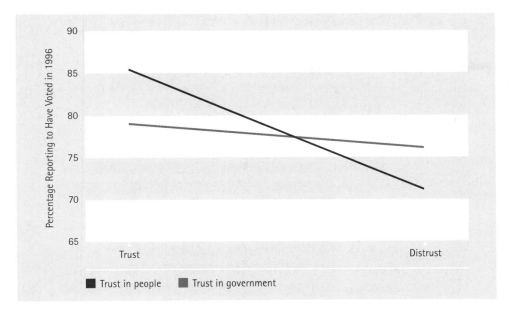

Figure 6.6

**Turnout Is Not Closely Related to Trust in Government, But It Is Related to Trust in People**
On the left side of the figure, reported turnout is indicated for those expressing trust in people and those expressing trust in government "just about always" or "most of the time." On the right side, reported turnout is shown for those expressing distrust in people and those expressing trust in the government "only some of the time" or "none of the time."

SOURCE: American National Election Studies.

icism about their fellow citizens is widespread. There is always a danger in arguments about the good old days (upon close examination, they often don't look so good), and we doubt that research can ever prove to everyone's satisfaction that people in the pre–New Deal era were more socially connected than people today, but given the societal changes that have taken place during the past century, the argument has some plausibility, and there is some research to support it.

Investigators have examined the social connectedness argument by looking for relationships between measures of social connectedness and turnout. Even relying on such crude indicators as marriage rates, home ownership, church attendance, and length of residence in a community, recent studies find that decreased social connectedness accounts for as much as one-quarter of the decline in presidential turnout.[42] (Interestingly, although being married is associated with higher turnout, being *newly* married is estimated to lower the odds of voting; apparently, voting is not high on the priority list of the newly married.[43])

A final point is of interest. Although citizens of other democracies generally vote at much higher levels than do Americans, turnout is on the decline elsewhere as well. In 17 of 19 advanced democracies around the world, turnout in the 1990s was lower than in the 1950s, although few have seen as big a decline as the United States has.[44] Some of the variables that are driving turnout down in the United States probably are at work in other countries as well.

### Section Summary

The decline in American voting rates has a number of contributing causes. Today's electorate is younger and less politically committed—less motivated to vote. And these less motivated individuals are less likely to be encouraged to vote by parties or campaign organizations in elections that are less competitive than they used to be. Moreover, individuals are also less likely to be stimulated to vote by spouses, church associates, and long-time neighbors than are the citizens in a less mobile, less atomized, more socially oriented country.

## Who Votes and Who Doesn't?

Low voting rates probably would not stimulate as much discussion as they do if all social and economic groups in America exhibited the same voting rates. But people differ in their ability to bear the costs of voting, in the strength of their feeling that

participation
**The Prepared Voter Kit**

**Figure 6.7**

**Group Differences in Turnout, 1996**

SOURCE: American National Election Studies.

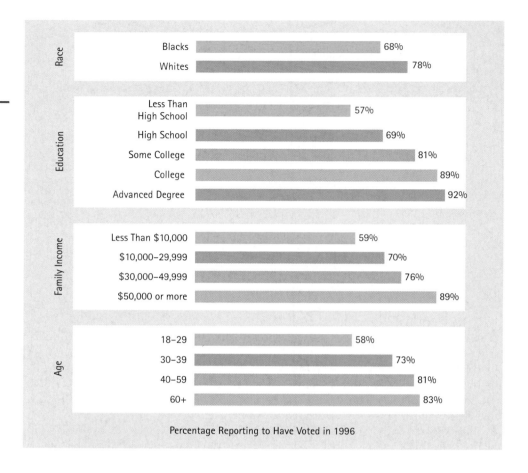

Percentage Reporting to Have Voted in 1996

voting is a duty, and in how often they are the targets of mobilization. Consequently, as Figure 6.7 indicates, turnout rates differ considerably across social and economic groups.[45]

Highly educated people are far more likely to vote than people with little formal education. Education instills a stronger sense of duty and gives people the knowledge, analytic skills, and self-confidence to meet the costs of registering and voting. Over and above education, income also has a significant effect. The wealthy are far more likely to vote than the poor. Affluence, too, reflects a set of skills and personal characteristics that help people overcome barriers to voting.

Studies of turnout in the 1970s concluded that, once disadvantages in education and income were factored out and their younger age was considered, blacks were at least as likely to vote as whites.[46] But more recent research finds that blacks are somewhat less likely to vote than whites, even taking into account differences in income and educational levels.[47] One suggestion is that African Americans were disillusioned by the failure of the Jesse Jackson campaigns in 1984 and 1988.[48] Other minorities, such as Latinos and Asians, still face language barriers, though the situation is gradually improving.[49]

Turnout increases with age, until very old age when the trend reverses. People presumably gain experience as they age, experience that makes it easier for them to overcome any barriers to vote. They also become more socially connected, as well as more settled down in a life situation that clarifies their political preferences.

Interestingly, the relationships between socioeconomic characteristics and turnout are consistently stronger in the United States than in other democracies. Indeed, in some countries there is almost no relationship between education and income on the one hand and voting on the other.[50] The reason is not that education and income have different effects than in the United States; it is that parties elsewhere are much more effective at mobilizing their supporters. In particular, European Social Democratic parties do a far better job of getting their less advantaged potential voters to the polls than does the Democratic party in the United States.

In sum, there is no question that the low turnout rates that exist in the United States result in an electorate that is somewhat wealthier, better educated, older, and whiter than the population at large. What are the implications of that fact?

**visual literacy**

**Voter Turnout: Who Votes? Do Americans Vote as Much as Other Citizens?**

## Is Low Turnout a Problem?

Given who votes and why, should the relatively low turnout rate in the United States be a cause for concern? Quite a few answers have been offered on both sides of this question. To a considerable degree, these differing views hinge on different beliefs about the motives for voting. We will briefly sketch three arguments on each side of the debate.

### Three Arguments Why Low Turnout Is Not a Problem

**A Conservative (With a Small "C") Argument**    Many of those concerned about low turnout implicitly assume that high turnout indicates enthusiasm about politics and commitment to making the political order work. Maybe not. Some skeptics suggest that high turnout may indicate tension or conflict, coupled with a belief that losing would be unacceptable. They cite the experience of Austria and Germany as their democratic governments crumbled and the Fascist parties took power in the 1930s.[51] Turnout in those elections reached very high levels, but this probably reflected disillusionment and desperation more than commitment and enthusiasm. The 1992 presidential election is a less extreme case in point. Turnout rose, but did this indicate a healthier political system? On the contrary, by many indications people were "mad as hell"—frustrated and upset with their government. Similarly, turnout rose a bit in 1994, but according to many pundits, it was the year of the "angry white male."

Generalizing from examples like these, some argue that low turnout indicates contentment, not estrangement. If so, low turnout is a sign of the health of a polity and contributes to political stability. Samuel Huntington goes so far as to argue that ". . . the effective operation of a democratic political system usually requires some measure of apathy and noninvolvement on the part of some individuals and groups."[52]

**An Elitist Argument**    On average, nonvoters are less educated than voters. Studies also show them to be less informed, less interested in politics, and less concerned about it. Given these facts, some argue that the quality of electoral decisions is higher if no special effort is made to increase turnout. For example, David Reisman once remarked, "Bringing sleepwalkers to the polls simply to increase turnout is no service to democracy."[53] Columnist George Will provides a more recent illustration of this elitist point of view:

> Here comes another campaign to encourage voting, alas. Last weekend, ABC News and Harvard's Kennedy School of Government sponsored a symposium on "the problem of declining voter participation." Problem? As more people are nagged to the polls, the caliber of the electorate declines. The reasonable assumption about electorates is: Smaller is smarter.[54]

Of course, this argument depends on nonvoters staying ignorant and unconcerned even if they were to vote. If, contrary to that assumption, the process of encouraging people to vote also informed them and raised their interest, the argument would be undercut.

**A Cynical or Radical Argument**    Some radicals contend that it is not the nonvoters but the voters who are a cause for concern. According to this viewpoint, elections don't matter—they are charades. Real decisions are made by power elites far from the popular arena. If so, voting is a merely symbolic act that makes the masses feel they have a say in how they are governed. Turnout doesn't matter because elections don't matter.

We disagree strongly with this latter argument. As we stress throughout this book, elections matter a great deal—in some cases, too much. In later chapters we will discuss some of the important issues facing Americans. Those discussions will make it clear that elections have had enormous effects on the shaping of public policy.

### Three Arguments Why Low Turnout Is a Problem

**The Voters Are Unrepresentative**    The most obvious concern arising from low turnout is that it produces an unrepresentative electorate. The active electorate is wealthier, whiter, older, and better educated than the potential electorate. People naturally assume that such an electorate is more Republican and more conservative than the voting-age population at large. Consequently, elections are biased, and public policies adopted by the winners are correspondingly biased.

Plausible as the argument seems, research suggests that it is overstated. Numerous studies have compared the policy views and the candidate preferences of voters and nonvoters. Typically, they differ little. Some studies have even found that at times the conservative candidate was more popular among nonvoters—Ronald Reagan in 1984, for example.[55] In general, nonvoters are less knowledgeable, less interested, and less committed, and therefore they are more susceptible to bandwagons, political advertising, and other transient forces.

After looking at the voting rates of rich and poor, minorities and whites, and so forth, people tend to assume that nonvoters and voters differ more than they do. But in the first place, although minorities and the poor vote less often than whites and the affluent, the difference is only a matter of degree. Thus blacks are less likely to vote than whites, but only about one-eighth of all the nonvoters are black. Similarly, the more highly educated are more likely to vote, but 25 percent of the nonvoters have some college education. Nonvoters are not all poor, uneducated, and members of minority groups. Plenty of nonvoters are affluent, well educated, and white. This is particularly true of movers: According to the U.S. Bureau of the Census, nearly one in five Americans moves during the two-year interval between national elections.[56]

In the second place, few groups are as one-sided in their political inclinations as African Americans, who vote more than 8:1 Democratic. If turnout among most other groups were to increase, the Democrats would get somewhat more than half the additional votes, but the Republicans would get a fair proportion as well.

Teixeira provides striking illustrations of these points. According to his calculations, if all the Hispanics and African Americans in the country had voted in 1988 at levels 10 percent higher than whites, and all the white poor had voted at levels 10 percent higher than the white rich, the Democratic candidate, Michael Dukakis, would still have lost by two and a half million votes.[57] Not all elections are so one-sided, of course, but given the improbability that the disadvantaged could ever be mobilized at such high levels, it is doubtful that realistic increases in turnout would produce a sea change in American politics.

Still, as Marxists might point out, there could be an element of "false consciousness" here: Because present nonvoters are uninformed and uncommitted, they fail to understand or act on their true interests. The political or social changes that could greatly increase their voting could also greatly increase their knowledge and interest and produce a different political outlook. This line of argument can be settled only by greatly increasing turnout and seeing whether the preferences of nonvoters change.

**Low Turnout Reflects a "Phony" Politics**    This argument emphasizes the character of political issues in present-day America. Essentially, the argument asserts that low turnout among the poor and minorities reflects a more general disengagement from an American politics that does not address "real" issues of concern to such people. What are real issues? Basically, they are economic issues: jobs, health care, housing, the income distribution, education. What the United States has is two middle-class parties obsessed with "phony" issues: rights of free expression, gun control, feminism, animal rights, capital punishment, gay rights—issues that have little relevance for the poor but great relevance for upper-middle-class elites. (We refer to such issues as **social issues** to distinguish them from traditional economic issues.) This argument often is made by Democrats who are liberals in the older economic sense. Richard Goodwin, a former aide to President Kennedy, comments:

> Now our public leaders are happy to debate the issues of abortion or gay rights or—God save us— "family values" as a welcome diversion from the serious flaws in American life; just as in the 1920s the nation was consumed with a struggle over the right to drink alcohol as the country approached its most serious economic crisis.[58]

In the 1980s a variant of this argument claimed that it was only the Democrats who were obsessed with such issues. Republicans, it was argued, shrewdly used social issues to deflect politics from real issues, such as redistribution of the wealth controlled by Republicans! By conducting political campaigns on the basis of more symbolic, lifestyle issues, Democrats fell for the Republicans' bait. But the rise of the Religious Right in the Republican party leaves little doubt that many activists in both parties are more concerned with social than with economic issues. As a result, some argue, the mass of poorer citizens unconcerned about such issues withdraws from an irrelevant politics based on them.

**Low Turnout Discourages Individual Development**   The final argument is in some respects a counter-argument to the elitist argument that low turnout is not a problem. Classical political theorists from Aristotle to John Stuart Mill emphasized that democracy has an important educational component. Participation in democratic politics stimulates individual development. Participants become better citizens and better human beings, which in turn enables them to take politics to a higher level. From the standpoint of this argument, low turnout signifies a lost opportunity to improve both the nonparticipants and politics itself.

Some are skeptical that political participation is such an ennobling experience, and certainly, the argument is more persuasive when applied to participation in intensive face-to-face processes like local board or council meetings than to impersonal processes like voting in a national election.[59] But the argument makes the important point that voting may not only affect who wins and what they do but may also affect the voters themselves—what manner of people they are and what they want.

## *Does Turnout Matter?*

There is considerable disagreement about whether low turnout in the United States is a problem and, if so, how serious a problem it is. Good-intentioned and well-informed people disagree and offer persuasive arguments in support of their positions. For our purposes, we point out once again that much of the disagreement arises from different assumptions about what motivates voters and nonvoters. Our view is that nonvoters and voters have diverse motives. Some nonvoters are content while others are alienated, and the same goes for voters. High turnout can indicate either high approval of the political order or serious dissatisfaction with it. Nonvoters don't have much information, but as we saw in Chapter 5, neither do many voters, so raising turnout will not "dilute" the electorate very much. Low turnout does make the actual electorate somewhat less representative than the potential electorate, but not so much as critics often assume. Some potential voters undoubtedly are discouraged by a politics that discusses issues of little relevance for them, but other citizens turn out to vote precisely because of their concern with such issues. And although participation fosters citizenship, we are doubtful that the simple impersonal act of casting a vote will foster it very much. In short, we find some validity in each of the arguments presented; we reject in its entirety only the argument that elections don't matter. Low turnout is a cause for concern, yes, a cause for despair, no.

**social issues**
Issues such as obscenity, feminism, gay rights, capital punishment, and prayer in schools that reflect personal values more than economic interests.

## Chapter Summary

Popular participation in democratic elections is the essence of democracy. But in most elections, a majority of the American electorate stays away from the polls; only in presidential elections does a majority usually turn out—and just barely a majority at that. When it comes to participation in more demanding ways, even fewer people get involved.

American turnout levels are significantly lower than in other modern democracies, and they are lower than they have been even in the recent past. The international difference is not hard to explain. In many ways the United States makes voting more costly than in other countries: Registration is left to the individual, voting is less convenient, and citizens are called on to vote much more often. In addition, mobilizing agents such as parties and unions are weaker in the United States than in other modern democracies; Americans get less encouragement from larger organizations than do citizens of other democracies.

The declining rate of participation in the United States is more difficult to understand. Reforms have lowered the costs of voting, and educational levels have gone up. But Americans seem less interested in politics and less inclined to think that voting makes a difference. The explanations for such disenchantment are a matter of much debate.

Different social and economic groups vote at very different rates. In particular, the poor, the less well educated, and minorities have lower turnout rates, giving rise to a concern that the actual electorate overrepresents the wealthy, the well educated, and whites. That is certainly true to some degree, but attempts to measure the actual political effects that would follow an expansion of the electorate suggest that these would be smaller than is usually supposed because the nonvoters are not nearly so homogeneous, and do not differ from voters as much, as is usually presumed.

*Participation* is a broad term that in this chapter we have largely restricted to voting in elections. In the next chapter we consider broader, often less direct forms of participation.

---

### On the Web

The League of Women Voters
www.lwv.org
A nonpartisan political organization that encourages the informed and active participation of citizens in government.
Project Vote Smart
www.vote-smart.org/
This wide-ranging site is supported by a nonpartisan group that gathers and distributes biographical histories,

voting records, campaign finances and promises, and performance evaluations of elected officials and candidates.
A History of the Suffrage Movement
www.rochester.edu/SBA/hisindx.html
An online history project with links dealing with the Nineteenth Amendment and the history of voting rights in the United States. This site is maintained by the University of Rochester.

---

## Key Terms

compositional effect, p. 180
eligible voting-age population, p. 170
franchise, p. 163

individual motivations for voting, p. 168
mobilization, p. 170
official turnout, p. 170
psychic benefits of voting, p. 169

registered voters, p. 171
social connectedness, p. 180
social issues, p. 185
suffrage, p. 164
voting-age population, p. 170

# Suggested Readings

Ansolabehere, Steven, and Shanto Iyengar. *Going Negative.* New York: Free Press, 1995. Based mostly on experiments, this important study finds that negative ads discourage moderates from voting.

Piven, Francis, and Richard Cloward. *Why Americans Don't Vote.* New York: Pantheon, 1988. This critical commentary on nonvoting in the United States contends that "have-nots" are systematically discouraged from voting.

Rosenstone, Steven, and John Mark Hansen. *Mobilization, Participation, and Democracy in America.* New York: Macmillan, 1993. Comprehensive statistical study of electoral and governmental participation from the 1950s to the 1980s, with particular emphasis on the decline in turnout.

Teixeira, Ruy. *The Disappearing American Voter.* Washington, DC: Brookings, 1992. Comprehensive statistical study of turnout from the 1960s to the 1980s, with particular emphasis on the turnout decline and the difference between turnout in the United States and in other democracies.

Verba, Sidney, and Norman Nie. *Participation in America: Political Democracy and Social Equality.* New York: Harper & Row, 1972. Classic older study of American participation, with special emphasis on the relationship between participation and equality.

Verba, Sidney, Kay Schlozman, and Henry Brady. *Voice and Equality: Civic Volunteerism in American Politics.* Cambridge, MA: Harvard University Press, 1995. A major extension of Verba and Nie. Fascinating discussion of the development of political skills in nonpolitical contexts such as churches. Strong on attention to differences involving race, ethnicity, and gender.

Wolfinger, Raymond, and Steven Rosenstone. *Who Votes?* New Haven, CT: Yale University Press, 1980. A statistical study that relies on huge Census Bureau samples, thus providing the best estimates of the relationships between demographic characteristics and voting, though in a limited number of elections (1972 and 1974).

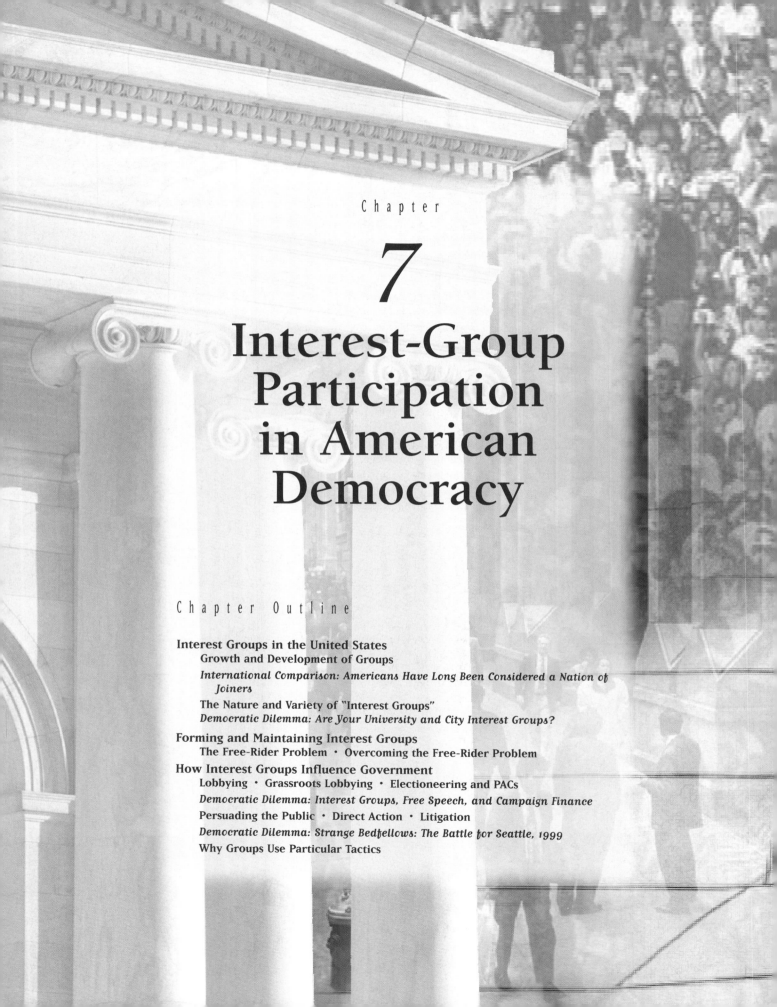

Chapter

# 7

# Interest-Group Participation in American Democracy

Chapter Outline

In February 1994, the House Education Committee was hard at work on an extension of the 1965 Elementary and Secondary Education Act, an important part of President Lyndon Johnson's Great Society legislation.[1] A subcommittee accepted an amendment by George Miller (D-CA) that would require school districts to have their teachers officially certified in subjects they teach. Districts that failed to meet this requirement would lose some of their federal education grants. This federal mandate would serve the public interest by boosting teacher qualifications, but there were political considerations as well. Teachers' unions favor such requirements, because raising teacher qualifications lowers competition for teaching positions from skilled individuals in other areas who are seeking a career change. Schools of education also favor such requirements, which increase the demand for their certification programs. Thus, for reasons of both public and private interest, public education constituencies supported the Miller proposal.

A home school advocate who had been following these obscure committee proceedings contacted Richard Armey (R-TX) to inquire whether the proposed mandate would affect home school teachers. Unbeknownst to many people, including most members of Congress at the time, between 500,000 and 1 million American children are educated at home, mostly by conservative Christian parents. Uncertain about the impact of the proposal, Armey sought the advice of the Home School Legal Defense Association. After consulting with their lawyers, the association decided that given the tendency of the courts to interpret legislative mandates broadly, there indeed was a danger that the proposed mandate might require formal certification of parents educating their children at home. The reaction was fierce and immediate. In a letter to Congress that illustrates the fevered pitch of political rhetoric today, the Home School Legal Defense Association charged that the House proposal was "the equivalent of a nuclear attack upon the home schooling community." Employing modern communications technologies, the interest group set out to mobilize the potential constituency of home schoolers and their ideological sympathizers. Electronic communications carried the warning to every corner of the United States, and in a matter of days the home school constituency generated more than half a million communications to Congress, typing up Capitol Hill switchboards and overwhelming fax machines. A few days later a second wave of electronic thunder rolled across Capitol Hill after the home school coalition convinced groups representing private schools that they, too, were endangered by the proposed mandate.

In the midst of this constituency explosion, many members of Congress—blithely unaware of what was going on in one of 275 committees and subcommittees—had gone home for the President's Day recess. Some of them were verbally ambushed at town meetings by constituents incensed by what they thought Congress was proposing to do to home schools. And when they tried to reach their offices to find out what was going on, they found the lines jammed! Armey could not get through from Texas, and other members had to call staff at their homes to learn the nature of the problem.

In the face of such an outcry, the House sounded a full retreat. Before galleries packed with home school advocates, the committee offered a floor amendment to kill the Miller provision and add statutory language specifically exempting home schools from the legislation's scope. This passed 424 to 1; only Representative Miller voted for his provision. Not completely satisfied, Armey introduced a further amendment declaring that the legislation did not "permit, allow, encourage or authorize any federal control over any aspect of any private, religious or home school." Just to be on the safe side, the Democratic-controlled House passed this amendment too, 374 to 53.

THIS EPISODE GRAPHICALLY ILLUSTRATES SEVERAL FEATURES of modern American democracy. First, although most citizens do not participate actively in politics as individuals, many are associated with groups that are very active in politics. Second, mobilizing ordinarily inactive citizens can be a highly effective way to exert political influence. Third, interest groups have adopted state-of-the-art technologies to supplement or even replace the more traditional strategies of group influence (lobbying office holders in Washington and working to elect sympathetic candidates). Fourth, elected officials are highly responsive to organized and aroused interests.

In this chapter we examine interest groups and how they influence government. Specifically, we consider these questions:

- What kinds of interest groups are there and how are they organized to communicate their views?
- What problems do interest groups face in mobilizing their members and how do they overcome these obstacles?
- How do interest groups influence government?
- How influential are interest groups?
- Do interest groups contribute to or detract from democratic government?

## Interest Groups in the United States

As we saw in Chapter 6, with the exception of voting, only small minorities of Americans participate directly in politics. But large majorities participate indirectly by joining or supporting **interest groups**—organizations or associations of people with common interests that participate in politics on behalf of their members. Although only half the adult population votes in presidential elections, more than three-quarters of Americans belong to at least one group; on average they belong to two; and they make financial contributions to four.[2] In comparison to citizens of other nations, Americans are joiners (see the accompanying International Comparison).

Of course, not all the groups with which people are associated are political groups—many are social clubs, charities, service organizations, church groups, and so forth—but there are literally thousands of groups that do engage in politics, and even seemingly nonpolitical groups often engage in political activity. For example, parent–teacher organizations often are active in school politics; neighborhood associations lobby about traffic, crime, and zoning policies; and even hobby or recreation groups mobilize when they perceive threats to their interests—witness the National Rifle Association!

**interest group**
Organization or association of people with common interests that engages in politics on behalf of its members.

### Growth and Development of Groups

Americans have a long-standing reputation for forming groups. In his classic book *Democracy in America*, Alexis de Tocqueville, the nineteenth-century French visitor to the United States noted that

## International Comparison

## Americans Have Long Been Considered a Nation of Joiners

Although Americans are less likely to vote than people in other democracies, they are more likely to join groups. International surveys conducted in the early 1990s found that of nine countries studied, only the Dutch joined groups at a rate comparable to that in the United States. In four of the countries surveyed, a majority of citizens reported belonging to no groups.[a]

Interestingly, the United States differs most from the rest of the world in the proportion of people who belong to religious organizations: Nearly half of all Americans report belonging to one. This is consistent with our discussion of the continued importance of religion in American political culture and of the role religion continues to play in American politics. The Dutch score so high because they are second only to the United States in religious group memberships, and they lead all countries surveyed in membership in educational, cultural, and environmental organizations.

*What do you think?*
- *Given that Americans value individualism, why do you think Americans are such joiners?*
- *Have Americans gone overboard on groups? Are there so many that they fragment the population and prevent people from seeing the things we have in common?*
- *Is there a negative relationship between the size and importance*

of government and the number and importance of groups—the more important a country's government, the less important its groups, and vice versa? Explain.

| | Percent Belonging to No Groups | Percent Belonging to Four or More Groups |
|---|---|---|
| Netherlands | 15 | 31 |
| United States | 18 | 19 |
| Germany | 33 | 8 |
| Canada | 35 | 16 |
| Britain | 46 | 9 |
| Italy | 59 | 4 |
| France | 61 | 4 |
| Mexico | 64 | 4 |
| Spain | 70 | 2 |

[a]Figures drawn from the World Values Surveys, 1990–1993, reported in *The Public Perspective*, April/May, 1995: 21.

Americans . . . are forever forming associations. They are not only commercial and industrial associations . . . but others of a thousand other types—religious, moral, serious, futile, very general and very limited, immensely large and very minute. . . . [A]t the head of any new undertaking, where in France you would find the government or in England some territorial magnate, in the United States you are sure to find an association.[3]

Moreover, if James Madison is to be believed, Americans—indeed, all people—come by their associative tendencies naturally. In his famous essay on factions ("Federalist 10") Madison writes,

The latent causes of faction are thus sown in the nature of man . . . [and] the most common and durable source of factions has been the various and unequal distribution of property. Those who hold and those who are without property have ever formed distinct interests in society. Those who are creditors and those who are debtors. . . . A landed interest, a manufacturing interest, a mercantile interest, a moneyed interest, with many lesser interests, grow up of necessity in civilized nations, and divide them into different classes, actuated by different sentiments and views.

However natural and long-standing the American propensity to form interest groups, there is no doubt that there are more organized groups today than ever before. In fact, one study found that 40 percent of the associations with Washington offices were formed after 1960.[4] Group formation in the United States has not been a steady, gradual process; rather, it has occurred in several waves, with the greatest wave of group formation in American history occurring in the 1960s and 1970s.

Before the Civil War, there were few national organizations in America. Life in general was local. The social organization of the United States was one of "island communities" not connected to each other by social and economic links.[5] There was no "national" economy; instead, regions produced and consumed much of what they used themselves. As the railroads connected the country after the Civil War, a national economy developed, and national associations were not far behind. The first two decades after the war saw the birth of national agricultural associations like the Grange and of trade unions like the Knights of Labor and the American Federation of Labor.

Another major wave of group organization occurred during the Progressive era, roughly 1890 to 1917. Many of today's most broad-based associations date from that era: the Chamber of Commerce, the National Association of Manufacturers, and the American Farm Bureau Federation, for example. The members of these associations have common economic interests, but other associations founded during the Progressive era had other goals. For example, the National Association for the Advancement of Colored People (NAACP) was formed as part of an effort to promote equality for black Americans, and the National Audubon Society was formed to promote conservation.

The 1960–1980 wave of group formation is by far the largest and the most heterogeneous. Thousands of additional economic groups formed, but these tended to be more narrowly based than earlier ones: The American Soybean Association, the National Corn Growers Association, the Rocky Mountain Llama and Alpaca Association, and numerous other specialized organizations joined the more general agricultural associations. Similarly, in the commercial and manufacturing sectors, numerous specialized groups joined the older, more broad-based groups.

Numerous nonprofit groups formed as well, many representing people who work in the public sector. What are sometimes called "government interest groups" proliferated as older national associations of mayors, governors, teachers, and social workers were joined by newer, more specialized associations like the National Association of State and Provincial Lotteries, the Association of State Drinking Water Administrators, and the U.S. Police Canine Association. Similarly, nongovernmental non–profit-sector groups now include all kinds of specialized occupational associations. Examples of particular interest to many readers of this book include the National Association of Student Financial Aid Administrators and the National Association of Graduate Admissions Professionals.

Innumerable shared interest groups have formed in recent decades. Some are actively political, working for particular points of view. Liberal groups such as the National Organization for Women (NOW, a feminist group) and People for the American Way (a civil liberties group) are deeply involved in politics, as are such conservative groups as the Christian Coalition (which promotes traditional morality) and Operation Rescue (an antiabortion group). Many "citizens" groups, such as Common Cause (a political reform group), Greenpeace (an environmental group), the National Taxpayers' Union (an antitax and antispending group), and numerous other environmental, consumer, and "watchdog" groups, are less than a generation old. A subset of such groups are called single-issue groups because of their narrow focus. Well-known examples include pro-choice and pro-life groups, the NRA, and some environmental groups.

www.longmanparticipate.com

participation

**Interest Groups and Gun Control**

### A "Single-Issue Group"—The National Rifle Association

The NRA was founded shortly after the Civil War to promote marksmanship, and it grew into an organization of hunters, target shooters, and gun collectors. By the mid-twentieth century, the NRA operated firearms and hunter safety programs and trained law enforcement officers. With a presence in every state, it takes the lead in opposing gun control legislation. Its PAC is usually one of the top ten contributors to congressional elections, and it employs some 80 lobbyists. The NRA is one of the best examples of a "single-issue group," a group focused on one issue to the exclusion of virtually everything else.

Other groups are not primarily political but have a political side. For example, the American Association of Retired Persons (AARP), established in 1958, has become the largest voluntary association that has ever existed, with upwards of 33 million members—and still growing! AARP is a major player whenever social security or Medicare is on the political agenda. Under the right circumstances almost any group may become involved in politics. Associations representing those who fish monitor water policy in particular and natural resources policies in general. Associations representing snowmobilers and mountain bikers make themselves heard when government threatens to restrict their use of public lands. Nearly every significant interest or activity in American society has groups that represent it.

Several factors contribute to the explosion of groups and associations during the past generation. First, the expansion of government activity has given people more reason to form groups. Business groups, for instance, may form in reaction to governmental regulation or because they see an opportunity to procure a government subsidy. Second, advances in communications technology have made groups easier to form. Simply learning about the existence of other people with common interests was difficult a generation ago, especially if they were scattered across wide geographic areas. Today, computer databases permit the generation of all kinds of specialized mailing lists, and once identified, people with common interests can communicate easily and cheaply via the Internet. Third, formation of a group to advance some interest may stimulate the formation of other groups opposed to that interest. The pro-life movement formed at least in part because of the activities of the pro-choice movement.[6] Similarly, the ranching, mining, lumber, and sporting interests that launched the "Sagebrush rebellion" were reacting to the success of the environmental movement. Mobilization of one interest stimulates counter-mobilization of opposing interests.

timeline
**Interest Groups in America**

## *The Nature and Variety of "Interest Groups"*

Robert Salisbury has called attention to the variety of groups, associations, and organizations included under the term *interest groups*.[7] Some have elaborate formal organizations with membership dues, journals, meetings, conventions, and so forth; the American Medical Association is a well-known example. Others are little more than an address where sympathizers send contributions; one study found that of 83 public interest groups examined, 30 had no membership.[8] Some, like Common Cause, are "membership groups" composed of numerous private individuals who make voluntary contributions. Others are associations consisting of corporate or institutional representatives who pay regular dues; trade associations and associations of universities are examples. Some large corporations maintain their own Washington offices, as do hundreds of state, city, and county governments and even universities. As you can see in the accompanying Democratic Dilemma, institutions, corporations, and governments are not really "groups" in the usual sense, although they certainly are "interests."

One researcher estimated that almost 80 percent of the interest groups in existence in the 1980s represented professional or occupational constituencies.[9] For such groups, economic matters are of crucial concern, but these groups are about equally divided between those representing profit-sector constituencies and those representing public and non–profit-sector constituencies, so they do not exert a uniformly conservative influence on government taxing and spending policies. The other 20 percent of American interest groups reflect the activities of citizens with particular interests, including those spawned by what are called social movements: broad-based reform or protest movements that bring new issues to the agenda. The civil rights movement, the environmental movement, the women's movement, and the religious right are important contemporary examples. We shall have more to say about these later in the chapter.

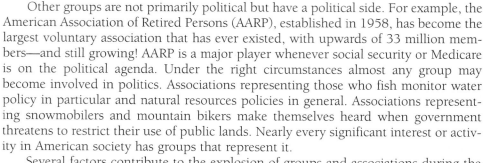

**Protecting a Hobby**
Associations representing hobbyists such as mountain bikers and snowmobilers make themselves heard when government threatens to restrict their use of public lands. *How hard or easy is it to organize a group of mountain bikers to lobby the government?*

## Democratic Dilemma

# Are Your University and City Interest Groups?

On hearing the term *interest group* you don't immediately think of a college, university, or town. But American universities and cities are in fact quite active in lobbying government.

Public universities, of course, get budget subsidies from state and local governments, but private universities lobby federal and state governments on matters ranging from student aid to building construction to research funding. Interestingly, a recent study showed that the top 10 universities in reported lobbying expenditures were all private. Stanford (number 8) officials noted that the data are unreliable because 400 of the 475 colleges and universities queried did not file reports, taking advantage of ambiguities and technicalities in the law to deny that their activities amounted to lobbying.

**University Lobbying (reported to IRS, fiscal year 1997)**

| | |
|---|---|
| 1. Boston University | $846,993 |
| 2. University of Miami | 693,289 |
| 3. Tufts | 494,880 |
| 4. Harvard | 470,000 |
| 5. Columbia | 440,000 |
| 6. Rochester Institute of Technology | 384,263 |
| 7. Drexel | 366,232 |
| 8. Stanford | 335,476 |
| 9. George Washington | 333,211 |
| 10. MIT | 297,815 |

Just as we do not ordinarily think of a university as an interest group, we do not usually think of cities and other governmental units as interest groups. But such units spend millions of dollars ($34 million in 1998) in attempts to shape federal programs and gain federal funding. The top 10 government spenders on lobbying in 1998 were as follows:

| | |
|---|---|
| 1. Commonwealth of Puerto Rico | $4,000,000 |
| 2. Commonwealth of Northern Mariana Islands | 1,300,000 |
| 3. City and County of Denver | 840,000 |
| 4. Los Angeles County | 720,000 |
| 5. Miami/Dade County | 690,000 |
| 6. City of Chicago | 500,000 |
| 7. City of Sacramento | 470,000 |
| 8. San Diego County | 460,000 |
| 9. Orange County, CA | 459,000 |
| 10. Metro Transit Authority of Harris County, TX | 420,000 |

*What do you think?*
- *How might cities or universities differ from other interest groups? How would they be similar?*
- *What local or state issues would be most important to your university or community?*

SOURCES: Betsy Carroll, "Stanford Ranked Eighth," *The Stanford Daily*, November 6, 1998, 1. "Spending on Lobbying Rises," *USA Today*, November 16, 1999, 11A.

## Forming and Maintaining Interest Groups

That so many people belong to so many groups and associations often leads people to overlook the difficulties many groups face.[10] But consider these facts:

There are about 104 million women over the age of 18 in the United States. Polls indicate that more than half have feminist sympathies. But the largest feminist group, NOW, has fewer than 300,000 members.

There are approximately 34 million African Americans in the United States, but the NAACP has only about 500,000 members—including whites.

About 40 million American households have at least one gun, but the membership of the NRA is only 2.8 million.

Majorities of Americans consistently support spending more on the environment, but the combined membership of seven large environmental groups is about 6.5 million (and this double- and triple-counts those who belong to more than one organization).[11]

As these examples suggest, millions of people do *not* join or support associations whose interests they share. Common interest may be a necessary condition for joining a group, but it is far from a sufficient one.

**Telephoning for Contributions**
This is a particularly challenging but necessary task for any interest group. *What sort of strategies might an interest group employ to persuade citizens to give money? Who would they call, members of the group or citizens-at-large?*

Why then do people join or decline to join groups? The question is important, because the answer bears on how well or how poorly interest groups represent the American citizenry. If some kinds of interests are not fairly represented, politics may be biased, despite the existence of thousands of groups with whom millions of people are affiliated.

Like voting, joining or supporting a group requires some investment of *resources*; that is, it involves costs. Contributing money or paying dues is the most obvious example, but the time required for group activities also can be a significant cost. People who have more resources will find participation easier. Thus it is no surprise that the affluent contribute more than the poor and that two-worker families with small children participate less than those whose family situations give them more free time.[12] More generally, a large institution or corporation has more resources to contribute than a solitary citizen. But whether rich or poor, one commits resources only if the *incentive* to do so—the expected benefit—justifies the investment.

Incentives take many forms, and different groups rely on different incentives. James Q. Wilson divides incentives into three categories.[13] The first he calls *solidary*. Some people join a group for social reasons: they simply wish to associate with particular kinds of people. Activity groups and church groups are examples. Where solidary incentives are dominant, membership in the group is an end in itself. Many groups (probably the majority) are composed of individuals who join for solidary reasons, but most such groups are nonpolitical. Conversely, it is unlikely that people join the National Taxpayers' Union to enjoy the company of other taxpayers, and people certainly do not send checks to such associations for social purposes!

A second category of incentives is *material*. Such incentives are economic rather than social: Some people join a group because membership confers tangible benefits. This is obviously the dominant incentive in economic groups and associations. IBM does not belong to various trade associations because its executives like to socialize with other computer executives—they have plenty of other opportunities to do that. IBM belongs because the trade associations are seen as a way of protecting and advancing corporate interests. Material incentives also play a role in some political groups. Those who join taxpayers' associations hope to reduce their taxes. Those who join groups that support government subsidies or services for people like themselves (realtors, the handicapped, the old, farmers) similarly hope to gain material benefits.

Finally, some people join groups for *purposive* reasons: People are committed to and wish to advance the group's social and political goals. They want to save the whales, to bring about a liberal or conservative Congress, to end abortion or to preserve freedom of choice. Given that many politically active groups espouse purposive goals, such incentives, along with the material incentives we have just discussed, would appear to be the dominant factor underlying the formation and persistence of most of the groups that are active in politics. Things are not so simple as they appear, however.

## The Free-Rider Problem

**free-rider problem**
Exists when people can enjoy the benefits of group activity without bearing any of the costs.

Groups that rely on purposive and material incentives face what is known as the **free-rider problem:** People can enjoy the benefits of group activity without bearing any of the costs. Thus they have an incentive to "free ride" on the efforts of others.[14] This problem arises when individuals perceive that attainment of the group goal has little relationship to their personal contribution. If you donate $20 to Greenpeace, does your contribution guarantee the survival of some identifiable baby seal? If you donate several hours of your time to march for the end of hunger, does your contribution measurably reduce the amount of malnutrition in the world? If you recycle everything you use and take care to buy only nonpolluting products, does your personal effort make any measurable difference in the amount of global pollution? Although most well-meaning people are reluctant to admit it, in each case the truthful answer is no.

These examples have two common elements. First, on reflection, people realize that their personal impact is virtually nonexistent. If you don't contribute, just as many baby seals will live or die, world hunger will be no different, and global pollution will be the same. So if your contribution makes no difference, why contribute? The second element makes matters worse: Individuals receive the benefit whether they contribute or not. If many others do contribute and do save some seals, reduce world hunger, or alleviate global pollution, you enjoy those outcomes even if you did not contribute. So if you get the same benefit regardless of your actions, why contribute? These two conditions are major obstacles to group formation and survival. When they hold, the temptation is for individuals not to participate themselves but rather, to free ride on the contributions of others. And if most people feel that way, the group may die or fail to form in the first place.

Two considerations affect the severity of the free-rider problem. First, other things being equal, the larger the group, the greater the problem. A few neighbors can pool their efforts to clean up a vacant lot that adjoins their properties. It is easy to identify who doesn't show up and subject them to social pressure. It would be unthinkable, however, for a large city to rely on volunteer effort to maintain city parks. Each resident's personal responsibility is small, and social pressure is less effective where people do not know each other. Thus cities pay city employees or private contractors to maintain their parks.

Second, other things equal, the free-rider problem is more serious the greater the distance and abstractness of the benefit the group seeks to achieve. It is much easier to see one's personal impact on cleaning up a vacant lot than on cleaning the atmosphere. It is much easier to see one's personal impact on feeding the poor in a specific locale than on reducing world hunger.

At issue here are what economists call **public goods**, as distinct from **private goods**. A tomato is a private good. In order to consume it, you must pay the cost, in the sense that you must grow it or purchase it. Moreover, if you consume it, others cannot. World peace, in contrast, is a public good. In order to enjoy it, you need not contribute in any way to achieving it. And if you enjoy it, others are in no way prevented from enjoying it as well. Economists believe that because free riders can enjoy or consume public goods even if they make no contribution to their provision, such goods typically are provided at lower than optimal levels.[15]

It is important to recognize that material goods can be public goods; therefore, groups and associations that seek material benefits also face free-rider problems. If

**public goods**
Goods that you can enjoy without contributing—by free riding on the efforts of those who do.

**private goods**
Goods that you must purchase to enjoy, and your consumption of which precludes that of others.

**Making a Statement**
Large numbers of Americans sometimes donate their time and effort to general causes, as in marches to end hunger. *What types of causes see this kind of mass support? And which types will engage in more direct lobbying of legislators?*

General Motors lobbies successfully for a tariff or quota on Japanese cars, Ford will enjoy the benefits (lower competition, higher prices) even if Ford did not aid GM in the lobbying effort. If members of the Corn Growers' Association pool their efforts to get a higher corn subsidy, even growers who are not members of the association reap the benefit of the higher subsidy. The free-rider problem is widespread. Only those groups based on social incentives escape it; because membership itself is the benefit in such groups, there is no incentive to free ride.

The most important implication of the free-rider problem for democratic politics lies in the kinds of groups best able to overcome it. Our discussion suggests that, other things being equal, small groups organized for narrow purposes have an organizational advantage over large groups organized for broad purposes. We call the former groups "special" interests and the latter "general" or "public" interests. For example, a small number of corporations will find it relatively easy to organize an association to lobby for regulations that raise prices; the millions of consumers who buy the products the corporations sell will find it much more difficult to organize an association to lobby against such anticompetitive regulations. The free-rider problem implies that in democratic politics special interests generally are advantaged relative to general interests.

## Overcoming the Free-Rider Problem

On first learning about the free-rider problem, some skeptics protest, "What if everyone felt that way?" Well, a great many people do; that is why so many groups mobilize such a small proportion of their potential constituencies. Consumers, taxpayers, environmentalists, conservatives, and liberals all enlist only a small proportion of the people who sympathize with their goals. Still, there are groups that represent broad purposive interests like these. How do these groups manage to overcome the free-rider problem? History reveals a number of useful strategies.

**Coercion**  If members of a labor union strike for higher wages, how can they prevent nonunion workers from enjoying the results? Historically, the answer has been coercion. Social pressure and even violence have been used to coerce reluctant workers to join unions or prevent them from crossing union picket lines. Because violence is costly to inflict and often brings violence in return, unions preferred to rely on a strategy of negotiating "closed shops" with management. Such agreements permit only union members to work, and they require workers to join the union as a condition of employment.

Milder forms of coercion are still widespread, although they are often unrecognized. For example, professional and occupational associations may lobby governmental jurisdictions to hire, approve, or certify only their members, thus making membership a condition of working or practicing in that jurisdiction. The practice of law usually requires membership in the state bar, the practice of specialized trades such as plumbing may require a state license, and teachers usually must be state-certified to teach in public schools. Such requirements are ways of coercing potential free riders into joining the associations that represent their trades and professions.

Although it has been very effective historically, coercion appears to be a declining means of overcoming the free-rider problem. The union movement has fallen on hard times, its membership declining from more than one-third of the workforce to less than one-sixth, as shown in Figure 7.1. Privatization is on the increase, and the general trend toward deregulation opens up occupations to competition.

**Social Movements**  There are also times when people do not think individualistically, as they do when they free ride. Consider the Patrons of Husbandry, more commonly known as the Grange. The first Grange chapter was established in 1867. As the railroads expanded after the Civil War, farmers and local communities became increasingly upset with railroad practices. Their discontent soon took organized form. In the spring of 1873 there were 3,360 Grange chapters, by fall the number had more

**The Grange**
The Grange was an important nineteenth-century social movement. It was built at the grassroots by farmers, starting in 1867.

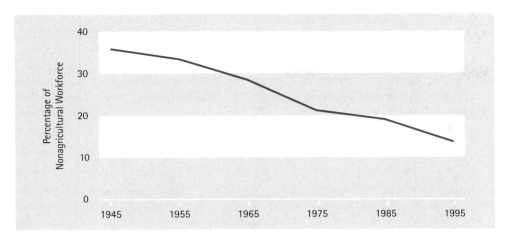

**Figure 7.1**

**Union Membership Has Declined Significantly Since Mid-Century**

SOURCE: George Kurian, *Datapedia of the United States: 1790–2000* (Lantham, MD: Bernham Press, 1994), p. 80; *Almanac of the 50 States,* 1997 edition (Palo Alto, CA: Information Publications, 1997).

than doubled to 7,325, and less than a year later it had exploded to 20,365. Political institutions yielded to this popular uprising and legislated against the financial power of the railroad corporations. Many states, especially in the Midwest, passed so-called Granger laws regulating railroad prices and practices.[16] Even the Republican-dominated House of Representatives thought it prudent to pass a national law in 1874.[17]

Such **social movements**—broad-based demands for government action on a problem or issue—have a long history in American politics. The abolitionist movement is one of the best known. Dedicated to ending slavery, this movement forced the issue onto the national agenda and played a role in the political upheaval of the 1850s and, ultimately, in the outbreak of the Civil War. Other nineteenth-century social movements included the Populists and labor in the 1880s and 1890s and the women's suffrage movement, which culminated in passage of the Nineteenth Amendment in 1920.

> **social movement**
> Broad-based demand for government action on some problem or issue, such as civil rights for blacks and women or environmental protection.

In modern times the civil rights movement is probably the best-known example of a social movement. As discussed in Chapter 17, the massive demonstrations of the 1960s evolved from a few sit-ins and boycotts in the 1950s. The movement culminated with the adoption of landmark federal legislation: the Civil Rights Act of 1964 and the Voting Rights Act of 1965.

Other movements soon followed. On April 22, 1970, Earth Day marked the sudden eruption of an environmental movement. Within the year we had an Environmental Protection Agency and a Clean Air Act. As we discuss in Chapter 17, the women's movement took off at about the same time, flexing its muscle in the 1972–1982 campaign for ratification of the Equal Rights Amendment (ERA), which succeeded in 35 states, 3 short of the three-fourths majority needed to adopt a constitutional amendment.[18] On the other side of the political spectrum, the ranks of the religious right swelled in the late 1970s and contributed to Ronald Reagan's presidential victories in the 1980s and to the Republican congressional resurgence of the 1990s.[19] The movement supports constitutional amendments to outlaw abortion and allow prayer in schools, but, like the feminists, the religious right has been unable as yet to achieve constitutional change.

Social movements build on emotional or moral fervor. Many of those active within them dedicate themselves to what they see as a higher cause. When individuals adopt a moral perspective, or when they think more collectively than individually, they may ignore the considerations that normally would lead them to free ride. As the examples cited demonstrate, social movements can mobilize interests and alter the policies and practices of government.

Still, social movements typically mobilize only small proportions of their prospective constituencies. Some people can be induced to think in moral or collective terms, but not many. Moreover, for most people, emotional and moral fervor are temporary conditions that they cannot sustain for long periods. Thus a social movement has a tendency to "run down" as its emotional basis subsides. Some scholars argue that conservative forces in politics often can stall social movements until they weaken, leaving things much as before. Murray Edelman, for example, suggests that under pressure from a social movement, Congress may pass a statute that establishes a regulatory agency or commission. But as the movement subsides, the regulators increasingly operate in an environment dominated by the more entrenched economic interests they are supposed to regulate. In the end, the payoff to the movement is more symbolic than substantive.[20] For a social movement to exert continued long-term influence, it must find a way to "institutionalize" itself—to spin off organized groups and formal associations that will continue to work for its interests.

**Selective Benefits**    Many groups that work to achieve collective goods also provide their members with valuable private goods. A professional association may make membership a condition of subscribing to a journal that contains occupationally useful information. A trade association may inform its members about important technological advances. Agricultural associations may provide their membership with information about new varieties of crops, new growing methods, and so forth. In short, people, corporations, and institutions may join associations less to support the collective goods that the association favors than for the specific private goods the association provides—selectively—to members: its **selective benefits**.

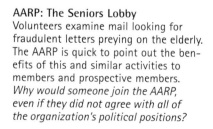

**selective benefits**
Side benefits of belonging to an organization that are limited to contributing members of the organization.

The American Association of Retired Persons (AARP) offers the most notable example of this strategy for overcoming the free-rider problem. For a mere $8 per year, members gain access to the world's largest mail-order pharmacy (where volume buying keeps prices low); low-cost auto, health, and life insurance; discounts on hotels, air fares, and car rentals; and numerous other benefits. Even a senior citizen who disagrees with the political positions of AARP finds it hard to forgo membership!

Selective benefits are not limited to direct economic ones or to information that indirectly produces economic benefits. Anything that people like and that can be selectively provided can be a selective benefit. Some environmental groups produce magazines full of beautiful pictures, organize outings and activities, rate outdoor clothing and equipment, and so forth. These and other benefits of membership often are sufficient to induce people to pay the modest amounts that membership requires.

In short, what you think of as the principal reason for a group's existence may not be the principal reason why many people belong. Just the opposite may be true—in

**AARP: The Seniors Lobby**
Volunteers examine mail looking for fraudulent letters preying on the elderly. The AARP is quick to point out the benefits of this and similar activities to members and prospective members. *Why would someone join the AARP, even if they did not agree with all of the organization's political positions?*

the minds of members—the political activity in which the group engages may be secondary to the selective benefits it provides.

**Patrons and Political Entrepreneurs** Discussions of the free-rider problem typically reflect a bottom-up notion of how groups form. The implicit assumption is that individual people, corporations, or institutions band together and form associations. Recent research, however, indicates that the process of group formation often is more top-down than bottom-up. Many groups owe their existence to a **political entrepreneur**, an individual or a small number of individuals who take the lead in setting up and operating the group.[21]

In the first place, some individuals, institutions, or corporations may be so rich or have such a stake in the group goal that it is worth their while to act independently or alone. Microsoft, General Motors, the State of California, and hundreds of other actors have their own Washington offices staffed by paid employees, because they have a great deal at stake and are sufficiently powerful that their activities and contributions can make a difference. Such large actors do not face a free-rider problem; for them, maintaining a lobbying arm is just a good business decision. Sometimes an association will be dominated by a single large firm that bears most of the costs but allows other members to free ride to give the appearance of a broad base of support. Ralston-Purina in the feed industry is an example.

Similarly, a rich individual with a deep commitment to the group goal may be able to make a difference. Your $20 contribution to Greenpeace may have no measurable impact, but if you are in a position to give a million dollars, you can probably save some seals. Foundations also support groups with grants and contracts. The W. Alton Jones Foundation and the Ford Foundation give millions of dollars a year to environmental groups.[22] Similarly, conservative foundations help to fund the Wise Use Movement that opposes traditional environmental groups.

In the second place, political entrepreneurs often set up and maintain a group for their own reasons. Their motives are varied. Some feel so strongly about a goal that they are willing to let others free ride on them. We call such people fanatical or dedicated, depending on whether we sympathize with their goals. An ascetic lawyer, Ralph Nader, did more than anyone else to organize the consumer movement and has devoted his life to it. A Missouri activist, Phyllis Schlafly, organized the anti-ERA cause. Ross Perot founded and subsidized his own political party. Many (though not all) such individuals have passed up opportunities to parlay their visibility into riches or political office, and this restraint suggests that their commitment to broader goals is genuine.

Of course, some political entrepreneurs do have ulterior motives. They may be aspiring politicians who see an opportunity to use new groups as the basis of future constituencies. Candidates for city and state offices often emerge from neighborhood associations and local protest groups. Perhaps these individuals were just swept along by political tides; on the other hand, their local work may have been a way to position themselves for future election campaigns.

In addition to wealthy patrons and dedicated or self-interested political entrepreneurs, the government itself did much to organize the new groups of the 1960s and 1970s. As the role of government expanded, federal bureaucracies needed new ways to implement programs through a decentralized federal system that mixed both public and private elements. One strategy was to stimulate and subsidize organizations: state and local elected officials; state and local employees such as social workers, police officers, and firefighters; public- and private-sector professionals such as educators, health providers, environmental engineers, and so forth. Once formed, the groups could be used to help develop standards and regulations and to publicize them and carry them out. In addition to the administrative utility of such groups, they were politically useful as well: Not surprisingly, groups and associations that receive federal funds are more than twice as likely to support expanded government activity—and, by implication, the elected officials who expand it—as groups that do not.[23]

> **political entrepreneurs**
> People willing to assume the costs of forming and maintaining an organization even when others may free-ride on them.

Note, incidentally, that although government has been a prominent source of support for the groups established since 1960, this is by no means a new governmental role. The Grange (discussed earlier) was founded by an employee of the U.S. Agriculture Department in 1867. The first local chapter was Potomac 1 and was composed of government workers and their wives.

The available evidence suggests that the top-down activities of patrons and political entrepreneurs are a more important means of overcoming the free-rider problem than the provision of selective benefits—AARP is not the typical case.[24] Wealthy individuals, government agencies, corporations, and private foundations have been important sources of support for non–profit-sector groups, especially citizens groups. About 90 percent of the latter have received such subsidies.

### Section Summary

The free-rider problem encountered by interest groups certainly can be overcome through coercion (as with picket lines of strikers); emotional or moral commitment to the group's cause (as in social movements); offering selective benefits (as does the AARP); and patrons and political entrepreneurs (Ralph Nader, foundations, and Ross Perot, for example). Not only are special interests represented in American politics, but general interests are represented as well. Still, there is little doubt that the free-rider problem creates a bias in the interest-group system. Political scientists have long found that the interest-group system is dominated by business interests, and this remains true today. Indeed, despite the large increase in the number of groups active in politics, including many citizens groups, a thorough analysis suggests that business dominance of the Washington interest-group universe is even more pronounced than it was several decades ago.[25]

## How Interest Groups Influence Government

The variety of groups, associations, and institutions that make up the interest-group universe engage in a wide array of political activities. We first discuss these political activities, which include government lobbying, grassroots lobbying, electioneering and political action committees, persuading the public, direct action, and litigation. Then we focus on why groups choose particular tactics over others.

### Lobbying

**lobbying**
Attempts by representatives of groups and associations to directly influence the decisions of government officials.

Many interest groups attempt to influence government the old-fashioned way: by lobbying public officials. **Lobbying** consists of attempts by group representatives personally to influence the decisions of public officials. Groups and associations draft bills for friendly legislators to introduce, testify before congressional committees and in agency proceedings, meet with elected officials and present their cases (sometimes at posh resorts where the official is the guest), and provide public officials with information. In these and other ways, group representatives try to influence those who make governmental decisions. Corporations account for the lion's share of traditional lobbying, spending upwards of $1.5 billion per year.[26]

**lobbyist**
One who engages in lobbying.

People who engage in lobbying are called **lobbyists**, although the term is usually reserved for those who do it as their primary job. Some lobbyists are so-called hired guns, people who will use their contacts and expertise in the service of anyone willing to pay their price, but some of the best known are closely associated with one party or the other. Many large groups and associations have their own staff lobbyists. Smaller groups and groups not often involved in politics may hire lobbyists on a part-time basis or share a lobbyist with other groups. Some groups simply have their own leaders engage in lobbying, although these individuals typically are not called lobbyists. There are federal and state laws that require lobbyists to register, but because of disagreement about what lobbying is and who is a lobbyist, as well as lack of enforce-

**Lobbyists at Work**
Three gentlemen collectively representing the Public Health Association, the Campaign for Tobacco Free Kids and the American Heart Association. *What strategies are most effective for these interest groups, focused on protecting the public health?*

ment, those who register are only a fraction of those engaged in lobbying.[27] For example, the *American Lobbyists Directory* lists 65,000 legally registered federal and state lobbyists, but estimates are that in Washington alone, there are upwards of 90,000.[28]

The term *lobbyist* has negative connotations (we doubt that many parents would want their child to grow up to be one). Movies, novels, and even the newspapers often portray lobbyists as unsavory characters who operate on the borders of what is ethical or legal—and often step across them. Research suggests that this is an exaggeration. Although there are examples of shady or corrupt behavior by lobbyists, given the number of lobbyists and the amount of lobbying that goes on, such transgressions are hardly the norm. Certainly, most analysts believe that corrupt behavior by interest-group lobbyists is less widespread today than in previous eras of American history. Numerous conflict-of-interest laws and regulations, along with an investigative media ever on the lookout for a hint of scandal, make outright corruption in today's politics relatively rare.

For the most part, lobbyists provide public officials with information and supporting arguments. They tend to deal with officials already sympathetic to their position and to support those officials' activities. Lobbyists have little incentive to distort information or lie; to do so would destroy their credibility and undermine their future effectiveness. Of course, they emphasize arguments and information favorable to their viewpoint, but they do not want to hurt their political allies by lying, concealing information, or otherwise exposing them to an embarrassing counterattack. Many political scientists think that lobbyists serve a useful purpose, injecting valuable information into the legislative process. As former Senator and President John Kennedy observed,

> Competent lobbyists can present the most persuasive arguments in support of their positions. Indeed, there is no more effective manner of learning all important arguments and facts on a controversial issue than to have the opposing lobbyists present their case.[29]

With the explosive growth of interest groups during the past generation, there is undoubtedly more old-fashioned lobbying than ever before. The number of corporate and trade association offices in Washington doubled between 1970 and 1980. Membership in the District of Columbia Bar Association more than tripled between 1973 and 1983. Registered lobbyists increased sixfold between 1960 and 1980.[30] In part, such developments were stimulated by the democratization of Congress and the

**simulation**
**You are a Lobbyist**

**The Five Commandments of Lobbying Congress**

1. Tell the truth.

2. Never promise more than you can deliver.

3. Know how to listen so that you accurately understand what you are hearing.

4. Staff are there to be worked with and not circumvented.

5. Spring no surprises.

From Bruce Wolpe and Bertram Levine, *Lobbying Congress* (Washington, DC: CQ Press, 1996), ch. 2.

expansion of government. Whereas in 1950 a group might lobby only one powerful committee chair or a key staffer, by 1980 it had to lobby numerous subcommittee chairs as well as the rank and file and many of their staff.

## Grassroots Lobbying

Today, Washington lobbying is often combined with so-called grassroots lobbying: Inside-the-beltway persuasion is supplemented with outside-the-beltway pressure. Whereas lobbying consists of attempts to influence government officials *directly*, **grassroots lobbying** consists of attempts to influence officials *indirectly* through their constituents. The home schooling example that opened this chapter illustrates the process. A Washington association communicates with its grassroots supporters, who in turn put pressure on their elected representatives. As one health care lobbyist put it recently,

> One of the perceptions about lobbying is that you go out drinking, and the guy's your buddy so he does you favors. . . . Those days are long gone. That sort of thing may work on tiny things like a technical amendment to a bill, but on big, important issues personal friendships don't mean a thing. I'll bet we could have done just as good a job as we did [on influencing health care reform] without ever going to the Hill or ever talking to a member of Congress. It is knowing when and how to ask the troops in the field to do it.[31]

**grassroots lobbying**
Efforts by groups and associations to influence elected officials indirectly, by arousing their constituents.

For several reasons, grassroots lobbying probably is more prevalent today than in the past. First, as we have noted, Congress is more decentralized. When only a few leaders need to be persuaded, an inside-the-beltway strategy of influence may suffice, but when dozens need to be persuaded, reaching out and touching their constituents may be more effective. Second, government in general is more open than in the past. It is not so easy for Washington insiders to make private deals; it is more important than ever to show that there is popular support for your group's position. Third, as the home schooling example vividly illustrates, the advent of modern communications technology makes grassroots mobilization easier than ever before.

One of the newest innovations in grassroots lobbying is "grass-tops" lobbying.[32] In this variation, an interest group makes an ad featuring a prominent local personality—especially one who is an important supporter of a member of Congress—and then plays the ad in the member's district. Such ads signal members in no uncertain terms that their actions are being closely watched by people who have the power to help or hurt them electorally.

By no means should anyone think that grassroots lobbying is a new tactic, however; it has been around for a long time. In a classic study of the Anti-Saloon League (a prohibition group), Peter Odegard noted that this group had more than 500,000 names on its mailing list nearly a century ago—long before dependable long-distance telephone service, let alone computers, the fax, and e-mail![33] Influencing government officials' views by reaching out to their constituents is nothing new, but the decentralized political institutions of the contemporary United States, along with rapid advances in communications technology, have made such a strategy more attractive than ever.

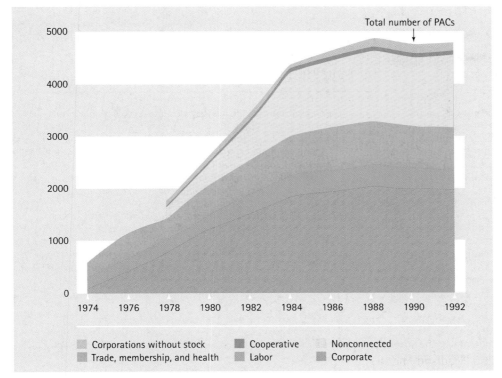

**Figure 7.2**

**PACs Formed Rapidly After the 1974 Federal Election Campaign Act (FECA) Reforms**

SOURCE: Paul Herrnson, *Congressional Elections* (Washington, DC: CQ Press, 1995), p. 106.

## Electioneering and PACs

Personal and grassroots lobbying are attempts to influence the views of public officials on specific matters. Another way to exert group influence is to affect the views of public officials in general by influencing who gets elected in the first place. Groups have always been involved in the electoral process, supporting some candidates and opposing others, but as the role of party organizations in campaigns and elections has eroded, and as campaigns have become more expensive, groups have become more active than ever before. Electioneering is probably the fastest-growing group tactic, and a principal vehicle of this tactic is the political action committee.

**Political action committees (PACs)** are specialized organizations for raising and spending campaign funds. Many are associated with an interest group or association. They come in as many varieties as the interests they represent.[34] Some, such as the realtors' RPAC and the doctors' AMPAC, represent big economic interests, but they represent thousands of smaller interests as well—the beer wholesalers, for example, have SixPAC. Numerous PACs represent interests that are at least partly noneconomic. Supporters of Israel donate to AIPAC and NATPAC. Supporters of abortion rights send money to NARAL-PAC, while their pro-life adversaries send money to National Right to Life PAC. (Pro-choice Republicans uncomfortable with the liberal positions of NARAL can give money to WISH LIST.) Gun control supporters contribute to Handgun Control Inc. PAC, whereas gun control opponents contribute to Gun Owners of America Campaign Committee. In addition to interest-groups PACs, scores of individual politicians have established personal PACs.[35] Like interest groups in general, PACs have enjoyed explosive growth in the past few decades. From a mere handful in 1970, they proliferated rapidly in the 1980s, as Figure 7.2 shows. Reflecting the overall contours of the interest-group system, far more PACs represent business and commercial interests than represent labor or citizen interests.

There is widespread public dissatisfaction with the role of PACs in campaign finance, although it is ironic that the proliferation of PACs is partly an unintended consequence of early-1970s attempts to reform the campaign finance laws[36] (see they accompanying Democratic Dilemma). As their numbers have proliferated, PACs have

> **political action committee (PAC)**
> Specialized organization for raising and contributing campaign funds.

## Democratic Dilemma

# Interest Groups, Free Speech, and Campaign Finance

Of all the things that contemporary Americans find unsatisfactory about their politics, campaign finance ranks near the top. People feel that free-spending special interests exercise too much influence over government actions and that free-spending candidates are able to buy elections. John McCain was able to capitalize on such sentiments to give Republican presidential nominee George W. Bush a scare in the early 2000 primaries.

Despite widespread dissatisfaction, however, and the efforts of public interest groups, little by way of reform has occurred. For one thing, any reforms have to be approved by elected officials whose electoral self-interest is at stake. This gives them a view of reform very different from that held by disinterested citizens. But another important part of the problem is that proposed reforms seem to be at least partly in conflict with constitutional freedoms. For example, in 1996 a proposal to ban PACs achieved considerable support in the House of Representatives, but opponents claimed that such a ban was patently unconstitutional.

In an important 1976 decision, *Buckley* v. *Valeo,* the U.S. Supreme Court held that Congress could not limit spending by either candidates or interest groups: Because it costs money to publicize one's views, limiting spending was equivalent to limiting expression.[a] Others disagree. Presidential candidate Bill Bradley argues that "I do not believe that a rich man's wallet is in free-speech terms the equivalent of a poor man's soapbox."[b] And an

expert campaign finance lawyer discounts constitutional arguments and characterizes the contemporary system of campaign finance as "felonious bribery."[c]

Campaign finance reform proposals raise difficult questions:

• *To what extent is it constitutionally permissible to regulate the campaign finance activities of interest groups?*

• *Should some rights of speech and expression be sacrificed to ensure the integrity of the electoral process?*

• *If the courts continue to strike down good-faith efforts, should the Constitution be amended to allow regulation of campaign spending?*

• *What criteria might we use to distinguish between constitutionally protected contributions to candidates who support the groups' viewpoint and the tendering of illegitimate bribes?*

---

[a] For background on the constitutional issues that arise in campaign finance reform debates, see Beth Donovan, "Constitutional Issues Frame Congressional Options," *Congressional Quarterly Weekly Report*, February 27, 1993: 431–437.

[b] Adam Clymer, "Senate Kills Measure to Limit Spending in Congress Races," *New York Times,* June 26, 1996, A16.

[c] Daniel Lowenstein, "Political Bribery and the Intermediate Theory of Politics," *UCLA Law Review* 32 (1985): 784–851.

played an increasingly prominent role in congressional campaign finance. Reflecting their business associations, most PACs tend to give instrumentally, which means donating to the members of key committees regardless of party. When the Democrats were in the majority in Congress, some of their members became highly dependent on business contributions, and critics charged that this dependence affected their legislative judgment.[37] When Democrats became a minority after the 1994 elections, they

**PAC-People**
PACs raise money for direct contributions to candidates. *What's in it for the interest groups contributing money to candidates?*

**Table 7.1**

**Business PAC Contributions Tend to Follow Political Power**

|  | Percentage of Contributions to Republicans Jan.–Feb. 1993 (Democratic majority) | Percentage of Contributions to Republicans Jan.–Feb. 1995 (Republican majority) |
| --- | --- | --- |
| American Dental Association | 27 | 90 |
| American Bankers Association | 52 | 87 |
| American Hospital Association | 53 | 81 |
| Ameritech | 35 | 79 |
| AT&T | 36 | 79 |
| American Institute of CPAs | 45 | 87 |
| Home Builders | 45 | 71 |
| Realtors | 75 | 91 |
| RJRNabisco | 69 | 81 |
| United Parcel Service | 55 | 78 |

SOURCE: Jonathan Salant and David Cloud, "To the 1994 Election Victors Go the Fundraising Spoils," *Congressional Quarterly Weekly Report*, April 15, 1995: p. 1057.

became much more favorable to campaign finance regulation that restricted PACs. (See Table 7.1.)

At the risk of sounding complacent, we suggest that, like interest-group corruption in general, the PAC problem in particular is somewhat exaggerated by the popular media. Most PAC contributions are small and are intended as a way of gaining access to public officials. Most research has failed to establish any significant relationship between contributions and votes.[38] There is even evidence that politicians extort PACs, pressuring them to buy tickets to fund-raisers and otherwise make contributions as a condition of continued access. For example, a former congressional staffer told one of us the following story:

> In our office we loved the FEC [Federal Election Commission] reports. We'd comb through them and list all the business groups who had contributed to our opponent. Then we'd call them up and say, "Hey, we noticed that you contributed to our opponent's campaign. The Congressman just wants you to know that there are no hard feelings. In fact, we're holding a fund-raiser in a few weeks; we hope you'll come and tell us your concerns."

Thus influence runs in both directions; elected officials are not just pawns to be moved around by interest groups. Campaign finance is a big question, and we will say more about it in later chapters.

**visual literacy**
**PACS and the Money Trail**

## *Persuading the Public*

This interest-group strategy overlaps somewhat with grassroots lobbying; the home school story was an example of interest groups persuading ordinary Americans that congressional actions directly threatened their interests. In recent years what has come to be called "issue advocacy" has grown in prominence: Groups conduct advertising campaigns designed to move public opinion in regard to some policy proposal. Estimates are that about $150 million was spent on issue advocacy in the 1996 presidential campaign and $260 million during the 1998 congressional campaigns, and preliminary figures suggest that these amounts were greatly exceeded during the 2000 campaigns.[39]

Many groups communicate with citizens even between campaigns and when no specific legislation or regulation is at issue. Their goal is to build general support for the group and its interests so that it will be more successful in the long run. Thus, in the 1970s, the Mobil Oil Corporation began paying to have columns printed on the Op-Ed page of the *New York Times*. Sometimes these were "advocacy ads" directed specifically at a government activity or proposed law, but more often they were what are now called "infomercials"—attempts to convey information and arguments favorable to business in general and the oil industry in particular.

One communications technique that is a product of modern electronic communications is **direct mail**.[40] Groups compile computerized mailing lists of people who might be favorably disposed toward their leader or cause and then send out printed or computer-generated materials soliciting financial contributions. Often, in an attempt to scare or provoke the recipient into contributing, the mailing exaggerates the threat the group faces. Some groups depend almost completely on direct-mail fund raising for their budgets. The citizens group Common Cause, for example, prides itself on its dependence on small contributions.[41] Once again, the rise of the Internet makes the direct-mail strategy both easier and cheaper. By tabulating who visits various Web sites, e-mail lists can be compiled and prospective supporters contacted for a much lower cost than that of traditional "snail mail" campaigns.[42]

Finally, any group likes to have favorable media coverage for its activities and points of view. Thus groups are always on the lookout for opportunities to get such coverage—to plant stories, to associate themselves with popular issues and candidates, and to position themselves as opponents of unpopular issues and candidates. In sum, whether we call it public relations or education, communication with a wider audience is a significant concern for many interest groups.

### Direct Action

As discussed in Chapter 2, the original 13 colonies cast off British authority in a violent revolution, the Constitutional Convention was in part stimulated by Shays's Rebellion, and the newly established federal government was tested by the Whiskey Rebellion. But these early conflicts were by no means the end of **direct action** by citizens opposed to government policies. In 1859, John Brown led an abolitionist raiding party against the federal arsenal at Harper's Ferry, West Virginia. Urban workers rioted against the Civil War draft in 1863. In the 1880s and 1890s, state or federal troops battled strikers from West Virginia to Idaho and from Michigan to Texas. In 1932, more than 20,000 veterans marched on Washington and were dispersed by federal troops. Protest—even violent protest—against social and economic conditions and related government policies is as American as apple pie.[43]

Seen against this background, the boycotts, sit-ins, marches, and demonstrations by civil rights, antiwar, feminist, environmentalist, gay rights, pro-choice, pro-life, and other activists are just more recent examples of a long tradition—and for the most part mild ones at that. As these examples suggest, forms of direct action are often used by social movements, given that their members have previously not been organized and lack the access to power and the resources to use other strategies. Direct action typically is used in combination with attempts to persuade larger constituencies. The media—TV in particular—find direct action newsworthy and thus communicate the protests to locales far beyond where they occur (see the accompanying Democratic Dilemma).

### Litigation

As we shall see in detail in Chapter 17, the modern civil rights movement followed a careful legal strategy, selecting cases to litigate that eventually led to the landmark ruling in *Brown* v. *Board of Education of Topeka, Kansas*. Drawing lessons from the success of the civil rights movement, environmentalists, feminists, and advocates for the handicapped, poor people, and other groups followed suit.[44] But litigation strategies are by no means limited to groups ordinarily thought of as liberal. In the 1970s the

**direct mail**
Computer-generated letters, faxes, and other communications to people who might be sympathetic to an appeal for money or support.

**direct action**
Everything from peaceful sit-ins and demonstrations to riots and even rebellion.

THANKS TO PHILLIPS, WEARY TRAVELERS WILL ALWAYS HAVE A PLACE TO STOP AND REFUEL.

**Good Corporate Citizens**
Persuading the public that you take care of migratory birds is part of being a good corporate citizen in this more environment friendly world. *Who is this advertisement aimed at? The public? Legislators?*

## Democratic Dilemma

# Strange Bedfellows: The Battle for Seattle, 1999

As we noted in Chapter 4, politics sometimes makes for strange bedfellows. A recent example came in the "Battle for Seattle" in December of 1999. The World Trade Organization (WTO), an organization dedicated to removing barriers to free trade, scheduled its "millennium round" of talks in Seattle. The meetings were expected to produce further trade agreements that would be a public relations boon to the Clinton administration, which lobbied behind the scenes to have the talks called "the Clinton round." By the time the meetings adjourned in a shambles, however, they had become a public relations disaster. Some suggested they should be remembered as the "Tear Gas Round."[a]

Ten thousand protesters disrupted the meetings, and a few ran wild in the streets of Seattle, smashing windows and looting stores. The protesters were mobilized by an extremely diverse set of groups. Labor unions claimed that trade agreements resulted in the export of American jobs to low-wage countries where workers were exploited. Though often opposed to labor, some environmental groups now joined them, contending that free-trade agreements in practice operated to override domestic environmental protection laws. Both attacked the WTO as a secretive international organization that operated in the shadows and threatened American sovereignty. This sort of argument normally is made by groups on the right wing of American politics, who at various times have charged that the United Nations, the Brookings Institution, and the Trilateral Commission are fronts for international conspiracies aimed at subjugating the United States. The WTO meetings brought all these strange bedfellows together. One militia member commented on the strangeness:

> "I'll be honest—I don't really know many people like the ones here," said Butch Razey, commander of the Yakima county Militia, who attended the protest on orders from superiors in Montana. "We're willing to die for our Constitution, and the patriots are all coming out because they know this is the beginning of world government. But I'll be honest—this will be the first time I'll be holding hands with a bunch of tree-huggers."[b]

Wrote one observer,

> As militia members milled with black-clad anarchists and topless environmentalists . . . , and trade unionists marched under "FREE MUMIA!" posters, it was clear that American protest had entered uncharted territory.[c]

Not since the 1960s have Americans seen these kind of militant protestors obviously dressed to sharpen their message about the WTO.

Encouraged by their success in Seattle, leaders of environmental and labor groups began planning additional collaboration when Congress considers future trade legislation. The militias' plans are unknown, but the protestors' Web site can be checked for future activities: www.al6.org.

*What do you think?*
- *Does the diversity of this coalition present any challenges to either of the major parties?*
- *Could this constituency be organized into an effective third party?*
- *Does this kind of protest represent democracy working (as politicians usually say) because people are expressing their opinion or does it represent democracy breaking down (as politicians may privately wonder) because the fringe can occasionally turn violent?*

[a]Charles Pope, "Will Labor–Green Alliance Succeed in 2000?" *Congressional Quarterly Weekly Report,* December 11, 1999: 2959.
[b]Charles Duhigg, "Seattle Dispatch: Means of Dissent," *The New Republic,* December 20, 1999: 14.
[c]*Ibid.*

Pacific Legal Foundation was set up to oppose environmental protection groups. The U.S. Chamber of Commerce established a National Chamber Litigation Center to support business interests in the courts. And the religious right founded the Christian Legal Society, which focuses on issues of church and state.[45] Liberal groups continue to be more active in the courts, perhaps because of the difficulty of constructing electoral majorities in support of their positions.

In addition to actually litigating cases, which is an expensive activity, interest groups also engage in other activities intended to influence the course of litigation. Although it is improper to lobby judges directly, groups stage demonstrations in front of courthouses, generate letters and telegrams to judges, and file ***amicus curiae*** (a Latin term meaning "friend of the court") briefs in cases in which they are not otherwise directly involved.

**amicus curiae**
Latin term meaning "friend of the court." It refers to legal briefs submitted by interested groups who are not directly party to a court case.

SECTION SUMMARY

> Interest groups have a variety of tactics for influencing government, ranging from the high-ly personal one-on-one contacts of high-powered Washington lobbyists to the impersonal electronic grassroots campaigns that are growing in frequency. Other methods include elec-tioneering; moving public opinion through issue advocacy; direct action such as marches, demonstrations, and sit-ins; and litigation. Some groups aim primarily at Congress, some at the courts, some at the executive, and some at public opinion. But the end goal of all groups is to affect the shape of public policies generated by the political system.

## Why Groups Use Particular Tactics

Different groups use different strategies or mixes of strategies. How they decide to allo-cate their resources depends both on their own characteristics and on the characteris-tics of the situation in which they are operating.

**Group Characteristics** How a group decides to deploy its resources depends on what kind of group it is, how much it has in the way of resources, and what kind of resources it has. A trade association representing profitable corporations will have a Washington office with a full-time staff of experts. This gives such associations the wherewithal to maintain close personal contact with government decision makers. A mass-membership group may find grassroots lobbying a more effective use of its resources. A public-interest law firm with no citizen membership will naturally follow a litigation strategy; indeed, the group may have been formed by lawyers precisely because they wished to engage in such activities. A social movement representing a disadvantaged constituency such as the poor may find that direct action is the only means of calling attention to its cause. Wealthy groups of any size or type may find campaign contributions and media campaigns to be useful investments.

Some suggest that groups with a federal structure—local chapters under a nation-al leadership—have a fund-raising advantage because contributions are solicited by people personally known to members rather than by an impersonal mailing. In addi-tion, such groups have chapters in many communities and therefore are constituents of a large number of representatives, and this may give them an advantage in grass-roots lobbying. Interest groups representing realtors, doctors, and banks are good examples.

In sum, size, composition, wealth, organizational structure, and other factors affect the activities in which groups engage; each group allocates its resources in the way it considers most efficient.

**Situational Characteristics** One of the reasons why the civil rights movement adopted a litigation strategy was that more traditional strategies were unavailable. African Americans were disenfranchised in much of the South and were politically discriminated against elsewhere. In the Congresses of the 1940s and 1950s, the path of civil rights legislation was blocked by senior committee chairmen from the South. African Americans as a group were not wealthy, and they were a small minority of the population. By choosing to litigate, they made a virtue out of necessity. Then, as the movement expanded and gained support, it was able to engage in direct action and, later, electioneering to advance its goals further.

In contrast, an industry or corporation interested in the fine details of a bill or reg-ulation may find it better to send an expert representative to discuss the matter with members of Congress and their staff or with regulators. In the former case, a campaign contribution may be a useful investment as well.

Direct mail and other modern advertising and persuasion techniques were developed largely by conservative groups, perhaps because for forty years Congress was controlled by Democrats who had little sympathy for their demands. Now that Congress is controlled by the Republicans, perhaps conservative groups are engaging in more direct lobbying. Conversely, having lost their access to the congressional leadership, liberal groups may be forced to shift their resources to alternative methods of exerting influence.

In sum, various situational characteristics—party control of Congress and the presidency, the economic situation, the mood in the country, what the interest group seeks to achieve—interact with characteristics of interest groups to determine what mix of strategies is adopted.

## How Influential Are Interest Groups?

The answer to this question is a matter of enormous disagreement. On the one hand, some critics believe that interest groups dominate American politics. One critic charges that the United States suffers from "demosclerosis," a condition in which interest groups clog the veins and arteries of the body politic.[46] Another claims that Americans have the best Congress money can buy.[47] Certainly the number of groups, the volume of their activities, and their massive expenditure of resources amount to strong circumstantial evidence that groups and associations are very influential in politics.

On the other hand, academic research yields less clear conclusions. Indeed, some of the most expert students of interest-group politics contend that a great deal of what groups do is canceled out.[48] There are so many groups, and so many *opposed* groups, that the efforts of one association's high-priced lobbyist only offset the efforts of another's, one group's media campaign only counteracts the effects of another's, one group's direct-mail barrage only neutralizes the effects of another's, and so on.

Also, it is likely that particular interests were more influential in the past than most individual interests are today. This is because changes in American politics have undermined the classic "subgovernments" that were dominated by particular interests.

### Subgovernments

Observers of American politics in the 1940s and 1950s developed the subgovernment model as a common pattern of policy making in America.[49] In the idealized **subgovernment**, policy was largely determined by three collective actors working hand in hand. A congressional committee provided an executive agency with program authorization and budgetary support, the agency produced outcomes favored by the interest-group constituency, and the interest groups provided campaign contributions and votes to the members of the congressional committee. Agriculture, public works, and business regulation were viewed as policy areas dominated by subgovernments. In the most extreme cases, subgovernments were called "iron triangles" (see Chapter 14) in recognition of the difficulty faced by outsiders who wished to influence the decisions of a powerful subgovernment.

The subgovernment model assigns to interest groups an important, if not dominant, role in the policy process. Interests control what members of Congress need most—electoral support—and provide it if the agencies controlled by Congress provide what the interest groups most need—favorable policies.

Whatever their importance in the past, subgovernments are less important today. First, as we shall see in Chapter 12, Congress has changed. The party caucuses and leadership are stronger and the committees weaker; particular committees no longer have strangleholds on their jurisdictions. Second, there are many more groups now, including many who oppose other groups. In particular, citizens groups representing consumers, environmentalists, and taxpayers are much more active now than they were a half-century ago. They oppose the excesses of special-interest politics and publicize their opposition. Third, as we discuss in Chapter 9, the media are different today.

**subgovernment**
A congressional committee, bureaucratic agency, and allied interest groups who combine to dominate policy making in some specified policy area.

In particular, they are very much on the lookout for stories of special-interest profiteering at the expense of general interests. In the spring of 1996, for example, the media helped kill a quiet attempt by the House Agriculture Committee to aid milk producers in raising prices by burying a helpful regulation in the agriculture bill then under consideration. Dan Rather discussed the "attempted rip-off of the consumer" on his evening news program, and in the wake of the publicity, the attempt collapsed.[50] Subgovernments thrived when they operated quietly, behind the scenes; they shrivel in the glare of publicity.

## Issue Networks

**issue network**
A loose constellation of larger numbers of committees, agencies, and interest groups active in a particular policy area.

In the view of many scholars, subgovernments have been superseded by **issue networks**—bigger, broader, and much looser connections of interest groups, politicians, bureaucrats, and policy experts who have a particular interest in or responsibility for a policy area.[51] Given the enormous number and variety of interest groups today, the proliferation of legislative staff and other policy experts, and the interactions between policies in one area and those in another, issue networks are much more open than subgovernments and much less stable in their composition. In the network model, interests are only one type of actor—they must compete with elected and appointed officials and experts for influence on public policy.

The academic consensus today clearly leans toward the network model, but not everyone agrees with the consensus, or with each other. On the one hand, some scholars suggest that even the term *network* may exaggerate the degree of organization that characterizes interest-group activity in Washington today.[52] But on the other hand, some scholars suggest that the demise of many traditional subgovernments should not make us overlook the influence of organized interests in new policy areas such as energy and social regulation. They go so far as to characterize the role of organized interests in these areas as "quasi-corporatist" and "neocorporatist," a reference to European **corporatist** systems in which important interest groups are given official representation in government decision-making bodies.[53] In short, judgments about the general importance of interest groups remain as divided as ever.

**corporatist**
The official representation of important interest groups in government decision-making bodies.

Probably the safest conclusion about the influence of interest groups is that influence is conditional: It ranges from weak to strong, depending on the conditions under which groups try to influence politics. Schlozman and Tierney conclude that groups are most influential when they act on low-profile issues, when they attempt to block action rather than originate it, when they are unopposed by other groups or politicians, and when they have plentiful resources.[54] Once again, the real world of American democracy is more complicated than many popular commentators suggest.

# Interest Groups and Democratic Politics

Even the generic term *interest group* has a negative connotation, and terms like *pressure group, vested interest,* and *special interest* have pronounced negative connotations.[55] Why do contemporary Americans hold interest groups in such low regard? After all, the Constitution protects the rights of citizens to form groups and to try to influence the government. Consider that the First Amendment not only guarantees freedom of religion, speech, and the press but also prohibits any law abridging the "right of the people peaceably to assemble and to petition the government for a redress of grievances." Americans have availed themselves of that right since the very beginning of the republic.

**pluralism**
A school of thought holding that politics is the clash of groups that represent all important interests in society and check and balance each other.

Political scientists generally have not held interest groups in as low regard as ordinary citizens have. In fact, one mid-century school of thought, **pluralism**, assigned groups a central place in American politics.[56] The pluralists believed that American politics consists of an interplay of numerous interests. Virtually everyone is represented in a dense network of groups, no single interest is dominant, and all are required to bargain and compromise. And groups exercise countervailing power; if one interest or set of interests becomes too powerful, others mobilize to counteract it. As a consequence, public policies tend to be moderate and to change incrementally. Thus the system tends toward an equilibrium that is representative of the broad range of interests in the country.

Pluralism is out of fashion today. Critics cite several problems in the pluralist account. We have already discussed the first, the unrepresentativeness of the interest-group universe. As critic E. E. Schattschneider once observed, "The flaw in the pluralist heaven is that the heavenly chorus sings with a strong upper-class accent."[57] Because of the free-rider problem, small special interests have an advantage over large general interests. In particular, economic groups procure narrow economic benefits at the expense of the broader population of consumers and taxpayers. This is probably one reason why the term *interest group* has negative connotations in the popular mind; people see that most groups do not represent the general interests of Americans.

A second objection to the pluralist account would still apply even if interest groups were more representative: The interest of the whole nation is not equal to the sum of the interests of the parts. In our discussion of public opinion, we pointed out that majorities of Americans want to cut government spending and reduce government regulation, but majorities oppose specific cuts and reductions. Thus, if Congress heeds the wishes of the individual constituencies, it will displease the entire country by maintaining a bigger budget and more intrusive government than a majority desires. Trade is another example. If the government erected a system of trade barriers to protect every American industry from foreign competition, the result would be retaliation against American exports, higher prices for consumers, and slower economic growth, if not worse. As Schattschneider long ago pointed out, a Congress operating according to pluralist principles enacted just such a trade policy in 1930—the Smoot-Hawley tariff, a policy that deepened and lengthened the Great Depression.[58] Simply adding up group interests is not enough. Ideally, politics harmonizes and synthesizes particular interests and incorporates them into the general interest of the nation (see the accompanying Election Connection).

A third criticism of pluralism is that a politics dominated by interest groups distorts political discussion and (ultimately) the political process. The reason is that group processes reinforce extremism and undercut moderation. Ordinary citizens have multiple attachments and affiliations, which generally serve to moderate their outlooks. A retired couple, for example, might naturally favor higher social security and Medicare expenditures. But if they also are parents and grandparents, they might oppose higher benefits for themselves if the result were higher taxes on their children or lower government expenditures on their grandchildren's schools. Leaders of interest groups, in contrast, are **fiduciaries**—people whose duty it is to act in someone else's interest. Typically, they see their job as the maximization of group benefits. Thus the leadership of a senior citizens group will be more supportive of higher benefits for the elderly than will many of its members. For example, AARP has been attacked as an organization composed of "tax-loving former teachers and government employees" who favor an "age-based welfare state."[59] This attack was levied by the National Taxpayers Union, an opposing interest group concerned with taxes.

This crowding out of moderate demands by more extreme ones is reinforced by the tendency of group activists and leaders to be more zealous in their views and more committed to group goals than nonmembers or even rank-and-file members; an example of which is shown in Table 7.2. Thus they push their demands beyond the point where ordinary members and sympathizers would stop. Activist supporters of the ERA agreed with the charges of the opponents that it would send women into combat on the same basis as men: "[C]ombat duty, horrendous as it might seem to all of us, must

**fiduciary**
Someone whose duty is to act in the best interest of someone else.

## Election Connection

# The Role of Interest Groups in the 1984 and 1992 Presidential Campaigns

In the summer of 1983, President Ronald Reagan was not a sure bet for reelection. The country was recovering from a serious recession, and most of the robust economic growth of Reagan's first term was yet to come. Moreover, the front runner for the Democratic nomination was former Vice-President Walter "Fritz" Mondale. Experienced and respected, Mondale was widely regarded as one of the bright spots of the Carter administration. As the primary season approached, the Mondale campaign busied itself by piling up endorsements from all the groups associated with the Democratic party.[a]

Mondale was endorsed by the American Federation of Teachers, the National Organization for Women, and the AFL-CIO. Environmental groups and peace groups offered their support. Civil rights groups came out in favor of their long-time ally, as did newer groups representing other ethnic minorities and gays. The party's elected officials were solidly behind Mondale. By the start of the primary season, the race for the nomination looked to be all but over.

Such impressions proved premature. Mondale stumbled badly; indeed, the Mondale bandwagon almost ran off the road. Senator Gary Hart did better than expected in the Iowa caucuses and, on the strength of the momentum developed there, beat Mondale in New Hampshire. Hart won in Maine, Wyoming, and Vermont and for a brief time became the front runner. Finally, Mondale staunched the bleeding with crucial primary victories in Alabama and Georgia. He recovered to win the nomination, but as a damaged candidate. President Reagan buried him in November.

Mondale's endorsement strategy played into a criticism frequently leveled at the Democratic party in the 1980s—that it had become a party of "special interests." Critics did not mean economic special interests (except for labor unions) but social and cultural special interests represented by liberals, minorities, feminists, welfare recipients, environmentalists, and the handicapped. Many of Mondale's critics sympathized with these groups, but they attacked him for having no larger vision for America. One of his primary opponents, Senator John Glenn, asked, "Will we offer a party that can't say no to anyone with a letterhead and a mailing list?" Mondale underlined the criticism when he gave in to the public demand of the National Organization for Women (NOW) that he choose a woman vice-presidential candidate.

Hart portrayed Mondale as a representative of the "old politics." Hart appealed to a younger, better educated segment of the population that was liberal on cultural issues but increasingly skeptical of demands for government intervention in the economy. In November, a third of Hart's primary supporters voted for Reagan.[b]

Many Democrats were well aware that the party had an image problem. Finally, Edward Kennedy (D-MA), a senator with impeccable liberal credentials, felt it necessary to face the negative public perception squarely. In a widely reported speech, he appealed to fellow Democrats:

> As Democrats we must understand that there's a difference between being a party that cares about labor and being a labor party. There's a difference between being a party that cares about women and being a women's party, and we can and must be a party that cares about minorities without being a minority party. We are citizens first and constituencies second.[c]

In the late 1980s, some "new" Democrats launched an organized effort to position the party closer to broad middle-class interests. In 1992 candidate Bill Clinton kept his campaign focused on the national economy and deliberately picked fights with some of the party's traditional constituency groups. In November he ended the party's 12-year exile from the White House.

*What do you think?*
- *Why should a large number of interest-group endorsements ever be a political negative? Don't they indicated that a candidate has a broad range of support?*
- *Although most people would agree that the tobacco companies and the oil companies are special interests, in what sense can minorities, feminists, the handicapped, and similar groups be labeled special interests?*
- *Is the Republican party a party of special interests?*

---

[a] The following account is based on the essays in Austin Ranney, ed., *The American Elections of 1984* (Durham, NC: Duke University Press, 1985); and Gerald Pomper, ed., *The Election of 1984* (Chatham NJ: Chatham House, 1985).
[b] CBS/*NYT* exit poll, *New York Times,* November 8, 1984, A19.
[c] *New York Times,* March 31, 1985, A24.

---

be assigned to persons on a gender-neutral basis."[60] Most American women and men preferred something less than such full equality. Today, environmental groups speak of a world on the brink of desolation, while their opponents scoff about imaginary threats. The minorities on the extremes of the pro-choice and pro-life debate polarize the debate and drown out the three-quarters of the population who could satisfactorily compromise on it. And the Home School Legal Defense Fund accuses Congress of a "nuclear attack" on home schoolers.

In the end, the general interests of a moderate population can get lost amid the bitter fighting of intense and extreme special interests. No one can deny that groups have a useful and legitimate role to play in articulating the interests of all components of American society, but many feel that groups somehow must be constrained. One of the first pluralists, James Madison, thought factions could be constrained by creating

**Table 7.2**

**Group Activists and Leaders Tend Toward More Extreme Views Than Nonmembers and Passive Members**

One study compared the views of 100 top leaders in environmental groups with the views of scientific experts—in this case cancer researchers. Both sets of people were asked to rate various cancer risks on a scale of 1–10, with 10 being the highest. Relative to expert judgments, environmentalists systematically overstated the risks of cancer from environmental causes.

| Carcinogen | Risk of Cancer | |
| | Environmentalists | Scientists |
| --- | --- | --- |
| Dioxin | 8.1 | 3.7 |
| Asbestos | 7.8 | 6.5 |
| EDB | 7.3 | 4.2 |
| DDT | 6.7 | 3.8 |
| Pollution | 6.6 | 4.7 |
| Dietary fat | 6.0 | 5.4 |
| Food additives | 5.3 | 3.2 |
| Nuclear power | 4.6 | 2.5 |
| Saccharin | 3.7 | 1.6 |

SOURCE: Stanley Rothman and S. Robert Lichter, "Environmental Cancer: A Political Disease," *Annals of the New York Academy of Sciences* 775 (1996): 234–235.

the extended republic, as he explained in "Federalist 10." He did not foresee several modern developments.

First is the tremendous expansion of society that contributed to the explosion of groups. The range of interests active today probably would shock someone like Madison, who thought in terms of broad interests such as land, labor and commerce, and debtors and creditors. Second is the prevalence of logrolling. Rather than check and balance each other, interest groups often cooperate, forming alliances and coalitions to exploit the general interests of consumers and taxpayers by getting higher prices and tax breaks.[61] Logrolling among interests is facilitated by a third development, the rise of professional politicians who, in seeking reelection, broker the group deals in return for the electoral support that interest groups provide.

But what can be done? As the critics look over the experience of democratic governments, they see only one means of controlling group demands that is both democratic and effective. Ironically, it is the institution that George Washington warned the country about—political parties, the subject of the next chapter.

## Chapter Summary

Only half the American citizenry votes in presidential elections, and only small minorities engage in other forms of political participation. But most Americans participate indirectly in politics by joining groups that attempt to influence government. In fact, Americans are more likely to participate indirectly through groups than are citizens of other democracies who vote at higher levels.

There has been a major increase in the number of interest groups in the past generation. Successful groups have found ways to overcome the free-rider problem, the tendency of people to benefit from group activity without contributing to its costs. Some of the groups rely on selective benefits that are available only to group members, while others depend on the efforts of dedicated or wealthy members who will bear a more than proportionate share of the costs of group maintenance. Some of the groups grew out of social movements composed of morally or emotionally committed members. Still others are not really groups but rather the representatives of one or two major members who believe that maintaining a political arm is a sound investment.

Group characteristics and their situations lead them to adopt a variety of political strategies. Grassroots lobbying involves attempts to influence elected officials indirectly by mobilizing constituents; traditional lobbying involves attempts to influence elected officials directly by speaking personally to them. Increasingly, groups engage in electioneering—contributing money to candidates or spending money independently to elect officials sympathetic to their interests and views. Groups also attempt to persuade or educate the public, and some resort to direct action—demonstrations, protests, and the like—to call attention to their positions. Finally, some groups end-run the political process and attempt to influence government through the courts.

Despite extensive study of interest groups, there is wide disagreement about how influential they are. In general, popular commentators view them as more powerful than do academic researchers. There is no doubt that groups engage in an incredible amount of political activity and invest a great deal of money and other resources, but it is difficult to say how effective they are. For every issue that appears to show that interest groups dominated the decision, skeptics can cite another issue where interest groups seemed to be ineffectual or to offset each other's efforts.

Although interest-group activity is constitutionally protected, many worry about its effects. First, special interests are better represented than general interests. Second, even if that were not so, the best interest of the nation as a whole is not merely the sum of the best interests of the particular parts. Third, interest groups over-represent the more extreme positions in the political debate and thus polarize political discussion and inject excessive conflict into the political process.

---

## On the Web

National Political Index
www.politicalindex.com/index.htm
The National Political Index is a Web site that provides an index of substantive political information for voters, political activists, political consultants, lobbyists, politicians, academicians, and media editors with a wide range of products, information, services, simulations, games, and polling in an interactive communications environment.

National Lobbyist Directory
www.lobbyistdirectory.com/
A state-by-state directory of lobbyists, containing names, addresses, and phone numbers.
Online Pennsylvania Lobbyist Directory
www.penncen.com/palobby/
A site that contains the names, phone numbers, and (where applicable), e-mail addresses and URLs for all registered Pennsylvania lobbyists.

---

## Key Terms

*amicus curiae,* p. 209
corporatist, p. 212
direct action, p. 208
direct mail, p. 208
fiduciary, p. 213
free-rider problem, p. 196
grassroots lobbying, p. 204

interest group, p. 191
issue network, p. 212
lobbying, p. 202
lobbyist, p. 202
pluralism, p. 212
political action committee
    (PAC), p. 205

political entrepreneurs, p. 201
private goods, p. 197
public goods, p. 197
selective benefits, p. 200
social movement, p. 199
subgovernment, p. 211

# Suggested Readings

Baumgartner, Frank, and Beth Leech. *Basic Interests.* Princeton, NJ: Princeton University Press, 1998. Comprehensive review, critique, and synthesis of the interest-group literature.

Freeman, Jo, and Victoria Johnson. *Waves of Protest.* Lanham, MD: Rowman and Littlefield, 1999. Useful collection describing the social movements active since the 1960s.

Heinz, John, Edward Laumann, Robert Nelson, and Robert Salisbury. *The Hollow Core: Private Interests in National Policy Making.* Cambridge, MA: Harvard University Press, 1993. The most recent major study of the Washington interest-group scene. Principal focus is on the characteristics and activities of group representatives and lobbyists.

Hertzke, Allen. *Representing God in Washington.* Knoxville, TN: University of Tennessee Press, 1988. Informative study of lobbying activities of religious groups, including (but not limited to) members of the Christian right.

Lowi, Theodore. *The End of Liberalism.* New York: Norton, 1969. Noted critique of "interest-group liberalism." Argues that a government of laws has been superseded by a process of bargaining between organized groups and public officials.

Mansbridge, Jane. *Why We Lost the ERA.* Chicago: University of Chicago Press, 1986. Thoughtful discussion of the narrow failure of the women's movement to win passage of the ERA. Argues that the movement overcame the free-rider problem by emphasizing the symbolism of the ERA, a strategy that precluded compromises that might have won passage of a weaker version.

Moe, Terry. *The Organization of Interests.* Chicago: University of Chicago Press, 1980. Analyzes the internal politics of groups and strategies used by political entrepreneurs for organizing and maintaining groups.

Petracca, Mark, ed. *The Politics of Interests.* Boulder, CO: Westview Press, 1992. Collection of current essays describing and assessing the activities of interest groups in American politics.

Schattschneider, E. E. *The SemiSovereign People.* New York: Holt, 1960. A delightful essay that remains timely. Argues that the pressure system of interest groups is biased and that the result is an artificially constricted range of political conflict in the United States.

Schlozman, Kay, and John Tierney. *Organized Interests and American Democracy.* New York: Harper & Row, 1981. Comprehensive study of the Washington interest-group universe circa 1980, as well as its expansion in the 1960s and 1970s.

Truman, David. *The Governmental Process.* New York: Knopf, 1951. Classic interpretation of American democracy as composed of the interplay of interest groups.

Walker, Jack. *Mobilizing Interest Groups in America.* Ann Arbor: University of Michigan Press, 1991. Describes the state of the Washington interest-group universe. Noted for discussion of outside support for establishment of groups.

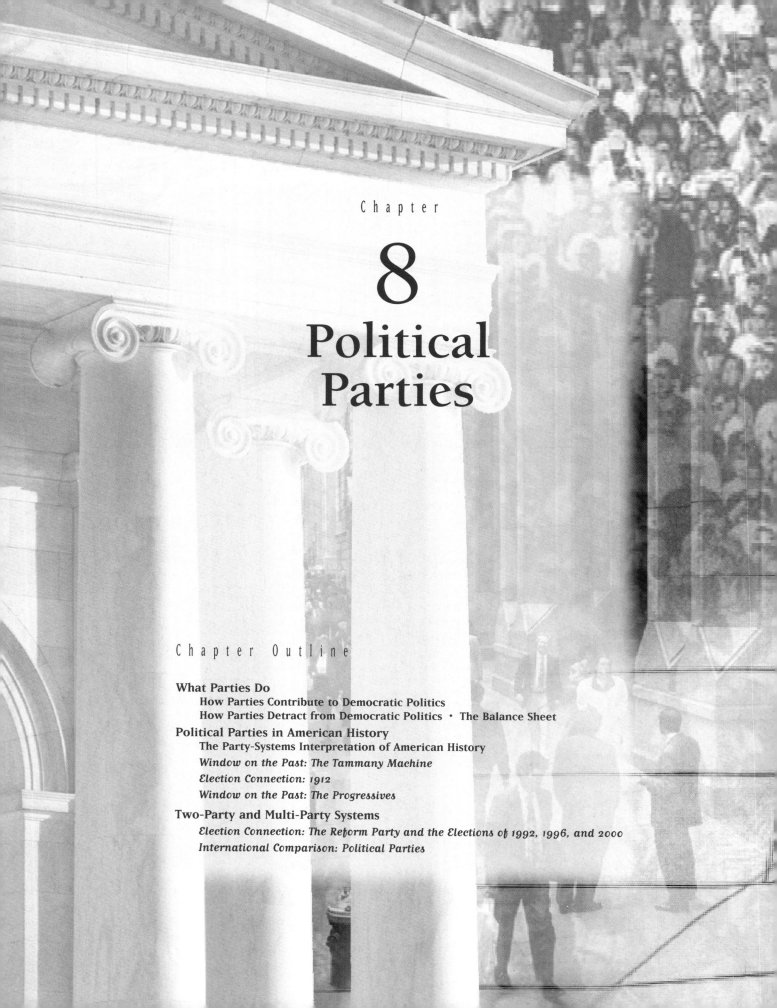

Chapter

# 8
# Political
# Parties

Chapter Outline

When George Washington left office in 1796, he warned his fellow citizens about "the spirit of party": "It agitates the community with ill-founded jealousies and false alarms, kindles the animosity of one part against another, foments occasional riot and insurrection." Washington's warning came too late—the spirit of party already was loose, never to be confined again. Treasury Secretary Alexander Hamilton's ambitious policies (a national bank, federal takeover of the states' Revolutionary War debts, and a generally active federal government) caused deep divisions within the Congress, and foreign policy problems encountered by the young republic reinforced these economic and philosophical divisions. Support for Hamilton's program was strongest in New England. It was generally endorsed by commercial interests and by those in favor of strong government under a strong executive. By the end of Washington's first term, critics of Hamilton vilified him and his followers as monarchists and British sympathizers.

Opposition to Hamilton was strongest in the South and West, especially among agrarian interests (many of whom were particularly outraged by Hamilton's tax on whiskey). Those philosophically averse to a strong executive also gravitated to the opposition, which was centered in the Virginia congressional delegation led by James Madison. Already called the Madison party by 1796, Madison and his followers were maligned as democrats and French sympathizers. Both Hamilton's and Madison's embryonic parties had their own newspapers, which they used to revile each other.[1]

In 1796 John Adams, Washington's vice-president, won the presidency. Thomas Jefferson, Washington's secretary of state, came in second in the electoral college voting and thus became the new vice-president. Over the course of the next few years, Jefferson and Madison laid the foundations of a new electoral alliance. Jefferson, who regularly glorified the "yeoman farmer," began to reach out to urban interests. In 1800 he and Madison concluded an alliance with the New York Republicans under Governor George Clinton and New York City political operative Aaron Burr. By all accounts a superb organizer, Burr delivered the New York legislature, which chose the presidential electors. New York's 12 electors were the key to the election—Jefferson and Burr finished only 8 votes ahead of President Adams.

THUS, WITHIN EIGHT YEARS OF THE ADOPTION OF THE CONSTITUTION, a two-party presidential race had been fought. The Constitution contains not a word about political parties, but they have been active in U.S. national politics almost since the founding. Indeed, some historians claim that the individual colonies had parties even earlier.[2]

All modern democracies have parties. Traditionally defined as groups of like-minded people who band together in an attempt to take control of government, **political parties** have dominated the connections between ordinary citizens and the public officials they elect. They nominate candidates for office, they help government administer the electoral process, and they mobilize voters. And after elections have determined the winners, parties also coordinate the actions of elected officials in the government. In this chapter we address the following questions about political parties:

**political parties**
Groups of like-minded people who band together in an attempt to take control of government.

- What do parties do that makes them essential to democratic politics?
- How have parties shaped the political history of the United States?
- Why does the United States have only two major parties?
- How influential are parties today in American politics?

## What Parties Do

To most political commentators in other advanced self-governed societies, democracy is unimaginable without parties. The European University Institute, a research arm of the European Community, has published a four-volume study on political parties. This study contains such observations as the following:

> Political parties have been considered the central institutions of democratic governments at least since the enfranchisement of the working class.[3]

> Competitive party systems of government have the special feature of being strongly associated with the values of liberal democracy or perhaps more accurately, to be regarded as its working mechanism.[4]

For contemporary Americans, claims like these are not self-evidently true. Americans are more likely to consider representative assemblies the central institutions of democratic government, and they associate the courts most closely with the values of liberal democracy. Americans inhabit a political world populated by nonpartisan local elections, the initiative, referendum and recall, town meetings, an independent judiciary, and other nonparty institutions that are viewed as important components of democracy. Not surprisingly, when asked directly about parties, most Americans do not sing their praises, and many Americans are more or less indifferent about them.[5] Indeed, surveys have shown that many Americans think that government would be better if there were none.

In contrast to voters and reformers, many American professors hold views of parties similar to the views of the European professors quoted above. E. E. Schattschneider, for example, devoted much of his life to making the case for the vital role played by political parties. In introducing his classic work, *Party Government*, he wrote, "This volume is devoted to the thesis that political parties created democracy and that modern democracy is unthinkable save in terms of the parties."[6]

In describing what political parties do, we begin with the views of those who approve of the role parties play in government and describe how they contribute positively to democracy. We then consider the views of critics who feel that parties detract from democratic politics.

### How Parties Contribute to Democratic Politics

*Why* are parties so important? What do parties do that makes most Europeans and some Americans think they are essential for democratic government? Could a healthy democracy have a nonpartisan politics that relied on the activities of individuals and groups? The general answer is that, except at the local level, such a democracy would be too disorganized to operate. Politicians create parties to *organize* political life, and parties do so by carrying on a series of activities.[7]

**Organizing and Operating the Government**   Often Congress is criticized for being disorganized and slow to move. Imagine what it would be like if there were no party leaders! Parties coordinate the actions of hundreds, indeed thousands, of public officials. At each level of government, executives count on the support of their fellow partisans in the legislature, and legislators trust the information they get from their fellow partisans in the executive branch. Parties also coordinate across levels of government, as when, in 1995, Democratic governors convinced some Democratic members of Congress that they should support far-reaching welfare reform proposals. Similarly, local officials appeal to their partisan allies in the state governments, and the latter appeal to their partisan allies in Congress. However disorderly American government often appears, many believe it would be absolutely chaotic without parties.

**Focusing Responsibility for Governmental Action**    Beyond shared views on policy issues, a major motivation for politicians to cooperate is summed up in Benjamin Franklin's observation that "we must all hang together, or most assuredly we will all hang separately." Franklin was exhorting colonial representatives to maintain unity or literally be hanged as traitors. By analogy, parties need to maintain unity or suffer electorally. Sharing the same label, party members correctly believe that they will be held to account for their *collective* performance.[8] This, in turn, gives them an incentive to fashion a party record that can be defended at the polls. After the Democrats won full control of national government in 1992, many Democratic members of Congress suspended their own reservations and supported President Clinton's policies because they believed they had to demonstrate to the country that the Democratic party could govern. Similarly, after the elections of 1994, many Republican members of Congress suspended their own reservations and supported the Contract with America because they believed in the importance of their campaign theme: "Promises made, promises kept."

**Developing Issues and Educating the Public**    Parties engage in a continual struggle for control of public offices, and they develop public issues as weapons in this struggle. They identify problems, publicize them, and advance possible solutions. Much of their motivation is political, of course, and the process is adversarial—somewhat like a court proceeding in which the opposing lawyers present their cases. But the competitive struggle for power generates information, educates the public, and shapes the policy agenda. Where parties are weak, as in the American South during the first half of the twentieth century, politics degenerates, taking on a more personal quality as factions contend for private benefits.[9]

visual literacy
**Comparing Political Party Platforms**

**Synthesizing Interests**    In Chapter 7 we explained how good public policy in a large, diverse republic must be more than the sum of the demands of individuals and groups. For one thing, some interests conflict; they cannot be simultaneously satisfied but must be compromised in some way. For another thing, satisfying every specific interest may detract from the general interest; granting every individual's spending demand can lead to deficits, inflation, high interest rates, and other national costs. Thus translating societal demands into public policy must go beyond simple addition to a more difficult and subtle kind of synthesizing or harmonizing of those demands. Because parties compete nationwide, they have incentives to offer platforms that offer a mix of benefits and burdens to all in the hope that a larger good will be the result. When they fail to do so, they suffer electorally. Thus, in 1984 the Democrats suffered because their platform was widely viewed as little more than a series of deals with interest groups. Similarly, in 1996 Republicans suffered because groups such as the religious right and the NRA were able to demand more extreme commitments than the bulk of the citizenry preferred.

**Recruiting and Developing Governmental Talent**    There is an old adage in politics: "You can't beat somebody with nobody." Even if an elected official appears vulnerable, voters may continue to return that incumbent to office unless offered a plausible alternative—someone with the background and qualifications to hold the office.[10] Thus parties are always on the lookout for promising candidates. They keep track of the weak members in the opposition and bring along potential replacements from their own ranks. Like predators in the natural environment, parties help to maintain the quality of public officials by weeding out the weak.

**Simplifying the Electoral System**    Imagine that there were no parties to winnow the field of candidates. Rather than choosing between two candidates for most offices, voters might be faced with many. Rather than being elected with majority support, the

**Full Slate of
Presidential Primary Candidates**
The Republican presidential contenders
mill around before a debate in Iowa
(l. to r. Orrin Hatch, Alan Keyes, Gary
Bauer, Steve Forbes, George W. Bush,
and John McCain). *How does narrowing
the choice to two major-party alternatives simplify the choice for voters?*

winner of, say, a five-candidate race might be elected by a plurality consisting of as little as 21 percent of the vote. Furthermore, the larger set of candidates would not run
with party labels. Although neither major party is completely homogeneous, the labels
"Democrat" and "Republican" nonetheless convey a good bit of information—and all
the information that some voters use. In the absence of parties, the information costs
imposed on voters would multiply manyfold.

## How Parties Detract from Democratic Politics

Despite these valuable organizational functions that political parties can perform,
Americans are traditionally suspicious of parties and, since the end of the nineteenth
century, have held them in relatively low esteem. There are two general reasons why
this is so.

First, that parties *can* perform valuable functions is no guarantee that they *will*
perform valuable functions. Politicians do not organize parties because they want to
simplify the electoral system, recruit talent, or synthesize interests for their own sake;
rather, they are interested in doing these things only insofar as such activities further
their chances of gaining power and implementing their preferred policies.[11] *Those who
organize and operate parties are motivated primarily by the desire to achieve their own political ends.* In particular, the motives for forming parties are primarily electoral:
Prospective public officials believe that forming a party will advance their chances of
winning office. Thomas Jefferson used a new party that came to be called the
Democratic–Republican party to wrest power from the Federalists. Abraham Lincoln
and others used the new Republican party to overthrow the Democratic majority.
Theodore Roosevelt established the Bull Moose party because he could not win the
nomination of the Republican party.

Once in office, public officials devote their efforts to maintaining their parties
because parties help them to govern by uniting members behind a single program.
Andrew Jackson used the spoils of victory to consolidate his party's majority, as did the
Republicans in the aftermath of the Civil War. Franklin Roosevelt used New Deal policies to strengthen the Democratic party in electorally critical local areas.[12] Ronald
Reagan actively supported efforts to strengthen the Republican national party, an
endeavor that left the Democrats far behind during the 1980s.

Although party leaders understandably may view their partisan activities as furthering the public interest, their opponents seldom agree. For this reason, there will always be a natural minority critical of party dominance—namely, the members of the party that is out of power.

But even partisans of the winning party may be critical of parties, for there is a second important reason for the relative unpopularity of parties. Party influence is a double-edged sword: Parties strong enough to perform the functions discussed above are also strong enough to abuse their power. Each of the positive functions that parties can perform can be corrupted, and unfortunately, American history provides numerous such examples.

**Capturing Governments and Dictating What They Do**    At a certain point, coordination becomes control. A strong party that controls its members can become the equivalent of an elected dictatorship, a charge the Progressives leveled at the urban machines that dominated many American cities a century ago. While continuing to face periodic elections, the machines kept a stranglehold on office by the calculated distribution of jobs, contracts, and other patronage. Such private payoffs purchased party control over public policy.

**Confusing Responsibility**    Because credit for good times and blame for bad times are valuable political currencies, the parties attempt to "manufacture" responsibility. Incumbent administrations are blamed for events they have no control over, just as they, in turn, take credit for outcomes not of their making. Worse, rather than helping to solve a public problem, opposition parties may deliberately act to undercut the governing party's attempts at solution, as the Republicans did with President Clinton's health care plan in 1994 and the Democrats did with the Republican plan to control entitlement spending in 1995. The temptation to torpedo the other party's initiatives is especially strong when **divided government** exists—when one party holds the presidency but does not control Congress. Under such conditions, parties can obstruct action, blaming each other for the failure of government to act, and voters are understandably unsure who really is responsible.[13] In short, parties often put their own electoral welfare over the good of the nation.

**Suppressing the Issues**    For various reasons, parties may choose not to develop new issues. Perhaps the leadership of both parties has gotten out of touch and fails to appreciate new developments in society. Or perhaps the internal harmony of parties is threatened by new issues: The parties suppressed the slavery issue during the first half of the nineteenth century, and the Democrats suppressed issues of racial equality in the first half of the twentieth. More generally, many historians attribute the periodic eruptions of third parties to popular frustration with the parties' refusal to deal with important issues. Third-party candidate Ross Perot's support in the 1992 presidential election came disproportionately from voters concerned about the deficit who believed that neither the Republicans nor the Democrats would do much about it.[14]

**Dividing Society**    Rather than synthesizing disparate interests into some larger whole, parties may do just the opposite. Seeking electoral advantage, they act divisively, creating or exacerbating cleavages and conflicts among citizens—just as Washington warned two centuries ago. During the 1980s, Democrats charged that Republican campaigns subtly inflamed racial resentments. We agree with that charge. For their part, Republicans charged that Democrats divided the country by catering to disparate groups—African Americans, Hispanics, gays, feminists, labor—and had no vision of a larger society. We agree with that charge too.

**Recruiting Hacks and Celebrities**    In theory, parties nominate seasoned members with long experience in office. In practice, parties have often nominated unqualified party hacks. For every Lincoln there was a Garfield, for every Roosevelt a Harding.

**divided government**
Said to exist when a single party does not control the presidency and both houses of Congress.

**Before and After, Celebrity Politician**
Bill Bradley has been famous for a long time. He went from New York Knick to New Jersey senator, and then presidential candidate. *While few might question Bill Bradley's abilities, what type of background makes for a good legislator? Or a good president?*

Moreover, in modern media and money-driven electoral politics, parties increasingly recruit celebrities—NBA (Rep. Tom McMillan, Sen. Bill Bradley) and NFL players (Rep. Jack Kemp), major-league pitchers (Rep. Jim Bunning), movie actors (Sen. Fred Thompson), entertainers (Rep. Fred Grandy, Rep. Sonny Bono), astronauts (Sen. John Glenn, Sen. Harrison Schmitt), and the wealthy (Sen. Herbert Kohl). Well known? Yes. Qualified? Sometimes.

**Oversimplifying the Electoral System**   The voter who must choose between two candidates, one labeled Democrat and one labeled Republican, has a clearer and apparently easier choice than the voter who can choose among many candidates with no labels. But what if she doesn't like that clear but restricted choice? What if she is a pro-choice Republican or a pro-life Democrat? That's just tough. If there are only two parties, she has only two alternatives to choose between. Her choice may be simple, but it may also be quite unsatisfactory.

## The Balance Sheet

Scholars value parties because they *can* make very useful contributions to democratic politics and government. Moreover, when evaluating party performance, scholars generally do not examine parties in the abstract; rather, they usually use the standard "relative to having no parties." Even if a party is performing poorly, what's the alternative? Reformers, on the other hand, see that parties often *do not* make useful contributions and, indeed, often abuse their power and detract from democratic government and politics. Moreover, reformers generally apply absolute standards, failing to ask whether there is an alternative institution that could replace parties and do a superior job.

Parties are among the most frequent targets of reform in American politics, and in the view of long-time observers like Austin Ranney and Nelson Polsby, such reforms are often misconceived.[15] In our view, an important reason for such inappropriate reforms is that reformers overlook the reasons why aspiring politicians form and maintain parties. Reformers fail to appreciate that parties inevitably act in accordance with their political interests. Attempting to force parties to behave contrary to their interests often leads to reforms that don't work, or to so-called unintended consequences, or to both.

SECTION SUMMARY

Parties can perform valuable functions. Political parties can contribute to democratic politics by

- organizing and operating government
- focusing responsibility for governmental action
- developing issues and educating the public
- synthesizing the interests of diverse groups
- •• recruiting and developing individuals to run for office
- simplifying the electoral system by defining the positions of candidates

However, parties can also can fail to perform these functions or undercut their performance by

- dictating government actions
- confusing responsibility for governmental action
- suppressing issues that do not lead to their own electoral success
- dividing society
- recruiting unsuitable candidates
- oversimplifying the electoral system by minimizing choices

Whether they contribute positively or negatively to the democratic process depends on how parties see their electoral interest.

## Political Parties in American History

Contemporary Americans' comparative lack of enthusiasm for parties is somewhat ironic, given that the United States pioneered the mass parties that are such an essential component of politics in modern Europe. When Washington issued his warning, his concern was directed at the political activities of elites—specifically, the followers of leaders like Hamilton and Madison within the national government. Such personal followings were the democratic counterparts of the "court" parties of monarchical governments, the groups of nobles who engaged in "palace intrigues" (and sometimes paid with their lives for their "treasonous" plotting).

American parties did not stay limited to the Washington elites for very long. During the administration of Andrew Jackson (1828–1836), the Democratic party spread outward from Washington and downward into the grassroots, a movement soon imitated by its adversaries, the Whigs. The kind of mass parties that were contesting American elections by the 1840s and 1850s did not become common in Europe until the end of the nineteenth century. As late as 1889 Lord Bryce, the famous English political commentator, could observe that "In America the great moving forces are the parties. The government counts for less than in Europe, the parties count for more."[16] Today, of course, the first part of the statement remains true: The government counts for less than in Europe in the sense that the public sector in the United States is smaller. But the second part of Bryce's statement can be turned around: The parties also count for less than in Europe. American parties now are weaker than most of their European counterparts, and weaker than those of other economically developed democracies such as Japan and South Korea.

Still, above the local level nearly all American public officials are elected as Democrats or Republicans (the Nebraska state legislature is formally nonpartisan). Unlike Europeans, Americans may not *believe* that parties are essential to democracy, but in practice, parties seem to be as pervasive as in Europe. Indeed, political historians of the past generation have developed general accounts of American history organized around the concept of "party systems."[17] These accounts describe the important role the political parties—appreciated or not—have played in American history.

## The Party-Systems Interpretation of American History

"Critical election" or "realignment" theorists view American political history as a succession of electoral eras often referred to as party systems.[18] Within each era, elections are similar, and the key points of similarity and dissimilarity are the **party alignments**—the social and economic groups that consistently support each party. The eras themselves are separated by one or more **critical elections,** or **realigning elections,** that alter the existing electoral alignment, often in response to some crisis. During these "critical periods," party elites polarize at the same time that intraparty conflicts break out. Third parties appear on the scene. Turnout rises as the general intensity of political life heightens. Some scholars see an additional characteristic of electoral eras, *periodicity.* They contend that critical or realigning elections come about once a generation, every 35 years or so. In this section we describe the six eras that make up the party-systems interpretation of American political history.

**The First Party System (Jeffersonian)**  Some historians date the first party system from the early 1790s to about 1824. The overriding issue during this period was the establishment of a national government and the delineation of its power. The commercial interests in the young republic, especially those located in New England, supported the Federalists, whereas the agricultural interests, especially those located in the South and West, supported the Jeffersonians, also called the Democratic–Republicans. The Jeffersonians were the dominant party, winning the presidency seven consecutive times from 1800 to 1824, but the system splintered when Jackson, the popular vote *and* electoral vote leader in 1824, was denied the presidency as the result of a so-called corrupt bargain.

Some historians object to characterizing the Democratic–Republican era as a party system because mass parties did not yet exist. Property qualifications prevented a majority of white males from voting, and women and slaves could not vote, so politics was primarily an elite game between personal factions, especially after the Federalists ceased to be a factor following the War of 1812. In the view of these skeptical historians, no party system, strictly speaking, came into existence until the 1830s.

**The Second Party System (Jacksonian Democracy)**  After his defeat in 1824, Jackson and his allies laid the groundwork for another presidential campaign. As part of their strategy, they sought to mobilize more of their potential voters. They succeeded with a vengeance: Between 1824 and 1828, turnout in the presidential election tripled, sweeping Jackson into office. Jackson's victory over the congressional caucus was complete when in 1832 he had himself renominated by a **national convention** that also chose Martin Van Buren as the vice-presidential nominee. To this day, conventions composed of delegates chosen in the states formally select the presidential nominees and the platforms on which they run.

The Jacksonian Democrats were often called simply the Democracy. This revitalized, greatly expanded successor to the Jeffersonian Democratic–Republicans was the world's first mass party; one of its principal architects, Martin Van Buren, is sometimes called the father of parties.[19] Jackson and Van Buren believed in the old adage "to the victors belong the spoils." They unabashedly defended the patronage system, freely and openly passing out government jobs and contracts to consolidate their hold on power. Until it splintered in the sectional conflicts of the 1850s, the Jacksonian Democracy lost only two presidential elections to the Whigs—in 1840 to William Henry Harrison and in 1848 to Zachary Taylor, both of whom were war heroes. The Democracy also controlled Congress through much of this period.

During this second party system, the dominant issues were economic and territorial (the tariff, the national banks, slavery, and the expansion of the Union), with major conflicts over the power of the federal government as opposed to states rights. As the system matured, new issues arose and sectional differences over economics and

**party alignment**
The social and economic groups that consistently support each party.

**critical election**
Election that marks the emergence of a new, lasting alignment of partisan support within the electorate.

**realigning election**
Another term for a critical election.

**national convention**
Quadrennial gathering of party officials and delegates who select presidential and vice-presidential nominees and adopt party platforms. Extension of the direct primary to the presidential level after 1968 has greatly reduced the importance of the conventions.

slavery intensified. By the late 1840s, dissatisfied citizens were challenging the system under the banners of third parties. The "Free Soilers" opposed the expansion of slavery into the territories, and a few years later the "Know Nothings" opposed the immigration of Catholics. Ultimately, in 1854–1856 a new party, the Republicans, displaced the Whigs as the second major party in the system. The badly split Democracy nominated both northern and southern candidates for president in 1860. Together with the Constitutional Union candidate, they received nearly 60 percent of the popular vote, but Abraham Lincoln led all candidates with nearly 40 percent, and with the winner-take-all electoral college system giving the leading candidate in a state its entire electoral vote, Lincoln received an electoral college majority.

**The Third Party System (Civil War and Reconstruction)** The third party system was the most competitive electoral era in American history.[20] The Democrats maintained a base in the House of Representatives during the Civil War, and they took control of the House in 1874 following the readmission of the South. Throughout the period, however, the Republicans controlled the Senate, partly through the strategy of admitting new western states to the Union. These states were very sparsely populated, but their small populations dependably elected Republican senators.[21] At the presidential level, the election results gave rise to the phrase "the period of no decision." From 1876 to 1892, no presidential candidate received as much as 51 percent of the popular vote. In two elections (that of Rutherford Hayes in 1876 and that of Benjamin Harrison in 1888), the electoral college chose a president who had come in second in the popular vote.

The dominant issue at the beginning of the period was Reconstruction, but after 1876, economic issues took center stage. The rise of large business organizations, industrialization and its associated dislocations, and a long agricultural depression generated the political issues of this party system. During this era, party organizations reached their high point. Bitter memories of the Civil War left many people committed to the party of the Union (Republicans) or the party of the rebels (Democrats), and these committed citizens voted a straight party line. Indeed, independents often were viewed contemptuously as "traitors." With feelings so strong and politics so competitive, the parties exerted tremendous effort in campaigns.[22] Moreover, there were thousands of immigrants to be fed and housed, employed, and marched to the polls. Parties reached such a high level of organization in many cities that they were referred to as **machines**[23] (see the accompanying Window on the Past).

Once again, the party system was unable to contain or adapt to new pressures. Partisan divisions rooted in the Civil War seemed increasingly outmoded as the United States emerged as an industrialized nation. The excesses and corruption of the urban machines spawned reform movements aimed at destroying their influence. The Depression of the 1890s, during the administration of Democrat Grover Cleveland, plunged much of the country into misery. Agricultural protest, common throughout the period, gave rise to a Populist party that seriously challenged the major parties in the South and West and ultimately fused with the Democrats to nominate William Jennings Bryan for president in 1896.[24] But the election showed that the electorate viewed the Populist vision of a worker–farmer alliance as less compelling than the Republican vision of a modern industrial state.

**The Fourth Party System (Industrial Republican)** The critical election of 1896 inaugurated a period of Republican dominance.[25] The Democrats were reduced to their base in the old Confederacy, while the Republicans were in firm control in many areas of the North and West. No longer needing the South for victory, the Republicans abandoned their black supporters and allowed the Democrats to finish erecting the system of political disenfranchisement that persisted into the 1950s.[26] In addition to region, important bases of political cleavage in the fourth party system were religion and ethnicity, as demonstrated in the first-ever major-party presidential nomination and subsequent defeat of a Catholic, Al Smith, in 1928.[27] The Democrats won the

**machine**
A highly organized party under the control of a boss, based on patronage and control of government activities. They were common in many cities in the late nineteenth and early twentieth centuries.

## Window on the Past

### The Tammany Machine

One of the most famous machines in American history was the Tammany Hall Machine, which ruled New York City from the 1850s until the 1930s. Newspaper reporter William Riordan wrote a classic little book about George Washington Plunkitt, one of the Tammany ward bosses at the turn of the century. Although the machines were vilified by the Progressives, Riordan's book makes the important point that the machines gained and maintained their power by using it to provide jobs, services, and assistance for thousands of poor constituents. Here is Riordan's description of a typical Plunkitt day:[a]

2 A.M.: Aroused from sleep by the ringing of his doorbell; went to the door and found a bartender, who asked him to go to the police station and bail out a saloonkeeper who had been arrested for violating the excise law. Furnished bail and returned to bed at three o'clock.

6 A.M.: Awakened by fire engines passing his house. Hastened to the scene of the fire, according to the custom of the Tammany district leaders, to give assistance to the fire sufferers, if needed. Met several of his election district captains who are always under orders to look out for fires, which are considered great vote-getters. Found several tenants who had been burned out, took them to a hotel, supplied them with clothes, fed them, and arranged temporary quarters for them until they could rent and furnish new apartments.

8:30 A.M.: Went to the police court to look after his constituents. Found six "drunks." Secured the discharge of four by a timely word with the judge, and paid the fines of two.

9 A.M.: Appeared in the Municipal District Court. Directed one of his district captains to act as counsel for a widow against whom dispossess proceedings had been instituted and obtained an extension of time. Paid the rent of a poor family about to be dispossessed and gave them a dollar for food.

11 A.M.: At home again. Found four men waiting for him. One had been discharged by the Metropolitan Railway Company for neglect of duty, and wanted the district leader to fix things. Another wanted a job on the road. The third sought a place on the subway and the fourth, a plumber, was looking for work with the Consolidated Gas Company. The district leader spent nearly three hours fixing things for the four men, and succeeded in each case.

3 P.M.: Attended the funeral of an Italian as far as the ferry. Hurried back to make his appearance at the funeral of a Hebrew constituent. Went conspicuously to the front both in the Catholic church and the synagogue, and later attended the Hebrew confirmation ceremonies in the synagogue.

7 P.M.: Went to district headquarters and presided over a meeting of election district captains. Each captain submitted a list of all the voters in his district, reported on their attitude toward Tammany, suggested who might be won over and how they could be won, told who were in need, and who were in trouble of any kind and the best way to reach them. District leader took notes and gave orders.

8 P.M.: Went to a church fair. Took chances on everything, bought ice cream for the young girls and the children. Kissed the little ones, flattered their mothers and took their fathers out for something down at the corner.

9 P.M.: At the clubhouse again. Spent $10 on tickets for a church excursion and promised a subscription for a new church bell. Bought tickets for a baseball game to be played by two nines from his district. Listened to the complaints of a dozen pushcart peddlers who said they were persecuted by the police and assured them he would go to Police Headquarters in the morning and see about it.

10:30 P.M.: Attended a Hebrew wedding reception and dance. Had previously sent a handsome wedding present to the bride.

12 A.M.: In bed.

---

[a] William Riordan, *Plunkitt of Tammany Hall* (New York: Dutton, 1963), pp. 91–93.

THE MILLENNIUM. THE TIGER AND THE LAMB LIE TOGETHER

**The Tammany Tiger**
A cartoonist's more negative view of the Tammany Hall Machine preying on the innocent. *The Tammany machine was very effective at organizing (and holding) power. But does this sort of organization further democracy?*

## *Election Connection*    1912

In 1912 the incumbent president, Republican William Howard Taft, finished a distant third in the popular vote and won only eight votes in the electoral college. Democrat Woodrow Wilson was the winner, and former President Theodore Roosevelt came in second, running as the Progressive party or "Bull Moose" candidate.

The young "Teddy" Roosevelt had become president in 1901, rising from the vice-presidency when President William McKinley was assassinated shortly after his term began. An energetic, colorful, and popular president, Roosevelt managed to straddle the split in the Republican party between the old-guard pro-business conservatives and the emerging Progressives. After serving out McKinley's term, he was easily elected in his own right in 1904. Although he had not served two full terms, Roosevelt chose not to run in 1908, turning the nomination over to his vice-president and friend, Taft, who won a comfortable victory.

Taft was neither as energetic nor as colorful as Roosevelt, nor was he a very astute politician. Although his policies originally were little different from Roosevelt's, he antagonized important elements of the party. Moreover, as the party split widened, Taft increasingly allied himself with the old guard, whereas Roosevelt had increasingly favored the Progressives.

Roosevelt returned home from safari in 1910 (despite his reputation as a conservationist, he shot over 3000 animals in Africa, including 13 rhinos and 5 elephants).[a] Former supporters begged him to reenter the political fray and take the nomination from Taft. In 1912 Roosevelt hammered Taft in the primaries, but they meant little in that era. At the convention, he was hammered in turn by professional party operatives and southern delegations loyal to Taft. Outraged, his supporters formed a new Progressive Party, held a convention later in the summer, and nominated Roosevelt, who told them that he felt as strong as a bull moose.

The split was fatal to the Republican Party. Although Woodrow Wilson received less than 42 percent of the popular vote, he was elected president as Republicans divided their votes between Taft and Roosevelt. Wilson was reelected in 1916.

Teddy Roosevelt, Noted Conservationist, on Safari in 1910

Wilson's two victories were the only ones by Democratic presidential candidates in the entire fourth party system—1896 to 1928.

*What do you think?*
- *In the 2000 primaries John McCain compared himself to Theodore Roosevelt. How does his failure to gain the nomination contrast with Roosevelt's?*
- *On the whole do you think the two-party system has served the United States well, or would it be better to have more major parties running candidates in U.S. elections?*

[a] John Garrity, *The American Nation: A History of the United States* (New York: Harper & Row, 1966), p. 664.

presidency only twice during the fourth party system: in 1912, when Woodrow Wilson emerged the victor in a three-way race with President William Howard Taft and ex-President Theodore Roosevelt, and again in 1916, when Wilson was narrowly reelected on a platform of keeping the United States out of World War I (see the accompanying Election Connection).

The fourth party system was a period of reform in American politics, but as noted in the accompanying Window on the Past, some commentators see a dark side to the reforms, during which wealthy and influential corporate and social elites called **Progressives** pushed many ordinary citizens out of politics.[28] Turnout in elections plummeted after the Progressives instituted the personal registration system and the secret ballot. The Progressives aimed body blows at the parties by trying to take away the two principal party resources: control of public employment and control of nominations. Civil Service reforms begun at the national level with the Pendleton Civil Service Act of 1883 were extended wherever possible, diminishing the spoils the parties had available to distribute to their members. The **direct primary** system, which allowed voters instead of party leaders to choose nominees for office, weakened party control of nominations and hence the control parties could exercise over office holders. The Progressives attacked the urban machines with demands for nonpartisan elections, and they provided ways to end-run elected officials with the initiative, ref-

**Progressives**
Middle-class reformers of the late nineteenth and early twentieth centuries who weakened the power of the machines and attempted to clean up elections and government.

**direct primary**
A method of choosing party candidates by popular vote of all self-identified party members. This method of nominating candidates is virtually unknown outside the United States.

## Window on the Past    The Progressives

The reform movement of the Progressives arose, in the 1890s, in the wake of rapid industrialization and urbanization. This attempt to bring order to a nearly chaotic society culminated in major innovation to almost every facet of public and private life in the United States. Progressives sought to improve the political system, the economy, and the standards of everyday living, thereby restoring economic competition and equality of opportunity. In the words of progressive Senator Robert M. La Follette, "The supreme issue, involving all the others, is the encroachment of the powerful few upon the rights of the many."

Because of the somewhat contradictory nature of the various branches within progressivism, controversy continues today over the membership and goals of this extremely diverse movement. It is viewed by some as primarily an urban, middle-class operation designed as a kind of protection against being squeezed out of power by an ever-growing working class on the one hand and the increasing power of big business on the other. Others claim the source of the movement to have been the workers themselves, and still others credit business leadership. Progressives have alternately been called altruistic reformers bent on improving the quality of American life (especially for the disadvantaged) and selfish, condescending meddlers bent more on social control than on social reform.

Whatever their motivations, Progressives tackled any number of the nation's ills, with varying degrees of success. Although Progressives accepted industrial capitalism, they were outraged by some of its consequences. Convinced of their ability to improve these conditions, Progressives became active in government reform, notably the destruction of political machines in favor of a more genuine democracy. They employed such measures as direct primaries and elections, the initiative, the referendum, and the recall. As with most movements within progressivism, this transformation of politics and government originated on the local level and only gradually spread into state and federal arenas.

The great trusts, so powerful as to be immune to the discipline of the individual consumer, were attacked and broken down via regulation and tariff reform. A variety of taxation reforms were introduced in an effort to distribute the nation's wealth more evenly. Additional specific legislative achievements encompassed such issues as child labor, industrial working conditions, workers' compensation, and women's suffrage.

Following an era of relatively passive chief executives who served as administrators rather than as policy shapers and leaders, progressivism marked the return of such strong, active presidents as Theodore Roosevelt and Woodrow Wilson. It was also characterized by great faith in the ability and skills of professionals to remedy society's ills.

SOURCE: Excerpted from Nancy Unger, "Progressivism (circa 1890s to 1917)," in L. Sandy Maisel, ed., *Political Parties and Elections in the United States: An Encyclopedia* (New York: Garland, 1991), Vol. 1, pp. 888–889.

erendum, and recall. Such reforms were aimed at real corruption, but one of their consequences was to weaken the mobilizing agents that brought many low-income and low-status people into politics.

After World War I, the Progressives' influence declined. For a time the country appeared to have achieved a new, permanent state of prosperity, but then came the great stock market crash of 1929, followed by the Depression of the 1930s with unemployment levels over 20 percent. The Republicans lost the House of Representatives in the mid-term elections of 1930, and the critical elections of 1932 and 1936 established a new party system.

**The Fifth Party System (New Deal)**    The fifth party system was a class-based party alignment that resembled electoral alignments in modern European democracies. After Roosevelt's first term, the Democrats became the party of the "common" people (blue-collar workers, farmers, and minorities), while the Republicans became, more than ever, the party of business and the affluent. The former accounted for a lot more voters than the latter, leading to a period of Democratic election dominance not seen since before the Civil War. Only Republican war hero Dwight Eisenhower was able to crack the Democratic monopoly in 1952 and 1956, and only from 1952 to 1954 did the Republicans control Congress as well as the presidency.

During the New Deal party system, the United States fought to overcome the Great Depression, defeated Germany and Japan in World War II, and presided over the "cold war" that followed. Foreign policy was formulated in a relatively nonpartisan fashion during this period, leaving politics to the domestic economic issues that favored Democrats. But once again, the Democratic party could not deal with racial divisions. In 1936 Roosevelt won repeal of the 104-year-old **two-thirds rule.** By requiring that the Democratic nominee receive a two-thirds majority of the delegates at the national convention, the rule had given the South a veto over the nominee. With its elimination, the South was increasingly unable to resist the growing national pressure for racial justice. Just as the inability to reconcile its northern and southern wings splintered the Jacksonian Democracy in the 1850s, the inability to reconcile its northern and southern wings splintered the New Deal Democrats a century later. By 1968 the Democratic party was at war with itself, and Republican Richard Nixon was elected president.

**The Sixth Party System (Divided Government)** For much of the past generation, scholars have debated whether the United States has a sixth party system, and if so, when it arose and what kind of party system it is. What puzzles scholars is that the Democrats lost five of the six presidential elections from 1968 to 1988, but they never lost control of the House of Representatives between 1954 and 1994, and they lost the Senate only from 1980 to 1986. Although such divided government had been common in the second and third party systems, it had nearly always occurred when the incumbent administration lost control of Congress during the mid-term election. What characterizes the sixth party system is a high rate of **ticket splitting**, with voters supporting the presidential and congressional candidates of different parties in the same election.

In retrospect, 1964 may well have been a critical election, in that political alignments changed permanently in its aftermath. Although they went down to a serious defeat, the Republicans made deep inroads in the Democrats' southern base, inroads that Richard Nixon widened and deepened in 1968 and 1972. Moreover, the third-party campaigns of George Wallace revealed how much resentment the racial issue had caused—even in the North. So long as the civil rights movement was aimed at the South, and it worked for political, economic, and social rights and equality of *opportunity*, it enjoyed widespread support. But once it moved north and began demanding some degree of equality of socioeconomic *condition*, large segments of white America withdrew their support. Many blue-collar and urban whites joined southerners in abandoning Democratic presidential candidates.

Race was not the only issue that damaged the Democrats, of course. The war in Vietnam led to a popular reaction against the party and spawned a protest movement that split the party internally. And as the first wave of the baby boom entered college, "social" issues began to take on importance as young people challenged traditional norms about drug use and sexual behavior in ways that alarmed their more traditionally oriented elders. Once again, the Democrats were split between their old and new wings, while Republicans allied themselves with more conservative "middle America."

Today, most commentators believe that the New Deal party system is gone, though they are in less agreement about precisely what has replaced it—or even *whether* it has been replaced. Some scholars, such as Joel Silbey, argue that there can be no further party systems or **realignments** because the American parties have grown too weak to organize the system or to realign. Silbey argues that the United States is now in a nonparty period.[29] Others disagree; although conceding that this is an unusual party system, historically speaking, they believe that the right issue or leader might once again realign the system into one that resembles the earlier party systems.[30]

timeline

**Parties that Made American History**

**two-thirds rule**
Rule governing Democratic national conventions from 1832 to 1936. It required that the presidential and vice-presidential nominees receive at least two-thirds of the delegates' votes.

**ticket splitting**
Occurs when a voter does not vote a straight party ticket.

**realignment**
Occurs when the pattern of group support for political parties shifts in a significant and lasting way, such as in the latter half of the twentieth century, when the white South shifted from Democratic to Republican.

Table 8.1

The Party-Systems Interpretation of American Electoral History

First (Jeffersonian) Party System: 1796–1824*
    7 Democratic–Republican presidential victories
    1 Federalist victory

Second (Jacksonian) Party System: 1828–1856
    6 Democratic victories
    2 Whig victories

Third (Civil War and Reconstruction) Party System: 1860–1892
    7 Republican victories
    2 Democratic victories

Fourth (National Republican) Party System: 1896–1928
    7 Republican victories
    2 Democratic victories

Fifth (New Deal) Party System: 1932–1964
    7 Democratic victories
    2 Republican victories

Sixth (Divided Government) Party System: 1968–??
    5 Republican victories
    3 Democratic victories

*Years are approximate.

## Section Summary

Political historians have developed accounts of American history organized around the concept of party systems, emphasizing the role that political parties have played in history. Via the party-systems approach, American history can be divided into six periods, each dominated by two parties, as summarized in Table 8.1.

## Two-Party and Multi-Party Systems

Given the history from Jefferson to the present, Americans understandably regard a **two-party system** as a natural state of affairs. As the description of party systems showed, for the entire two centuries of the country's history, two major parties have dominated elections for national office, although third parties regularly arise (see Table 8.2). Several third parties, such as the Reform party described in the accompanying Election Connection, have influenced the outcomes of some American elections, but nearly all third parties disappear.[31] Only once has a third party replaced a major party—the Republicans displaced the Whigs in the 1850s. Often third parties are a reaction to a particular problem, and they fade when the problem does. If the problem persists, the third party usually is absorbed or "co-opted" by a major party, as were the Populists in the 1890s, who joined with the Democrats.

But Americans are in a minority as far as the rest of the world is concerned. Most democracies have **multi-party systems**, as shown in the accompanying International Comparison. A single party rarely wins majority control of government; rather, two or more minority parties that together constitute a legislative majority must form a **coalition government**.

Many scholars believe that the electoral system strongly affects whether a country has two parties or more. An **electoral system** is the way in which a country's constitution or laws translate popular votes into control of public offices.[32] The United States relies almost exclusively on the **single-member, simple plurality (SMSP) system**.

**two-party system**
System in which only two significant parties compete for office. Such systems are in the minority among world democracies.

**multi-party system**
System in which more than two parties compete for control of government. Most of the world's democracies are multi-party systems.

**coalition government**
Occurs when two or more minority parties must join together in order to elect a prime minister. Such governments are common in multi-party systems.

**electoral system**
A means of translating popular votes into control of public offices.

**single-member, simple plurality (SMSP) system**
Electoral system in which the country is divided into geographic districts, and the candidates who win the most votes within their districts are elected.

**Table 8.2**

**Third Parties in American History**

| Candidate (party, year) | Showing | Subsequent Events |
|---|---|---|
| Martin Van Buren (Free Soil party, 1848) | 10.1 percent 0 electoral votes | Party drew 5 percent in 1852; supporters then merged into Republican Party |
| James B. Weaver (Populist party, 1892) | 8.5 percent 22 electoral votes | Supported Democrat William Jennings Bryan in 1896 |
| Theodore Roosevelt (Progressive party, 1912) | 27.4 percent 88 electoral votes | Supported GOP nominee in 1916 |
| Robert M. La Follette (Progressive party, 1924) | 16.6 percent 13 electoral votes | La Follette died in June 1925 |
| Strom Thurmond (States' Rights Democratic party, 1948) | 2.4 percent 38 electoral votes | Democrats picked slate acceptable to South in 1952 |
| Henry A. Wallace (Progressive party, 1948) | 2.4 percent 0 electoral votes | Party disappeared |
| George C. Wallace (American Independent party, 1968) | 13.5 percent 46 electoral votes | Ran in Democratic primaries in 1972 until he was injured in assassination attempt |
| John B. Anderson (National Unity Campaign, 1980) | 6.6 percent 0 electoral votes | Withdrew from elective politics |
| H. Ross Perot (Independent, 1992) | 18.7 percent 0 electoral votes | Formed new party (Reform) to take part in 1996 and 2000 presidential elections |
| H. Ross Perot (Reform party, 1996) | 8.5 percent 0 electoral votes | Adopted a lower profile |
| Patrick Buchanan (Reform party, 2000) | <1 percent 0 electoral votes | Finished in national politics? |
| Ralph Nader (Green party, 2000) | 3 percent 0 electoral votes | Failed to qualify for federal funding in 2004 |

Note: The list includes significant third-party candidates who received at least 2 percent of the popular vote. Other third parties that won at least 2 percent of the vote include the Liberty party (1844); the Greenback party (1880); the Prohibition party (1888, 1892); and the Socialist party (1904, 1908, 1912, 1916, 1920, 1932).

SOURCE: Adapted from Kenneth Jost, "Third-Party Prospects," *The CQResearcher*, December 22, 1995, 1148. Updated with 1996 and 2000 election returns.

Elections for office take place within geographic units (states, congressional districts, cities, and so on), and the candidate who wins the most votes wins the election. When only two candidates run, one candidate will win a majority; when more than two run, a simple plurality determines the winner. This electoral system is characteristic of the "Anglo-American democracies" (England and its former colonies). It is often called the "first past the post" system: Just as in a horse race, the winner is the one who finishes first, no matter how many others are in the race or how close the finish.

In most of the world's democracies, however, the electoral system is some version (there are many variations) of **proportional representation (PR).** In such systems, elections may (Germany) or may not (Israel) take place within geographic units, but even if they do, each unit elects a number of officials, with each party winning seats in proportion to the vote it receives.

To illustrate the operation of these differing electoral systems, consider an example. Great Britain has a SMSP system, but for decades a small third party, currently called the Liberal Democrats, has survived. Suppose the vote were to be divided as follows within a parliamentary constituency:

Conservative: 39%

Labour: 44%

Liberal Democrat: 17%

**proportional representation (PR)**
Electoral system in which parties receive a share of seats in parliament that is proportional to the popular vote they receive.

## Election Connection

# The Reform Party and the Elections of 1992, 1996, and 2000

In the 1992 presidential election, H. Ross Perot, a colorful Texas multimillionaire, got 19 percent of the vote in a three-way race with Bill Clinton and George Bush. This was the best showing by a third candidate since Theodore Roosevelt's Bull Moose insurgency in the 1912 election.

After preliminary preparations Perot announced on CNN's *Larry King Live!* in early 1992 that he would run for president if his supporters could get his name on the ballot in all 50 states. His candidacy caught on, and his poll numbers rose rapidly—by May several polls showed a statistical dead heat among the three candidates. With visibility came critical examination, however, and with doubts rising about his personality and temperament and his campaign starting to slip in the polls, Perot withdrew from the race in July at the conclusion of the Democratic convention. His supporters continued to work, however, and after they qualified his name for the ballot in all 50 states, Perot reentered the race. In total, Perot spent $65 million of his personal fortune.

**Jesse Ventura,
Governor of Minnesota**

Surveys showed that Perot supporters tended to be people who had not previously been involved in politics. They were "between" the two parties in terms of their policy stands: neither as socially conservative as Republicans nor as socially liberal as Democrats. They did not want to spend more money on new programs like traditional Democrats, nor did they want to cut taxes like many Republicans. Instead, they wanted to attack budget deficits, Perot's signature issue.[a]

After the election Perot transformed his campaign organization, "United We Stand, America" into a citizen watchdog group and continued to speak out on national politics. In 1994 he urged his supporters to "send a message," helping the Republicans capture control of Congress. In late 1995 Perot announced on CNN

that he would encourage the formation of a third party. The new Reform Party would not compete in the 1996 primaries but would compete in the general election. The Federal Election Commission announced that, on the basis of its 1992 showing, the party would be eligible for $30 million in federal matching funds.

Perot did much worse in 1996, winning only 9 percent of the vote. But the party did not fade away as many expected. In 1998 the Reform Party ran more than 180 candidates for a variety of offices and even managed to elect a governor, former professional wrestler Jesse Ventura, in Minnesota. With $12.6 million in federal matching funds available for 2000 and a network of supporters in place, the Reform Party nomination was still worth something. The party split badly in late 1999. Ventura continued to resist appeals that he run for president. Multimillionaire real estate developer Donald Trump considered running, then decided against it. Social conservative Pat Buchanan *did* declare, creating a dilemma for many Reform Party supporters who are not social conservatives. Buchanan won the nomination but received less than 1 percent of the popular vote in 2000.

*What do you think?*
- *Will the Reform Party go the way of most third parties and die out? Why will it, or won't it, survive?*
- *Has its impact been large or small, particularly in budget matters?*

_____

[a]"The Perot Phenomenon," *The Public Perspective* September/October 1992: 91–95.

---

The Labour candidate, having won a plurality, would win the seat with a minority of the overall vote. The Conservatives and the Liberal Democrats would have nothing to show for the 56 percent they won. In fact, the current Labour government, which holds 63 percent of the seats in Parliament, received only 44 percent of the nationwide vote in the 1997 elections. This is not unusual: *SMSP electoral systems tend to manufacture majorities or at least to exaggerate their size.*

When elections are conducted under PR electoral arrangements, geographic units tend to be much larger and are assigned multiple representatives. If the preceding distribution of the vote had occurred in a unit assigned 20 members of parliament, the Conservatives would have been given 8 seats, Labour 9, and the Liberal Democrats 3, an allocation of seats roughly proportional to the number of votes received. Under PR, parties win majorities of seats only when they win majorities of votes.

In the SMSP electoral system, winning is everything—finishing in any position but first wins nothing. Thus, if small parties have more in common with each other

## International Comparison

## Political Parties

| Significant Parties | Description | Seats |
|---|---|---|
| **United States** | | **1996** |
| Democratic party | Favors government assistance for workers, the poor, and minorities; economically and socially left of center | 206 |
| Republican party | Favors reliance on individualism and the free market; federalism; economically and socially right of center | 228 |
| **Canada** | | **1997** |
| Bloc Québécois | Seeks negotiated sovereignty of the Québec province | 44 |
| Liberal Party of Canada | Favors comprehensive social security and Canadian autonomy | 155 |
| New Democratic party | Social Democrats | 21 |
| Progressive Conservative party | Favors individualism and free enterprise | 20 |
| Reform Party | Favors decentralization of federal government and fiscal reform | 60 |
| **France** | | **1997** |
| Rassemblement pour la République (RPR) | Gaullist conservative party | 134 |
| Union pour la Democratie Française (UDF) | Non-Gaullist centrist coalition | 106 |
| Parti Socialiste (PS) | Socialist party | 242 |
| Parti Communiste Français (PCF) | Communist party | 34 |
| Mouvement des Radicaux de Gauche (MRG) | Left-wing radical party | 12 |
| National Front (FN) | Extreme right-wing nationalist party | 1 |
| **Germany** | | **1994** |
| Christian Democratic Union (CDU)/ Christian Social Union (CSU) | Conservative party (CSU is the Bavarian version of the CDU) | 294 |
| Free Democratic Party (FDP) | Centrist party; supports individualism and the free market | 47 |
| The Greens | Left-wing party focusing on ecological issues, social justice, and comprehensive disarmament | 49 |
| Party of Democratic Socialism (PDS) | Re-formed from the Communist party in areas of the former East Germany; favors public ownership of means of production | 30 |
| Social Democratic party | Socialist party | 252 |
| **India** | | **1998** |
| Bharatiya Janata party (BJP) | Radical, right-wing Hindu party | 181 |
| Indian National Congress | Socialist party; favors government control of industry | 141 |
| United Front | Coalition of the National Front, which includes liberal centrist parties, and the Left Front, which includes Communist parties | 97 |

than with the largest party, they have an incentive to join together in a single opposing party to challenge the plurality winner, because dividing the opposition among more than one candidate plays into the hands of the largest party. Citizens, in turn, realize that voting for a small party is tantamount to "wasting" their vote, because such a party has no chance of coming in first.[33] Thus they tend to support one of the two larger parties. These calculations by parties and voters work against third parties.

In PR systems, of course, so long as a party finishes above some legally defined threshold, it wins seats in proportion to its vote. Because it is not necessary to finish first in order to win something, party leaders have more incentive to maintain their separate organizations. And because all votes count, voters are not motivated to abandon small parties. Thus, a multi-party system persists.

As shown by the British example above, the correlation between electoral system and number of parties around the world is not perfect—third parties do survive in SMSP systems. The correlation is strong, however. One study found that the average number of parties in proportional representation systems was 3.7, while the average number in SMSP systems was 2.2.[34]

## Political Parties, *continued*

| Significant Parties | Description | Seats |
|---|---|---|
| **Israel** | | **1996** |
| Hadash | Socialist party | 5 |
| Israel Labour party | Left-of-center party; favors negotiated peace with Arab neighbors and Palestinians in occupied territories | 34 |
| Likud ("Consolidation") | Right-of-center party; emphasizes security issues in peace negotiations and favors continued Jewish settlement of occupied territories | 32 |
| Meretz ("Vitality") | Favors civil rights, electoral reform, and Palestinian self-determination | 9 |
| National Religious party | Favors strict adherence to Jewish religion and tradition, but moderate by Israeli religious standards | 9 |
| Shas (Sephardic Torah Guardians) | Ultra-orthodox Jewish party | 10 |
| The Third Way | Centrist party; tries to merge Labour & Likud ideology | 4 |
| United Arab List | Muslim Party | 4 |
| United Torah Judaism | Jewish religious party | 4 |
| Yisrael Ba'aliya | Russian immigrant party | 7 |
| **Japan** | | |
| Japanese Communist party (JCP) | Communist party | 26 |
| Democratic party | Splinter party from LDP and NFP | 52 |
| Liberal Democratic party (LDP) | Favors a strong welfare state, government promotion of industry and Japanese culture | 239 |
| New Frontier party (NFP) | Amalgamation of nine opposition parties | 156 |
| Social Democratic party of Japan (SDPJ) | Seeks collective security system with China, U.S., CIS | 15 |
| **Venezuela** | | **1993** |
| Acción Democrática (AD) | Socialist party | 55 |
| Partido Social-Cristiano (COPEI) | Christian Democrats | 54 |
| Convergencia Nacional (CN)/ Movimento al Socialismo | Coalition for national unity against the government in power and corruption; socialist movement | 50 |
| Causa Radical | Grassroots, left-wing workers' party | 40 |

Note: The table shows major parties winning seats in the indicated legislative elections. The National Front is included among French political parties because, although it received one seat in the last parliamentary election, it received almost 15 percent of the vote in the first round of balloting and has previously held several seats.

One factor that affects the survival of third parties in SMSP systems is whether their votes are geographically concentrated. If they receive, say, 20 percent of the nationwide vote but it is distributed evenly across the country, they win nothing. On the other hand, if their vote is regionally concentrated so that they are the first or second party in some constituencies, they may persist indefinitely. For example, modern Canadian elections have been dominated by two major parties, the Liberals and the Progressive Conservatives, which compete nationwide and ordinarily win most of the seats in Parliament. But in recent elections, two smaller parties have established regional footholds. In the French-speaking province of Québec, the Parti Québécois is the dominant party, and in some western provinces, Reform is the strongest party.

## Section Summary

Americans regard the two-party system as natural and the occasional appearance of a third party as the exception. But this is a misperception. Most democracies have more than two major parties. An important factor in determining the number of parties is the electoral system. Single-member, simple plurality systems winnow out small parties, whereas proportional representation systems allow many of them to survive.

## How Strong Are American Parties Today?

Given the preceding discussion of parties in American history, you may be surprised to learn that during the past three decades, some scholars have argued that the parties were declining or even dying. In a 1970 book, Burnham discussed "The Onward March of Party Decomposition."[35] (He titled a more popular 1969 article "The End of American Party Politics."[36]) Broder titled a 1971 book *The Party's Over.*[37] This thesis of party decline dominated research on American parties for well over a decade, but by the mid-1980s, a revisionist view had begun to emerge. Kayden and Mahe titled a 1985 book *The Party Goes On*, and less than two decades after Burnham first wrote, Sabato published *The Party's Just Begun.*[38] In works with less catchy titles, other scholars claim their colleagues mistake "change" for "decline."[39] How can professional students of politics arrive at such widely differing viewpoints?

Part of the answer is that people have different conceptions of what a party is. Parties are multifaceted, and although we defined parties earlier, no definition we have ever read captures all or even most of the facets. Scholars often skirt the definitional problem by subdividing the concept and talking about different aspects, a practice we follow here.[40]

In most of the world, *party* means an organization of like-minded people officially united in an effort to elect their members to office. In many other democracies, parties are very well-defined organizations. People join them in the same way they join clubs in the United States: They pay dues, receive official membership cards, and have a right to participate in various party-sponsored activities (such as nominating candidates). Americans who travel abroad often are surprised to find that parties elsewhere have buildings, full-time professional staffs, and even newspapers and television stations.

The term *party* also may refer to the officials elected to government—the members of the parliament and cabinet in most democracies. This is especially the case where elected officials dominate the party leadership and the grassroots, as in the British Conservative party. In most other countries, the parties are much more united in their governments than in the United States, and party candidates run much more centralized campaigns than in the candidate-centered politics of the United States.

Historically, the United States did not have true national party organizations. Rather, what passed for national organizations were temporary associations of state parties that briefly joined together every four years to work for the election of a president. In the aftermath of the Progressive reforms, these state and local organizations themselves declined. Similarly, party members in government have generally not been terribly cohesive. Both parties (but especially the Democrats) have suffered from regional splits, and both parties have incorporated conflicting interests—agricultural versus commercial, and so forth.[41]

Because neither party as organization nor party as unified corps of elected officials fits U.S. experience very well, modern American commentators have discussed party primarily in a third sense, as the adherents to the party—its supporters in the electorate—ordinary citizens who identify themselves as Democrats or Republicans.

For some decades it appeared that political parties in the United States were in decline whatever the sense in which one used the concept. By mid-century, state and local party organizations had withered. Meanwhile, party cohesion and presidential support in Congress had declined; in 1963 James MacGregor Burns complained that the United States had a four-party system, with presidential Democrats and Republicans often opposed by congressional Democrats and Republicans.[42] The number of adherents to the two parties began dropping as well; in the mid-1960s the proportion of those calling themselves "independents" rose. But by the mid-1980s, the first two of these trends had clearly reversed: Party organizations were growing more active again, and party was becoming more important in government. A comparable reversal has not occurred among party in the electorate, though declining trends have at least bottomed out.

We will discuss party in the electorate in Chapter 10 when we consider voting behavior. And we will discuss parties in the government when we talk about Congress and the presidency in Chapters 12 and 13. Here we focus on the party organizations, the most common concept of party around the world.

## The Decline of Party Organizations

Party organizations were at their strongest at about the time the Progressive movement began. The decline of American party organizations was in considerable part a consequence of deliberate public policies. As we noted earlier, the two principal resources that party organizations depend on are control of patronage and control of nominations for office. The first was gradually eliminated by regular expansions of civil service protection and, after World War II, by unionization of the public sector, which gave government workers an additional layer of protection from partisan politics (the largest union in the AFL-CIO today is the American Federation of State, County and Municipal Employees). Today the president personally controls fewer than 4000 appointments.[43] At the height of the spoils system—and with a much smaller federal government—presidents controlled well over 100,000 appointments.[44] Similarly, governors and big-city mayors who once controlled tens of thousands of jobs today control only a few thousand.

Party control over nominations was greatly weakened by the spread of the direct primary, one of the most important Progressive reforms. As we describe in Chapter 10, the United States is the only world democracy that relies on open, popular elections to decide nominations. In all other democracies, much smaller groups of party activists and officials choose party nominees.

Deprived of their principal resources, modern American parties had few sticks and carrots to work with. Electoral defeat did not mean that tens of thousands of people would lose their jobs; hence they were less inclined to work for parties and support them through thick and thin. Similarly, outsiders could challenge parties for their nominations, and if they won, the parties had no choice but to live with the fact. Controlling neither the livelihoods of ordinary voters nor the electoral fates of public officials, the party organizations atrophied.

However, deliberate political reforms are not the entire explanation for the weakening of American parties. Other factors also have contributed to their decline. These were less deliberate actions than they were independent developments that indirectly weakened the parties. For one thing, the communications revolution lessened the need for traditional parties. Candidates could raise funds through direct-mail appeals and then use such funds to reach voters directly by computer-generated mail and television. Elections have become less labor-intensive and more capital- and technology-intensive.[45] Technological developments have diminished the need for party workers and party support. In certain European countries, the parties have preserved their influence in some part by gaining control of modern communications. In Italy, for example, the Christian Democrats, Social Democrats, and Communists each had their own TV network.

A second development that undercut U.S. parties was the post–World War II increase in mobility—social, economic, and residential. Better educated voters had less need of parties to make sense of politics and guide their behavior. In a booming economy, voters had less need of parties to help them get jobs. And as the suburbs grew, the traditional, urban-based parties came to represent an ever-smaller proportion of the population, while the new, decentralized suburbs went largely unorganized.

Still a third development that may have weakened parties was the so-called reapportionment revolution set off by the Supreme Court's "one-person one-vote decisions" in the 1960s.[46] Prior to these Court decisions, political jurisdictions tended to coincide with natural communities. In the lower houses of many state legislatures, for example, every county had a seat. Thus a natural association existed between legislators and their local parties. In the aftermath of the reapportionment revolution, however, districting plans often cut across cities, counties, and other jurisdictions in the pursuit of numerical equality, racial balance, and other considerations. Today, legislators might have parts of several counties in their districts. The same is true of cities and towns. Such fragmentation makes each local party less important to the legislator, and in turn, any given local party has less interest in its legislator.

## The Revival of Party Organizations?

Despite the preceding story of decline, by the 1980s it was becoming clear that creative politicians had begun using the nearly empty party vessels for new ends. Most observers credit Republicans such as William Brock, chairman of the Republican National Committee (RNC) from 1976 to 1982, for leading the way. Through most of American history, a traditional organization chart of American parties would have given a misleading impression. Although organization charts of the parties normally look hierarchical, as shown in Figure 8.1, in practice the parties were anything but. On the contrary, through most of their 150-year history, the national committees were the weakest level of party organization, becoming active only during presidential years, when they served as organizing structures for the independent state and city organizations. Similarly, although powerful state organizations existed in some states, in many others the state organization was only a loose confederation of local organizations. That has changed greatly in the past quarter-century; today, the national committees are active and well financed, they have been joined by senatorial and congressional campaign committees, and together these national committees have helped rejuvenate party organization at lower levels.

In brief, Brock and the Republicans first saw the possibilities of adapting parties to the modern age. They used direct-mail technology to raise large sums of money. They hired full-time political operatives and experts on polling, fund raising, campaigning, and the media. They retained lawyers who knew how to exploit loopholes

### Figure 8.1

**Parties Are Not as Hierarchical as This Organization Chart Suggests**

SOURCE: Adapted from John Bibby, *Politics, Parties, and Elections in America* (Chicago: Nelson-Hall, 1992), p. 82.

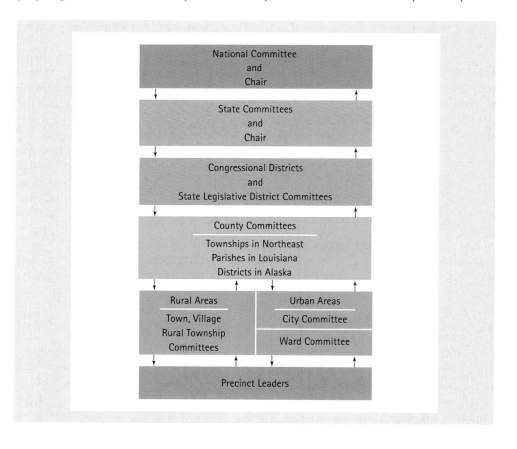

*Democratic Dilemma*

## "Soft Money" and Campaign Finance

Federal election law limits the amount that can be given directly to candidates. Consider an election for U.S. Representative. Individual contributions are limited to $1000 per candidate per election. Thus you can contribute $1000 to a candidate in the primary and another $1000 in the general election (and if state law is such that a run-off may be held after the primary, you can contribute $1000 in that election too). Interest-group and PAC contributions are limited to $5000 per candidate per election, so they can contribute a maximum of $15,000 to a candidate if three elections are necessary. The national and the state parties are permitted to contribute another $15,000 in each election. Such limits are easily evaded, however.

As we saw in a previous Democratic Dilemma, the courts have held that political contributions are a form of speech. Thus restrictions on campaign contributions and expenditures potentially violate First Amendment rights of free speech and expression. The courts have compromised the issue by upholding limits on contributions to specific candidates, but not limits on spending for other purposes. The result is that interest groups, PACs, and even wealthy individuals are allowed to spend unlimited amounts of money "independently" of the campaign. They can produce a commercial, publish an ad, or rent a billboard denouncing one candidate, supporting another, or advocating a position, all so long as they have not coordinated their activity with a candidate.

Similarly, parties can spend unlimited amounts of money on "generic" political activity. They can conduct polls on behalf of all their nominees. They can mount voter registration drives and "get out the vote" drives. They can pay for producing and broadcasting attack ads denouncing the other party and its candidates and for positive ads praising their own candidates and positions. So long as the ads or other activities are not explicitly coordinated with the candidates' campaigns, they are legal. Moreover, contributions to the parties for such purposes are not limited. Such contributions and the resulting spending are known as "soft money," and the amount spent in this way grew rapidly in 1990s campaigns.

Many public interest groups are critical of the expanding role of soft money. According to Ellen Miller of the Center for Responsive Politics, "there are unprecedented amounts of soft money and unprecedented opportunities to abuse the law. Soft money is an addiction; the more there is, the more they want it."[a] Critics advocate closing the loopholes that permit soft money, even to the extent of supporting proposals that First Amendment lawyers view as unconstitutional. Thus far, they have not been successful. On the contrary, a June 1996 Supreme Court decision not only upheld "soft money" contributions by parties but also affirmed the right of parties to spend unlimited amounts "independently" on behalf of their candidates.[b] Turned loose by that decision, the parties set new records as they raised more than 260 million in the 1996 campaign, three times what they had raised in 1992.[c]

Naturally enough, the political parties vigorously defend their expanding role in campaign financing. Some political scientists agree, noting that party spending adds a desirable broadening or coordinating force to a campaign finance system that otherwise would be dominated by the contributions of thousands of individual contributors and interest groups, each seeking its particular goals.

*What do you think?*
- *Does the soft money loophole allow too much to be spent on campaigns?*
- *Should spending by parties be reduced? Or does party spending produce an electoral process that is less fragmented and less influenced by interest groups than would be the case if soft money and independent party expenditures were restricted? (See Election Connection, Money in 1996, p. 296, for more on campaign finance reform.)*
- *Rather than attempt to limit spending, should we abandon all spending limits and instead simply have the law mandate full disclosure of all contributions?*

[a] Peter Stone, "Some Hard Facts About Soft Money," *National Journal* March 23, 1996, 672.
[b] Jonathan Salant, "Ruling Loosens Reins on Parties," *Congressional Quarterly Weekly Report*, June 29, 1996, 1857.
[c] Rebecca Carr, "As Soft Money Grows, So Does Controversy," *Congressional Quarterly Weekly Report*, November 16, 1996, 3272–3273.

---

in the campaign finance laws, as well as specialists skilled in computers and other technologies. These consultants and services were made available at low cost to Republican party organizations and candidates nationwide. Moreover, the RNC stretched the boundaries of campaign finance laws to funnel "soft money" to poor state and local organizations, rejuvenating them in the process (see the accompanying Democratic Dilemma). By the late 1980s, there were reports of Republican congressional campaign committees actively recruiting candidates for office, a level of national intervention that would have been unthinkable half a century ago. For their part, the Democrats imitated the Republicans, although later and less successfully until the Clinton presidency.

State and local party organizations have become more active as well; indeed, there are data to suggest that the resurgence of local organizations began earlier, in the 1960s.[47] In contrast to a generation ago, most state parties have permanent headquarters, usually in the state capital, and they employ full-time directors and other staff. Many state organizations now conduct statewide polls. They too provide campaign aid and recruit candidates more actively than they did a few decades ago. A major study of party organization leaves no doubt that in terms of personnel and activities, the state and local party organizations have a more tangible existence today than they did at mid-century.[48] In sum, the process of party decline seems to have been arrested right about the time that the thesis of party decline was advanced!

Still, the debate is not over. Some knowledgeable observers remain skeptical of the party resurgence thesis. John Coleman asks whether the parties are resurgent or "just busy."[49] Others grant that the parties are more active now than in earlier decades but argue that the newer activities do not make them stronger "parties" in any traditional sense. According to these critics, the party organizations essentially have become large campaign consulting firms, taking advantage of economies of scale to provide electioneering services to their associates. But despite increased recruiting efforts, such parties still do not have the control over the candidates that they had in the United States a century ago or that they have in most other democracies today; rather, U.S. candidates continue to have the upper hand over the parties. The new parties cannot deny anyone a nomination or demand their loyalty once elected. If a party-recruited candidate is defeated in a primary, the party normally supports the victor. And only rarely are "rebels" in office threatened with loss of party support. Indeed, in 1995, when Speaker Newt Gingrich suggested in a memo that rebellious freshmen members of the House Agriculture Committee would have their committee assignments changed, it was the Speaker who was forced to back down![50] The reasons are obvious. Independence is highly valued in the United States. If a party tried to discipline a member, it would probably only ensure his or her reelection. Moreover, despite the impressive efforts of the newly constituted parties, they contribute only a fraction of the resources spent on electioneering. Candidates have personal organizations and raise their own war chests. Contributions by the parties to members of Congress, for example, make up under 10 percent of all congressional campaign expenditures, although the amount spent "independently" is growing.

## Section Summary

American party organizations historically have been much more decentralized than those of other democracies, and elected officials have generally been much less united. This was particularly true during the 1950s and 1960s, and that situation resulted in a thesis of party decline. But those trends appear to have reversed in recent years, leading to a thesis of party renewal. Those skeptical of party renewal argue that what Americans call parties today are not really parties but giant political action committees—super-PACs—or large campaign consulting firms. You can call these new campaign organizations parties, but that does not make them parties in the traditional sense. The debate goes on.

## *Parties Versus Interest Groups*

Some political theorists believe that the power of interest groups is negatively correlated with the power of parties—when parties are strong, groups are weak, and vice versa.[51] The argument follows from two premises: first, that parties have incentives to synthesize narrow interests in order to make the broad appeals necessary to win elections; and second, that strong parties can provide electoral resources and deliver the vote, thus freeing their candidates from dependence on interest-group resources on the one hand, and insulating them from interest-group reprisals on the other.

This argument implicitly assumes two-party politics rather than multi-party politics, because in the latter, parties often make very narrow appeals. Indeed, in multi-party systems, there may be little difference between small parties and large interest groups. But within the two-party context, the argument has considerable plausibility. As discussed in the preceding chapter, interest groups proliferated in the Progressive era, when the parties were systematically attacked by reformers, and again in the 1960s and 1970s, when American parties reached their nadir, before their recent recovery. Just as nature is said to abhor a physical vacuum, so it may be that political vacuums cannot persist. When parties do not fill them, groups or some other source of influence will.

If this argument is valid, then the real alternative to party domination of the electoral process is not popular influence but interest-group influence. Rather than reflect the broad appeals of parties, elections will reflect the narrow views of special interests. Of course, interest groups are not the only competitors of parties in modern societies. As we will see in Chapter 9, another potential competitor is the media.

## Chapter Summary

Although the Constitution makes no mention of them, political parties have been part of American politics from the beginning. Indeed, American political history often is told in terms of "party systems," wherein each party has dependable support among particular social groups, so that elections tend to be similar within each system. Such electoral eras end with "critical" or "realigning" elections that alter the group alignments and usher in a new party system. At present, the United States has a party system that is less stable and more confusing than most of those that have preceded it.

The basic reason why parties have played such an important role in American history—as well as in the histories of all modern democracies—is that they perform coordinating functions that are essential in large-scale representative democracies. Parties coordinate the actions of numerous office holders and focus responsibility for their actions. Parties develop issues and educate the public, and they synthesize the disparate interests of a heterogeneous nation–state. Parties recruit and develop governmental talent and simplify the choices of voters who would otherwise be overwhelmed by the task of choosing among numerous candidates for office.

Despite these important functions that parties perform, most Americans do not hold them in especially high regard. One reason is that parties perform their functions as part of the continual struggle for political supremacy. Thus they act in accordance with partisan self-interest and historically have behaved dictatorially, corruptly, and divisively. The question reformers must face, however, is what alternative is there to party influence and activity, however imperfect parties may be?

The United States has the world's longest-lived two-party system. Most modern democracies have multi-party systems. One important reason for the difference is the electoral system prevalent in the United States: Our winner-take-all SMSP system gives opposition parties incentives to unite and their supporters incentives not to waste their votes on small parties that can't win. In contrast, most other democracies have PR systems, which give parties seats in parliaments roughly in proportion to the votes they receive.

Parties in the United States are not nearly so strong as they were in earlier periods, particularly in the late nineteenth century. Like other American institutions and processes, the parties have been democratized. Few "bosses" remain, party processes are open to all who register, and those elected under the party flag often go their own way when it suits them or their constituents. But despite much discussion of party decline, the Democratic and Republican parties continue to dominate American elections and to organize government. And despite periodic third-party insurgencies, that dominance is likely to continue.

**On the Web**

The Republican Party
www.rnc.org
The Internet home of the GOP. This site offers information on virtually all aspects of the Republican party—from its platform to its local, district organizations.

The Democratic Party
www.democrats.org
The Internet home of the Democratic party. This site offers information on virtually all aspects of the Democratic party—from its platform to its local, district organizations.

The Reform Party
www.reformparty.org
Politics1: The Internet home of the Reform party.
A Directory of U.S. Political Parties
www.politics1.com
*Politics1* and *The Politics1 Report* newsletter are published as a nonpartisan public service to promote fully informed decision making by the American electorate. Politics1 is unaffiliated with any political party, campaign, candidate, or organization.

# Key Terms

coalition government,
    p. 233
critical election, p. 227
direct primary, p. 230
divided government, p. 224
electoral system, p. 233
machine, p. 228

multi-party system, p. 233
national convention, p. 227
party alignment, p. 227
political parties, p. 220
Progressives, p. 230
proportional representation (PR),
    p. 234

realigning election, p. 227
realignment, p. 232
single-member, simple plurality
    (SMSP) system, p. 233
ticket splitting, p. 232
two-party system, p. 233
two-thirds rule, p. 232

# Suggested Readings

Aldrich, John. *Why Parties?* Chicago: University of Chicago Press, 1995. Wide-ranging rational-choice account of how and why politicians form and transform political parties.

Bibby, John F. *Politics, Parties, and Elections in America,* 4th ed. Belmont, CA: Wadsworth, 1999. Up-to-date textbook on party politics in the contemporary United States.

Burnham, Walter, D. *Critical Elections and the Mainsprings of American Politics.* New York: Norton, 1970. Influential statement of critical-elections theory. Suggests that party decomposition may make classical realignments obsolete.

Epstein, Leon. *Political Parties in the American Mold.* Madison: University of Wisconsin Press, 1986. Capstone work by a prominent student of American parties. Argues that modern parties have adapted and continue to play an important political role but that their future prospects are limited by ambivalent feelings in the American electorate.

Jewell, Malcolm E., and Sarah M. Morehouse. *Political Parties and Elections in the American States,* 4th ed. Washington, DC: Congressional Quarterly, 2000. Textbook on parties and elections at the subnational level.

Key, V. O., Jr. *Southern Politics.* New York: Vintage, 1949. Another classic. Again, the material is dated, but the theoretical arguments about the nature of politics in systems with weak or nonexistent parties remain relevant today.

Key, V.O., Jr. *Politics, Parties and Pressure Groups,* 5th ed. New York: Crowell, 1964. A classic text. Although dated, it can still be read both for historical interest and for theoretical observations about party politics in a democracy.

Maisel, L. Sandy, ed. *Political Parties and Elections in the United States: An Encyclopedia.* New York: Garland, 1991. Useful reference that provides short discussions of specific topics in the history of party politics in America.

Mayhew, David. R. *Placing Parties in American Politics.* Princeton, NJ: Princeton, 1986. Comprehensive study of state party organization in the twentieth century.

Sundquist, James. L. *Dynamics of the Party System,* rev. ed. Washington, DC: Brookings, 1983. History of national politics since the 1840s told from a party-systems perspective.

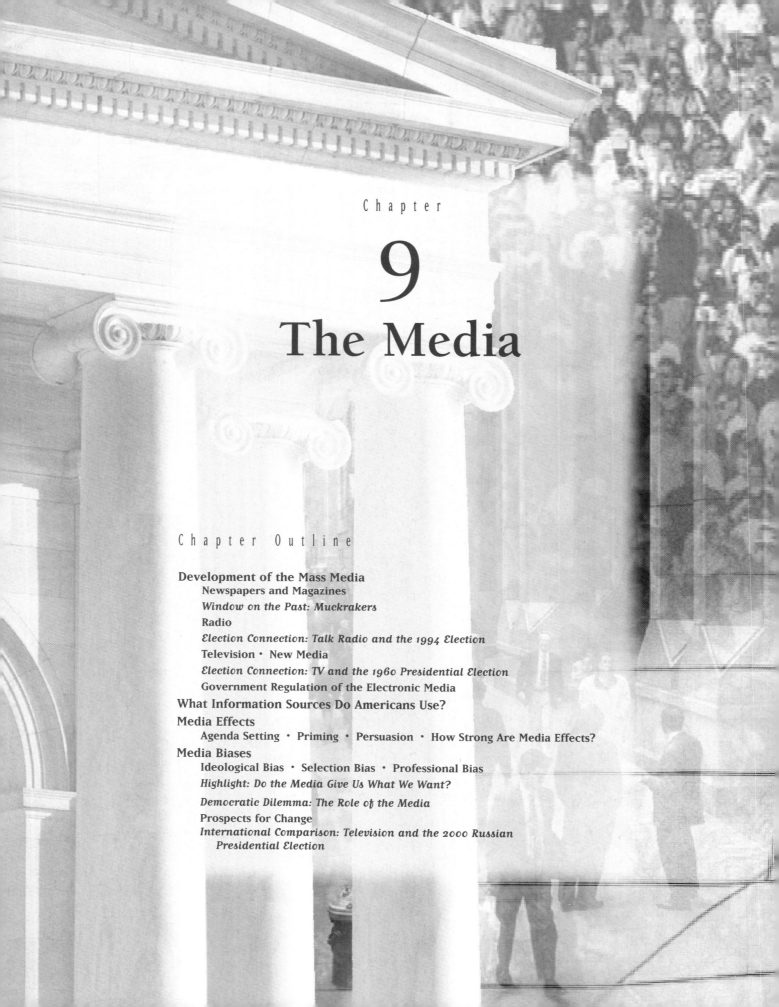

Chapter

# 9
# The Media

Chapter Outline

More than three decades ago, hundreds of thousands of young Americans fought in the Vietnam war. More than 58,000 died, and ten times that number were wounded. Vietnam has been called the first media war. Events associated with the war provide striking illustrations of the way the media affect public opinion.

### A Tale of Two Battles—I: Tet

In the 1964 election, Democrat Lyndon B. Johnson (LBJ) routed Republican Barry Goldwater. Running as the peace candidate, LBJ pledged to keep the United States out of the growing hostilities in Vietnam, promising that "Asian boys will fight Asian wars." Little by little, however, U.S. involvement deepened, and by late 1967 more than 500,000 troops were in Vietnam. With criticism of the war growing, the administration launched what it called a "progress initiative," a public relations campaign intended to build support for the war. Top officials announced that they could see "light at the end of the tunnel." The commanding general predicted that troop withdrawals might begin within two years.

And then came Tet. On January 30, 1968, as the Vietnamese New Year (Tet) celebration began, the North Vietnamese army and the indigenous Viet Cong guerrillas launched offensives all across South Vietnam, attacking 36 provincial capitals, 64 district capitals, 5 of the 6 largest cities, and numerous hamlets. Even the U.S. embassy in Saigon nearly was overrun. American forces were rocked by the surprise attacks.

Before Tet, criticism of the war had been confined to the political fringes, but now it spread to establishment circles. In the aftermath of the offensive, editorial comment turned pessimistic, and *Newsweek* published a "searching reappraisal." The tone of news coverage turned sharply critical, with increasingly negative stories about low troop morale, drug abuse, and corruption in the South Vietnamese government. CBS anchorman Walter Cronkite—the most trusted man in America according to the polls—was startled by the Tet footage. He announced that he would go to Vietnam to see the situation for himself. Upon returning to the United States, Cronkite broadcast a special report to the nation, contending that the war had become a bloody stalemate, with no military victory in sight:

> . . . it is increasingly clear to this reporter that the only rational way out, then, will be to negotiate, not as victors, but as an honorable people who lived up to their pledge to defend democracy and did the best they could.[1]

According to some accounts, LBJ said to his aides, "It's all over."[2] A journalist later wrote that "It was the first time in history that a war had been declared over by an anchorman."[3] Johnson fell 8 points in the polls immediately after Tet and continued to slide for six weeks. Popular support for administration policy dropped from 60 percent to 40 percent, and optimism about victory faded. On March 12, Senator Eugene McCarthy (D-MN), a peace candidate, got 42 percent of the vote in the New Hampshire Democratic primary. Four days later, Robert Kennedy announced he would oppose Johnson's renomination. On March 31, LBJ announced he would not seek reelection.

At first glance, this story is encouraging: Adverse developments occurred, the media reported the facts, the public responded, and leaders were replaced—the system worked! But within a few years, some people took a second look and reached a different conclusion.[4] As emotions subsided, as documents were declassified, and as former enemies communicated, revisionists made a persuasive case that the media got Tet wrong—that Tet in fact was just what the military said it was at the time: a major defeat for the enemy.[5]

Military planners had expected the North to launch a last major assault to break the stalemate and force negotiations.[6] Most of the initial Tet assaults were repulsed, with heavy casualties for the attackers. While LBJ's poll numbers plummeted, the North Vietnamese and the Viet Cong suffered nearly 60,000 combat deaths, compared to 4,000 for the United States and 5,000 for the South Vietnamese. The Viet Cong, who bore the brunt of the fighting, were decimated. They had expected a popular uprising, and when it did not occur, they were left exposed and outgunned. But this military defeat was turned into a psychological victory by the spin the media put on the facts. The initial surprise attacks were described as American defeats, even though most ended in bloody retreats. The media ignored the good performance of the South Vietnamese army, botched several big stories, and overlooked others.

Some conservatives accuse the media of losing the war, but more disinterested analysts believe the media's failings reflected inexperience and ignorance, not ideology. The point is simply that the media misconstrued Tet, making it look far worse than it was, just as they misconstrued the prior situation, making it look better than it was. Nevertheless, the evidence suggests that media accounts significantly affected public opinion,[7] supporting the views of those who believe in the awesome power of the media to "create reality."[8]

### A Tale of Two Battles—II: Chicago

Domestic politics grew increasingly turbulent after Tet. Elimination of graduate student deferments in the spring meant that the **draft**—the involuntary induction of young men into the military—now would reach deeper into the middle class. Partly in consequence, the antiwar movement grew rapidly. As the Democratic convention drew near, 10,000 demonstrators gathered in Chicago to protest the impending nomination of LBJ's vice-president, Hubert Humphrey, who had not entered a single primary and who was expected to continue Johnson's policies.

The level of tension that existed then exceeds anything familiar to observers of contemporary politics. Widespread violence was fully expected; Mayor Richard Daley called out extra police, asked for state and federal troops to go on standby, and threatened to treat protesters harshly. After some preliminary skirmishes, violence erupted. In what an investigative commission later described as a police riot, waves of armored police charged demonstrators, sometimes clubbing innocent

**draft**
(also called conscription) The involuntary induction of citizens into military service.

**The 1968 Democratic Convention in Chicago**
The Democrats did not get a positive "bounce" from their 1968 national convention. Outside the convention hall, Chicago police wielded clubs, tear gas, and Mace in pitched battles with thousands of antiwar protesters. Contrast this picture with the more recent "infomercial" conventions described below. *Why does a party work to tightly control the convention? Is this realistically possible?*

bystanders in the process. More than 500 protesters needed medical attention. Hard-bitten British reporters who had covered civil war in Northern Ireland wrote that the Chicago police had literally gone berserk.[9]

For the media covering the convention, however, the situation was heaven-sent. There were charges and retreats, snarling police dogs, horses, motorcycles—lots of action and great pictures. Bleeding protesters were eager to vent their spleen over the airwaves. Inside and outside the convention, public figures used the harshest rhetoric: In prime time, from the podium of the convention, Senator Abraham Ribicoff of Connecticut accused Mayor Daley of using Gestapo tactics in the streets outside. It was a night made for TV.

But reporters were not only reporting. By and large their sympathies were with the protesters. As Tom Wicker of the *New York Times* put it, "these were our children in the streets, and the Chicago police beat them up."[10] Over the course of the evening, the media lost all semblance of balance. Longtime NBC anchor Chet Huntley condemned the police. Walter Cronkite choked back tears.

Over and above the rhetoric, of course, TV was showing dramatic footage. The scene was hazy with tear gas, the sound of sirens filled the background, and throughout the evening the airwaves carried the continuous chant of the demonstrators: "The whole world is watching, the whole world is watching." Indeed, much of the United States was watching. But most were cheering. When the major poll results came in, American elites were stunned. Popular majorities believed that the Chicago police had acted appropriately; in fact, more believed that the police should have used greater force than thought their actions were excessive![11]

In other words, with the full power of the media telling them that atrocities were being committed in the streets of Chicago, the American people tuned it all out, stared at their TVs, and cheered for the police. So much for the awesome power of television. The simple fact was that most Americans at the time—many of them veterans of World War II and their families—didn't like demonstrators, whom they regarded as unpatriotic at best and subversive at worst. The protesters had gone to Chicago looking for trouble, and they had found it, whatever the media thought.

How powerful are the media, then? Are they an overwhelming force that brings down presidents, or a lot of sound and fury that ordinary Americans ignore? The answer is that, depending on the circumstances, the media are both, and everything in between. Media influence is a *contingent influence*; that is, it depends on other conditions present in a situation. Under some conditions, the media can have extremely powerful effects on public opinion, even to the extent of determining who wins elections and what governments do. But under other conditions, media effects are sharply limited. We discuss such contingencies in this chapter. We begin our analysis of the role of the media by answering these questions:

- How did the media evolve and attain their present position as an important component of American democracy?

- What kinds of media do Americans rely on for political information?

  Then we consider two important questions:

- In what ways do the media affect public opinion today?

- What types of bias characterize media reports today?

Our general point of view is that the relationship between the media and politics is ever-changing. Politicians strive to use the media for their own ends, and the media cooperate or not according to their ends. New developments in either the political or the technical realm can alter the equilibrium between these two important actors.

## Development of the Mass Media

The term **mass media** refers to means of communication that are technologically capable of reaching most people and are economically affordable to most. Failure to meet either criterion restricts a medium's reach to smaller parts of the population. Mass media have existed for less than two centuries. Their evolution is bound up with the evolution of American democracy: New developments in the media require politicians to adapt as part of a never-ending struggle to control the information that reaches their constituents. Information is power, and politicians contend with the media for control of it. In this section we trace the development of the major forms of mass media: print (newspapers and magazines) and broadcast (radio and television). We also look at the emergence of such new media as cable TV and the Internet. In each case we focus on control of the message: Who is responsible for the information transmitted? Because some fear that the media can wield a powerful influence on public opinion, some forms, particularly broadcast media, have been regulated in the interest of fairness.

**mass media**
Means of communication that are technologically capable of reaching most people and economically affordable to most.

### Newspapers and Magazines

At the time of the American Revolution, most of the colonies' newspapers were weeklies; the first daily paper began publication in Philadelphia in 1783.[12] These early papers were published by printers who, like Benjamin Franklin, also published books, almanacs, and official documents. They reprinted material from European newspapers and from each other, as well as letters and essays from their readers.

As party politics developed, both fledgling parties realized the importance of having a means of communicating with their constituents. Hamilton and the Federalists established a "house" paper, the *Gazette of the United States*, and the Jeffersonians responded with the *National Gazette*. These newspapers were unabashedly partisan: they printed the party line, viciously attacked the opposition, and depended for economic survival on government printing contracts. Modern presidents try to influence voters by "going public," speaking directly to the citizenry through the media. Although early presidents did not speak in their own voice, to the extent that the technology allowed, they have been going public since the beginning of the republic.[13]

Improvements in the manufacturing of paper and type and the invention of the steam-driven printing press made it cheaper and easier to publish papers. In 1833 the *New York Sun* began daily publication, selling for a mere penny. (Before that time the going price for a newspaper was an exorbitant six cents!) The rise of the penny press marks the birth of the mass media in the United States. Newspapers now were cheap enough to be purchased and read by millions of ordinary people. Within two years the circulation of the *Sun* was third in the world behind the two largest London newspapers.

As readership expanded, the newspapers began to acquire their modern characteristics. The first was an emphasis on local news—the older, more expensive weeklies focused more on national and international news and developments. The second was sensationalism; then, as now, crime and sex sold newspapers. The third was the rise of the human-interest story; more abstract discussions of politics and economics were left to the older weeklies. Still, the new penny papers were overwhelmingly partisan: According to the 1850 census, only 5 percent of the country's newspapers were neutral or independent.[14] Politicians worked hand in hand with the editors of friendly papers and withheld information from those allied with the opposition.

After the Civil War, an independent press began to develop. One-sided editorial positions remained common, but no longer were most newspapers regularly aligned with one or the other of the parties. Papers took critical positions on many late-nineteenth-century developments and advocated policy changes of various kinds. This was the heyday of the political machine, however, and party bosses were less dependent on newspapers than politicians in earlier decades. Party bosses used their own networks of party workers to communicate with constituents, most of whom were more influenced by jobs and contracts than by editorials.

More than ever, late-nineteenth-century newspaper circulation depended on sensationalism. Indeed, the 1890s are remembered for their "yellow journalism"—a term derived from the colorful comics pages of the sensation-seeking papers of the era. But again, conditions were changing. Around the turn of the century, many newspapers became large enterprises. Hearst, Scripps, and others bought up independent papers and consolidated them in great chains. Thus the typical paper no longer was the voice of a lone editor. The partisanship of newspapers continued to decline and the professionalism of journalists to increase. Some newspapers were important participants in the Progressive movement, publishing "muckraking" exposés of shocking conditions in American industry and corruption in government, as described in the accompanying Window on the Past. Magazines like *The Nation* and *The Atlantic* aimed at the new, educated middle class also appeared.

Today, newspapers and magazines continue to be an important part of the mass media: More than 10,000 newspapers and 12,000 periodicals are currently published. Large city papers like the *New York Times* and the *Los Angeles Times* have circulations of more than 1 million per day, and the *Wall Street Journal* reaches nearly 2 million. A relatively new entry, *USA Today*, has a circulation of about 1.5 million. *Time, Newsweek,* and *U.S. News and World Report* together sell about 10 million copies per week. These publications maintain their own Washington bureaus and send reporters all over the world. But even smaller city papers can get up-to-the-minute national and international news by subscribing to news services like the Associated Press (AP) and Reuters.

## *Window* on the *Past*    Muckrakers

In the late nineteenth century, the new, nonpartisan press opened its pages to a group of social critics later called "muckrakers" after Theodore Roosevelt's ambivalent characterization: "Men with the muckrake are often indispensable to the well-being of society, but only if they know when to stop raking the muck."[a] Roosevelt thought muckrakers often were too zealous and was comparing them to the man in *Pilgrim's Progress* (a popular nineteenth-century volume) "who was offered a celestial crown for his muckrake but who could neither look up nor regard the crown he was offered but continued to rake to himself the filth of the floor."[b]

The muckrakers published numerous exposés of the political and economic corruption common in the period, and as with investigative journalists today, some people in politics naturally resented their stories. Among the best-known muckrakers were Lincoln Steffens, Ida Tarbell, and Upton Sinclair. Steffens's articles in *McClure's Magazine* were later compiled as *The Shame of the Cities.*[c] The flavor of muckraker writing is apparent in the first page of his article on Minneapolis, "The Shame of Minneapolis: The Rescue and Redemption of a City That Was Sold Out."

> Whenever anything extraordinary is done in American municipal politics, whether for good or for evil, you can trace it almost invariably to one man. The people do not do it. Neither do the "gangs," "combines," or political parties. These are but instruments by which bosses (not leaders; we Americans are not led, but driven) rule the people, and commonly sell them out. But there are at least two forms of the autocracy which has supplanted the democracy here as it has everywhere it has been tried. One is that of the organized majority by which, as in Tammany Hall in New York and the Republican machine in Philadelphia, the boss has normal control of more than half the voters. The other is that of the adroitly managed minority. The "good people" are herded into parties and stupefied with convictions and a name, Republican or Democrat; while the "bad people" are so organized or interested by

*McClure's Magazine*

> the boss that he can wield their votes to enforce terms with party managers and decide elections. St. Louis is a conspicuous example of this form. Minneapolis is another. Colonel Ed Butler is the unscrupulous opportunist who handled the non-partisan minority which turned St. Louis into a "boodle town." In Minneapolis "Doc" Ames was the man.

### What do you think?
- *Was Roosevelt right? Are muckrakers indispensable?*
- *Do journalistic exposés do any good beyond furthering the author's reputation?*

[a] Address on laying the cornerstone of the House Office Building, April 14, 1906.
[b] From "Muckraker," in Jay Shafritz, *The HarperCollins Dictionary of American Government and Politics* (New York: Harper Perennial, 1992), p. 373.
[c] Lincoln Steffens, *The Shame of the Cities* (New York: McClure, 1904).

**Yellow Journalism**
William Randolph Hearst's *New York Journal* went on the warpath after the explosion of the *Maine* in Cuba (ultimately leading to the Spanish-American War). Many people feared that the Spanish were responsible, and Hearst's papers played on that fear. *What sort of coverage do media outlets give similar tragedies today? Compare this to the coverage of the Gulf War. How is the coverage different? Similar?*

The most important modern trends in the newspaper industry are the decline in the number and independence of papers. Afternoon newspapers have all but disappeared. Mergers have resulted in most cities now being served by one or two papers, as opposed to several a half century ago, and chains have continued to gobble up independent newspapers; the largest, Gannett, owns 74 papers with a combined circulation of nearly 7 million. Moreover, some media conglomerates own TV and radio stations and networks as well as newspapers. Some observers worry that the print media in particular, and the mass media in general, are becoming increasingly homogeneous as a result of common ownership and increased pressure to make profits for the larger enterprise.

## Radio

In the 1930s, the print monopoly of mass communications began to erode. The first radio stations were established in the 1920s, the first radio news agencies in the 1930s. Politicians quickly made use of this exciting new technology. Although he was known as "silent Cal," President Coolidge (1924–1928) took to the airwaves to reach voters. In the 1930s, Franklin Roosevelt helped calm a worried nation with his famous "fireside" chats, while radio demagogues, such as the anti-Semitic Father Coughlin, exerted a less calming influence. (Roosevelt also established a press relations office in the White House, recognizing that an increasingly professional media required an equally professional political response.)

Radio spread rapidly throughout the country. Today there are more than 14,000 stations that reach nearly 85 percent of the population at some time on an average day. Virtually every household has at least one radio, and the average is over five. And, of course, there are millions of cars on the road, nearly all of which contain radios. Because of its local orientation, and because it is relatively cheap, radio continues to be an important way for lower-level public officials to reach people.

At the national level, radio is an important means of political communication as well. Radio enjoyed something of a resurgence in the 1980s. President Reagan had a regular Saturday broadcast, and President Clinton adopted a similar practice.

Probably the most important recent political development in radio communications was the rapid increase in talk shows. Talk shows have existed for half a century, but until recently most were local productions. The development of satellite technology and the lowering of long-distance telephone rates removed the geographic limits on such shows, and today many of them are syndicated by large networks. Rush

*Election Connection*

## Talk Radio and the 1994 Election

**Talk Radio**
Steve Forbes adjusts his earphones while taking calls at a New Hampshire radio station shortly before that state's first primary.

The Republican takeover of Congress in the 1994 elections catapulted talk radio into the forefront of political discussion. According to one popular interpretation, 1994 was the year of the "angry white male," especially disaffected followers of Ross Perot, whom Rush Limbaugh, G. Gordon Liddy, and other Clinton-hating talk radio hosts had mobilized against the Democratic Congress. As San Francisco "shock jock" Geoff Metcalf put it, "I'd vote for PeeWee Herman before I'd vote for Clinton."

Talk radio certainly blossomed during the 1990s. And talk radio does have a conservative slant—a number of the highest-rated shows are hosted by well-known conservatives. But studies show that the audience for talk radio is more diverse than the popularity of conservative hosts might suggest; it is not nearly so heavily male and Republican as the stereotype. In 1995 only about half the listening audience consisted of white males, and only a fifth were angry white male Republicans. More recently a 1999 study showed even less of an imbalance between men and women, and, interestingly, there were more independent listeners than Republicans and Democrats combined.[a]

Talk show listeners are more highly educated than the general population and have slightly higher incomes. They are significantly more likely to be registered to vote and are more likely to participate in government in such ways as writing to public officials and attending political meetings. All in all, talk radio appears to be neither so different nor so threatening as some commentators assume.[b] In fact, talk radio was less prominent in the 1996 election than in 1994, and it was rarely mentioned in 1998. Perhaps the political use of talk radio has already peaked.[c]

[a] Diana Owen, "Who's Talking? Who's Listening? The New Politics of Radio Talk Shows," in Stephen Craig, ed., *Broken Contract* (Boulder, CO: Westview, 1996), pp. 127–146. Louis Bolce, Gerald De Maio, and Douglas Muzzio, "Dial-In Democracy: Talk Radio and the 1994 Election," *Political Science Quarterly* 111 (1996): 457–481. "The Talk Radio Research Project," *Talkers Magazine,* posted at **http://www.talkers.com.**
[b] Owen, "Who's Talking? Who's Listening?
[c] Ronald Elving, "On Radio, All Politics Is a Lot Less Vocal," *Congressional Quarterly Weekly Report,* May 10, 1997: 1102.

Limbaugh's show is perhaps the best-known example. This conservative commentator began broadcasting nationally in 1988 and, as of 2000, reaches about 20 million listeners on more than 600 stations.[15] Many local stations pair his show with one that is locally produced. In recent years, liberals have established more such shows in an attempt to compete for the radio audience, but as noted in the accompanying Election Connection, conservative viewpoints continue to have a wide edge. The talk format is a very popular radio format. The five most popular formats are (1) country and western, (2) adult contemporary, (3) talk, news, and business, (4) oldies and classic hits, and (5) religion.[16]

## Television

Today, the term *mass media* is associated first and foremost with television. There are more than 1500 television stations in the United States, and about 99 percent of all households have at least one TV set, the average being four. Like radio, TV is as close to being a universal medium of communications.

The first TV station went on the air in 1939, but TV grew very slowly during World War II. Afterward it spread rapidly; by 1960, 90 percent of all households had TVs. The industry was organized in three large networks—NBC, CBS, and ABC—that were established earlier as radio broadcasting networks. The networks pay local affiliates to carry programs the networks offer. The affiliates, in turn, make advertising time available for the networks to sell. The difference between what the networks pay the affiliates and what they get for the advertising time is their profit. Of course, the price the networks can charge for advertising time depends critically on the popularity of their shows, which is why ratings are such an important consideration when it comes to programming decisions.

The Eisenhower campaign was the first to take advantage of TV for communicating political messages, producing simple commercials that are amusing when viewed today. But it was the Kennedy administration that elevated TV above the print medium and used it effectively during the campaign (see the Election Connection that follows.) And during his short presidency, Kennedy held regularly televised press conferences that enabled him to go over the heads of the media and communicate directly with voters. Kennedy once commented to a reporter, "When we don't have to go through you bastards we can really get our story to the American people."[17]

When network TV reached its height in the 1980s, about 85 percent of all the commercial TV stations in the country were affiliated with one of the big-three networks. But the network system began to fray after government deregulated the cable industry in the 1970s. The percent of households with cable increased from 20 percent in 1980 to 67 percent in 2000. Prime-time network programming has lost more than a quarter of its audience as cable stations have proliferated, leading some scholars to suggest that the United States is in transition from an era of broadcasting to an era of narrowcasting.[18] Still, although the combined ratings of the ABC, CBS, and NBC evening news telecasts have fallen by 30 percent since the mid-1980s, they continue to draw an audience of about 70 million people on an average weekday.[19] Its coverage has declined over the past two decades, but network TV continues to be the largest single source of information available to Americans.

### New Media

During the 1992 campaign, Bill Clinton and Ross Perot irritated the establishment media by appearing on such nontraditional outlets as *Larry King Live!*, the *Arsenio Hall Show*, and even *MTV*. Clinton played his sax on *Arsenio Hall*, Perot virtually announced his candidacy on *Larry King Live!*, and even President Bush felt compelled to appear on *Larry King Live!* and *MTV* to compete with Clinton. Two years after the election, Vice-President Gore returned to *Larry King Live!* to debate Ross Perot over NAFTA, an important trade agreement, and Gore's performance was credited with helping to save the Clinton administration from an embarrassing congressional defeat.

Cable TV is the most widespread example of the **new media**. Although CNN and ESPN may seem no different from ABC and CBS to young Americans today, they are relatively newly established—both in 1979. The term *new media* includes a wide range of technological innovations of the past two decades, including VCRs, fax, cellular phones, satellite dishes, and CDs, but increasingly it is coming to mean anything connected with the internet.[20] Whenever you send e-mail or surf the Internet, you are using the new media.

**new media**
Cable and satellite TV, fax, e-mail, and the Internet—the consequences of the technological advances of the past few decades.

Except for cable TV, the new media are not yet mass media. For example, in 2000 less than half of American homes had personal computers, and only 70 percent of those had modems—although some people have access to the Internet at work or at various public sites. Surveys indicate as of summer 2000 about half of the American population has access to the Internet.[21] Even those with Internet access do not rank political Web sites high on their interest lists: One survey during the height of the 2000 primary season found that only 11 percent of Internet users had ever visited a candidate's Web site, a figure far lower than the number who had seen a candidate on network TV's evening news, or even CNN.[22]

But radio and TV also started small, and given the explosive growth of the Internet, it is likely that after another election cycle or two, the Internet will be a true mass medium. Consider that in 1992 neither presidential candidate had an official Web site; by 2000, Web sites were standard in campaigns as far down as the local

## Election Connection

# TV and the 1960 Presidential Election

As Dwight Eisenhower's second term drew to a close, it was unclear whether the presidency would revert to the Democratic control that was the norm during the New Deal party system or continue under Republican control. The prospective Republican candidate was Richard Nixon, Eisenhower's vice-president. On the Democratic side, the identity of the nominee was much less certain. One of the aspiring Democrats was John Kennedy, a young Massachusetts senator.

Kennedy had several liabilities. By the standards of the time, he was relatively inexperienced, especially in foreign affairs, and he had little by way of legislative accomplishment to show for his years in the Senate. In addition, Kennedy was a Catholic. Every president (and vice-president) prior to 1960 had been a Protestant. The only previous Catholic nominee, Al Smith in 1928, had lost badly—even in states in the Democratic "solid South." Although Kennedy was a personable, attractive candidate, many in the party feared that nominating a Catholic was a losing proposition.

To convince party leaders of his electability, Kennedy took his case to the people, previewing the kind of campaign that is now the norm. In 1960 only 16 states held primaries, and these chose only a small fraction of the convention delegates. Primaries were mostly "beauty contests" in which candidates could show strength and indirectly influence the professionals who would choose the nominee. Kennedy entered seven primaries.

In Wisconsin, Kennedy beat Senator Hubert Humphrey, who also had decided to take the primary route, but the voting pattern was troublesome. Kennedy lost the Protestant congressional districts and won Catholic districts, fueling fears that a Catholic still could not win a national election in a heavily Protestant country. This set up West Virginia, 95 percent Protestant, as the critical battleground. Kennedy took the direct approach, discussing the religion issue in a half-hour statewide telecast. Never giving up the offensive, Kennedy barnstormed the state, but according to Theodore White,

> Above all, over and over again there was the handsome, open-faced candidate on the TV screen, showing himself, proving that a Catholic wears no horns. The documentary film on TV opened with a cut of a PT boat spraying a white wake through the black night, and Kennedy was a war hero; the film next showed the quiet young man holding a book in his hand in his own library receiving the Pulitzer Prize, and he was a scholar; then the young man held his golden-haired daughter of two, reading to her as she sat on his lap, and he was the young father; and always, gravely, open-eyed, with a sincerity that could not be feigned, he would explain his own devotion to the freedom of America's faiths and the separation of church and state.[a]

**The Kennedy–Nixon Debates**
It is part of American political mythology that John F. Kennedy's confident appearance in the televised debates with Richard Nixon helped him win the election.

Kennedy beat Humphrey in Protestant West Virginia and went on to win the nomination. TV was not the only explanation for his victory—he had the Kennedy family fortune behind him, and by all accounts, used it freely—but more than any previous candidate, he had used TV as a critical part of the campaign.

The next task was to defeat a more formidable foe, Vice-President Nixon, viewed by many as more knowledgeable and experienced than Kennedy. Nixon and Kennedy agreed to a series of four debates to be carried by radio and, for the first time, TV.

A mythology has grown up about the debates. It is too much to say that they were the key to Kennedy's winning the election, although in what was to be the closest election in American history, everything was critical. The audience for the debates was huge, approaching World Series figures. Both candidates performed creditably, and the discussion was more substantive than TV debates generally are today. But winning debating points was not Kennedy's aim. By showing him side by side with Nixon, the debates helped Kennedy establish that he belonged in the race. He projected a cool, confident image that contrasted favorably with Nixon's more nervous, less comfortable appearance. Through the debates, Kennedy was able to partially offset Nixon's perceived advantage in maturity and experience and to overcome the hesitation of some Democrats who had been reluctant to vote for him.[b]

In November, Kennedy's Catholicism cost him votes in some areas and gained him votes in others, but the losses were concentrated in the South, where the Democrats had plenty of votes to spare. On the plus side, religion may have gained him the critical states of New Jersey and Illinois, the latter by a thin 9000-vote margin.[c] Kennedy became the first Catholic president, and the religious issue—at least in its Protestant versus Catholic form—was laid to rest.

*What do you think?*
- *How did Kennedy's visual appearance contribute to the perception (among TV viewers) that he won the debate?*
- *What characteristics are important to the TV audience?*

---

[a]Theodore H. White, *The Making of the President, 1960* (New York: Signet, 1961), p. 128.
[b]Nelson Polsby and Aaron Wildavsky, *Presidential Elections: Strategies of American Electoral Politics* (New York: Scribner, 1964), pp. 119–121.
[c]Angus Campbell, Philip Converse, Warren Miller, and Donald Stokes, "Stability and Change in 1960: A Reinstating Election," in *Elections and the Political Order* (New York: Wiley, 1966), Ch. 5.

**Drudge**
By reporting scandal and intrigue Matt Drudge has inserted his brand of journalism into events as important as Vice Presidential selections and impeachment, though as this screenshot shows, he does not concentrate exclusively on politics.

level. Use of the Web for raising money grew rapidly in the recent primary campaigns as well. In absolute terms the amount raised was small: In 1999 the four leading presidential candidates (Bradley, Bush, Gore, and McCain) raised a total of $139 million, less than 3 percent of which came from online contributions.[23] But the proportion raised online increased over the course of the year. Moreover, after McCain's upset victory in the New Hampshire primary, online contributions soared—in the month after New Hampshire, he raised $5.6 million, a quarter of his total fund raising.[24] Some

**The Future of Newspapers?**
*Why did people switch from newspapers to television to get their news? Could anything (like the Internet) drive out television broadcasts?*

skeptics contend that such figures are inflated because they include not just donors who voluntarily visit Web sites but also contributors who are reached by telephone and directed to Web sites.[25] But given the ease of contributing online, especially after e-check technology becomes widespread, online fund raising no doubt will continue to grow.[26]

Network TV has a large, heterogeneous audience. Thus it encourages politicians to make general appeals. In contrast, the newer media allow politicians to communicate more specific information to specialized audiences. Once again, an innovation in the media realm is altering the existing equilibrium between politicians and the media, this time apparently in favor of politicians. The new media give them a greater capacity to communicate to voters without having their messages constrained and edited by the traditional mass media. The struggle for control of information continues.

timeline

**300 Years of
U.S. Media**

## Government Regulation of the Electronic Media

One of the reasons why newspapers spread so rapidly in the United States was that freedom of the press was closer to being an absolute doctrine here than in other countries. That was not the case when it came to radio and TV, however. After the invention of radio, it soon became apparent that if they were left to their own devices, stations would broadcast on the same frequencies and interfere with each other. To deal with this problem, Congress created the Federal Radio Commission in 1927, followed by the Federal Communications Commission in 1934. These commissions were charged with regulating the industry by issuing licenses to operate and specifying the conditions of operation. When television became commercially viable, Congress added regulation of television to the FCC's responsibilities.

Because the government was allocating a limited public resource, granting it to some and denying it to others, the courts upheld the right of government to regulate what was said over the airwaves in ways that never would have been allowed in the case of print. And politicians certainly had incentives to regulate: After all, to be denied access to radio (and later to TV) could severely handicap their electoral chances. And to restrict access to some points of view could keep those points of view from receiving a fair public hearing. Thus the legislation creating the FCC established an **equal-time rule** specifying that if a station sells time to a legally qualified candidate, it must sell time to all such candidates. Later the rule was expanded, so that, for example, when the networks carry the president's State of the Union speech, they also must carry a reply from the opposition. From 1949 to 1987, the FCC also enforced a **fairness doctrine** that required stations to devote a reasonable amount of time to matters of public importance and to air contrasting viewpoints on those matters. Eventually the doctrine also required stations to give public figures who were attacked an opportunity to reply.

In the 1970s, technological advances began to undercut the rationale for government regulation. Soon thereafter, the Bell Telephone monopoly of telecommunications was broken up, and new technologies such as fiber optics and microwave transmission created a virtually unlimited number of radio and television channels, easing fears that a few large networks could deny a hearing to issues or candidates they opposed. In 1987 a deregulation-minded FCC staffed by appointees of President Reagan repealed the "fairness doctrine." And more deregulation was to come.

By the mid-1990s, technological developments had made the 1930s structure of communications regulation hopelessly obsolete. After three years of hard work, the Congress overwhelmingly approved a major telecommunications act in 1996, a genuinely bipartisan effort in the conflict-ridden 104th Congress. As much as practically and politically possible, the act sought to replace government regulation with competition. It created a giant national market for telecommunications services. Previously, local phone service had been separated from long-distance service, and both had been separated from cable technology. The new legislation abolished the local phone monopolies but allowed the local companies to compete in offering long distance.

**equal-time rule**
Promulgated by the FCC, required any station selling time to a candidate to sell time to other candidates at comparable rates.

**fairness doctrine**
Promulgated by the FCC, required stations to carry some public affairs programming and to balance the points of view expressed.

Cable rates were deregulated, but telephone companies were permitted to offer video services. As a result of the act's removal of long-standing barriers between sectors of the industry, far-reaching change in the telecommunications field is expected in the years ahead. Some of today's new media may soon become old media.

Despite this general trend toward deregulation, recent years have seen a rise in the number of proposals for regulation of the Internet. Some people would like to regulate content, making it difficult for children to reach pornographic, hate-filled, violent, or otherwise objectionable Web sites, for example. The courts probably will rule against most such attempts to restrict content transmitted over the Internet. Various others would like to regulate e-commerce. For example, many state governors are unhappy that purchases made over the Internet are often not subject to state sales tax, which has the effect of denying their states revenue and putting state merchants at a competitive disadvantage. This is a touchy subject, and both George W. Bush and Al Gore finessed it during the 2000 campaign by supporting the current moratorium on Internet taxation, which expires in October 2001.

### Section Summary

There have been enormous changes in how citizens get political information in the United States, from short newspapers printed by hand on crude presses to the amazing technology of the computer age. Print was joined by radio and broadcast TV, and both have been joined by the new media: cable TV and the Internet. Politicians adapt to each stage in the evolution of the media, attempting to use prevailing media to best advantage. On the one hand, the proliferation of new media enables politicians to reach specialized audiences with little filtering by journalists, but on the other hand, the Internet's creation of a "global village" means that anything a politician does or says can spread to every corner of the country very quickly.

## What Information Sources Do Americans Use?

Communication is a two-way street. No one can make people read newspapers, listen to radio, watch TV, or visit a home page. Citizens are free to consume or ignore the information provided. When we examine the media choices of ordinary Americans, however,

**Figure 9.1A**

**TV Is the Primary Source of News for Contemporary Americans**

SOURCE: Data are taken from the Roper Organization, *America's Watching: Public Attitudes Toward Television* (1997).

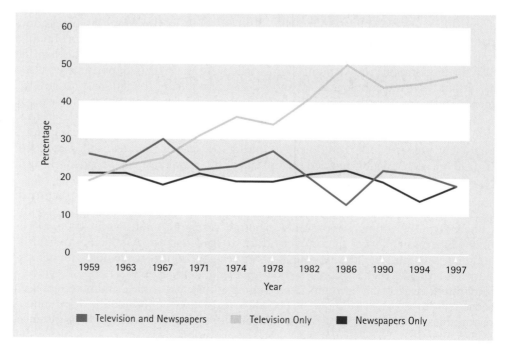

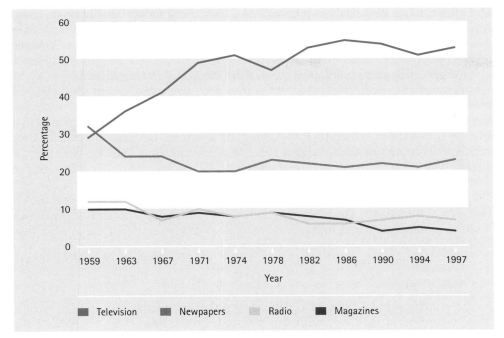

**Figure 9.1B**

**Contemporary Americans Consider TV Their Most Credible Source of News**

SOURCE: Data are taken from the Roper Organization, *America's Watching: Public Attitudes Toward Television* (1997).

there are few surprises. For the most part, media companies are profit-making enterprises, so their growth or decline should reflect the tastes and choices of the popular audience.

Surveys show that TV supplanted newspapers as the public's principal source of information in the early 1960s. As shown in Figure 9.1A, nearly 60 percent of Americans today rely primarily on television. A much smaller 20 percent rely primarily on newspapers, and the remaining 20 percent use both. Figure 9.1B shows that a comparable percentage reports TV to be the most credible source of information. In short, TV is the dominant provider of information in American society.

An important qualification to this conclusion about the dominance of TV is that citizens' reliance on different kinds of media varies with the focus of their attention.[27] In presidential campaigns, people rely more on TV than on newspapers by a margin of 3 to 1. But in statewide races for governor and senator, TV's edge is only 5 to 3. And in local election contests, newspapers have an edge over TV as the principal source of information: The national networks do not cover local races in small cities and towns, except under unusual circumstances. Whether newspapers can maintain their importance in this niche as local cable stations proliferate remains to be seen.

Individuals vary in predictable ways in their absorption of information.[28] Well-educated individuals are more likely than the less well educated to rely on newspapers. As one would expect, the younger generation relies more on TV than its elders. Minorities rely on TV and newspapers less than whites (but they pay more attention to racial and ethnic publications and radio stations than do whites). Newspaper supporters argue that print is more informative than TV, but research fails to support that argument once the characteristics of the audience (such as education) are taken into account.[29] That is, people of comparable levels of education tend to learn about the same amount, whether they rely on print or television.

## Media Effects

The rapid spread of radio in the 1930s coincided with the rise of fascism in Europe. Some worried that this was more than coincidence. Before 1930, political leaders had communicated with constituencies indirectly, speaking and writing to lower-level leaders who in turn communicated with the grassroots. But demagogues like Hitler and Mussolini spoke directly to their audience, giving rise to fears that radio was contributing to the creation of a "mass society" in which charismatic leaders could sway vast numbers of lonely individuals no longer tightly integrated into churches, unions, local communities, and other social networks.[30] Stimulated by such concerns, researchers conducted numerous studies of the media's ability to persuade.

Contrary to expectations, research on the effects of mass communication proved mostly negative. Americans, at least, were remarkably resistant to attempts to change their views. Many studies found selective perception: People ignored information that was not consistent with their predispositions and absorbed information that was. Thus exposure to communications tended more to reinforce than to change what people already believed.[31] By 1960, a **minimal-effects thesis** had become widely accepted: The mass media, it was assumed, had only a slight impact on American public opinion.[32]

After the rapid spread of TV, however, younger generations of researchers took a new look at the subject. This newer research has documented important media effects, such as agenda setting and priming, that are more subtle than the kind of mass persuasion earlier studies had sought to document.

### Agenda Setting

Public opinion scholar Bernard Cohen argued that the media may not tell people *what* to think, but that they tell people what to think *about*.[33] The media set the agenda, even if they do not determine how the issues will be decided. We know that many people are relatively uninformed about many issues. By choosing to focus on one issue or problem rather than another, the media can induce people to think about that issue or problem. In recent years, for example, various catastrophes in Third World countries have gone largely unnoticed in the developed countries until the media—particularly television—turned its attention to them. In October of 1984, the international community launched a massive relief effort to alleviate famine in Ethiopia after the British Broadcasting Corporation (BBC) showed heart-rending footage. During the preceding year the *New York Times* had published 4 front-page articles on the famine, the *Washington Post* had published 3, and the Associated Press (AP) wire service had carried 228 stories.[34] But not until TV decided to cover the story and send tragic pictures into American living rooms did people in great numbers become aware of the problem and support a governmental effort to help.[35] Similar responses followed media coverage of Somalia, Rwanda, and other more recent scenes of human tragedy. Some observers have wondered whether the United States would have intervened in Kosovo but for the images transmitted by TV. Media analysts have even given government responses like these a nickname, the **CNN effect**, after the tendency for a problem to be addressed once the Cable News Network covers it.

**Agenda setting** is well documented, although much of the evidence is not conclusive.[36] That is, if unemployment rises, the media increasingly focus on unemployment, and people in growing numbers begin to think of unemployment as a major national problem, is this agenda setting, or are the media and the people both responding to the same real conditions? Similarly, some careful studies of the CNN effect conclude that the independent impact of the media has been exaggerated; astute government officials use the media to place problems on the national and international agendas.[37] A study of failed attempts to pass national health care plans concluded that "peaks in the volume and substantive focus of media reporting coincided with upsurges in discussions of real-world developments and fierce political debate over policy reforms."[38] Thus, to attribute heightened public concern to media coverage in all cases where the two coexist undoubtedly overestimates agenda setting by the media. Because of such ambiguities, experimental studies that raise viewer concern about subjects *not* high on the national agenda provide some of the best evidence of agenda setting.[39]

---

**minimal-effects thesis**
Theory that the mass media have little or no effect on public opinion.

**CNN effect**
Purported ability of TV to raise a distant foreign affairs situation to national prominence by broadcasting vivid pictures.

**agenda setting**
Occurs when the media affect the issues and problems people think about, even if the media do not determine what positions people adopt.

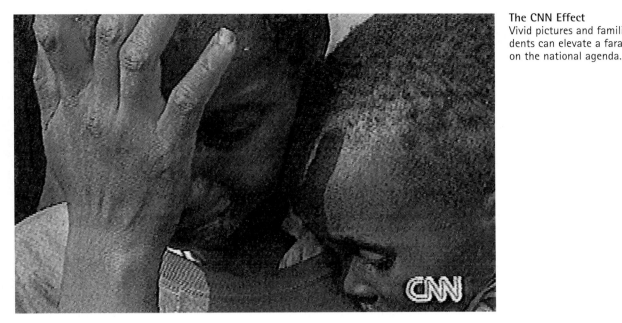

**The CNN Effect**
Vivid pictures and familiar correspondents can elevate a faraway situation on the national agenda.

## Priming

As we related in Chapter 5, in February of 1991, the American ground offensive in Kuwait began, and within a week the Iraqis had been driven back across their border, with great loss of life. President Bush's approval ratings soared, reaching unprecedented levels (near 90 percent) in the immediate aftermath of the war. Within a year, however, Bush's ratings had plummeted. What happened? In the spring of 1991, his ratings were based primarily on his handling of the war in the Gulf, but when the war ended, the media turned to other stories, chiefly the struggling economy. Gradually, Bush's ratings became dependent on his handling of the economy, which was viewed far less positively than his handling of the war.[40]

Bush's fall from favor is an example of **priming**—events and the media primed people to evaluate him according to his handling of the war in February 1991, but in terms of the economy later. We emphasize that the media were not totally responsible for this shift in standards of public evaluation. War pushes everything else off the agenda of public opinion: Husbands and wives and sons and daughters in danger make all other concerns seem minor in comparison. Thus both the media and the public were reacting to the reality of the war. Similarly, after the war, both the media and the public were reacting to the reality of the struggling economy. Still, studies suggest that the media overemphasized the economic difficulties facing the country, thus heightening public pessimism as well as the attention people paid to an issue on which President Bush was vulnerable.[41]

**Framing** and priming are related notions.[42] In Chapter 5 we explained that Americans tend to be more supportive of abortion when the issue is framed as a question of a woman's freedom to choose, and less supportive when it is framed as the act of destroying a potential life. How issues and arguments are framed can produce important differences in public opinion. For example, if the issue of crime is framed as a problem that presidents can and should do something about, it is more likely to have a political impact than if it is framed as an uncontrollable by-product of family and religious breakdown that presidents can do little about. During the 1996 campaign, Robert Dole attacked President Clinton for appointing judges who were soft on criminals. He was attempting to frame the issue in a way that reflected negatively on the president. Inducing people to think along certain lines rather than others can affect their positions on issues and their evaluations of public officials.

**priming**
Occurs when the media affect the standards people use to evaluate political figures or the severity of a problem.

**framing**
Occurs when the media induce people to think about an issue from one standpoint rather than others.

## *Persuasion*

In 1984 *The New Yorker* published a cartoon in which a man sits up in bed and comments, with surprise, "I went to bed a Democrat, but woke up a Republican."[43] Seldom do people undergo such political conversions, and there is little evidence that the media have the ability to convert people in dramatic ways, at least in large numbers. Nevertheless, by setting the agenda, priming, and framing, the media can subtly influence people's views and choices. By emphasizing issues that help a candidate, the media can provide an advantage, and vice versa. By emphasizing some aspect of elected officials' performances, the media can help or hurt them. If persuasion occurs, it is generally the end result of a chain of subtle influences rather than the direct product of media attempts to convert people to an alternative point of view.

## *How Strong Are Media Effects?*

The view that the mass media would enable demagogues to manipulate public opinion clearly overstated the influence of the media. Similarly, the "minimal-effects thesis" understated the effects of the media. The media can affect the agenda—what people think about—and can prime people to think about some issues and conditions rather than others. Effects like agenda setting, priming, and framing depend on both the characteristics of the audience and the nature of the information. People who are uninterested in and uninformed about politics are most susceptible to agenda setting. Because political independents are more likely to be uninformed, they can more easily be swayed as political attention shifts from issue to issue. On the other hand, partisans are more easily primed—encouraged to think in terms of certain issues. One study found that Democrats tend to prime on civil rights and unemployment, Republicans on defense and inflation. Partisans were predisposed to think in terms of issues and problems that were at the core of their party's concerns.[44]

But the characteristics of the information being communicated probably are at least as important as the characteristics of the people receiving it. When the problem or event is far away—well beyond personal experience—and the mass media provide the only information we have, their influence will be greater than when information is closer to home and people have some personal basis for arriving at opinions.[45] The Tet and Chicago examples support this view. The media provided the only available information about the events in South Vietnam, and inasmuch as there was no alternative source of information, the media had considerable ability to affect the public's view of the war. In the case of Chicago, however, Americans were being shown protesters they had seen demonstrating on their local college campuses, at local public buildings such as draft offices, and in city streets. Many people had developed strong views about protesters and protests; there was little opportunity for the media's interpretation of the events in Chicago to alter such predispositions. Thus the media *can* have a major impact on public opinion, but *whether* they do so depends on both whom they are reaching and what they are focusing on. Media influence is *contingent*; there is no across-the-board or automatic media effect.

## **Media Biases**

Politicians constantly attempt to set the agenda, prime people to think in certain ways, and frame arguments to advance their position. Those tactics have been used at least since humans have been able to communicate. Of course, when politicians try to change public opinion, we presume that they are biased. They are expected to present one case—theirs—and we can discount their arguments and appeals accordingly.

But the modern media purport to be objective. They are supposed to report events and describe issues and conditions. If, through agenda setting, priming, and framing, they alter public opinion, it is important that they do so in a neutral way. If they fail to maintain neutrality, they become players in the political process, not disinterested chroniclers of that process. Many observers believe that the media do have characteristic biases, which fall into several general categories. The most common charge is that the media show political bias, but most media critics believe that selection bias and professional bias are more serious.

## Ideological Bias

Conservatives often complain about the "liberal media." There is no doubt that liberal viewpoints are over-represented among practicing journalists, but how much those viewpoints influence political coverage is far less certain.

Numerous studies report that journalists are more Democratic than the population at large: Even George McGovern and Walter Mondale got majorities of the vote among journalists when Republicans Nixon and Reagan were winning by landslides. More recently, a survey of Washington bureau chiefs and congressional correspondents reported that in 1992, 89 percent voted for Clinton, compared to 43 percent of the electorate.[46] More detailed analyses indicate that journalists hold views that are more liberal than those of other college-educated professionals, especially on so-called social issues—abortion, drugs, crime, the death penalty, feminism, gay rights, and so forth.[47]

But do such biases show through in the news? Some studies find evidence of partisan bias on the part of reporters. For example, a team of researchers carefully watched tapes of the network evening news programs broadcast during the 1984 campaign. Their aim was to evaluate the **spin**—the positive or negative slant—that reporters and anchors put on their reports. They found that President Reagan got 10 seconds of bad spin for every second of good spin. In contrast the Democratic candidate, Walter Mondale, had a 3 to 2 ratio of good to bad spin.[48] On a less serious note, a study of the jokes told by late-night TV talk show hosts Johnny Carson and David Letterman during the 1988 campaign found that Republicans were skewered twice as often as Democrats.[49]

> **spin**
> The positive or negative slant that reporters or anchors put on their reports.

Despite such suggestive findings, there really is not much evidence of a consistent liberal bias in media coverage of politics. Although journalists and editors report predominantly liberal sentiments, readers of their newspapers do not perceive predominantly liberal viewpoints.[50] And although Democrats got more good spin than Republicans in 1984, more than three-fourths of the coverage had no spin at all. A study of newspaper, television, and Web coverage of the 2000 campaign during October found that Al Gore received significantly more negative coverage than George W. Bush.[51] Michael Robinson, who has conducted a number of spin studies, suggests that the media are harder on incumbents (Democrat Carter in 1980, Republican Reagan in 1984) than on challengers. And the studies indicate a tendency to pile on apparent losers (Democrat Carter in 1980, Republican Bush in 1992). Similarly, late-night TV hosts focus on whoever offers the best material, regardless of ideology. In the 2000 primary season they were easy on Republican John McCain, tougher on Republican George W. Bush, and toughest of all on Democratic President Clinton, even though he wasn't running![52] As of mid-September 2000, George W. Bush had been the butt of 50 percent more late night jokes than Al Gore.

Bill Clinton's early ups and downs with the national media provide a good example of the media's partisan inconsistency. The Gennifer Flowers feeding frenzy nearly destroyed Clinton's 1992 nomination hopes. However, after the 1992 campaign, many critics and even some in the media community charged that the media had been overly sympathetic to Clinton and too hard on Bush.[53] But within six months, the press had turned on Clinton again, filing one story after another about scandal, incompetence, and disarray within the administration.[54] The media focused on Clinton's $200 haircuts, parties with actress Sharon Stone, the Whitewater real estate scandal, the suicide of a top aide, and other subjects that reflected negatively on the administration,

**Figure  9.2**

Newspapers Endorse Republican
Presidential Candidates More Often
than Democratic Candidates

SOURCE: Harold Stanley and Richard Niemi,
*Vital Statistics of American Politics*, 5th ed.
(Washington, DC: CQ Press, 1995), p. 73.

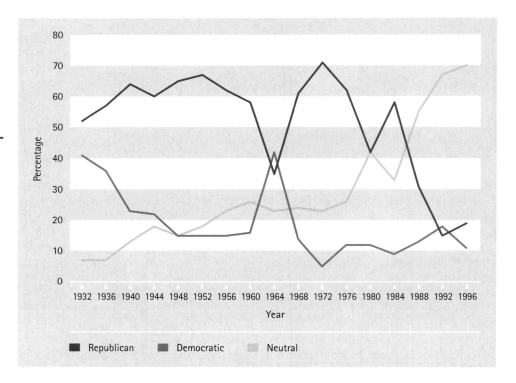

while not recognizing programmatic victories that were genuine accomplishments in the eyes of disinterested observers.[55]

Although they get less publicity, critics on the left of the political spectrum also charge that the media are ideologically biased, only they see a conservative bias. After all, even if reporters and editors are liberal, Figure 9.2 shows that the endorsements of the newspapers they work for go disproportionately to Republican candidates. Since 1930, only Lyndon Johnson and Bill Clinton have been endorsed by more newspapers than their Republican opponents.[56]

Moreover, whatever the personal views of the journalists and editors, the TV stations, major newspapers, and newsmagazines are profit-making enterprises. They are managed by rich executives, they have stockholders who demand a return on their investment, and they must avoid offending major corporations to whom they sell advertising. All of these circumstances exert a conservative pull. The eminent journalist Ben Bagdikian argues that "All of broadcast and printed news is pulled by a dominant current into a continuous flow of business conservatism. . . . It has a sufficiently powerful effect to shrink other ideas and news of tax-supported social needs necessary in any self-correcting democracy."[57] In the most recent version of this line of criticism, questions have been raised about whether superstar news media personalities ("buckrakers") are unduly influenced by corporate interests who pay them honoraria.

In sum, an analysis of network TV and national print coverage of politics will uncover instances of partisan and ideological bias, and these probably favor the liberal side of issues more often than not. But few disinterested observers believe there is an overwhelming liberal bias in the media. Less often recognized conservative forces exist as well, particularly on economic issues. Moreover, the weakening of the dominance of the big-three networks should reduce any existing liberal bias. Local news and public affairs programs are more likely to reflect more conservative local sentiments than the network news operations headquartered in New York,

**Dilbert**
Americans generally get "bad" rather than "good" news, though they often express a preference for positive stories. *Why does the media lead with controversy and mayhem? Is it what the people really want despite their complaints?*

Washington, and Los Angeles. Cable channels broadcast programs produced by conservative and evangelical groups. Talk radio has a conservative slant. The Internet is open to all points of view, and libertarians are especially well represented there. In short, as network dominance weakens, the communications channels of the future will be more open to alternative points of view than were the airwaves in the past.

Of course, this is not to say that bias is not a serious problem. It is only to say that other forms of bias—selection bias and professional bias—may be more serious than ideological bias. Both liberals and conservatives worry about these.

## Selection Bias

Periodically, frustrated citizens write to the editor to complain that all their newspaper ever prints is bad news. People working hard and contributing to their communities is not news; one sociopath who runs amok is. Why not more good news? The answer is that to a considerable extent, the media *define* news as bad news.[58] A government program that works well is not news; one that is mismanaged, corrupt, or a failure *is* news. An elected official who is doing a good job is not newsworthy; one who is incompetent or mired in a scandal is. Far more pervasive than ideological bias is a bias toward the negative in the media. An emphasis on the negative is a kind of **selection principle**; that is, reporters and editors consider some kinds of stories more newsworthy than others.

Professor Larry Sabato argues that the negative tone of the media has become much more prominent in recent decades. He contends that presidents from Franklin Roosevelt to John Kennedy enjoyed the support of a press with a "lapdog" mentality. Johnson and Nixon were subject to far greater scrutiny from a press with a "watchdog" mentality. Succeeding presidents, he maintains, suffer mean treatment from a press with a "junkyard dog" mentality.[59] Some observers believe that the negative tone of press coverage has contributed to the increased cynicism of the American public toward politics and government.[60] The claim is that politics today is no worse than in previous eras—perhaps it is better—but that media treatment makes things *seem* worse.

Another selection bias is that "news" is that which is new, and especially that which is exciting and unusual as well. Thus events and crises make better news than gradual developments or persistent conditions, which do not lend themselves to the kind of hit-and-run coverage favored by the contemporary media. Heroes and villains are wanted, not abstract social and economic developments. This bias is particularly characteristic of TV, which is even more fast-paced than print. TV needs dramatic events, colorful personalities, bitter conflicts, short and snappy comments (sound bites), and above all, compelling pictures—a frequently heard maxim is "If it bleeds, it leads." The result can be insufficient treatment for stories that do not fit the needs of the media and distorted treatment of stories to make them fit those needs.[61]

**selection principle**
Rule of thumb according to which stories with certain characteristics are chosen over stories without those characteristics.

Our remaining correspondents fly from earthquake to famine, from insurrection to massacre. They land running, as we were all taught to do, and they provide surprisingly good coverage of whatever is immediately going on. . . . [But] we miss anticipation, thought, and meaning. Our global coverage has become a comic book: ZAP! POW! BANG-BANG.[62]

Numerous observers have pointed to such selection biases as a factor in the largest (in financial terms) policy debacle in American history—the Savings and Loan (S&L) disaster of the 1980s, which ultimately is expected to cost taxpayers a total of 200 billion dollars.[63] Democrats and Republicans, Congress and the executive—all share the blame. As early as 1981, accountants, prominent economists, and a top government regulator began to issue warnings, eventually declaring the S&L industry bankrupt. But by the time the government finally acted to close down insolvent S&Ls in 1989, many had been operating recklessly for years, secure in the knowledge that their losses would be covered by the Federal Savings and Loan Insurance Corporation—that is, by taxpayers.

Only after the debacle did the media pick up the story. Why? There are many contributing reasons, but several have to do with the needs of the media. For one thing, the story was about financial policies that journalists themselves found uninteresting, certainly much less interesting than investigating the sex lives of politicians. As one journalist commented, "It was a 'numbers' story, not a 'people' story."[64] For another thing, even if journalists had been interested in the story, it was complex and did not lend itself to short, simple coverage. The problem was particularly acute for TV. It was hard to summarize the developing S&L crisis in a 30-second story, and interesting pictures were difficult to come by. Not until housing developments were being auctioned off for a song, S&L executives indicted, and members of Congress investigated did the media have the kind of story (and pictures) that it liked.

When the media finally did pick up the story, they distorted it, emphasizing fraud and corruption when, in fact, experts estimate that only a small proportion of the losses were a result of fraud. Most of the problem came from the ordinary operation of the political process.[65] Every congressional district has S&Ls, as well as industries that depend on them, such as real estate and construction. These interests are important components of many local economies. Moreover, S&L executives, realtors, and construction interests are generous contributors to political campaigns. They lobbied Congress and the executive branch, who obliged them with favorable legislative changes and protected them from regulators when they got into trouble. Economists and other experts warned that these policies would lead to economic disaster; when they did, the press emphasized the corruption of individuals rather than a political process that ignored the predictable long-term effects of policies for short-run electoral gain. Thus the media even missed the opportunity to articulate a useful lesson that might avoid such a problem in the future.

## Professional Bias

A third kind of media bias arises from the demands of the journalism profession today. A few journalists are experts who work specific "beats"—the business reporter, education reporter, health reporter, Supreme Court reporter, and so on. But most reporters and journalists are generalists who lack specific substantive expertise. They operate on tight deadlines and must start from scratch on each new story. Thus, on many subjects more complex than scandals and conflicts, they are dependent on experts and other outside sources for information and interpretation. Ironically, despite the familiar image of the investigative reporter, studies find that reporters uncover only a small fraction of the scandals they report—probably less than one-quarter.[66] Government agencies reveal the lion's share, and they generally do so officially, not through surreptitious "leaks."

Moreover, as journalists themselves recognize, the news media have increased their emphasis on entertainment.[67] Especially in the case of TV, looks and personali-

participation

**Where Do You Get Your News, and How Reliable is It?**

## Highlight       Do the Media Give Us What We Want?*

Humorist Dave Barry writes: I am getting tired of listening to the public carp about the news media. Every time I turn on the TV, they're interviewing some typical heartland Americans—five or six hard-working, salt of the earth agricultural guys wearing bib overalls and baseball-style caps imprinted with the brand name of a pesticide, drinking coffee in a diner in some soy-bean-infested region. One of these guys always says something like: "I'm sick of the media. All they want to talk about is scandals and sex! We want 'em to cover the issues! And don't sensationalize. Stick to the facts." And the other guys nod in agreement . . . the antimedia remarks they make are echoed by many Americans. Probably, if anybody asks you what you think of the news media, you say, "I think they go too far. They should stop covering sex and go back to covering important issues, such as the economy." You make a strong point. Let me respond by saying this: Liar, liar, pants on fire. You don't want to read about the economy. You love to read about sex. *Everybody does.*

Let's consider two headlines. FIRST HEADLINE: "Federal Reserve Board Ponders Reversal of Postponement of Deferral of Policy Reconsideration." SECOND HEADLINE: "Federal Reserve Board Caught in Motel with Underage Sheep."

Be honest, now. Which of these two stories would you read? There's no need to answer: We in the newspaper business already know. You want sex. Nobody ever reads the stories about the company. We can prove it. Every day for the past six months, as an experiment, all major daily newspapers in the United States have been running stories with headlines referring to the Indonesian currency crisis. But guess what? There is no Indonesian currency crisis. We're not even sure that there is any such place as Indonesia. And you never noticed! You were too busy reading stories about the "issues" that you really care about, such as who took Monica Lewinsky to her junior prom.

* Excerpted from Dave Barry, "Scandal Sheep," *The Boston Globe Magazine,* March 15, 1998: 12–13.

ties are more important today than a generation ago. With the growth of the new media, competitive pressures are greater than ever and have resulted in a race to the bottom as network news becomes more like infotainment (a mixture of news and entertainment) and major newspapers become more like tabloids.

The lack of internal expertise and the competitive pressure for ratings and sales contribute to an unattractive feature of modern political coverage: "pack journalism," in which reporters unanimously decide something is the big story and attack it like wolves tearing apart wounded prey. Sabato calls the more extreme manifestations of this behavior feeding frenzies.[68] Normal people, observing such behavior, are puzzled by the media's obsession with seemingly minor matters, but to journalists under great competitive pressure, there is safety in numbers. One can hardly be faulted for working on the same story as other prominent journalists. Far better to focus on what turns out to be an overblown, inconsequential story than "run the risk of going down in history as 'the reporter who missed the next Watergate.'"[69] Indeed, there is every indication that the "pack" mentality extends to editorial offices, where each news show or newspaper fears missing a big story.

**Calvin and Hobbes**
As the public gets more reports of scandal and problems, some worry that the electorate grows more cynical. *Does excessive coverage of scandal "packaged as soap opera and horse race" lead the public to distrust government and politicians?*

## Democratic Dilemma

## The Role of the Media

Many critics of the way the mass media cover politics and government implicitly view the media as educational institutions. They consider the most important function of the media to be providing accurate information that citizens can use to inform their opinions and votes. Moreover, the media can present alternative interpretations of the information and its implications for public policy. In short, the media facilitate democratic deliberation.

Many in the news media share this view of their role. They emphasize their importance to democracy, as indicated by the guarantees in the First Amendment. They defend their aggressive pursuit of news by pointing out that they are the watchdogs in modern democracy—the people have "a right to know" what they have uncovered. But critics charge that the media invade people's privacy, report news that people have no need to know, and weaken democracy by their negativity, emphasis on conflict, and avoidance of detailed coverage of the issues.

Both points of view are valid. The problem is that although we want them to act like an educational institution, the news media are part of profit-making enterprises. All the significant newspapers and news magazines are located in the private sector, as are about three-quarters of the TV stations. And the public broadcasting channels have smaller audiences than the commercial channels. In a sense, we are criticizing a segment of the entertainment industry for not behaving like educational institutions.

Americans are not enthusiastic about public media: The very phrase *government-controlled media* makes people suspicious. The Republican-organized 104th Congress even considered killing the Public Broadcasting Service that produces programs for "educational TV." PBS survived largely because of its identification with popular shows like *Sesame Street* and *Barney.* Many other democracies have a far greater public presence in the mass media. The British Broadcasting Corporation (BBC) is the best-known example, but public ownership and public regulation are common throughout the world.

Given the importance of information in today's world, consider the following questions:

* *Should Americans rethink their historical bias against public media?*
* *Would it be a good idea to expand PBS and give it generous public subsidies so that it could provide more public affairs programming without worrying about the bottom line?*
* *Has the government abdicated its responsibility by granting use of the airwaves to private, profit-making corporations while requiring little or no public service in return? Why or why not?*

**simulation**

**You are the News Editor**

**comparative**

**Comparing News Media**

## Prospects for Change

However justified, criticisms of the media's coverage of politics and government miss an important point. The news media in the United States are neither educational institutions nor public institutions; rather, most are private, profit-making enterprises. As one journalist commented, "What few people recognize is that the purpose of the media is not to educate, it is to impress—to make an impression. There isn't the time or space to educate."[70] To complaints that their coverage falls short of what many would like to see, defenders of the media generally respond that they try to provide the kind of coverage people want. Indeed, modern newspapers use focus groups and other measures of reader interest to better serve their readers.[71] If tabloid journalism is on the rise, it is because media executives see that approach as what the modern public wants.

Of course, the media have always claimed that they are more than profit-making businesses. They claim to be providing an essential public service (see the accompanying Democratic Dilemma). When they publish sensitive or private information, they justify their behavior with public interest images (they are the guardians of the First Amendment, the public has a right to know, the free flow of information is the pillar of democracy). Many people believe that such an exalted self-image carries with it the responsibility to give the public what it needs as well as what it wants.

Of course, the media are private-sector corporations protected by the First Amendment and hence cannot be forced to change their practices; this is in sharp contrast to countries in which government influence over the media is accepted (see the accompanying International Comparison). Perhaps the main hope of citizens is that media executives may be wrong about what people want. Certainly Americans are not happy with media behavior today. As Table 9.1 shows, popular evaluations of the media have declined sharply since the mid-1980s, and growing percentages

## International Comparison

## Television and the 2000 Russian Presidential Election

Supporters of publicly owned or operated media often hold up the British Broadcasting Corporation (BBC) as an example of high-quality, objective television journalism, but skeptics can point out disturbing examples of media abuse when government owns the medium or is involved with its operation. In the 2000 Russian elections, for example, supporters of acting President Vladimir Putin were determined to ensure that he receive an absolute majority of the vote in the first round of voting so that he could claim a popular mandate.[a]

On the eve of the election, the ORT television network, 51 percent of which is owned by the government, broadcast a series of damaging reports against candidate Grigori Yavlinsky, most of whose support was thought to overlap with Putin's. The broadcasts exploited prejudices still widespread in Russia: anti-Semitism, distrust of foreigners, and intolerance of gays. One broadcast alleged that Yavlinsky's campaign was bankrolled by rich Jewish businessmen (he is half-Jewish and has dual Russian and Israeli citizenship). A second reported on gay support for Yavlinsky. A third alleged without evidence that Yavlinsky was supported by German think tanks. The Putin campaign denied any involvement, suggesting that ORT was merely reporting the facts that the Russian people had a right to know.

Disinterested observers believed otherwise, especially because another one of the network's principal owners, Boris Berezovsky, is a major supporter of Putin. Although the effects of the broadcasts cannot be measured, Putin won his majority and was elected to a full term as president.

Although extreme, this example raises disturbing questions about government involvement in the media.

- *Is this kind of heavy-handed government interference in media operations likely in a developed democracy such as the United States, or is it a concern only in a country like Russia, where democratic practices only recently have been introduced?*
- *Even if abuses like these are unlikely, are the dangers of government abuse of the media so great that the U.S. government should not own any news media?*
- *Are there institutional or constitutional safeguards that could prevent this kind of abuse from occurring in the United States?*

---

[a]This account is drawn from Michael R. Gordon, "Russian TV Assails Putin Rival," *San Francisco Chronicle*, March 26, 2000, A13.

---

believe that the media are unprofessional, uncaring, immoral, and even harmful to democracy.

Do the media underestimate the American citizen? During the 1992 presidential campaign, people in the media were stunned by the ratings earned by Ross Perot's "infomercials"—as many as 10 million households tuned in.[72] TV producers defend sound-bite journalism with the observation that the average voter has an attention

**visual literacy**
**What's in an Ad?**

## Table 9.1

Negative Evaluations of the Media Are on the Increase

| News Organizations Generally Are: | 1985 | 1999 |
|---|---|---|
| Moral | 54% | 40% |
| Immoral | 13% | 38% |
| Care about people they report on | 35% | 21% |
| Don't care | 48% | 67% |
| Highly professional | 72% | 52% |
| Not professional | 11% | 32% |
| Protect democracy | 54% | 45% |
| Hurt democracy | 23% | 38% |
| Care about how good a job they do | 79% | 69% |
| Don't care | 11% | 22% |

SOURCE: "Big Doubts About New Media's Values," The Pew Research Center for the People & the Press, February 1999. http://www.people-press.org.

span of less than 30 seconds, but Perot treated voters as intelligent adults and held the interest of many for 30 minutes with lengthy expositions accompanied by charts and figures! As the network system declines, as more independent stations begin operating, and as the new media continue to advance, we may see the development of numerous specialized informational channels whose emphasis differs from the emphasis on entertainment that increasingly shapes the modern mass media. Thus the selection biases we have discussed might gradually be undermined by technological change.

### SECTION SUMMARY

Because time and space are scarce and the amount of potential news is large, the media must decide what to cover and what to ignore. Such decisions raise questions of bias. Charges of partisan and ideological bias are common, but many media critics believe such political biases are less important than selection biases and professional biases, which reflect judgments about what is news. Negativity, an emphasis on conflict, a preference for the dramatic, a tendency to explain everything in personal terms—these are biases that give citizens a distorted picture of public affairs. Although many people are unhappy with media practices, change is unlikely. The mass media are profit-making enterprises that increasingly bring entertainment values into news and public affairs coverage in an attempt to maximize ratings. The new media—especially the Internet—offer dissatisfied citizens the opportunity to find alternative sources of information.

## The Media and Electoral Politics

The mass media play an important role in democratic politics. Ideally, they transmit information about problems and issues, helping voters make intelligent choices about the candidates who compete for their votes. Many critics feel that the general biases we have discussed cause media coverage of elections to fall far short of the ideal.

### Campaign Coverage

Nowhere do critics of the mass media find more to criticize than in the media's coverage of political campaigns. Numerous studies report that the various selection and professional biases of the media come together to produce campaign coverage that is characterized by sins of both omission and commission. We illustrate these in more detail when discussing presidential campaigns in Chapter 10, but we summarize them briefly here.

Critics complain that the media provide too little coverage of policy issues: the nature of social and economic problems, the contrasts among the programs the candidates advocate, unbiased appraisals of officials' performance, and so forth. Instead, critics charge, the media devote too much attention to "character" issues that have little to do with the ability of the candidates to govern. Thus the press dwells on whether a candidate was suspended from school, had an extramarital affair, accepted a free vacation from an interest group, and the like. Such matters have some relevance, to be sure, and the media defend their attention to them as providing indications of how the candidate would govern, but reporting on such matters should not crowd out more substantive election coverage.

Not only do the media concentrate on candidate character at the expense of genuine policy and performance issues, but media interest in such issues stems less from an attempt to evaluate the quality of the candidates than from a wish to handicap the race. Critics assail the media for "horse race" coverage of campaigns. Specifically, coverage focuses on which candidate is leading, which candidate is dropping back, which one is coming up on the rail, what the latest polls say, who got what endorsement, and how a new announcement on a key issue will affect the polls more than on the candidates' qualifications and the positions they espouse. Positions, in fact, are viewed as tactical moves that can affect the candidates' standing in the larger horse race.

This tendency to cover political campaigns as "games" or "horse races" has become much more pronounced over the past generation, and the attention devoted to substance has declined.[73] Increasingly, journalists interpret what candidates say rather than allowing candidates to speak for themselves. One study that compared network newscasts in 1968 with those in 1988 found that the average sound bite for presidential candidates who appeared on the news had fallen from 42 seconds to less than 10.[74] Although the media consciously tried to make sound bites longer in 1992 and 1996, the situation has improved little, and candidates still do not get enough time to explain their positions on complex issues. Modern candidates adapt to media needs and practices by simplifying their appeals accordingly.

Observers of contemporary political campaigns are not the only ones who are critical of media coverage. The candidates themselves are critical—so much so that they are finding ways to get around the contemporary media. As previously noted, in the 1992 campaign Larry King usurped the role played by the traditional network anchors. In addition, candidates appeared on the *Arsenio Hall Show*, *ABC Prime Time*, and even *MTV*. Establishment reporters complained that the candidates were insulating themselves from the hard questioning of seasoned political reporters, but the candidates enjoyed the opportunity to talk about issues rather than the trivia that often fascinates political journalists. The growth of the new media gives today's candidates the means to act on sentiments that candidates probably have felt for decades, if not centuries: Recall President Kennedy's observation about the filtering effect of the media.

## The Conventions

Before presidential candidates were chosen in the primaries, the national conventions were important political events. Party leaders came together, made deals, hammered out a platform, nominated candidates, and (if successful) left with a unified party prepared to battle the opposition. In recognition of the importance of the conventions, CBS and NBC provided gavel-to-gavel coverage from 1956 to 1976 and regularly assigned their top anchors and reporters to the events.

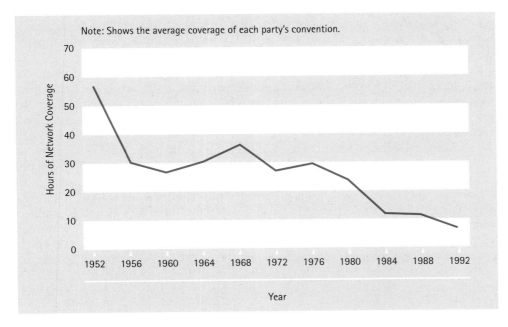

Note: Shows the average coverage of each party's convention.

**Figure 9.3**

**The Networks Increasingly Ignore the National Political Conventions**

SOURCE: Adapted from Harold Stanley and Richard Niemi, *Vital Statistics of American Politics*, 5th ed. (Washington, DC: CQ Press, 1995), p. 69.

The process of nominating presidential candidates via state primaries and caucuses was institutionalized in 1972. Since then, the conventions have not been nearly so important as in earlier eras, and media coverage has dropped accordingly (see Figure 9.3). In consequence, the parties now treat the conventions as huge infomercials in an attempt to take advantage of their diminishing time on the screen. Attractive speakers are slotted for prime time, and the entire convention schedule is arranged with the media in mind. The parties showcase their candidates in hopes of producing a postconvention "bounce" upward in the polls. Recent conventions that produced large bounces for the candidates were the 1988 Republican convention (for Bush) and the 2000 Democratic convention (for Gore).[75] Media coverage is a double-edged sword, however; if coverage emphasizes a divided party or unpopular elements of the party, it will cause the candidate to drop in the polls. The 1968 Chicago Democratic convention discussed at the beginning of this chapter is the classic modern example. Similarly, in 1992 Pat Buchanan's "raw meat" speech to the Republican convention turned off many moderates and hurt President Bush's chances for reelection.

The conventions probably will be even less important in the future. As one commentator observed after the 1996 events, "the more the party managers tried to package their message to please television, the less the major networks were interested."[76] In 1996 Ted Koppel and his *Nightline* team abandoned the Republican convention after two days, the networks cut coverage to about an hour a night, and ratings were off 25 percent from 1992. In 2000 MTV provided more coverage than the three major networks combined.[77] The networks appear to be abandoning convention coverage to cable channels and the Internet.

## The Presidential Debates

One of the high points of modern presidential campaigns is the series of debates between the two—sometimes three—major candidates. No other campaign events earn such high ratings. In fact, more people watch the debates than vote.

The first televised debates were held during the 1960 campaign between candidates Richard Nixon and John Kennedy. One of the surprising findings in studies of the debates was that people who listened to them on the radio evaluated Nixon's performance more favorably than people who watched them on TV, an indication that visual images could have impacts different from the words with which they were associated.[78] No debates were held in 1964, 1968, or 1972, but they have been held in every election since. Although the format and arrangements usually are matters of considerable controversy, debates now appear to be an institutionalized part of presidential campaigns.

Studies show that performance in the debates can sway the undecided voter. For example, in 1984 President Reagan appeared tired and confused in his first debate with Walter Mondale. His unexpectedly poor performance raised the issue of his age (then 73) and resulted in a slight drop in the polls. Knowing how important the next encounter was, Reagan came in alert, prepared, and full of good humor. He dispelled the concerns raised in the first debate and gained 4 points in the polls.[79]

As in campaign coverage generally, the first question the media raise about debates is "Who won?" If a candidate has misspoken, that often becomes the subject of a "feeding frenzy." In 1992 President Bush and Governor Clinton tried a new format. A media personality, ABC's Carole Simpson, moderated a studio show in which uncommitted voters asked questions of the candidates. The questions asked by ordinary citizens were much more substantive than those typically asked by reporters, a welcome development in the eyes of many media critics. But how did the media view it? According to the *New York Times*, "Historic it was. Also responsible, civic-minded, worthwhile, and informative. Also dull as C-SPAN at midnight."[80] Even for the *New York Times*, "responsible, civic-minded, worthwhile, and informative" no longer are sufficient.

### SECTION SUMMARY

Election coverage illustrates the media biases discussed earlier. Substantive discussion gets short shrift in favor of conflict, scandal, the "horse race," and personal character. Candidates get blamed for the low level of their campaigning, but they have adapted their campaign styles to the practices of the mass media; moreover, what substance they emphasize is often ignored by the media in favor of topics the audience may find more entertaining.

## Media Coverage of Government

Media coverage of government exhibits problems and biases analogous to those evident in media coverage of campaigns. From the standpoint of the mass media, much of the routine work of government is dull; hence the media focus on what they consider more exciting.

### Emphasis on the President (and Other Personalities)

The president is a single individual with personality and character; therefore, he (no woman has thus far been president) is inherently more interesting than a collectivity like Congress or an abstraction like the bureaucracy. The president receives the lion's share of the evening news coverage.[81] And not only does Congress play second fiddle in terms of media coverage, but coverage of the Congress has declined in recent decades.[82] The problem, of course, is that the president is only one part of the government, and, as we will see in Chapter 13, his powers are fairly limited. Thus the media prime citizens to focus on the president to a degree that is disproportionate to his powers and responsibilities.

The exception to this generalization is one that proves the rule. For six months after the 1994 elections, the media virtually forgot about President Clinton as pack journalism turned its attention to House Speaker Newt Gingrich and the new Republican majority in Congress. For once, the media could represent Congress via a single personality. If the Republican takeover of Congress had not been associated with a colorful personality like Gingrich, the media in all likelihood would have devoted less attention to Congress.

This focus of the media on personalities seems to be a universal tendency. Note that it is similar to building sports coverage around superstars such as Vince Carter, Sammy Sosa, and Keyshawn Johnson. An effective governmental team, like a winning sports team, requires teamwork, but the media find individual heroics and failures to be more compelling stories. Unfortunately, in framing coverage in terms of individuals, the media probably encourage individualism and discourage teamwork, reinforcing tendencies already present in modern entrepreneurial politics. Moreover, such media coverage primes citizens to think about government in terms of the heroic exploits and tragic failures of individuals rather than in terms of institutions and processes that are operating effectively or less well.[83]

### Emphasis on Conflict

Every time Speaker Gingrich made a controversial comment, he was assured of media coverage. Indeed, because he was so likely to make the kind of comments the media love, and to offer them up in convenient sound bites, they followed him in hopes of being fed.

In 1995, when President Clinton and Speaker Gingrich appeared on the same platform in New Hampshire and engaged in an intelligent, mature discussion, citizens were very receptive, and even Clinton and Gingrich seemed to enjoy it. Journalists found it dull. How could they report an intelligent discussion? They would have

**Monica**
Monica Lewinsky is led through a sea of reporters after turning over handwriting, fingerprint, and voice samples. *When is a scandal an appropriate story?*

preferred the Speaker to level a serious charge or offer a personal criticism that could have provided a 10-second sound bite. According to David Broder, the dean of American political commentators,

> It is conflict—not compromise—that makes news. A piece of videotape showing Democratic Rep. Pete Stark of California denouncing the Republicans for "cutting" Medicare will play over and over. Tape of a Democrat praising a Republican for the successful "culmination of a long, bipartisan effort to reexamine and refocus the federal role in the education and training of America's workers" will never make it out of the editing room.[84]

### Emphasis on Scandals and Gaffes

However favorable the coverage of Clinton's election, the honeymoon with the media ended quickly. In the first months of his presidency, the public was bombarded with stories about Whitewater, aide Vince Foster's suicide, $200 haircuts, parties with Sharon Stone, the White House travel office, Hillary Clinton's investments, and numerous other matters that you do not remember. The reason you do not remember is that, however important these matters were to the individuals involved at the time, they were not important for the overall operation of government. Hence they have been appropriately forgotten.

The same study that found coverage of Congress to be declining also found that the focus of coverage had changed. Policy stories outnumbered scandal stories by 13 to 1 from 1972 to the mid-1980s, but since then the ratio has plunged to 3 to 1.[85] Is Congress that much worse, or have the media become increasingly interested in scandal?

### Emphasis on the Negative

Media on the lookout for conflicts, scandals, and gaffes naturally emphasize the negative. What government does well is less newsworthy than what government does badly. Quiet compromises that improve public policies are less newsworthy than noisy arguments that accomplish nothing.

Thus network coverage of Congress has gone from highly negative to almost completely negative. According to one count, three of every four evaluations of Congress were negative in 1972, and that ratio rose to nine of ten by 1992.[86] Again we may ask whether Congress has become that much worse or whether the change is due to an increasing media emphasis on the negative. Even entertainment shows now portray government officials more negatively than they did a generation ago.[87]

## Exaggerated Concern with the Press

Because the press has become the principal link between citizens and their government, in their concern about that link, elected officials often lose sight of the people. According to a former Clinton White House official,

> When I was there, absolutely nothing was more important than figuring out what the news was going to be. . . . There is no such thing as a substantive discussion that is not shaped or dominated by how it is going to play in the press. . . . When you put together a press that is only interested in "horse race" and "inside baseball" and a White House staff that is interested only in the press, you've got the worst of both worlds.[88]

### SECTION SUMMARY

Media coverage of government reflects the general media biases discussed earlier. Coverage emphasizes the personal, the dramatic, and the conflictual, not the impersonal, the routine, and the consensual. Coverage of character and scandal crowds out coverage of policies and outcomes. Much of the work of government is far from entertaining; attempting to make it so results in a distorted view of how government operates.

## Chapter Summary

The mass media are less than two centuries old. TV has superseded print as the most important form of mass communication, but recent technological developments have produced new media, such as cable TV and the Internet, that are weakening the traditional broadcast system and encouraging various forms of narrowcasting aimed at smaller, more specialized audiences. Trends in the print medium seem to be going in the opposite direction, with mergers reducing the number of papers, large chains absorbing others, and larger conglomerates absorbing media corporations.

Although the mass media can have important effects on public opinion, such effects are not automatic but contingent—they depend on other conditions present in the situation. For example, where people have strong predispositions, the effects of the mass media are limited. Also, where people have alternative sources of information, such as their personal experience, media effects are limited.

Media effects on public opinion fall into several categories. Agenda setting occurs when media coverage affects what issues or problems people think about. Priming occurs when the media encourage people to evaluate political figures in terms of one set of considerations rather than another. Framing occurs when the media present problems or issues in such a way that people are stimulated to think about them in terms of one frame of reference rather than another. Finally, outright persuasion occurs when the media change people's minds about issues or candidates, whether suddenly or as the result of more complicated processes of agenda setting, priming, and framing.

Frequently, critics charge the media with one or another form of bias. Surveys show that reporters and editors are more Democratic and liberal than the population at large, but research results offer little reason to believe that media coverage of elections and government has a significant liberal bias. Moreover, other critics charge that economic considerations lead the media in a conservative direction, at least on economic issues. More important than ideological biases are biases that arise from the definition of what is news, and especially what is considered good TV news. The media reflect an emphasis on the negative and an emphasis on conflict. The media focus on dramatic incidents and colorful personalities rather than on more abstract forces and developments, even where the latter are far more important. The media oversimplify complex situations and reduce complicated arguments and positions to sound bites. Such media biases are understandable. In contrast to the situation in many other countries, the media in the United States are organized and operated from the private sector. This means that, like other private enterprises, the media must look at the bottom line—what will sell. Thus the role of the mass media in serving the public interest exists in constant tension with their role as profit-making enterprises serving their stockholders.

## On the Web

ABC News Political Nation
abcnews.go.com/sections/politics
News, campaign coverage, chat rooms, and multimedia reports from an industry leader.

The Pew Research Center for the People and the Press
www.people-press.org
Surveys of American public opinion particularly as related to the media and the way the media cover campaigns and government.

Politics Now
www.politicsnow.com
A collaboration of *Newsweek*, ABC News, the *Washington Post*, the *National Journal*, the *Los Angeles Times* and the *Associated Press*.

CNN and Time AllPolitics
www.cnn.com/ALLPOLITICS/
An online portal that contains breaking news, features, documents, quizzes, and links to other Net resources from AOL Time Warner.

## Key Terms

agenda setting, p. 262
CNN effect, p. 262
draft, p. 249
equal-time rule, p. 259

fairness doctrine, p. 259
framing, p. 263
mass media, p. 251
minimal-effects thesis, p. 262

new media, p. 256
priming, p. 263
selection principle, p. 267
spin, p. 265

## Suggested Readings

Ansolabehere, Steven, Roy Behr, and Shanto Iyengar. *The Media Game.* New York: Macmillan, 1993. A readable survey of the influence of television in modern American politics.

Davis, Richard. *The Web of Politics: The Internet's Impact on the American Political System.* New York: Oxford University Press, 1999. A first look at how the Internet is changing American politics.

Graber, Doris, *Processing the News,* 2nd ed. New York: Longman, 1988. Detailed study of how Americans process the news they receive from TV and print sources. Finds that although attention is haphazard, most people learn about important political matters.

Iyengar, Shanto, and Donald Kinder. *News That Matters.* Chicago: University of Chicago Press, 1987. An exemplary experimen-

tal study that demonstrates the existence of agenda setting and priming.

Jamieson, Kathleen. *Packaging the Presidency.* New York: Oxford University Press, 1996. Critical survey of the evolution of presidential campaign advertising from the Eisenhower years to the present.

Neumann, W. Russell. *The Future of the Mass Audience.* Cambridge,

England: Cambridge University Press, 1991. Thoughtful examination of the effects of technological change on mass communications. Concludes that new media will not fragment the audience as much as many think.

Patterson, Thomas. *Out of Order.* New York: Vintage, 1994. A critical discussion of the way the print media define news when they cover presidential campaigns. Recommended by President Clinton.

Sabato, Larry. *Feeding Frenzy.* New York: Free Press, 1991. Entertaining critique of the most extreme manifestations of "pack journalism."

West Darrell. *Air Wars*, 2nd ed. Washington, DC: Congressional Quarterly, 1997. Readable study of the evolution and consequences of television advertising in campaigns since 1952.

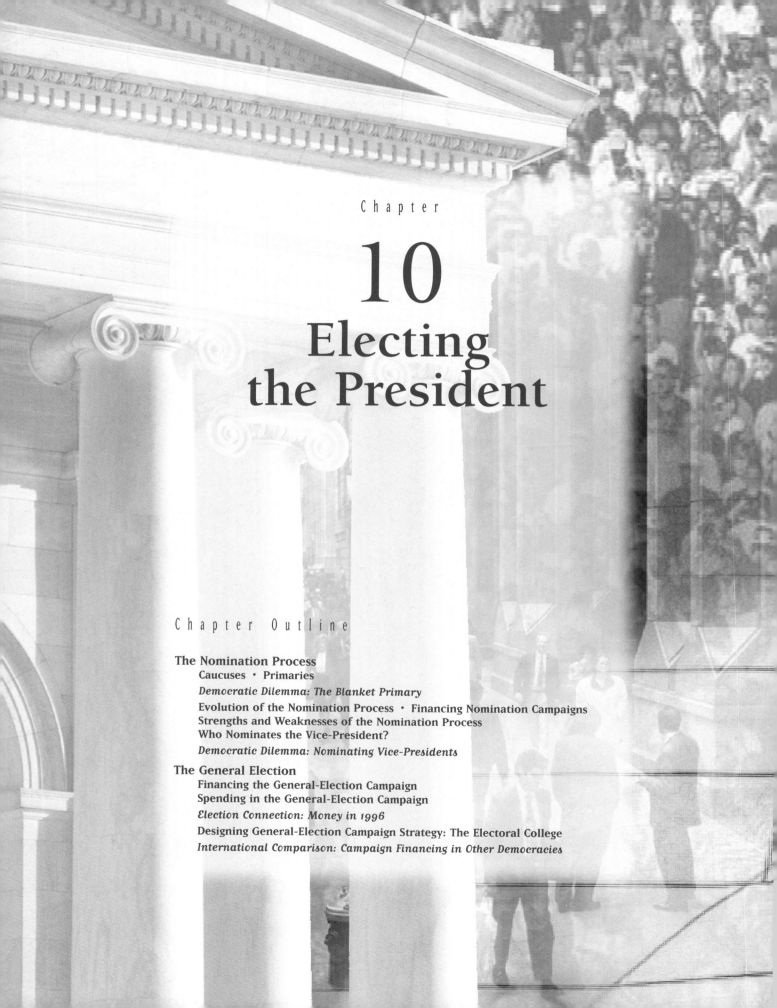

Chapter

# 10
# Electing
# the President

Chapter Outline

The 1990s saw the full flowering of the permanent campaign in U.S. politics. Bill Clinton won the 1992 election, but if his victory marked the end of that campaign, it is only a slight exaggeration to say that it also marked the beginning of the next one. Realizing that Clinton was a "minority president"—he received only 43 percent of the popular vote—Republicans in Congress quickly served notice that they would oppose his agenda. Senate Republicans killed Clinton's economic stimulus program by refusing to allow it to come to a vote. Then both Senate and House Republicans voted *unanimously* against Clinton's budget, which passed by one vote in the House and only by virtue of Vice-President Gore's tie-breaking vote in the Senate.[1]

A few months later Clinton delivered on his campaign promise to send Congress a plan for national health insurance. Although most observers anticipated some kind of bipartisan compromise, congressional Republicans soon decided that their best electoral strategy was to oppose all health care plans that were on the table. With the Democrats themselves divided, national health care was officially pronounced dead in September 1994. As the Republicans had foreseen, the public did not blame them for killing the health care plan; the public blamed the Democrats, who controlled the presidency and both houses of Congress. The complete failure of health care reform suggested that the Democrats were incapable of governing. Other defeats in Congress followed, and in a stunning reversal, the Democrats lost control of both the House and Senate in the 1994 elections. Six days after the elections, one Republican senator, Arlen Specter (PA), already was campaigning in New Hampshire, and another, Phil Gramm (TX), had filed a statement of candidacy. Republicans thought Clinton was a goner.

But Clinton did not call himself "the comeback kid" for nothing. He had recovered politically by early 1996, and he never trailed in the 1996 trial heats. Because the election was a foregone conclusion, many insiders began to speculate about the 2000 election before the 1996 elections had even been held! Would Vice-President Al Gore be the Democratic nominee, or would his way be blocked by Minority Leader Richard Gephardt or some other contender? The 1996 campaign began within a week of the 1994 elections, but the race for the 2000 nomination began even *before* the 1996 elections!

Because the polls showed that the race was too close to call, speculation about 2004 was not as widespread as in 1996, nor did it begin quite so early. Still, within a month of Gore's nomination the first pieces speculating about 2004 had appeared.[2] And speculation about 2004 was well underway before the outcome of the 2000 race had been decided.

**honeymoon**
Period early in a president's term when partisan conflict and media criticism are minimal.

TRADITIONALLY, NEWLY ELECTED PRESIDENTS ENJOY A HONEYMOON, a period in which the opposition and the media suspend criticism and give the new president a chance to organize his administration and begin governing. Modern presidents have no more than a year—the first year after their election—in which electoral considerations do not

**The Accelerating Cycle**
*How soon is too soon to consider the next presidential race (or the one after that)?*

dominate the national arena. In the second year of the administration, members of Congress are gearing up for their own campaigns, and in the third and fourth years of the administration, the prospective presidential candidates are gearing up for theirs. Nearly everything a president proposes after the first year is given an electoral spin by media eager for an exciting contest and by competitors for the presidential nomination. In fact, the recent elections we have described suggest that contemporary presidents do not even have a year in which governing has priority over electioneering. This chapter takes an in-depth look at how Americans choose their presidents. We begin with the nomination process:

- How are presidential candidates nominated in the United States?
- How did our unusual nominating process come to be?
- What are the pros and cons of the American nominating process?

Then we turn to the general election:

- How does the electoral college affect the nature of the campaign?
- How do Americans vote in presidential elections?
- Why is the importance of the media and the campaign often exaggerated?
- What issues and other factors have influenced the most recent presidential elections?

## The Nomination Process

The United States is unusual among world democracies for its lengthy and participatory process of nominating candidates for chief executive; one British correspondent calls it "a bizarre ritual."[3] In most democracies, nominees are chosen by party activists and leaders—a small minority of dues-paying, card-carrying, meeting-attending *members* of the party. But in the United States every citizen, whatever his or her history of party support, can participate in a **caucus**—a meeting of candidate supporters—or a **primary election**—a preliminary election—to choose national convention delegates committed to particular candidates. At the presidential level, nearly three-quarters of

**caucus**
Meeting of candidate supporters that chooses delegates to a state or national convention.

**primary election**
Preliminary election that narrows the number of candidates by determining who will be the nominees in the general election.

**The Iowa Democratic Caucus**
Attending the Democratic caucus was important to Rachelke Tsachor, so she packed her dinner and ate it at Longfellow School in Iowa City as the caucus began. *Is this typical of the American voter? How do the primaries and caucuses differ from the general election?*

the states choose their delegates in primary elections, and the other quarter choose them in caucuses. Because caucus states tend to be smaller, the lion's share of the delegates are chosen in primaries.

## Caucuses

In caucus states, supporters of the respective candidates meet in each voter precinct to start the process of delegate selection. Generally they gather in public places such as town halls or public schools, but sometimes they meet on private property such as in a restaurant. These precinct gatherings are only the beginning, however, because the process has a number of stages. For example, the Iowa caucuses early in the election year are the first major test for the candidates. But these caucuses choose only delegates to the county conventions that are held in March, which then choose delegates to the May congressional district conventions and the June state convention!

Democratic caucuses are constrained by national party rules that require proportional representation for the supporters of different candidates, as well as equal numbers of male and female delegates, where possible. Any registered Democrat is eligible to participate. Republican caucuses are less open. Some limit participation to party officials and workers, and they are freer to adopt their own rules (some use variants of proportional representation and some continue to use winner-take-all voting procedures).[4]

Caucus turnout is extremely low—typically in single digits. About 6 percent of the voting-age population participated in the 2000 Iowa caucuses. This was not an unusually low figure; the 12 percent turnout in the 1988 Iowa caucuses, when both parties had competitive contests, is believed to be the highest caucus turnout ever recorded. Caucus participants of both parties are unrepresentative of the general population in terms of income and education, and ideologically they tend to be more extreme than their party's broader base of identifiers.

## Primaries

Primaries take many forms across the states. In **closed primaries** only party members can vote—and only in the primary of the party in which they are registered. Independents cannot vote at all. Some of the most populous states, such as New York, Pennsylvania, and Florida, have closed primaries. In **semi-closed primaries** independents can vote in one of the party primaries. States with semi-closed primaries include Massachusetts, New Jersey, and Oregon. In **open primaries** any registered voter can vote in any party's primary. Most of the southern states have open primaries, along

**closed primaries**
Primaries in which only party members can vote—and only in the party in which they are registered.

**semi-closed primaries**
Primaries in which independents can vote in one of the party primaries.

**open primaries**
Primaries in which any registered voter can vote in any party's primary.

## Democratic Dilemma

# The Blanket Primary

In the 2000 elections, the states of Alaska, California, and Washington chose candidates for office using what are called blanket primaries.[a] Any registered voter can participate in such primaries, and all receive the same ballot. All the candidates for a given office—Democratic, Republican, and minor party—are listed together and a voter can vote for any party's candidate for each office to be filled. Thus a voter could vote for a Republican Senate candidate, a Democratic House candidate, a Libertarian gubernatorial candidate, a Peace and Freedom secretary of state candidate, and so on. Because such primaries ignore considerations of party membership and party loyalty, they have been called "free love" primaries: Voters can switch from party to party and don't have to make any commitments!

The California parties sued to overturn the state's blanket primary which had passed by a popular initiative over their bipartisan opposition in 1998, on the grounds that it violated their constitutional right of free association. Lower court decisions were appealed to the Supreme Court. In June of 2000 in *California Democratic Party* v. *Jones*, the Supreme Court overturned the California blanket primary, sending its supporters back to the drawing board to attempt to devise some constitutionally permissible alternative.

Supporters of the blanket primary make two arguments. First, they claim that it increases turnout because members of a party with no exciting contests might be drawn to the polls by an exciting race in the other party. Second, they claim that blanket primaries moderate politics because conservative Republicans usually win in Republican primaries, liberal Democrats in Democratic primaries. Allowing everyone into a party's primary increases the likelihood that moderates can win.

Opponents of the blanket primary argue that it allows parties to be "hijacked by drive-by voters with no durable interest in the parties, acting on transitory whims, or even to make mischief by burdening a party with a weak candidate."[b]

*What do you think?*
- *Do the goals of boosting turnout and encouraging moderation outweigh restricting the parties' rights of free association?*
- *Given that two major parties together control the electoral process, is it right to exclude people who are not party members (one-third of the voting age population) from choosing candidates?*

---

[a] In California, however, although voters could vote for any presidential candidate, delegates were allocated in proportion to the votes cast by party members only.

[b] George Will, "'Blanket' Primary Can Hijack a Party," *San Francisco Chronicle*, May 1, 2000: A23.

---

with Ohio, Wisconsin, and other states in the upper Midwest. A few states—Washington, California (below the presidential level), and Alaska—have "blanket primaries" in which any registered voter not only can vote but can also switch from one party to another, office by office.

The type of primary a state holds was significant in the 2000 primary season because of the candidacy of John McCain. McCain won in New Hampshire, a semi-closed-primary state, because he received heavy support among independents, who voted in the Republican primary. Then he scared George W. Bush in South Carolina and won in Michigan—both open-primary states—where he received support among independents and even some Democrats. The parties generally would prefer to control participation in their primaries. Indeed, the California parties sued to have their state's blanket primary declared an unconstitutional restriction of the parties' rights of free association and the Supreme Court upheld their argument in the summer of 2000 (see the accompanying Democratic Dilemma).

## Evolution of the Nomination Process

The direct primary is an American invention, a Progressive reform that swept across the states in the early twentieth century. Despite their adoption at the state and local levels, however, primaries did not determine presidential nominations for another half-century.[5] As late as 1968, Vice-President Hubert Humphrey won the Democratic nomination without entering a single primary. Although some states had held presidential primaries since the turn of the century, these were treated as "beauty contests" in which a prospective candidate could demonstrate popular appeal to party leaders. These leaders—mayors, governors, and other public and party officials—controlled the delegates to the national conventions where nominations actually were made.

Humphrey's nomination divided the Democratic party. Many Democratic activists had supported "peace" candidates Eugene McCarthy and Robert Kennedy, who opposed the war in Vietnam.[6] These candidates won most of the primaries that were held, driving President Lyndon Johnson from the race in the process, and their supporters—already stunned by Robert Kennedy's assassination—were outraged that the nomination went to Johnson's vice president. The antiwar faction gained the upper hand in the party and adopted the current process.[7] The Republicans already had been moving toward greater popular participation in their nominating process. In 1964 Senator Barry Goldwater, an insurgent from Arizona, won the nomination by edging out New York Governor Nelson Rockefeller, the candidate of the party establishment, in the California primary.[8]

The new nomination process was a fact by 1976, when the previously unknown Jimmy Carter won the Democratic nomination. Carter probably was the first to recognize that the new process had transformed presidential politics; in many ways his campaign became a model for those that followed.

The past two decades have seen much tinkering with the rules, but the broad outlines of the system have not changed. In 2000 all of the Republican delegates and about 80 percent of the Democratic delegates were chosen in primaries and caucuses. (The Democrats generally reserve about 20 percent of their slots for elected officials and party leaders called *superdelegates*.) The general pattern today is for candidates to build extensive organizations in the states where the first caucuses and primaries are held. Here the emphasis is on "retail politics," face-to-face contact with voters, which resembles the dealings of neighborhood merchants with their customers. Candidates strive to exceed "expectations" and to build "momentum" so that they can raise money and thereby qualify for federal matching funds to continue their campaigns in later, more expensive contests.[9]

### Financing Nomination Campaigns

**matching funds**
Public moneys (from $3 check-offs on income tax returns) that the Federal Election Commission distributes to primary candidates according to a prespecified formula.

Most presidential candidates depend on federal **matching funds** in their campaigns. The federal government provides public subsidies to candidates for the party nominations.[10] The money comes from the voluntary check-offs on Americans' income tax returns, and the subsidies are distributed by the Federal Elections Commission (FEC). Qualifying candidates have their fund-raising matched, dollar for dollar, up to a prespecified maximum spending limit—hence the name *matching funds*. Eligibility is not automatic, however. To be eligible, a candidate must raise at least $5000 in each of 20 states, in contributions no larger than $250, in the year in which he or she announces or in the preceding year. Most serious candidates do not find it very difficult to raise $100,000 in this way. Even minor party candidates have qualified, although they generally do not raise much money after they do.

Staying eligible is harder than becoming eligible, however. To stay eligible, and continue to receive matching funds throughout the primary season, candidates must comply with spending limits in each state, and they must be at least minimally successful. A candidate who fails to receive at least 10 percent of the vote in two consecutive primaries loses eligibility and can regain it only by getting 20 percent or more of the vote in a later primary. Thus a struggling campaign may find itself deprived of funds just when it most needs them.

Most candidates take matching funds, but there have been some notable recent exceptions. In both 1996 and 2000, multimillionaire Steve Forbes declined to accept federal funds so that he would not be subject to the spending limits that accompany them. In 2000 the FEC spending limit for the nomination campaign was $40.5 million, so having already raised $70 million before the primary season began, George W. Bush joined Forbes in declining to accept matching funds and the associated restrictions.[11] By the time he defeated John McCain and clinched the nomination, Bush had already spent $63 million, half again as much as he would have been permitted to spend had he accepted matching funds.[12]

## *Strengths and Weaknesses of the Nomination Process*

Despite its participatory nature, many observers are critical of the presidential nomination process.[13] Their concerns fall into two broad categories, one procedural, the other political.

**Procedural Concerns**  The nomination process is sequential: Candidates organize and campaign in one state, then pack up and move on to the next one. The problem, critics complain, is that the process starts too early and lasts too long. A Pew poll taken in January 2000, as the candidates were gearing up for Iowa and New Hampshire, found that 58 percent of the respondents felt that the campaign is too long, and about 50 percent that it started too early.[14] Unlike presidential candidates, ordinary Americans are not preoccupied with elections. For example, the January 2000 candidate debate carried by NBC in prime time drew an audience of 4.7 million. That was only a bit larger than the audience for reruns of *Buffy the Vampire Slayer* and only 60 percent as large as the audience for *WWF Smackdown!*[15] Candidates may be sending messages a year before the general election, but voters are not tuned in to receive them. Consequently, some candidacies die before anyone knows they were born.

Critics who think the process begins too early suggest that it be compressed into a few regional primaries or even a single national primary held much closer to the general election. Others reply that it is precisely the early-starting, drawn-out character of the process that gives outsiders a chance to compete.[16] Jimmy Carter was the former governor of a medium-sized state, Jesse Jackson a civil rights leader, Pat Buchanan a political pundit, Bill Clinton the governor of a small state. If the primary process is helpful to the candidacies of those outside establishment party and government circles, then, depending on what you think of such candidacies, you may view this feature of the nomination process as either positive or negative.

Those who believe that the nomination process starts too early naturally tend to believe that it lasts too long. By the time the process is over, the candidates may have been pounding on each other for months. Every personal flaw and past mistake has been exposed by the media and the attacks of campaign rivals. The nominees already are "damaged goods," and they have yet to face the candidate of the other party! Is it any surprise that many Americans are unhappy with the presidential candidates among whom they must choose?

**The Grueling Presidential Marathon**
Running for president is a physically, mentally, and emotionally exhausting experience.

**Figure 10.1**

**In 1996 and 2000 the Presidential Nominations were Decided Earlier than Ever**

SOURCE: Data compiled by Sam Abrams through various news reports.

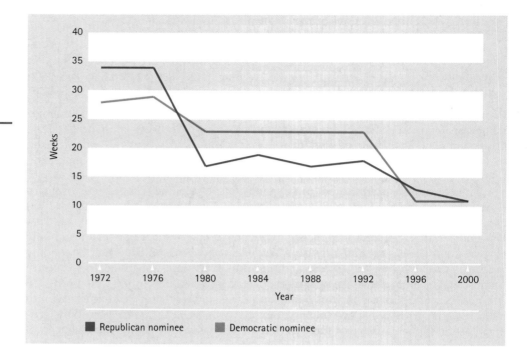

The response is that the process shines a bright light on candidates and reveals a great deal of information about them. Is it better that voters be ignorant of cheating on spouses, alcohol or drug abuse, questionable business dealings, and other short-comings that often went unknown before the modern nomination process? The reply to this defense is that because no one is perfect, the process surely discourages good people who are unwilling to give up every shred of personal privacy. Indeed, some have suggested—jokingly?—that anyone willing to expose every aspect of his or her life to media scrutiny is not the kind of person Americans should want to elect.

And so the procedural argument goes, back and forth. The structure of the nomination process has positive and negative qualities, and any change is soon criticized. For example, in 1996 and 2000 the primaries were "front-loaded"; many states moved their primaries to early dates in hopes that the nomination contests would be decided more quickly and the winners would have more time to unify their parties and plan for the fall election campaign.[17] As Figure 10.1 shows, these hopes were fulfilled. Critics charged that this front-loading gave an advantage to well-known, establishment candidates who could raise large sums of money to pay for a national campaign.

**Political Concerns**  A second set of criticisms of the nomination process focuses on the *politics* of the process. The reformers who instituted the process claimed they were giving "power to the people"—the new process would empower ordinary citizens at the expense of the party "bosses." As we noted in earlier chapters on political parties and interest groups, however, taking power away from one elite seldom empowers unorganized citizens. Rather, other elites are more often the beneficiaries. Thus weaker parties may mean stronger interest groups, not empowered citizens. In the case of the nomination process, many commentators fear that taking power from party leaders and government officials who were viewed as unrepresentative may only have empowered two groups who are equally or more unrepresentative: political activists and the media.

**Political activists** gained influence from the changes in the nomination process. These are people who are more interested in and committed to political issues than are average citizens. As noted, caucus turnout is extremely low, and although it is

**political activists**
People who voluntarily participate in politics; they are more interested in and committed to particular issues and candidates than are ordinary citizens.

## Table 10.1

**Party Activists Are Not Moderates**

Surveys find that, on most issues Democratic activists tend to be more liberal than Democratic identifiers, and Republican activists more conservative than Republican identifiers. Here is how national convention delegates compared to their parties' supporters in 1996. Democratic delegates were more extreme than identifiers on eight of ten issues, Republican delegates more extreme on nine of ten issues.

| Issue | Democratic Delegates | Democratic Identifiers | Republican Identifiers | Republican Delegates |
|---|---|---|---|---|
| Government should do more to | | | | |
|    solve the nation's problems | 76% | 53% | 20% | 4% |
|    regulate the environment and safety practices of business | 60 | 66 | 37 | 4 |
|    promote traditional values | 27 | 41 | 44 | 56 |
| Abortion should be permitted in all cases | 61 | 30 | 22 | 11 |
| Assault weapons should be banned | 91 | 80 | 62 | 34 |
| Necessary to have laws to protect racial minorities | 88 | 62 | 39 | 30 |
| Affirmative action programs should be continued | 81 | 59 | 28 | 9 |
| Organized prayer should be permitted in public schools | 20 | 66 | 69 | 57 |
| Trade restrictions are necessary to protect domestic industries | 54 | 65 | 56 | 31 |
| Children of illegal immigrants should be allowed to attend public school | 79 | 63 | 46 | 26 |

SOURCE: From *New York Times*/CBSNews Poll results distributed by Michael Kagay at the Annual Meeting of the American Political Science Association, San Francisco, August 31, 1996.

higher, turnout in the primaries is still much lower than turnout in general elections: Of the 18 states that voted while the nominations were still undecided in 2000, 12 set turnout records, but the average turnout was only 13.6 percent![18] Being more dedicated, activists naturally are more likely to vote in primaries than are ordinary citizens, so caucuses and primaries give their views more weight. Even more important, the activists work in campaigns and give money to candidates; they help mobilize other voters. None of this would be a cause for concern if the activists were like everyone else, but in some important respects the activists are different. Not only are their views more intense than those of nonactivists, but as shown in Table 10.1, their views often are more extreme as well.

Thus pundits doubt that it was any coincidence that a pro-life Tennessee congressman like Al Gore became pro-choice before deciding to seek the Democratic nomination in 1988. Could any pro-life candidate possibly win a majority of delegates in Democratic caucuses and primaries in which feminist and other pro-choice activists play an important role? Conversely, was it any coincidence that cosmopolitan figures like the senior George Bush in the late 1970s and Steve Forbes in the late 1990s became pro-life social conservatives as they anticipated entering a Republican nomination process in which activists of the religious right play a major role?

Because participation in primaries, and especially caucuses, is so low, small groups of dedicated activists can exert more influence in the nomination contests than they can in general elections, where turnout is much higher. Consequently, some worry that the primary process confers an advantage on candidates who appeal to activists by taking positions far from the center of the political spectrum where the mass of Americans are located. Democratic candidates generally are more liberal, and Republican candidates generally more conservative, than the average voter, and whoever is elected is between a rock and a hard place; the winner must either attempt to fulfill unpopular campaign promises or flip-flop and go back on those commitments.[19] In the former case a candidate disappoints voters, and in the latter case, activists.

Although examples are easy to cite, some research suggests that the preceding argument is exaggerated. Primary electorates, at least, do not appear to be significantly unrepresentative, even if convention delegates and campaign workers may be.[20] And even convention delegates may temper their views in the interests of winning.[21] Certainly, neither the Democrats nor the Republicans have yet nominated any genuine "extremists" for president. The evidence is not conclusive, however; and even if presidential primaries are not wildly unrepresentative in most states, it seems likely that in the caucuses and in the fund-raising arena, unrepresentative activists exercise disproportionate influence.[22]

Another consequence of the enhanced influence of activists in the nominating process is that they skew the political debate. To someone following the process, it might seem that the most important issue facing the United States are so-called hot-button issues such as abortion and gun control. Although issues like these are important, ordinary voters do not view them as the crucial issues facing the country. Yet such issues often steal the spotlight from general and far-reaching issues of concern to all Americans: education, medical care, and economic prosperity.

The media are the second group that gained influence from the nomination process—the television, radio, and newspaper reporters, commentators, and editors who interpret confusing primary and caucus developments for the American people. As we saw in Chapter 9, there is widespread dissatisfaction with media coverage of elections, especially the caucuses and primaries.

Some critics claim that the press trivializes elections by focusing on matters other than public policies and government performance. The press focuses on the "horse race"—who is ahead and by how far, who is coming up on the rail, and who is fading from contention. Is the campaign play-by-play more important than the implications of the campaign for the country? Recall the concept of framing that we discussed in Chapter 9. Professor Thomas Patterson has documented a striking shift in how the media "frame" campaigns. In the 1960s, before the primary era, media coverage was about evenly split between a "policy" frame and a "game" frame. In 1972, the first year of the new system, coverage shifted to the game frame by a proportion of 2 to 1. Since 1976, the game frame has had a 4 to 1 edge.[23] For the media, campaigns have become the political equivalent of "March Madness."

Not only do the media focus on the race, but in explaining who is winning and why, they tend to focus on what many observers regard as trivia—scandals, gaffes, and campaign feuds. Accounts of modern presidential campaigns are littered with stories like Jimmy Carter's revelation to *Playboy* magazine that he had felt "lust in his heart" and Bill Clinton's affairs. Critics charge that the media are more concerned with sleaze than with real questions of government policy.

Of course, the media have a response to these criticisms of their behavior: Newspapers, newsmagazines, and television networks cannot be expected to behave like nonprofit educational enterprises, because they are profit-making enterprises, which must compete for advertising dollars. If they focus on the horse race and on sleaze, it is because that is what voters want to hear and read about. Despite what voters tell pollsters, who gets higher ratings—the long, informative newscasts on public television or the tabloid shows? Look in the mirror, defenders of the media say, "the media only give us what we want."

A second criticism of the media is that the pressure to provide news often leads the media to *manufacture* news by exaggerating the importance of many campaign events and developments. Thus, as Figure 10.2 amusingly illustrates, Iowa, the first caucus state, and New Hampshire, the first primary state, receive a disproportionate share of news coverage. Some critics ask whether two sparsely populated, rural, mostly white states should play such an important role in determining whether candidacies are viable, or indeed in determining who is the front runner.[24]

Finally, some observers complain that the media no longer are mere reporters of the nomination process but have become important players in that process. Again, in the 1960s, Patterson found that 20 percent or fewer of all campaign stories were

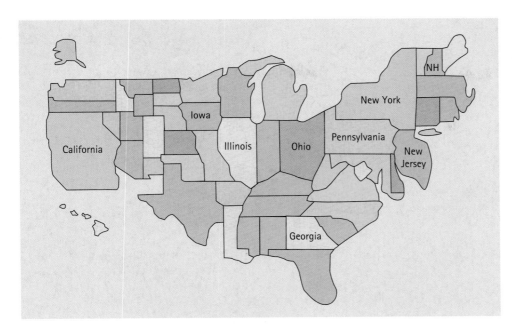

Figure 10.2

**The Contrast Between Electoral Votes and News Coverage of Primaries**
(a) States in proportion to electoral votes, 1984. (b) States in proportion to news coverage of primaries, 1984.

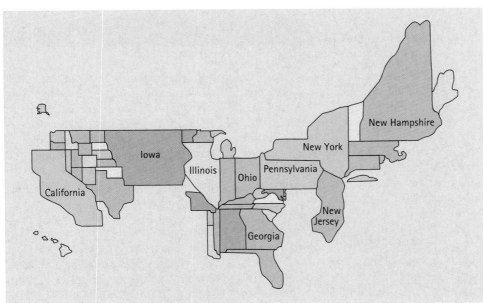

"interpretive"; the rest were "descriptive." In 1972 the ratio shifted to 50:50, and in the 1988 and 1992 elections, the ratio shifted further to 80 percent interpretative and 20 percent descriptive.[25] Rather than tell Americans what the political participants think, the media now tell Americans what the media think.

For example, in every campaign there is a widely publicized "expectations" game. The question is not so much whether candidates win or lose but how they perform relative to "expectations." And who sets these expectations? The media, the critics answer. The classic example occurred in 1972, when Senator Edmund Muskie's campaign never recovered from his showing in the New Hampshire primary. Muskie won the primary over George McGovern 46 percent to 37 percent. But New Hampshire was next to Muskie's home state—Maine—so the media expected him to do well, whereas they thought that South Dakotan McGovern's showing was unexpectedly strong. The momentum that McGovern took out of New Hampshire carried him to the Democratic nomination.

**The Expectations Game**
*Should the media's "expectations" play such a large role?*

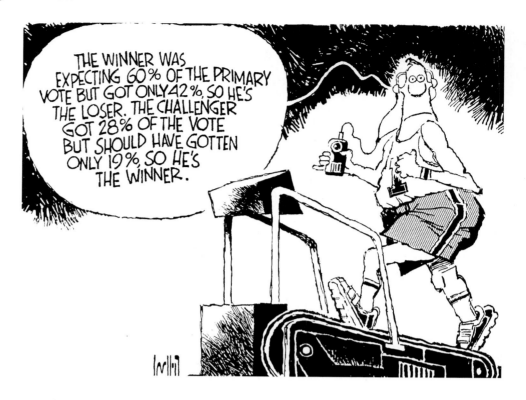

The response to this charge is that by interpreting campaign events, the press performs a legitimate and useful task. The media are not the only ones that put a spin on campaign developments, but they may be the only ones without a vested interest in putting a political spin on the results. After all, how do we define victory in an election where numerous candidates are running and no one wins a majority? In fact, it is the candidates and their managers who start the expectations game, downplaying their strength and exaggerating that of their competitors in an effort to foster low expectations that they can easily exceed. The media counteract the more biased and self-interested spin of the campaigns.

In sum, the modern nomination process for selecting presidential nominees has given increased influence to the media. Some critics regard this as a minus, believing that the media are neither qualified nor motivated to cover campaigns in a way that would inform the American public. Others believe that this is an unreasonable standard by which to measure media behavior and point out that the media in fact perform a number of positive functions. The question is not whether the media are performing well or badly according to some absolute standard but, rather, how their performance compares with any practical alternative.

Whatever your view of the pros and cons of the American nomination process, it is now well established and is unlikely to change, except in marginal ways, in the foreseeable future. The system "works" in the sense that it determines a winner for each party, and it is democratic in the most basic sense that—so far—the nominees are the candidates who win the largest share of the popular vote in their parties' primaries.

## Who Nominates the Vice-President?

Since 1968, one candidate in each party has won a majority of convention delegates by the end of the caucus and primary season. Consequently, the national conventions no longer are the important party meetings they were in earlier eras. As we saw in Chapter 9, they are media events: Party leaders today try to use the conventions to showcase their stars and rising stars and to unify the party by compromising on the platform and giving the losers a chance to speak. Of course, having

*Democratic Dilemma*

# Nominating Vice-Presidents*

The vice-presidency traditionally is the butt of jokes and derision. For example, Texan John Nance Garner, vice-president in Franklin D. Roosevelt's first term, once commented that the vice-presidency "was not worth a bucket of warm spit." Nevertheless, the office is extremely important. Under the Constitution, the vice-president is first in line to succeed the president should the latter die or otherwise be unable to serve—not an uncommon occurrence. In just the past half-century, Harry Truman became president upon FDR's death in 1945, Lyndon Johnson became president after the assassination of John Kennedy in 1963, and Gerald Ford became president after Richard Nixon resigned in 1974.

Moreover, even when presidents survive their terms, vice-presidents frequently become presidential contenders in later years. Richard Nixon was Eisenhower's vice-president. Vice-president Hubert Humphrey was the 1968 Democratic presidential nominee. Former Vice-president Walter Mondale became the Democratic presidential nominee in 1984. George Bush was Ronald Reagan's vice-president. And Clinton's vice-president, Al Gore, was the Democratic nominee in 2000.

Given this history, many are troubled by the seemingly haphazard way in which presidential candidates choose their vice-presidential running mates. Some choices clearly have been questionable. In 1968 Richard Nixon chose Maryland Governor Spiro Agnew, who resigned in 1973 when faced with corruption charges. In 1972 Democratic nominee George McGovern chose Senator Tom Eagleton of Missouri. When it was revealed that Eagleton had been treated for emotional problems, he was dropped from the ticket, an episode that damaged the already struggling McGovern campaign. In 1984 Walter Mondale felt politically obligated to choose a woman, but the excitement generated by the choice of Representative Geraldine Ferraro evaporated in the face of questionable financial dealings by her and her husband. In 1988 George Bush chose Dan Quayle, a young, relatively inexperienced senator from Indiana, who was a liability in the campaign and thereafter.

Although presidential campaigns have been more thorough in checking the backgrounds of vice-presidential possibilities in recent years, many feel that the process is unsatisfactory.

*What do you think?*

- Should the occupant of such an important office be determined entirely by the personal preferences and political calculations of the presidential nominee?
- Should the presidential candidates with the second highest number of delegates in each party automatically be named the party's vice-presidential nominees?
- Should vice-presidential candidates be selected via an entirely separate nomination process?

---

*For background see William Mayer, "A Brief History of Vice-Presidential Selection," in *Pursuit of the White House 2000*, William Mayer, ed. (Chatham, NJ: Chatham House, 2000), pp. 313–374.

realized that the conventions now do little of importance, the media increasingly ignore them.

Before the establishment of the contemporary nomination process, the conventions chose the vice-presidential candidates as well as the presidential candidates. The choice usually was an effort to "balance" the ticket ideologically or geographically, and the convention often chose the runner-up for the presidential nomination, who, by definition, was supported by a significant fraction of the party. Today, the choice of vice-presidential candidates is completely in the hands of the presidential nominees, although they still attempt to choose a nominee who will help the ticket, or at least not hurt it.[26] The presidential nominees simply announce their choices, and the conventions accept them. Sometimes the presidential nominees keep the choice secret, hoping to inject some excitement into an otherwise dull convention, but in 2000 both Bush and Gore made their choices before the convention. Given that vice-presidents quickly become viewed as serious presidential candidates, the fact that choosing them often has been something of an afterthought concerns some people[27] (see the accompanying Democratic Dilemma).

## SECTION SUMMARY

Presidential nominees win national party convention delegates in a succession of caucuses and primaries whose rules differ from state to state. A few primaries are closed to all but registered party members, others are wide open, and almost everything in between exists in some state. Today's nomination process gives average Americans more say in the choice of presidential candidates than the citizens of other democracies have in the choice of their candidates for chief executive. Nevertheless, the process is widely criticized. Critics say it

**A Ground-Breaking Choice**
Vice-Presidential nominee Joseph Lieberman was the first Jew to run on a major party ticket.

begins too early, lasts too long, and gives disproportionate influence to unrepresentative political activists and to the mass media. Defenders have counter-arguments to each criticism. Thus, although the parties regularly tinker with the process, major reform remains only a slim (if tantalizing) possibility.

## The General Election

Labor Day traditionally is the official start date for the fall campaign, although today's nominees do not take so much of a break after the summer conventions as they did in the past. From the start of the campaign until election day—the first Tuesday after the first Monday in November—the candidates maintain an exhausting pace, and the campaign dominates the news.[28]

### Financing the General-Election Campaign

From the mid-1970s to the mid-1990s, presidential campaign funding was a very simple proposition. Under the terms of the 1974 Federal Elections Campaign Act (FECA), the general-election campaign is publicly funded. Unlike in the primaries, however, federal funds are not matching funds. Rather, the FEC gives major-party candidates a subsidy (Bush and Gore received approximately $67.5 million each in 2000), and in return the candidates agree not to raise and spend any more. Thus, from 1974 to 1992, most observers believed that the nominees of the major parties were adequately and equally funded.

In the 1990s, however, campaigns increasingly relied on soft money. Recall that soft money is money contributed by interest groups, labor unions, and individual donors that is not subject to federal regulation. The reason why these contributions are not regulated is that the money is not given to the candidates, who are subject to FECA restrictions, but to party committees, which legally can take contributions of any size and spend as much as they take in. As Figure 10.3 demonstrates, softmoney contributions to the parties exploded in the 1990s. In 1992 the parties raised about half as much in soft money as their candidates received in public funds. In 1996 soft money raised by the parties far exceeded public funds. And preliminary estimates suggest that in 2000, soft money did exceed the publicly provided funds.

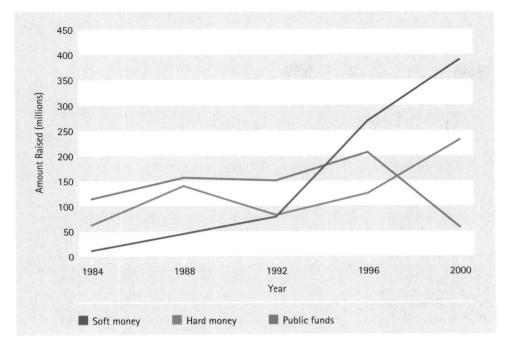

**Figure 10.3**

**In the 1990s Reliance on Soft Money in Presidential Elections Increased Dramatically with No End in Sight**

SOURCE: The Federal Election Commission. Note that the Federal Election Commission began requiring the parties to disclose their soft money in 1991. Figures for 1991 through 1996 are from the FEC. Figures for the 1984 and 1988 cycles are based on voluntary disclosures by the parties and on published estimates. Figures for 2000 are estimates. Public funding declined in 2000 because Bush, Forbes, and the Republican Party declined federal matching funds.

## Spending in the General-Election Campaign

Campaign consultants oversee the expenditure of the large sums of money raised by the campaigns—and they profit personally from such spending. These specialists in modern candidate-based campaigns have replaced the party leaders who supervised the party-based campaigns of earlier eras. Modern campaigns retain pollsters expert in measuring surges and slumps in public opinion during the campaign. Media consultants design the campaign ads or "spots," stage "media events" (appearances designed to allow reporters to get a story, not candidates to meet voters), and schedule the candidate's time so as to maximize coverage. Derided by critics as "handlers" and "hired guns," some campaign consultants have become celebrities in recent decades.

The most important category of general-election spending is for what the FEC calls electronic media—TV and radio advertising, with the lion's share going to television. In 1996 over 60 percent of both Clinton's and Dole's general election spending was for electronic media.[29] Although campaign advertising is widely criticized, studies have consistently found that it is informative, in that those exposed to ads know more about the candidates and where they stand than those not exposed to ads.[30] Indeed, contrary to popular perceptions that everything is getting worse, research suggests that the issue content of ads actually has increased in recent years.[31]

Another, less positive recent trend is in the tone of campaign advertising: It has grown increasingly negative.[32] Rather than make a positive case for themselves, candidates make a negative case against their opponents. However, not all negative ads are bad; pointing out the failures and flaws of an opponent is a perfectly legitimate part of the campaign.[33] But too often, the campaign debate is filled with exaggerations, distortions, and, on occasion, outright lies.

Negative advertising seems to work, in the sense that people remember more of what they have seen from negative than from positive spots.[34] Thus candidates will continue to "go negative." What is good for individual candidates, however, may have harmful consequences for the larger political process. Much of what people remember may be inaccurate, and as we have noted previously, there is evidence that attack ads reduce turnout. In particular, they reduce turnout among the independent, more moderate segment of the population. Candidates, then, are playing to the more committed and more extreme voters, making campaigns more polarized as well as more negative.[35]

simulation

**You are a Professional Campaign Consultant**

timeline

**Presidential Candidates and Their Television Ads**

## Election Connection

# Money in 1996

For most of the 1996 campaign, President Clinton appeared headed for an easy win—a double-digit margin according to most of the polls. But in the end, his margin of victory was only 8 points, and he failed to reach the psychologically important 50 percent mark. Once again Clinton was a "minority president."

The most likely explanation for Clinton's late fade was the campaign finance scandal that began to break in the last week of the campaign. Asian Americans had made large soft-money contributions to the Democratic National Committee. There is nothing illegal about that, and the Clinton defense at first implied that critics were bigoted. But a number of the contributions looked suspicious, as though foreign corporations were funneling money through American citizens, and that *is* illegal (although contributions by U.S. subsidiaries of foreign corporations are legal). The Democratic National Committee began returning questionable contributions, and soon Vice President Al Gore found himself mixed up in a series of flip-flops associated with his fund-raising activities. In the aftermath of the election, embarrassing new revelations filled the media. Large contributors had been taken on U.S. trade missions, invited to White House coffees, and (in some cases) even invited to stay a night in the Lincoln bedroom. Both parties essentially had "sold" photo-ops and invitations to social functions where high-level politicians were present.

When the final reports were filed, it turned out that the party committees had raised about $260 million in the 1995–1996 campaign season, the Republicans taking in about 140 million and the Democrats about 120 million.[a] These sums were three times higher than the corresponding amounts in the 1992 campaign, a rather clear indication that the June 1996 Supreme Court decision had opened the floodgates.

Post-election stories began to link large contributions and White House policy changes, giving rise to an outcry for reform. In his February State of the Union Address, President Clinton endorsed a bipartisan campaign finance bill. The McCain–Feingold Bill, named after its sponsors Arizona Senator John McCain, a

Republican, and Wisconsin Representative Russell Feingold, a Democrat, proposed to eliminate soft money, prohibit PAC contributions, and provide low-cost broadcast time to candidates who accept spending limits. Congress killed an earlier version of the bill in June 1996 and has declined to pass various other versions since.

Legislation is unlikely to settle the debate over campaign finance. The debate is a perennial one, and every step toward reform seems to create a new problem. As noted earlier, PACs were a response to the 1974 FECA amendments, and soft money is actually a product of a 1979 law designed to give the parties a greater role in the campaign process.[b] The problem is especially difficult because attempts to restrict spending run afoul of free-speech considerations, and any proposed regulation or restriction threatens the electoral self-interests of incumbents and the partisan self-interests of the contending parties. Whatever is done about campaign finance between 2000 and 2004, we suspect that the issue will live on. As presidential candidate Bill Bradley put it, "Money invades politics like ants in the kitchen—without closing all the holes, there is always a way in."[c]

*What do you think?*
- *Given the American Constitution and the incentives facing politicians, is it possible to close all the holes Bradley refers to?*
- *Should reformers push for a constitutional amendment that allows restrictions on campaign spending?*
- *Are there reforms short of constitutional amendments that will improve the present state of campaign financing?*
- *Should the law simply require full disclosure of contributors and their contributions and trust the voters in the ballot booth to discourage illegitimate activity?*

[a] Rebecca Carr, "As Soft Money Grows, So Does Controversy," *Congressional Quarterly Weekly Report*, November 16, 1996, 3272.
[b] Jonathan Salant, "Despite Attempts, Loopholes in Law Remain Unplugged," *Congressional Quarterly Weekly Report*, November 16, 1996, 3274–3275.
[c] Carr, "As Soft Money Grows," p. 3272.

Soft-money scandals marred the 1996 Clinton–Gore campaign, as described in the accompanying Election Connection. In the aftermath of the campaign, calls for reform once again sounded. This is a perennial problem in the United States, a by-product of the First Amendment, private-sector media, and traditionally weak parties. In few other countries is campaign finance such a recurring issue (see the accompanying International Comparison).

### Designing General-Election Campaign Strategy: The Electoral College

**popular vote**
The total vote cast for a candidate across the nation.

**electoral vote**
Cast by electors, with each state receiving one vote for each of its members of the House of Representatives and one vote for each of its senators.

The candidate who wins the most votes—the so-called **popular vote,** or the actual votes cast—does not necessarily become president. Three times in American history (John Quincy Adams in 1824, Rutherford Hayes in 1876, and Benjamin Harrison in 1888), the candidate who came in second became president; 2000 may be a fourth occurrence. Recall that the Constitution stipulates that the president and vice-president are chosen by the electoral college, a collection of electors chosen by the voters. In the electoral college, each state receives an **electoral vote** equal to the sum of its House and Senate seats (and the District of Columbia gets three votes under the terms of the Twenty-Third Amendment). Thus Hayes and Harrison became presidents because they won a majority of the electoral vote despite losing the popular vote. If no one receives a majority of the electoral vote, then the election is decided by the House of Representatives, which is how Adams defeated Andrew Jackson.

## Campaign Financing in Other Democracies

Campaign finance is rarely a major issue in other democracies. There are a number of reasons for this contrast with the United States.

In the first place, much more money is spent in American elections—even relative to the size of the electorate—than in other countries. Nationwide, the total amount spent in the 1996 elections (the last presidential election for which we have complete data) was more than $3 billion. Only Japan comes close to spending as much (relative to the size of its electorate).

The total cost of campaigns depends on both the number of campaigns and the amount spent on each. As we have noted, there are far more elections in the United States than elsewhere, because there are more offices, and terms of office are short. Additionally, the cost of campaigns is higher. One reason is the candidate-centered electoral system. Like the United States, high-spending Japan has candidate-centered elections: Each candidate constructs a personal organization that funds the campaign. Most other democracies have party-centered elections. The national party and its leaders conduct a single campaign on behalf of all the party candidates. Rather than having hundreds of individual candidates running duplicate campaigns, the parties take advantage of what economists call economies of scale. Another factor that contributes to the expense of American campaigns is that increasingly they are fought over the airwaves, and TV campaigns are expensive—not only the time itself, but the services of the consultants, ad people, and so forth.[a] In most other democracies, candidates still rely more on the campaign work of party members than attempting to reach voters directly through broadcasting.

A second reason why campaign finance is a lesser concern in other democracies is that spending is heavily regulated. In Britain individual candidates are not permitted to buy television or radio time! Even the parties cannot make media buys. They are limited to a small number of publicly financed addresses by national party leaders. In Germany the law requires TV networks to give the parties free airtime during campaigns, but it is illegal for candidates to buy any additional radio or TV ads.[b] Of course, if limits such as these were adopted in the United States, the courts would strike them down as violations of the First Amendment right of free speech.

Finally, many other democracies provide at least some degree of public financing of all elections.[c] For example, in Austria, Belgium, Denmark, Finland, Germany, Mexico, Sweden, and Turkey, the parties receive public subsidies in proportion to the number of votes they received in the last election or the number of seats they hold in parliament. In-kind subsidies, especially free media time, also are common. Many democracies even provide subsidies for the major parties *between* elections. In the United States, public financing has progressed only as far as presidential elections; attempts to extend it even to Congress have failed. And imagine the popular reaction if anyone were to propose that the Democratic and Republican National Committees receive public subsidies between elections!

In sum, the structure of electoral processes, the Constitution, and popular attitudes all interact to create a campaign finance problem more severe in the United States than elsewhere. Contrasts with other democracies raise a number of questions.

*What do you think?*
- *Should all legitimate candidates receive free TV time?*
- *Should all campaigns be publicly financed?*
- *Should the United States adopt constitutional amendments that permit regulation of how much candidates can spend and what they can spend it on?*

[a] "Money and Politics," *The Economist*, February 8, 1997: 23.
[b] Charles Lane, "Kohl Train," *The New Republic*, February 14, 2000: 17.
[c] Richard Katz, "Party Organizations and Finance," in Lawrence LeDuc, Richard Niemi, and Pippa Norris, eds., *Comparing Democracies* (Thousand Oaks, CA: Sage, 1996), pp. 129–132.

Because every state has two senators, whereas the number of House seats depends on the state's population, the electoral college gives a theoretical advantage to small states. For example, with 2 senators but only 1 seat in the House, Wyoming has 3 electoral votes—approximately 1 per 151,000 residents. With 2 senators but 52 seats in the House, California has 54 electoral votes, approximately 1 per 550,000 residents, a ratio only one-third as large as Wyoming's. In the 2000 election, if a candidate had won a plurality in each of the 40 least populated states, which together include only 46 percent of the U.S. population, he would have won a majority of the electoral college and become president.

Most observers agree, however, that in practice, the electoral college has a large-state bias that overwhelms the small-state bias just described. The reason is the traditional **winner-take-all voting.** In the electoral college, the candidate who wins the state receives *all* of the state's electoral votes (except for Maine and Nebraska, which give the winner of each congressional district that electoral vote and the statewide winner the two other votes). Thus, if you carry a large state by a tiny margin, you get all of its electoral votes, whereas even if you win a small state by a landslide, you get only a few electoral votes. This is why candidates often win bigger electoral college majorities than their popular majorities, as illustrated in Figure 10.4. In 1996 Clinton won 49 percent of the popular vote but 70 percent of the electoral vote. And this is also the reason why, in a tight election like 2000, the popular-vote winner can lose in the electoral college.

**winner-take-all voting**
Any voting procedure in which the side with the most votes gets all of the seats or delegates at stake.

## Figure 10.4

Bill Clinton Won an Overwhelming Electoral College Majority in 1996, Despite Winning Only 49 Percent of the Popular Vote

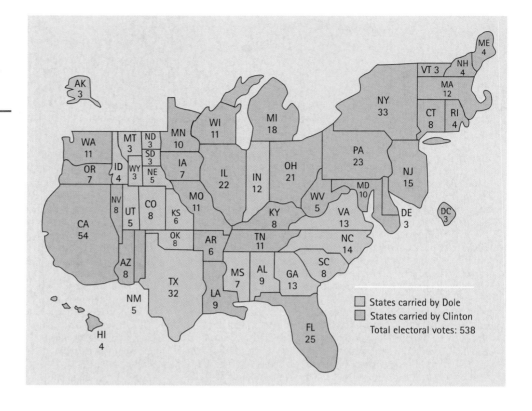

**visual literacy**

**American Electoral Rules: How Do They Influence Campaigns?**

For more than a century the popular and electoral vote winners were the same, so the electoral college received little attention although some observers periodically argued that it could produce the "wrong winner."[36] The confusion of 2000, however, has brought the electoral college to the forefront of national attention, and proposals for reform no doubt will be offered in the coming years.[37]

The media tend to portray the campaign as a contest for the popular vote, reporting nationwide polls almost daily as the election draws near, but the campaigns themselves are focused on the electoral vote. It does not matter whether you are ahead in the national polls if you are not ahead in states that compose an electoral college majority. In fact, the electoral college was particularly unkind to the Democrats throughout the 1970s and 1980s. Between 1968 and 1988, 21 states with 191 electoral votes voted six consecutive times for the Republican candidate. Another 17 states with 176 electoral votes voted five times (with the single exception of 1976) for the Republicans. Only the District of Columbia, with 3 electoral votes, was as loyal to the Democrats. This base in the electoral college—the Republican "L" depicted in Figure 10.5—was the basis for the much talked-about Republican "lock" on the presidency.[38] Although Democratic candidates often were competitive in national polls, in each election they had to formulate a strategy to win every state outside the Republican base and perhaps chip a few out of it.

### Section Summary

The general-election campaign fills the period between Labor Day and election day. The campaign is organized around the goal of winning a majority in the electoral college, which on rare occasions has chosen a president who came in second in the popular vote. To win the states necessary for a majority, candidates conduct expensive campaigns designed by experts in modern campaign methods—especially public opinion polling and media advertising. Although campaigns have received public funding since the 1970s, the parties today raise even larger sums in soft money that they use to conduct modern media campaigns.

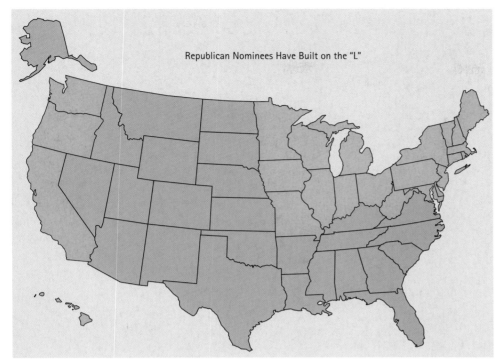

Republican Nominees Have Built on the "L"

**Figure 10.5**

**The Republican "L"**
The base on which GOP majorities were built in presidential elections in the 1970s and the 1980s was a wide swath of states called "the Republican L." It takes in the Rocky Mountain region, the Plains states, and the entire South. With Alaska thrown in, these states have a total of 233 electoral votes (270 are needed to win). Bill Clinton cracked the "L" but it reemerged in 2000.

SOURCE: "Republican Nominees Have Built on the "L," *Congressional Quarterly Guide to the 1996 Republican National Convention*, August 3, 1996, p. 9.

## Voting Behavior in Presidential Elections

In general, candidates' strategies take some states for granted, concede that they will lose others no matter what they do, and concentrate their efforts in the ones that are "up for grabs." Why do some states consistently support one party or the other for long periods of time? The reason is that there is considerable continuity in how citizens vote. This continuity, or "electoral inertia," explains why candidates know ahead of time that they will probably lose some states and win others. It is also why the impact of campaigns and the media is limited in the context of the general election. To explain these observations, we need to take a close look at *when* and *how* Americans decide how to vote for presidential candidates.

### When Americans Decide

Many people decide how they will vote before the campaign begins. As shown in Figure 10.6, typically, one-third to one-half of the electorate reports deciding how to vote *before the primaries*. This decision is easy enough for people who always vote the party line, and it is also easy for voters who know the identity of at least one of the nominees—usually an incumbent president who seeks reelection. Another portion of the electorate reports deciding how to vote between the start of the primaries and the end of the conventions. All told, from one-half to two-thirds of the electorate decides how to vote by the end of the conventions—before the fall campaign gets under way. The figure was 51 percent in 1988, when no incumbent ran, and 63 percent in 1996, when Clinton sought reelection. Hence a large fraction of the electorate (typically more than half) are not much affected by the campaign, already having made up their minds.

### How Americans Decide

How can people make up their minds before policies and programs are debated in the fall campaign? The answer is simply that Americans decide how to vote not only on the basis of the short-term considerations that dominate the campaign (the candidates

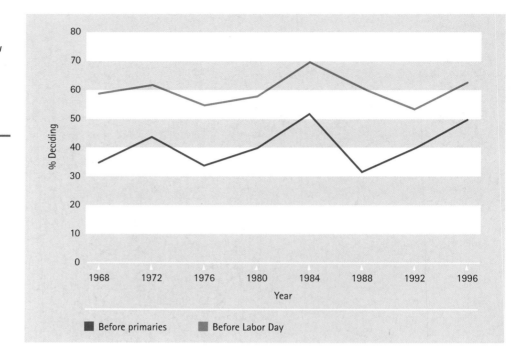

and the positions they advocate) but also on the basis of longer-term considerations that arise years before the campaign gets under way. The considerations that determine how Americans vote fall into four general categories: party loyalties, public policies, government performance, and the qualities of the candidates.

**Party Loyalties** About two-thirds of the American electorate view themselves as Democrats or Republicans, the remainder as independents. Political scientists call this allegiance to one party or the other **party identification,** or party ID for short.[39] Party ID is a long-term force that provides continuity from election to election. For example, the Civil War and Reconstruction created many "yellow dog" Democrats in the South—people who wouldn't vote for a Republican if the Democratic nominee were a yellow dog. Similarly, the Great Depression left many northerners intensely committed to the New Deal Democratic party of Franklin Roosevelt. Such deeply held allegiances underlie the "party systems" that we discussed in Chapter 8. The traumatic events of the 1960s—Vietnam and civil disorders—shook the party identifications that underpinned the New Deal party system. The number of voters holding strong party identifications declined, and the number professing independence increased, especially among young people. Since the mid-1960s surveys typically record more independents than Republicans and occasionally almost as many independents as Democrats.

Party identification underlies the well-known tendencies of various groups to support candidates of one party or the other. For example, Table 10.2 shows that African Americans and Jews are heavily Democratic in their voting. Union members, urban residents, and Catholics also have traditionally been Democratic groups, although the support of union members and Catholics has fluctuated in recent decades. On the other hand, the wealthy, rural residents, southerners, and protestants—especially evangelicals—tend to vote Republican..

At one time, party ID was considered to be much like a religious affiliation. Not only was it resistant to change but it was also learned early in childhood and had little policy or ideological content. Just as children learn to call themselves Catholics, Jews, or Muslims before they know the doctrines of their religion, so children learned to call themselves Democrats or Republicans before knowing what the party stands for. Today it is recognized that party ID responds to political events and conditions, although it is a lagging indicator.[40] For example, some southerners continued to call

**party identification**

A person's subjective feeling of affiliation with a party.

Table 10.2

Groups Differ in Their Support for the Parties

| Groups | Percentage Voting for Bush in 2000 |
|---|---|
| White | 54 |
| Hispanic | 35 |
| African-American | 9 |
| Poor (< $15,000/year) | 37 |
| Wealthy (> $100,000/year) | 54 |
| Union member | 34 |
| Not a union member | 52 |
| Protestant | 56 |
| Catholic | 47 |
| Jew | 19 |
| Big city resident | 26 |
| Suburban resident | 49 |
| Rural resident | 59 |
| Lives in the East | 39 |
| Lives in the Midwest | 49 |
| Lives in the South | 55 |
| Lives in the West | 46 |

SOURCE: Excerpted from VNS Exit Polls posted on the MSNBC website, November 8, 2000.

themselves Democrats long after they had begun voting for Republicans. There is some evidence, too, that younger people are more likely to change their party ID than older people.[41] During the 1980s, for example, younger Americans led the resurgence of identification with the Republican party.[42]

As shown in Figure 10.7, between the 1936 and 1984 elections, more Americans consistently considered themselves Democrats than Republicans. Republican candidates such as Eisenhower and Nixon were able to win by capturing a majority of the independents and some Democrats. After Reagan's reelection in 1984, the gap between the parties began to close. Taking into account that Republicans are more likely to vote than Democrats, today's electorate contains about equal numbers of Democrats and Republicans. For the strongest partisans, the campaign is irrelevant; come hell or high water, they will vote their party ID.

**Public Policies** For the most politically interested voters, policies and programs are the essence of politics. There are problems and conflicts in the United States and in the world. Problems cry out for solutions and conflicts for resolution. Elections decide these solutions and resolutions. For people with this view of politics, the campaign is a long-running debate—a chance to educate the electorate about alternative paths the country might choose and to persuade voters to follow one of them.

Surprisingly, research has found that although policy concerns are important, in most elections they are not the dominant factor.[43] One reason is that public policy debates often are complex, and people have limited information. To cite one extreme example, President Clinton's 1993 health care proposal required 1342 printed pages, and that was just one of the competing proposals! How could voters possibly be expected to have detailed views about such complex issues?

Figure 10.7

**The Democratic Advantage in Party Identification Has Eroded**

SOURCE: American National Election Studies.

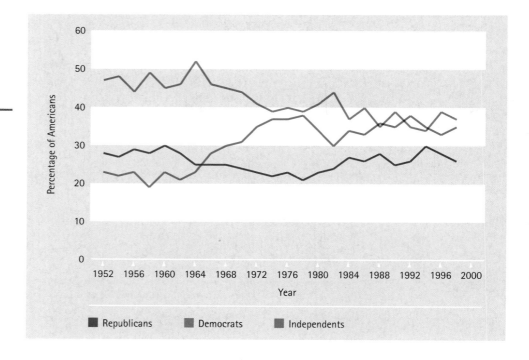

Moreover, voters often are unsure where the candidates stand, because candidates equivocate and otherwise confuse voters about their positions. Research on the 1968 election, for example, found that views on U.S. policy in Vietnam (whether to escalate the war, maintain the status quo, or withdraw) were only minimally related to the presidential vote. How could that be true when disagreement about the war was tearing the country apart? The answer is that the positions of the candidates gave the voters no basis on which to choose. The Democratic nominee, Humphrey, supported the status quo, but he kept wavering; and the Republican, Nixon, refused to reveal his position, saying that he had a "secret plan" to end the war. In the end, befuddled voters guessed that both candidates supported the same policy.[44]

Some may find it troubling that preferences about specific policies do not dominate presidential elections, but it really depends on what theory of democracy you hold. Recall our discussion of popular and responsible theories in Chapter 1. *Popular theories* treat elections as expressions of the popular will and assume that elections provide mandates for the elected. In order for elections to work that way, citizens must decide how to vote on the basis of policy issues. In contrast, *responsible theories* view elections as occasions when citizens endorse or reject parties and leaders. Elections provide opportunities for leadership, not mandates. In such theories, citizens can vote largely on the basis of outcomes rather than on the basis of the policies that produce those outcomes.

There are some important exceptions to the finding that public policies are not the dominant factor in most elections. The first such exceptions are social or cultural issues. Candidates announce that they favor prayer in schools or that they oppose abortion. Such issues are "easy" in the sense that the desired outcome and the policy that achieves it are one and the same: Pray in schools, stop abortions.[45] Such issues are different from policy issues such as health insurance or education, where a chain of actions is required to bring about a particular outcome.[46] Social issues are as much about values held by different groups in society as they are about specific public policies. Indeed, such values often are incorporated into the party identifications of citizens—they are part of the **party images,** the associations that voters make between the parties and particular issues.[47] Campaign appeals based on such issues serve to solidify a candidate's base and reach out to sympathetic members of the other party.

**party image**

A set of widely held associations between a party and particular issues and values.

Second, voters may be upset about a problem and eager for government to do *something* about it. Thus candidates talk about "getting tough on crime," "cleaning up the welfare mess," and "getting guns out of the hands of children." These are important political issues, to be sure, but often they do not involve much by way of specific policy proposals; rather, voters are asked to choose between general approaches such as "soft" and "tough." Moreover, such issues at least implicitly reflect voters' unhappiness with the government *performance* that has allowed such problems to fester.

**Government Performance**  Real elections are a mix of the considerations emphasized in popular theory and responsible theory, but a great deal of research confirms the importance of government performance as emphasized in responsible theory.[48] Performance voting demands less of voters than policy voting. To make judgments about performance, voters do not have to watch C-SPAN or read the *New York Times*. Voters can make judgments about economic conditions from their own experiences and those of their friends and neighbors. They can make judgments about other social conditions by observing the conditions of their communities, schools, and workplaces.

Voting by looking backwards at performance (often called **retrospective voting**) may outweigh voting by looking forward at alternative policies (often called **prospective voting**). The 1984 campaign provided a classic illustration. Public opinion surveys showed that on many issues, more voters were closer to the Democratic nominee, Walter Mondale, than to President Reagan. A majority believed that tax increases were inevitable (Mondale's position), a majority were dubious about "Star Wars" (the missile defense system dear to Reagan's heart), a majority rejected Reagan's call for further increases in defense spending, and a majority were doubtful about Reagan's Central America policy.[49] Nevertheless, Reagan carried 49 states. Was this just an expression of his winning personality? Probably not. Analysis of the election returns showed that a majority of voters approved of Reagan's performance as president, regardless of many of the specific policies he followed.

Voters hardly can be blamed for adopting shortcuts like performance voting. The future is uncertain, the experts disagree, and time is limited, so how can one make an intelligent decision about complex policy alternatives? Moreover, candidates are not always clear about their intentions. At least good performance by government suggests competent leadership, and voters certainly are behaving reasonably in voting for competence.[50] To return to an earlier example, although voting in 1968 was not related to Vietnam policy preferences, people who disapproved of President's Johnson's performance voted against Vice-President Humphrey.

From the perspective of our discussion of voting behavior, the important point to remember is that government performance is a medium-term consideration. It is something that reflects four years of activity, not something that suddenly arises when the campaign begins. The campaign can attempt to put some "spin" on government performance, but it is difficult to make a bad economy or unpopular war into a positive accomplishment for the incumbent administration, no matter how good the media experts and campaign consultants.

**The Qualities of the Candidates**  Not surprisingly, the individual candidates are the major source of change in how people vote from election to election.[51] Not since 1956, when Adlai Stevenson fought a rematch with Dwight Eisenhower, have Americans had the same choice of candidates in two presidential elections. In a country that exhorts voters to "support the person not the party," the qualities of the candidates are extremely important influences on how people vote. But it is important to keep several cautions in mind.

First, when we say that candidate qualities are important influences on how people vote, we are not using *qualities* as a synonym for *personalities*. Personality is overrated, especially by the losers. It is more comforting to blame your loss on the winning personality of your opponent than to admit that voters reject what you believe in

**retrospective voting**
Voting on the basis of the past performance of the incumbent administration.

**prospective voting**
Voting on the basis of the candidates' policy promises.

Some critics charged that Gore ran a poor campaign in 2000, rarely mentioning the economic successes of the Clinton administration. *Why do you think that Gore's theme was "I'm going to fight for you." instead of "You've never had it so good."?*

or that they think you are incompetent. In fact, detailed analyses of what people like and dislike about the candidates indicate that most of the qualities they mention have some legitimate relevance to governing: intelligence, integrity, experience, character, and their opposites.[52]

Second, after the election there is a tendency to downgrade the loser's personal qualities and upgrade the winner's. For example, in the spring of 1988, many Democrats considered Michael Dukakis an attractive candidate—a tough, competent manager. But after he lost, he was criticized for being an unemotional policy wonk. Dukakis hadn't changed, but many in the Democratic party found it easier to blame their messenger than to admit that the electorate had rejected their message, a tendency reinforced by the media's habit of explaining politics in personal terms.

Robert Dole provides a more recent example. After his defeat in 1996, many Republicans concluded that Dole was a terrible candidate who had run an uninspired campaign. Although there is some truth to such charges, his critics seemed to forget that Dole had been viewed very differently less than two years earlier. In the aftermath of the Republican takeover of Congress in 1994, Dole was viewed as the "grownup" in Washington, a mature, responsible, experienced public official who would fill the leadership vacuum, negotiate the necessary compromises, and keep the government functioning. Reports mentioned his quick wit and warm—if private—personality. Did Dole change in two years? No, he was the same Dole, but a national presidential campaign calls for different strengths than Washington negotiations, and even more important, he was trying to unseat an incumbent who had peace and prosperity behind him.

There are some striking contrasts between what voters actually thought of the candidates in a given campaign and how popular history views the candidates. The 1960 contest between John F. Kennedy and Richard Nixon is the best example. Although revisionist historians have debunked much of the Kennedy mystique, you are probably familiar with the Kennedy legend—the charismatic leader of a new "Camelot." On the contrary, 1960 survey data show that Nixon was more favorably regarded as a candidate than Kennedy.[53] Kennedy owed his narrow victory primarily to the fact that he was a Democrat, and at the time there were more Democrats than

Republicans.[54] Did the data indicate that Nixon had a more attractive personality than Kennedy? No. Nixon was viewed as more experienced and better qualified for the job. But what lives on in political folklore about the candidates may have little resemblance to the reality of citizens' opinions when they voted.

Finally, we should remember that what people think about the candidates is partly based on the other considerations already discussed. Most citizens with a strong Democratic party ID are going to like the Democratic candidate—any Democratic candidate; people with strong positions on certain policies probably are going to like any candidate who shares those policy commitments and to dislike any candidate who does not; people who think the president has performed very well probably are going to like him as a president, whether they'd like him as a neighbor or not.

Thus, the identities of the candidates and their personal qualities are important influences on how people vote. But there is a tendency to overestimate the effect of the candidates, because (1) we tend to rewrite history in terms of the personalities on the political stage at a particular time and (2) impressions of the candidates are influenced by the policies they advocate and their performance records, as well as by the partisanship of the voters.

## Limited Media Influence on Presidential Elections

The media are less influential in the general-election campaign than in the primaries. In Chapter 9, we pointed out that media influence is *contingent*. The primaries, especially the early primaries, maximize the opportunity for media influence, but in the general election, media coverage runs up against voter predispositions—the party identifications that many hold, and the impressions of government performance that voters have been forming for four (or even eight) years, not just the few months of the campaign.[55] In the primaries, neither predisposition exists. Primary voters choose only among Democrats or only among Republicans, so party ID is not relevant. Nor is presidential performance of any use: Normally, all the candidates in the incumbent party's primaries defend the president's record, whereas all the candidates in the other party's primaries criticize that record. Consequently, citizens use other information to choose among the candidates, and the media in most cases provide it. The general election differs in that many voters have all the information they need: their own partisan identification, that of groups they like or dislike, and their impressions of government performance.

The importance of the campaign itself is similarly exaggerated. Contrary to what the media imply, many elections are decided before the campaign begins; conditions in the preceding four years and the government's response to them determined the outcome. The 1964, 1972, 1984, and 1996 campaigns are the clearest examples but not the only ones. Political scientist James Campbell has calculated that between 1948 and 1996, the campaigns probably were decisive in 1948 and 1960, two exceedingly close elections. The campaigns "may have possibly been decisive" in 1976 and 1980. In the other nine elections, the outcome was largely predetermined.[56]

Certainly campaigns do matter.[57] But instead of the exaggerated view that campaigns decide election outcomes, we suggest the more complex view that campaigns themselves are determined by broader forces. Campaigns are constrained by what goes on between elections. A card game provides a good analogy. Who wins a hand depends on both the skill with which the participants play and the deal of the cards. No matter how skillfully you play, it may not be sufficient to overcome a bad draw.

In politics, some cards are dealt years, even decades, before the election. The Democrats drew the Herbert Hoover Depression card in 1932 and played it successfully until the 1950s. The Republicans drew the McGovern "liberal" card in 1972 and were still trying to play it in 1996. Other cards are drawn in the four years since the last election. Good economic conditions are aces dealt to the incumbent party; poor conditions are aces dealt to the opposition. The same is true for international embarrassments and costly wars.

The luck of the draw strongly affects the campaign. We praise and criticize campaigns, while often forgetting that the candidates were limited in what they could do by social and economic realities. Did the fact that Dukakis lost to Vice-President Bush in 1988 while Clinton beat President Bush in 1992 indicate that Dukakis ran a poor campaign and Clinton a brilliant one? In retrospect, Dukakis surely could have done some things better.[58] But Clinton's brilliant campaign probably also reflects the fact that an economic recession made the Bush administration a much fatter target in 1992 than the Reagan–Bush administration was in 1988.

The Dole campaign in 1996 is the most recent example of this common confusion of political cause and effect. Despite suggestions in the media, Robert Dole did not lose the election because he ran a poor campaign.[59] The opposite is more nearly true: His campaign was poor because he had no chance to win the election. As noted below, the economy and the image that the Republican party projected in 1995–1996 put Dole well behind before the campaign ever began.

The importance of the campaign in presidential elections emerges in close contests. If, on the basis of party ID and presidential performance, the race is about even when the campaign begins, then the campaign will determine the outcome by winning over the marginal, or undecided, voters. Under such conditions, the favorability of media coverage and the expertise of media advisers may in fact win or lose the election. But the point to remember is that many elections, such as the election in 2000, do not begin as even contests. Rather, what elected officials have done between elections has largely determined the outcome.

### SECTION SUMMARY

Presidential candidates take some states for granted and focus on states that are "up for grabs." The reason why some states are predisposed toward one candidate or another is that many people decide how to vote on the basis of long-standing party loyalties, issues that arose long before the campaign began, and the performance of the incumbent administration. Newer policy issues and the identities of the candidates add an element of uncertainty to every campaign, but they often do not overcome the effects of those long-term considerations. For that reason, many Americans already know how they will vote before the campaign begins. Because of these patterns of voter behavior, the effects of the media—and, indeed, those of the campaign itself—are limited in the general election. Candidates who run fine campaigns may still lose because the long-term factors are stacked against them.

## The Contemporary Presidential Election Scene

The New Deal party system splintered in the 1960s. The racial and social turmoil created by the civil rights revolution and the war in Vietnam forced President Lyndon Johnson from the race in 1968 and enabled Republican Richard Nixon to win two terms. It was the beginning of a Republican streak that saw them win five of the six presidential elections between 1968 and 1988. Not until the 1990s were the Democrats able to overcome the problems that first arose in the 1960s. We will survey these ups and downs in party fortunes in light of our discussion of American voting behavior in the previous section.

### The 1970s and 1980s: Republican "Lock"

The so-called Republican lock on the presidency reflected developments that gave Republicans a clear advantage on two of the four major factors that determine how Americans vote: performance and issues. This advantage forced Democratic candidates to defend unpopular policies and eventually eroded the long-standing Democratic advantage in party ID. Although the Democrats enjoyed a brief recovery when the American public passed a harsh judgment on Republican performance after the Watergate scandal and the recession of 1973–1974, the extremely narrow margin of

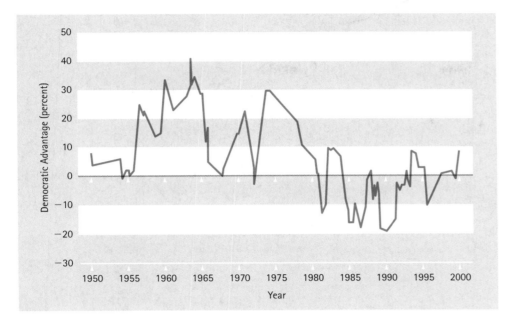

**Figure 10.8**

**Until the 1980s the Democrats Generally Had Been Viewed as the Party of Prosperity**
Respondents were asked the question "Which political party—the Republican or the Democratic party—would do a better job of keeping the country prosperous?" The "Democratic advantage" is the percentage responding Democratic minus the percentage responding Republican.

SOURCE: Harold Stanley and Richard Niemi, *Vital Statistics on American Politics*, 2000 ed. (Washington, DC: CQ Press, 2000), p. 146.

Jimmy Carter's victory suggested the severity of the Democrats' problems. The poor performance of the Carter administration gave the presidency back to the Republicans, who then won three consecutive elections—1980, 1984, and 1988. During this period, Republican performance and policies beat the Democrats on each of the major issue fronts in contemporary politics: economic, foreign and defense, racial, and social.

**The Economy** As recorded in Figure 10.8, for almost half a century, Americans viewed Democrats as the party of prosperity. But in the early 1970s, the post–World War II economic expansion gave way to an inflationary era that economists blamed on President Johnson's attempt to wage war in Vietnam and implement major new domestic programs without raising taxes. Although Republican Presidents Nixon and Ford did little to stem the rising tide of inflation, it reached frightening levels (13 percent) under Democratic President Carter.

An economically pinched electorate naturally became less generous—less supportive of government programs to aid the needy and less willing to tolerate further increases in their tax burden. By the late 1970s, a tax revolt had begun. As the party that favored government spending, the Democrats were on the wrong side of the issue. And as the party in power when economic conditions hit bottom, the Democrats took the blame for the downturn in the economy.

**National Defense and International Relations** Although mid-century Americans viewed the Democrats as the party of prosperity, they viewed Republicans as more capable in the international arena. The Vietnam war reinforced that view, while splitting the Democratic Party and strengthening its pacifist wing. Americans are not imperialists; they tend to be skeptical of international interventions. But during the 1970s, the United States faced a series of foreign challenges, and voters were not confident that the Democratic party could deal with them. The final humiliation came when Iranian militants seized 90 hostages from the American embassy in Tehran and held them for more than a year. This hostage crisis destroyed any remaining hopes for President Carter's reelection and reinforced the popular perception that the Democrats were unable to counter world threats to America's interests.

**Race** Slavery split the Democratic party in the 1850s, and the continuing issue of race helped do so again a century later. When President Johnson signed the 1964

**Figure 10.9**

**Blacks and Whites Differ Greatly in Their Views about Race Relations and Racial Policy**

SOURCE: "An American Dilemma" (Part II), *The Public Perspective*, February/March 1996: 20, 23, 26.

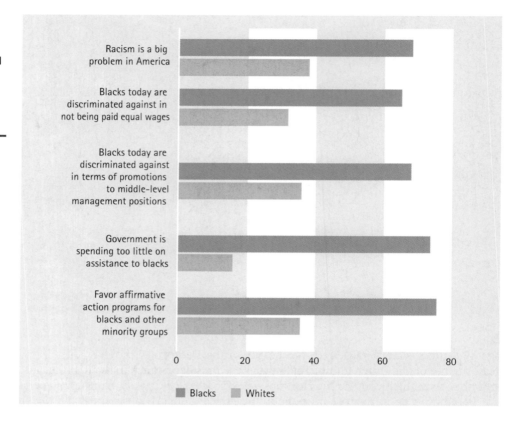

Civil Rights Act, he commented that he was "giving the South to the Republicans for a long time to come." Johnson may not have realized that his strong support of civil rights would hurt Democratic candidates not only in the South but in the North as well.

There is great disagreement today about the nature of the racial issue. Some believe that white support of Republican candidates and white opposition to policies aimed at helping blacks simply show the continued strength of racism in the United States.[60] Others disagree, arguing that racial prejudice has greatly declined but that many policies proposed to help minorities—such as affirmative action—are inconsistent with traditional American values.[61] Figure 10.9 illustrates the great gulf between black and white opinion. Whites feel that enormous progress has already been made and, to a lesser degree, that African-Americans fail to recognize how much racism has declined. Blacks see continued racism and focus on how much remains to be accomplished before racial equality is a reality. To their electoral misfortune, the Democrats were caught in the middle of such disagreements between the white majority and their most loyal constituency.

**Social Issues** As noted in Chapter 5, the New Deal Democrats were a liberal party, but *liberal* then had primarily economic connotations. In the 1960s, liberalism took on new meanings, becoming more closely associated with racial issues such as busing, welfare, and affirmative action; and later, liberalism came to be linked to sexual permissiveness and gay rights.

A majority of Americans took "conservative" stances on such issues, and the more prominent such issues became, the more fertile the ground they provided for a popular reaction. That reaction came in the late 1970s in the form of the "new right," a socially conservative movement associated with evangelical religious groups. Given that culturally liberal points of view had met with a warmer welcome in the Democratic party than in the Republican, the reaction typically took an anti-Democratic form.

## *The 1990s: Democratic Resurgence*

In 1992 Bill Clinton was elected with 43 percent of the vote in a three-way election. Although analysts disagree somewhat on whether Ross Perot cost Clinton or Bush more votes, there is little doubt that Clinton still would have won in a two-way race.[62] Turnarounds in each of the four issue areas we have just discussed contributed to Clinton's win.

Most fundamentally, the recession rejuvenated the Democrats' image as the party of prosperity. The struggling economy was the foundation of Clinton's campaign. He promised to get the economy moving again, and he appealed to middle-class concerns with his support of health care for all. Fortunately for the Democrats, the end of the Cold War meant that foreign threats did not interfere with the voters' preoccupation with the economy. With the collapse of the Soviet threat, national defense and foreign policy vanished from the list of voter concerns in 1992 and have remained off the list since, to Republicans' dismay.

Meanwhile, Clinton took a more conservative stance on race, distancing himself from prominent black leaders, such as Jesse Jackson, and even criticizing an African American entertainer, Sister Souljah, for the lyrics in some of her songs. He defused social issues by aligning himself with "Middle America." Clinton talked about personal responsibility and family values, promised "to end welfare as we know it," prayed, allowed a convicted murderer in Arkansas to be executed, and in other ways tried to dispel the cultural liberal image that had dogged the Democrats for a generation.

After the Democrats lost Congress in 1994, President Clinton looked electorally dead. He maintained such a low profile that in a press conference in April 1995, one reporter had the audacity to ask him whether he was "still relevant" to American politics. Within a year, however, Clinton rose from the political grave. Throughout 1996, his reelection never seemed in doubt, and he won handily. Clinton's reversal of fortune was based on several favorable developments.

**The Economy**  The economy grew steadily throughout Clinton's first term, and by the 1996 elections, most Americans were economically optimistic—indeed, as optimistic as they had been in 1984 when they overwhelmingly reelected Republican Ronald Reagan.[63] Both inflation and unemployment were very low, and the stock market was at an all-time high. Incumbents who run during times of economic prosperity tend to be successful, and Clinton was no exception. The relatively high level of economic satisfaction meant that the Dole campaign was paddling upstream against a strong current.

**The Republican Congress**  Even the Republican national chairman conceded that the Republican Congress overplayed its hand during 1995–1996, reading too much into the election returns, as new majorities often do.[64] By attacking restrictive environmental regulations, Congress exposed the Republican party to the charge that it was anti-environment, a charge that is especially damaging among independent voters. By passing a welfare reform bill with numerous provisions viewed as harsh, the new Congress exposed the party to the charge that it lacked compassion, a charge especially damaging among women. And perhaps most important, the Republican Congress made a serious tactical error in shutting down the government in the winter of 1995–1996, when President Clinton would not accept their budget. The polls indicated that Congress lost the battle of the budget and, in doing so, quite probably cost Dole any chance of winning the election. Clinton took the position that it was necessary to reelect him in order to check and balance the Republicans in Congress. Ironically, by the end of the campaign, the Republican party was running ads arguing that it was necessary to reelect congressional Republicans in order to check and balance Clinton![65]

**The Gender Gap**  If only men had voted in 1996, Robert Dole would have won the election, the first time this had been true. As Figure 10.10 shows, since the 1980

**Figure 10.10**

**Since 1980 Women Have Consistently Voted More Democratic than Men**

SOURCE: The Gallup Organization.

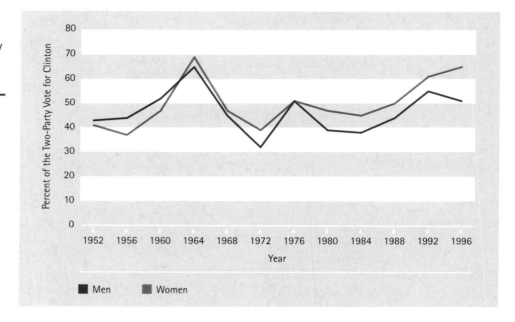

election, women have been more likely than men to vote Democratic for president, but the gap was larger in 1996 than ever before. In 2000 the gap was almost as large.

The gender gap is widely misunderstood. Given the growing influence of the Women's Movement in the 1970s, the near-successful campaign for the Equal Rights Amendment (ERA), and the rise of the abortion issue, many pundits understandably attributed the emergence of the gender gap to different male and female positions on "women's issues." On the contrary, men and women differ little in their views of abortion and issues related to equality of opportunity for women—such issues do not underlie the gender gap.[66] Rather, differences in voting appear to stem more from long-standing gender differences on issues of military force, the use of violence, and government activities in support of the disadvantaged.[67] Note that in the 1950s, women were more likely than men to favor Republican Eisenhower, who ended the Korean War and declined to become involved in Vietnam.

There is considerable disagreement about why women and men differ on issues. Some argue that women's values are different from men's. If so, do they reflect childhood socialization, maternal experience, biology, or some combination of factors?[68] From an electoral standpoint, the origins of gender differences are less important than the fact that they exist. Women are more supportive of the disadvantaged than are men, less supportive of force and coercion than are men, and more likely than men to favor an activist government, as indicated in Table 10.3. Given the images of the contemporary Republican and Democratic parties, the gender gap follows.[69]

The actions of the Republican Congress helped to widen the gender gap and defeat Robert Dole. By adopting an approach to welfare that was viewed as punitive, by taking an aggressive stance on Medicaid and Medicare reform, and by proposing cutbacks in environmental and safety regulation—in these and similar ways, the Republicans heightened the attention that voters gave to issues that divided men and women.

In addition, the close association between the Republican party and the religious right probably served to widen the gender gap. Although the religious right emphasizes family values, its ideal seems to be the patriarchal family with a stay-at-home mother. Though appealing to some women, such an ideal is not appealing to others, a large number of whom are unmarried or divorced, and most of whom work. The gender gap is wider among single men and women than among married men and women—a marriage gap.[70]

**Table 10.3**

Women's and Men's Attitudes Differ

| | Women | Men |
|---|---|---|
| **Role of Government** | | |
| Consider self conservative | 29% | 43% |
| Government should provide fewer services | 30 | 45 |
| Poverty and homelessness are among the country's most important problems | 63 | 44 |
| Government should guarantee medical care for all | 69 | 58 |
| Favor affirmative action programs for blacks and other minority groups | 53 | 41 |
| **Force/Violence** | | |
| American bombers should attack all military targets in Iraq, including those in heavily populated areas | 37 | 61 |
| Handguns should be illegal except for use by police and other authorized persons | 48 | 28 |
| Favor death penalty | 76 | 82 |
| Approve of caning the teenager in Singapore who committed acts of vandalism | 39 | 61 |
| Approve of the way the Justice Department took Elian Gonzalez from his Miami relatives | 35 | 52 |

SOURCE: *The Public Perspective*, August/September 1996: 10–27; *The Public Perspective*, July/August 1994: 96. Gallup Tuesday Briefing, May 2, 2000.

**The Issues That Weren't**   Almost as interesting as the issues that swayed votes in the 1990s are the issues that did not play a major role in the presidential campaigns. Where was crime, an issue that Republicans used to define Democrats—negatively— in the 1970s and 1980s? What about "hot-button" issues like welfare, immigration, race, and affirmative action? Part of the reason why such issues did not loom large in the campaigns of the 1990s is that President Clinton co-opted them, moving close enough to the Republicans to neutralize the issues. He was criticized by Democratic liberals for this strategy of "triangulation"—positioning himself between liberal congressional Democrats and conservative congressional Republicans—but the campaign and election suggest that his strategy was effective.[71]

**Money**   Not all issues in campaigns are policy issues. In particular, President Clinton's win in 1996 was marred by a series of campaign finance scandals involving large illegal contributions by foreign interests. Many Democratic politicians felt that the late revelations were sufficiently damaging to enable the Republicans to keep control of the House of Representatives by a narrow margin. After the election, the media reported new revelations of presidential fund raising that apparently resulted in privileged access to major economic interests in return for large contributions.

### *The Y2K Election*

Prophets of doom predicted that the U.S. economy would melt down when the calendar changed from 1999 to 2000. The economy did just fine, but no one anticipated that the polity would melt down later in the year. The outcome of the 2000 presidential election is stranger than fiction. As we go to press, we do not know who will be our next president—an uncertainty that may hang over the country for weeks. If Governor Bush ultimately prevails, he will head the first unified Republican government since 1954,

## Highlight

## Humor: Campaign Finance

Basically, our campaign finance system works this way: Donors give money to politicians, who then use the government to do favors for the donors. It's exactly like buying a hamburger, except that under our laws, everyone must pretend that nobody is buying anything and nobody is selling anything. The donors must pretend that they're giving money solely because they support good government; the politicians must pretend that the favors will benefit the entire nation. If Burger King operated this way, a typical transaction would go like this:

CUSTOMER: Here's some money. But I don't want a burger. I'm just supporting quality fast food.

COUNTER PERSON: Fine. Because we don't sell burgers here at Burger King, although there might be a burger here that you can have, for the good of the entire nation.

CUSTOMER: Would it have extra pickles?

COUNTER PERSON: Of course it would. The entire nation needs extra pickles.

If you think this scenario is amusing, you would have enjoyed the campaign finance hearings, during which the fact that the federal government is basically for sale was largely disregarded in favor of endless nit-picky discussion about exactly how President Clinton and Vice-President Gore grubbed for money, and especially whether they grubbed for money *on* federal property (bad) or *off* (OK), and whether they grubbed for money from foreign sleazebags (bad) or domestic sleazebags (OK).

The politicians in Congress, who of course have spent the majority of their adult lives grubbing for money, expressed great shock upon learning how campaign financing works. So did Clinton and Gore. They had no idea! So, now, everybody in Washington is fed up with the current system. Democrats and Republicans agree: It's time for *real* reform, darn it. No more messing around. And thus it appears that, after years of stalling, this nation really and truly will have meaningful campaign finance reform, just as soon as we establish a viable trout farm on Jupiter.

Excerpted from Dave Barry, "Direct Deposit," *Boston Globe Magazine*, November 30, 1997: 12–13.

---

while if Vice-President Gore wins, he will continue the Democratic-headed divided government that appeared in 1994.

The election underscores our earlier discussion of the importance of the Electoral College in shaping campaign strategy. If you are a citizen of Kansas or Utah, California or Massachusetts, you might scarcely have known an election was taking place. Your states were written off by one party and taken for granted by the other. But if you were a citizen of Florida, Pennsylvania, Missouri, Michigan, or other "battleground" states you were bombarded with campaign ads, and the candidates visited your state numerous times.

The election also underscores our discussion of the difference between primary and general election campaigns. In the primaries hot-button issues like abortion and gun control were prominent, but exit polls showed that such issues were of only minor importance in the general election. Instead, broad issues of concern to the great body of Americans—the economy, health care, social security and education—took center stage. Gore had to back away from his primary position on guns because it was unpopular in many of the battleground states; similarly, Bush deemphasized his ties to social conservatives. Instead the candidates talked long and in some detail about restructuring social security, reforming public education, and the future mix of taxing and spending that they advocated.

In several ways the 2000 voting is a puzzle. As suggested by our discussion of the importance of government performance for voting, most political scientists expected an easy win for Gore. The 1990s was a decade of unprecedented prosperity and there is peace in the world—relatively speaking. President Clinton's approval ratings are exceptionally high by historical standards, people feel optimistic about the economy, and people feel that the country is on the right track. Historically, incumbent administrations do not lose under such conditions. Why then did Gore underperform?

Firm answers must await detailed analyses, but several possibilities will receive close attention in the year ahead. The first is that Gore did not receive much credit for the good times. Polls indicated that people attributed prosperity more to the creativity of American business and the efforts of Alan Greenspan than to the Clinton Administration. In addition, some commentators suggested that times had been good for so long that Americans took prosperity for granted. Still others argued that Gore had run a poor campaign. Earlier we argued that the effects of campaigns are exaggerated. Both parties have plenty of money and talent; thus, they will do the best they can given the larger political and economic environment. Their campaign efforts balance each other, and the larger environment determines the outcome. But if one candidate chooses not to make maximum use of his opportunities, the campaign can make a bigger difference. Gore chose not to emphasize the Clinton Administration's record, in essence throwing away his trump card. As one critic sarcastically observed, Gore's theme was "You've never had it so good, and I'm mad as hell about it."[72]

A second possibility is what is called the "Clinton factor." One explanation for why Gore chose not to emphasize the administration record was that his campaign feared that disapproval of the President's personal behavior would hurt Gore. Clinton's personal ratings are much lower than his job ratings, and a majority of the country does worry that the country is on the wrong track morally, whatever the state of the economy. Whether such fears were justified remains to be seen.

Finally, some observers felt that Gore's personality turned off some voters who agreed with him on the issues, an effect that may have been heightened by the tendency of the media to emphasize personality at the expense of substance. Some commentators have criticized voters as victims of the MTV—Oprah—Leno—Letterman reduction of politics to entertainment. But leaders must inspire confidence and trust in the citizenry, so personality considerations can not be dismissed out-of-hand.

All in all, the 2000 elections will provide topics for political discussion for years to come. For the latest see **www.ablongman.com/fiorina.**

## *Beyond 2000*

Our view is that contemporary elections are sufficiently different from those of the 1970s and 1980s to suggest that what was known as the sixth party system has evolved into something new. We think that politics today looks much like the so-called era of no decision that prevailed from the 1870s to the 1890s. During that period—a time of social and economic change—presidential elections were won and lost by the narrowest of margins, and control of Congress shifted back and forth. No dependable majority existed.

The situation today looks similar. For nearly two decades, disagreement about how to handle large budget deficits led to repeated complaints of gridlock and paralysis. With the budget deal of 1997 that produced the first balanced budget since 1967, that problem has been resolved, at least temporarily. But problems with major entitlements such as social security and Medicare still loom, and attempts to reform the tax system and the public schools will prove very contentious. Neither party has earned the allegiance of a majority of the American people, and as a consequence, control of Congress and the presidency is up for grabs.

## *Chapter Summary*

The American nomination process is far more open than the nomination processes of other democracies. It gives rank-and-file voters more influence than in other countries where party leaders and elected officials dominate the process, and it gives "outsider" candidates a chance by enabling them to contest the early, smaller primaries and caucuses. The process begins long before the election itself and sometimes lasts months before a nominee is determined. It also heightens the influence of party issue activists and the media. But whatever its positive effects and whatever its drawbacks, the system is now well established and is unlikely to change except at the margins.

The presidential campaign is often misunderstood. It is not an independent force that determines election outcomes; rather, the campaign itself is shaped by events and conditions in the years leading up to the election. Candidates who run good campaigns are usually those who have good records that are easy to defend or those whose opponents have bad records that are hard to defend. Candidates who run bad campaigns are generally those who face the opposite situations.

The reason why campaigns are limited in their impact is that most voters do not make up their minds on the basis of the campaign. Many of them decide well before the campaign ever begins. They do so on the basis of long-standing party identifications, evaluations of government performance, and the associations between the parties and particular values and positions. Only a minority decide how to vote late in the campaign and on the basis of the particular candidates and the particular things they say. Campaigns determine outcomes when party identification, government performance, and the deeper issues leave both candidates evenly matched. The Gore campaign in 2000 may be the exception that proves the rule.

---

### On the Web

The United States Electoral College
www.nara.gov/fedreg/ec-hmpge.html
A detailed explanation of the electoral college as well as an historical database of presidential election data. The site is maintained by the National Archives and Records Administration and has links to other government data sets pertaining to elections on all levels of government.

Common Cause
www.commoncause.org/index.html
Common Cause is a nonprofit, nonpartisan citizen's lobbying organization promoting open, honest, and accountable government. This site contains a searchable database of special-interest soft-money contributions to the Democratic and Republican national party committees, as well as a database of materials that focus on the impact of big money in politics.

Presidential Election Statistics
www.multied.com/elections/
A graphical presentation on each of the U.S. presidential elections, providing both electoral and popular votes. This site is run by MultiEducator Incorporated, an online education company that offers free access to many of its files over the internet.

American National Election Studies
www.umich.edu/~nes/
Probably the single most important source of data for students of American elections. This impressive collection of election surveys conducted from the 1950s to the present is the source of many of the figures and tables that appear in this book.

---

## Key Terms

caucus, p. 283
closed primaries, p. 284
electoral vote, p. 296
honeymoon, p. 282
matching funds, p. 286

open primaries, p. 284
party identification, p. 300
party image, p. 302
political activists, p. 288
popular vote, p. 296

primary election, p. 283
prospective voting , p. 303
retrospective voting, p. 303
semi-closed primaries, p. 284
winner-take-all voting, p. 297

# Suggested Readings

Abramson, Paul, John Aldrich, and David Rohde. *Change and Continuity in the 1996 Elections.* Washington, DC: CQ Press, 1998. This quadrennial publication provides a comprehensive overview of voting behavior in national elections.

Asher, Herbert. *Presidential Elections and American Politics*, 5th ed. New York: Brooks/Cole, 1997. An excellent survey of presidential campaigns and how voters reacted to them in the second half of the twentieth century.

Brown, Clifford, Lynda Powell, and Clyde Wilcox. *Serious Money.* Cambridge, England: Cambridge University Press, 1995. A detailed empirical study of who contributes to presidential campaigns and why.

Carmines, Edward, and James Stimson. *Issue Evolution: Race and the Transformation of American Politics.* Princeton, NJ: Princeton University Press, 1989. An important argument about the importance of race for realigning American politics in the 1960s.

Holbrook, Thomas. *Do Campaigns Matter?* Thousand Oaks, CA: Sage, 1996. A scientifically rigorous study of the impact of presidential campaigns.

Mayer, William, ed. *In Pursuit of the White House 2000: How We Choose Our Presidential Nominees.* Chatham, NJ: Chatham House, 2000. An informative collection of essays covering all facets of the contemporary nominating process.

Miller, Arthur, and Bruce Gronbeck, eds. *Presidential Campaigns and American Self-Images.* Boulder, CO: Westview, 1994. This collection of essays presents a balanced and sophisticated view of campaigns.

Polsby, Nelson, and Aaron Wildavsky. *Presidential Elections*, 10th ed. Chatham, NJ: Chatham House, 2000. A classic text that covers all aspects of presidential elections.

Pomper, Gerald, *et al. The Election of 1996.* Chatham, NJ: Chatham House, 1997. This quadrennial publication by a group of knowledgeable authors complements Abramson, Aldrich, and Rohde, offering less detail about voting behavior but a broader view of the campaigns and the activities of elites.

Wayne, Stephen. *The Road to the White House, 1996.* New York: St. Martin's, 1997. Provides useful background on stages of the presidential nomination and election process, along with specific discussions of how the 1996 campaigns played out.

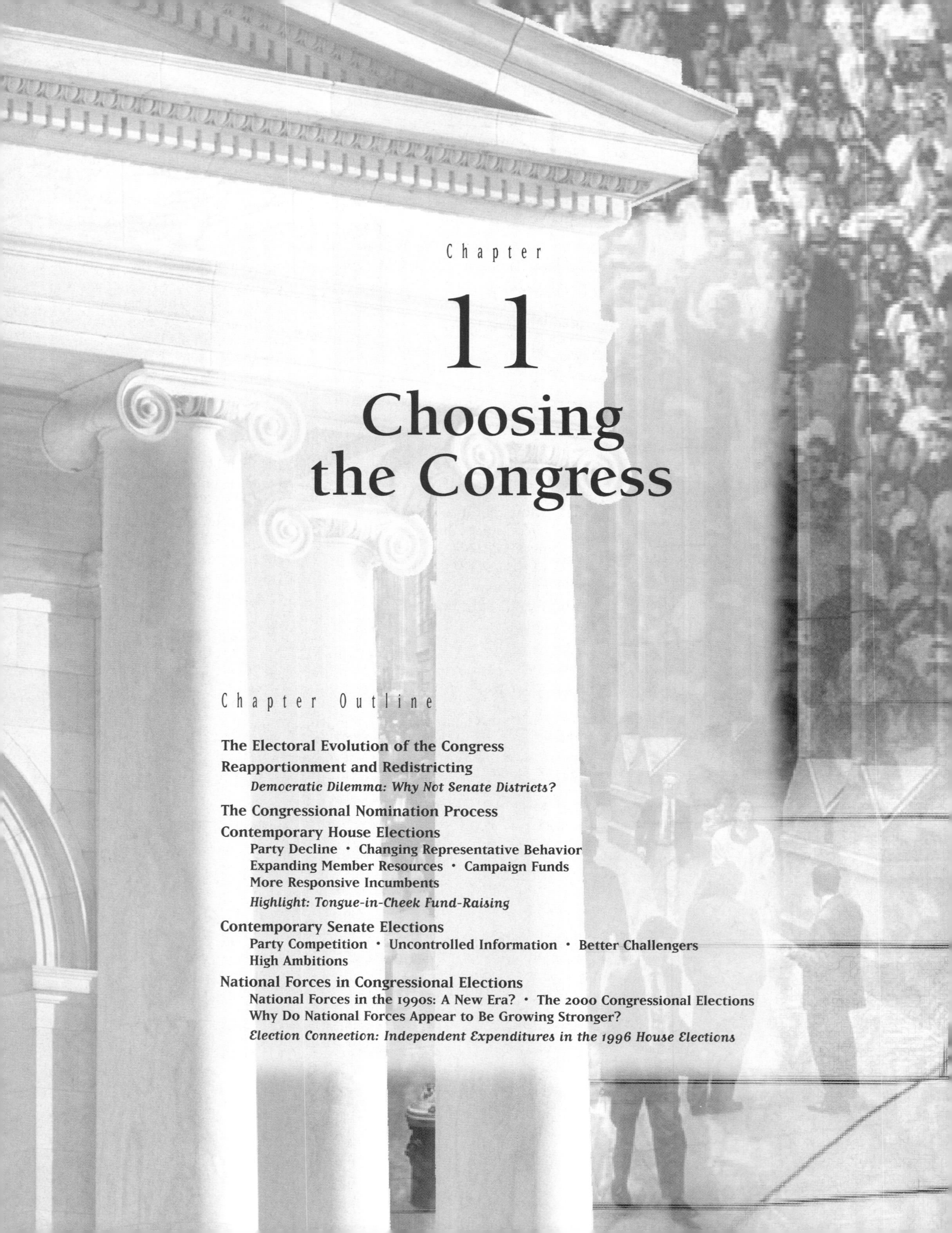

Chapter

# 11
# Choosing the Congress

Chapter Outline

**Do Congressional Elections Produce a Representative Body?**

Women

*International Comparison: Women in Politics*

Minorities

*Democratic Dilemma: Affirmative Action Redistricting*

Elections, Parties, and Group Representation

**Chapter Summary**

**On the Web**

**Key Terms**

**Suggested Readings**

In 1992 Bill Clinton broke the Republican "lock" on the presidency. But 1992 was noteworthy for a second reason as well: It was the so-called year of the woman. Four new female senators were elected, and the number of women representatives rose from 28 to 47. One of the newcomers to the House of Representatives was Democrat Marjorie Margolies-Mezvinsky, commonly known as MMM, the first Democrat in 76 years to be elected from the Pennsylvania 13th district, an affluent suburban area near Philadelphia with a 2 to 1 Republican registration edge. A well-known local newscaster, MMM jumped into the race when the Republican incumbent announced his retirement. She won the Democratic primary handily, then narrowly defeated her Republican opponent in November by less than 1 percent of the vote. Normally, a member's first election is the hardest. Once in office, members can utilize the advantages of incumbency to expand their support among constituents, and so long as they behave prudently and don't give potential challengers a damaging issue, they can anticipate reelection with very high probability. MMM was an exception to this pattern.

Eight months after the election, the House of Representatives held the fate of the Clinton presidency in its hands. The final version of the president's deficit reduction plan lay before the House. A sweeping package of spending cuts and tax increases, the plan would chart the course of governmental economic policy for the next five years. Earlier in the year, the House and Senate had passed the Clinton plan without a single Republican vote. Differences in the two chambers' versions of the legislation had been ironed out, and now final passage was at hand. Or was it?

Again, not a single Republican would support the plan: The income tax increases were unacceptable to them, and even though these tax increases fell entirely on affluent Americans, some Democrats were opposed to the plan because it included small increases in gasoline taxes and other elements that they disliked. Democratic leaders worked feverishly to muster a majority. Speaker Thomas Foley exhorted his partisans: "Tonight is the time for courage. Tonight is the time to put away the old, easy ways. Tonight is the time for responsibility. Tonight is the night to vote."[1]

President Clinton himself worked the phones, calling undecided Democrats and telling them that he had to have their vote—his presidency was at stake. For Representative Margolies-Mezvinsky, the situation was a political nightmare. She already had voted against each of Clinton's three key economic proposals, including the deficit reduction package that was once again on the floor. On that earlier occasion she had announced, "I promised the voters of Montgomery County that I would not vote for an across-the-board tax increase—and tonight I kept that promise."[2] Since then she had reassured her constituents that she would continue to oppose the plan. Now she was under intense pressure from the president and Democratic leaders to reverse her stand.

At the conclusion of electronic voting, the tally stood at 216-216. A majority of the full house (218 of 435) is required to pass the budget. Pat Williams, a Democrat from Montana, had agreed to support the president, if necessary, so MMM's vote would decide the fate of the plan and, by implication, the fate of the Clinton presidency. Surrounded by supportive Democrats and "with the demeanor of someone being marched to her own hanging," she approached the well of the house to cast a written vote, while gleeful Republicans chanted "Goodbye, Marjorie!"[3] MMM may have saved the Clinton presidency, but the cost was her political life.

In 1994 President Clinton himself appeared in her district to help her campaign for reelection, and the Democratic leadership helped her raise more than $1,600,000 in campaign funds, but it wasn't enough. The Republican whom MMM defeated in 1992 was her opponent again. Although he raised less than two-thirds as much money as MMM did, she could not overcome her damaging vote and the national Republican tide. She received only 45 percent of the vote.

ELECTIONS ARE NEVER FAR FROM THE MINDS OF MEMBERS OF CONGRESS. Members of the House of Representatives put their fates on the line every second November, but even that two-year interval between elections is deceptive. Many representatives face primaries in the spring of election years, so primary campaigns are under way scarcely more than a year after members have taken the oath of office. In response to such realities, representatives campaign for reelection more or less continuously. Surprisingly, the situation isn't much different for senators. Although senators are elected for six-year terms, one-third are elected every two years, so at any given time one-third of the Senate is operating with the same short time horizon as members of the House. Moreover, Senate campaigns are so expensive that the average incumbent must raise an average of just over $15,000 every week for six years, a time-consuming, psychologically draining activity that keeps all of them aware of their need to maintain political support, even if their actual reelection campaign is years away.

The great majority of congressional incumbents win reelection, but as the unhappy experience of Representative Margolies-Mezvinsky illustrates, the advantage of incumbency is not automatic. Even if you are an incumbent and even if you spend much more than your challenger, one politically damaging decision may cost you your seat. That simple fact colors all aspects of congressional life.

In this chapter we focus on the members of the United States Congress:

- How do they get elected and reelected?
- What is the advantage of incumbency?
- How do House and Senate elections differ?
- How have recent congressional elections changed?
- How representative is the body that congressional elections determine?

Before considering these questions, we review what the framers of the Constitution expected when they designed the Congress and how accurate their expectations have proved to be. Then we look at how the Constitution and subsequent court decisions shape the constituencies that select members of Congress.

simulation

**You are a
Professional
Campaign
Consultant**

## The Electoral Evolution of the Congress

The founders intended the House of Representatives to be highly sensitive to popular wishes as expressed in elections. Madison wrote that the House should have "an

Young Representative Abraham Lincoln (Whig-IL) in 1846

**rotation**

The practice whereby a member of Congress stepped down after a term or two so that someone else could have the office.

immediate dependence on, and an intimate sympathy with, the people. Frequent elections are unquestionably the only policy by which this dependence and sympathy can be effectually secured."[4] An electorally sensitive Senate, however, was not the founders' intent. The Constitution originally provided for senators to be chosen by state legislatures, not elected by the people. According to Madison, the insulated Senate was "to consist in its proceeding with more coolness, with more system, and with more wisdom, than the popular branch."[5] Not until adoption of the Seventeenth Amendment to the Constitution in 1913 did all senators face popular election, although many states adopted various popular-voting procedures as early as the mid-nineteenth century.

Thus the framers were half right (the House) and half wrong (the Senate) in their expectations about the electoral sensitivity of the Congress. In terms of the actual history of the two chambers, however, neither has worked out exactly as the framers planned. At first, the House indeed was the *amateur* political body the framers expected. Unstable in its membership and tumultuous in its operation, the House operated more or less according to plan. More than 40 percent of the members of the First Congress did not return for the Second. In fact, turnover levels often were as high as 50 percent until after the Civil War.[6] But contrary to Madison's argument, frequent elections were not the cause. Until the late nineteenth century, many more representatives quit than were defeated. In the first place, job conditions were not very attractive, especially after the national government moved to Washington, DC, an uninhabited, swampy area with a less than desirable climate.[7] Many members found life in Washington less comfortable than life in the cities and towns of their home states. In the second place, the national government was not very important in the early years of the republic. Ambitious politicians, especially outside the South, often found state governments to be better outlets for their energies than the small and limited national government.[8] Even those members willing to serve multiple terms sometimes were prevented from doing so by **rotation** practices, whereby the counties, towns, or political factions in a congressional district "took turns" holding the congressional seat. Abraham Lincoln, for example, was elected to the House in 1846 but stepped down after one term in accordance with local rotation agreements.[9] The result of these and other considerations was that average service in the House of Representatives did not reach three years until after 1900.

Also contrary to Madison's expectations, the early Senate was far from being a stable body whose members served for long periods. In the first ten years of the repub-

**Figure 11.1**

**Congress Became a Career in the Twentieth Century**

SOURCES: Nelson W. Polsby, "The Institutionalization of the U.S. House of Representatives," *American Political Science Review* (March 1968): 146. Norman J. Ornstein *et al.*, eds., *Vital Statistics on Congress, 1995–1996* (Washington, DC: Congressional Quarterly, 1996), p. 60.

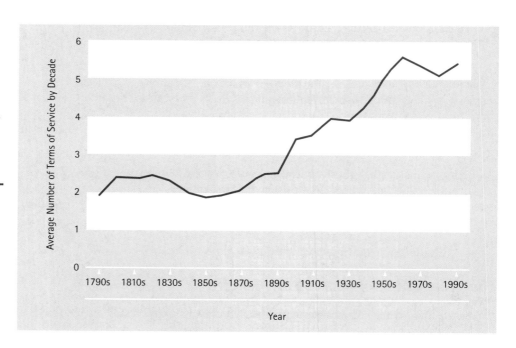

lic, more than one-third of the Senators failed to serve out their terms, and until 1820 more Senators *resigned* during their term than were denied reelection by their state legislatures. Although they had the opportunity to stay longer than members of the House, for the reasons noted earlier many chose to pass it up.[10]

Today, things are much different. The Congress is the world's foremost example of what political scientists call a **professional legislature:** Its members are full-time legislators who stay for long periods, as shown in Figure 11.1. Relatively few members quit voluntarily, and many intend to remain in Congress indefinitely. In fact, many people in the United States think that the membership of Congress is *too* stable and support institutional changes such as term limits in order to shake up what they see as an unresponsive institution. Such views conflict with our description of the contemporary Congress as an electorally sensitive if not hypersensitive institution. Given the electoral advantage that contemporary incumbents appear to enjoy, it might seem strange to argue that Congress is such an electorally sensitive institution, but contemporary incumbents fare so well precisely *because* they are so electorally aware; they anticipate threats to their reelection and act to avoid them.

## Reapportionment and Redistricting

How are the constituencies that are represented in Congress defined? In the Senate, representation is simple and never changes. The Constitution gives every state two senators, regardless of population, and this provision can be amended only with the consent of every state (Article 5). Because smaller states cannot be expected to give up their political advantage, equal representation in the Senate is essentially an amendment-proof feature of American democracy.

Things are more complicated in the House. The Constitution requires that a census be held every decade. After the census, the 435 seats in the House of Representatives are apportioned among the states according to their populations; hence the term **reapportionment,** which refers to the new allocation of seats as a result of population shifts. In recent decades, northeastern states have lost House seats and southern and southwestern states have gained them, as population has shifted from the frost belt to the sun belt. Given the different political leanings of these regions, the net effect has been to strengthen Republican representation in the House.

Currently, six states have such small populations that they have only one representative, a minimum guaranteed by Article I. After the others learn how many House seats they have received, they set to work **redistricting**—drawing the boundaries of the new districts. In most states the legislature does the work, but in five states bipartisan commissions do the job, and in several others some combination of legislators and outside appointees draws the lines. The redistricting process is often highly contentious, because political careers depend on which voters get placed in which districts. Charges of **gerrymandering**—drawing the lines for partisan or other political advantage—are hurled back and forth, and often the courts are drawn into the process.

Districts must be of nearly equal population, the result of Supreme Court decisions beginning with *Wesberry v. Sanders* in 1964 (previously, districts varied widely in population). Subsequent decisions have refined the standard to one of precise numerical equality. (This standard in practice is often absurd; census data are only approximate even on the day they are recorded, and actual populations are changing all the time.)

**simulation**

**You are Redrawing District Lines After the Census**

**professional legislature**
Legislature whose members serve full-time and for long periods.

**reapportionment**
The allocation of House seats to the states after each decennial census.

**redistricting**
Drawing new boundaries of congressional districts, usually after the decennial census.

**gerrymandering**
Drawing boundary lines of congressional districts in order to confer an advantage on some partisan or political interest.

### SECTION SUMMARY

Congress consists of 535 members. Two senators represent each state, yielding a 100-person Senate. Each of the 435 members of the House represents a district, and the boundaries of most of these districts change every ten years after the census.

## Democratic Dilemma

# Why Not Senate Districts?

Most states have more than one U.S. representative, whom they elect from single-member districts within the states. In the early nineteenth century, a few states used multimember districts, but a federal statute in 1842 required the use of single-member districts in House elections.[a] In contrast, two U.S. senators represent each state, making states multimember districts. This feature of Senate elections is universally considered to be an unchangeable feature of the constitutional order.

But not everyone agrees. Terry Smith, a law professor at Fordham University, has recently argued that nothing in the Constitution, the Seventeenth Amendment to the Constitution (which provides for direct election of senators), or the debates surrounding the adoption of the Constitution and the Seventeenth Amendment precludes the creation of Senate districts.[b] (Indeed, Smith notes that in the early decades of the nineteenth century, some states explicitly required their legislatures to choose senators from two different portions of the state and that other states did so informally well into the twentieth century.

Smith argues that dividing states into two equally populated halves and assigning a senator to each would have a number of advantages. First, Senate constituencies would be smaller in both geographic and population terms. Therefore, senate elections would be less expensive, and the candidates' need for special-interest money would be correspondingly lower. Second, Senate districts

would make the election of racial and ethnic minorities more likely. States such as New York, Illinois, and California could center one Senate district around a minority-dominated urban area (such as New York City, Chicago, or Los Angeles), which would be more likely to elect a minority than would the entire state. Furthermore, each senator would represent only half as many people as at present, allowing for closer contact with constituents.

*What do you think?*
* *Who are your two senators?*
* *Why should each state have two instead of one? If each had one, there would still be equal state representation in the Senate, as the Constitution requires.*
* *Would it be better to have just one senator represent half the number of people in your state?*
* *Is there any argument in favor of two senators running statewide, other than 200 years of tradition that may be outmoded in the modern world?*

---

[a] Although even in the twentieth century, an entire state delegation sometimes had to run at-large (statewide) when the legislature could not agree on a redistricting plan in time for the election.
[b] Terry Smith, "Rediscovering the Sovereignty of the People: The Case for Senate Districts," *North Carolina Law Review* 75 (1996): 1–74.

## The Congressional Nomination Process

The congressional nomination process is much simpler than the presidential one: A nominee for the House or Senate must win at most one primary election, not a sequence across many states. In a few states party conventions can nominate candidates, but in most states the candidates are chosen in primaries. Some states hold their Senate and House primaries on the same day, and under the same rules, as their presidential primaries. Other states hold them at different times or under different rules.[11]

**filing deadline**
The latest date on which a candidate for office may file official papers or pay required fees to state election officials.

The dates of **filing deadlines** and primary elections also vary widely across states.[12] The filing deadline is the latest date on which a candidate who wishes to be on the ballot must file official documents and/or pay fees with state election officials. In 2000 Texas had the earliest filing deadline, January 3, and Louisiana had the latest, August 18. The earliest primaries were in California, Maryland, and Ohio on March 7, and the latest was in Hawaii on September 23. Thus some candidates know whether they will have an opponent and who it is as much as nine months earlier than others.

**open seat**
A House or Senate race with no incumbent (because of death or retirement).

The hardest-fought primaries occur when a seat becomes **open** because an incumbent dies, retires or opts to run for another office. If both parties have strength in the area, the primaries in both parties are hotly contested. If only one party is strong, its primary will be a donnybrook, because the winner is viewed as the next member of Congress. Few incumbents lose primaries: In the ten elections held since 1980, a total of 50 House incumbents and 6 Senate incumbents were defeated, and not many more even had tough races. This does not prove that primaries are unimportant. It may indicate instead that incumbents behave in such a way as to keep their constituencies satisfied and preempt a strong primary challenge.

Once elected, the new representative or senator is the incumbent, the target of future challengers. How do incumbents survive as many elections as most of them do?

# Contemporary House Elections

Although journalists and politicians often comment that incumbency is the single most important factor in winning House elections, that claim is not accurate. Rather, party long has been and continues to be the single most important factor in House elections. Most strikingly, the Democrats maintained unbroken control of the House of Representatives between 1954 and 1994, even while all but three of their 1954 incumbents departed.[13] In many House districts it is almost inconceivable that a member of a party other than that of the present incumbent could win. Such districts are called safe seats.

Of course, the parties do not control nominations and campaigns as they did in earlier periods of American history, and when deciding how to vote, voters are not so much influenced by party loyalties as in earlier times. Party organizations and party loyalties may not be *as* important as in earlier periods, but they are still very important. One reason why party remains the most important factor in House elections is that many voters know little, if anything, about the candidates. Compared to presidential, senatorial, and even most gubernatorial elections, House elections are "low-information" elections. Only a third of the citizenry can recall the name of the incumbent, and even fewer can remember anything he or she has done for the district. Only 10 percent or so can remember how the incumbent voted on a particular bill. Challengers are even less well known. Having little information on which to base their vote, many people simply vote for the candidate of the party with which they generally sympathize. In House elections, 70 percent or more of all voters who identify with a party typically support the House candidate of that party.[14]

If not the single most important factor in House elections, incumbency clearly is the second most important factor. Moreover, incumbency has grown in importance while party has declined. Statistical studies of House elections have found that the **incumbency advantage**—the electoral benefit of being an incumbent after controlling for other relevant political characteristics—has grown from about 2 percent before 1964 to as high as 12 percent in some recent elections.[15] The increase has not been smooth; rather, as shown in Figure 11.2, the incumbency advantage surged in the late 1960s, leveled off, peaked in 1986, then declined in the 1990s. At least five factors underlie this development: the weakening of parties, changes in the activities of

**incumbency advantage**
The electoral advantage a candidate enjoys by virtue of being an incumbent, over and above his or her other personal and political characteristics.

The second election of each decade is not plotted because in those years decennial redistricting altered the districts of some incumbents, making incumbency advantage impossible to calculate.

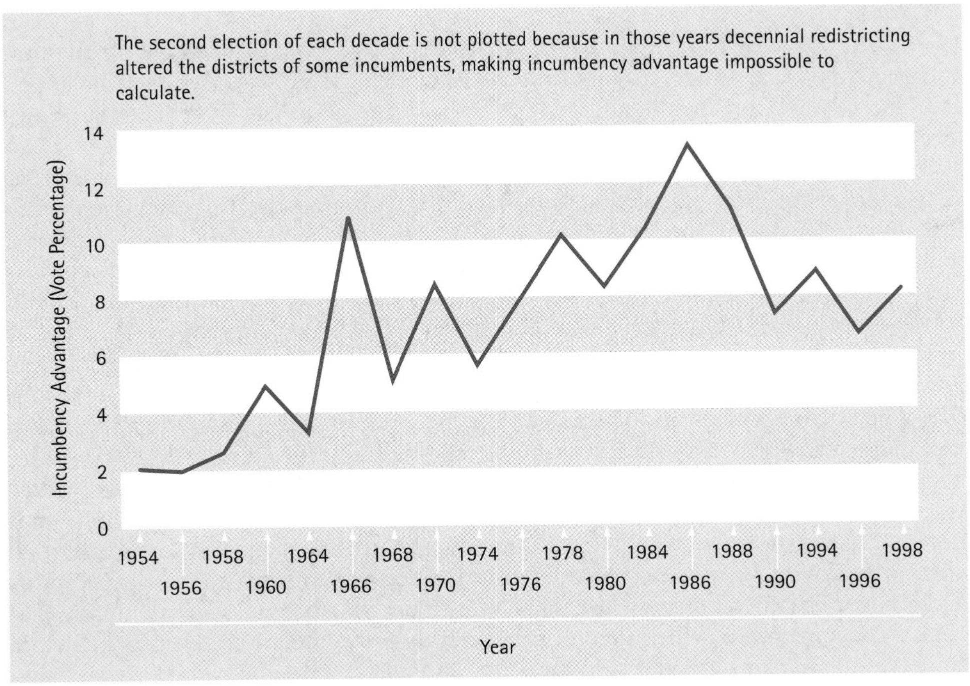

**Figure 11.2**

The Advantage of Incumbency Surged in the Mid-1960s

SOURCE: Calculated by the authors using the Gelman–King method.

representatives, the growth in resources available to incumbents, campaign funding disparities, and more responsive incumbents.

### Party Decline

Although 70 percent of all party identifiers support the candidate of their party today, the figure was more than 80 percent until 1964, and more voters had a party allegiance in the 1950s than do today.[16] As party affiliations weakened, voters became more "available," more susceptible to other sorts of appeals.[17] Thus, the weakening of parties created an environment in which other factors, such as the incumbent's personal characteristics and activities, could exert a stronger influence on voter behavior.

Moreover, realizing that more voters were "up for grabs" than before, incumbents adjusted their behavior to fit the new reality. Their own partisan constituencies became somewhat less secure, so incumbents moved to offer voters additional, more personal reasons to support them. Similarly, the partisan constituencies of the opposition became somewhat more vulnerable, so incumbents began to court them. The result is that challenger-party identifiers began to defect to incumbents at much higher rates in the late 1960s, and since then, their defection rates have often been close to 50 percent. In contrast, defection rates of incumbent-party identifiers have stayed below 10 percent.[18]

### Changing Representative Behavior

You may think of members of Congress primarily as *lawmakers*. Indeed making laws is the principal business of Congress and the major responsibility that the Constitution bestows on the Congress. But members of Congress do much more than make laws. Indeed, the official title of members of the House is "representative," and at least in the contemporary era, most people's view of representation involves other activities in addition to making national laws.[19]

One activity that occupies a great deal of the time and effort of members of Congress is **district service**—making sure that their congressional districts get a fair share (or more) of federal programs, projects, and expenditures.[20] Some members of Congress are famous for their efforts to bring such economic benefits to their districts. Although critics of Congress often label such benefits "pork barrel," constituents generally approve when their representatives and senators "bring home the bacon"—and reward them at the ballot box for their successes.

Another activity to which modern representatives devote a great deal of attention is **constituent assistance,** usually called "casework." Citizens, groups, and businesses frequently encounter difficulties in qualifying for government benefits or subsidies or in complying with federal regulations. When their problems are not solved through normal channels, they appeal to members of Congress for assistance. About one in six voters reports having contacted a representative for information or help with a problem. In overwhelming numbers, they report satisfactory resolution of their problems and, again, show their gratitude at the polls.[21] In other countries, such assistance is often provided by an administrative official called an **ombudsman;** in the United States, members of Congress act as ombudsmen.[22]

District service and constituent assistance often are included together under the general term **constituency service.** The activities share two important characteristics that shed some light on the advantage of incumbency. First, they are nonpartisan and nonideological. Road projects and grants to schools and local governments are neither liberal nor conservative, Democratic nor Republican. Similarly, Democratic incumbents willingly help Republican businesses deal with federal regulators, and Republican incumbents willingly help Democratic constituents qualify for federal benefits. When members of Congress take positions on issues, they please some groups and antagonize others; on controversial issues, their positions may lose them as many votes as they gain. But when incumbents bring home an economic benefit or help a constituent, nearly everyone approves. Such activities carry significant electoral bene-

**district service**
Efforts of members of Congress to make sure that their districts get a share of federal projects and programs.

**constituent assistance**
Efforts of members of Congress to help individuals and groups when they have difficulties with federal agencies.

**ombudsman**
Official whose job it is to mediate conflicts between citizens and government bureaucracies.

**constituency service**
The totality of Congress members' district service and constituent assistance work.

**How Nice to See You!**
Constituents receive an enthusiastic welcome on Capitol Hill.

fits but entail little, if any, electoral cost. Small wonder that by a 5 to 1 margin in one survey, House administrative assistants ranked constituency service over their members' legislative records as the most important factor in maintaining their electoral base.[23]

The second characteristic that both forms of constituency service share is that they have grown in importance. As the federal government expanded during the 1960s and 1970s, subsidizing and regulating more and more activity, the contacts between citizens, groups, and firms and the government multiplied. The opportunities for members of Congress to engage in constituency service increased correspondingly. In 1978, for example, three times as many citizens reported having contacted their representative for assistance as reported having done so in 1958.[24] Thus, at the same time that strength of party affiliation was declining, an expanding federal government was stimulating constituent demand for assistance that members of Congress were able and willing to provide. These activities enabled them to reinforce their own base and make inroads into that of the opposition.

In sum, representatives present themselves to constituents as guardians of district economies and ombudsmen for constituents, as well as framers of national laws. An expanding federal government increased the demand for constituency service—and thereby the opportunity for members of Congress to respond to such demands. Because such activities are generally applauded, incumbents were able to add to their reservoir of goodwill and undercut their opposition.

## Expanding Member Resources

Some observers compare members of Congress to CEOs (chief executive officers) of small businesses.[25] Each member heads an office system—one in Washington and one or more in the district—and directly employs an average of 18 personal staff assistants, more than 40 percent of whom are assigned to district offices.[26] (Senators have even bigger staffs, although their size depends on their states' population.) Although these offices have many responsibilities, no one doubts that much of their effort is directed toward the representative's reelection. Indeed, it has been said that Capitol Hill is the headquarters of 535 political machines.

**Figure 11.3**

**Personal Staffs of Representatives and Senators Have Expanded**

SOURCE: Norman J. Ornstein *et al.*, eds., *Vital Statistics on Congress, 1999–2000* (Washington, DC: American Enterprise Institute, 2000), p. 131.

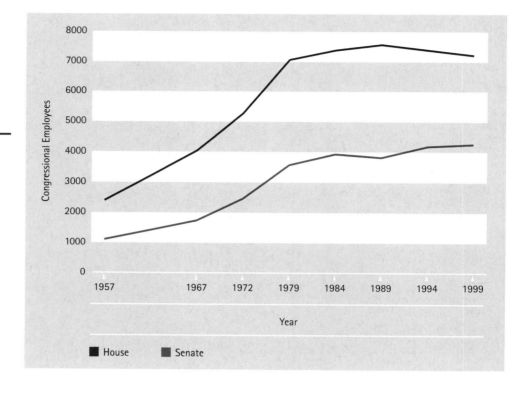

Such was not always the case. In 1950 the average representative had three staff employees. And as late as 1960, nearly a third of the representatives did not have a permanent district office. As shown in Figure 11.3, the 1960s and 1970s were a period of great growth in congressional staff resources. Travel subsidies and other perks also expanded greatly.[27] In 1960 members were reimbursed for only three trips to their districts per year, by 1976 the number had increased to 26, and today there is no limit except the overall budget allocated to each member. Of course, before the jet plane, few members could go home every weekend, as they do today, and many went home only once or twice a session. Improvements in transportation made possible a change in behavior, and Congress authorized the funds to support that change.

Use of the **frank**—the free use of the U.S. mail for official business—has also grown. Although Congress has long subsidized communication with constituents, technological advances such as computerized mailing lists have allowed members to take greater advantage of the privilege in recent years. Congressional use of the frank increased much faster than the rate of population increase or the increase in incoming mail that must be answered. Not surprisingly, congressional mailings to constituents are much higher in even-numbered (election) years than in odd-numbered years. Figure 11.4 shows this pattern.

Representatives naturally are taking political advantage of new technologies as well. More and more members have homepages on the Web—especially younger members, Republicans, and members who represent affluent, highly educated constituents.[28] Although this technology has great potential for communicating information about legislation to constituents, thus far House offices appear to be using it mostly to advertise their members.[29]

Members of Congress are frequently criticized for providing themselves with these resources—often called perks, for "perquisites of office." Under pressure from public interest groups, Congress has adopted some restrictions on the use of the frank. For example, newsletters cannot be mailed within 90 days of an election, and members cannot include more than two personal photos per page. No one has seriously suggested that cutbacks of staff, offices, or travel be imposed, however.

The increased resources enjoyed by incumbent representatives are related to the weakening of party and the increase in constituency service. As traditional party orga-

---

**frank**

Name given to representatives' and senators' free use of the U.S. mail for sending communications to constituents.

**participation**

**The Net Election: Campaigning on the Internet**

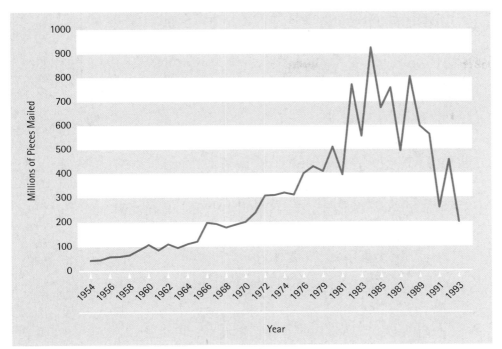

**Figure 11.4**

**Mail Franked by Senators and Representatives**

SOURCE: Norman J. Ornstein *et al.*, eds., *Vital Statistics on Congress, 1999–2000* (Washington, DC: American Enterprise Institute, 2000), p. 165.

nization became increasingly unreliable, members had incentives to vote themselves the resources to substitute for the declining organizations. Similarly, as they realized that reliance on traditional partisan voting was becoming increasingly unreliable, they had incentives to vote themselves the resources necessary to meet the increasing demand for constituency service. The resources controlled by incumbents are necessary for them to do their jobs well, of course, but these resources can easily be put to other uses, such as promoting the members and advertising their activities. An incumbent representative today has free access to resources that would cost more than $1 million per year if purchased on the open market.[30] This level of support undoubtedly contributes to the advantage of incumbency.

### Campaign Funds

House elections have become increasingly expensive: Average total spending in each House race was more than half a million dollars in 1998, with 87 candidates spending over a million dollars.[31] Moreover, as Figure 11.5 shows, the gap between incumbents' spending and that of their challengers is wide and has grown wider since 1980. For many of today's reformers, the explanation of the advantage of incumbency is simple and self-evident: money.

Money certainly affects candidate visibility, and congressional challengers are seriously underfunded. Nevertheless, research on the influence of money in congressional elections paints a surprisingly complicated picture. Although money contributes significantly to the electoral advantage that incumbents enjoy, its contribution often is exaggerated.

First, researchers have found that campaign spending has what economists call *diminishing returns*: The more a candidate spends, the less the impact of an additional dollar of spending. In particular, for an incumbent who already has perquisites of office worth as much as a million dollars a year, an extra $100,000 has less impact than it would if spent by a challenger who lacked the taxpayer-provided resources of an incumbent. Sophisticated advocates of campaign finance reform oppose low spending limits because such limits would hurt challengers, who have little name recognition, much more than incumbents, who already enjoy the visibility and perquisites of office.[32]

**Figure 11.5**

**House Campaign Funding, Incumbent Versus Challenger**

SOURCE: Norman J. Ornstein *et al.*, eds., *Vital Statistics on Congress, 1999–2000* (Washington, DC: American Enterprise Institute, 2000), p. 81.

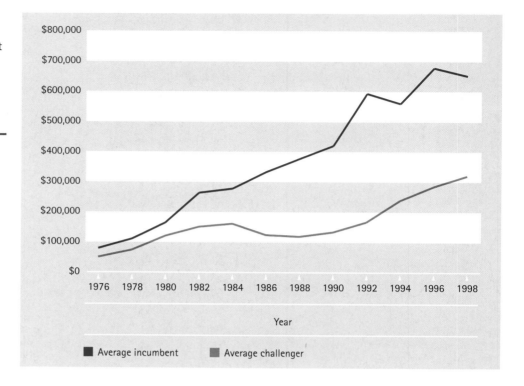

Second, the surge in the incumbency advantage (the mid-1960s) did not occur at the same time as the explosion of spending in congressional campaigns. House elections in the late 1960s and early 1970s were not nearly so expensive as they are today. Indeed, heavy spending by an incumbent was regarded as a sign not of electoral strength but of weakness—a signal that an incumbent was in trouble.[33] That remains true today: Of the ten highest-spending representatives in 1998, four lost. Moreover, the growth of PACs took place *after* the adoption of campaign finance reform laws in 1974, when incumbents had already developed a significant advantage. Although there is no doubt that spending levels are now so high that incumbents benefit from spending, the great majority of incumbents probably would still be reelected if campaign spending were slashed.

An important effect of campaign spending today is one that is difficult to observe, let alone measure. Because it takes so much money for a challenger to mount a serious campaign—$600,000 in the estimation of political scientist Gary Jacobson—many potentially strong challengers probably are discouraged from entering the race.[34] If the incumbent has a widely advertised million-dollar "war chest," the prospect of a challenge is all the more daunting. Why mortgage your house and your children's college education for what is at best a long shot? Thus incumbents' ability to raise substantial campaign funds may be most important as a deterrent: More than actually buying the election, money may scare potential opponents out of the arena if challengers have not been otherwise scared off.[35]

**THATCH** by Jeff Shesol

This deterrent effect of campaign funds probably has been reinforced by the decline of parties. In today's candidate-centered system, the individual candidate bears the risk of running and losing. A losing challenger may have given up her job, exhausted her savings, and gone deeply into debt. In earlier party-centered systems the party assumed such risks, allowing candidates to run and lose without suffering financial and political ruin. Once again, the weakening of parties creates a context in which other factors take on greater importance—to the advantage of incumbents.

In recent years the topic of campaign finance reform has received enormous attention, and members of Congress have grappled with a wide variety of reform proposals. One presidential hopeful, John McCain, even made it the centerpiece of his campaign in 2000. Although the negative effects of the present system are somewhat exaggerated, citizens are disgusted with the present system of campaign finance and cynical about government in general and the Congress in particular as a result of it. Some reform is appropriate, but thus far little has been accomplished.

The problem is that the reforms that would probably do the most good have the least likelihood of adoption. Many observers believe that public financing of congressional elections is the most constructive proposal that could be adopted. By relieving members of the burden of fund raising, it would give them more time to spend on more publicly productive activities, and it would insulate them from the influence of special interests. The problem is that if campaign subsidies are set too low, they will benefit incumbents, who already enjoy high visibility and the perks of office. But setting subsidies high enough to make challengers credible (perhaps half a million dollars in House races, not counting primaries) would no doubt allow expenditures too large for a cynical public to accept—not that incumbents would ever vote to give their challengers that much funding anyway.[36]

All in all, the great advantage in campaign spending that incumbent representatives enjoy surely contributes to the extraordinary advantage of incumbency, but it is far from the only explanation. Even if spending disparities were wiped out overnight, incumbents would still do very well. And as we will discuss later in this chapter, recent developments in interest-group and party spending seem likely to erode the great advantage that incumbents enjoyed in the 1980s and 1990s.

## More Responsive Incumbents

Many critics of Congress believe that there is something wrong with high rates of reelection. That is true if members' electoral success reflects the operation of some illegitimate factor—selling out to PACs, for example. But as we have noted, one reason for members' success is that they work very hard at helping their constituents and serving their districts. Another source of their success is that these legislators are extremely sensitive to the wishes of their constituents, perhaps even more so than members of Congress from earlier eras.

One reason for this sensitivity is that members of Congress today have more and better information than members of Congress did previously. Not only do their offices have fax machines, e-mail, World Wide Web pages—technologies undreamt of a few decades ago—but the members also physically return to their districts 30 to 50 times a year. Only a generation ago, one often heard a derisive phrase "the Tuesday to Thursday Club" applied to a minority of East Coast members who lived close enough to Washington to go home to their districts on Friday and return to the capitol on Monday. Today, jet transportation enables most of the Congress to belong to the Tuesday to Thursday club. Important business is rarely scheduled for Mondays or Fridays because so many members are traveling on those days. With members spending so much time in their districts, is it any surprise that they are highly attuned to the sentiments of constituents?

Moreover, members have access to survey research today. Again, as recently as a generation ago, only a few well-funded interest groups ever conducted a poll in a congressional district, and then usually only to gauge a candidate's chances. Today, with the growth of the survey research industry and the arrival of computer-assisted

## *Highlight*    Tongue-in-Cheek Fund-Raising

All members of Congress who plan to run for reelection spend a significant amount of time raising money, but many find it an unpleasant, if not demeaning, task. Some find ways to inject a bit of humor into the process, as this fund-raising letter from Massachusetts Democratic Representative Barney Frank illustrates.

February 1998

Dear Liz and Gary:

Fortunately, having been in electoral politics for 25 years, serving as a State Representative and then as a Member of the U.S. House of Representatives, I've had a good deal of experience in choosing the lesser evil. And that is what I am doing right now as I dictate this letter. Indeed, this letter is in fact the lesser evil in question—I am about as eager to write it as you are to read it. But writing it wins out over the greater evil which is to try to get reelected in 1998 without any campaign funds.

I believe I am mellowing as I get older and am somewhat nicer than I used to be, but I concede that I am not yet at the point where I can win reelection on charm alone—which brings me to this letter, which in turn I hope brings you to send me some money.

I realize that fundraising is in lower repute this year than it has ever been, but since the various recipients of this letter and I have been engaged in campaign fundraising—that is I have been engaged in fundraising and the recipients have, fortunately for me, been willing to engage in fund giving (semantically I suppose the opposite of fundraising should be fundlowering but that does not seem fully opposite)—and I will now confess that while dictating I have entirely lost track of where this sentence was going so I will simply end it.

To return to the point I was trying to make, it's an election year, I am running for reelection, and while I do not anticipate having to spend millions of dollars, I will have to spend more than I now have so if you think it is a good idea for me to be reelected, I hope you will send me some money.

*Barney*

Paid for by the Barney Frank for Congress Committee
Box 260, Newtonville, MA 02160

---

telephone interviewing, more members can afford to conduct surveys to learn the views of constituents. Today's members probably make fewer mistakes based on bad information than their predecessors did.

Contemporary members of Congress also may have greater incentive to act in accordance with the superior information they now have. In the modern Congress, every vote cast is closely watched by interest groups who rate members; moreover, years after a vote, opponents engaged in opposition research may bring it up in a campaign. In the House, more votes are public now than a generation ago. Until 1971, many votes were cast by standing, voice (aye–nay), and "tellers" (depositing colored cards in boxes)—procedures that camouflaged the member's individual positions. But rules changes that year made it easy to demand a roll call, and the number of roll calls in an average session more than doubled. A damaging roll call vote need not be a highly visible one that saves a president, as in Margolies-Mezvinsky's case. An obscure vote may come back to haunt a member years later if the policy supported proved a failure or had negative consequences.[37] More recorded votes mean more electoral danger.

A third reason why members may be more responsive today than in the past is that there are fewer constraints that might keep members from acting on the information and the incentives they have. Once again, party decline is an important factor here. Except under the most unusual circumstances, such as those that Rep. Margolies-Mezvinsky encountered, members of Congress are not forced to cast votes that will damage them in their districts. When party and constituency collide, constituency trumps party—absent exceptional circumstances. If members are forced to toe the party line, they are more likely to be defeated when constituents disagree with the party position or disapprove of the president's performance, because party unity leaves constituents with no choice but to vent their disagreement or disapproval on the party as a whole. Today, members of Congress distance themselves from their party and president whenever they think it politically advantageous. Thus one of the reasons why fewer are defeated is that fewer give their constituents such reasons to defeat them.

### SECTION SUMMARY

Party is still the single most important factor in congressional elections. The proportion of party identifiers supporting their party's candidate has declined only a bit since the 1950s. Since then, the incumbency advantage has grown in importance. This is due, at least in part, to the efforts to diligently serve constituents' needs. In fact, members of Congress have gone to some lengths to provide themselves with the resources (staff, offices, franking, etc.) to help constituents. Members use all of these resources—and survey research tools—to stay in close touch with their constituents, and increase their reelection chances. Fund-raising has become an increasingly important part of the member's job: since the 1970s the average incumbent is spending more than six times as much on campaigns.

## Contemporary Senate Elections

The importance of incumbency in House elections contrasts with its importance in Senate elections. As Figure 11.6 shows, although incumbent senators are elected more often than not, they are defeated much more frequently than are representatives, and in a few elections (such as 1980), barely more than half survive. Despite their 6-year terms, the average length of time a senator serves is the same as the average tenure of a representative: about 11 years.[38] Senate elections differ from House elections in terms of the extent of party competition, the sources of information, the quality of

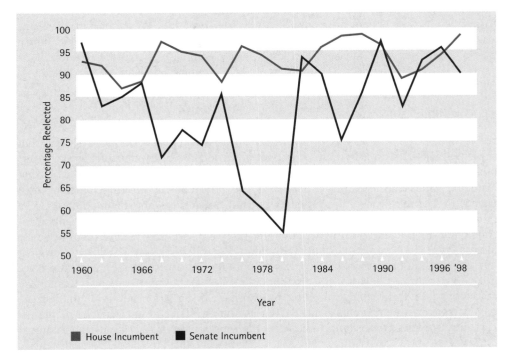

**Figure 11.6**

**Representatives Get Reelected More Often Than Senators**

SOURCE: Norman J. Ornstein *et al.*, eds., *Vital Statistics on Congress, 1995–1996* (Washington, DC: Congressional Quarterly, 1996), pp. 60–61.

challengers, and the ultimate ambitions of senators. Each of these makes the position of Senate incumbents less secure than that of House incumbents.

## Party Competition

The two parties compete more evenly in Senate races than in House races.[39] Each senator has a state for a constituency, and in general, states are more heterogeneous than the smaller congressional districts included in them. This difference is significant because social and economic diversity provides a basis for party competition.[40] For example, an urban, heavily minority House district will be dominated by the Democrats, and a rural, white district usually will be dominated by the Republicans. But if a state includes both kinds of districts, each party has a natural base on which to compete for the Senate seats. Few states are reliably "safe" for either party, whereas a majority of the smaller, more homogeneous House districts are "safe" seats. Thus, part of the reason why senators lead less secure electoral lives than representatives is simply that they have larger, more diverse constituencies that are more difficult to please.

## Uncontrolled Information

Senators receive far more media coverage than representatives. One study found that the average senator appeared on the network evening news 33 times during the course of a session, compared to 5 times for the average representative. Every senator had at least one appearance, whereas a quarter of the House got no coverage whatsoever.[41] Given the popular image of politicians as publicity seekers, greater media exposure might appear to benefit senators, but the source of the information is an important consideration. Nearly all the information that constituents receive about House incumbents comes *from* House incumbents—newsletters, press releases, and so forth.[42] Naturally, such information has an entirely positive slant: Representatives are not going to spread negative information about themselves! Senators also would like their constituents to receive nothing but positive information about them, but the media are not under Senate control. The media publicize controversial statements, personal embarrassments, and fights with the president and other politicians; controversy and conflict are newsworthy. And such coverage inevitably puts the senator in a negative light in the eyes of at least some constituents.

## Better Challengers

The office of senator enjoys a higher status than the office of representative. After all, the Senate is commonly referred to as the "upper" chamber, whereas the House is referred to as the "lower" chamber (reflecting sensitive House feelings, members of Congress refer to the "other" chamber). Naturally, potential challengers are more willing to risk a race for the more prestigious Senate than a race for the less prestigious House. Moreover, Senate seats are scarce. Every two years, all 435 House seats are available, compared to 33 or 34 Senate seats; a state with 20 House seats has 40 House elections in a four-year period, but only 2 Senate elections. Thus, far fewer credible challengers are needed to make Senate races competitive.

The combination of greater attractiveness and greater scarcity attracts Senate challengers who are on average stronger than House challengers.[43] Senate challengers are better known and better liked than House challengers, and the funding gap between incumbents and challengers is smaller, as shown in Figure 11.7, partly because the challengers are more highly regarded and partly because the incumbents are apt to be less highly regarded (as a result of their having less control of press coverage and more heterogeneous constituencies, as explained earlier).

## High Ambitions

Another reason why senators are associated with more controversial matters than representatives is that many of them have higher ambitions. Pundits have commented that every senator looks in the mirror and sees a president. The political system depends, of course, on ambitious office seekers putting themselves on the line.[44] But higher ambition has its risks. No senator can seek the presidential nomination solely on the basis of the pork barrel projects brought home to his or her state. Presidential ambitions require senators to take positions on larger national and international issues to demonstrate vision, expertise, and leadership. But such issues are controversial, and

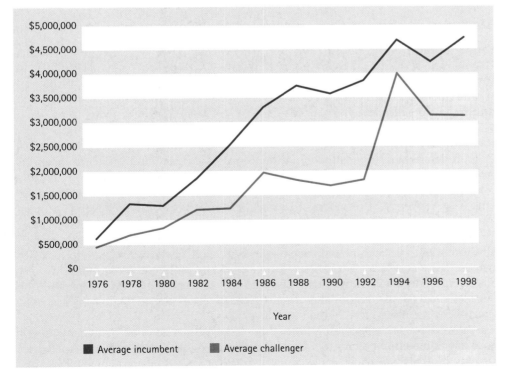

Figure 11.7

**Senate Incumbents' Spending Advantage**

SOURCE: Norman J. Ornstein *et al.*, eds., *Vital Statistics on Congress, 1999–2000* (Washington, DC: American Enterprise Institute, 2000), p. 81.

■ Average incumbent     ■ Average challenger

**Table 11.1**

**How House and Senate Elections Compare**

| Factor | House | Senate |
|---|---|---|
| Competition | Many safe districts | Few safe states |
| Incumbency advantage | Highly significant | Smaller and more variable |
| Challengers | Weaker on average | Stronger on average |
| Local issues | More important | Less important |
| Constituency service | More important | Less important |
| National issues | Less important, but importance is increasing | More important |
| Campaign funding | Challengers extremely disadvantaged | Challengers less disadvantaged |
| Electoral turnover | Lower | Higher |

senators' comments and votes on them are bound to offend some constituents; moreover, involvement with broader national and international issues leaves senators vulnerable to the charge that they are neglecting their states. In recent years, senators have been defeated partly as a result of charges that they had become the "Senator from Angola" or were "more interested in Africa than Iowa."[45]

SECTION SUMMARY

Incumbent senators have a tougher time electorally than representatives. This is because they typically face stronger challengers nominated by parties who are competitive state-wide, because they cannot control the information about them that constituents receive, and because the higher ambitions many of them harbor require them to play a more visible role in national politics. Table 11.1 compares the factors that influence House and Senate elections.

## *National Forces in Congressional Elections*

Former Speaker of the House Thomas P. "Tip" O'Neill (D-MA) once commented that "all politics is local." O'Neill's remark partly reflected the parochial politics of Massachusetts, but it also is a reminder that although members of Congress are national lawmakers, they are elected and reelected by people in thousands of localities, to whom they are ultimately responsible.

The tendency of representatives and senators to distance themselves from party and presidential positions that are locally unpopular makes modern congressional elections less subject to the kind of **national forces**—across-the-board electoral effects generated by presidents, party performance, and economic conditions—that were common in American history until the mid-twentieth century.[46] Presidential **coattails**—the tendency of presidents to carry their own party's candidates for Congress into office—have declined in strength.[47] More voters today split their tickets, voting for presidential and congressional candidates of different parties.[48] Moreover, as parties have weakened and incumbency has strengthened, fewer voters seem to treat off-year elections as referenda on the performance of the president. Until 1998, in every off-year election between the Civil War and 1994 except one (1934), the party of the president lost House seats—and usually Senate seats—but as Figure 11.8 shows, fewer were lost more recently than earlier.

As we have seen, beginning in the mid-1960s, congressional incumbents developed entrepreneurial politics to a fine art. They voted themselves perks to replace the resources formerly provided by local party organizations, they used constituency service to construct a nonpartisan, nonideological layer of support, and they developed

**national forces**
Electoral effects felt across most states and congressional districts, most often generated by especially strong or weak presidential candidates, party performance, or the state of the economy.

**coattails**
Positive electoral effect of a popular presidential candidate on congressional candidates of the party.

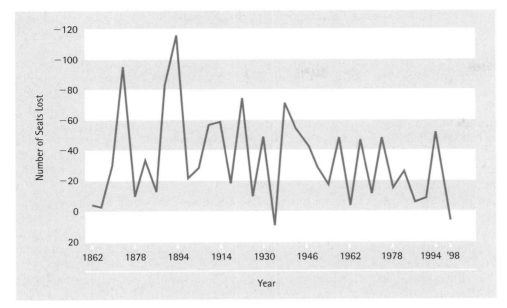

**Figure 11.8**

**Incumbent Administrations Do Not Lose as Many House Seats in Mid-Term Elections Today as in the Past**

SOURCE: Norman J. Ornstein *et al.*, eds., *Vital Statistics on Congress, 1995–1996* (Washington, DC: Congressional Quarterly, 1996), p. 55.

fund-raising capacities that dwarfed those of potential opponents. Add to this the research showing that presidential coattails and mid-term effects were declining, and members of the House appeared to be well on their way to insulating themselves from the kinds of national forces that in earlier times often determined which party controlled Congress.

## National Forces in the 1990s: A New Era?

The 1994 elections challenged the prevailing view of incumbent insulation. The 52-seat Democratic loss in the House, the largest loss since 1946, seemed to illustrate late-nineteenth-century electoral conditions more than late-twentieth-century conditions. Coupled with an 8-seat loss in the Senate, the election results suggested that a strong national tide had destroyed the insulation of the Democratic Congress, the advantages of incumbency notwithstanding. With the benefit of hindsight, it appears that national forces clearly were more important in 1994 than in other recent elections, but the changes were somewhat exaggerated.[49]

Even though incumbent losses in 1994 were severe and were entirely on the Democratic side, 85 percent of the Democratic House incumbents who ran were reelected. Some of the new Republicans announced that they intended to act as courageous lawmakers and not engage in mundane political activities like bringing home the bacon. Representative Michael Flanagan (R-IL), who had upset a scandal-tainted incumbent, "practically bragged that he would bring home less federal largesse, saying, 'Pork has not served this district well.'"[50]

A year later Rep. Flanagan had changed his tune: His press release read, "These are good projects, not pork."[51] In the end, Flanagan's about-face could not save him (his district was too Democratic), but there is little doubt that the Republicans saved their majority in 1996 by time-honored techniques—putting distance between themselves and an unpopular leader (Newt Gingrich) and highlighting their activities on behalf of their districts.[52] In the 1996 elections, the Republican majorities pulled through as ticket splitting and the incumbency advantage helped 91 Republican House candidates to win districts carried by President Clinton.

The 1998 elections underscored the exceptional nature of 1994. Most observers initially anticipated a quiet election. Only 33 House seats were open, few senators seemed vulnerable, and as the year began, the economy was booming and President Clinton's approval ratings were high. Both parties tried and failed to develop an issue that captured the imagination of the electorate. Early in 1998 most experts expected some Democratic losses in Congress (consistent with historical experience) but expected those losses to be minimal, as in such incumbency-dominated elections as 1986 and 1988.

Then, in late January, the Monica Lewinsky scandal erupted. For a few days the media speculated that President Clinton might be forced to resign, but the president's performance ratings held and the issue seemed to die away. In the spring, a quiet "status quo" election again seemed likely. But the Lewinsky scandal erupted again with greater fury in August, and candidates and pundits everywhere began to reassess the situation. Republicans dreamed that popular revulsion toward the president would give them a landslide, and Democrats feared Republicans might be right. Many Democratic candidates distanced themselves from the president; some even canceled fund-raisers at which he was to appear.[53]

But the president's approval ratings held. Some observers believed that congressional Republicans overplayed their hand, playing to their base among social conservatives but alienating moderate voters who might have supported them had they appeared less partisan. In a stunning surprise, Democrats actually gained five seats, the first time since 1934 that the president's party had gained in the mid-term election. Only one Democratic incumbent lost, as did four Republican incumbents, for an all-time record incumbent reelection rate of 98.5 percent. In the Senate the parties broke even. And of particular interest to many, of the three Democratic women senators (Boxer—CA; Mosley-Braun—IL; Smith—WA) elected in 1992 and once thought to be vulnerable, only one lost. The "year of the other woman" did not undo the "year of the woman."

## The 2000 Congressional Elections

The Republicans retained their congressional majorities in the 2000 elections, but just barely. When the final results are in, the Republican majority in the House might be fewer than six, and depending on the outcome of a tight race in the state of Washington, there is a possibility that the parties may exactly tie in the Senate.

Most observers felt that the elections had no national theme like the Republican Contract in 1994 and the Clinton impeachment in 1998. With control of both chambers at stake party leaders urged members to run on their own records and even to highlight their differences with the leadership where it was electorally advantageous. For example, Democratic party committees even backed some pro-life candidates like Robert Casey of Pennsylvania. The results were reminiscent of the incumbency-dominated elections of the 1970s and 1980s. Only eight House incumbents lost out of 412 who ran. As usual, Senators had a rougher time with five of 28 defeated and another undecided as this book goes to press.

On the other hand, the parity demonstrated in the presidential voting showed up just as clearly in the congressional voting. Exit polls reported that in total, virtually equal numbers of Americans voted for Democratic and Republican House and Senate candidates. Preliminary analysis also suggests that districts tended to cast similar votes for President and Representative. In these respects the 2000 congressional elections look like the more nationalized 1990s elections.

For updates on the 2000 Congressional elections see www.ablongman.com/fiorina.

## Why Do National Forces Appear to Be Growing Stronger?

Although the changes represented by the 1994 elections may have been exaggerated, the evidence nonetheless suggests that congressional elections are more nationalized now than in Tip O'Neill's day when "all politics was local." Two related reasons contribute to this development. The first is more unified, and more distinct, political parties. The congressional parties are more homogeneous today than they were a generation ago, and the differences between Republicans and Democrats are greater.[54] Thus voters today usually are presented with a clear choice between two candidates who

**Election Connection**

## Independent Expenditures in the 1996 House Elections

For nearly two decades, PACs occupied center stage in congressional campaign finance debates. The 1996 campaign was different: PACs and their activities barely made the radar screen. Instead, attention focused on a new development—the large independent-expenditure campaigns mounted on behalf of congressional candidates. Independent expenditures have become more important as parties and interest groups push the envelope of campaign finance practices, and the courts decline to restrain them.

Most of the action was in House campaigns; it was generally conceded that the Republicans would hold the Senate, but Democrats believed they had a reasonable shot at recapturing the House. Anticipating tough campaigns, House candidates raised and spent over $400 million in hard money, a 25 percent increase over the previous record set in 1994. But although these direct candidate expenditures made up the lion's share of what was spent, they were not what got the publicity.

In early 1996, the AFL-CIO announced that it would spend $35 million dollars in an attempt to defeat Republican House candidates.[a] The union organization targeted many of the freshmen first elected in 1994, as well as seats with no incumbent in 1996. The campaign included negative ads attacking Republican positions on the so-called $M^2E^2$ issues—Medicare and Medicaid, the environment and education—as well as such other issues as health care and the minimum wage.

The Republicans responded, of course. The Republican National Committee spent millions of dollars of their soft money on ads, attacking "big-labor bosses" who were trying to "buy Congress." The U.S. Chamber of Commerce organized a coalition of 31 organizations that spent $7 million on ads designed to offset the union ads, and conservative religious groups spent a reported

$10 million. (The image of a national war between two well-organized coalitions should not be overdrawn, however; some of the Republican candidates on the national "hit list" received contributions and support from individual union PACs![b] House elections continue to be predominantly decentralized, district-oriented affairs.)

In the end, the AFL-CIO effort fell a bit short, and ironically, it may have been the campaign finance scandals that erupted during the last two weeks of the campaign that prevented the Democrats from winning the few additional seats they needed to recapture the House. Whatever the 1996 electoral impact, however, the dramatic increases in soft-money contributions, much of which funded independent expenditures, signaled the end of the campaign finance system that prevailed between 1976 and 1996.[c]

*What do you think?*
- *Should Congress pass campaign finance laws?*
- *These laws might affect freedom of speech. How much of a restriction should be tolerated?*
- *On the other hand, the supporters of a candidate can be relevant to voters.*
- *What information should be made public about these independent expenditures?*

---

[a] The following account is drawn from Anthony Corrado, "Financing the 1996 Elections," in Gerald Pomper *et al.*, eds., *The Elections of 1996* (Chatham, NJ: Chatham House, 1997), pp. 162–164.
[b] Jonathan Salant, "Some on Labor 'Hit List' Get Labor Contributions," *Congressional Quarterly Weekly Report*," October 5, 1996, 2884–2885.
[c] Corrado, "Financing the 1996 Elections."

---

hold distinct positions on national issues. Such clear differences are less likely to be overwhelmed by local factors or by the candidate's personal characteristics, which were more important in the preceding three decades.

The second reason lies in recent developments in campaign finance, namely soft money and independent expenditures, much of which goes to promote national issues in congressional campaigns. In 1998, the most recent election for which data are available, the Republicans raised more than $100 million in soft money, the Democrats more than $75 million. These numbers were vastly exceeded in the 2000 elections: The Republicans are estimated to have raised $215 million and the Democrats $180 million.[55] The parties spend much of this money on "issue advocacy," mostly TV commercials praising their own candidates or attacking the other party's candidates. In 1998 Republican congressional committees spent about $26 million on such ads, including $11 million on an ad blitz that that tied Democrats to the Lewinsky scandal.

Interest groups also engage in issue advocacy. In 1998, for example, the NRA spent $2.3 million on ads, and they are by no means the biggest spenders. Indeed, perhaps the most important recent development on the campaign finance front is the proliferation of *truly* independent expenditures by groups (see the accompanying Election Connection). Previously, there was some degree of coordination between groups on the one hand and parties and candidates on the other—they simply had to avoid being explicit about their conversations in order to preserve legal deniability. But in 1998, groups began running ads without the knowledge of (and sometimes in defiance of) the wishes of candidates. In a spring special election in California, for example, pro-life groups attacked the Democratic candidate even though the Republican candidate did not want to make abortion an issue in the race. Groups supporting term limits also jumped in. As the campaign progressed, the Sierra Club, the Christian Coalition, and various pro-business groups joined abortion groups and term limits groups in spending independently.[56]

The parties also got into the act. Locked in a tight reelection race, Senator Russell Feingold (D-WI), a well-known campaign finance reformer, refused as a matter of principle to accept outside contributions. When the national Democratic party, fearful of losing his seat, made an independent ad buy to support him, he demanded that they cease spending. In the end Feingold won the race—and the argument.

The long-term implications of truly independent spending are significant. Candidates prefer to control the campaign agenda as much as possible. Both candidates may prefer that an issue not come up, either because the district is so split that neither candidate feels he or she can profit from the issue or, more innocently, because the issue is not important in their districts and needlessly muddies the political waters. Groups reject such viewpoints. They argue that the agenda does not belong to the candidates and that they have every right to force candidates—and voters—to address their issues.

Although many people are troubled by these developments, two things can be said in their favor. The first is that they help to redress the imbalance between incumbents and challengers. Parties and interest groups can inject large sums into campaigns where credible challengers are running, thus helping to offset incumbents' large advantage in PAC and individual contributions. Second, campaigns in which the parties and national interest groups actively participate will be more issue-oriented than those in which they are absent. Many people believe this is the way elections should be.

## *Do Congressional Elections Produce a Representative Body?*

Members of Congress generally are qualified people. In contrast to times past, today's Congress contains few political "hacks"—people there only because of their connection to some political "boss." Current members are hard-working, well-educated, bright, and personally interested in public policy. Moreover, despite media portrayals, today's members are less corrupt than ever before. Although scandals are reported more commonly now than in the past, that probably reflects changing perspectives in the media—the rise of the "junkyard dog" mentality—rather than increased corruption in the Congress.

Still, some people look at the membership of Congress and are troubled. They see a supposedly representative body that does not mirror the diversity of the United States. The Congress consists overwhelmingly of white male professionals. The House that sat in 1999–2000 had only 56 women (its historical high-water mark), and the 37 African American, 18 Hispanic, and 5 Asian members were less than their proportions of the larger population.[57] Comparable proportions of the Senate are much lower: 9 women, 1 African American, no Hispanics, and 2 Asian Americans (the senators from Hawaii). As shown in Figure 11.9, the numbers have been rising in recent decades, but the rate of increase, except for the 1992 surge, has been slow.

The subject of the gender, racial, and ethnic diversity of the Congress has been a matter of considerable controversy in recent years. The concept of representation means different things to different people. For some, personal characteristics such as the gender or race of a representative are unimportant: So long as he or she is responsive to the needs and aspirations of constituents, they feel well represented.[58] Others disagree. They contend that almost by definition, a male representative cannot be responsive to the needs and aspirations of women ("They just don't get it!"), and that white representatives cannot be responsive to the needs and aspirations of blacks and other minorities. Those who hold such views believe that Congress must be *descriptively* similar to the country in order to be a truly representative body. Still others con-

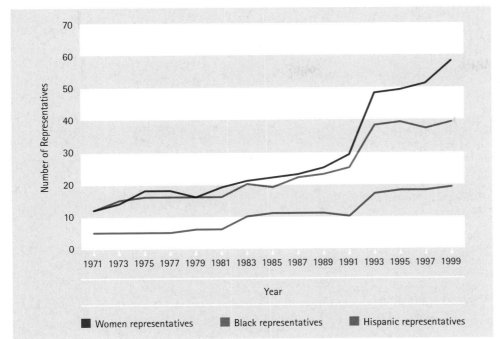

**Figure 11.9**

**Women and Minority Members of Congress**

SOURCE: Harold W. Stanley and Richard G. Niemi, *Vital Statistics in American Politics, 1999–2000*. (Washington, DC: CQ Press, 2000).

cede that white male representatives might be able to represent women and minorities but believe nonetheless that women and minority representatives have important symbolic value. If they have a visible presence in the councils of government, they will both provide valuable role models for women and minorities in the population and enhance the legitimacy of government actions.[59]

Those who believe in either the actual or the symbolic importance of diversifying the Congress are not likely to see their frustration alleviated soon. The Congress is not like a business that hires employees or a university that admits students. Its members are chosen by millions of citizens voting independently (and secretly) in hundreds of elections. Voters can be urged to practice affirmative action, but such appeals are unlikely to be very effective. Because the electoral obstacles faced by women and minorities are different, they require separate discussions.

## Women

The United States ranks quite low among world democracies in the proportion of women in the lower chamber of its national legislature (see the accompanying International Comparison). But gender prejudice does not seem to be the major reason. Societal prejudice against women serving in public office is low and has been diminishing.[60] Women suffer politically in that they have only recently gained admission to the networks that move politicians upward to higher office—men have had a long head start. Despite some well-publicized examples of TV anchors and other personalities moving laterally into Congress, these are exceptions, not the rule. Winning a seat is usually the result of a series of successful efforts: beginning with a local office or community organization, moving through state office, and ultimately winning an open seat or defeating a vulnerable incumbent. Along the way, the member-to-be of Congress learns the art of politics, makes valuable political allies, becomes acquainted with those who bankroll campaigns, and generally acquires the experiences, characteristics, and resources that constitute the "qualifications" that someday will make her a "credible" challenger. The most common base for congressional candidates is the state legislature. As Figure 11.10 demonstrates, women are making rapid progress in this arena, and as the pool of women in state legislatures and other lower offices grows, their representation in Congress will follow.

# *International Comparison*

# Women in Politics

Since the 1950s, the role of women in the United States has undergone a revolutionary change. Gender inequalities are still apparent, as in the salaries and wages that women earn compared to those earned by men and the unequal division of housework and child care responsibilities between wives and husbands, but the expectations of young women today are similar to those of young men, and the career opportunities of today's young women far exceed those of their mothers, let alone their grandmothers. In most other countries, women face educational and occupational barriers of one sort or another; consequently, American women are better represented in business and the professions than in other developed democracies.[a]

There is one arena, however, in which American women continue to trail women in other countries—politics. A recent study found that, compared to women in other democracies, American women are considerably less likely to hold national office. The accompanying table shows the proportion of women elected to the lower (more important) house of a country's parliament, compared to the proportion of women in the U.S. House of Representatives.

The United States trails all but a few of the advanced industrial democracies, occupying a cluster that includes Belgium, the United Kingdom, and Australia. Only France and Japan rank significantly lower. Undoubtedly there are many reasons for the differences, but one seems to be the electoral system. The countries with highest proportions of women tend to have some version or another of proportional representation (PR). In such systems, party leaders submit lists of candidates who will be elected in proportion to the party's vote. Judging by the results, these lists appear to have significant numbers of highly ranked women. Countries with simple-plurality or related systems tend to have lower proportions of women. Apparently, women are less successful where they have to contend for a specific, geographically defined seat.

[a]"Jill-in-a-Box," *The Economist,* July 18, 1998: 9.

**The Japanese Diet**
Women are even rarer in the Japanese Diet than in the U.S. Congress. Why might women be elected in larger numbers in some countries?

**Women Legislators in the Lower House**

| | Year of Election | Women Members (Percentage) | Electoral System |
|---|---|---|---|
| Sweden | 1994 | 40.3 | PR |
| Norway | 1993 | 39.4 | PR |
| Finland | 1991 | 39.0 | PR |
| Denmark | 1990 | 33.0 | PR |
| Netherlands | 1994 | 31.3 | PR |
| Germany | 1994 | 26.3 | Other |
| Austria | 1990 | 21.3 | PR |
| New Zealand | 1993 | 21.2 | Plurality |
| Canada | 1993 | 18.0 | Plurality |
| Switzerland | 1991 | 17.5 | PR |
| Argentina | 1993 | 16.3 | PR |
| Spain | 1993 | 16.0 | PR |
| Italy | 1994 | 15.1 | Other |
| Costa Rica | 1994 | 14.0 | PR |
| Poland | 1993 | 13.0 | Plurality |
| Ireland | 1992 | 12.1 | Other |
| Columbia | 1994 | 11.0 | PR |
| Hungary | 1994 | 10.9 | Other |
| United States | 1994 | 10.8 | Plurality |
| Philippines | 1992 | 10.6 | Plurality |
| Bangladesh | 1991 | 10.3 | Plurality |
| Czech Republic | 1992 | 10.0 | PR |
| Russia | 1993 | 9.6 | PR |
| Belgium | 1991 | 9.4 | PR |
| Israel | 1992 | 9.2 | PR |
| United Kingdom | 1992 | 9.2 | Plurality |
| Portugal | 1991 | 8.7 | PR |
| Australia | 1993 | 8.2 | Other |
| Mexico | 1991 | 7.6 | Other |
| India | 1991 | 7.3 | Plurality |
| France | 1993 | 6.1 | Other |
| Uruguay | 1989 | 6.1 | PR |
| Brazil | 1990 | 6.0 | PR |
| Japan | 1993 | 2.7 | Other |

SOURCE: Adapted from Pippa Norris, "Legislative Recruitment," in Lawrence LeDuc, Richard Niemi, and Pippa Norris, eds., *Comparing Democracies* (Thousand Oaks, CA: Sage, 1996), pp. 191–92.

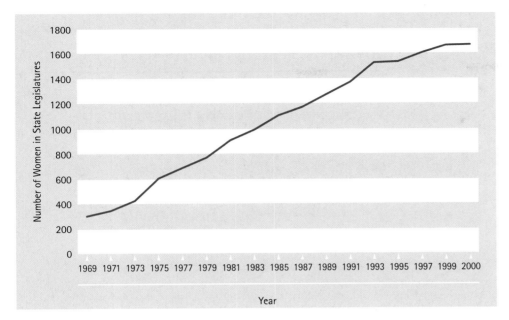

**Figure 11.10**

**The Number of Women in State Legislatures Has Increased Steadily**

SOURCE: "America at the Polls 1998," *The Public Perspective*, December/January 1999: 28.

Thus we believe that the under-representation of women in Congress will naturally lessen as women's career patterns become more like those of men. Some feminists may reject this analysis, believing that women should strive to be elected as *women,* politicians with a "different voice," not because they have learned to play the electoral game the same way men do. We recognize this viewpoint, but in our view such a strategy will not succeed, simply because American women are unlikely to vote as a block rather than as a complex combination of all their identities.

## Minorities

The prospects for further increasing minority representation in Congress are less favorable than for women, especially the prospects for African Americans. The critical difference is that in racially diverse constituencies, **bloc voting**—in which groups vote as blocs—often occurs. When it does, a black candidate can be elected only where African Americans are a majority of the electorate. In the 103rd Congress, for example (the first Congress after the most recent redistricting), 32 of the 39 black members came from districts in which African Americans were in the majority, and in 5 of the remaining 7 districts, African Americans plus Latinos made up a majority. Similarly, 15 of the 17 Latino members of the 103rd Congress came from majority-Latino districts; none came from districts with a white majority.

Given this high degree of racially polarized voting, efforts to increase minority representation in Congress have been made largely through the redistricting process. The 1982 amendments to the Voting Rights Act and subsequent court decisions have been interpreted to require the creation of **majority-minority districts** wherever possible. In such districts, a racial or ethnic minority constitutes a majority of the population. Given the lower turnout rates that prevail among minority groups, the rule of thumb is that for a minority candidate to be elected to Congress, about 65 percent of the population in such districts should belong to minority groups.

Efforts to create majority-minority districts, sometimes called **affirmative action redistricting,** have generated considerable controversy. Some of the districts that have been created have unusual shapes, uniting areas of different cities connected only by a highway. Such districts have provoked charges of racial gerrymandering. In 1993 the Supreme Court ruled in *Shaw* v. *Reno* that majority-minority districting had limits: A district created on no basis other than to include a majority of minorities might raise constitutional questions. And more recently, the Court declared redistricting plans in Georgia, North Carolina, and Texas to be unconstitutional racial gerrymanders (see the accompanying Democratic Dilemma).

**bloc voting**
Voting in which nearly all members of one group (such as African Americans) vote for a candidate of their race, whereas nearly all members of another group (such as whites) vote against that candidate.

**majority-minority districts**
District in which a minority group is the numerical majority.
Affirmative action redistricting

**affirmative action redistricting**
The process of drawing district lines to maximize the number of majority-minority districts.

## *Democratic Dilemma*    Affirmative Action Redistricting

In the 1980s, the Voting Rights Act was put to a new use. With the right of minorities to cast a vote seemingly secure, civil rights activists turned their attention to the outcomes of elections.[a] Although barriers to voting had been overturned, in many areas racially polarized voting prevented minorities from actually winning any elections. The proposed remedy came to be the creation of majority-minority districts.

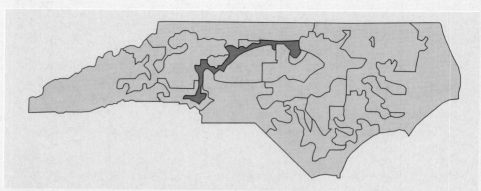

Congress encouraged such districts in 1982 amendments to the act, and the Supreme Court continued in the same direction in a 1986 decision, *Thornburg* v. *Gingles.* Ultimately, the Justice Department began to deny approval to redistricting plans that did not provide for the creation of the maximum number of majority-minority districts.

In 1993 the Court began to draw back. A North Carolina plan contained two districts with unusual shapes. As shown in the figure, one followed Interstate 95 across the state to pick up black residential areas in the state's major cities. In *Shaw* v. *Reno*, a splintered Court sent the plan back to the lower courts, expressing concern over "bizarrely shaped" districts drawn only to include people of a particular race. In 1995 the Court went further in *Miller* v. *Johnson*. By a 5 to 4 majority, the Court ruled that Georgia's plan was a "racial gerrymander" that violated the equal protection clause of the Constitution.[b] In 1996 the Court affirmed *Miller* in *Shaw* v. *Hunt*, striking down the North Carolina plan that a lower court had approved.[c] The decision again was by a 5 to 4 majority. Although the Court has not explicitly rejected the use of racial considerations in redistricting, it appears that the current Court will reject plans that use race as a "predominant factor" in drawing districts. However, the Court has left itself a loophole

because it has shown no inclination as yet to strike down the large amount of race-dominated districting that is required by its own interpretation of the Voting Rights Act in *Thornburg*. Furthermore, the current majority is fragile, and one law professor has commented that the current state of the law depends "on Justice O'Connor's personal opinion about when race-consciousness goes too far."[d]

*What do you think?*
- *How could these districts actually harm the substantive representation of minority interests?*
- *How does the "equal protection" clause of the Constitution support arguments both for and against majority-minority districts?*

[a]This discussion is partly based on personal communications with Daniel Lowenstein, Professor of Law, UCLA.
[b]Holly Idelson, "Court Takes a Harder Line on Minority Voting Blocs," *Congressional Quarterly Weekly Report,* July 1, 1995, 1944–1946.
[c]Holly Idelson, "Minority-District Decisions Lay No Clear Guidelines," *Congressional Quarterly Weekly Report,* June 15, 1996, 1679–1681.
[d]Pamela Karlan, quoted in Idelson, p. 1679.

Even racial liberals are not all of the same mind on the issue of majority-minority districting. Those who support creating such districts value the increased representation of African American and Latino representatives. Those opposed are naturally cautious about something supported by Republicans and likely to work against Democrats. During the Bush administration, the Justice Department aggressively pushed majority-minority redistricting plans, and Republicans have typically joined minorities in challenging plans that did not create the maximum number of such districts. The political logic is clear: Republicans believe that by concentrating minority groups in urban districts, they can push white Democratic incumbents outward into the suburbs where they are more vulnerable to Republican challengers. Republicans understandably prefer fewer Democrats to more Democrats, regardless of race.

The dilemma posed by majority-minority districting became very evident after the 1996 elections. Were it not for the majority-minority districting after the 1990 census, the Democrats might have won control of the House.[61] Democrats ask whether it is better to have somewhat fewer African Americans who would all be subcommittee or committee chairs in a Democratic House, or to have somewhat more African American members who are all back-benchers in a Republican House?

Whatever your view of such trade-offs, there is an upper limit on the number of majority-minority districts that can possibly be created: Racial minorities by definition consist of *minorities* of people, and redistricters cannot cross state boundaries to concentrate them. Indeed, given the recent court decisions, the United States may already be near that limit. If the maximum number of majority-minority districts that can be created is little more than the number that currently exist, then the upper limit for minority representatives will be correspondingly low unless minorities can break through and win in districts where they are not majorities. From that standpoint, the kind of racial bloc voting assumed in (and perhaps even encouraged by) majority-minority districting works *against* the long-term prospects for minority candidates to win in nonminority districts. That is, the floor for minority representation ensured by majority-minority districting might also set a ceiling on the number of minority representatives. Thus many were encouraged when two black incumbents whose districts were redrawn were able to win reelection in white-majority districts in 1996.[62]

A second potentially negative effect of affirmative action redistricting is less obvious: It may work to marginalize minority members of Congress, particularly black representatives. The homogeneity of African American views should not be overstated.[63] Nevertheless, blacks are overwhelmingly Democratic in their allegiance, more liberal in general, and far more supportive of federal social programs in particular.[64] Representatives of such a group are correspondingly liberal. Indeed, members of the Congressional Black Caucus (CBC), all of whom are Democrats, are among the most liberal members of Congress, as measured by numerous interest-group ratings. But liberal records compiled as U.S. representatives may preclude African Americans from being credible challengers in gubernatorial, senatorial, and ultimately presidential elections, where statewide constituencies are much more heterogeneous in general and more conservative in particular.[65] A minority member of the House who faithfully represents a majority-minority district may thereby compile a record that makes it impossible for him or her to contend statewide or nationwide.

In sum, the subject of minority representation in Congress is a difficult one, and existing court-imposed methods of encouraging more minority representation are controversial. Each person must decide whether the gains that accrue from ensuring some level of minority representation exceed the costs. Unfortunately, the latter are highly uncertain and, to a considerable extent, subjective. Thus people of good faith may disagree.

## Elections, Parties, and Group Representation

Some part of the difficulty in increasing minority representation reflects the basic fact that the single-member district, simple plurality (SMSP) electoral system is not designed to produce a descriptively representative legislative body. The SMSP system puts all minorities, racial and otherwise, at a disadvantage. If you receive fewer votes than the leading candidate—even if you get 49 percent of the vote—you win nothing. Republicans in Democratic districts and vice versa, liberals in conservative districts and vice versa, African Americans in white districts and vice versa, pro-lifers in pro-choice districts and vice versa—all are unrepresented if the majority elects a representative who shares the majority sentiment. In a sense, U.S. courts have been trying to coax a more proportional result from an electoral system not designed to be proportional. Not surprisingly, their efforts have met with limited success. Recognizing these realities, some academic critics have raised questions about the electoral system itself. President Clinton's 1993 nomination of Lani Guanier to the office of assistant attorney general for civil rights would have provided an opportunity for the general public to hear some of this debate, but some of her proposals proved too controversial, and her nomination was withdrawn before hearings were held.

It is conceivable that minorities (and women) would be better represented if the old-style party machines were still in existence. After all, the "balanced ticket" was a common strategy of the political party: To construct a coalition of diverse groups, the party recognized each group when putting together a slate of candidates.[66] Historians believe that because of racial prejudice, minorities generally did not fare so well as whites in the urban machines, which were based largely on white ethnic groups. But it is at least arguable that if every city in the United States still had a respectable machine, there would be more African Americans in Congress. As Professor V.O. Key, Jr., argued in his classic work *Southern Politics,* a disorganized politics advantages the economic "haves" and disadvantages the economic "have nots." The urban machines integrated earlier ethnic groups into the American political structure, but the machines were crumbling when the large post–World War II migration of African Americans from the rural South to northern cities took place. Today, local party organization has weakened, and candidates fend for themselves. The demise of the machines and the rise of candidate-centered politics may be an additional disadvantage imposed on African Americans.

## Chapter Summary

Members of the House of Representative are reelected at very high rates—more than 90 percent in all recent elections, including the Republican landslide of 1994. Upon close examination, this high level of incumbent success does not violate the founders' intention of an electorally sensitive House. On the contrary, because representatives are so electorally sensitive, they work very hard at serving their districts, try very hard to represent constituents' policy concerns, and in general attempt to eliminate any basis for a strong challenge against them. Contrary to the charges of many critics, electoral success does not lead members of the House to be lazy and unresponsive. On the contrary, members are reelected *because* they are so hard-working and responsive.

Senators too are hard-working and responsive (probably more responsive than the framers intended), although they do not enjoy the same electoral success as members of the House. On average, their constituencies—states—are more competitive than House districts; they face stronger challengers; and their ambitions and prominence make them the object of media coverage that they do not control and exposes them to expectations and ambitions that carry risks as well as rewards.

For most of the past generation, the impact of national forces on congressional elections was lower than earlier in American history, as incumbents managed to distance themselves from national leaders, de-emphasize potentially damaging issues, and emphasize their personal records. In recent elections, national forces have grown stronger, reflecting the greater distinctiveness of today's parties and the increased emphasis on national issues by parties and interest groups engaging in issue advocacy.

The single-member district, simple plurality electoral system provides strong incentives for representatives to be *responsive* to the wishes of majorities in their districts. But the system in no way ensures that the composition of the Congress will be *descriptively representative* of the diversity of the country's population. On the contrary, if people vote as ethnic or racial blocs, the system will not elect a proportional number of ethnic and racial minorities. The courts have encouraged districting arrangements that would produce more proportional outcomes, but these efforts have met with limited success and have involved procedures such as majority-minority districts that are controversial and politically divisive. At this time, such procedures may be the only way to ensure some reasonable representation of minorities, but in the long run, they may work against minority representation by encouraging bloc voting and establishing ceilings on minority representation rather than floors.

For women, the problems are different and the most promising solution is time: As women increasingly win lower offices, the pool of qualified women candidates will inevitably expand. As the pool expands, the proportion of women candidates for Congress will increase.

**On the Web**

Legislative Histories
www.lib.umich.edu/libhome/Documents.center/legishis.
html
A site designed by the University of Michigan for students
doing research on the U.S. Congress. The site includes
pointers to historical sources and present-day resources,
and includes a concise tutorial on the legislative process.
The U.S. Government Legislative Branch Directory
lcweb.loc.gov/global/legislative/congress.html

A comprehensive list of Internet resources from and about
the U.S. Congress, selected and organized by the Library
of Congress.
Voter Information Services
www.vis.org/
A site that includes scorecards, voting records, and various
public interest groups' ratings for members of the U.S.
Congress.

## Key Terms

affirmative action redistricting, p. 341
bloc voting, p. 341
coattails, p. 334
constituency service, p. 324
constituent assistance, p. 324
district service, p. 324

filing deadline, p. 322
frank, p. 326
gerrymandering, p. 321
incumbency advantage, p. 323
majority-minority districts, p. 341
national forces, p. 334

ombudsman, p. 324
open seat, p. 322
professional legislature, p. 321
reapportionment, p. 321
redistricting, p. 321
rotation, p. 320

## Suggested Readings

Brady, David. *Critical Elections and Congressional Policy Making.* Stanford, CA: Stanford University Press, 1988. Prize-winning account that ties together congressional elections, processes, and policy making.

Butler, David, and Bruce Cain. *Congressional Redistricting.* New York: Macmillan, 1992. Readable account of the redistricting process, with comparisons to practices in other democracies.

Campbell, James. *The Presidential Pulse of Congressional Elections.* Lexington, KY: University of Kentucky Press, 1993. Detailed analysis of national forces operating in mid-term elections.

Canon, David. *Actors, Athletes, and Astronauts.* Chicago: University of Chicago Press, 1990. Interesting study of how political amateurs run for and occasionally win a seat in Congress.

Fenno, Richard. *Home Style.* Boston: Little, Brown, 1978. Influential study of how House members interact with constituents, earning their trust.

Fiorina, Morris. *Congress—Keystone of the Washington Establishment,* 2nd ed. New Haven, CT: Yale University Press, 1989. A critical look at the implications of constituency service for national policy making.

Grofman, Bernard, and Chandler Davidson, eds. *Controversies in Minority Voting.* Washington, DC: Brookings, 1992. This collection of essays offers a balanced perspective on the uses to which the Voting Rights Act has been put.

Herrnson, Paul. *Congressional Elections,* 2nd ed. Washington, DC: CQ Press, 1997. The most up-to-date study of congressional campaigns.

Hibbing, John. *Congressional Careers.* Chapel Hill: University of North Carolina Press, 1991. Detailed study of career development of modern U.S. representatives after their initial election.

Jacobson, Gary. *The Politics of Congressional Elections,* 4th ed.

New York: Longman, 1997. The definitive text on modern congressional elections.

Kahn, Kim and Patrick Kenney. *The Spectacle of U.S. Senate Campaigns.* Princeton, NJ: Princeton University Press, 1999. Detailed study of how candidate strategies, media practices, and voter decisions interact in contemporary Senate campaigns.

Mayhew, David. *Congress—The Electoral Connection.* New Haven, CT: Yale University Press, 1974. Influential work that shows how much of congressional structure and behavior can be explained by the assumption that reelection is the most important goal of members.

Thernstrom, Abigail. *Whose Votes Count? Affirmative Action and Minority Voting Rights.* Cambridge, MA: Harvard University Press, 1987. Critical study of majority-minority districting and other uses to which the Voting Rights Act, as amended, has been put.

Chapter

# 12
# The Congress
# and Its Work

Chapter Outline

In April 1992 a Los Angeles jury acquitted four police officers who had brutally beaten an African American, Rodney King, after an early-morning chase. The acquittal triggered violent rioting that resulted in 60 deaths and a billion dollars in property damage. Originally misinterpreted by the media as a simple race riot, the disturbances soon were recognized as a multi-ethnic conflict reflecting the tensions of urban poverty and joblessness, mixed with ethnic and racial rivalries. Understandably, many Americans turned to the national government to do something about "the crisis of the cities." Whatever their personal views of the riots, with an election only six months away, many in Congress felt compelled to respond.[1]

Jack Kemp, secretary of Housing and Urban Development in the Bush administration, long had advocated an urban policy of "enterprise zones." These are designated areas in which investors receive favorable tax treatment. The goal is to stimulate economic development in run-down areas that investors otherwise would avoid. Although the program had previously met with a cool reception in the Democratic Congress, which favored more direct government aid, it now became the vehicle through which Congress would respond to the urban crisis. The Democrats proposed new government spending in the zones to reinforce the tax incentives, and the legislative dance began.

The House passed a bill providing for 50 zones, 25 of which were to be located in rural areas. The Senate decided on 115 zones, with 40 allocated to rural areas and 40 to cities with populations of less than 500,000. Were these appropriate responses to the "crisis of the cities"? Why so many zones, and why zones in rural areas and small cities (as well as Native American reservations, in one version of the Senate bill)? The reason is that senators and representatives from rural states and districts will not support a bill that provides nothing for *their* constituencies. Eventually, the House position prevailed: 50 zones split evenly between urban and rural. The bulk of the direct spending was allocated to the urban zones, but much of it was earmarked for smaller cities, rather than the urban concentrations people think of when they hear the phrase *crisis of the cities.*

By this time the legislation had become tangled up in election-year politics. Six months after the riots, and a week before the elections, Congress included the urban legislation in a huge tax bill that it submitted to then-President Bush. By bundling together a number of controversial pieces of legislation, the Democratic Congress hoped to force Bush to accept programs he opposed in order to get other things he wanted. The strategy failed: Bush vetoed the bill. The crisis of the cities would have to wait.

THE PRECEDING EPISODE DISPLAYS SEVERAL COMMON CHARACTERISTICS OF CONGRESS. On the one hand, individual members are quick to respond to a societal problem. On the other hand, the Congress as a whole is slow to decide what to do about the problem, in part because members use their positions within the Congress to seek benefits for their constituencies. The struggle distorts the purpose of the legislation, and when all is said and done, it is not clear whether the legislative response would make a major contribution if it *were* enacted. This chapter examines the workings of our most powerful, most complicated, most democratic, but least respected political institution. Specifically, we consider:

- the party and committee organization that Congress has developed
- the complex process of lawmaking
- the ambivalent feelings that Americans have about Congress
- attempts to reform Congress by limiting its members' terms

Before proceeding to these topics, we first review some basic features of the Congress.

## Congress—The First Branch

Congress is called the first branch of government because the Constitution prescribes the powers and structure of Congress in Article I. Table 12.1 lists the powers that the Constitution gives to Congress. The most important are the "power of the purse"—the power to tax and spend—and the "power of the sword"—the power to make war.

Like many of the world's parliaments, Congress is **bicameral,** consisting of two chambers, the House of Representatives and the Senate. Unlike most of the world's bicameral parliaments, however, both chambers have roughly equal powers. In other countries, the upper chamber of parliament typically has only ceremonial duties or, at most, powers that are much weaker than those of the lower chamber. The equal status of the two chambers in the United States creates a certain amount of interchamber rivalry. A Speaker of the House once commented that "The Senate is a nice quiet place where good Representatives go when they die."[2] The Senate has a quick response to such jibes: In all of American history, only one Senator has given up a Senate seat to run for the House, and that was in 1811 (Henry Clay).

Although their constitutional powers are roughly equal, historically, the political power and importance of the two chambers have waxed and waned. In the decades prior to the Civil War, when turnover in the House was very high, the Senate was clearly the more important body. The country's most prominent statesmen—Henry Clay, John C. Calhoun, Daniel Webster, Stephen Douglas, and others—spent their

**bicameral**
A legislature that contains two chambers.

**Table 12.1**

**The Principal Powers of Congress**

| |
|---|
| To levy taxes |
| To borrow money |
| To regulate commerce |
| To decide requirements for citizenship |
| To make monetary policy |
| To establish a postal system |
| To establish federal courts below the Supreme Court |
| To declare war |
| To raise an army and a navy |
| To call up the state militias |
| To make all laws that shall be necessary and proper for executing the other powers of Congress |

SOURCE: U.S. Constitution, Article I.

time in the Senate. After the Civil War, political leadership moved to the House, where shifting party control more accurately reflected national sentiments and where strong Speakers mobilized their party majorities.

For most of the twentieth century the two chambers have been equal in importance. Political circumstances may make one chamber enjoy greater prominence for a time, but eventually the equal power of the other chamber asserts itself. For example, after the Republican takeover of Congress in the 1994 elections, national attention fixed on the successful efforts of House Republicans to pass the Contract with America. Ultimately, however, only 10 of 21 specific proposals passed by the House were adopted by Congress, a pointed reminder that the Congress is genuinely bicameral.

Each chamber of Congress divides itself into specialized committees that do the legislative work and oversee the executive branch. The committees, in turn, divide themselves into even more specialized subcommittees. And in each chamber, Democrats and Republicans select party leaders who coordinate the work of the committees and the operation of the legislative process in general. We discuss the committee system and the party leadership at length a little later in the chapter.

The legislative branch also includes tens of thousands of people in addition to the 535 members of the House and Senate. The members have personal staffs that total more than 7,000 in the House and 4,000 in the Senate, and each chamber hires thousands of staff members to support the committees. Many of these staffers are clerical workers, and others are policy experts who play an important role in the shaping of legislation, especially long-time staff who speak for important members. Additional staff employees support the party leaders who coordinate the flow of bills through the legislative process. All in all, about 17,000 people are employed as congressional staff.

In addition to staff employed by members and committees, thousands of others work in various support agencies of Congress. The Library of Congress employs nearly 5,000 as does the General Accounting Office (GAO), the watchdog agency of Congress that oversees the operation of the executive branch. A smaller number of people work for the Congressional Budget Office (CBO). This agency provides Congress with expert economic projections and budgetary information. In total, the legislative branch of government consists of some 30,000 people. Table 12.2 provides a summary listing.

**The Jefferson Room**
The Jefferson Room of the Library of Congress serves the needs of many of the staffers and bureaucrats that work for Congress. *What do 30,000 staffers and researchers do for the members of Congress?*

**Table 12.2**

**The Legislative Branch**
Members of Congress are only a fraction of the legislative branch.

**House**

| | |
|---|---|
| Committee staff | 1267 |
| Personal staff | 7216 |
| Leadership staff | 179 |
| Officers of the House staff | 974 |

**Senate**

| | |
|---|---|
| Committee staff | 910 |
| Personal staff | 4272 |
| Leadership staff | 219 |
| Officers of the Senate staff | 990 |

| | |
|---|---|
| **Joint Committee Staffs** | **104** |

**Support Agencies**

| | |
|---|---|
| General Accounting Office | 3275 |
| Congressional Research Service | 747 |
| Congressional Budget Office | 232 |

**Miscellaneous**

| | |
|---|---|
| Architect | 2012 |
| Capitol police | 1251 |

SOURCE: Norman Ornstein, Thomas Mann, and Michael Malbin, *Vital Statistics on Congress, 1999–2000* (Washington, DC: Congressional Quarterly, 2000), pp. 129–130.

## The Organization of Congress: Parties and Committees

The House and Senate are not undifferentiated collections of people who sit in their seats all day debating and voting as the urge strikes them. Like other large decision-making bodies, the two chambers have evolved an extensive division of labor—the committee system—as well as a means of organizing large numbers of people to make decisions—the party leadership structure. The Constitution says nothing about either: Elected officials have developed parties and committees to meet their needs.[3] Both are more important in the House than in the Senate. The House is much larger, so it needs more internal organization to facilitate its work. The House operates in a more hierarchical, more follow-the-rules fashion than the Senate, which, being much smaller, can operate more by way of informal coordination and negotiation.[4]

### The Congressional Parties

Although parties do not dominate Congress to nearly the extent to which they dominate the parliaments of other democracies, they are still the principal organizing force in the Congress. (See the accompanying International Comparison.)

**Speaker of the House** The Constitution stipulates that the House shall elect a Speaker. Though technically a constitutional officer, in practice the **Speaker** is always the leader of the majority party in the House and is usually elected on a straight party-line vote. Despite being a partisan leader, the Speaker ordinarily does not vote on legislation. Only on close contests involving matters vital to the party does the Speaker

comparative
**Comparing Legislatures**

Speaker
The presiding officer of the House of Representatives; normally, the Speaker is the leader of the majority party.

## Presidential Versus Parliamentary Systems of Government

The United States is one of the distinct minority of world democracies that have a presidential form of government—a government in which the chief executive is elected directly by the people rather than chosen by the legislature. Most world democracies are parliamentary in form—the parliament chooses the chief executive from among its members. (A few countries, such as France, have hybrid systems.)

Legislatures are stronger and more independent in presidential systems. In parliamentary systems, legislatures tend to be arenas that choose the executive and then do little more than rubber-stamp the executive's program. Indeed, in parliamentary systems, legislatures generally are not called legislatures, because they do little legislating; instead they are called parliaments, because they do a lot of talking. To highlight the difference between the two systems, consider the case of the China Trade Bill passed by the house in May of 2000.

Although the China Trade Bill was strongly supported by President Clinton and Vice-President Gore, the opposition was led by the Democratic Whip, David Bonior of Michigan, *the number 2 person in the Democratic congressional leadership*. The number 1 person, Minority Leader Dick Gephardt of Missouri, also opposed the legislation, although he did not actively try to persuade fellow Democrats to oppose it. Few American commentators found this situation disturbing or even noteworthy.[a] Bonior represents a Michigan rust-belt district in which unions are strong. He has consistently opposed trade agreements frowned on by organized labor. And Gephardt's opposition was perfectly in keeping with the positions of unions and other Democratic constituencies, such as human rights groups and environmentalists.

In sharp contrast, in, say, Britain, the world's oldest parliamentary democracy, Bonior's and Gephardt's actions would have been unthinkable. Once the prime minister and cabinet decide on an important party policy, they expect virtually unanimous support from the party rank and file in Parliament. High-ranking members such as Bonior and Gephardt who opposed the policy would have been expected to resign their party positions or, failing that, would have been removed. And rather than attempt to buy off opponents, as Clinton did, the executive would have threatened to punish them.

One important reason why the executive can impose such discipline is that in most parliamentary systems, elections do not occur at fixed time intervals as they do in the United States. Rather, the government chooses when to call elections, subject to some constitutional provision that they must occur at least once within some interval of time. Thus a prime minister could declare a vote on a proposal like the China Trade Bill a "vote of confidence," meaning that if it fails to pass, he or she will dissolve Parliament and call a new parliamentary election. (Alternatively, when the government suffers a serious defeat, the opposition may offer a "vote of no confidence." If it passes, a new election is held.)

Although a serious defeat for the U.S. president can cripple his presidency, there is no way to replace him or elect a new Congress before the next scheduled election. Citizens of other democracies consider this a strange feature of American democracy, and most view it as a defect.

*What about you?*
- *Do you think that members of Congress, rather than voters, should choose the president?*
- *Do you think that members of the party leadership in Congress should show complete loyalty to a president of their party?*
- *Do you think the president should have the constitutional power to order new elections if Congress doesn't do what he or she wants?*
- *Is a parliamentary form of government generally more efficient but less responsive than a presidential form?*

[a]"Key Democrat Ready to Oppose China Trade Bill," *San Francisco Chronicle*, April 18, 2000, A3.

---

**timeline**

**The Speaker of the House**

vote. In 1995, for example, even with the Republicans in control of the House for the first time in 40 years, a new, aggressive Speaker (Newt Gingrich) participated in only 58 of 845 recorded votes.[5]

Until the late nineteenth century, the Speaker was the only formal party leader in the House. Indeed, from the end of Reconstruction to the turn of the century, the Speaker often rivaled the president as the most powerful public official in the United States (see the accompanying Window on the Past). Many scholars refer to this period of congressional history as a period of "party government." Powerful Speakers awarded the chairmanships of important committees to their close allies, made all committee assignments, and punished disloyal members by removing them from committees on which they had previously served.[6] Moreover, as the presiding officer of the House and chairman of the Rules Committee, which determines legislative procedure, the Speaker controlled the floor. Speakers ruled. Then came the revolt.

In 1910 a coalition of Democrats and unhappy Republicans removed Republican Speaker "Boss" Cannon from the Rules Committee, expanded the committee, and gave the House as a whole the power to elect the members.[7] A year later, after the Democrats captured the House, they stripped the Speaker of the power to make committee assignments and vested that power in the House as a whole (although, practically speaking, in the majority party). The office of Speaker never regained the powers removed at this time. In the months immediately following the 1994 elections,

## Window on the Past

### When Speakers Ruled the House

During the latter part of the nineteenth century, the House of Representatives was arguably the most powerful of the three branches of government. Presidents of the period were undistinguished, and the public image of the Senate was poor, partly because of its unrepresentative partisan balance and partly because of its unrepresentative membership, which included numerous party bosses and millionaire industrialists.

In this unusual context, a series of strong Speakers organized their party members into energetic, cohesive, lawmaking majorities.[a] First was James G. Blaine (R-ME), who from 1869 to 1875 raised party loyalty to a moral principle and ruthlessly manipulated committee assignments to maintain discipline and to pass the legislation he wanted. Republicans had no monopoly on strong leadership, however. In the 1880s, Speaker John Carlisle (D-KY) claimed for the Speaker absolute discretion in the power to recognize members to make speeches or offer amendments. The authority of the Speaker to control floor proceedings is one of the few powers that has persisted almost unchanged to the present.

Thomas "Czar" Reed (R-ME) is considered by many to be the greatest Speaker ever. In the 1890s he raised the power of the House majority to new heights. Soon after taking office, Reed destroyed the ability of the minority to obstruct House action. According to the Constitution, in order to pass legislation, a *quorum* of the House—one-half plus one—must be present. In Reed's time, members of the minority would offer some trivial motion and then refuse to vote, thus appearing to be absent. (This was known as the "disappearing quorum.") Because some members of the majority party were invariably absent as well, the House could not proceed as a result of the apparent lack of a quorum. First, Reed announced that he would no longer entertain "dilatory motions"— motions intended only to obstruct action. Then he instructed the clerk of the House to record Democrats in the chamber who didn't vote as "present," thus counting them toward the number needed for a quorum. An uproar ensued. Democrats reacted by rushing from the chamber so that they were physically absent. Reed countered by ordering the sergeant at

arms to lock the doors! Eventually, the Democrats gave in, and when they returned to majority status, Speaker Charles Crisp (D-GA) took full advantage of "Reed's rules."

Reed also made the Rules Committee a powerful tool of the Speaker. With Reed himself as chair, the three majority members would arrange floor procedures that paved the way for their legislative program. Then Reed reportedly would announce to the two minority members, "Gentlemen, we have decided to perpetrate the following outrage."

Joseph "Boss" Cannon was the last of the great Speakers. Pushing the envelope of all the powers he had inherited, Cannon dominated the House in the first decade of the twentieth century. But times were changing. The Republican party was split between regular and progressive wings, and maintaining party discipline led Cannon to an increasingly punitive use of his powers.[b] Dissident Republicans who chafed under the iron rule of the majority eventually joined with Democrats in a revolt that stripped the Speaker of his most important powers.[c] In 1910 to 1911, the Speaker lost the power to make committee assignments and was removed from the Rules Committee. Procedural reforms also guaranteed ordinary members some right to have their proposals considered. The era of the strong Speakers was over.

When Newt Gingrich moved boldly in the weeks following the 1994 elections, elevating some members with lower seniority to committee chairmanships over members with higher seniority, some commentators likened his behavior to that of Reed and Cannon. But such comparisons ceased as the power of individual members today soon circumscribed what Gingrich and the leadership could do.

[a] For colorful accounts of these congressional leaders, see Neil McNeil, *Forge of Democracy* (New York: McKay, 1963).

[b] Nelson Polsby, Miriam Gallagher, and Barry Rundquist, "The Growth of the Seniority System in the U.S. House of Representatives," *American Political Science Review* 63 (1969): 787–807.

[c] Charles Jones, "Joseph G. Cannon and Howard W. Smith: An Essay on the Limits of Leadership in the House of Representatives," *Journal of Politics* 30 (1968): 617–646.

Joseph "Boss" Cannon

Newt Gingrich

Speaker Gingrich moved boldly and decisively, in a manner reminiscent of late-nineteenth-century Speakers. But the appearance was deceptive. The new Republican majority allowed Gingrich to exercise more authority than he formally possessed. As the session wore on, Gingrich's ability to rule the House diminished.[8] In the next Congress his difficulties increased, and when the Republicans unexpectedly lost seats in the 1998 elections, Gingrich took the fall. He resigned under pressure less than four years after some had proclaimed a "brave Newt world."

**majority leader**

The Speaker's chief lieutenant in the House and the most important officer in the Senate. He or she is responsible for managing the floor.

**minority leader**

Leader of the minority party, who speaks for the party in dealing with the majority.

**Party Leadership: House**  Next in line to the Speaker, who presides, is the **majority leader,** who leads the majority party on the floor. Majority leaders are elected by the members of the majority party. They are responsible for the day-to-day leadership of the party: scheduling legislation; coordinating committee activity; negotiating with the president, the Senate, and the minority; and otherwise working to build and maintain the coalitions required to pass legislation. Unlike the Speaker, the majority leader votes on legislation. The minority counterpart of the majority leader is the **minority leader,** the floor leader of the minority party. Although we generally think of the floor leaders as principally occupied with all the work needed to build coalitions to pass or obstruct legislation, Barbara Sinclair stresses that another important job of the leaders is simply to maintain "peace in the family." Different points of view flourish within parties, and it falls to the leadership to prevent minor spats and quarrels from developing into destructive feuds.[9]

**whips**

Members of Congress who serve as informational channels between the leadership and the rank and file, conveying the leadership's views and intentions to the members, and vice versa.

The majority and minority leaders are assisted by **whips,** whose job is to link the leadership to the party rank and file. The whip communicates leadership positions and strategies, counts votes, and carries rank-and-file views back to the Speaker and the majority and minority leaders. The whip offices are rather large, with deputy, assistant, regional, and zone whips (upwards of 25 in the Democratic party, about 20 in the Republican party). Their title conjures up an image of party leaders "whipping" their members into line (the title derives from "whippers-in" of the hounds in a fox hunt), but in practice the whips engage in communication and cajolery far more than in coercion.

Many party members participate in the leadership via the whip organizations. Others participate via membership in party committees such as the Democratic Steering and Policy Committee, the Republican Policy Committee, and the Republican Steering Committee. These party committees provide a forum for discussion of the issues and development of a party program, and occasionally they endorse legislation. When the Democrats are in the majority, the Speaker chairs the Democratic Steering Committee and appoints many of its members. Given that this committee appoints the members of the standing committees, this gives the Speaker an important lever for influencing the behavior of members in their committees. In contrast, the Republicans elect a chair of their Policy Committee and also a chair of their Steering Committee, which makes their committee assignments.

**caucus**

All Democratic members of the House or Senate. Members in caucus elect the party leaders, ratify the choice of committee leaders, and debate party positions on issues.

**conference**

What Republicans call their caucus.

**president pro tempore**

President of the Senate, who presides in the absence of the vice-president.

Finally, the members of both parties belong to their party **caucus** (the Republicans call theirs the **conference**). These meetings of the full party membership elect the party leadership and approve the slates of committees nominated by the Steering Committees. Sometimes they debate policies and attempt to develop party positions on policies. In Woodrow Wilson's time, they even adopted resolutions requiring party members to support particular policy proposals. This power is rarely used today.

**Party Leadership: Senate**  With two members from each state—an even number—some tie-breaking mechanism is necessary, and the Constitution obliges by making the vice-president the president of the Senate and giving him a tie-breaking vote *when necessary.* The Constitution also provides for a **president pro tempore,** who presides in the absence of the vice-president, which is nearly all the time. This office is mainly honorific, without real power. Ordinarily it goes to the most senior member of the majority party.

The Senate too has majority and minority leaders and whips, but Senate leaders today are not so strong as those in the House. Indeed, one of the main jobs of the leaders is to hammer out **unanimous-consent agreements.** So called because they are agreed to by all senators with any interest in a proposal, these agreements specify the terms of debate—the amendments that will be in order, how long they will be debated, when votes will be taken, and so forth.[10] Such agreements are necessary because (unbelievable as it may sound) a single member can hold up consideration of a bill or resolution. The reason is the Senate's tradition of unlimited debate: the **filibuster.** According to present rules, debate cannot be ended unless a **cloture** motion is adopted, and that requires the support of 60 senators. The existence of the filibuster means that a simple majority of senators is not a winning coalition. A minority of 41 can prevent the Senate from acting on a measure. Together with malapportionment (because states differ so much in population), the filibuster gives an advantage to minority points of view. The Senate is less of a majoritarian institution than the House.

Table 12.3 recaps the congressional party leadership, listing the top positions and the members who occupied them in the 106th Congress (1999–2000).

**Ups and Downs of the Congressional Parties**   Although the party leadership today is not so strong as it was in the period before the revolt against "Boss" Cannon, it is

**unanimous-consent agreement**
Agreement that sets forth the terms and conditions according to which the Senate will consider a bill; these are individually negotiated by the leadership for each bill.

**filibuster**
Delaying tactic by which one or more senators refuse to allow a bill or resolution to be considered, either by speaking indefinitely or by offering dilatory motions and amendments.

**cloture**
Motion to end debate; requires 60 votes to pass.

## Table 12.3

**Party Organization and Leaders of the 106th Congress**

| Leadership Position | Occupant |
|---|---|
| **House Republicans** | |
| Speaker | J. Dennis Hastert, R-IL |
| Majority leader | Dick Armey, R-TX |
| Majority whip | Tom DeLay, R-TX |
| Conference chairman | J.C. Watts, R-OK |
| Conference vice-chairman | Tillie Fowler, R-FL |
| Conference secretary | Deborah Pryce, R-OH |
| **House Democrats** | |
| Minority leader | Richard A. Gephardt, D-MO |
| Minority whip | David E. Bonior, D-MI |
| Caucus chairman | Martin Frost, D-TX |
| Caucus vice-chairman | Robert Menendez, D-NJ |
| **Senate Republicans** | |
| Majority leader | Trent Lott, R-MS |
| Assistant majority leader | Don Nickles, R-OK |
| Conference chairman | Connie Mack, R-FL |
| Conference secretary | Paul Coverdell, R-GA |
| Chief deputy whip | Judd Gregg, R-NH |
| **Senate Democrats** | |
| Minority leader and conference chairman | Tom Daschle, D-SD |
| Minority whip | Harry Reid, D-NV |
| Conference secretary | Barbara Mikulski, D-MD |
| Chief deputy whip | John B. Breaux, D-LA |
| Assistant floor leader | Dick Durbin, D-IL |

SOURCE: Updated lists for the 108th Congress are available at the respective Web sites, **www.house.gov** and **www.senate.gov.**

**Figure 12.1**

**The Congressional Parties Are More Unified Today Than a Generation Ago**
The graph shows the percentage of all recorded votes on which a majority of voting Democrats opposed a majority of voting Republicans. Numbers for each year have been averaged over each Congress.

SOURCE: Norman Ornstein, Thomas Mann, and Michael Malbin, *Vital Statistics on Congress, 1999–2000* (Washington, DC: Congressional Quarterly, 2000), p. 201.

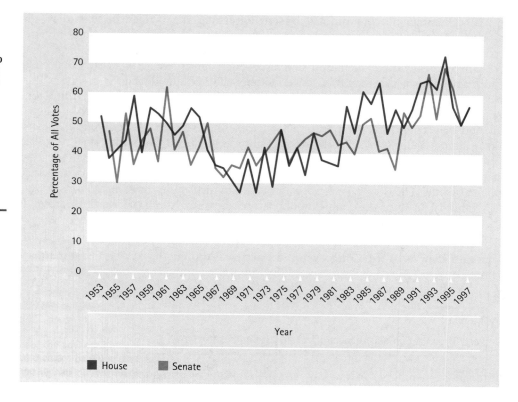

stronger than it was for half a century after the revolt. From the 1920s to the 1970s, Speakers were far weaker and less active than in the preceding half-century. Scholars refer to this mid-century period of weak party leadership as the era of "committee government," an allusion to the fact that committees operated much as they pleased with little constraint from the party leadership.[11] Beginning in the mid-1970s however, a series of reforms and political developments strengthened the Speakership in particular and the party leadership in general.

In 1975 the Democratic caucus, including a large number of new members (the "class of '74"), deposed three standing committee chairmen, two of them because their arrogant and arbitrary styles were found unacceptable. For example, when the freshmen invited the chair of the Armed Forces Committee, F. Edward Hebert (D-LA), to speak to them, he patronized them, reportedly addressing them as "boys and girls."[12] His arrogance cost him his position.

Shortly thereafter, the power to make Democratic committee assignments was transferred to a Steering Committee in which the leadership was highly influential. Moreover, the Speaker was given the power to appoint the Democratic members of the Rules Committee, making it virtually part of his office. Figure 12.1 shows how, paralleling these institutional changes, party unity in roll call voting recovered from the low levels to which it had sunk in the 1960s.

When the Republicans took control of Congress in 1994, partisanship surged. They had chafed under Democratic control for decades, and now the time for payback was at hand. Democrats personally disliked Speaker Gingrich and bitterly opposed his program. Republicans, in turn, united in support of the leader who had brought them majority status. The congressional parties looked stronger in the mid-1990s than they had looked at any time since the late nineteenth century.

Why does party power rise and fall? One reason uncovered by recent scholarship emphasizes the homogeneity of the parties. When parties are relatively homogeneous, members are willing to give more power to party leaders because they have little fear that the leaders will act in ways that endanger their reelection prospects. That is, if all party members agree about some issue, anyone can decide for all. But when the parties are heterogeneous, members are reluctant to give power to party leaders who may act in ways opposed by many of the rank and file—and that are electorally dangerous to them.[13]

Thus political scientist David Brady argues that the strong congressional parties of the late nineteenth century reflected the homogeneity of their constituencies.[14] The two parties represented different kinds of interests, and neither had many members who represented the kinds of interests represented by the other party. Only when the Republican party split into progressive and regular wings did the movement to weaken the Speakership gain momentum. Conversely, the weak parties of the mid-twentieth century reflected the internal divisions of the parties, especially of the majority Democrats. After labor and liberal groups gained control of the presidential wing of the Democratic party during the New Deal, and especially after civil rights split the party in the 1960s, southern Democrats became unwilling to accept party leadership that would reflect the view of the northern majority. After the split over Vietnam and the emergence of these social issues, the cohesiveness of the party and the willingness of the southerners to accept northern leadership hit bottom.[15]

What changed that situation was largely what had caused it: the civil rights revolution and, especially, the 1965 Voting Rights Act guaranteeing everyone—particularly southern African Americans—the right to vote. As the electoral influence of southern African Americans increased, some southern Democrats moderated their views to accommodate newly enfranchised black constituents. Consequently, southern Democrats in the 1990s are not so different from northern Democrats as were southern Democrats in the 1960s. Moreover, some white southern voters reacted to black empowerment (and to the social issues) by voting Republican and replacing Democratic members of Congress with Republicans. Consequently, the Democratic House contingent from southern and border states is only half as large today as it was in the 1960s. The upshot of these changes is that both congressional parties are more homogeneous now than a generation ago and consequently are more willing to support strong leaders committed to particular national policies.[16] Especially in the House, the Democrats are now a liberal, urban party, whereas the Republicans are a conservative, suburban and rural party.

But why would members be willing to tolerate *any* party constraints at all? After all, members are elected by the citizens of states and districts far from Washington, where the congressional leadership has no influence. Nor does the local party have much influence. Forty years ago, Speaker Sam Rayburn could phone a local party boss like Chicago's Mayor Daley and request his help in getting the Chicago House delegation to support Rayburn. Daley had the power—control of nominations, workers, and money—to deliver the votes. But in few areas today does the local party organization have much influence over the member of Congress. Why would members tolerate party institutions that constrain them in any way?

Part of the answer is that although the electoral fates of members of Congress are largely dependent on their personal efforts, they are not completely so. An effective congressional party contributes to members' electoral prospects in two ways. First, although presidential coattails have weakened, they still exist, and a successful president provides coattails that can help members running for reelection. Conversely, as the Democrats found to their sorrow in 1994, an unsuccessful president can hurt the party, especially in the mid-term elections. Thus members of the president's party have an incentive to work together to help him succeed, and members of the opposing party have an incentive to work together to make him fail. Second, an effective congressional party also helps members among those voters who know nothing about their representative and vote instead on the basis of impersonal factors, including party images. An ineffective congressional party contributes to the impression that the party is incompetent, and in so doing, it costs all party members votes.

Members of Congress, then, are willing to tolerate party constraints partly because such constraints contribute indirectly to their electoral success. Just as most people believe they are better off obeying traffic signals that add a few minutes to their travel time, so members of Congress feel it is wise to give the parties some authority over them in exchange for general support provided by the party or the president.

Another source of party influence has grown in importance in recent years: The Congressional parties are increasingly active in campaign funding. The House and Senate campaign committees are controlled by the leadership, and most members of the leadership have established their own PACs.[17] Members who have received campaign contributions from party leaders naturally feel some obligation to support party leaders when such support does not threaten their own electoral prospects.

Finally, electorally independent members willingly accept some party discipline because they see it as necessary to attain other goals. For some, reelection is an end in itself, but most wish to accomplish something while in office and view party organization as necessary to accomplish anything in a body as unwieldy as Congress. Members are willing to accept some restrictions on their individual freedom of action in return for getting legislation passed.

## The Committee System

Congress does its work through its committees. Members introduce thousands of bills and resolutions every year. Nearly all are referred to committees for consideration, and most never emerge. Since 1980, for example, 6,000 to 8,000 bills have been introduced in each two-year session of the House of Representatives, but only 10 to 15 percent eventually passed. A few unsuccessful proposals died on the floor, but most of the 85 to 90 percent that failed never made it out of committee. Floor majorities can discharge a proposal from a recalcitrant committee via a rarely used **discharge petition,** which requires 218 signatures, but in most cases, favorable action by a committee is necessary for a proposal to become law.

**Standing committees** have fixed memberships and jurisdictions, and they persist from one Congress to another. The Appropriations, Commerce, and Foreign Relations Committees are examples. **Select committees,** by contrast, are temporary committees created to deal with specific issues. Both houses of Congress had standing committee systems in place by 1825.[18] The number of committees tends to expand until at some point the system is reorganized when majorities come to believe it has grown unwieldy and out of alignment with contemporary problems. The Legislative Reorganization Act of 1946 gave the committee system the shape it largely retains today, more than half a century later. In the 106th Congress (1999–2000) there were 19 standing committees in the House and 17 in the Senate; see Table 12.4. These "full" committees are subdivided into more than 150 subcommittees. There also are 4 "joint" committees with membership from both houses, and a small number of select committees.

**House Committees** House committees fall into three levels of importance. Both parties agree that the Rules, Appropriations, and Ways and Means Committees are highest in importance. The Rules Committee is the right arm of the Speaker. By granting or withholding rules, it controls the flow of legislation to the floor and the conditions of debate. The other two committees deal with spending and taxing, broad powers that enable them to affect nearly everything government does. A member who serves on such a committee is ordinarily allowed no other assignment, except that he or she is eligible to serve on the Budget Committee. Committees at the second level of importance deal with nationally significant policy areas: agriculture, armed services, energy, and so forth. A member ordinarily serves on only one such major policy committee and on a third-level committee of lesser importance. These less important committees include "housekeeping" committees, such as Government Reform and Oversight, and committees with narrow policy jurisdictions, such as Veterans' Affairs. The Budget Committee has a special status. Members can serve for only four years in any ten-year period, and its membership is drawn from other committees and from the leadership.

**Senate Committees** The Senate committee system is simpler than that of the House; it has just major and minor committees. Like their House equivalents, Appropriations

## Table 12.4

### Standing Committees of the 106th Congress

| Committee | Size (Party Ratio) | Number of Subcommittees | Chair | Ranking Member |
|---|---|---|---|---|
| **Senate** | | | | |
| Agriculture | 18 (R10/D8) | 4 | Richard G. Lugar, R-IN | Tom Harkin, D-IA |
| Appropriations | 28 (R15/D13) | 13 | Ted Stevens, R-AK | Robert C. Byrd, D-WV |
| Armed Services | 20 (R11/D9) | 6 | John W. Warner, R-VA | Carl Levin, D-MI |
| Banking, Housing and Urban Affairs | 20 (R11/D9) | 5 | Phil Gramm, R-TX | Paul S. Sarbanes, D-MD |
| Budget | 22 (R12/D10) | | Pete V. Domenici, R-NM | Frank R. Lautenberg, D-NJ |
| Commerce, Science, and Transportation | 20 (R11/D9) | 7 | John McCain, R-AZ | Ernest F. Hollings, D-SC |
| Energy and Natural Resources | 20 (R11/D9) | 4 | Frank H. Murkowski, R-AK | Jeff Bingaman, D-NM |
| Environment and Public Works | 18 (R10/D8) | 4 | Bob Smith, R-NH | Max Baucus, D-MT |
| Finance | 20 (R11/D9) | 5 | William V. Roth Jr., R-DE | Daniel Patrick Moynihan, D-NY |
| Foreign Relations | 18 (R10/D8) | 7 | Jesse Helms, R-NC | Joseph R. Biden, Jr., D-DE |
| Governmental Affairs | 16 (R9/D7) | 3 | Fred Thomspson, R-TN | Joseph I. Lieberman, D-CT |
| Health, Education, Labor, and Pensions | 18 (R10/D8) | 4 | James M. Jeffords, R-VT | Edward M. Kennedy, D-MA |
| Indian Affairs | 14 (R8/D6) | | Ben Nighthorse Campbell, R-CO | Daniel L. Inouye, D-HI |
| Judiciary | 18 (R10/D8) | 7 | Orrin G. Hatch, R-UT | Patrick J. Leahy, D-VT |
| Rules and Administration | 16 (R9/D7) | | Mitch McConnell, R-KY | Christopher J. Dodd, D-CT |
| Small Business | 18 (R10/D8) | | Christopher S. Bond, R-MO | John Kerry, D-MA |
| Veterans' Affairs | 12 (R7/D5) | | Arlen Specter, R-PA | John D. Rockefeller IV, D-WV |
| **House** | | | | |
| Agriculture | 51 (R27/D24) | 4 | Larry Combest, R-TX | Charles W. Stenholm, D-TX |
| Appropriations | 61 (R34/D27) | 13 | C.W. Bill Young, R-FL | David R. Obey, D-WI |
| Armed Services | 60 (R32/D28) | 7 | Floyd D. Spence, R-SC | Ike Skelton, D-MO |
| Banking and Financial Services | 60 (R32/D27/I1) | 5 | Jim Leach, R-IA | John J. LaFalce, D-NY |
| Budget | 43 (R24/D19) | | John R. Kasich, R-OH | John M. Spratt, Jr., D-SC |
| Commerce | 53 (R29/D24) | 5 | Thomas J. Bliley Jr., R-VA | John D. Dingell, D-MI |
| Education and Workforce | 49 (R27/D22) | 5 | Bill Goodling, R-PA | William L. Clay, D-MO |
| Government Reform | 44 (R24/D19/I1) | 8 | Dan Burton, R-IN | Henry A. Waxman, D-CA |
| House Administration | 9 (R6/D3) | | Bill Thomas, R-CA | Steny H. Hoyer, D-MD |
| International Relations | 49 (R26/D23) | 5 | Benjamin A. Gilman, R-NY | San Gejdenson, D-CT |
| Judiciary | 37 (R21/D16) | 5 | Henry J. Hyde, R-IL | John Conyers, Jr., D-MI |
| Resources | 52 (R28/D24) | 5 | Don Young, R-AK | George Miller, D-CA |
| Rules | 13 (R9/D4) | 2 | David Dreier, R-CA | Joe Moakley, D-MA |
| Science | 47 (R25/D22) | 4 | F. James Sensenbrenner Jr., R-WI | George E. Brown, Jr., D-CA |
| Select Intelligence | 16 (R9/D7) | 2 | Porter J. Goss, R-FL | Julian C. Dixon, D-CA |
| Small Business | 36 (R19/D17) | 5 | James M. Talent, R-MO | Nydia M. Velazquez, D-NY |
| Standards of Official Conduct | 10 (R5/D5) | | Lamar Smith, R-TX | Howard L. Berman, D-CA |
| Transportation and Infrastructure | 75 (R41/D34) | 6 | Bud Shuster, R-PA | James L. Oberstar, D-MN |
| Veterans' Affairs | 31 (R17/D14) | 3 | Bob Stump, R-AZ | Lane Evans, D-IL |
| Ways and Means | 39 (R23/D16) | 5 | Bill Archer, R-TX | Charles B. Rangel, D-NY |

SOURCE: Updated lists for the 108th Congress are available at the respective Web sites, **www.house.gov** and **www.senate.gov**.

**A Packed House**
Most committee hearings are sparsely attended. But when the House Judiciary Committee considers the impeachment of a president the room is very full.

and Finance are major committees, but the Senate Rules Committee is a minor committee with nothing like the power of its House counterpart (the Senate leadership itself discharges the tasks performed by the House Rules Committee). Budget is also a major committee, as is Foreign Affairs, reflecting the constitutional responsibilities of the chamber in that area (advise and consent to treaties, confirm ambassadors).

Committee power in the Senate is widely distributed: Chairs of major committees cannot chair any other committee or subcommittee, and chairs of minor committees can chair only one other panel. Each senator serves on one minor and two major committees, and every senator gets to serve on one of the four major committees named above. On average, senators sit on more committees than representatives. In part this reflects a simple size difference: The Senate has nearly as many committees as the House but less than one-fourth as many members to staff them. But in addition, senators represent entire states, which are typically more heterogeneous than congressional districts; thus, they cannot afford to focus their attention on one or two subjects, as many representatives can. Having more committee assignments creates conflicting loyalties and makes it difficult to specialize in a few subjects, as many House members do. As a result, senators' legislative lives are not so closely tied to a particular committee as are the lives of representatives.[19]

**How Committees Are Formed**  The committee system is formally under the control of the majority party in the chamber. Each committee has a ratio of majority to minority members at least as favorable to the majority as the overall division of the chamber. The more important committees are stacked in favor of the majority. In the 106th Congress, for example, the Republicans had a 9 to 4 advantage over the Democrats on the House Rules Committee, a ratio far greater than their 223 to 211 edge in the chamber. In contrast, the party ratio on the less important Judiciary Committee was 20 to 15. Party committees nominate members for assignment, and party caucuses approve those assignments, so the potential for party control of committees exists. In practice, however, the committees exercise a considerable degree of independence.

Part of the reason is the use of **seniority** to choose committee chairs. The majority-party member with the longest continuous service on the committee almost invariably chairs the committee. Often called a "norm" because the use of seniority is not an

**seniority**
Practice by which the majority party member with the longest continuous service on a committee becomes the chair.

official rule and is nowhere written down, seniority became the mode of selecting Senate committee chairs in the 1880s and House chairs after the 1910 revolt. The practice of seniority includes the right to continued reappointment to a committee. Thus, once a member is initially appointed to a committee, he or she automatically rises on its seniority ladder. Given sufficient longevity, members eventually become chairs, perhaps decades after their initial appointment. Physically or mentally failing members sometimes are moved aside, and on occasion the caucus rejects a nomination for chair, but the system gives committee chairs in particular, and committee members in general, a degree of independence or autonomy.

After the 1994 elections gave Republicans control of Congress for the first time in 40 years, Speaker Gingrich passed up the most senior committee member when he named the Republican chairs of Appropriations, Commerce, and Judiciary.[20] Whether this represents a one-time deviation from seniority because of an electoral upheaval or the beginning of a long-term move away from seniority is something to watch in the years ahead.

**Committee Reforms**  By the 1950s, party influence in Congress had become so weak that many observers believed the chairs of the standing committees held the real power. A few of them behaved autocratically, creating and abolishing subcommittees and varying their jurisdictions, monopolizing subcommittee chairmanships, controlling committee staff and budgets, and even refusing to call meetings and to consider legislation they opposed. To make matters worse, because members from safe southern seats had built up considerable seniority, many of the chairs were more conservative than the younger, mostly northern Democrats who held more liberal views.[21] Eventually, the rank and file, operating through the party caucuses, curbed the power of the standing committee chairs and injected more democracy into the committee system. Much of this effort took place in the Democratic caucus.[22]

In the early 1970s, a caucus resolution limited House committee chairs to holding one subcommittee chair (previously some committee chairs hoarded subcommittee chairs as well). A "subcommittee bill of rights" guaranteed subcommittees their existence, jurisdictions, budgets, and staff. Moreover, power was distributed by allowing the Democratic members of the committee to choose among available subcommittee chairs in order of their seniority on the committee—subject to a vote of all committee Democrats. The Senate had treated junior members somewhat better since the 1950s, but in recent decades it too moved in the same direction as the House, spreading power more evenly across the membership.

Many contemporary observers were unsure whether the preceding changes were reforms. Did Congress simply decentralize power from approximately 40 standing committees to approximately 300 standing committees and subcommittees, many of them as small as eight or nine members? Had a period of "committee government" given way to a period of even more decentralized "subcommittee government?"[23] For more than a decade, political scientists debated the net impact of the reforms. Today the prevailing view is that the reforms adopted in the late 1970s to strengthen the party leadership more than offset the subcommittee reforms. The committee system appears to have been more subject to party influence in the last decade than a generation ago. An out-of-the-mainstream chair of an important committee or subcommittee would run a greater risk of being overthrown today than at any time since the revolt against Cannon. Moreover, when the Republicans took control in 1995, their leadership acted to restrict the independence of subcommittees.

**Theories of the Committee System**  Why does the standing committee system exist at all? Members of Congress are elected as equals. Why would a majority give to a minority exceptional influence in a policy area—the power to decide whether legislation should be considered at all, the power to shape the legislation if it is considered, and the power to review its implementation? Why not consider everything on the chamber floor (the so-called *Committee of the Whole*), where all members participate on an equal basis?

**log-rolling**
Colloquial term given to politicians' trading of favors, votes, or generalized support for each other's proposals.

**distributive theory**
Theory that sees committees as an expression of a standing log-roll in which members get to serve on the committees most important to them.

**informational theory**
Theory that sees committees as means of providing reliable information about the actual consequences of the legislation that members could adopt.

And if the size of the membership would make that process too unwieldy, why not consider legislation in select committees specifically created for the particular bill or resolution? Why give a minority—sometimes an unrepresentative minority—more or less permanent influence over a policy area? The various answers to these questions are interpretations or theories of the committee system.

The first theory views the committee system as a comprehensive **log-rolling** process in which members implicitly trade votes.[24] According to this interpretation, members choose committees in order to satisfy constituency interests. For example, members from urban districts seek membership on committees that deal with banking, housing, or labor, whereas members from rural districts have little interest in such issues and opt instead for committees that deal with agriculture and resources. Once appointed to committees whose work is relevant to their constituencies, members are in a position to use the process to bestow benefits on those constituencies. Studies have documented how districts and states whose members serve on particular committees receive a disproportionate share of projects and grants from programs in the jurisdictions of those committees.[25] And to cite more anecdotal evidence, Senator Robert Byrd (D-WV) became infamous for using his chairmanship of the Senate Appropriations Committee to lavish federal largesse on West Virginia (see the accompanying Window on the Past). According to this **distributive theory** of the committee system, members join committees that deal with matters important to their constituencies and then use their strategic position to deliver for those constituencies. Members are willing to go along with committees that deal with issues they care little about because they expect others to reciprocate when their own committees deal with issues they do care about.

An alternative interpretation is that committees primarily serve a knowledge function.[26] This **informational theory** stresses that members frequently are uncertain about the outcomes that policies will produce. Hence they wish some members to become experts in each subject area and to reveal their knowledge to the broader membership. One way to do this is to give committees disproportionate influence, subject to the condition that they do their job conscientiously and do not abuse their power. Committee members can utilize their position to gain a bit extra for themselves, but only to the extent that they specialize and give the chamber useful, reliable information.

These two theories are not incompatible. Each describes an important aspect of the committee system. Indisputably, members wish to serve their constituencies and regard committees as important means (though certainly not the *only* means) for doing so. But just as certainly, members often are unsure exactly how they can best serve their constituencies. If they adopt the wrong policy and the results are disastrous, it could come back to haunt them in a future campaign.[27] Thus members need and value information. The distributive theory appears most applicable to the committees responsible for straightforward matters such as handing out money—subsidies, grants, and funding for projects. Here members of Congress will allow interested colleagues to turn public institutions into private preserves, so long as they receive similar privileges in areas of importance to *their* constituencies. In contrast, where policy making involves great uncertainty or large costs and benefits—telecommunications regulation, for example—members will wish to have reliable information and will hold committees to a higher standard.

The distributive theory also seems somewhat less applicable today than in the period of "committee government." When government revenues were rising steadily and congressional party influence was weak, there was little to prevent members from using the committee system for their narrow ends. But with the budget deficits of the 1980s and 1990s, with stronger congressional parties, and with considerable uncertainty surrounding much of the policy agenda (health care, environmental protection, the Internet revolution), committee members are less free to pursue their narrow constituency interests. The incentives still are present, but the opportunities are more limited.

# *Window* on the *Past*

## Senator Robert Byrd, Pork-Meister

Democratic Senator Robert C. Byrd of West Virginia chaired the Senate Appropriations Committee from 1989 until 1994, when the Democrats lost control of the Senate. He had vowed to steer $1 billion homeward after assuming the powerful chairmanship of the Appropriations Committee, and he exceeded his best expectations.

Byrd met his five-year goal in less than three years and afterward continued to deliver almost unprecedented federal largesse to West Virginia. At least $510.8 million in projects and earmarked funds for his rural home state cropped up in fiscal 1992 spending bills moving through the Senate. The money was to come from various agencies and programs and not just the Interior appropriations that Byrd oversaw as a subcommittee chairman. A rundown of the funding for West Virginia in key Senate appropriations bills for 1992 includes:

*Transportation*
$165 million for a corridor G highway improvement project to "demonstrate methods of eliminating traffic congestion and to promote economic benefits" for western West Virginia.
$12.3 million for a highway demonstration construction project for a $185-million FBI complex, which Byrd had earlier won for Clarksburg. The bill also allots $600,000 for a study.
$14 million for an upgraded approach radar system for the Eastern West Virginia Airport in Martinsburg.

*Defense, Military Construction*
$32.9 million to begin moving 21 CIA offices to Harpers Ferry and to Prince William County, VA.
$9.6 million to build a Guard and reserve center at Huntington Air Force Base and $25.1 million to house C-130 cargo airplanes at Martinsburg Air Force Base.
$5.4 million to alter the operations center at the Naval Radio Telescope Observatory in Green Bank.

*Commerce, Justice, State*
$48 million to develop and install in 1995 an automated fingerprint identification system for the new FBI headquarters in Clarksburg.

*Agriculture*
$600,000 for two West Virginia research services to study a replacement for lime fertilizer and to develop sensors to cut the costs of handling fruit.
$750,000 for the Appalachian Export Center for Hardwoods at West Virginia University in Morgantown.
$9 million for the construction of North and South Mill Creek Dam No. 7.
$3.5 million for the Huntington area hit by spring floods.

*Treasury, Postal Service*
$25 million for the construction of a federal building and courthouse in Beckley.

*Energy and Water*
$58 million for corridors G and H.
$26 million for two flood control projects in Mingo County that are part of an ongoing Army Corps of Engineers program in West Virginia and Kentucky.
$2.4 million for Army Corps of Engineers water project studies on several West Virginia and Kentucky sites.
$2 million to build a riverfront park in Charleston.

*Interior*
$4.5 million to Mercer County as the second Forest Service grant for the Hardwoods Training and Flexible Manufacturing Center.
$13.7 million in Bureau of Land Management funds for construction of the Harpers Ferry National Educational Training Center and $2 million to acquire the site.
$2.5 million to restore the current funding level for the Generic Center for Respirable Dust.

*VA, HUD, Independent Agencies*
$22.5 million for the National Technology Center at the Wheeling Jesuit College.
$7.5 million for construction and an educational program at Wheeling Jesuit College using multimedia aids such as simulated space missions and a video library.
$10 million for a validation center for NASA computer software at West Virginia University in Morgantown.
$2.1 million to convert abandoned buildings into a job training center in Elkins, an Alzheimer's clinic and adult day care center in Parkersburg, and a rural health care clinic in McDowell County.

SOURCE: Adapted from "Byrd's Eye View," *Congressional Quarterly Weekly Report*, September 21, 1991, 2682.

SECTION SUMMARY

The Congress is a highly differentiated institution. Each chamber is organized along party lines, but within each chamber the work is divided among expert committees and subcommittees. The party leadership works with the committee leadership to put the pieces together again to pass budgets, tax bills, and other major public policies. Reflecting political conditions in the outside electoral arena, the strength of both parties and committees has varied over time.

## How a Bill Becomes a Law

Congress makes the laws that govern the United States. In addition to the specific legislative powers set out in Article I, the "necessary and proper" clause authorizes Congress "to make all laws which shall be necessary and proper for carrying into execution the foregoing powers, and all other powers vested by this Constitution. . . ." How do the 2 parties in 2 chambers organized into over 250 committees and subcommittees get together and pass laws? Although no flowchart can possibly convey the complexity of getting a major bill through Congress, we will outline the process, describing the stages that important legislation goes through. Figure 12.2 lays out the process in idealized form, but any particular bill or resolution may have a different and even more complicated history.

To start things off, a bill or resolution is introduced by a congressional **sponsor** and one or more cosponsors. The House Speaker or Senate presiding officer, advised by the chamber's parliamentarian (an expert on rules and procedures), refers the proposal to an appropriate committee. In some cases sponsors are not serious but are acting only to please some constituency or interest group. If they *are* serious, they may draft their bill in such a way as to increase its chances of being referred to a friendly committee—often theirs—rather than to a less friendly one. This strategic possibility exists because committee jurisdictions often overlap. In recent years the Speaker of the House has made increasing use of **multiple referrals,** sending the bill simultaneously to more than one committee or dividing it among several committees. Complex legislation and overlapping committee jurisdictions raise the likelihood of multiple referrals.

Once the bill goes to committee, the chair gives it to an appropriate subcommittee. Here the work begins. If the subcommittee takes the bill seriously, the staff will schedule hearings at which witnesses will speak in favor of the bill or in opposition to it. Witnesses can be other members of Congress, members of the executive branch, representatives of groups and associations, or ordinary citizens. Sometimes hearings are genuine attempts to gather information. More often, hearings are carefully choreographed: The subcommittee staff stacks the witness list in favor of the position of the subcommittee chair. As one study observed, "committees neither seek nor receive complete information. Rather, they seek to promote certain views of their issues to bolster their abilities to produce favorable legislation."[28]

After hearings, the subcommittee begins **markup** of the bill—revising it, adding and deleting sections, and preparing it for report to the full committee, assuming that a majority of the subcommittee supports it. The full committee may repeat the process, holding its own hearings and conducting its own markup, or it may largely accept the work of the subcommittee.[29] If a committee majority supports the bill after committee markup, the bill is nearly ready to be reported to the floor—but not quite.

Let's consider first what happens in the House. Bills that are not controversial, because they either are trivial or have extremely narrow impact, can be called up at specified times and passed unanimously with little debate. Many somewhat more important bills are considered under a fast-track procedure called **suspension of the rules.** Upon being recognized, the committee chair moves to consider a bill under suspension. If a two-thirds majority of those voting agrees, the bill will be considered.

**sponsor**
Representative or senator who introduces a bill or resolution.

**multiple referrals**
Said to occur when party leaders give more than one committee responsibility for considering a bill.

**markup**
Process in which a committee or subcommittee considers and revises a bill that has been introduced.

**suspension of the rules**
Fast-track procedure for considering bills and resolutions in the House; debate is limited to 40 minutes, no amendments are in order, and a two-thirds majority is required for passage.

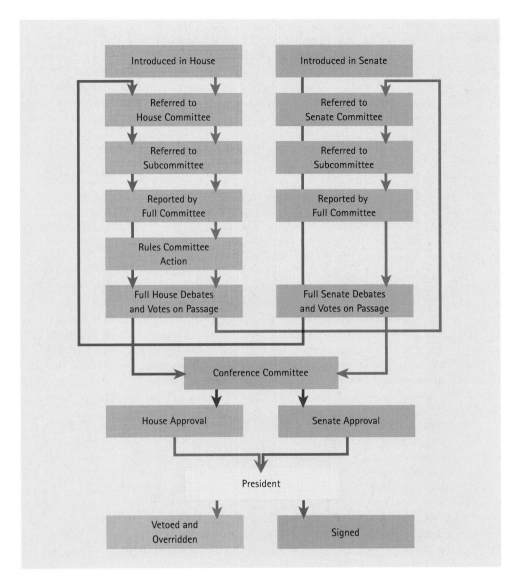

**Figure 12.2**

**How a Bill Becomes a Law**
There's a bit more detail involved than passage by Congress and a presidential signature.

Debate is limited to 40 minutes, no amendments are in order, and a two-thirds majority is required for passage. There is some risk in considering a bill under suspension: Even if a majority supports it, it could fail because the majority is smaller than two-thirds. Indeed, opponents of the bill sometimes support the motion to suspend the rules precisely in order to raise the threshold for passage to two-thirds.

Legislation that is important, and therefore usually controversial, goes to the Rules Committee before going to the floor. The Rules Committee, too, may hold hearings, this time on the type of **rule** it should grant. In these hearings only members of Congress may testify. The rule specifies the terms and conditions of debate. A rule specifies the time that the supporters and opponents will be allowed to speak, and it may prohibit any amendments (a *closed rule*), allow any amendments (an *open rule*), or specify the amendments that are in order (a *restrictive rule*). In recent years three-quarters of all bills that came from the Rules Committee have been granted restrictive rules. Sometimes rules are unusual. For example, so-called *king of the mountain rules* allow a number of (often conflicting) amendments to be offered, but they specify that only the last amendment that receives a majority is adopted. Naturally, the committee orders the amendments so that the one it favors goes last. This kind of rule allows some members to play a little game with constituents and interest groups. The

**rule**
Specifies the terms and conditions under which a bill or resolution will be considered on the floor of the House—in particular, how long debate will last, how time will be allocated, and the number and type of amendments that will be in order.

members can vote for several conflicting amendments, thereby satisfying each of their supporters, all the while knowing that the last vote is the only one that matters.

Assuming that the Rules Committee recommends a rule, the floor then chooses to accept or reject the rule. Rules rarely are rejected, but that does not mean that the floor goes along with anything the Rules Committee proposes. Rather, in shaping the rule, the committee anticipates the limits of what the floor will accept. Sometimes committee members miscalculate and are embarrassed when a floor majority rejects the rule. Most of the time the rule is approved, and the bill is finally under consideration by the full chamber. After debate and voting on amendments, the floor then decides whether to adopt the "perfected" bill.

In the Senate, the process is a bit simpler. For uncontroversial legislation, a motion to pass a bill by unanimous consent is sometimes all that is necessary. More important and controversial legislation will require the committee and party leaders to negotiate unanimous-consent agreements, which are complicated bargains analogous to the rules granted by the House Rules Committee. Assuming that they succeed and thereby avoid a filibuster, the bill eventually comes to a floor vote.

If a majority votes to adopt the bill, are we at the end of the process? Not at all. Before the bill can be sent for the president's signature, it must pass both chambers in identical form. But the bill may have started in one chamber before going to the other, or it may have proceeded simultaneously through both. In either case, it is extremely unlikely that the House and Senate have passed exactly the same bill. In fact, their versions of the legislation may be in serious conflict. Sometimes, with less controversial matters, one house will simply adopt the other's version as is. Sometimes the two chambers may send proposals back and forth (this is called messaging) and iron out the points of difference. But for major legislation, each chamber appoints conferees to participate in a **conference committee.**

One participant-observer likens a bill's making it to conference to a college basketball team's making it to the "Final Four." Only, according to Paul Light, "conferences have very few rules and absolutely no referees. Games almost never start on time, and no one gets called for traveling."[30] In theory, each chamber's conferees are committed to their chamber's version of the legislation, but in practice this is not likely. Conferences for some complex bills involve hundreds of members who support some parts of the bill, oppose other parts, and care little about still other parts. This makes the situation ideal for bargaining. When a majority of each chamber's conferees agree to the final compromise, the bill is reported back to the parent chambers, where another floor vote in each chamber is required for passage.[31]

Now, you may think that we have finally reached the end of the process. The bill will be sent to the president and, barring a presidential veto, will become law. While this is formally true, it does not guarantee that the bill will have any effect. The reason is that we have been describing only the **authorization process.** All government action—paying subsidies, issuing regulations, buying bombers, inspecting workplaces, whatever—must be authorized; there must be statutory authority for the government's activity. That authority is contained in the bills passed by the authorization process. But before the government actually can carry out its activities, money must be appropriated for it to do so.

The Constitution grants Congress the power of the purse and makes the House the lead actor: All tax bills must originate in the House, and by custom and tradition, all appropriations bills do too. The **appropriations process** parallels the authorization process. Thirteen appropriations subcommittees in each chamber hold hearings and mark up the bill (the subcommittee chairs are commonly referred to as "the Cardinals of Capitol Hill").[32] The full committees may also do so, but they usually defer to their subcommittees. In the House, appropriations bills are *privileged;* they take precedence over other legislation, and a motion to take up an appropriations bill can be offered at any time. But in practice, appropriations bills, too, usually pass through the Rules Committee. Thus appropriations subcommittees in both chambers must report bills,

**conference committee**
Group of representatives from both the House and the Senate who iron out the differences between the two chambers' versions of a bill or resolution.

**authorization process**
Term given to the entire process of providing statutory authority for a government program or activity.

**appropriations process**
Process of providing funding for governmental activities and programs that have been authorized.

**simulation**

**You are a Member of Congress**

the rank and file in both chambers must pass them, and a conference committee must agree on every dollar before the government actually has any money to spend.

## Section Summary

Before Americans feel the impact of a new government policy, that policy must run the legislative gauntlet four times (an authorization process in both House and Senate and an appropriations process in both House and Senate). To succeed, it must win the approval of party leaders and committee leaders at each stage, and it must win majorities of voting members a dozen times (three times—subcommittee, committee, floor—in each of the four stages). In addition, the two chambers must agree on the results of the authorization and appropriations processes, and the president must accept their agreements. Small wonder that of approximately 12,000 bills introduced in each recent Congress, only about 600 ultimately became law, and even fewer were funded at the level their proponents believed was necessary.

# Evaluating Congress

It is easy to get so wrapped up in the detail of Congress and its operations that we lose sight of the reason for our interest in the institution. The reason, of course, is that Congress is the first branch, arguably the most powerful and most important of our three branches of government. It is the branch that bears primary responsibility for representing the needs and values of the American public and for developing legislation to improve their well-being. How well does Congress meet its responsibilities?

## Criticisms of Congress

The most common criticism of the congressional process should be obvious: *It is lengthy and inefficient.* Legislation may take months or even years to wend its way through the process, and there is much duplication of effort—both within and between the chambers. Moreover, after all is said and done, Congress often produces a compromise that leaves no one satisfied. To those who want quick, decisive action, Congress-watching is enough to put their teeth on edge. Of course, that is what the framers intended. They wished to ensure that laws would pass only after they had been thoroughly considered and majorities were convinced that they were needed.

But that raises a second criticism: *The congressional process works to the advantage of policy minorities, especially those content with the status quo.* Proponents of legislation must build many winning coalitions—in subcommittee, full committee, appropriations committee, and conference committee, and on the floor, in both chambers. Opponents have it much easier. A minority that controls only a single stage of the process may be able to frustrate the majority. Of course, a determined majority cannot be stopped indefinitely, except by a Senate filibuster, but it can be held at bay for a long time. Moreover, potential majorities sometimes decide not to act, calculating that the costs of overcoming all the obstacles are not worth the effort. Because changing the status quo requires positive action, the congressional process handicaps majorities who support change and helps minorities who are content to block change. In a word, the congressional process is *conservative* with a small *c*.

Two other criticisms focus on what Congress does when it acts, rather than on its failure to act. Given that members are trying to please constituencies, *they constantly are tempted to use their positions to extract constituency benefits*, even when important national legislation is at stake (see the accompanying Democratic Dilemma). President Jimmy Carter got so upset trying to deal with Congress on national energy policy that he wrote in his diary, "Congress is disgusting on this particular subject."[33] President Clinton's lobbying on behalf of the North American Free Trade Agreement (NAFTA) was likened to an "oriental bazaar." Members not only demanded special treatment for constituency interests but even traded votes for concessions on unrelated issues. Besides its appearing unseemly (unless *you* are part of the constituency getting the concession), many observers charge that Congress defeats, distorts, and otherwise damages national interests in pursuit of its members' parochial interests. Of course, others point out that such trading of favors may simply be the price of passing any general national legislation.[34] As long as the president and congressional leadership do not "give away the store," taking a "cut" for one's constituents is a standard feature of legislative politics.

Finally, the nature of the congressional process is such that *sometimes the very process of passing legislation ensures that it will not work*. This is especially true of proposals that target resources on small portions of the population. For example, in the aid-to-the-cities effort described in the introduction to this chapter, the process of getting the legislation through Congress spread the available resources across small cities and rural areas, leaving too little to make much difference to the major cities, even if it had been enacted.[35]

**distributive tendency**
Tendency of Congress to spread the benefits of any program widely and thinly across the districts of the members.

Examples like these illustrate the charge that Congress regularly shows a **distributive tendency.** Every member wants a "fair share" of the federal pie for his or her district, and by *fair,* the legislators mean "as much as possible." Even if the district or state is relatively affluent or does not have the problem a program addresses, its representatives and senators are reluctant to pass up an opportunity to deliver local benefits. Taken to extremes, this tendency can be almost comical. Consider, for example, the Economic Development Administration created in the 1960s to subsidize the construction of infrastructure—roads, utilities, industrial parks, and so forth—in depressed areas. By the time the program was killed by the Reagan administration, it had been repeatedly expanded by Congress to the point where more than 80 percent of all the counties in the United States were officially classified as "economically depressed" to make them eligible for federal subsidies.[36]

The distributive tendency reflects the difficulty Congress has with redistribution. All too often, federal programs are not targeted for the most needy areas or focused on people for whom they would do the most good. Instead, members want a piece of the action whether their districts really need it or not. Federal programs distribute money on the basis of complex formulas that include population, economic conditions, and characteristics of the people and area. These formulas are of great importance to members of Congress. Indeed, members' staffs use state-of-the-art spreadsheets to show

**All Politics Is Local?**
Like many members of Congress, former Speaker Tip O'Neill saw government programs through the eyes of his constituents.

## *Democratic Dilemma*

## Delegates or Trustees?

The SMSP system not only makes voters outside a representative's district irrelevant to his or her chances of reelection, it also encourages a philosophy of representation that holds that it is representatives' responsibility to work first and foremost for the people in their districts. Thus, most members of Congress, much of the time, in genuine good conscience, will work to advance the interests of their districts even at the expense of the districts of other members.[a]

The debate over *whom* a representative should represent—the constituency or the whole country—goes back centuries in political philosophy. It is often intertwined with another debate about *how* the representative should act.[b] Edmund Burke posed the question most sharply in a classic speech in 1774.[c] Is it the representative's duty to act as a **delegate** of the constituency, who follows the wishes of those who have elected him or her, or as a **trustee**, who decides according to his or her own best judgment? Many people have difficulty maintaining consistency when they think about this question. Here is a simple thought experiment:

> Representative A believes that the United States should constitutionally prohibit abortion, but she represents a suburban district with a pro-choice majority. Should she vote for or against a constitutional amendment prohibiting abortion?

> Representative B believes the Constitution implies a right to abortion, but she represents a Catholic district with a pro-life majority. Should she vote for or against a constitutional amendment prohibiting abortion?

Our classroom experiments show that some pro-choice students would like the representative to behave as a delegate in the first example and as a trustee in the second, whereas some pro-life students have the opposite preference. This is not necessarily hypocrisy, although for some people it may be. Rather, representation is a complicated notion.

*What do you think?*
- *Should members of Congress generally act as delegates or as trustees?*
- *Does the issue under consideration make a difference? That is, should representatives behave as delegates on some issues and trustees on others?*
- *Should representatives behave differently from senators?*

[a] For a critical evaluation of such a philosophy of representation, see Dennis Thompson, *Ethics in Congress* (Washington, DC: Brookings, 1995), Chs. 3–4.
[b] Heinz Eulau, John Wahlke, William Buchanan, and Leroy Ferguson, "The Role of the Representative: Some Empirical Observations on the Theory of Edmund Burke," *American Political Science Review* 53 (1959): 742–756.
[c] "Speech to the Electors of Bristol," Peter Standlis, ed., *Selected Writings and Speeches* (New York: Doubleday, 1963).

how much their districts would gain or lose under alternative formulas. And too often, those estimates become the basis for supporting or opposing policies.

Bashing federal programs is a popular sport. Sometimes it is warranted—programs may be badly designed, poorly implemented, or incompetently administered. But federal programs often fail because they were born to fail: They are not focused on where they will do the most good, and resources are not sufficiently concentrated to have a major impact. Consequently, money is spent and the citizenry has little to show for it. But this is not because of incompetence or corruption. It is because members of Congress, ostensibly working in their constituents' interest, spread resources so broadly and thinly that they have little impact.

**delegate**
Role a representative plays when following the wishes of those who have elected him or her.

**trustee**
Role a representative plays when acting in accordance with his or her own best judgment.

**A Congressional Debate**
Disrespect for Congress is nothing new, as this 1798 print of the congressional floor shows.

participation
**Write to Your Congressperson**

## Why Americans Like Their Members of Congress So Much More Than Congress Itself

More than people in other democracies, Americans are proud of their political institutions. They revere the Constitution, honor the law, and respect the presidency and the courts. But there is an exception to this generalization, and it is the Congress. Congress is often the butt of jokes. Humorist Mark Twain once observed that "it could probably be shown with facts and figures that there is no distinctly native American criminal class except Congress."[37] Congress has been defined as "a creature with 535 bellies, and no brain." Critics regularly remark that "the opposite of progress is Congress."

Disparaging quips like these reflect popular sentiments. As Figures 12.3 and 12.4 show, surveys consistently report that only a minority of Americans trust the Congress to do what is right or have confidence in Congress, and they view members as having ethical standards only a bit higher than car salespersons. The reputation of Congress has been repeatedly tarnished by scandals. Ironically, this most electorally sensitive institution is the one whose image is the most negative.[38] Majorities of Americans doubt the competence and integrity of the Congress.[39]

This negative perception of Congress contrasts with the generally positive view Americans have of their particular members of Congress. After all, at the same time that popular majorities express doubts about the collective Congress, they reelect 90 percent or more of all incumbents who run. This gap between electoral approval of individual members and unhappiness with the collective Congress is so striking that political scientists have given it a name, "Fenno's paradox," after Professor Richard Fenno, who first pointed out that citizens invariably rate their members of Congress far more favorably than the Congress as a whole (see Figure 12.5).[40] Members take advantage of this disparity by adopting an unusual electoral strategy: "Members run *for* Congress by running *against* Congress."[41] They criticize the institution and claim that they are different from the other members who are the ones to blame for the things people dislike about Congress.

## Figure 12.3

**Public Confidence in Congress Trails Confidence in Many Other Institutions**

SOURCE: The Gallup Poll, June 10, 2000.

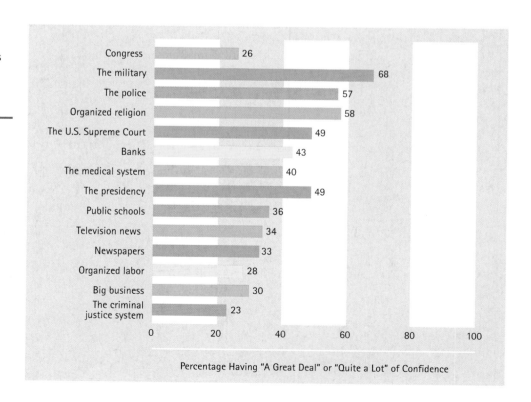

| Institution | Percentage |
|---|---|
| Congress | 26 |
| The military | 68 |
| The police | 57 |
| Organized religion | 58 |
| The U.S. Supreme Court | 49 |
| Banks | 43 |
| The medical system | 40 |
| The presidency | 49 |
| Public schools | 36 |
| Television news | 34 |
| Newspapers | 33 |
| Organized labor | 28 |
| Big business | 30 |
| The criminal justice system | 23 |

Percentage Having "A Great Deal" or "Quite a Lot" of Confidence

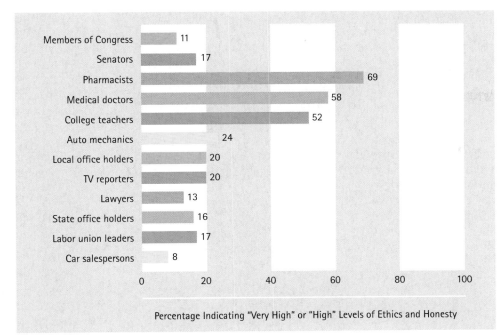

**Figure 12.4**

**The Public Rates the Honesty and Ethics of Members of Congress Lower Than Those of Other Occupations**

SOURCE: The Gallup Poll, November 4–7, 1999.

Fenno's observations are not puzzling in the light of a good understanding of the operation of Congress and the incentives underlying congressional operations. Americans dislike Congress but nevertheless reelect the great majority of their senators and representatives because they judge the collective Congress and the individual member by different standards.[42] They judge the Congress by how well it solves major problems and meets the serious challenges the country faces. Polls show that

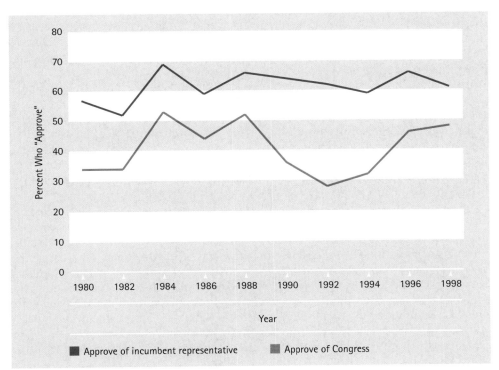

**Figure 12.5**

**Americans Rate Their Representatives Much More Positively Than the Congress**

SOURCE: American National Election Studies Guide to Public Opinion and Electoral Behavior (http://www.umich.edu/~nes/nes-guide/nesguide.htm)

Americans generally take a dim view of how well the Congress solves those problems and meets those challenges. The Congress, they believe, rarely meets its collective responsibilities. Moreover, citizens take an equally dim view of how they think Congress operates—sluggishly, conflictually, inefficiently, and sometimes corruptly. But citizens judge their representatives and senators positively for doing the very things that make the collective Congress perform poorly. Members respond to narrow—special—interests that are part of their constituencies, they look for opportunities to channel benefits to constituencies, they go to bat for constituents seeking exemptions from general policies, and they try to extract constituency concessions from major legislative efforts. Even though many of these activities detract from the national good, local constituencies appreciate them and reward members for engaging in them.

But the collective good suffers. An old country maxim states that "if you want to make an omelet, you've got to break some eggs." Constituencies want the omelet, but they oppose contributing any of their eggs, and indeed, they applaud when their members of Congress steal eggs from other districts and states.

## Reforming Congress: Limit Their Terms?

In the early 1990s a reform movement swept over much of the United States. It proposed that public officials, especially legislators, be limited by law to some maximum number of terms, usually amounting to 6 to 12 years of service. The strength of the movement reflects popular frustration with American government in general and with legislative bodies in particular. By 1997, 21 states had limited the terms of their state legislators. Twenty-three states also tried to limit congressional service, but the Supreme Court held in *U.S. v. Thornton* (1995) that such attempts were unconstitutional. Still, some candidates elected to Congress have pledged to support congressional term limits, Ross Perot's United We Stand organization supports term limits, and congressional limits were the announced position of the Republican party.

Whether Republican or Democratic, conservative or liberal, few political scientists favor term limits.[43] They generally believe that term limits would accomplish little and would probably do some harm. In their view, those who advocate term limits misunderstand what is wrong with Congress in particular and with legislatures in general.

The argument for term limits assumes that incumbents are virtually unbeatable and that their electoral strength is illegitimate—the product of responsiveness to special interests. Thus a mechanism like term limits is needed to turn incumbents out of office and increase legislative responsiveness to popular majorities. As we discussed in Chapter 11, however, incumbents are not unbeatable, nor is their success illegitimate. Rather, incumbents win so often because they work so hard. In large part, they succeed because they are so responsive to constituents and work so diligently on their behalf.

The popular perception is that legislatures are performing poorly. But legisla*tures* often perform poorly because legisla*tors* perform so well, at least in terms of responding to their constituencies. That is the irony underlying Fenno's paradox: If individual members single-mindedly serve their constituencies, it often detracts from the general welfare. Failure to understand this irony generates the support for term limits. If your member is doing a good job, simple logic implies that the problem must be everyone else's member, and because you cannot vote in other districts, imposing term limits is the only way to get rid of other districts' members. The problem is that every constituency is a special interest from the standpoint of other constituencies, and your member is a pork-barreling tool of special interests from the standpoint of other districts.

**visual literacy**

**Why is It So Hard to Defeat an Incumbent?**

Would term limits change that? Supporters argue that professionals interested in reelection would be replaced by "citizen legislators" who would deliberate and take a broad view of the public interest. Syndicated columnist George Will argues, "Term limits would increase the likelihood that people would come to Congress from established careers, with significant experience in the private sector."[44] This claim is not persuasive. What kind of people can devote six to ten years to serve in Congress? How can people sacrifice years out of their careers? In all likelihood, Congress would still be populated with professional politicians. They would not be professional members of Congress, however; rather, professional politicians would probably rotate from municipal to state to federal offices and back. Would the responsiveness of such people to special interests—and local constituencies—be less than it is today? It might be even greater than now, because the professionals would be continually worried about their next positions. Another source of temporary legislators might be special interests themselves (corporate, ideological, and other), who could subsidize employees to serve temporary stints in Congress and then return to their permanent employment. Would that be an improvement?

Term limits would not be the end of the world—both advocates and opponents exaggerate the probable effects. But term limitation does not address the real problem with Congress. The real problem is that professional politicians chosen in single-member districts have compelling incentives to please the special interests within their districts and, as campaign funds become increasingly important, special interests outside their districts. They have much less compelling incentives to consider the consequences of their activities for the larger, more general interests of the country.

## Chapter Summary

The United States Congress is the world's most powerful legislature. It is also the most professionalized; its members are full-time, professional legislators. It has an extensive division of labor—the committee system—that is the envy of parliamentarians in other countries who have much less power and responsibility. Nevertheless, citizens hold Congress in much lower esteem than they hold their individual representatives and senators, whom they reelect regularly.

This discrepancy arises because members of Congress depend for their election on specific constituencies. Thus they have strong incentives to serve those constituencies, and those incentives often are inconsistent with behavior that would best serve the larger interest of the nation. In particular, members organize the committee system not just to deal efficiently and effectively with major national problems but also to enable them to serve their constituencies. Members hesitate to give the party leadership enough power to mount an efficient and effective response to national problems in part because that power might be used to prevent them from serving constituency interests or even to force them to oppose constituency interests. The structure of Congress is an uneasy compromise between what it takes to get the job done and what it takes to get reelected.

The result is that Congress is slow and inefficient, and what emerges from the complex legislative process may not be very effective policy. This makes citizens frustrated with Congress, but they fail to see that it is precisely the efforts of their own representatives to serve their specific interests that makes it so difficult for Congress as a whole to serve the national interest. Citizen frustration has produced a powerful reform movement that seeks to limit the terms of legislators. Most political scientists are skeptical, believing that term limits are not an appropriate solution to what ails Congress. Members have powerful incentives to behave as they presently do, and term limits do not specifically attack those incentives.

## On the Web

*Roll Call* Online
www.rollcall.com
*Roll Call* is widely regarded as the leading source for congressional news and information both inside the Beltway and beyond. Since 1955, *Roll Call* has been the newspaper of Capitol Hill, giving members of Congress a way to communicate with one another across the aisle, between chambers, and beyond party affiliations.
THOMAS Online: Legislative Information on the Internet
thomas.loc.gov
Acting under the directive of the 104th Congress to make federal legislative information freely available to the Internet public, a Library of Congress team brought the THOMAS World Wide Web system online in January 1995. THOMAS is the most comprehensive congressional Web site on the net. It posts the full text of all congressional proceedings and contains historical information on Congress from its inception to the present.

Congressional Quarterly
www.cq.com
Congressional Quarterly is a world-class provider of information on government, politics, and public policy. It is extremely successful in its mission to "...project the highest levels of accuracy, comprehensiveness, nonpartisanship, readability, timeliness and analytical rigor."
Congressional Democrats
www.democraticleader.gov
Congressional Republicans
www.gop.gov
These Web sites of the congressional parties in the House contain mixtures of political and policy information.

## Key Terms

appropriations process, p. 366
authorization process, p. 366
bicameral, p. 349
caucus, p. 354
cloture, p. 355
conference, p. 354
conference committee, p. 366
delegate, p. 369
discharge petition, p. 358
distributive tendency, p. 368

distributive theory, p. 362
filibuster, p. 355
informational theory, p. 362
log-rolling, p. 362
majority leader, p. 354
markup, p. 364
minority leader, p. 354
multiple referrals, p. 364
president pro tempore, p. 354
rule, p. 365

select committee, p. 358
seniority, p. 360
Speaker, p. 351
sponsor, p. 364
standing committee, p. 358
suspension of the rules, p. 364
trustee, p. 369
unanimous-consent agreement,
  p. 355
whips, p. 354

## Suggested Readings

Arnold, R. Douglas. *The Logic of Congressional Action*. New Haven, CT: Yale University Press, 1990. An excellent discussion of how the incentives that motivate members interact with characteristics of public policy problems to shape legislation.

Cox, Gary, and Mathew McCubbins. *Legislative Leviathan*. Berkeley: University of California Press, 1993. Important revisionist work that argues that parties were more significant in the mid-century congresses than most analysts believed.

Davidson, Roger, and Walter Oleszek. *Congress and Its Members*, 5th ed. Washington, DC: CQ Press, 1996. A comprehensive and readable text that relates the electoral and institutional arenas.

Deering, Christopher, and Steven Smith, *Committees in Congress*. Washington, DC: CQ Press, 1997. The most thorough and up-to-date discussion of the congressional committee system.

Dodd, Larry, and Bruce Oppenheimer, eds. *Congress Reconsidered*, 7th ed. Washington, DC: CQ Press, 2000. An excellent collection of articles on Congress. Many pieces in earlier editions still merit reading.

Kingdon, John. *Congressmen's Voting Decisions*, 3rd ed. Ann Arbor: University of Michigan Press, 1989. Classic study of how representatives decide to vote on the floor.

Oleszek, Walter. *Congressional Procedures and the Policy Process*, 4th ed. Washington, DC: CQ Press, 1995. The most accessible treatment of the myriad rules and procedures that govern the national legislative process.

Ornstein, Norman, Thomas Mann, and Michael Malbin. *Vital Statistics on Congress, 1999–2000*. Washington, DC: American Enterprise Institute, 2000. This biennial compilation of congressional statistics is to Congress watchers what *The Bill James Baseball Sourcebook* is to baseball fans.

Rohde, David. *Parties and Leaders in the Post-Reform House*. Chicago: University of Chicago Press, 1991. Important work that traces the strengthening of the congressional parties in recent decades.

Sinclair, Barbara. *Legislators, Leaders, and Lawmaking: The U.S. House of Representatives in the Postreform Era*. Baltimore, MD: Johns Hopkins University Press, 1995. Organized around an argument similar to that of Cox and McCubbins, this is the most up-to-date treatment of Democratic leadership in the modern House.

Smith, Steven. *Call to Order: Floor Politics in the House and Senate*. Washington, DC: Brookings, 1989. Detailed study of the increasing importance of the chamber floors in the contemporary Congress.

———. *The American Congress*, 2nd ed. Boston: Houghton Mifflin, 1999. The newest comprehensive textbook on Congress. Incorporates changes that occurred after the Republicans assumed control in 1994.

Chapter

# 13
# The Presidency: Powers and Practice

Chapter Outline

**Presidential Expectations and Presidential Performance**

The morning after election day is a dangerous time for a new president-elect. Euphoria can sweep aside caution. As President Calvin Coolidge once said, "One of the first lessons a president has to learn is that every word he says weighs a ton."[1]

The day after Bill Clinton first won the presidency, a reporter asked him whether he would issue an executive order allowing gays to join the armed forces. Unhesitatingly, the president-elect said, "Yes."[2] With that one word, the president-elect had created a political problem for himself. Though gays thought his stand morally courageous, Clinton paid a political price for his policy commitment.

The political miscalculation was in some ways understandable. Gays had by 1992 become a significant political force. By taking pro-gay positions, Clinton had received as much as $3.5 million in campaign dollars from the gay community and gained an estimated 72 percent of its vote.[3] That Clinton, as president, had the legal authority to permit gays in the military also seemed beyond question. Congress had never passed a law on the subject, and the ban was based solely on an order issued by President Reagan.

But Clinton still might have thought more about the political consequences before responding positively to the reporter's question. Gay access to the military had marginal popular appeal. Though it was acceptable to 45 percent of the electorate, 47 percent remained opposed. And of those opposed, eight out of ten said they held strong opinions.[4]

With no military experience, Clinton was vulnerable on defense policy issues. Further, the president-elect's promise to gays annoyed senior military officers, who were quoted as saying the policy would "wreck morale" and "undermine recruiting."[5] General Colin Powell, a hero of the Persian Gulf War, said that "the presence of homosexuals in the force would be detrimental to good order and discipline."[6] The president-elect could, of course, simply ignore opposition from within the military. After all, he was **commander in chief,** and the armed forces have to obey executive orders. But these orders can be overturned by congressional legislation.

**commander in chief**
The president in his constitutional role as head of the armed forces.

Attention shifted to Capitol Hill, where members of Congress quickly sensed the emergence of a controversial issue. In a single day the congressional switchboard was swamped by nearly half a million phone calls, mainly in opposition.[7] Delighted at the president's predicament, one Republican legislator exclaimed, "You would think that someone who has not served a day in uniform would be particularly careful to consult his military chiefs."[8]

Clinton appointed a presidential task force to review the issue. It recommended a compromise formula known as "Don't ask, don't tell." Although individuals were not to be asked questions about their sexual preferences when joining the armed forces, gays could be asked to leave the armed services if they told anyone they were gay or if they were observed engaging in impermissible behavior. The compromise was more satisfactory to Republicans than to gay rights advocates. One political commentator wondered whether "there is *any* principle for which Bill Clinton will fight."[9] By 1998 the number of individuals in the armed services dismissed for homosexual activity had actually increased 92 percent, and the following year Clinton himself admitted that the policy had not worked well in practice.[10]

PRESIDENTS FREQUENTLY SEEM UNPRINCIPLED because they are often forced into compromises and modifications of their original campaign positions. Their problems are due both to the constituency pressures they face and to the limits on their powers. In this chapter we consider the pressures on the presidency and its strengths and weaknesses as an office by focusing on the following questions:

- What are the president's constituencies, and how do they influence his actions?
- What constitutional powers do presidents exercise, and what are the limitations on these powers?
- What factors contribute to presidential success and failure in office?

## Presidential Constituencies

Presidents often find it challenging to strike the right balance between their national constituencies, created by the general election, and their partisan constituencies, shaped by presidential primaries. President Clinton's desire to allow gays to serve in the armed forces was popular with many members of his own party, yet the policy did not have the broad national support that a presidential proposal generally needs. Both national and partisan constituencies play a role in presidential decision making.

### National Constituency

Presidents have one unique political asset: They fill the only position elected by a national constituency. Only presidents can persuasively claim to be speaking for the country as a whole, and they can use this national constituency to powerful effect. In late 1995, after budget negotiations between the president and Congress deadlocked, much of the government was shut down for nearly a month. National parks were closed and government bills went unpaid. In the midst of the crisis, President Clinton asked Congress to place the national interest above partisan objectives. Republican Speaker of the House Newt Gingrich replied by saying it was the president who should put the country's future ahead of his own. Each appealed to a national constituency, but the president, in part because he was the *president*, proved to be more persuasive. According to polls, most Americans sided with the president and blamed Congress for the deadlock. House Republicans lost seats in the 1996 elections, and Gingrich lost authority within his party. In late 1998, he left Congress.

Although the president's national constituency is a great political asset, it creates problems as well. In the eyes of the voters, presidents are held responsible for many events and conditions over which they have little control. Presidents are expected to conduct foreign policy, manage the economy, administer a complex bureaucracy, promote desired legislation, respond to disasters, and address an endless variety of real and imagined social problems.[11]

Though presidents are sometimes given credit for prosperity and success, they are more often blamed when things go bad. President George H. W. Bush, for example, enjoyed a succession of foreign policy triumphs equaled by only a few of his predecessors. He oversaw the fall of the Berlin wall, the collapse of the Soviet Union, and a spectacular victory in the Persian Gulf War. Yet when the economy faltered, Bush was drummed from office. Clinton presided over one of the longest periods of economic expansion in history, but his vice-president, Albert Gore, had to fight for every vote he received.

**Republican Turned Reformer**
Before running on the Reform Party ticket, Patrick Buchanan served as gadfly to a number of more moderate presidential candidates in Republican primaries. *Why do candidates like Buchanan, who have a small band of followers, sometimes do well in primary elections?*

## Partisan Constituencies

In addition to a national constituency, presidents have a party constituency to which they must be responsive. They need to keep the support of their party's most active members who work in and help finance their campaigns. If they do not satisfy their party constituency, they may encounter difficulties with the party faithful in presidential primaries. In 1992, when George Bush was thought to have been insufficiently conservative, he was challenged by Pat Buchanan during the primary election campaign. In the 2000 primaries, when Democratic party activists considered Vice-President Al Gore to be too moderate on health and environmental policies, many turned to Bill Bradley.

A party constituency usually takes more extreme issue positions than does the national constituency. Republican activists support tighter controls on abortion than do most voters. Democratic activists support more comprehensive government health care programs than the typical voter does. Presidents have to find some way to balance the demands of their most ardent supporters with the more moderate concerns of the general-election voters who determine the outcome of national elections.

## Partisan Support in Congress

Even if presidents can balance their national and party constituencies, they usually cannot take action on their pledges without considering their level of support in Congress. On most issues, presidents gain more support from members of their own party than from the opposition. As can be seen in Figure 13.1, members of the president's party in both the House and the Senate vote with their leader somewhere between 70 and 80 percent of the time. Opposition-party members vote with presidents somewhere between 40 and 50 percent of the time. As a consequence, when presidents have larger majorities in Congress, they are more likely to get their proposed legislation approved.[12]

Recent events provide a clear illustration of the importance to presidents of a party majority in Congress. During the first two years of President Clinton's presidency, he enjoyed a Democratic party majority in both the Senate and the House. During this time Congress approved several significant components of Clinton's election platform, including laws that eased voter registration requirements, provided medical and family leave for new parents, and reduced the budget deficit. After Democrats lost their majority in the 1994 elections, Clinton was forced to scale back his own agenda and

**Figure 13.1**

**Partisan Support
for the President in Congress**
Each party in Congress supports its own president more often than a president of the opposing party. *What do you think happens when presidents face divided government?*

SOURCE: This figure is based on data for the period 1954–1998, taken from Norman Ornstein, Thomas E. Mann, and Michael Malbin, *Vital Statistics on Congress, 1999–2000* (Washington, DC: Congressional Quarterly, 2000).

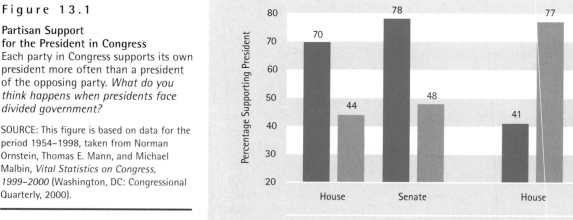

## International Comparison

## U.S. Presidents and British Prime Ministers

British prime ministers receive the support of nearly every party member in Parliament on all major issues. Over 90 percent of the time, party members go along with the prime minister. These extraordinary high levels of party support are due to a rule that forces prime ministers to resign from office if they fail to get a majority on critical votes. When that happens, a new election is usually called, and members of Parliament must immediately run for reelection—something they usually like to delay for as long as possible.

Because the American president can lose votes in Congress and still remain in power, members of Congress balance party loyalty against their own convictions as well as constituency and interest-group pressures. Bill Clinton, for example, could not per-

suade his party to pass his health care reform. Had he been a British prime minister, he could have forced either passage or new elections.

*Which system makes more sense to you?*
- *Is the British system better because it allows the government to take swift, unified action? Or is the U.S. system better because it blocks unnecessary policies?*
- *Would you rather be a U.S. president or a British prime minister?*

SOURCE: Jack Brand, *British Parliamentary Parties: Policy and Power* (New York: Oxford University Press, 1992), Ch. 2.

---

accepted Republican welfare proposals with which he did not altogether agree (see Chapter 1). He even suffered impeachment by the House of Representatives as a result of the Lewinsky scandal.

Partisanship is not as pervasive in the United States as it is in many European countries (see the accompanying International Comparison). Still, political scientists have debated whether it is good or bad to have **divided government**, control of the presidency by one party and control of one or both Houses of Congress by the other. Some argue that a president needs a majority of his own party in Congress in order to solve national problems. Others suggest that when government is divided, each party provides a beneficial check on the other (see the accompanying Democratic Dilemma).

> **divided government**
> The control of the presidency by one party and the control of one or both houses of Congress by the other.

### SECTION SUMMARY

Presidents are the only U.S. officials elected by the whole country, and they can use this fact to political advantage. But they must also take care to address the needs of important constituencies within their own parties. If party regulars or congressional majorities rebel against presidents, it can be difficult for presidents to pursue their agendas successfully.

## Separate Institutions Sharing Power

In addition to frequent partisan divisions of government, presidents also face the fundamental divisions of power between the executive and legislative branches that are written into the constitution. Presidents are seldom in a position to force members of Congress to support them; they usually have to coax, beg, plead, and compromise to gain the necessary votes. Even when the same party controls both the presidency and Congress, presidents do not find it easy to get their proposals approved. For instance, Jimmy Carter was unable to persuade a Democratic Congress to enact most of his energy policy.[13] Over 80 percent of the time, presidents either fail to secure passage of their major legislative agendas or must make important compromises to win congressional approval.[14] As presidential scholar Charles Jones has observed, "Presidents don't pass laws; they work with, alongside of, or against the House and Senate."[15]

When President Clinton was unable to open the military to gays, he was not the first president to be frustrated by Congress. Theodore Roosevelt sighed, "Oh, if I could only be president and Congress too for just ten minutes."[16] Harry Truman expressed the frustration of many presidents when he predicted what would happen to his successor, General Dwight Eisenhower: "He'll sit here and he'll say, 'Do this! Do that!' *And*

## Democratic Dilemma

# Is Divided Government Good or Bad?

Scholars disagree on the issue of divided government. Some see it as an unfortunate and harmful phenomenon, others as a harmless or even beneficial result of popular elections.

James Sundquist argues that divided government often prevents the government from taking necessary action because it makes it harder for the president to enact his policy agenda. "When the president sends a recommendation to the opposition-controlled Congress," says Sundquist, "the legislators are virtually compelled to reject or profoundly alter it; otherwise they are endorsing the president's leadership . . . [and] strengthening him or his party for the next election." Sundquist proposes a novel solution to this problem: Four-year House terms and eight-year Senate terms, with elections coinciding with presidential elections. Sundquist claims that if the president and Congress were elected at the same time, divided government would be less likely.

Others believe that the concern about divided government is unwarranted and such radical solutions unnecessary. Morris Fiorina suggests that divided government may be the result of conscious decisions by the voters to send mixed signals. If this is so, "who are we to recommend that they make a clear choice?" Perhaps voters believe that Republicans are too extreme on some issues and Democrats are too extreme on others. (For more on divided government, see Chapter 8.)

*Whom do you believe?*
- *Do you think divided government produces harmful gridlock? Or do you think it serves as a check against extreme action by either party?*
- *Are good policies blocked?*
- *Are bad policies prevented?*

**George W. Bush and Senator Trent Lott**
*Did concern about unified Republican government cause some voters to vote against Bush in the 2000 election?*

SOURCES: James L. Sundquist, *Constitutional Reform and Effective Government* (Washington, DC: Brookings, 1986), pp. 75–76, 240. Morris Fiorina, *Divided Government* (New York: Macmillan, 1992), pp. 128–29.

*nothing will happen.* Poor Ike—it won't be a bit like the Army. He'll find it very frustrating."[17] Presidents find their position particularly exasperating because they feel they have a duty to take decisive action. "I don't want to sound sanctimonious about this," said President George H. W. Bush, "but I was elected to govern."

Those who wrote the Constitution ensured that presidents would govern only with the help of Congress (see Table 2.5). Most delegates to the constitutional convention wanted to strengthen the executive branch beyond what was provided for by the Articles of Confederation. Alexander Hamilton even proposed electing a president for life. But the founders realized that voters would never ratify a constitution that created a strong executive who might become another King George. The result is a government of "separated institutions sharing powers."[18] We now turn to the many ways in which the Constitution has shaped presidential power and practice. (Our emphasis in this chapter will be on the president's powers with respect to domestic affairs.)

### The Power to Inform and Persuade

PRESIDENTIAL POWER: *The President "shall from time to time give to the Congress Information of the State of the Union."*

CONGRESSIONAL CHECK: *None*

The Constitution requires presidents to give Congress information about the state of the Union. Because the line between information and persuasion is thin, presidents have interpreted this requirement as authority to persuade Congress and the public at large to support their policies. Modern presidents rely on hundreds of public speeches each year to set forth their vision of the country's future, but the most prestigious and formalized address is the **State of the Union address,** which is given annually, usually in late January or early February.

**State of the Union address**

Annual speech delivered by the president in fulfillment of the constitutional obligation of reporting to Congress on the state of the Union.

**Early Use of Persuasion Power** The power to persuade is used much more publicly today than it was in the early years of the republic, as Figure 13.2 illustrates. Early presidents seldom spoke in public, and when they did, their remarks were of a general nature. To fulfill their obligation to report on the state of the union, Thomas Jefferson and his nineteenth-century successors sent written messages to Congress. Early presidents found other ways of persuading Congress. Instead of using public rhetoric, Jefferson, a master politician, invited members of Congress to the Executive Mansion (later called the White House) for dinners at which he would persuade them to support his political agenda.[19] He also communicated his views through friendly newspaper editors. Though active behind the scenes, early presidents avoided open involvement in day-to-day politics.[20] Not until Woodrow Wilson addressed a joint session of both houses of Congress in 1913 did it become a regular practice for presidents to report in person on the state of the union.[21]

In fact, the unwritten rule against presidential rhetoric was at one time so strong that it became a basis for presidential impeachment. President Andrew Johnson, who succeeded to the presidency upon the assassination of Abraham Lincoln, publicly criticized specific members of Congress. In the list of impeachment charges brought against Johnson, one seems particularly strange to modern Americans:

> That said Andrew Johnson, President of the United States, unmindful of the high duties of his office and the dignity and propriety thereof . . . did . . . deliver with a loud voice certain intemperate, inflammatory, and scandalous harangues, and did therein utter loud threats and bitter menaces . . . against Congress.[22]

Today we would think that such a president, though not very politically prudent, was merely exercising the right of free speech.

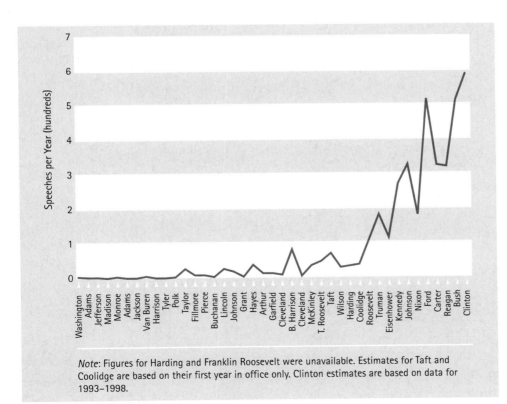

*Note:* Figures for Harding and Franklin Roosevelt were unavailable. Estimates for Taft and Coolidge are based on their first year in office only. Clinton estimates are based on data for 1993–1998.

**Figure 13.2**

**Growth in Presidential Speech Making**

SOURCES: Data on Washington through McKinley are taken from Jeffrey Tulis, *The Rhetorical Presidency* (Princeton, NJ: Princeton University Press, 1987), p. 64. For Theodore Roosevelt, see Robert V. Friedenberg, *Theodore Roosevelt and the Rhetoric of Militant Decency* (New York: Greenwood Press, 1990). For Taft, see *Presidential Addresses and State Papers of William Howard Taft,* Vol. 1, 1910 (New York: Doubleday). For Wilson, see Albert Shaw, ed. *Messages and Papers of Woodrow Wilson,* Vols. 1 and 2 (New York: Review of Reviews Corporation, 1924). For Coolidge, see Claude M. Feuss, *Calvin Coolidge: The Man from Vermont* (Hamden, CT: Archon Books, 1965). For Presidents Truman through Reagan, see Roderick Hart, *The Sound of Leadership* (Chicago: The University of Chicago Press, 1987). For Hoover, Bush, and Clinton, information is taken from *The Public Papers of the President,* various years.

**Establishing a Modern Tradition**
In 1916 Woodrow Wilson (right of center) became the first president to address joint sessions of both houses of Congress regularly. *Why do you think Wilson began the practice of personally delivering the State of the Union speech to Congress? Why have all presidents since Wilson followed this practice?*

**bully pulpit**
The nature of the president's status as an ideal vehicle for persuading the public to support the president's policies.

**Modern Persuasion Power** More than any other president, Theodore ("Teddy") Roosevelt changed the definition of what was permissible in presidential rhetoric. Roosevelt liked to achieve results by using what he called the "**bully pulpit**" available to presidents. (*Bully* was nineteenth-century slang for "excellent"). Roosevelt suggested that, like a preacher, the president could use his position to move his "congregation"— the public—to action. He mobilized support through bold gestures, forceful speeches, presidential trips, and dramatic turns of phrase. Roosevelt's rhetoric may have been his most lasting contribution to presidential politics. As one historian has noted, "the number of laws [Roosevelt] inspired was certainly not in proportion to the amount of noise he emitted."[23] Yet Roosevelt's popular appeal was such that a cartoon depicting the president sparing the life of a bear cub while hunting resulted in the emergence of the term "Teddy Bear."

Presidents since Teddy Roosevelt have increasingly used the bully pulpit to persuade Congress and the public, as Figure 13.2 illustrates.[24] Franklin Delano Roosevelt's "fireside chats" over the radio enabled him to sidestep the print media, which he accused of being controlled by Republican publishers. John Kennedy had a compelling rhetorical style that both inspired and challenged his audience. In his inaugural speech, the young president challenged Americans: "Ask not what your country can do for you, ask what you can do for your country."[25]

President Reagan, the first president with experience as a professional actor, used television more effectively than any of his predecessors. He understood that there is but "a thin line between politics and theatricals."[26] Pictures were worth a thousand words, and body language spoke more convincingly than verbal formulations.[27] As Reagan once said, "I've wondered how people in positions of this kind . . . manage without having had any acting experience."[28]

**veto power**
Presidential rejection of congressional legislation. May be overridden by a two-thirds vote in each congressional chamber. Most state governors also have veto power over their legislatures.

## The Veto Power

PRESIDENTIAL VETO POWER: *Before any law "shall take effect," it must be "approved by" the president.*

CONGRESSIONAL CHECK: *Unless "repassed by two-thirds of the Senate and House of Representatives."*

The president's **veto power** is more concrete than the power to inform: It gives presidents the capacity to prevent bills passed by Congress from becoming law. Before the

DRAWING
THE LINE
IN MISSISSIPPI

**A Popular President**
Although President Theodore Roosevelt was an avid hunter, it was his decision to spare the life of a bear cub in 1902 that led to the emergence of the term "Teddy Bear."

Civil War, presidents seldom used the veto. President Washington cast only two vetoes. The average number cast by presidents between Madison and Lincoln was only a little more than four. As Figure 13.3 shows, presidents from Franklin Roosevelt on have been much more willing to use the veto power.

This presidential power to say "No" can be checked. But Congress usually fails to muster the necessary two-thirds vote in each chamber to pass an **override**, which makes the bill a law despite the president's opposition. Since the Kennedy administration, Congress has overridden approximately only one out of every ten vetoes.[29] Only 1 of President Clinton's 32 vetoes was overridden.

The veto power is of little help to presidents in their attempts to initiate policy change. During the energy crisis of the late 1970s, President Carter wanted an energy policy that was the "moral equivalent of war," but when confronted by opposition from senators from Texas, Louisiana, and other oil-producing states, he was forced to sign a law much altered from his original proposals. Carter might have vetoed the legislation, but once having put the issue on the agenda, he could hardly block the action Congress saw fit to take.

Though the veto can seldom be used to initiate policy, it can be successfully employed as a weapon in negotiations with Congress or to protect the status of existing executive orders. In late 1999, though President Clinton had suffered the disgrace of impeachment and was ineligible for reelection, he used the veto to force Republicans in Congress to give in on some of his policy objectives. By vetoing a massive tax cut plan passed by Congress, Clinton both gained the upper hand in budget negotiations and increased his political support. One Republican strategist acknowledged the president's advantages: "We've learned that it's nearly impossible to frame the national debate from the lower chamber of the legislative branch."[30]

If Congress enacts a law ten days before it adjourns, a president may exercise a **pocket veto** by simply not signing the bill into law. Congress has no opportunity to override a pocket veto. Nearly all of President Reagan's vetoes were pocket vetoes. Because these vetoes could not be overridden, Reagan was able to use them to convey

**override**
Congressional passage of a bill by a two-thirds vote over the president's veto.

**pocket veto**
Presidential veto after congressional adjournment, executed merely by not signing a bill into law.

## Figure 13.3

**Trends in Presidential Use
of the Veto Power**
Currently presidents use the veto less
than at mid-century but more than in
the 1800s. *Why did presidents become
more assertive?*

SOURCES: Figures from 1789–1996 are
taken from Gary L. Galemore, "Presidential
Vetoes, 1789–1996: A Summary Overview,"
Congressional Research Service Report for
Congress, 97-163 GOV. Figures from
1997–1999 are taken from Library of
Congress, "Legislation: Bills, Amendments,
and Laws," **http://lcweb.loc.gov/global/
legislative/bill.html**, accessed December 7,
1999.

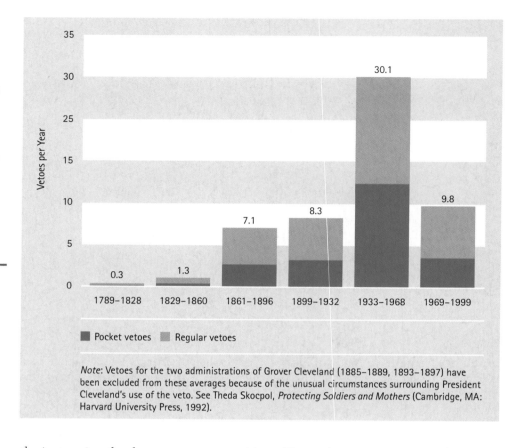

*Note*: Vetoes for the two administrations of Grover Cleveland (1885–1889, 1893–1897) have
been excluded from these averages because of the unusual circumstances surrounding President
Cleveland's use of the veto. See Theda Skocpol, *Protecting Soldiers and Mothers* (Cambridge, MA:
Harvard University Press, 1992).

**line item veto**
Presidential authority to negate particular provisions of a law, granted by
Congress in 1996 but struck down by
the Supreme Court in 1998.

the impression that he was a strong president. The pocket veto strategy works only at
the very end of a congressional session, however; if Congress remains in session for
more than ten days after passing a bill, the president must explicitly cast a veto to prevent the bill from becoming law. As the distinction between campaigning and governing has disappeared, Congress has remained in session virtually throughout the entire
year, giving Bush and Clinton few opportunities to cast pocket vetoes. This is yet
another example of the way elections increasingly influence American government.

Although Congress is sometimes able to override vetoes, it more often counters
the president's veto power indirectly, by incorporating policies that presidents oppose
into large bills that contain items presidents feel they must approve. When faced with
such a package, the president finds it difficult to cast a veto. For example, Clinton
reluctantly signed a bill requiring the discharge of HIV-positive soldiers from the
armed services because the provision was incorporated into an important defense bill.

Because Congress can artfully package laws in such a way as to make the veto unus-
able, many people favor giving the president the **line item veto**, the authority to negate
particular provisions of a law while letting the remainder stand. As discussed in Chapter
3, many state governors already have this power. The presidential line item veto became
a popular idea among congressional Republicans during the Reagan and Bush administrations, a time when Democratic Congresses were packaging laws in ways that
Republican presidents found difficult to veto. In 1995 the shoe was slipped onto the
other foot: A line item veto would have given Democratic President Bill Clinton the
power to veto expenditures approved by a Republican Congress. As did presidents
before him, Clinton welcomed this proposed enhancement of presidential power, and
he supported Republican efforts to amend the Constitution. But supporters could still
not get the two-thirds majority in Congress necessary to pass a constitutional amendment. Because some legal scholars had argued that the Constitution already allowed a
line item veto, proponents decided to enact a simple piece of legislation giving presidents a line item veto over certain expenditures and minor tax items. In 1997 President

Clinton exercised his new power, vetoing tax loopholes for financial companies, special Medicaid spending for the State of New York, and other minor items.

New York City, together with others adversely affected, challenged the legislation's constitutionality, and in 1998 the Supreme Court struck down the law by a margin of 6 to 3. "If the Line Item Veto Act were valid," said Justice John Stevens, "it would authorize the president to create a different law, one whose text was not voted on by either house of Congress." This is contrary to the "procedures designed by the framers . . . of the Constitution." The justices concluded that it would require a constitutional amendment to give presidents the line item veto.

## The Appointment Power

PRESIDENTIAL POWER: *The president "shall appoint Ambassadors, other public Ministers and Consuls . . . and all other Officers of the United States."*

CONGRESSIONAL CHECK: *Appointments are subject to the "Advice and Consent of the Senate," which is taken to mean that a majority must approve the nomination.*

The appointment power enables presidents to appoint thousands of public officials to positions of high responsibility within their **administration,** which consists of those responsible for directing the executive branch of government.

> **administration**
> The president and his political appointees responsible for directing the executive branch of government.
>
> **cabinet**
> Top administration officials; mostly heads of executive branch departments.
>
> **secretary**
> Head of a department within the executive branch.

**The Cabinet** The president's **cabinet** consists of the key members of the administration. Most are heads of government departments and carry the title **secretary.** The terms are left over from the days when a *secretary* was a confidential assistant who kept secrets under lock and key in a wooden *cabinet.* Originally, the president's cabinet had but four departments, and the secretaries met regularly with the president, giving him confidential political guidance on a broad range of policies. It was in cabinet meetings, for example, that Abraham Lincoln developed his strategy for fighting the Civil War.

Over the years, government began to perform a much broader range of functions. As the number of departments grew from 4 to 15 (see Table 14.1), the cabinet lost its capacity to provide confidential advice to presidents. In President Nixon's words, "Cabinet government is a myth and won't work. . . . No [president] in his right mind submits anything to his cabinet."[31] Today the cabinet meets only occasionally, primarily for ceremonial purposes or to help the president make some kind of political statement.

**The White House Staff** Many of the modern president's closest advisers are not cabinet secretaries but White House aides who deal in matters with utmost confidentiality. At one time the president's personal staff was small and informal. Abraham Lincoln had just two young assistants; otherwise, he communicated personally with his cabinet. Even President Franklin Roosevelt originally had only a handful of personal assistants. To address organizational problems caused by the growing size of the federal government, Roosevelt in 1936 asked a committee of three specialists in public administration headed by Louis Brownlow to recommend ways to improve the organization of the federal government. Saying "the President needs help," the Brownlow Committee recommended sweeping changes throughout the government, including additional appointments to the president's personal staff. Brownlow said presidential staff members "should be possessed of high competence, great physical vigor, and a passion for anonymity." Though Congress rejected most of the other Brownlow recommendations, it agreed to enlarge the White House staff.[32]

Brownlow envisioned only a "small number of executive assistants," but the president's staff has steadily evolved in size and complexity.[33] The number of aides has grown from 48 in 1944 to over 400 today (see Figure 13.4). Its organization is now complex enough to confuse even well-informed citizens. One basic distinction to remember is the difference between the **White House Office,** the main subject under discussion here, and the much larger **Executive Office of the President (EOP).**

> **White House Office**
> Political appointees who work directly for the president, many of whom occupy offices in the White House.
>
> **Executive Office of the President (EOP)**
> Agency that houses both top coordinating offices and other operating agencies.

**Figure 13.4**

**Size of the White House Office**
*Why have presidents since FDR relied on hundreds of White House staffers?*

SOURCES: White House Office staff, 1943–1993, from Harold W. Stanley and Richard G. Niemi, *Vital Statistics on American Politics,* 4th ed. (Washington, DC: CQ Press, 1994), pp. 267–269; staff figures for 1994–1996 taken from U.S. Office of Personnel Management, *Federal Civilian Workforce Statistics.*

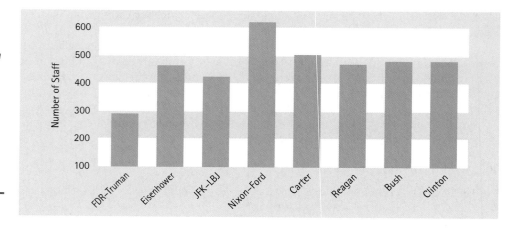

**chief of staff**
Head of White House staff. Has continuous, direct contact with the president.

Although the names make it seem as though they are much the same thing, the White House Office is just one component of the EOP, which also includes other important coordinating bodies as well as operating agencies (see Table 13.1).

In Franklin Roosevelt's day, no single person headed the White House staff. Even as late as the Carter administration, White House aides worked together as "spokes in a wheel," each having direct access to the president. But today presidents usually place one person in charge.[34] This person, the **chief of staff**, meets with the president several times a day and communicates decisions to other staff, cabinet officers, and members of Congress.

The best chiefs are usually Washington insiders. Though little acclaimed, Ronald Reagan's 1987–1988 chief, Howard Baker, was one of the most powerful and effective. A former Senate majority leader and presidential aspirant, Baker served at a time when he had forsaken all political ambition. Skilled at reaching compromises, Baker helped boost Reagan's popularity, despite the fact that the aging president himself had lost much of his former vitality.

**Table 13.1**

**Executive Office of the President, Budget and Staff Levels**

| | Budget (Millions)* | Staff* |
|---|---|---|
| Office of Management and Budget | $60.6 | 518 |
| White House Office | 52.3 | 400 |
| Office of National Drug Control Policy | 48.0 | 124 |
| Office of Administration | 28.3 | 192 |
| Office of the U.S. Trade Representative | 24.2 | 178 |
| White House Residence/Operating Expenses | 8.1 | 91 |
| National Security Council | 6.8 | 60 |
| Office of Policy Development | 4.0 | 31 |
| Office of Science and Technology Policy | 5.0 | 39 |
| Council of Economic Advisers | 3.7 | 35 |
| Office of the Vice-President | 3.5 | 23 |
| Council on Environmental Quality | 2.7 | 22 |

SOURCE: Executive Office of the President, *Budget of the United States Government, Fiscal Year 2000,* Appendix.
*As of 1999.

Newcomers to Washington are usually less successful. Typically, they become lightning rods—people to be blamed when things go wrong. John Sununu, former governor of New Hampshire, was forced to leave the job of chief of staff when he was blamed for urging President Bush to sign an unpopular tax increase.[35] Thomas McLarty from Arkansas resigned when he was blamed for the Clinton administration's poor beginning.[36]

Although Brownlow expected White House aides to have "no power to make decisions," modern presidents have regularly used their staffs to shape their public policy proposals.[37] Within the White House staff, more than anywhere else, presidents can count on the loyalty of those around them simply because, unlike the careers of department secretaries, those of staff members are closely intertwined with that of the president.

The White House staff is more potent than ever in part because presidents have more need for political help. Presidents today need pollsters who can keep them in touch with changes in public opinion.[38] They also need assistants who can help them communicate with the media, interest groups, and members of Congress. Once a major piece of legislation arrives for consideration on the chamber floor, White House aides are in regular contact with many legislators. In 1992, as part of the White House effort to enact legislation that would engage young people in a national service program, one aide personally contacted 67 Senate offices.[39] So intense is the work inside the White House that most staff jobs demand 7-day, 100-hour work weeks. As a result, many positions go to those young in years and spirit.

Quite apart from the president's genuine need for lots of political help, the White House staff is an excellent place to reward loyal campaign workers. After the presidency has been won, those who worked on the campaign often expect something in return. The White House Office is a convenient place for the president to put campaign workers, because the president has exclusive control over appointments to his personal staff. Not even the chief of staff must be confirmed by the Senate.

During presidential election years, the number of people working at the White House sometimes provokes strong criticism from the opposition party. When running for president, Bill Clinton promised to cut the White House staff by 25 percent. But when it came time to make the cuts, Clinton found his White House Office too valuable to be the target of cost-cutting efforts. Thus the president made staff cuts elsewhere in the Executive Office of the President. Because of the confusion in the public's mind between the White House Office and the EOP, it was difficult for Republicans to criticize him for breaking this campaign promise.

**Scandals in the White House Office**    The highly personal and partisan nature of the White House staff can be a weakness as well as a strength. A White House full of personal friends and fellow partisans has at times so shielded the presidents from external criticism that the chief executive has lost touch with political reality. And sometimes staff members have used the power of the presidential office for improper—even illegal—purposes, paving the way for scandals of presidential proportions.

Scandals are hardly new to American politics. When lawmakers discovered that Abraham Lincoln's wife and her assistants outspent housekeeping funds, the president successfully pleaded with Congress to appropriate more money secretly rather than to carry out an investigation.[40] But the intensity and significance of White House scandals have escalated in recent decades.[41] In addition to the Lewinsky scandal discussed later, two major and many more minor scandals have captured the attention of the nation and carried the potential for presidential impeachment.

The most serious was the Watergate scandal during the Nixon administration. In 1972, at the instigation of members of the White House staff, five men broke into Democratic party headquarters at the Watergate condominium complex in Washington, DC, apparently to obtain information on Democratic party campaign strategies. Nixon's chief of staff, Bob Haldeman, knew that "hush money" was paid to keep the burglars from revealing White House involvement. When tapes of Nixon's own conversations indicated that the president himself had been involved in the "cover-up," the House initiated impeachment proceedings, and the president was forced to resign.

In the Iran–Contra scandal, staffers in the Reagan White House illegally sold arms to the Iranian government and gave the profits, also illegally, to a group of guerrillas known as Contras who were fighting to overthrow a left-wing government in Nicaragua. White House aides were prosecuted and some Democrats talked of impeachment, but no direct evidence implicating the president was found.

Certain factors make the White House staff particularly prone to scandal. News organizations and opposition leaders have a vested interest in uncovering a White House scandal. Any misdoing by the White House Office immediately embarrasses the president and could lead to presidential defeat, resignation, or impeachment. Furthermore, presidential campaigns often attract young, bold, ambitious risk takers. These types of people are not necessarily prepared to exercise the restraint and caution that a job on the White House staff demands. As an exasperated congressman exclaimed upon learning that a Clinton aide (formerly a campaign worker) had erroneously obtained FBI files on prominent Republicans, "we have political operatives, incompetents and even teen-agers involved in this process."[42]

## The Power to Recommend

> PRESIDENTIAL POWER: *The president may recommend to Congress for "their consideration such Measures as he shall judge necessary and expedient."*

> CONGRESSIONAL CHECK: *Only Congress may enact measures into law.*

The power to recommend gives the president the power of initiation—the power to set the political agenda.[43] Presidents can shut down old policy options, create new possibilities, and change the political dialogue. Ronald Reagan placed defense increases and budget and tax cuts on the policy agenda; Bill Clinton proposed major health care reform, welfare reform, and reduction of class size in public schools.

## Election Connection — Roosevelt's First Hundred Days

When Franklin D. Roosevelt campaigned for president in 1932 in the midst of the Great Depression, he promised the voters that he would bring "Recovery, Relief, and Reform." As soon as he became president, he called Congress into special session and persuaded it to pass dozens of new laws within 100 days. These laws included the following legislation, which provided the foundation for what became known as the New Deal.

- Emergency Banking Relief Act (stabilized embattled banks)
- Emergency Conservation Work Act (created the Civilian Conservation Corps, a public works program)
- Federal Emergency Relief Act (general assistance to the unemployed)
- Agricultural Adjustment Act (price supports for farmers)
- Tennessee Valley Authority Act (built power plants in the Tennessee Valley)
- National Industrial Recovery Act (managed labor and competition in the private sector and set up additional public works programs)
- Glass–Steagall Banking Recovery Act (insured bank deposits)

One senator declared that if the president had asked Congress "to commit suicide tomorrow, they'd do it."

Although some of the legislation had been so hastily drafted that it later had to be reconsidered, Roosevelt's bill-passing record has haunted presidents ever since. At the end of every president's first 100 days, newspaper reporters compare his bill-passing record to Roosevelt's. The comparison is inevitably unfavorable.

*Is this a fair comparison to make? After all, FDR came into office in a time of national emergency, when Congress and the public were willing to take drastic action. Should Roosevelt's record be used as a model, or should it be thought of as an exception?*

SOURCES: Thomas Bailey, *The American Pageant* (Boston: D.C. Heath, 1956), p. 836; William E. Leuchtenburg, *In the Shadow of FDR: From Harry Truman to Bill Clinton* (Ithaca, NY: Cornell University Press, 1993).

---

However, this power does not go unchecked. Congress can—and often does—ignore or greatly modify a presidential recommendation. Congress rejected Clinton's health care proposals and greatly modified his proposals on welfare reform. Nor is the power to initiate limited to the president. In 1994, congressional Republicans campaigned on a "Contract with America" that set the policy agenda for the next two years, although, except for welfare reform and a law banning unfunded state mandates, only a small portion of the "contract" became law.

**Early Use of the Power to Recommend** Presidential use of the power to recommend was exercised with great restraint in the decades preceding the Civil War.[44] At that time, the preservation of national unity required a taciturn president. Because the president was the symbol of the nation as a whole, and because the nation was divided into free and slave states, presidents dared not talk about slavery, the most important political question of the period. This principle of silence was extended to other issues as well, and in general presidents were expected to remain publicly silent on an issue once deliberations about it had begun on Capitol Hill.[45]

**Modern Use of the Power to Recommend** The presidential power to recommend expanded rapidly after the end of the Civil War. The country was growing swiftly, and many social and economic problems were becoming national in scope. The nation's strongest presidents have had their greatest impact not so much by making decisions as by opening up new possibilities. For example, Theodore Roosevelt made conservation a major public concern. Franklin Roosevelt called for a New Deal that would protect Americans from economic downturns and persuaded Congress to pass dozens of bills within 100 days of his inauguration (see the accompanying Election Connection). Reagan focused attention on reducing the size of government.

**Timing Presidential Initiatives** Presidents have the best chance of initiating policy in the first months after their election. As Figure 13.5 shows, presidents make most new proposals at the very beginning of their first term. This is the time when presidential popularity is at a peak, and both Congress and the country are eager to hear what solutions the new president is bringing to the country's problems. As one of

Figure 13.5

**The Presidential Legislative Agenda:
It's Largest in the First Year**
*Why do presidents try to get the most
done in their first year in office?*

SOURCES: Calculations are based on data
drawn from Lyn Ragsdale, *Vital Statistics on
the Presidency* (Washington, DC: CQ Press,
1996).

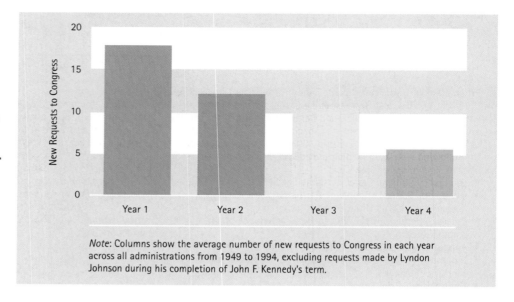

*Note:* Columns show the average number of new requests to Congress in each year
across all administrations from 1949 to 1994, excluding requests made by Lyndon
Johnson during his completion of John F. Kennedy's term.

Lyndon Johnson's top aides noted, "You've got to give it all you can that first year. . . .
You've got just one year when they treat you right. . . . You can't put anything through
when half of the Congress is thinking about how to beat you. So you've got one
year."[46]

Because the beginning of a presidential term is so important, the **transition** period between the previous presidency and the new one is critical. The transition period
consists of the approximately 75 days between election day (the first Tuesday after the
first Monday in November) and January 20, Inauguration Day. It is the one moment
when incoming presidents have power without responsibility. They do not yet have
the burdens of office, but they have the time and resources to set the stage for a vigorous start. If the transition is well organized, this is the best of all times for building
public support.

In a highly successful transition, Reagan asked his top advisers to prepare an
extensive array of tax cuts, increases in the defense budget, and cuts in domestic
expenditures and government regulation. Bill Clinton's transition was much more
troublesome. The issue of gays in the military dogged him throughout, and his nominee for attorney general asked that her name be withdrawn because of a controversy
surrounding her failure to pay social security taxes for a household employee.

The transition period is typically followed by the presidential **honeymoon**—the
first several months of a presidency, when reporters are kinder than usual, Congress
more inclined to be cooperative, and the public receptive to new approaches.[47] Ronald
Reagan's reputation as a strong president owes much to his accomplishments during
his honeymoon period. Controlled by the opposition party, Congress at first seemed
prepared to defy his wishes, but when Reagan survived an assassin's bullet with spirit
and self-confidence, his popularity soared and Congress acquiesced to many of his
requests.

Some have wondered whether presidential honeymoons have gone the way of
rotary-dial telephones and wooden tennis rackets. As public expectations have risen
and presidents have become ever more exposed to media scrutiny, chief executives can
no longer count on a period of good will before facing determined opposition.[48]
Certainly, Bill Clinton's honeymoon hardly lasted the time it took him to traverse the
Inauguration Day parade route from the Capitol to the White House. "By Memorial
Day," one scholar has noted, "Clinton gave an address at the Vietnam War memorial
that was met by a highly vocal and hostile crowd."[49] Only later did Clinton recover
from one of the most "shallow and brief" of presidential honeymoons.[50] Presidents

**transition**
The period after a presidential candidate has won the November election
but before the candidate assumes
office as president on January 20.

**honeymoon**
The first several months of a presidency, when reporters are more forgiving than usual, Congress more
inclined to be cooperative, and the
public receptive to new approaches.

**visual literacy**

**Presidential Success
in Congress**

**Two Very Different Honeymoons**
Presidents Reagan and Clinton experienced very different transition and honeymoon periods. Whereas Reagan was able to get his tax and budget proposals through Congress, Clinton became bogged down in issues such as gays in the military. *What advice would you give a president who wanted to have a successful honeymoon period?*

sometimes also enjoy a brief second honeymoon after their reelection. Ronald Reagan managed to use this moment to initiate a major tax reform. Clinton used his second honeymoon to achieve a balanced budget.

## The President as Chief of State

> PRESIDENTIAL POWER: *The President "shall receive Ambassadors and other public Ministers . . . and shall Commission all the Officers of the United States."*
>
> CONGRESSIONAL CHECK: *None.*

In bestowing one of the very few unchecked powers granted to the president, this constitutional clause seems to say little more than that presidents may welcome visitors and administer oaths of office. Yet the words endow presidents with an invaluable political resource, the capacity to act with all the dignity countries accord their heads of state. In many countries, the political leader and the head of state are institutionally separated (see the accompanying International Comparison). In the United States, the president fills both roles.

According to Walter Bagehot, a nineteenth-century analyst of British politics, governments have both efficient and dignified aspects.[51] The **efficient aspect** of government involves the making of policy, administration of the laws, and the settling of political disputes. This is the nuts and bolts of day-to-day policy making, the kind of activity enjoyed by the Washington insider, often derisively called a "policy wonk." It is also hard work that often generates conflict. But government also has a **dignified aspect** that Bagehot thought equally important to its long-term effectiveness. Governments must express the unity of the people, their high moral purposes, their hopes for the future, and their capacity to defend themselves against foreign aggressors. Ceremonial occasions provide opportunities for expression of the dignified aspect of government that helps sustain public trust and loyalty.

The dignified aspect of the presidency has always seemed somewhat inconsistent with the egalitarian ideals of American democracy. One of the issues discussed in the very first Congress was in what manner President George Washington should be addressed. A Senate committee recommended that he be addressed as "His Highness the President of the United States of America, and Protector of Their Liberties." When the House of Representatives objected to the royal language, the Senate agreed to address Washington simply as "the President of the United States." Washington himself preferred the simpler title. He wrote privately to a friend, "Happily the matter is

**efficient aspect**
According to Walter Bagehot, the aspect of government that involves making policy, administering the laws, and settling disputes.

**dignified aspect**
According to Walter Bagehot, the aspect of government, including royalty and ceremony, that generates citizen respect and loyalty.

## International Comparison — The Chief of State in Other Countries

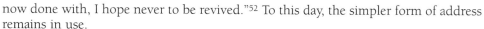

In many countries the political leader and the chief of state are institutionally separated. In Great Britain, for example, the dignified chief of state is the queen. She symbolizes the unity of the nation, represents her country on formal international occasions, and presides over national holidays. The efficient aspect of British government is headed by the country's prime minister. Though powerful, prime ministers lack royal dignity. Their residence is a modest home tucked away on a small London side street. Before assuming ministerial responsibilities, they must first accept on bended knee Her Majesty's request that they form a government.

The division of political responsibilities in Japan is much the same. The emperor of Japan is the dignified chief of state; the elected prime minister is—in ceremonial terms—nothing more than the emperor's efficient minister. Of course, the dignified queen and emperor have very little real power, but their presence as a symbol of the unity of the nation reminds people that the ministers can be ejected by the voters at any time.

In the United States, presidents are expected to combine both the efficient and dignified aspects of government. In addition to their political and policy tasks, presidents are expected to be the symbol of national unity. When queens and emperors assemble, the United States is represented by its president. On days of national celebration, such as Independence Day and Thanksgiving, it is the president who is called upon to express national hopes and dreams. Presidents live in the White House, which, though modest by the standards of European and Japanese castles, has become an increasingly grand focal point of Washington society.

*What do you think?*
- *Do you think the dignified aspect of national leadership is necessary? What needs does it fill?*
- *What are the advantages and disadvantages of combining the efficient and dignified aspects of leadership in one person?*

---

www.longmanparticipate.com

comparative

**Comparing Chief Executives**

**An Informal President**
President Jimmy Carter was uncomfortable with the dignified aspect of the presidency, adopting a casual style even when meeting with chiefs of state. He donned his trademark sweater for negotiations with Egyptian President Anwar Sadat.

now done with, I hope never to be revived."[52] To this day, the simpler form of address remains in use.

Early American presidents were expected to play only a limited role in the efficient aspect of government so that they could enhance the dignity of the national government and serve as a unifying symbol for a far-flung country. By remaining distant from day-to-day legislative politics, presidents tried to retain the respect and admiration of citizens from throughout the nation. As presidents have become increasingly engaged in the efficient aspect of government, they have sometimes found it more difficult to maintain their dignity. In the words of one novelist, presidents must learn to "appreciate the gentle absurdity of Dignity skating on the thinnest of ice with the placid sangfroid of the truly courageous."[53]

The Watergate crisis during the presidency of Richard Nixon took a particularly severe toll. As president, Nixon enjoyed the pomp and circumstance of office. He liked to listen to the presidential song, "Hail to the Chief," and to review at strict attention ranks of marching soldiers. Nixon's vaguely royal pretensions seemed harmless enough initially, but after Watergate many people began to feel that an all-too-royal president was endangering democratic practice.

After Nixon's resignation, his successors de-emphasized the splendor of the office. Gerald Ford adopted a folksy, informal manner. Jimmy Carter wore a sweater, carried his own suitcases, and remained on a first-name basis with ordinary voters. At the same time, Carter became deeply involved in the efficient aspects of government, working late into the night on policy issues and foreign policy crises. Carter's relaxation of presidential dignity had its costs. When American diplomats were taken hostage in Iran, many blamed the president for appearing too weak.

Ronald Reagan worked assiduously to restore grandeur to the presidential office. White House social events once again became formal affairs. The unveiling of a restored Statue of Liberty was carefully designed to celebrate the country's past and future. At the same time, Reagan withdrew from day-to-day legislative politics. By emphasizing the dignity of the office, Reagan acquired the title "the Teflon President," because bad news never seemed to stick to him.

In the first year of his presidency, Bill Clinton took quite the opposite tack. Instead of emphasizing broad themes, he became known as a policy wonk. Toward the end of his first year in office, President Clinton met with a group of scholars who advised him

"to pull back from the immediate details of policies and programs . . . and to explain what is at stake morally and politically in these policies." The president responded by making a series of speeches condemning violence on television and crime in the streets and calling for an end to the "great crisis of the spirit that is gripping America today."[54] The change helped him gather greater public support in subsequent years, though by the time of his impeachment, many believed that his personal transgressions had robbed him of his moral authority. In short, if not carried to royalist extremes, a president's dignity can be a valuable political asset.

**The First Lady** The historical role of the president's spouse, traditionally called the **First Lady,** was to reinforce the dignified aspect of the presidency. In keeping with the traditional role women have played in American society, First Ladies typically hosted social events, visited the sick, promoted children's issues, and loyally stood by their husbands in times of trouble. Yet some were able to use this dignified role to make contributions that will long be remembered. Jacqueline Kennedy invigorated Washington art and culture and restored the White House. Lady Bird Johnson committed herself to the beautification of Washington. Nancy Reagan's "Just Say No" educational program may have done more to reduce drug use than billions of dollars spent in antidrug enforcement efforts.[55]

Few First Ladies were as effective at managing the dignified aspect of the presidency as Barbara Bush. Her gray hair and unflappable demeanor gave her a grandmotherly appeal that crossed political boundaries. Her book about her dog Millie became a national best-seller, out-selling her husband's memoirs by a wide margin.

Not all First Ladies have been content to confine themselves to the dignified aspect of the presidency, however. Eleanor Roosevelt promoted civil rights and other social causes supported only off-handedly by her husband.[56] But it has been Hillary Rodham Clinton who has given the role of the First Lady a dramatically new definition. At the beginning of Clinton's first term, she was appointed to lead the presidential health care task force.[57] Her policy involvement won the praise of some, but it took a toll on her popularity with the public in general. Hillary Clinton was initially less popular than her predecessor, Barbara Bush. To enhance her public image, Hillary Clinton began de-emphasizing her policy responsibilities and enlarged her dignified

**First Lady**
Traditional title of the president's spouse.

**A Gathering of First Ladies**
Claudia (Lady Bird) Johnson, Betty Ford, Rosalynn Carter, Nancy Reagan, Barbara Bush, and Hillary Rodham Clinton make a rare joint appearance. *How has the role of the First Lady changed in recent decades?*

role by concentrating on children's issues. Her popularity rose further as a result of the Lewinsky scandal, when she defended her husband in a time of adversity.

In 1999 Hillary Clinton became the first First Lady to embark on her own independent career in elective politics. As she ran for a New York senate seat, she scaled back her White House hostess duties and increased her appearances at campaign events. It was now Bill Clinton's turn to be supportive of his wife: "If I can help her in any way, I will. I think it's wonderful."[58]

It remains to be seen whether Hillary Clinton has permanently redefined the role of the First Lady. And perhaps the role of presidential spouse will be redefined most profoundly when the position is referred to as First Gentleman.

**The Vice-President** Traditionally, the vice-president's impact on policy has been so limited that the office suffered in dignity as well. The nation's first vice-president, John Adams, wrote to his wife, "My country has in its wisdom contrived for me the most insignificant office that ever the invention of man contrived. . . . I can do neither good nor evil." Harry Truman, when vice-president, allowed that the job was "about as useful as a cow's fifth teat."[59]

Jokes about the vice-presidency have a basis in reality. The only formal responsibility of the office is to preside over the United States Senate and cast a vote in case of a tie. Otherwise, the vice-president's duties and influence depend entirely upon the will of the president. As Vice-President Hubert Humphrey put it, "He who giveth can taketh away and often does."[60]

Presidents have traditionally been reluctant to delegate responsibility to vice-presidents, because they constitute a potential political problem. Presidents cannot fire their vice-presidents, as they can other aides. If a vice-president decides to criticize the president or pursue an independent policy line, the president can do little about it. When Vice-President Nelson Rockefeller pushed more liberal policies than those favored by Gerald Ford, he proved an embarrassment to the president and was not chosen to be Ford's running mate in 1976. Some claim the Rockefeller controversy cost Ford his reelection.

The vice-presidential selection process accentuates the potential for conflict, because vice-presidents often come from a wing of the party opposite that of the president.[61] An aide to John Kennedy admitted that Lyndon Johnson was picked for vice-president because "he was the leader of that segment of the party where Kennedy had very little strength—the South."[62] Carter's assistant said, "Mondale was chosen to run . . . precisely *because* he . . . was from a different area of the country and represented the other wing of the Democratic party."[63] To win moderate votes, Al Gore selected Joe Lieberman as his running mate despite the fact that Lieberman had previously supported school vouchers and social-security reform, policies Gore opposed.

But if presidents have powerful incentives to limit the vice-presidential role, one can no longer dismiss vice-presidents as political lightweights. For one thing, no person is more likely to become president of the United States than the vice-president, who can succeed to the office through death, by resignation, or by winning the next election. Twelve of the 41 presidents of the United States held the office of vice president, and no fewer than half of the last 8 presidents were vice-presidents.

Perhaps because of the greater awareness that the vice-president may one day gain the highest office, the role of the vice-president has steadily broadened. Vice-presidents now travel extensively in foreign countries, attend state funerals, speak at political party and interest-group conventions, and act as substitutes for the president on state occasions. Their efficient role has also been enhanced. For example, as vice-president, Albert Gore played a key role in shaping the Clinton administration's environmental policy. Richard Cheney, George W. Bush's vice-presidential choice, was selected for his familiarity with national-security issues.

### Inherent Executive Power

> PRESIDENTIAL INHERENT EXECUTIVE POWER: *"The executive power shall be vested in a President."*

Some claim that this statement adds nothing to presidential power beyond the specific powers granted to the president. But many presidents have found in this clause the basis for a claim to additional rights and privileges. As will be discussed in Chapter 20, presidential claims to **inherent executive power** have been invoked most frequently in making foreign policy. But presidents have asserted inherent executive power on other occasions as well. Teddy Roosevelt placed 46 million acres of public land into the National Forest system just before signing a bill denying presidents the power to place any more land in the National Forest system.[64] After leaving office, Roosevelt admitted, "My belief was that it was not only the [president's] right but his duty to do anything that the needs of the Nation demanded unless such action was forbidden by the Constitution or by its laws."[65]

**inherent executive power**
Presidential authority inherent to the executive branch of government, though not specifically mentioned in the Constitution.

**executive order**
A presidential directive that has the force of law, though it is not enacted by Congress.

**Executive Order** One way in which presidents use their inherent executive powers is by issuing **executive orders**—directives that carry the weight of law even though they were not enacted by Congress. The Supreme Court ruled in 1936 that executive orders are constitutional, and since then they have increased in frequency and importance.[66] Executive orders were used by Harry Truman to desegregate the armed forces, by Lyndon Johnson to institute the first affirmative action program, by Ronald Reagan to forbid homosexuality in the military, and by Bill Clinton to impose sanctions on Haiti after a military coup in that country. Executive orders may not run contrary to congressional legislation, and they may be overturned by Congress. When President Clinton proposed to issue an executive order reversing the ban on gays in the military, it was the threat of congressional action reversing such an order that forced the president to reach the "Don't ask, don't tell" compromise discussed in the opening section of this chapter. Figure 13.6 shows how sharply the use of executive orders among modern presidents has increased.

timeline

**The Executive Order over Time**

**Executive Privilege** The most controversial invocation of inherent executive powers has been the doctrine of **executive privilege,** the right of the president to deny Congress information it requests on the grounds that the activities of the executive branch must be kept confidential. George Washington was the first to invoke

**executive privilege**
The right of members of the executive branch to have private communications among themselves that need not be shared with Congress.

**Figure 13.6**

**Significant Executive Orders, 1900–1996**
A "significant" executive order is defined as an order that receives mention in a Congressional hearing, on the floor of Congress, or in the pages of the *New York Times. Why do you think modern presidents have issued more executive orders than earlier presidents?*

SOURCE: William Howell, "The President's Powers of Unilateral Action: The Strategic Advantages of Acting Alone." (Stanford University dissertation, 1999).

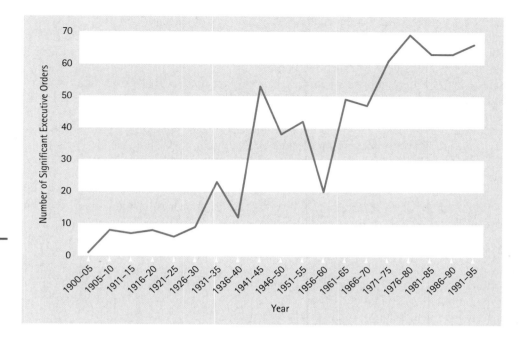

executive privilege when he refused to provide Congress information about an ill-fated military expedition on the grounds that its "disclosure . . . would injure the public."[67] Ever since, presidents have claimed authority to withhold from Congress information on executive decision making. The Watergate scandal brought the question before the Supreme Court, which sanctioned the doctrine of executive privilege, saying that privileged communication among aides to the president was "fundamental to the operation of government and inextricably rooted in the separation of powers under the Constitution."[68]

Although Congress could not simply demand access to any and all conversations taking place among the president's advisers, the Supreme Court went on to say that executive privilege could not be invoked to cover up criminal conduct. Communication that might be privileged under other circumstances loses that status when wrongdoing occurs. Nor can it be left to the executive branch to decide whether the communication is part of a cover-up. The disputed documents must be submitted to the court for its examination behind closed doors. When the Supreme Court examined the Watergate documents, sufficient evidence of criminal conduct was found that President Nixon was forced to release the documents. Because of this ruling, the Clinton administration reluctantly released many (but not all) documents connected with the Whitewater/Lewinsky scandal.

### The Impeachment Power

CONGRESSIONAL IMPEACHMENT POWER: *Presidents may be impeached by a majority of the House of Representatives for "high crimes and misdemeanors." The president is removed from office if the Senate convicts by a two-thirds vote.*

**impeachment**
Recommendation by a majority of the House of Representatives that a president, other executive-branch official, or judge of the federal courts be removed from office; removal depends on a two-thirds vote of the Senate.

Nothing makes more clear the subordination of presidents to Congress than the fact that the House of Representatives can impeach and the Senate can convict and remove presidents from office. Though seldom used, the constitutional power of **impeachment** is no dead letter. Andrew Johnson was impeached in 1868, though the Senate, by one vote, failed to convict him.[69] Richard Nixon resigned in the face of almost certain impeachment in 1974. And President Clinton's affair with Monica Lewinsky, a White House intern, led to the first impeachment and trial of a president in over a century.

In 1994 a three-judge panel appointed Kenneth Starr as independent counsel with the authority to investigate charges related to the questionable Whitewater land

**President on Trial**
President Clinton's was the first impeachment and trial of a U.S. president in 130 years. *Was this a frivolous extension of partisan politics or a reasoned response to a serious scandal?*

deal in which Clinton had been involved while governor of Arkansas. Separately, an Arkansas public employee, Paula Jones, sued Clinton for sexual harassment. In 1998 the scandals merged. Starr concluded that Clinton had obstructed justice and committed perjury when, in the Jones case, he denied under oath having sexual relations with Lewinsky.

The president claimed his denial was not perjury, because the Lewinsky affair did not include sexual relations, as Clinton narrowly defined the term. The electorate seemed to take his side: When Republicans lost ground in the 1998 congressional elections, pundits interpreted the results as reflecting voter disgust with Republicans for exaggerating and prolonging the issue. Afterwards, Newt Gingrich resigned as Speaker of the House. But on December 19, 1998, the House voted (along mostly partisan lines) to impeach the president, making him only the second U.S. chief executive to face removal from office by Congress.

In early 1999 the Senate began its trial of the president, with Chief Justice William Rehnquist presiding. Representative Henry Hyde of Illinois, one of the House members acting as prosecutors in the trial, argued that the president's actions, far from being a private matter, endangered the integrity of his office. Perjury and obstruction of justice, Hyde said, "are public acts. And when committed by the chief law enforcement officer of the land . . . they do become the concern of Congress."[70]

Clinton's own lawyers put up a spirited defense, and after five weeks of testimony from both sides, the Senate was ready to vote. In considering their actions, most Senators believed that if they were to overturn a national election by removing Clinton from office, they needed more serious cause. After all, polls showed that two-thirds of the public still thought the president should stay.[71] On February 12, the Senate voted for acquittal. Republican Senator Susan Collins explained her vote this way:

> As much as it troubles me to acquit this President, I cannot do otherwise and remain true to my role as a Senator. To remove a popularly elected president . . . is an extraordinary action that should be undertaken only when the President's misconduct so injures the fabric of democracy that the Senate is left with no option. . . .[72]

The Clinton scandals have altered the American presidency in important respects. First, presidents are now at risk of being sued by their political opponents. Before the Jones case, no president had ever been sued. Clinton argued that the Jones suit should be delayed until his term in office had ended. Otherwise, he maintained, it would interfere with his constitutional duties. But the Supreme Court ruled that presidents could be sued for alleged wrongful conduct that is not part of their presidential duties. No one, not even the president, is above the law. In the opinion it issued, the Supreme Court said that lawsuits were unlikely to interfere with presidential responsibilities. But others are not so sure. In this age of media-driven politics, will new lawsuits produce still more scandals for future presidents?

Second, it has become clear that the advice presidents receive from their government attorneys is not necessarily confidential. The president's attorney claimed the right to keep conversations about Lewinsky confidential. But the courts said that conversations between government attorneys and presidents were not protected unless they involved official duties. In the future, presidents can be expected to hire private legal advisers.

Finally, some scholars have argued that the partisan nature of Clinton's impeachment is a sign that the practice is more likely to be used in the future as a political weapon. From this perspective, threatened impeachment has now become a more powerful check on the executive branch. Others disagree, however, noting that the circumstances of the scandal were unique. "If Watergate was a 'long national nightmare,'" suggests one presidential scholar, the Lewinsky scandal "seems more like a drug-induced hallucination."[73]

**independent counsel**
(Originally called special prosecutor) Legal officer appointed by a court to investigate allegations of criminal activity against high-ranking members of the executive branch. Law expired in 1999.

**Independent Counsel** As the Clinton scandal illustrated, the establishment of the office of **independent counsel** in 1978 enhanced the impeachment power of Congress. An independent counsel (originally called a special prosecutor) was to be appointed whenever allegations of criminal conduct were made against high-ranking officials of the executive branch. Appointed by judges, the counselors were independent in the sense that, once the scope of the investigation had been defined, they were independent of officials in the executive branch. No fewer than 20 independent-counsel investigations took place between 1978 and 1999.[74]

The law was allowed to expire in 1999. Not many members of Congress favored renewing it. Even Kenneth Starr, the independent counselor in the Lewinsky case, testified before Congress against the law. In the absence of an independent-counsel law, the attorney general will begin ethics investigations of top officials at her or his discretion.[75] This change may make high-profile investigations less likely.

SECTION SUMMARY

Presidents are granted various powers by the Constitution, including the power to inform and to try to persuade Congress, to veto bills, to appoint officials, to recommend policies, and to act as chief of state. But the Constitution grants Congress important checks on these presidential powers, such as the power to override vetoes, approve nominations, and even remove the president from office. The result is that, in effect, Congress and the president share power, a situation that can prove frustrating to both.

## Presidential Expectations and Presidential Performance

Presidents are expected to be strong, yet presidential powers are limited. As a result, presidents seldom satisfy the hopes and aspirations of the voting public. Presidential successes are quickly forgotten, whereas their failures are often magnified by time. To sustain their reputation and effectiveness, presidents are often forced to act with Machiavellian cleverness (see the accompanying Window on the Past).

Presidents in the past were often able to cover ruthless actions with a cloak of dignity that the role of chief of state allowed them to wear. But as the life of the president becomes more open to the media, it grows ever more difficult to keep the cloak of

## *Window* on the *Past*

### Lincoln, the Great Machiavellian

Presidents often find themselves in tough situations not much different from the circumstances faced by sixteenth-century rulers of northern Italian cities, who were constantly threatened by foreign invasions and internal coups. The strategic advice that the great political philosopher Niccolò Machiavelli gave these rulers has remarkable applicability to modern presidents. Most Americans believe Lincoln was their greatest president, but few realize the extent to which his behavior was Machiavellian. Machiavelli's advice can be reduced to three maxims, all of which Lincoln followed.

**Maxim I: Be energetic, decisive, and sudden.**

At the very beginning of his presidency, Lincoln recognized the benefits of sudden, decisive action. Even before he took the Oath of Office, seven southern states seceded from the Union. Lincoln knew that the more time the Confederate states had to organize an armed force, the more likely it was that the secession would become permanent. Lincoln was also concerned that Congress would be reluctant to initiate military action. Lincoln moved quickly while Congress was in recess. Just days after his inauguration, he ordered the U.S. Navy to resupply the troops at South Carolina's Fort Sumter. The Confederates, claiming the fort as theirs, shot at northern ships as they entered the harbor. Blaming the southerners for having started the war (though he had invited the attack), Lincoln appealed to northerners to join a volunteer army. Now that blood had been shed, new recruits poured into Washington.

**Maxim II: Make plans in secret.**

Lincoln wrote the Emancipation Proclamation that freed the southern slaves two months before announcing it and chose not to announce the proclamation until the Union army had won a significant victory. Otherwise the proclamation might have appeared to be an act of desperation. It might even have caused loyal slave states, such as Kentucky and Missouri, to defect to the Confederacy.

Niccolò Machiavelli

**Maxim III: Only one ruler is possible.**

According to ancient legends, Rome was founded by two brothers, Romulus and Remus. When the two became rulers of the city, Romulus killed Remus. Machiavelli thought the killing was justified, because the existence of two rulers invites a destructive contest for power.

When Lincoln assumed office, he was thought to be little more than a lightweight, story-telling attorney from a small, frontier town. Most cabinet members thought they were more qualified to serve as president than Lincoln was. But he proved tougher and more shrewd than any of the others. On one occasion, when every member of the cabinet opposed him, he declared the vote as follows: "Seven nays, one aye—the ayes have it."

SOURCES: Harvey Mansfield, Jr., *Taming the Prince: The Ambivalence of Modern Executive Power* (New York: Free Press, 1989); James McPherson, *The Battle Cry of Freedom: The Civil War Era* (New York: Oxford University Press, 1988), pp. 264–75, 505; Frederic Austin Ogg and P. Orman Ray, *Introduction to American Government,* 10th ed. (New York: Appleton-Century-Crofts, 1951), p. 394.

dignity tightly wrapped. As Bill Clinton said one year into his presidency, "It is difficult for people to function in an environment in which they feel that their character, their values, and their motives are always suspect, and where the presumption here is against them."[76]

## Presidential Reputations

**beltway insider**
Person living in the Washington metropolitan area who is engaged in, or well informed about, national politics and government.

To meet public expectations despite their limited power, presidents need to protect their professional reputation among members of Congress and other **beltway insiders,** the politically influential people who live inside the highway that surrounds Washington, DC.[77] Presidential reputations inside Washington are shaped by the quality of the people who serve the presidents and the frequency with which presidents win political contests. They also depend on the president's ability to let go of issues that cannot be won. As Lincoln put it, "When you have got an elephant by the hind legs and he is trying to run away, it is best to let him run."[78]

## Presidential Popularity

**presidential popularity**
Evaluation of president by voters, usually as measured by a survey question asking the adult population how well they think the president is doing his job.

In addition to guarding their professional reputation, presidents need to maintain their popularity with the general public. As Lincoln also shrewdly observed, "With public sentiment, nothing can fail; without it, nothing can succeed."[79] **Presidential popularity** is measured by asking the adult population how well they think the president is doing his job. Pollsters now ask the same question almost every week, so it provides a decent barometer of the public's current assessment of the president's performance.

All presidents experience fluctuations in their popularity over the course of their terms. Their support rises and falls with changes in the country's economic conditions and in response to foreign policy crises. But in addition to these external factors, presidential popularity tends to decline over time as public expectations go unfulfilled.[80] A study of the first term of eight recent presidents indicates that, apart from any specific economic or foreign policy events, their popularity fell by nearly 8 points in their first year in office and by 15 points by the middle of their third year (see Figure 13.7). Their popularity recovered in their fourth year, when a presidential campaign was under way, probably because at that time presidents made special efforts to communicate positive news about their administrations. Presidents regained popularity when reelected, but once again it trailed off.

President Clinton had lower than average public support at the beginning of his first term, but it did not decay over time. During his first year, only 48 percent of Americans thought he was doing a good job; the percentage rose slightly to 52 percent in his second and third years and to 53 percent his fourth year.[81] Despite the Lewinsky scandal, Clinton's popularity was even higher in his second term, beginning in 1997 at 58 percent and rising above 60 percent for all of 1998 and most of 1999.[82] The usual tendency for presidential support to drop was probably offset in this case by steady economic growth.

Presidential popularity and professional reputation were at one time regarded as two quite separate phenomena. Unpopular presidents could still have the respect of beltway insiders if they husbanded their political resources carefully. But the distinction between popularity and reputation has become clouded.[83] Presidents are the focus of seemingly inexhaustible but utterly exhausting television, radio, and newspaper coverage. They are the objects of what has been called the "politics of high exposure." As soon as they have addressed one problem, they are urged to resolve the next. As one commentator put it, "Getting the public's attention, particularly on a subject that the polls show is already gnawing at people, is no trick for a President. . . . The trick is holding that attention."[84]

The one kind of attention presidents (or would-be presidents) are likely to hold is the kind they don't want. When George Bush became nauseated at a state dinner in Tokyo, the embarrassing consequences were graphically reported in news headlines. When Al Gore, campaigning for president, said he "took the initiative in creating the

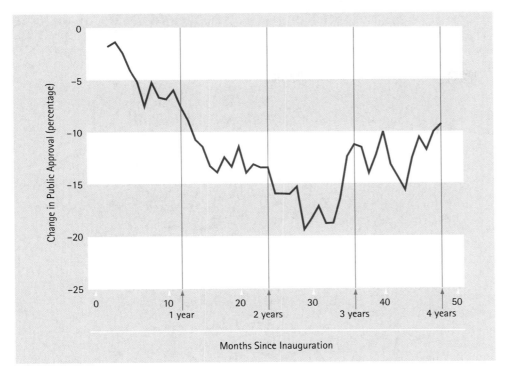

**Figure 13.7**

**Decline in Presidential Popularity Over the First Term**
The president's popularity typically declines until the year before the next election.

SOURCE: This figure is taken from Paul Brace and Barbara Hinckley, *Follow the Leader: Opinion Polls and the Modern Presidents* (New York: Basic Books, 1992), p. 33, Figure 2.3.

Internet," Republican Senate leader Trent Lott mocked him by issuing a news release claiming that Lott had invented the paperclip.[85] And when Gore's opponent, George W. Bush, was unable to name three obscure foreign leaders, some declared that he was unfit for the top job.

If these kinds of incidents cause a president's popularity to slip, weekly polling results transmit this information to beltway insiders. If the president's reputation is slipping in Washington, the news media just as quickly communicate insider opinions to the wider public. As a result, the president now has to work both the inside and the outside of the beltway at the same time.[86]

## Great Presidents

All presidents are challenged by problems and opponents both at home and abroad, and all find it difficult to preserve both professional reputation and public popularity throughout their terms of office. Yet some presidents are remembered as "Great Presidents," because they achieve many of the objectives they set for themselves; others are seemingly unable to tackle the problems they face. Why do some succeed and others fail?

In a study of presidential character, James Barber argued that certain personality traits make for successful presidents (see Figure 13.8).[87] He said that effective presidents both like their job and readily adapt their policies to changing circumstances. He called these presidents "active-positives." For Barber, Franklin Roosevelt was the ideal active-positive president. He loved his job as president, and he brought great energy to it. He changed his mind frequently—but always with an eye to solving governmental problems. No wonder he was reelected three times. Clinton also seemed to have an active-positive approach to the job.

Barber argued that most other modern presidents lacked one or the other of these two character traits. President Eisenhower brought a positive attitude, but Barber thought he was too passive. Instead of taking the initiative, he waited for others to pose solutions to problems. Barber claimed that both Lyndon Johnson and Richard Nixon brought an active-negative attitude to the job. Both were grimly determined to do their duty to the end. Though both brought energy to the job, neither

Figure 13.8

**Presidential Character**
*Does presidential effectiveness depend on presidential attitudes and energy?*

SOURCE: Adapted from James Barber, *The Presidential Character: Predicting Performance in the White House*, 4th ed. (Englewood Cliffs, NJ: Prentice-Hall, 1992).

|  | PRESIDENT HAS **HIGH** ENERGY LEVEL. | PRESIDENT HAS **LOW** ENERGY LEVEL. |
|---|---|---|
| **PRESIDENT ENJOYS THE JOB.** | Active-Positive<br><br>Examples<br>Thomas Jefferson<br>Franklin Roosevelt | Passive-Positive<br><br>Examples<br>James Madison<br>Dwight Eisenhower |
| **PRESIDENT IS DISCOURAGED BY THE JOB.** | Active-Negative<br><br>Examples<br>John Adams<br>Lyndon Johnson | Passive-Negative<br><br>Examples<br>George Washington<br>Calvin Coolidge |

www.longmanparticipate.com

participation

**Rate the Presidents**

could adapt to new circumstances. As a result, each pursued a policy position long after a more adaptive president would have changed course. Johnson led the country ever more deeply into the Vietnam War; Nixon tried to "cover up" Watergate misdeeds when he might have been better advised to let the problem come immediately to the surface.

Critics of Barber's schema say he placed too much emphasis on presidential activity.[88] Bill Clinton was an active policy wonk, but he was not always successful in achieving his goals. Eisenhower appeared to be passive, but presidential analyst Fred Greenstein shows that he governed with a "hidden hand."[89] Though Ike let others grab the headlines, he steered the ship from behind, staying out of controversy and preserving his popularity. Reagan was hardly a policy wonk—on the contrary, he seldom

**A President's Resignation**
The epitome of the active-negative president, grimly determined to do his duty until the end, Richard Nixon doggedly repeats his "V for victory" sign upon leaving office on August 9, 1974.

let the presidency interfere with a good afternoon nap.[90] Yet his use of the power of the dignified presidency, together with his focus on fundamental goals, made him a powerful political force.

Presidential success may depend less on personality than on the circumstances under which the newly elected come into office.[91] Presidential scholar Stephen Skowronek says that most are so hemmed in by the checks placed upon them that they simply cannot accomplish the job the public expects. As a result, presidents become "great" only when political circumstances allow them to repudiate the past and move in a sharply different direction. By rejecting the old way of doing things, they are able to discard political baggage that would limit presidential action.

Franklin Roosevelt is once again the archetypal effective president. Running for office in 1932 in the midst of the recession, he declared "these unhappy times call for . . . plans . . . that build from the bottom up and not from the top down, that put their faith once more in the forgotten man." After an election that realigned the American party system, Roosevelt pushed through a huge volume of important legislation in his first 100 days in office.

Roosevelt was not the first effective president who profited by breaking with the past (see Table 13.2). Thomas Jefferson discarded the program of John Adams and the Federalist party, a party so badly defeated it never returned to national power. Republican Abraham Lincoln attacked slavery. Ronald Reagan halted the growth in government that had occurred under his predecessors, saying "Government is not the solution to our problem. Government *is* the problem."[92] Whether a president is able to repudiate the past successfully is somewhat beyond the president's control, however. Congress and the public must also agree that a new direction is needed.

Skowronek's model is not perfect. Many people think Theodore Roosevelt was one of the country's most successful presidents, but he did not become president through a pivotal election or at a time of crisis. And some people think other presidents— Eisenhower (for managing the Cold War) and Johnson (for initiating the Great Society)—deserve inclusion at the top of the list of presidents. But Skowronek does show that presidents are often most effective when they exercise their power to initiate new approaches. It is often left to other, less effective presidents to try to follow this lead.

If Skowronek's theory is correct, the new administration is unlikely to be among the most successful. The prosperous economy and public satisfaction with President Clinton's approach to policy suggest that neither Congress nor the American people are ready for significant policy shifts.

## Table 13.2

**Do Failed Policies and Presidents Lead to the Election of Presidents Who Succeed by Repudiating the Past?**

| Year | Failure | Leads to . . . | Very Successful President |
|------|---------|----------------|---------------------------|
| 1789 | Articles of Confederation | → | George Washington |
| 1800 | John Adams | → | Thomas Jefferson |
| 1828 | John Q. Adams | → | Andrew Jackson |
| 1860 | James Buchanan | → | Abraham Lincoln |
| 1932 | Herbert Hoover | → | Franklin Roosevelt |
| 1980 | Jimmy Carter | → | Ronald Reagan |

SOURCE: Based on Stephen Skowronek, *The Politics Presidents Make* (Cambridge, MA: Harvard University Press, 1993).

## Chapter Summary

Presidents must meet the high expectations of their national and partisan constituencies, despite the fact that Congress checks many of their most important powers.

- Presidents can initiate legislation, but Congress often rejects or substantially modifies their proposals.
- Presidents can appoint executive and judicial officers, but the Senate must approve them.
- Presidents may invoke inherent executive power, including the right of executive privilege, but Congress can impeach them.
- Though the president can veto congressional bills, Congress may override the veto by a two-thirds vote.
- Presidential leadership depends most heavily on the power of the chief executive to initiate and persuade—capacities that derive as much from the dignity of the office as from any specific clauses in the Constitution.

To achieve their goals, presidents must preserve their professional reputation and their political popularity. Because their popularity tends to slip over time, it is at the beginning of their presidency—during the transition and honeymoon periods—that they have the most capacity to initiate change. Great presidents emerge not so much because they have the right personal qualities as because they come to office when the country thinks it is time for a change.

---

### On the Web

The White House
www.whitehouse.gov
The official Web site of the White House offers current and historical information about U.S. presidents.

Center for the Study of the Presidency
www.thepresidency.org
The Center for the Study of the Presidency publishes *Presidential Studies Quarterly* and showcases academic information and links.

National Archives and Records Administration
www.nara.gov/nara/president/address.html
The National Archives and Records Administration provides information about and links to presidential libraries.

---

## Key Terms

administration, p. 387
beltway insider, p. 402
bully pulpit, p. 384
cabinet, p. 387
chief of staff, p. 388
commander in chief,
    p. 378
dignified aspect, p. 393
divided government, p. 381
efficient aspect, p. 393

Executive Office of the President
    (EOP), p. 387
executive order, p. 397
executive privilege, p. 397
First Lady, p. 395
honeymoon, p. 392
impeachment, p. 398
independent counsel (originally
    called special prosecutor),
    p. 400

inherent executive power, p. 397
line item veto, p. 386
override, p. 385
pocket veto, p. 385
presidential popularity, p. 402
secretary, p. 387
State of the Union address, p. 383
transition, p. 392
veto power, p. 384
White House Office, p. 387

# Suggested Readings

Barber, James. *The Presidential Character: Predicting Performance in the White House,* 4th ed. Englewood Cliffs, NJ: Prentice-Hall, 1992. Argues that presidential character affects presidential success.

Jones, Charles. *The Presidency in a Separated System.* Washington, DC: Brookings, 1994. Examines the role of the president under divided government.

Kernell, Samuel. *Going Public: New Strategies of Presidential Leadership,* 3rd ed. Washington, DC: CQ Press, 1997. Describes the increasing tendency of presidents to use popular appeals to influence legislative processes.

Korn, Jessica. *The Power of Separation: American Constitutionalism and the Myth of the Legislative Veto.* Princeton, NJ: Princeton University Press, 1996. Identifies the many ways in which power is shared between Congress and the executive.

Moe, Terry. "The Politicized Presidency," in John Chubb and Paul E. Peterson, eds., *The New Direction in American Politics.* Washington, DC: Brookings, 1985. Insightful essay on the evolution of the White House staff.

Nelson, Michael, ed., *The Presidency and the Political System,* 5th ed. Washington, DC: CQ Press, 1997. Important contemporary essays on the presidency.

Neustadt, Richard E. *Presidential Power and the Modern Presidents.* New York: Free Press, 1990. Modern classic on the limits to presidential power.

Skowronek, Stephen. *The Politics Presidents Make: Leadership from John Adams to George Bush.* Cambridge, MA: Harvard University Press, 1993. Provocative analysis of the historical development of the presidency.

Sundquist, James L. *The Decline and Resurgence of Congress.* Washington, DC: Brookings, 1981. Authoritative description of the growth in presidential powers and responsibilities as well as congressional response to that trend.

Tulis, Jeffrey. *The Rhetorical Presidency.* Princeton, NJ: Princeton University Press, 1987. Contrasts modern presidential rhetoric with that of early presidents. Argues against a rhetorical presidency.

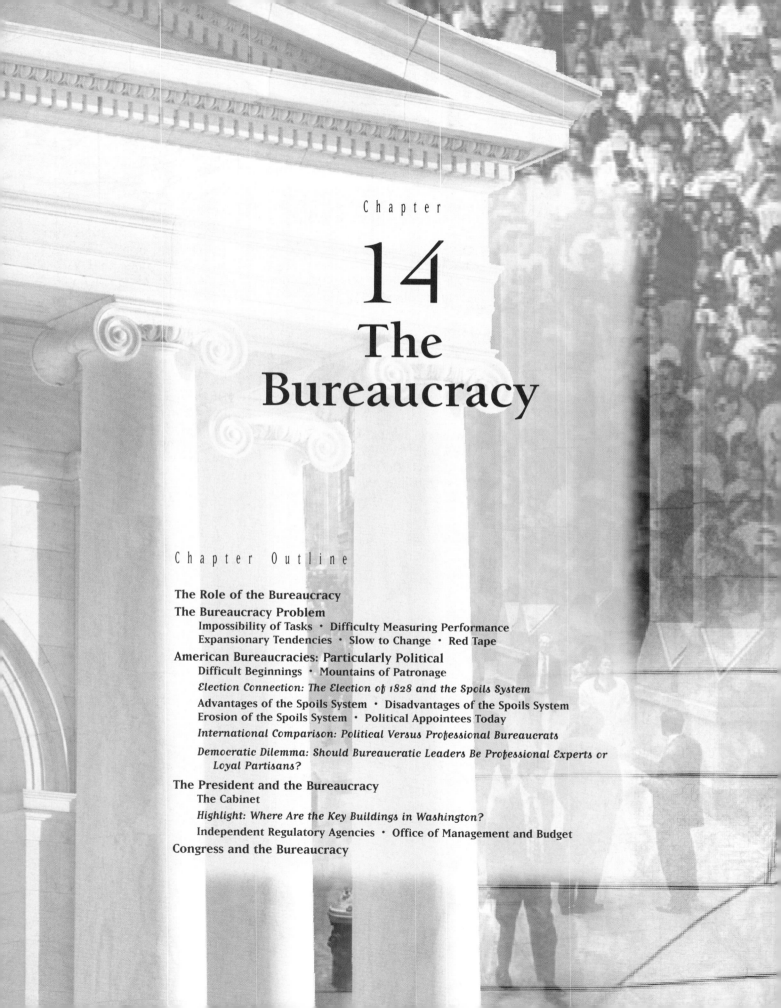

Chapter

# 14
# The
# Bureaucracy

Chapter Outline

W e can no longer afford to pay more for—and get less from—our government," declared Bill Clinton and Al Gore in their first presidential campaign. "It is time . . . to shift from top-down bureaucracy to entrepreneurial government."[1] To accomplish this, Vice-President Gore issued a report on "reinventing government" containing hundreds of proposals expected to save over $100 billion. The federal government would no longer order "designer bug sprays" or pay more for computer disks than those who buy at discount stores.[2] Gore's plan was well received. According to one poll, 95 percent of the public believed that the government wasted "a great deal" or "quite a lot" of the taxpayers' dollars.[3] "Make no mistake about this," the president said. "This is one report that will not gather dust in a warehouse."[4]

Among other things, Gore proposed to "transfer [the] law enforcement functions of the Drug Enforcement Administration [DEA] and the Bureau of Alcohol, Tobacco and Firearms [ATF] to the Federal Bureau of Investigation [FBI]." The missions of the three overlapped. ATF enforced laws regulating the sale and use of alcohol, tobacco, and firearms, DEA enforced drug laws, and the FBI's job included similar responsibilities and many more. In 1992 DEA received $758 million to fight narcotics; the FBI got $205 million.

Duplication of efforts was not just inefficient; it was dangerous. "It is not uncommon for agents from one . . . agency to believe the other to be the criminal element," said a draft version of the Gore study. It concluded that "this . . . could result in life-threatening situations."[5] In part because ATF and the FBI had overlapping responsibilities, in 1993 they bungled an attempt to seize a weapons stockpile held by the Branch Davidians, a religious sect based in Waco, Texas. When agents sought to overrun the Branch Davidian compound after a 51-day siege, the sect's leaders set fire to the building, causing the deaths of 81 adults and children.[6]

Despite the president's commitment to the consolidation of law enforcement, Gore's proposal failed to get off the ground. Within days of its announcement, the idea was scuttled by critics in Congress and in government agencies. ATF was located within the Department of the Treasury, headed by Secretary Lloyd Bentsen—the most powerful member of the first Clinton cabinet—who let it be known he did not want to give up part of his turf. The DEA also had its supporters. Representative Charles Rangel, head of the House Caucus on Drugs, said the merger "would be a monumental mistake."[7] Many government employees, familiar with the cultures of DEA and of the FBI, also considered a merger between the two inconceivable. DEA agents often arrived at work in jeans, ponytails, and earrings, whereas their counterparts in the FBI dressed like Wall Street bankers. Said one DEA agent, "An FBI guy's idea of [going] undercover is to loosen his tie."[8] In the end, the reorganization was abandoned.

⭐ PRESIDENT CLINTON WAS NOT THE FIRST PRESIDENT to try—and fail—to reform the structure of the executive branch. Agency officials feel threatened by changes in their job descriptions, and Congress is also wary of such efforts. As one member of Congress observed, "We all know that the toughest things in Washington are the turf wars. . . . No [congressional] committee likes their authority cut back."[9]

The DEA, ATF, and FBI are all part of the federal bureaucracy. **Bureaucracies** are hierarchical organizations of officials with responsibility for specific tasks. They are essential to government action but are often criticized as being inefficient or too large. In this chapter we discuss how bureaucracies have developed and describe how they fit into modern American politics. In particular, we answer these questions:

- What role does the bureaucracy play in government, and what problems impede its performance?
- How has today's bureaucracy been shaped by the history of our nation, and what changes have been made to reform the bureaucracy?
- What influence do the president and Congress have on the bureaucracy?
- How is the bureaucracy organized, and how do elections affect its operation?

**bureaucracy**
Hierarchical organization designed to perform a particular set of tasks.

## The Role of the Bureaucracy

Bureaucracies are essential to governmental action. Laws become effective only when a government agency implements them. Without some kind of organization, government cannot build roads, operate schools, put out fires, fight wars, distribute social security checks, or do the thousands of other things Americans expect from their government.

As the range of governmental responsibilities has grown, the number of bureaucrats in the United States has also greatly increased. The most growth has occurred at state and local levels, where the vast majority of civilian government workers are employed, including school teachers, police officers, and sanitation workers (see Figure 14.1). In addition, many private contractors perform tasks paid for by government agencies. Though the number of employees who work directly for the federal government is smaller, we shall focus most of our attention on federal bureaucracies,

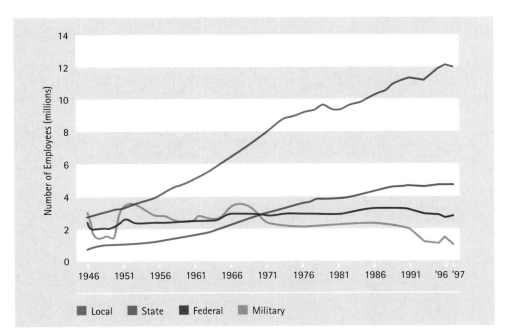

**Figure 14.1**

**Government Employment, 1946–1997**
The number of state and local employees has increased, but the number of federal employees has remained about the same. Note that federal government employment figures include civilians only. Military employment figures include only active-duty personnel.

SOURCES: U.S. Bureau of the Census, *Historical Statistics of the United States: Colonial Times to 1970* (Washington, DC: GPO, 1975), pp. 1100, 1141; Advisory Commission on Intergovernmental Relations, *Significant Features of Fiscal Federalism, 1994* (Washington, DC: ACIR, 1994), Table E; Harold W. Stanley and Richard G. Niemi, *Vital Statistics on American Politics*, 4th ed. (Washington, DC: CQ Press, 1994), pp. 359–360; *Statistical Abstract of the United States, 1999*, Tables 534 and 578.

## Figure 14.2

### The Federal Bureaucracy

SOURCES: *Statistical Abstract of the United States, 1999,* Table 547 (budget figures for Agriculture), Table 566 (employment figures); *United States Government Manual 1999/2000* (Washington, DC: GPO, 1999), structure of FDIC; www.fdic.gov (accessed January 11, 2000; budget data for FDIC); www.ftc.gov (accessed January 14, 2000; budget data for FTC).

| The President | | |
|---|---|---|
| **14 Departments** <br> Directed by cabinet secretaries appointed by president, confirmed by Senate | **63 Independent Agencies** <br> Directed by administrators, boards, or commissions appointed by president, confirmed by Senate | **27 Government Corporations** <br> Directed by boards or commissions usually appointed by president, confirmed by Senate |
| EXAMPLE <br> **Department of Agriculture** | EXAMPLE <br> **Federal Trade Commission** | EXAMPLE <br> **Federal Deposit Insurance Corporation** |
| PURPOSE <br> Oversees agricultural programs | PURPOSE <br> Prevents unfair and anti-competitive business practices | PURPOSE <br> Insures bank deposits |
| OFFICIAL HIERARCHY <br> Secretary (1) <br> Deputy secretary (1) <br> Undersecretary (7) <br> Assistant secretary (2) <br> Deputy undersecretary (7) <br> Lower-level and civil service officials (105,646) | OFFICIAL HIERARCHY <br> Chairman (1) <br> Commissioners (4) <br> Office and Bureau Directors (8) <br> Lower-level and civil service officials (991) | OFFICIAL HIERARCHY <br> Chairman of board (1) <br> Other members of board of directors (4) <br> Division directors (8) <br> Office directors (5) <br> Lower-level employees (7,778) |
| BUDGET <br> $63.4 billion | BUDGET <br> $117 million | BUDGET <br> $1.2 billion |

**agency**
Basic organizational unit of federal government. Also known as *office* or *bureau.*

**department**
Organizational unit into which many agencies of the federal government are grouped.

**government corporation**
Independent organization created by Congress to fulfill functions related to business.

**administrative discretion**
Power to interpret a legislative mandate.

because their policies and regulations are far-reaching and their impact is felt throughout the country.

The **agency**, also known as the *office* or *bureau,* is the basic organizational unit of the federal government. It is the entity specifically assigned by Congress to carry out a task. There are hundreds of agencies within the federal government, but most are grouped under one of 14 **departments**, collections of federal agencies that report to a secretary who serves in the president's cabinet. Some 63 agencies are free-standing entities that report either to the president or to a board.[10] The Central Intelligence Agency and the Environmental Protection Agency are examples of independent agencies. Finally, there are 27 **government corporations**, independent organizations created by Congress to fulfill functions related to business.[11] Examples of government corporations include the Federal Deposit Insurance Corporation, which insures bank deposits, and the National Railroad Passenger Corporation, which runs Amtrak. Figure 14.2 illustrates how the federal bureaucracy is organized.

Bureaucracies can have great influence over policy because of their **administrative discretion**, the power to interpret their legislative mandates. Congress can enact general rules, but it cannot anticipate every circumstance, nor can it apply these rules to every individual case. Congress may decide to provide benefits to the disabled, but it is up to a bureaucrat (in this case, an official within the Social Security Administration) to decide whether a particular handicap precludes employment.[12] Congress may decide to give loans to college students from families of moderate income, but it is up to a bureaucrat (in this case, an officer within the Department of Education) to decide what family resources count as income.

## The Bureaucracy Problem

If a bureaucracy is working ideally, it is organized in such a way as to achieve its assigned task efficiently. People hired to work in the bureaucracy are selected for their ability to do the job. Each reports to his or her superior, and ultimate authority is exercised by the head of the agency. The bureaucracy supplies each worker with the materials and supplies necessary to get the job done. The ideal is best exemplified by sol-

**Unexpected Bureaucrats**
These handlers feeding sea lions at the National Zoo are as much members of the federal bureaucracy as are IRS employees.

diers on parade, marching together in lockstep formation. When all works perfectly, bureaucracies exhibit unity, focus, and power.[13]

Although the ideal bureaucracy has tremendous potential, many factors inhibit perfection. Bureaucracies face impossible tasks, their performance is difficult to measure, they have a tendency to expand, they are slow to change, and they are often mired in red tape. Taken together, these factors create what is known as the bureaucracy problem.[14]

## Impossibility of Tasks

Most governmental tasks are difficult to accomplish. If they were easy, someone other than the government would have undertaken the job! Tasks are usually complex, and goals may remain vague and indefinite.[15] Schools are expected to teach students—but there is no end to what students might learn. Transportation agencies are expected to achieve smooth-flowing traffic—but to avoid all bottlenecks in most large cities, one would have to pave almost everything. The Environmental Protection Agency is supposed to protect the environment from pollutants—but nearly all human activity increases pollution in some way. Because their responsibilities are so complicated, bureaucracies are often blamed for problems even if they do the best possible job.

## Difficulty Measuring Performance

It is often difficult to measure the performance of government bureaucracies.[16] If the streets and parks are strewn with garbage and litter, one is tempted to criticize the government. Yet city garbage collectors may be doing a good job but having trouble keeping up with the behavior of inconsiderate citizens. Because it is hard to measure the performance of most government bureaucracies, it is difficult for supervisors to tell whether work is being performed carefully and promptly. If officials are unsure about how to gauge a bureaucracy's performance, they will have trouble trying to improve it. As a result, bureaucracies often have a reputation for inefficiency.

## Expansionary Tendencies

Once they are created to address a problem, bureaucracies generally try to expand so they can address it better. Government agencies almost always feel they need more

**An Impossible Task?**
The Environmental Protection Agency (EPA) faces the difficult task of protecting the environment from pollutants. *What kinds of groups and individuals do you think might exert pressure on the EPA?*

money, more personnel, and more time to perform their tasks effectively.[17] Bureaucrats experience policy problems up close, so they often sincerely believe that they need more resources to address them. But because they focus on specific issues, they can lose sight of the big picture. Congress cannot grant unlimited funds to every bureaucracy that wants them; trade-offs and choices have to be made.

There is nothing new about this debate between bureaucrats and Congress. "You may blame the War Department for a great many things," General Douglas MacArthur said back in 1935, "but you cannot blame us for not asking for money. That is one fault to which we plead not guilty." In much the same vein, the head of the Forest Service once exclaimed to a congressional committee: "Mr. Chairman, you would not think that it would be proper for me to be in charge of this work and not be enthusiastic about it and not think that I ought to have more money, would you? I have been in it for thirty years, and I believe in it."[18]

### Slow to Change

Any large governmental organization has standard procedures through which it makes its decisions. And most standard procedures are essential if large numbers of people are to coordinate their work toward some common end. If procedures were not standardized, those working within the bureaucracy would be so confused they would soon be unable to do anything.

Standard procedures nonetheless make bureaucracies sluggish and slow to adjust to new circumstances.[19] Schools still provide long summer holidays that were originally allowed so that children could help harvest crops on family farms. The U.S. customs service issued forms in the 1970s that "have not changed to any great extent since 1790, and merchant vessels today are required to report on the number of guns mounted."[20] As one humorist observed, "Bureaucracy defends the status quo long past the time when the quo has lost its status."[21]

### Red Tape

Everyone complains about governmental red tape, but, as one analyst has observed, "One person's red tape may be another's treasured procedural safeguard."[22] People often complain, for example, that it takes forever to get a bridge repaired. But bridge repair can be politically complicated. The design of the replacement bridge must be acceptable to neighbors. If the bridge is regarded as an historical landmark—and a surprising number of bridges are so designated—the approval of an historical commission must be obtained. After the design is approved, the agency, when letting contracts, must advertise the job and allow time for the submission of bids. To avoid accusations of political favoritism, the choice of contractors must be made according to published criteria. And the repairs themselves must be subject to careful inspection to make sure the bridge does not collapse upon completion. Once again, a common bureaucratic problem is not caused by malice or ignorance but by important considerations of politics and safety.

At times, exceptions can be made. After the 1994 Los Angeles earthquake destroyed many bridges and roadways, seriously crippling metropolitan traffic, the Department of Transportation waived the usual procedural safeguards and promised the contractor extra payment if the work could be done ahead of schedule. The end result: a record-breaking restoration of key roadways within 85 days.[23] But red tape was eliminated in this case only because the public insisted that time was of the essence.

## American Bureaucracies: Particularly Political

The bureaucracy problem exists in all countries, but American bureaucracies have special problems that are rooted in the country's unusual political history. As we discuss in this section, U.S. bureaucracies had a difficult beginning, were built with patronage, and were only slowly modernized by a "bottom-up" civil service reform.

### Difficult Beginnings

American bureaucrats lack the noble heritage of their counterparts in Europe and Japan, where government departments evolved out of the household of the king, queen, or emperor. In the late 1600s, King Louis XIV constructed a great French administration within the Palace of Versailles. Japan's powerful bureaucracy owes its prestige to a time-honored relationship with the emperor. The extraordinarily efficient German administration, which became a model for the world, descended from the household of the King of Prussia. The lineage of federal bureaucrats in the United States is less distinguished. As one scholar has pointed out, "In England, France and Germany, . . . it is considered an honor simply to serve the state. . . . In the United States civil servants, instead of being regarded with honor, are often considered tax eaters, drones, grafters, and bureaucrats."[24]

The American Revolution was fought against King George's bureaucrats, who had been appointed to oversee the governments of the colonies. The resulting suspicion of appointed officials carried over to the time that the Constitution was being written, when the framers could not even agree on where to put the people who were to run the new national government. Finally, as part of a compromise, they agreed to locate the District of Columbia, the new home of the federal government, on the Maryland–Virginia border near the small city of Georgetown.

Thomas Jefferson believed that the location would attract virtuous Virginians to federal jobs, leading to "a favourable bias in the Executive officers."[25] In fact, the land Congress had chosen was swampy and miserable. Visitors complained that it was thick with "contaminated vapour," which produced "agues and other complaints."[26] If the government was to attract quality workers, its location would not be its main selling point.

**The Dream and the Reality**
The original plans for the District of Columbia called for federal workers to live in a city reminiscent of 17th-century France (top), but the location they chose turned out to be so swampy and miserable (bottom) that initially few people opted to live there. *How has this shaped American attitudes toward federal bureaucracies?*

www.longmanparticipate.com

comparative

**Comparing
Bureaucracies**

### Mountains of Patronage

Not only did the disreputable living conditions in the District of Columbia diminish the prestige of the federal government, but bureaucrats received a second blow after the election of 1828, when President Andrew Jackson handed out to followers political **patronage**, consisting of government jobs, contracts, and other favors (see the

**patronage**
Jobs, contracts, or favors given to political friends and allies.

## Election Connection

# The Election of 1828 and the Spoils System

With the election of Andrew Jackson in 1828, patronage became a staple of American national politics. Jackson replaced 2000 government workers with his own supporters, creating what came to be known as the spoils system. Jackson saw patronage as critical for building his campaign organization, but he also elevated patronage to the level of political principle. In Jackson's view, one person was as good as the next. Almost anyone could do government work, and therefore everyone should take a turn. Government offices should rotate, giving new people a chance to learn the skills and duties of public service.

By replacing learned experts with ordinary citizens, Jackson felt he was making government more democratic. The spoils system ensured that the government administrators were in tune with the views of the people. It also got rid of malcontents in the bureaucracy who might

frustrate the new government. But it often meant the appointment of unsavory political cronies to positions such as New York customs collector, a job with a wealth of opportunities for personal enrichment. Jackson's appointee to that post absconded to England when it became clear that he could not account for a million dollars worth of customs fees.

*What do you think?*
* *Corruption aside, do you believe expertise is the most important criterion for selection of a bureaucratic worker? Or did Jackson have a point when he argued that ordinary people should be represented in federal agencies?*
* *What sorts of jobs are best suited for experts, and what kinds for nonexperts?*

President Andrew Jackson's use of the spoils system was lampooned by political cartoonists.

**spoils system**
A system of government employment in which workers are hired on the basis of party loyalty.

accompanying Election Connection). The practice of hiring workers on the basis of party loyalty became known as the **spoils system** when New York Senator William Marcy attacked President Jackson for seeing "nothing wrong in the rule that to the victor belong the spoils."[27]

Politicians in both political parties quickly discovered that the spoils system suited their needs.[28] Local, state, and national elections occurred frequently, making campaign tasks numerous and time-consuming. By handing out patronage, party politicians found it easier to find campaign workers to take on such thankless jobs as passing out pamphlets, organizing rallies, and getting people out to vote. The New York machine politician George Washington Plunkitt explained the logic of patronage this way: "You can't keep an organization together without patronage. Men ain't in politics for nothin'. They want to get somethin' out of it."[29] Patronage also made it easier for parties to raise large amounts of cash to fund their frequent election campaigns. Every Pennsylvania state employee during this period received the following letter from the Republican State Committee: "Two percent of your salary is _____. Please remit promptly. At the close of the campaign we shall place a list of those who have not paid in the hands of the head of the department you are in."[30] These practices were not conducted in secret; politicians felt they were a natural and legitimate part of politics.

Plunkitt defended patronage, or graft, by making the fine distinction between its dishonest and honest varieties. Dishonest graft wasted the taxpayers' money. Honest graft simply paid a friend to build a bridge or roadway that needed to be constructed anyway. Or, as the patronage-prone Chicago Mayor Richard J. Daley once said when asked to explain why he had given the city's insurance business to one of his sons, "If a man can't put his arms around his sons, then what kind of a world are we living in? . . . I make no apologies to anyone. There are many men in this room whose fathers helped them, and they went on to become fine public officials."[31] Mayor Daley's sons did well for themselves. Richard M. Daley was elected to a fourth term as Chicago mayor in 1999, and President Clinton appointed William Daley his Secretary of

**Family Ties**
The Mayors Richard Daley, father and son, in a moment of family resemblance.

Commerce in 1997. In 2000 William Daley was asked to run Al Gore's presidential campaign.

## Advantages of the Spoils System

Looking back on American political history, many scholars have found much to praise in the old spoils system.[32] For one thing, it helped immigrants adjust to the realities of urban life in the United States. "I think there's got to be in every ward somebody that any bloke can come to—no matter what he's done—and get help," said one Boston politician. "Help, you understand; none of your law and your justice, but help."[33] Some of the help took the form of jobs in city government. Irish immigrants were particularly good at using politics as a way of getting ahead. In Chicago, the percentage of public school principals of Irish background rose from 3 percent in the 1860s to 25 percent in 1914. In San Francisco, it climbed from 4 percent to 34 percent over a similar period.[34]

Contemporary affirmative action programs have many of the same pluses and minuses as the old-fashioned spoils system. When African Americans became part of urban governing coalitions, they gained better access to government jobs by invoking the principle of affirmative action.[35] Nationwide, African Americans are more likely to get a job in government than in the private sector (see Figure 14.3), a sign that politics still seems to help some disadvantaged groups get a toehold on the ladder to success. However, government employment for Hispanics still lags behind their position in the private sector, probably because the percentage of Hispanics who vote and otherwise participate in politics remains comparatively low (see Figure 14.4).

## Disadvantages of the Spoils System

If the spoils system helped incorporate immigrants into American politics and society, it nonetheless contributed to the negative image suffered by American bureaucracies. Education, training, and experience counted for little, and jobholders changed each time a new party came to power. As one Democratic leader joked after his party had been in power for years, a bureaucrat was "a Democrat who holds some office that a Republican wants."[36]

The many decades of patronage politics have left an antibureaucratic legacy that continues to the present day. Three-fourths of all Americans think "people in the

## Figure 14.3

**Black Representation in State and Local Government Workforce Is Higher Than in Private Sector**
Note that government figures are from 1997; private-sector figures are from 1998.

SOURCE: *Statistical Abstract of the United States 1999*, Table 537 (government workers), Table 675 (private sector).

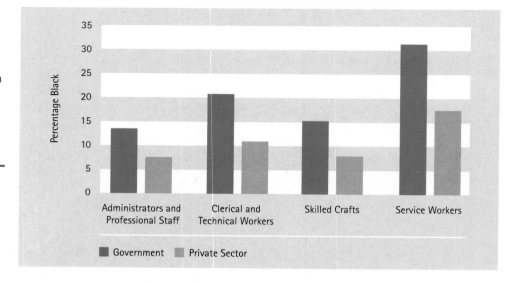

## Figure 14.4

**Hispanic Representation in State and Local Government Workforce Is Lower Than in Private Sector**
Note that government figures are from 1997; private-sector figures are from 1998.

SOURCE: *Statistical Abstract of the United States 1999*, Table 537 (government workers).

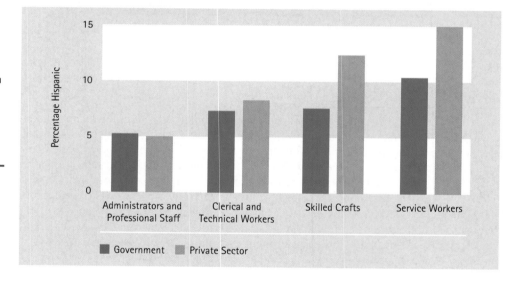

participation
**Who Wants to be a Bureaucrat?**

**mugwumps**
A group of civil service reformers organized in the 1880s who maintained that government officials should be chosen on a merit basis.

government waste a lot of money we pay in taxes" (see Figure 14.5). When Americans were asked how they would rate the credibility of federal government workers, only 20 percent found them credible. (Americans were otherwise quite lenient in their evaluations; even accountants scored above 50 percent! See Figure 14.6.)

## Erosion of the Spoils System

The mountains of patronage created by the spoils system were gradually eroded by civil service reformers who, in the 1880s, were called **mugwumps**. A group of professors, journalists, clerics, and business leaders, mugwumps said government officials should be chosen on the basis of merit, not for their political connections. Originally a sarcastic term of abuse, the name is a modification of a Native American word meaning "great man" or "chief." Mugwumps were also scorned for refusing to back either party. It was said that their "mugs" peered over one side of the fence while their "wumps" stuck out over the other. Mugwumps, in turn, accused politicians of appointing political hacks. One clergyman accused the mayor of Boston of appointing saloon keepers and bartenders to public office.

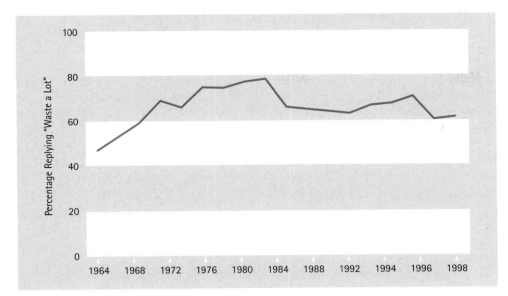

**Figure 14.5**

**The Public Thinks There
Is a Lot of Waste in Government**
Survey respondents were asked the following question: "Do you think that
people in the government waste a lot
of money we pay in taxes, waste some
of it, or don't waste very much of it?"
*What do you think? Is the public is
justified in its belief that the government wastes a lot of money?*

SOURCE: National Election Study,
1948–1998 Cumulative Data File, conducted
by the Center for Political Studies at the
University of Michigan.

Even though the mountains of patronage did not erode easily, mugwumps won a
succession of victories that gradually changed the system. Their first major breakthrough came in 1881 when President James Garfield was assassinated by a mentally
disturbed man said to be a disappointed office seeker. Public scrutiny focused on the
new president, Chester A. Arthur, who had once served as the New York customs collector and seemed the personification of the spoils system. In 1883, as the demand for
reform swept the country, Congress passed—and Arthur signed—the **Pendleton Act**,
which created a Civil Service Commission to set up qualifications, examinations, and
procedures for filling many government jobs.

**Pendleton Act**
Legislation in 1881 creating the Civil
Service Commission.

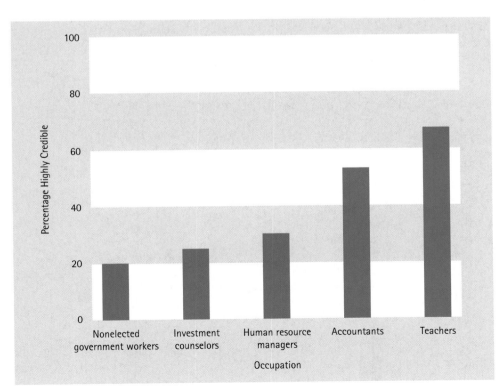

**Figure 14.6**

**Government Workers Are
Thought to Be Less Credible
Than Other Occupational Groups**

SOURCE: Gallup/Employee Benefit Research
Institute Poll, April 1994 (USGALLUP.EBRI56).

**civil service**

A system in which government employees are chosen according to their educational qualifications, performance on examinations, and work experience.

**Hatch Act**

1939 law prohibiting federal employees from engaging in political campaigning and solicitation.

timeline

**Evolution of the Federal Bureaucracy**

**Civil service** reform occurred from the bottom up. Requirements initially applied mainly to lower-level, less skilled jobs—those who swept the floors and typed government forms. Gradually, higher-level positions were included in the civil service; such additions were especially plentiful when the party in power expected defeat in the next election. By making a job part of the civil service, soon-to-be-ousted presidents "blanketed in" their supporters, making it impossible for their successors to replace them with patronage workers from the other party. Civil service reform became nearly complete when, in 1939, Congress passed the **Hatch Act**, which barred federal employees from political campaigning and solicitation. The mountains of patronage were all but worn away.

## Political Appointees Today

In the arid expanses of Arizona and New Mexico stand mesas—often called islands in the desert—that tower over surrounding flatland. All that remain of ancient plateaus, long eroded by wind and water, mesas are ecologically distinct from the surrounding desert.

Just as one finds geological mesas in the deserts of the West, one can locate patronage mesas that have survived decades of civil service reform. One of the most heavily populated patronage mesas is also the most prestigious, for it includes thousands of policy makers at the top levels of the federal government. It consists of most members of the White House staff, the heads of most departments and agencies, and the members of most government boards and commissions. Political appointees also predominate in the upper levels of individual agencies and departments, inhabiting offices bearing such titles as deputy secretary, undersecretary, deputy undersecretary, assistant secretary, deputy assistant secretary, and special assistant.

This high-level patronage mesa is becoming increasingly crowded. The estimated number of top-level agency appointees grew from less than 500 in 1960 to nearly 2500 in 1998 (see Figure 14.7). Adding the White House staff, the total number of high-ranking patronage positions is estimated to be close to 3000.[37] No other industrial democracy gives its leader as much patronage power (see the accompanying International Comparison).

The president's ability to recruit political allies for the top echelon of government has both advantages and disadvantages. On the positive side, it allows newly elected presidents to enlist many new people with innovative ideas. For example, President Reagan's dramatic tax and expenditure cuts were designed by think-tank experts and

**Figure 14.7**

Growth of High-Level Patronage Appointments, 1960–1998

SOURCES: Paul Light, *Thickening Government* (Washington, DC: Brookings, 1995), p. 9, Table 1-2; Paul Light, "The Changing Shape of Government," Brookings Institution Policy Brief 45 (Washington, DC: Brookings, February 1999), p. 1.

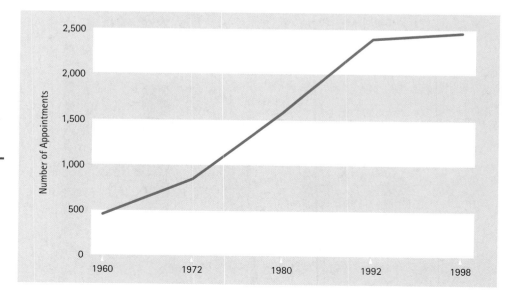

## Political Versus Professional Bureaucrats

Most high-level administrative positions in Europe and Japan are occupied by well-educated, highly experienced, professional civil servants who refrain from participating actively in politics. Most achieve their positions by studying in prestigious training programs and spending years–even decades–in dedicated government service.

In the United States, high government officials often get their jobs only after gaining prominence outside government in business, law, medicine, education, or a policy institute. Usually, they have worked in a presidential campaign, made financial contributions, or given other evidence of party loyalty. For example, President Clinton's secretaries of commerce were not long-time government experts on trade policy but Ron Brown, Mickey Kantor, and William Daley, each of whom played key roles in the Clinton and Gore campaigns. Similarly, President George H.W. Bush, when selecting his secretary of transportation, turned not to a long-time government servant who had worked on roads or airports but to Andrew Card, who had managed his political campaign in Massachusetts. Secretary Card, in turn, chose as his special assistant a loyal political aide who had been a member of the Massachusetts state legislature. Secretary Card admitted that his aide could not answer any questions on transportation policy but argued that he would nonetheless be an invaluable adviser because he was "a politician in the very positive sense of the

word." As one wag put it, "One of the principal qualifications for a political job is that the applicant know nothing much about what he is expected to do."

The less professional, more political orientation of high-level appointees in the United States is due in part to the fact that the bureaucracy must respond to both the president and Congress. In most other industrial democracies, the legislative branch has less direct influence over the bureaucracy. Where the bureaucracy has only one master, bureaucrats can be professionals instead of politicians.

*Do you think the bureaucracy should be reformed so that it has only one master? What would such reforms look like? What are the advantages and disadvantages of the tug of war between Congress and the president over the bureaucracy?*

SOURCES: Harry Eckstein, "The British Political System," in Samuel Beer and Adam Ulam, eds., *Patterns of Government: The Major Political Systems of Europe* (New York: Random House, 1962), pp.158–68; Hugh Heclo, *Modern Social Politics in Britain and Sweden: From Relief to Income Maintenance* (New Haven, CT: Yale University Press, 1974); Paul Pierson, *Dismantling the Welfare State* (New York: Cambridge University Press, 1994); Kent Weaver, Bert Rothman, and Terry M. Townsend, as quoted in Chuck Henning, *The Wit and Wisdom of Politics: Expanded Edition* (Golden, CO: Fulcrum Publishing, 1992), p.11.

---

leaders from business and industry. The wholesale changeover in personnel also helps presidents introduce their political agendas with minimal resistance from an entrenched executive branch. President Clinton's economic recovery package and health reforms were designed without the aid or obstruction of leftover Bush advisers. Indeed, it is the power of appointment that makes presidents the most dynamic element in the American political system.

Yet the arrival of so many new faces at about the same time complicates the coordination of government. European and Japanese governments are marked by close, informal, long-time associations among leading administrators. In the United States, the average presidential appointee leaves office after only a little more than two years; almost a third leave in less than 18 months.[38] A member of Woodrow Wilson's cabinet once admitted that "the average head of a department is not highly competent and has not first-rate executive ability,"[39] a view echoed many years later by public administration expert Leonard White, who observed, "The previous experience of federal Secretaries does not usually prepare them to exercise quick and effective leadership."[40]

The rapid turnover in high-level governmental personnel is so pervasive that it has been called a government of **in-and-outers**—people who come in, go out, and come back in again with each change in administration.[41] Because they cannot count on long-term employment with the government, most political appointees begin planning ways of making a satisfactory departure shortly after they arrive. For some people, it will mean returning to their old positions in the business, legal, or academic world. For others, it will be a matter of using connections inside the beltway to win new financial opportunities in the private or nonprofit sectors. One deputy secretary leaving the Clinton administration just a year after joining it was asked whether he had any regrets. "Yes," he replied. "I should have rented" instead of incurring the costs of

**in-and-outers**
Political appointees who come in, go out, and come back in again with each change in administration.

## Democratic Dilemma

# Should Bureaucratic Leaders Be Professional Experts or Loyal Partisans?

Presidents often must choose between knowledgeable professionals and long-time political associates. The first bring more expertise to the task of government; the second are more loyal to presidents. Presidential scholars differ about what presidents need most. With whom do you agree?

Hugh Heclo argues that a corps of knowledgeable professionals will bring the bureaucracy closer to the ideal of "neutral competence," with bureaucrats giving their "cooperation and best independent judgment" to the president and other top officials. The advantages of such a system are:

- improvement in the capacity of elected leadership to direct the bureaucracy, because competent bureaucrats are at the helm;
- accumulation of long-term, informal knowledge in the bureaucracy; and
- preservation of continuity from administration to administration.

Terry Moe, on the other hand, argues that because civil servants make up so much of the bureaucracy, presidents have difficulty exercising leadership. Presidents can work against this phenomenon by appointing loyal partisans to as many offices as possible and centralizing policy making in the White House, which is full of political appointees. Career bureaucrats are bad for presidents, argues Moe, because they:

- are independent (that is, they cannot be fired);
- resist change; and
- develop ties to vested interests.

Political appointees on the other hand, owe their livelihood to the president and thus have incentives to advance the president's program. It is therefore in the president's interest to keep career bureaucrats at bay.

*If you were the president, with which view would you probably agree?*

SOURCES: Hugh Heclo, "OMB and the Presidency—the Problem of 'Neutral Competence,'" *Public Interest* 38 (Winter 1975): 80–98; Terry Moe, "Presidents, Institutions and Theory," in George C. Edwards III, John H. Kessel, and Bert A. Rockman, eds., *Researching the Presidency: Vital Questions, New Approaches* (Pittsburgh, PA: Pittsburgh University Press, 1993), pp. 337–386.

buying a house in Washington. In 2000, vice-presidential candidate Richard Cheney, former Secretary of Defense under George H. W. Bush, was the top-ranking "outer" seeking to return to government.

These rapid changes in personnel create a government that lacks the continuity necessary for sustained policy focus (see the accompanying Democratic Dilemma). The newcomers bring energy and ideas, but by the time their ideas are turned into plans that can be brought to fruition, they themselves are gone, succeeded by another energetic group with an altogether different set of priorities. The newcomers also run the risk of trying to make too many changes at once. Clinton's inexperienced health policy experts tried to introduce such massive changes that their efforts collapsed under the weight of their own ambitions.[42]

With rapid change in personnel, governmental memory becomes as limited as that of an antiquated computer. One Japanese trade specialist who negotiated with the United States observed that the Japanese "look at politics in their historical perspective. . . . However, in the case of the U.S., almost all of their negotiators seem like they came in just yesterday."[43] At one point in 1994, the differing styles of top Japanese and U.S. bureaucrats created a relationship so abrasive that the two countries broke off trade negotiations on the eve of a summit meeting between their leaders.

Worst of all, the denial of most top-level positions to nonpolitical civil servants makes the civil service a less attractive career for intelligent, ambitious young people. In Japan, many of the top students graduating from the country's most prestigious law schools go directly into government service, and the most gifted reach the highest levels of government. But the peak of the U.S. government is not part of a large mountain that employees can gradually ascend over a lifetime career. Instead, the top-level mesa positions are ordinarily cut off from the surrounding civil service desert, reachable only by a patronage-filled presidential helicopter.

If young people knew that years of work in the civil service could eventually be rewarded by promotion to high-level policy positions, many more might consider this an attractive career option. But the best advice that can be given to a young person who wants to achieve a high policy-making position in government is to do an internship with a member of Congress, build connections with a political party, achieve distinction outside the government, and wait for the right moment to *rent* a Washington home.

## SECTION SUMMARY

Bureaucratic organizations are characterized by a set of difficulties collectively known as the bureaucracy problem. They face hard tasks, they tend to expand their budgets and resist change, they produce too much red tape, and supervisors have trouble measuring the success or failure of programs. There are often no easy solutions to these problems. Though the bureaucracy problem exists everywhere, the unique history of the spoils system in the United States has produced a longstanding suspicion of government agencies, as well as residual pockets of patronage.

## The President and the Bureaucracy

CONSTITUTION, ARTICLE II, SECTION 3: *The President "shall take Care that the Laws be faithfully executed."*

The Constitution charges the president with enforcement of the laws. Presidents fulfill this obligation by overseeing the federal bureaucracy, which is formally responsible to the chief executive. The president's cabinet is the most visible and long-standing connection between the president and the bureaucracy; however, the president also exercises power through appointments to independent agencies and through the powerful Office of Management and Budget.

Despite these means of control, even presidents can be frustrated by the bureaucracy problem. As an exasperated President Harry Truman once said, "I thought I was the president, but when it comes to these bureaucrats I can't do a d—ed thing."[44]

### The Cabinet

Most federal agencies are located in one of the major departments. The president appoints secretaries to head these departments. The secretaries, along with a few other top-ranking officials, form the president's cabinet (see Chapter 13). The four original departments are known as the **inner cabinet**, because their secretaries typically have ready access to the president.[45] Even the locations of their offices are close to the White House, as you can see from the accompanying map of Washington, DC. These departments are:

- *State*, responsible for foreign policy
- *Defense*, originally called War, responsible for the military
- *Treasury*, responsible for tax collections, payments, and debt service
- *Justice*, headed by the attorney general, who is responsible for law enforcement

> **inner cabinet**
> The four original departments (State, Defense, Treasury, and Justice) whose secretaries typically have the closest ties to the president.

A major function of the remaining departments of the cabinet, which are known as the **outer cabinet**, is to provide interest-group access to the executive branch of government.[46] The Interior Department's job was originally to regulate the use of federal land, particularly in the West. Today, it maintains close ties to ranchers, timber companies, mining interests, and others who depend on federal lands for their livelihood. The Agriculture Department serves farmers; the Commerce Department helps business and industry, especially firms with overseas contracts; Labor defends unions; Health and Human Services heeds the American Association for Retired Persons; and Education pays attention to teacher organizations (see Table 14.1).

> **outer cabinet**
> Newer departments that have fewer ties to the president and are more influenced by interest-group pressures.

The connections between departments and interest groups can change overnight, however, if an event activates the public spotlight. During the first Clinton administration, the Department of Commerce worked hard to open foreign markets to U.S. businesses. Secretary Ronald Brown routinely escorted prominent corporate executives on trade missions throughout the world. In 1996 he literally gave his life to the

# *Highlight*

# Where Are the Key Buildings in Washington?

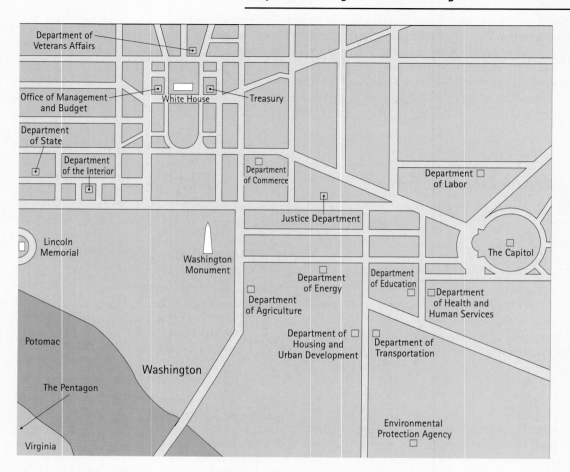

The physical location of the headquarters of the inner cabinet suggests the comparatively close ties these departments have to the president. Treasury is located next door to the White House. The walks from State and Justice to the White House are also shorter than to Capitol Hill. Defense, almost a world unto itself, is headquartered in the Pentagon in nearby Virginia.

Many of the departments of the outer cabinet are located on the foot of Capitol Hill. There they hunker, almost on bended knee, faceless and humorless, in the shadow of the magnificent Capitol building. Transportation, Education, Agriculture, Housing and Urban Development, and Health and Human Services all stumble over one another near the Hill's left foot in an unappealing corner of Washington that tourists seldom see. Labor pays homage at the Hill's right foot. The Environmental Protection Agency, though housed in a bedraggled part of town, still sits on a spot closer to the Hill than to the White House. The Department of the Interior stands as an exception to this pattern. It is located near the White House, despite its close ties to the interest-group community. The Office of Management and Budget (OMB), the nerve center of the executive branch, stands at the president's side, physically as well as metaphorically.

cause when a military plane crashed in Bosnia, killing Brown, 13 business leaders, and other government officials. Brown's trade missions had won applause in business circles, but his successor, William Daley, though the son of a machine politician, terminated them when the practice became tainted by reports that many of those accompanying Brown were contributors to the Clinton campaign.[47]

Presidents exercise their control over the cabinet departments primarily by appointing political allies to top positions. But once they become agency heads, allies often more closely identify with their turf than with the president's program. As FDR's

**Table 14.1**

Establishment Year and Interest-Group Allies of Each Cabinet Department
*Why have outer cabinet departments formed alliances with outside groups?*

| Department | Year | Interest-Group Allies |
|---|---|---|
| **INNER CABINET** | | |
| State | 1789 | |
| Treasury | 1789 | |
| Justice (attorney general) | 1789 | |
| Defense | 1789 (as War) | |
| **OUTER CABINET** | | |
| Interior | 1849 | Timber, miners, ranchers |
| Agriculture | 1889 | Farm bureau, other farm groups |
| Commerce | 1913 | U.S. Chamber of Commerce, other business groups |
| Labor | 1913 | Labor unions |
| Health and Human Services | 1953 | American Association of Retired Persons |
| Housing and Urban Development | 1965 | National League of Cities, Urban League |
| Transportation | 1966 | Auto manufacturers, truckers, airlines |
| Energy | 1977 | Gas, oil, nuclear power interests |
| Education | 1979 | Teachers' unions |
| Veterans Affairs | 1987 | American Legion, Veterans of Foreign Wars |
| Environmental Protection Agency | Not an official department | Sierra Club, other environmental groups |

top budget adviser put it, "Cabinet members are vice presidents in charge of spending, and as such they are the natural enemies of the President."[48] The bureaucracy problem, which tends to encourage sluggishness, red tape, and budgetary expansion (see above), can be particularly frustrating for presidents, who are often interested in speed and efficiency.

## Independent Regulatory Agencies

Not all agencies are members of cabinet departments. Some of the most important of these, the **independent regulatory agencies**, have quasi-judicial regulatory responsibilities, which are meant to be carried out in a manner free of presidential interference. These agencies are generally headed by a several-member board or commission appointed by the president and confirmed by the Senate. Independence from the president, which is considered desirable to insulate such agencies from partisan politics, is achieved by giving board members appointments that last for several years (see Table 14.2). In a number of cases, presidents may not be able to appoint a majority of board members until well into their second term in office.

**independent regulatory agencies**
Agencies that have quasi-judicial responsibilities.

Most independent regulatory agencies were established by Congress in response to widespread public pressure to protect workers and consumers from negligent or abusive business practices. The Federal Trade Commission (FTC) was created in 1914 in response to the discovery of misbranding and adulteration in the meatpacking industry. The FTC was given the power to prevent price discrimination, unfair competition, false advertising, and other unfair business practices. Congress formed the Securities and Exchange Commission in 1934 to root out fraud, deception, and inside manipulation on Wall Street after the stock market crash of 1929 left many Americans suspicious of speculators and financiers.

**T a b l e   1 4 . 2**

**Independent Agencies and Their Interest-Group Allies**

| Independent Agency | Board Size | Length of Term (years) | Interest-Group Allies |
|---|---|---|---|
| National Credit Union Administration | 3 | 6 | Credit unions |
| Federal Reserve Board | 7 | 14 | Banks |
| Consumer Product Safety Commission | 5 | 5 | Consumers Union |
| Equal Employment Opportunity Commission | 5 | 5 | Civil rights groups |
| Federal Deposit Insurance Corporation | 5 | 3* | Banks |
| Federal Energy Regulatory Commission | 4 | 4 | Oil/gas interests |
| Federal Maritime Commission | 5 | 5 | Fisheries |
| Federal Trade Commission | 5 | 7 | Business groups |
| National Labor Relations Board | 5 | 5 | Unions |
| Securities and Exchange Commission | 5 | 5 | Wall Street |
| Tennessee Valley Authority | 3 | 9 | Regional farmers and utilities |

*One member, the comptroller of the currency, has a 5-year term.

When originally formed, most regulatory agencies aggressively pursued their reform mandates. But as the public's enthusiasm for reform fades, many agencies find their most interested constituents to be members of the very community they are expected to regulate. Thus the independent commissions, too, have tended to become connected to organized interest groups.[49] In one instance, a regulator's legal fight to keep his job was financed by those subject to his regulation. The three-person board of the National Credit Union Administration has responsibility for overseeing the nation's 12,000 credit unions. When the term of board member Robert Swan expired, President Clinton nominated another to take his place. Arguing that he should keep his job until the new member was confirmed by the Senate (an event itself delayed by partisan bickering), Swan, with the financial help of the members of the National Association of Federal Credit Unions, filed suit in federal court. One critic cautioned that if Swan wins the suit, "He will be . . . beholden to the very people about whom he casts judgment." Swan nonetheless won strong support on Capitol Hill; House Speaker Newt Gingrich even wrote to the president that Swan's ouster might violate "laws relating to the tenure of government employees in independent agencies."[50] A federal appeals court settled the issue in late 1996, ruling in Clinton's favor.[51] Swan lost his job, but not before drawing attention to the close connections between regulatory agencies and those they regulate.

### Office of Management and Budget

Before 1921, every federal agency sent its own budget to Congress to be examined by an appropriations subcommittee. Without anyone to review all the requests, no one, not even the president, knew whether agency requests exceeded government revenues. When President Woodrow Wilson asked for a bureau to coordinate these requests, Congress at first refused to create one, saying such a bureau encroached on congressional authority. However, when federal deficits ballooned during World War I, Congress, under pressure to make government more efficient, relented and gave the president the needed help.

Originally known as the Bureau of the Budget, the agency is now called the **Office of Management and Budget (OMB)**, a name that reflects its enlarged set of responsibilities. Although development of the president's budget is still its most important job,

# DOONESBURY                                            by Garry Trudeau

Doonesbury by Gary Trudeau
Reagan's first budget director, David Stockman, gave OMB's a more politicized image.
SOURCE: Doonesbury copyright © 1981 G. B. Trudeau. Reprinted with permission of Universal Press Syndicate. All rights reserved.

OMB also sets personnel policy and reviews every piece of proposed legislation that the executive branch submits to Congress to ensure that it is consistent with the president's agenda. Agency regulations, too, must now get OMB approval. Even preliminary drafts have to be reviewed by OMB before they are unveiled to the public. One bureau chief claimed that OMB has "more control over individual agencies than . . . [the departmental] secretary or any of his assistants [do]."[52]

OMB was once considered to be a professional group of technicians, who searched for budget cuts. But OMB became more political as budget deficits took center stage in the electoral politics of the 1980s and 1990s.[53] Former Congressman David Stockman, Reagan's OMB director, led the fiscal side of the Reagan revolution.[54] Clinton's first OMB director, Leon Panetta, had also been a former member of Congress, and later became the White House chief of staff, an admittedly political office. As discussions over surpluses, rather than deficits, begin to characterize the debate in Washington, OMB's position may become less dominant than in the recent past. But it is unlikely to return to its technical, nonpolitical days.

Although OMB has given presidents greater control over agencies, the latter can still make **end runs** around OMB by appealing to their allies on Capitol Hill. When OMB tried to cut the budget of the Customs Service, the chair of the House subcommittee responsible for its appropriations objected: "I am getting the feeling there is somebody in the Office of Management and Budget that is carrying on an endless vendetta against the U.S. Customs Service."[55]

To check OMB's growing power, in 1974 Congress created the **Congressional Budget Office (CBO)**, an organization under the control of Congress that evaluates the president's budget as well as the budgetary implications of all other legislation. CBO's sophisticated analyses of budget and economic trends have caused its influence in Washington to grow to the point where it now stands as a strong rival to OMB. In the health care policy debate, for example, it proved to be a "critical player in the game" whose estimates of the costs of health care reform doomed both presidential and congressional proposals.[56]

**Office of Management and Budget (OMB)**
Agency responsible for coordinating the work of departments and agencies of the executive branch.

**end run**
Effort by agencies to avoid OMB controls by appealing to allies in Congress.

**Congressional Budget Office (CBO)**
Congressional agency that evaluates the president's budget as well as the budgetary implications of all other legislation.

## SECTION SUMMARY

Presidents use bureaucracies to enforce the law in accordance with their constitutional mandate, appointing key allies to top bureaucratic positions. But departments and agencies often also become allied with interest groups in the areas that they oversee. Presidents can supervise executive branch budgets and priorities more closely through the Office of Management and Budget, an agency that is itself monitored by the Congressional Budget Office.

## Congress and the Bureaucracy

It is a truism that no one should have more than one "boss." When two or more people can tell someone what to do, signals get confused, delays ensue, and accountability is undermined. Government bureaucrats in Japan and most European countries generally abide by this rule. Members of the civil service report to the heads of their departments, who report to the head of the government. Members of parliament have little to say about administrative matters.

Officially, federal bureaucrats in the United States have only one boss—the president, who according to the Constitution is the head of the executive branch. But they also have many bosses in Congress. One House subcommittee chair declared, quite frankly, "I've been running the medicare system, or our committee has, for the past nine years. We're its board of directors."[57] With Congress divided into House and Senate, and each chamber divided into many committees, bureaucrats often find themselves reporting to multiple committees, all considering themselves "boards of directors." Further, the pressures on bureaucracies have intensified in an era of high exposure and perpetual campaigns. As Martha Derthick has observed, "[Although] the U.S. Constitution has not changed . . . the presidency ha[s] become much more vigilant and intrusive . . . [while] Congress has become more critical."[58]

### Senate Confirmations

senatorial courtesy

An informal rule that the Senate will not confirm nominees within or from a state unless they have the approval of the senior senator of the state from the president's party.

Congressional influence begins with the very selection of executive department officers. The Senate's confirmation power has long given senators a voice in administrative matters, traditionally by the practice of **senatorial courtesy**. This custom consists of an informal rule that the Senate will not confirm nominees for positions within a state unless they have the approval of the senior senator of the state from the president's party. For example, there are 93 U.S. attorneys in the Department of Justice, appointed by the president to positions throughout the United States. A senator could block the approval of a U.S. attorney in his or her home state if for some reason the senator found the nominee unsatisfactory. Through the practice of senatorial courtesy, senators can protect their political bases by controlling patronage and shaping administrative practices within their states.

In recent years, the mass media have linked senatorial confirmations and election strategies even more closely. In an age when strong visual images are needed for the television screen, confirmation processes make for good political theater. Nominees have private lives to be examined. They can be asked embarrassing questions during their confirmation hearings. Conflicts between nominees and senators can elevate a little-known senator to the national stage.

Because the confirmation process has greater potential to affect elections than ever before, senators want more than just the usual "courtesy" traditionally extended to senators from the nominee's home state. Senators now want to be assured that presidential nominees take acceptable policy positions, do not have private investments that conflict with their public duties, have not violated any laws, and have not acted contrary to conventional moral norms. The Senate rejected George Bush's nomination of John Tower as secretary of defense because of an acknowledged drinking problem. It forced Bill Clinton to withdraw the nomination of Zoe Baird as attorney general because she had not paid the required social security taxes for her housemaid. It denied confirmation of Henry Foster as Clinton's surgeon general because he had performed 39 abortions. Former Massachusetts Governor William Weld's nomination as ambassador to Mexico was scuttled in 1997 because it was alleged that the governor, when district attorney, had not prosecuted drug dealers aggressively.

Senate rejections of presidential nominees are still the exception, not the rule. Yet the new, more election-driven confirmation process has had important consequences for government administration. To decrease the likelihood that the Senate will reject a nominee, the White House must interview the potential nominee at length, ask the

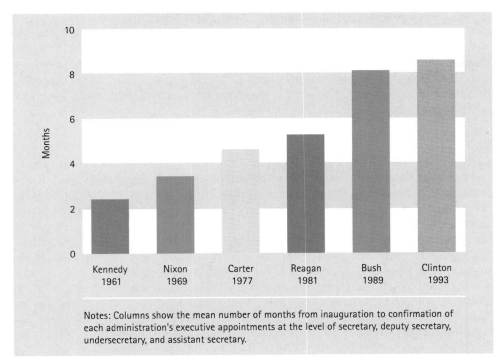

**Figure 14.8**

**Average Time It Takes Presidential Appointees to Be Confirmed**
*Why has it taken longer in recent years for presidential appointees to be confirmed? What role might elections have played in this trend?*

SOURCE: Paul Light, *Thickening Government* (Washington, DC: Brookings, 1995), p. 68.

Notes: Columns show the mean number of months from inauguration to confirmation of each administration's executive appointments at the level of secretary, deputy secretary, undersecretary, and assistant secretary.

FBI to undertake an extensive background check, and defend the nominee against exhaustive senatorial scrutiny. When John Kennedy was president, the average nominee was confirmed in less than two and a half months. The confirmation of Bill Clinton's average nominee required eight and a half months (see Figure 14.8).

Prolonging the confirmation process strengthens congressional control over administrative matters. As long as agency heads await confirmation, they hesitate before taking actions that might offend members of Congress. Bill Clinton was without half his administrative team throughout much of his first year as president, the very year in which he was expected to set the country on a new course.

Under Article II of the Constitution, presidents may make **recess appointments** without Senate confirmation "during the Recess of the Senate." Recess appointees may serve until the end of the next session of Congress, at which point they must resign if they have not been confirmed. Nothing in the Constitution precludes presidents from using the recess appointment repeatedly for the same person, even if that person is never confirmed. When Theodore Roosevelt could not secure confirmation of an African American as a customs collector in Charleston, South Carolina, the president reappointed him to the office during Senate recesses. Congress has since placed a check on the recess appointment power by passing legislation prohibiting payment of salary to appointees who serve more than a year without Senate confirmation. As a result, presidents today seldom exercise this power over Congressional objections.[59] One exception occurred in 1999, when President Clinton used a recess appointment to make businessman James Hormel the first openly gay U.S. ambassador. The Senate had been holding up Hormel's confirmation as ambassador to Luxembourg for almost two years, and several senators protested loudly at Clinton's action.[60] A loss of salary meant little to Hormel, a multimillionaire. But some observers worried that the law would discourage less wealthy people from seeking presidential appointments.

**recess appointment**
An appointment made when the Senate is in recess.

## Agency Reorganization

Not only do presidents and Congress struggle over the appointment of agency heads, but Congress often opposes presidential proposals to reorganize executive agencies. Congress resists change because each agency reports to a specific congressional committee, and these committees are frequently protective of their power. They therefore typically resist governmental reorganization, no matter how duplicative or antiquated existing organizational structures might be.[61] For example, Jimmy Carter wanted to shift worker training programs from the Department of Labor to the newly created Department of Education. But powerful senators defeated the proposal because they wanted to keep the programs within their committee's jurisdiction.[62] As we saw at the beginning of this chapter, the same thing occurred when Vice-President Gore proposed to move the DEA and ATF to the FBI.

## Legislative Detail

Congress also exercises its powers by writing detailed legislation outlining an agency's specific legal responsibilities. In European countries, most legislation is enacted in a form close to the draft prepared by the executive departments.[63] In Japan, 90 percent of all successful legislation is drafted by an executive agency.[64] In the United States, most legislation proposed by presidents is extensively revised by Congress, mainly by the committee with jurisdictional responsibility for the agency.[65] American bureaucracies therefore have much less authority over their own legislative mandates than bureaucracies elsewhere.

Sometimes conflicting legislative mandates can have nonsensical results. For over a decade, critics have ridiculed laws that give the Agriculture Department the authority to regulate sausage pizzas, but the Food and Drug Administration the authority to regulate cheese pizzas. FDA operates under legislation authored by the House Commerce Committee and the Senate Human Resources Committee, while the Agriculture Department receives its mandates from the House and Senate Agriculture committees. Neither set of committees wishes to relax its control over its agency, so the odd division of agency responsibilities remains unresolved. The result, according to one report, "hinders the government's efforts to efficiently and effectively protect consumers from unsafe food."[66]

Even if the statute itself does not dwell on administrative issues, agency operations can be influenced by committee reports accompanying the legislation. These reports are considered by the courts as evidence of congressional intent and have frequently been given the force of law. Even in the absence of court action, agencies pay attention to committee reports. In the words of one observer, "That language [in the reports] isn't legally binding, but the agencies understand very well what happens if they ignore it."[67]

The issue of legislative detail can be seen as a balancing act between administrative discretion, on the one hand, and congressional control, on the other. If the agency is mindful of congressional intent, Congress may allow it more freedom to act on its own. If an agency neglects a committee's wishes, Congress may enact legal restrictions or even use more forceful methods, such as its control over the agency's budget, to get its way.

## Budgetary Control

Every year each agency prepares a budget for the president to submit to Congress. Each agency must defend its budget before an appropriations subcommittee in both the House and the Senate, and those who offend committee members jeopardize their funding.

**earmark**
A specific congressional designation of the way money is to be spent.

To ensure that agencies spend monies in ways consistent with congressional preferences, significant portions of many agency budgets are subject to an **earmark**, a very specific designation of the way money is to be spent, sometimes even specifying particular congressional districts (see the accompanying Election Connection). Earmarking seems to be on the increase. At one time Congress let the scientific research community decide national research priorities, but between 1980 and 1995, the amount of research dollars earmarked for specific projects skyrocketed from $11 million to $875 million,[68] often for pet projects at a representative's home university. In 1999, Congress approved 324 earmarks, worth $475 million, for EPA projects in which

## Election Connection

### Congressional Legislation: A Matter of Detail

To help get re-elected, members of Congress try to get what they want out of bureaucracies through the practice of earmarking, designating specific ways in which money is to be spent. Here, in italics, is the specific language the Senate has substituted for the equally specific language of the House, which has been crossed out.

*What do you think?*
- *If you were an agency official, would you prefer more or less earmarking?*
- *Why do members of Congress care whether the money is spent for the Cumberland Gap tunnel or the Pittsburgh Busway?*

SOURCE: Department of Transportation Appropriations Act, Fiscal Year 1994, with the amendments of the Senate numbered H.R. 2750, 103rd Congress, 1st Session (GPO 1993), p. 40, as reprinted in Allen Schick, *The Federal Budget: Politics, Policy, Process* (Washington, DC: Brookings, 1995), p. 150.

9      ADDITIONAL HIGHWAY PROJECTS

10      APPALACHIAN CORRIDOR IMPROVEMENT PROJECT

11      For 80 percent of the expenses necessary to continue

2      construction on (130) ~~Kentucky Corridor B~~ *West Virginia*

13      *Corridor L* of the Appalachian Development Highway Sys-

14      tem, as authorized by section 1069(y) of Public Law 192–

15      240, (131) ~~$3,800,000~~ *$62,200,000.*

16      (132) ~~CUMBERLAND GAP TUNNEL PROJECT~~

17      ~~For 80 percent of the expenses necessary for the~~

18      ~~Cumberland Gap Tunnel Project, as authorized by~~

19      ~~1069(e) of Public Law 102-240, $10,000,000.~~

20      (133) *PITTSBURGH BUSWAY*

21      *For 80 percent of the expenses necessary for the Pitts-*

22      *burgh Busway, as authorized by section 1069(e) of Public*

23      *Law 102-240, $28,000,000.*

Congress members or their constituents were interested.[69] The greatest "earmarker" of all time may be the former chair of the Senate Appropriations Committee, Robert Byrd, beloved by his constituents for earmarks requiring numerous agencies to locate their operations in his home state of West Virginia. For example, he once slipped into an emergency bill a provision that shifted the 2600-employee FBI fingerprinting center from downtown Washington to Clarksburg, West Virginia.[70]

## Legislative Oversight

In addition to earmarking, committees hold hearings to ensure that agencies are not straying from their congressional mandates. The increase in such oversight hearings in recent decades has expanded committee control over administrative practice. The number of days each year that committees hold oversight hearings nearly quadrupled between the 1960s and the 1980s.[71] At these hearings, members of the administration are asked to testify about agency experiences and problems. Witnesses representing outside groups are given opportunities to praise or criticize the bureaucrats. Through the oversight process, committees obtain information that can be used to revise existing legislation or modify agency budgets.

## Iron Triangles and Issue Networks

Congress has such power over bureaucracies that many agencies seek to build coalitions of allies among congressional committees and interest groups simply in order to survive. These connections have become so intimate that some political scientists say government in the United States is run by **iron triangles**.[72] Interest groups form the base of the triangle, because they have the membership and money that can influence the outcome of congressional elections, and agencies listen to group demands to obtain committee backing (see Figure 14.9a).

**iron triangle**
Close, stable connection among agencies, interest groups, and congressional committees.

The relationship is said to be an *iron* triangle because the connections among the threesome remain a lot more stable than in the proverbial love triangle. In the case of the iron triangle, each of the three parties can deliver something the other needs. Compromises are readily arranged because interests are mutual. Most oversight hearings are in fact three-way love fests. Agency work is adored by the groups it serves, and members of Congress add words of endearment. When a congressional scholar asked congressional committee staff whether they considered their committee to be agency advocates, nearly two-thirds said "yes." In response to this question, one staff person replied,

> I think any subcommittee . . . whatever its subject is, they're advocates. I mean the Aging Subcommittee is advocating for aging programs, the Arts for arts, you know, Education for education, Health for health. They wouldn't be doing their work if they weren't interested.

Added another:

> The trouble of it is we get in bed with agency people in some respects. We're hoping that they'll distribute good projects in our state, you know, and it's a kind of a working with them so that, you know, there'll be more, more and better of everything for everybody.[73]

These relationships often transcend partisan divisions. With the Republican takeover in 1995, the House leadership initially placed tight restrictions on committees in order to weaken the committee–agency relationship. Infuriated at the loss of committee power, Democrats on one committee complained that "the Republican leadership has decided that the considered judgment of expert committees no longer matters."[74] But within a year the Republican leadership found it necessary to loosen its controls, and the natural tendency for committees to support "their" agencies reasserted itself. For example, in 1995 House Republican leaders proposed elimination of all funding for the public broadcasting corporation. "We were read our last rites," said the corporation's president. But after Republican members of the key congressional subcommittee were besieged by letters and faxes from constituents, who feared the demise of *Sesame Street* and *Mister Rogers' Neighborhood*, they voted to keep the agency alive, though at a reduced level of funding.[75]

Some iron triangles are no longer as rigid as they once were. As the number of interest groups and policy experts has expanded, congressional committees and government agencies have been bombarded with competing demands from multiple sides, which together form **issue networks** (see Figure 14.9b).[76] For example, nuclear energy policy was at one time of interest mainly to just four companies that built nuclear reactors and to the utility companies that used the electricity. After an accident

**issue networks**
Loose, competitive relationships among policy experts, interest groups, congressional committees, and government agencies.

**Congress Keeps Watch**
Though some say bureaucracies should be insulated from public scrutiny, others point out that Senate oversight hearings on the Internal Revenue Service (IRS) in 1998 resulted in significant reforms. *With which view do you agree?*

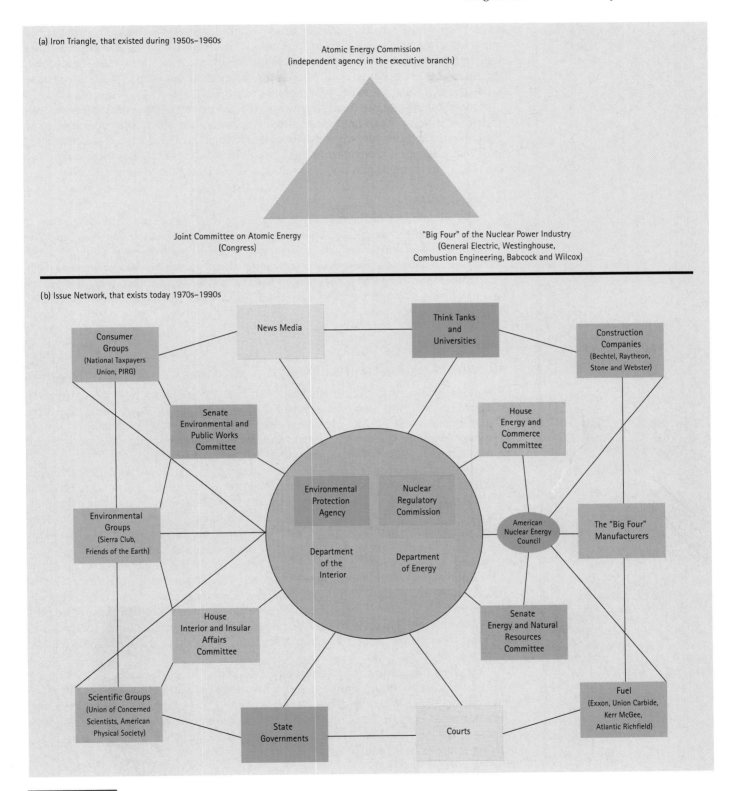

**(a) Iron Triangle, that existed during 1950s–1960s**

Atomic Energy Commission
(independent agency in the executive branch)

Joint Committee on Atomic Energy
(Congress)

"Big Four" of the Nuclear Power Industry
(General Electric, Westinghouse,
Combustion Engineering, Babcock and Wilcox)

**(b) Issue Network, that exists today 1970s–1990s**

Consumer Groups (National Taxpayers Union, PIRG)

News Media

Think Tanks and Universities

Construction Companies (Bechtel, Raytheon, Stone and Webster)

Senate Environmental and Public Works Committee

House Energy and Commerce Committee

Environmental Protection Agency

Nuclear Regulatory Commission

Department of the Interior

Department of Energy

American Nuclear Energy Council

The "Big Four" Manufacturers

Environmental Groups (Sierra Club, Friends of the Earth)

House Interior and Insular Affairs Committee

Senate Energy and Natural Resources Committee

Scientific Groups (Union of Concerned Scientists, American Physical Society)

State Governments

Courts

Fuel (Exxon, Union Carbide, Kerr McGee, Atlantic Richfield)

## Figure 14.9

**Change of Nuclear Energy Policy Arena from Iron Triangle to Issue Network**
*Why has the policy-making environment changed from a triangle to a web?*

SOURCE: Based on information in Seong-Ho Lim, "Changing Jurisdictional Boundaries in Congressional Oversight of Nuclear Energy Regulation: Impact of Public Salience" (paper presented before the Annual Meeting of the American Political Science Association, 1992); Frank R. Baumgartner and Bryan D. Jones, "Agency Dynamics and Policy Subsystems," *Journal of Politics* 53 (November 1991): 1044–1074.

at the Three Mile Island reactor in Pennsylvania, however, the subject attracted the attention of environmental, safety, and antinuclear groups, all of whom pressed for tighter regulation of nuclear reactors. With the interests of the groups divided, the media took a greater interest in the issue, and conflict between congressional committees and the Department of Energy intensified.[77]

Many scholars argue that the concept of issue networks presents a more realistic picture of the way Washington works today than does the older concept of iron triangles. In past decades, the three points of the triangle provided a good description of how many agencies, Congress, and interest groups did business, but increasingly, our current, more complicated politics looks less like a triangle and more like a web.

### SECTION SUMMARY

Congress oversees the bureaucracy in a variety of ways, including Senate confirmation of many appointees, specific legislation, budgetary control, and legislative oversight. Depending on its level of satisfaction with an agency, the congressional committee with jurisdiction over it may choose to exert more or less control. Often, relationships among interest groups, congressional committees, and agencies become so close that the parties are said to form iron triangles. In recent years, many of these iron triangles have given way to more complex issue networks.

## *Elections and the Bureaucracy*

For more than a century, reformers have tried to separate politics from administration. Government should serve the people, they argue, not the special interests. Departments should make decisions according to laws and regulations, not in response to political pressure. Agencies should treat every applicant alike, not respond more favorably to those who contribute to political parties.

These reform principles are worthy of respect. When politics interfere, bureaucracies can be inefficient and ineffective. The post office, long a patronage reserve, is said to deliver snail mail. The customs service, its name once synonymous with political spoils, is still slow to report international economic transactions. The Department of Housing and Urban Development, always a political thicket, has at times so badly mismanaged its property it has had to blow up buildings it constructed.[78]

Many of the more effective federal bureaucracies are less politically charged.[79] The National Science Foundation, protected from political pressures by an independent board, is known for the integrity with which it allocates dollars among competing scientific projects. The Federal Bureau of Prisons does a better job than many state prisons of maintaining security without depriving prisoners of rights; it has succeeded in part because members of Congress, respectful of prison leadership, have left the agency alone.[80]

But even though agency autonomy has worked in some instances, electoral pressures have also played a positive role and in any case are an essential feature of modern bureaucracies.[81] Public pressure exerted through elections has affected the way bureaucracies keep secrets, enforce the law, manage their budgets, and make decisions. In the end, elections create pressures that force many agencies to balance competing interests by striking compromises.

### *Bureaucratic Secrecy*

Bureaucracies like to protect their secrets. Inside knowledge is power. Secrecy can cover mistakes. In Europe, where administrators are less exposed to electoral pressure, they work hard to guard their private information. In Britain it is a crime for civil servants to divulge official information, and political appointees swear themselves to secrecy upon taking office.

Electoral pressures have sharply curtailed the amount of secrecy in American government. In the view of one specialist, "secrecy has less legitimacy as a governmental practice in the United States than in any other advanced industrial society with the possible exception of Sweden," in large part because "Congress has done a great deal to open up the affairs of bureaucracy to greater outside scrutiny."[82] The **sunshine law**, passed in 1976, required that federal government meetings be held in public, unless military plans, trade secrets, or personnel questions are under discussion. Under the Freedom of Information Act of 1967, citizens have the right to inspect unprotected government documents. If the government feels the requested information needs to be kept secret, it must bear the burden of proof when arguing its case before a judge.

> **sunshine law**
> A 1976 law requiring that federal government meetings be held in public.

Secrecy is hard for agencies to preserve, even when it is both permitted and essential. The tear-gas attack on the Branch Davidians was announced ahead of time by an enterprising reporter for a Waco, Texas, radio station, who had gleaned the information from federal officials. Because the attack was no longer a surprise, the leaders of the Branch Davidians had time to organize their self-immolation (see the opening of this chapter).

General Norman Schwarzkopf did a better job at preserving secrecy when U.S. troops invaded Kuwait in 1991. The army planned an end run around Iraqi forces, surprising the enemy from behind. The surprise depended on keeping not only the enemy but also the international press from finding out about the operation.

## Bureaucratic Coercion

Bureaucracies are often accused of using their coercive powers harshly and unfairly. Police officers stop young drivers for traffic violations that are often ignored when committed by older drivers. Bureaucratic zealots trap sales clerks into selling cigarettes to heavily bearded 17-year-olds. Disabled people are refused benefits because they do not fill out their applications correctly.

Although such abuses occur, they happen less frequently because agencies are held accountable to the electorate. In 1998, for example, Republican senators sensed popular discontent with the Internal Revenue Service (IRS), the government's tax collection agency. The agency's approval rating was an embarrassingly low 38 percent.[83] The Senate Finance Committee held a series of hearings that brought to light a litany of agency failings. The IRS had lost $150 billion in 1995 because of mistakes, unreported income, or improper deductions. Taxpayers were overbilled an average of $5 billion per year.[84] The technology the agency used was so outdated that even IRS Commissioner Charles Rossotti admitted, "I have never seen a worse situation in a large organization."[85] And one rogue agent even tried to frame an ex-senator on money-laundering and bribery charges.[86]

As a result of the hearings, Congress enacted a law restructuring the agency, making it harder for the IRS to accuse taxpayers of wrongdoing and bringing its tax collection systems up to date.[87]

## Agency Expansion

Though agencies generally try to increase their budgets, elections brake such tendencies, if only because politicians get blamed for raising taxes. "As a general rule," says analyst Martha Derthick, "Congress likes to keep bureaucracy lean and cheap."[88] The number of people working for the federal government, as a percentage of the workforce, has declined (see Figure 14.1), in good part because elected officials are under public pressure to cut bureaucracy.

www.longmanparticipate.com

**visual literacy**

**The Changing Face of the Federal Bureaucracy**

## Administrator Caution

Federal agencies are sometimes accused of going beyond their legislative mandates. But most federal agencies are more likely to err on the side of caution. The worst thing any agency can do is make a major mistake that captures national attention. As one official explained, "The public servant soon learns that successes rarely rate a headline, but government blunders are front-page news. This recognition encourages the development of procedures designed less to achieve successes than to avoid blunders."[89]

In 1962 it was discovered, to widespread horror, that thalidomide, a sedative available in Europe, increased the probability that babies would be born with serious physical deformities. Congress immediately passed a law toughening the procedures the Food and Drug Administration (FDA) needed to follow before approving prescription drugs for distribution.[90] Two decades later, in keeping with this policy, the FDA refused to approve the sale of several experimental drugs to terminally ill people suffering from AIDS. Patients desperate to try anything did not share the FDA's concern for ascertaining proven effectiveness. When the FDA's refusal to allow experimentation became a public issue, the agency began to allow AIDS patients to try the untested drugs, once again responding to potential electoral pressures.

## Compromised Capacity

Agency effectiveness is often undermined by the very terms of the legislation that created it. For legislation to pass Congress, a broad coalition of support is necessary. To build this support, proponents must strike deals with those who are at best lukewarm to the idea. Such compromise can cripple a program at birth.[91]

The politics of charter schools illustrate the restraint that compromises can place on organizational effectiveness. School reform advocates have begun to establish charter schools—new schools free of most state regulations. Reformers expect charter schools to provide alternatives to and competition for traditional public schools. School boards and teacher organizations oppose the establishment of these schools, claiming they will attract students away from their local schools. Many state legislatures, under pressure from both sides, have compromised on the issue by passing legislation allowing charter schools but restricting their number, funding, and autonomy. It remains to be seen whether charter schools can prosper within the constraints imposed by these legislative compromises.[92]

## Muddling Through

American bureaucracies do not perform as badly as most Americans think. One survey examines the actual experiences of clients encountering government bureaucracies and then compares their reactions to these experiences with the impressions that these same people have of government bureaucracies in general. The differences between actual experiences and general impressions are striking:

> Seventy-one percent of all the clients said that their [own] problems were taken care of, but only 30 percent think that government agencies [generally] do well at taking care of problems. Eighty percent said that they were treated fairly, but only 42 percent think that government agencies treat most people fairly.
>
> In other words, most Americans . . . decide that their [good] experiences represent an exception to the rule. People who have had *bad* experiences, however, are likely . . . to think that everyone else is getting unfair treatment too.[93]

When all the pluses and minuses are added up, the average government bureaucracy probably deserves something like a B minus. A few agencies, like NASA during the race to the moon, merited an A plus, though its reputation has since slipped. A few others, like the customs service, don't deserve a passing grade. But the general tendency is toward a bland, risk-free mediocrity. Too much imagination generates too much controversy, which invites political retribution. The best way to survive politically is to try to muddle through.[94]

The forest service, which is responsible for managing most of the millions of acres owned by the federal government, does a pretty good job of muddling through. Although its rangers are professionally trained, talented individuals, its political problems are vexing. Ranchers, miners, and timber companies want to exploit the land's natural resources. Others want to use the land for hiking, camping, and fishing. Environmentalists want to convert as much of the land as they can into wilderness areas for the benefit of future generations.

To balance these pressures, the forest service came up with the doctrine of multiple use. It proposed to manage the land in such a way that its multiple uses could be blended together and harmonized. Timber harvests should be accompanied by reforestation. Especially scenic areas should be preserved for recreational activities. Mining should be as inconspicuous as possible.

But the doctrine of multiple use did not so much resolve conflicts as institutionalize them. As a result, the forest service is under constant pressure. Ranching, timber, and mining interests have clout at the local level, where local political leaders make the potent claim that the local economy will suffer unless these interests are protected. Environmentalists have the greatest influence on those chosen in elections affected by the national media, which dramatically depict the desecration of the American landscape.

Any attempt to balance these interests antagonizes one or more sides of the dispute. Only by muddling through can the forest service survive politically and manage the federal lands as well as it does.[95]

## SECTION SUMMARY

Although a few bureaucracies are insulated from public pressures, elections affect most agencies in fundamental ways. On the positive side, U.S. bureaucracies are less secretive and more accountable than bureaucracies in other countries. On the other hand, they often internalize conflict in an attempt to please everyone, making it more difficult to chart an authoritative course.

## *Chapter Summary*

Government bureaucracies are essential, and bureaucratic problems are inevitable. But American bureaucracies have specific troubles that can be attributed to the electoral climate in which they have evolved. With the creation of the spoils system, bureaucrats were often regarded as slow, inefficient, corrupt political hacks. Gradually, civil service reforms eliminated the worst of the abuses. But the reforms were bottom-up, not top-down. The highest levels of government continue to be filled with political appointees—generally capable but not always experienced government administrators.

As chief executive, the president is nominally in charge of the bureaucracy, appointing key officials and exerting control through the Office of Management and Budget. But Congress also influences federal agencies via the confirmation process, detailed legislative enactments, the budget process, and legislative oversight. To survive, agencies build ties to key interest groups, who form the base of what are known as iron triangles. Today, some of these iron triangles are being transformed into more complex issue networks.

Elections influence agencies in diverse ways. On the one hand, they keep agencies from becoming too secretive and coercive. On the other hand, they can also make agencies too cautious or force them to operate under compromised laws that undermine their effectiveness. Most of the time, agencies respond to politics by muddling through, for which they deserve more credit than they usually get.

## On the Web

FedWorld
www.fedworld.gov
Most U.S. government agencies and departments have informative Web sites that can be reached through FedWorld.
Office of Management and Budget
www.whitehouse.gov/OMB/
The Office of Management and Budget offers copies of budget documentation, testimony before Congress, and regulatory information.
Congressional Budget Office
www.cbo.gov

The Congressional Budget Office provides copies of its reports on the economy, the budget, and current legislation.
General Accounting Office
www.gao.gov
The General Accounting Office, the investigative arm of Congress, assists Congress in its oversight of the executive branch.
National Performance Review
www.npr.gov
The National Performance Review site provides information about the current wave of "reinventing government" initiatives.

## Key Terms

administrative discretion, p. 412
agency, p. 412
bureaucracy, p. 411
civil service, p. 420
Congressional Budget Office (CBO) , p. 427
department, p. 412
earmark, p. 430
end run, p. 427

government corporation, p. 412
Hatch Act, p. 420
independent regulatory agencies, p. 425
inner cabinet, p. 423
in-and-outers, p. 421
iron triangle, p. 431
issue networks, p. 432
mugwumps, p. 418

patronage, p. 415
Pendleton Act, p. 419
Office of Management and Budget (OMB), p. 427
outer cabinet, p. 423
recess appointment, p. 429
senatorial courtesy, p. 428
spoils system, p. 416
sunshine law, p. 435

## Suggested Readings

Chubb, John, and Terry Moe. *Politics, Markets and America's Schools*. Washington, DC: Brookings, 1990. Brilliant, controversial account of the way in which politics interferes with effective management of public schools.

DiIulio, John. *Governing Prisons: A Comparative Study of Correctional Management*. New York: Macmillan, 1990. Shows how politics affects the management of prisons.

Heclo, Hugh. "Issue Networks and the Executive Establishment," in Anthony King, ed. *The New American Political System*. Washington, DC: American Enterprise Institute, 1978. Describes the shift from iron triangles to issue networks.

Kaufman, Herbert. *The Forest Ranger*. Baltimore, MD: Johns Hopkins University Press, 1981. Classic study of a government agency.

Kettl, Donald F. and John J. DiIulio Jr., eds. *Inside the Reinvention Machine: Appraising Governmental Reform*. Washington, DC: Brookings, 1995. Preliminary evaluation of the Clinton/Gore "reinventing government" initiative.

Light, Paul. *Thickening Government: Federal Hierarchy and the Diffusion of Accountability*. Washington, DC: Brookings, 1995. Identifies and explains the growth in higher-level governmental positions.

Morone, James A. *The Democratic Wish: Popular Participation and the Limits of American Government.* New York: Basic Books, 1990. Account of the ways in which democratic movements have shaped the development of public administration in U.S. history.

Niskanan, William A. *Bureaucracy and Representative Government.* Chicago: Aldine-Atherton, 1971. Develops the argument that government bureaucracies seek to maximize their budgets.

Wilson, James Q. *Bureaucracy: What Government Agencies Do and Why They Do It.* New York: Basic Books, 1989. Comprehensive treatment of public bureaucracies.

Young, James. *The Washington Community 1800–1828.* New York: Harcourt, 1966. Engaging, insightful account of political and administrative life in Washington during the first decades of the nineteenth century.

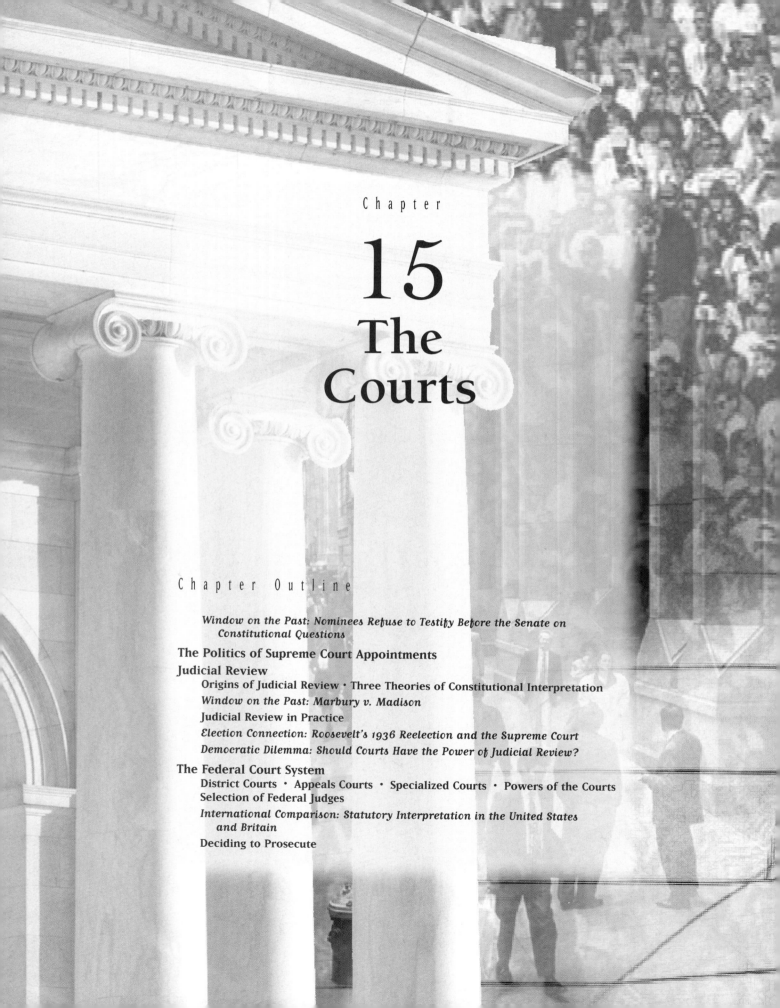

Thurgood Marshall, the Supreme Court's first black justice, once jested, "I have a lifetime appointment and I intend to serve it. I expect to die at 110, shot by a jealous husband."[1] He nonetheless resigned in June 1991, reluctantly concluding that at age 83 he could no longer continue a civil rights struggle he had fought for decades. Asked by reporters why he was stepping down, an impatient Marshall declared, "I'm old! I'm getting old and coming apart."[2]

Marshall's retirement set in motion the process of replacing him on the Court. As mandated by the Constitution, the president nominates Supreme Court justices, but each nominee must then be confirmed by a majority of the Senate. At times the nomination process can explode into conflict, especially when issues of race or gender are at the forefront, as they were bound to be in the case of Marshall's seat. After days of public and media speculation about possible candidates, President Bush nominated Clarence Thomas, an African American who had brought a conservative definition of equal opportunity to his work as chair of the Equal Employment Opportunity Commission (EEOC). In stark contrast to the man he would replace, Thomas was opposed to affirmative action programs that gave preferential treatment to minorities because "they assume that I am not the equal of someone else, and if I'm not the equal, then I'm inferior."[3]

The Democrat-controlled Senate viewed the nominee with great suspicion, but at first it seemed that Thomas's political savvy would allow him to escape much criticism. For one thing, he had not publicly expressed his views on controversial constitutional questions, which made it more difficult for his opponents to criticize his legal opinions.

Thomas also realized that silence was golden during the nomination process. Anything he said might be used as ammunition by those opposing him. At the traditional confirmation hearings before the Senate Judiciary Committee, when Thomas was asked no fewer than 70 times for his opinion on the constitutionality of laws against abortion, his replies were studiously ambiguous.[4] By refusing to respond clearly to these questions, Thomas withheld from his opponents weapons they needed to defeat his candidacy.

Still another factor was significant. Civil rights groups and liberal Democrats were uneasy in their opposition to Thomas, hesitant to denounce an African American when they had so frequently called on presidents to appoint more minorities. Moreover, opinion polls indicated that three-quarters of the black population supported Thomas's appointment, despite his conservative views.[5] Massachusetts Senator Edward Kennedy, opposed as he was to the Thomas nomination, was forced to admit, "In many ways he exemplifies the promise of the Constitution and the American ideal of equal opportunity."[6]

But Thomas ended up being the center of a political uproar after all—as the result of testimony by a soft-spoken woman named Anita Hill. An attorney and former employee of Thomas's at the EEOC, Hill had left the high-pressure world of Washington politics to assume an academic position at the University of

Oklahoma. She had left Washington, she told a friend, because Thomas had sexually harassed her.

Judiciary Committee staffers approached Hill, who told them her story. Within days, her accounts of sexual harassment had been leaked to the media. Eventually, in hearings televised across the country, millions had an opportunity to hear Hill's account of the lewd and suggestive phrases she claimed to have heard from the mouth of a future justice of the Supreme Court. Thomas angrily denied all charges and called the televised Senate exploitation of the Hill allegations nothing less than a "high-tech lynching."[7]

The confirmation battle spilled out of the Washington beltway to involve men and women of all races and creeds all across the country. For the 14 Judiciary Committee senators forced to listen to the sensational testimony, it was a political nightmare. In some strange twist of politics, it was not just Thomas, but the Senate itself, that was on trial. When one senator explored Anita Hill's credibility through close cross examination, women's groups attacked him for his unfair, aggressive style.

In the end, the Senate confirmed Thomas by a close vote. More Americans believed Thomas than Hill, and a clear majority continued to favor Thomas's confirmation.[8] The strong support Thomas received from African American voters was particularly significant.[9]

Though Thomas was confirmed, the process had a dramatic effect on the next election. The more women thought about the outcome, the more unhappy they became. The percentage of women who believed Thomas had harassed Hill increased from 27 to 51 percent over the following year.[10] The number of women elected to the House of Representatives increased by almost 70 percent in 1992, from 28 to 47, and 4 new women were elected to the Senate. In the presidential election, Bush's support among women was 5 percentage points less than his support among men, enough of a difference to cost Bush the election.[11] It was the costliest nomination to the Supreme Court a president had ever made.

IN RECENT YEARS, THE COURTS HAVE BEEN INCREASINGLY INFLUENCED by electoral considerations, even though the founders meant the courts to be more isolated from public pressures than other political institutions. This chapter describes the U.S. judicial system, which is headed by the Supreme Court and also includes other federal and state courts. In discussing the role the courts play in affecting public policy, we will answer the following questions:

- How are people chosen to sit on the Supreme Court?
- What power does the Supreme Court wield to influence policy?
- What is the structure of the federal court system?
- What is the role of state courts?
- How does the Supreme Court decide the outcome of specific cases?
- What are the checks on the power of the Supreme Court?
- How are the courts used to advance political agendas?

**Window on the Past**

**Nominees Refuse to Testify Before the Senate on Constitutional Questions**

Much to the chagrin of opposition senators, Supreme Court nominees often refuse to testify on issues that might be brought up before the Court. Both conservative judge Clarence Thomas and liberal nominee Thurgood Marshall refused to answer many questions.

Exchange Between Senator Joseph Biden (D-DE) and Clarence Thomas (1991)

THOMAS: . . . what I have attempted to do is not agree or disagree with existing cases.

BIDEN: You are doing very well at that.

THOMAS: . . . I do not approach these cases with any desire to change them . . .

BIDEN: If you had a desire to change [the decision in *Roe* v. *Wade*] would you tell us?

THOMAS: I don't think so.[a]

Exchange Between Senator Sam Ervin (D-NC) and Thurgood Marshall (1967)

ERVIN: If you are not going to answer a question about anything which might possibly come before the Supreme Court some time in the future, I cannot ask you a single question about anything that is relevant to this inquiry.

MARSHALL: All I am trying to say, Senator, is I do not think you want me to be in the position of giving you a state-ment on the Fifth Amendment, and then, if I am confirmed and sit on the Court, when a Fifth Amendment question comes up, I will have to disqualify myself.

ERVIN: If you have no opinions on what the Constitution means at this time, you ought not to be confirmed. Anybody that has been at the bar as long as you have certainly ought to have some very firm opinions about the meaning of the Constitution.

MARSHALL: . . . I do have an opinion as of this time. But I think it would be wrong for me to give that opinion at this time.[b]

*What do you think?*

- *Do you think the nominees are correct to refrain from testifying on specific constitutional issues?*
- *Does such an attitude preserve the integrity of the Court, or does it detract from the Senate's ability to perform its duty in the confirmation process?*
- *What types of information should senators and the public know about prospective Supreme Court justices?*

---

[a]David Brock, *The Real Anita Hill: The Untold Story* (New York: Free Press, 1993), pp. 90–91.
[b]Paul Simon, *Advice and Consent* (Bethesda, MD: National Press Books, 1992), p. 278.

## The Politics of Supreme Court Appointments

CONSTITUTION, ARTICLE II: *"The President shall nominate . . . and by and with the Advice and Consent of the Senate, shall appoint . . . Judges of the Supreme Court."*

The judicial system is supposed to be politically blind. Justice is expected to fall, like the rain, equally on rich and poor, Democrat and Republican, black, white, Latino, Asian, and Native American. Judges are appointed for life because they are expected to decide each case with an open mind and to avoid discussing specific cases in public. Chief Justice Warren E. Burger went so far as to claim that "Judges . . . rule on the basis of law, not public opinion, and they should be totally indifferent to pressures of the times."[12] Adopting a posture both convenient and consistent with this under-standing of the impartial role of the justice, most Supreme Court nominees, like Thomas, tell judiciary committee senators that they cannot comment on specific issues that might come before the court (see the accompanying Window on the Past).

Despite this ideal, however, the process by which justices are selected is a politi-cal one, and it has become more so in recent decades. Justices are nominated by the president, evaluated by the Senate judiciary committee, and confirmed by a vote of the full Senate. The court's **chief justice** must also be nominated and confirmed in this manner, even if he or she is already a member of the Court. Because of this process,

**chief justice**
Head of the Supreme Court.

**The Supreme Court**
Originally conceived by President and Chief Justice William Howard Taft to instill public respect for the judicial branch, the Supreme Court building resembles a Greek temple built to house ancient gods.

elected officials, as well as interest groups and the media, all have a voice in choosing members of the Court. These players pay close attention to the electoral consequences of their actions, so elections inevitably affect nominations to the Court, and confirmation battles affect elections.

For at least the first half of the twentieth century, presidential nominations to the Supreme Court were confirmed by the Senate as a matter of course. Most nominees were approved quietly without even testifying before the Judiciary Committee. One of Harry Truman's nominees declined an explicit invitation to testify but was confirmed anyway.[13] Earl Warren, the Eisenhower appointee who would write the opinion in the landmark 1954 school desegregation decision, *Brown* v. *Board of Education* (see Chapter 17), was also confirmed without giving testimony.[14]

This long-time separation of Supreme Court nominations from political disputes owed a great deal to the efforts of William Howard Taft. Taft was the only person ever to serve both as president (1909–1913) and as chief justice of the Supreme Court (1921–1930). Before Taft, political factors openly affected the confirmation decisions. In the nineteenth century, the Senate rejected a third of the presidents' nominees.[15] But Taft worked hard both as president and as chief justice to enhance the quality of nominees, minimize the significance of confirmation procedures, and elevate the prestige of the Court. He also made sure that the new Supreme Court building, eventually completed in 1935, was designed to resemble a Greek temple, so that Americans would respect their laws with the same reverence with which the ancient Greeks venerated their gods.

Taft was so successful that until 1968, the Senate confirmed every twentieth-century nominee but one, most without significant dissent. But in the past 50 years, the Senate has regained some of the power it had lost. Since 1955, every Supreme Court nominee has appeared before the judiciary committee, and the Senate's propensity to reject presidential nominees has steadily increased, as Table 15.1 indicates. One of the most celebrated cases involved Robert Bork, a Reagan nominee rejected by the Senate in 1987. A staunch conservative, Bork had produced a great many journal articles and speeches, which interest groups and Senate opponents used to attack him in a concerted national campaign. The Reagan administration was caught off guard by the new tactics. "We didn't anticipate this would be conducted like a federal election," one aide complained.[16]

Bork's rejection has in fact given American politics a new word, **borking**, which means politicizing the nomination process through an organized public campaign portraying the nominee as a dangerous extremist. Judicial appointments have become

**borking**
Politicizing the nomination process through an organized public campaign that portrays the nominee as a dangerous extremist.

Table 15.1

Presidential Nominees to the Supreme Court Not Confirmed by the Senate, 1900–2000

| Nominee | Year | President | Main Reason for Rejection/Withdrawal |
|---------|------|-----------|--------------------------------------|
| John Parker | 1930 | Hoover | Antilabor |
| Abraham Fortas (sitting justice nominated to be chief justice) | 1968 | Johnson | Too liberal; resigned from Court in 1969 over alleged financial abuses |
| Homer Thornberry | 1968 | Johnson | No vacancy when Fortas not confirmed for chief justice |
| Clement Haynesworth | 1970 | Nixon | Alleged financial abuses |
| G. Harrold Carswell | 1970 | Nixon | Racially conservative |
| Robert Bork | 1987 | Reagan | Controversial conservative record |
| Douglas Ginsburg | 1987 | Reagan | Smoked marijuana with students |

so influenced by estimates of their effects on the next election that pundits had to invent this new word to describe what was happening. Both Congress and the media now subject each nomination to scrutiny.

Not every Supreme Court nomination will be subject to borking. If the same party controls both Congress and the presidency, borking is less likely. Thus, for example, Bill Clinton was able to appoint both Ruth Bader Ginsburg in 1993 and Stephen Breyer in 1994 without significant controversy. Even so, Clinton had to be careful to pick moderates rather than well-known liberals. Although Ginsburg was one of the first to develop a legal case against sex discrimination, as a lower-court judge she had taken moderate positions on other issues, making her acceptable to conservatives. Ginsburg was respectfully questioned by the Senate Judiciary Committee and confirmed by the overwhelming margin of 96 to 3.

Even if the Senate is controlled by the opposition, presidents may avoid borking by choosing a nominee whose views are unknown, a "stealth" strategy named after the bomber that cannot easily be detected by radar. In 1990 President Bush nominated stealth candidate David Souter, a New Hampshire state supreme court justice who had never written an opinion or treatise on any major constitutional question. Legal scholars lamented such conflict avoidance. One law professor protested that to sidestep a political firestorm, "no president will nominate anyone who has written anything very interesting."[17] Indeed, Souter was easily confirmed because Washington insiders could not be sure where he stood on most issues.

Although many think the increasing politicization of judicial appointments destroys "the public's belief in the fairness of those on the bench and . . . undermine[s] confidence in the Court,"[18] future trends seem clear. The United States is unlikely to go back to the older way of selecting Supreme Court justices. Modern methods of communication—televised hearings, fax machines, 800 numbers, radio talk shows, and the Internet—ensure that presidents will choose justices with an eye to the public controversies they might create, and senators and interest groups will conduct detailed evaluations of each appointee. By a margin of 5 to 1, Americans agree that the "Senate should carefully scrutinize a presidential nominee."[19] The selection of Supreme Court justices is likely to continue to be strongly affected by electoral considerations.

simulation

**You are Appointing a Supreme Court Justice**

SECTION SUMMARY

Though the Supreme Court is not subject to election, nominations to the Court are considered amid intense pressure from interest groups and the media. For the last 40 years, the Senate has been more willing to scrutinize and, at times, reject presidential selections for the high court. This has at times prompted presidents to nominate less controversial judges to sit on the Court.

# Judicial Review

CONSTITUTION, ARTICLE VI: *"This Constitution, and the Laws of the United States which shall be made in Pursuance thereof . . . shall be the supreme Law of the Land."*

Many Americans believe Supreme Court nominees should be carefully scrutinized, in part because the Supreme Court's great political authority includes the power of **judicial review**, the power of the courts to declare null and void laws of Congress and of state legislatures that they find unconstitutional. The power of judicial review can be exercised by any court, federal or state, but all lower court decisions are subject to review by the Supreme Court, if it chooses to do so. The significance of the courts' power of judicial review for a democratic society can hardly be overestimated. Judicial review gives judges, appointed for life, the power to negate laws passed by the elected representatives of the people, causing Senator George W. Norris to complain, "The people can change Congress but only God can change the Supreme Court."[20]

Although the Constitution affirms that it is the "supreme law of the land," it says nothing explicit about judicial review. The founders provided for a Supreme Court but offered few details about its powers (see Chapter 2, page 50). From what little they said at the Constitutional Convention, it seems the delegates did not expect the Court to be particularly powerful. As political scientist Robert McCloskey once observed, "The United States began its history . . . with a Supreme Court whose birthright was most uncertain."[21]

## Origins of Judicial Review

Despite its uncertain status during the first years of the new republic, in 1803 the Supreme Court successfully asserted the power of judicial review for the first time in the most important of all its decisions, **Marbury v. Madison** (see the accompanying Window on the Past). In the case, Chief Justice John Marshall used a small question of political patronage as an occasion to assert that the Supreme Court could declare laws of Congress null and void. This authority has been acknowledged and accepted ever since.

In asserting the power of judicial review, Marshall's reasoning was simple and straightforward. Any new law overrides older laws on the same subject, except when the older law has been issued by a higher governmental entity. If a city passes a law declaring its speed limit to be 30 miles an hour, an older law that sets a speed limit of 40 miles an hour is automatically void, unless the old law was passed by a higher level of government, such as the state. Then the state law, even if it is from an earlier date, takes precedence. The highest law of the land, according to Marshall, is the Constitution. It was established by the people, and no entity subject to the Constitution, not even Congress itself, can enact legislation that contravenes the will of the people, as expressed in the Constitution.

## Three Theories of Constitutional Interpretation

The reasoning is impeccable as long as one assumes that judges only examine a law of Congress, compare it to the Constitution, and determine whether or not the law runs counter to constitutional language. The simplest case, perhaps, would be a law that postponed a constitutionally mandated election day. But very few issues of constitutionality are that simple. To help decide which laws are unconstitutional, the Supreme Court has developed three distinct theories of constitutional interpretation: original intent, living constitution, and plain meaning of the text.

The first is the theory of **original intent**, which determines the constitutionality of a law by ascertaining the intentions of those who wrote the Constitution. To establish the intentions of the founders, judges examine such documents as the notes that James Madison wrote down at the Constitutional Convention, the *Federalist Papers*, and the speeches made during the ratifying campaign in 1787 and 1788. Among today's sitting justices, Justice Thomas relies most frequently on the theory of original intent. For example, he favors overturning *Roe v. Wade* because he finds nothing in the Constitution that gives women the right to choose an abortion. On the contrary, he

**judicial review**
Power of the courts to declare null and void laws of Congress and of state legislatures they find unconstitutional.

*Marbury* v. *Madison*
Supreme Court decision (1803) in which the court first exercised the power of judicial review.

**original-intent**
A theory of constitutional interpretation that determines the constitutionality of a law by ascertaining the intentions of those who wrote the Constitution.

# *Window* on the *Past*

## Marbury v. Madison

On the evening of March 3, 1801, the United States was hours away from going through its first peaceful transition of power from one party to another. After a bitter presidential race, Federalist leader John Adams would leave the presidency the next day, and Thomas Jefferson, of the arch-rival Democratic–Republicans, would take his place (see the discussion of the Election of 1800 in Chapter 3).

But before the Federalists relinquished command, they were determined to leave their mark on the government. On March 2, Adams nominated 42 new justices of the peace for Washington, DC; the Senate approved the appointments the next day; and that evening, as the skies grew dark in the nation's capital, Secretary of State John Marshall stamped their official commissions with the Great Seal of the United States.

The appointments had been so hastily arranged, however, that no one in the outgoing administration had time to deliver the commissions to the appointees. Jefferson found the stack of documents lying on a table in the State Department when he arrived and ordered that they not be delivered. Without the commissions, the new justices of the peace could not take office.

According to the Judiciary Act of 1789, the jilted appointees could request a writ of *mandamus* (a court order) to be granted the appointments. Furthermore, said the act, the Supreme Court would have original jurisdiction in such cases—that is, it would be the first and only court to which such cases would be brought. On the basis of this law, one appointee, William Marbury, sued Jefferson's secretary of state, James Madison, for what he believed was his rightful office.

The Supreme Court heard arguments in *Marbury v. Madison* in early 1803. Ironically, John Marshall, who had prepared Marbury's commission, was now the Court's chief justice. (To avoid complicating

Appointed by John Adams to serve as chief justice (1801–1835), John Marshall was also a Revolutionary War soldier, a supporter of the Constitution at the Virginia ratifying convention, a Federalist member of Congress, and secretary of state. Can you name another key court decision that Marshall wrote?

the issue further, Marbury's lawyer declined to call Marshall himself as a witness in the dispute.)

The case offered no easy solution. The justices were sure that if they issued the writ of *mandamus,* Madison would successfully ignore it, making the Court seem weak and ineffectual. On the other hand, if they declined to issue the writ, they would appear to be caving in to pressure from the Jeffersonians.

On February 24, Marshall read the opinion of the Court to an anxious, crowded audience of Federalists and Democratic–Republicans. First, he scolded the Jeffersonians for denying Marbury what was clearly his rightful position. Withholding the appointment, he said, was "violative of a vested legal right." Next, he argued that the laws of the United States must provide recourse for someone whose legal rights had been so violated.

But then Marshall asked a crucial question: Was the Supreme Court the proper place to address Marbury's complaint? His stunning conclusion was that it was not. Why? The Constitution granted the Supreme Court original jurisdiction *only* in "all Cases affecting Ambassadors, other public Ministers and Consuls, and those in which a State shall be Party." By giving the Court original jurisdiction in the case of judicial appointees, Section 13 of the Judiciary Act of 1789 had violated the Constitution and was therefore void.

Marshall's brilliant decision had transformed a situation that looked sure to sap the power of the Court into one that strengthened it tremendously. By denying the Supreme Court's jurisdiction in the case, he invoked the power of judicial review for the first time, ensuring that the judiciary would always be an authoritative force in American politics.

SOURCE: Jean Edward Smith, *John Marshall: Definer of A Nation* (New York: Holt, 1996), Ch. 13; *Marbury* v. *Madison* 5 U.S. 137 (1803).

says that at the time the Constitution was ratified, many states outlawed abortion, making it clear the framers had no intention of denying the states this authority.

Critics of original-intent theory say that many issues now before the courts were never contemplated by those who wrote the Constitution. Additionally, constitutional language may be the result of compromises between those who held contradictory beliefs. And even if the founders were united in their opinions, should their views count more than ours? Should the perspectives of 55 men gathered together in Philadelphia in the summer of 1787 constrain the actions of the U.S. government more than 200 years later?

Those who criticize original-intent theory offer instead a **living-constitution theory** of judicial review, which says that a law's constitutionality ought to be judged in light of the entire history of the United States as a nation. The determining factors should include not only the opinions expressed at the time the Constitution was written but also ideas and judgments shaped by American experience since then. In the words of Justice Oliver Wendell Holmes, Jr., constitutional questions must be "considered in the light of our whole experience and not merely in that of what was said a hundred years ago."[22] The living-constitution theory is practical and helps the Constitution adapt to modern circumstances; however, it reduces constitutional interpretation to the judge's personal understanding of the meaning of American history. And because no two judges' interpretations of the country's history are likely to be the same, constitutional interpretation becomes highly subjective.

These difficulties have given rise to what has been called the **plain meaning of the text theory** of constitutional interpretation, which determines the constitutionality of a law in light of what the words of the Constitution obviously seem to say. Justice William Douglas pointed out that the First Amendment requires that "Congress shall make no law . . . abridging freedom of speech," adding "The First Amendment is couched in absolute terms—freedom of speech shall not be abridged . . . No leeway is granted."[23]

Plain meaning has two clear advantages. Unlike original-intent theory, it does not require extensive inquiry into obscure debates undertaken in the distant past. The constitutional text itself is taken as a guide to action. Nor does this approach require that judges evaluate the meaning of the totality of the American experience and apply it to the case at hand.

But plain-meaning theory has its own limitations. The Constitution is a very short document that left many issues undecided and used ambiguous language in order to win ratification. Words that appear plain do not always have a clear meaning. Even Justice Douglas agreed to some limitations on free speech—for example, he agreed that one private person cannot libel another with impunity. (See Chapter 16.)

More recently, Justice Sandra Day O'Connor relied on plain-meaning theory to overturn a federal law on the grounds that the federal government cannot order states to follow a regulatory program. She said no such power could be found in the Constitution, and the Tenth Amendment "made explicit" that all powers not delegated to Congress are reserved to the states. "Some truths," she wrote, "are so basic that, like the air around us, they are easily overlooked." But Justice John Stevens argued that O'Connor's interpretation of the law was far from a basic truth, pointing out that Congress under the Articles of Confederation had the authority to compel states to take certain actions. He said the Constitution was written to strengthen, not weaken, the powers of Congress. "The Tenth Amendment surely does not impose any limit on Congress' exercise of the powers delegated to it," he wrote.[24] If two noted jurists, O'Connor and Stevens, do not agree on the content of the Tenth Amendment, its meaning can hardly be plain and clear.

**living-constitution theory**
A theory of constitutional interpretation that places the meaning of the Constitution in light of the total history of the United States.

**plain meaning of the text theory**
A theory of constitutional interpretation that determines the constitutionality of a law in light of what the words of the Constitution obviously seem to say.

## Judicial Review in Practice

Disagreements about theories of judicial review are not just academic; the manner in which the Court interprets the Constitution can have serious consequences for the nation. In three celebrated instances, the Supreme Court created constitutional crises by declaring laws unconstitutional, thereby defying the declared will of Congress and the president.

The first case, *Dred Scott* v. *Sandford* (1857), declared unconstitutional the Missouri Compromise law, passed in 1820.[25] The law drew a line coinciding with the Arkansas–Missouri border, north of which there could never be slavery (see Figure 15.1). Missouri, the exception, was allowed to legalize slavery. The Missouri Compromise had been so successful at preventing a breakup of the union that few even considered the possibility that the Supreme Court would dare call it unconstitutional. But instead of respecting Congress's capacity to find satisfactory compromises, the Supreme Court denied the power of Congress to prohibit slavery in the territories, claiming it was an unconstitutional restriction on property rights. Few Supreme Court decisions have been more disastrous. If it did not by itself cause the Civil War, it certainly kindled fiery sentiments. The *Dred Scott* decision alarmed many northerners, who feared that slavery would, in practice, be extended throughout the Union. For southerners, it helped justify armed resistance.

In the late nineteenth century, the Supreme Court once again unwisely used its power of judicial review to declare a law unconstitutional, this time to block legislation designed to curb the abuses of industrial capitalism. In *Lochner* v. *New York* (1905), the Supreme Court said the State of New York could not regulate the number of hours bakers worked because to do so deprived them of the "right" to work as long and as hard as they pleased. The New York legislature had passed the law at issue, limiting the work week to 60 hours to protect workers from unscrupulous employers. In his dissent from the Court's decision, Oliver Wendell Holmes insisted that the Constitution be interpreted as a living document:

> This case is decided upon an economic theory which a large part of the country does not entertain. A Constitution is not intended to embody a particular economic theory. It is made for people of fundamentally differing views.[26]

Holmes's dissent in *Lochner* eventually became the view of the Supreme Court. Today, it is accepted that government can regulate working conditions.

A third unfortunate use of the power of judicial review occurred after Franklin Delano Roosevelt became president in 1933. Coming to power in the midst of a depression, Roosevelt and his Democratic party allies in Congress passed a host of new legislation, known as the New Deal, which was designed to stimulate economic recovery. Republicans felt that New Deal policies interfered with the natural workings of the economy and would only prolong the depression.

The Supreme Court, which included a majority of justices appointed by Republican presidents, declared many of the New Deal laws unconstitutional. In

**Dred Scott**
This painting depicts Dred Scott, a slave whose master had brought him outside slave-owning states. Scott sued for his freedom, arguing that when he set foot in a free state, he became free. In an infamous decision, the Supreme Court ruled that Scott had no right to sue and that Congress had no right to prohibit slavery in the territories.

**Figure 15.1**

**The Missouri Compromise**
The *Dred Scott* decision invalidated the Missouri Compromise, an 1820 agreement that averted a sectional crisis by fixing a line (pictured) south of which slavery would be permitted. Areas north of the line would be free.

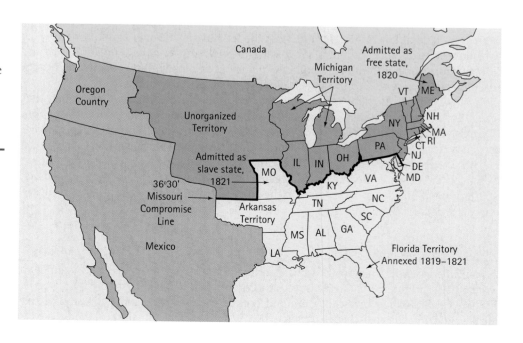

### Election Connection

### Roosevelt's 1936 Reelection and the Supreme Court

In 1936, seven of the nine Supreme Court justices had been appointed by Republican presidents, most of whom initially resisted President Franklin Roosevelt's efforts to expand federal power as part of the New Deal. As late as 1935, the Supreme Court, in *Schechter*, declared unconstitutional a federal regulation of economic activity within a state.[a]

The Roosevelt Democrats were furious at decisions that seemed to deny the country's elected officials the right to govern. Never before had judicial review placed the Supreme Court in such direct conflict with the president and Congress. But Roosevelt overplayed his hand. Instead of trying to change Supreme Court views gradually by appointing justices who shared his New Deal philosophy, he tried to "pack the Court" by adding six new justices over and above the nine already on the Court (one for each of those over 70 years old who refused to retire). Although the Constitution does not specify the number of justices that shall serve on the Supreme Court–its actual size had varied between five and ten–many felt the courts should not be subjected to such direct political manipulation. Roosevelt's court-packing scheme went nowhere in Congress.

Although Roosevelt lost the battle, he won the war. Shortly after his great reelection victory in 1936, Chief Justice Charles Evans Hughes and Justice Owen Roberts, who had previously voted to restrict federal power, changed their views. This time the issue involved the recently passed Wagner Act, a New Deal law that protected union organizers.[b] Despite the fact that the new law regulated activities within a state, a Court majority, in a 5 to 4 vote, declared it constitutional.

The change of heart by Hughes and Roberts has been called "the switch in time that saved nine." The New Deal majority that emerged on the Court was soon augmented and solidified by Roosevelt's own appointees.

*Should the Court respond to changing political conditions?*

---

[a]*Schechter Poultry Corp.* v. *United States* 295 U.S. 495 (1935). The Court also said Congress could not delegate its power to regulate to the executive branch, unless clear standards were established. This rule was also overturned by later Court decisions.
[b]*NLRB* v. *Jones & Laughlin Steel Co.* 301 U.S. 1 (1937).

---

*Schechter Poultry Corp.* v. *United States* (1935), the Supreme Court found the National Industrial Recovery Act, which managed labor and competition in the private sector, an unconstitutional intrusion on the power of the states to regulate commerce inside their own borders.[27] In what was known as the "sick chicken" case, the Court, with all the precision of a medieval theologian calculating the number of angels that can dance on the head of a pin, said the law regulated the sale of poultry *after* it arrived within the State of New York, not while the chicks were being transported across a state line. Because Congress could regulate only commerce between states, not commerce within a state, the Court declared the law unconstitutional (see Chapter 3, page 70). The decision placed the Supreme Court at odds with the president and Congress, creating a constitutional crisis that was not resolved until several justices switched their votes on such cases in the wake of Roosevelt's overwhelming reelection (see the accompanying Election Connection).

Cases such as *Dred Scott, Lochner,* and *Schechter Poultry* have led some to argue that judicial review should be abandoned because it is antidemocratic. But others see judicial review as a valuable protection against majority infringement on minority civil rights and civil liberties (see the accompanying Democratic Dilemma). Despite the controversy, judicial review has become a well established practice in American government. It survives in part because it is seldom used to defy the strongly held views of the president and Congress. On only 143 occasions between 1803 and 1999 did the Supreme Court decide that a federal law was unconstitutional.[28] Most of these decisions affected old laws no longer supported either by a majority of Congress or by the president.

Political scientist Robert Dahl has gone so far as to claim that "The Supreme Court is inevitably a part of the dominant political leadership. The main task of the Court is to confer legitimacy on [the government's] fundamental policies."[29] Though some scholars think the Court is less sensitive to political pressure than Dahl claims, a recent study has identified changes in Supreme Court policy that parallel swings in public opinion. These policy shifts are not so pronounced as those in Congress, the study finds, but justices still seem to pay "attention to what the public wants."[30] The *Dred Scott* and *Schechter Poultry* cases are the exception, not the rule. Bartender Mr. Dooley, the Irish cartoon figure, was not wide of the mark when he observed years ago that "th' supreme court follows th' illiction returns."

timeline

**Umpiring the Government**

## Democratic Dilemma

## Should Courts Have the Power of Judicial Review?

Some scholars say the Supreme Court must have the power of judicial review to protect civil liberties; others say such power is antidemocratic.

John Ely argues that although "Majoritarian democracy is the core of our entire system," a majority may at times unjustly "deal itself benefits at the expense of the minority." Voters and their elected representatives may, for example, restrict the political rights of unpopular groups. Preserving these rights is essential in a democracy, but "we cannot trust elected officials to do so." Only the courts, through the wise use of constitutional law, can play this crucial role.

Others believe this optimism about the role of the judiciary is unfounded. "If judicial review is a means to check legislative encroachments," asks John Agresto, "what means exist to check the encroachments of the judiciary, a judiciary that has increasingly taken on itself the attributes and powers of legislation?" In fact, although we may look to the Court to rule on questions of constitutional law, the Court often creates wholly new public policies in areas such as abortion, welfare, schools, racial busing, and

employment. Most recently, the Court said Congress could not ban guns from school grounds—only the states could do so. Critics like Agresto suggest that we should rein in the power of the courts, limiting the incidence of such "unreviewed judicial legislation."

*What do you think?*
- *Do you believe the Court's independence and judicial review authority work to preserve democracy?*
- *Or do you think the Court is likely to take this power too far, using it to create policies that neither the people nor their elected representatives prefer?*
- *How do you think Chief Justice John Marshall would respond? Franklin Roosevelt? Dred Scott?*

SOURCES: John H. Ely, *Democracy and Distrust: A Theory of Judicial Review* (Cambridge, MA: Harvard University Press, 1980), pp. 7, 106, 183. John Agresto, *The Supreme Court and Constitutional Democracy* (Ithaca, NY: Cornell University Press, 1984), p.163. Excerpted with ellipses deleted.

### SECTION SUMMARY

Judicial review, the power to declare laws unconstitutional, is the key power of the judicial branch, because it gives courts the authority to overturn the decisions of the people's elected representatives. Since *Marbury* v. *Madison*, all have agreed that the courts have this power, but many still disagree on how it should be used. Should justices interpret the Constitution according to the original intent of the founders, the living-constitution theory, or the plain meaning of the text? Conflicts about what the Constitution means have been at the center of key controversies in American history.

## The Federal Court System

CONSTITUTION, ARTICLE III, SECTION 1: *"The judicial power . . . shall be vested in one supreme Court, and in such inferior Courts as the Congress may from time to time ordain and establish."*

Although the Supreme Court provides the linchpin for the nation's system of courts, resolving difficult constitutional and other legal questions, most of the day-to-day work of the federal judicial branch is carried out at lower tiers. Indeed, the vast majority of Supreme Court cases are heard first in the lower federal courts or in the state courts. These lower courts are less visible institutions, but they are no less affected by political and electoral forces. In this section we describe the federal court system. (In the next section we discuss the state courts, which handle the majority of court cases in the United States.)

### District Courts

The Constitution established a Supreme Court, leaving it to Congress to decide what lower federal courts were needed in addition to the state courts already in existence. The first Congress enacted the Judiciary Act of 1789, which, though it has been updated in many ways, still provides the basic framework for the modern federal court system.

Most federal cases are initially filed in one of the 94 **federal district courts**, the lowest tier of the federal court system. As Figure 15.2 shows, the vast majority of fed-

**federal district courts**
The lowest level of the federal court system and the courts in which most federal trials are held.

eral legal proceedings begin and end in these district courts, which are also called trial courts.

As this name suggests, the main responsibility of the district courts is to hold trials. In all trials there are two sides: the **plaintiff**, the person bringing the suit, and the **defendant**, the person against whom the complaint is made.

Trials settle alleged violations of the civil and criminal code. The **civil code** regulates the legal rights and obligations of citizens with regard to one another. Alleged violations of the civil code are stated by individuals, who ask the court to award damages and otherwise offer relief for injuries they claim to have suffered. For example, you can act as plaintiff and sue your landlord for not supplying heat to your apartment. You can ask for monetary damages and a guarantee that this will not happen in the future. In these civil cases, redress for injury depends on your taking legal action against the defendant. People cannot be imprisoned for violating the civil code (though they can be imprisoned for noncompliance with a court order issued in conjunction with a civil suit).

Violations of the **criminal code** are offenses against society as a whole and are enforced by the government itself, acting as plaintiff and initiating charges against suspects. If convicted, the criminal owes a debt to society, not just to the injured party. The debt may be paid by fine, imprisonment, or, in the case of capital crimes, execution. Table 15.2 summarizes the differences between civil and criminal cases.

The same action can simultaneously be a violation of both the criminal and the civil code. After a jury found former football star O. J. Simpson not guilty of criminal charges in conjunction with the murder of his ex-wife, Nicole Brown Simpson, her relatives filed civil charges, alleging that the family should be compensated for pain and suffering caused by her wrongful death. The plaintiffs were able to secure a guilty verdict in the civil suit and a monetary award of $33.5 million despite the finding of not guilty in the criminal prosecution, because in civil suits, the accused can be forced to testify and the standards of proof are lower. In civil suits, one is not considered innocent until proven guilty beyond a reasonable doubt. Juries need only decide whose case is better supported by the preponderance of the evidence.

**High Profile Plaintiff**
In 1997, several New York police officers tortured prisoner Abner Louima in a police station bathroom. After the officers were prosecuted in criminal court, Louima filed a civil suit against New York City, the police union, and his attackers.

**plaintiff**
One who brings legal charges against another.

**defendant**
One accused of violating the civil or criminal code.

**civil code**
Laws regulating relations among individuals. Alleged violators are sued by presumed victims, who ask courts to award damages and otherwise offer relief.

**criminal code**
Laws regulating relations between individuals and society. Alleged violators are prosecuted by government.

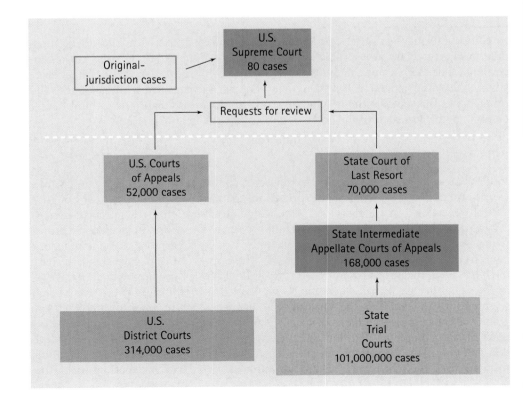

**Figure 15.2**

**Federal and State Court Systems**

**Table 15.2**

**Differences Between Civil and Criminal Trials**

|  | Criminal Trial | Civil Trial |
|---|---|---|
| Plaintiff is | The government | Private person or group |
| At issue | Duty of citizens to obey the law | Legal rights and obligations of citizens to one another |
| Type of wrongdoing | Transgression against society | Harm to private person or group |
| Remedy | Punishment (fine, imprisonment, etc.) | Compensation for damages |
| Standard of proof | Beyond a reasonable doubt | Preponderance of the evidence |
| Can defendant be forced to testify? | No | Yes |

## Appeals Courts

**circuit court of appeals**
Court to which decisions by federal district courts are appealed.

**plenary session**
Activities of a court in which all judges participate.

The federal district courts are organized into 13 circuits, including 11 numbered circuits, a DC circuit, and a federal circuit, each of which has a **circuit court of appeals**, the court to which all district court decisions may be appealed (see Figure 15.3). Originally, circuit judges traveled a circuit, going by stagecoach from district to district and listening to appeals from lower-court decisions. Depending on the size of the circuit, the courts of appeals have between 6 and 28 judges. The senior appeals-court judge assigns 3 judges, usually chosen by lot, to review each case that has been appealed. In exceptionally important cases, a **plenary session** may be held in which all of the appeals judges in the circuit participate. Courts of appeals confine their review to points of law under dispute; they ordinarily take as given the facts of the case, as stated in the trial record and decided by district judges. They do not accept new evidence or hear additional witnesses. Though decisions by the appeals court may be taken up by the Supreme Court, most appeals-court decisions are final.

simulation
**You are a Young Lawyer**

## Specialized Courts

In addition to the 94 district courts, there are two trial courts with nationwide jurisdiction over specialized issues. The Court of International Trade handles cases concerning international trade and customs. And the U.S. Court of Federal Claims hears suits concerning federal contracts, money damages against the United States, and other issues that involve the federal government. Cases originating in either of these courts may be appealed to the court of appeals for the federal circuit.

## Powers of the Courts

**statutory interpretation**
The judicial act of interpreting and applying the law to particular cases.

Judicial review is only the most sweeping and controversial of judicial powers. The courts also engage in **statutory interpretation**, the application of the laws of Congress and of the states to particular cases. American courts have great discretion in exercising this power, much more than their counterparts in Great Britain (see the accompanying International Comparison). For example, Congress passed a vague and general law protecting endangered species in 1973. The Supreme Court gave this law sharp teeth by saying that Congress intended to protect all species, the tiny snail darter as well as the eagle. In reaching this decision, Chief Justice Warren Burger wrote that "it may seem curious to some that the survival of a relatively small number of three-inch fish among all the countless millions of species extant would require the permanent halting of a virtually completed dam for which Congress has expended more than $100 million." But the law, Burger said, required "precisely that result."[31] Though dissenting Justice Powell thought it was "absurd" to think Congress had any such intention, the

comparative
**Comparing Judiciaries**

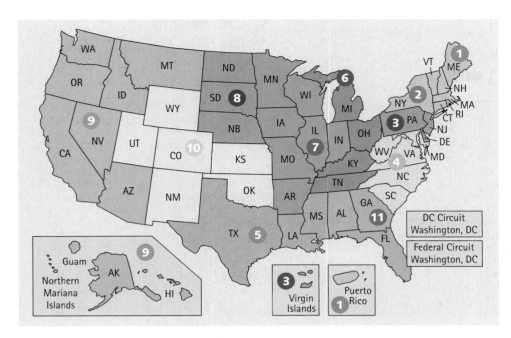

**Figure 15.3**

**Courts of Appeals Circuit Boundaries**
*What is the role of the federal appeals court?*

SOURCE: Robert A. Carp and Ronald Stidham, *The Federal Courts,* 2d ed. (Washington, DC: CQ Press, 1991), p.18.

Court majority argued that all it was doing in this instance was interpreting and applying an act of Congress. Yet its decision has had far-reaching consequences.

If a court finds that an injury has been suffered, it is up to the court to fashion a **remedy**, the compensation for the injury. Often the remedy simply involves monetary compensation to the injured party. But a judge may also direct the defendant to alter future behavior. To overcome racial segregation in schools, courts have ordered school boards to institute magnet schools, to set up special compensatory programs, and to bus children from one part of a city to another. As Justice Lewis Powell put it, courts have the right, if racial segregation is sufficiently severe, to "virtually assume the role of school superintendent and school board."[32]

**remedy**
Court-ordered action designed to compensate plaintiffs for wrongs they have suffered.

## Selection of Federal Judges

All federal judges hold lifetime positions after their nomination by the president and confirmation by the Senate. Because of long-standing agreements among senators, known as **senatorial courtesy,** any presidential nominee must be acceptable to the senior senator of the state involved who is of the same political party as the president. Political influences play a major role in the selection of federal judges. As shown in Figure 15.4, most share the same partisan identification as the president who nominates them; 94 percent of Ronald Reagan's nominees were Republican, 90 percent of Jimmy Carter's nominees were Democrats.[33] Though most judges would not acknowledge it publicly, political loyalty is often the key to appointment. As one judge admitted,

**senatorial courtesy**
An informal rule that the Senate will not confirm nominees within or from a state unless they have the approval of the senior senator of the state from the president's party.

> I worked hard for Franklin Roosevelt. . . . In 1939 I began running for the Senate, and the party convinced me it would be best if there wasn't a contest for the Democratic nomination. So I withdrew. . . . They gave this judgeship as sort of a consolation prize. . . .[34]

Although most lower-court nominees are confirmed, rejections do occur. Rejection is usually a result of some financial or personal problem uncovered during the confirmation process. Ideological and partisan considerations play a minor role. Robert Bork, for example, was easily confirmed as an appeals-court judge, even though he was later rejected as a nominee to the Supreme Court. But ideological battles over lower-court judges have become increasingly important. Clinton declined to nominate a liberal Washingtonian, Peter Edelman, as an appeals-court judge because Republicans in the Senate said they would block the appointment. In a similar case,

## Statutory Interpretation in the United States and Britain

When interpreting statutes, British judges exercise much less discretion than American judges. British judges have less leeway because they operate within a less fragmented governmental system. In Britain, the party of the prime minister exerts effective control over Parliament. Every piece of legislation passed by the party in power is carefully examined by specialists, who ensure that new legislation is internally coherent and consistent with existing laws. If a judge says government administrators have misinterpreted the law, the party in power can also, if it chooses, quickly pass new legislation. Political scientist Shep Melnick points out that as a result, "it is not surprising that British judges seldom question the interpretive authority of administrators."[a]

American judges work within a more decentralized governmental context. To get a majority when writing legislation, members of Congress are tempted to use ambiguous language that may include phrases that come close to contradicting one another. In Melnick's words, "The openness and messiness of the legislative process in the United States ensures that when judges scrutinize a statute and its history, they will seldom discover a single, coherent purpose or intent."[b] In the voting-rights legislation of 1982, for example, Congress forbade electoral arrangements that gave minorities "less opportunity than other members of the electorate to elect representatives of their choice" but, a few sentences later, said that nothing in the legislation required minorities be elected

"in numbers equal to their proportion in the population." The "less opportunity" forbidden in the first phrase seemed permitted by the second phrase saying that "equal numbers" need not be elected.[c]

When courts are asked to sort out the meaning of this kind of vague and potentially contradictory language, the office of the solicitor general may express the opinion of the presidential administration. But if the courts ignore the solicitor general, the administration must try to persuade Congress to enact a new law—a far more difficult task for American presidents than for British prime ministers. Knowing this, U.S. courts feel free to interpret laws in any way not plainly contrary to the intent of Congress. As Supreme Court Justice William Brennan once said, "the Court can virtually remake congressional enactments."[d]

*The U.S. system is certainly more complex than the British one. Is it better?*

---

[a]R. Shep Melnick, *Between the Lines: Interpreting Welfare Rights* (Washington, DC: Brookings, 1994), p.13. (Ellipses deleted.)
[b]Melnick, *Between the Lines.*
[c]As quoted in Bernard Grofman, Lisa Handley, and Richard G. Niemi, *Minority Representation and the Quest for Voting Equality* (New York: Cambridge University Press, 1992), p.39. (Ellipses deleted.)
[d]Melnick, *Between the Lines*, p.13.

---

when Daniel Manion was nominated by Ronald Reagan to serve on an appeals court, Democrats opposed and nearly defeated the appointment because they said the nominee was too conservative.

Short of rejection, opposition-party senators may exert their power by simply refusing to bring a nomination to a vote. In the late 1990s, partisan conflict over judicial nominations became bitter and vocal, as President Clinton complained of congressional foot-dragging and Republicans criticized his judicial nominations as too liberal. In 1997 the Senate approved only about 45 percent of Clinton's nominees (a 20-year low) and delayed action on the rest. Even Chief Justice William Rehnquist issued a written statement pressing the Senate to act, arguing that "vacancies cannot remain at such high levels without eroding the quality of justice."[35]

One reason parties are willing to do battle over nominations is that there are important ideological differences between potential judicial appointees. Overall, district judges' decisions reflect the political orientation of the president who nominated the particular judge. According to one study, Reagan-appointed judges were tougher toward those accused of crime than were Carter-appointed judges.[36] More generally, as shown in Figure 15.5, judges appointed by Democratic presidents are more likely than those appointed by Republican presidents to hand down liberal decisions.

Congress may threaten judges with impeachment and removal from office if their behavior is inappropriate or their decisions run contrary to dominant opinion. In practice, few judges have been impeached, and successful impeachments have nearly always been the result of financial abuse of the office. But movements to impeach judges who handed down unpopular decisions have regularly surfaced. Those opposed to school desegregation campaigned for years for the impeachment of Earl Warren. Recently, some conservatives in Congress have defended the use of impeachment to restrain judicial activism. Congressman Tom DeLay (R-TX) argues that "impeachment properly applied is a tool for keeping judicial power in check."[37]

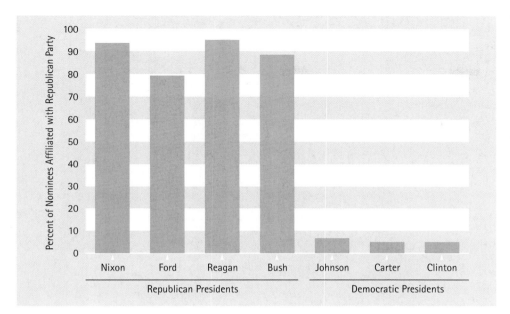

**Figure 15.4**

**Partisan Affiliation of District Judges**
*Why do Republican presidents usually appoint Republican judges and Democratic presidents appoint Democratic judges?*

SOURCE: Sheldon Goldman, "Reagan's Judicial Legacy: Completing the Puzzle and Summing Up," *Judicature* 72 (April–May 1989): 321–322.

## Deciding to Prosecute

Suspected violations of the federal criminal code are usually investigated by the Federal Bureau of Investigation, though other federal agencies, such as the Secret Service and the Bureau of Alcohol, Tobacco and Firearms, also exercise investigative powers. The evidence collected is given to prosecutors in the office of a **U.S. attorney**, who is responsible for prosecuting violations of the federal criminal law. Appointed by the president and confirmed by the Senate, the 93 U.S. attorneys act as the government's chief litigators. If persuaded that a prosecution is warranted, a U.S. attorney asks a grand jury consisting of 16 to 23 citizens to indict, or bring charges against, the suspect. Because accused people cannot defend themselves before a grand jury, the U.S. attorney's advice usually determines the outcome. As one wit observed, "Under the right prosecutor, a grand jury would indict a ham sandwich."[38] After the indictment, government prosecutors may find it more difficult to convince the trial jury to convict the defendant, however.

> **U.S. attorney**
> Person responsible for prosecuting violations of the federal criminal code.

U.S. attorneys have a particularly high political profile. They usually share the president's party affiliation, and, though expected to be incorruptible, they often are sensitive to the political needs of their superiors in Washington. Because routine law enforcement is left in the hands of state officials, U.S. attorneys concentrate on high-visibility, attention-grabbing activities. If they are particularly successful, they may become candidates for higher office. For example, New York Mayor Rudolph Giuliani achieved prominence as a federal attorney who successfully prosecuted Wall Street inside-trader Ivan Boesky and tax-evading hotel magnate Leona Helmsley. Sometimes one can get ahead politically just by initiating a high-profile investigation. Former Governor William Weld of Massachusetts won fame as a U.S. attorney by investigating the mayor of Boston. He launched the investigation, he later admitted, because "I had picked up enough anecdotal stuff to persuade me there was a spiritual" violation of the law. Though the investigation attracted widespread media attention, which certainly helped Weld obtain the governorship, he eventually dropped the charges when no actual crime could be identified.[39] But it was Thomas Dewey who turned the office of U.S. attorney to greatest political advantage. After winning fame by prosecuting labor racketeers, he became governor of New York and, in 1948, won the Republican presidential nomination, though he lost the election to Harry Truman.[40]

**Figure 15.5**

**Decision Making by Democratic and Republican Judges**
*Why do judges appointed by Democratic presidents make more liberal decisions?*

SOURCES: Robert A. Carp and Ronald Stidham, *The Federal Courts*, 2d ed. (Washington, DC: CQ Press, 1991), p.116; *U.S. News and World Report*, May 26, 1997: 24.

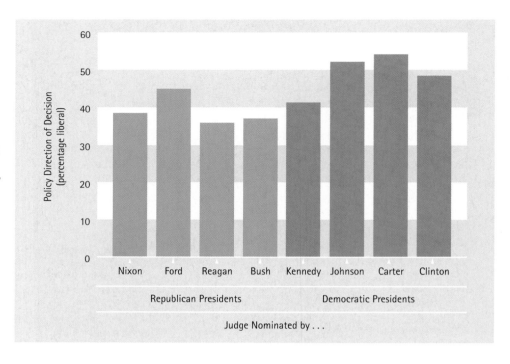

*McCulloch v. Maryland*
Decision (1819) in which the Supreme Court first declared a state law unconstitutional.

## State Courts

Every state has its own judicial arrangements, but in most the basic structure has the same three tiers found in the federal system: trial courts, courts of appeals, and a court of last resort, usually called the state supreme court. Decisions of state supreme courts may be appealed to the federal Supreme Court if the case involves a federal statute or the interpretation of the federal Constitution.

For the first few decades under the Constitution, the relationship between state and federal legal and judicial systems remained vague. Then, in an early key decision, **McCulloch v. Maryland** (1819), the Supreme Court made it clear that the power of judicial review applied to state as well as federal laws (see Chapter 3, page 70). Maryland had imposed a tax on the congressionally chartered Bank of the United States. When a bank cashier, James McCulloch, refused to pay the tax, he was convicted of violating the law. But the Supreme Court overturned the conviction. Chief Justice Marshall argued that "the power to tax involves the power to destroy" and that no state had the power "to retard, impede, burden or in any manner control, the operations of the constitutional laws enacted by Congress."[41]

The Supreme Court's power to review state laws and decisions of state courts is essential for maintaining basic uniformity in the laws of the United States. Over the decades, the Supreme Court has found over 1100 state statutes and state constitutional provisions contrary to the federal Constitution.[42] The judicial power to declare state laws unconstitutional is much less controversial than the power to declare laws of Congress unconstitutional. As Justice Holmes once said,

> I do not think the United States would come to an end if we lost our power to declare an act of Congress void. I do think the Union would be imperilled if we could not make that declaration as to the laws of the several states. For one in my place sees how often a local policy prevails with those who are not trained to national views.[43]

### State Trial Courts: The Judicial Workhorses

Most judicial activity takes place within state trial courts under the control of state and local governments, which go by many different names in the various states (district courts, county courts, courts of common pleas, and so forth). In fact, 99 percent of all civil and criminal cases originate in these courts.

State courts are influenced by political factors at least as much as are federal courts. In 37 of the 50 states, both appellate and trial judges are subject to election. In the remaining states, judges are appointed by the state legislature, the governor, or a governmental agency. Exactly which judges are elected varies from state to state. In New York, trial court judges are elected but appellate judges are appointed.[44] In Georgia it is the reverse.

Though many state judges are subject to election, most judicial campaigns "are waged in obscurity, with the result that most voters are unfamiliar with the names, not to speak of the issues, involved in the campaign."[45] As a result, judicial elections have traditionally been dominated by organized groups and party politicians interested in controlling court patronage. During the 1960s, 73 out of Chicago's 80 circuit court judges were active in Democratic party politics. Political scientist Milton Rakove described how the party–judicial connection worked:

> Without question the surest and safest road to a seat on the bench is through the party organization. Having a judge on the bench from [their] ward organizations gives the precinct captains access to the county judicial system which can be used on behalf of the ward's constituents. Many sitting judges continue to attend ward organization meetings and ward fund-raising affairs.[46]

Even today, Chicago observers bemoan "the political shenanigans that taint judicial elections and undermine public confidence in the justice system."[47] But parties seem to have a bigger impact on court patronage than on judicial decisions; most studies find few differences between the decisions of Democratic and Republican state judges.[48]

Interest groups have also had a growing influence on judicial elections, especially as the cost of running campaigns for judgeships has increased. In 1996, for example, the candidates for two Alabama supreme court seats spent a combined total of over $2 million on the race, nearly ten times what they would have spent only a decade earlier.[49] Much of the money to fund judicial races is donated by single-issue groups that may have an interest in the way certain cases are decided.

## Prosecuting State Cases

The process of bringing civil and criminal cases before state and local courts is comparable to the federal process. In civil cases, most states follow rules similar to the federal code of civil procedure. Upon receiving information from the police on criminal wrongdoing, prosecutors in the office of the local **district attorney** determine whether the evidence warrants presentation before a grand jury for prosecution. In large cities the district attorney has enormous responsibilities. In Los Angeles, for example, the district attorney's office prosecutes 300,000 cases a year.

**district attorney**
Person responsible for prosecuting criminal cases.

Because they are responsible for the prosecution of all criminal cases, some of which have high visibility in local news media, many prosecutors earn recognition that wins them election or appointment to the judiciary. About 10 percent of all judges once worked in a district attorney's office.[50] Many local district attorneys are interested in moving to other elected offices as well. For example, the decision to try the Los Angeles police officers accused of beating motorist Rodney King in 1991 was made by District Attorney Ira Reiner. Less than a year before, Reiner had run for state attorney general, a steppingstone to the governor's mansion. He hoped prosecution of the police officers would help his political ambitions. When the jury failed to convict the police officers, however, the voters blamed Reiner for a sloppy prosecution and, at the earliest opportunity, threw him out of office.

In early 2000, Paul Howard, a Georgia district attorney, was up for reelection. He pressed for the arrest and trial of Baltimore Ravens football star Ray Lewis after two murders outside a suburban Atlanta bar. But prosecutors could find no evidence linking Lewis to the crime, and Lewis' attorney criticized them for "indicting before investigating."[51] After prosecutors dropped charges and released Lewis, some observers blamed the botched investigation on the district attorney's desire for notoriety. "Because Howard tried to ride to fame on the back of Ray Lewis," one critic wrote, "he has damaged—not enhanced—his chances for reelection."[52]

## Relations Between State and Federal Courts

Most cases are heard in state courts, but any case can be shifted to a federal court if it can be shown that a federal law or constitutional principle is involved. The federal courts have higher prestige than state courts; to become a federal judge is to hold a position of great honor. But as Justice Sandra Day O'Connor, herself a former state judge, acutely observed, "When the state court judge puts on his or her federal court robe, he or she does not become immediately better equipped intellectually to do the job."[53]

**double jeopardy**
Placing someone on trial for the same crime twice.

The same act can simultaneously be a violation of both state and federal laws. Although the Fifth Amendment to the Constitution forbids **double jeopardy**—being tried twice for the same crime—something very close to double jeopardy can occur if a person is tried in both federal and state courts for the same action. In 1897 the Supreme Court permitted dual prosecutions, saying "an act denounced as a crime by both national and state sovereignties is an offense against the peace and dignity of both."[54] In recent years the chances for such prosecution has been rising, because Congress, under pressure to do something about crime, has passed new laws essentially duplicating state laws.

Despite the recent wave of anticrime legislation, dual state and federal prosecutions remain unusual. Most of the time, federal and state officials reach an agreement allowing one or the other to take responsibility. Generally speaking, the federal government takes over the prosecution only when the case has national implications. (From this comes the popular phrase "Don't make a federal case out of it.") For example, the 1995 bombing of a federal building in Oklahoma, in which 168 people lost their lives, constituted a violation of both state and federal laws. Although state officials began the investigation, federal investigators quickly took charge, and the accused, Timothy McVeigh and Terry Nichols, were convicted in a federal courtroom.

Later, when Nichols failed to receive the federal death penalty for his role in the crime, state prosecutors leveled state murder charges against him. His case was scheduled to go to trial in late 2000.

If the state prosecution fails to result in a conviction in a sensational case where a federal law has been broken, the federal U.S. attorney may also bring charges. In 1992 the State of California, as we noted above, was unable to win a conviction in the trial of four police officers charged with beating Rodney King, an event that had been videotaped. The failure to convict officers for what seemed to be a well-documented offense provoked three days of civil disorder in Los Angeles's minority communities.

To help calm the city, the U.S. attorney decided to bring federal charges against the officers, despite the fact that the state had already tried them once for the alleged offense. After hearing all the evidence, the jury in the federal trial convicted two officers and acquitted the other two. The decision to hold a second trial was almost certainly affected by public and media pressure. Though the decision was made by the U.S. attorney serving Los Angeles, it was made only at the request of the attorney general and with the apparent approval of President Bush. The president was at that moment in the midst of the presidential election campaign—in which his opponent, Bill Clinton, was accusing Bush of having helped create the racial climate that led to a failure to convict in the first trial.

### SECTION SUMMARY

The state and federal judicial systems are similar in structure, though there are variations from state to state. In the federal system, district courts hold trials and decide civil and criminal cases, which can then be appealed to an appeals court, or, ultimately, to the Supreme Court. The state courts have comparable systems of trial courts, appellate courts, and courts of last resort. Federal and local prosecutors are responsible for bringing criminal cases before the courts, and they may use their positions as springboards to higher office. Most state and local judges are elected, whereas federal judges and U.S. Supreme Court justices are appointed by the president and confirmed by the Senate. Since *McCulloch* v. *Maryland*, the U.S. Supreme Court has asserted its power to invalidate state laws that conflict with the federal Constitution.

## The Supreme Court in Action

The Supreme Court sits atop a massive pyramid of judicial activity. Each year prosecutors and private citizens bring more than 27 million criminal trials and civil suits before the state and federal courts.[55] Yet in the 1999–2000 term, the nation's high court heard only 80 cases. In this section, we explain how the Court exerts its substantial influence through such a small number of cases and describe how justices make decisions and write opinions. First, we discuss two important rules of court procedure. Next, we discuss the important players involved in the Court's activity. Finally, we consider the process of decision making itself.

### Stare Decisis

A small number of Supreme Court decisions can have a far-ranging impact because lower federal and state courts are expected to follow the principle of **stare decisis**. The phrase is Latin for "let the decision stand." This is to say that in deciding cases, judges should adhere to **precedents**, prior decisions, as well as their written justifications, which are known as court **opinions**. Jonathan Swift used his biting satire to define *stare decisis* somewhat differently:

> Whatever has been done before may legally be done again; and therefore [judges] take special care to record all the decisions formerly made against common justice and the general reason of mankind. These, under the name of precedents, they produce as authorities, to justify the most iniquitous of opinions.

Despite Swift's lampoon, *stare decisis* is a powerful judicial principle that can be ignored only at risk to the stability of the legal system. Only if court decisions are consistent with one another over time can a country live under a rule of law, where citizens know what it is that they are expected to obey. In the words of one judge, "We cannot meddle with a prior decision [unless it] strikes us as wrong with the force of a five-week-old unrefrigerated dead fish."[56] Because of *stare decisis*, a single Supreme Court decision can affect thousands of lower-court decisions, providing the broad legal framework within which judges rule on many specific cases.

When reaching a decision that seems contrary to a prior decision, courts try to find a **legal distinction** between the case at hand and earlier court decisions, usually by emphasizing that the facts of the current case differ. The process of drawing a legal distinction can in some cases become the refined art of perceiving a distinction when others can see no difference. As one wit has put it, the Supreme Court "could find a loophole in the Ten Commandments."[57] Or, as an attorney once bragged, "Law school taught me one thing: how to take two situations that are exactly the same and show how they are different."[58] If the legal distinctions drawn by a lower court seem unconvincing to the losing side, it may file an **appeal** to the next-higher court asking for a reversal of the lower court's decision. If the higher court thinks the lower court has strayed too far from legal precedents, it may decide on a **reversal**, or overturning, of the lower-court decision.

### Certs

At one time the Supreme Court was, by law, forced to review many appeals, but the workload became so excessive that in 1925 Congress gave the Court the power to refuse review of almost any case it did not want to consider. Today nearly all cases argued before the Court arrive upon the grant of what is known as a **cert** by court insiders. Cert is a shorthand of the Latin phrase **writ of *certiorari***, which means "to be informed of," and when a cert is granted, it means the Court has agreed to consider the case.[59] Approximately 95 percent of the time, the Supreme Court denies cert to a filed petition. The Court rejects most certs because it is only practical to consider a fraction of the approximately 7000 cases appealed to it each year. As one clerk for a Supreme Court justice put it, "You almost get to hate the guy who brings the cert petitions around. He is really a nice guy, but he gets abuse all the time."[60]

---

**stare decisis**
In court rulings, reliance on consistency with precedents. See also *precedent*.

**precedent**
Previous court decision or ruling applicable to a particular case.

**opinion**
In legal parlance, a court's written explanation for its decision.

**legal distinction**
The legal difference between a case at hand and previous cases decided by the courts.

**appeal**
The procedure whereby the losing side asks a higher court to overturn a lower-court decision.

**reversal**
The overturning of a lower-court decision by an appeals court or the Supreme Court.

**cert**
See writ of *certiorari*.

**writ of *certiorari* (cert)**
A document issued by the Supreme Court indicating that the Court will review a decision taken by a lower court.

www.longmanparticipate.com

visual literacy
**Case Overload**

The number of certs granted by the Supreme Court has fallen markedly in recent years. In the 1970s the Supreme Court decided as many as 400 cases annually.[61] But as we have noted, in the 1999–2000 term, only 80 cases were decided. After a period in which many controversial decisions were issued, the Court seems to want to reduce its visibility in American politics. "Do I make policy?" asked Justice Anthony Kennedy. "Was I appointed for life to go around . . . suggesting answers to the Congress? That's not our function."[62]

Certs are granted only for those cases that raise the most important legal or constitutional issues. As the old saying goes, the Supreme Court cares less about justice than about the law. In the words of one chief justice,

> The Supreme Court is not, and never has been, primarily concerned with the correction of errors in lower court decisions. . . . To remain effective the Supreme Court must continue to decide only those cases which present questions whose resolution will have immediate importance far beyond the particular facts and parties involved."[63]

To issue a cert requires the vote of four justices. The justices look for a nebulous quality known as "certworthiness" when considering which cases to accept for full-scale argument before the Court. The mere fact that an issue is controversial does not necessarily mean the Court will grant a cert. The justices may decide to let the issue percolate in the lower courts for a few years until the matter is ripe for decision.

The case for cert is strongest if two lower courts have reached opposite conclusions on cases in which the facts seem virtually identical. In such cases, the Supreme Court feels a responsibility to clarify the law so that its effect is uniform throughout the United States. In 1998 for example, the Supreme Court granted cert in a case involving media "ride-alongs" with law enforcement officials. In a Maryland case, the 4th Circuit Court of Appeals had ruled that police did not violate criminal defendants' privacy by bringing reporters along to witness an arrest. In a similar Montana case, however, the 9th Circuit Court of Appeals ruled that the press should not be allowed to be present when law enforcement officials searched a private home. Resolving the apparent contradiction between the two decisions, the Supreme Court ruled that police may be sued for inviting the press into private homes but that filming officers and suspects in public places is permissible.[64]

### The Role of the Chief Justice

**associate justice**
One of the eight justices of the Supreme Court who are not the chief justice.

The members of the Supreme Court consist of eight **associate justices** and the chief justice, who heads the Court and is responsible for organizing its work. Though the chief justice has only one vote and many of the chief's tasks are of a ceremonial or housekeeping nature, certain responsibilities give the office added influence. For one thing, the chief justice, if voting with the majority, assigns the responsibility for writing the majority opinion. Because the Court's opinion is often as important as the actual decision, this assignment power can have far-reaching consequences; some cases are "destined for the history books, whereas others are, in [former Justice Lewis] Powell's term, 'dogs.'" Powell's biographer tells us that Warren Burger, not the most popular of chief justices, was suspected by his colleagues of voting with the majority, even when privately opposed, simply in order to exercise his assignment power.[65]

Some chief justices have used their position to facilitate compromise and achieve consensus. In the case of *Brown* v. *Board of Education of Topeka, Kansas* (1954), the landmark decision desegregating schools, Chief Justice Earl Warren was able to win the support of two judges who were initially inclined to dissent. To achieve the unanimity he thought crucial, Warren agreed to write a less than sweeping opinion. *Brown* banned segregation in schools but not in other public places, and it specified delay in the implementation of the ruling. Warren was willing to make these compromises because he thought only a unanimous Court could order such a major social change—which at the time ran contrary to strongly held opinions of many southern whites.[66]

## The Role of the Solicitor General

A powerful figure who regularly appears before the Supreme Court is the **solicitor general**, the government official responsible for presenting before the Court the position of the presidential administration. Involvement of the solicitor general is a signal that the president and attorney general have strong views on the subject, raising its visibility and political significance. Because the Court pays close attention to the position of the solicitor general, the occupant of this office is sometimes referred to as "the tenth justice." Seventy percent of the solicitor general's cert petitions are accepted by the Court.[67]

Solicitor generals are employees of the Justice Department and as such report to the attorney general. However, they are always carefully selected by the president for their legal skills and are "in fact what the Attorney General is in name—the chief legal officer of the United States government as far as the courts are concerned."[68] The solicitor general presents the case for the government whenever it is party to a suit. In other important cases, the solicitor general may submit an *amicus curiae* brief—literally, a brief submitted by a "friend of the court." (*Amicus curiae* briefs can also be submitted by others who wish to inform the court of a legal issue presented by a particular case.) When the office of the solicitor general files an *amicus curiae* brief, it finds itself on the winning side approximately three-quarters of the time, a batting average envied by even the most successful private attorneys.[69]

> **solicitor general**
> Government official responsible for presenting before the courts the position of the presidential administration.

## The Role of Clerks

Much of the day-to-day work within the Supreme Court building is the job of **law clerks**, young, influential aides hired by each of the justices. Recently out of law school, most will have spent a year as a clerk with a lower court before being asked to help a Supreme Court justice. Each justice has between two and four law clerks.[70] The role of the law clerk has grown in recent years. Not only do clerks initially review certs, but they also draft many opinions. As a result, says one critic, "the standard opinion style has become that of the student-run [law] reviews: colorless, prolix, platitudinous, always error on the side of inclusion, full of lengthy citations and footnotes—and above all dull."[71] Law clerks have become so important to the Court's routine that some claim that a junior Supreme Court of bright but unseasoned attorneys, unconfirmed by the Senate or anybody else, is the true "Supreme Court" of today. Others reply that well-trained graduates of the country's most prestigious law schools may be better judges than aging Titans who refuse to leave office well beyond the age of normal retirement. The truth probably lies between these two extremes: The brilliance of the young clerks and the political and legal experience of the justices are probably better in combination than either would be without the other.[72]

> **law clerk**
> Young, influential aide to a Supreme Court justice.

## Supreme Court Decision Making

Before reaching its decisions, the Supreme Court considers **briefs**, written legal arguments submitted by the opposing sides. (Unfortunately for judges, briefs are often anything but brief.) The justices then listen to oral arguments from attorneys on both sides in a plenary session, attended by all justices, the chief justice presiding. Open to the public, these plenary sessions are held on Mondays, Tuesdays, and Wednesdays from October through May. If a controversial case is to be heard, such as one involving abortion rights, the courtroom overflows, and outside, "competing protesters square . . . off at the courthouse steps, chanting, singing and screaming at each other."[73] During the half-hour allotted to each side to present its case, attorneys often find themselves interrupted by searching questions from the bench. Former law professor Antonin Scalia is especially well known for his willingness to turn the plenary session into a classroom seminar. Yet it is not always clear how closely the justices attend to the responses. As Chief Justice John Marshall said many years ago, "The acme of judicial distinction means the ability to look a lawyer straight in the eye for two hours and not hear a damned word he says."[74]

> **brief**
> Written arguments presented to a court by lawyers on behalf of clients.

After hearing the oral argument, the justices usually reach a preliminary decision the same week in a private conference presided over by the chief justice. There are "three levels of elbow room about the conference table." The most ample is for the chief justice and senior associate justice, who sit at opposite ends. The next best is grabbed by the three most senior justices sitting on one side, leaving the four most junior crowded together across from them. No outsiders, not even a secretary, are permitted to attend. The only record consists of handwritten notes taken by individual justices.

From the outside, it may appear that the private conferences are opportunities for great minds to gather and discuss fundamental legal questions. But in most instances, the justices have already discussed the case with their law clerks and enter the conference room with their intentions firmly fixed. The justices express their views and preliminary votes in order of seniority, beginning with the chief justice.[75] If the chief justice is in the minority, the writing of the opinion is assigned by the senior associate justice in the majority.[76]

The justice assigned the responsibility for preparing the court opinion circulates a draft version among the other eight. Revisions are then made in light of comments received from the other justices. On rare occasions, the justice writing the opinion has "lost a court"—that is, one or more justices voting with the majority at the first conference have changed their minds. To keep a majority, the justice writing the opinion may produce an extremely bland opinion that gives little guidance to lower-court justices. In a 1993 sexual harassment case, *Harris* v. *Forklift Systems*, for example, the majority hardly created any precedent at all, saying only that courts should look at the "totality of the circumstances" in order to decide whether harassment in the workplace had occurred.[77]

Justices who vote against the majority may prepare a **dissenting opinion** that explains their disagreement. **Concurring opinions** may be written by those members of the majority who agree with the basic decision but disagree with some aspect of the reasoning included in the majority opinion or who wish to elaborate by raising further considerations. Two hundred years ago, when John Marshall was chief justice, the court was usually unanimous, and the chief justice wrote most opinions. Today, as Figure 15.6 shows, the Court is seldom unanimous in its judgments, and quite apart from the dissenting opinions, so many concurring opinions are filed that it is sometimes difficult to ascertain exactly what the majority has decided. For example, in an important case involving racial quotas, only the justice who wrote the majority opinion, Lewis Powell, took the middle position allowing affirmative action programs but forbidding racial quotas.[78] The other eight justices expressed, in their concurring and dissenting opinions, views that were either more conservative or more liberal than Powell's (see the discussion in Chapter 17, page 522). As a result, it has been difficult to determine exactly what the Supreme Court decided in this case.

Though the proliferation of dissenting and concurring opinions has caused considerable confusion about overall Supreme Court rulings, these opinions themselves often have a clearer and more convincing style than majority opinions—in part because they are signed by only one or two justices, making compromise language unnecessary. In *Harris* v. *Forklift Systems*, the sexual harassment case mentioned above, Justice Ginsburg, though agreeing with the decision, wrote a crisp concurring opinion that proposed a simple, straightforward standard for ascertaining whether harassment had occurred: Harassment, she wrote, exists whenever discriminatory conduct makes it more difficult for a person to perform well at a job. Convincingly written concurring and dissenting opinions, such as Ginsburg's, sometimes become even more influential than majority opinions.

Once the Court reaches a decision, it usually sends, or **remands**, the case to a lower court for implementation. Because the Supreme Court regards itself as responsible for establishing general principles and an overall framework, it seldom becomes involved in the detailed resolution of particular cases. This leaves a great deal of legal responsibility in the hands of lower courts.

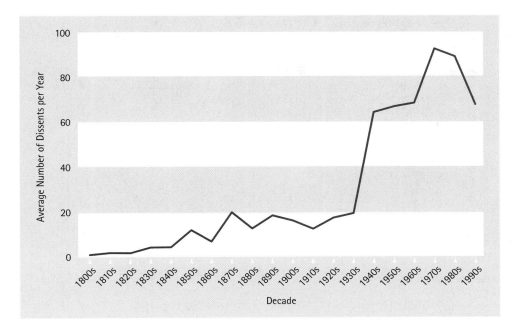

**Figure 15.6**

**Number of Supreme Court Dissents**
This graph shows the rising number of dissenting opinions written by members of the Supreme Court over the decades. *Why do you think dissents have increased? Do dissenting voices make the Court look stronger or weaker, in your view?*

SOURCE: Data from Gregory Calderia and Christopher J.W. Zorn, *Of Time and Consensual Norms on the Supreme Court*, Inter-University Consortium on Political and Social Research, Study No. I01142. See Gregory Calderia and Christopher J.W. Zorn, "Of Time and Consensual Norms on the Supreme Court," *American Journal of Political Science* 42:3 (July 1998): 874–902.

## Voting on the Supreme Court

Justices of the Court fall into quite predictable voting blocs. An exception to this pattern, Justice John Stevens, has "long been considered a maverick" who has often "confound[ed] the categorizers."[79] But the remainder of the judges currently serving on the Supreme Court can be divided into three fairly well-defined blocs.

The more liberal justices, consisting of Souter and the two Clinton appointees, Ruth Bader Ginsburg and Stephen Breyer, favor a certain amount of **judicial activism**, a doctrine that means that the principle of *stare decisis* should sometimes be sacrificed in order to adapt the Constitution to changing conditions. Ginsburg and Breyer contend that too rigid an application of the principle of *stare decisis* would place the country in a straitjacket and make it unable to adapt. Judicial activists also see the Court as a mechanism for preserving minority rights and fundamental freedoms that may be trampled upon by electoral majorities.

A second bloc of three conservative **restorationists**, including Thomas, Scalia, and Rehnquist, believe in overturning earlier liberal decisions. They think the only way the original meaning of the Constitution can be restored is by ignoring the doctrine of *stare decisis* until earlier liberal decisions have been reversed. For example, they favor reversing *Roe* v. *Wade*, the decision that declared laws forbidding abortion unconstitutional.

The moderates who hold crucial swing votes on the Court, Justices O'Connor and Kennedy, favor **judicial restraint**, a doctrine that means courts should, if at all possible, avoid overturning prior court decisions. If the law is to be changed, it should be changed not by the courts but by the people's elected representatives. O'Connor and Kennedy are willing to uphold prior decisions even when they do not necessarily agree with them. Although they may not agree that *Roe* v. *Wade* was a correct decision, these justices have expressed a reluctance to reverse it.

Most of the time, justices vote along lines anticipated by those who nominated and confirmed them. Both statements made in testimony before Congress and other information available at the time the justice is confirmed generally provide a clear indication of the justice's future voting pattern. According to one study, information about the political views of Supreme Court justices at the time they were being confirmed by the Senate allows one to predict correctly the justices' decisions in civil liberties cases over 60 percent of the time.[80] That the future behavior of the typical justice is predictable may suggest that the justices do not decide each case on its facts

**judicial activism**
Doctrine that says the principle of *stare decisis* should sometimes be sacrificed in order to adapt the Constitution to changing conditions.

**restorationist**
Judge who thinks that the only way the original meaning of the Constitution can be restored is by ignoring the doctrine of *stare decisis* until liberal decisions have been reversed.

**judicial restraint**
Doctrine that says courts should, if at all possible, avoid overturning a prior court decision.

**The Justices of the Supreme Court**
In this composite, the justices of the Supreme Court are pictured from left to right according to their judicial philosophies. On the left are John Paul Stevens, David Souter, Ruth Bader Ginsburg, and Stephen Breyer. In the middle are Anthony Kennedy and Sandra Day O'Connor.

To the right are Chief Justice William H. Rehnquist, Antonin Scalia, and Clarence Thomas. *When the next justice is appointed, where do you think the new justice's picture will be positioned?*

and merits. But predictability does allow elected officials—both presidents and senators—to shape the future direction of the Supreme Court, thereby maintaining some degree of popular control of the courts.

Not every prediction of future behavior is correct, however. The justice who most surprised those who favored his selection was Harry Blackmun, thought to be a judicial conservative. Yet Blackmun wrote the famous opinion in *Roe* v. *Wade* declaring state laws forbidding abortion unconstitutional. Blackmun himself once said, "Having been appointed by a Republican President and being accused now of being a flaming liberal on the court, the Republicans think I'm a traitor, I guess, and the Democrats don't trust me. And so I twist in the wind . . . beholden to no one, and that's just exactly where I want to be."[81]

On the present Court, Justice David Souter was appointed by a conservative president, Bush, and became one of the more liberal justices. This may have been a consequence of Bush's "stealth strategy" in nominating him (see page 446). Because Souter had produced few legal writings, the president found it easy to get the Senate to confirm him—but hard to predict how he would act once on the Court.

### SECTION SUMMARY

Supreme Court decisions are influenced by tradition and the justices' philosophies about the law. *Stare decisis* and the process of granting writs of *certiorari* ensure that the Court decides few cases but that these cases carry great weight. The chief justice enjoys added influence on the Court, in part by assigning the task of writing opinions. In granting certs and hearing cases, justices pay close attention to the solicitor general, who represents the executive branch before the courts. Clerks do much of the day-to-day work of the Supreme Court, evaluating appeals, researching decisions, and writing drafts of opinions. Justices fall into three voting blocs on the basis of their attitudes about the role the Court should play in policy making.

## *Checks on Court Power*

Although court decisions have great impact, their consequences can be limited by other political actors. As political scientist Jack Peltason has put it, "Judicial decision making is one stage, not the only nor necessarily the final one.[82] Alexander Hamilton, writing in the *Federalist Papers,* explained why this was to be expected under the Constitution:

> The judiciary will always be the least dangerous to the political rights of the Constitution. The executive not only dispenses honors but holds the sword of the community. The legislature not only commands the purse, but prescribes the rules. The judiciary, on the contrary, has no influence over either the sword or the purse. It may truly be said to have neither *force* nor *will,* but merely judgment; and must ultimately depend on the aid of the executive arm even for the efficacy of its judgments.[83]

Other branches of government can alter or circumscribe court decisions in three important ways: by constitutional amendment, by statutory revision, and by nonimplementation.

## Constitutional Amendment

The power to amend the Constitution is the formal constitutional check on the Supreme Court's power of judicial review. But this constitutional check has been used on only a few occasions. The Eleventh Amendment overturned an early Court decision that gave citizens of one state the ability to sue another state. The Sixteenth Amendment allowing an income tax was prompted by a Court decision that seemed to prohibit one. Many amendments under consideration by Congress today have been generated by Supreme Court decisions, including amendments to ban abortions, allow school prayer, and prohibit flag burning. It is unclear whether any of these proposed amendments will win the support necessary for them to become part of the Constitution, because for amendments to pass, supporters must ordinarily win a two-thirds vote in Congress and the backing of three-quarters of the states. In practice, the complexities of the amendment process make it the weakest check on court power.

participation
**The Court and School Prayer**

## Statutory Revision

Congress can reverse court decisions without resorting to a constitutional amendment if the court decision involves only the interpretation of a statute. In such cases, Congress can simply pass a clarifying law that reverses a court interpretation of earlier legislation. In the case of *Wards Cove Packing Co.* v. *Atonio,* for example, the Supreme Court gave a narrow interpretation to a congressional law banning race and gender discrimination. The Court said that Congress intended that women and minorities bringing a discrimination complaint had to bear the burden of proof, a difficult assignment in these kinds of cases. Under pressure from women's groups and civil rights organizations, Congress responded in 1991 by passing a law that said the burden of proof had to be borne by the business, thereby reversing the Supreme Court decision.

   Although passing new legislation is much easier than amending the Constitution, it still is only a partial check on court power. Republicans in Congress tried in 1995 to amend the Endangered Species Act so as to narrow its impact on businesses. But a storm of protest from environmentalists and a threatened presidential veto weakened Republican resolve, and the legislation, as interpreted by the courts, remains on the books unscathed.

## Nonimplementation

Court decisions can also be checked simply by being ignored. When told of a Supreme Court decision he did not like, President Andrew Jackson reportedly replied, "Justice Marshall has made his decision, now let him enforce it."[84] Although outright refusal to obey a Supreme Court decision by a president is today unlikely, strong resistance to lower-court decisions by state and local governments can occur. After the Supreme Court declared Bible reading in public schools unconstitutional, the practice in most Tennessee school districts continued unchanged. As one school board attorney explained, "My personal conviction is that the Supreme Court decisions are correct, and I so told the Board and Superintendent, but I saw no reason to create controversy. If the Board had made public a decision abolishing devotional exercises, there would have been public outcry."[85]

Flat-out refusal to obey a court order is rare because it undermines the authority of the judicial branch, but there are less open ways in which elected officials and the public can avoid carrying out court decisions. Public opposition frustrated the implementation of a New Jersey state supreme court ruling that required every school district in the state to spend the same amount of money per pupil. Committed to equal school financing arrangements and feeling obliged to obey the court decision, Democratic Governor James Florio and his Democratic colleagues in the state legislature passed a new law carrying out the decision by shifting funds from wealthier school districts to poorer ones. Parents in the communities that lost money responded by voting the governor and his allies in the legislature out of office and electing a new governor, Christine Todd Whitman, who promptly signed legislation repealing some of the shift in funds. The court decision was not fully implemented.

**receiver**
Court official who has the authority to see that judicial orders are carried out.

To ensure implementation of judicial orders, courts sometimes appoint a **receiver**, an official who has the authority to see that judicial orders are carried out. For example, in 1996 a Massachusetts judge found the State Department of Mental Retardation guilty of willfully abusing its authority over a school that served severely disabled students. Because the state agency had a long history of misusing its authority over this school, the judge, to prevent future abuse, replaced state supervision of the school with that of a court-appointed receiver.

But even the monitoring power of the courts can be checked by elected officials. For two decades, the Correction Department in the city of New York had been overseen by a court monitor who enforced judicial orders ensuring respect for the civil rights of prisoners. Judge Harold Baer, Jr., reluctantly withdrew the monitor in 1995 after Congress and the president, concerned that the rights of the guilty were taking precedence over the rights of victims, enacted a law limiting court authority in such matters. "Although the court's [my] concerns with this new legislation are myriad," Judge Baer wrote, "I am constrained under the law to uphold it."[86]

### Section Summary

The founders believed the judicial branch would be naturally weak because it had "no influence over either the sword or the purse." Indeed, elected officials and the public may check the power of the courts by passing constitutional amendments, enacting new legislation, or ignoring court decisions altogether. This is not to say that the courts lack power, however—such checks are often difficult and costly to exercise.

## Litigation as a Political Strategy

The courts have increasingly been used by interest groups to place issues on the political agenda, particularly when elected officials have not responded to group demands. This strategy was first used successfully by civil rights groups, a topic discussed in detail in Chapter 17. But the technique has since spread and become a common political phenomenon,[87] a development fully consistent with Alexis de Tocqueville's observation over a century and a half ago that "there is hardly a political question in the United States which does not sooner or later turn into a judicial one."[88]

Disabled Americans owe many of their current legal rights in the United States to an extraordinarily successful use of litigation as a political strategy. As late as 1970, school officials told many parents of disabled children that their sons and daughters were not qualified to attend public school. Challenging such denial of equal educational opportunity, advocacy groups won, in 1972, two federal court rulings that gave the disabled a right to an "appropriate education." Anticipating further litigation, many school officials felt that a federal law might clarify the situation. Under pressure from advocacy groups and with the acquiescence of lobbyists representing local school officials, Congress within two years passed a law said to be the "most significant child welfare legislation" of the decade. Although President Ford had opposed the legislation, it passed in both House and Senate by such lopsided margins that he signed it into law, fully aware that a veto was futile.[89]

To advance an issue, advocacy groups often file **class action suits** on behalf of all individuals in a particular category, whether or not they are actually participating in the suit. For example, in the late 1990s groups of former smokers in several states filed class action suits against the major tobacco companies for lying to consumers about the harms caused by smoking. In the first such case to reach a verdict favorable to plaintiffs, a jury ordered the five major tobacco companies to pay millions of dollars in damages to up to 500,000 ill Florida smokers.[90] Class action suits are justified on the grounds that the issue affects many people in essentially the same way, and it should not be necessary for each member of the class to bring a separate individual suit in order to secure relief.

> **class action suit**
> Suit brought on behalf of all individuals in a particular category, whether or not they are actually participating in the suit.

Attorneys have been accused of abusing their power to file class action suits by filing problematic claims and then reaching settlements that mainly benefit lawyers, not clients. In 1989 a pop duo calling themselves Milli Vanilli issued a hit album called "Girl You Know It's True," which won a Grammy award and sold over 10 million copies. When their producer admitted that the two had not truly sung any of their songs but had instead been lip-synching in videos and at concerts, attorneys shouted fraud and filed class action suits, naming their own children as plaintiffs. Some two years later, the case was settled when the distributor agreed to rebate customers $1 for each single record, $2 for each video cassette, and $3 for each compact disc, provided that they had a sales receipt (something only the most compulsive sales-slip collector was likely to possess). The distributor also agreed to make a modest contribution to some charities. The big winners: a few lawyers for the defendants who collected $670,000 in fees.[91]

## SECTION SUMMARY

Civil rights groups pioneered the ever more popular strategy of using litigation to place new issues on the political agenda. Many other groups have followed their lead, including Americans with disabilities. Advancement of such group issues often entails class action suits, filed on behalf of all people in a particular category.

## *Chapter Summary*

The courts are the branch of government most removed from political influences. Federal judges are appointed for life. They are expected only to apply the law, not to revise it. Constrained by the principle of *stare decisis*, they are expected to rely on legal precedents when reaching their decisions. They have been accused of sometimes using the power of judicial review to frustrate the popular will. In the famous *Dred Scott* and *Schechter Poultry* cases, the Supreme Court may well have done so.

Yet the courts are not immune to electoral pressures. Although many important political issues eventually reach the Supreme Court, the day-to-day work of the judiciary is carried out by state and lower federal court judges, who interpret the civil and criminal code. Many state judges and district attorneys are elected officials, and political factors also influence the operation of the lower courts in many other ways.

When justices are selected for the Supreme Court, their political and judicial philosophies are closely evaluated by both presidents and Congress. Once appointed, most Supreme Court justices decide cases in ways that are consistent with views they were known to have at the time of their selection. Most of the time, court decisions are broadly responsive to contemporary political currents. If court decisions challenge deep-seated political views, they may be modified by new legislation, frustrated by nonimplementation, or even reversed by constitutional amendment.

The judicial system may not work perfectly, but it is probably better than most alternatives. If the law were more removed from politics, the law would control people instead of the reverse. But if federal judges did not have the distance from politics that lifetime appointment gives many of them, justice could be perverted to narrow, partisan ends.

## On the Web

Supreme Court
www.supremecourtus.gov
The official web site of the U.S. Supreme Court contains information on the Court's docket, the text of recent opinions, the rules of the Court, and links to related Web sites.

Legal Information Institute
www.law.cornell.edu
The Legal Information Institute at Cornell Law School includes information on federal and state laws, rules of civil and criminal procedure, and a searchable database of Supreme Court decisions.

Legal Information Site
www.findlaw.com
This all-purpose legal information site includes various searchable databases and links.

Federal Judiciary
www.uscourts.gov
The Federal Judiciary homepage provides a concise guide to the federal court system, a regular newsletter, and annual reports on the state of the judiciary written by Chief Justice William Rehnquist.

Department of Justice
www.usdoj.gov/osg/
The Solicitor General's Office in the U.S. Department of Justice offers copies of briefs it has filed in federal court cases.

National Center for State Courts
www.ncsc.dni.us
The National Center for State Courts showcases statistical information on the caseload of state court systems, as well as links to state-level legal associations.

## *Key Terms*

appeal, p. 461
associate justice, p. 462
borking, p. 445
brief, p. 463
cert, p. 461
chief justice, p. 444
circuit court of appeals, p. 454
civil code, p. 453
class action suit, p. 469
concurring opinion, p. 464
criminal code, p. 453
defendant, p. 453
dissenting opinion, p. 464
district attorney, p. 459

double jeopardy, p. 460
federal district courts, p. 452
judicial activism, p. 465
judicial restraint, p. 465
judicial review, p. 447
law clerk, p. 463
legal distinction, p. 461
living-constitution theory, p. 449
*Marbury* v. *Madison*, p. 447
*McCulloch* v. *Maryland*, p. 458
opinion, p. 461
original-intent theory, p. 447
plain meaning of the text theory, p. 449
plaintiff, p. 453

plenary session, p. 454
precedent, p. 461
receiver, p. 468
remand, p. 464
remedy, p. 455
restorationist, p. 465
reversal, p. 461
senatorial courtesy, p. 455
solicitor general, p. 463
*stare decisis*, p. 461
statutory interpretation, p. 454
U.S. attorney, page 457
writ of *certiorari*, p. 461

# *Suggested Readings*

Agresto, John. *The Supreme Court and Constitutional Democracy.* Ithaca, NY: Cornell University Press, 1984. Makes a powerful case against judicial review.

Bork, Robert. *The Tempting of America.* New York: Free Press, 1990. Bork's defense of his legal position and his interpretation of the Senate confirmation process.

Bronner, Ethan. *Battle for Justice: How the Bork Nomination Shook America.* New York: Norton, 1989. Fascinating case study of the Senate refusal to confirm Robert Bork's nomination to the Supreme Court.

Carp, Robert A., and Ronald Stidham, *The Federal Courts,* 2nd ed. Washington, DC: CQ Press, 1991. Lucid description of the federal court system and its political context.

Jeffries, John C., Jr., *Justice Lewis F. Powell, Jr.: A Biography.* New York: Scribner, 1994. Superb biography by Powell's law clerk that provides inside information on the thinking that went into some of the most important Supreme Court decisions.

Massaro, John. *Supremely Political: The Role of Ideology and Presidential Management in Unsuccessful Supreme Court Nominations.* Albany: State University of New York Press, 1990. Engaging account of the politics of Supreme Court nominations.

McCloskey, Robert G. *The American Supreme Court.* Chicago: University of Chicago Press, 1960. Excellent, though somewhat dated, analysis that shows the close connection between public opinion and court decisions.

Melnick, R. Shep. *Between the Lines: Interpreting Welfare Rights.* Washington, DC: Brookings, 1994. Insightful analysis of the Court's role in the interpretation and elaboration of statutory law.

Murphy, Walter F. *Elements of Judicial Strategy.* Chicago: University of Chicago Press, 1964. A political analysis of the courts.

O'Brien, David M. *Storm Center: The Supreme Court in American Politics,* 4th ed. New York: Norton, 1996. Up-to-date account of the political role of the Supreme Court.

Perry, H. W., Jr. *Deciding to Decide: Agenda Setting in the United States Supreme Court.* Cambridge, MA: Harvard University Press, 1991. Comprehensive explanation of the process by which the Supreme Court decides whether to review a case.

Pritchett, C. Herman. *The American Constitution.* New York: McGraw-Hill, 1959. Dated, but still authoritative, account of constitutional issues.

Simon, James F. *The Center Holds: The Power Struggle Inside the Rehnquist Court.* New York: Simon & Schuster, 1995. Describes the recent split between conservative and moderate justices.

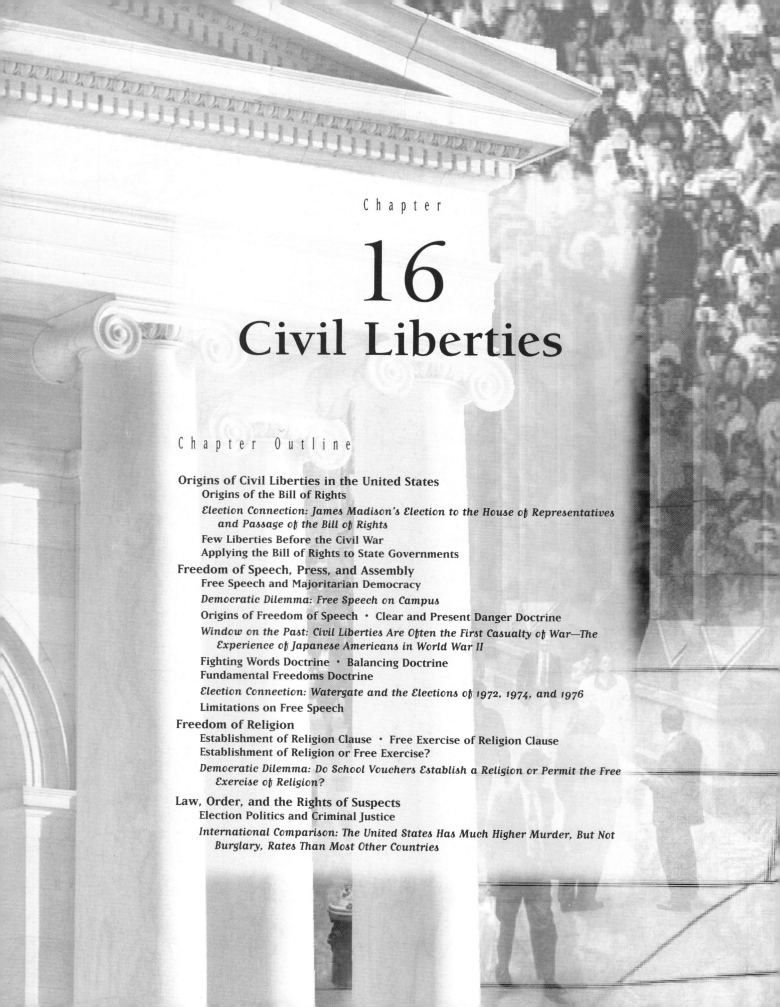

Chapter

# 16
# Civil Liberties

O n a crisp January night in 1993, a group of African American women at the University of Pennsylvania were celebrating. Unfortunately, their ardor invited only a stream of invective from the windows above that included racial and sexually demeaning slurs. Someone was said to have yelled, "Shut up, you black water buffaloes! Go back to the zoo where you belong!" When the women complained to campus administrators, an ensuing investigation identified only one individual, Eden Jacobowitz, who admitted to having participated in the outcry. Jacobowitz, an Israeli, denied any racial animosity and claimed he was upset only because the women failed to quiet down. He admitted to calling the women "water buffaloes" but said the term was nothing more than a translation of a "mild Hebraic epithet for a rude person." He also admitted replying, when invited to join the party below, "If you're looking for a party, there's a zoo a mile from here!"[1] The university's Judicial Inquiry Office felt that the campus code prohibiting racial epithets had been violated; Jacobowitz objected that the university's code violated his right of free speech.

At almost the same time, Professor Leonard Jeffries complained that his right of free speech had been violated by the City College of New York. Jeffries, the head of the college's black studies department, had claimed in a 1991 speech that there was a "conspiracy, planned and plotted and programmed out of Hollywood," a conspiracy that included Jews and the Mafia, to cause "the destruction of black people." A month after the speech, the president of City College sent a letter to the university community stating that Jeffries's rhetoric "contained clear statements of bigotry and anti-Semitism." The following year, the Board of Trustees removed Jeffries as head of black studies. He sued to be reinstated as department chair on the grounds that his right to free speech had been infringed. A federal jury found in favor of Jeffries, but the ruling was ultimately struck down by a federal appeals court.[2]

IN AN EFFORT TO PROMOTE AN ATMOSPHERE OF TOLERANCE and respect for men and women from diverse racial and religious backgrounds, many colleges and universities have established guidelines that limit the use of "fighting words" on sensitive topics. The desirability of such regulations has been a subject of national debate. In this chapter we place such debates in a larger constitutional context by describing the evolution of civil liberties under the U.S. Constitution. The concept of **civil liberties**, the fundamental freedoms that together preserve the rights of a free people, is never mentioned in the Constitution, nor has it ever been explicitly defined by the Supreme Court. But specific rights that together make up the civil liberties of U.S. citizens are to be found in the Bill of Rights—the first ten amendments to the Constitution—and again in amendments added to the Constitution after the Civil War.

Civil liberties should be distinguished from civil rights (considered in Chapter 17), which concern the rights of citizens to equal treatment under the law. This distinction may seem confusing because at times both categories of protection may be referred to as "rights." But civil liberties are fundamental *freedoms* from government *interference*, while civil rights are fundamental *guarantees* of equal *treatment* by the government. In this chapter we focus on civil liberties and answer the following questions:

**civil liberties**
Fundamental freedoms that together preserve the rights of a free people.

- How did civil liberties originate and evolve in the United States?
- What do the freedoms of speech, press, and assembly mean in practice?
- What are the two components of the Constitution's guarantee of freedom of religion, and how may they conflict with one another?
- What rights do accused criminals possess under the law?
- How do conflicting views of citizens' right to privacy shape modern court decisions and policy disputes?

## Origins of Civil Liberties in the United States

The evolution of civil liberties in the United States has been shaped by Supreme Court decisions. But as we shall see, these liberties have also been affected by political debates and election outcomes. Civil liberties have not been created simply by the actions of a small number of justices; rather, they reflect basic values shared by most citizens (see Chapter 4). In this section we discuss the constitutional beginnings of civil liberties and how Americans' understanding of these liberties has evolved since then.

### Origins of the Bill of Rights

The liberties of Americans were among the rallying cries of the American Revolution. Not only did the Declaration of Independence assert fundamental rights to "Life, Liberty and the pursuit of Happiness," but many states incorporated similar principles into their constitutions and statutes. For example, the Virginia assembly passed a bill of rights a month before the proclamation of the Declaration of Independence. Among its provisions was the pronouncement that "freedom of the press" was "one of the great bulwarks of liberty."[3]

Despite their expressed commitment to basic freedoms, the colonial revolutionaries trampled on the liberties of the Tories, who opposed the revolution. They closed Tory newspapers, threatened well-known Tory editors, confiscated their property, and so intimidated the royalists that some 80,000 to 100,000 people fled to Canada, England, and the West Indies.[4] Even John Adams, a future president of the United States, vowed that "the [Tory] presses will produce no more seditious or traitorous speculations."[5]

**Not Much Free Speech**
Many a Tory editor was hanged in effigy before and during the American Revolution. *Why was free speech limited at the time of the American Revolution?*

**Election Connection**

## James Madison's Election to the House of Representatives and Passage of the Bill of Rights

Despite harboring doubts about the necessity of the Bill of Rights, James Madison emerged in the first Congress as the driving force behind its passage. Madison's willingness to defer to the desire of others can be explained by the same constituency pressures that shape the views of modern-day members of Congress. Though a Federalist, Madison came from Virginia, the home state of the acclaimed Virginia Bill of Rights and of the country's most influential Anti-Federalists, George Mason and Patrick Henry. Henry had successfully fought to prevent Madison from being selected as one of Virginia's two senators, and Madison had won a seat in the House of Representatives only by promising to work for the passage of a Bill of Rights.

That Madison was influenced more by election pressures than by constitutional scruples is evident from the fact that at the Constitutional Convention itself, he had seen little need for such a document. Even after the convention, Madison wrote, "I have never thought the omission [of a bill of rights] a material defect, nor been anxious to supply it even by subsequent amendment, for any other reason than that it is anxiously desired by others."

In Madison's hands, the meaning of the Bill of Rights underwent a significant transformation. Whereas the Anti-Federalists had wanted amendments that would protect states' rights, the Bill of Rights, as written by Madison, mentions states rights in only two out of eight amendments, focusing all the other amendments on the rights of individuals. By focusing on the rights of individuals, Madison avoided the central issue of contention between Federalists and Anti-Federalists—the balance of power between the states and the new national government. The ten amendments Congress eventually agreed on were quickly and quietly ratified in 1791 by all but two states, apparently because few people thought they would have much practical effect.

*If, as historians believe, Madison promoted the Bill of Rights under electoral pressure, should this change our understanding of these rights? Should it change how the courts interpret them today?*

SOURCES: Robert A. Rutland, *The Birth of the Bill of Rights* (Chapel Hill: University of North Carolina Press, 1955); Stanley Elkins and Eric McKitrick, *The Age of Federalism* (New York: Oxford University Press, 1993); Thornton Anderson, *Creating the Constitution: The Convention of 1787 and the First Congress* (University Park: Pennsylvania State University Press, 1993), p. 176.

---

Nor did those who drafted the Constitution include explicit protection for individual civil liberties. When Anti-Federalist Charles Pinckney offered a motion at the Constitutional Convention to guarantee freedom of the press, the Federalist majority voted the measure down—on the grounds that states should be responsible for regulating speech and the press.[6] Only when ratification of the Constitution seemed in danger did Federalists agree to add a Bill of Rights in the form of a series of amendments to the Constitution (see Chapter 2). The first Congress reluctantly approved the ten amendments that make up the Bill of Rights in 1790 only at James Madison's insistence (see the accompanying Election Connection). Most voted for the amendments, it seems, because they thought the provisions would have little effect.

### Few Liberties Before the Civil War

Initially, the Bill of Rights was applied only to the national government, not the states. The First Amendment, for example, focused solely on the national government, saying that "Congress shall make no law" abridging speech or religious practice. No limitations were placed on state governments. As a result, the Episcopalian Church remained the official state church in Virginia, and the Puritan religion remained the established religion in Massachusetts.

Many of the other provisions in the Bill of Rights did not specifically mention either the national or the state governments, leaving open the possibility that they applied to both. For example, the Fifth Amendment said that "no person shall . . . be deprived of life, liberty, or property, without due process of law." But when the owner of Barron's Wharf complained that the City of Baltimore had deprived his company of property without "due process of law," the Supreme Court, in 1833, said the Fifth Amendment limited the powers of the federal government but not those of the states. The Bill of Rights, wrote Chief Justice John Marshall, "contain[s] no expression indicating an intention to apply them to the state governments. This court cannot so apply them."[7]

It would have been difficult for Marshall to apply the Bill of Rights to the states prior to the Civil War, because doing so would have forced the country to confront the slavery issue head-on. Were slaves people who had liberties granted to them by the First Amendment, or were they property that belonged to their masters, according to the Fifth Amendment? These questions would eventually provoke the Civil War, but during the early 1800s both the Supreme Court and most elected leaders avoided the issue.

The main use of the Bill of Rights prior to the Civil War, ironically enough, was to justify continued enslavement. In the extraordinary *Dred Scott* decision, Chief Justice Roger Taney reached the conclusion that the Fifth Amendment precluded Congress from denying Dred Scott's master his right of property. As for Dred Scott, the slave, he was not regarded as a person within the meaning of the Fifth Amendment.

## Applying the Bill of Rights to State Governments

CONSTITUTION, FOURTEENTH AMENDMENT: *"No State shall . . . deprive any person of life, liberty, or property, without due process of law."*

The Civil War transformed the spirit, meaning, and application of the Bill of Rights. Once slavery had been abolished, the words in the first ten amendments could begin to be applied to all Americans. To give the Bill of Rights new meaning, the Constitution was altered by three **civil rights amendments,** the Thirteenth, Fourteenth, and Fifteenth Amendments, which abolished slavery, redefined civil rights and liberties, and guaranteed the right to vote to all adult male citizens, respectively. Ordinarily, the complex procedures for amending the Constitution would have made it impossible to enact amendments that changed the Constitution so fundamentally (see Chapter 2). But the civil rights amendments were approved at a time when those who had fought for the South were excluded from political participation. Congress was controlled by those who had remained loyal to the Union, and southern states were denied readmission to the Union until they had ratified these amendments.

Of all the provisions in the civil rights amendments, the one that has had the greatest significance for civil liberty is the **due process clause** of the Fourteenth Amendment, which says that a person cannot be deprived of life, liberty, or property without due process of law. As we noted above, the phrase was already found in the Fifth Amendment, but the Fourteenth Amendment greatly expanded civil liberties by making one apparently minor change—saying that no *state* may "deprive any person of life, liberty, or property, without due process of law." By specifically mentioning state governments, the due process clause of the Fourteenth Amendment guaranteed that neither the federal government nor the states could interfere with civil liberties.

Despite the explicit language in the Fourteenth Amendment applying the due process clause to the states, the Supreme Court has never interpreted this clause as saying that states must abide by each and every provision of the Bill of Rights. Instead, the Court has taken an approach known as **selective incorporation,** a process by which it decides on a case-by-case basis whether a particular denial of a liberty listed in the Bill of Rights is also a violation of the due process clause of the Fourteenth Amendment. Over the years, nearly all of the provisions in the Bill of Rights have been incorporated. But a few exceptions remain, such as the Second Amendment, which says that inasmuch as "a well-regulated militia" is necessary to "the security of a free state, the right of the people to keep and bear arms shall not be abridged." Although the National Rifle Association (NRA) has argued that state laws banning or restricting the use of guns are contrary to the Constitution, the Supreme Court has maintained that this amendment only guarantees the state governments' right to have a militia.

**civil rights amendments**
The Thirteenth, Fourteenth, and Fifteenth Amendments, which abolished slavery, redefined civil rights and liberties, and guaranteed the right to vote to all adult male citizens.

**due process clause**
Found in the Fifth and Fourteenth Amendments to the Constitution; forbids deprivation of life, liberty, or property without due process of law.

**selective incorporation**
The case-by-case incorporation, by the courts, of the Bill of Rights into the due process clause of the Fourteenth Amendment.

## Section Summary

Though the Revolutionary War was fought amid the rhetoric of liberty, the Constitution initially did not contain a detailed enumeration of citizens' rights. The Bill of Rights was added only as a compromise between Federalist and Anti-Federalist forces at the time of ratification, and it had little effect until after the Civil War. At that time, the Fourteenth

Amendment was added to the Constitution, and its due process clause enabled the Supreme Court to begin applying the Bill of Rights to the states. Since then, the Court has practiced selective incorporation, deciding on a case-by-case basis how to extend the rights guaranteed in the Constitution.

## *Freedom of Speech, Press, and Assembly*

CONSTITUTION, FIRST AMENDMENT: *"Congress shall make no law . . . abridging the freedom of speech, or of the press; or the right of the people peaceably to assemble, . . ."*

Of the liberties listed in the Bill of Rights, one trio is paramount: freedom of speech, press, and assembly. Though each has its own nuance, the three are closely intertwined. If free speech is to be effective, it must be communicated through a free press. Unless an audience can be assembled to listen, speakers might as well keep silent. Because of the close connection among the three liberties, we shall treat them as one—which we refer to as free speech.

Even though the beginnings of free speech date back to the colonial period, the doctrine of free speech, as we know it today, is not as deeply entrenched in the American tradition as Fourth of July speakers often proclaim. Despite the First Amendment, people have been jailed for expressing controversial thoughts as long ago as 1798 and as recently as 1968. In this section we discuss the value of free speech for democratic governance and outline the history of how this section of the First Amendment has been interpreted by the Supreme Court. Finally, we point out key limitations of free speech in such areas as commercial speech, libel, and obscenity law.

### *Free Speech and Majoritarian Democracy*

Free speech is vital to the workings of free elections in a democratic society. In the absence of free speech, government officials could manipulate public opinion without fear of contradiction. Elections have little meaning when candidates cannot express their opinions without fear of punishment.

**tyranny of the majority**
Stifling of dissent by those voted into power by the majority.

Even so, elections are won by candidates backed by a majority of the voters, and majorities can at times be as tyrannical as single-minded despots. Indeed, the greatest threat to the rights of the people, said James Madison, is the **tyranny of the majority**—the suppression of minority opinions by those voted into power by a majority.[8] The larger a majority gets, the more sure it is that its views are correct, and the more capable it is of punishing dissenters. As British historian Lord Acton said, "The one pervading evil of democracy is the tyranny of the majority, or rather of that party, not always the majority, that succeeds, by force or fraud, in carrying elections."[9]

Because of such fears about unscrupulous political coalitions, the authors of the Bill of Rights believed that free speech should be placed outside the reach of even very powerful majorities. Enshrining free-speech rights in the Constitution meant that majorities would have to tolerate dissent—at least unless they could muster the strength to change the Bill of Rights.

The classic defense of free speech was provided by the English civil libertarian John Stuart Mill, who insisted that in the free exchange of ideas, truth would eventually triumph over error. This argument, said Mill, applied not just to politics, but to many aspects of life. Galileo's declaration that the Earth was not at the center of the universe eventually became accepted as true, though informed opinion initially regarded his claims as preposterous. Modern events seem to bear out Mill's argument. Fifty years ago, geologists laughed at Alfred Wegener's suggestion that the world's continents gradually drifted over long distances. Hardly a decade ago, the claim that dinosaurs were destroyed by an asteroid was dismissed out of hand by paleontologists.

But if these examples illustrate the value of free speech in scientific debates, must we tolerate even offensive and vicious error? It is not easy to accept the idea of people enjoying the freedom to spread doctrines of racial hatred (see the accompanying

## *Democratic Dilemma*

# Free Speech on Campus

College campuses are supposed to foster creativity and intellectual growth. But in the 1980s and 1990s, many colleges and universities adopted speech codes, under which faculty members and students could be punished for uttering offensive words or promoting unacceptable ideas.

Some argue that such codes are essential for intellectual activity to thrive on campus. Racist or sexist language, say proponents of speech codes, only serves to stifle discussion and put many students on edge. Take, for example, the true story of a farm science professor who used a *Playboy* centerfold to illustrate different cuts of meat. Is this a legitimate exercise of freedom of expression, or is it offensive and punishable behavior?

Or, to take another example provided by Sharon Gwyn, of Stanford University, who speaks from personal experience:

> When I was in sixth grade, my teacher gave us the word "slavery" in a spelling test. He recited a sentence to clarify its meaning: "Sharon is lucky she is not in slavery." As my stomach began to lurch, my hands held tighter to my pencil. . . . My teacher merely smiled; he never apologized. . . . If I was hurt in a situation of that level, think of how the person who is the target of a racial epithet must feel.

Others maintain that offensive language and behavior, though sometimes painful, are part of intellectual growth. Says Jason Shepard, an openly gay student at the University of Wisconsin, "Racism, sexism, homophobia are all parts of our society, whether we like it or not. We can't erect a wall around our university and pretend those things don't exist."

Philosophy professor Lester Hunt agrees:

> Some people, like me, teach subjects that concern all the hot-button areas—race, gender, you name it—and what the [speech] code does is threaten you with punishment if you say the wrong thing. That makes it difficult or impossible to teach these subjects effectively.

*What do you think?*
- *Should colleges and universities restrict certain types of speech on campus?*
- *Which approach creates the best environment for learning?*

SOURCES: Gwyn's remarks are quoted from the *New York Times,* May 12, 1989, B12; other material: Mitchell Zuckoff, "A New Word on Speech Codes; One School That Led Way Is Rethinking Its Rules," *Boston Globe,* October 21, 1998, A1.

Democratic Dilemma). Are their beliefs not founded on false premises that could never be shown to be true? To such contentions, Mill replied that "he who knows only his own side of the case, knows little of that."[10] Mill argued further that error suppressed becomes more powerful by virtue of its suppression. Only if error is allowed to express itself can its proponents be denied the privilege of a false martyrdom.

## *Origins of Freedom of Speech*

Speech and press during the early colonial period were governed by the **prior restraint doctrine,** which said the government could not censor an article before it was published. However, the prior restraint doctrine did not prevent prosecution after the fact. Instead, the publisher could be convicted for bringing the government's "dignity into contempt," even if what he said were true. Thus in 1734, when John Peter Zenger published a true and accurate critique of an incompetent, unprincipled New York governor, the governor put Zenger in jail at excessive bail for ten months while he was awaiting trial. In one of the great early victories for freedom of the press, the jury found Zenger innocent after his attorney argued that the issue at stake was "the Liberty—both of exposing and opposing arbitrary Power . . . by speaking and writing Truth."[11]

> **prior restraint doctrine**
> Legal doctrine that gives individuals the right to publish without prior restraint—that is, without first submitting material to a government censor.

## *Clear and Present Danger Doctrine*

Despite victories such as the Zenger case, the early history of free speech in the United States is not filled with instances of the Supreme Court protecting minorities from the tyranny of the majority, as the authors of the Bill of Rights might have hoped. For many years the judiciary did not give minorities much protection. Instead, the Supreme Court's view of what free speech entails has moved along at about the same speed as—or perhaps a little slower than—that of the rest of the country. In the words of one scholar, "the Court has seldom lagged far behind or forged far ahead of

America."[12] Nonetheless, progress toward free speech in the United States can best be traced by noting the evolution in Court doctrine.

The first major Supreme Court decision affecting freedom of speech arose out of the conscription of young men into the army during World War I. Wartime creates conditions that test the boundaries of civil liberties. As the country mobilizes to fight a common foe, elected officials are often under public pressure to identify pacifists or other dissenters as being in league with the enemy. As Alexis de Toqueville wrote, "All those who seek to destroy the liberties of a democratic nation ought to know that war is the surest and shortest means to accomplish it."[13]

The occasion for the ruling was the conviction of Charles Schenck, a socialist who had mailed anticonscription materials to draft-age men during the war. The jury decided that Schenck had violated the 1917 Espionage Act, which made it illegal to obstruct armed forces recruitment.

**clear and present danger doctrine**

The principle that people should have complete freedom of speech unless their language endangers the nation.

When asked to review Schenck's conviction, the Supreme Court, in *Schenck* v. *United States* (1919), enunciated the **clear and present danger doctrine**, the principle that people should have complete freedom of speech unless there is a "clear and present danger" that their language will provoke "evils that Congress has a right to prevent." The Supreme Court, no more sympathetic to socialists than Congress had been when it passed the Espionage Act, upheld Schenck's conviction. The Schenck case nevertheless marked the first time the Court moved to limit the regulation of speech by proposing a definite standard. Justice Oliver Wendell Holmes made the common-sense observation that no person has the right falsely to cry "Fire" in a crowded theater: Such a cry creates a clear and present danger to the public safety. In the same way, he argued, Congress could regulate speech only when there was a clear and present danger that the speech would provoke serious evils. His example seemed to capture succinctly the appropriate balance between the right of free speech and the need to maintain social order.

The meaning of clear and present danger, however, is open to different interpretations. If this standard is applied to the two race-related controversies on college campuses discussed at the beginning of this chapter, some might decide that in neither instance was anything said that was tantamount to crying "Fire" in a crowded theater. Others might reply that, if racial and ethnic slurs came to be widely used, they would constitute a clear and present danger to society; to keep that from happening, speech should be restricted before the danger becomes too present.

Holmes himself took this second, more restrictive point of view. He said that Schenck's actions constituted a clear and present danger to the successful prosecution of the war because, if successful, the mailing of antidraft pamphlets to draft-age men could endanger the war effort.[14] Holmes ignored the fact that few prospective servicemen paid much attention to Schenck and his associates.

But even though Holmes initially used the clear and present danger doctrine to suppress dissent, the doctrine became the foundation upon which a free-speech tradition was gradually built. During the 1930s, when the public was more tolerant of dissenting opinion, the Supreme Court, reflecting the changing political climate, explicitly defended the civil liberties of minorities. Two cases decided in 1931, *Stromberg* v. *California* and *Near* v. *Minnesota*, were particularly important, because for the first time they gave court protection to extremely unpopular opinions. Yetta Stromberg had encouraged children attending a camp operated by the Young Communist League to pledge allegiance to the flag of the Soviet Union, a violation of California's "red-flag" law.[15] The Supreme Court overturned her conviction, saying that the California law limited "free political discussion." Also in 1931, the Supreme Court, in *Near* v. *Minnesota*, overruled the Minnesota legislature after it shut down a newspaper for publishing "malicious, scandalous and defamatory" material. The action of the legislature was regarded by the Court as "the essence of censorship."[16] Because neither Stromberg nor the Minnesota newspaper constituted a clear and present danger, said the Court, their civil liberties should not be curtailed.

## Window on the Past

### Civil Liberties Are Often the First Casualty of War— The Experience of Japanese Americans in World War II

Responding to public concern that Japanese Americans might act as spies for Japan during World War II, President Franklin Roosevelt ordered 70,000 Japanese American citizens and another 40,000 resident Japanese to leave their homes and live in "relocation centers." Those who swore loyalty to the United States were released, but if they lived close to either coast, they were told they could not return home. Earl Warren, the California attorney general and later chief justice of the Supreme Court, gave a racial rationale for these actions: "When we are dealing with the Caucasian race we have methods that will test the loyalty of them. . . . But when we deal with the Japanese . . . we cannot form any opinion that we believe to be sound."[a]

Discriminatory actions by elected officials at a time when popular opinion was ferociously anti-Japanese is perhaps understandable. More difficult to rationalize is the inability of the Supreme Court to protect this minority against the tyranny of the majority. In *Korematsu* v. *United States* (1944), the Court found relocation

centers constitutional. But in his dissent from the Court's decision, Justice Frank Murphy condemned the relocation as "one of the most sweeping and complete deprivations of constitutional rights in the history of this nation."[b] To rectify the injustice, Congress in 1988 finally voted to compensate many Japanese Americans who had been relocated.

*Most people agree that the detention and relocation of Japanese Americans during World War II was unjust. But are there circumstances under which concerns for public safety should override individual liberties? For example, would authorities be justified in detaining all residents of a specific town if they had clear evidence that an unknown resident was plotting a serious and immediate terrorist attack? Who ought to have the authority to decide when such action can be taken? The courts? The president? Congress?*

[a] Robert Goldstein, *Political Repression in Modern America: 1870 to the Present* (New York: Schenkman, 1978), pp. 266–267.
[b] *Korematsu* v. *United States* 323 US 244 (1944).

## Fighting Words Doctrine

The toleration that emerged during the 1930s did not survive the onset of World War II (see the accompanying Window on the Past). In 1940 Congress responded to public outrage against fascism by enacting the Smith Act, which forbade advocating the overthrow of the government by force. Even some university administrators forbade demonstrations against the draft, arguing that such demonstrations would reflect poorly on their schools. Columbia University President Nicholas Butler justified the ban in these words: "Before academic freedom comes university freedom to pursue its high ideals, unembarrassed by conduct which tends to damage its reputation."[17]

Instead of acting as a bulwark against majority tyranny during World War II, the Supreme Court endorsed these limitations on free speech. In *Chaplinsky* v. *New Hampshire*, the court enunciated the **fighting words doctrine** that some words constitute violent acts. Walter Chaplinsky, a member of the Jehovah's Witnesses religious group, had asked a policeman to guard him from a threatening crowd objecting to his pacifist address. When the policeman gave him no protection but instead cursed him and asked him to "come along," Chaplinsky called the policeman "a God damned racketeer" and "a damned Fascist." Enunciating the fighting words doctrine, the Supreme Court upheld Chaplinsky's conviction on the grounds that he had used threatening words that are not speech but "by their very utterance inflict injury or intend to incite an immediate breach of the peace."[18] In sum, this new fighting words doctrine seriously qualified the Court's earlier inclination to protect most speech

> **fighting words doctrine**
> The principle, endorsed by the Supreme Court in *Chaplinsky* v. *New Hampshire* (1942), that some words constitute violent acts.

under the clear and present danger doctrine. As mentioned earlier, it was this doctrine that many university administrators invoked in the early 1990s when they tried to enforce racial and ethnic tolerance on campus.

### Balancing Doctrine

The end of World War II did not automatically restore civil liberties to dissident groups. Instead, those who were regarded as Communist sympathizers suffered harassment by government officials responding to public concern about the growing conflict between the United States and the Soviet Union. Senator Joseph McCarthy of Wisconsin gained political popularity by accusing artists, teachers, and government officials of having ties to the Communist party. As part of the anti-Communist crusade, Congress voted to require that all employees of the federal government take an oath swearing loyalty to the United States. Students also had to take this oath when applying for student loans.

Once again, it was up to the courts to protect the free speech of minority dissidents. But instead of taking special care to protect free speech, the Supreme Court enunciated the **balancing doctrine**, the principle that freedom of speech had to be balanced against other competing public interests at stake in particular circumstances. The Court developed this doctrine when considering a case in which 11 leaders of the Communist party had been convicted under the Smith Act for espousing the revolutionary overthrow of the government. In *Dennis* v. *United States* (1951), the Court said the convictions had been constitutional, arguing that the "balance . . . must be struck in favor" of the governmental interest in resisting subversion. The balancing doctrine was used to reinterpret and place limits on the clear and present danger doctrine. The Court explicitly said that clear and present danger "cannot mean that before the Government may act, it must wait until . . . the [revolutionary] plans have been laid and the signal is awaited."[19] If the government waited too long to act, it might be too late.

It was elected political leaders, not judges, who resisted the threat that McCarthyism posed to the country's civil liberties. A disgusted President Eisenhower refused to act on McCarthy's most outrageous accusations, and McCarthy's Senate colleagues finally inquired into the senator's methods of operation, later censuring him for his inappropriate conduct.

**balancing doctrine**
The principle enunciated by the courts that freedom of speech must be balanced against other competing public interests at stake in particular circumstances.

**Senator Joseph McCarthy**
Senator Joseph McCarthy, right, built a career in the 1950s on investigating alleged Communist sympathizers. *His methods outraged many, but should civil liberties be balanced against other important governmental interests, such as national security?*

## Fundamental Freedoms Doctrine

After an elected president and Congress had exposed and discredited McCarthy, public opinion became increasingly supportive of protecting the free-speech rights of all Americans, even radicals and Communists (see Figure 16.1). Reflecting these changes in public opinion, the Supreme Court gradually became committed to the **fundamental freedoms doctrine,** the principle that some constitutional provisions ought to be given special preference because they are basic to the functioning of a democratic society. The doctrine has its origins in a Supreme Court opinion written in 1938 by Justice Harlan Stone, who said that some freedoms, such as freedom of speech, have a "preferred position" in the Constitution; any law threatening these freedoms must be placed under strict scrutiny by the Supreme Court.[20]

Although no single court case specifically set forth the fundamental freedoms doctrine, it became the Supreme Court's governing principle during the 1960s in the midst of the Vietnam War. Under its guidance, the Court was more effective at defending dissenters against government repression than in any previous war. As one civil libertarian wrote in 1973, "The truly significant thing in recent years has not been the attempt of the current administration to suppress criticism, but rather the marked inability of the administration to do so effectively."[21] In virtually every case that came before it, the Court ruled against efforts to suppress free speech. For example, it overturned the expulsion from the University of Missouri of a student who had distributed a newspaper containing a picture of a policeman raping the Statue of Liberty. Said the Court: "The mere dissemination of ideas—no matter how offensive to good taste—on a state university campus may not be shut off" in the name of decency.[22]

In one of its most significant decisions, *New York Times* v. *United States* (1971), the Supreme Court rejected an attempt by the Nixon administration to prevent, on grounds of national security, the *New York Times* from publishing the "Pentagon Papers," a lengthy and detailed Defense Department document revealing many mistakes made by government officials in their conduct of the Vietnam War. The *Times* objected that the government was trying to exercise prior restraint, a violation of the freedom of the press outlawed since the days of Peter Zenger. The Supreme Court ruled in the newspaper's favor on the grounds that the "Pentagon Papers" did not, in fact, include highly sensitive material. In subsequent years, the Nixon administration's entanglement in the Watergate scandal served to reinforce public and legal support of civil liberties (see the accompanying Election Connection).

**fundamental freedoms doctrine**
Court doctrine stating that laws impinging on the freedoms that are fundamental to the preservation of democratic practice—the freedoms of speech, press, assembly, and religion—are to be scrutinized by the courts more closely than other legislation. These are also termed the *preferred freedoms.*

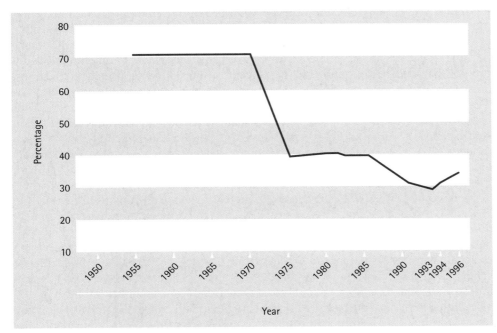

**Figure  16.1**

**Percentage Opposed to Allowing Communists to Make a Speech**
The public has become more willing to grant rights even to extremists. *Do you believe that this is a sign that people are becoming more tolerant? Or is their changed attitude merely a reflection of the end of the Cold War?*

SOURCES: Benjamin L. Page and Robert Y. Shapiro, *The Rational Public: Fifty Years of Trends in Americans' Policy Preferences.* (Chicago: University of Chicago Press, 1992), p. 87; National Opinion Research Center, General Social Survey.

## Watergate and the Elections of 1972, 1974, and 1976

Many consider civil liberties to be fundamental to a democracy because only in the context of freedom of expression can fair elections take place. The Watergate scandal that destroyed the Nixon presidency reinforced how important civil liberties are to elections—and how dangerous executive power can be to fundamental freedoms.

As part of its campaign for reelection in 1972, the Nixon administration engaged in a wide variety of activities that violated the privacy of prominent political opponents and undermined the political process. Nixon operatives tapped telephones without court authorization, scrutinized income tax returns for politically motivated reasons, and broke into an office belonging to the psychiatrist of the insider who had leaked the controversial Pentagon Papers. One aide even suggested fire-bombing the Brookings Institution, a Washington think tank, to cover up a political burglary there. Later, police apprehended five burglars breaking into Democratic party headquarters at the Washington, DC, Watergate complex. When it became clear that the burglary had been authorized by the president and his top aides, Nixon was forced to resign as president of the United States.

The public outrage prompted by the Watergate revelations placed civil liberties on more solid ground than ever before. Nixon's party was overwhelmingly defeated in the congressional elections in 1974, and it lost control of the White House in 1976. Elected officials became aware that serious violations of civil liberties could provoke adverse electoral consequences.

*What safeguards can be put in place to prevent the U.S. president, the most powerful official in the country, from violating civil liberties? If fair elections are themselves undermined by such behavior, can the other institutions of government check the presidency?*

SOURCE: Fred Emery, *Watergate: The Corruption of American Politics and the Fall of Richard Nixon* (New York: Simon & Schuster, 1994).

**Gregory Johnson and the Flag**
Gregory Johnson's conviction for torching the American flag in 1984 was overturned by the Supreme Court. *Is flag burning protected free expression, as the Court argued, or is the flag a unique national symbol that is worthy of special treatment?*

The fundamental freedoms doctrine has now become firmly established. Nothing better illustrates the contemporary Supreme Court's strong commitment to this principle than its rulings with respect to flag burning.[23] During the 1984 Republican national convention in Dallas, Gregory Johnson was arrested for burning an American flag to protest the policies of the Reagan administration. Five years later, Johnson's case came before the Supreme Court. The Court, in *Texas* v. *Johnson* (1989), overturned his conviction, saying the principal purpose of free speech is to invite dispute and the mere burning of the flag was "expressive conduct" that did not breach the peace.[24]

Unlike earlier court decisions, the Supreme Court in the flag-burning case went well beyond popular opinion of the day. In a spirited dissent to the case, Chief Justice Rehnquist quoted Ralph Waldo Emerson and the national anthem, arguing that "For more than 200 years, the American flag has occupied a unique position as the symbol of our Nation, a uniqueness that justifies a governmental prohibition against flag burning."[25] President George Bush called for a constitutional amendment that would prohibit flag desecration, and over 70 percent of the public supported him. Almost immediately, Congress passed a law making it a federal offense to burn the flag. The very day the law was passed, activists set fire to flags in Seattle and Washington, DC, preparing the ground for another court decision. The next year the Supreme Court, in *United States* v. *Eichman* (1990), declared the new law unconstitutional.[26] Many thought it an indication that the commitment to free speech was now very broadly based when Antonin Scalia, one of the Court's most conservative justices, voted with the majority.

If anything, Supreme Court conservatives have become champions of free speech. In *R. A. V.* v. *City of St. Paul* (1990), Scalia wrote a majority opinion that gave protection to speech criticizing other ethnic groups. The City of St. Paul had passed an ordinance forbidding the placement on public or private property of a symbol that "arouses anger, alarm or resentment in others on the basis of race, color, creed, religion or gender." When on the summer solstice of 1990 a group of teenagers were caught placing a "crudely made cross" made of "broken chair legs" inside the fence of the yard of a black neighbor and setting fire to it, the City of St. Paul charged them with violating the city ordinance. The Supreme Court unanimously agreed with the defendants that

**Liquor advertisement.**
Despite the first amendment's guarantee, commercial speech, such as advertisements for alcohol and tobacco products, may be regulated. *What is the rationale behind this exception?*

the ordinance violated their right of free speech, saying that ordinary trespassing laws were adequate to deal with the alleged intrusion on a person's property.[27]

## Limitations on Free Speech

Although free speech has now been firmly established as one of the country's fundamental freedoms, this does not mean that all speech is free of government control. In particular, three types of speech are subject to regulation: commercial speech, libel, and obscenity.

**Commercial speech**—advertising or other speech made for business purposes—may be regulated. According to the Court, regulation of commercial speech is needed so that companies will not take advantage of consumers by providing false or misleading information. Also, commercial speech can be controlled to discourage the consumption of substances the government regards as harmful. For example, cigarette advertising on television and radio is forbidden, despite the complaints by tobacco companies that this prohibition interferes with their right to free speech.

**commercial speech**
Advertising or other speech made for business purposes; may be regulated.

**Libel**—a false statement defaming another—is not constitutionally protected if made by one private person about another. But what if press reports about public figures are erroneous? Can a newspaper then be successfully sued? This issue was raised by a fund-raising advertisement placed in the *New York Times* on March 29, 1960, by a civil rights group. The advertisement reported on student demonstrations against segregation in Montgomery, Alabama. In addition to containing several relatively innocuous errors (student demonstrators sang the national anthem, not "My Country 'Tis of Thee," as claimed), the advertisement implied that the local police were part of a "wave of terror" directed at protesters. "When the entire student body protested to state authorities by refusing to reregister," read the advertisement, "their dining hall was padlocked in an attempt to starve them into submission."

**libel**
False statement defaming another.

Pointing out that the police had never padlocked the dining hall, the local official charged with supervising the police department, Montgomery County Commissioner J. L. Sullivan, sued for libel. An all-white Alabama jury found the *New York Times* and those who placed the ad guilty to the tune of half a million dollars per allegation.[28]

The Supreme Court's decision in this case reflected national public opinion, which at the time was very supportive of the civil rights movement. In *New York Times* v.

**Talk Show Host Oprah Winfrey After a Victory in Court**
A Texas court ruled in Winfrey's favor after she was sued by cattlemen for condemning beef on her show.

*Sullivan* (1964), the Court reversed the libel conviction, holding that untruthful statements made about public figures were not actionable for libel unless the errors were made knowingly or with reckless disregard for the truth. In the Court's view, the errors in the advertisement were reasonable mistakes that showed no reckless disregard for truth.

Some wonder whether the *Sullivan* decision, by freeing the media from legal responsibility for "accidental" errors and falsehoods, granted it too much power. Certainly, the news media have adopted an aggressive, investigative style which at times has led them to make erroneous accusations. In 1993 the CBS newsmagazine program, *Eye to Eye,* placed at risk severely disabled students by stationing a reporter with a hidden camera in their school, seeking (but not finding) evidence of wrongdoing. The year before, ABC's *Primetime Live* had an employee, again with a hidden camera, submit a fake résumé to gain a job in the meat section of a grocery store that it accused of selling doctored and outdated fish. A federal jury found ABC liable for $5.5 million in damages due to fraud, but an appeals court threw out the award in late 1999, granting the grocery store only a symbolic $2 for trespassing and encouraging employee disloyalty.[29] Though these cases prompted some editorial writers to question journalistic ethics, legal efforts to restrain the media must still clear very high hurdles.

**obscenity**
Publicly offensive language or portrayals with no redeeming social value.

**Obscenity**—publicly offensive language or portrayals with no redeeming social value—is not protected under the First Amendment. Whether explicit sexual material is obscene depends on whether it has some social or cultural purpose. The Warren Court, in *Redrup* v. *New York* (1967), came close to saying that it would not uphold any obscenity conviction unless the obscenity involved a juvenile, was forced upon unwilling adults, or "pandered" to the most disgusting of prurient interests. But just a few years later, in *Miller* v. *California* (1973), a more conservative Court said that obscenity is a matter to be settled according to local community standards, though this was later qualified to mean local standards as long as they take into account the "national consensus of protected expression."[30] Overall, the Court seems to have said that local communities may ban hard-core pornography if they wish to do so. Less explicit sexual material may not be outlawed, particularly if presented within an artistic or literary context.

With the growth of the Internet, the distinction between national and local standards is rapidly disappearing, and sexually explicit material has become generally

**visual literacy**
**What Speech is Protected by the Constitution?**

**Blue Ribbon Campaign**

Join EFF    Act Now    Sign Up    About EFF

The Campaign for Online Freedom of Expression

Ranked by WebCrawler as one of the 4 most-linked-to sites on the Web.

**Click Flag for Regional Campaign**

| Australia | Bulgaria | Canada | France | P.R. of China | Portugal | UK | USA |
|---|---|---|---|---|---|---|---|

**Online Free Expression News**    FREE SPEECH ONLINE / BLUE RIBBON CAMPAIGN

■ **ALERT: BANKRUPTCY REFORM ACT with unrelated Internet censorship section**, H.R. 833, needs to be stopped immediately. The entire METHAMPHETAMINE ANTI-PROLIFERATION ACT OF 1999, including censorship provisions as mentioned below, is attached to this bill as a rider. the Bankruptcy Reform Act is now in conference committee between House and Senate. This is the last chance to remove the language before it hits the President's desk. It could make talking about harm reduction or even linking to pages that talk about drug usage or basic chemistry illegal. This bill needs letters and phone calls to your senators and congresspeople immediately. A very sneaky backdoor bit of legislating while people are watching MAPA below. (June 14, 2000)

**The Blue Ribbon Campaign**
In response to the 1996 Communications Decency Act (later ruled unconstitutional), Internet activists mobilized against it. *What are some of the new challenges for civil liberties in the Internet age?*

available. In 1996 Congress passed the Communications Decency Act, which prohibited posting or sending on the Internet obscene material that might be viewed by minors. But the following year, the Supreme Court struck down this law as unconstitutional, arguing that its restrictions were too broad.[31] Since the ruling, antipornography advocates have focused on moving less restrictive laws through Congress and on promoting software designed to screen out objectionable sites.

## SECTION SUMMARY

In a country governed by popular majorities, it may seem odd to place some issues beyond the control of majority rule. But theorists such as John Stuart Mill have argued that prohibiting majorities from regulating free speech is essential to the functioning of a healthy democracy. For one thing, elections would not be free and fair if only certain points of view were allowed to be heard. Even before the Revolution, courts on occasion acted to protect individual liberty for this and other reasons. But the Supreme Court went farthest in its protection of free speech in the twentieth century, beginning with the enunciation of the clear and present danger doctrine, which said speech should be free unless it was obvious that it would lead to substantial evils. The Court has suffered lapses in its commitment to free speech ideals, most notably in its adoption of the fighting words doctrine and the balancing doctrine to justify wartime restrictions on speech. Beginning in the 1960s, the Court seemed to settle on the fundamental freedoms doctrine, which protects free speech in strong terms. However, commercial speech, libel, and obscenity are not protected by free speech rules in order to protect consumers, individual reputations, and community standards, respectively.

## *Freedom of Religion*

CONSTITUTION, FIRST AMENDMENT: *"Congress shall make no law respecting an establishment of religion, or prohibiting the free exercise thereof."*

Freedom of religion is guaranteed by two clauses in the First Amendment. The **establishment of religion clause** denies the government the power to establish any single religious practice as superior. The **free exercise of religion clause** protects the right

**establishment of religion clause**
Denies the government the power to establish any single religious practice as superior.

**free exercise of religion clause**
Protects the right of individuals to practice their religion.

of individuals to practice their religion. When interpreting these clauses, the Supreme Court, as we shall see, has often been influenced by the political and electoral context in which its decisions have been made.

### Establishment of Religion Clause

The constitutional prohibition against government establishment of religion may seem stark, but one can point out many gray areas and seeming contradictions in the way it has been enforced. The motto "In God We Trust" appears on U.S. currency, yet courts have ruled against nativity scenes in village squares. Each session of Congress opens with a prayer, but public schools cannot begin their day in a similar fashion.

Religious issues often arise in conjunction with the provision of public education, in good part because many think schools need to teach not only reading and arithmetic but morals and values as well. The issue is one of the oldest in American politics. Massachusetts passed the nation's first compulsory schooling law in 1852, because many Protestants felt something had to be done about the waves of Catholic immigrants arriving in Boston from Ireland and Germany. Distressed by the changing composition of the city's population, the Boston School Committee urged,

> We must open the doors of our school houses and invite and compel them to come in. There is no other hope for them or for us. . . . In our schools they must receive moral and religious teaching, powerful enough if possible to keep them in the right path amid the moral darkness which is their daily and domestic walk.[32]

Catholic parents did not think they were allowing their sons and daughters to live in "moral darkness" and saw little reason why their children should acquire their moral and religious training in public schools run by Protestants, so they requested instead public monies to help fund Catholic schools. But Catholic demands for government financing only heightened Protestant fears of immigrants and "the power of the Catholic pope." The anti-Catholic forces were so strong that in 1875 they nearly succeeded in passing a constitutional amendment that explicitly forbade state aid to religious schools.[33]

Although the proposed amendment failed to pass, Supreme Court decisions interpreting the establishment of religion clause reflected the views of the Protestant majority, which opposed aid to religious schools. As a result, the Court has for the most part followed Thomas Jefferson's **separation of church and state doctrine,** which says that a wall should separate the government from religious activity. For example, in *Meek* v. *Pittenger* (1975), the Court struck down most forms of aid that Pennsylvania provided to religious schools as part of its federally funded compensatory education program.[34] The Court said public monies cannot be used to pay religious-school teachers, for curricular materials, or for any other expense, except for textbooks and the cost of transporting students to school.

For many years, public schools observed Protestant religious celebrations despite the separation of church and state doctrine. But in recent years the doctrine has been applied quite rigorously to most forms of state-supported religious activity. School prayer, a sacred moment of silence, reading from the Bible as a sacred text, and the celebration of religious holidays—all once widely practiced—have all been banned.[35]

Evangelical religious groups, concerned by the growing secularization of society, have reacted to these Court decisions by advocating an amendment to the Constitution allowing prayer in schools. A majority of the public have said they support such an amendment,[36] and Republican presidential candidates have generally campaigned in favor of its adoption. But supporters have been unable to win the necessary two-thirds vote in Congress. In 1990, however, a more conservative Supreme Court relaxed the ban on prayer in school somewhat, saying students may form Bible-reading or school prayer clubs as long as other clubs are allowed to use school property.[37] Banning religious groups while allowing secular ones to organize was said to infringe upon students' right to free exercise of their religion.

**separation of church and state doctrine**
The principle that a wall should separate the government from religious activity.

Other recent decisions have also opened up windows in the wall of separation between church and state. In 2000 the Supreme Court ruled that states could provide private religious schools with computer equipment.[38] More importantly, in *Agostini* v. *Felton* (1997) the Supreme Court ruled that public school teachers could provide specialized nonreligious instruction in religious schools, so long as this instruction is "made available generally without regard to the sectarian–nonsectarian or public–nonpublic nature of the institution benefitted" and that any aid to individuals occurred "only as a result of the genuinely independent and private choices of individuals." By justifying its decision in terms of the "private choices of individuals," the Court once again showed a concern for the right to the free exercise of religion, the subject to which we now turn.

## Free Exercise of Religion Clause

If the establishment of religion clause seems to bar state involvement in religion, the free exercise of religion clause seems to instruct states not to interfere with religious practices. Once again, this issue often arises in the context of education policy. The Supreme Court has often protected private religious schools from hostile action by state legislatures. For example, during the 1920s anti-immigrant sentiments were so strong in Nebraska that the legislature tried to close private religious schools that provided instruction in foreign languages. In 1923 the Supreme Court ruled that the law violated the free exercise clause of the First Amendment, because it prevented parents from exercising "the right of the individual to . . . establish a home and bring up children [and] to worship God according to the dictates of his own conscience."[39]

But the Supreme Court has in some cases allowed state interference with religious practice. In 1940, with war breaking out in Europe and patriotic fervor on the rise, the Court upheld a West Virginia statute requiring that Jehovah's Witnesses salute the American flag in public school ceremonies, despite the fact that it was against the group's religion to salute a secular symbol. The Court said that schools could interfere with religious liberty in this case, because saluting the flag promoted "national unity, [which] is the basis of national security."[40] Yet just three years later the Court, apparently realizing it had unduly curbed religious liberty, reversed the West Virginia decision. "Compulsory unification of opinion," wrote Justice Robert Jackson in the midst of the war against Nazism, "achieves only the unanimity of the graveyard."[41] Extending this line of reasoning, the Court in 1972 disallowed the application of a compulsory-attendance law to two Amish children, whose parents opposed on religious grounds their continued attendance in a public school.[42]

## Establishment of Religion or Free Exercise?

The case of the Amish children raises the issue of what the courts ought to do when the establishment clause and the free exercise clause come into conflict with one another. Some might argue that by allowing the Amish to be exempt from certain laws to ensure that they could exercise their religion freely, the Court was violating the establishment clause by giving the Amish preferential treatment. A similar quandary arises when one considers the case of overseas members of the armed services. Should the army hire chaplains to ensure soldiers' right of free religious exercise? Or does the army violate the establishment clause by employing religious leaders?

The debate over school choice, which divided presidential candidates in 2000, involves weighing the establishment of religion clause against the free exercise clause.[43] Republican candidate George W. Bush favored giving families vouchers that would allow parents to choose among public schools and religious private schools. Democrat Al Gore argued that choice should be limited to public schools. A key point of contention was whether vouchers increasing parental choice would be a violation of the establishment clause.

## Democratic Dilemma

# Do School Vouchers Establish a Religion or Permit the Free Exercise of Religion?

Voucher programs, which have been implemented by several cities and states, give parents of school-aged children yearly stipends to pay for their children's education. In many cases, they may use these stipends to pay for tuition at private religious schools. So far, the Supreme Court has not made a definitive ruling on the constitutionality of such programs.

Those for vouchers make the following arguments:

1. Vouchers are consistent with the free exercise of religion clause, because they allow families to choose the moral and religious environment in which their children are to be raised. The absence of prayer in school conveys as distinctive a religious message as its presence. Because schools cannot avoid providing religious and moral instruction, parents should be given a choice among schools. For example, they should be allowed to choose a school that teaches sex education programs in a manner with which they agree.
2. The main purpose of vouchers is educational, not religious. Vouchers force schools to respond to the needs and interests of the young people who attend them, not those of the adults who work there. Schools will become more effective under a system of vouchers because the competition among them will drive inefficient, ineffective schools out of business.

Those against vouchers make the following arguments:

1. Tuition voucher plans violate the establishment of religion clause. By allowing parents to use state-provided vouchers to pay for the cost of education in religious schools, the government provides financial support to religious groups. The wall of separation between church and state is thereby breached.
2. Apart from constitutional questions, vouchers are bad policy. The contribution that the public school has made to democracy will be undermined. Schools will no longer serve as a melting pot that blends together students from diverse racial and religious backgrounds. Voucher plans turn public schools into charity schools reserved for poor minorities. Middle-class parents will add their own monies to tuition vouchers in order to educate their children in ethnically and socially isolated settings.

*What do you think?*
- *Do you believe voucher programs are constitutional?*
- *How about a law that gives parents tax credits for private school tuition?*
- *Or a state grant program that gives public money to both public and private schools?*

The Supreme Court has yet to decide whether school vouchers establish a religion or simply permit its free exercise (see the accompanying Democratic Dilemma). In 1998 it allowed a Milwaukee private school voucher program to continue by refusing to review a lower-court case.[44] Some observers argue that opinion on the Court is so evenly divided that the outcome will hinge on the appointments to the Supreme Court made by the new president. If so, this will demonstrate, once again, the close connection between politics and court rulings.

### Section Summary

The establishment and free exercise clauses are the twin guarantors of freedom of religion in the United States. They promise that the government will neither impose religious practices on citizens nor interfere with such practices. But when the Supreme Court has considered individual cases, it has discovered that enforcing the separation of church and state is not always as easy as it sounds. Some of the hardest cases, such as that of public vouchers for private religious schools, involve instances in which the establishment and free exercise clauses are in conflict. Such cases are not the province of courtroom argument alone; they are also debated regularly in national election campaigns.

## Law, Order, and the Rights of Suspects

Elections also affect court interpretations of the procedural rights of the accused. These procedural rights are often thought to conflict with the need for government to maintain social order. Many public officials believe procedural obstacles protecting the rights of suspects unduly handicap the efforts of the police to find and prosecute criminals. They seem to share the view of the ancient jurist who once said, "The judge is condemned when the criminal is absolved."[45] But others think that unless procedural safeguards are carefully observed, innocent people will be unjustly convicted. "I think it a less evil," said Justice Oliver Wendell Holmes, "that some criminals should escape than that the government should play an ignoble part."[46] In this section we first summarize the role that elections play in this debate and then review the rights of the accused, including the rights of suspects against unreasonable police intrusion, as well as their rights at and after criminal trials.

## Election Politics and Criminal Justice

Politics affects criminal justice routines, because almost everyone worries about being a victim of a crime. According to the Federal Bureau of Investigation, 83 percent of all Americans will become crime victims at some point in their lifetime.[47] Most of these crimes—thefts, burglaries, and robberies—take place in the United States at more or less the same rate as in other major industrial countries. But many people in the United States today are especially afraid of personal injury and violent death, and their fears are not unfounded. The murder rate in the United States is far in excess of that of most other countries (see the accompanying International Comparison).

In recent years, the news media have magnified public concern about crime. Coverage of murder, rapes, carjackings, and muggings surged in the mid-1990s (see Figure 16.2). Even if these stories do not touch most people directly, they create an atmosphere in which many feel they are witnessing a crime rate that is escalating out of control. In response to public demands to solve the problem, politicians often feel they must "do something." As one senator remarked, "There is a mood here that if someone came to the floor and said we should barbwire the ankles of anyone who jay-walks, I suspect it would pass."[48] (See the accompanying Democratic Dilemma.)

Whether crime rates are actually rising or falling is not so easy to determine, because many crime statistics are notoriously unreliable. The best evidence on trends in crime rates comes from statistics on homicides, because most murders are reported and are correctly classified. Most victims of homicides are men. Black men are more likely to be murdered than white men. But for older men, both black and white, the murder rate has been falling since the 1980s. On the other hand, the murder victimization rate among younger men, especially younger black men, rose steeply in the early 1990s (see Figure 16.3) and then declined noticeably in the late 1990s.

The way the police and the courts treat suspects was severely scrutinized during the 1960s, when civil rights groups focused public attention on the rights of the dis-

simulation
**You are the Police Officer**

comparative
**Comparing Civil Liberties**

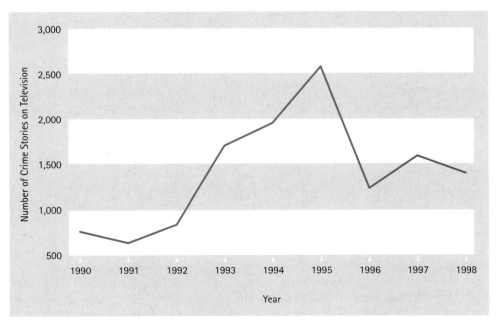

**Figure 16.2**

**TV Crime News**
Television coverage of crime increased in the mid-1990s but declined more recently. Compare this graph to the actual incidence of crime shown in Figure 16.3. *Are the news media accurately reflecting crime rates, in your view?*

SOURCES: "News of the Nineties: The Top Topics and Trends of the Decade," *Media Monitor* 11/3 (July/August, 1997); "1998 Year in Review," *Media Monitor* 13/1 (January/February 1999).

*International Comparison*

## United States Has Much Higher Murder, but Not Burglary, Rates Than Most Other Countries

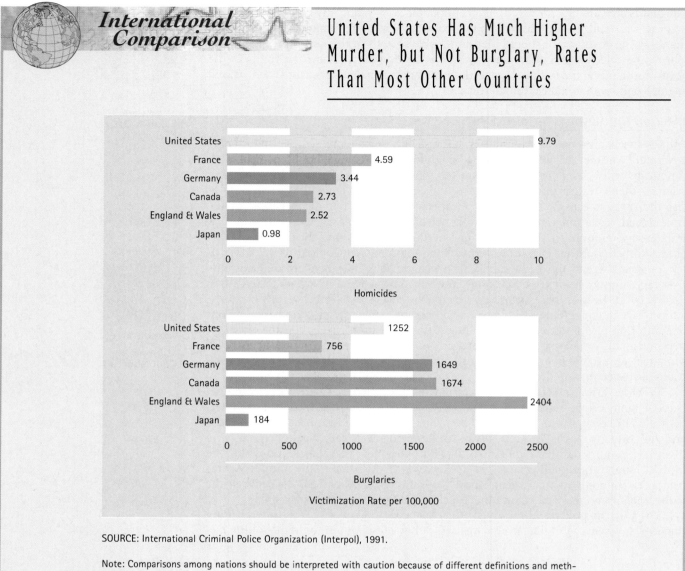

Homicides

Burglaries

Victimization Rate per 100,000

SOURCE: International Criminal Police Organization (Interpol), 1991.

Note: Comparisons among nations should be interpreted with caution because of different definitions and methods of calculation.

advantaged. Influenced by political currents at the time, the Supreme Court, under the leadership of Chief Justice Earl Warren, issued a series of decisions (discussed below) that substantially extended the meaning of the Bill of Rights.

As the rights of the accused were being extended by these Warren Court decisions, many law enforcement officials claimed that the courts had forgotten about the rights of victims. An increasing number of voters agreed, favoring rigorous enforcement of laws and harsh punishments for criminials, including the death penalty. (See Figure 16.4.) Court procedures soon became a campaign issue, and many who sought office called for tougher law enforcement. Richard Nixon's successful 1968 campaign was the first to become known as the "law and order" election. Since then, the issue has arisen in both national and local campaigns. In the 2000 presidential race, both George W. Bush and Al Gore campaigned as "law and order" candidates. Bush, as governor of Texas, allowed the executions of a number of death row inmates during the presidential campaign, including born-again Christian Karla Faye Tucker and great-grandmother Betty Lou Beets. Though activist groups denounced Bush's failure to grant clemency in these cases, Gore, a death penalty supporter, did not.

## Democratic Dilemma

# Can Crime Be Reduced While Protecting Civil Liberties?

The best way to lower crime rates is a matter of great dispute. Four quite different approaches have been suggested.

1. James Q. Wilson says crime is best reduced by incarcerating repeat offenders. "Wicked people exist," he frankly asserts. "Nothing avails except to set them apart from innocent people." He calls for a strategy of "incapacitating a larger fraction of the convicted serious robbers" and other criminals.[a] Wilson recommends more money for police, courts, and prisons so that the necessary resources are made available to find, convict, and imprison serious criminals.

2. Sociologist William J. Wilson argues that crime can be reduced in minority communities only when job opportunities are enhanced.[b] In many central cities, many males continue to be unemployed. Starved of legitimate economic opportunities, young men steal, commit burglaries, and sell drugs to get the cash they need. Once they have a criminal record, these young men find it even more difficult to obtain a job within the economic mainstream. Without jobs, they do not have the resources or self-esteem to form stable family relationships.

3. Still others attribute the high levels of violence and murder in the United States to the ready availability of guns in American society, which they would subject to strict regulation. They point out that the victims of most violent crimes know their assailants. Violence is usually not premeditated or a by-product of a professional robbery, but rather the result of actions taken in anger. Easy access to guns has increased the deadliness of angry encounters. Opponents of gun control argue that gun laws are obeyed only by the law-abiding; besides, they deprive citizens of their Second Amendment rights.

4. Finally, many blame high rates of crime and violence on the widespread availability and use of illegal narcotics. Police estimate that one-third of all major crimes are drug-related. Some people feel that the criminal consequences of drug use can best be reduced through the legalization of drugs. When she was the U.S. surgeon general, Joycelyn Elders said, "We would markedly reduce our crime rate if drugs were decriminalized."[c] But her statement was immediately rebutted by President Clinton, and she soon resigned her position. Drug decriminalization remains highly controversial, and has virtually no mainstream political support.

*What do you consider to be the most important cause of crime? Which solution sounds most reasonable to you?*

---

[a]James Q. Wilson, *Thinking About Crime* (New York: Basic Books, 1975), pp. 199, 205, 209.

[b]William J. Wilson, *The Truly Disadvantaged: The Inner City, the Underclass, and Public Policy* (Chicago: University of Chicago Press, 1987).

[c]*Dayton Daily News,* November 27, 1994, 16A.

---

Although most anticrime talk is tough, former New York Mayor Ed Koch found a way of making his case in a more humorous vein: "A judge I helped elect was mugged recently. And do you know what he did? He called a press conference and said: 'This mugging of me will in no way affect my decisions in matters of this kind.' And an elderly lady got up in the back of the room and said: 'Then mug him again.'"[49]

After Earl Warren's retirement in 1969, the Supreme Court, responding to changing political circumstances, began to temper its decisions on the rights of those accused of a crime. Yet, as we shall see in the remainder of this section, the post-Warren Court did not reverse but only qualified the major Warren Court decisions (see Table 16.1). Most debate over the rights of those suspected of criminal activity has focused on five constitutional provisions: (1) search and seizure, (2) immunity against self-incrimination, (3) impartial jury, (4) legal counsel, and (5) double jeopardy. These are the topics of the remainder of this section.

## Search and Seizure

CONSTITUTION, FOURTH AMENDMENT: *"The right of the people to be secure in their persons, houses, papers, and effects, against unreasonable searches and seizures, shall not be violated, and no Warrants shall issue, but upon probable cause."*

Your house cannot be searched without your permission unless a search warrant, based on evidence that a crime has probably been committed, is properly issued by a court. The Supreme Court, under Earl Warren, decided in **Mapp v. Ohio** (1961) that any improperly obtained evidence cannot be used in court.[50] But in *Washington* v. *Chrisman* (1982), a more conservative Court ruled that this protection did not extend to dormitory rooms on a college campus.[51]

Conservative modifications of the principle enunciated in *Mapp* have continued. In early 2000, a unanimous Court ruled that officers may sometimes stop and search people simply because they turn and run when they see police approaching. Running

> **Mapp v. Ohio**
> Supreme Court decision saying that any evidence obtained without a proper search warrant may not be introduced in a trial.

**Figure 16.3**

**Homicide Rates in the United States**
Rates rose in the 1980s and early 1990s but fell in the latter half of the 1990s.

SOURCE: Bureau of Justice Statistics, *Homicide Trends in the U.S.*, www.ojp.usdoj.gov/bjs/homicide/homtrnd.htm#contents, accessed March 24, 2000.

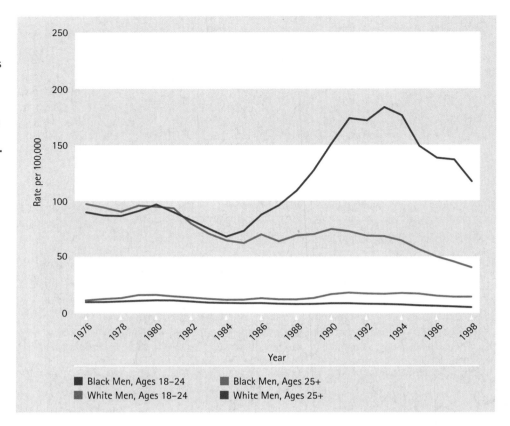

**Figure 16.4**

**Most People Think Courts Should Be Tougher on Criminals**
*Why has support for the death penalty dropped in recent years?*

SOURCE: Benjamin I. Page and Robert Y. Shapiro, *The Rational Public: Fifty Years of Trends in Americans' Policy Preferences.* (Chicago: University of Chicago Press, 1992), p. 92; General Social Survey.

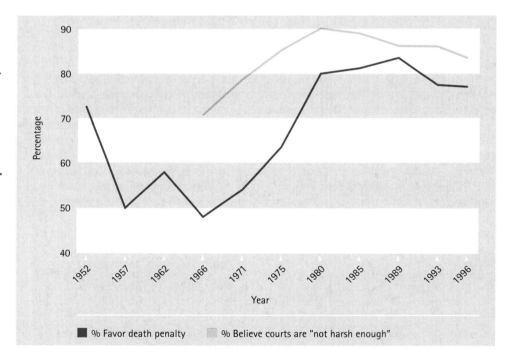

away, argued the Court, is cause for "reasonable suspicion," which can justify such a search. "Headlong flight—whenever it occurs—is the consummate act of evasion," Chief Justice William Rehnquist wrote in his opinion. "It is not necessarily indicative of wrongdoing, but it is certainly suggestive of such."[52] Though such a decision might have provoked much political controversy in the 1960s or 1970s, neither presidential campaign in 2000 seemed to take notice.

**Table 16.1**

Key Changes in the Rights of the Accused

| Constitutional Provision | Amendment | Extensions by Warren Court | Limitation by Post-Warren Court |
|---|---|---|---|
| Search and seizure | 4 | *Mapp* v. *Ohio*, 1961 Improperly collected evidence cannot be introduced in court. | *Washington* v. *Chrisman*, 1982 But campus dorm rooms can be searched. |
| No self-incrimination | 5 | *Miranda* v. *Arizona*, 1966 Officers must tell suspects their rights before questioning. | *Harris* v. *New York*, 1971 But if suspects testify, evidence obtained without "reading them their rights" can be introduced. *Dickerson* v. *U.S.*, 2000 *Miranda* reaffirmed. |
| Impartial jury | 6 | *Sheppard* v. *Maxwell*, 1966 Establishes guidelines to protect jurors from biased news coverage. | *Nebraska Press Association* v. *Stuart*, 1976 But pretrial publicity does not necessarily preclude a fair trial. |
| Legal counsel | 6 | *Gideon* v. *Wainwright*, 1963 Poor defendants are guaranteed legal counsel. | No limitation |
| No double jeopardy | 5 | *Benton* v. *Maryland*, 1969 Applies to state as well as federal trials. | No limitation |

## Immunity Against Self-Incrimination

CONSTITUTION, FIFTH AMENDMENT: *"Nor shall [any person] be compelled in any criminal case to be a witness against himself."*

The Fifth Amendment protects individuals from torture and coerced confessions by saying that persons cannot be forced to testify against themselves. In **Miranda v. Arizona** (1966), the Warren Court put teeth into this constitutional provision by requiring police officers to tell suspects, before questioning them, that they need not reply and that they may request the presence of an attorney. If suspects are not so "Mirandized," then any information obtained may not be presented in court. After Richard Nixon made the *Miranda* decision an issue in his 1968 presidential campaign, the Supreme Court softened the ruling when it decided, in *Harris v. New York* (1971), that information gathered in violation of the *Miranda* decision may be introduced in evidence if defendants testify in their own defense.

In 2000 the Supreme Court finally ruled on a 1968 law passed by Congress that some believed overturned the *Miranda* decision. In a 7–2 decision, the Court affirmed the *Miranda* ruling. Chief Justice Rehnquist, writing for the majority, pointed out that "*Miranda* has become embedded in routine police procedure to the point where the warnings have become part of our national culture." Reluctant to reverse earlier Supreme Court decisions and modern police practices, the majority chose judicial restraint in the case. Many commentators found it particularly interesting that Rehnquist, usually a judicial restorationist who had in the past specifically questioned the *Miranda* decision, joined the moderates on the Court in favor of judicial restraint when asked to overturn prior decisions. Some even felt that Rehnquist's reference to "culture" indicated the decision had been influenced by the TV ritual of "reading suspects their '*Miranda*' rights" on cop shows such as CBS's *NYPD Blue*. In a heated dissent, Justice Antonin Scalia, who remained a judicial restorationist in this case as in others, objected that the *Miranda* requirements had no basis in the Constitution. He argued that according constitutional force to the original *Miranda* decision simply on

*Miranda* v. *Arizona*
Supreme Court decision stating that accused persons must be told by police that they need not testify against themselves.

the grounds that an earlier court had (in his view, wrongly) so decided would give the courts an "immense and frightening antidemocratic power" to declare federal laws unconstitutional simply on the grounds that they wanted laws to be consistent not with the Constitution but simply with previous court decisions, whether rightly or wrongly decided.[53] (See Chapter 15, judicial restraint, restorationists, p. 465.)

## Impartial Jury

CONSTITUTION, SIXTH AMENDMENT: *"The accused shall enjoy the right to a speedy and public trial, by an impartial jury."*

The requirement that a jury be impartial is difficult to meet when a crime becomes newsworthy, because jurors may be biased by media accounts of the alleged crime both before and during the trial. The Warren Court considered these issues in *Sheppard* v. *Maxwell* (1966), a case that grew out of the trial of medical doctor Sam Sheppard, who was accused of murdering his wife. (The case became the basis for the television show and movie *The Fugitive*.) Sheppard complained about the excessive news coverage to which jurors were exposed, including the fact that the media were positioned in the courtroom in such a way that they could listen in on his conversations with his attorneys.[54] The Supreme Court overturned his conviction and set forth the following guidelines in an effort to ensure impartial juries in the future.

1. Trials should be postponed until public attention has subsided.
2. Jurors should be questioned to screen out those with detailed knowledge or fixed opinions.
3. Judges should instruct jurors emphatically to consider only the evidence presented in the courtroom, not any evidence obtained from an external source.
4. A court may **sequester** jurors during a trial—that is, keep them away from all sources of information about the crime other than that presented in the courtroom.[55]
5. Courts should consider changing the **trial venue**—the place where the trial is held—in order for the case to be heard by a jury less exposed to pre-trial publicity.

Although these constitutional safeguards designed to prevent the jury from becoming biased have never been reversed, the post-Warren Court, in *Nebraska Press Association* v. *Stuart* (1976), handed down a decision reflecting the country's more conservative political mood. It said that "pre-trial publicity—even pervasive, adverse publicity—does not inevitably lead to an unfair trial."[56]

Sometimes a change in venue to avoid publicity can have a dramatic effect on the outcome of a trial. In 1992, black motorist Rodney King was videotaped by an amateur cameraman as he was beaten by Los Angeles police after he tried to get away when an officer asked him to stop. When the officers were brought to trial, a state appeals court ordered a change of venue to escape the racial passions that had been aroused in Los Angeles. The trial court judge chose as the new venue a state court in Simi Valley, on the northwestern fringe of the Los Angeles metropolitan area. The judge picked Simi Valley because its docket was short and extra space was available for the expected avalanche of reporters. Many residents of Simi Valley were former police officers and army personnel, so the jury ended up containing several people associated with law enforcement. The jury found three of the four officers innocent of all charges, and it could not agree on charges against the fourth.

## Legal Counsel

CONSTITUTION, SIXTH AMENDMENT: *". . . and to have Assistance of Counsel for his defense."*

The Warren Supreme Court ruled in *Gideon* v. *Wainwright* (1963) that all citizens accused of serious crimes, even the indigent, are constitutionally entitled to legal representation. If the accused is too poor to hire an attorney, then the court must assign one.

**Ernesto Miranda**
Ernesto Miranda, the namesake of the "Miranda Rights" that are read to all suspects before questioning. The Supreme Court ruled that Miranda's confession was inadmissible in court because he had not been advised of his right not to answer questions. *Are Miranda rights now part of American culture?*

**sequester**
To house jurors privately, away from any information other than that presented in the courtroom.

**trial venue**
Place where a trial is held.

*Gideon* v. *Wainwright*
Supreme Court decision in 1963 giving indigent people accused of crimes the right to court-appointed counsel.

It was easier to enunciate this right than to put it into practice. At one time, courts asked private attorneys to donate their services in order to defend the poor. But donating time to help suspected crooks was not popular among the members of the legal profession. As a result, most states have created the office of **public defender**, an attorney whose full-time responsibility is to provide for the legal defense of indigent criminal suspects. When the public defender was originally established, it was thought that full-time, paid attorneys would provide higher-quality representation. But this solution, too, has had its problems. For one thing, the job of a public defender is thankless, pay is low, and defenders are forced to deal with "rotten case after rotten case."[57] One of the public defenders' biggest problems is winning respect from those with whom they work. From the perspective of the police, defenders simply throw up roadblocks to prevent conviction of the guilty. Surprisingly, defendants are hardly more grateful. Defendants, like most other people, think that anything free probably is not worth much. One felon, when asked by a judge whether he had had an attorney, replied, "No, I had a public defender."[58] Public prosecutors probably appreciate the work of the public defender more than anyone else. As fellow attorneys, they know that those working on the other side are just doing their job. Still, there is a general impression, perhaps unfair in many cases, that public defenders are "crummy lawyers . . . an inferior breed."[59]

> **public defender**
> Attorney whose full-time responsibilities are to provide for the legal defense of indigent criminal suspects.

## Double Jeopardy

CONSTITUTION, FIFTH AMENDMENT: *"Nor shall any person be subject for the same offence to be twice put in jeopardy of life or limb."*

The Warren Court ruled in *Benton v. Maryland* (1969) that states cannot try a person twice for the same offense, thereby placing the defendant in **double jeopardy**. Despite this rule, the Supreme Court, in an old decision that has never been overturned, has said that a person can be tried in federal courts, even if acquitted in a state court. "An act denounced as a crime by both national and state sovereignties is an offense against the peace and dignity of both."[60] As mentioned in Chapter 15, both may prosecute without putting the defendant in double jeopardy.

> **double jeopardy**
> Fifth Amendment provision that prohibits prosecution for the same offense twice.

Prosecution by both federal and state governments is most likely in high-visibility cases. For example, when the State of California was unable to win a conviction in the trial of the four police officers charged with beating Rodney King, the officers were tried again under federal law.

The decision to bring the officers to a second trial was undoubtedly influenced by the consequences of the case for national elections. Three days of civil disorder broke out in Los Angeles's minority communities after the initial failure to win a conviction. In his campaign for president, Bill Clinton blamed the Bush administration for creating an atmosphere that fostered racial conflict. Although the decision to bring a second prosecution was made by the federal U.S. attorney serving Los Angeles, it was made only at the request of the attorney general (probably with the approval of President Bush). The decision to prosecute a second time calmed the city, and the issue dropped out of the presidential campaign. In the federal trial, the jury split the difference, convicting two officers and acquitting the other two.

## Rights in Practice: The Plea Bargain

If a case is newsworthy, constitutional procedures are generally observed: The public is looking on, and those participating in the trial must take political pressures into account. But the reality of justice in most criminal cases is very different. Hardly anyone accused of a crime is actually tried by a jury, and nearly all those convicted of a crime testify against themselves. The accused have their rights, to be sure, but very few of the accused actually choose to exercise them. Most of the time, it is to their advantage *not* to do so.[61]

Trial court judges depend on the willingness of prosecutors and defenders to settle cases before going to trial. The number of people accused of crimes is high, the list

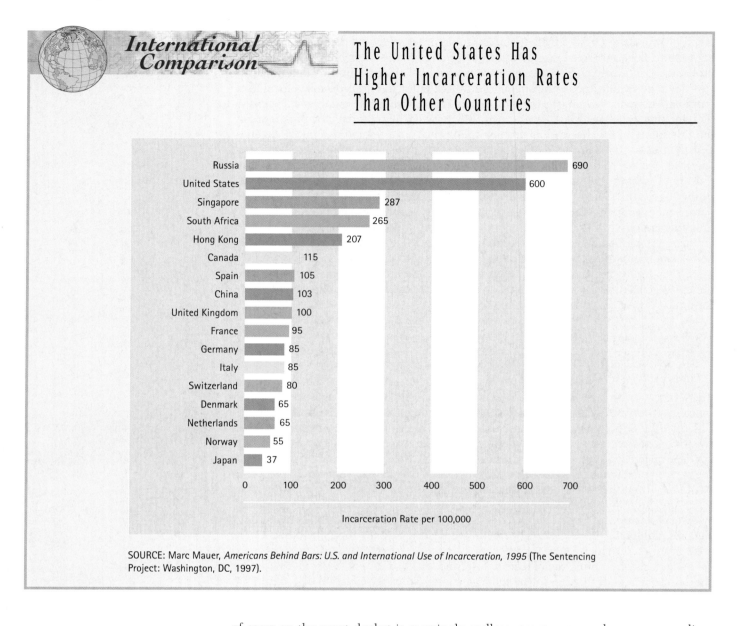

**International Comparison**

## The United States Has Higher Incarceration Rates Than Other Countries

| Country | Incarceration Rate per 100,000 |
|---|---|
| Russia | 690 |
| United States | 600 |
| Singapore | 287 |
| South Africa | 265 |
| Hong Kong | 207 |
| Canada | 115 |
| Spain | 105 |
| China | 103 |
| United Kingdom | 100 |
| France | 95 |
| Germany | 85 |
| Italy | 85 |
| Switzerland | 80 |
| Denmark | 65 |
| Netherlands | 65 |
| Norway | 55 |
| Japan | 37 |

SOURCE: Marc Mauer, *Americans Behind Bars: U.S. and International Use of Incarceration, 1995* (The Sentencing Project: Washington, DC, 1997).

**plea bargain**
Agreement between prosecution and defense that the accused will admit having committed a crime, provided that other charges are dropped and the recommended sentence is shortened.

of cases on the court docket is seemingly endless, court personnel resources are limited, and court time is precious. Judges are expected to preside over efficient courtrooms, settle cases quickly, and keep the court docket short. To speed the criminal justice process, defenders and prosecutors are usually expected to try to arrange a **plea bargain**—an agreement between prosecution and defense that the accused will admit to having committed a crime, provided that other charges are dropped and a reduced sentence is recommended. The Supreme Court has approved of this transformation of the rights of the accused into chips that can be used "to cop a plea." In the words of Justice Burger, plea bargaining is "an essential component of the administration of justice. Properly administered, it is to be encouraged."[62]

Extensive use of the plea bargain has become an issue in electoral politics, with many candidates insisting that those convicted should serve longer sentences. One popular proposal, enacted in a number of states, is known as "three strikes and you're out." After having been convicted of three felonies, a convict must receive life imprisonment, whether or not a plea bargain is struck. As a result of these tough new laws, incarceration rates are rising and prison costs are becoming one of the fastest growing items in state budgets. The United States now seems to have the largest incarceration rate in the world (see the accompanying International Comparison).

Whether a higher incarceration rate is the best way to reduce crime has become a subject of considerable debate. Even some judges now argue that the laws are too severe. In a recent case, a Michigan judge rejected prosecutors' pleas to imprison with adults a boy who had killed at age 11. Handing down a seven-year sentence to be served in a juvenile facility, Judge Eugene Moore chastised the legislature for writing laws that were not "helping to prevent [crimes] and rehabilitate" criminals. The speaker of the Michigan House of Representatives told the judge, in effect, to mind his own business: "We don't need judges on a soapbox; we need judges who will uphold the law."[63]

## SECTION SUMMARY

The Constitution guarantees those accused of crimes an impartial jury, legal counsel, and protection against unreasonable searches, self-incrimination, and being tried twice for the same crime. Like the other freedoms discussed in this chapter, however, the Supreme Court's protection of these rights has waxed and waned on the basis of politics and pressures. In the mid-1960s, when public attention was focused on protecting the rights of minorities, the Court made many of its landmark civil liberties decisions, such as the *Mapp* v. *Ohio* ruling against unauthorized searches and the *Miranda* ruling against self-incrimination. When concerns about crime dominated electoral politics in the 1980s and 1990s, the Court qualified its earlier decisions somewhat, though it did not reverse them. In practice, those accused of crimes often agree to plea bargains, waiving their right to trial by an impartial jury in exchange for a reduced charge.

# The Right of Privacy

CONSTITUTION, NINTH AMENDMENT: *"The enumeration in the Constitution, of certain rights, shall not be construed to deny or disparage others retained by the people."*

The civil liberties discussed thus far are explicitly mentioned in the Bill of Rights. In addition, the Supreme Court has enunciated another liberty, the **right of privacy**—the right to be free of government interference in those aspects of one's personal life that do not affect others. Although the right of privacy is not explicitly mentioned in the Constitution, the Ninth Amendment says that some rights may be retained by the people even though they may not be explicitly mentioned in the Constitution. Questions about privacy issues are growing as technology makes personal information more readily available to all. (See the accompanying International Comparison.)

Some constitutional scholars believe that the judicial power to identify any right not explicitly mentioned in the Constitution should be exercised with great caution, because abuse of this power would give a nonelected judiciary the authority to override the will of elected public officials, who presumably are carrying out the will of the majority. "Where constitutional materials do not clearly specify [a right]," judicial scholar Robert Bork has said, "the judge must stick close to the text and history, and their fair implications, and not construct any new rights."[64]

Nevertheless, in the 1960s and 1970s the Court went a long way toward constructing a right to privacy. In this section, we consider the Court's rulings on this issue, first with regard to private sexual behavior and then concerning the explosive issue of abortion.

## Regulation of Sexual Behavior

The modern right to privacy owes its existence to the Supreme Court's ruling in *Griswold* v. *Connecticut* (1965).[65] Estelle Griswold, executive director of Planned Parenthood, was fined $100 for violating a Connecticut law prohibiting the use of any instrument for the purpose of contraception. Declaring the law unconstitutional, Justice William Douglas discerned "a right of privacy older than the Bill of Rights." "Would we allow the police to search the sacred precincts of marital bedrooms for tell-

**right of privacy**
Right to keep free of government interference those aspects of one's personal life that do not affect others.

participation
**Protect Your Online Privacy**

## *International Comparison*     Privacy in the Information Age

The Internet and related technologies have sparked an information revolution, changing the daily lives of millions by making research, shopping, dining, and even obtaining medical care faster and more convenient. But technology also reduces the privacy of individuals. One popular Web site, for example, allows customers to uncover all publicly available information about anyone, with the click of a mouse, for under $40. This includes phone numbers, neighbors' phone numbers, professional licenses, any bankruptcy filings, civil procedures involving the person, property ownership and value, and a summary of other assets.

And private firms are not the only ones in the information collection business: Intelligence-gathering agencies from the United States, Britain, Canada, Australia, and New Zealand jointly administer a communications system called Echelon, which monitors international satellite telecommunications traffic for suspicious or threatening words or phrases.

In the United States, consumer credit records and other financial data are covered by 1970s-era laws that allow customers to review their files and demand corrections. But the European Union has gone much further, enacting a Data Protection Directive that requires the "unambiguous consent" of consumers before any company or government agency can use personal financial data. In addition, the data cannot be exported or used for any purpose other than the original one. Each EU country will also appoint a "privacy commissioner" to handle consumer grievances.

*Do you believe that new technology poses a threat to privacy? Does the private sector or government represent the greater threat? If you believe there is a threat, what legal measures do you think can be taken to protect individuals?*

SOURCE: "The Surveillance Society," *The Economist*, May 1, 1999.

tale signs of the use of contraceptives?" asked Douglas. "The very idea is repulsive to the notions of privacy surrounding the marriage relationship."[66] In a dissent, Justice Potter Stewart declared the Ninth Amendment "but a truism" that could hardly be used to "annul a law passed by the elected representatives of the people."

Despite Stewart's objection, there is little doubt that a national majority agreed with the Supreme Court that a married couple should have the right to use contraceptives. But would the Supreme Court be equally protective of the right of privacy when the actions in question were not approved by a majority of the public? This question arose in 1986 in *Bowers* v. *Hardwick*, when the Court was asked to declare unconstitutional a Georgia law prohibiting sodomy under which two homosexuals had been convicted. Noting that laws against sodomy existed at the time the Constitution was written, the Court majority found no reason to think that the writers of the Ninth Amendment intended to exempt homosexual behavior from state reg-

**Gay Civil Unions**
A couple celebrates after the Vermont legislature voted to legalize gay civil unions in April 2000. *Does the right to privacy include gay marriage?*

ulation. In dissent, Justice Blackmun said the freedom to enjoy intimate associations is "central to any concept of liberty."[67] More recently, state courts in Georgia, Louisiana, and Maryland have invalidated antisodomy laws on the grounds that they interfere with the right to privacy.[68] Legal activists have vowed to bring such cases to the Supreme Court, so the verdict in *Bowers* may be revisited in the years ahead.

Although these rulings may not appear to be consistent with one another, they are consistent with one measure: public opinion. In 1986, when *Bowers* was decided, a majority of those surveyed believed that homosexual relations should be outlawed. But by 1999, polls found that Americans favored legalizing homosexual behavior by a margin of 50 to 43 percent. Similarly, 83 percent of people thought gays and lesbians should have equal rights in the workplace—a figure up nearly 25 percentage points from the early 1980s. If the Supreme Court accepts recent lower-court decisions, it will once again have shifted with changing public sentiment.[69]

## Abortion: Right to Life or Right to Choose?

Although the Court has left uncertain the range of sexual acts to which the right of privacy extends, it ruled, in *Roe* v. *Wade* (1973), that the right of privacy was broad enough to include at least a partial right of abortion. The case arose out of a request from Norma McCorvey, using the pseudonym Jane Roe. Roe, seeking to terminate a pregnancy, asked for a judgment declaring unconstitutional the Texas law prohibiting abortion. Writing for the Court majority, Justice Harry Blackmun said that the woman's right of privacy was so fundamental that it could be abridged only when the state interest in doing so was compelling. Dissenting justices objected to judicial interference with a state legislature's right to balance a woman's rights against the welfare of her unborn child (see the accompanying Window on the Past).

*Roe* v. *Wade* launched two powerful political movements that have helped to shape American politics in the three decades since the Court's decision. The "right to life" crusade was organized by Catholic and other religious groups opposed to abortion on two grounds. These groups believe that inasmuch as human life begins at conception, abortion cannot be distinguished from infanticide. They also believe human sexuality is and should always be intimately connected with procreation. Separating the two undermines the moral basis of family and society. In short, opponents of abortion do not regard the issue as a question of a woman's personal preference; the welfare of both the fetus and society are also at stake.

These "right-to-life" supporters became actively engaged in state and national politics, lobbying legislatures to impose as many restraints on abortion as the courts would allow. Responding to right-to-life groups, Congress in 1976 enacted legislation preventing coverage of abortion costs under government health insurance programs, such as Medicaid. In 1980 the Republican party promised to restore the "right to life," and in subsequent years, Republican presidents began appointing to the Supreme Court justices who were expected either to reverse *Roe* v. *Wade* or to limit its scope.

In response to these political pressures and to the change in its membership, the Supreme Court began to declare constitutional certain restrictions on abortion. The Court ruled in 1980 that the law Congress had enacted prohibiting the public funding of abortions was constitutional.[70] In 1989 it said that states could require the doctor to ascertain the viability of a fetus before permitting an abortion, if the woman was 20 or more weeks pregnant.[71] By 1990 judicial observers believed that four justices on the Supreme Court were prepared to overturn *Roe* and that any new appointment by a Republican president would create the majority needed to reverse the decision.

Opposition to "right-to-life" groups was at first weak and uncertain, mainly because many of those who supported a woman's constitutional "right of choice" thought it had been permanently protected by the Supreme Court decision. But as the

**Jane Roe**
Shown here in 1973, when *Roe* v. *Wade* was decided, Norma McCorvey (whose privacy at the time was protected via the pseudonym Jane Roe) in 1995 made the surprise announcement that she had become a pro-life advocate.

## Court Reasoning in <u>Roe</u> v. <u>Wade</u>

When the Supreme Court ruled on the legality of abortion in 1973, it invoked the right of privacy as a justification. Do you believe the Court's reasoning is persuasive? Or do you agree with Justice Byron White's dissent?

[T]he Court has recognized that a right of personal privacy, or a guarantee of certain areas or zones of privacy, does exist under the Constitution. . . . This right of privacy. . .is broad enough to encompass a woman's decision whether or not to terminate her pregnancy. The detriment that the State would impose upon the pregnant woman by denying this choice altogether is apparent.

—Justice Harry Blackmun,
majority opinion, *Roe* v. *Wade*

The Court apparently values the convenience of the pregnant mother more than the continued existence and development of the life or potential life which she carries. . . . I find no constitutional warrant for imposing such an order of priorities on the people and legislatures of the States. In a sensitive area such as this, I cannot accept the Court . . . interposing a constitutional barrier to state efforts to protect human life.

—Justice Byron White,
dissenting in *Roe* v. *Wade*

SOURCE: *Roe* v. *Wade* 410 US 113 (1973).

"right-to-life" movement gained momentum and it became more likely that *Roe* v. *Wade* would be overturned, the "right-to-choose" movement gained in strength and aggressiveness. By 1984 it was able to secure the Democratic party's commitment to the "right-to-choose" principle.

Both sides of the controversy waited anxiously for the 1992 court decision in *Planned Parenthood* v. *Casey*.[72] The organization challenged a Pennsylvania law that placed a number of restrictions on the right to abortion that went well beyond what seemed permissible under *Roe* v. *Wade*. Right-to-life groups saw the case as an opportunity to return to the states the authority to decide whether abortions were legal. Right-to-choose groups feared that many, if not all, of the recently enacted impediments to abortion would be declared constitutional. The Court majority satisfied neither side entirely, finding a compromise that upheld some of the Pennsylvania restrictions on abortion but left intact the principle that states cannot simply outlaw all abortions.

The majority based its decision on nothing other than the principle of *stare decisis*, the rule stating that court decisions, once made, should be followed by subsequent judges if at all possible (see Chapter 15, page 461). To do otherwise, argued the court, is to make a mockery of the law. In the words of Judge Sandra Day O'Connor, "Where . . . the Court decides a case in such a way as to resolve the sort of intensely divisive controversy reflected in *Roe* . . . the promise of constancy, once given, binds its maker for as long as . . . the understanding of the issue has not changed so fundamentally as to render the commitment obsolete." In other words, the Court said it was not changing its mind. In 2000, the Court reaffirmed its position when it ruled that states could not simply ban a particular type of abortion, in this case a partial birth abortion.[73]

Either by accident or design, the Court majority once again adopted a position very close to that of the average American voter. It permitted restrictions (such as a requirement that teenagers obtain parental consent) endorsed by a majority of voters

timeline

**The History of the Right to Privacy**

but rejected those most people think are not warranted (such as a requirement that a married woman obtain the consent of her husband). Even in matters as sensitive as the right of privacy, the Court seems to be influenced by majority opinion, as expressed in the outcome of recent elections.

## SECTION SUMMARY

One of the most controversial legal debates in recent years revolves around whether the Constitution contains right of privacy and how far that right should extend. The right owes its legal existence to several cases involving the regulation of sexual behavior, which most people now seem to agree ought to be free from government interference. Much more controversial, however, is the question of whether the practice of abortion ought to be considered a privacy issue, or whether the issue ought instead to be framed in terms of an unborn person's right to life. The Supreme Court's rulings have paralleled public opinion on these issues, allowing some regulation of abortion, but not an outright ban.

## *Chapter Summary*

The Bill of Rights remained pretty much a dead letter until the Civil War ended slavery. Only as key provisions of the Bill of Rights were selectively incorporated into the due process clause of the Fourteenth Amendment did they become effective components of the country's constitutional makeup.

Although the courts are expected to protect civil liberties against majority tyranny, most of the time the Supreme Court has followed, not led, public opinion. In 1919 the Supreme Court said speech could not be prohibited unless it created a clear and present danger to a peaceful society, but it initially applied the doctrine in such a way as to convict a socialist for his political speech. Though it protected minority dissent during the 1930s, it later elaborated the fighting words doctrine, which declared certain phrases to be the equivalent of violent acts. Not until McCarthyism had been rejected by elected officials did a Court majority say free speech was a fundamental freedom that required special protection.

Freedom of religion is protected by two separate clauses in the First Amendment. The establishment of religion clause prohibits the propagation of religious beliefs by public institutions and direct aid to churches, religious schools, and other religious institutions. The free exercise of religion clause prevents the government from interfering with the religious activities of citizens. At times the two clauses come into conflict. For example, the Supreme Court has yet to decide whether school vouchers that permit families to choose between religious and secular schools violate the establishment clause or are permitted under the free exercise clause.

When balancing the rights of the accused against the need to maintain social order, Supreme Court decisions have fluctuated with changes in public opinion. During the 1960s, the Warren Court expanded the rights of the accused by tightening rules under which police and prosecutors could obtain evidence, question suspects, and hold trials. After "law and order" became a campaign issue, the Supreme Court modified, though it did not reverse, many of these decisions.

The Court has also discerned a right of privacy, despite the fact that no such right is mentioned explicitly in the Bill of Rights. This right of privacy is broad enough to include a woman's right to terminate a pregnancy. But it is not absolute. As interpreted by the Court, the right of privacy does not preclude regulation of abortions, especially among children and after the first trimester of pregnancy. Nor has the Supreme Court extended it to include homosexual acts, though some state courts have done so. The right of privacy discerned by the Court comes very close to the viewpoint held by most Americans. The country's definition of civil liberties seems to depend as much on the thinking of its citizens as on its judicial system.

---

**On the Web**

American Civil Liberties Union
www.aclu.org
The sometimes controversial American Civil Liberties Union has a detailed Web site outlining its agenda for promoting civil liberties, as well as describing the history and present status of the law.

Freedom Forum
www.freedomforum.org
The Freedom Forum is an international foundation that promotes freedom of the press and of religion.

Electronic Frontier Foundation
www.eff.org
Center for Democracy and Technology
www.cdt.org
The Electronic Frontier Foundation and the Center for Democracy and Technology follow issues and provide information about free speech and privacy on the Internet.

Program on Educational Policy and Governance
http://data.fas.harvard.edu/pepg
Harvard University's Program on Educational Policy and Governance provides reports of studies on existing school choice programs.

---

## Key Terms

balancing doctrine, p. 482
civil liberties, p. 474
civil rights amendments, p. 477
clear and present danger doctrine, p. 480
commercial speech, p. 485
double jeopardy, p. 497
due process clause, p. 477
establishment of religion clause, p. 487

fighting words doctrine, p. 481
free exercise of religion clause, p. 487
fundamental freedoms doctrine, p. 483
*Gideon* v. *Wainwright*, p. 496
libel, p. 485
*Mapp* v. *Ohio*, p. 493
*Miranda* v. *Arizona*, p. 495
obscenity, p. 486

plea bargain, p. 498
prior restraint doctrine, p. 479
public defender, p. 497
right of privacy, p. 499
selective incorporation, p. 477
separation of church and state doctrine, p. 488
sequester, p. 496
trial venue, p. 496
tyranny of the majority, p. 478

## Suggested Readings

Bork, Robert H. "Neutral Principles and Some First Amendment Problems." *Indiana Law Journal* 47 (1971): 1–35. Argues for a narrow definition of constitutional rights that limits the majority will.

Casper, Jonathan D. *American Criminal Justice: The Defendant's Perspective.* Englewood Cliffs, NJ: Prentice-Hall, 1972. Discusses the day-to-day realities of the criminal justice system.

Friedman, Lawrence M. *Crime and Punishment in American History.* New York: Basic Books, 1993.

Readable overview of the changing nature of the American system of criminal justice.

Garrow, David J. *Liberty and Sexuality.* New York: Macmillan, 1994. Comprehensive account of the legal debate over abortion before and after *Roe.*

Goldstein, Robert. *Political Repression in Modern America: 1870 to the Present.* New York: Schenkman, 1978. Comprehensive account of violations of freedom of speech, press, and assembly in the United States.

Goldstein, Robert. *Saving "Old*

*Glory": The History of the Desecration Controversy.* Boulder, CO: Westview, 1995. Authoritative political and constitutional history of the flag-burning controversy.

Lewis, Anthony. *Make No Law: The Sullivan Case and the First Amendment.* New York: Random House, 1992. Excellent, readable case study of the politics of the *Sullivan* decision and the evolution of free-speech doctrine.

Macedo, Stephen. *The New Right v. The Constitution.* Washington, DC: Cato Institute, 1987. Thoughtfully asserts the responsibility of the courts to protect all liberties, not just fundamental freedoms, from legislative intrusion.

McIntyre, Lisa J. *The Public Defender: The Practice of Law in the Shadows of Repute.* Chicago: University of Chicago Press, 1987. Careful sociological study of this little-appreciated courtroom player.

Meiklejohn, Alexander. *Free Speech and Its Relation to Self-Government.* New York: Harper, 1948. Influential, early statement of the absolutist position.

Pritchett, C. Herman. *Constitutional Civil Liberties.* Englewood Cliffs, NJ: Prentice-Hall, 1984. Definitive, if somewhat dated, discussion of civil liberties constitutional law in a political context.

Rosenberg, Gerald N. *The Hollow Hope: Can Courts Bring About Social Change?* Chicago: University of Chicago Press, 1991. Casts doubt on the proposition that the courts play a major, independent role in shaping policy.

Skolnick, Jerome. *Justice Without Trial.* New York: Wiley, 1966. Classic study of the way in which police and courts resolve low-visibility criminal cases.

Wilson, James Q. *Thinking About Crime.* New York: Basic Books, 1975. Makes a persuasive, realistic, conservative case for ways of controlling crime.

Wilson, William J. *The Truly Disadvantaged: The Inner City, the Underclass, and Public Policy.* Chicago: University of Chicago Press, 1987. Places urban crime in the context of economic deprivation and social dislocation.

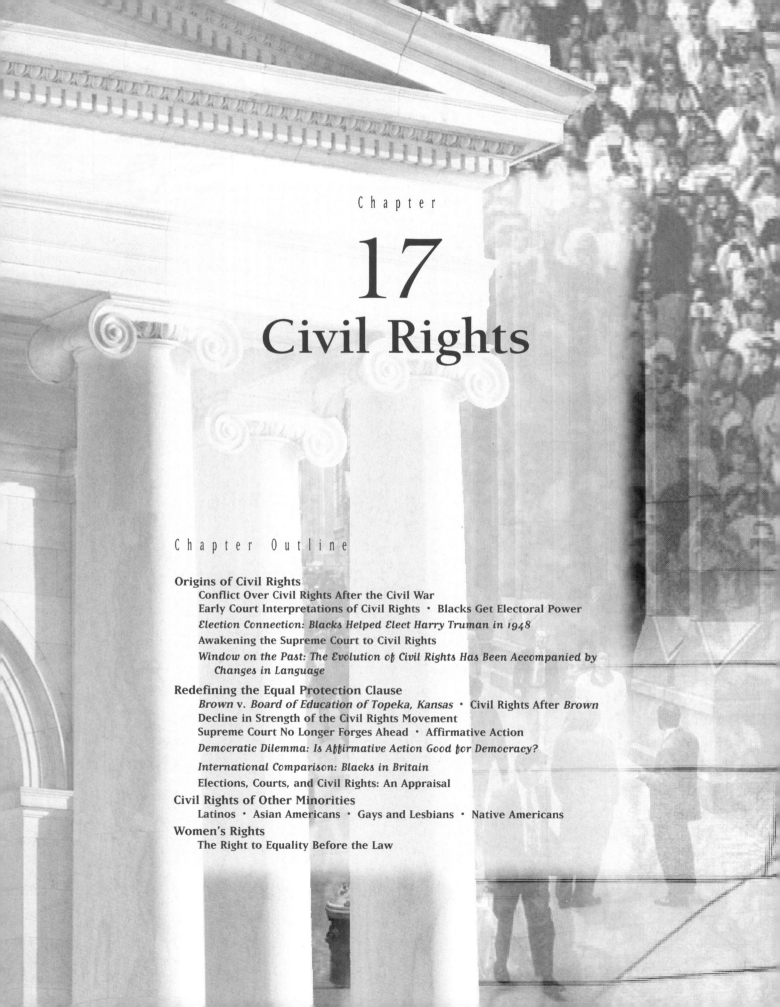

Chapter

# 17
# Civil Rights

The scene reminded observers of the protests of the 1960s. On a cool Wednesday night in November 1996, hundreds of University of California-Berkeley students gathered for an angry rally in the center of campus. Sixty then marched to the University's Campanile clock tower and occupied the structure, some chaining themselves to its stone walls. Meanwhile, 300 UC-Santa Cruz students surrounded their student services building, forcing the closure of the registrar's office. The next day, a group of San Francisco State students blocked traffic on a crowded city street. Less than a week later, UC-Riverside protesters stormed the administration building, shackled the doors shut from the inside, and presented a list of demands to the chancellor.[1]

What prompted the wave of protests was not a war or even an autocratic university decision, but a popular vote. On Tuesday November 5, 1996, the voters of the state of California passed Proposition 209, an amendment to the state constitution that banned giving preferential treatment to "any individual or group on the basis of race, sex, color, ethnicity or national origin in the operation of public employment, public education, or public contracting."[2] Though it might have seemed uncontroversial at first glance, this measure was meant to dismantle a series of California programs that took race into consideration in policy making. It codified a recent decision by the University of California's Board of Regents to end all consideration of race as a factor in its admissions decisions.

Many minority college students feared that because of the vote, the educational opportunities they had been granted would not be available for future generations. "I've made it through UC, but I have little brothers and sisters that could be denied access," said one protester.[3] But supporters of the proposition argued that giving preferential treatment to members of minority groups was insulting and counterproductive. Ward Connerly, an African American member of the UC Board of Regents, backed the constitutional amendment and the change in University of California policy. "For decades we have relied on government to secure our rights . . . but the time has indeed come to let go. We cannot forever look through the rearview mirror at America's mistakes."[4]

The University of California's decision to alter its admissions policies took effect in 1997. The University said that instead of considering race in the admissions process, it would make efforts to recruit more minority applicants, increasing the size and quality of the admissions pool. Results have been mixed. In early 2000, University officials trumpeted statistics that showed the number of minority applicants had increased since the policy change, and in 2000 "underrepresented groups" made up 17.6 percent of the incoming UC class, just short of the 18.8 percent before the change. However, critics complained that these satisfactory figures masked a more troubling trend, in which minority students were much less likely to attend the UC's most elite campuses.[5] It is still too soon to judge what lasting impact the new admissions system will have on California's university system.

THE DEBATE OVER PROPOSITION 209 RAISES BROADER QUESTIONS. What does it mean to say the Constitution is colorblind? When may people be legally classified by race, ethnicity, or gender? Do the courts define the issues, and then elected officials follow? Or is it the other way around? In this chapter we shall discuss the struggle for civil rights for African Americans, other minority groups, women, and the disabled. In most cases we shall find that in characterizing the legal meaning of civil rights, the Supreme Court followed trends initiated by the public debates and coalition building that make up electoral politics. As Justice Ruth Bader Ginsburg once observed, "With prestige to persuade, but not physical power to enforce, and with a will for self-preservation, the Court generally follows, it does not lead, changes taking place elsewhere in society."[6] Nonetheless, the Court has played a major role by codifying civil rights policy into constitutional doctrine. We explore these issues by answering the following questions:

- How did African Americans' struggle for civil rights begin, and how did the Supreme Court become involved?

- How has the Supreme Court's interpretation of the Fourteenth Amendment's equal protection clause shaped the development of civil rights?

- What steps have other groups, such as women and other minorities, taken to ensure their civil rights, and how have the courts and elected officials responded?

## *Origins of Civil Rights*

CONSTITUTION, FOURTEENTH AMENDMENT: *"No state shall . . . deny to any person within its jurisdiction the equal protection of the laws."*

Although the terms *civil rights* and *civil liberties* are often used interchangeably, there is an important distinction between them. Civil liberties are the fundamental freedoms that together preserve the rights of a free people (see page 474). **Civil rights** embody the right to equal treatment under the law. In Chapter 16 we emphasized how important the due process clause of the Fourteenth Amendment has been to the protection of civil liberties in the United States. The civil rights of Americans are guarded by a no less important provision in the Fourteenth Amendment, the **equal protection clause,** which says that no state can deny any of its people equal protection under the law.

Because most people have personal experience with the relationships among races, genders, and ethnic groups, differing interpretations of the meaning of the equal protection clause have generated intense political controversy.[7] Many members of minority groups rely on this constitutional guarantee as a primary protection of their right to equal opportunity. But the meaning of civil rights for disadvantaged groups is shaped as much by majority opinion as by minority demands, because elected leaders, though often sensitive to the rights of minorities, never forget they are elected by majorities.

Because minorities, by definition, cannot by themselves control the outcome of elections, they have often pursued a legal strategy, bringing apparent violations of civil rights to the attention of the courts. But legal strategies do not always work. Judges, too, are concerned about preserving credibility with majorities. If judges defy public opinion regularly, they might undermine confidence in the courts. Also, if judges persist in deviating from the majority view, elected officials will eventually appoint judges willing to reverse direction. As a result, the Supreme Court has not provided steady leadership on civil rights questions. As one legal scholar has noted, "For every case destructive of racial segregation, other cases can be cited with greater force to support the view of judicial power as fundamentally unfriendly to civil rights, unnecessarily illiberal in its judgment, and oppressive in its results."[8]

In this section, we first describe actions taken in the years following the Civil War that affected the civil rights of African Americans, then review the Supreme Court's early rulings on these efforts, and finally examine the changes in political power that led up to the Court's major rulings on civil rights in the mid-twentieth century.

**civil rights**
Embody the right to equal treatment under the law.

**equal protection clause**
Fourteenth Amendment clause specifying that no state can deny any of its people equal protection under the law.

timeline
**The Fourteenth Amendment**

## Conflict Over Civil Rights After the Civil War

**black codes**
Restrictive laws that applied to newly freed slaves but not to whites.

At the end of the Civil War, some southern states passed **black codes,** restrictive laws that applied to newly freed slaves but not to whites. "Persons of color . . . must make annual written contracts for their labor," one of the codes said, adding that if blacks ran away from their "masters," they had to forgo a year's wages.[9] Other black codes denied African Americans access to the courts or the right to hold property, except under special circumstances. Northern abolitionists, who thought the fight against slavery had been won, urged Congress to override these black codes. Congress responded by passing the Civil Rights Act of 1866, which gave citizens "of every race and color . . . the same right . . . to full and equal benefit of all laws." Almost the same words were incorporated into the equal protection clause of the Fourteenth Amendment, which won final ratification two years later.

**Reconstruction**
Period after the Civil War when southern states were subject to a federal military presence.

The federal government's civil rights stance was imposed on southern whites during **Reconstruction,** a period after the Civil War when southern states were subject to a federal military presence. During this period, blacks exercised their right to vote, while that right was denied to many whites who had served in the Confederate army. In addition, Congress established a Freedman's Bureau, which was designed to provide blacks with education, immediate food relief, and inexpensive land from former plantations.[10]

Reconstruction was motivated both by moral outrage at racial injustice and by northern postwar bitterness toward the Confederacy. But as the years progressed, moral commitment evaporated and war memories faded. The programs of the Freedman's Bureau ultimately proved to be a disappointment to many blacks and abolitionists. Northerners were thrown on the defensive by charges of fraud, corruption, and mismanagement in the new southern state governments. Though not always justified, complaints were effectively leveled against both black elected officials and new arrivals from the North—derisively called carpetbaggers, after the luggage in which they kept their clothing.

The close election of 1876 brought Reconstruction to an end. Republican presidential candidate Rutherford B. Hayes claimed victory, but the outcome depended on allegedly fraudulent vote counts reported by several southern states. The compromise resolving the dispute gave each side what it most wanted. Republicans were given the presidency, but Democrats won removal of the federal army from the South and control of future southern elections.

With the ending of Reconstruction, whites gradually restored many of the old racial patterns.[11] Although black men were still voting in significant numbers as late as the 1880s, the Ku Klux Klan, a fraternity dedicated to white supremacy, tried to keep them from voting by holding great parades of hooded figures, by burning crosses, and by lynching those they accused of crimes.

**poll tax**
Fee that allowed one to vote.

Their tactics were reinforced by formal restrictions on the right to vote. State legislatures enacted laws requiring voters to pass a literacy test, meet strict residency requirements, and pay a **poll tax,** a fee that allowed one to vote. Although the laws themselves avoided specific mention of African Americans, blacks were in fact the target. As the chair of the suffrage committee in Virginia bluntly admitted, "I expect the [literacy] examination with which the black men will be confronted to be inspired by the same spirit that inspires every man in this convention. I do not expect an impartial administration of this clause."[12] States also enacted what became known as a

**grandfather clause**
Racially restrictive provision of certain southern laws after Reconstruction permitting a man to vote if his father or grandfather could have voted.

**grandfather clause,** a law that exempted men from voting restrictions if their fathers and grandfathers had voted before the Civil War. Of course, only whites benefited from this exemption.

**white primary**
Primary elections, held by the Democratic party after Reconstruction, that excluded nonwhites from participation in many southern states.

The most successful restriction on the right to vote was the **white primary,** elections held by the Democratic party that excluded nonwhites from participation. Republicans were perceived by southerners as the hated instigators of Reconstruction, so Democrats won nearly all southern elections at that time. As a result, the winner of the white primary nearly always won the general election.[13] Because blacks were denied a meaningful vote, only 10 percent of adult African American males were registered to vote in most of the states of the old Confederacy in 1910.[14]

African Americans were also subject to **Jim Crow laws,** state laws that segregated the races from each other. (The name comes from a stereotypical, belittling characterization of African Americans in minstrel shows popular at the time). Jim Crow laws required African Americans to attend segregated schools, sit in separate areas in public trains and buses, eat in different restaurants, and use separate public facilities.

### Early Court Interpretations of Civil Rights

With little public support for civil rights, the Supreme Court of the day took a very restrictive view of the Fourteenth Amendment's equal protection clause. Two Court decisions were of particular significance. In a decision that has been given the ironic title the *Civil Rights Cases* (1883), the Court declared the Civil Rights Act of 1875 unconstitutional.[15] This law, written just before Reconstruction came to an end, had abolished segregation in restaurants, train stations, and other public places. In declaring the law unconstitutional, the Supreme Court developed the **state action doctrine,** the principle that only the actions of state and local governments, not those of private individuals, must conform to the equal protection clause. The Court said that Congress could prevent state and local governments from discriminating against blacks but that it had no constitutional authority to tell private individuals whom to serve in their restaurants, railroads, and hotels. The Court maintained that by attempting to do so, the Civil Rights Act of 1875 unconstitutionally violated the right of businesses to do what they wished with their property.

The second major decision by the courts, ***Plessy v. Ferguson*** (1896), had even more sweeping consequences. It developed the **separate but equal doctrine,** the principle that segregated facilities were constitutional as long as they were equivalent. Homer Plessy had challenged a Louisiana law that required separation of the races in buses, railroad cars, and waiting rooms at train stations. Plessy argued that his inability to use white facilities denied him equal protection before the law. But the Supreme Court majority said the Louisiana statute was constitutional, because the mere fact that the racial groups were being separated did not stamp African Americans with a "badge of inferiority." In a famous dissent, Justice Harlan protested that "Our Constitution is color-blind, and neither knows nor tolerates classes among citizens. In respect of civil rights, all citizens are equal before the law." Laws enforcing segregation, argued Harlan, violated this ideal.[16]

### Blacks Get Electoral Power

Because of the court decisions in the *Civil Rights Cases* and *Plessy* v. *Ferguson,* legally sanctioned segregation remained intact until well into the middle of the twentieth century. Significant gains in dismantling the old system of segregation took place only after African Americans gained electoral clout by moving in large numbers from southern states, where they could not vote, to northern states, where they could. During World War I, industrial northern cities faced a labor shortage, and many African Americans gave up sharecropping in Mississippi and Alabama for factory work in the sweatshops of New York, Chicago, and Detroit. When World War II created another shortage of factory workers, blacks left southern farms for northern big-city tenements in even larger numbers, as Figure 17.1 illustrates.

Northerners were not much more tolerant of blacks than were southerners. Most northern blacks attended segregated schools, ate in segregated restaurants, and shopped in segregated stores. Housing was even more segregated than in the South. But at least African Americans in the North could vote.

Unlike those who governed the South, northern machine politicians who dominated big city politics were not fussy about the color or religion of the voters they organized. Machine politicians had long represented poor, downtrodden immigrants who

**Figure 17.1**

**Percentage of African Americans Living Outside South, By Decade, 1910 to 1999**
*What explains the northern migration of blacks from 1910 to 1970, and their recent return to the South?*

SOURCE: U.S. Bureau of the Census, *Current Population Survey Reports.*

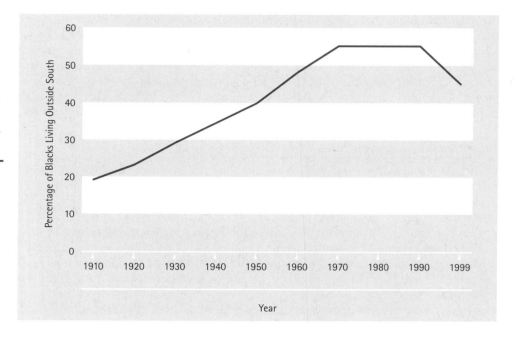

had little material wealth or social prestige. Any warm body who could walk into a voting booth was worth courting for a machine politician. The tough, shrewd political organizer knew that black votes counted as much as the vote of any other resident of the city.[17]

By the 1930s, African Americans used their votes to win a small place in the politics of a few big cities. African American politicians won election to city councils and became neighborhood leaders in party organizations, obtaining jobs and other benefits for their constituents.[18] By 1944 two African Americans, William Dawson of Chicago and Adam Clayton Powell of New York, had been elected to the House of

**Civil Rights Workers**
Tear gas clouds, laid by the Mississippi Highway Patrol, rained confusion on early civil rights marchers in Canton, Mississippi. *Did these marchers or the courts contribute more to the end of formal segregation?*

## Election Connection

## Blacks Helped Elect Harry Truman in 1948

In 1948 African Americans had their first opportunity to shape presidential politics. For many decades, partly because Republican President Abraham Lincoln had issued the Emancipation Proclamation, African Americans had favored Republican party candidates. But during the thirties, the Republican stranglehold on the black vote began to loosen. Franklin Roosevelt's programs for the poor had induced many black voters to switch to the Democratic party. By 1948 it was no longer clear which party would gain the most black votes.

The 1948 election was hotly contested, and the outcome was decided by just a few thousand votes. Because the African American vote might go to either political party and could prove decisive for the outcome of the election, appeals to the black voter became an explicit part of President Harry Truman's campaign strategy. In the words of his top political analyst, "the northern Negro vote today holds the balance of power in Presidential elections for the simple arithmetical reason that the Negroes not only vote in a block but are geographically concentrated in the pivotal, large and closely contested electoral states such as New York, Illinois, Pennsylvania, Ohio, and Michigan."

Truman himself had never been known as a civil rights enthusiast. On the contrary, he came from the former slave state of Missouri, and his private language was sprinkled with racial slurs. But Truman had exceptional political instincts. The election year had hardly begun before Truman delivered the strongest civil rights message any president had ever presented. He called for the abolition of poll taxes, more effective protection of black voting rights, the creation of a Fair Employment Practices Commission with authority to stop racial discrimination, and an end to racial segregation within the armed forces.

Some have claimed that Truman's civil rights strategy was responsible for his reelection. The two-thirds support he received from African Americans helped him carry the "large, pivotal" states of Ohio by 7000 votes, Illinois by 33,000 and California by 17,000. Had he lost these states, his Republican opponent, Thomas Dewey, would have been elected. Although no single factor determines the outcome of any presidential election, African Americans had become a significant force in national politics for the first time since 1876. Significantly, it was in that same year the NAACP began to win key Supreme Court decisions.

Although in 1948 the African American vote was in question, in more recent elections, Democrats have received overwhelming majorities of the black vote. *Does this allow Democrats to take African Americans for granted? Do you think key groups must be willing to vote for either party if they are to exert electoral influence? What are some other ways of exerting electoral influence, besides threatening to vote for the other party?*

SOURCES: David McCullough, *Truman* (New York: Simon & Schuster, 1992), pp. 586–590; Patricia Gurin, Shirley Hatchett, and James S. Jackson, *Hope and Independence: Blacks' Response to Electoral and Party Politics* (New York: Russell Sage, 1989), pp. 36–38.

---

Representatives. But the biggest political breakthrough for African Americans occurred in 1948, when many gave them credit for casting the decisive votes electing Harry Truman president (see the accompanying Election Connection). This growing electoral clout, and the increasing rhetorical support President Truman gave to the cause of civil rights, lent added force to civil rights lawsuits that activists began to bring before the Supreme Court.

## Awakening the Supreme Court to Civil Rights

The legal case against segregation was gradually developed by the **National Association for the Advancement of Colored People (NAACP)**, a civil rights organization that relied heavily on a legal strategy to pursue its objectives. Formed in 1909, the NAACP bears a name that strikes readers today as odd but is rooted in the historical moment when it was established (see the accompanying Window on the Past). The NAACP chose the courtroom strategy because its leaders thought the electoral strength of African Americans was too small to effect dramatic change.

But a legal strategy carried out without the support of black votes was not very effective. Despite the care with which cases were prepared by the NAACP's lead attorney, Thurgood Marshall (who later became the first black Supreme Court justice), the organization initially had but few successes in the courtroom. It could get neither the poll tax nor education requirements outlawed. The Court did strike down one version of the white primary in 1927,[19] but it did so in such a convoluted way that its decision had no practical consequence. For all of the legal efforts of the NAACP, only 12 percent of the southern black adult population was registered to vote in 1947.[20]

> **National Association for the Advancement of Colored People (NAACP)**
> Civil rights organization, dating from 1909, that relied heavily on a legal strategy to pursue its objectives.

**The Evolution of Civil Rights Has Been Accompanied by Changes in Language**

The well-known newspaper columnist Miss Manners tells us that it is respectful to refer to people by the name they wish to be called. This can readily be done for individuals, but when members of a group cannot themselves agree by what name they wish to be called, selecting a respectful reference is more difficult.

In the case of the descendants of immigrants to the United States from Africa, the name deemed respectful has evolved over the years. At the turn of the century, many preferred *colored people,* so the National Association for the Advancement of Colored People took a name that now seems unusual. When *colored people* came to be used by some whites in an abusive way, *Negro* became the respectful reference; hence Martin Luther King, Jr., referred to the *Negro* in his "I Have a Dream" oration. But at the very moment King was speaking, *Negro* was beginning to be regarded as a deprecatory reference, and the simpler word *black* was frequently substituted. Thus King, in the same "Dream" speech, also

refers to blacks. Significantly, he uses *Negro* when referring to the past, *black* when speaking of his dream about the future:

> Five score years ago, a great American, in whose symbolic shadow we stand, signed the Emancipation Proclamation. This momentous decree came as a great beacon light of hope to millions of Negro slaves. . . . But . . . we must face the tragic fact that the Negro is still not free. . . .

> I have a dream that . . . little black boys and black girls will be able to join hands with little white boys and white girls as brothers and sisters.

Recently, *African American* has become the identification preferred by many; it places more emphasis on national origin than skin color. Because the preferred designation may be changing, we are following the lead of Martin Luther King by using both the established referent, *black,* and the referent *African American* that may be replacing it.

Later, as blacks moved north and became politically effective in that part of the country, the NAACP's legal strategy became more potent. In an important 1944 case, *Smith* v. *Allwright,* the Court outlawed the white primary, saying parties were not private organizations but integral parts of a state electoral system.[21] After this decision, black voting in the South gradually began to increase.

In 1948, the very year blacks helped elect Harry Truman, the Court outlawed **restrictive housing covenants,** legal promises by those buying houses that they would not resell to an African American. Under the state action doctrine enunciated by the court in the *Civil Rights Cases,* the contract seemed a private matter, not subject to constitutional scrutiny. But in its 1948 ruling in *Shelly* v. *Kramer,* the Court held that although the contracts themselves were indeed private, any state *enforcement* of such covenants was a public act that violated the equal protection clause.[22] By making this decision, the Court greatly narrowed the range of activities in which segregation could be legally practiced, laying the groundwork for a redefinition of the equal protection clause.

**restrictive housing covenant**

Legal promise by home buyers that they would not resell to an African American; enforcement declared unconstitutional by Supreme Court.

### Section Summary

The civil rights of Americans are protected by the equal protection clause of the Fourteenth Amendment, which says that states cannot deny people equal protection of the laws. Though the Fourteenth Amendment was added to the Constitution in the aftermath of the Civil War, its meaning and strength have evolved over more than a century of lawmaking and court decisions. After Reconstruction, many southern states acted to restrict the legal rights of

African Americans through such means as poll taxes, grandfather clauses, the white prima-ry, and Jim Crow laws, which segregated people by race. In *Plessy* v. *Ferguson*, the Supreme Court ruled that Jim Crow laws were constitutional, as long as the separate facilities for blacks were equivalent to white facilities. As African Americans gained political strength in the aftermath of World War II and Harry Truman's election to the presidency, the attitude of the Court began to change. The NAACP pressed the Court to expand civil rights in a number of key cases.

**Linda Brown**
Linda Brown, in whose case the Supreme Court declared racial segrega-tion in schools unconstitutional, stands in front of the school that refused to admit her. *What compromises were made within the Supreme Court to obtain a unanimous decision in* Brown?

## Redefining the Equal Protection Clause

Though Harry Truman's election and the Court's decisions in *Smith* v. *Allwright* and *Shelly* v. *Kramer* offered some hope, the legal rights of African Americans in the United States had changed little from the 1890s to the 1940s. Most blacks lived in segregat-ed neighborhoods, many could not vote, and violence and intimidation directed against blacks continued.

From the mid-1950s to the early 1970s, the status of African Americans changed dramatically, however, through both legal victories and popular mobilization. By no means were all problems solved in this period, but blacks made great advances in redefining and strengthening the constitutional guarantee of "equal protection of the laws." In this section, we review the history of the civil rights movement that began in the 1950s, consider the debate over affirmative action, and assess the current state of civil rights for African Americans.

### Brown v. Board of Education of Topeka, Kansas

Civil rights groups tried hard to reverse the separate but equal doctrine set forth in *Plessy* v. *Ferguson*, but for decades the Supreme Court resisted. In one extraordinary case, the Court admitted that educational facilities for blacks and whites were unequal, because whites were allowed to keep their high school in operation after a nearby black high school had been shut down.[23] Yet the Court allowed the white school to continue to operate, saying that blacks would gain little from a decision to shut down a white school, and ignoring the possibility that blacks and whites might share the same facility.

The NAACP seemed more successful in 1938 when it won a suit on behalf of a black law student denied access to Missouri's all-white law school.[24] Missouri had no black law school but offered to pay students' tuition to attend a law school in an adja-cent state. When the Court ruled that this policy was unconstitutional, Missouri and other southern states responded by creating all-black law schools of inferior quality, leaving blacks worse off than they were before the decision.

After blacks demonstrated their electoral influence in the 1948 presidential elec-tion, the NAACP proved more effective in the courtroom, as the Supreme Court began to reconsider the separate but equal doctrine enunciated in *Plessy*. First, in 1950, the Court declared that an all-black law school was inherently unconstitutional because it could not be an effective "proving ground for legal learning and practice."[25] By focus-ing on law schools, the NAACP had shrewdly aimed at the weakest point in the sep-arate but equal doctrine. Most Supreme Court justices were attorneys, and they knew from personal experience the importance of a law school's reputation for one's subse-quent career.

Once the law school decision provided an opening wedge, the NAACP attacked the separate but equal doctrine directly by encouraging Oliver Brown to file suit say-ing his daughter, Linda, was being denied equal protection by Topeka, Kansas, by being forced to attend an all-black school. The fact that the black schools in Topeka seemed to be just as good as the white schools was irrelevant, argued the NAACP. This suit led to the Supreme Court's ***Brown v. Board of Education of Topeka, Kansas*** deci-sion in 1954 that finally declared racial segregation unconstitutional.[26]

*Brown* v. *Board of Education of Topeka, Kansas*
1954 Supreme Court decision declar-ing racial segregation in schools unconstitutional.

Chief Justice Earl Warren, a former California governor, was keenly aware of the political significance of the Brown decision, so he asked the justices to delay it for a year, using the extra time to try to get a unanimous vote. At first it seemed that Warren would fail in this effort, because two members of the Court thought a decision to reverse *Plessy* v. *Ferguson* would violate the principle of *stare decisis*, a rule that says courts should adhere to the doctrines set forth in prior decisions (see Chapter 15, page 461). But Warren argued that the *Brown* decision could be distinguished from the *Plessy* decision, because the *Plessy* case had involved buses and trains, not schools.

To distinguish segregation in school from segregation in train stations, Warren cited psychological studies provided by the NAACP to show that racial separation created a sense of inferiority among black children. One study showed, for example, that black children favored white dolls over black ones.[27] Focusing on the particularly harmful effects of segregation on children allowed Warren to limit his opinion to schools, thereby avoiding a direct repeal of *Plessy*. By so limiting the effect of the decision, Warren was able to obtain a unanimous vote from the justices, but in pursuing a legal doctrine Warren might have done better to have followed Harlan's dissent in *Plessy* that simply said, "the Constitution is color-blind." Since the *Brown* decision, many have argued that the constitutionality of racial segregation should depend not on its psychological effects, which may vary from person to person, but on whether racial criteria are valid grounds for classifying individuals.

Years later, the Supreme Court did provide this very rationale for its finding that segregation was unconstitutional. In 1973 it said that any legal distinction based on race or on membership in any other ethnic group that had been discriminated against in the past was a **suspect classification,** which required strict scrutiny by the courts to make sure that its use did not violate the Fourteenth Amendment's equal protection clause. This concept, which is now the standard tool with which the courts adjudicate civil rights cases, soon became crucial for ensuring that racial and ethnic minorities received equal protection before the law.[28]

> **suspect classification**
> Categorization of a particular group that will be closely scrutinized by the courts to see whether its use is unconstitutional.

In 1954, however, Chief Justice Warren realized he could not get a unanimous Court to back such a sweeping statement outlawing all forms of segregation, and so in *Brown*, he settled for less by focusing on segregation's psychological effects on young children. Also to preserve court unanimity, Warren postponed consideration of the exact way in which school boards were to rectify their segregated practices. The following year, the Court handed down a separate ruling on this issue, calling for school desegregation "with all deliberate speed," a phrase that appeared to have contradictory meanings. *Deliberate* implied a slow, methodical pace, whereas *speed* suggested a need for prompt compliance. Most southern school boards focused on deliberation, enacting as little desegregation as possible.

In spite of its defects, scholars believe *Brown* to be among the most important decisions the Supreme Court has ever made.[29] In this decision, the Supreme Court declared unconstitutional a system of racial segregation that from the earliest colonial settlements had organized social life in a large part of the United States. Within two years, the border states of Maryland, Kentucky, and Missouri, as well as Kansas and the District of Columbia, eliminated formal segregation in their schools.

## Civil Rights After Brown

*Brown* also energized civil rights activists around the country. The impact on young people and church leaders was particularly noticeable. Immediately after the decision, three new civil rights organizations, the Congress of Racial Equality (CORE), the Student Nonviolent Coordinating Committee (SNCC), and the Southern Christian Leadership Conference (SLCL), rose to prominence. Consisting mainly of college students and ministers, the groups held demonstrations, led boycotts, undertook voter registration drives, and appealed to the federal government for intervention into southern racial practices.[30]

One year after *Brown*, a more militant phase of the civil rights movement erupted. Rosa Parks, of Montgomery, Alabama, engaged in an extraordinarily successful act of **civil disobedience**—a peaceful, well-publicized violation of a law designed to dramatize that law's injustice. Her arrest for refusing to vacate her seat in the white section of a segregated bus prompted a bus boycott led by a young Baptist minister, Martin Luther King, Jr., who had just earned his Ph.D. in theology. He was only 27 years old at the time, but he had the resourcefulness and rhetorical capacity necessary to give the event national significance.[31] Using boycotts, protests, and acts of civil disobedience, the southern civil rights movement gained strength by winning sympathetic coverage in the northern press.[32]

The civil rights movement met intense opposition from southern government officials. In March 1956, nearly every southern member of Congress signed the Southern Manifesto, committing each official to resist the implementation of the *Brown* decision by "all lawful means."[33] Southern resistance to court-ordered integration was so consistent and complete that, in the states of the Old Confederacy, hardly any school desegregation actually occurred. When school began in the fall of 1964, ten years after the *Brown* decision, only 2.3 percent of black students in the states of the Old Confederacy attended integrated schools.[34]

Yet the protests and demonstrations gradually had their effect. For one thing, southern African Americans were registering to vote. The percentage registered more than doubled from 12 percent in 1947 to 28 percent in 1960. At the same time, African Americans were becoming a more powerful political force in the large industrial states of the North. With civil rights demonstrators focusing national attention on racial issues, presidential candidates had to balance southern resistance against the need to get black votes in big northern states.

John Kennedy's victory over Richard Nixon in the breathtakingly close election of 1960 owed much to his success in attracting the black vote. When the 1960 election campaign began, Kennedy realized that he needed to improve his civil rights credentials, especially because he had won the Democratic nomination by defeating two candidates with stronger civil rights records: Hubert Humphrey and Adlai Stevenson. To strengthen his support in the black community, Kennedy placed a well-publicized phone call to Coretta Scott King expressing sympathy for the plight of her husband, Martin Luther King, who had been jailed in Birmingham after participating in a student sit-in. That phone call took on great symbolic significance and helped mobilize Kennedy's supporters in the black community. He captured enough black votes to win such crucial states as Ohio, Michigan, and Illinois.

Once in office, Kennedy introduced civil rights legislation, which received vigorous support from civil rights demonstrators. In the largest of these demonstrations, 100,000 black and white demonstrators marched on the Washington Mall in the summer of 1963, calling for congressional passage of the proposed legislation and other reforms. From the steps of the Lincoln Memorial, King delivered his powerful and moving "I Have a Dream" oration. Suddenly, a plurality of Americans viewed civil rights as the country's most important problem.[35] Just a few months later, Kennedy's assassination generated an unprecedented outpouring of moral commitment to racial justice (see Figure 17.2).

Elected political leaders responded quickly to this transformation in the public mood. The new president, Lyndon Johnson, though himself a southerner, called upon Congress to memorialize the dead president by enacting his civil rights legislation, which had been stalled in the Senate since the previous summer. After intense debate, majorities of both Republican and Democratic members of Congress voted in favor of the Civil Rights Act of 1964, the most sweeping civil rights legislation passed since Reconstruction. This act banned segregation in all places of public accommodation, prohibited federal money from being used to support segregated programs, and created the Equal Employment Opportunity Commission (EEOC) to guard against employment discrimination. The legislation brought about major changes in race

**civil disobedience**
A peaceful, well-publicized violation of a law designed to dramatize that law's injustice.

Rosa Parks

## Figure 17.2

**Evaluation of Civil Rights as the Country's Most Important Problem**
Many people saw civil rights as an important problem in the wake of the Kennedy assassination and civil rights demonstrations. Today (not shown) only around 3 percent view race relations as the most important problem. *Does this reflect real progress, or a lack of attention to current problems?*

SOURCE: Gerald Jaynes and Robin M. Williams, Jr., eds, *A Common Destiny: Blacks and American Society* (Washington, DC: National Academy Press, 1989), p. 224.

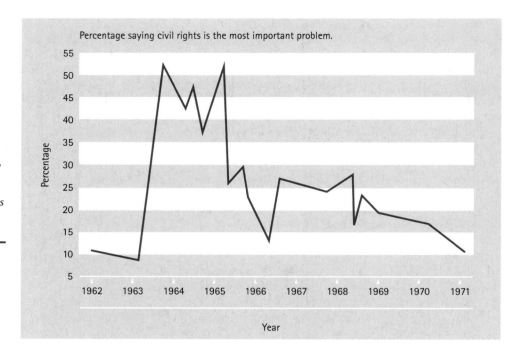

relations throughout the South. Enticed by new federal funds facilitating desegregation, and intimidated by the new enforcement powers of federal officials, many southern schools desegregated. The percentage of black students in southern schools that included whites increased dramatically from 2.3 percent in 1964 to 91.3 percent in 1972.

Buoyed by economic prosperity and his civil rights achievements, Lyndon Johnson won a sweeping election victory in the fall of 1964. Not one to rest on his accomplishments, Johnson soon engineered congressional passage of the Voting Rights Act of 1965, which guaranteed black voting rights by stationing federal exam-

## Figure 17.3

**Changes in Black and White Participation in Presidential Elections, by Region**
*Why do you think blacks still vote at lower rates than whites? Why do southern and northern blacks now vote at similar rates?*

SOURCE: U.S. Bureau of the Census, *Current Population Survey Reports*. (*South* is defined as the states that formed the Confederacy.)

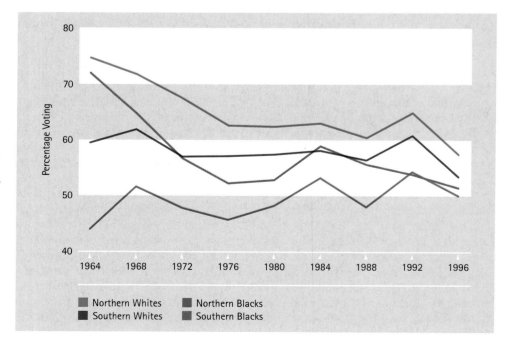

**I Have a Dream**
Martin Luther King, Jr., delivers his "I Have a Dream" speech at the March on Washington in August 1963. *Why did the civil rights movement lose support just a few years later?*

iners in southern registration halls and polling places.[36] As a result, the percentage of voters among southern black adults jumped upward after 1964, as shown in Figure 17.3.[37] By 1992 southern blacks were as likely to vote as northern blacks, though their voting rate still lagged behind whites. Nonetheless, the number of elected officials of African American descent rose from less than 500 in 1965 to over 8800 in 1998.[38]

## Decline in Strength of the Civil Rights Movement

Segregation and discrimination were not limited to the South. Most northern blacks lived in racially isolated neighborhoods, sent their children to predominantly black schools, and found it hard to get good jobs. Even as Congress was passing the Voting Rights Act of 1965, Martin Luther King shifted the focus of the civil rights movement by mounting a series of civil rights demonstrations in Chicago.[39] This decision changed the way the public viewed the civil rights movement. As school busing and job discrimination became a northern issue as well, support for civil rights protests among many northern whites dwindled.[40] At the same time, new black leaders, such as black nationalist Malcolm X, took a more militant position, affirming black culture and denying the value of integration. Civil violence began to break out in black neighborhoods, beginning in Los Angeles in 1964 and spreading to other cities over the next three years. When Martin Luther King was assassinated by a white man in Memphis, Tennessee, in the spring of 1968, violent racial disturbances broke out simultaneously in dozens of cities throughout the country. National guard and army units were called upon to quell wholesale theft and property destruction.

After these events, the white majority began to view the problem of civil rights as less important, as Figure 17.2 indicates. As long as civil rights issues were being addressed by nonviolent demonstrations in the South, African Americans appealed successfully to the moral instincts of northern whites. But once whites realized that the problem was national in scope, and that civil disobedience could turn violent, many had second thoughts. Opposition to busing, affirmative action, and other programs of racial integration split the biracial political coalition that had elected Harry Truman and John Kennedy.

Figure 17.4

**Percentage of Delegates to Republican and Democratic National Conventions Who Are African American**
*Why has African American participation in Democratic party politics risen dramatically?*

SOURCES: "The Democratic Delegates," *San Francisco Examiner,* August 27, 1996, A9; Robert Zauser, "Small Number of Black Delegates Illustrates Problem for Republicans," *Philadelphia Inquirer,* August 16, 1996, A22.

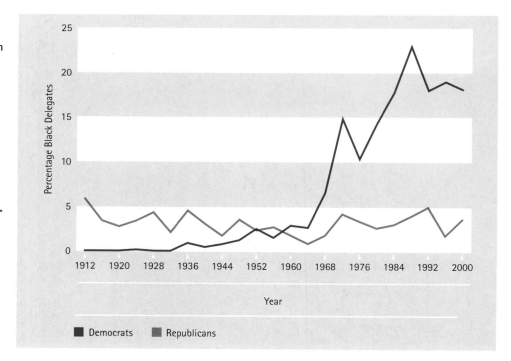

Race issues now began to divide the two political parties further. When Senator Barry Goldwater voted against the Civil Rights Act of 1964, he was among a minority of Republicans to do so. But by 1968, Republicans were pursuing what was known as a "southern strategy," an appeal to all those who thought the civil rights movement had gone too far. Meanwhile, blacks solidified their allegiance to the Democratic party.[41] The percentage of delegates attending the Democratic convention who were black grew from 6.7 to 14.6 percent between 1968 and 1972 (see Figure 17.4).

### Supreme Court No Longer Forges Ahead

Encountering increasing popular resistance to further legislative initiatives, civil rights groups once again turned to the courts for assistance. African American leaders hoped the Supreme Court would remain a bulwark against this shift in public opinion. But the courts, following the direction in which public opinion was moving, also adopted a more conservative attitude. For example, the Supreme Court drew a distinction between two types of segregation. **De jure segregation,** the legal separation of the races practiced in the South, was said by the Court to violate the equal protection clause of the Constitution. But segregation in the North was said to be **de facto segregation,** occurring as the result of private decisions made by individuals—such as their choice of residence.

In *Milliken v. Bradley* (1974), the Supreme Court considered the constitutionality of the most pervasive form of *de facto* segregation.[42] Bradley argued that the State of Michigan (under governor William Milliken) tolerated racial segregation by allowing virtually all-white suburban school districts to surround the City of Detroit, whose schools were predominantly black. In rejecting Bradley's argument that the whole metropolitan area ought to be desegregated, the Court ruled that suburban school districts in the North had never practiced *de jure* racial segregation. The segregation that had occurred was *de facto,* simply the result of private decisions to live in Detroit or its suburbs.

Writing for the majority, Warren Burger, who had replaced Earl Warren as chief justice, said that the lower courts, in siding with Bradley, were trying to produce "the

---

*de jure* **segregation**
Racial segregation that is legally sanctioned.

*de facto* **segregation**
Segregation that occurs as the result of decisions by private individuals.

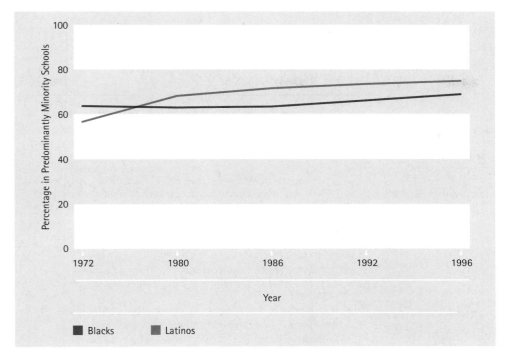

**Figure 17.5**

**Percentage of African American and Latino Students in Segregated Schools, 1972–1996**
*In your opinion why has segregation increased in the 1980s and 1990s?*

SOURCE: Gary Orfield and John T. Yun, *Resegregation in American Schools* (Cambridge, MA: The Civil Rights Project, Harvard University, 1999), Table 9.

racial balance which they perceived as desirable." But the Constitution only forbids segregation; it "does not require any particular racial balance." Dissenting from the decision, Justice Thurgood Marshall, the former NAACP attorney, responded, "Negro students will continue to perceive their schools as segregated educational facilities and this perception will only be increased when whites flee . . . to the suburbs to avoid integration." After the *Milliken* decision, little additional school desegregation took place in either the North or the South. In recent years, school segregation among African Americans and Latinos has actually increased, as Figure 17.5 illustrates.

## Affirmative Action

Civil rights groups also called upon government agencies, universities, and businesses to rectify past discrimination by taking affirmative steps to provide increased educational and job opportunities for African Americans. In response to these demands, many organizations have instituted policies of **affirmative action,** programs designed to enhance opportunities for race- or gender-based groups that have suffered discrimination in the past. Affirmative action programs vary in their size and significance. In some cases, these programs may consist of nothing more than special advertising, recruitment, and counseling initiatives designed to help members of disadvantaged groups learn about available opportunities. In other cases, universities and employers may also take note of a person's membership in a disadvantaged group as one factor among many to be considered in admissions or hiring decisions. The strongest form of affirmative action involves setting aside a **quota,** or a specific number of positions, for members of disadvantaged groups (see the accompanying Democratic Dilemma).

The constitutionality of affirmative action programs was considered by the Supreme Court in 1978 in a case that involved Allen Bakke, a Norwegian American, who sued for admission to the medical school of the University of California at Davis.[43] Out of an entering class of 100, Davis reserved 16 spots for minority students, leaving the remaining 84 for general applications. Two years in a row, Bakke fell just short of being admitted. He went to court, arguing that by prohibiting him from

**affirmative action**
Programs designed to enhance opportunities for groups that have suffered discrimination in the past.

**quota**
Specific number of positions set aside for a specific group; said by the Supreme Court to be unconstitutional.

## *Democratic Dilemma*

## Is Affirmative Action Good for Democracy?

Few issues stir more passions in the United States than the issue of affirmative action. In the 1978 *Bakke* case, the Supreme Court took a middle position, arguing that some types of affirmative action were acceptable under the Constitution, whereas others were not. Far from settling the issue, however, the case set the stage for decades of public controversy.

An opponent of affirmative action might argue as follows:

The Constitution is colorblind and gender-neutral. When race or gender is used as a criterion for allocating educational and job opportunities, this confers advantages on some individuals at the expense of others. Those who are helped are regarded with suspicion, because they are thought to have received their opportunity for reasons other than their individual merit. As a result, affirmative action perpetuates group antagonisms as well as feelings of group superiority and inferiority. In the end, ethnic and gender classification is self-defeating. If it is difficult to fire people because they are members of a particular group, they will not be hired in the first place.

A proponent of affirmative action, on the other hand, might argue as follows:

The Constitution has historically been neither colorblind nor gender-neutral: It permitted the slave trade and counted slaves as only three-fifths of a person. It permitted denial of the vote to women. Racism and sexism permeate institutions and practices so thoroughly that the only way discrimination can be alleviated is through race- and gender-conscious policies designed to reverse the unfair practices of the past. The equal protection clause of the Fourteenth Amendment does not preclude classification by race. The clause requires only that race classifications not harm those groups against whom discrimination has historically been practiced.

*What do you think?*

- *Is affirmative action a necessary remedy for past discrimination, or does it simply reinforce harmful race and gender distinctions?*
- *If you take a middle view, as the Supreme Court did in* Bakke, *exactly what kinds of classifications are acceptable?*
- *Is a university admissions policy that sets lower SAT-score standards for minorities all right?*
- *Is it constitutional for a law to require governments to hire minority-owned contractors to work on municipal improvement projects?*

competing for the 16 minority slots, the university had denied him equal protection of the law.

The Supreme Court's decision in *Regents of the University of California* v. *Bakke* was unusually complex. Four justices rejected Bakke's claim to admission, arguing that the Constitution allowed quotas when they were needed to remedy "past societal discrimination." Four other justices believed that Bakke ought to be admitted to Davis and said that any and all forms of affirmative action were illegal, violating either the equal protection clause or the Civil Rights Act of 1964. This left the Court in a 4-4 tie and created the opportunity for Justice Lewis Powell, the ninth justice, to write a "majority" opinion that struck a compromise between the two extremes.

Powell believed that some kinds of affirmative action programs were justified if the goal was, for example, to create "diversity" that would be beneficial to all. A college or university has a justifiable interest in having a diverse group of students, Powell wrote, and decisions encouraging such diversity were constitutional. For this reason, race sometimes may play a role in university admissions decisions. But on the other hand, he argued, Davis's system of quotas violated the equal protection clause. Powell's judgment, and therefore the Court's, was that the University of California-Davis admissions system was unconstitutional and that Bakke should be admitted to medical school.

Though Powell was the only justice to agree fully with his "majority" opinion, it has remained the guiding Court doctrine, in large part because it took a middle position that seemed to have broad public support. A majority of Americans have supported programs designed to encourage diversity but have opposed specific quotas.

During the 1990s, all forms of affirmative action came under increasing criticism. In 1995 the University of California Board of Regents voted to end the use of race as a factor in its admissions policies, a decision that took on broader significance when the state later passed Proposition 209, banning affirmative action (see the opening to

**Allen Bakke**

Allen Bakke was admitted to medical school following the Supreme Court decision in his favor and is now a doctor. *Do you believe it is appropriate to consider race in university admissions?*

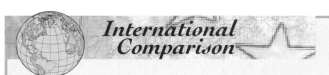

## International Comparison

## Blacks in Britain

Racism might seem like a uniquely American problem. But other countries have also had to consider how to combat it and how to guarantee the civil rights of ethnic and racial minorities. British sociologist Stephen Small points out several problems that blacks (who make up about 4 percent of the population) face in his country: "One problem is the racialized nature of immigration legislation which has increasingly restricted [blacks'] entry to the country. Another problem is the perception on the part of white English people that black people are somehow 'not English' even if born in England."

Britain's major civil rights legislation is the Race Relations Act of 1976. This act prohibits discrimination by private employers and created a Commission for Racial Equality to enforce the law and increase public awareness of race issues. In the late 1990s, the inadequacy of the act was highlighted by an official inquiry into police misconduct surrounding the 1993 racially motivated murder of an 18-year-old black man, Stephen Lawrence. Though police obtained the names of five suspects within hours of the murder, no arrests were made in the case until spring 2000. The judicial inquiry into the matter blamed its mishandling on "professional incompetence, institutional racism, and failure of leadership."

The implications went beyond any single case. One black clergyman summed up the problem by pointing out that blacks in Britain "have been overpoliced and to a large extent underprotected." Police often fail to take note of the racist nature of some

crimes, recording only 10 percent of actual cases. Blacks are five times more likely than whites to be stopped and searched by police (one black motorist finally decided to sue the London police after being stopped 34 times). They also have greater odds of being charged with crimes, denied bail, injured while in prison, and jailed if found guilty.

The report on the Lawrence case has inspired many proposals for reform. One such proposal has been to extend the Race Relations Act to cover government agencies, rather than just the private sector. Members of Britain's growing Muslim minority have lobbied for laws that ban discrimination on the basis of religion. And the London police force has promised to require more training for its officers and to appoint more blacks to high posts. Just as in the United States, however, there are few quick fixes. As one police officer pointed out in defense of his colleagues, "We have a society that has institutional racism."

*In your opinion, are race relations better or worse in the United States than in other industrial societies?*

SOURCES: Stephen Small, *The Black Experience in the United States and England in the 1980s* (New York: Routledge, 1994), p. 178; Alexander MacLeod, "To Confront Racism, Britain Redefines It," *Christian Science Monitor*, March 1, 1999, 6; "Stephen Lawrence's Legacy," *The Economist*, January 30, 1999: 51; "A Tragedy and a Shame," *The Economist*, February 27, 1999: 53.

---

this chapter). That same year, voters in Washington State passed a similar measure, and two years later, a federal court ordered Texas to eliminate race-based preferences from its state university admissions system. As alternatives to affirmative action, Texas, California, and Florida have all begun programs that require public universities to accept all students who graduated near the top of their high school class.[44] Florida officials said that minority university admissions rose 12 percent since the end of affirmative action.[45]

The views of the two leading presidential candidates in 2000 reflected this growing national ambivalence toward affirmative action. George W. Bush opposed race-based preferences, pointing to Texas's change in policy as a model. Al Gore, while agreeing with President Clinton in supporting some kinds of affirmative action, stressed his opposition to quotas.

### Elections, Courts, and Civil Rights: An Appraisal

Significant problems still beset African Americans in the United States as well as elsewhere (see the accompanying International Comparison). Chief among them is the persistence of poverty in the black community. Despite a booming economy, poverty rates among blacks remain more than triple those of whites.[46] Black unemployment is double the national average.[47] And teen pregnancy and infant mortality rates are far higher among African Americans than among others.[48] Critics argue that though middle- and upper-class blacks have made progress, these successes have not translated into wide-reaching economic gains for all African Americans.

But there is increasing reason for optimism about the status of African Americans in the United States. The victories of the civil rights movement have promoted

comparative

**Comparing Civil Rights**

**Defending "Dixie"**
Symbolizing Southern pride to some and racial hatred to others, South Carolina's practice of flying the Confederate flag over the statehouse became an issue in the 2000 presidential campaign. The flag was later moved elsewhere as part of a compromise.

advancement in almost every sector. The percentage of black men and women in professional and managerial positions increased markedly in the decades following the passage of the Civil Rights Acts.[49] Blacks have also made political gains, winning an increasing number of mayoral elections, state legislative races, and seats in Congress, and they have made noticeable educational advances. The percentage of blacks between the ages of 18 and 24 who have dropped out of high school fell from 27 percent in 1975 to 17 percent in 1997. And between 1980 and 1990, the test scores of black high school seniors improved by 9 percent (compared with negligible gains among whites in the same period), though some of these gains have been lost in the 1990s.[50]

The economic boom of the late 1990s also proved beneficial to blacks. Although it is still high, the poverty rate among African Americans shrank in 1998 to its lowest level since the Bureau of the Census began collecting data in 1959.[51] Unemployment declined as well. It is too early to tell whether these economic gains will endure, but they are encouraging nonetheless.

## Section Summary

The NAACP's litigation strategy bore its most significant fruit with the Supreme Court decision in *Brown* v. *Board of Education of Topeka, Kansas*. This pivotal decision rejected *Plessy* v. *Ferguson's* separate but equal doctrine and paved the way for the Court's strict scrutiny of any law that classified people by race. In the aftermath of *Brown*, activists around the country, including Martin Luther King, Jr., took part in boycotts, voter registration drives, and protests to pressure the government into enacting further civil rights protections. These efforts largely won over the sympathy of the American public and culminated in the Civil Rights Act of 1964 and the Voting Rights Act of 1965.

After 1965 the public began to view civil rights demands less favorably, and the Supreme Court also began to take a more conservative view. The Court drew a distinction between *de jure* and *de facto* segregation, arguing that the Constitution did not require the government to produce the optimal "racial balance" in all circumstances. In *University of California Regents* v. *Bakke*, the Court ruled that race-based quotas were unconstitutional, although college admissions officers and others might legally take race into account if they wanted to increase diversity. In the 1990s, attacks on affirmative action grew more frequent.

The civil rights victories of the mid-twentieth century led to significant political and educational gains among African Americans. Economic problems remain, however, with poverty and unemployment figures for black Americans remaining far above those for whites.

**visual literacy**
**Race and the Death Penalty**

## *Civil Rights of Other Minorities*

Most of the civil rights issues and rulings discussed thus far apply as much to other racial and ethnic groups as they do to African Americans. The civil rights of other ethnic groups nonetheless assume of distinctive legal and political significance under two circumstances: (1) when groups eligible for affirmative action need to be defined, and (2) when language or other group-specific issues arise.

The Supreme Court has never specifically delineated the groups in American society whose treatment over the course of U.S. history makes them eligible for affirmative action. Neither the 1964 nor the 1965 civil rights legislation identified any groups other than blacks as deserving affirmative action to redress historical grievances. But after the civil rights movement defined many issues in terms of equal protection under the Constitution, groups representing other ethnic minorities began to make similar civil rights claims, and Congress, through voting rights legislation, has given them recognition.

The pace of this process and the degree to which each group receives recognition in law has in large part depended on how effectively each group has been able to

**Courting the Latino Vote**
George P. Bush, whose mother is of Mexican descent, campaigned for his uncle, George W. Bush, in the Latino community in 2000. *Why has the importance of the Latino vote lagged behind that of African Americans?*

mobilize its members in elections. Latinos, Asian Americans, and gays and lesbians have recently begun to exert their influence on national electoral politics. But until very recently American Indians remained a small, politically inactive voting bloc.

## Latinos

Latinos have in recent years been numerically the most rapidly growing minority group in the United States. In 1980 they made up only 6.4 percent of the U.S. population, but by the year 2000 they had grown to about 11 percent, approaching in size the 12 percent that are African American.[52] In contrast to African Americans, who have been politically assertive for nearly 50 years, Latinos are only beginning to make a significant political impact. There are several reasons for this difference. A sizable percentage of the Latino population lacks citizenship, and even among Latino citizens, voting rates are much lower than among African Americans, partly because most Latinos have not experienced a prolonged—and unifying—civil rights struggle. Many new Latino immigrants also plan to return to their countries of origin and therefore care more about the politics of the home country than about politics in the United States.[53]

Building a broad-based political coalition is further complicated by the fact that Latinos come from many different countries and differ from one another in important cultural and political respects. For example, Mexican Americans in California and Texas who are concerned about job discrimination and working conditions may have a hard time identifying with Cuban Americans in Florida who are primarily concerned with the restoration of democracy in their home country. Latino voters are also much less likely than African Americans to vote as a bloc. Whereas 85 percent of blacks consider themselves Democrats, only 55 percent of Latinos do.[54]

In recent years, however, Latinos have become increasingly active and influential in politics. One of the earliest groups to draw attention to the civil rights concerns of Latinos was the Mexican American Legal Defense and Education Fund (MALDEF), which has focused on voting, education, and immigration issues (see Chapter 4 for discussion of immigration). In 1974, in response to MALDEF complaints, the Supreme Court interpreted the 1964 Civil Rights Act to mean that schools must provide special educational programs for those not proficient in the English language.[55]

**participation**

**Statehood for Puerto Rico and the District of Columbia?**

MALDEF and other advocacy groups also argued that Latinos and other language minorities were discriminated against because ballots and other voter registration materials were published only in English. Congress responded to these demands in 1982 by requiring that ballots be printed in the language of any protected minority that constitutes more than 5 percent of a county's population, thereby extending protection not only to Latinos but also to Asian Americans and American Indians.[56]

Latinos have also begun to make their influence felt in elections—first in state and local politics, later in national campaigns—although their voter turnout remains low relative to other groups.[57] A key turning point came in 1994 when California voters passed Proposition 187, which would have denied state and local public services to illegal aliens (see the Election Connection in Chapter 4). Though courts blocked the measure before it could be implemented, the bitter campaign over its passage energized the California Latino community. Republican support for the proposition helped California Republican candidates win narrowly in 1994, but in 1996 and 1998, Democrats scored resounding victories there, carrying large majorities of the Latino vote.[58]

Cuban politics took center stage in 1999 when fishermen off the Florida coast rescued six-year-old Elian Gonzalez and brought him to Miami. Gonzalez's mother hoped to defect to the United States with her son, but she perished in an accident at sea. Elian's uncle and other relatives in Miami embraced the boy, and sought to become his legal guardians. But the U.S. Immigration and Naturalization Service (INS) insisted the boy be returned to his father in Cuba, and after a seven-month legal battle, he was.

The political struggle over Elian took many twists and turns. At first it energized Cuban Americans, who believed that the child's predicament would dramatize the struggle against Castro and secure them a stronger place in American politics. When Vice-President Gore broke with the Clinton administration position and appeared to take the side of the Miami relatives, Cuban Americans thought their prayers had been answered.

But the longer the Elian case dominated the media, the more public opinion swung away from the Miami relatives. Most voters felt the boy should live with his natural father, even if meant returning to Cuba. Indeed, some began to wonder why the United States maintained its strict trade embargo on Cuba, especially as it stepped up trade with China, another Communist nation.

The Elian case revealed both the extent to which an ethnic group can mobilize itself for political action and the clear limits to what such a group can achieve once a majority of Americans take another point of view. Sometimes strong political mobilization can backfire.

Still, both presidential candidates courted the Latino vote in 2000. George W. Bush repeatedly repudiated Proposition 187 and cited his more moderate record on immigration in Texas. He also stressed his support for some bilingual education programs and his opposition to English-only mandates. Bush's Hispanic nephew, George P. Bush, made pleas on his uncle's behalf in the Latino community. Both Al Gore and George Bush peppered their speeches with Spanish while campaigning in such key states as California, Florida, and New York.

### Asian Americans

Like Latinos, Asian Americans have only recently begun to make their voices heard in national electoral politics. They constitute only 4 percent of the population, and over 60 percent are foreign born.[59] Like Latinos, they represent many different nationalities and have differing, even conflicting, foreign policy concerns. Asians are also less likely to support affirmative action programs and more likely to vote Republican than other ethnic minorities.[60]

In 1996 activists in the Asian American community flexed their political muscle by mounting a coordinated fund-raising and voter registration drive.[61] That year, Gary

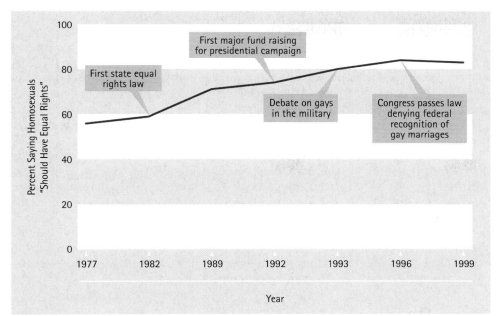

**Figure 17.6**

**Public Opinion on Gay Rights Has Changed as Gay and Lesbian Political Activism Increased**

SOURCE: The Gallup Poll, **www.gallup.com,** accessed April 12, 2000.

Locke of Washington state was elected the first Asian American governor of a state other than Hawaii. But the Clinton campaign's fund-raising scandals, in which several Asians and Asian Americans were involved, caused many to worry about a backlash against the Asian American community, especially after presidential candidate Al Gore was accused of committing perjury when he denied knowing that his visit to a Buddhist temple constituted participation in a fund-raising event. When, at the same time, a Chinese American scientist was jailed—and even placed in isolation—on thin evidence, awaiting trial for alleged spying for the Chinese government, activists voiced public concern about stereotyping of Asian Americans and about a "chilling effect" on Asian American political participation.[62] Eventually, the government dropped all but one less serious charge.

The major civil rights victory for Asian Americans in recent years has been the compensation paid to Japanese Americans for their internment in relocation camps during World War II (see page 481). Because of the diversity of the Asian American community, a unified political agenda for the future has yet to take shape. Some Asian American activists and political organizations are concerned with issues such as immigrant rights and expanding the Supreme Court's definition of a suspect classification to include Asian language speakers.[63] However, other Asian Americans favor the elimination of quotas and affirmative action programs from which they are excluded.

## Gays and Lesbians

Some of the most contentious political debates in the late 1990s surrounded the rights of gays and lesbians. It is no accident that at the same time, homosexuals were more engaged in electoral politics than ever before. Though the first local law protecting against discrimination on the basis of sexual orientation was passed in 1973, and the first such state law in 1982, it has only been since 1992 that the gay and lesbian community has exerted significant influence in national elections.[64] That year, gay and lesbian donors gave an estimated $3.5 million to the Clinton campaign, persuading Clinton to promise, among other things, an end to the ban on gays in the military (see Chapter 13).[65]

Since the early 1990s, according to one estimate, the number of openly gay government officials has tripled.[66] At the same time, the country is undergoing an increasingly vocal debate over the rights that should be accorded gays, a debate that is being fought in election and referendum campaigns.

In the last decade the American public grew to believe that equal job opportunities ought to be accorded gays, as Figure 17.6 shows. Laws barring employment discrimination on the basis of sexual orientation have been passed in 11 states and have bipartisan support in Congress.[67] In 2000 Vermont became the first state to legally recognize same-sex civil unions.

But public opinion remains conservative on other issues regarding homosexuality. Large majorities disapprove of gay marriages and have serious reservations when asked whether gays should be allowed to serve as teachers or youth leaders. Thirty-two states have passed laws banning same-sex marriages. In Hawaii, where a state court decision in 1993 legalized same-sex unions, voters overwhelmingly passed a constitutional amendment in 1998 that outlawed them again. And in 2000 the Supreme Court ruled that the Boy Scouts could legally dismiss a gay scout leader on the grounds that homosexuality was "inconsistent" with the organization's values.[68]

### Native Americans

The rights and liberties of descendants of indigenous tribes are not protected by the Bill of Rights, because, at the time of the writing of the Constitution, these people were considered members of a foreign nation. As one authority on Indian rights has put it, "No constitutional protections exist for Indians in either a tribal or an individual sense."[69]

The relations between Native Americans and the government are instead governed by laws of Congress and by the many treaties that have been signed by the United States and American Indian tribes. Over the long course of American history the United States government, under political pressure from those migrating westward, ignored or broke many of the treaties it made with indigenous tribes. Still, the Supreme Court today interprets some of these treaties as binding.[70] As a result, members of these tribes have certain rights and privileges not available to other groups. For example, Court interpretations of treaties have given tribes in the Pacific Northwest special rights to fish for salmon.

One economically significant tribal right recognized in recent years has been the authority to provide commercial gambling on tribal property. The Court has said that tribal grounds are governed by federal, not state, law. Federal law does not disallow gambling on tribal grounds except if it is forbidden everywhere within a state. In several cases, tribes have used resources from these gambling operations to secure political influence.

**Women's Rights Across the Century** (left) Women's rights issues in the United States at first focused on women's right to vote. (right) In August 1970, 50 years after women had won the franchise, 10,000 women's liberationists marched to a "Women's Strike for Equality" rally at New York City's Bryant Park. *Why did the women's rights movement begin in the 1970s, when women had voting rights as early as 1920?*

Most of the rights contained in the Bill of Rights have been applied to members of tribes through congressional legislation. To protect tribal religious freedom, Congress in 1978 passed the American Indian Religious Freedom Resolution. Tribal leaders have argued that the resolution gives them special access to traditional religious sites in national parks and other government-owned lands. But the federal courts have interpreted the resolution narrowly, saying it does not make indigenous Americans "supercitizens." Rather, it gives them religious freedoms comparable to those granted to other citizens.[71]

## Section Summary

The civil rights victories of the 1960s apply for the most part to members of all minority groups. But many minority groups have group-specific issues that are not covered by broader civil rights laws and court decisions. The extent to which minority groups have managed to achieve recognition in law and by the courts has paralleled their influence in American politics and elections. Latinos and Asian Americans have had difficulty forming broad-based coalitions because of many internal divisions. Gays and lesbians, on the other hand, have achieved significant influence in elections despite their small absolute numbers. Native Americans, not clearly covered by constitutional guarantees, have secured protection of most basic rights through special congressional legislation.

## Women's Rights

Although gender is not mentioned in the equal protection clause of the Fourteenth Amendment, the meaning of the clause has been gradually redefined to refer to equal rights for women as well as for racial and ethnic groups. As one constitutional scholar has written, "It is in the very nature of ideas to grow in self-awareness, to work out all their implications over time. . . . The very content of the great clauses of the Constitution, their coverage, changes."[72] But the changes in the meaning of the equal protection clause were not won simply by actions taken in courtrooms. They were part of a broad struggle for women's rights played out as much among the electorate as in the legal arena.

The first struggle for women's rights focused on the right to vote (see page 165). Once the Nineteenth Amendment was passed in 1920, the women's movement became dormant for nearly 50 years, finally to be awakened in the late sixties by the civil rights movement.[73] Since the late sixties, women's groups have achieved four civil rights objectives: the right to equal treatment before the law, tough enforcement of this right, the right not to be sexually harassed in the workplace, and access to state-funded military academies. In the following discussion, we will show that achievement of these objectives required both electoral involvement and courtroom presentations.

### The Right to Equality Before the Law

As unlikely as it may seem, it was a conservative southerner, Howard Smith of Virginia, who proposed an amendment to Title VII of the Civil Rights Act of 1964 that would prohibit discrimination on the basis of sex as well as race, religion, or national origin. Although the amendment passed overwhelmingly, the National Organization for Women (NOW) was formed because activist women became concerned that the gender provision in Title VII would not be enforced (see the accompanying Window on the Past). To guarantee enforcement of women's civil rights, NOW, together with other women's organizations, backed the **Equal Rights Amendment,** a proposed amendment to the Constitution that banned gender discrimination. This amendment was expected to give the courts the tools necessary to strike down gender inequities.

At first it seemed that women's groups would succeed in winning passage of this constitutional amendment. Responding to its female constituency, Congress passed

**Equal Rights Amendment (ERA)**
Proposed amendment to the Constitution that banned gender discrimination.

## Window on the Past
### The Civil Rights of Women and African Americans— Cooperation and Conflict

From its very beginning, the struggle for women's civil rights has been shaped by the African American struggle for equal rights. Many of those who first fought for women's rights came out of the struggle for equality for black Americans. Yet these causes have come into conflict on two critical occasions.

1. Elizabeth Cady Stanton organized the first public meeting on behalf of women's rights in Seneca Falls, New York, in 1848, because she had been refused the right to participate in an antislavery convention. Because she included in her demands the women's right to vote, her own husband—who would later become Abraham Lincoln's secretary of state—refused to participate in the meeting. The women's first efforts to petition for equal property rights in New York were received by an all-male legislative committee in the following words: "Ladies always have the best place and choicest tidbit at the table. . . . [Yet men] have presented no petitions for redress." To which Sojourner Truth, an ex-slave who became the first black advocate for women's rights, responded, "Nobody ever . . . gives me the best place—and aren't I a woman?" Raising her work-weary arm, she cried, "I have ploughed and planted and gathered into barns—and aren't I a woman?. . . I have borne thirteen children, and seen most of 'em sold into slavery, and when I cried out with my mother's grief, none but Jesus heard me—and aren't I a woman?" Stanton tried to get members of Congress to forbid gender discrimination and to give women the right to vote when they wrote the Fourteenth and Fifteenth Amendments at the end of the Civil War, but she was unsuccessful because male antislavery leaders did not want to reduce the chances of securing ratification of the amendments by also raising the gender question. So bitter was Stanton about the exclusion of women from the rights guaranteed by the two amendments that she campaigned against them, despite the fact she supported racial equality.

2. The modern women's movement was also shaped by race politics.

Ironically enough, a conservative southerner's tactical effort to deflect the civil rights movement was the initial stimulus. In the heat of the debate over the Civil Rights Act of 1964, Representative Howard Smith, one of the most shrewd and effective opponents of the civil rights movement, offered an amendment adding "sex" to the Title VII provision of the legislation that prohibited discrimination on the basis of race, religion, or national origin. Just as radical Republicans had kept women's rights out of the Fourteenth Amendment 100 years earlier, so liberals opposed the Smith Amendment to Title VII of the Civil Rights Act of 1964 on the grounds that it would weaken the racial focus of the civil rights legislation. But unlike the situation in 1867, women in 1964 had the vote, and most members of Congress dared not vote to prohibit discrimination on the basis of gender. So amid great hilarity—one representative said that in his household he always had the last two words, "yes, dear"—and with little appreciation of the significance of what they were about to enact, the Civil Rights Act of 1964 was amended so as to ban gender as well as racial discrimination.

When the head of the Federal Equal Employment Opportunity Commission was called upon to enforce Title VII and refused to do so, calling it a "fluke" that was "conceived out of wedlock," a number of women working within the commission urged the formation of a national organization that would campaign for its enforcement. They also persuaded Betty Friedan, author of the recently published book *The Feminine Mystique,* to head it. Friedan then persuaded the founders to call the organization the National Organization for Women (NOW).

SOURCES: Eleanor Flexner, *Century of Struggle: The Women's Rights Movement in the United States* (Cambridge, MA: Harvard University Press, 1975), Ch. 5; Jo Freeman, *The Politics of Women's Liberation* (New York: Longman, 1975), pp. 53–54; *Congressional Record,* House, February 8, 1964, p. 257.

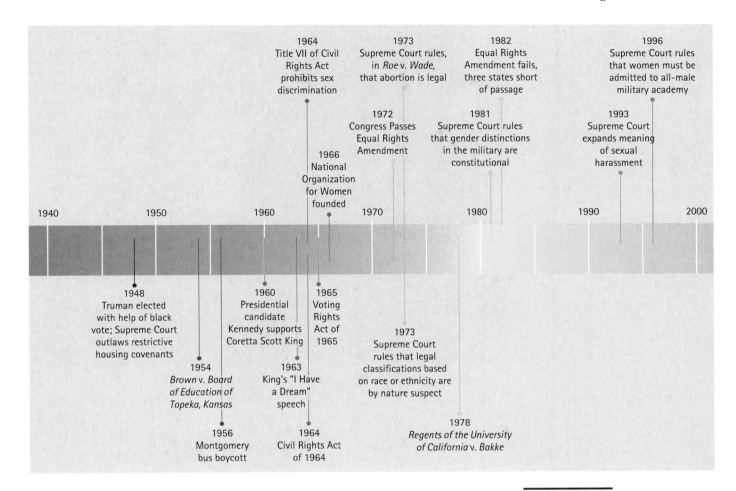

Figure 17.7

Important Events of the
Civil Rights Movement
and the Women's Movement

the ERA by overwhelming majorities by the spring of 1972. Within a year a majority of states had voted to ratify it.[74] But at the very moment the ERA was about to become a part of the U.S. Constitution, it encountered increasing resistance led by groups of conservative women who were concerned, among other things, that the amendment would require government funding of abortions and the application of the military draft to women.[75] With women divided, the amendment was ratified by 35 states but failed to win approval from the 3 additional legislatures necessary to achieve the three-fourths required to ratify a constitutional amendment.

As discouraging as the ERA defeat was for its supporters at the time, in retrospect it seems that they won the war by losing the battle. Fifty years earlier, the women's movement had collapsed immediately following passage of the Nineteenth Amendment. This time, the women's movement continued to forge on, perhaps part-ly because the Equal Rights Amendment did not pass. Because the prolonged cam-paign for the ERA became a lengthy political and educational struggle, the movement did not wither away. In the 25 years after the ERA campaign began in earnest, women's place in politics changed more dramatically than in any previous quarter-century. More women were elected to public office in the 1990s than ever before.[76] In 2000 the House of Representatives included 56 women, the Senate had 9, and 2 of the 9 Supreme Court justices were female.

## Initial Court Response to Women's Rights

The ERA also had an impact on Supreme Court decisions. Before the ERA campaign, the Court had done little, if anything, for women's rights. As late as 1961, in an

**Women in the Military**
Classifications by gender still exist in the military. *Are these gender distinctions justified?*

opinion ironically signed by the same Chief Justice who wrote the *Brown* decision, Earl Warren, the Court unanimously upheld a Florida law that made a clear gender distinction. It said that men were to be asked to serve on juries but that women were to serve on a jury only if they volunteered for duty.[77]

Court opinions changed after the House of Representatives had voted overwhelmingly in favor of the ERA's passage. The Supreme Court, in *Craig v. Boren* (1976), declared unconstitutional an Oklahoma law that allowed women to drink at age 18 but denied that privilege to men until the age of 21. Oklahoma defended the law on the grounds that young men were more likely than young women to drive when drunk and were therefore more likely to have accidents. But the Supreme Court rejected the statistical evidence Oklahoma had presented as irrelevant on the grounds that the law constituted "invidious gender-based discrimination" that constituted "a denial [to males] of equal protection of the laws in violation of the Fourteenth Amendment."[78] (Oklahoma subsequently made 21 the legal drinking age for both men and women.)

Although the Supreme Court said that gender discrimination violates the equal protection clause, it has never said that gender, like race, is a suspect classification, which will be strictly scrutinized by the courts to see whether its use is constitutional. Instead, the Court has said only that it will rule against a law that includes gender distinctions unless those distinctions have "a substantial relationship to an important objective."[79]

National defense remains the most important arena in which classifications by gender remain intact. According to federal law, men must register for the draft but women need not, and men carry out combat assignments whereas women are not allowed to do so (though many "noncombat" positions now assigned to women may actually place women in danger of enemy fire). The Supreme Court ruled gender distinctions within the military constitutional in *Rostker v. Goldberg* (1981) on the grounds that on military matters, "Congress' constitutional power" is broad and "the lack of competence on the part of the courts is marked."[80] The ruling was consistent with the view of a majority of the voters, who favored certain restrictions on female participation in military combat.[81]

## Discrimination in the Workplace

The Supreme Court has said that "business necessity" may at times make it difficult to recruit and retain members of disadvantaged groups. The Court has reasoned that some types of positions must be performed by a person of a particular gender or that qualified members of disadvantaged groups are not readily available for the type of work that needs to be performed.[82] In *Ward's Cove Packing Co. v. Antonio* (1989), the Court also said that Congress, in Title VII of the Civil Rights Act of 1964, intended that those discriminated against bear the burden of proof when showing that race or gender discrimination, not business necessity, caused a particular employment practice.[83] Although the case involved Alaskan salmon workers, women's organizations believed that the case had broad implications for gender discrimination as well. Burden of proof is not a small matter in discrimination cases, because it is often difficult to provide conclusive evidence one way or another.

In his dissenting opinion, Justice Harry Blackmun denounced the restrictive interpretation given Title VII by the Supreme Court in *Ward's Cove* in the strongest possible language, saying, "One wonders whether the majority [of the Court] still believes that . . . discrimination is a problem in our society, or even remembers that it ever was."[84] Sharing Blackmun's concern about the decision, women's and civil rights groups pressed Congress to shift the burden of proof from plaintiffs to businesses, thereby overturning the Supreme Court decision. Congress responded to these demands and enacted them into law as part of the Civil Rights Act of 1991, signed by President George Bush. In sum, it was elected officials, not the Court, that took the lead on this gender discrimination issue.

## Sexual Harassment

The Supreme Court did not rule on the meaning of sexual harassment in the workplace until *Meritor Savings Bank* v. *Vinson*, a case decided in 1986.[85] In this case, Michelle Vinson said that she had been psychologically damaged as a result of sexually abusive language used in her presence. In deciding in Vinson's favor, Justice Rehnquist wrote a very narrow opinion that strongly implied that sexual harassment would be considered illegal only if it caused psychological damage to the victim. In other words, the Court said sexual harassment had to be experienced as personally devastating before it constituted a violation of Title VII.

Sexual harassment became a major political issue in 1991, when Clarence Thomas was nominated to serve on the Supreme Court (see Chapter 15, page 442–443). The issue so energized the women's movement that 1992, the election year that followed, became known as the "year of the woman"; the number of women elected to the House of Representatives increased by 19, and 4 more women were elected to the Senate. Responding to the change in the political atmosphere, the Supreme Court, in the unanimous 1993 decision *Harris* v. *Forklift Systems*, expanded its definition of sexual harassment.[86] Teresa Harris resigned her position at Forklift Systems Inc., a heavy equipment rental firm, because her employer called her "a dumb ass woman" and made other derogatory remarks. Although she had complained and he had promised to restrain his remarks, her boss subsequently suggested in front of other employees that Hardy had had intercourse with a client in order to land a contract. She quit and sued. Lower courts denied her compensation, because no psychological damage could be shown. But Justice Sandra Day O'Connor wrote, in the majority opinion, that Title VII "comes into play before harassing conduct leads to a nervous breakdown." Justice Ruth Bader Ginsburg went further, writing in her concurring opinion that gender discrimination exists whenever it is more difficult for a person of one gender than of another to perform well on a job. Once again, the Supreme Court moved forward in the wake of public pressure and political events.

## Single-Sex Schools and Colleges

Single-sex schools have long been a significant part of American education. As late as the 1950s, well-known private colleges, such as Princeton and Yale, limited their admissions to men. Although these colleges now admit approximately equal numbers of men and women, single-sex education survives at many private women's colleges. These colleges assert that women learn more in an environment where many can assume leadership roles. Hillary Rodham Clinton, who graduated from Wellesley, a Massachusetts women's college, said it "was very, very important to me and I am so grateful that I had the chance to go to college at a place where women were valued and nurtured and encouraged."[87] Arguments have recently been made for all-male education as well. In 1989 the Dade County, Florida, school system established an all-male elementary school serving African American boys.[88] The school system claims the school has succeeded in increasing student attendance and test scores, while reducing hostility among the students. Despite the claims of those who favor single-sex education, many believe that education that is separated by gender cannot be equal.

Although the pros and cons of single-sex education are still under debate, the Supreme Court in 1996 cast doubt on its constitutionality. In *United States* v. *Virginia*, the Court ruled that women must be admitted to Virginia Military Institute (VMI), even though the state had recently established a separate military education program for women.[89] The Court said the newly established military training program for women did not match the history, reputation, and quality of VMI. It remains unclear, however, whether the Court will extend its decision to private schools or to state programs beyond those that prepare young people for military careers.

## The Future of Women's Rights

Despite many gains, the women's movement has not yet realized all of its civil rights agenda. Sexual harassment remains a burning issue within the military and in many business firms. Only a few women have broken through what is known as the **glass ceiling**—the invisible barrier that has limited their opportunities for advancement to the highest ranks of politics, business, and the professions. Very few women are chosen as college presidents, as heads of major corporations, or as partners in major law firms. And no woman has yet been nominated for president by either major political party.

The changing American family has also left many women in difficult circumstances. The percentage of children raised in single-parent families headed by a woman has increased sharply in the past quarter-century, and these households are much more likely to be poor than households headed by males or couples. Women's issues are likely to remain an important feature in American politics in the twenty-first century.

> **glass ceiling**
> The invisible barrier that has limited women's opportunities for advancement to the highest ranks of politics, business, and the professions.

### Section Summary

After remaining dormant from the 1920s to the 1960s, the movement for women's rights gained inspiration from the civil rights movement. As in the civil rights movement, legal victories for women paralleled their organized popular involvement in electoral politics. Despite the failure to secure ratification of the Equal Rights Amendment, the women's movement succeeded in persuading Congress to prohibit discrimination against women. In addition, they have witnessed court decisions against gender discrimination in the workplace, legal protections against sexual harassment, and provision for the admission of women to state-funded military academies. These legal changes followed—they did not lead—changes in public opinion.

**Max Cleland**
*Are the rights of the disabled more effectively protected by the courts or by elected officials? Why?*

## Americans with Disabilities

Disabled people constitute about 9 percent of the working-age population.[90] Ironically, they have one political advantage that both women and minorities lack: Every person runs the risk of someday becoming disabled. The rights of disabled people thus have broad appeal. Yet this advantage is offset by a number of political limitations. Disabilities differ in kind and severity, making coordinated efforts more difficult. The disabled are also more scattered and less visible than ethnic minorities. The more severely mentally disabled neither vote nor engage directly in politics and hence must depend on others to defend their rights. The cost of helping people with disabilities is another drawback. It is estimated that the annual cost of disability payments and health care services for this group exceeds $275 billion.[91] Although many people are, in principle, sympathetic to the needs of the disabled, they do not necessarily like to pay the taxes needed to fund appropriate services.

Only after the civil rights movement of the 1960s sensitized the country to the needs of minorities were the civil rights of the disabled taken seriously. Previously, programs for the disabled were seen as charitable activities to be supported by private donations. Mentally disabled people were closeted away in "insane asylums" and "homes for the incurable." Organizations representing the disabled were fragmented into those interested in the blind, the deaf, the mentally ill, and so forth.

The needs of the disabled were first successfully cast in terms of civil rights not by an interest group but by one individual, Hugh Gallagher, a wheelchair-bound polio victim who in the mid-sixties served as a legislative aide to Alaska Senator E. L. Bartlett. Gallagher constantly faced great difficulty using public toilets and gaining access to such buildings as the Library of Congress. At his prodding, Congress in 1968—just four years after the 1964 Civil Rights Act—enacted a law requiring that all future public buildings constructed with federal monies provide access for the disabled. Similar language was subsequently inserted into the transportation legislation in 1970.[92]

Once elected officials had responded to the demands of the disabled, the courts, too, became more sensitive. Previously, many retarded children were denied access to public education on the grounds that they were not mentally competent. But in the early seventies, federal courts in Pennsylvania and the District of Columbia required that states provide disabled children with equal educational opportunity.[93] These decisions generated a nationwide movement for disabled children, culminating in the passage in 1975 of federal legislation that guaranteed all handicapped children the right to an appropriate education.[94]

Encouraged by both judicial and legislative victories, groups representing the physically and mentally challenged became increasingly energetic and assertive. Legislative victories in education, transportation, and construction of public buildings finally culminated in the Americans with Disabilities Act of 1991, signed by George Bush. This act made it illegal to deny employment to individuals on the grounds that they are handicapped. To the extent feasible, the workplace is to be adapted to the capacities of the disabled person.

Because of these legislative changes, opportunities for the disabled have greatly increased. Twenty years ago, public toilets for the disabled hardly existed; sidewalks and staircases had no ramps; buses and trains were inaccessible to those in wheelchairs; colleges and universities were designed in ways that all but precluded attendance by the physically challenged; and developmentally disabled children were denied a public education. Unlike President Franklin Roosevelt, who 50 years ago felt it necessary to avoid being photographed in the wheelchair to which he was confined, Robert Dole referred constantly to his disabled arm during his 1996 campaign for the presidency. Meanwhile, Georgia voters elected wheelchair-bound Vietnam Veteran Max Cleland to the Senate, and President Clinton appointed David Tatel, who is blind, to a federal appeals court.

The courts themselves have shown considerable reluctance to interpret the rights of the disabled in sweeping terms. For example, in 1979 the Supreme Court unanimously ruled against a nearly deaf woman who complained that she had been denied admission to a nurses' training program for which she was otherwise qualified. The Court ruled that deafness might preclude the woman from understanding instructions in a hospital setting, just as blindness fundamentally limits an otherwise qualified bus driver.[95] Most of the expansion in the rights of the disabled has thus occurred as the result of congressional legislation rather than court interpretation.

Yet the disabled, too, have begun to encounter increasing political resistance. Educators complain that too many school dollars are set aside for special-education programs. Architectural changes in public buildings and adaptations in transportation are said to be far too expensive to justify the limited amount of usage they receive. Ordinary citizens grumble as they drive past empty parking spots reserved for the disabled. It remains to be seen whether such complaints are a sign that the rights of the disabled are soon to be subjected to more limits or whether the extensions enacted in recent years will continue.

**simulation**
**You are
the Mayor**

### Section Summary

Judicial and legislative victories for the disabled in the 1970s paved the way for their major civil rights victory: the Americans with Disabilities Act of 1991. This law prohibits discrimination against the disabled in employment and requires buildings and other public facilities to be accessible to disabled people, to the extent feasible. Because of this legislation, opportunities for the disabled have greatly increased. Yet public concern about increasing costs of regulations and programs designed to meet the needs of the disabled may limit future gains.

## Chapter Summary

Civil rights groups have achieved many of their advances by persuading majority populations of the justice of their causes through participation in political demonstrations and electoral politics.[96] The 1954 *Brown* decision, to be sure, had an impact of its own, but even this decision came only after blacks had demonstrated political clout in the 1948 presidential election. Otherwise, the Supreme Court has usually followed the moods and trends of the rest of the country. When the country abandoned Reconstruction in the latter part of the nineteenth century, the Supreme Court, in *Civil Rights Cases* and *Plessy* v. *Ferguson*, ruled against civil rights demands. When blacks moved north and thereby acquired the right to vote, the Supreme Court reversed these decisions and redefined the equal protection clause, banning discrimination against African Americans, Latinos, Asians, and members of other minority groups. Yet the most notable progress toward racial desegregation occurred as the result of legislation passed by bipartisan majorities in Congress in 1964 and 1965.

When civil rights groups called for metropolitan-wide desegregation and affirmative action programs in the North, many northern whites, no less than southern whites, felt threatened by racial change. Supreme Court decisions in the 1970s reflected this new mood. The Court said *de facto* segregation was not contrary to the Constitution, and the Court also forbade quotas as part of affirmative action programs.

Latinos, Asian Americans, gays and lesbians, and American Indians have achieved varying degrees of legal rights, based in large part on their electoral clout. In general, these groups have only begun to exert their strength in national elections, though they were influential in some states and localities much earlier.

The modern women's rights movement grew out of the civil rights movement. Once women's groups became active, they achieved striking changes in legal doctrine, even though they did not succeed in securing passage of the ERA. The Supreme Court outlawed most forms of gender discrimination, though women are not allowed in combat positions within the military. The Court has declared gender discrimination and sexual harassment in the workplace contrary to the Civil Rights Act of 1964 and has ruled state-funded, single-sex military training unconstitutional.

The civil rights movement also helped focus attention on the rights of the disabled. Once again, the most important steps forward were taken not by the courts but by Congress, which acted in response to electoral-based political pressure.

## On the Web

U.S. Department of Justice
www.usdoj.gov
The U.S. Department of Justice's Civil Rights division provides information on its enforcement of existing civil rights law.

U.S. Commission on Civil Rights
www.usccr.gov
Established in 1957, the U.S. Commission on Civil Rights monitors discrimination in many sectors of American society.

Martin Luther King, Jr., Papers Project
www.stanford.edu/group/King/
The Martin Luther King, Jr., Papers Project at Stanford University maintains a Web site with many of King's speeches and sermons, as well as several scholarly articles and book chapters.

National Association for the Advancement of Colored People
www.naacp.org
The NAACP is the nation's oldest civil rights organization.

National Organization for Women
www.now.org
The country's largest feminist organization, NOW's goal is "to take action to bring about equality for all women."

National Council of La Raza
www.nclr.org
The National Council of La Raza monitors issues of concern to Hispanic Americans.

Human Rights Campaign
www.hrc.org
This is the official Web site for the Human Rights Campaign (a leading gay rights organization).

Leadership Education for Asian Pacifics, Inc.
www.leap.org
Leadership Education for Asian Pacifics, Inc. (LEAP) houses the Asian Pacific American Public Policy Institute, which authors numerous reports on Asian Americans.

National Council on Disability
www.ncd.gov
The National Council on Disability is an independent federal agency that makes recommendations to the president and Congress regarding Americans with disabilities. The agency's site provides links to other relevant federal agencies, press releases, and in-depth reports.

## Key Terms

affirmative action, p. 521
black codes, p. 510
Brown v. Board of Education of Topeka, Kansas, p. 515
civil disobedience, p. 517
civil rights, p. 509
de facto segregation, p. 520
de jure segregation, p. 520
equal protection clause, p. 509

Equal Rights Amendment, p. 529
glass ceiling, p. 534
grandfather clause, p. 510
Jim Crow laws, p. 511
National Association for the Advancement of Colored People (NAACP), p. 513
Plessy v. Ferguson, p. 511

poll tax, p. 510
quota, p. 521
Reconstruction, p. 510
restrictive housing covenant, p. 514
separate but equal doctrine, p. 511
state action doctrine, p. 511
suspect classification, p. 516
white primary, p. 510

## Suggested Readings

Browning, Rufus, Dale Rogers Marshall, and David H. Tabb. *Protest Is Not Enough: The Struggle of Blacks and Hispanics for Equality in Urban Politics.* Berkeley: University of California Press, 1984. Excellent analysis of the importance of electoral politics for black advances.

Deloria, Vine, Jr. "The Distinctive Status of Indian Rights." In Peter Iverson, ed., *The Plains Indians of the Twentieth Century.* Norman: University of Oklahoma Press, 1985, pp. 237–248. Discusses the constitutional status of the rights of indigenous peoples.

Flexner, Eleanor. *Century of Struggle: The Women's Rights Movement in the United States.* Cambridge, MA: Harvard University Press, 1975. Engaging history of the suffragist movement.

Foner, Eric. *A Short History of Reconstruction.* New York: Harper, 1990. An abridgment of Foner's classic historical study of Reconstruction.

Ginsburg, Ruth Bader. "Employment of the Constitution to Advance the Equal Status of Men and Women," In Shlomo Slonim, ed., *The Constitutional Bases of Political and Social Change in the United States.* New York: Praeger, 1990, pp. 186–196. Succinct overview of court interpretations of women's rights.

Higgenbotham, A. Leon, Jr. *Shades of Freedom: Racial Politics and Presumptions of the American Legal Process.* New York: Oxford University Press, 1996. A former jurist's sharp critique of the racial bias in American legal practice.

Hochschild, Jennifer L. *The New American Dilemma.* New Haven, CT: Yale University Press, 1984. Identifies the tension between racial desegregation and electoral politics in the United States.

Katzman, Robert A. *Institutional Disability: The Saga of Transportation Policy for the Disabled.* Washington, DC: Brookings, 1986. Discusses the ways in which legislative and judicial policy making for the disabled have interacted.

Katznelson, Ira. *Black Men, White Cities.* New York: Oxford University Press. Compares the political involvement of blacks in American and English cities.

Key, V. O., Jr. *Southern Politics.* New York: Random House, 1949. Classic study of the effects of racial conflict on southern politics.

Lipsky, Michael. "Protest as a Political Resource." *American Political Science Review* LXII (December 1968): 1144–1158. Shows the limits of protest as a political bargaining tool.

Lublin, David. *The Paradox of Representation: Racial Gerrymandering and Minority Interests in Congress.* Princeton, NJ: Princeton University Press, 1997. Discusses dilemmas of affirmative action in redistricting.

Mandel, Ruth B. "The Political Woman." In Sherri Matteo, ed., *American Women in the Nineties: Today's Critical Issues.* Boston: Northeastern University Press, 1993, pp. 34–65. Describes the increasing involvement of women in politics.

Mansbridge, Jane J. *Why We Lost the ERA.* Chicago: University of Chicago Press, 1986. Insightful, readable case study.

Rosenberg, Gerald N. *The Hollow Hope: Can Courts Bring About Social Change?* Chicago: University of Chicago Press, 1991. Argues that courts are generally unable to act contrary to majority opinion.

Skerry, Peter. *Mexican Americans: The Ambivalent Minority.* New York: Free Press, 1993. Engaging but controversial book that questions the effectiveness of Mexican American political leadership.

Skocpol, Theda. *Protecting Soldiers and Mothers: The Political Origins of Social Policy in the United States.* Cambridge, MA: Harvard University Press, 1992. Analyzes the way women's groups have influenced U.S. social policy.

Tate, Kathryn. *From Protest to Politics.* Cambridge, MA: Harvard University Press, 1993. Explains black political choices in the 1980s.

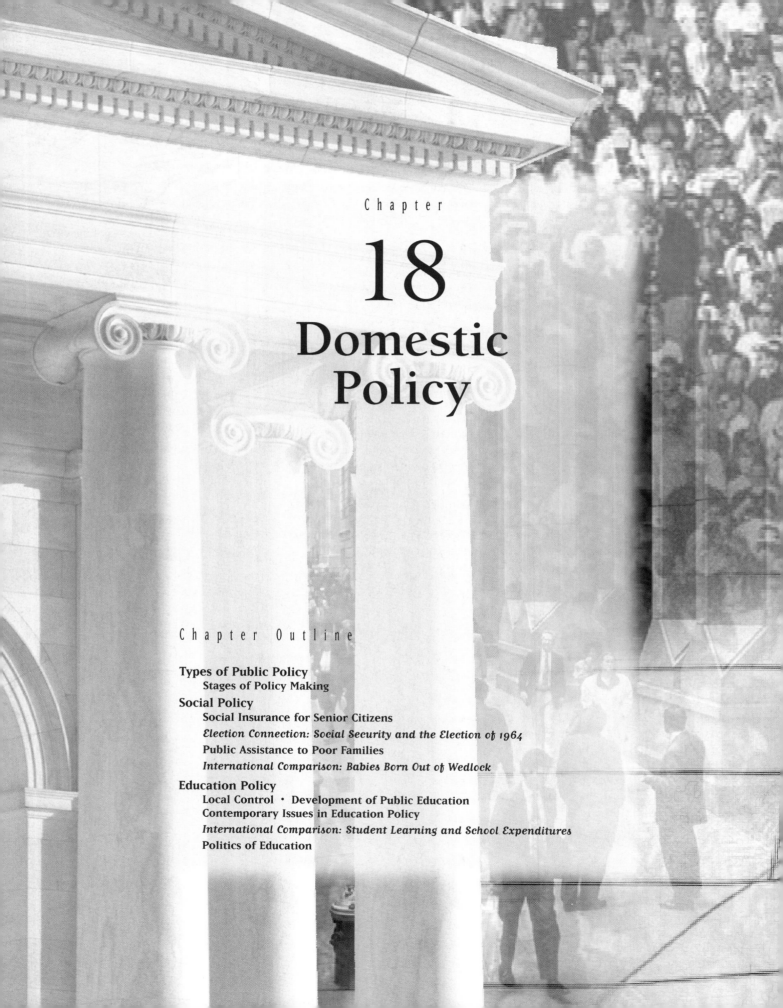

Chapter

# 18
# Domestic
# Policy

Chapter Outline

For decades the United States government had been running large and politically controversial budget deficits. But suddenly, in 1998, the deficit disappeared and a budget surplus appeared—almost out of nowhere. As a growing economy was quickly making many Americans more prosperous, it was also generating much more revenue for the government.

What should the government do with the newly available money that no one had anticipated? Some recommended making tax cuts. "Let's give this money back to the people who earned it," they said. Others maintained that it was time to help the truly needy—the poor, the disabled, and disadvantaged children. Still a third voice advocated using this money to help senior citizens, insisting that social security must first be saved, then Medicare, and only then could we do other things.

As the debate continued, the economy—and the budget surplus—grew and grew. By the summer of 2000, projections of the total expected surplus from 2000 to 2010 reached over $2 trillion. It gradually became clear that the winner of the debate over how to expend these sums would realize a massive victory.

After the 2000 elections, the winner was clear. Both the Gore and Bush presidential campaigns stressed the need to shore up the social security and Medicare budgets. These programs for the elderly would win the lion's share of the budget surplus. Tax cuts would come next. And advocates for increased funding of programs for needy families would have to take a place in line.

WHY WILL THE BULK OF THE SURPLUS GO TO PROGRAMS SERVING SENIOR CITIZENS rather than to programs for needy families with children? Are the elderly's social needs greater? Are families with children less deserving? Or are senior citizens better organized and do they exercise more voting power?

To provide a way of thinking about these questions, this chapter will examine the electoral and political forces that shape domestic policy. In this chapter we shall discuss the various stages through which all domestic policies proceed and then consider three major types of domestic policy: social policy, education policy, and regulatory policy. For each, we shall examine the political factors that help shape policy outcomes. In doing this, we address the following questions:

- What is domestic policy and how is it made?
- What are the major social policies in the United States, how have they developed over time, and who are the major political actors in debates over these policies?
- How does politics shape education policy?
- What is regulatory policy and how is it formulated?

## Types of Public Policy

*Public policy* is a term applied to all government programs and regulations. **Domestic policy** consists of all government programs and regulations that directly affect those living within a country. It includes everything from education and health care to transportation and garbage collection—hundreds of different kinds of governmental activity. Foreign policy involves relations with other nations (see Chapter 20). However, the distinction between domestic and foreign policy is not always sharp and clear. Some

**domestic policy**
Government programs and regulations that directly affect those living within a country.

domestic policies, such as immigration policy, affect relations with other countries. Some foreign policies, such as foreign trade regulations, have major domestic consequences. In addition to the distinction between foreign and domestic policy, one can also divide domestic policies into economic policies and other policies. Economic policies are among the most complex and important, and we devote Chapter 19 to a discussion of economic policy. In this chapter we concern ourselves with noneconomic domestic policy.

Most policies, whether domestic or foreign, develop through a series of stages known as the policy-making round.

## Stages of Policy Making

The making of policy is a complex, never-ending round of events. To clarify what is often a very messy process, political scientists have divided the policy-making round into six stages; these are shown in Figure 18.1. At each stage, electoral forces are at work.

The first stage is **agenda setting,** making an issue visible enough that important political leaders take it seriously.[1] When elected officials think a problem is serious and might even affect an election, the issue has reached the agenda stage. The second stage consists of **policy deliberation,** the debate and discussion over issues placed on the policy agenda.[2] At this stage, groups and policy experts try to convince leaders not only that their proposals are a good way to deal with the problem but also that they are popular with the electorate. Next comes **policy enactment,** the passage of a law by public officials. Enactment may involve passage by Congress, a state legislature, or a city council and signing into law by a president, governor, or mayor. Elected officials who vote for the law usually expect that its passage will enhance their popularity, though there are celebrated instances when political leaders sacrifice their career for what they see as the good of the country. The fourth stage is **policy implementation,** the translation of the legislation into an actual set of government programs or regulations.[3] When fashioning the details, bureaucrats are expected to carry out the intentions of the legislative branch and not to stray too far from what is politically acceptable. At the fifth stage, government produces **policy outputs,** the provision of services to citizens or the regulation of their conduct. Beneficiaries usually think well of those who established the program; those who are hurt by the policy outputs probably feel otherwise. Finally, **policy outcomes** are the effects of policy outputs on individuals and businesses.[4] These outcomes often give rise to new issues, which are then placed on the policy agenda, completing the policy-making round.

**agenda setting**
Making an issue so visible that important political leaders take it seriously.

**policy deliberation**
Debate and discussion by groups and political leaders over issues placed on the policy agenda.

**policy enactment**
Passage of a law by public officials.

**policy implementation**
Translation of legislation into a set of government programs or regulations.

**policy output**
Provision of services to citizens or regulation of their conduct.

**policy outcome**
Effect of policy outputs on individuals and businesses.

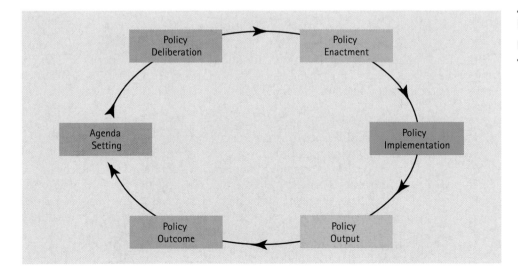

**Figure 18.1**
**Policy-Making Stages**

**Temporary Assistance for Needy Families (TANF)**

Welfare reform law passed by Congress in 1996.

The enactment of the 1996 welfare reform law, **Temporary Assistance for Needy Families (TANF)**, illustrates the way politics affects the various stages of the policy round. The first stage, placing the issue on the policy agenda, occurred when Bill Clinton scored points in his 1992 campaign for president by promising to "end welfare as we know it." The second stage, policy deliberation, occurred when interest groups, policy experts, members of Congress, and the media debated many different ways of redesigning welfare policy. Throughout the debate, polls reported that a majority of the public supported welfare reform, increasing the likelihood that something would be approved. The third stage, policy enactment, saw Congress shift responsibility for welfare policy from the federal to state governments. President Clinton signed the bill into law in part because voters supported the idea even though he had expressed strong reservations about many provisions. The fourth stage, policy implementation, began in early 1997 when many state governments started revising their welfare plans, often in response to electoral pressures at the state level. The fifth stage, policy outputs, took place when many families left or were removed from the welfare rolls.

We now know a few of the initial policy outcomes. Welfare rolls declined dramatically; about half as many people received assistance in 1999 as in 1994. Many of these former welfare recipients found jobs because the program was implemented at a time when the economy was growing rapidly and new job opportunities were plentiful. Others were shifted to programs serving the disabled. However, some of the most disadvantaged, those with few job skills, were left destitute, and many of those who initially found jobs left them within a year.[5] These numbers may grow if the economy falters. If this problem becomes severe, it could place welfare reform back on the policy agenda, producing a new policy-making round.

The political forces that shape public policies differ from one policy to the next. In the remainder of this chapter we shall describe the political factors shaping three major types of public policy: social policy, education policy, and regulatory policy.

### Section Summary

A public policy is any government program or regulation and can deal with domestic issues or with foreign affairs. The government makes policy through a complicated and recurring process called the policy-making round. This process has many stages, from the early agenda setting to the final policy outcomes. At each stage, elections influence the process.

## Social Policy

**social policy**

Domestic policy programs designed to help those thought to be in need of government assistance.

**Social policy** is a type of domestic policy that consists of programs designed to help those thought to be in need of government assistance. People may be regarded as needy because they are old, infirm, young, disabled, unemployed, poor, or some combination of these. One of the central issues in the making of social policy is finding an appropriate balance between government assistance to the elderly and to the young. As the chapter opening emphasizes, the elderly have done particularly well in securing government help.

One can observe the different effects of social policy on the young and the old by comparing some basic statistics concerning changes in the nation's poverty rate. As shown in Figure 18.2, poverty among senior citizens fell from 25 percent in 1970 to 10.5 percent in 1998, but poverty among families with children increased from 15 percent to 20 percent over this same period of time. The poverty rate among families with children in the United States is twice as high as in most other advanced industrial societies;[6] the poverty rate among senior citizens is about the same in the United States as elsewhere.[7]

Poverty is not just a matter of money; it pervades many aspects of life. For example, the chances of being in good health are different for senior citizens and children.

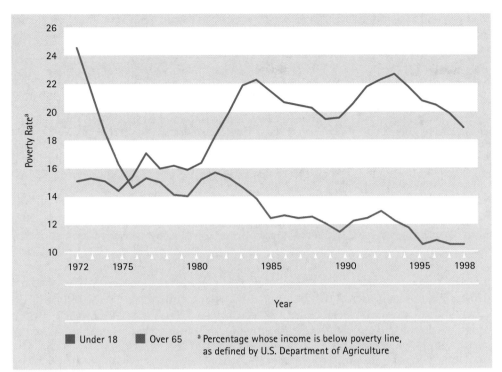

**Figure 18.2**

**U.S. Poverty Rates for Senior Citizens and Children, 1970–1998**
*Why have poverty rates fallen for seniors and risen for children?*

SOURCE: U.S. Census Bureau, *Historical Poverty Tables — People*, Table 3: Poverty Status by Age, Race and Hispanic Origin http://www.census.gov/hhes/poverty/hist-pob/hstpov3.html, accessed July 24, 2000.

Of the seven countries with the largest economies, the United States has the highest infant mortality rate. But if one becomes a senior citizen, one has a better chance of living longer in the United States than in any of the other six countries. As one analyst put it, the United States is the "healthiest place to grow old but the riskiest [in which] to be born."[8]

In the next two sections, we shall explain how this strange phenomenon came to be. First we shall describe the development of social programs for senior citizens and the powerful political support that sustains them. Then we shall describe the development of social programs for children and the more limited support that they enjoy.

## Social Insurance for Senior Citizens

The improvement in the well-being of senior citizens today is due in good part to the country's social policy. As the population has aged, the government has expanded programs to meet the retirement income and medical needs of the elderly. The amount spent on social programs for senior citizens grew from under $4000 per senior citizen in 1960 to over $16,500 in 1995. (Unless otherwise indicated, all dollar figures in this chapter are expressed in 1999 dollars so as to adjust for inflation.) In this section we describe the conditions that led to this dramatic increase in social insurance.

**Origins and Development of Social Insurance Programs** Demands for aid to senior citizens escalated during the Great Depression of the 1930s, when poverty among the elderly was particularly acute. Approximately 5 million senior citizens rallied behind the proposals of Dr. Francis E. Townsend, a Californian who promised to end the depression by giving everyone over 60 years old the equivalent in today's dollars of $2400 a month, provided that they spent it immediately.[9] Always quick to recognize potential electoral threats, President Franklin Roosevelt checked Townsend's soaring popularity by appointing an advisory committee to recommend better ways of meeting the needs of the elderly. The committee recommended a program of **social insurance**, a program that provides benefits in return for contributions made by

**social insurance**
Program that provides benefits in return for contributions made by workers.

Social policy was set on a new course after the election of Lyndon Johnson over Barry Goldwater in 1964. When Goldwater suggested that social security be made a voluntary program, Democrats accused him of seeking to destroy it. Though Goldwater denied wanting to do anything other than strengthen the program, both election analysts and Goldwater himself thought this issue did him more harm than any other.

Johnson won 60 percent of the vote, and the Democratic party captured a large majority of both houses of Congress. Although other factors also contributed to Johnson's overwhelming victory, the outcome was interpreted as providing a mandate for more social insurance. Over the next two years, Congress passed

the Medicare program for senior citizens, passed the Medicaid program for low-income families, passed an educational program for low-income children, and generally laid the groundwork for a rapid expansion of the welfare state over the next dozen years.

*What are three reasons why the social security program is so popular? Can you imagine a vast expansion of social insurance, such as the one that occurred in the 1960s occurring today? Why or why not?*

SOURCES: John D. Pomfret, "Campaign Issues—VI" *New York Times*, October 30, 1964, 24; "Goldwater Sees Signs of Victory" November 1, 1964, 75.

---

**social security**
Social insurance program for senior citizens.

**Medicare**
Program that provides social security recipients a broad range of medical benefits.

workers. Consistent with the committee's recommendations, in 1935 Congress enacted the landmark Social Security Act, which created a broad range of social programs, including a social insurance program for senior citizens generally known as **social security.**[10]

The social security program initially cost the government very little. Most of those who first retired under the program received minimal benefits because they had paid into the program only for a limited number of their working years. Also, retirement costs were low because, in 1935, average life expectancy for those reaching the age of 65 was only 12.6 years. In contrast, a worker retiring at 65 today is expected to live more than 17 years.

Gradually, the program expanded. The number of people covered went up; so did the length of their retirement. Benefits increased in size and cost. Two major changes deserve particular attention. In 1965, the year after Democrats won an overwhelming election victory against Republican Barry Goldwater, a presidential candidate accused of opposing social security, Congress enacted **Medicare,** which provides social security recipients a broad range of medical benefits (see the accompanying Election Connection). In 1972, an election year, Congress gave senior citizens a large increase in their monthly social security check and linked, or indexed, this amount to the cost of living. If inflation goes up 10 percent, so does the paycheck.[11] Passed at a time when prices were rising, this new benefit soon became very popular.

The popularity of both social security and Medicare is due in part to the fact that they are based on the insurance principle—that is, the principle that people receive benefits in return for contributions they have made. In the case of social security, the insurance principle works in the following way: People become eligible for benefits by paying a portion of their regular salary—a payroll tax—to social security during their working years. To get social security benefits, beneficiaries need only prove that they are over the age of 65 (or, if they agree to a lower monthly check, the age of 62). Because of the insurance principle, a retiree does not have to show a need. People can receive benefits even if they own a vacation house overlooking the ocean and have millions in the bank. Upon reaching the age of 65, even billionaire Microsoft founder Bill Gates will be eligible to receive a social security check.

Although social security is called an insurance program, it differs from a true insurance program in one fundamental respect: It operates at a loss. In private insurance programs, most people pay more in initial payments and forgone interest than they receive in benefits; if this were not so, the insurance company could not make a profit. But, from the beginning, social security has given most people more in benefits than they contributed in their social security tax. A couple who retired in 1995 can

expect to receive about $471,000 in social security and Medicare benefits over the remaining years of their lives, even though the worker in the family made tax contributions of only $184,000. The windfall for the average single person is less, but even this retiree will get back some $64,000 more than the amount contributed in taxes.[12]

How is this magic possible? How can benefits exceed contributions? Why have social security and Medicare not gone broke? Up until now, there have been three reasons:

1. Workers have grown in number, as women and "baby boomers" have entered the workforce and unemployment rates have fallen. This means more people are contributing to the social security program.
2. Workers today produce more and earn more than their predecessors did. This means that more money is available to distribute to retirees.
3. Workers today pay a higher percentage of their earnings in social security taxes than their predecessors did. Essentially, younger generations have been asked to pay more to cover the expenses of older ones. As economist Lester Thurow has pointed out, "the current generation of retirees . . . did not have to pay [much] into the system but gets benefits financed by those behind them."[13] The practice is not new. Jonathan Swift saw the same thing happening in England three centuries ago. "'Tis pleasant to observe," he said, "how free the present Age is in laying taxes on the next."[14]

Unfortunately, some of these circumstances may be changing:

1. Experts do not expect the number of workers to increase much in the next couple of decades. The massive baby boom generation will reach retirement age from 2010 to 2030. As they leave the workforce, the number of retirees will grow faster than the number of workers. As a result, the cost of retirement programs will increase, as Figure 18.3 shows.
2. Rates of growth in economic productivity may not always be as high as they were in the 1990s. Although the recent economic prosperity has greatly enhanced the viability of the social security program, a serious economic recession could quickly change the picture. Then workers in the future would not be producing enough to cover the higher cost of social security caused by the retirement of the baby boomers.

**Figure 18.3**

**Projected Cost of
Social Insurance for Senior Citizens**
*Why will costs of programs for senior
citizens rise rapidly in the coming
years?*

SOURCE: Neil Howe and Richard Jackson,
*The Graying of the Welfare State*
(Washington, DC: National Taxpayers Union
Foundation, 1999).

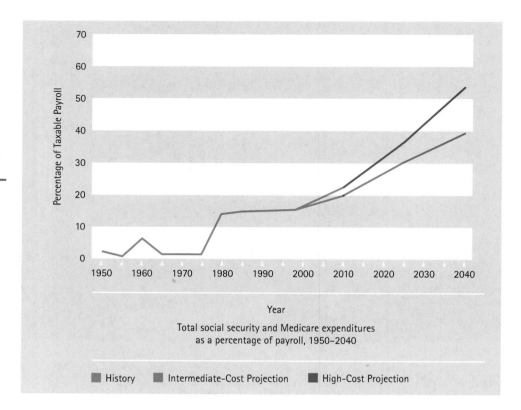

Total social security and Medicare expenditures
as a percentage of payroll, 1950–2040

■ History    ■ Intermediate-Cost Projection    ■ High-Cost Projection

3. Workers may be less willing to pay higher taxes. It will be difficult to increase
   taxes to cover the retirement costs of the baby boomers.

For these reasons, political leaders were delighted to discover an unanticipated
budget surplus in the late 1990s that could be set aside to shore up social security.
Promises to senior citizens could be kept without increasing taxes on working voters.
In the next section, we describe the predicament from which political leaders have
narrowly escaped—at least for the time being.

**Politics of Social Insurance**    Many subway systems use dangerous middle, or
"third," rails that provide the electricity that drives the trains. Social security and
Medicare are said to be the "third rail" of American politics—"touch it and you die."
Richard Morin put it another way: "The bottom line on the public's attitude is: Spend
whatever is needed—particularly on me—just don't bill us for it."[15]

*The Risks of Change to Social Security*—Most public officials know they will be punished
by the voters if they are perceived as threatening social security programs. In 1981
President Ronald Reagan suggested offhandedly that Congress might need to place
limits on the growth in social security. Two days later, the Senate condemned the idea.
Every senator, both Republican and Democrat, disavowed the president's position.
Even so, Republicans lost control of the Senate the following year, and a number of
pundits attributed the loss to Reagan's remark on social security (though a downturn
in the economy was also a factor).

Only once, in 1983, did Congress make significant cuts in social security benefits.
A commission that included leaders from both political parties recommended cuts that
would become effective, for the most part, only in the distant future.[16] Because the recommendations were bipartisan and because cuts were postponed into the next century, the reductions did not produce an electoral fallout. But at all other times, presi-

dential candidates, leaders in Congress, and both parties have opposed cutting social security, even though it is the most costly single program in the entire federal budget. In 1995, both Republican House Speaker Newt Gingrich and Democratic President Clinton called for massive spending cuts for almost every domestic program. Yet both leaders insisted that social security be completely spared from the budgeteers' ax.

*Complexities of Medicare*—The politics of Medicare are much the same, making it difficult to keep the cost of the program from growing rapidly. The program, which cost little more than $30 billion in 1970, grew to nearly $212 billion in 1999.[17] Numerous factors contribute to the rapidly rising cost of Medicare. Though doctors and hospitals are often accused of price gouging, other factors play a more important role. The number of elderly is growing rapidly, increasing the demand for medical services. Doctors can now diagnose and treat more crippling injuries and life-threatening diseases (through magnetic resonance imaging, bone marrow transfusions, and other high-tech, high-cost procedures). Hospitals and doctors try to offer the latest in technology and service. Patients expect error-free medicine, and they sue doctors when mistakes are made, which drives up doctors' insurance costs (and the fees doctors must charge to cover them).

Congress controlled some of these costs by placing limits on doctor and hospital fees, ending the duplication of high-cost technologies, refusing to pay for expensive, highly experimental treatments, and encouraging the formation of health maintenance organizations (HMOs)—which have strong incentives to rein in costs. These actions slowed and even halted the rising cost of Medicare, at least for a while. In 1999, for example, Medicare costs declined slightly from 1998 levels.[18]

Although costs were contained in the late 1990s, they are expected to rise again when the baby boom generation retires and needs more medical services. Stronger proposals, such as raising medical premiums and requiring patients to pay a larger share of the costs, have provoked political controversy. When Republicans made these suggestions in 1995, they said they were doing so only to save the program from bankruptcy. They claimed that President Clinton's failure to reduce cuts doomed Medicare over the long run. Clinton and his Democratic allies in Congress responded that Republicans were cutting medical services in order to cut rich people's taxes. Cuts in Medicare became a central issue in the 1996 election. President Clinton was able to use the issue so successfully that he carried Florida, a normally Republican state but one to which many retirees have migrated.

*The Influence of Senior Citizens*—The electoral impact of the social security issue is likely to remain central to American politics. At a time when overall voter turnout has been declining, senior citizen turnout rates are high and have been climbing. Between 1972 and 1996 turnout among voters aged 18 to 24 dropped by 17 percent, while turnout among voters over 65 climbed by 3.5 percent.[19] Sixty percent of voters over 65 said they voted in the 1998 congressional elections, but only 17 percent of those between the ages of 18 and 24 reported voting.[20] One study of the 2000 presidential primaries found that political advertisements are between 3 and 6 times more likely to be targeted to voters over 50 than to younger voters.[21]

Senior citizens are also much more likely than young people to back up their votes by other political actions, such as writing letters to elected officials and contributing money to political campaigns.[22] Over 33 million people have joined the American Association of Retired Persons (AARP), the largest interest group in the United States.

AARP is a large influential organization. Upon reaching the age of 50, any person can become a member of AARP for $8 per year. Members are eligible for a wide range of travel and other discounts worth much more than their annual dues. They also receive a magazine that keeps them up to date on policy proposals that might affect their social security and Medicare benefits. AARP employs more than 1100 people, works with over 160,000 volunteers, and has an annual budget that exceeds $500 million.[23]

**Supporting Medicare**
*Why are there fewer public demonstrations in favor of programs for the poor?*

**visual literacy**
**Where the
Money Goes...**

Figure 18.4

**Both Young and Old Support Senior Citizens' Programs**
*Why do the young support programs for the elderly even though they do not yet receive benefits from such programs?*

SOURCES: Survey by the Luntz Research Companies/Mark A. Siegal and Associates, September 8–10, 1994; *The Public Perspective: People, Opinions, & Polls,* February/March 1995.

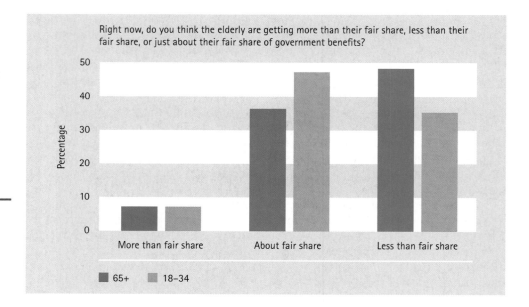

*Broad Support*—AARP has the advantage of promoting a cause that few voters strongly oppose. In fact, young people are just about as likely to support social security as those over the age of 65. Only 7 percent of younger adults think the elderly are getting more than their fair share of government benefits, and 48 percent think the elderly are getting *less* than their fair share (see Figure 18.4).

There are three main reasons for the broad support social security enjoys. First, most people hope to benefit from social security and Medicare someday themselves. In addition, many have parents who currently receive these benefits, relieving their children of financial responsibility. Finally, most people think that because senior citizens contributed to social security, they now deserve the benefits they were promised, and few are aware that these benefits are usually in excess of the contributions.

## Public Assistance to Poor Families

If the interests of the elderly are well protected by AARP and both political parties, the same cannot be said for the interests of poor families with children. Programs designed for poor families are neither as lavish nor as user-friendly as those designed for the elderly. Neither political party is strongly committed to expanding them, and no association comparable to the AARP defends the interests of poor families with children.

**public assistance**
Programs that provide to low-income households a limited income and access to essential goods and services.

**Origins and Development of Public Assistance Programs** Public assistance consists of programs that provide low-income households with limited income and access to essential goods and services. Together, the programs form what is often known as the "safety net" that catches those who fall into financial difficulty. The sheer number of major public assistance programs actually exceeds the number of major programs for the elderly. Public assistance programs include Temporary Assistance for Needy Families, food stamps, the Earned Income Tax Credit, rent subsidies, and Medicaid.

*Temporary Assistance for Needy Families (TANF)*—As mentioned earlier in this chapter, this program, enacted by Congress in 1996, gave the states the responsibility for designing income-maintenance programs for poor families. However, state programs are subject to certain limitations. For example, no family may receive more than two consecutive years of assistance, and no family may receive more than five years of assistance altogether.

timeline
**The Evolution of Social Welfare Policy**

TANF has replaced the long-standing public assistance program known as **Aid to Families with Dependent Children (AFDC)**, which was established in 1935 as part of the Social Security Act. AFDC was designed to serve widows, but as the number of unmarried women increased, the size of the program grew sharply and the social composition of beneficiaries changed markedly. Branded "the welfare program," AFDC was criticized by liberals and conservatives alike. Conservatives claimed that it discouraged recipients from working, an argument that became increasingly potent as the percentage of working women increased.[24] Liberals believed that the benefits were too low and that program eligibility and administrative restrictions were too harsh: Recipients lost their benefits as soon as they earned more than a very minimal amount, and administrators inquired into the personal lives of the poor.[25] TANF has so far proved to be a more popular welfare program, because welfare rolls have fallen and poverty rates have not increased. Whether it will remain popular over the long run remains to be seen.

*Food Stamps*—This public assistance program provides recipients with coupons that can be used to purchase food. Enacted by Congress on an experimental basis in the early seventies, it has been gradually enlarged so that today it is larger than TANF. The **food stamps** program has been more popular than AFDC was, because most Americans feel everyone should be provided with enough to avoid going hungry— especially when agricultural surpluses exist.

*Earned Income Tax Credit (EITC)*—This program returns the taxes paid to those who have little income. Initially proposed by Republicans in the early seventies as a way of simultaneously helping the poor and rewarding work, the **Earned Income Tax Credit** program was greatly expanded during the first year of the Clinton administration. An eligible person who fills out a tax return can receive an EITC reimbursement even if no taxes have been paid. In 1999, a family of four could receive a credit of as much as $3800 a year.[26]

*Supplemental Security Income (SSI)*—**Supplemental Security Income** provides disabled people of low income with income assistance. Created in 1972, SSI succeeds programs of aid to the blind and the deaf established by the Social Security Act of 1935. As of January 2000, the average monthly benefit for SSI's 6.6 million recipients was $377.[27]

**Aid to Families with Dependent Children (AFDC)**
Public assistance program established in 1935 as part of the Social Security Act; replaced in 1996 by Temporary Assistance to Needy Families (TANF).

**food stamps**
Public assistance program that provides recipients with stamps that can be used to purchase food.

**Earned Income Tax Credit (EITC)**
Provision that gives back tax payments to those who have little income.

**Supplemental Security Income (SSI)**
Provides disabled people of low income with income assistance.

**Seeking Welfare and Food Stamp Assistance**
The food stamp program is more popular than AFDC was. *Why do you think it was the more popular program?*

**rent subsidies**
Help in paying rent for low-income families, provided that they select designated housing.

**Medicaid**
Program that provides medical care to those of low income.

*Rent Subsidies*—This policy helps low-income families pay their rent, provided that they select designated housing. The **rent subsidies** program was established in the early 1970s to replace public housing programs, which had been criticized for encouraging racial segregation and creating large concentrations of poverty.

*Medicaid*—This program pays for medical services for the poor. A person becomes eligible only if he or she has no more than a minimal income and few assets other than a home. **Medicaid** was established in 1965, at the same time as Medicare, in response to Republican objections to Medicare on the grounds that it was designed to serve the middle class but not the poor. The cost of Medicaid benefits has risen rapidly—from around $12 billion in 1970 to $108 billion in 1999.

Although Medicaid serves poor families, regardless of age, over one-quarter of all Medicaid costs cover the medical expenditures of low-income senior citizens.[28] Thus Medicaid is an important supplement to the better-known Medicare program discussed earlier.

**Limitations on Public Assistance Programs** This list of public assistance programs that help poor families with children seems impressive, but actual expenditures are only one-tenth as much as what is spent on the elderly. Federal social programs for the elderly amounted to over $13,000 per capita in 1990, whereas public assistance programs for families with children amounted to little more than $1300 per capita (see Figure 18.5). In addition, programs for families with children are more restrictive than programs for senior citizens. Six factors make programs for families with children less user-friendly.[29]

*Fewer Cash Benefits*—In 1990 the elderly received nearly 67 percent of their benefits in cash,[30] whereas only 41 percent of the benefits received by poor families with children were cash benefits.[31] Senior citizens have the better arrangement, because most people prefer cash income to benefits in the form of goods or services. Cash income enables one to purchase what one wants, when, where, and from whom one wishes.

*Less Indexation*—Nearly all benefits to the elderly, including social security and other retirement pensions, are indexed to changes in the cost of living. Although some programs for families with children are also indexed, the main welfare program, TANF (previously AFDC) is not. Instead of keeping pace with increases in the cost of living, benefits under this program fell by 43 percent between 1975 and 1993 in the average state. Following welfare reform in 1996, average benefit levels dropped another 7 percent in real terms.[32]

*Assistance, Not Insurance*—Unlike social security, which distributes benefits automatically according to age and contributions made to an insurance fund, programs for families with children are paid out only after family income has been carefully scrutinized. To become eligible for benefits, a low-income family must demonstrate that it has virtually no other means of livelihood. To show minimal income, the family head must visit a government agency, wait patiently in line with appropriate documents in hand, and then reveal to a government official the family's complete fiscal record. To receive cash benefits, the potential recipient must document that the family does not own a home, has virtually no savings, and has hardly any income.

*State, Not National, Programs*—Families with children receive benefits that vary from one state to another. Only EITC benefits are uniform throughout the country. For the other major programs—TANF, food stamps, SSI, housing assistance, and Medicaid—eligibility rules and benefit levels vary from state to state. In the case of TANF, the benefits can be eight times as much in one state as in another.[33]

Because public assistance programs are state-operated, families with children who move from one state to another have to reconnect to public assistance programs. This

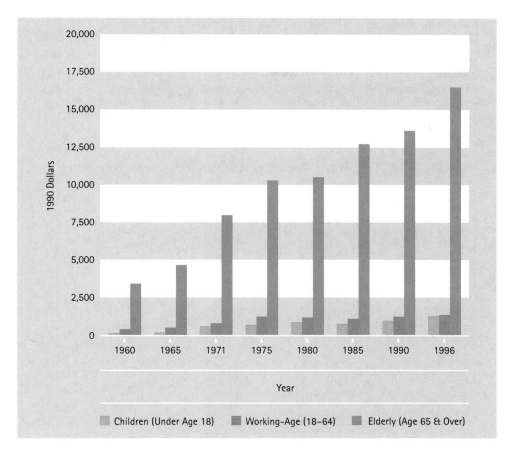

**Figure 18.5**

**Federal Entitlement Expenditures by Beneficiary Age Group, Per Capita, 1960–1996**

NOTE: Figures in constant 1996 dollars.
SOURCE: Neil Howe and Richard Jackson, *1998 Chartbook: Entitlement and the Aging of America* (Alexandria, VA: National Taxpayers Union Foundation, 1998), Chart 3-3, p. 35.

means that poor families may not be able to respond quickly to job opportunities or changing family circumstances.[34]

These restrictions do not apply to senior citizens because social security is a national program. Senior citizens can move from New Jersey to Florida (or even overseas) without jeopardizing the amount or delivery of their social security check.

*Benefits Cannot Supplement Income*—The benefits that poor families with children receive are a substitute for other income; they do not supplement it. In most states, families are not eligible for income assistance if they have savings of more than $1000, a car worth more than $1500, or anything other than a very modest home (the exact value varies from state to state). Under the AFDC program, families lost a dollar in benefits for every dollar they earned. The rules are now changing under TANF, but if the old pattern holds, a recipient whose combined income is at the poverty line will continue to suffer a $.51 loss in benefits (from AFDC, food stamps, and EITC combined) for every dollar earned over the first $2400.[35]

By comparison, senior citizen benefits supplement the recipient's own resources. Senior citizens may receive their Medicare and social security benefits even if they are working full-time, have savings, earn dividends and interest on their investments, and are homeowners. Restrictions on outside income for social security beneficiaries have actually decreased recently. Before the year 2000, social security recipients between 65 and 69 years old lost $1 in benefits for every $3 they earned in wages above $17,000 per year. But Republicans and Democrats in Congress, eager to please elderly voters in an election year, repealed this "earnings penalty" unanimously.[36]

**Politics of Public Assistance** Programs for poor families with children are poorly funded and restrictively designed because, unlike the elderly, children and the poor

## International Comparison — Babies Born Out of Wedlock

Data from other countries suggest that cultural forces have a more powerful effect on family life than does either welfare policy or employment opportunities. Over half the babies are born out of wedlock in Sweden, a country with a waning religious tradition. Only 8 percent of newborns are born to unmarried women in Italy, a Catholic country that places heavy emphasis on family ties. In Japan, an even more traditional society, babies are almost never born out of

wedlock. The United States falls between these extremes with a rate roughly comparable to that of Canada, France, Britain, and Germany.

*In your view, did welfare policy cause out-of-wedlock births in the United States to increase? Or were cultural changes more important?*

SOURCE: *Statistical Abstract of the United States,* 1998, Table 1347.

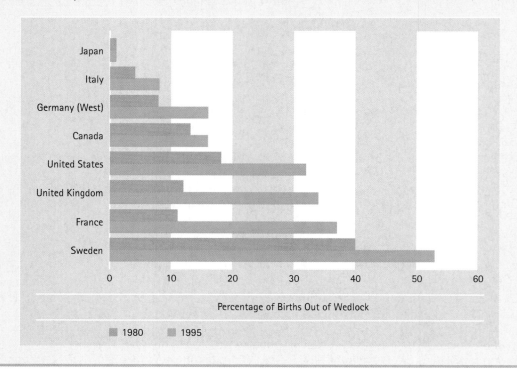

do not exercise direct political power. Instead, they are dependent on others who offer only limited help: policy analysts who offer competing explanations for the persistence of poverty; a weak network of interest groups that fight among themselves; a divided public; and opportunistic political parties.

*Policy Debate*—Before the government can design solutions, it has to decide what the problem is. But policy experts disagree about the causes of poverty among families with children. Three different theories have influenced the welfare debate.

*Liberal theory* argues that poverty rates among children have risen because the government has not maintained an adequate level of governmental assistance. Sociologist Theda Skocpol points out that lower poverty rates in European countries are due in part to government programs that aid low-income families.[37] She advocates the establishment of a similar family allowance program that would guarantee all families with children a basic stipend not unlike the social security checks that the elderly receive.

*Conservative theory* finds the explanation for rising poverty rates in what is identified as a "culture of poverty," in which young people are encouraged to place short-term pleasures ahead of long-term goals. Flashy clothes, adventure, crime, and sexual promiscuity are emphasized, to the detriment of the discipline, patience, and hard work necessary for long-term success. Policy analyst Charles Murray has argued that this culture of poverty has been strengthened and reinforced by welfare policies that reward sloth and irresponsibility. The work ethic is undermined by government programs that give as much money in welfare benefits as can be obtained from an entry-level job. Because they can count on government aid, young people bear more children out of wedlock and think less about responsible parenting.[38]

Conservatives point out that between 1970 and 1991, the percentage of women with children who were living without a mate more than doubled—from 11 percent to 27 percent. These female-headed families are particularly at risk of living in poverty. Many women find it difficult to both work and raise children. Mothers who do work find it hard to get full-time jobs at good wages. Nearly two-thirds of all children living in poverty are living in single-parent families headed by a woman.[39] Liberals respond by noting that poverty rates among families with children are much lower in other countries, despite the fact that the frequency of out-of-wedlock births is often just as high (see the accompanying International Comparison). Apparently, the availability of family allowances softens the economic impact on single-parent families. Conservatives argue that the drop in welfare rolls under TANF's restrictive rules proves that their theory is correct. But liberals point out that the booming economy of the late 1990s could also be responsible for the reduction in the numbers of public assistance recipients. They say that the real test of TANF will not come until the country experiences an economic downturn.

Offering a third explanation, sociologist William J. Wilson attributes a growing culture of poverty to *changes in the postindustrial economy*. Physically demanding blue-collar jobs, which can be performed by unskilled workers with minimal education, are declining in number. These jobs have been lost to technology or have moved overseas.[40] As a result, unemployment rates among young men without a high school degree have exploded, climbing from 8 percent in 1969 to 22 percent in 1985.[41] According to Wilson, when young men cannot find work, they refuse to take on the responsibilities of marriage and child rearing. Young women don't want to marry men with few prospects. Wilson believes his view has been substantiated by trends in the late 1990s. As the economy has blossomed, less-well-educated males are finding new job opportunities, marriage rates are up, and, at the same time, welfare rolls are declining.

*Group Organization*—No group speaking on behalf of children has a mass membership of a size remotely comparable to that of AARP. Instead, many small, competing groups take stances as varied as the alternative explanations for rising poverty rates. The most significant pro-welfare group, the Children's Defense Fund, headed by Marion Wright Edelman, fought welfare reform to no avail. Though the group had a budget in 2000 of $13 million and a staff of 150, it lacks a large membership that can effectively lobby Congress.[42]

On the conservative side, Gary L. Bauer, a Republican candidate for president in 2000, built the Family Research Council into a 250,000-member organization committed to the protection of family values. The group favored the welfare reform bill, a stance reflecting its conviction that welfare programs, by helping unwed mothers make ends meet, discourage family formation and allow fathers to neglect family responsibilities.

Groups with larger memberships do take positions on children's issues, but these groups are also divided about policy choices. For example, the Christian Coalition and Planned Parenthood both take stands on issues relevant to children, but inasmuch as they disagree on abortion policy and many other issues, they generally work at cross-purposes.

Still other groups adopt positions on issues that affect children's welfare, but these groups typically have other objectives more central to their mission. For example, the Urban League has long emphasized the importance of youth programs, but its fundamental objective remains protection of the civil rights of African Americans. The AFL-CIO supports most legislation intended to promote child welfare, but its main

**Spokeswoman for Children**
Marian Wright Edelman, founder of the Children's Defense Fund. *Why does Edelman have less clout in Washington than does the head of the AARP?*

concern is protection of the interests of labor. Though many women's groups care about children's issues, they tend to remain focused on issues of gender discrimination and sexual harassment. In short, the interest-group chorus on children's issues sings separate songs in different keys. They are unable to focus on a common cause in the way AARP does.

*Public Opinion*—The general public wavers between liberal and conservative explanations for rising poverty rates. In 1992, when the country was emerging from a recession, half the population thought poverty was mainly due to circumstances beyond a person's control, and less than a third thought it was mainly due to a lack of effort. But for the rest of the 1990s, when the economy was booming, more people thought poverty was due to a lack of effort than thought it was due to circumstances beyond a person's control.[43] With the passage of TANF, welfare has become a less potent political issue. Conservatives no longer have a national welfare program to criticize, because policies vary from one state to the next. Welfare rolls are also falling, and the cost to the government has been stabilized. Liberals, meanwhile, have found it difficult to criticize TANF because poverty rates have also been dropping. The issue is likely to remain less controversial unless a downturn in the economy makes poverty a visible and urgent problem again.

*Political Parties*—Because public opinion on welfare policy fluctuates, so do the positions of the political parties. Most of the time, the Democratic party takes a more liberal position, the Republicans a more conservative one. Hillary Clinton, for example, was once a member of the liberal Children's Defense Fund's board of directors. Gary Bauer of the Family Research Council is a former Reagan adviser and ran for president himself in 2000.[44] But despite these underlying partisan differences, party leaders often search for the middle ground. As a result, their positions shift over time, and they do not always disagree. In fact, both parties have adjusted their positions over the years, largely in response to changes in the public mood.

When the country was building the Great Society in the 1960s and 1970s, Democrats took the lead, but Republicans were not far behind. Republican presidents signed into law several welfare programs for children. President Nixon proposed the food stamp and SSI programs. Republicans proposed, and President Ford signed, the law creating the Earned Income Tax Credit. Republicans in Congress initiated the Medicaid program.

As the public mood shifted in a conservative direction, the positions of both parties changed accordingly. In 1995 it was the Republicans who took the lead, proposing cuts in many of the programs they had once sponsored.[45] Although some Democrats opposed the cuts, a majority voted in favor of welfare reform, and President Clinton signed the bill into law. Today, both parties take credit for the passage of TANF.

participation

**Making a Difference: Welfare Reform**

### SECTION SUMMARY

Social policy is a type of domestic policy designed to help individuals in need of special assistance. Most major U.S. social policies can be divided into two categories: programs that help the old and programs that help the young. Policies designed to aid the elderly, including social security and Medicare, may be affected by economic downturns and budget constraints but are resistant to major change or elimination. This is because policy makers fear being punished at the polls by well-organized, ably led elderly voters who benefit from the programs.

Policies designed to help the young, such as Medicaid, food stamps, and Temporary Assistance to Needy Families (TANF), are much smaller in size and scope than the huge Medicare and social security programs. They are also much more vulnerable to change or elimination. This is both because policy experts cannot agree on the causes of poverty and because elected officials have little to fear politically from disappointed beneficiaries of these programs. Advocates for the poor and for children are smaller, more divided, and less well funded than advocates for the elderly. Although the public overwhelmingly favors aid to senior citizens, it is more fickle in its support of welfare programs.

## Education Policy

Although social policy has long been one of the domestic policies of great interest to voters, education policy has recently become almost as significant in the public debate. Historically, Americans have supported a large, well-financed educational system. Equal opportunity meant equal access to good schools. But the commitment to public schools, though still strong, has been modified by increasing concern about the quality of education provided in traditional public schools (see Figure 18.6). In this section we discuss the history of locally controlled public education in the United States, current policy regarding education, and the groups that shape this increasingly visible policy debate.

### Local Control

Responsibility for education is divided among local school boards, state departments of education, and the federal Department of Education, but the bulk of control over education policy remains at the state and local level. Keeping control of public schools in the hands of local communities is an important issue for many parents and educators who do not want faraway politicians making decisions about their children's lives. Former Secretary of Education Lamar Alexander provided a vehement expression of this point of view. Testifying before Congress, he accused those in favor of federal involvement of holding "the deeply erroneous belief that American parents, teachers, communities, and states are too stupid to raise their own children, run their own schools, and make their own decisions."[46]

Today, 95 percent of the cost of public education is paid for out of state and local budgets, each contributing approximately half the cost (though the exact percentage paid varies widely from one state to another). The 5 percent contribution by the federal government is spent mainly on programs enhancing equal opportunity, such as

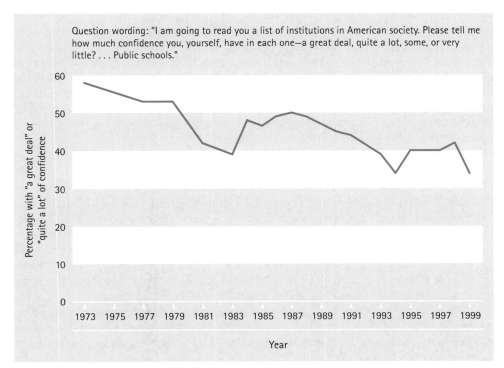

Question wording: "I am going to read you a list of institutions in American society. Please tell me how much confidence you, yourself, have in each one—a great deal, quite a lot, some, or very little? . . . Public schools."

Percentage with "a great deal" or "quite a lot" of confidence

Year

**Figure 18.6**

**Fewer Americans Have Confidence in Public Schools**
*What accounts for the decrease in confidence in public schools over the last few decades?*

SOURCE: Gallup Poll, various years.

special education for the disabled and compensatory programs for disadvantaged children.[47] Core education programs are generally paid for out of state and local dollars.

## Development of Public Education

The public's commitment to its schools is deeply rooted. As early as 1785, Congress set aside the revenue from the sale of one-sixteenth of the land west of the Appalachian Mountains to help pay for "the maintenance of public schools."[48] Support for public schools intensified with the flood of immigrants that arrived in the nineteenth century. As immigrants gained the right to vote, they won access to public education. In Chicago and San Francisco, for example, children from immigrant backgrounds were no more likely to suffer from crowded classrooms than were children from native-born families. On the other hand, where racial minorities lacked adequate political representation, they were given second-class schools. Before gaining the right to vote, African Americans in the South and Chinese in California were segregated into badly maintained, inferior schools.[49]

Despite the discriminatory treatment of racial minorities, public schools did much to build American democracy. The percentages of young people enrolled in American schools far surpassed those in European countries. Public schools helped foster a common language among people from disparate parts of the world. Open to most, if not all, citizens, they reinforced a distinctive American identity built around the concepts of liberty and equality. They also educated the workforce that operated the new machines that were to make the country the world's greatest industrial power.

## Contemporary Issues in Education Policy

Despite the strength of the American educational tradition, Americans seem to be increasingly dissatisfied with traditional public schools. Within the United States itself, financial support for elementary and secondary education (as a percentage of GDP) has increased only slightly over the past 25 years.[50] Teacher salaries, relative to salaries in other occupations, have hardly improved at all.[51]

Other nations, once far behind in school spending, have now nearly caught up. Governments in the United States spend 3.5 percent of the U.S. Gross Domestic Product on primary and secondary education. Although Japan and Germany still spend less than the United States, countries such as Canada, Sweden, and France spend more (see the accompanying International Comparison).

American schools also seem to be doing an inferior job at converting dollars into schools that help students learn.[52] Students in American schools are learning less in reading, science, math, and geography than are students in most other industrial countries (see the International Comparison). Not surprisingly, the public's assessment of the quality of its schools has slipped. The percentage of Americans who expressed "a good deal" or "quite a lot" of confidence in the public schools dropped from 58 percent in 1973 to 36 percent in 1999.[53] (See Figure 18.6.)

As in other social policy areas, liberals and conservatives diagnose the problem differently and offer competing solutions. Liberals argue that schools could be more effective if they were given more resources.[54] Maintaining educational expenditures at the same level as in the past is not enough. Liberals point out that between 1985 and 1995, government spending on health care jumped 50 percent—from 4.2 to 6.3 percent of GDP.[55] But government spending on education inched up from only 4.7 percent to 5 percent of GDP.[56] In other words, government has committed itself to helping pay more of the costs of medical care in order to extend the last years of life, while doing little additional to enhance the capacities of those in the first years of life. Some say this is another sign that domestic policy is skewed to the advantage of the elderly.

Others respond by saying that money is neither the problem nor the solution. They cite studies showing that the amount young people learn in school is seldom affected by the amount of money a school has.[57] The problem is not financial but bureaucratic. Lacking goals, public schools have become cafeterias, where students

## International Comparison

# Student Learning and School Expenditures

Student math scores are lower in the United States than in other industrial countries, yet Americans pay more for schools than many other countries. *Do you believe that test scores would improve if the United States spent more on education? Why or why not?*

SOURCE: U.S. Department of Education, National Center for Education Statistics, *Digest of Education Statistics, 1999*, May 2000 (NCES 2000-031), Table 419, p. 471.

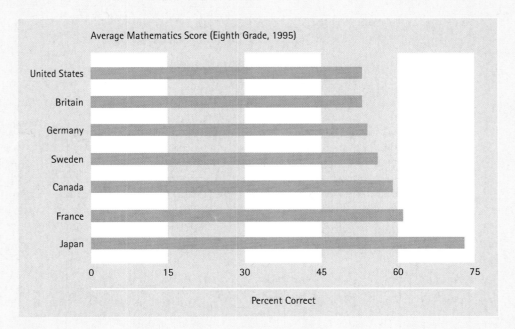

Average Mathematics Score (Eighth Grade, 1995)

Percent Correct

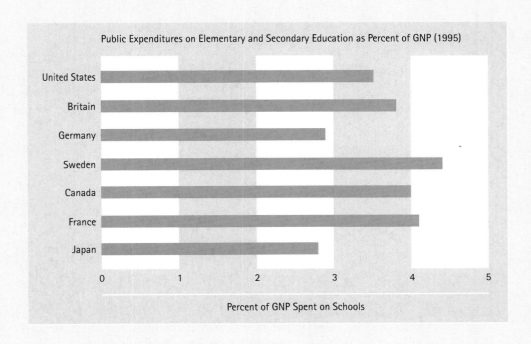

Public Expenditures on Elementary and Secondary Education as Percent of GNP (1995)

Percent of GNP Spent on Schools

**Campaigning on Education**
*Can presidential decisions have a significant effect on school policies? Why or why not?*

take whatever courses they want. Lacking competition, public schools have gone stale. They better serve the interests of the adults teaching in and administering the school than those of the students who are its presumed clientele.

Critics of American education offer two widely contrasting solutions. Some propose national standards, together with a national curriculum, that clearly define the country's educational goals.[58] The George H. W. Bush administration began an effort to create such national standards in 1991. The project ran into difficulty when it attempted to define exactly what students should learn in school. Do students need to learn about Paul Revere's ride? Or about the traditions and way of life of Native Americans? When committees of experts were created to resolve these kinds of issues, they decided to ask students to learn nearly everything any expert recommended. Although this helped the committees reach a consensus, the end result was a curriculum so comprehensive that even a Ph.D. student couldn't master it. The project eventually collapsed under the weight of its own ambitions, but the issue continues to percolate. In 2000 George W. Bush supported a compromise testing system in which states would be required to test students but would set the standards themselves. Al Gore supported a more lenient system of voluntary national tests.[59]

Other critics recommend redesigning the educational system so that students and parents have their choice of schools, just as senior citizens, under Medicare, have their choice of doctors and hospitals.[60] The government would give each family a voucher, which could then be used to purchase education from any school the family preferred. Those opposed to the idea say it will enhance racial, religious, and ethnic divisions and make it more difficult for students from disadvantaged backgrounds to achieve equal educational opportunity (see Chapter 16, page 490).[61]

simulation

**Federally Funded Vouchers and the Future of Public Education**

Voucher programs are being tried in Milwaukee, Cleveland, and Florida. They will probably not be implemented on a larger scale until the Supreme Court resolves the debate over their constitutionality (see Chapter 16). Charter schools have been proposed as an alternative to school vouchers, and they have received backing from both Republican and Democratic leaders. These schools are public schools in that they receive a charter from a state government agency. However, they are not subject to the same state regulations as traditional public schools, and only a few find their policies subject to negotiation with teachers' unions. As in the case of voucher programs, charter schools compete with traditional schools for students. In 2000, there were over 1600 charter schools operating in 34 states. However, less than 2 percent of all public school students attend a charter school.

## Politics of Education

In the past, public schools were, like motherhood and apple pie, beyond partisan dispute. But in recent years, the two political parties have begun to disagree over a broad range of educational issues. Republicans have increasingly supported testing, vouchers, and charter schools, whereas Democrats have won strong support from the two largest teacher groups, the National Education Association and the American Federation of Teachers, by maintaining a steadfast commitment to traditional public schools.

Despite the partisan controversy, both parties remain strongly committed to public education. Campaigning for president, George W. Bush proposed a series of education initiatives involving testing, vouchers, and charter schools. Gore was quick to point out that for all his rhetoric, Bush suggested spending only a small amount more on education.[62] Yet a majority of Republicans, especially those elected at state and local levels, have continued to support public schools, whether traditional or charter. And in the 2000 campaign, both George W. Bush and Al Gore advocated expanding charter school programs. For all the current discontent, Americans still think schools are crucial for achieving the American dream. As long as the electorate feels this way, schools will continue to have bipartisan support.

## Section Summary

Education policy has in recent years become a more important issue in national politics, even though it has historically been—and continues to be—primarily a local issue. For over a century, Americans have felt that public schools taught the virtues of citizenship, the fundamentals of national identity, and the skills to succeed in a dynamic economy. Now, however, other nations are catching up and even surpassing the United States in education spending, and the public has expressed rising concern about the quality of the public schools. Liberals argue for increased funding, whereas conservatives have called for a shift in the way schools work, promoting ideas such as school choice, charter schools, and national standards. However, party differences narrow in the heat of a political campaign; no candidate for public office wants to run the risk of seeming to be anti-education.

## Regulation

On May 11, 1996, 110 people boarded ValuJet's Flight 592 from Miami to Atlanta, many of them students returning from spring break. Over 100 oxygen generators, mislabeled as empty, were also loaded onto the plane. Shortly after takeoff, a fire broke out in a cargo hold. The oxygen generators exploded, fueling the fire, and the plane nose-dived into the Florida Everglades, killing all aboard.

The oxygen generators never should have been loaded onto the plane. According to regulations issued by the Federal Aviation Administration (FAA), ValuJet was not authorized to carry hazardous materials.[63] Hours after the Florida Everglades disaster, Anthony Broderick, an FAA administrator, assured the public that ValuJet was a safe airline. But several weeks later, investigators discovered that the company had not followed FAA procedures. Broderick was fired, all 51 ValuJet aircraft were grounded, and Congress began a massive investigation.

The ValuJet disaster raises questions about the government's regulatory policies. Does the federal government have the responsibility to ensure the public safety? What other kinds of activities should be regulated? How should this responsibility be exercised? In the remainder of this chapter, we discuss why and how the federal government regulates many aspects of our lives.

### The Rise of Federal Regulation

Government **regulation** consists of rules and standards that control economic, social, and political activities. Regulation dates back to feudal times. For example, businesses in sixteenth-century England "were required to set prices and render service in a socially responsible manner."[64] In the United States, the basis for federal regulation is found in the Constitution, which gives Congress the power "to regulate Commerce." Regulations under the authority of the commerce clause were originally applied to the railroad industry, with the passage of the Interstate Commerce Act of 1887. They have

**regulation**
Rules and standards that control economic, social, and political activities.

**The ValuJet Accident**
Searchers look for bodies and wreckage of the ill-fated ValuJet Flight 592, which crashed in the Everglades. The crash led to heightened scrutiny of federal regulations affecting airline safety. *Are airline regulations today too strict or too lax?*

since been applied by Congress to regulate everything from civil rights to national insurance standards. Since the New Deal, the Supreme Court has generally found regulatory policies constitutional (see Chapter 3).[65]

Government regulations increased in number and significance at three distinct periods in the country's history: the progressive era, the New Deal era, and the Great Society era. Each period is marked by a strong political movement that identified major abuses in certain sectors of society, and each produced legislation that created a host of new government agencies (see Figure 18.7).

During the progressive era of the 1890s and early 1900s, writers and journalists known as muckrakers exposed the worst abuses of industrialization. Initially, the spotlight was turned on the power of large corporations, such as Standard Oil Company, which exercised almost complete control over the oil industry. When the public demanded antitrust legislation, Congress enacted the Sherman Act (1890), which made it a crime to "restrain" or "monopolize" trade. This law still plays a major role in government–industry relations. Microsoft, producer of computer operating systems and software, was found guilty under this statute for creating a monopoly and restraining trade. Microsoft appealed the decision, however, saying its practices are aimed at making its products as convenient for consumers to use as possible. In 2000 the appeal was still under consideration.

The muckrakers also publicized other abuses, leading to the creation of additional regulatory agencies. For example, Upton Sinclair's best-selling novel *The Jungle* detailed horrible sanitation conditions in the meat-packing industry and resulted in the passage of the Meat Inspection Act of 1906.

The second regulatory wave occurred during the 1930s, when the government tried to prevent practices that were thought to have caused the Great Depression. The eight major new regulatory agencies created at this time, as listed in Figure 18.7, formed an important component of Franklin Roosevelt's New Deal. The new agencies included the Civil Aeronautics Board, the predecessor to the FAA, which later played such a controversial role in the ValuJet disaster.

A third wave of regulatory innovation took place during the 1960s and 1970s as part of the Great Society. During this period, the issues were consumer safety, occupational safety, and environmental protection. In 1965 Ralph Nader, an enterprising young lawyer, published a best-selling book, *Unsafe at Any Speed*, that revealed serious safety problems with a popular sports car, the Corvair. His efforts were so effec-

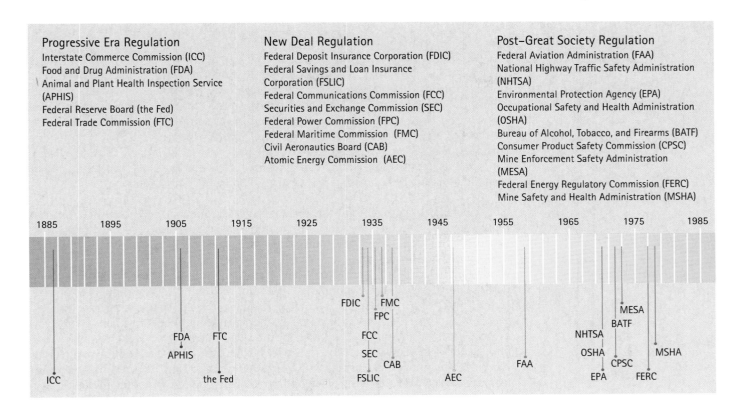

**Figure 18.7**

**Establishment of Major Federal Regulatory Agencies Occurred in Three Waves**

SOURCE: Marcia Lynn Whicker, *Controversial Issues in Economic Regulatory Policy* (Newbury Park, CA: Sage Publications, 1993).

tive that General Motors halted production and new government regulations required manufacturers to install seat belts in all cars. Nader founded several consumer advocacy organizations, hiring young people who came to be known as "Nader's Raiders." In time, they found safety problems in many domains, including other consumer products, occupational environments, and industrial pollutants. In the ensuing years, Congress passed 61 significant pieces of new regulatory legislation and established or substantially enhanced the role of 9 regulatory agencies. Nader has remained politically active; in 2000, he ran for president as the candidate of the Green Party and received 3 percent of the vote, including 5 percent of the vote in Oregon.

The most important of the new agencies formed was the **Environmental Protection Agency (EPA)**, which has the main responsibility for issuing regulations designed to protect the environment from unwanted pollutants. Its controls on air and water pollution have done much to improve air and water quality in many metropolitan areas. As one analyst has pointed out,

> Air pollution from lead, by far the worst atmospheric poison, declined 89 percent during the 1980s; from carbon monoxide, also poisonous, went down 31 percent. In 1992, the number of Americans living in counties that failed some aspect of air-quality standards was only half [those] who lived in dirty air in 1982.[66]

**Environmental Protection Agency (EPA)**

Agency responsible for issuing regulations designed to protect the environment from unwanted pollutants.

## Justifications for Regulation

As a result of these waves of regulatory expansion, the government now regulates many business and social activities. According to Murray Weidenbaum, a former chairman of the Council of Economic Advisors,

> No business, large or small, can operate without obeying a myriad of government rules and restrictions. Costs and profits can be affected as much by a directive written by a government official as by a management decision in the front office or a customer's decision at the checkout counter.[67]

Why have the regulatory responsibilities of government expanded so dramatically during the past century? Scholars have identified three broad types of circumstances in which they find government regulation most easily justified: natural monopoly, externalities, and protection of the uninformed.

**natural monopoly**
A situation in which a public service is best provided by a single company.

**Natural Monopoly** In a **natural monopoly**, a public service is best provided by a single company. To make sure that the company does not take advantage of its monopoly power and charge consumers unnecessarily high prices, natural monopolies are usually subject to regulation. For example, regulations control the charges set by telephone companies that until recently have had exclusive rights in a particular region. Regulations also control the prices of gas, electricity, cable television, and other utilities that have exclusive rights in a particular state or locality. Otherwise, it is likely that these companies would charge excessively high rates.

**externalities**
Consequences of activities that affect those not directly engaged in them.

**Negative Externalities** An **externality** is any consequence of an activity that has an impact on those not responsible for the action. An externality may be positive or negative. If neighbors plant beautiful flowers in their front yard, then they provide those nearby with a positive externality. But if the same neighbors pile unsightly, reeking junk on their front lawn, then those nearby suffer a negative externality. Because neighbors—and corporations—may not care about the consequences of their actions for others, the government may regulate to prevent or adjust for externalities.

One of the best examples of an externality is air pollution. A company may try to keep its costs low by using cheap fuel, even though burning that fuel emits black soot into the air. The black soot does not seriously affect the company, though it threatens the health of, and creates a nuisance for, those living nearby. To prevent companies from imposing this externality on others by polluting their environments, the EPA has imposed numerous regulations on industry to control the emission of pollutants.

A recent controversy over government regulation of externalities took place over the use of U.S. national park land. Until the year 2000, over 180,000 snowmobile aficionados used the national parks each winter, sometimes racing through the woods at speeds in excess of 60 miles per hour. Environmentalists protested this use of public property, arguing that "the national parks should be places where the public can go to escape traffic. . . And clearly these snow machines are loud, they're polluting, and they cause conflict with other visitors." In April 2000, the National Park Service sided with the environmentalists, announcing a sweeping ban on snowmobile use in the nation-

**Snowmobiling in Yellowstone**
*Do snowmobilers in U.S. national parks represent an externality-producing nuisance that must be regulated?*

al parks, with only minor exceptions. As in many other cases of regulation, those being regulated became very upset. Fumed one angry rider, "It's part of a planned campaign by this administration to limit access to public lands."[68]

**Protecting the Uninformed**  Regulations are also used to protect those who cannot be expected to be well informed, most notably consumers. For example, many government rules forbid the marketing of unsafe products or the use of deceptive advertising and labeling.

The need for regulation is especially great in the case of medications. When citizens catch the flu, they cannot be expected to research the side effects of every cold medication on the market. Thus government regulation is necessary to ensure that drugs sold over the counter meet specified safety standards.

Regulation of drugs began during the progressive era. In 1906 Congress created the Food and Drug Administration (FDA), which was given the power to regulate the production and labeling of goods sold in interstate commerce. The initial legislation gave the FDA only limited powers. To garner public support for stronger regulatory authority, in the 1920s the FDA established a museum known as the Chamber of Horrors that contained such atrocities as:

> Samples seized from goods on public sale—samples of patent medicines to cure every known disease, with testimonials from their users, accompanied by copies of their death certificates; and samples of cosmetics—eye-lash beautifiers containing poisonous aniline dyes, hair removers containing thallium acetate, and hair tonics, freckle removers, ointments, and salves containing mercury or other dangerous ingredients—together with photographs of women who had been blinded, paralyzed, or permanently disfigured by their use.[69]

The museum effectively aroused public concern. The FDA now monitors the production of everything from drugs to cosmetics to therapeutic devices such as muscle developers and sun lamps.

## Politics of Regulation

When and how regulations are imposed are political decisions. Regulations are thus shaped by election pressures on Congress, government agencies, and even the courts.

**Congress**  Members of Congress often create regulatory agencies in order to escape criticism when things go wrong. Laws often win passage in response to a well-publicized incident or disaster. In 1984 the Union Carbide chemical plant explosion in Bhopal, India, which killed thousands, resulted in the Emergency Planning and Community Right-to-Know Act, which required plants to disclose possible dangers to the surrounding community. The *Exxon Valdez* oil spill in 1989 that polluted the pristine waters of an Alaskan sound sparked enactment of the Oil Pollution Act of 1990, which established rules for future oil spill prevention and rapid response. With each disaster, congressional representatives demonstrate their responsiveness to public concerns by passing yet another regulatory act. The end result is that regulations often duplicate and overlap one another.

Though regulation may help reassure the public after a crisis or disaster has occurred, it is inherently unpopular with at least some. Regulations require some people to follow restrictive procedures in order to avoid injuring others. For example, the regulations that prohibit snowmobiles in national parks may win the approval of environmentalists, but they almost certainly will alienate devotees of the sport. Because compelling people to do something is likely to make them upset or angry, members of Congress usually employ a strategy known as **blame avoidance**, a set of political techniques designed to disguise their actions and shift the blame to others. In the case of regulatory policy, Congress avoids blame by not directly imposing the regulations but handing that job off to a regulatory agency.

**blame avoidance**
Set of political techniques employed by political leaders to disguise their actions and shift blame to others.

When creating a regulatory agency, Congress often defines its task in general terms. As one group of policy analysts has said about the EPA, its "discretion [is] truly enormous. It produce[s] hundreds of pages of regulations, embodying dozens of significant policy choices, all on the basis of the most elliptical statutory language and the sparsest of legislative records."[70] Congress justifies leaving the terms of reference vague on the grounds that the authors of the legislation cannot anticipate every circumstance requiring regulatory action. Legislators can correctly claim that only those who know the facts in detail can come up with the appropriate regulation. But Congress has also discovered that it can avoid "unpleasant truths" by keeping regulatory legislation broad and general.[71] Different members of Congress may then interpret the law in contrasting ways. Some may claim they have satisfied the concerns of environmentalists and consumers; others will insist they have not imposed undue burdens on business and industry.

When Congress deliberated over the Clean Air Act of 1990, it could have decided to reduce air pollution greatly by making one or two clear decisions, such as increasing the gasoline tax (thereby discouraging unnecessary gas consumption) or subjecting minivans, four-wheelers, and other light trucks to the same antipollution standards that passenger cars must meet (thereby reducing the rapid growth in pollution caused by the booming popularity of these vehicles). But had Congress taken either step, members would have been blamed for raising taxes or driving up the cost of light trucks. To avoid blame, Congress chose to state the clean-air goals that it wanted to achieve in general terms and then require the EPA to figure out ways of achieving them.

In rare cases where the public has become upset at the vagueness of congressional legislation, Congress has taken further (though still less than specific) steps. One such measure has been to set specific goals and then to include a **hammer**—a harsh penalty—if these goals are not met somehow. For example, the Clean Air Act of 1990 says that if certain goals are not met in particular metropolitan areas by a specific deadline, then the "sale of all gasoline in the designated area must cease."[72] Such draconian penalties make Congress *appear* tough, but in fact they are typically so impractical that they would never be used, and the legislation still usually includes no guidelines regarding how the goals should be met.

**Agency Discretion**  Because of the very ambiguity of much congressional legislation, agencies often enjoy considerable freedom in deciding how to execute their mandates. When Congress charged the EPA with improving air quality in metropolitan areas, the agency had to decide the following kinds of questions: Should automobile manufacturers be required to build and sell some electric cars within ten years? Should every vehicle be checked at a state-run inspection station? Should inner-city highways be subject to a toll during rush hour? Should states be told they cannot build new roads? Although EPA officials have considered each of these difficult questions, nothing in the Clean Air Act of 1990 provides precise answers.

The autonomy afforded to regulatory agencies is not limitless. There exists a **zone of acceptance**—a range within which Congress will accept whatever an agency decides is the correct interpretation of the statutes.[73] When an agency goes beyond this informal and ambiguous zone, political opposition arises and the agency backtracks. For example, all of the clean-air options mentioned above provoked controversy, and as a result, the EPA has been slow to implement them.

**Courts**  Although regulatory policies are enacted by Congress and executed by agencies, courts interpret the meaning of congressional statutes and decide whether their application in specific cases conforms to congressional intent. Courts exercise considerable discretion when performing this role, because they are often asked to interpret vague, and even contradictory, laws passed by Congress.

Court interpretations of the 1973 Endangered Species Act illustrate how federal judges influence public policy. The law protects any species on federal lands that is found by the U.S. Fish and Wildlife Service to be threatened with extinction. The species' natural habitat is to be safeguarded from threatening human activity, no mat-

**hammer**
Harsh penalty set by Congress if a regulatory agency does not achieve a statutory objective.

**zone of acceptance**
Range within which Congress allows agencies to interpret and apply statutes.

## Window on the Past        The Spotted Owl Dispute

One of the most controversial court interpretations of a statute has involved the northern spotted owl. This small creature lives in the old-growth forests of the Pacific Northwest, and only some 3000 pairs remain. The species can be saved from extinction only by preserving forests whose habitat is dark enough to allow the spotted owl to evade its main predator, the great horned owl.

Environmentalists called for the protection of the spotted owl partly because they can, at the same time, preserve from logging the old-growth forests, with their marvelous redwoods, cedars, and Douglas firs. Only 10 percent of the original forests remain. To safeguard these, environmentalists asked the Fish and Wildlife Service to declare the spotted owl an endangered species. After extensive investigation, the Fish and Wildlife Service announced that logging on federally owned ancient forests would have to be reduced by 50 percent.

Timber interests prized these great trees for the quality of the wood they produced. The industry saw little need to protect an owl that few had ever seen. "There are millions of owls in the world," said their political ally, Oregon Republican Representative Denny Smith. "This little puppy just happens to be a passive kind of owl that's being run over by the great horned owl." The thousands of workers in the industry cherished not only their jobs but also the logging way of life to which they had become accustomed. Bumper stickers appeared, calling on the reader to "Save a Logger. Kill a Spotted Owl." Local taverns advertised "Spotted Owl Stew" for dinner.

The issue came before federal judge William Dwyer, who issued an injunction halting all logging on federally owned, old-growth forests until the government offered a clear plan that would protect the spotted owl.

The spotted owl became a major campaign issue in the 1992 presidential election, in part because Bush and Clinton both considered Washington and Oregon to be important swing states. Bush called the Endangered Species Act a "broken law," asserting "it's time to put people ahead of owls." Governor Clinton sought votes from both environmentalists and loggers by accusing the Bush administration of not coming up with a reasonable plan to resolve the conflict.

After the Clinton victory in both states, officials in his administration, after meeting with both sides, reduced the logging operations by two-thirds and restricted logging entirely in over 3 million acres of ancient forests. At the same time, the federal government allocated over $1 billion for retraining programs for loggers and to stimulate the economy of distressed logging communities.

Both sides found it difficult to accept the compromise. Environmentalists condemned loopholes in the plan, and timber interests claimed the aid was simply a way of paying off displaced loggers. But Judge Dwyer found the compromise consistent with the requirements of the Endangered Species Act.

Subsequently, a Republican Congress voted in favor of allowing the timber industry to carry out a two-year program that salvaged fallen trees. Despite the intense opposition of environmentalists, who said fallen trees were part of the ecology, Clinton signed the bill, though he later said he regretted having done so.

*Should courts have the power to ban logging to safeguard a small animal in danger of extinction? Or should such issues be left to Congress? How would regulation change if Congress had to approve each regulatory decision?*

SOURCES: Timothy Egan, *The Good Rain* (New York: Random House, 1991); *New York Times,* June 23, 1990, A1; *New York Times,* January 9, 1992, A14; *New York Times,* May 22, 1990, A20; *New York Times,* September 15, 1992, A25. See also Kathie Durbin, *Tree Huggers* (Seattle, WA: Mountaineers Books, 1996).

## Democratic Dilemma

# How Much Regulation Is Needed?

At what point do government regulations become excessive? The contemporary debate over the FDA drug approval policy indicates how difficult it is to answer this question.

Since 1981, upwards of 430,000 Americans have died from AIDS. In 1988 the average AIDS patient lived only 18 months after diagnosis; more than 85 percent died within 3 years. However, there existed only one FDA-approved drug on the market, Azidothymidine (AZT), to combat this deadly disease. Pharmaceutical companies were investing millions of dollars to develop new drugs, but partly because of the lengthy approval process, these drugs were slow to reach AIDS patients. This sparked outrage by AIDS activists across the country. Patsy Stewart, who contracted AIDS in the early 1990s, expressed their view:

> I believe that pharmaceutical research offers the best hope of beat-
> ing this disease. But it now takes nearly 15 years to develop a new
> drug, in part because the FDA micro-manages the development
> process.

When David Kessler became the head of the FDA in 1991, he initiated numerous programs to streamline the drug approval process. A succession of new drugs were quickly approved. The FDA permitted patients in the advanced stages of AIDS to undergo experimental treatment with certain drugs, such as Pentamidine.

Pharmaceutical companies proposed new "home testing devices" to help combat the spread of the disease.

Though the increased speed of drug approval satisfied some, others have recently criticized the FDA for being too lax in its oversight. One controversy surrounded experimental gene therapy procedures, in which doctors use genetically altered viruses to deliver DNA to patients' cells in an effort to cure or treat diseases. After an 18-year-old patient at the University of Pennsylvania's Institute of Gene Therapy died after being treated for a liver disorder, investigators discovered a number of regulatory violations. Following a public outcry, the Clinton administration announced new measures to tighten FDA supervision of gene therapy procedures.

*Should FDA regulations be further relaxed? Or do these regulations serve as important safeguards against the proliferation of potentially dangerous drugs and procedures? Who should decide these questions?*

SOURCES: Margaret S. Rivas, "The California AIDS Initiative and the Food and Drug Administration: Working at Odds with Each Other?" *Food, Drug, Cosmetic Law Journal*, January 1991, 107; Patsy Stewart, "Reform FDA's Lengthy Drug Approval Process," *Tampa Tribune*, May 31, 1996, 14; Marlene Cimons, "Tougher Gene Therapy Protections Urged," *Los Angeles Times*, May 24, 2000, A6.

---

ter what the economic consequences of such protection. In voting for this legislation, most members of Congress probably thought they were protecting large mammals and birds, such as wolves, whooping cranes, and eagles. And, indeed, the Endangered Species Act has been successful in protecting the American bald eagle. In 1963 there were only 417 nesting pairs; by 1999 the numbers had increased to 5800, and President Clinton announced that the animal would be removed from the endangered species list.[74] However, the Fish and Wildlife Service greatly expanded the scope of the legislation when it found nearly 1000 species to be in danger of extinction. And the federal courts have interpreted the law as applicable to even little-known species. Judges have halted the growth of suburbs in order to protect desert kangaroo rats; they have prevented the construction of a billion-dollar dam in order to save a tiny snail darter; and they have halted logging operations in order to safeguard the spotted owl (see the accompanying Window on the Past).

### Deregulation

Although regulation is an inevitable part of modern society, it can be carried to an excess. Regulations intended to protect consumers may have the opposite effect. For example, regulating drugs may prevent some patients from getting the treatment they need (see the accompanying Democratic Dilemma). Furthermore, regulation is expensive. Salaries for bureaucrats, lawyers, and investigators generate an annual price tag that runs to billions of dollars. Regulatory policies may also limit the ability of businesses to compete effectively. The additional paperwork, inspections, procedures, and mandates imposed by regulatory agencies can make the difference between a business that thrives and provides good jobs to Americans and one that cannot remain solvent and is forced to reduce its workforce.

To address these concerns, Congress has introduced in many areas policies of **deregulation**, the removal of government rules that once governed an industry. It has

**deregulation**
Removal of government rules that once controlled an industry.

systematically authorized the partial deregulation of the trucking, banking, and communications industries.[75] Banks may now provide customers with insurance and stock market investments. Regional telephone companies may now offer long-distance and cellular service.

Perhaps the most celebrated deregulation occurred within the airline industry. At one time, a government agency approved the air fare set for every route a plane flew. Though it was originally enacted to prevent price gouging by airlines that had a monopoly in a particular city, many policy analysts claimed that the effect of the law was precisely the opposite of its intent: Regulators were letting airlines charge excessively high prices. President John F. Kennedy placed airline deregulation on the political agenda when he called for "greater reliance on the forces of competition and less reliance on the restraints of regulation" in the industry.[76] Alfred Kahn pushed the issue forward when President Carter appointed him chair of the Civil Aeronautics Board. Opposed to the regulation of airline prices and flight patterns, Kahn announced his intention to eliminate many regulations. Kahn stripped away many of the pricing regulations that had governed the airline industry for decades.[77] The action led to enactment of the Airline Deregulation Act.

Most policy outcomes were favorable. Airline competition increased, companies became more efficient, service to remote areas increased, and air fares fell.[78] Although some worried about the effect on safety,[79] the number of deaths per passenger mile also declined. Yet the ValuJet crash suggests that some regulation must remain in place to ensure that airline companies, in their eagerness for profits, do not cut corners too closely.[80] Complete deregulation is unlikely, because the public will always expect government to act in the wake of disasters or to prevent costly externalities.

## Section Summary

Regulation is a key component of U.S. public policy. Throughout American history, increases in regulation have accompanied key periods of public activism, such as the progressive era and the rise of consumer advocacy in the 1960s and 1970s. In addition to protecting the uninformed public from hazardous products, regulation may be justified in the case of a natural monopoly or when an activity generates significant negative externalities. Congress tends to pass new regulations to win public approval in the wake of well-publicized disasters but uses several techniques to escape blame by those being regulated. One way to avoid blame is to keep the law vague, giving executive department agencies broad discretion on which specific rules to implement. Congress has sometimes deregulated certain activities in response to complaints about inefficient or excessive regulation.

## *Chapter Summary*

Domestic policy involves government spending on social, education, and other policies as well as government regulation of these activities. Many domestic policies divide the two political parties. Democrats typically want to spend more on social and education policy, and they usually favor more regulation. Republicans usually favor less spending and less regulation.

But beyond these partisan differences, there are also differences in the way these policies affect different interest groups and portions of the electorate. This allows the policy-making process to vary from one policy to another and results in policy outcomes that at times seem self-contradictory. Social policies designed to aid the elderly are far more popular and more extensive than similar policies designed to aid poor children. The public wants national candidates to address education policy but does not want to relinquish local control over public schools. And Congress is quick to pass regulatory legislation in the wake of disasters but otherwise tends to write vague legislation, leaving interpretation to the agencies and the courts. Only through a clear understanding of the policy process can one understand these complex, even contradictory outcomes.

## On the Web

Medicare
www.medicare.gov
The official government information site for Medicare.

Social Security Administration
www.ssa.gov
The Social Security Administration (SSA) Web site provides information on the characteristics of the social security program.

Health Care Financing Administration
www.hcfa.hhs.gov
The Health Care Financing Administration (HCFA) administers the Medicare and Medicaid programs.

American Association of Retired People
www.aarp.org
The American Association of Retired People (AARP) maintains a large Web site describing its volunteer programs and lobbying efforts and offering health and recreation tips for seniors.

U.S. Department of Education
www.ed.gov
This Web site of the U.S. Department of Education provides statistical information on the state of education in the United States and describes national education programs.

Harvard University Program on Education Policy and Governance
http://data.fas.harvard.edu/pepg/
Harvard's Program on Education Policy and Governance researches issues of school choice and vouchers.

American Federation of Teachers
www.aft.org
The American Federation of Teachers (AFT) is one of the most powerful lobbying organizations on education issues.

Environmental Protection Agency
www.epa.gov

Occupational Safety and Health Administration
www.osha.gov

Food and Drug Administration
www.fda.gov
The Environmental Protection Agency (EPA), the Occupational Health and Safety Administration (OSHA), and the Food and Drug Administration (FDA) are three of the largest and most important regulatory agencies in the U.S. government.

Public Citizen
www.publiccitizen.org
Ralph Nader's Public Citizen lobbies for consumer protection regulations. The site contains facts and figures and links to papers and other publications.

Heritage Foundation
www.regulation.org
This, the conservative Heritage Foundation's regulation Web site, advocates decreased regulation. The site contains facts and figures and links to papers and other publications.

## Key Terms

Aid to Families with Dependent Children (AFDC), p. 551
agenda setting, p. 543
blame avoidance, p. 565
deregulation, p. 568
domestic policy, p. 542
Earned Income Tax Credit (EITC), p. 551
Environmental Protection Agency (EPA), p. 563
externalities, p. 564

food stamps, p. 551
hammer, p. 566
Medicaid, p. 552
Medicare, p. 546
natural monopoly, p. 564
policy deliberation, p. 543
policy enactment, p. 543
policy implementation, p. 543
policy outcome, p. 543
policy output, p. 543

public assistance, p. 550
regulation, p. 561
rent subsidies, p. 552
social insurance, p. 545
social policy, p. 544
social security, p. 546
Supplemental Security Income (SSI), p. 551
Temporary Assistance for Needy Families (TANF), p. 544
zone of acceptance, p. 566

# Suggested Readings

Burtless, Gary, ed. *Does Money Matter? The Effect of School Resources on Student Achievement and Adult Success.* Washington, DC: Brookings. Excellent collection of essays that debate the current state of public education.

Derthick, Martha, and Paul Quirk. *The Politics of Deregulation.* Washington, DC: Brookings, 1985. Engaging accounts of the political circumstances that enable the federal government to eliminate existing regulations.

Jencks, Christopher, and Paul E. Peterson, eds. *The Urban Underclass.* Washington, DC: Brookings, 1991. Collection of essays analyzing and providing information on the underclass debate.

Kingdon, John. *Agenda, Alternatives and Public Policies.* Boston: Little, Brown, 1984. Discusses the policy-making process, paying special attention to how problems become issues on the political agenda.

Landy, Marc K., Marc J. Roberts, and Stephen R. Thomas. *The Environmental Protection Agency: Asking the Wrong Questions from Nixon to Clinton,* expanded edition. New York: Oxford University Press, 1994. Thorough, critical analysis of EPA policy making.

Melnick, R. Shep. *Regulation and the Courts.* Washington, DC: Brookings, 1983. Case studies of the central role the courts play in interpreting government regulations.

Murray, Charles A. *Losing Ground: American Social Policy: 1950–1980.* New York: Basic Books, 1984. Makes the case that government welfare benefits help to create poverty. Suggests ending welfare.

Pierson, Paul. *Dismantling the Welfare State? Reagan, Thatcher and the Politics of Retrenchment.* New York: Cambridge University Press, 1994. Insightful analysis of political battles over cuts in welfare expenditure.

Skocpol, Theda. *Protecting Soldiers and Mothers: The Politics of Social Provision in the United States.* Cambridge, MA: Harvard University Press, 1993. Fascinating, comprehensive historical analysis of the evolution of the U.S. welfare state.

Tyack, David. *The One Best System: A History of Urban Education.* Cambridge, MA: Harvard University Press, 1974. Classic historical account of the expansion of public education.

Weidenbaum, Murray L. *Business, Government and the Public.* Englewood Cliffs, NJ: Prentice-Hall, 1990. Examines when and how the government interferes with business affairs.

Whicker, Marcia. *Controversial Issues in Economic Regulatory Policy.* Newbury Park, CA: Sage Publications, 1993. Provides a comprehensive summary of the arguments for and against government regulation.

Wilson, James Q. *The Politics of Regulation.* New York: Basic Books, 1980. Comprehensive text on regulatory politics and policy.

Wilson, William J. *The Truly Disadvantaged: The Inner City, the Underclass, and Public Policy.* Chicago: University of Chicago Press, 1987. Argues that poverty has been caused by the internationalization of the economy and the disappearance of blue-collar jobs. Maintains that government should provide jobs.

Chapter

# 19
# Economic Policy

Republicans were optimistic. The year was 2000, the beginning of a new century. In many ways, the voters were unhappy with what was happening in Washington. The Lewinsky scandal had denied President Clinton the dignified place in history to which he had aspired. Indeed, he had become just the second president to be impeached by the House of Representatives and forced to defend himself in a Senate trial. The Democrats' nominee for president, Clinton's loyal vice-president Al Gore, looked vulnerable. A stodgy candidate who lacked Clinton's skill with the mass media and tactical finesse, Gore trailed his Republican opponent George W. Bush by a significant margin in polls taken in the summer of 2000.

Yet Gore had one ace up his sleeve that proved decisive on election day: The country had enjoyed eight years of uninterrupted economic growth during the Clinton administration. During those years, the size of the country's economy had grown by an average of 5.3 percent per year,[1] unemployment rates had plunged from 7 percent to 3.9 percent—the lowest level in three decades[2]—and the value of stocks on Wall Street had nearly tripled.[3] Never before had Americans enjoyed such prosperity for such an extended period of time.

**gross domestic product**
The measure of the total value of economic activity in a nation in one year.

Republicans insisted that Clinton and Gore were no more responsible for the booming economy than a crowing rooster is responsible for the rising sun. They claimed the steady rise in the **gross domestic product (GDP),** the official measure of the total value of economic activity in the United States, had resulted instead from increased productivity, the expanding new technology industries, and the decisions made by Alan Greenspan, head of the Federal Reserve Board. Republicans asked voters to ignore economic factors over which Clinton had exercised little control and to focus on the moral leadership the president had failed to provide.

Despite Republican claims and despite the unprecedented prosperity, the results of the election were far closer than experts from either party had predicted. Still, the close results of the 2000 election suggests that it was a rare exception to an ancient law of politics: Voters like governments that fatten their wallets.

ELECTED OFFICIALS PLACE GREAT EMPHASIS ON FORMULATING AND IMPLEMENTING the policies that affect economic conditions. And elections are often decided on the basis of economic factors. But were the voters correct to reward the Democrats for the prosperity of the 1990s? How much control do the president and Congress have over the economy? Who is Alan Greenspan and why is he so important? To answer these and related questions, we consider the following specific topics:

- How does the state of the economy affect presidential elections?
- What kinds of policies does the government use to manage economic fluctuations?
- How has the economic prosperity of the 1990s affected the federal budget and national policy debates?
- How does the U.S. tax system work?
- How does the relationship between the U.S. government and the economy compare to that in other nations?

## Economic Growth and the Business Cycle

Economies grow as the result of technological innovations, investments in physical capital (factories, agricultural production, communication systems, and so on), and investments in human capital (education, worker training, and the like). As a result of technological change and investments in physical and human capital, the U.S. economy has grown enormously, and many of those who have invested in American industry have reaped huge rewards. For example, if you had purchased $25 worth of stock in a cross section of American companies in the late 1920s, that stock would be worth about $1100 today.

In any given year, however, short-term fluctuations in the economy can adversely affect stock values. For example, that $25 investment would have lost over two-thirds of its value from 1929 to 1933, the early years of the Great Depression, and would not have regained its original value until the mid-1950s.

Few economic downturns are as severe as the Great Depression. But **recessions**, slowdowns in economic activity, occur relatively often, if unpredictably. Economists refer to these periodic episodes of economic slowdown, followed by recovery, renewed expansion and rising prices, as the **business cycle.** Figure 19.1 provides an illustration of this phenomenon.

Governments try to set economic policies to minimize the disruptions caused by the business cycle so that most people keep their jobs and prices remain stable. In other words, they try to avoid two major problems: inflation and unemployment. **Inflation**—a rise in the price level—makes consumers pay more money for an equal amount of goods and services. As a result, the general public becomes unhappy if inflation rates are high. **Unemployment**—which occurs when people willing to work at prevailing wages cannot find jobs—harms a smaller number of people but in ways that are marked and visible. It also makes it difficult for many people who have jobs to change jobs or win wage increases.

Political leaders try to avoid both misfortunes, but they are not always successful. For a long time, the two conditions were thought to be closely related: lower

**recession**
A slowdown in economic activity, officially defined as a decline that persists for two quarters (six months).

**business cycle**
The alternation of periods of economic growth with periods of economic slowdown.

**inflation**
A sustained rise in the price level such that people need more money to purchase the same amount of goods and services.

**unemployment**
The circumstance that exists when people who are willing to work at the prevailing wage cannot get jobs.

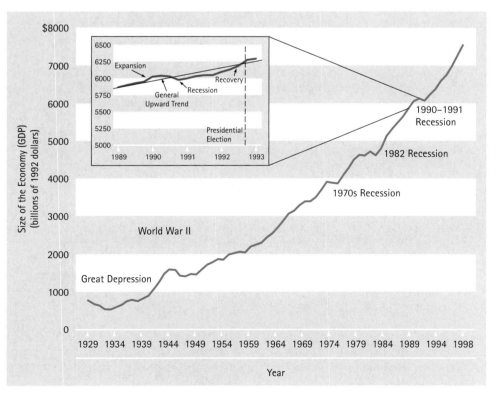

**Figure 19.1**

**Long-Term Growth and the Business Cycle in the United States**
Though the general economic trend may be upward over the long run, expansions and recessions that characterize the business cycle can—in the short term—harm both citizens and elected officials.

SOURCES: U.S. Census Bureau, *Statistical Abstract of the United States: 1999*, p. 881, Table 1434; U.S. Department of Commerce, Economics and Statistics Administration, "National Income and Product Accounts," http://www.bea.doc.gov/bea/dn/gdplev.htm, accessed July 27, 2000.

## Election Connection

### 1980

In 1980 Jimmy Carter became the first elected president since Herbert Hoover to lose his bid for reelection. Ironically, the struggling economy that helped him win office in 1976 led to his defeat four years later.

In 1976 Carter added together the inflation and unemployment rates and named the resulting sum the "misery index," suggesting that it was a measure of the misery suffered by the average American. The misery index was 12.5 in 1976, up from 8.9 in 1972. Partly as a result of the poor economic conditions summarized by the index, Carter narrowly defeated the unelected incumbent, Gerald Ford.

Carter was unlucky enough to hold office in the 1970s, an era of "stagflation"—low growth (economic stagnation) and high inflation. During his administration, inflation raged at double-digit levels, interest rates exceeded 15 percent, and even the unemployment rate seemed stuck at a relatively high level. In the late 1970s, the Gallup Poll reported that the Democrats had lost their traditional advantage of being perceived as the party best able to keep the country prosperous. In 1980, the misery index stood at 18.2, one-third higher than when Carter defeated Ford.

Ronald Reagan campaigned across the country asking crowds, "Are you better off today than you were four years ago?" And the crowds yelled back "No!" In the final days of the campaign, undecided voters moved decisively to Reagan and he won easily. In the next few years, stern decisions by the Federal Reserve smashed inflation. In 2000, the misery index had fallen to 7.7.

*Is it fair to judge a president's performance on the basis of the misery index? Why do many voters place economic issues ahead of other issues in evaluating candidates?*

SOURCE: Data are taken from *OECD Economic Outlook*, no. 58, December 1995 (Paris: Organisation for Economic Cooperation and Development).

---

unemployment was assumed to mean higher inflation, and vice versa.[4] But economists no longer believe the relationship is so close. In fact, President Carter had the misfortune to run for reelection at a time of "stagflation," when both inflation and unemployment were high. He suffered a humiliating defeat. For the next three elections, Republicans reminded the public of the economic chaos of the Carter years (see the accompanying Election Connection).

### Economic Conditions and Political Fortunes

As Carter's experience shows, people tend to blame those in charge when times are hard. President George Bush also suffered from economic adversity in 1992. His popularity ratings fell 40 percentage points during a recession in the second half of his administration—from 78 percent in July 1990, when the rate of unemployment first began to rise, to 38 percent two years later, when unemployment peaked.

Bush and Carter were not the only presidents to have lost popularity when the economy faltered. Presidents Eisenhower and Nixon suffered similar fates, losing significant public support when recessions hit. Some critics called Ronald Reagan the "Teflon president" because they believed that none of the usual political dirt and grease stuck to him; but even Ronald Reagan's popularity dropped precipitously during the 1981–1982 recession.[5]

Terrible economic times in American history are associated with massive election losses for the party of the president. The depression of the 1890s ushered in an era of Republican dominance, and the Great Depression of the 1930s did the same for the Democrats. Indeed, Republican President Herbert Hoover (1929–1933) became one of history's most unpopular presidents simply because he was in office when the Great Depression began. For decades afterwards, Democrats ran against the party of Hoover, using the Depression issue to help them win the next five elections.

Prosperity, in contrast, strengthens a president's position for reelection, as Figure 19.2 illustrates. Riding booming economies, Lyndon Johnson trampled Barry Goldwater in 1964, Richard Nixon crushed George McGovern in 1972, and Ronald Reagan trounced Walter Mondale in 1984. Of course, a healthy economy does not guarantee presidential popularity. For example, prosperity did not keep Johnson's popularity from falling sharply in response to the rising casualty rate in Vietnam.[6] Nonetheless, presidents usually do better electorally when the economy is strong.

National economic conditions may influence congressional elections as well.[7] In 1930, Democrats captured control of Congress when voters blamed Republicans for the onset of the Great Depression. The Eisenhower recession of 1958 inflated the narrow Democratic majorities in the House and Senate. The huge Democratic majorities of 1974 were due both to the Watergate scandal and to an economic downturn.[8] When the economy dragged Carter under in 1980, the Republicans took control of the Senate and made large gains in the House. To be sure, economics is not the only force at work in congressional elections. The Democrats suffered serious congressional losses in 1966, even though the economy was fine. That election turned on Vietnam and racial tensions. Similarly, the Republicans captured control of both House and Senate in 1994, even though unemployment fell during Clinton's first two years.

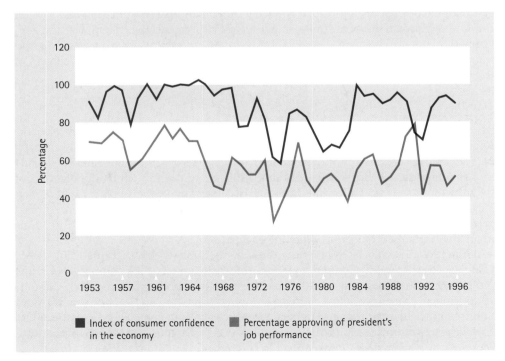

**Figure 19.2**

**How Americans Feel About the Economy Influences What They Think About the President**
*When does the economy not have a major impact on the public's view of the president?*

NOTE: The figure displays data for the first quarter of each year.

Although it may seem surprising, the condition of the national economy also affects state election outcomes. When times are bad, the party of the president suffers significant losses in gubernatorial and state legislative elections.[9] State officials can do little about national economic conditions, but unhappy voters take out some of their frustration on members of the president's party throughout government. Thus state elected officials take great interest in the economic policies followed by national officials of their party.

But the economy is most critical for presidential elections, so it is the president who pays the closest attention to economic policy. Traditionally, presidents try to shape immediate economic conditions by using two major policy tools, fiscal policy and monetary policy. We discuss these policy tools in the next two sections.

## SECTION SUMMARY

The business cycle is an irregular but recurring feature of the economy. Elected officials work to minimize its negative effects by keeping a close watch on both inflation and unemployment, both of which can upset voters by disrupting their economic security. Elected officials at all levels, but especially presidents, know that voters will punish them if the economy turns sour. This is reason enough for them to pay close attention to national economic policy.

## *Fiscal Policy*

**fiscal policy**
The sum total of government taxing and spending decisions, which determines the level of the deficit or surplus.

**deficit**
The amount by which annual spending exceeds revenue.

**surplus**
The amount by which annual revenue exceeds spending.

**budget**
The government's annual plan for taxing and spending.

A government's **fiscal policy,** the sum total of government taxation and spending, determines whether government revenues exceed expenditures. When yearly spending exceeds tax receipts, the government runs a **deficit.** When the amount collected in taxes exceeds spending, the government enjoys a **surplus.** When the two are exactly the same, the budget is said to be balanced. The nation's fiscal policy is formulated in a **budget,** the government's annual plan for taxing and spending. The budget sets funding levels for all government programs. In 2000, the federal budget amounted to about $1.8 trillion, or 17 percent of the nation's GDP.[10] Since the 1970s, the president has proposed a budget to Congress each year, but Congress usually makes major changes to the president's plan before passing it (see the accompanying Window on the Past). The largest portion of the federal budget—22 percent—goes to the social security program, as Figure 19.3 indicates. Medicare and Medicaid claim 17 percent, and national defense accounts for 15 percent of the nation's spending. Interest paid on the sizable national debt consumes an additional 11 percent. Everything else the government spends money on—from highway funds, to education programs, to child nutrition, to housing subsidies, to foreign aid, constitutes the remaining 35 percent of the budget.[11]

### *Use of the Budget Deficit*

According to an influential English economist of the 1920s and 1930s, John Maynard Keynes, there is nothing sacred about a balanced government budget; on the contrary, he said, budget deficits can lift an economy out of a recession. If government spends money when no one else does, it can jump-start the economy, which then can begin to grow on its own. Following this line of reasoning, which came to be called **Keynesianism,** Franklin Roosevelt broke with the traditional belief in a balanced budget (held by his predecessor Herbert Hoover) and ran large deficits during the 1930s in an attempt to get the country moving again.

After World War II, Keynesian thinking became widely accepted. In 1946, Congress established a **Council of Economic Advisors (CEA)** composed of three prominent economists who would advise the president about the state of the national and international economy, present economic forecasts, and make recommendations about the budget. Because deficits were thought to create jobs, whereas surpluses held prices down, these expert economists tried to help presidents "fine-tune" the economy to ensure steady prosperity. On the recommendation of the CEA to stimu-

**Keynesianism**
Economic policy based on the belief that governments can control the economy by manipulating demand, running deficits to expand it and surpluses to contract it.

**Council of Economic Advisors (CEA)**
Three economists who head up a professional staff that advises the president on economic policy.

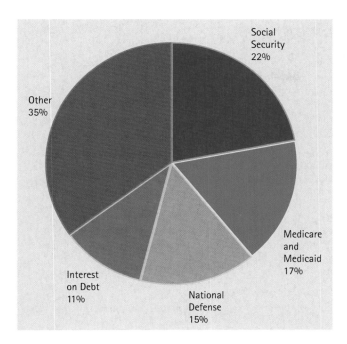

**Figure 19.3**

**Major Components
of the Federal Budget**

SOURCE: *A Citizen's Guide to the Federal
Budget: Budget of the United States
Government, Fiscal Year 2000* (Washington,
DC: Office of Management and Budget,
1999).

late a sluggish economy, John Kennedy urged Congress to pass a deficit-creating tax cut. Some credit the cut, passed in 1964, with stimulating the mid-1960s economic boom.[12] Conversely, to slow down the inflation rate, Lyndon Johnson followed CEA advice and persuaded Congress to pass a tax increase in 1968. Despite the tax, inflation continued. Some said that the cut failed to have the desired effect because the tax increase was not big enough.[13] Others said that failure of the tax increase to stop inflation proved Keynes's theory wrong.

## Decline of Fiscal Policy

Administrations today are much less likely to use fiscal policy as a tool for managing the economy than they were during the Kennedy–Johnson era. For example, the CEA has declined in importance—so much so that some Republicans in the House of Representatives proposed its abolition in 1995. Several factors have contributed to the decline in the economic significance of fiscal policy; these factors include divided government, monetarism, budget deficits, and internationalization.

**Divided Government** Fiscal policy and divided government do not mix well together. An economic policy must be implemented quickly if it is to alleviate the economic conditions it is aimed at. But when government is divided between the two parties, it is difficult to enact fiscal policy quickly in response to changing economic conditions.

Fiscal policy is a product of the taxing and spending decisions recommended by presidents and passed by Congress. Even under the most favorable conditions, it takes considerable time for the two institutions to iron out their differences and adopt a budget. Getting them to work together when each is controlled by different parties is even more difficult.[14] In the divided-government administrations of the 1980s, it typically took eight months for Congress to act on a president's annual budget, and then it took many more months for the taxing and spending decisions to take effect. Meanwhile, the economy can change direction dramatically. Thus the economic conditions that seem to require fiscal policy measures often have changed by the time the specific policy takes effect. For example, Bush's 1990 tax increase was supposed to check inflation in a growing economy, but it took effect in the midst of a recession, when unemployment was the greater concern.

timeline

**Growth of
the Budget and
Federal Spending**

**John Maynard Keynes**
John Maynard Keynes, responsible for
the school of macroeconomics that
came to be called "Keynesianism." *Why
is Keynesian thinking on fiscal policy less
influential today?*

## *Window on the Past*    Constructing the 2000 Federal Budget

The practice of developing the federal budget is a long and complicated process that resembles the legendary labyrinth containing the Minotaur, a monster to whom young Athenian men and women were sacrificed.[a] Much gets lost within the intricate passages. In the legend, only Daedalus and his son Icarus escaped by devising wings and flying out.

That anything escapes through the budget labyrinth seems equally miraculous. To illustrate, consider the rules for constructing the federal budget and the way the budget was created for fiscal year 2000, which, by law, began not on January 1, 2000, but three months earlier, on October 1, 1999.

Budget construction begins within the executive branch along lines set forth in the Budget and Accounting Act of 1921. The process starts a year and a half before the beginning of the fiscal year. Thus, budgeting for fiscal year 2000 began in the spring of 1998, when federal agencies developed preliminary guidelines. They submitted their budget requests during the summer of 1998 to the Office of Management and Budget (OMB). During the fall of 1998, OMB reviewed the requests and made modifications. This was followed by a period of negotiation between the departments and OMB, with final decisions made by the president.

The Budget and Accounting Act requires that the president's budget be submitted to Congress no later than the first Monday in February prior to the beginning of the new fiscal year. But no law requires Congress to pay any attention to what the president has recommended, and when a different party controls Congress the president's budget is likely to arouse strong opposition. When Clinton submitted his budget to Congress in February 1999, the Republican leaders in Congress frankly announced they were not inclined to pay much heed to what the president had proposed. For one thing, Republicans believed the president had been weakened by his impeachment and pending Senate trial. For another, they believed that taxes should be cut substantially in light of the budget surplus. Clinton had proposed only minor, focused tax reductions.

To construct its own budget, Congress followed the procedures laid down in the 1974 Budget and Impoundment Control Act, which created two budget committees, one for the Senate, the other for the House. The other congressional committees were asked to submit the estimated cost of their proposed activities to the budget committees by March 15. The budget committees are then expected to recommend to their respective chambers a budget resolution that specifies the total amount that the government plans to raise and spend in each of the next five years. The resolution also allocates funding to 20 broad categories of spending for the next fiscal year.

The budget resolution, which Congress is expected to approve by April 15, usually generates controversy, because it often requires that committees rewrite existing law to adopt difficult spending and tax changes that will reconcile government policy with the resolution. This process is referred to as reconciliation.

*(continued on next page)*

---

**monetarism**

An economic school of thought that rejects Keynesianism, arguing that the money supply is the most important influence on the economy.

**Monetarism**  The second factor that has reduced the significance of fiscal policy is the increased influence of **monetarism,** a school of economic thinking that says that the money supply, not budget deficits, is the most important influence on the economy. Monetarists argued that deficits are paid for by borrowing money from investors. Thus every dollar the government spends is one less dollar to be invested in other productive activities. Budget deficits do not add any extra stimulus—they just transfer available dollars from the private sector to the government.

Even Keynesians favored only temporary deficits; they did not believe that a government budget could be continually in deficit. Over the long run, a nation's economy can grow only if people save money and invest it in productive enterprises. The problem is that when a government borrows money, it soaks up some of the country's

## Window on the Past    Constructing the 2000 Federal Budget, *continued*

*(continued from previous page)*

But if reconciliation is not complicated enough, the budget maze is still more intricate. Since 1990, Congress has operated under a pay-as-you-go rule, which says that any proposal to cut taxes or increase spending must be coupled with an offsetting proposal that will cover the cost of the tax cut or expenditure. With this added complexity, the difficulty of adopting a budget resolution on schedule is just as hard as escaping the Minotaur. In fact, Congress has met the statutory deadline for adoption only once since the 1974 law went into effect.

Once the budget resolution is enacted, the appropriations subcommittees use the funding targets agreed to in the budget resolution as a framework for writing the 13 detailed appropriations bills. Congress is then expected to pass these bills by October 1, the start of the new fiscal year. In practice, this almost never happens on schedule, and parts of the government must operate under continuing resolutions, temporary funding measures passed by Congress to keep the government operating.

In 1999, the Republican Congress had passed only 5 of the 13 appropriations bills by October, and Clinton vetoed one of these. The president also rejected a Republican-sponsored $800-billion ten-year tax cut bill. In addition, the two sides clashed over a proposed delay in the payment of the earned income tax credit, a benefit for lower-income families. Congressional Republicans lost this debate to the president when Republican presidential candidate George W. Bush objected to the proposal.[b]

Finally, after weeks of continuing resolutions, late-night negotiations over budget targets, and partisan acrimony, the budget bill was given its wings and took flight from the labyrinth when Clinton signed the bill into law on November 29, 1999.[c] This was nearly two months after the start of the fiscal year, and a year and a half after the fiscal 2000 budget process had begun.

This example may seem extreme in the amount of bickering that occurred, but in reality it is about average. Worse conflicts and delays occurred in 1985, 1987, and 1990. In 1995, partisan battles forced two extended government shutdowns and left the nation without a budget for nearly four months. In 1998, Congress skipped the budget resolution stage, technically violating the law.

*Does the labyrinthine nature of the budget process make it easier to understand why fiscal policy is now seldom used to manage the national economy? Why or why not? Some reformers have proposed changing the budget process so that Congress would write budgets for several years at a time. Do you think this change would make the process more or less acrimonious?*

---

[a] The following summary account is drawn from Allen Schick, *The Federal Budget* (Washington, DC: Brookings, 1995); and Steven Smith, *The American Congress* (Boston, MA: Houghton Mifflin, 1995), Ch. 11.

[b] Tim Weiner, "Criticism Appears to Doom Republican Budget Tactic," *New York Times*, October 1, 1999, A20.

[c] Richard W. Stevenson, "Clinton Signs Final Budget Bill and Turns to Next Year," *New York Times*, November 30, 1999, A20.

---

savings, and with less savings to finance investment, economic growth slows. Thus most economists today agree that persistent deficits result in lower long-term economic growth.

**Growing Budget Deficits** Fiscal policy was also undermined by the large budget deficits of the 1980s. In the 1960s, when regulation of the economy by means of fiscal policy was a popular idea, the federal **debt**—the accumulation of annual deficits—was still declining from the peak to which it had climbed in World War II. Thus modest adjustments in fiscal policy could be made from one year to the next without creating long-term problems. But in the 1970s large defense expenditures, coupled with growing social welfare spending, regularly produced unbalanced budgets in which

**debt**
The accumulation of yearly deficits.

total expenditures exceeded tax revenues by significant amounts. In the 1980s **supply-side economics,** implemented by the Reagan administration, further exacerbated the situation.[15] The central tenet of supply-side economics (called "Reaganomics" by critics) held that lowering tax rates would stimulate so much additional productive economic activity that the government would raise more in revenues even if tax rates were lower. The theory proved incorrect. Large tax cuts enacted during the 1980s, coupled with increases in defense spending and continued high spending for social programs, led to sustained deficits unprecedented in American history (see Figure 19.4). At a time when budget deficits were already high, it was politically infeasible to propose still higher ones, no matter what the economic situation.

**Internationalization** Fiscal policy has been further limited by the internationalization of the economy. Economic activity has become increasingly linked to overseas markets, so the reactions of economic actors to government policies are no longer limited to conditions in their own countries. If American investors think the government is spending too much, they can move billions of dollars to markets in Europe or Asia. Investors in other countries can do the same. Thus advances in communications have enabled investors in stocks and bonds to penalize governments for poor economic policies. If a government adopts taxation or spending policies that investors dislike, they can, for example, sell their bonds and their money to more accommodating countries, thus imposing economic costs on the government that adopts unfavorable policies. James Carville, President Clinton's 1992 campaign manager, offered a humorous recognition of the power of investors in the stock and bond markets when he commented that "I used to think if there was reincarnation, I wanted to come back as the president or the Pope . . . but now I would like to come back as the bond market. You can intimidate everybody."[16]

These changes in the international economy gave rise to another school of economic thinking called "rational expectations." According to this theory, firms, investors, and other private economic actors rationally anticipate what government plans to do and then act in ways that offset what the government subsequently does.[17] For example, if the government plans to run a budget deficit in order to stimulate the economy, rational investors anticipate inflation and, to protect their investments, demand a higher interest rate on government bonds and other investments. But high-

## Figure 19.4

**The Federal Deficit or Surplus, 1950–2005**
*What accounts for the large deficits of the 1980s and the sudden surpluses of the late 1990s?*

SOURCE: Office of Management and Budget, *The Budget of Fiscal Year 2001, Historical Tables,* p. 22, Table 1.2.

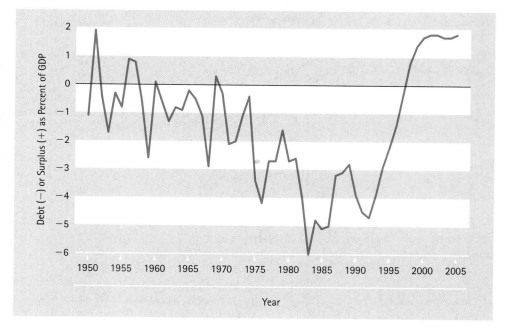

er interest rates dampen economic growth, which offsets the intended stimulus effect of the budget deficit. In other words, government objectives are undermined by investors in the bond market.

Of course, people are not perfectly informed, and even professional economic forecasters cannot predict economic developments very well, but rational-expectations arguments were sensible enough to raise doubts about the ability of government to manage the economy, especially when government plans become widely known during the lengthy public process of setting fiscal policy. By 2000, governments appeared especially sluggish at a time when the communications revolution was making it possible for investors to react very quickly to changes in government policy.

visual literacy

**Evaluating Federal Spending and Economic Policy**

### SECTION SUMMARY

During much of the twentieth century, elected officials tried to manipulate the economy by using fiscal policy—that is, by altering the government's taxing and spending decisions. Economist John Maynard Keynes was a strong proponent of this method, arguing that budget deficits could propel an economy out of recession. Though government policy makers focused on fiscal policy until at least the 1970s, a confluence of factors discredited its use. These included divided government, the rise of an alternative monetarist theory, persistent budget deficits, and the growing internationalization of the U.S. economy.

## Monetary Policy: The Federal Reserve System

Although fiscal policy was once a significant method of regulating the economy, today **monetary policy,** adjusting interest rates by varying the supply of money, is the government's most important tool in this regard. The essence of monetary policy is raising or lowering interest rates, which governments do by subtracting money from or adding money to the economy. When the supply of money is increased, its price—interest rates—comes down, which encourages people to borrow more. As they spend and invest the borrowed money in new productive activity, the economy grows and unemployment falls. Conversely, when the supply of money goes down, interest rates go up, and people borrow less. With less to be spent and invested, the economy slows and inflationary pressures ease.

Monetary policy is thought to be an effective tool for managing the economy partly because, unlike fiscal policy, it can be altered quickly in response to changing economic circumstances. Interest rates can be adjusted on a monthly, weekly, or even daily basis as the need arises (although it may take months before the policy change actually affects economic conditions).

Commonly referred to as the Fed, the **Federal Reserve System** is a government authority that manages the government's monetary policy. Created in 1913, the Fed is headed by a board consisting of 7 governors appointed by the president and confirmed by the Senate, each Fed governor holding office for 14 years. The Fed acts on the economy through the operations of its 12 regional banks, each of which oversees member banks in its part of the country. Figure 19.5 illustrates the structure of the Fed and its relationship to the federal government.

Often the Fed is said to be the most powerful agency in the government after the Executive Office of the President. Its decisions affect interest rates, employment levels, and economic growth rates. The great American humorist Will Rogers once remarked that "there are two things that can disrupt the American economy. One is a war. The other is a meeting of the Federal Reserve Board." Surprisingly, in view of its importance, the Fed's activities are relatively unknown to many Americans.

The most important decisions affecting the day-to-day workings of the economy are made by the Fed's Open Market Committee. This committee considers whether interest rates are too high or too low and what adjustments should be made. The

**monetary policy**
The actions taken by government to affect the level of interest rates by varying the supply of money.

**Federal Reserve System**
The country's central bank, which executes monetary policy by manipulating the supply of funds that lower banks can lend.

**Figure 19.5**

The Structure of the
Federal Reserve System
*Do banks have too much say?*

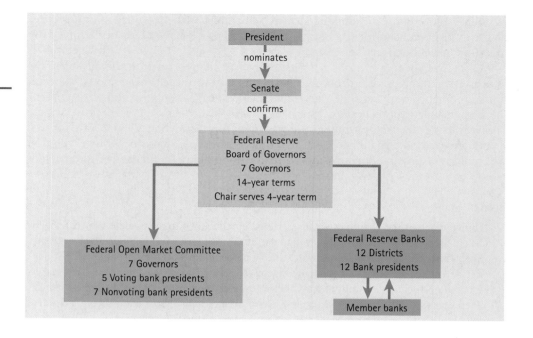

committee consists of the 7 governors, all of whom vote, and the 12 regional bank presidents, only 5 of whom have a vote (the New York bank president always has a vote; the remaining 4 votes rotate among the other 11 banks).

## The Fed Chair

If the Fed is the second most powerful agency in Washington, the chair of the Federal Reserve Board, currently Alan Greenspan, ranks among the most powerful persons in government (see the accompanying Window on the Past). The chair's great power derives from close ties to the president, direct access to up-to-date economic information supplied by Fed staff, and the power to approve the appointment of the 12 presidents of the Federal Reserve Banks (upon the recommendation of the member banks

**Fed Chair**
Alan Greenspan testifying before congressional committee. *Why is Congressional influence over the Fed less than its influence over most agencies?*

*Window* on the *Past*

## The Second Most Powerful Man in the United States

Most Americans cannot name the man pictured here, but there are those who feel that he is one of the most powerful persons in the country. He is Alan Greenspan, the current chair of the Federal Reserve.

Greenspan was appointed by President Ronald Reagan and was reappointed to a second four-year term by President George Bush in 1992. Greenspan's second term was to end in 1996. Would President Clinton reappoint this life-long conservative Republican?

Greenspan had many critics in the Democratic party who felt that he had been too concerned about inflation, and he had kept economic growth needlessly slow by holding interest rates higher than necessary to avert inflation. Senator Tom Harkin (D-IA) opposed Greenspan's reappointment, charging that "under the Greenspan Fed, job growth and the living standards of average Americans have been sacrificed on the altar of high interest rates and slow growth policies."[a] Certainly the political importance of the appointment was widely appreciated.

**Alan Greenspan**
*What are the sources of his influence over economic policy?*

Despite these and other criticisms from some elected officials, Greenspan enjoyed broad support in the financial community. Ignoring liberal critics, President Clinton reappointed Greenspan twice, in 1996 and 2000. His current term expires in 2004.

[a] Andrew Taylor, "Greenspan, Rivlin Confirmed," *Congressional Quarterly Weekly Report*, June 22, 1996: 1746.

in each region). In addition, the chair inherits a job held in the past by powerful, prestigious people. Martin Eccles, head of the Fed during the 1930s, is acclaimed for taking actions to get the country out of the Great Depression, William McChesney Martin received credit for keeping the American economy on an even keel after World War II, and Paul Volcker is remembered for bringing the double-digit inflation of the late 1970s to an end. Greenspan is adding to this tradition by becoming known as the person who managed the sustained economic growth of the 1990s.

## Who Controls the Fed?

Surprisingly, in an elections-dominated political system, this key government agency is relatively insulated from electoral pressures. The Fed's power, independence, and objectivity are symbolized by its Washington home, a magnificent quasi-palace fronted by a remote—almost forbidding—facade, and located two miles from Capitol Hill, adjacent to the National Academy of Sciences. Of course, the Fed is not immune to political pressure, but it is more insulated than most government agencies.

**Congressional Influence** Like all other government agencies, the Fed was created and its powers defined by congressional statutes. Nominees to the Federal Reserve Board must be approved by the Senate, and the Fed must make quarterly reports to the banking committees of the House and Senate.

But despite these legal obligations to Congress, the Fed is remarkably free of congressional influence. For one thing, the Fed's budget is not congressionally determined. Instead, the Fed raises its own revenue by creating money (almost literally) and using this money to buy U.S. Treasury bonds, from which it earns interest. Creating money and buying Treasury bonds are a necessary part of the Fed's job—they are among the ways the Fed puts money into and takes money out of the economy. But Fed investments have a side benefit for the agency. Every year Fed investments earn billions of dollars (nearly $27 billion in 1998). Most of this money is turned over to the federal Treasury, but the Fed keeps about a tenth for its own operations.[18] As a result, the Fed does not need to ask Congress for an appropriation the way most agencies do. The Fed owns squash courts in its building near the Washington Monument and bowling alleys on Wall Street, the most expensive real estate in the world—a reflection of the fact that it can almost literally manufacture its own money.

The Fed is also relatively free of congressionally determined salary schedules and personnel controls. Consequently, it is able to hire a better-trained, more professional, more prestigious staff than other government agencies. In fact, the Fed is the one agency of the United States government that has a civil service that resembles the type found in Europe and Japan (see Chapter 13). Instead of political appointees that rotate in and out of office, the Fed staff consists of expert, career appointees.

In general, congressional influence on the Fed is exerted indirectly. Congress "jawbones" the Fed when it feels that monetary policy is not appropriate for prevailing conditions. Individual members make critical speeches, and committees hold hearings at which the Fed chair is asked to testify. In these ways, some members make known their belief that monetary policy is too restrictive, and others announce their conviction that monetary policy is too loose. In these pronouncements there is an implied warning that if the Fed is not responsive, more serious attempts to influence the Fed may be forthcoming. But members of Congress usually cannot agree on any specific course of action.

Although observers usually agree that Congress does not exercise significant control over the Fed, there is less of a consensus on the influence of other groups and institutions. Three distinct interpretations of the source of influence over Fed operations have been offered: banker dominance, presidential control, and Fed independence.

**Banker Dominance**    The first interpretation, held by many liberal critics of the Fed, is that the banks control the Fed.[19] Just as interest groups underpin other iron triangles (see Chapter 14), so the banking industry, which has a huge stake in Fed decisions, forms the primary base of support for the Fed. Bankers influence the appointment of the Board of Governors, and they nominate the Federal Reserve bank presidents, who cast five votes on the Open Market Committee.

As evidence of banker dominance, proponents point to the apparent policy bias of the Fed, which is generally viewed as being less concerned about reducing unemployment than about lowering inflation rates. To put it another way, the Fed seems to be more worried about rising prices than about staving off recessions. The Fed "can't stand prosperity." When jobs are plentiful and people are spending freely, the Fed typically responds by raising interest rates and slowing down the economy: "Just when the party gets going, the Fed takes away the beer."[20]

The Fed defends itself against such accusations of policy bias by saying that unless inflation is checked quickly, much stronger action will eventually have to be taken, creating more hardship in the long run. The Fed offers as evidence its policy in the late 1970s, when it mistakenly let inflation get out of control. Only after the deep and painful recession of 1981–1982 were inflation and interest rates brought down to an acceptable level.

**Presidential Dominance**    A second interpretation emphasizes not the bankers, but the president, as the main source of influence. And indeed, most observers believe that the president, who appoints its members and chairs, has a great deal more influence than Congress.[21] But how much influence do presidents have, and to what ends do they use it?

Some political scientists suggest that presidents try to manipulate Fed policy for their own political purposes. These scholars note that the chair of the Federal Reserve Board, in order to win reappointment, must be sensitive to signals from the White House. Even more important, the Fed's very desire to appear nonpolitical creates a dependence on the president. If the president publicly criticizes the Fed, it becomes the subject matter of news commentaries and talk shows because the Fed's actions have become matters of partisan controversy. The best way for the Fed to appear independent is for its chair to listen carefully to suggestions coming from presidents and their advisors and to avoid acting in such a way as to provoke controversy.

There are two versions of the presidential control interpretation—the partisan and the election cycle.[22] The **partisan interpretation** distinguishes between the constituencies of Republican and Democratic presidents.[23] The Republican constituency includes more upper-income business and professional people, who traditionally are less worried about unemployment (which less frequently strikes them) than about inflation. The Democratic constituency includes more lower-income, blue-collar workers traditionally more concerned about rising unemployment (which normally hits them hardest). Indeed, studies show that inflation rates tend to rise under Democratic presidents and fall under Republican presidents, and that stocks and bonds earn higher returns under Republican administrations.[24] But during the 1990s, inflation and unemployment rates both remained low, and stock prices also soared— a confluence of events that not only runs contrary to the partisan interpretation but also, in the words of one observer, "has flouted several economic laws."[25]

> **partisan interpretation**
> The argument that Democratic administrations set economic policy to benefit lower-income, wage-earning groups and that Republican administrations set economic policy to benefit higher-income, business and professional groups.

There are other reasons to doubt the more extreme version of the partisan interpretation. Most citizens, regardless of income, occupation, or partisan affiliation, dislike both rising unemployment and rising prices; they don't want to lose their jobs, but neither do they want to see the purchasing power of their wages eroded by inflation. Similarly, investors dislike inflation, but if growth slows and unemployment rises, their investments will earn lower returns. Thus, whatever their party, presidents are better off striking a balance between the two goals rather than focusing on either one and neglecting the other. Nevertheless, Democrats and Republicans strike different balances, reflecting their different constituencies. Republican administrations seem more willing to accept a little more unemployment in order to avoid inflation. Democrats strike the opposite balance. They appear more likely to accept somewhat higher inflation in order to avoid unemployment. To keep from provoking presidents, the Fed probably tends to slant its decisions in the direction of these well-known partisan preferences. But the effect is too small to call it presidential control.

The second version of the presidential dominance view, the **election-cycle interpretation,** says that presidents deliberately manipulate the economy to engineer their reelections. They tolerate slow growth, even a recession, early in their term of office so they can step on the gas and "rev up" the economic engine when the election payoff is greatest.

> **election-cycle interpretation**
> The argument that, whatever their party, presidents attempt to slow the economy early in their terms and then expand it as their opportunity for reelection approaches.

Richard Nixon's first term is a clear example of presidential manipulation. The Nixon administration pulled out all the stops and achieved a huge increase in household income during the election year 1972.[26] Nixon was reelected overwhelmingly. Reagan's first term is another example consistent with presidential manipulation of the economy. During the first two years of his administration, the country suffered a deep recession as the Fed squeezed high inflation out of the economy. During the last two years, the Fed lowered interest rates and the economy took off. Economic growth in the election year of 1984 was the best in the entire decade, and Reagan was overwhelmingly reelected.

But if Nixon's and Reagan's first terms fit the election-cycle interpretation, Carter's and Bush's directly contradict it. Carter may have tried to increase growth, but the economy was stagnant throughout his administration, and the year he sought

**Figure 19.6**

**Presidential Elections
and Economic Growth**
*Why does the economy usually grow
more the year a president is running
for reelection?*

SOURCE: Data are calculated from *The
Economic Report of the President*
(Washington, DC: Government Printing
Office, February 1994).

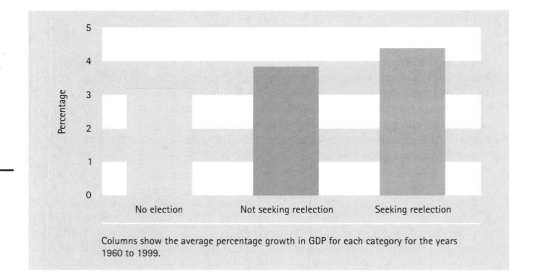

Columns show the average percentage growth in GDP for each category for the years
1960 to 1999.

reelection was a recession year. Bush also seems to have done things exactly backwards. At the beginning of his term the country enjoyed steady growth, but later the
economy reversed and Bush's fortunes shifted with it. Bush's timing could not have
been worse.

Combining information for all years since World War II yields some evidence, but
not a lot, that presidents manipulate the economy to their political advantage. In years
when presidents themselves are running for reelection, growth rates are, on average,
somewhat higher, but not a lot higher, than in other years (see Figure 19.6).

**An Independent Fed**  Fed supporters say the agency is independent of both politics
and external pressure groups.[27] The independence of the Fed is guaranteed by the fact
that board members are appointed for 14-year terms. They can be removed only
through the impeachment process. Because board members serve such long terms,
presidents may not be able to appoint a majority of the board until they have been in
office 6 years. And because the chair of the Fed serves a 4-year term, in the worst case
a president may not be able to appoint a new chair until the fourth year of an
administration.

There are other reasons for the Fed's independence. Business confidence in government economic policy is strengthened by the belief that Fed decisions are above
politics. The board acts on the advice of a strong, independent staff. The chair is usually more knowledgeable about economic policy than any other presidential
appointee. Monetary policy is too arcane to engage the general public; consequently,
Fed-bashing is not a very effective campaign tactic.

Further, those who say the Fed is independent usually believe this is a good idea.
They say that an independent Fed has improved the management of the economy. In
particular, they emphasize that the country has had fewer and shorter recessions since
the Fed was established than it had earlier in history.

Perhaps it is impossible to conclude that anyone tightly controls the Fed. The Fed
operates with a considerable amount of independence, mainly because it tries to
achieve not only what presidents want but also what nearly everyone desires: steady,
stable economic growth. Presidents need good economic news their first year, because
that is when they are getting their political agenda off the ground. They need good
economic news their second year to help the congressional candidates of their party.
It is dangerous for a president to encourage a recession in the third year because it
could spill over into the election campaign, and of course, no president wants a recession in the election year.

*Democratic Dilemma*

# An Independent Federal Reserve

In Homer's *Odyssey*, when the hero's ship passes the Isle of the Sirens, Odysseus orders his crew to block their ears, lest they be lured by the Sirens' irresistible singing and wreck the ship on the rocks. But Odysseus himself wants to hear the Sirens, and he has the crew tie him to the mast so that he can hear the singing but will be unable to steer the ship toward certain doom.

The moral of this episode is that people sometimes are better off preventing themselves from doing what they would otherwise like to do. Some people view the Federal Reserve in these terms. They argue that although it is undemocratic to have monetary policy set by a small elite that is not subject to election or even oversight by Congress, that's the whole point of an insulated, independent agency.

Before the Federal Reserve was established in 1913, monetary policy was the subject of intense political controversy. Battles over whether to issue more or less money, paper versus metal currency, gold versus silver, and so on were important parts of nineteenth-century history.[a] (In 1896 presidential hopeful William Jennings

Bryan based his campaign on his opposition to a policy of linking the U.S. currency to gold reserves, thundering "You shall not crucify mankind on a cross of gold!") According to defenders of the Fed, only when monetary policy is taken out of politics is it possible to set policy rationally and with a long-term view. If the Federal Reserve were subject to democratic control, they argue, politicians would be tempted to manipulate policy for short-term electoral gain, and the country would be worse off in the long run. In essence, the Federal Reserve System ties presidents to the figurative mast, leaving them powerless to heed the Sirens of public opinion on monetary policy.

*What do you think? In a democracy, can citizens decide that some policies will not be decided democratically? Is it acceptable to place so much power beyond the reach of electoral accountability?*

[a] James Livingston, *Origins of the Federal Reserve System* (Ithaca, NY: Cornell University Press, 1986).

The Fed's emphasis on steady, moderate growth is pretty much what the president wants, so the president can usually leave the Fed alone. A case in point is the relationship President Clinton had with Fed chair Alan Greenspan. Ronald Reagan first appointed Greenspan as Fed chair, and Clinton sought to reassure financial markets in the election year of 1996 by renominating him.[28] Because both Greenspan and Clinton were interested in stable growth, each felt it was in his interest to leave the other alone. Greenspan's management of the economy won him such universal acclaim that 2000 presidential candidate John McCain quipped that "I would not only reappoint Mr. Greenspan. If Mr. Greenspan were to die, God forbid, I would do like in the movie *Weekend at Bernie's* and stuff him and prop him up."[29] Perhaps the Fed is an example of the proposition that good public policy in a democracy is not necessarily produced by the most democratic processes (see the accompanying Democratic Dilemma).

## SECTION SUMMARY

In the last few decades, most policy makers came to agree that the most important government tool for managing the economy is monetary policy—that is, adjusting interest rates by varying the supply of money in the economy. The Federal Reserve System, created in 1913, is the institution charged with making decisions about monetary policy. The Fed is more independent of Congress than other government agencies, which has led observers to disagree over who controls it. Some argue that the president, who nominates Fed governors, has substantial indirect power over the Fed's decisions. Others argue that the banking community, from which Fed governors are usually appointed, holds the most sway. The truth may be that each of these outside actors has some influence. But the Fed's independence gives it the luxury of being isolated from both politics and external pressure groups—and considerable freedom to make policy on its own.

## *Deficits and Surpluses*

During the 1980s and most of the 1990s, the budget deficit was a major issue in American politics. Elected officials struggled to find a way to satisfy public demands for a reduced deficit without angering voters by raising taxes or cutting spending. Ross Perot made deficit reduction the centerpiece of his independent campaign for the presidency in 1992, and stalemates between the president and Congress over how to balance the budget forced the federal government to shut down several times in the winter of 1995–1996.

In 1997 Clinton and a Republican Congress finally agreed on a balanced budget. But the achievement was due almost entirely to unexpected economic growth that by itself dramatically cut budget deficits. Suddenly it became easy to balance the budget while at the same time cutting taxes and increasing social spending. In 1992 the deficit had hit a record high of $290 billion dollars, but in 1998 the budget was in surplus by $70 billion.[30] Some estimates showed the cumulative surplus for 2000–2010 reaching over $2 trillion.[31]

Of course, the government may never achieve such a surplus because elected officials may divide the extra money into various combinations of tax cuts and spending increases. As one might predict, Democrats tend to argue for a larger proportion of spending increases, whereas Republicans tend to argue for tax cuts. Republican presidential candidate George W. Bush promised in 2000 to make sure much of the surplus was "returned to the American people, who earned it and deserve it." Al Gore advocated fewer tax cuts and more "investments in our future," in the form of spending on education, health, and other programs.[32] The politics of surpluses is unlikely to be as contentious and difficult as the politics of deficits—too much money is always a better problem than too little—but serious differences between the parties remain. These differences will define the budget debate in the early twenty-first century.

participation

**Dealing with a Surplus: Having a Say**

## The "T" Word: Taxes

Hardly anyone likes to pay taxes. As Figure 19.7 shows, most people think that their tax bill is too high. With the budget running annual surpluses, some voters may feel they have an additional reason to believe they are paying too much to the government. As a result, tax policy is a major topic of public concern, and various aspects of the American tax system are subject to heated debate.[33] In this section we discuss the three most important issues in this debate: the tax burden, the breadth of the tax base, and the progressivity of the tax structure.

**F i g u r e   1 9 . 7**

**Public Opinion About Taxes**
*Do you think taxes are too low or too high? Why?*

SOURCE: Surveys by the National Opinion Research Center.

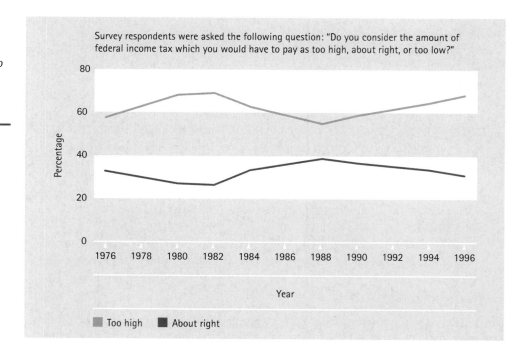

Survey respondents were asked the following question: "Do you consider the amount of federal income tax which you would have to pay as too high, about right, or too low?"

■ Too high    ■ About right

**Protesting the Tax Burden**
*Why are antitax sentiments widespread in the United States, when the country's taxes are lower than in many comparable nations?*

## The Tax Burden

In considering changes in tax policy, officials must take into account the **tax burden**, the total level at which Americans are taxed. Federal individual income tax receipts, as a percentage of the nation's GDP, rose by over 60 percent between 1950 and 1970.[34] Although they stabilized after 1970, the steep increase in the earlier period put the tax burden issue high on the country's political agenda. Some advocates of higher government spending argue that Americans have become selfish over the course of the past generation and are increasingly unwilling to tax themselves for good purposes. Others, writing in defense of taxpayers, point to the stagnation of personal incomes that began in the early 1970s. So long as standards of living were rising, people were willing to absorb higher taxes, but once living standards stagnated, frustrated citizens increasingly vented their unhappiness on the tax system. At any rate, many Americans came to feel that the tax burden was too high, and elected officials responded—from Reagan's tax cuts to President Bush's 1988 campaign pledge of "no new taxes."

The rapid growth of the economy in the late 1990s dampened the tax burden issue. In part because of the size of the budget surplus, each candidate in the 2000 presidential race advocated some tax cuts. George W. Bush proposed lowering tax rates for all taxpayers.[35] Al Gore proposed a more modest tax cut, geared toward favorable tax treatment of the middle class designed to encourage spending on education and savings.[36] But the candidates discovered that many voters were more interested in cutting the national debt than in seeing their tax bills cut. To the surprise of political commentators, the public had become more fiscally responsible than their leaders! The demand for tax cuts could re-emerge, however, if budget surpluses continue to rise or if economic conditions should worsen.

## The Tax Base

Even though the tax burden is the most frequently discussed topic, it is not necessarily the most important. At least as critical is the breadth of the **tax base**: the income, property, wealth, or economic activity that is taxed. Many economists argue that taxes are less intrusive if they are broad-based—that is, imposed on all economic activity at the same rate. Thus the amount you pay in taxes should depend only on the amount you make, not on how you make it. Whether you make your money growing crops, making movies, writing wills, or running a charity should not matter. Nor should the

**tax burden**
The total amount of tax that a household pays.

**tax base**
Types of activities, types of property, or kinds of investments that are subject to taxation.

amount you pay in taxes depend on whether you spend money on groceries, cars, beer, or medical insurance. If everything is taxed alike, then tax policy will not distort the economy. That is, it will not influence the choices people make.

Broad-based taxes are more easily recommended than enacted into law, however. Frequently, good reasons can be given for not taxing some particular activity, and there are numerous organized groups that offer good (and often not-so-good) reasons to persuade elected officials to give favorable treatment to the activities of their members. In response to these pressures, national and state legislators have enacted thousands of **tax preferences** that exempt particular types of economic activity from taxation. Critics say these tax preferences distort economic activity and cost the government billions of dollars in forgone revenues. Here are some major examples of tax preferences and the economic distortions that critics say they foster:

> **tax preferences**
> Special tax treatment received by certain activities, property, or investments.

- *Tax credits for college tuition* ($7.3 billion).[37] In 1997 Congress allowed a tax credit for college tuition, a tax break popular with college students. Critics say colleges, realizing that students have more tuition dollars, will simply boost tuition.
- *Deductions for mortgage interest on owner-occupied homes* ($59 billion). Developers and brokers claim that this tax preference encourages home ownership, said to be good for families and community stability. Critics say the preference primarily benefits higher-income people who can afford huge mortgages and subsidizes their over-investment in big houses and vacation homes.
- *Deductions for charitable contributions* ($25.5 billion). Defenders of this tax preference claim that it encourages public support for the arts, education, and the needy. But critics say many charities are actually businesses that provide services to those who "give" them money.

Tax preferences are the classic "slippery slope." Once government grants them to any group, it abandons the principle of neutral taxation and encourages other groups to lobby for their own preferences. Tax preferences distort the economy by encouraging people to make economic decisions on the basis of tax considerations. Moreover, granting preferences to some activities requires that taxes be higher on other activities that lack defenders strong enough to get their own tax break. Yet it is unlikely that all tax preferences will be eliminated. Some activities—home ownership, education, charities—are so popular most people think they should get a tax break.

> **sin tax**
> Tax intended to discourage unwanted behavior.

Not all special treatment is favorable. The government also sometimes imposes **sin taxes,** taxes intended to discourage unwanted behavior. The most prominent examples of sin taxes are the taxes on the consumption of cigarettes and alcohol. Critics of such measures argue that they fall primarily on the poorest segments of the population and fail to have a significant impact on the consumption of addictive products.

## Tax Progressivity

> **progressive tax**
> A tax structured so that higher-income people pay a larger proportion of their income in taxes.
>
> **regressive tax**
> A tax structured so that higher-income people pay a smaller proportion of their income in taxes.

If some economists think the breadth of the tax base is the most important tax issue, others think that tax progressivity is. Taxes are said to be **progressive taxes** if people with higher income pay a higher tax rate. The most important progressive tax is the federal income tax. In 2000, individual taxable incomes up to $25,750 were being taxed at a 15-percent rate. For example, if your annual income was $20,000, you paid 15 percent, or $3000, in taxes. Additional income between $25,750 and $62,450 was being taxed at a 28-percent rate. If you made $50,000 a year, your total tax was $10,653, three and one-half times the amount paid by those earning $20,000. Rates on additional income rose to as high as about 43 percent.

Taxes that require low-income people to pay a higher rate are called **regressive taxes.** The payroll or social security tax is a regressive tax, because in 2000 it was levied only on the first $76,200 a person earns. Because all earnings in excess of that figure are exempt from the tax, higher-income people pay a smaller share of their income for social security than do lower-income people.

For example, if you made $40,000 per year, you would pay 6.2 percent of your income, or $2480, in social security taxes. If you made $1 million, you would pay 6.2 percent in taxes on the first $76,200 you made, or $4724. In the second case, the amount paid is larger, but note that it makes up only half a percent of total income, whereas in the first case, 6.2 percent of total income goes for the tax.

There are numerous taxes levied in the United States. The federal personal income tax and some state personal income taxes are progressive. Social security and state sales taxes are regressive. Property taxes vary a great deal but generally fall in between. When all taxes levied by federal, state, and local governments are taken into account, it is difficult to say whether the tax structure in the United States is progressive or not.[38]

Progressive taxes traditionally have been defended by liberals, who claim that progressive rates reduce income inequality in the society. Thus Bill Clinton and the congressional Democrats pushed through an increase in the taxes paid by high-income taxpayers over united Republican opposition in 1993. Progressive taxes traditionally have been opposed by conservatives, who claim that progressive rates discourage investment and hard work by the most productive members of society. Thus the tax cut passed by a Republican Congress in 1999 (but vetoed by President Clinton) made bigger reductions in taxes paid by high-income groups.

## Tax Reform

Debates over tax reform traditionally focus on the breadth and progressivity of the tax system. In 1986 Congress passed a widely acclaimed reform that lowered individual income tax rates, raised corporate rates, and broadened the tax base by eliminating many tax preferences. The federal income tax burden for a typical family of four dropped from 10.5 to 8.9 percent of total income without reducing government revenue.[39]

In recent years, many members of Congress have proposed even more sweeping tax reforms. The best known is the **flat tax**, a proposal that would eliminate progressive income tax rates and would tax all income groups above a certain minimum at the same rate.[40] Advocates argue that it is unfair to require some people to pay a higher percentage of their income in taxes than others. Supporters of a flat tax also defend it on the grounds of efficiency—the more progressive taxes are, the greater the incentive for the wealthy to hire accountants, lawyers, and lobbyists to help them avoid taxes. Indeed, the wealthy are not the only ones who pay: As of 1990, a majority of Americans used professional tax preparers, and taxpayers spent at least $75 billion a year on record keeping, filling out forms, complying with audits, and paying for accountants and lawyers.[41]

**flat tax**
A tax that is neither progressive nor regressive; everyone pays at the same rate.

**Campaigning for a Flat Tax**
Steve Forbes campaigned for the Republican presidential nomination on a radical reform of the tax system: replacing the graduated income tax with a "flat tax." *Why were tax issues less important in 2000 than in many previous elections?*

In the 1996 and 2000 Republican primaries, *Fortune* magazine publisher Steve Forbes based his presidential campaign on his advocacy of the flat tax. Although he enjoyed some success in 1996 and helped publicize the idea of a flat tax, the philosophy was dismissed by most of the other candidates, and Forbes fared worse in the 2000 race than he had 4 years earlier.

The debate over tax reform is likely to remain fractious and many-sided, even in an era of surpluses, because people want to use the tax system to achieve different goals—goals that often conflict. They want to raise revenue, to reduce income inequality, to discourage some kinds of behavior, and to give breaks so as to promote other kinds of activity, such as education and home ownership.

### Section Summary

Economic policy in the United States underwent a major shift in the late 1990s from an environment characterized by deficits to one characterized by surpluses. Deficit politics was marked by acrimony and confrontation between the two parties. Both parties claimed to want to eliminate deficits, but Democrats generally favored raising taxes, whereas Republicans favored making cuts in spending. Surpluses will probably reduce the number of direct confrontations between the two parties, but serious disagreements over how to use the additional funds remain.

Federal income tax receipts as a percent of GDP grew rapidly between 1950 and 1970, but they have remained more or less constant over the past several decades. Despite the recent consistency of the tax burden, controversies over altering the details of specific taxes have continued. In response to pressures from organized groups, Congress and the president have enacted a series of tax preferences to exempt certain activities or institutions from some taxes. The income tax system is also progressive; it taxes wealthy people at a higher rate than lower-income people. The social security tax, however, is regressive, hitting lower-income earners harder. Some have advocated ridding the system both of tax preferences and tax progressivity and replacing them with a single flat tax. Drastic change in the tax system is unlikely in the near future, however, because most Americans, enjoying a prosperous economy, seem willing to share some resources with the government. Nonetheless, Republicans and Democrats have begun debating what kinds of tax cuts should result from the budget surplus.

# The U.S. Economy: An International Comparison

Even though we have focused on government and the economy, the truth is that the extent to which the economy can be controlled by government is limited—and has become much more so in recent years. When the Fed loosens or tightens the money supply, it is reacting to national and global economic forces that may overcome its best efforts. Indeed, all over the world, countries with very different political systems are struggling to meet economic challenges similar to those in the United States. Relative to other advanced democracies, the United States is dealing reasonably well with its economic challenges and difficulties. In this section we shall place U.S. taxes, national debt, and employment opportunities in comparative perspective.

## Taxes

The tax burden in the United States compares very favorably with that in the world's other developed countries. As of 1998, the tax burden in the United States was among the lowest of 13 major industrialized countries: about 34 percent of GDP. At the other extreme, the public sector in Sweden taxes away over 60 percent of the country's GDP. Taxes in Holland, Belgium, France, and Italy all exceed 45 percent of GDP (see Figure 19.8).

   To be sure, other countries provide more services in exchange for the money they extract in taxes. The most important example is health care; about half of it is paid for by the private sector in the United States, whereas it is almost entirely government-provided in other countries.

   If their tax rates and the overall tax burden are the lowest in the developed world and are continuing to fall, why were Americans, until recently, so unhappy with taxes, and why did presidential candidates in 2000 promise further tax cuts?

   We doubt that there is any single explanation for the American aversion to taxes. Part of the answer may lie in the nature of the American tax system. The United States relies more heavily than most other countries on income and payroll taxes to raise revenues; nearly two-thirds of total tax revenues come from such sources, a figure exceeded only by Switzerland and Belgium. Other countries rely more heavily on con-

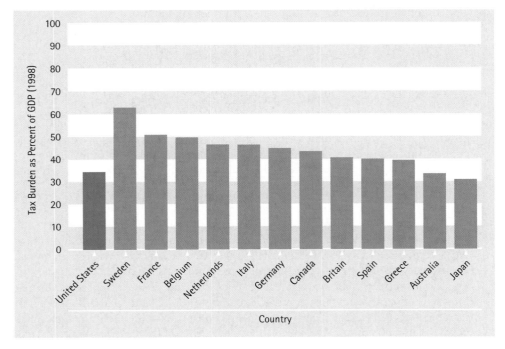

**Figure 19.8**

**U.S. Tax Burden Less Than in Many Other Democracies**
*Why are U.S. taxes lower than taxes in other countries?*

SOURCE: U.S. Bureau of the Census, *Statistical Abstract of the United States, 1999*, Table 1372.

**Figure 19.9**

**U.S. Debt Is Smaller
Than the Debt of Other Countries**

SOURCE: U.S. Bureau of the Census,
*Statistical Abstract of the United States,
1999,* Table 1372.

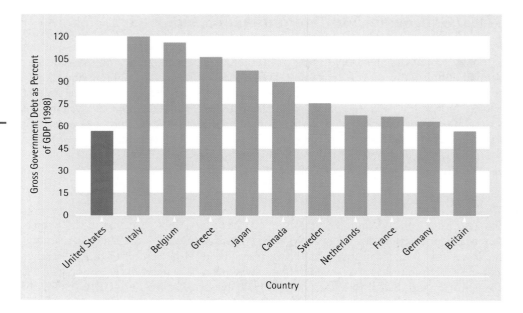

sumption taxes, such as a sales tax known as the value-added tax (VAT), which is hidden in the prices of goods and services. Thus their voters may not realize the full tax cost of the services they receive, despite the fact that the VAT affects low-income families the most. Ironically, Sweden, Germany, and Italy—with their large welfare states—rely heavily on the VAT, a tax that American liberals view as regressive. Only Japan, with its minimal provision of social services, relies less on sales taxes than the United States.

U.S. historical experience is probably more important for explaining the views of Americans than the type of tax levied, however. In Chapter 4 we saw that, more than the citizens in other countries, Americans are economic individualists who wish to keep the role of government limited. They expect less from government, and they wish to keep more of their money for their own use.

## National Debt

Five and one half trillion dollars, the size of the national debt in 2000, is an almost unimaginable number. But such numbers are meaningful only relative to baselines, and the natural baseline—the size of the American economy—was $8.5 trillion. Relative to the size of the economy, the public debt in the United States is moderate. For example, as a proportion of GDP, France, Germany, and Japan all have larger national debts than the United States—and Italy's debt is over twice as large (see Figure 19.9).

Certainly, this is not to say that concern about the debt during the 1980s was unwarranted. That so much debt accumulated in such a short period of time is worrisome, but the debt in other democracies has increased even more rapidly. For example, between 1990 and 1998, the total U.S. debt grew only marginally, while France's debt increased by over 65 percent.[42]

## Employment Opportunities

The United States has done a better job than most countries of incorporating new workers into the economy. In 2000, for example, the unemployment rate in Western Europe hovered around 10 percent—over twice the rate in the United States.

The situation in 2000 is the result of changes that date back to the 1980s. At that time, the workforce in the Western world expanded rapidly as the baby boom generation reached working age and as women moved into the workforce in greater numbers. The American economy absorbed these new workers far more successfully than did European economies, creating three times more new jobs per 1000 people than did France and West Germany. Moreover, European countries were able to keep their

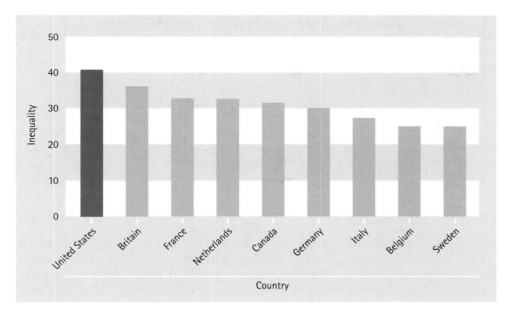

**Figure 19.10**

**Income Inequality Greater in United States Than in Many Other Countries**
*Why is inequality greater in a wealthy country like the United States?*

NOTE: The bars represent the value of the Gini index for each country. A Gini index value of zero represents complete equality; a value of 100 represents complete inequality. Data were collected from 1991 to 1997.

SOURCE: *2000 World Development Indicators* (Washington, DC: World Bank, 2000), Table 2.8, pp. 66–68.

unemployment rates as low as they did only by introducing policies that would be unacceptable in the United States. For example, policy in Germany and Switzerland induced so-called guest workers to return to their countries of origin. The United States, in contrast, allowed immigration to increase during the 1980s. Some countries absorbed new workers by expanding their public sectors. The Swedes, for example, dealt with the surge of women into the labor force by doubling public-sector employment.[43] In the United States, public-sector employment grew very slowly.

Some critics object that many of the jobs that have been created in the United States are low-skill, low-paying "McJobs," but the evidence suggests that such claims are exaggerated. According to an extensive jobs study by the Organization of Economically Developed Countries (OECD), four-fifths of the net job increase in the United States came in the professional, technical, managerial, and administrative categories—again, a performance far superior to western European democracies.[44]

Compared to most other countries, the American economy is less restricted by government policies and regulations. This gives it a greater capacity to adapt to changing economic conditions. For example, changes in the world economy have had an adverse effect on workers in the manufacturing sector. In 1950 these industries accounted for 34 percent of U.S. jobs, and by 2000 this figure had shrunk to 15 percent. Amazingly, the United States produces no more steel today than it did in the early 1960s.[45]

But these adverse consequences have been offset by gains in the service, communications, and technology industries. In the late 1990s, the U.S. information technology sector grew at stunning rates, and officials estimated that by 2006, nearly half the U.S. workforce would be employed by industries closely connected to the technology sector. The United States is better equipped than most of its European peers to handle this rapid transition to a high-technology economy. For example, the proportion of people with access to the Internet is about four times greater in the United States than in Germany or France.[46]

### Inequality

The price of limited government seems to be greater social inequality. Compared to other advanced democracies, income inequality in the United States is higher (see Figure 19.10). Moreover, after declining between 1930 and 1970, inequality rose until, in the 1990s, it was higher than at any time since the 1930s. Some social critics see in such trends a "class war" of the rich against the poor,[47] but there seems to be no great popular demand for government to intervene directly to reverse the trend toward inequality. Candidates who advocate a greater role for government and a greater degree of income redistribution regularly run for office, but the American people have usually not elected them. Nor have they demanded such policies from their representatives in Congress and the state legislatures.

### SECTION SUMMARY

The United States has lower taxes, a smaller national debt, and lower unemployment rates than many comparable industrialized countries. And the United States has been more successful in adapting to economic change than many of its peers. But there is a higher degree of income inequality in this country than in most others.

## Chapter Summary

People care a lot about whether they can find a job and what they have to pay for the things they buy. When times are bad, the president takes the blame. When times are good, the president usually—but not always—gets the credit. Presidents' popular standing and their odds of reelection are significantly influenced by national economic conditions. To a somewhat lesser extent, this is also true of members of Congress and even state-level elected officials.

Given these political facts of life, presidents give economic policy top priority. To achieve this objective, they give the agency responsible for monetary policy, the Federal Reserve, a good deal of independence. Although they may try to shape policy on occasion, presidents generally realize that the Fed needs independence to do its job well. And when the Fed does a good job by keeping economic growth steady, the president usually gets the credit.

For half a century, presidents tried to use fiscal policy—the management of budget deficits and surpluses—to manage the economy. But the importance of fiscal policy for managing the economy has been reduced by a combination of factors, including divided government, declining faith in Keynesian theory, a rising public debt, and the globalization of economic activity.

Debates over tax reform typically involve discussion of the tax burden, whether tax preferences should be eliminated in order to broaden the tax base, and whether the progressivity of the tax system needs to be raised or lowered. Although the two parties fought for much of the 1980s and 1990s over whether to increase taxes to eliminate the deficit, in the late 1990s the parties began debating how much of the new budget surplus to devote to tax cuts.

The United States has a lower tax burden, a smaller national debt, and lower unemployment rates than many other countries. It is also quick to adapt to economic change. But Americans seem more willing to tolerate economic inequality than people in other nations are.

### On the Web

The Federal Reserve
www.federalreserve.gov
The Federal Reserve System maintains an informative Web site, complete with publications, congressional testimony, and economic data.
U.S. Department of Commerce
www.commerce.gov
The Department of Commerce houses the Economics and Statistics Administration and the Bureau of Economic

Analysis, which provide regular data and analysis on the U.S. economy.
National Bureau of Economic Research
www.nber.org
The National Bureau of Economic Research publishes an excellent series of working papers by eminent economists.

## Key Terms

budget, p. 578
business cycle, p. 575
Council of Economic Advisors
    (CEA), p. 578
debt, p. 581
deficit, p. 578
election-cycle interpretation, p. 587
Federal Reserve System, p. 583
fiscal policy, p. 578

flat tax, p. 593
gross domestic product (GDP),
    p. 574
inflation, p. 575
Keynesianism, p. 578
monetarism, p. 580
monetary policy, p. 583
partisan interpretation, p. 587
progressive tax, p. 592

recession, p. 575
regressive tax, p. 592
sin tax, p. 592
supply-side economics, p. 582
surplus, p. 578
tax base, p. 591
tax burden, p. 591
tax preferences, p. 592
unemployment, p. 575

## Suggested Readings

Birnbaum, Jeffrey H., and Alan S. Murray. *Showdown at Gucci Gulch.* New York: Random House, 1987. Fast-paced case study of the passage of the 1986 tax reforms.

Bradford, David F. *Untangling the Income Tax.* Cambridge, MA: Harvard University Press, 1986. Everything you ever wanted to know about income taxes, presented in a reasonably comprehensible fashion.

Greider, William. *Secrets of the Temple.* New York: Simon & Schuster, 1987. Long, well-researched, and engagingly written, if uneven, book on the history of the Federal Reserve Board.

Hibbs, Douglas, A., Jr. *The American Political Economy.* Cambridge, MA: Harvard University Press, 1987. Provides detailed statistical evaluations of partisan and election-cycle interpretations of presidential management of the economy.

Kettl, Don. *Deficit Politics.* New York: Macmillan, 1992. Short, readable book on budget deficits.

Krugman, Paul. *Peddling Prosperity.* New York: Norton, 1994. Written for the noneconomist, this critique of many of those who have influenced recent economic policy provides a comprehensible discussion of schools of economic thought and an overview of economic trends of the past several decades.

Weaver, R. Kent. *Automatic Government: The Politics of Indexation.* Washington, DC: Brookings, 1988. Explains how government benefits came to be indexed.

Weir, Margaret. *Politics and Jobs: The Boundaries of Employment Policies in the United States.* Princeton, NJ: Princeton University Press, 1992. Broad historical and political analysis of government efforts to guarantee full employment.

# 20

# Foreign and Defense Policy

Put foreign affairs first, the Italian thinker Nicolò Machiavelli advised his prince. If you fail at foreign policy, nothing you do in the domestic sphere will matter. If living today, Machiavelli might add that in matters of war and peace, military success is not enough. In the world of the modern presidency, leaders must not only succeed but also do so quickly. As the following story shows, voters don't have much patience.

In the late 1970s, the Carter administration viewed the Iranian Shah, Mohammed Reza Pahlavi, as a loyal, anticommunist ally in the oil-rich but politically unstable Persian Gulf region. Though known for his ruthless suppression of internal dissent, the Shah was, experts believed, capable of using his country's oil wealth to modernize its industry and economy. Muslim fundamentalists, led by Ayatollah Ruhollah Khomeini, opposed the Shah because they feared his pro-U.S. policies were undermining the country's religious traditions. Khomeini's followers held ever-larger demonstrations in the streets of Tehran, the Iranian capital. At first U.S. officials considered them little more than a political irritant, but with striking speed, the Muslim revolutionaries proved the experts wrong. They seized power, declared an Islamic republic, and forced the Shah to flee to the United States. On the night of November 4, 1979, angry demonstrators stormed into the U.S. embassy in Tehran, taking more than 60 American officials hostage.

Invading a foreign embassy and seizing diplomatic personnel transgresses the most ancient and fundamental principle of international law. For hundreds of years, countries have established diplomatic ties with one another so that they can learn about each other, communicate about differences, and reach agreements. The residence and offices of the ambassador, known as the embassy, are respected as the sovereign territory of the guest nation. Its privacy is not to be violated by the host nation—even if war breaks out between the two countries. When that occurs, the countries break diplomatic relations, and each side allows the other's ambassador and staff to depart peacefully. For a country to do otherwise would only invite retaliation against its own diplomatic personnel.

Revolutionaries, however, are not known for their respect for law, domestic or international. When they seize power, they act first and only later consider the possible ramifications of their actions. The Muslim revolutionaries of Tehran refused to return the U.S. ambassador and other diplomatic personnel until the Shah had been returned to Iran and the country had been paid damages for alleged wrongs.

Demanding the return of the hostages, President Jimmy Carter broke diplomatic relations with Iran, imposed a trade embargo, and froze all Iranian economic assets in the United States, expecting that these strong actions would force the new Iranian government to recognize its international obligations. But after five months passed without release of the hostages, Carter ordered a secret rescue operation, which failed when a U.S. helicopter and its crew crashed in a desert sandstorm. Carter decided that any further military action would only endanger the lives of the hostages.

Time and economic pressure finally took their toll. The hostages were released 14 months after they had been captured. Carter paid a high price for his patience, however. At the beginning of the crisis, public opinion rallied around the president. His standing in the polls jumped by as much as 27 percentage points. But as the crisis persisted into the summer and fall of an election year, the president himself seemed to have been taken hostage. Television interviews with the hostages' families made Americans familiar with individual captives. Yellow ribbons, banners, and bumper stickers expressed public concern, and the news media began counting the number of days the hostages had been held. Because the president seemed incapable of bringing the problem to resolution, his support in opinion polls fell dramatically. On election day, Carter carried only six states (plus the District of Columbia) and won but 41 percent of the popular vote. Few television scenes have ever been more ironic than those showing hostages leaving Tehran while Ronald Reagan was viewing his inaugural parade. Carter's economic sanctions finally forced the release of the hostages, but his success had come too late.

PRESIDENT CARTER'S HANDLING OF THE IRANIAN HOSTAGE SITUATION provides a telling example of the conduct and consequences of American foreign policy. Presidents play a preeminent role in the making of foreign policy, and they may be rewarded and punished accordingly by the voting public—especially if there is a high-profile crisis abroad. In this chapter, we explore how America conducts foreign policy and examine the changing connections between foreign policy and electoral politics. In doing so, we answer the following questions:

- What characteristics of foreign policy enable presidents to exercise greater influence over it than over domestic policy?

- What constitutional responsibilities over foreign affairs are granted to the president and Congress?

- How do various agencies in the executive branch help design and coordinate foreign policy?

- How has America's history shaped modern debates over the country's foreign policy goals?

## Elections, Presidents, and Foreign Policy

**Foreign policy** is the conduct of relations among nation–states. The most important foreign policy issues involve war and peace. Of all foreign policy objectives, the most critical is to prevent the country from being attacked or invaded by a foreign power. But foreign policy also involves economic trade among nations, as well as such mundane matters as issuing passports to citizens who wish to travel abroad.

In a classic essay, political scientist Aaron Wildavksy developed the **two-presidency theory,** which explains why presidents exercise greater power over foreign affairs than over domestic policy.[1] On domestic matters, presidents are usually subject to pressure politics and congressional checks. On foreign policy questions, however, presidents have a degree of autonomy that enables them to manage the external relations of the country fairly free of short-term political pressures. In this section we describe four reasons why foreign policy differs from domestic policy: (1) the need for fast action; (2) the voters' focus on presidents; (3) the limited role of interest groups; and (4) the congressional role.

**foreign policy**
Conduct of relations among nation states.

**two-presidency theory**
Theory that explains why presidents exercise greater power over foreign affairs than over domestic policy.

## Figure 20.1

**"Rally 'round the Flag" Effects**
Presidents' gains in popularity
average 8 percentage points in the
months following a crisis. *Why do
you think President Clinton did not
experience as large a boost in public
support after foreign policy crises as
his predecessors?*

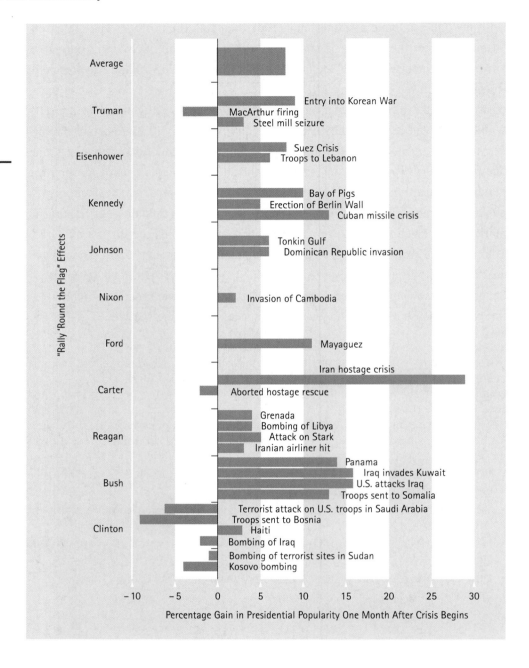

Percentage Gain in Presidential Popularity One Month After Crisis Begins

### Need for Fast Action

On domestic issues, the president may negotiate with Congress over the course of several years, but foreign policy questions often require rapid, decisive action. As Alexander Hamilton observed, governments require a single executive leader in order to achieve "decision, activity, secrecy, and dispatch."[2] Or, in the words of humorist Artemus Ward, "Thrice is he armed that has his quarrel just—And four times he who gets his fist in first."[3] Following this principle, President Bush in 1991 quickly placed U.S. troops in Saudi Arabia to forestall an invasion by Iraq (see Figure 20.1). Congress did not consider the issue until six months later.

### Voters' Focus on Presidents

On key domestic issues, members of Congress know that voters hold them to account, but on foreign affairs, Wildavksy points out, voters "expect the president to act."[4] In the early days of a crisis, voters often ignore those who criticize presidential actions.

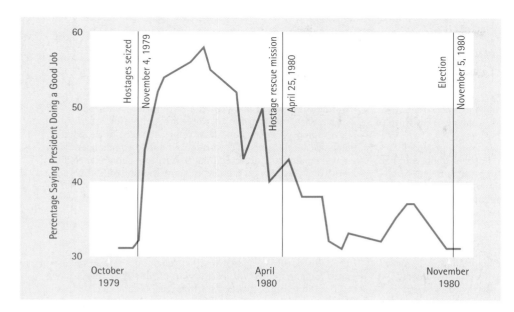

**Figure 20.2**

**Shifts in Carter's Popularity During the Hostage Crisis**

SOURCE: Michael Nelson, ed., *Congressional Quarterly Guide to the Presidency, 1989,* (Washington, DC: CQ Press), 1471.

When Edward Kennedy ran against Carter for the Democratic nomination during the first months of the hostage crisis, he made little political headway. And despite being weakened by an impeachment crisis in the spring of 1999, President Clinton received broad public and congressional support when he bombed Serbian army positions in Kosovo.

The tendency among the public to back presidents in foreign crises, often called the **"rally 'round the flag" effect,** shows up in opinion polls in almost every instance in which the United States becomes involved in a foreign policy emergency.[5] Support for the president nearly always goes up in the first days of a conflict with another nation. Figure 20.1 shows the crises that presidents from Truman to Clinton have faced and the changes in opinion polls that occurred after those crises. Between 1950 and 1999, public support for presidents increased by an average of 8 percentage points in the month after a foreign policy crisis occurred.

Although voters support presidents initially, they nonetheless demand quick results. Though Carter won public backing in the first month of the hostage crisis, his popularity later took a nose-dive, as Figure 20.2 illustrates.

The public seems especially ready to hold presidents accountable when war breaks out and American casualties mount. The public supported U.S. entry into both the Korean and Vietnam Wars. But when the conflicts dragged on, both Harry Truman, in the case of the Korean War, and Lyndon Johnson, in the case of Vietnam, lost so much public support that they announced they would not run for reelection. The opposition party won the next election in each instance.[6]

Not only do voters demand quick results, but they soon forget foreign policy victories. If the economy steadily improves, presidents receive credit for the progress year after year. But unless a foreign policy accomplishment immediately precedes an election, there are few electoral dividends. Before too long, voters forget and turn to domestic concerns. For example, during the first three years of the Bush presidency, the United States won both the Cold War and the Persian Gulf War. Yet one year later, the voters, deciding that domestic issues were more important, voted Bush out of office (see the accompanying Election Connection).

As presidents have come to be exposed to increasing media coverage, the number of crises have increased and grace periods have shortened. Satellite television and the Internet supply details about international events to a broader public audience than ever before. Struggles that might have been unknown or ignored in the past are now regularly served along with microwave dinners. Americans can now see intense and personal images of conflict and suffering anywhere on the planet.

**"rally 'round the flag" effect**
The tendency for the public to back presidents in moments of crisis.

## Election Connection

# Foreign Policy Success Comes Too Soon

No matter how spectacular a president's foreign policy successes may be, the public quickly forgets about them. For presidential reelection strategies, a foreign policy success should occur close to election day.

A decade after President Carter's Iranian hostage debacle, a second crisis exploded in the Persian Gulf. Iran's neighbor Iraq had long coveted the oil riches of Kuwait, its small, defenseless neighbor, and Saddam Hussein, Iraq's shrewd, unpredictable leader, often asserted historical claims to Kuwait. But when the Iraqi army overran Kuwait on the night of August 2, 1990, the United States was taken by surprise.

Having captured Kuwait, Hussein controlled 10 percent of the world's oil reserves. With his army poised to march into neighboring Saudi Arabia, Hussein stood within reach of another 10 percent. At the request of the Saudis, President Bush first ordered 200,000 troops to Saudi Arabia and then succeeded in winning United Nations support for a trade embargo against Iraq. Bush's advisers next debated the wisdom of using military force to drive the Iraqi army from Kuwait.

Carter's experience with Iran came immediately to their minds. From that episode, it was clear that it would take months, maybe years, for economic sanctions to cripple the Iraqi economy. And the stalemate would undoubtedly undermine Bush's political popularity. Yet Bush also had to consider the price of military action. If American soldiers were to die by the tens of thousands in an all-out war, the public might never forgive the president.

For Bush the choice was not difficult. He persuaded the United Nations to demand departure of Iraqi troops from Kuwait by January 15, 1991, a date that postponed the final decision on going to war until after the November congressional elections. In the new, heavily Democratic Congress, most Democratic congressional leaders recommended that the president delay military action until the effectiveness of economic sanctions could be tested. One critical senator said, "It doesn't pass my Dover, Delaware, test. How many bodies will be coming back through Dover?"[a] One Republican senator accused Democratic leaders of "wanting it both ways. If it works, they want to be with the President. If not, they want to be against him."

Despite the opposition of the Democratic leadership, a majority of both the House and the Senate voted in favor of Bush's ultimatum. Within days of the key votes on Capitol Hill, American planes bombed Baghdad and Iraqi troops adjacent to the Saudi border. General Norman Schwarzkopf, the field commander, faked a naval landing and attacked Iraqi troops from behind, encircling and virtually destroying the enemy army. The United States suffered fewer than 2000 combat fatalities. Only the decision not to march to Baghdad and capture Saddam Hussein himself made the victory less than complete.

The victory boosted Bush's popularity ratings to the highest levels ever achieved by a modern American president. As the summer of 1991 approached, Bush seemed politically invincible. Democrats openly wondered whether their opposition to the use of armed force in Iraq would "keep us out of the White House forever." The White House chief of staff gloated, "I can't believe that [Democrats] are going to expect everyone to ignore the vote they cast on the most important issue this country has had to deal with in 40 years." But within a year, public memories of the Persian Gulf war had faded, and the news media turned their attention to domestic problems. The economy was languishing. The deficit was burgeoning. Success in foreign affairs had come too early, too quickly, and too easily to propel President Bush into a second term.

*What do you think?*
- *Do you think the public is unreasonable to forget foreign policy successes at election time?*
- *Should voters place more weight on foreign policy and less on domestic policy?*

[a] Senator John Glenn of Ohio, as quoted in Jill Zuckman, "In Congress, Big Majority Isn't Voting for Invasion," *Boston Globe,* May 18, 1994, 7.

SOURCES: James Baker, III, with Thomas M. DeFrank, *The Politics of Diplomacy: Revolution, War, and Peace, 1989–1992* (New York: Putnam 1995). "Parties Split Into Postwar Camps after Giving Victory Cheer," *Congressional Quarterly* 49 (March 9, 1991): 611. *New York Times,* January 4, 1991, 1. *Washington Post,* December 7, 1990, A25.

President Bush sent troops to Somalia to end internal warfare that was causing mass starvation. Foreign policy expert George Kennan attributes public support for the policy to "the exposure of the Somalia situation by the American media, above all, television. . . . The [public] reaction was . . . occasioned by the sight of the suffering of the starving people."[7] Similarly, President Clinton felt responsible for resolving political disorder that was causing widespread suffering in Haiti. He sent in troops to enforce a plan to restore democracy there after a period of military rule. In the words of one commentator, decisions such as these are "less the result of a rational weighing of need or what is remediable than . . . of what gets on nightly news shows."[8]

At the same time as pressure to intervene has risen, presidents seem not to be enjoying as much of a benefit from doing so. President Clinton has not received the same "rally 'round the flag" boost enjoyed by his predecessors. During the major foreign policy crises of the Clinton administration, the president's popularity averaged a downward shift of an average of 3 points, rather than the average 8-point boost that previous presidents enjoyed.

Not only do voters seem increasingly reluctant to rally around the flag, but they now seem to expect results within a year after the United States becomes deeply

**Patriotic Fervor**
The Gulf War stirred a wave of patriotic fervor, boosting President Bush's approval ratings to the highest ever for a modern president. *Why did this support evaporate so rapidly that Bush lost the 1992 election?*

involved in a crisis. They become especially unhappy if U.S. soldiers are dying in foreign fields for more than a year without any "light at the end of the tunnel." When President Clinton kept soldiers in Somalia for more than a year, the death of just 18 soldiers cost the president public support, and U.S. troops were withdrawn shortly thereafter. When President Clinton sent 20,000 troops to Bosnia in 1995, he promised to remove them within a year, a date conveniently set just beyond the date of the next presidential election. Immediately after his reelection, Clinton, now a second-term president no longer vulnerable to punishment by the voters, announced that the troops would have to remain longer. In the year 2000, 6,000 U.S. troops remained as part of an international peacekeeping force, and one key general suggested that such troops would be needed in the region for "at least a generation."[9] Surprisingly, public support for the action did not wane, probably because no American soldiers had been killed in combat.

### Limited Role of Interest Groups

On domestic issues, many groups with large constituencies constantly mobilize voters and urge members of Congress to take action. But on foreign policy questions, "the interest group structure is weak, unstable, and thin."[10] The most important body influencing foreign affairs is the Council on Foreign Relations, a prestigious group that includes former secretaries of state, former ambassadors, foreign policy experts, and prominent business leaders. But the organization influences government action by the quality of its advice, not by its ability to mobilize votes.

On some occasions, organized groups capable of mobilizing large numbers of voters play a role in foreign policy issues. For example, the hundreds of thousands of people living in Florida whose families fled Cuba in the 1950s when communist leader Fidel Castro came to power have persuaded the U.S. government not to recognize the legitimacy of the Castro regime, despite the fact that nearly every other country now does. In the 2000 presidential election race, both major party candidates were quick to sympathize with the plight of young Elian Gonzalez, a six-year-old Cuban boy whose mother had died trying to bring her son to America. After Attorney General Janet Reno sent a team of federal agents to take the boy away from the Miami relatives who had refused to relinquish him, Vice-President Al Gore even broke with the administration position, saying that the case ought to have been handled in family court.

Middle East policies are also shaped by group pressures. James Baker, former Secretary of State, has observed that the conflict between Israel and Palestine is "a perpetual fixture of domestic politics" as a result of "the political power of the American Jewish community."[11] Because a strong domestic constituency is vitally interested, Congress regularly becomes actively engaged. The American Israel Public Affairs Committee (AIPAC) boasts on its Web site that *Fortune* magazine has ranked it the second most influential lobbying group in Washington, second only to the American Association of Retired Persons.[12] With strong support in Congress, Israel receives 20 percent of all U.S. foreign aid.[13] But although U.S. Middle East policies are, in the words of one former State Department official, influenced by "what we can get through [Capitol] Hill,"[14] they are also shaped by the country's interest in protecting access to oil reserves located in Arab countries. As a result, U.S. support for Israel seldom is as complete as Jewish organizations would prefer, and relations between the United States and Israel are often uneasy.

But these examples are "exceptions that prove the rule." Most nationality groups are not large enough or concentrated enough or sufficiently attentive to events overseas to have a decisive effect on U.S. foreign policy. Civil rights groups have long taken an interest in race relations in South Africa, but they have never been as effective at mobilizing supporters for the South African cause as for affirmative action questions and other domestic issues.

## Congressional Role

Although Congress plays a central role in the formation of domestic policy, when it comes to foreign affairs members of Congress follow a "self-denying ordinance." They do not think it is their job to determine the nation's defense policies."[15] This was particularly true in the years immediately after World War II. During these years, Congress's prestige with respect to foreign policy was seriously damaged because it had left the country unprepared for World War II. Just four months before the Japanese attacked Hawaii's Pearl Harbor, the incident that provoked U.S. involvement in the war, a bill requiring young men to register for service in the armed forces passed the House of Representatives by only a single vote. After the war, Congress, embarrassed by its earlier mistakes, let the president make most major foreign policy decisions.

After the Vietnam War, however, Congress played a more assertive foreign policy role, and conflict between Congress and the president intensified.[16] For example, Congress began to cut the defense requests of Republican presidents by an average of 5 percent, as Figure 20.3 shows. Congress also called for more strenuous efforts to secure arms reduction agreements with the Soviet Union. Some Congressional leaders even opposed the use of force against Iraq in the Persian Gulf War, though a majority of Congress eventually backed the president.

The great victory in the Persian Gulf has erased some of the bad memories from the Vietnam War and helped boost the prestige of the executive. In recent years, Congress has begun to defer somewhat more to the president on foreign policy questions. For example, it acquiesced to the placement of troops in Somalia under Bush and in Bosnia under Clinton.[17]

### SECTION SUMMARY

The president has more influence over the conduct of foreign affairs than over domestic matters. This is due in part to the nature of foreign policy itself. The conduct of relations with other nations often requires quick, decisive action that only the president can provide. In times of conflict, voters tend to flock to support the president's actions—at least at first. Interest groups also play a much more limited role in foreign policy than in domestic policy, and Congress defers to presidential leadership.

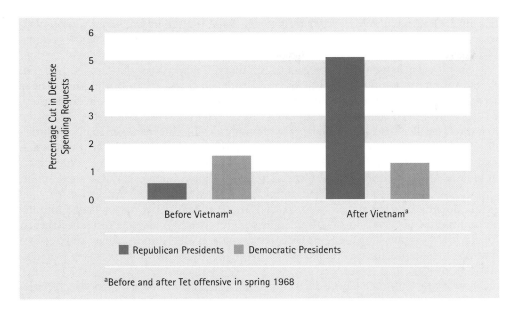

**Figure 20.3**

**Growing Partisanship in Congress**
After Vietnam, Democratic Congresses cut Republican presidential defense spending requests. *What accounts for Congress's increasing assertiveness in foreign affairs?*

NOTE: Data from 1947–1991.

SOURCE: Ralph Carter, "Budgeting for Defense," in Paul E. Peterson, ed., *The President, the Congress, and the Making of Foreign Policy* (Norman, OK: Oklahoma University Press, 1993), p. 165.

## Foreign Policy Responsibilities of the President and Congress

CONSTITUTION, ARTICLE I, SECTION 8: "The Congress shall have power to . . . declare war, . . . raise and support armies, . . . provide and maintain a navy, . . . [and] make rules for the government and regulation of the land and naval forces."

CONSTITUTION, ARTICLE II, SECTION 2: "The President shall be commander in chief of the army and navy."

CONSTITUTION, ARTICLE II, SECTION 1: "The executive power shall be vested in a President of the United States."

Although the president plays the dominant role in the making of foreign policy, the Constitution gives clear responsibilities to Congress as well. As a consequence, the constitutional debate over the power of Congress and of the presidency has continued from the early years of the republic down to the present day. In this section we review how the power to wage war has evolved through history, describe congressional attempts to limit presidential war powers, and consider the treaty-making power, which the Constitution divides between the president and the Senate.

### War Power

The debate over which institution ought to control the nation's war power predates even the ratification of the Constitution. Writing in support of the new form of government, Alexander Hamilton argued that "Of all the concerns of government, the direction of war most peculiarly demands the exercise of power by a single hand."[18] Yet the Constitution gives Congress the authority to declare war and to raise and maintain the armed forces. The president's constitutional powers are less clearly defined; the Constitution says only that the president is commander in chief and exercises executive power. Chief Justice John Marshall interpreted these powers broadly: "The President is the sole organ of the nation in its external relations, and its sole representative with foreign nations."[19] But Congressman Thaddeus Stevens, a great defender of congressional prerogatives, proclaimed that "though the president is commander-in-chief, Congress is his commander, and God willing, he shall obey."[20] The issue has been debated ever since.

Prior to the Civil War, presidents seldom acted on their own on military matters. President James Madison refused to attack Great Britain in 1812 until Congress had declared war. And in 1846, President James K. Polk, though he provoked war by placing troops in disputed territory, did not actually order troops into battle against Mexico until Congress had declared war.

Faced with a national emergency, Abraham Lincoln was the first to give an expanded interpretation of the role of commander in chief. When the southern states seceded from the Union, Lincoln proclaimed a blockade of southern ports and enlisted 300,000 volunteers before Congress convened. A few decades later, Theodore Roosevelt further broadened the role of commander in chief by exercising executive powers in a much less urgent situation. He sent naval ships to Japan even when Congress refused to appropriate enough money for the trip. He said that the president, in his role as commander in chief, would send the ships. Congress, if it wished, could appropriate enough funds to get them back. Congress did.

Following Lincoln and Roosevelt's lead, modern presidents have felt free to initiate military action even in the absence of congressional approval. President Truman fought the Korean War without any congressional declaration whatsoever. More recently, President Clinton ordered the bombing of Kosovo without securing congressional approval.

Two major Supreme Court decisions have set the boundaries within which presidents exercise their authority as commander in chief. In 1936 the Court was asked, in **U.S. v. Curtiss-Wright**, whether Congress could delegate to the president the power to determine whether arms could be sold to Bolivia and Paraguay, countries engaged in a border dispute. In his decision in favor of presidential power, Justice George Sutherland wrote that the authority of presidents on foreign policy questions was greater than their authority on domestic issues. Sutherland referred to "the very delicate, plenary and exclusive power of the president as the sole organ of the federal government in the field of international relations." He went on to say that the president had "a degree of discretion and freedom . . . which would not be admissible were domestic affairs alone involved."[21]

*Curtiss-Wright* was qualified by the 1951 **Youngstown Sheet and Tube Co. v. Sawyer** case, in which the Supreme Court placed limits on the executive power of the president. Trade unions in the steel industry had gone on strike during the Korean War. Claiming that the steel industry was crucial for national defense, President Truman ordered the federal government to seize control of the steel mills and commanded the strikers to return to work. In doing so, Truman ignored alternative procedures for handling strikes that had recently been enacted by Congress. When the steel companies disputed Truman's claim of executive power in this case, the Supreme Court ruled against the president, saying he should have instead observed the congressionally defined procedures. Justice Robert Jackson wrote that when a president "takes measures incompatible with the expressed or implied will of Congress, his power is at its lowest ebb."[22]

When the *Curtiss-Wright* and *Youngstown* cases are considered together, the Court seems to have said that presidents have more constitutional discretion with respect to foreign than domestic questions. However, presidents may not act contrary to the clearly expressed will of Congress.[23]

## War Powers Resolution

The issue of executive authority arose again during the Vietnam War. Presidents Eisenhower and Kennedy had sent soldiers to Vietnam to serve as "advisers" to the South Vietnamese army, which was engaged in a war against communist guerrillas trained in North Vietnam. Neither Eisenhower nor Kennedy had received congressional authorization to send these advisers, and as the war intensified, U.S. military personnel became ever more directly involved. Then, in the summer of 1964, North Vietnamese torpedo boats attacked several U.S. destroyers stationed in Tonkin Bay off the coast of Haiphong, Vietnam's second largest city. President Lyndon Johnson denounced the action as an unlawful attack on U.S. ships which he said were sailing in international waters. He asked Congress for a resolution authorizing him to respond

---

*U.S. v. Curtiss-Wright*
Supreme Court decision in which Congress is given the authority to delegate foreign policy responsibilities to the president.

*Youngstown Sheet and Tube Co. v. Sawyer*
Case in which the Supreme Court placed limits on the executive power of the president.

with armed force. Congress overwhelmingly passed the **Tonkin Gulf Resolution,** which gave the president the authority to "take all necessary measures" to repel any attacks and to "prevent further aggression."[24] The resolution became the legal basis for a war that would last for eight more years. Only much later was it revealed that Johnson had misled Congress by inaccurately claiming that the United States had not invaded North Vietnam's territorial waters.

The experience of a long and discouraging war in Vietnam prompted Congress to rethink its broad approval of the president's authority over military action. In 1970 it repealed the Tonkin Gulf Resolution. As a further precaution against presidential usurpation of congressional prerogatives, Congress in 1973 passed, over President Nixon's veto, the **War Powers Resolution,** which required that the president formally notify Congress any time he orders U.S. troops into military action. The resolution further specifies that troops must be withdrawn unless Congress approves the presidential decision within 60 days after notice of the military action has been received.

Other than George Bush, who asked for congressional authorization of the Persian Gulf War, no president has asked for congressional authorization for military action. President Reagan invaded Grenada, bombed Libya, and placed military troops in Lebanon without notifying Congress. President Bush attacked Panama and moved troops into Somalia. President Clinton bombed Iraq, deployed troops in Bosnia, and bombarded Serb positions in Kosovo without notifying Congress as called for by the War Powers Resolution. On five separate occasions, individual members of Congress have sued in federal courts, attempting to force the president to abide by that resolution. In each case, however, judges have dismissed the suits.[25] In 1999, 26 members of Congress failed in an attempt to force President Clinton to obtain congressional approval of the Kosovo air strikes.[26]

Some believe that these failed efforts, coupled with presidential refusal to notify Congress of military engagements, have made the War Powers Resolution a dead letter without any legal significance. But other analysts have pointed out that Congress can, by majority vote, pass a resolution that takes formal notice of any military engagement, and once it has done so, the 60-day clock begins to tick, after which troops must be withdrawn. Though lawsuits have been filed by individual representatives, Congress as a whole has never been willing to challenge presidential refusal to observe the War Powers Resolution by passing this type of measure. Until such a direct conflict between the president and Congress takes place, the exact significance of the War Powers Resolution will remain unclear.

**Tonkin Gulf Resolution**
Congressional resolution giving the president the authority to send troops to Vietnam.

**War Powers Resolution**
1973 congressional resolution requiring the president to notify Congress formally upon ordering U.S. troops into military action.

**A Slow Buildup**
Initially serving as military advisers, U.S. soldiers gradually became more involved in the fight against communism in Southeast Asia. *Why did this war induce Congress to pass the War Powers Resolution?*

## Treaty Power

CONSTITUTION, ARTICLE II, SECTION 2: "[The President] shall have power, by and with the advice and consent of the Senate, to make Treaties, provided two-thirds of the Senators present concur."

**treaties**
Official agreements with foreign countries that are ratified by the Senate.

The power of the president to negotiate **treaties**—official agreements with foreign countries that are ratified by the Senate—is the most circumscribed of all presidential powers. A treaty does not take effect until it wins approval by a two-thirds Senate vote. Because this super-majority can be difficult to achieve unless a treaty has overwhelming public support, presidents have often felt constrained by senatorial pressures when negotiating with foreign countries. Prior to 1928, the Senate rejected or withheld approval of 14 percent of the treaties presidents had negotiated.[27]

No president was more frustrated than Woodrow Wilson by this constitutional check on presidential power. When negotiating the Versailles treaty that ended World War I, President Wilson pursued one objective above all others: the establishment of a **League of Nations,** an international organization created to settle international disputes, which became the precursor to the United Nations. Wilson felt that such an organization was essential if future world wars were to be avoided. The other nations at the Versailles conference and a considerable portion of the public supported Wilson's ideas. But the Senate voted down the treaty, primarily because many believed the League of Nations would undermine U.S. sovereignty. The United States, alone among the countries that had fought in the war, did not add its signature to the document and remained outside the League of Nations. Shocked and dismayed, Wilson lost both his political efficacy and his personal health.

**League of Nations**
International organization created after World War I to settle international disputes; precursor of the United Nations.

Eighty years later, President Clinton faced similar difficulties with Congress. In October 1999, the Senate considered the Comprehensive Nuclear Test Ban Treaty, which was negotiated in 1996. The multinational agreement would have prohibited the testing of nuclear weapons and enacted more stringent monitoring systems to ensure compliance. Proponents of the treaty argued that it was essential to slowing the spread of nuclear weapons around the world. But critics, including many Senate Republicans, were skeptical of its effectiveness and worried that it would hamper the nation's ability to modernize its armed forces. After negotiations broke down between Republican leaders and the Clinton administration, the Senate voted against ratification, 51 to 48.

**executive agreement**
Agreement with foreign countries that requires only a presidential signature.

Because one-third-plus-one of the Senate can block passage of a treaty, presidents often negotiate **executive agreements,** legal contracts with foreign countries that require only a presidential signature. Though nothing in the Constitution explicitly gives the president the power to make executive agreements, the practice has long been established. The first executive agreement—limiting the size of both countries' naval forces on the Great Lakes—was signed by President James Monroe with Great Britain in 1817. In 1937 the Supreme Court affirmed the constitutionality of executive agreements.[28] Since that decision, presidents have increasingly relied on this method as a vehicle for negotiating with other nations. Most executive agreements either are extensions of treaties ratified by the Senate or involve routine presidential actions that have otherwise been authorized by Congress. But presidents sometimes use executive agreements to implement major foreign policy decisions. For example, President Clinton relied on an executive agreement to coax newly independent Ukraine into giving up its nuclear arsenal in exchange for economic aid.[29] In recent years, about 20 executive agreements have been signed for every treaty submitted to the Senate for its approval (see Figure 20.4).

participation
**America's Place
in the World**

### SECTION SUMMARY

Since Abraham Lincoln, presidents have interpreted their constitutional position as commander in chief of the armed forces as granting them broad powers over military matters. In its *Curtiss-Wright* decision, the Supreme Court validated this presidential interpretation of the Constitution, though the Court ruled in *Youngstown* that presidents cannot contradict

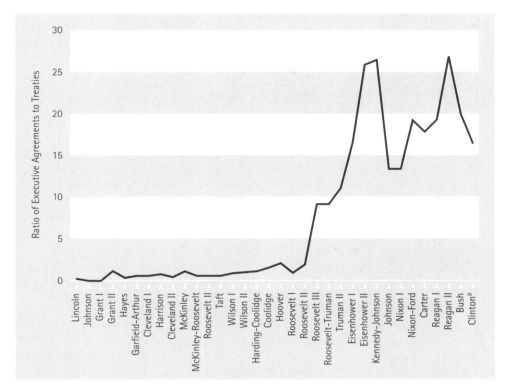

Figure 20.4

**Growing Presidential Power: Executive Agreements Are Replacing Treaties**
*Why have presidents increasingly turned to executive agreements? Does this behavior deny the Senate its constitutional role in foreign policy?*

SOURCES: Gary King and Lyn Ragsdale, *The Elusive Executive: Discovering Statistical Patterns in the Presidency* (Washington, DC: CQ Press, 1988), pp. 131–140; U.S. Bureau of the Census, *Statistical Abstracts of the United States* (U.S. Government Printing Office, 1996), Table 1294, 792; fax from Randall J. Snyder, Law Librarian, Office of the Legal Advisor, Department of State, Washington, DC, December 1996.

[a] 1993–1995

the expressed will of Congress. During the Vietnam War, Congress granted the president a broad military mandate under the Tonkin Gulf Resolution, but it later reversed course and passed the War Powers Resolution, which restricts the president's power to wage war without congressional approval. The effectiveness of the War Powers Resolution is questionable, however, inasmuch as presidents seldom request congressional authorization for military activities abroad. Presidents must submit treaties to the Senate for ratification by a two-thirds majority, but they have relied increasingly on executive agreements, rather than treaties, to make pacts with other nations.

## Institutions Responsible for Foreign Policy

The critical institutions that are today responsible for foreign policy took shape in the early years of the **Cold War**, the 43-year conflict between the United States and the Soviet Union from 1946 to 1989. At the beginning of the Cold War there emerged the modern Department of State, the Department of Defense, the Central Intelligence Agency, and the office of the National Security Adviser. These organizations' relationships to one another and to the president are shown in Figure 20.5. In this section, we begin with a description of the Cold War itself, discuss the emergence of each of these institutions, and consider their changing roles during the post–Cold War era.

> **Cold War**
> The 43-year period (1946–1989) during which the United States and the Soviet Union threatened one another with mutual destruction by nuclear warfare.

### The Cold War

The country's greatest foreign policy challenge accompanied the beginning of the Cold War. In the months following World War II, Germany was divided into eastern and western parts, and Korea was split into a North and South, one-half of each country under western influence, the other within the communist domain. In short order, the Soviet Union consolidated its control over much of Eastern Europe, establishing communist governments in Poland, Hungary, Bulgaria, and Romania. In 1948 Soviet-backed communists seized control of Czechoslovakia, and the following year communist forces won China's civil war. Armed barriers preventing movement across

**Figure 20.5**

**The Foreign Policy Institutions**
*Why does the Army Chief of Staff report both to the Joint Chiefs and to the Secretary of the Army?*

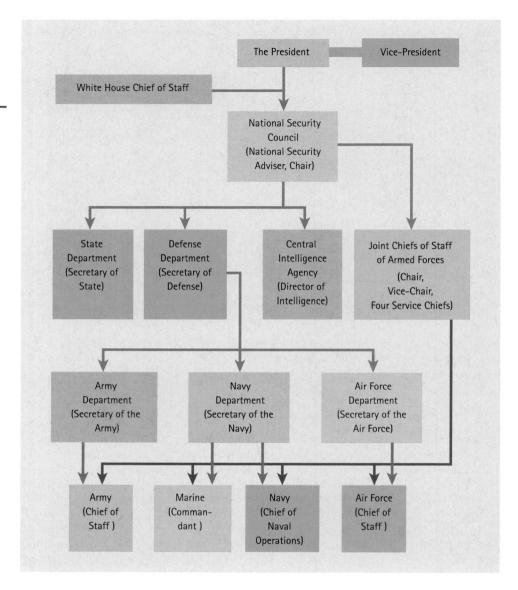

iron curtain
Armed barrier during the Cold War that prevented movement across national borders between communist Eastern Europe and democratic Western Europe.

containment
U.S. policy that attempted to stop the spread of communism in the expectation that this system of government would eventually collapse on its own.

national borders that became known as the **iron curtain** divided Europe into East and West (see Figure 20.6). British Prime Minister Winston Churchill coined the term in 1946 when he said, "From Stettin in the Baltic to Trieste in the Adriatic an iron curtain has descended across the Continent."[30] In 1961 a huge concrete wall was built through the middle of Berlin, dramatically symbolizing the division of the world into its communist and western parts.

The Cold War began at a time when the prestige of the executive branch had been greatly enhanced by its successful prosecution of World War II. As a result, President Truman was able to mobilize bipartisan support for his foreign policy and recruit to key positions the most talented group of foreign policy advisers the country had ever assembled. They decided on a strategy of **containment**, a policy that attempted to stop the spread of communism in the expectation that this system of government would eventually collapse on its own. The policy, designed by George Kennan, a brilliant State Department specialist, won bipartisan support.[31] Though it took nearly 50 years, containment proved successful. Unrest began in the communist-dominated countries of East Europe during the 1980s and spread to the Soviet Union by the end of the decade. When East Germany allowed demonstrators to tear down the Berlin Wall in 1989, the Cold War finally came to an end.

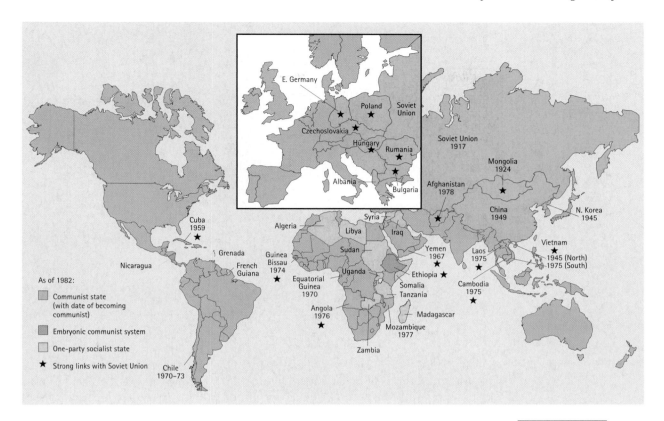

 caption area labels:
As of 1982:
- Communist state (with date of becoming communist)
- Embryonic communist system
- One-party socialist state
- ★ Strong links with Soviet Union

## State Department

It was during the Cold War that the modern professional State Department emerged out of the patronage-ridden entity that preceded it. However, the State Department itself, the agency responsible for conducting diplomatic relations, dates back to the administration of George Washington and his secretary of state, Thomas Jefferson.

Ever since this time, the **secretary of state** has been the president's official foreign policy adviser. In most administrations, the secretary of state is also the nation's chief diplomat. For example, the secretary of state during the first term of the Clinton administration, Warren Christopher, played a major role in negotiating a peace agreement between Israel and the Palestinians. The job of chief diplomat is extremely

**Figure 20.6**

**Spread of Communism after World War II**
*How did the spread of Communism influence the organization of the State Department? The Defense Department? The CIA?*

**The Berlin Wall**
Built during the presidency of John F. Kennedy, the Berlin Wall (left) symbolized what Churchill called the Iron Curtain. The wall, and the curtain, crumbled in 1989 (right).

**Secretary of State Madeline Albright, with Palestinian Leader Yasir Arafat**
*How does a modern secretary of state use the resources of the State Department to influence United States foreign policy?*

**secretary of state**
Officially, the president's chief foreign policy advisor and head of the Department of State, the agency responsible for conducting diplomatic relations.

**ambassador**
The head of a diplomatic delegation to a major foreign country.

**embassy**
The structure that houses ambassadors and their diplomatic aides in the capital cities of foreign countries.

challenging. As former Secretary of State George Marshall once commented, "In diplomacy, you never can tell what a man is thinking. He smiles at you and kicks you in the stomach at the same time."[32] Or as one pundit put it, "Diplomacy is the art of saying 'nice doggie' until you can find a rock."[33]

Reporting to the secretary of state are **ambassadors,** who head the diplomatic delegations to major foreign countries. Ambassadors are responsible for the management of major U.S. **embassies** abroad, which house diplomatic delegations in the capital cities of foreign countries. Consulates are maintained in important cities that are not foreign capitals. If you wish to travel abroad, you must first obtain a passport from the State Department. If you encounter difficulty while traveling in a foreign country, your first phone call might well be made to the closest embassy or consulate.

Although embassies and consulates help American tourists and businesses, their most important political responsibility is to report back to the State Department detailed information on the government and politics, as well as the economic and social conditions, of the host country. The ambassador also conveys to the host country the views of the United States government, as instructed by the State Department. An ambassador must be able to listen to others carefully and communicate no more than what the president wants to convey. As the British diplomat Sir Henry Wotton put it, "an ambassador is an honest man sent to lie abroad" for his country.[34]

Before the Cold War, U.S. ambassadorial appointments were as important for rewarding those who helped presidents win election as for the diplomacy they carried out. The most prestigious ambassadorships were given to long-time political supporters who had raised large sums of money for the president's election. The grandest appointment of all was ambassador to the Court of St. James, the U.S. embassy in London. The holder of this distinguished position could be expected to be invited to the most elegant of the queen's official gatherings.

Appointments to the Court of St. James often went to truly worthy public figures who happened also to be loyal partisans. But many other ambassadorial and diplomatic positions were handed out to individuals with considerably less diplomatic skill. As one historian put it, "Most diplomats earned their appointments through party affiliation, personal wealth, or social position, seldom through training. Many lacked knowledge; some lacked dignity, although few were as tactless as John Randolph, who allegedly commented, when presented to the Czar in 1830, 'Howaya Emperor? And how's the madam?'"[35] Even today, some ambassadorial positions remain frankly political. President Clinton named an undistinguished Boston mayor ambassador to the Vatican. He also appointed as ambassador to Ireland the sister of influential Senator Edward Kennedy, despite the fact that she had little foreign policy experience.

But patronage today is more the exception than the rule. Those appointed to less prestigious diplomatic positions are nearly always trained career officers who are familiar with the language and customs of the host country.

Ever since the 1920s these officers have been organized into a **foreign service,** which consists of the diplomats who staff U.S. embassies and consulates. After World War II, the foreign service was strengthened as part of the effort to fight the Cold War. In particular, Dean Acheson, President Truman's secretary of state, did much to improve the professional caliber of the foreign service. A reporter at the time declared, "For the first time in the memory of living man, the American foreign office comes somewhere near being adequate to the needs of the country."[36]

The State Department and the foreign service are today key, if rather stodgy, components of the foreign policy system. Washington policy makers often call the Department of State "Foggy Bottom" because of its location near the foggy banks of the Potomac River. (Some people think the name especially apt, given the hazy quality of many State Department memos.) Diplomatic service tends to place a higher premium on etiquette than imagination. Historian Arthur Schlesinger once wrote, "At times it almost looked as if the [foreign] service inducted a collection of spirited young Americans at the age of 25 and transmuted them in 20 years into bland . . . denizens of a conservative men's club."[37] Schlesinger's suggestion that the foreign service tended to be a men's club was on target, for as recently as 1995 only about one-quarter of foreign service positions were held by women.[38] With the appointment by Clinton of Madeleine Albright as the country's first female secretary of state, we may see more changes in the gender composition of the State Department.

## *Defense Department*

Since the first decades of the country's independence, Americans have been concerned about the ill effects of a large military. Though the nation has sometimes looked to popular generals, such as George Washington and Dwight Eisenhower, for political leadership (see the accompanying Window on the Past), Congress and the president have always made certain that the military was controlled by civilian appointees. As one analyst puts it, freedom "demands that people without guns be able to tell people with guns what to do."[39] The Cold War posed new challenges for this ideal of civilian control. To ensure the country's continued international leadership and carry out the policy of containment, Congress provided for the largest military establishment in the nation's history. In an effort to handle better this large peacetime standing army, the military went through several major organizational changes.

At the close of World War II, the army and navy were two separate departments, each with its own air force and each with its own seat in the president's cabinet. With the onset of the Cold War, to coordinate civilian control of the armed forces better, the 1947 National Security Act created a single **Department of Defense** that contained within it the Departments of Army, Navy, and Air Force, each with its own civilian secretary appointed by the president. The secretaries for the army and the air force are each responsible for their respective branches of the armed services. The secretary of the navy is responsible for both the naval forces and the marines. All three secretaries report to the **secretary of defense,** the president's chief civilian adviser on defense matters and overall head of all three departments.

Subordinate to the civilian leadership of the secretary of defense and the other three appointed secretaries, military professionals direct the armed forces. At one time, each armed force had its own military leadership, and they acted more or less independently of each other. To achieve better coordination, Congress formally created the **Joint Chiefs of Staff** in 1947. The Joint Chiefs consist of the heads of all the military services—the army, navy, air force, and marine corps—together with a chair and vice-chair nominated by the president and confirmed by the Senate. Omar Bradley, the first

**foreign service**
Diplomats who staff U.S. embassies and consulates.

**Department of Defense**
Cabinet department responsible for managing the U.S. armed forces.

**secretary of defense**
The president's chief civilian adviser on defense matters and overall head of the army, navy, and air force.

**Joint Chiefs of Staff**
The heads of all the military services, together with a chair and vice-chair nominated by the president and confirmed by the Senate.

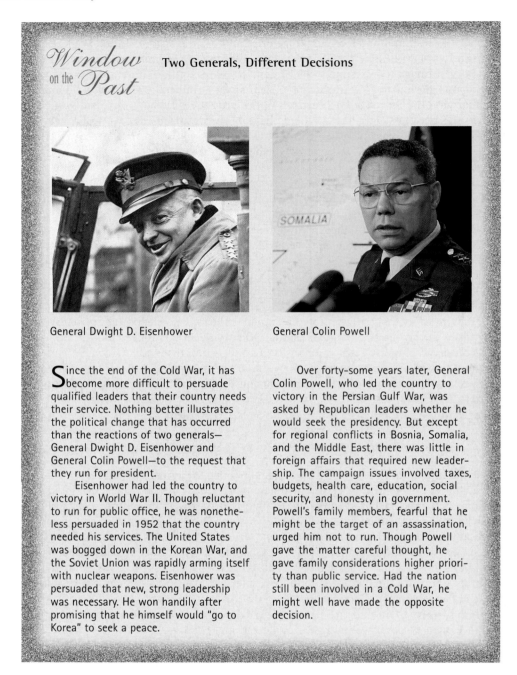

*Window on the Past*    **Two Generals, Different Decisions**

General Dwight D. Eisenhower

General Colin Powell

Since the end of the Cold War, it has become more difficult to persuade qualified leaders that their country needs their service. Nothing better illustrates the political change that has occurred than the reactions of two generals— General Dwight D. Eisenhower and General Colin Powell—to the request that they run for president.

Eisenhower had led the country to victory in World War II. Though reluctant to run for public office, he was nonetheless persuaded in 1952 that the country needed his services. The United States was bogged down in the Korean War, and the Soviet Union was rapidly arming itself with nuclear weapons. Eisenhower was persuaded that new, strong leadership was necessary. He won handily after promising that he himself would "go to Korea" to seek a peace.

Over forty-some years later, General Colin Powell, who led the country to victory in the Persian Gulf War, was asked by Republican leaders whether he would seek the presidency. But except for regional conflicts in Bosnia, Somalia, and the Middle East, there was little in foreign affairs that required new leadership. The campaign issues involved taxes, budgets, health care, education, social security, and honesty in government. Powell's family members, fearful that he might be the target of an assassination, urged him not to run. Though Powell gave the matter careful thought, he gave family considerations higher priority than public service. Had the nation still been involved in a Cold War, he might well have made the opposite decision.

chairman of the Joint Chiefs of Staff, suggested that the organization was essential if the country were to achieve a unified, effective military force: "Our military forces are one team—in the game to win regardless of who carries the ball. This is no time for 'fancy dans' who won't hit the line with all they have on every play unless they can call the signals."[40]

Rivalries among the armed services have been so intense that it took decades to achieve what Bradley promised in 1949, but eventually a unified command structure was created in each of the regions of the world. This unified structure proved extraordinarily effective during the Persian Gulf War when General Norman Schwarzkopf, an army general, directly controlled not only the actions of the army but also those of the navy, air force, and marines, achieving one of the most coordinated military attacks the United States has ever mounted. Back in Washington, Chairman of the Joint Chiefs of Staff Colin Powell provided key military advice to President Bush.

The post–Cold War world offers a number of serious challenges for the Defense Department. Some experts worry that the military has become so large and institutionalized that it is slow to adapt to the changing world. Most of the armed forces are operating with weapons systems and technology designed to battle the Soviet Union, rather than engage in the smaller regional conflicts in which the U.S. military has become involved in the last decade. "We are probably severely under-investing in preparations to meet emerging challenges," says one Washington observer.[41]

In part, the military has been slow to change because of its own strategy for winning public backing of its programs. During the Cold War, when the Defense Department wished to ensure Congressional approval of a weapons system or military base, it enlisted the help of defense contractors and former military personnel to lobby Congress for support of the projects. As a result, many military production facilities and bases were placed in key congressional districts. Today, these key members of Congress are reluctant to allow the military to change its ways, because this might mean a loss of jobs to their constituents. With increasing frequency, the Defense Department is in the awkward position of receiving ample funds for projects that no longer need the money, and getting insufficient resources for important new weapons systems. At a congressional hearing in 1998, Chairman of the Joint Chiefs of Staff Henry Shelton scolded Congress for not closing enough military bases.[42]

Accentuating these specific funding issues has been the fact that the overall military budget declined significantly in the 1990s. At the beginning of the Cold War, the United States invested heavily in its armed forces. Throughout the 1950s, approximately 10 percent of the total GDP was devoted to defense expenditures. The percentage reached as high as 14 percent during the Korean War and was 6 percent as recently as the mid-1980s. After the fall of the Berlin Wall, Congress began to cut the defense budget, responding to the decline in public concern about the communist threat. In 1998 and 1999, as Figure 20.7 shows, defense expenditures dropped to 3.2 percent of GDP—the lowest level since before World War II.

**visual literacy**
**Evaluating Defense Spending**

## Central Intelligence Agency

"I only regret that I have but one life to lose for my country," said the Revolutionary War hero Nathan Hale, after he had been caught spying and was about to be hanged by the British. A statue in Hale's memory stands at the entrance of the main offices of the **Central Intelligence Agency (CIA)**, the agency primarily responsible for gathering and analyzing information about the political and military activities of other nations. The subject of many a spy novel, it is lovingly referred to as "the Company" or "the Pickle Factory" by members of the intelligence community.[43]

But if spying is an ancient and honorable practice, its organization into an independent agency that reports directly to the president is of fairly recent vintage. The need for better-organized intelligence became clear during World War II, especially on December 7, 1941, at Hawaii's Pearl Harbor, called a "day of infamy" by President Roosevelt. It was a day of particular disrepute for the intelligence community, inasmuch as naval officers at Pearl Harbor were completely unaware that Japan had both the capability and the intention of destroying half the U.S. naval force. (The chief naval official in Hawaii had an appointment with the Japanese envoy on that infamous day.)

The U.S. government made haphazard efforts to improve intelligence capabilities in the wake of the Pearl Harbor attack, but it was not until the Cold War began that Congress established a systematic, centralized system of intelligence gathering. The National Security Act of 1947 created the CIA as a separate agency, independent of both the Department of State and the Department of Defense. Although State and Defense (as well as other departments) continue to have their own sources of intelligence, the 1947 law made the CIA the main intelligence collection agency. It also gave the CIA the authority to conduct secret operations abroad at the request of the president.

It is the CIA's authority to conduct clandestine, or covert, operations that has been most controversial, because critics argue that only the armed forces ought to conduct

**Central Intelligence Agency (CIA)**
Agency primarily responsible for gathering and analyzing information about the political and military activities of other nations.

**Figure 20.7**

**Defense Expenditures Have Declined as a Percentage of GDP, 1950–1999**

SOURCE: *Statistical Abstract of the United States, 1999*, Tables 574 and 1444.

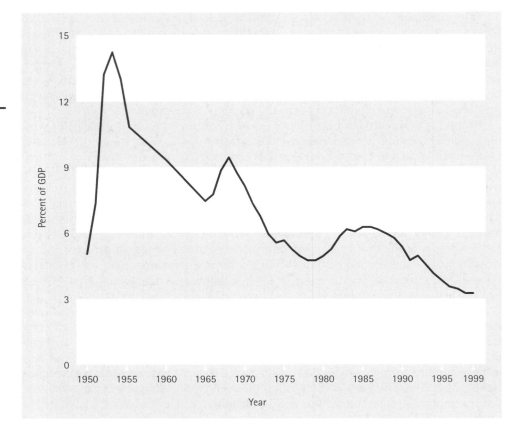

secret military activities. The CIA's most notorious covert operation was the ill-fated attempt in 1961 to dislodge communist leader Fidel Castro from Cuba.[44] In an effort to overthrow Castro, the CIA helped Cuban exiles plan an invasion on the shores of the Cuban **Bay of Pigs** that was expected to foment a popular insurrection. President Kennedy approved the invasion attempt but decided against giving it naval or air support. The effort failed, leaving in doubt the CIA's ability to conduct large-scale military operations. Though the Bay of Pigs was the CIA's most visible covert operation, the agency drew criticism for covert activities in Chile in the early 1970s, in Nicaragua in the 1980s, and in other nations.

Despite intelligence errors and flawed operations in Cuba and elsewhere, the CIA has become one of the pillars of the foreign policy establishment. It recruited brilliant analysts whose interpretations of Soviet intentions informed U.S. Cold War policy. It utilized as informers people who held high-ranking positions within the Soviet government. It placed spies inside terrorist cells throughout the world. And though the CIA has many critics, it played a crucial role throughout the Cold War.[45] Today the agency helps identify and squelch potential terrorist operations, assesses the threat of nuclear proliferation, and helps monitor other nations' compliance with arms control agreements. In 1999, the CIA even assisted in efforts to document war crimes committed by the Serbian military in Kosovo, referring the results to international authorities.[46]

## National Security Council

**Bay of Pigs**
Location of CIA-supported effort by Cuban exiles in 1961 to invade Cuba and overthrow Fidel Castro.

**National Security Council (NSC)**
White House agency responsible for coordinating U.S. foreign policy.

Because so many departments and agencies needed to work together to formulate U.S. Cold War policy, President Truman decided he needed a coordinating mechanism to help resolve differences in viewpoints and recommendations. The **National Security Council (NSC),** created by Congress in 1947 and placed inside the White House

Executive Office of the President, is responsible for coordinating U.S. foreign policy. Meetings of the NSC are generally attended by the president, the vice-president, the secretary of state, the secretary of defense, the head of the Central Intelligence Agency, the chair of the military Joint Chiefs of Staff, the president's chief of staff, and such other persons as the president designates.[47] The council is assisted by a staff located in the White House under the direction of the National Security Adviser (NSA). The NSA has often played simply a coordinating role as someone who reconciles interagency disagreements or, if that proves impossible, reports them to the president. But inasmuch as the NSA has more access to the president than any member of the foreign policy team, the adviser can wield great influence. During the Nixon administration, National Security Adviser Henry Kissinger became the president's most influential aide, overshadowing the secretary of state. Similarly, Clinton's NSA, Samuel R. Berger, emerged as a more influential adviser than Secretary of State Madeline Albright. Though Albright had significant influence, said one expert, Berger was in control: "There is no dispute who runs the show on foreign policy."[48]

The office of the NSA has not escaped controversy. The most notorious event in which it played a major part has become known as the **Iran–Contra affair**, an allegedly illegal diversion of funds from an Iranian arms sale to antigovernment rebels in Nicaragua known as the Contras. In this case, the NSA office, officially responsible only for policy coordination, actually attempted to conduct a covert operation of the type conducted by the CIA. The Iran–Contra affair developed out of a bitter confrontation between the president and Congress. To dislodge communist Nicaraguan leaders from power, the Reagan administration supported the organization and funding of a rebel group known as the Contras. But in 1984 Congress, wary of getting bogged down in a Central American guerrilla conflict, passed a law that its author said "clearly ends U.S. support for the war in Nicaragua." At this point, President Reagan privately asked his NSA, Robert McFarlane, to "assure the Contras of continuing administration support."[49] Telling President Reagan, "I certainly hope none of this discussion will be made public in any way," McFarlane then solicited contributions for the Contras from wealthy individuals and from small, oil-rich U.S. allies in the Persian Gulf.[50] Meanwhile, in a separate effort to secure the release of several American hostages held by terrorists in the Middle East, McFarlane helped orchestrate a secret arms sale to Iran—an action that was in clear violation of U.S. antiterrorist policy. An NSC staffer diverted the profits from this arms sale to the Contras in Nicaragua.

In 1987 these secret activities became public and culminated in the Iran–Contra scandal. The NSC staff appeared to have ignored both administration antiterrorist policy and clear congressional directives. Congress held hearings on the scandal, and an independent prosecutor conducted a thorough investigation, though no convictions withstood court appeals. A specially appointed presidential commission recommended that, in the future, the office of the NSA limit itself to a coordinating role and not involve itself in covert operations. By following these guidelines, the NSA has since avoided political controversy.

> **Iran–Contra affair**
> An allegedly illegal diversion of funds from the sale of arms to Iran to a guerrilla group in Nicaragua.

## SECTION SUMMARY

The major organizations responsible for foreign policy formation in the United States took their modern form during the first years of the Cold War and are now working to adapt to the post–Cold War period. The State Department comprises the nation's diplomatic corps, including the secretary of state, ambassadors, and other foreign service officers. The country's military forces are housed in the Defense Department, under the command of a civilian secretary of defense and civilian secretaries of each of the armed services. In 1947 Congress reorganized the military into its present form and created the Central Intelligence Agency and the National Security Council. The CIA serves as the primary (though not the only) source of U.S. intelligence. The National Security Council and its staff coordinate foreign policy among the various foreign-policy-making agencies.

## Ideals and Interests in American Foreign Policy

The way in which the president and his advisers resolve foreign policy questions is shaped by a long-standing tension that exists between American philosophical ideals and the country's practical need to defend itself against foreign aggression. Alexander Hamilton, in the *Federalist Papers*, made the best case for placing the highest priority on the country's practical interests: "No Government [can] give us tranquility and happiness at home, which [does] not possess sufficient stability and strength to make us respectable abroad."[51] The idealist point of view was best expressed by Abraham Lincoln, who reminded his fellow citizens that one purpose of the American experiment was to spread liberty throughout the world. "The Declaration of Independence . . . [gave] liberty, not alone to the people of this country, but hope to the world for all future time."[52]

Under the best of circumstances, as in the waging of World War II, ideals and practical interests were readily combined. But at other times, as we shall see, the United States has been forced to make hard choices. In this section we first review the historical roots of the tension between ideals and interests, highlighting the conflict between the ideal of spreading democracy and the conflicting argument that the U.S. ought either to remain neutral and uninvolved in world affairs or to act simply to protect its immediate interests. The history of U.S. involvement in Latin America illustrates this conflict. Next, we show that these same conflicts are present in debates over contemporary American foreign policy making, including policy regarding international organizations, regional conflicts, Russia, and human rights.

### The Democratic Ideal

It is a stated goal of U.S. foreign policy to spread democracy throughout the world. Of course, over the course of its history the United States has not been so naive and innocent that its affirmation of democratic ideals is unconnected to its underlying national interests. The country acquired land and possessions when opportunities were ripe. The United States drove American Indians from their homelands, coming close to committing genocide in the process. The country has defended itself against attack and threat of attack by other world powers. But more than most nations, the United States has expressed its national interest in a language that identifies its cause with that of people throughout the world.

Its idealism is rooted in its revolutionary, anticolonial heritage. The United States is founded not on the racial or ethnic characteristics of its people but on the ideals that inspired the Declaration of Independence and the Bill of Rights. Liberty, democracy, and inalienable rights help define what it is to be an American. So important are these ideals to the country's self-definition that they cannot be ignored when framing its relations with other countries.

**Monroe Doctrine**
Policy that declared the Western Hemisphere to be free of European colonial influence (1819).

The **Monroe Doctrine**, declaring the Western Hemisphere to be free of European colonial influence, provides an early statement of U.S. foreign policy ideals. In 1823, at a time when European countries were establishing colonies throughout the world, President Monroe declared that "The American continents . . . are henceforth not to be considered as subjects for future colonization by any European power."[53] The Monroe Doctrine was particularly idealistic, because it was enunciated at a time when the United States lacked the military power to enforce the doctrine.

A century later, America fought in two world wars in the name of democracy. When asking his countrymen to enter World War I, President Woodrow Wilson claimed it was necessary because "the world must be made safe for democracy."[54] He promised that this would be the war to end all wars, but unfortunately, it was not. When World War II broke out, the United States was asked, this time by President Roosevelt, to fight for the four freedoms: "freedom of speech . . . everywhere in the world; freedom . . . to worship God . . . in his own way—everywhere in the world; freedom from want . . . everywhere in the world; and freedom from fear . . . anywhere in the world."[55] All in all, Woodrow Wilson may have been right when he said,

timeline

**The Evolution of Foreign and Military Policy**

"Sometimes people call me an idealist. Well, that is the way I know I am an American. America is the only idealist nation in the world."[56]

## National Interests

Though American ideals have helped shape and justify the country's foreign policy, that policy also reflects the country's practical self-interests. One of the oldest U.S. foreign policy principles, **isolationism,** is in fact explicitly self-centered. Isolationism is a principle that says the United States should remain separate from the conflicts taking place among other nations. Isolationists often quote a phrase from George Washington's Farewell Address, made when he retired from the presidency: "Tis our true policy to steer clear of permanent alliances, with any portion of the foreign world."[57] Washington meant to say that our alliances should not be permanent, but he was often interpreted as saying that alliances should not be made at all.

For more than a century after Washington made this speech, the United States pursued an essentially isolationist foreign policy. Until airplanes and nuclear missiles shrank the size of the globe, the United States was, in the words of Winston Churchill, "splendidly isolated." Asian wars took place across the wide Pacific, making them all but irrelevant to U.S. concerns. Even the narrower Atlantic Ocean placed the United States months away from most European controversies. When the United States did enter a war, it usually emerged successful shortly afterward, which seemed to prove that the United States did not need the help of others (see the accompanying International Comparison).

Such a large proportion of Americans sympathized with the isolationist argument that the United States became involved in World Wars I and II only reluctantly and belatedly. World War I broke out in August 1914, but the United States remained, for over two and one-half years, as "splendidly isolated" from the European tangle as it possibly could be. In language reminiscent of George Washington's Farewell Address, President Wilson initially called for the United States to be "neutral in fact as well as in name. . . . We must be impartial in thought as well as in action."[58] The United States did not declare war until well after the Germans began torpedoing U.S. commercial ships delivering supplies to Britain.

At the beginning of World War II, the United States once again declared its neutrality. In his campaign for reelection in the fall of 1940, President Roosevelt promised American "mothers and fathers" that the country's neutrality would be preserved: "I have said this before, but I shall say it again and again and again: Your boys are not going to be sent into any foreign wars."[59] But soon after the election, Roosevelt lent arms to the British and began to make preparations for war, declaring "we must be the great arsenal of democracy."[60]

## Latin America

The conflict between U.S. ideals and its national interests has been particularly intense in debates over U.S. policy toward its immediate neighbors in Latin America. Most of the time, the nation's practical self-interests, not its democratic ideals, shaped its policy toward the region. The one phrase that best expresses how the U.S. in fact conducted its Latin America policy was popularized by President Theodore Roosevelt: "Speak softly but carry a big stick."

Long before Roosevelt, the United States was wielding a heavy stick upon its neighbors. As early as 1846, President James K. Polk asked Congress to declare war on Mexico. The war was a complete mismatch between the United States, an emerging industrial power, and Mexico, a still technologically undeveloped nation. The United States won easily, seizing from Mexico land that is now Texas, Arizona, New Mexico, and parts of California and Colorado.

Fifty years later, when the Cubans revolted against a weak Spanish government, President William McKinley employed U.S. military might in a war against Spain.

**isolationism**
A foreign policy that keeps the United States separate from the conflicts taking place among other nations.

## International Comparison

## United States Lucky in War

Isolationist sentiments have been fed by the country's wartime successes, which have fostered the belief that the United States is invincible. After the War of 1812 and until the Vietnam War, the United States had an impressive military record. The Mexican War, the Spanish–American War, and World Wars I and II all ended in overwhelming victories. Few, if any, other world powers have achieved such an unbroken string of successes. Japan and Germany can never forget their humiliating defeats in World War II. The French cannot forget the ease with which German troops captured Paris in both 1870 and 1940. The Russians cannot readily dislodge the memory of their defeat by Japan in 1905 or the collapse of their army in 1917. Only the British have nearly as enviable an historical record as the Americans, and even Britain suffered more than one defeat at the hands of the French.

Not only has the United States won its wars, but it has done so quickly. The Mexican War, though spread over three years, consisted of three short and decisive campaigns. The Spanish–American War was over in eight months. Even U.S. involvement in the two world wars was of relatively short duration. Within six months of the arrival of U.S. troops in Europe, an armistice brought World War I to an end. The pattern was not altogether different in World War II. Little more than a year after U.S. troops landed in Normandy, Germany was defeated. Japan struggled for an addi-

tional two months until nuclear bombs dropped over Hiroshima and Nagasaki forced surrender. American civilians have never suffered significantly from foreign attack. Not since the British burning of Washington, DC, in 1814 has the mainland of the United States been invaded by foreign troops. Apart from the bombing of Pearl Harbor, the United States has been free of aerial raids. During World War II, German tanks overran Europe and Russia, German airplanes bombed Britain, and U.S. airplanes all but destroyed German and Japanese cities. As the graph here shows, even U.S. troop casualties have been small.

*What effect have the loss in Vietnam and the victory in the Persian Gulf had on U.S. foreign policy debates?*

SOURCES: R. Ernest Dupuy and Trevor N. Dupuy, *The Harper Encyclopedia of Military History: From 3500 B.C. to the Present* (New York: HarperCollins, 1993). Y. Takenob, *The Japan Year Book: 1919–1920* (Tokyo: Japan Year Book Office, 1921). B. R. Mitchell, *International Historical Statistics: Europe 1750–1988* (New York: Stockton Press, 1992). B. R. Mitchell, *International Historical Statistics of the Americas: 1750–1988* (New York: Stockton Press, 1993). B. R. Mitchell, *International Historical Statistics: Africa and Asia* (New York: New York University Press, 1982). Raymond E. Zickel, ed., *Soviet Union: A Country Study* (Washington, DC: U.S. Government Printing Office, 1991).

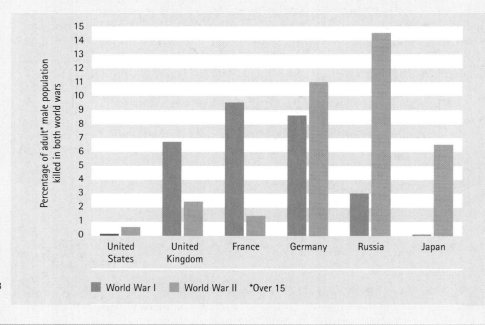

NOTE: Population figures are from the following years: France, 1911, 1936; Germany, 1910, 1939; United Kingdom (including Scotland), 1911, 1931; United States, 1910, 1940; Russia, 1913 (estimated), 1939; Japan, 1913, 1940.

Although the Monroe Doctrine was involved, the United States was mainly interested in asserting its influence over Cuba. Once again, the battle was hardly a contest. The United States had become one of the most powerful industrialized countries of the world, while Spain's days of glory had long passed. In the treaty that ended the war, the victorious United States gained several important Spanish colonial possessions, including Puerto Rico, Guam, and the Philippines.

The United States also repeatedly used military force to impose its will on weaker countries in the Caribbean and Latin America. The most significant case occurred when Theodore Roosevelt wanted to build the Panama Canal, which would shorten the distance ships needed to travel between the East Coast and California. At the time,

Panama was a part of Colombia, which resisted Roosevelt's requests to build the canal. To get around Colombian opposition, President Roosevelt fomented a Panamanian rebellion and then ordered naval ships to support the revolt. Panama became an independent country, and the canal was dug. The canal remained under direct U.S. control until it was turned over to Panama on December 31, 1999.

In short, U.S. foreign policy toward its immediate neighbors to the south has historically been dictated more by its national interests than by its national ideals. True, the Monroe Doctrine called for the liberation of Latin America from colonial powers. But the United States has not been adverse to invading countries and seizing territory when it served U.S. interests to do so.

## Contemporary Foreign Policy Issues

The tension between ideals and interests that has long been part of the American foreign policy tradition continues to shape policy debates today. On the one side, **idealists** say that U.S. foreign policy should be guided primarily by democratic principles—the spread of liberty, equality, human rights, and respect for international law throughout the world. On the other side, **realists** say that U.S. foreign policy best protects democracy when it guards its own economic and military strength.

One can find both idealists and realists in each political party and in all government agencies, and some people are idealistic on one issue, yet realistic on another. But some general tendencies seem to exist. Idealists are more likely to associate themselves with the Democratic party, and Republicans tend to be realists. The idealists are more likely to be found in the State Department, the realists in the Defense Department.

The debate between idealists and realists appears in all three of the following issues: the role of international organizations, intervention in regional conflicts, and the role of human rights in relations with Russia and China.

**idealists**
Those who say that U.S. foreign policy should be guided primarily by democratic principles—the spread of liberty, equality, human rights, and respect for international law throughout the world.

**realists**
Those who say that U.S. foreign policy best protects democracy when it safeguards its own economic and military strength.

**Role of International Organizations** At the end of World War II, the victorious nations agreed to establish the **United Nations,** an international organization whose purpose is to preserve world peace and foster economic and social development throughout the world. Though the United Nations has been more successful than its predecessor, the ill-starred League of Nations, idealists and realists within the United States often find themselves at odds concerning the usefulness of the United Nations and other international organizations as vehicles for the conduct of U.S. foreign policy.

Idealists recommend that the United States work through the United Nations and other international organizations to achieve closer international cooperation. Idealists argue that these goals not only place American foreign policy on a high ethical plane but they are an important tool for promoting peace and stability. If countries work together in international organizations, they are less likely to engage in warfare.[61]

Realists are reluctant to give the United Nations or other international organizations responsibility for the conduct of U.S. policy. They insist that decisions to intervene in world affairs must be predicated not on some vague ideal but on a calculation of the extent to which the United States has a substantial and visible interest at stake.[62] These decisions must be made on a case-by-case basis by the United States alone. Realists point out, for example, that the United Nations has condemned Israel, a U.S. ally, for its treatment of Arab Palestinians. They also criticize U.N. officials for wasteful and inefficient administration.

**United Nations**
Organization of all nation-states, whose purpose is to preserve world peace and foster economic and social development throughout the world.

**Regional Conflicts** Conflicts among countries in specific regions of the world often occur. For example, the breakup of Yugoslavia in Eastern Europe at the end of the Cold War provoked bitter strife among Bosnians, Serbs, and Croats. Idealists supported the Clinton administration's decision to send troops to separate the warring parties in Bosnia, and to conduct aerial bombing to end the Serbian invasion of Kosovo. By using whatever force it takes to bring regional conflicts under control, idealists argue, the United States keeps them from escalating. Perhaps even more important, the United States, through such actions, tries to prevent genocide by punishing governments that engage in so-called ethnic cleansing and by capturing war criminals and referring them to international tribunals.

According to realists, the United States should avoid getting involved in regional conflicts unless U.S. interests are directly at stake. The United States cannot become the world's police force without stretching its own economic and military resources too far. Realists opposed President Bush's decision to send troops into Somalia and Clinton's decision to send them to Bosnia and Kosovo. If the United States continues to involve itself in such minor conflicts, they argue, it will eventually find itself unprepared or unable to defend its true interests when they are threatened.

**Russia, China, and Human Rights**  Many countries regularly violate basic human rights and democratic procedures. The South African government for decades suppressed the anti-apartheid movement. In 2000, the Indonesian government tolerated the massacre of Christians in East Timor. Idealists and realists differ on how to handle such human rights violations. These differences have not only shaped the debate over relations with less powerful nations but also with Russia and China, two of the world's leading countries.

Idealists say that the United States should use its economic and military muscle to promote human rights throughout the world. South Africa abolished apartheid and granted suffrage to blacks only because of prolonged international pressure. South Korea, Taiwan, and other countries in Asia have established more democratic regimes in response to expressed U.S. concerns. So have many countries in Latin America. To achieve similar objectives, idealists advocate conducting relations with Russia and China with an eye to each nation's record on human rights. Because China crushed a democratic movement in Beijing's Tiananmen Square in 1989 and has jailed many dissidents and religious groups for their political and religious beliefs, idealists have argued that the United States should use economic and political means to force the Asian nation to alter its policies. Similarly, they argue that the United States must sanction Russia for its ongoing war in Chechnya, in which many civilians have been killed and allegations of atrocities are widespread.

Realists recommend that the United States exercise caution before supplementing diplomatic efforts to promote human rights with economic or military pressure. They argue that progress toward democracy is achieved largely through internal political

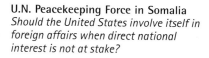

**U.N. Peacekeeping Force in Somalia**
*Should the United States involve itself in foreign affairs when direct national interest is not at stake?*

struggle. It can seldom be imposed successfully from abroad. Violations of human rights and democratic norms are so frequent and widespread that consistent application of an interventionist doctrine would compel constant U.S. involvement in the affairs of other countries. With regard to Russia and China, constant U.S. pressure on human rights would actually be counterproductive, they argue (see the accompanying Democratic Dilemma). The best way to encourage a stable and democratic China, say realists, is to accept the country into the international economic and political community. Trade or diplomatic sanctions would only make the proud nation more angry and belligerent. In the same vein, Russia has gone through severe upheavals over the past decade, and to withdraw U.S. support for economic and political reforms would further destabilize the country. In the long run, realists maintain, it is best not to harp on each instance of human rights abuse but to further U.S. idealistic goals by encouraging the spread of free markets and international trade, the subject to which we now turn.

simulation

**The China Dilemma**

## The Politics of World Trade: New Alliances?

When the Cold War began, U.S. foreign policy makers were concerned with economic as well as political and military questions. Believing that stable economies and the growth of free markets would aid in the effort to contain communism, the Truman administration helped negotiate a new international economic system. International banks were created to loan money to needy countries, United Nations organizations handled world health and refugee problems, and an international trade agreement reduced tariffs around the world. In late 1947, for example, 23 countries founded the General Agreement on Tariffs and Trade (GATT) in Geneva, Switzerland.

Believing that it might be difficult to persuade Congress to approve GATT, Truman signed on to the measure anyway, proclaiming that it was an executive agreement that did not need Senate approval. This action set the pattern for the conduct of trade policy ever since, though the full Congress still sometimes votes on major trade questions.[63]

During the Cold War, most of the public saw trade policy as arcane and uncontroversial. But in the 1990s, when the Cold War had come to an end, trade became a much more publicized and contentious issue. First came the 1993 battle over the North American Free Trade Agreement (NAFTA), which eliminated trade barriers among the United States, Canada, and Mexico. Negotiated by President Bush and promoted by President Clinton, NAFTA won only a narrow majority in Congress after fierce lobbying by all sides.

More significant than the publicity surrounding NAFTA was the unusual profile of the coalitions on both sides of the debate. Though it was promoted by a Democratic president, only 40 percent of Democratic members of Congress supported the measure.[64] Opponents included labor unions, environmental groups, consumer groups, and isolationist politicians. They worried that trade agreements would cost workers jobs, harm the environment, and lead to the nullification of U.S. laws and standards. Proponents included business groups and those who favored greater ties with other nations. Realists found themselves strangely allied with those who favored international organizations. Isolationists banded together with liberal idealists. Perhaps Patrick Buchanan, later Reform party candidate for president, best expressed this marriage of isolationism with idealism when he wrote, "NAFTA's defeat would be a declaration of independence for a new generation of Americans, a shot heard round the world that the Old Republic is back, that we Americans are, once again, going to start looking out for America first."[65]

The battle over NAFTA proved to be only the beginning of a very public debate over the status of world trade. In 1994, negotiators from 104 nations officially transformed GATT into the World Trade Organization (WTO), a trade body much more powerful than GATT, with enforcement and dispute resolution mechanisms. Opposition to the organization was significant and vocal and was led by the same

## Should U.S. Foreign Policy Focus on Promoting Human Rights and Democratic Practices or on Defending U.S. Interests?

Many countries violate human rights to varying degrees. Particularly egregious violations of human rights are regularly practiced by China's authoritarian government. Since 1950, China has forced many Tibetans, including the revered Dalai Lama, to seek refuge abroad. During the Tiananmen Square massacre of 1989, over 700 pro-democracy demonstrators were killed and 10,000 dissidents were arrested; 31 leaders were subsequently tried and executed. The families of each of those executed received a bill for the cost of the bullet used to kill their relative. Harry Wu, who spent 19 years in a Chinese labor reform camp, has chronicled the dual function of these camps: "Politically, they suppress dissidents to reinforce the system of dictatorship, while economically they exploit prisoners to earn foreign exchange for the Chinese Communist regimes."[a]

Idealists and realists differ in their response to such human rights violations. Idealists argue that the United States should abet the cause of human rights by placing trade restrictions on Chinese products. In the words of one commentator, "Americans are troubled that their country contributes heavily to oppression. They know that the profits of Chinese goods sold in the United States, and the benefits of American investments, go in substantial part directly to the Chinese Army, policy and politburo."[b] In part because of China's dismal human rights record, the International Olympic Committee rejected China's bid to host the Summer Games in 2000.

Realists say that trade sanctions would only isolate U.S. businesses from one of the world's largest and fastest-growing markets. The best way to foster human rights in China is to tie its economy closely to ours. They claim that when free markets develop, democratization soon follows. Former Secretary of Commerce Mickey Kantor explained the Clinton posture toward China in the following terms: "Not mutually assured destruction and a policy of containment, but mutually assured prosperity and a policy of engagement."[c] Both presidential candidates in 2000 supported legislation passed by Congress in 2000 that permanently lifted trade restrictions on China, though both Bush and Gore suggested that they would raise the issue of human rights in talks with Chinese leaders.

*What do you think?*
- *Is the issue of human rights important enough to warrant economic sanctions on China?*
- *Or would such sanctions be counterproductive and contrary to the national interest of the United States?*

[a]Harry Wu, *Bitter Winds: A Memoir of My Years in China's Gulag* (New York: Wiley, 1996), p. 284.
[b]A. M. Rosenthal, "What Can I Do?" *New York Times,* December 6, 1995, A23.
[c]David Nyhan, "Clinton Wields the Velvet Glove on China," *Boston Globe,* November 29, 1996, A31.

---

groups that opposed NAFTA. Tens of thousands of protesters disrupted a meeting of WTO trade ministers in Seattle in 1999, blocking streets and preventing delegates from attending the meetings. World trade became the subject of public controversy like never before. As California State Senator Tom Hayden said, "the WTO, which was unknown in this country yesterday, is going to be a household word now. . . .This is a great turning point."[66]

The debate over world trade may be only in its early stages. But it shows signs of creating new political coalitions and of involving more interest groups and members of the public than a typical foreign policy issue would. Regardless of the details, trade issues seem sure to define a major part of post–Cold War American foreign policy.

### Section Summary

Two opposing views about the goals of U.S. foreign policy have shaped debates about its conduct since the American Revolution. In the early years of the republic, those who believed that the United States should concern itself with the worldwide spread of democratic ideals argued against isolationists, who believed that the country should make few alliances and involve itself in foreign affairs only if vital national interests required. The Monroe Doctrine was issued so that Latin American countries would remain free of European colonial influence and become democratic nations. However, in nineteenth-century wars against Mexico and Spain, the United States proved more interested in tangible benefits, such as land and commercial investments, than in the spread of democracy.

## *Window on the Past*

### Idealism, Realism, and the United States in the Philippines

Since President Monroe declared Latin America free of European influence, the United States had considered itself the enemy of colonial empires. But in 1898 a war that began as an effort to free Cuba from Spanish rule became the basis for the creation of an American colonial regime. As American politicians grappled with how to govern the Philippines, the odd combination of idealism and realism that characterizes much of U.S. foreign policy became strikingly evident.

When the United States declared war on Spain in 1898, the focus of the war was on the Spanish colony of Cuba. But Assistant Secretary of the Navy Theodore Roosevelt wasted no time in directing the U.S. fleet against Spanish forces in the Philippines, halfway around the world. The Americans smashed the enemy fleet in Manila Bay, and within a few months had won control of the islands. Despite celebrations in the streets back in Washington over the navy's great victory, most had little understanding of the Philippines themselves. President William McKinley privately admitted, "I could not have told where those darned islands were within 2000 miles."[a]

Once possessed of the islands, the United States had to decide what to do with them. Those on both sides of the debate used idealist and realist arguments to bolster their cases. Anti-imperialists such as writer Mark Twain and labor leader Samuel Gompers argued that colonialism was cruel and immoral. Furthermore, in more practical terms, the maintenance of a colony would require expending resources that could be better employed close to home. Businessman Andrew Carnegie feared that the country would needlessly be drawn into "the vortex of international militarism."[b]

Those who favored holding the islands, including Roosevelt and influential Massachusetts Senator Henry Cabot Lodge, countered that the colony would be a stepping stone to worldwide power, and as such would serve the national interest admirably. They also made the paternalistic argument that the United States had a moral duty to tutor the people of the Philippines in the ways of democracy—at least until they were fit to govern themselves.

In the end, the United States settled on keeping the Philippines. But the residents of the territory did not view their new rulers with the anticipated warmth and conciliation. Rebels waged a four-year guerrilla war against the occupying American forces, a conflict that swung U.S. public opinion against maintaining permanent control of the islands. In 1901, military governor William Howard Taft granted the territory significant local autonomy. Finally, in 1946, the Philippines gained their full independence.

*Why did both sides in the debate over the Philippines feel that it was necessary to use both idealist and realist arguments? Which arguments do you find most convincing in the case—realist or idealist ones?*

SOURCE: Alan Brinkley, *The Unfinished Nation: A Concise History of the American People,* Second Edition (New York: Knopf, 1997), pp. 569–578; David Traxel, *1898: The Birth of the American Century* (New York: Random House, 1998).

[a] Traxel, pp. 138–139
[b] Traxel, p. 315

In the twentieth century, foreign policy experts have continued to fall into two camps. Realists argue that the United States should be wary of international organizations, shun involvement in regional conflicts, and build economic ties with China and Russia, even if these countries violate human rights. Idealists, on the other hand, favor involvement in international organizations, promote intervention in regional conflicts when moral principles are at stake, and argue that China and Russia ought to be punished for human rights violations.

The twenty-first century politics of world trade may signal the drawing of new foreign policy battle lines, as labor and environmental groups oppose business groups, as idealist interest groups find themselves allied with isolationists, and as realists promote the WTO, an international organization.

## *Chapter Summary*

Electoral considerations alone help account for the fact that presidents dominate policy making on foreign policy questions more than on domestic ones. Voters expect presidents to take the lead. In the short run, they tend to support presidents in crises no matter what action is taken. Only later, if things do not turn out well, do voters penalize presidents for choosing the wrong policy.

Other factors reinforce the president's dominant role in foreign policy. Fast action is often needed; interest-group pressures are less intense than on domestic issues; the Supreme Court has interpreted the powers of the president broadly; and Congress tends to defer to the executive. However, Congress became more assertive, and foreign policy more partisan, in the years following the end of the Vietnam War when Congress passed the War Powers Resolution, which attempted to place controls on the president's role as commander in chief.

The three agencies that shape U.S. foreign policy, the Department of State, the Department of Defense, and the Central Intelligence Agency, together with the head of the Joint Chiefs of Staff, all sit on the National Security Council, which is managed by a National Security Adviser responsible to the president for overall foreign policy coordination.

Both idealistic and realistic factors help shape American foreign policy. On the one hand, the United States feels responsible for promoting the democratic experiment abroad. On the other hand, the United States, like any other country, has its own interests to protect. Idealist and realist considerations both play a role in current debates over international organizations, regional conflicts, and the human rights records of Russia and China. World trade may prove to be an atypically public and intense foreign policy issue.

---

### On the Web

Department of State
www.state.gov
Department of Defense
www.defenselink.mil
Central Intelligence Agency
www.odci.gov
The Web pages of the Department of State, the Department of Defense, and the Central Intelligence Agency provide publications and other information about the structure and conduct of U.S. foreign policy.
U.S. Trade Representative
www.ustr.gov
The U.S. trade representative, located in the Executive Office of the President, is the U.S. government's chief trade negotiator.

United Nations
www.un.org
World Trade Organization
www.wto.org
Learn about the United Nations and the World Trade Organization at their Web sites.
Council on Foreign Relations
www.cfr.org
Founded in 1921, the Council on Foreign Relations promotes understanding of international politics and publishes the journal *Foreign Affairs*.
Senate Committee on Foreign Relations
www.senate.gov/~foreign/
The U.S. Senate's Committee on Foreign Relations provides information on treaties presented to the Senate for its approval, as well as nominations and hearings on foreign policy.

# Key Terms

ambassador, p. 616
Bay of Pigs, p. 620
Central Intelligence Agency (CIA), p. 619
Cold War, p. 613
containment, p. 614
Department of Defense, p. 617
embassy, p. 616
executive agreement, p. 612
foreign policy, p. 603
foreign service, p. 617

idealists, p. 625
Iran–Contra affair, p. 621
iron curtain, p. 614
isolationism, p. 623
Joint Chiefs of Staff, p. 617
League of Nations, p. 612
Monroe Doctrine, p. 622
National Security Council (NSC), p. 620
"rally 'round the flag" effect, p. 605
realists, p. 625

secretary of defense, p. 617
secretary of state, p. 616
Tonkin Gulf Resolution, p. 611
treaties, p. 612
two-presidency theory, p. 603
United Nations (U.N.), p. 625
*U.S. v. Curtiss-Wright*, p. 610
War Powers Resolution, p. 611
*Youngstown Sheet and Tube Co.* v. *Sawyer*, p. 610

# Suggested Readings

Allison, Graham. *Essence of Decision*. Boston: Little, Brown, 1971. Fascinating account of the Cuban missile crisis, the closest the United States and the Soviet Union ever came to nuclear confrontation.

Baker, James, III, with Thomas M. DeFrank. *The Politics of Diplomacy: Revolution, War, and Peace, 1989–1992*. New York: Putnam, 1995. Thoughtful reflections of George Bush's secretary of state.

Corwin, Edward S. *Total War and the Constitution*. New York: Knopf, 1947. Classic, if dated, discussion of constitutional arrangements as they affect foreign policy.

Huntington, Samuel. *The Clash of Civilizations*. New York: Simon & Schuster, 1996. Argues that future world conflicts will occur between clusters of nations that share a common cultural heritage.

Jeffreys-Johnes, Rhodri. *The CIA and American Democracy*. New Haven, CT: Yale University Press, 1989. A solid history of the CIA.

Johnson, Loch K. *America's Secret Power: The CIA in a Democratic Society*. New York: Oxford University Press, 1989. Informed critique of CIA power and tactics.

Koh, Harold Hungju. *The National Security Constitution: Sharing Power after the Iran–Contra Affair*. New Haven, CT: Yale University Press, 1990. Analyzes the constitutional authority of the president and Congress on matters of foreign policy.

Leffler, Melvyn P. *A Preponderance of Power: National Security, the Truman Administration, and the Cold War*. Stanford, CA: Stanford University Press, 1992. Historical account of the establishment of U.S. Cold War strategy under Truman.

Mann, Thomas E., ed. *A Question of Balance: The President, the Congress and Foreign Policy*. Washington, DC: Brookings, 1990. Essays arguing that too much power over foreign policy has shifted from the president to Congress.

Peterson, Paul E., ed. *The President, the Congress, and the Making of Foreign Policy*. Norman, OK: Oklahoma University Press, 1994. Essays describing changes in presidential and congressional policy-making roles.

Silverstein, Gordon. *Imbalance of Powers: Constitutional Interpretation and the Making of American Foreign Policy*. New York: Oxford University Press, 1996. Argues that the president's constitutional authority over foreign policy has not been ceded to Congress.

Weissman, Stephen R. *A Culture of Deference: Congress's Failure of Leadership in Foreign Policy*. New York: Basic Books, 1995. Argues that Congress defers too much to presidential authority in foreign affairs.

Wildavsky, Aaron. "The Two Presidencies." In Steven A. Shull, ed., *The Two Presidencies: A Quarter Century Assessment*. Chicago: Nelson-Hall, 1991, pp. 11–25. Explains how politics differs between foreign and domestic issues.

# Appendix I

## The Declaration of Independence

*In Congress, July 4, 1776*
*The Unanimous Declaration of the Thirteen United States of America*

WHEN IN THE COURSE of human events it becomes necessary for one people to dissolve the political bands which have connected them with another, and to assume, among the powers of the earth, the separate and equal station to which the Laws of Nature and of Nature's God entitle them, a decent respect to the opinions of mankind requires that they should declare the causes which impel them to the separation.

We hold these truths to be self-evident, that all men are created equal, that they are endowed by their Creator with certain unalienable Rights, that among these are Life, Liberty and the pursuit of Happiness. That to secure these rights, Governments are instituted among Men, deriving their just powers from the consent of the governed. That whenever any Form of Government becomes destructive of these ends, it is the Right of the People to alter or to abolish it, and to institute new Government, laying its foundation on such principles and organizing its powers in such form, as to them shall seem most likely to effect their Safety and Happiness. Prudence, indeed, will dictate that Governments long established should not be changed for light and transient causes; and accordingly all experience hath shewn that mankind are more disposed to suffer, while evils are sufferable, than to right themselves by abolishing the forms to which they are accustomed. But when a long train of abuses and usurpations, pursuing invariably the same Object evinces a design to reduce them under absolute Despotism, it is their right, it is their duty, to throw off such Government, and to provide new Guards for their future security.—Such has been the patient sufferance of these Colonies; and such is now the necessity which constrains them to alter their former Systems of Government. The history of the present King of Great Britain is a history of repeated injuries and usurpations, all having in direct object the establishment of an absolute Tyranny over these States. To prove this, let Facts be submitted to a candid world.

He has refused his Assent to Laws, the most wholesome and necessary for the public good.

He has forbidden his Governors to pass Laws of immediate and pressing importance, unless suspended in their operation till his Assent should be obtained; and when so suspended, he has utterly neglected to attend to them.

He has refused to pass other Laws for the accommodation of large districts of people, unless those people would relinquish the right of Representation in the Legislature, a right inestimable to them and formidable to tyrants only.

He has called together legislative bodies at places unusual, uncomfortable, and distant from the depository of their Public Records, for the sole purpose of fatiguing them into compliance with his measures.

He has dissolved Representative Houses repeatedly, for opposing with manly firmness his invasions on the rights of the people.

He has refused for a long time, after such dissolutions, to cause others to be elected; whereby the Legislative Powers, incapable of Annihilation, have returned to the People at large for their exercise, the State remaining in the mean time exposed to all the dangers of invasion from without, and convulsions within.

He has endeavored to prevent the population of these States; for that purpose obstructing the Laws of Naturalization of Foreigners; refusing to pass others to encourage their migration hither, and raising the conditions of new Appropriations of Lands.

He has obstructed the Administration of Justice, by refusing his Assent to Laws for establishing Judiciary powers.

He has made Judges dependent on his Will alone, for the tenure of their offices, and the amount and payment of their salaries.

He has erected a multitude of New Offices, and sent hither swarms of Officers to harass our people, and eat out their substance.

He has kept among us, in times of peace, Standing Armies without the Consent of our legislatures.

He has affected to render the Military independent of and superior to the Civil power.

He has combined with others to subject us to a jurisdiction foreign to our constitution, and unacknowledged by our laws, giving his Assent to their Acts of pretended Legislation:

For quartering large bodies of armed troops among us:

For protecting them, by a mock Trial, from punishment for any Murders which they should commit on the Inhabitants of these States:

For cutting off our Trade with all parts of the world:

For imposing Taxes on us without our Consent:

For depriving us in many cases, of the benefits of Trial by Jury:

For transporting us beyond Seas to be tried for pretended offences:

For abolishing the free System of English Laws in a neighboring Province, establishing therein an Arbitrary government, and enlarging its Boundaries so as to render it at once an example and fit instrument for introducing the same absolute rule into these Colonies:

For taking away our Charters, abolishing our most valuable Laws, and altering fundamentally the Forms of our Governments:

For suspending our own Legislatures, and declaring themselves invested with power to legislate for us in all cases whatsoever.

He has abdicated Government here, by declaring us out of his Protection and waging War against us.

He has plundered our seas, ravaged our Coasts, burnt out towns, and destroyed the lives of our people.

He is at this time transporting large Armies of foreign Mercenaries to compleat the works of death, desolation and tyranny, already begun with circumstances of Cruelty and perfidy scarcely paralleled in the most barbarous ages, and totally unworthy the Head of a civilized nation.

He has constrained our fellow Citizens taken Captive on the high Seas to bear Arms against their Country, to become the executioners of their friends and Brethren, or to fall themselves by their Hands.

He has excited domestic insurrections amongst us, and has endeavored to bring on the inhabitants of our frontiers, the merciless Indian Savages, whose known rule of warfare, is an undistinguished destruction of all ages, sexes and conditions.

In every stage of these Oppressions We have Petitioned for Redress in the most humble terms: Our repeated Petitions have been answered only by repeated injury: A Prince, whose character is thus marked by every act which may define a Tyrant, is unfit to be the ruler of a free people.

Nor have We been wanting in attention to our British brethren. We have warned them from time to time of attempts by their legislature to extend an unwarrantable jurisdiction over us. We have reminded them of the circumstances of our emigration and settlement here. We have appealed to their native justice and magnanimity; and we have conjured them by the ties of our common kindred to disavow these usurpations, which would inevitably interrupt our connections and correspondence. They too have been deaf to the voice of justice and consanguinity. We must, therefore, acquiesce in the necessity, which denounces our Separation, and hold them, as we hold the rest of mankind, Enemies in War, in Peace Friends.

We, therefore, the Representatives of the United States of America, in General Congress, Assembled, appealing to the Supreme Judge of the world for the rectitude of our intentions, do, in the Name, and by Authority of the good People of these Colonies, solemnly publish and declare, That these United Colonies are, and of Right ought to be Free and Independent States; that they are Absolved from all Allegiance to the British Crown, and that all political connection between them and the State of Great Britain, is and ought to be totally dissolved: and that as Free and Independent States, they have full power to levy War, conclude Peace, contract Alliances, establish Commerce, and to do all other Acts and Things which Independent States may of right do. And for the support of this Declaration, with a firm reliance on the protection of divine Providence, we mutually pledge to each other our Lives, our Fortunes and our sacred Honor.

JOHN HANCOCK

NEW HAMPSHIRE
*Josiah Bartlett,*
*Wm. Whipple,*
*Matthew Thornton.*

MASSACHUSETTS BAY
*Saml. Adams,*
*John Adams,*
*Robt. Treat Paine,*
*Elbridge Gerry.*

RHODE ISLAND
*Step. Hopkins,*
*William Ellery.*

CONNECTICUT
*Roger Sherman,*
*Samuel Huntington,*
*Wm. Williams,*
*Oliver Wolcott.*

NEW YORK
*Wm. Floyd,*
*Phil. Livingston,*
*Frans. Lewis,*
*Lewis Morris*

NEW JERSEY
*Richd. Stockton,*
*In. Witherspoon,*
*Fras. Hopkinson,*
*John Hart,*
*Abra. Clark.*

PENNSYLVANIA
*Robt. Morris,*
*Benjamin Rush,*
*Benjamin Franklin,*
*John Morton,*
*Geo. Clymer,*
*Jas. Smith,*
*Geo. Taylor,*
*James Wilson,*
*Geo. Ross.*

DELAWARE
*Caesar Rodney,*
*Geo. Read,*
*Tho. M'kean.*

MARYLAND
*Samuel Chase,*
*Wm. Paca,*
*Thos. Stone,*
*Charles Caroll of*
    *Carollton.*

VIRGINIA
*George Wythe,*
*Richard Henry Lee,*
*Th. Jefferson,*
*Benjamin Harrison,*
*Thos. Nelson, jr.,*
*Francis Lightfoot Lee,*
*Carter Braxton.*

NORTH CAROLINA
*Wm. Hooper,*
*Joseph Hewes,*
*John Penn.*

SOUTH CAROLINA
*Edward Rutledge,*
*Thos. Heyward, Junr.,*
*Thomas Lynch, jnr.,*
*Arthur Middleton.*

# Appendix II

## The Constitution of the United States of America

WE THE PEOPLE of the United States, in Order to form a more perfect Union, establish Justice, insure domestic Tranquility, provide for the common defence, promote the general Welfare, and secure the Blessings of Liberty to ourselves and our Posterity, do ordain and establish this Constitution for the United States of America.

ARTICLE I

SECTION 1. All legislative Powers herein granted shall be vested in a Congress of the United States, which shall consist of a Senate and House of Representatives.

SECTION 2. The House of Representatives shall be composed of Members chosen every second Year by the People of the several States, and the Electors in each State shall have the Qualifications requisite for Electors of the most numerous Branch of the State Legislature.

No person shall be a Representative who shall not have attained to the Age of twenty five Years, and been seven Years a Citizen of the United States, and who shall not, when elected, be an Inhabitant of that State in which he shall be chosen.

Representatives and direct Taxes shall be apportioned among the several States which may be included within this Union, according to their respective Numbers which shall be determined by adding to the whole Number of free Persons, including those bound to Service for a Term of Years, and excluding Indians not taxed, three fifths of all other Persons. The actual Enumeration shall be made within three Years after the first Meeting of the Congress of the United States, and within every subsequent Term ten Years, in such Manner as they shall by Law direct. The Number of Representatives shall not exceed one for every thirty Thousand, but each State shall have at Least one Representative; and until such enumeration shall be made, the State of New Hampshire shall be entitled to chuse three, Massachusetts eight, Rhode-Island and Providence Plantations one, Connecticut five, New-York six, New Jersey four, Pennsylvania eight, Delaware one, Maryland six, Virginia ten, North Carolina five, South Carolina five, and Georgia three.

When vacancies happen in the Representation from any State, the Executive Authority thereof shall issue Writs of Election to fill such Vacancies.

The House of Representatives shall chuse their speaker and other Officers; and shall have the sole Power of Impeachment.

SECTION 3. The Senate of the United States shall be composed of two Senators from each State chosen by the Legislature thereof, for six Years; and each Senator shall have one Vote.

Immediately after they shall be assembled in Consequence of the first Election, they shall be divided as equally as may be into three Classes. The Seats of the Senators of the first Class shall be vacated at the Expiration of the second year, of the second Class at the Expiration of the fourth Year, and of the third Class at the Expiration of the sixth Year, so that one third may be chosen every second Year and if Vacancies happen by Resignation, or otherwise, during the Recess of the Legislature of any State, the Executive thereof may make temporary Appointments until the next Meeting of the Legislature, which shall then fill such Vacancies.

No Person shall be a Senator who shall not have attained to the Age of thirty Years, and been nine Years a Citizen of the United States, and who shall not, when elected, be an Inhabitant of that State for which he shall be chosen.

The Vice President of the United States shall be President of the Senate, but shall have no Vote, unless they be equally divided.

The Senate shall chuse their other Officers, and also a President pro tempore, in the Absence of the Vice President, or when he shall exercise the Office of President of the United States.

The Senate shall have the sole Power to try all Impeachments. When sitting for that Purpose, they shall be on Oath or Affirmation. When the President of the United States is tried, the Chief Justice shall preside: And no Person shall be convicted without the Concurrence of two thirds of the Members present.

Judgment in Cases of Impeachment shall not extend further than to removal from Office, and disqualification to hold and enjoy any Office of honor, Trust or Profit under the United States; but the Party convicted shall nevertheless be liable and subject to Indictment, Trial, Judgment and Punishment, according to Law.

SECTION 4. The Times, Places and Manner of holding Elections for Senators and Representatives, shall be prescribed in each State by the Legislature thereof; but the Congress may at any time by law make or alter such Regulations, except as to the Places of chusing Senators.

The Congress shall assemble at least once in every Year, and such Meeting shall be on the first Monday in December, unless they shall by Law appoint a different Day.

SECTION 5. Each House shall be the Judge of the Elections, Returns and Qualifications of its own Members, and a Majority of each shall constitute a Quorum to do Business; but a smaller Number may adjourn from day to day, and may be authorized to compel the Attendance of absent Members, in such Manner, and under such Penalties as each House may provide.

Each House may determine the Rules of its Proceedings, punish its Members for disorderly Behaviour, and with the Concurrence of two thirds, expel a Member.

Each House shall keep a journal of its Proceedings, and from time to time publish the same, excepting such Parts as may in their judgment require Secrecy; and the Yeas and Nays of the Members of either House on any question shall, at the Desire of one fifth of those present, be entered on the Journal.

Neither House, during the Session of Congress, shall, without the Consent of the other, adjourn for more than three days, nor to any other Place than that in which the two Houses shall be sitting.

SECTION 6. The Senators and Representatives shall receive a Compensation for their Services, to be ascertained by Law, and paid out of the Treasury of the United States. They shall in all Cases, except Treason, Felony and Breach of the Peace, be privileged from Arrest during their Attendance at the Session of their respective Houses, and in going to and returning from the same; and for any Speech or Debate in either House, they shall not be questioned in any other Place.

No Senator or Representative shall, during the Time for which he was elected, be appointed to any civil Office under the Authority of the United States, which shall have been created, or the Emoluments whereof shall have been increased during such time; and no Person holding any Office under the United States, shall be a Member of either House during his Continuance in Office.

SECTION 7. All Bills for raising Revenue shall originate in the House of Representatives; but the Senate may propose or concur with Amendments as on other Bills.

Every Bill which shall have passed the House of Representatives and the Senate, shall, before it become a Law, be presented to the President of the United States; If he approves he shall sign it, but if not he shall return it, with his Objections to that House in which it shall have originated, who shall enter the Objections at large on their journal, and proceed to reconsider it. If after such Reconsideration two thirds of that House shall agree to pass the Bill, it shall be sent, together with the Objections, to the other House, by which it shall likewise be reconsidered, and if approved by two thirds of that House, it shall become a Law. But in all such Cases the Votes of both Houses shall be determined by Yeas and Nays, and the Names of the Persons voting for and against the Bill shall be entered on the Journal of each House respectively. If any Bill shall not be returned by the President within ten Days (Sundays excepted) after it shall have been presented to him, the Same shall be a Law, in like Manner as if he had signed it, unless the Congress by their Adjournment prevent its Return, in which Case it shall not be a Law.

Every Order, Resolution, or Vote to which the Concurrence of the Senate and House of Representatives may be necessary (except on a question of Adjournment) shall be presented to the President of the United States; and before the Same shall take Effect, shall be approved by him, or being disapproved by him, shall be repassed by two thirds of the Senate and House of Representatives, according to the Rules and Limitations prescribed in the Case of a Bill.

SECTION 8. The Congress shall have Power To lay and collect Taxes, Duties, Imposts and Excises, to pay the Debts and provide for the common Defence and general Welfare of the United States; but all Duties, Imposts and Excises shall be uniform throughout the United States;

To borrow Money on the credit of the United States;

To regulate Commerce with foreign Nations, and among the several States, and with the Indian Tribes;

To establish a uniform Rule of Naturalization, and uniform Laws on the subject of Bankruptcies throughout the United States;

To coin Money, regulate the Value thereof, and of foreign Coin, and fix the Standard of Weights and Measures;

To provide for the Punishment of counterfeiting the Securities and current Coin of the United States;

To establish Post Offices and post Roads;

To promote the Progress of Science and useful Arts, by securing for limited Times to Authors and Inventors the exclusive Right to their respective Writings and Discoveries;

To constitute Tribunals inferior to the supreme Court;

To define and punish Piracies and Felonies committed on the high Seas, and Offences against the Law of Nations;

To declare War, grant Letters of Marque and Reprisal, and make Rules concerning Captures on Land and Water;

To raise and support Armies, but no Appropriation of Money to that Use shall be for a longer Term than two Years;

To provide and maintain a Navy;

To make Rules for the Government and Regulation of the land and naval Forces;

To provide for calling forth the Militia to execute the Laws of the Union, suppress Insurrections and repel Invasions;

To provide for organizing, arming, and disciplining, the Militia, and for governing such Part of them as may be employed in the Service of the United States, reserving to the States respectively, the Appointment of the Officers, and the Authority of training the Militia according to the discipline prescribed by Congress;

To exercise exclusive Legislation in all Cases whatsoever, over such District (not exceeding ten Miles square) as may, by Cession of particular States, and the Acceptance of Congress, become the Seat of the Government of the United States, and to exercise like Authority over all Places purchased by the Consent of the Legislature of the State in which the Same shall be for the Erection of Forts, Magazines, Arsenals, dock-Yards, and other needful Buildings;—And

To make all Laws which shall be necessary and proper for carrying into Execution the foregoing Powers, and all other Powers vested by this Constitution in the Government of the United States, or in any Department or Officer thereof.

SECTION 9. The Migration or Importation of such Persons as any of the States now existing shall think proper to admit, shall not be prohibited by the Congress prior to the Year one thousand eight hundred and eight, but a Tax or duty may be imposed on such Importation, not exceeding ten dollars for each Person.

The Privilege of the Writ of Habeas Corpus shall not be suspended, unless when in Cases of Rebellion or Invasion the public Safety may require it.

No Bill of Attainder or ex post facto Law shall be passed.

No Capitation, or other direct, Tax shall be laid, unless in Proportion to the Census or Enumeration herein before directed to be taken.

No Tax or Duty shall be laid on Articles exported from any State.

No Preference shall be given by any Regulation of Commerce or Revenue to the Ports of one State over those of another; nor shall Vessels bound to, or from, one State, be obliged to enter, clear, or pay Duties in another.

No Money shall be drawn from the Treasury, but in Consequence of Appropriations made by Law; and a regular Statement and Account of the Receipts and Expenditures of all public Money shall be published from time to time.

No Title of Nobility shall be granted by the United States: And no Person holding any Office of Profit or Trust under them, shall, without the Consent of the Congress, accept of any present, Emolument, Office, or Title, of any kind whatever, from any King, Prince, or foreign State.

SECTION 10. No state shall enter into any Treaty, Alliance, or Confederation; grant Letters of Marque and Reprisal; coin Money; emit Bills of Credit; make any Thing but gold and silver Coin a Tender in Payment of Debts; pass any Bill of Attainder, ex post facto Law, or Law impairing the Obligation of Contracts, or grant any Title of Nobility.

No State shall, without the Consent of the Congress, lay any Imposts or Duties on Imports or Exports, except what may be absolutely necessary for executing its inspection Laws: and the net Produce of all Duties and Imposts, laid by any State on Imports or Exports, shall be for the Use of the Treasury of the United States, and all such Laws shall be subject to the Revision and Controul of the Congress.

No State shall, without the Consent of Congress, lay any Duty of Tonnage, keep Troops, or Ships of War in time of Peace, enter into any Agreement or Compact with another State, or with a foreign Power, or engage in War, unless actually invaded, or in such imminent Danger as will not admit of delay.

ARTICLE II

SECTION 1. The executive Power shall be vested in a President of the United States of America. He shall hold his Office during the Term of four Years, and, together with the Vice President, chosen for the same Term, be elected as follows.

Each State shall appoint, in such Manner as the Legislature thereof may direct, a Number of Electors, equal to the whole Number of Senators and Representatives to which the State may be entitled in the Congress; but no Senator or Representative, or Person holding an Office of Trust of Profit under the United States, shall be appointed an Elector.

The Electors shall meet in their respective States, and vote by Ballot for two Persons, of whom one at least shall not be an Inhabitant of the same State with themselves. And they shall make a List of all the Persons voted for, and, of the Number of Votes for each; which List they shall sign and certify, and transmit sealed to the Seat of the Government of the United States, directed to the President of the Senate. The President of the Senate shall, in the Presence of the Senate and House of Representatives, open all the Certificates, and the Votes shall then be counted. The Person having the greatest Number of Votes shall be the President, if such Number be a Majority of the whole Number of Electors appointed; and if there be more than one who have such Majority, and have an equal Number of Votes, then the House of Representatives shall immediately chuse by Ballot one of them for President; and if no Person have a Majority, then from the five highest on the List the said House shall in like Manner chuse the President. But in chusing the President, the Votes shall be taken by States, the Representation from each State having one Vote; A quorum for this Purpose shall consist of a Member or Members from two thirds of the States, and a Majority of all the States shall be necessary to a Choice. In every Case, after the Choice of the President, the Person having the greatest Number of Votes of the Electors shall be the Vice President. But if there should remain two or more who have equal Votes, the Senate shall chuse from them by Ballot the Vice President.

The Congress may determine the Time of chusing the Electors, and the Day on which they shall give their Votes; which Day shall be the same throughout the United States.

No Person except a natural born Citizen, or a Citizen of the United States, at the time of the Adoption of this Constitution, shall be eligible to the Office of President; neither shall any Person be eligible to that Office who shall not have attained to the Age of thirty five Years, and been fourteen Years a Resident within the United States.

In Case of the Removal of the President from Office, or of his Death, Resignation, or Inability to discharge the Powers and Duties of the said Office, the Same shall devolve on the Vice President, and the Congress may by Law provide for the Case of Removal, Death, Resignation or Inability, both of the President and Vice President, declaring what Officer shall then act as President, and such Officer shall act accordingly, until the Disability be removed, or a President shall be elected.

The President shall, at stated Times, receive for his Services, a Compensation, which shall neither be encreased nor diminished during the Period for which he shall have been elected, and he shall not receive within that Period any other Emolument from the United States, or any of them.

Before he enter on the Execution of his Office, he shall take the following Oath or Affirmation—"I do solemnly swear (or affirm) that I will faithfully execute the Office of President of the United States, and will to the best of my Ability, preserve, protect and defend the Constitution of the United States."

SECTION 2. The President shall be Commander in Chief of the Army, and Navy of the United States, and of the Militia of the several States, when called into the actual Service of the United States; he may require the Opinion, in writing, of the principal Officer in each of the executive Departments, upon any Subject relating to the Duties of their respective Offices, and he shall have Power to grant Reprieves and Pardons for Offences against the United States, except in Cases of Impeachment.

He shall have Power, by and with the Advice and Consent of the Senate, to make Treaties, provided two thirds of the Senators present concur; and he shall nominate, and by and with the Advice and Consent of the Senate, shall appoint Ambassadors, other public Ministers and Consuls, Judges of the supreme Court, and all other

Officers of the United States, whose Appointments are not herein otherwise provided for, and which shall be established by Law: but the Congress may by Law vest the Appointment of such inferior Officers, as they think proper, in the President alone, in the Courts of Law, or in the Heads of Departments.

The President shall have Power to fill up all Vacancies that may happen during the Recess of the Senate, by granting Commissions which shall expire at the end of their next Session.

SECTION 3. He shall from time to time give to the Congress Information of the State of the Union, and recommend to their Consideration such Measures as he shall judge necessary and expedient; he may, on extraordinary Occasions, convene both Houses, or either of them, and in Case of Disagreement between them, with Respect to the Time of Adjournment, he may adjourn them to such Time as he shall think proper; he shall receive Ambassadors and other public Ministers; he shall take Care that the Laws be faithfully executed, and shall Commission all the Officers of the United States.

SECTION 4. The President, Vice President and all civil Officers of the United States, shall be removed from Office on Impeachment for, and Conviction of, Treason, Bribery, or other high Crimes and Misdemeanors.

ARTICLE III

SECTION 1. The judicial Power of the United States, shall be vested in one supreme Court, and in such inferior Courts as the Congress may from time to time ordain and establish. The Judges, both of the supreme and inferior Courts, shall hold their Offices during good Behaviour, and shall, at stated Times, receive for their Services, a Compensation, which shall not be diminished during their Continuance in Office.

SECTION 2. The judicial Power shall extend to all Cases, in Law and Equity, arising under this Constitution, the Laws of the United States, and Treaties made, or which shall be made, under their Authority;—to all Cases affecting Ambassadors, other public Ministers and Consuls;—to all Cases of admiralty and maritime Jurisdiction;—to Controversies to which the United States shall be a Party;—to Controversies between two or more States;—between a State and Citizens of another State;—between Citizens of different States,—between Citizens of the same State claiming Lands under Grants of different States,—and between a State, or the Citizens thereof, and foreign States, Citizens of Subjects.

In all Cases affecting Ambassadors, other public Ministers and Consuls, and those in which a State shall be Party, the supreme Court shall have original Jurisdiction. In all the other Cases before mentioned, the supreme Court shall have appellate Jurisdiction, both as to Law and Fact, with such Exceptions, and under such Regulations as the Congress shall make.

The Trial of all Crimes, except in Cases of Impeachment, shall be by Jury; and such Trial shall be held in the State where the said Crimes shall have been committed; but when not committed within any State, the Trial shall be at such Place or Places as the Congress may by Law have directed.

SECTION 3. Treason against the United States, shall consist only in levying War against them, or in adhering to their Enemies, giving them Aid and Comfort. No Person shall be convicted of Treason unless on the Testimony of two Witnesses to the same overt Act, or on Confession in open Court.

The Congress shall have Power to declare the Punishment of Treason, but no Attainder of Treason shall work Corruption of Blood, or Forfeiture except during the Life of the Person attainted.

ARTICLE IV

SECTION 1. Full Faith and Credit shall be given in each State to the public Acts, Records, and judicial Proceedings of every other State. And the Congress may by general Laws prescribe the Manner in which such Acts, Records and Proceedings shall be proved, and the Effect thereof.

SECTION 2. The Citizens of each State shall be entitled to all Privileges and Immunities of Citizens in the several States.

A Person charged in any State with Treason, Felony, or other Crime, who shall flee from Justice, and be found in another State, shall on Demand of the executive Authority of the State from which he fled, be delivered up, to be removed to the State having Jurisdiction of the Crime.

No Person held to Service or Labour in one State under the Laws thereof, escaping into another, shall, in Consequence of any Law or Regulation therein, be discharged from such Service or Labour, but shall be delivered up on Claim of the Party to whom such Service or Labour may be due.

SECTION 3. New States may be admitted by the Congress into this Union; but no new State shall be formed or erected within the Jurisdiction of any other State; nor any State be formed by the Junction of two or more States, or Parts of States, without the Consent of the Legislatures of the States concerned as well as of the Congress.

The Congress shall have Power to dispose of and make all needful Rules and Regulations respecting the Territory or other Property belonging to the United States; and nothing in this Constitution shall be so construed as to Prejudice any Claims of the United States, or of any particular State.

SECTION 4. The United States shall guarantee to every State in this Union a Republican Form of Government, and shall protect each of them against Invasion, and on Application of the Legislature, or of the Executive (when the Legislature cannot be convened) against domestic Violence.

ARTICLE V

The Congress, whenever two thirds of both Houses shall deem it necessary, shall propose Amendments to this Constitution, or, on the Application of the Legislatures of two thirds of the several States, shall call a Convention for proposing Amendments, which, in either Case, shall be valid to all Intents and Purposes, as Part of this Constitution, when ratified by the Legislatures of three fourths of the several States, or by Conventions in three fourths thereof, as the one or the other Mode of Ratification may be proposed by the Congress; Provided that no Amendment which may be made prior to the Year One thousand eight hundred and eight shall in any Manner affect the first and fourth Clauses in the Ninth Section of the first Article; and that no State, without its Consent, shall be deprived of its equal Suffrage in the Senate.

ARTICLE VI

All Debts contracted and Engagements entered into, before the Adoption of this Constitution, shall be as valid against the United States under this Constitution, as under the Confederation.

This Constitution, and the laws of the United States which shall be made in Pursuance thereof; and all Treaties made, or which shall be made, under the Authority of the United States, shall be the supreme Law of the Land; and the Judges in every State shall be bound thereby, any Thing in the Constitution or Laws of any State to the Contrary notwithstanding.

The Senators and Representatives before mentioned, and the Members of the several State Legislatures, and all executive and judicial Officers, both of the United States and of the several States, shall be bound by Oath or Affirmation, to support this Constitution; but no religious Test shall ever be required as a Qualification to any Office or public Trust under the United States.

ARTICLE VII

The Ratification of the Conventions of nine States, shall be sufficient for the Establishment of this Constitution between the States so ratifying the Same.

Done in Convention by the Unanimous Consent of the States present the Seventeenth Day of September in the Year of our Lord one thousand seven hundred and Eighty seven and of the Independence of the United States of America the Twelfth. In witness whereof we have hereunto subscribed our Names,

Go. WASHINGTON
Presid't. and deputy from Virginia

Attest
WILLIAM JACKSON
Secretary


Articles in addition to, and amendment of the Constitution of the United States of America, proposed by Congress and ratified by the Legislatures of the several states, pursuant to the Fifth Article of the original Constitution.

*(The first ten amendments were passed by Congress on September 25, 1789, and were ratified on December 15, 1791.)*


## AMENDMENT I

Congress shall make no law respecting an establishment of religion, or prohibiting the free exercise thereof; or abridging the freedom of speech, or of the press; or the right of the people peaceably to assemble, and to petition the Government for a redress of grievances.


## AMENDMENT II

A well regulated Militia, being necessary to the security of a free State, the right of the people to keep and bear Arms, shall not be infringed.


## AMENDMENT III

No Soldier shall, in time of peace be quartered in any house, without the consent of the Owner, nor in time of war, but in a manner to be prescribed by law.


## AMENDMENT IV

The right of the people to be secure in their persons, houses, papers, and effects, against unreasonable searches and seizures, shall not be violated, and no warrants shall issue, but upon probable cause, supported by Oath or affirmation, and particularly describing the place to be searched, and the persons or things to be seized.


## AMENDMENT V

No person shall be held to answer for a capital, or otherwise infamous crime, unless on a presentment or indictment of a Grand Jury, except in cases arising in the land or naval forces, or in the Militia, when in actual service in time of War or public danger; nor shall any person be subject for the same offence to be twice put in jeopardy of life or limb; nor shall be compelled in any criminal case to be a witness against himself, nor be deprived of life, liberty, or property, without due process of law; nor shall private property be taken for public use, without just compensation.

### AMENDMENT VI

In all criminal prosecutions, the accused shall enjoy the right to a speedy and public trial, by an impartial jury of the State and district wherein the crime shall have been committed, which district shall have been previously ascertained by law, and to be informed of the nature and cause of the accusation; to be confronted with the witnesses against him; to have compulsory process for obtaining witnesses in his favor, and to have the assistance of counsel for his defence.

### AMENDMENT VII

In Suits at common law, where the value in controversy shall exceed twenty dollars, the right of trial by jury shall be preserved, and no fact tried by a jury, shall be otherwise re-examined in any Court of the United States, than according to the rules of the common law.

### AMENDMENT VIII

Excessive bail shall not be required, nor excessive fines imposed, nor cruel and unusual punishments inflicted.

### AMENDMENT IX

The enumeration in the Constitution, of certain rights, shall not be construed to deny or disparage others retained by the people.

### AMENDMENT X

The powers not delegated to the United States by the Constitution, nor prohibited by it to the States, are reserved to the States respectively, or to the people.

### AMENDMENT XI
### (Ratified on February 7, 1795)

The Judicial power of the United States shall not be construed to extend to any suit in law or equity, commenced or prosecuted against one of the United States by Citizens of another State, or by Citizens or Subjects of any Foreign State.

### AMENDMENT XII
### (Ratified on June 15, 1804)

The Electors shall meet in their respective states, and vote by ballot for President and Vice-President, one of whom, at least, shall not be an inhabitant of the same state with themselves; they shall name in their ballots the person voted for as President, and in distinct ballots the person voted for as Vice-President, and they shall make distinct lists of all persons voted for as President, and of all persons voted for as Vice-President, and of the number of votes for each, which lists they shall sign and certify, and transmit sealed to the seat of the government of the United States, directed to the President of the Senate;—The President of the Senate shall, in the presence of the Senate and House of Representatives, open all the certificates and the votes shall then be counted;—The person having the greatest number of votes for President, shall be the

President, if such number be a majority of the whole number of Electors appointed; and if no person have such majority; then from the persons having the highest numbers not exceeding three on the list of those voted for as President, the House of Representatives shall choose immediately, by ballot, the President. But in choosing the President, the votes shall be taken by states, the representation from each state having one vote; a quorum for this purpose shall consist of a member or members from two-thirds of the states, and a majority of all the states shall be necessary to a choice. And if the House of Representatives shall not choose a President whenever the right of choice shall devolve upon them, before the fourth day of March next following, then the Vice-President shall act as President, as in the case of the death or other constitutional disability of the President.—The person having the greatest number of votes as Vice-President, shall be the Vice-President, if such number be a majority of the whole number of Electors appointed, and if no person have a majority, then from the two highest numbers on the list, the Senate shall choose the Vice-President; a quorum for the purpose shall consist of two-thirds of the whole number of Senators, and a majority of the whole number shall be necessary to a choice. But no person constitutionally ineligible to the office of President shall be eligible to that of Vice-President of the United States.

### AMENDMENT XIII
*(Ratified on December 6, 1865)*

SECTION 1. Neither slavery nor involuntary servitude, except as a punishment for crime whereof the party shall have been duly convicted, shall exist within the United States, or any place subject to their jurisdiction.

SECTION 2. Congress shall have power to enforce this article by appropriate legislation.

### AMENDMENT XIV
*(Ratified on July 9, 1868)*

SECTION 1. All persons born or naturalized in the United States, and subject to the jurisdiction thereof, are citizens of the United States and of the State wherein they reside. No State shall make or enforce any law which shall abridge the privileges or immunities of citizens of the United States; nor shall any State deprive any person of life, liberty, or property, without due process of law; nor deny to any person within its jurisdiction the equal protection of the laws.

SECTION 2. Representatives shall be apportioned among the several States according to their respective numbers, counting the whole number of persons in each State, excluding Indians not taxed. But when the right to vote at any election for the choice of electors for President and Vice President of the United States, Representatives in Congress, the Executive and Judicial officers of a State, or the members of the Legislature thereof, is denied to any of the male inhabitants of such State, being twenty-one years of age, and citizens of the United States, or in any way abridged, except for participation in rebellion, or other crime, the basis of representation therein shall be reduced in the proportion which the number of such male citizens shall bear to the whole number of male citizens twenty-one years of age in such State.

SECTION 3. No person shall be a Senator or Representative in Congress, or elector of President and Vice President, or hold any office, civil or military, under the United States, or under any State, who, having previously taken an oath, as a member of Congress, or as an officer of the United States, or as a member of any State legislature, or as an executive or judicial officer of any State, to support the Constitution of the United States, shall have engaged in insurrection or rebellion against the same, or given aid or comfort to the enemies thereof. But Congress may by a vote of two-thirds of each House, remove such diability.

SECTION 4. The validity of the public debt of the United States, authorized by law, including debts incurred for payment of pensions and bounties for services in suppressing insurrection or rebellion, shall not be questioned. But neither the United States nor any State shall assume or pay any debt or obligation incurred in aid of insurrection or rebellion against the United States, or any claim for the loss or emancipation of any slave, but all such debts, obligations and claims shall be held illegal and void.

SECTION 5. The Congress shall have power to enforce, by appropriate legislation, the provisions of this article.

AMENDMENT XV
*(Ratified on February 3, 1870)*

SECTION 1. The right of citizens of the United States to vote shall not se denied or abridged by the United States or by any State on account of race, color, or previous condition of servitude.

SECTION 2. The Congress shall have power to enforce this article by appropriate legislation.

AMENDMENT XVI
*(Ratified on February 3, 1913)*

The Congress shall have power to lay and collect taxes on incomes, from whatever source derived, without apportionment among the several States, and without regard to any census or enumeration.

AMENDMENT XVII
*(Ratified on April 8, 1913)*

The Senate of the United States shall be composed of two Senators from each State, elected by the people thereof, for six years; and each Senator shall have one vote. The electors in each State shall have the qualifications requisite for electors of the most numerous branch of the State legislatures.

When vacancies happen in the representation of any State in the Senate, the executive authority of such State shall issue writs of election to fill such vacancies: Provided, That the legislature of any State may empower the executive thereof to make temporary appointments until the people fill the vacancies by election as the legislature may direct.

This amendment shall not be so construed as to affect the election or term of any Senator chosen before it becomes valid as part of the Constitution.

AMENDMENT XVIII
*(Ratified on January 16, 1919)*

SECTION 1. After one year from the ratification of this article the manufacture, sale, or transportation of intoxicating liquors within, the importation thereof into, or the exportation thereof from the United States and all territory subject to the jurisdiction thereof for beverage purposes is hereby prohibited.

SECTION 2. The Congress and the several States shall have concurrent power to enforce this article by appropriate legislation.

SECTION 3. This article shall be inoperative unless it shall have been ratified as an amendment to the Constitution by the legislatures of the several States, as provided in the Constitution, within seven years from the date of the submission hereof to the States by the Congress.

AMENDMENT XIX
*(Ratified on August 18, 1920)*

The right of citizens of the United States to vote shall not be denied or abridged by the United States or by any State on account of sex.

Congress shall have power to enforce this article by appropriate legislation.

AMENDMENT XX
*(Ratified on February 6, 1933)*

SECTION 1. The terms of the President and Vice President shall end at noon on the 20th day of January, and the terms of Senators and Representatives at noon on the 3d day of January, of the years in which such terms would have ended if this article had not been ratified; and the terms of their successors shall then begin.

SECTION 2. The Congress shall assemble at least once in every year, and such meeting shall begin at noon on the 3d day of January, unless they shall by law appoint a different day.

SECTION 3. If, at the time fixed for the beginning of the term of the President, the President elect shall have died, the Vice President elect shall become President. If a President shall not have been chosen before the time fixed for the beginning of his term, or if the President elect shall have failed to qualify, then the Vice President elect shall act as President until a President shall have qualified; and the Congress may by law provide for the case wherein neither a President elect nor a Vice President elect shall have qualified, declaring who shall then act as President, or the manner in which one who is to act shall be selected, and such person shall act accordingly until a President or Vice President shall have qualified.

SECTION 4. The Congress may by law provide for the case of the death of any of the persons from whom the House of Representatives may choose a President whenever the rights of choice shall have devolved upon them, and for the case of the death of any of the persons from whom the Senate may choose a Vice President whenever the right of choice shall have devolved upon them.

SECTION 5. Sections 1 and 2 shall take effect on the 15th day of October following the ratification of this article.

SECTION 6. This article shall be inoperative unless it shall have been ratified as an amendment to the Constitution by the legislatures of three-fourths of the several States within seven years from the date of its submission.

AMENDMENT XXI
*(Ratified on December 5, 1933)*

SECTION 1. The eighteenth article of amendment to the Constitution of the United States is hereby repealed.

SECTION 2. The transportation or importation into any State, Territory, or possession of the United States for delivery or use therein of intoxicating liquors, in violation of the laws thereof, is hereby prohibited.

SECTION 3. This article shall be inoperative unless it shall have been ratified as an amendment to the Constitution by conventions in the several States, as provided in the Constitution, within seven years from the date of the submission hereof to the States by the Congress.

AMENDMENT XXII
*(Ratified on February 27, 1951)*

No person shall be elected to the office of the President more than twice, and no person who has held the office of President, or acted as President, for more than two years of a term to which some other person was elected President shall be elected to the office of the President more than once. But this Article shall not apply to any person holding the office of President when this Article was proposed by the Congress, and shall not prevent any person who may be holding the office of President, or acting as President, during the term within which this Article becomes operative from holding the office of President or acting as President during the remainder of such term.

AMENDMENT XXIII
*(Ratified on March 29, 1961)*

SECTION 1. The District constituting the seat of Government of the United States shall appoint in such manner as the Congress may direct:

A number of electors of President and Vice President equal to the whole number of Senators and Representatives in Congress to which the District would be entitled if it were a State, but in no event more than the least populous State; they shall be in addition to those appointed by the States, but they shall be considered, for the purposes of the election of President and Vice President, to be electors appointed by a State; and they shall meet in the District and perform such duties as provided by the twelfth article of amendment.

SECTION 2. The Congress shall have power to enforce this article by appropriate legislation.

AMENDMENT XXIV
*(Ratified on January 23, 1964)*

SECTION 1. The right of citizens of the United States to vote in any primary or other election for President or Vice President, for electors for President or Vice President, or for Senator or Representative in Congress, shall not be denied or abridged by the United States or any State by reason of failure to pay any poll tax or other tax.

SECTION 2. The Congress shall have power to enforce this article by appropriate legislation.

AMENDMENT XXV
*(Ratified on February 10, 1967)*

SECTION 1. In case of the removal of the President from office or of his death or resignation, the Vice President shall become President.

SECTION 2. Whenever there is a vacancy in the office of the Vice President, the President shall nominate a Vice President who shall take office upon confirmation by a majority vote of both Houses of Congress.

SECTION 3. Whenever the President transmits to the President pro tempore of the Senate and the Speaker of the House of Representatives his written declaration that he is unable to discharge the powers and duties of his office, and until he transmits to them a written declaration to the contrary, such powers and duties shall be discharged by the Vice President as Acting President.

SECTION 4. Whenever the Vice President and a majority of either the principal officers of the executive departments or of such other body as Congress may by law provide, transmit to the President pro tempore of the Senate and the Speaker of the House of Representatives their written declaration that the President is unable to discharge the powers and duties of his office, the Vice President shall immediately assume the powers and duties of the office as Acting President.

Thereafter, when the President transmits to the President pro tempore of the Senate and the Speaker of the House of Representatives his written declaration that no inability exists, he shall resume the powers and duties of his office unless the Vice President and a majority of either the principal officers of the executive department or of such other body as Congress may by law provide, transmit within four days to the President pro tempore of the Senate and the Speaker of the House of Representatives their written declaration that the President is unable to discharge the powers and duties of his office. Thereupon Congress shall decide the issue, assembling within forty-eight hours for that purpose if not in session. If the Congress, within twenty-one days after receipt of the latter written declaration, or, if Congress is not in session, within twenty-one days after Congress is required to assemble, determines by two-thirds vote of both Houses that the President is unable to discharge the powers and duties of his office, the Vice President shall continue to discharge the same as Acting President; otherwise, the President shall resume the powers and duties of his office.

### AMENDMENT XXVI
*(Ratified on July 1, 1971)*

SECTION 1. The right of citizens of the United States, who are eighteen years of age or older, to vote shall not be denied or abridged by the United States or by any State on account of age.

SECTION 2. The Congress shall have power to enforce this article by appropriate legislation.

### AMENDMENT XXVII
*(Ratified on May 7, 1992)*

No law varying the compensation for the services of Senators and Representatives shall take effect until an election of Representatives shall have intervened.

# Appendix III

## The Federalist No. 10

*November 22, 1787*

*James Madison*

### TO THE PEOPLE OF THE STATE OF NEW YORK.

Among the numerous advantages promised by a well constructed Union, none deserves to be more accurately developed than its tendency to break and control the violence of faction. The friend of popular governments, never finds himself so much alarmed for their character and fate, as when he contemplates their propensity to this dangerous vice. He will not fail therefore to set a due value on any plan which, without violating the principles to which he is attached, provides a proper cure for it. The instability, injustice and confusion introduced into the public councils, have in truth been the mortal diseases under which popular governments have every where perished; as they continue to be the favorite and fruitful topics from which the adversaries to liberty derive their most specious declamations. The valuable improvements made by the American Constitutions on the popular models, both ancient and modern, cannot certainly be too much admired; but it would be an unwarrantable partiality, to contend that they have as effectually obviated the danger on this side as was wished and expected. Complaints are every where heard from our most considerate and virtuous citizens, equally the friends of public and private faith, and of public and personal liberty; that our governments are too unstable; that the public good is disregarded in the conflicts of rival parties; and that measures are too often decided, not according to the rules of justice, and the rights of the minor party; but by the superior force of an interested and over-bearing majority. However anxiously we may wish that these complaints had no foundation, the evidence of known facts will not permit us to deny that they are in some degree true. It will be found indeed, on a candid review of our situation, that some of the distresses under which we labor, have been erroneously charged on the operation of our governments; but it will be found, at the same time, that other causes will not alone account for many of our heaviest misfortunes; and particularly, for that prevailing and increasing distrust of public engagements, and alarm for private rights, which are echoed from one end of the continent to the other. These must be chiefly, if not wholly, effects of the unsteadiness and injustice, with which a factious spirit has tainted our public administrations.

By a faction I understand a number of citizens, whether amounting to a majority or minority of the whole, who are united and actuated by some common impulse of passion, or of interest, adverse to the rights of other citizens, or to the permanent and aggregate interests of the community.

There are two methods of curing the mischiefs of faction: the one, by removing its causes; the other, by controlling its effects.

There are again two methods of removing the causes of faction: the one by destroying the liberty which is essential to its existence; the other, by giving to every citizen the same opinions, the same passions, and the same interests.

It could never be more truly said than of the first remedy, that it is worse than the disease. Liberty is to faction, what air is to fire, an aliment without which it instantly expires. But it could not be a less folly to abolish liberty, which is essential to political life, because it nourishes faction, than it would be to wish the annihilation of air, which is essential to animal life, because it imparts to fire its destructive agency.

The second expedient is as impracticable, as the first would be unwise. As long as the reason of man continues fallible, and he is at liberty to exercise it, different opinions will be formed. As long as the connection subsists between his reason and his self-love, his opinions and his passions will have a reciprocal influence on each other; and the former will be objects to which the latter will attach themselves. The diversity in the faculties of men from which the rights of property originate, is not less an insuperable obstacle to a uniformity of interests. The protection of these faculties is the first object of Government. From the protection of different and unequal faculties of acquiring property, the possession of different degrees and kinds of property immediately results: and from the influence of these on the sentiments and views of the respective proprietors, ensues a division of the society into different interests and parties.

The latent causes of faction are thus sown in the nature of man; and we see them every where brought into different degrees of activity, according to the different circumstances of civil society. A zeal for different opinions concerning religion, concerning Government and many other points, as well of speculation as of practice; an attachment to different leaders ambitiously contending for pre-eminence and power; or to persons of other descriptions whose fortunes have been interesting to the human passions, have in turn divided mankind into parties, inflamed them with mutual animosity, and rendered them much more disposed to vex and oppress each other, than to cooperate for their common good. So strong is this propensity of mankind to fall into mutual animosities, that where no substantial occasion presents itself, the most frivolous and fanciful distinctions have been sufficient to kindle their unfriendly passions, and excite their most violent conflicts. But the most common and durable source of factions, has been the various and unequal distribution of property. Those who hold, and those who are without property, have ever formed distinct interests in society. Those who are creditors, and those who are debtors, fall under a like discrimination. A landed interest, a manufacturing interest, a mercantile interest, a monied interest, with many lesser interests, grow up of necessity in civilized nations, and divide them into different classes, actuated by different sentiments and views. The regulation of these various and interfering interests forms the principal task of modern Legislation, and involves the spirit of party and faction in the necessary and ordinary operations of Government.

No man is allowed to be a judge in his own cause; because his interest would certainly bias his judgment, and, not improbably, corrupt his integrity. With equal, nay with greater reason, a body of men, are unfit to be both judges and parties, at the same time; yet, what are many of the most important acts of legislation, but so many judicial determinations, not indeed concerning the rights of single persons, but concerning the rights of large bodies of citizens, and what are the different classes of legislators, but advocates and parties to the causes which they determine? Is a law proposed concerning private debts? It is a question to which the creditors are parties on one side, and the debtors on the other. Justice ought to hold the balance between them. Yet the parties are and must be themselves the judges; and the most numerous party, or, in other words, the most powerful faction must be expected to prevail. Shall domestic manufactures be encouraged, and in what degree, by restrictions on foreign manufactures? are questions which would be differently decided by the landed and the manufacturing classes; and probably by neither, with a sole regard to justice and the public good. The apportionment of taxes on the various descriptions of property, is an act which seems to require the most exact impartiality; yet, there is perhaps no legislative act in which greater opportunity and temptation are given to a predominant party, to trample on the rules of justice. Every shilling with which they over-burden the inferior number, is a shilling saved to their own pockets.

It is in vain to say, that enlightened statesmen will be able to adjust these clashing interests, and render them all subservient to the public good. Enlightened statesmen will not always be at the helm: Nor, in many cases, can such an adjustment be made at all, without taking into view indirect and remote considerations, which will rarely prevail over the immediate interest which one party may find in disregarding the rights of another, or the good of the whole.

The inference to which we are brought, is, that the causes of faction cannot be removed; and that relief is only to be sought in the means of controlling its effects.

If a faction consists of less than a majority, relief is supplied by the republican principle, which enables the majority to defeat its sinister views by regular vote: It may clog the administration, it may convulse the society; but it will be unable to execute and mask its violence under the forms of the Constitution. When a majority is included in a faction, the form of popular government on the other hand enables it to sacrifice to its ruling passion or interest, both the public good and the rights of other citizens. To secure the public good, and private rights, against the danger of such a faction, and at the same time to preserve the spirit and the form of popular government, is then the great object to which our enquiries are directed: Let me add that it is the great desideratum, by which alone this form of government can be rescued from the opprobrium under which it has so long labored, and be recommended to the esteem and adoption of mankind.

By what means is this object attainable? Evidently by one of two only. Either the existence of the same passion or interest in a majority at the same time, must be prevented; or the majority, having such co-existent passion or interest, must be rendered, by their number and local situation, unable to concert and carry into effect schemes of oppression. If the impulse and the opportunity be suffered to coincide, we well know that neither moral nor religious motives can be relied on as an adequate control. They are not found to be such on the injustice and violence of individuals, and lose their efficacy in proportion to the number combined together; that is, in proportion as their efficacy becomes needful.

From this view of the subject, it may be concluded, that a pure Democracy, by which I mean, a Society, consisting of a small number of citizens, who assemble and administer the Government in person, can admit of no cure for the mischiefs of faction. A common passion or interest will, in almost every case, be felt by a majority of the whole; a communication and concert results from the form of Government itself; and there is nothing to check the inducements to sacrifice the weaker party, or an obnoxious individual. Hence it is, that such Democracies have ever been spectacles of turbulence and contention; have ever been found incompatible with personal security, or the rights of property; and have in general been as short in their lives, as they have been violent in their deaths. Theoretic politicians, who have patronized this species of Government, have erroneously supposed, that by reducing mankind to a perfect equality in their political rights, they would, at the same time, be perfectly equalized and assimilated in their possessions, their opinions, and their passions.

A republic, by which I mean a government in which the scheme of representation takes place, opens a different prospect, and promises the cure for which we are seeking. Let us examine the points in which it varies from pure democracy, and we shall comprehend both the nature of the cure and the efficacy which it must derive from the union.

The two great points of difference, between a democracy and a republic, are, first, the delegation of the government, in the latter, to a small number of citizens, elected by the rest; secondly, the greater number of citizens, and greater sphere of country, over which the latter may be extended.

The effect of the first difference is, on the one hand, to refine and enlarge the public views, by passing them through the medium of a chosen body of citizens, whose wisdom may best discern the true interest of their country, and whose patriotism and love of justice, will be least likely to sacrifice it to temporary or partial considerations. Under such a regulation, it may well happen, that the public voice, pronounced by the representatives of the people, will be more consonant to the public good, than if pronounced by the people themselves, convened for the purpose. On the other hand the effect may be inverted. Men of factious tempers, of local prejudices, or of sinister designs, may by intrigue, by corruption, or by other means, first obtain the suffrages, and then betray the interest of the people. The question resulting is, whether small or extensive republics are most favorable to the election of proper guardians of the public weal, and it is clearly decided in favor of the latter by two obvious considerations.

In the first place, it is to be remarked that, however small the republic may be, the representatives must be raised to a certain number, in order to guard against the cabals of a few; and that however large it may be, they must be limited to a certain number, in order to guard against the confusion of a multitude. Hence, the number of representatives in the two cases not being in proportion to that of the constituents, and being proportionally greatest in the small republic, it follows, that if the proportion of fit characters be not less in the large than in the small republic, the former will present a greater option, and consequently a greater probability of a fit choice.

In the next place, as each Representative will be chosen by a greater number of citizens in the large than in the small Republic, it will be more difficult for unworthy candidates to practise with success the vicious arts, by which elections are too often carried; and the suffrages of the people being more free, will be more likely to center on men who possess the most attractive merit, and the most diffusive and established characters.

It must be confessed, that in this, as in most other cases, there is a mean, on both sides of which inconveniences will be found to lie. By enlarging too much the number of electors, you render the representatives too little acquainted with all their local circumstances and lesser interests; as by reducing it too much, you render him unduly attached to these, and too little fit to comprehend and pursue great and national objects. The Federal Constitution forms a happy combination in this respect; the great and aggregate interests being referred to the national, the local and particular, to the state legislatures.

The other point of difference is, the greater number of citizens and extent of territory which may be brought within the compass of Republican, than of Democratic Government; and it is this circumstance principally which renders factious combinations less to be dreaded in the former, than in the latter. The smaller the society, the fewer probably will be the distinct parties and interests composing it; the fewer the distinct parties and interests, the more frequently will a majority be found of the same party; and the smaller the number of individuals composing a majority, and the smaller the compass within which they are placed, the more easily will they concert and execute their plans of oppression. Extend the sphere, and you take in a greater variety of parties and interests; you make it less probable that a majority of the whole will have a common motive to invade the rights of other citizens; or if such a common motive exists, it will be more difficult for all who feel it to discover their own strength, and to act in unison with each other. Besides other impediments, it may be remarked, that where there is a consciousness of unjust or dishonorable purposes, communication is always checked by distrust, in proportion to the number whose concurrence is necessary.

Hence it clearly appears, that the same advantage, which a Republic has over a Democracy, in controlling the effects of faction, is enjoyed by a large over a small Republic—is enjoyed by the Union over the States composing it. Does this advantage consist in the substitution of Representatives, whose enlightened views and virtuous sentiments render them superior to local prejudices, and to schemes of injustice? It will not be denied, that the Representation of the Union will be most likely to possess these requisite endowments. Does it consist in the greater security afforded by a greater variety of parties, against the event of any one party being able to outnumber and oppress the rest? In an equal degree does the increased variety of parties, comprised within the Union, increase this security? Does it, in fine, consist in the greater obstacles opposed to the concert and accomplishment of the secret wishes of an unjust and interested majority? Here, again, the extent of the Union gives it the most palpable advantage.

The influence of factious leaders may kindle a flame within their particular States, but will be unable to spread a general conflagration through the other States: a religious sect, may degenerate into a political faction in a part of the Confederacy but the variety of sects dispersed over the entire face of it, must secure the national Councils against any danger from that source: a rage for paper money, for an abolition of debts, for an equal division of property, or for any other improper or wicked project, will be less apt to pervade the whole body of the Union, than a particular member of it; in the same proportion as such a malady is more likely to taint a particular county or district, than an entire State.

In the extent and proper structure of the Union, therefore, we behold a Republican remedy for the diseases most incident to Republican Government. And according to the degree of pleasure and pride, we feel in being Republicans, ought to be our zeal in cherishing the spirit, and supporting the character of Federalists.

Publius

# Appendix IV

## The Federalist No. 51

*February 6, 1788*
*James Madison*

TO THE PEOPLE OF THE STATE OF NEW YORK.

To what expedient then shall we finally resort for maintaining in practice the necessary partition of power among the several departments, as laid down in the constitution? The only answer that can be given is, that as all these exterior provisions are found to be inadequate, the defect must be supplied, by so contriving the interior structure of the government, as that its several constituent parts may, by their mutual relations, be the means of keeping each other in their proper places. Without presuming to undertake a full development of this important idea, I will hazard a few general observations, which may perhaps place it in a clearer light, and enable us to form a more correct judgment of the principles and structure of the government planned by the convention.

In order to lay a due foundation for that separate and distinct exercise of the different powers of government, which to a certain extent, is admitted on all hands to be essential to the preservation of liberty, it is evident that each department should have a will of its own; and consequently should be so constituted, that the members of each should have as little agency as possible in the appointment of the members of the others. Were this principle rigorously adhered to, it would require that all the appointments for the supreme executive, legislative, and judiciary magistracies, should be drawn from the same fountain of authority, the people, through channels, having no communication whatever with one another. Perhaps such a plan of constructing the several departments would be less difficult in practice than it may in contemplation appear. Some difficulties however, and some additional expense, would attend the execution of it. Some deviations therefore from the principle must be admitted. In the constitution of the judiciary department in particular, it might be inexpedient to insist rigorously on the principle; first, because peculiar qualifications being essential in the members, the primary consideration ought to be to select that mode of choice, which best secures these qualifications; secondly, because the permanent tenure by which the appointments are held in that department, must soon destroy all sense of dependence on the authority conferring them.

It is equally evident that the members of each department should be as little dependent as possible on those of the others, for the emoluments annexed to their offices. Were the executive magistrate, or the judges, not independent of the legislature in this particular, their independence in every other would be merely nominal.

But the great security against a gradual concentration of the several powers in the same department, consists in giving to those who administer each department, the necessary constitutional means, and personal motives, to resist encroachments of the others. The provision for defense must in this, as in all other cases, be made commensurate to the danger of attack. Ambition must be made to counteract ambition.

The interest of the man must be connected with the constitutional right of the place. It may be a reflection on human nature, that such devices should be necessary to control the abuses of government. But what is government itself but the greatest of all reflections on human nature? If men were angels, no government would be necessary. If angels were to govern men, neither external nor internal controls on government would be necessary. In framing a government which is to be administered by men over men, the great difficulty lies in this: You must first enable the government to control the governed; and in the next place, oblige it to control itself. A dependence on the people is no doubt the primary control on the government; but experience has taught mankind the necessity of auxiliary precautions.

This policy of supplying by opposite and rival interests, the defect of better motives, might be traced through the whole system of human affairs, private as well as public. We see it particularly displayed in all the subordinate distributions of power; where the constant aim is to divide and arrange the several offices in such a manner as that each may be a check on the other; that the private interest of every individual, may be a sentinel over the public rights. These inventions of prudence cannot be less requisite in the distribution of the supreme powers of the state.

But it is not possible to give to each department an equal power of self defense. In republican government the legislative authority, necessarily, predominates. The remedy for this inconveniency is, to divide the legislature into different branches; and to render them by different modes of election, and different principles of action, as little connected with each other, as the nature of their common functions, and their common dependence on the society, will admit. It may even be necessary to guard against dangerous encroachments by still further precautions. As the weight of the legislative authority requires that it should be thus divided, the weakness of the executive may require, on the other hand, that it should be fortified. An absolute negative, on the legislature, appears at first view to be the natural defense with which the executive magistrate should be armed. But perhaps it would be neither altogether safe, nor alone sufficient. On ordinary occasions, it might not be exerted with the requisite firmness; and on extraordinary occasions, it might be prefidiously abused. May not this defect of an absolute negative be supplied, by some qualified connection between this weaker department, and the weaker branch of the stronger department, by which the latter may be led to support the constitutional rights of the former, without being too much detached from the rights of its own department?

If the principles on which these observations are founded be just, as I persuade myself they are, and they be applied as a criterion, to the several state constitutions, and to the federal constitution, it will be found, that if the latter does not perfectly correspond with them, the former are infinitely less able to bear such a test.

There are moreover two considerations particularly applicable to the federal system of America, which place that system in a very interesting point of view.

First. In a single republic, all the power surrendered by the people, is submitted to the administration of a single government; and usurpations are guarded against by a division of the government into distinct and separate departments. In the compound republic of America, the power surrendered by the people, is first divided between two distinct governments, and then the portion allotted to each, subdivided among distinct and separate departments. Hence a double security arises to the rights of the people. The different governments will control each other; at the same time that each will be controlled by itself.

Second. It is of great importance in a republic, not only to guard the society against the oppression of its rulers; but to guard one part of the society against the injustice of the other part. Different interests necessarily exist in different classes of citizens. If a majority be united by a common interest, the rights of the minority will be insecure. There are but two methods of providing against this evil: The one by creating a will in the community independent of the majority, that is, of the society itself, the other by comprehending in the society so many separate descriptions of citizens, as will render an unjust combination of a majority of the whole, very improbable, if not impracticable. The first method prevails in all governments possessing an hereditary or self appointed authority. This at best is but a precarious security; because a power independent of the society may as well espouse the unjust views of the major, as the rightful interests, of the minor party, and may possibly be turned against both parties. The second method will be exemplified in the federal republic of the United States. While all authority in it will be derived from and dependent on the society, the society itself will be broken into so many parts, interests and classes of citizens, that the rights of individuals or of the minority, will be in little danger from interested combinations of the majority. In a free government, the security for civil rights must be the same as for religious rights. It consists in the one case in the multiplicity of interests, and in the other, in the multiplicity of sects. The degree of security in both cases will depend on the number of interests and sects; and this may be presumed to depend on the extent of country and number of people comprehended under the same government. This view of the subject must particularly recommend a proper federal system to all the sincere and considerate friends of republican government: Since it shows that in exact proportion as the territory of the union may be formed into more circumscribed confederacies or states, oppressive combinations of a majority will be facilitated, the best security under the republican form, for the rights of every class of citizens, will be diminished; and consequently, the stability and independence of some member of the government, the only other security, must be proportionally increased. Justice is the end of government. It is the end of civil society. It ever has been, and ever will be pursued, until it be obtained, or until liberty be lost in the pursuit. In a society under the forms of which the stronger faction can readily unite and oppress the weaker, anarchy may as truly be said to reign, as in a state of nature where the weaker individual is not secured against the violence of the stronger: And as in the latter state even the stronger individuals are prompted by the uncertainty of their condition, to submit to a government which may protect the weak as well as themselves: So in the former state, will the more powerful factions or parties be gradually induced by a like motive, to wish for a government which will protect all parties, the weaker as well as the more powerful. It can be little doubted, that if the state of Rhode Island was separated from the confederacy, and left to itself, the insecurity of rights under the popular form of government within such narrow limits, would be displayed by such reiterated oppressions of factious majorities, that some power altogether independent of the people would soon be called for by the voice of the very factions whose misrule had proved the necessity of it. In the extended republic of the United States, and among the great variety of interests, parties and sects which it embraces, a coalition of a majority of the whole society could seldom take place on any other principles than those of justice and the general good; and there being thus less danger to a minor from the will of the major party, there must be less pretext also, to provide for the security of the former, by introducing into the government a will not dependent on the latter; or in other words, a will independent of the society itself. It is no less certain than it is important, notwithstanding the contrary opinions which have been entertained, that the larger the society, provided it lie within a practicable sphere, the more duly capable it will be of self government. And happily for the republican cause, the practicable sphere may be carried to a very great extent, by a judicious modification and mixture of the federal principle.

Publius

# APPENDIX V

## *Presidents of the United States*

| President | Year | Party | Most Noteworthy Event |
| --- | --- | --- | --- |
| George Washington | 1789–1797 | Federalist | Establishment of Federal Judiciary |
| John Adams | 1797–1801 | Federalist | Alien-Sedition Acts |
| Thomas Jefferson | 1801–1809 | Dem.-Republican | First President to Defeat Incumbent/Louisiana Purchase |
| James Madison | 1809–1817 | Dem.-Republican | War of 1812 |
| James Monroe | 1817–1825 | Dem.-Republican | Monroe Doctrine/ Missouri Compromise |
| John Quincy Adams | 1825–1829 | Dem.-Republican | Elected by "King Caucus" |
| Andrew Jackson | 1829–1837 | Democratic | Set up Spoils System |
| Martin Van Buren | 1837–1841 | Democratic | Competitive Parties Established |
| William H. Harrison | 1841 | Whig | Universal White Male Suffrage |
| John Tyler | 1841–1845 | Whig | Texas Annexed |
| James K. Polk | 1845–1849 | Democratic | Mexican-American War |
| Zachary Taylor | 1849–1850 | Whig | California Gold Rush |
| Millard Fillmore | 1850–1853 | Whig | Compromise of 1850 |
| Franklin Pierce | 1853–1857 | Democratic | Republican Party Formed |
| James Buchanan | 1857–1861 | Democratic | Dred Scott Decision |
| Abraham Lincoln | 1861–1865 | Republican | Civil War |
| Andrew Johnson | 1865–1869 | Republican | First Impeachment of President |
| Ulysses S. Grant | 1869–1877 | Republican | Reconstruction of South |
| Rutherford B. Hayes | 1877–1881 | Republican | End of Reconstruction |
| James A. Garfield | 1881 | Republican | Assassinated by Job-seeker |
| Chester A. Arthur | 1881–1885 | Republican | Civil Service Reform |
| Grover Cleveland | 1885–1889 | Democratic | Casts 102 Vetoes in One Year |
| Benjamin Harrison | 1889–1893 | Republican | McKinley Law Raises Tarrifs |
| Grover Cleveland | 1893–1897 | Democratic | Depression/Pullman Strike |
| William McKinley | 1897–1901 | Republican | Spanish-American War |
| Theodore Roosevelt | 1901–1909 | Republican | Conservation/Panama Canal |
| William H. Taft | 1909–1913 | Republican | Judicial Reform |
| Woodrow Wilson | 1913–1921 | Democratic | Progressive Reforms/ World War I |
| Warren G. Harding | 1921–1923 | Republican | Return to Normalcy |
| Calvin Coolidge | 1923–1929 | Republican | Cuts Taxes/Promotes Business |
| Herbert C. Hoover | 1929–1933 | Republican | Great Depression |
| Franklin D. Roosevelt | 1933–1945 | Democratic | New Deal/ World War II |
| Harry S Truman | 1945–1953 | Democratic | Beginning of Cold War |
| Dwight D. Eisenhower | 1953–1961 | Republican | End of Korean War |
| John F. Kennedy | 1961–1963 | Democratic | Cuban Missile Crisis |
| Lyndon B. Johnson | 1963–1969 | Democratic | Great Society/Vietnam War |
| Richard M. Nixon | 1969–1974 | Republican | Watergate Scandal |
| Gerald R. Ford | 1974–1977 | Republican | War Powers Resolution |
| James Earl Carter | 1977–1981 | Democratic | Iranian Hostage Crisis |
| Ronald Reagan | 1981–1989 | Republican | Tax Cut/ Expenditure Cuts |
| George Bush | 1989–1993 | Republican | End of Cold War/Persian Gulf War |
| William J. Clinton | 1993–2001 | Democratic | Deficit Reduction |

Refer to www.ablongman.com.fiorina

# GLOSSARY

**administration**   The president and his political appointees responsible for directing the executive branch of government.

**administrative discretion**   Power to interpret a legislative mandate.

**advice and consent**   Support for a presidential action by a designated number of senators.

**affirmative action**   Programs designed to enhance opportunities for groups that have suffered discrimination in the past.

**affirmative action redistricting**   The process of drawing district lines to maximize the number of majority-minority districts.

**agency**   Basic organizational unit of federal government. Also known as *office* or *bureau.*

**agenda setting**   Making an issue so visible that important political leaders take it seriously.

**Aid to Families with Dependent Children (AFDC)**   Public assistance program established in 1935 as part of the Social Security Act; replaced in 1996 by Temporary Assistance to Needy Families (TANF).

**ambassador**   The head of a diplomatic delegation to a major foreign country.

*amicus curiae*   Latin term meaning "friend of the court." It refers to legal briefs submitted by interested groups who are not directly party to a court case.

**Annapolis Convention**   1786 meeting to discuss constitutional reform.

*Anti-Federalists*   Those who opposed ratification of the Constitution.

**appeal**   The procedure whereby the losing side asks a higher court to overturn a lower-court decision.

**Appropriations process**   Process of providing funding for governmental activities and programs that have been authorized.

**aristocracy**   Government by a few leaders made eligible by birthright.

**Articles of Confederation**   The first (1781–1789) basic governing document of the United States and forerunner to the Constitution.

**associate justice**   One of the eight Justices of the Supreme Court who are not the chief justice.

**authorization process**   Term given to the entire process of providing statutory authority for a government program or activity.

**balancing doctrine**   The principle enunciated by the courts that freedom of speech must be balanced against other competing public interests at stake in particular circumstances.

**Bay of Pigs**   Location of CIA-supported effort by Cuban exiles in 1961 to invade Cuba and overthrow Fidel Castro.

**beltway insider**   Person living in the Washington metropolitan area who is engaged in, or well informed about, national politics and government.

**bicameral**   A legislature that contains two chambers.

**Bill of Rights**   The first ten amendments to the Constitution, which protect individual and state rights.

**black codes**   Laws that applied to newly freed slaves but not to whites.

**blame avoidance**   Set of political techniques employed by political leaders to disguise their actions and shift blame to others.

**bloc voting**   Voting in which nearly all members of one group (such as African Americans) vote for a candidate of their race, whereas nearly all members of another group (such as whites) vote against that candidate.

**block grants**   Federal grants to a state and/or local government that impose minimal restrictions on the use of funds.

**borking**   Politicizing the nomination process through an organized public campaign that portrays the nominee as a dangerous extremist.

**brief**   Written arguments presented to a court by lawyers on behalf of clients.

*Brown v. Board of Education of Topeka, Kansas*   1954 court decision declaring racial segregation in schools unconstitutional.

**budget**   The government's annual plan for taxing and spending.

**bully pulpit**   The nature of the president's status as an ideal vehicle for persuading the public to support the president's policies.

**bureaucracy**   Organization designed to perform a particular set of tasks.

**business cycle**   The alternation of periods of economic growth with periods of economic slowdown.

**cabinet**   The combined heads of all departments of the executive branch.

**campaign consultant**   An expert in the tools of modern candidate-based campaigns, especially polling and the media.

**categorical grants**   Federal grants to a state and/or local government that impose programmatic restrictions on the use of funds.

**caucus**    All Democratic members of the House or Senate. Members in caucus elect the party leaders, ratify the choice of committee leaders, and debate party positions on issues.

**Central Intelligence Agency (CIA)**    Agency primarily responsible for gathering and analyzing information about the political and military activities of other nations.

**cert**    *See* writ of *certiorari.*

**checks and balances**    Constitutional division of power into separate institutions, giving each institution the power to block the actions of the others.

**chief justice**    Head of the Supreme Court.

**chief of staff**    Head of White House staff. Has continuous, direct contact with the president.

**circuit court of appeals**    Court to which decisions by federal district courts are appealed.

**citizen duty**    The belief that it is a citizen's duty to be informed and to participate in politics

**citizenship**    Status held by someone entitled to all the rights and privileges of a full-fledged member of a political community.

**civic republicanism**    A political philosophy that emphasizes the obligation of citizens to act virtuously in pursuit of the common good.

**civil code**    Laws regulating relations among individuals. Alleged violators are sued by presumed victims, who ask courts to award damages and otherwise offer relief.

**civil disobedience**    A peaceful, well-publicized violation of a law designed to dramatize that law's injustice.

**civil liberties**    Fundamental freedoms that together preserve the rights of a free people.

**civil rights**    Right to equal treatment under the law.

**civil rights amendments**    The Thirteenth, Fourteenth, and Fifteenth Amendments, which abolished slavery, redefined civil rights, and guaranteed the right to vote to all adult male citizens.

**civil service**    A system in which government employees chosen according to their educational qualifications, performance on examinations, and work experience.

**class action suit**    Suit brought on behalf of all individuals in a particular category, whether or not they are actually participating in the suit.

**clear and present danger doctrine**    The principle that people should have complete freedom of speech unless their language endangers the nation.

**clericalism**    The exercise of political power by religious leaders and organizations, such as established religions.

**closed primaries**    Primaries in which only party members can vote—and only in the party in which they are registered.

**closed-ended question**    Survey question that asks people to choose their answer from a set of prespecified alternatives.

**cloture**    Motion to end debate; requires 60 votes to pass.

**CNN effect**    Purported ability of TV to raise a distant foreign affairs situation to national prominence by broadcasting vivid pictures.

**coalition government**    Occurs when two or more minority parties must join together in order to elect a prime minister. Such governments are common in multi-party systems.

**coattails**    Positive electoral effect of a popular presidential candidate on congressional candidates of the party.

**Cold War**    The 43-year period (1946–1989) during which the United States and the Soviet Union threatened one another with mutual destruction by nuclear warfare.

**colonial assembly**    Lower legislative chamber elected by male property owners in a colony.

**colonial council**    Upper legislative chamber whose members were appointed by British officials upon the recommendation of the governor.

**commander in chief**    The president in his constitutional role as head of the armed forces.

**commerce clause**    Constitutional provision that gives Congress power to regulate commerce "among the states."

**commercial speech**    Advertising or other speech made for business purposes; may be regulated.

**communism**    An extreme type of socialism based on the work of Karl Marx, who taught that history is a product of the struggle between those who exploit and those who are exploited.

**compositional effect**    A change in the behavior of a group that arises from a change in the group's composition, not from a change in the behavior of individuals in the group.

**concurring opinion**    A written opinion prepared by judges who vote with the majority but who wish to disagree with or elaborate on some aspect of the majority opinion.

**conference**    What Republicans call their caucus.

**conference committee**    Group of representatives from both the House and the Senate who iron out the differences between the two chambers' versions of a bill or resolution.

**Congressional Budget Office (CBO)**    Congressional agency that evaluates the president's budget as well as the budgetary implications of all other legislation.

**Connecticut Compromise**    Constitutional convention proposal that created a House proportionate to population and a Senate in which all states were represented equally.

**constituency**    Those legally entitled to vote for a public official.

**constituency service**    The totality of Congress members' district service and constituent assistance work.

**constituent assistance**    Efforts of members of Congress to help individuals and groups when they have difficulties with federal agencies.

**Constitution**    Basic governing document of the United States.

**containment**    U.S. policy that attempted to stop the spread of communism in the expectation that this system of government would eventually collapse on its own.

**cooperative federalism**    The theory that all levels of government can work together to solve common problems. Also known as *marble-cake federalism.*

**corporatist**    The official representation of important interest groups in government decision-making bodies.

**Council of Economic Advisors (CEA)**    Three economists who head up a professional staff that advises the president on economic policy.

**criminal code**    Laws regulating relations between individuals and society. Alleged violators are prosecuted by government.

**critical election**    Election that marks the emergence of a new, lasting alignment of partisan support within the electorate.

*de facto* **segregation**    Segregation that occurs as the result of decisions by private individuals.

*de jure* **segregation**    Racial segregation that is legally sanctioned.

**debt**    the accumulation of yearly deficits.

**Declaration of Independence**    Document signed in 1776 declaring the United States to be a country independent of Great Britain.

**defendant**    One accused of violating the civil or criminal code.

**deficit**    The amount by which annual spending exceeds revenue.

**delegate**    Role a representative plays when following the wishes of those who have elected him or her.

**democracy**    System in which governmental power is widely shared among the citizens, usually through free and open elections.

**department**    Organizational unit into which many agencies of the federal government are grouped.

**Department of Defense**    Cabinet department responsible for managing the U.S. armed forces.

**deregulation**    Removal of government rules that once controlled an industry.

**devolution**    Return of governmental responsibilities to state and local governments.

**dignified aspect**    According to Walter Bagehot, the aspect of government, including royalty and ceremony, that generates citizen respect and loyalty.

**Dillon's rule**    Legal doctrine that local governments are mere creatures of the state.

**direct action**    Everything from peaceful sit-ins and demonstrations to riots and even rebellion.

**direct democracy**    Type of democracy in which ordinary people are the government, making all the laws themselves.

**direct mail**    Computer-generated letters, faxes, and other communications to people who might be sympathetic to an appeal for money or support.

**direct primary**    A method of choosing party candidates by popular vote of all self-identified party members. This method of nominating candidates is virtually unknown outside the United States.

**discharge petition**    Means by which a House majority (218) may take a bill out of a committee that refuses to report it.

**dissenting opinion**    Written opinion presenting the reasoning of judges who vote against the majority.

**distributive tendency**    Tendency of Congress to spread the benefits of any program widely and thinly across the districts of the members.

**distributive theory**    Theory that sees committees as a standing log-roll in which members get to serve on the committees most important to them.

**district attorney**    Person responsible for prosecuting criminal cases.

**district service**    Efforts of members of Congress to make sure that their districts get a share of federal projects and programs.

**diversity**    A concept relative to time and place; currently refers primarily to ethnic and racial distinctions among people (as opposed to, say, class or occupational differences.

**divided government**    Said to exist when a single party does not control the presidency and both houses of Congress.

**divine right**    Doctrine that says God selects the sovereign for the people.

**domestic policy**    Government programs and regulations that directly affect those living within a country.

**double jeopardy**    Placing someone on trial for the same crime twice.

**dual sovereignty**    A theory of federalism saying that both the national and state governments have final authority over their own policy domains.

**due process clause**    Found in the Fifth and Fourteenth Amendments to the Constitution; forbids deprivation of life, liberty, or property without due process of law.

**earmark**    A specific congressional designation as to the way money is to be spent.

**Earned Income Tax Credit (EITC)**    Provision that gives back tax payments to those who have little income.

**efficient aspect**    According to Walter Bagehot, the aspect of government that involves making policy, administering the laws, and settling disputes.

**election-cycle interpretation**    The argument that, whatever their party, presidents attempt to slow the economy early in their terms and then expand it as their opportunity for reelection approaches.

**electoral college**   Those chosen to cast a direct vote for president by a process determined by each state.

**electoral incentive**   Desire to obtain or retain elected office.

**electoral system**   A means of translating popular votes into control of public offices.

**electoral vote**   Cast by electors, with each state receiving one vote for each of its members of the House of Representatives and one vote for each of its senators.

**eligible voting-age population**   All people in the United States over the age of 18 minus those not eligible to vote because of mental illness, criminal conviction, or noncitizenship.

**embassy**   The structure that houses ambassadors and their diplomatic aides in the capital cities of foreign countries.

**end run**   Effort by agencies to avoid OMB controls by appealing to allies in Congress.

**Environmental Protection Agency (EPA)**   Agency responsible for issuing regulations designed to protect the environment from unwanted pollutants.

**equal protection clause**   Fourteenth Amendment clause specifying that no state can deny any of its people equal protection under the law.

**Equal Rights Amendment (ERA)**   Proposed amendment to the Constitution that banned gender discrimination.

**equality of condition**   The notion that all individuals have a right to a more or less equal part of the material goods that society produces.

**equality of opportunity**   The notion that individuals should have an equal chance to advance economically through individual talent and hard work.

**equal-time rule**   Promulgated by the FCC, required any station selling time to a candidate to sell time to other candidates at comparable rates.

**establishment of religion clause**   Denies the government the power to establish any single religious practice as superior.

**executive agreement**   Agreement with foreign countries that requires only a presidential signature.

**Executive Office of the President (EOP)**   Agency that houses both top coordinating offices and other operating agencies.

**executive order**   A presidential directive that has the force of law, though it is not enacted by Congress.

**executive privilege**   The right of members of the executive branch to have private communications among themselves that need not be shared with Congress.

**exit poll**   Survey of actual voters taken as they leave the polling stations.

**externalities**   Consequences of activities that affect those not directly engaged in them.

**fairness doctrine**   Promulgated by the FCC, required stations to carry some public affairs programming and to balance the points of view expressed.

**fascism**   Rule by a charismatic dictator supported by a strong party that permeates society; generally supports capital against labor and is associated with extreme nationalism.

**federal district court**   The lowest level of the federal court system and the court in which most federal trials are held.

**Federal Reserve System**   The country's central bank, which executes monetary policy by manipulating the supply of funds that lower banks can lend.

**federalism**   Division of sovereignty between at least two different levels of government.

**Federalists**   Those who wrote and campaigned on behalf of ratification of the Constitution.

**Federalist Papers**   Essays that were written in support of the Constitution's ratification and have become a classic argument for the American constitutional system.

**fiduciary**   Someone whose duty is to act in the best interest of someone else.

**fighting words doctrine**   The principle, endorsed by the Supreme Court in *Chaplinsky* v. *New Hampshire*(1942), that some words constitute violent acts.

**filibuster**   Delaying tactic by which one or more senators refuse to allow a bill or resolution to be considered, either by speaking indefinitely or by offering dilatory motions and amendments.

**filing deadline**   The latest date on which a candidate for office may file official papers or pay required fees to state election officials.

**First Continental Congress**   The first quasi-governmental institution that spoke for nearly all the colonies (1774).

**First Lady**   Traditional title of the president's spouse.

**fiscal policy**   The sum total of government taxing and spending decisions, which determines the level of the deficit or surplus.

**flat tax**   A tax that is neither progressive nor regressive; everyone pays at the same rate.

**focus groups**   Small groups used to explore how ordinary people think about issues and how they react to the language of political appeals.

**food stamps**   Public assistance program that provides recipients with stamps that can be used to purchase food.

**foreign policy**   Conduct of relations among nation states.

**foreign service**   Diplomats who staff U.S. embassies and consulates.

**framing**   Stating an argument in such a way as to emphasize one set of considerations and deemphasize others.

**franchise**    The right to vote.

**frank**    Name given to representatives' and senators' free use of the U.S. mail for sending communications to constituents.

**free exercise of religion clause**    Protects the right of individuals to practice their religion.

**free-rider problem**    Occurs when people can enjoy the benefits of group activity without bearing any of the costs.

**fundamental freedoms doctrine**    Court doctrine stating that laws impinging on the freedoms that are fundamental to the preservation of democratic practice—the freedoms of speech, press, assembly, and religion—are to be scrutinized by the courts more closely than other legislation. These are also termed the *preferred freedoms*.

**general election**    Final election that selects the office holder.

**general revenue sharing**    The most comprehensive of block grants, which gives money to state and local governments to be used for any purpose whatsoever.

**gerrymandering**    Drawing boundary lines of congressional districts in order to confer on advantage on some partisan or political interest.

*Gideon v. Wainwright*    Supreme Court decision in 1963 giving indigent people accused of crimes the right to court-appointed counsel.

**glass ceiling**    The invisible barrier that has limited women's opportunities for advancement to the highest ranks of politics, business, and the professions.

**government**    The institution in society that has a "monopoly of the legitimate use of physical force."

**government corporation**    Independent organization created by Congress to fulfill functions related to business.

**grandfather clause**    Racially restrictive provision of certain southern laws, permitting a man to vote if his father or grandfather could have voted.

**grassroots lobbying**    Efforts by groups and associations to influence elected officials indirectly, by arousing their constituents.

**gross domestic product**    The measure of the total value of economic activity in a nation in one year.

**hammer**    Harsh penalty set by Congress if a regulatory agency does not achieve a statutory objective.

**Hatch Act**    1939 law prohibiting federal employees from engaging in political campaigning and solicitation.

**honeymoon**    Period early in a president's term when partisan conflict and media criticism are minimal.

**idealists**    Those who say that U.S. foreign policy should be guided primarily by democratic principles-the spread of liberty, equality, human rights, and respect for international law throughout the world.

**ideology**    System of beliefs in which one or more organizing principles connect the individual's views on a wide range of issues.

**impeachment**    Recommendation by a majority of the House of Representatives that a president, other executive-branch official, or judge of the federal courts be removed from office; removal depends on two-thirds vote of the  Senate.

**implementation**    The way in which grant programs are administered at the local level.

**in-and-outers**    Political appointees who come in, go out, and come back in again with each change in administration.

**incumbency advantage**    The electoral advantage a candidate enjoys by virtue of being an incumbent, over and above her or his other personal and political characteristics.

**independent counsel** (originally called special prosecutor)    Legal officer appointed by a court to investigate allegations of criminal activity against high-ranking members of the executive branch.Law expired in 1999.

**independent regulatory agencies**    Agencies that have quasi-judicial responsibilities.

**individual motivations for voting**    The tangible and intangible benefits and costs of exercising one's right to vote.

**inflation**    A sustained rise in the price level such that people need more money to purchase the same amount of goods and services.

**information cost**    The time and mental effort required to absorb and store information, whether from conversations or the media.

**informational theory**    Theory that sees committees as means of providing reliable information about the actual consequences of the legislation that members could adopt.

**inherent executive power**    Presidential authority inherent to the executive branch of government, though not specifically mentioned in the Constitution.

**initiative**    Proposed laws or state constitutional amendments placed on the ballot via citizen petition.

**inner cabinet**    The four original departments (State, Treasury, Justice, and Defense) whose secretaries typically have the closest ties to the president.

**interest group**    Organization or association of people with common interests that engages in politics on behalf of its members.

**intergovernmental grant**    Grant from the national government to a state or local government.

**Iran–Contra affair**    An allegedly illegal diversion of funds from the sale of arms to Iran to a guerrilla group in Nicaragua.

**iron curtain**    Armed barrier during the Cold War that prevented movement across national borders between communist East Europe and democratic West Europe.

**iron triangle**    Close, stable connection among agencies, interest groups, and congressional committees.

**isolationism**    A foreign policy that keeps the United States separate from the conflicts taking place among other nations.

**issue networks**    Loose, competitive relationships among policy experts, interest groups, congressional committees, and government agencies.

**issue public**    Group of people particularly affected by or concerned with specific issues.

**Jim Crow Laws**    Laws passed by southern states, after Reconstruction, enforcing segregation.

**Joint Chiefs of Staff**    The heads of all the military services, together with a chair and vice-chair nominated by the president and confirmed by the Senate.

**judicial activism**    Doctrine that says the principle of *stare decisis* should sometimes be sacrificed in order to adapt the Constitution to changing conditions.

**judicial restraint**    Doctrine that says courts should, if at all possible, avoid overturning a prior court decision.

**judicial review**    Power of the courts to declare null and void laws of Congress and of state legislatures they find unconstitutional.

**Keynesianism**    Economic policy based on the belief that governments can control the economy by manipulating demand, running deficits to expand it and surpluses to contract it.

**laboratories of democracy**    Doctrine that state and local governments contribute to democracy by providing places where experiments are tried and new theories tested.

**law clerk**    Young, influential aide to a Supreme Court justice.

**League of Nations**    International organization created after World War I to settle international disputes; became the precursor of the United Nations.

**legal distinction**    The legal difference between a case at hand and previous cases decided by the courts.

**libel**    False statement defaming another.

**liberalism**    A philosophy that elevates and empowers the individual as opposed to religious, hereditary, governmental, or other forms of authority.

**line item veto**    Presidential authority to negate particular provisions of a law, granted by Congress in 1996 but struck down by the Supreme Court in 1998.

**living-Constitution theory**    A theory of constitutional interpretation that places the meaning of the Constitution in light of the total history of the United States.

**lobbying**    Attempts by representatives of groups and associations to directly influence the decisions of government officials.

**lobbyist**    One who engages in lobbying.

**log-rolling**    Colloquial term given to politicians' trading of favors, votes, or generalized support for each other's proposals.

**machine**    A highly organized party under the control of a boss, based on patronage and control of government activities. They were common in many cities in the late nineteenth and early twentieth centuries.

**majority**    50 percent plus one.

**majority-minority districts**    District in which a minority group is the numerical majority.

**majority leader**    The Speaker's chief lieutenant in the House and the most important office in the Senate. He or she is responsible for managing the floor.

**mandate**    Implied authorization by the electorate to implement the party platform.

*Mapp* **v.** *Ohio*    Supreme Court decision saying that any evidence obtained without a proper search warrant may not be introduced in a trial.

**marble-cake federalism**    The theory that all levels of government can work together to solve common problems. Also known as *cooperative federalism*.

**Marbury v. Madison**    Supreme Court decision (1803) in which the court first exercised the power of judicial review.

**markup**    Process in which a committee or subcommittee considers and revises a bill that has been introduced.

**mass media**    Means of communication that are technologically capable of reaching most people and economically affordable to most.

**mass public**    Ordinary people for whom politics is a peripheral concern.

**matching funds**    Public moneys (from $3 check-offs on income tax returns) that the Federal Election Commission distributes to primary candidates according to a prespecified formula.

**Mayflower Compact**    First document in colonial America in which the people gave their expressed consent to be governed.

*McCulloch* **v.** *Maryland*    Decision of 1819 in which the Supreme Court declared unconstitutional the state's power to tax a federal government entity.

**measurement error**    The natural uncertainty that comes from using a population subsample— dictated by statistical theory.

**Medicaid**    Program that provides medical care to those of low income.

**Medicare**    Program that provides social security recipients a broad range of medical benefits.

**minimal-effects thesis**    Theory that the mass media have little or no effect on public opinion.

**minority leader**    Leader of the minority party, who speaks for the party in dealing with the majority.

*Miranda* **v.** *Arizona*    Supreme Court decision stating that accused persons must be told by police that they need not testify against themselves.

**mobilization**   The efforts of parties, groups, and activists to encourage their supporters to participate in politics.

**monetarism**   An economic school of thought that rejects Keynesianism, arguing that only monetary policy affects the state of the economy.

**monetary policy**   The actions taken by government to affect the level of interest rates.

**Monroe Doctrine**   Policy that declared the Western Hemisphere to be free of European colonial influence (1819).

**mugwumps**   A group of civil service reformers organized in the 1880s who maintained that government officials should be chosen on a merit basis.

**multiculturalism**   The idea that ethnic and cultural groups should maintain their identity within the larger society and respect one another's differences.

**multi-party system**   System in which more than two parties compete for control of government. Most of the world's democracies are multi-party systems.

**multiple referrals**   Said to occur when party leaders give more than one committee responsibility for considering a bill.

**National Association for the Advancement of Colored People (NAACP)**   Civil rights organization, dating from 1909, that relied heavily on a legal strategy to pursue its objectives.

**national convention**   Quadrennial gathering of party officials and delegates who select presidential and vice-presidential nominees and adopt party platforms. Extension of the direct primary to the presidential level after 1968 has greatly reduced the importance of the conventions.

**national forces**   Electoral effects felt across most states and congressional districts, most often generated by especially strong or weak presidential candidates, party performance, or the state of the economy.

**National Security Council (NSC)**   White House agency responsible for coordinating U.S. foreign policy.

**natural monopoly**   A situation in which a public service is best provided by a single company.

**necessary and proper clause**   Constitutional clause that gives Congress the power to take all actions that are "necessary and proper" to the carrying out of its delegated powers. Also known as the *elastic clause.*

**New Deal**   Programs created by the Franklin Roosevelt administration that expanded the power of the federal government for the purpose of stimulating economic recovery and establishing a national safety net.

**New Jersey Plan**   Small-state proposal for constitutional reform.

**new media**   Cable and satellite TV, fax, e-mail, and the Internet—the consequences of the technological advances of the past few decades.

**nullification**   A doctrine developed by John Calhoun that says that states have the authority to declare acts of Congress unconstitutional.

**obscenity**   Publicly offensive language or portrayals with no redeeming social value.

**Office of Management and Budget (OMB)**   Agency responsible for coordinating the work of departments and agencies of the executive branch.

**official turnout**   Defined by the Census Bureau as the number of people voting for president divided by the size of the voting-age population.

**oligarchy**   Government by a few who gain office by means of wealth, military power, or membership in a single political party.

**ombudsman**   Official whose job it is to mediate conflicts between citizens and government bureaucracies.

**open-ended question**   Survey question that allows people to answer in their own words.

**open primaries**   Primaries in which any registered voter can vote in any party's primary.

**open seat**   A House or Senate race with no incumbent (because of death or retirement).

**opinion**   In legal parlance, a court's written explanation for its decision.

**Original-intent**   A theory of constitutional interpretation that determines the constitutionality of a law by ascertaining the intentions of those who wrote the Constitution.

**outer cabinet**   Newer departments that have fewer ties to the president and are more influenced by interest-group pressures.

**override**   Congressional passage of a bill by a two-thirds vote over the president's veto.

**partisan interpretation**   The argument that Democratic administrations set economic policy to benefit lower-income, wage-earning groups and that Republican administrations set economic policy to benefit higher-income, business and professional groups.

**party identification**   A person's subjective feeling of affiliation with a party.

**party identification**   A person's subjective feeling of affiliation with a party.

**party image**   A set of widely held associations between a party and particular issues and values.

**Patriots**   Political group defending colonial American liberties against British infringements.

**patronage**   Appointing individuals to public office in exchange for their political support. Widely practiced in the eighteenth and nineteenth centuries and continues to present day.

**patronage**   Jobs, contracts, or favors given to political friends and allies.

**Pendleton Act**   Legislation in 1881 creating the Civil Service Commission.

**permanent campaign** Condition that prevails when the next election campaign begins as soon as the last has ended and the line between electioneering and governing has disappeared.

**plain meaning of the text** A theory of constitutional - interpretation that determines the constitutionality of a law in light of what the words of the Constitution obviously seem to say.

**plaintiff** One who brings legal charges against another.

**plea bargain** Agreement between prosecution and defense that the accused will admit having committed a crime, provided that other charges are dropped and the recommended sentence is shortened.

**plenary session** Activities of a court in which all judges participate.

*Plessy v. Ferguson* Court decision declaring separate but equal public facilities constitutional.

**pluralism** A school of thought holding that politics is the clash of groups that represent all important interests in society and check and balance each other.

**pocket veto** Presidential veto after congressional adjournment, executed merely by not signing a bill into law.

**policy deliberation** Debate and discussion by groups and political leaders over issues placed on the policy agenda.

**policy enactment** Passage of a law by public officials.

**policy implementation** Translation of legislation into a set of government programs or regulations.

**policy outcome** Effect of policy outputs on individuals and businesses.

**policy output** Provision of services to citizens or regulation of their conduct.

**political action committee (PAC)** Specialized organization for raising and contributing campaign funds.

**political activists** People who voluntarily participate in politics; they are more interested in and committed to particular issues and candidates than are ordinary citizens.

**political culture** Collection of beliefs and values about the justification and operation of a country's government.

**political efficacy** The belief that one can make a difference in politics by expressing an opinion or acting politically

**political elite** Activists and office holders who are deeply interested in and knowledgeable about politics.

**political entrepreneurs** People willing to assume the costs of forming and maintaining an organization even when others may free-ride on them.

**political parties** Groups of like-minded people who band together in an attempt to take control of government.

**political socialization** The set of psychological and sociological processes by which families, schools, religious organizations, communities, and other societal units inculcate beliefs and values in their members.

**poll tax** Fee that allowed one to vote.

**popular model of democracy** Type of representative democracy in which ordinary people participate actively and closely constrain the actions of public officials.

**popular vote** The total vote cast for a candidate across the nation.

**precedent** Previous court decision or ruling applicable to a particular case.

**president *pro tempore*** President of the Senate, who presides in the absence of the vice-president.

**presidential popularity** Evaluation of president by voters, usually as measured by a survey question asking the adult population how well they think the president is doing his job.

**primary** Preliminary election in which eligible voters select a party's nominee.

**primary election** Preliminary election that narrows the number of candidates by determining who will be the nominees in the general election.

**priming** Occurs when the media affect the standards people use to evaluate political figures or the severity of a problem.

**prior restraint doctrine** Legal doctrine that gives individuals the right to publish without prior restraint—that is, without first submitting material to government censor.

**private goods** Goods that you must purchase to enjoy, and your consumption of which precludes that of others.

**professional legislature** Legislature whose members serve full-time and for long periods.

**progressive tax** A tax structured so that higher-income people pay a larger proportion of their income in taxes.

**progressives** Middle-class reformers of the late nineteenth and early twentieth centuries who weakened the power of the machines and attempted to clean up elections and government.

**proportional representation (PR)** Electoral system in which parties receive a share of seats in parliament that is proportional to the popular vote they receive.

**proposition** A shorthand reference to an initiative or a referendum.

**proprietary colony** Colony governed either by a prominent English noble or by a company. See *royal colony.*

**prospective voting** Voting on the basis of the candidates' policy promises.

**psychic benefits of voting** Intangible rewards of voting, such as satisfaction with doing one's duty and feelings of solidarity with the community.

**public assistance**   Programs that provide to low-income households a limited income and access to essential goods and services.

**public defender**   Attorney whose full-time responsibilities are to provide for the legal defense of indigent criminal suspects.

**public goods**   Goods that you can enjoy without contributing—by free-riding on the efforts of those who do.

**public opinion**   Those opinions that are held by private persons and that governments find it prudent to heed in the aggregate.

**quota**   Specific number of positions set aside for a specific group; said by the Supreme Court to be unconstitutional.

**"rally 'round the flag" effect**   The tendency for the public to back presidents in moments of crisis.

**realigning election**   Another term for a critical election.

**realignment**   Occurs when the pattern of group support for political parties shifts in a significant and lasting way, such as in the latter half of the twentieth century, when the white South shifted from Democratic to Republican.

**realists**   Those who say that U.S. foreign policy best protects democracy when it safe-guards its own economic and military strength.

**reapportionment**   The allocation of House seats to the states after each decennial census.

**recall election**   Attempt to remove an official from office before the completion of the term.

**receiver**   Court official who has the authority to see that judicial orders are carried out.

**recess appointment**   An appointment made when the Senate is in recess.

**recession**   A slowdown in economic activity, officially defined as a decline that persists for two quarters (six months).

**reconstruction**   Period after the Civil War when southern states were subject to a military presence.

**redistricting**   Drawing new boundaries of congressional districts, usually after the decennial census.

**referendum**   A law or state constitutional amendment that is proposed by a legislature or city council but does not go into effect unless the required majority of voters approve it.

**registered voters**   Those legally eligible to vote who have registered in accordance with the requirements prevailing in their state and locality.

**regressive tax**   A tax structured so that higher-income people pay a smaller proportion of their income in taxes.

**regulation**   Rules and standards that control economic, social, and political activities.

**remand**   To send a case to a lower court to determine the best way of implementing the higher court's decision.

**remedy**   Court-ordered action designed to compensate plaintiffs for wrongs they have suffered.

**rent subsidies**   Help in paying rent for low-income families, provided that they select designated housing.

**representative democracy**   An indirect form of democracy in which the people choose representatives who determine what government does.

**responsible model of democracy**   Type of representative democracy in which public officials have considerable freedom of action but are held accountable by the people for the decisions they make.

**restorationist**   Judge who thinks that the only way the original meaning of the Constitution can be restored is by ignoring the doctrine of *stare decisis* until liberal decisions have been reversed.

**restrictive housing covenant**   Legal promise by home buyers that they would not resell to an African American; enforcement declared unconstitutional by Supreme Court.

**retrospective voting**   Voting on the basis of the past performance of the incumbent administration

**reversal**   The overturning of a lower court decision by an appeals court or the Supreme Court.

**right of privacy**   Right to keep free of government interference those aspects of one's personal life that do not affect others.

**rotation**   The practice whereby a member of Congress stepped down after a term or two so that someone else could have the office.

**royal colony**   Colony governed by the king's representative with the advice of an elected assembly. See *proprietary colony*.

**rule**   Specifies the terms and conditions under which a bill or resolution will be considered on the floor of the House—in particular, how long debate will last, how time will be allocated, and the number and type of amendments that will be in order.

**sampling error**   The error that arises in public opinion surveys as a result of relying on a representative but small sample of the larger population.

**Second Continental Congress**   Political authority that directed the struggle for independence beginning in 1775.

**secretary**   Head of a department within the executive branch.

**secretary of defense**   The president's chief civilian advisor on defense matters and overall head of all the Army, Navy, and Air Force.

**secretary of state**   Officially, the president's chief foreign policy advisor and head of the Department of State, the agency responsible for conducting diplomatic relations.

**select committee**   Temporary committee appointed to deal with a specific issue or problem.

**selection bias**    The error that occurs when a sample systematically includes or excludes people with certain attitudes.

**selection principle**    Rule of thumb according to which stories with certain characteristics are chosen over stories without those characteristics.

**selective benefits**    Side benefits of belonging to an organization that are limited to contributing members of the organization.

**selective incorporation**    The case-by-case incorporation, by the courts, of the Bill of Rights into the due process clause of the Fourteenth Amendment.

**semi-closed primaries**    Primaries in which independents can vote in one of the party primaries.

**senatorial courtesy**    An informal rule that the Senate will not confirm nominees within or from a state unless they have the approval of the senior senator of the state from the president's party.

**seniority**    Practice by which the majority party member with the longest continuous service on a committee becomes the chair.

**separate but equal doctrine**    Rule stating that the equal protection clause was not violated by the fact of racial segregation alone, provided the separated facilities were equal.

**separation of church and state doctrine**    The principle that a wall should separate the government from religious activity.

**separation of powers**    A system of government in which different institutions exercise different components of governmental power.

**sequester**    To house jurors privately, away from any information other than that presented in the courtroom.

**Shays's Rebellion**    Uprising in western Massachusetts in 1786 led by Revolutionary War captain Daniel Shays.

**simple random sample**    A sample in which every individual in the population has an equal probability of being included.

**sin tax**    Tax intended to discourage unwanted behavior

**single-issue voter**    Voter who cares so deeply about some particular issue that a candidate's position on this one issue determines his or her vote.

**single-member, simple plurality (SMSP)**    Electoral system in which the country is divided into geographic districts, and the candidates who win the most votes within their districts are elected.

**social connectedness**    The degree to which individuals are integrated into society—families, churches, neighborhoods, groups, and so forth.

**social insurance**    Program that provides benefits in return for contributions made by workers.

**social issues**    Issues such as obscenity, feminism, gay rights, capital punishment, and prayer in schools that reflect personal values more than economic interests.

**social movement**    Broad-based demand for government action on some problem or issue, such as civil rights for blacks and women or environmental protection.

**social policy**    Domestic policy programs designed to help those thought to be in need of government assistance.

**Social security**    Social insurance program for senior citizens.

**socialism**    A philosophy that supports government ownership and operation of the means of production as well as government determination of the level of social and economic benefits that people receive.

**socialization**    The end result of all the processes by which individuals form their beliefs and values in the home, schools, churches, communities, and workplaces.

**solicitor general**    Government official responsible for presenting before the courts the position of the presidential administration.

**sovereignty**    Fundamental governmental authority.

**Speaker**    The presiding officer of the House of Representatives; normally, the Speaker is the leader of the majority party.

**spending clause**    Constitutional provision that gives Congress the power to collect taxes to provide for the general welfare.

**spin**    The positive or negative slant that reporters or anchors put on their reports.

**spoils system**    A system of government employment in which workers are hired on the basis of party loyalty.

**sponsor**    Representative or senator who introduces a bill or resolution.

**Stamp Act Congress**    A meeting in 1765 of delegates from 13 colonies to oppose the Stamp Act; the first political organization that brought leaders from several colonies together for a common purpose.

**stamp tax**    Passed by Parliament in 1765, it required people in the colonies to purchase a small stamp to be affixed to legal and other documents.

**standing committee**    Committee with fixed membership and jurisdiction, continuing from Congress to Congress.

*stare decisis*    In court rulings, reliance on consistency with precedents. See also *precedent*.

**state action doctrine**    Rule stating that only the actions of state and local governments, not those of private individuals, must conform to the equal protection clause.

**State of the Union address**    Annual speech delivered by the president in fulfillment of the constitutional obligation of reporting to Congress on the state of the Union.

**statutory interpretation**    The judicial act of interpreting and applying the law to particular cases.

**subgovernment**   A congressional committee, bureaucratic agency, and allied interest groups who combine to dominate policy making in some specified policy area.

**suffrage**   Another term for the right to vote.

**sunshine law**   A 1976 law requiring that federal government meetings be held in public.

**Supplemental Security Income (SSI)**   Provides disabled people of low income with income assistance.

**supply-side economics**   Economic policy based on the belief that governments can keep the economy healthy by supplying the conditions (especially low taxes and minimal regulation) that encourage private economic activity.

**supremacy clause**   Constitutional provision that says the laws of the national government "shall be the supreme Law of the Land."

**surplus**   The amount by which annual revenue exceeds spending.

**survey research**   The scientific design and administration of public opinion polls.

**suspect classification**   Categorization of a particular group that will be closely scrutinized by the courts to see whether its use is unconstitutional.

**suspension of the rules**   Fast-track procedure for considering bills and resolutions in the House; debate is limited to 40 minutes, no amendments are in order, and a two-thirds majority is required for passage.

**tax base**   Types of activities, types of property, or kinds of investments that are subject to taxation.

**tax burden**   The total amount of tax that a household pays.

**tax preferences**   Activities, property, or investments that receive special tax treatment.

**taxation without representation**   Levying of taxes by a government in which the people are not represented by their own elected officials.

**Temporary Assistance for Needy Families (TANF)**   Welfare reform law passed by Congress in 1996.

**three-fifths compromise**   Constitutional provision that counted each slave as three-fifths of a person when calculating representation in the House of Representatives; repealed by the Fourteenth Amendment.

**ticket splitting**   Occurs when a voter does not vote a straight party ticket.

**Tonkin Gulf Resolution**   Congressional resolution giving the president the authority to send troops to Vietnam.

**Tories**   Those colonists who opposed independence from Great Britain.

**transition**   The period after a presidential candidate has won the November election but before the candidate assumes office as president on January 20.

**treaties**   Official agreements with foreign countries that are ratified by the Senate.

**trial venue**   Place where a trial is held.

**trustee**   Role a representative plays when acting in accordance with his or her own best judgment.

**two-party system**   System in which only two significant parties compete for office. Such systems are in the minority among world democracies.

**two-presidency theory**   Theory that explains why presidents exercise greater power over foreign affairs than over domestic policy.

**two-thirds rule**   Rule governing Democratic national conventions from 1832 to 1936. It required that the presidential and vice-presidential nominees receive at least two-thirds of the delegates' votes.

**tyranny of the majority**   Stifling of dissent by those voted into power by the majority.

**Unanimous-consent agreement**   Agreement that sets forth the terms and conditions according to which the Senate will consider a bill; these are individually negotiated by the leadership for each bill.

**unemployment**   The circumstance that exists when people who are willing to work at the prevailing wage cannot get jobs.

**unfunded mandates**   Federal regulations that impose burdens on state and local governments without appropriating enough money to cover costs.

**unitary government**   System under which all authority is held by a single, national government.

**United Nations**   Organization of all nationstates, whose purpose is to preserve world peace and foster economic and social development throughout the world.

**U.S. attorney**   Person responsible for prosecuting violations of the federal criminal code.

***U.S.v. Curtiss-Wright***   Supreme Court decision in which Congress is given the authority to delegate foreign policy responsibilities to the president.

**veto power**   Presidential rejection of congressional legislation. May be overridden by a two-thirds vote in each congressional chamber. Most state governors also have veto power over their legislatures.

**Virginia Plan**   Constitutional proposal supported by convention delegates from large states.

**Voting-age population**   All people in the United States over the age of 18.

**War on Poverty**   One of the most controversial of the Great Society programs. Designed to enhance the economic opportunity of low-income citizens.

**War Powers Resolution**   1973 congressional resolution requiring the president to notify Congress formally upon ordering U.S. troops into military action.

**Whigs**   Political opposition in eighteenth-century England that developed a theory of rights and representation.

**whips**    Members of Congress who serve as informational channels between the leadership and the rank and file, conveying the leadership's views and intentions to the members, and vice versa.

**White House Office**    Political appointees who work directly for the president, many of whom occupy offices in the White House.

**white primary**    Primary elections, held by the Democratic party, that excluded nonwhites from participation in many southern states.

**winner-take-all voting**    Any voting procedure in which the side with the most votes gets all of the seats or delegates at stake.

**writ of *certiorari* (cert)**    A document issued by the Supreme Court indicating that the Court will review a decision taken by a lower court.

***Youngstown Sheet and Tube Co.v. Sawyer***    Case in which the Supreme Court placed limits on the executive power of the president.

**zone of acceptance**    Range within which Congress allows agencies to interpret and apply statutes.

# ENDNOTES

## TO OUR COLLEAGUES

1. *Pluralist Democracy in the United States: Conflict and Consent* (Chicago: Rand McNally, 1967).

2. Robert Dahl, *The New Political (Dis)Order* (Berkeley, CA: IGS Press, 1994): 1.

3. Ibid., 5.

4. "The Civic Culture: Prehistory, Retrospect, and Prospect," Center for the Study of Democracy Research Monograph No. 1, University of California, Irvine, 1996: 14.

5. James Stimson, "Opinion and Representation," *American Political Science Review* 89(1995): 181.

6. James Barnes, "Clintonís Horse Race Presidency," *National Journal* (5/29/93): 1310.

7. The Transition to Governing Project, directed by Norman Ornstein and Thomas Mann.

## CHAPTER 1

1. For an informative collection of public opinion data on welfare, see "Welfare: The American Dilemma," *The Public Perspective,* February/March 1995: 39–46.

2. For a dispassionate academic work, see Lawrence Mead, *The New Politics of Poverty* (New York: Basic Books, 1992). The most prominent conservative critiques were those of George Gilder, *Wealth and Poverty* (New York: Bantam, 1981) and Charles Murray, *Losing Ground: American Social Policy, 1950–1970* (New York: Basic Books, 1984).

3. Martin Gilens, "Race and Poverty in America: Public Misperceptions and the American News Media," *Public Opinion Quarterly* 60 (1996): 515–541.

4. For background on Clinton's promises and actions, see "Clinton, Congress Talk of Welfare Reform," *1993 CQ Almanac* (Washington, DC: Congressional Quarterly Inc., 1994), pp. 373–375; and "Welfare Reform Takes a Back Seat," *1994 CQ Almanac* (Washington, DC: Congressional Quarterly Inc., 1995), pp. 364–365.

5. Details of the 1995–1996 welfare reform debate appear in "Welfare Bill Clears Under Veto Threat," *1995 CQ Almanac* (Washington, DC: Congressional Quarterly Inc., 1996): 7–35 to 7–52.

6. Jeffrey Katz, "After 60 Years, Most Control Is Passing to States," *Congressional Quarterly Weekly Report,* August 3, 1996: 2190.

7. *Ibid.,* p. 2195.

8. "Half a Million Voters' Choices," *Governing,* April 1995: 15.

9. Herbert Jacob and Kenneth Vines, "Courts," in Virginia Gray, Herbert Jacob, and Kenneth Vines, eds., *Politics in the American States: A Comparative Analysis,* 4th ed. (Boston: Little, Brown, 1983), p. 238.

10. Thomas Cronin, *Direct Democracy* (Cambridge, MA: Harvard University Press, 1989); and David Magleby, *Direct Legislation* (Baltimore, MD: Johns Hopkins University Press, 1984).

11. Anthony King, *Running Scared: Why America's Politicians Campaign Too Much and Govern Too Little* (New York: Free Press, 1996), pp. 2–3.

12. Joseph S. Nye, Jr., Philip D. Zelikow, and David C. King, eds., *Why People Don't Trust Government* (Cambridge, MA: Harvard University Press, 1997).

13. H. H. Gerth and C. W. Mills, trans., *From Max Weber* (New York: Oxford University Press, 1946), p. 78.

14. Chuck Henning, *The Wit and Wisdom of Politics: Expanded Edition* (Golden, CO: Fulcrum, 1992), p. 91.

15. The novel *Primary Colors,* in which the main character is modeled on Bill Clinton, emphasizes this dimension of the Clinton personality.

16. Jimmy Carter, *A Government as Good as Its People* (New York: Simon & Schuster, 1977), p. 102.

17. "Federalist 51."

18. Hobbes, *Leviathan* (New York: Dutton, 1973), p. 65.

19. Henning, *Wit and Wisdom,* p. 89.

20. "How to Run a Referendum," *The Economist,* November 23, 1996: 66.

21. Good surveys of democratic theory include J. Roland Pennock, *Democratic Political Theory* (Princeton, NJ: Princeton University Press, 1979); and Giovanni Sartori, *The Theory of Democracy Revisited* (Chatham, NJ: Chatham House, 1987).

22. James Marone, *The Democratic Wish: Popular Participation and the Limits of American Government* (New York: Basic Books, 1990), p. 5. Marone is summarizing the claims of others; he himself is a critic of popular democracy.

23. Benjamin Barber, *Strong Democracy* (Berkeley, CA: University of California Press, 1984).

24. Alexis de Tocqueville, *Democracy in America,* 2nd ed., Henry Reeve, trans., 2 vols. (Cambridge, MA: Sever & Francis, 1863), I, pp. 318–319, as quoted in Marone, *The Democratic Wish,* p. 86.

25. John Adams, *The Political Writings of John Adams,* George Peek, Jr., ed. (New York: Macmillan, 1985), p. 89.

26. Marone, *The Democratic Wish,* pp. 5–6.

27. "Federalist 51."

28. Sidney Blumenthal, *The Permanent Campaign* (New York: Simon & Schuster, 1982).

29. Hugh Heclo, "The Permanent Campaign: A Conspectus," in *Campaigning to Govern or Governing to Campaign?* Thomas Mann and Norman Ornstein, eds. (Washington, DC: Brookings, 2000).

30. Woodrow Wilson, *Congressional Government* (Cleveland, OH: Meridian Books, 1956), p. 39.

31. Richard Boyd, "Decline of U.S. Voter Turnout: Structural Explanations," *American Politics Quarterly* 9 (1981): 133–159.

32. Frank Sorauf, *Political Parties in the American System* (Boston: Little, Brown, 1964); and Martin Wattenberg, *The Decline of American Political Parties, 1952–1984* (Cambridge, MA: Harvard University Press, 1986).

33. Gary Jacobson finds that national swings in House elections are much more heterogeneous than at mid-century. See "The Marginals Never Vanished: Incumbency and Competition in Elections to the U.S. House of Representatives, 1952–1982," *American Journal of Political Science* 31 (1987): 126–141.

34. Norman Ornstein, Thomas Mann, and Michael Malbin, *Vital Statistics on Congress, 1997–1998* (Washington, DC: Congressional Quarterly, Inc., 1998), Table 3.1.

35. John Broder, "Governors Join Ranks of Full-Time Campaign Money-Raisers," *New York Times,* December 5, 1999, 22.

36. John Alford and John Hibbing, "Electoral Convergence of the Two Houses of Congress," Paper presented at the Norman Thomas Conference on Senate Exceptionalism, Vanderbilt University, Nashville, TN, October 21–23, 1999.

37. Susan A. Macmanus, *Young v. Old: Generational Combat in the 21st Century* (Boulder, CO: Westview Press, 1996), Ch. 2.

38. R. Douglas Arnold, *The Logic of Congressional Action* (New Haven, CT: Yale University Press, 1990).

39. Benjamin Ginsberg and Martin Shefter, *Politics by Other Means: The Declining Importance of Elections in America* (New York: Basic Books: 1990); and Terry Moe, "The

Politics of Bureaucratic Structure," in John Chubb and Paul Peterson, eds., *Can the Government Govern?* (Washington, DC: Brookings, 1989), pp. 267–329.

40. John Dewey, as quoted in Marone, *The Democratic Wish,* p. 322.

41. Marone, *The Democratic Wish.*

42. Henning, *Wit and Wisdom,* p. 94.

43. "A League of Evil," *The Economist*, September 11, 1999, 7.

44. Henning, *Wit and Wisdom,* p. 58.

45. Charles Masters, "Riviera Tramps Run Risk of 'Tourist Cleansing' Round-Ups," *Daily Telegraph,* July 27, 1996, International Section, 15.

CHAPTER 2

1. Herbert J. Storing, ed., *The Complete Anti-Federalist: Maryland and Virginia and the South,* Volume 5 (Chicago: University of Chicago Press, 1981), p. 210; Selections from speech—ellipses deleted to make the text more readable.

2. Storing, *Complete Anti-Federalist,* p. 207.

3. James Madison, "Federalist 10," in Alexander Hamilton, John Jay, and James Madison, writing under the pseudonym Publius, *The Federalist Papers* (Baltimore, MD: Johns Hopkins University Press, 1981), pp. 16, 23.

4. Owen S. Ireland, *Religion, Ethnicity and Politics: Ratifying the Constitution in Pennsylvania* (University Park, PA: Pennsylvania State University Press, 1995).

5. Thomas A. Bailey, *The American Pageant: A History of the Republic* (Boston: D.C. Heath, 1956).

6. Gordon S. Wood, *The Radicalism of the American Revolution* (New York: Knopf, 1992), p. 80.

7. Jack p. Greene, "The Role of the Lower Houses of Assembly in Eighteenth-Century Politics," in Jack p. Greene, ed., *The Reinterpretation of the American Revolution 1763–1789* (New York: Harper & Row, 1968), pp. 86–109.

8. Merrill D. Peterson, *Thomas Jefferson and the New Nation* (New York: Oxford University Press, 1970), pp. 22–23.

9. Wood, *Radicalism,* p. 55.

10. J. Franklin Jameson, *The American Revolution Considered as a Social Movement* (Princeton, NJ: Princeton University Press, 1926).

11. Edmund S. Morgan and Helen M. Morgan, *The Stamp Act Crisis: Prologue to Revolution* (Chapel Hill: University of North Carolina Press, 1953), p. 106.

12. Morgan and Morgan, *Stamp Act Crisis,* p. 106.

13. Bernard Bailyn, *The Origins of American Politics* (New York: Knopf, 1968), p. 12.

14. Thomas Hobbes, *Leviathan* (New York: Oxford University Press, 1996). Originally published in 1651.

15. John Locke, *Two Treatises on Civil Government* (London: Dent, 1924). Originally published in 1690.

16. J. H. Plumb, *The Origins of Political Stability* (Boston: Houghton Mifflin, 1967).

17. For a discussion of the influence of James Harrington on colonial thought, see Samuel H. Beer, *To Make a Nation: The Rediscovery of American Federalism* (Cambridge, MA: Harvard University Press, 1993).

18. John Bartlett, *Familiar Quotations,* 15th ed., (Boston: Little, Brown, 1980), pp. 334, 342, 414.

19. Thomas Paine, *Common Sense* (New York: Penguin, 1986). Originally published in 1776.

20. C. L. Becker, *Freedom and Responsibility in the American Way of Life* (New York: Knopf, 1945), p. 16, as quoted by Louis Hartz, *The Liberal Tradition in America* (New York: Harcourt, 1955), p. 61.

21. Robert J. Dinkin, *Voting in Revolutionary America: A Study of Elections in the Original Thirteen States, 1776–1789* (Westport, CT: Greenwood Press, 1982); and Robert J. Dinkin, *Voting in Provincial America: A Study of Elections in the Thirteen Colonies, 1689–1776* (Westport, CT: Greenwood Press, 1977).

22. Willi Paul Adams, *The First American Constitutions: Republican*

*Ideology and the Making of the State Constitutions in the Revolutionary Era* (Chapel Hill: University of North Carolina Press, 1980), pp. 245, 308–311.

23. Adams, *First American Constitutions,* p. 207.

24. Bailey, *American Pageant,* p. 136.

25. Charles A. Beard, *An Economic Interpretation of the Constitution of the United States* (New York: Free Press, 1913).

26. Robert E. Brown, *Charles Beard and the Constitution* (Princeton, NJ: Princeton University Press, 1956); and Forrest McDonald, *We the People* (Chicago: University of Chicago Press, 1958).

27. John p. Roche, "The Founding Fathers: A Reform Caucus in Action," *American Political Science Review* 55 (December 1961): pp. 799–816.

28. Winton U. Solberg, ed., *The Federal Convention and the Formation of the Union of the American States* (New York: Bobbs-Merrill, 1958), p. 79.

29. Solberg, *Federal Convention,* p. 78.

30. Solberg, *Federal Convention,* pp. 131–134.

31. Max Farrand, *The Framing of the Constitution of the United States* (New Haven, CT: Yale University Press, 1913), p. 113.

32. Thornton Anderson, *Creating the Constitution: The Convention of 1787 and the First Congress* (University Park, PA: Pennsylvania State University Press, 1993).

33. Arthur M. Schlesinger, Jr., ed., *History of American Presidential Elections, 1789-1968,* Vol. 2 (New York: McGraw-Hill, 1971), p. 1244.

34. Anderson, *Creating the Constitution,* p. 148.

35. Anderson, *Creating the Constitution,* p. 148.

36. Henry Steele Commager, ed., *Documents of American History* (New York: Appleton-Century-Crofts, 1958), p. 104; and Willi Paul Adams, *The First American Constitutions: Republican Ideology and the Making of the State Constitutions in the*

*Revolutionary Era* (Chapel Hill: University of North Carolina Press, 1980).

37. Arthur M. Schlesinger, *Prelude to Independence* (New York: Knopf, 1958), p. 299.

38. C. M. Kenyon, "Men of Little Faith: The Anti-Federalists on the Nature of Representative Government," in Jack P. Greene, *The Reinterpretation of the American Revolution, 1763–1789* (New York: Harper & Row, 1968), pp. 526–67; and Herbert J. Storing, ed., *The Anti-Federalist* (Chicago: University of Chicago Press, 1986).

39. John Jay, Alexander Hamilton, and James Madison, writing under the pseudonym Publius, *The Federalist Papers* (New York: New American Library, 1961).

40. Jane Mansbridge, *Why We Lost the ERA* (Chicago: University of Chicago Press, 1986).

41. Charles A. Beard, *An Economic Interpretation of the Constitution of the United States.*

42. Bernard Bailyn, *The Ideological Origins of Revolution* (Cambridge, MA: Harvard University Press, 1967); and Gordon S. Wood, *The Creation of the American Republic, 1776–1787* (Chapel Hill: University of North Carolina Press, 1969).

43. Beard, *Economic Interpretation,* Ch. 9.

44. Second Inaugural Address, 1865, as quoted in John Bartlett, *Familiar Quotations,* 16th ed. (Boston: Little, Brown, 1992), p. 450.

CHAPTER 3

1. John Bartlett, *Familiar Quotations: Revised and Enlarged,* 15th ed. (Boston: Little, Brown, 1980), p. 452.

2. Alexis de Tocqueville, *Democracy in America,* Vol. I, ed. Philips Bradley (New York: Knopf, 1945), p. 169.

3. Timothy Conlan, "And the Beat Goes On: Intergovernmental Mandates and Preemption in an Era of Deregulation," *Publius* 21 (Summer 1991): 57.

4. On the costs of environmental mandates, see Richard C. Feiock, "Estimating Political, Fiscal and Economic Impacts of State Mandates: A Pooled Time Series Analysis of Local Planning and Growth Policy in Florida." Paper prepared for the annual meeting of the American Political Science Association, 1994.

5. Colleen M. Grogan, "The Influence of Federal Mandates on State Policy Decision-Making." Paper prepared for the annual meeting of the American Political Science Association, 1994; Teresa Coughlin, Leighton Ku, and John Holahan, *Medicaid Since 1980* (Washington, DC: Urban Institute, 1994); and John Holahan et al., "Explaining the Recent Growth in Medicaid Spending," *Health Affairs* 12 (Fall 1993): 177–193.

6. Gregory S. Lashutka, "Local Rebellion: How Cities Are Rising Up Against Unfunded Mandates," *Commonsense* 1 (Summer 1994): 66.

7. Jean E. Smith, *John Marshall: Definer of a Nation* (New York: Henry Holt, 1996), pp. 440–446.

8. *McCulloch* v. *Maryland* (1819), 4 Wheaton 316, as reprinted in Henry Steele Commager, ed., *Documents of American History,* 6th ed. (New York: Appleton-Century-Crofts, 1949), p. 217.

9. *McCulloch* v. *Maryland* (1819), as reprinted in Commager, p. 217.

10. Dan M. Berkovitz, "Waste Wars: Did Congress 'Nuke' State Sovereignty in the Low-Level Radioactive Waste Policy Amendments Act of 1985?" *Harvard Environmental Law Review* 11, (1987): pp. 437–440.

11. *New York Times,* January 18, 1991.

12. *New York* v. *U.S.,* 112 *Supreme Court Reporter,* 2414–47 301 U.S. 1 (1991).

13. *United States* v. *E. C. Knight Co.* (1895).

14. *NLRB* v. *Jones & Laughlin Co.,* 317 U.S. 111 (1937).

15. *Wickard* v. *Filburn* (1942).

16. *Helvering* v. *Davis,* 301 U.S. 548, 599 (1937).

17. *South Dakota* v. *Dole,* 483 U.S. 203 (1987).

18. Morton Grodzins, *The American System: A New View of Government in the United States,* ed. Daniel J. Elazar (Chicago: Rand McNally, 1966).

19. Calculated from data in Ester Fuchs, *Mayors and Money* (Chicago: University of Chicago Press, 1992), p. 210.

20. Chuck Henning, comp. , *The Wit and Wisdom of Politics: Expanded Edition.* (Golden, CO: Fulcrum, 1992), 208.

21. Chuck Henning, comp. , *The Wit and Wisdom of Politics: Expanded Edition.* p. 208.

22. James M. Perry, "GOP Congressman Shows How to Keep Power, Even While Under Indictment for Corruption," *Wall Street Journal,* June 14, 1994, A16.

23. Jeffrey L. Pressman and Aaron Wildavsky, *Implementation,* 3rd ed. (Berkeley: University of California Press, 1984); Martha Derthick, *New Towns in Town: Why a Federal Program Failed* (Washington, DC: Urban Institute, 1972); and Eugene Bardach, *The Implementation Game,* 4th ed. (Cambridge, MA: MIT Press, 1982).

24. Derthick, *New Towns in Town.*

25. Pressman and Wildavsky, *Implementation,* p. 118.

26. Paul E. Peterson, Barry Rabe, and Kenneth Wong, *When Federalism Works* (Washington, DC: Brookings, 1986).

27. Timothy Conlan, *New Federalism: Intergovernmental Reform from Nixon to Reagan* (Washington, DC: Brookings, 1988).

28. Executive Office of the President, Officer of Management and Budget, *Budget for Fiscal Year 2000, Historical Tables,* Table 12.3.

29. David McKay, *Domestic Policy and Ideology: Presidents and the American State, 1964–1987* (New York: Cambridge University Press, 1989), Ch. 4.

30. Peter J. Howe, "State's Share of Federal Dollars Drops," *Boston Globe,* July 2, 1994, 17.

31. Lynda McDonnell, "Will Our State Be a Magnet for Poor from Across Nation?" *Pioneer Press,* December 31, 1995, 1A, 10A.

32. Paul E. Peterson and Mark Rom, *Welfare Magnets: A New Case for a National Standard* (Washington, DC: Brookings, 1990).

33. Judith Havemann, "Welfare Reform 'Surplus' is $4.7 Billion" *Washington Post,* September 8, 1998, p. A2.

34. Peterson, *The Price of Federalism.*

35. James Bryce, *Modern Democracies* (New York: Macmillan, 1921), Vol. I, p. 132.

36. Robert R. Alford and Eugene C. Lee,"Voting Turnout in American Cities," *American Political Science Review* 62 (September 1968): 796–813.

37. Village politics are well described in A. J. Vidich and J. Bensman, *Small Town in Mass Society* (New York: Harper & Row, 1972). For descriptions of courthouse gangs in the county politics of the South, see V. O. Key, *Southern Politics* (New York: Random House, 1949).

38. Paul E. Peterson, *City Limits* (Chicago: University of Chicago Press, 1981).

39. *Statistical Abstract of the United States,* 1992, Table 22.

40. Greta Anand, "Circling of the Welcome Wagons: Selectman Candidates Rip Social Programs," *Boston Globe,* West Weekly Section, March 19, 1995, 1, 8.

41. "Money to Burn," *The Economist,* August 14, 1993: 23.

42. Steve Rushin, "The Heart of a City," *Sports Illustrated,* December 4, 1995.

43. Daniel Elazar, *American Federalism: A View From the States* (New York: Harper & Row, 1984).

44. Morris Fiorina, *Divided Government* (New York: Macmillan, 1992).

45. Calculated from U.S. Bureau of the Census, *State and Local Finance Estimates by State: 1995–1996,* **www.census.gov/govs/www/esti96.html** accessed November 11, 1999. Data on state expenditures combine expenditures by state and local governments. Because the sharing of responsibilities by state and local governments varies widely from state to

state, any interstate comparison that looks at state government expenditures alone can be quite misleading.

46. Peterson, *The Price of Federalism,* p. 105.

47. *Baker v. Carr,* 369 U.S. 186 (1962); *Reynolds v. Sims,* 377 U.S. 533 (1964).

48. See Gordon E. Baker, *The Reapportionment Revolution* (New York: Random House, 1966); and Timothy G. O'Rourke, *The Impact of Reapportionment,* (New Brunswick, NJ: Transaction Books, 1980).

49. The Council of State Governments, *The Book of the States: 1996–97 Edition,* Lexington, KY: Council of State Governments.

50. Thad Beyle, "Being Governor," in Carl E. Van Horn, ed., *The State of the States,* 2nd. ed. (Washington, DC: Brookings, 1993).

51. George Skelton, "Lessons from an Earlier Foreign Journey," *Los Angeles Times,* October 25, 1999.

CHAPTER 4

1. Joseph B. Mitchell, *Military Leaders of the American Revolution* (McLean, VA: EPM Publications, 1967), pp. 138–149.

2. Jan Stanislaw Kopczewski, *Kosciuszko and Pulaski* (Warsaw: Impress Publishers, 1976).

3. Louis des Cognets, Jr., *Black Sheep and Heroes of the American Revolution* (Princeton, NJ: Cognets, 1965), Ch. 15.

4. Carl J. Friedrich, *Problems of the American Public Service* (New York: McGraw-Hill, 1935), p. 12.

5. See Alvin Rabushka and Kenneth Shepsle, *Politics in Plural Societies* (Columbus, OH: Merrill, 1972).

6. John A. Garrity and Peter Gay, eds., *The Columbia History of the World* (New York: Harper & Row, 1972), p. 673.

7. Garrity and Gay, eds., *Columbia History of the World,* pp. 669–670.

8. Quoted in Marc Shell, "Babel in America; or, The Politics of Language Diversity in the United States," *Critical Inquiry* 20(1993): 109.

9. Richard McCormick, "Ethno-Cultural Interpretations of Nineteenth-Century American Voting Behavior," *Political Science Quarterly* 89(1974): 351–377.

10. Richard Wayman, "Wisconsin Ethnic Groups and the Election of 1890," *Wisconsin Magazine of History* 51(1968): 273. More generally, see Paul Kleppner, *The Third Electoral System, 1853–1892: Parties, Voters, and Political Cultures* (Chapel Hill, NC: University of North Carolina Press, 1979).

11. J. Morgan Kousser, *The Shaping of Southern Politics* (New Haven, CT: Yale University Press, 1974).

12. On the multicultural character of California after it was annexed to the United States, see Ronald Takaki, *A Different Mirror* (Boston: Little, Brown, 1993), Ch. 8.

13. John Miller, "Chinese Exclusion Act," *Congressional Record–Senate 1882*, 13, Pt. 2: 1484–1485.

14. This is Oscar Handlin's sardonic characterization. See his *Race and Nationality in American Life* (Boston: Little, Brown, 1957), p. 95.

15. Madison Grant, *The Passing of the Great Race* (New York: Scribner's, 1916), pp. 80–81.

16. *Abstracts of Reports of the Immigration Commission* (Washington, DC: Government Printing Office, Vol. 1, 1911). The quoted passages can be found on pp. 244, 251, 259, 259, 261, 265, and 229, respectively. The characterization of southern Italians is based on work by an Italian (presumably northern) sociologist, but the commission clearly agrees with the description.

17. Henry Cabot Lodge, "Immigration Restriction," *Congressional Record–Senate 1896*, 28, Pt. 3: 2817.

18. "Emergency" immigration restrictions passed in 1921 were fine-tuned and formalized in the National Origins Act of 1924 and the National Origins Quota Act of 1929.

19. Seymour Martin Lipset and Earl Raab. *The Politics of Unreason* (New York: Harper & Row, 1970), p. 111.

20. Alan Lichtman, *Prejudice and the Old Politics: The Presidential Election of 1928* (Chapel Hill, NC: University of North Carolina Press, 1979).

21. Spencer Rich, "A 20-Year High Tide of Immigration," *Washington Post National Weekly Edition,* September 4–10, 1995: 30.

22. George Borhas, "The New Economics of Immigration," *The Atlantic Monthly,* November 1996: 72–80.

23. National Research Council. *The New Americans: Economic, Demographic, and Fiscal Effects of Immigration.* Washington, DC: National Academy Press, 1977), Chs. 4–6.

24. David Kennedy, "Can We Still Afford to Be a Nation of Immigrants?" *The Atlantic Monthly,* November 1996: 67.

25. Arthur Schlesinger, Jr., *The Disuniting of America* (Knoxville, TN: Whittle, 1991).

26. Louis Hartz, *The Liberal Tradition in America* (New York: Harcourt, 1955).

27. On Madison's pessimistic view of human nature, see Richard Matthews, *If Men Were Angels* (Lawrence, KS: University of Kansas Press, 1995), especially Ch. 3.

28. Clinton Rossiter, *Conservatism in America* (New York: Knopf, 1962), pp. 67, 71.

29. Bernard Bailyn, *The Ideological Origins of the American Revolution* (Cambridge, MA: Harvard University Press, 1967).

30. Gordon Wood. *The Creation of the American Republic* (New York: Norton, 1972. J. G. A. Pocock, *The Machiavellian Moment* (Princeton, NJ: Princeton University Press, 1975).

31. Rogers Smith, "Beyond Tocqueville, Myrdal and Hartz: The Multiple Traditions in America," *American Political Science Review* 87(1993): 549–566. These inconsistencies were not lost on earlier thinkers, to be sure. Recall Jefferson's pessimistic predictions in his *Notes on the State of Virginia 1781–1785.* Also see Alexis de Tocqueville, *Democracy in America,* ed. J. p. Mayer (New York: Harper, 1969), pp. 340–363.

32. Samuel Huntington, *American Politics: The Promise of Disharmony* (Cambridge, MA: Harvard University Press, 1981).

33. I. A. Lewis and William Schneider, "Hard Times: The Public on Poverty," *Public Opinion,* June/July 1985: 2–8, 59–60.

34. "Income Tax Irritation." *Public Perspective* (July/August, 1990): 86.

35. Stanley Feldman, "Structure and Consistency in Public Opinion: The Role of Core Beliefs and Values," *American Journal of Political Science* 32(1988):416–440.

36. Paul Krugman, *Peddling Prosperity* (New York: Norton, 1994), Ch. 5.

37. Madison, "Federalist 10."

38. Everett Carll Ladd, *The American Ideology* (Storrs, CT: The Roper Center, 1994), pp. 56–57.

39. Sidney Verba and Gary Orren, *Equality in America* (Cambridge, MA: Harvard University Press, 1985).

40. "In (Blank) We Trust," The Economist, October 12, 1996: 32.

41. Mariana Servin-Gonzalez and Oscar Torres-Reyna, "Trends: Religion and Politics," *Public Opinion Quarterly* 63(1999): pp. 613–614.

42. Seymour Martin Lipset, *American Exceptionalism* (New York: Norton, 1996).

43. Robert Booth Fowler, *Religion and Politics in America* (Metuchen, NJ: American Theological Library Association, 1985), p. 27.

44. Huntington, *American Politics: The Promise of Disharmony.*

45. Frederick Jackson Turner, *The Frontier in American History* (New York: Holt, 1920).

46. Hartz, *The Liberal Tradition,* p. 89.

47. For a discussion, see Seymour Martin Lipset, "Why No Socialism in the United States?" in Seweryn Bialer and Sophia Sluzar, eds., *Sources of Contemporary Radicalism* (New York: Westview Press, 1977).

48. Sven Steinmo, "American Exceptionalism Reconsidered," in Larry C. Dodd and Calvin Jillson, eds., *The Dynamics of American Politics* (Boulder, CO: Westwood, 1994), pp. 106–131.

49. For a sympathetic description of the trials and ordeals of the immigrants, see Oscar Handlin, *The Uprooted,* 2nd ed. (Boston: Little, Brown, 1973).

50. Hartz, *The Liberal Tradition,* p. 18.

51. *Abstracts of Reports of the Immigration Commission*, p. 170.

52. William Bennett and Jack Kemp, "The Fortress Party?" *Wall Street Journal*, October 21, 1994: A14.

53. David Firestone, "Mayor Seeks Immigration Coalition," *New York Times*, October 11, 1996: B-3.

54. "The Effects of Ethnicity on Political Culture," in Paul Peterson, ed., *Classifying by Race* (Princeton, NJ: Princeton University Press, 1995), pp. 351–352.

55. Rodolfo de la Garza, Angelo Falcon, and F. Chris Garcia, "Will the Real Americans Please Stand Up: Anglo and Mexican American Support of Core American Political Values," *American Journal of Political Science* 40(1996): 335–351.

56. Lydia Saad, "Immigrants See United States as Land of Opportunity," *The Gallup Poll Monthly*, July 1995: pp. 19–33.

57. Gregory Rodriguez, quoted in Patrick McDonnell, "Immigrants Quickly Becoming Assimilated, Report Concludes," *San Francisco Chronicle*, July 7, 1999: A4.

58. Philip Martin and Elizabeth Midgley, "Immigration to the United States," Washington, DC: Population Reference Bureau, June 1999: 37.

## CHAPTER 5

1. For background on the Gulf War, see "Gulf Crisis Grows Into War with Iraq," *1990 Congressional Quarterly Almanac* (Washington, DC: Congressional Quarterly Inc., 1991): 717–756; and "1991 Begins with War in the Mideast," *1991 Congressional Quarterly Almanac* (Washington, DC: Congressional Quarterly Inc., 1992): 437–450.

2. Jon Krosnick and Laura Brannon, "The Impact of the Gulf War on the Ingredients of Presidential Evaluations," *American Political Science Review* 87(1993): 963–975.

3. Paul Quirk and Joseph Hinchliffe, "The Rising Hegemony of Mass Opinion," *Journal of Policy History* 10(1998): 19–50.

4. *Public Opinion and American Democracy* (New York: Knopf, 1961).

5. Carl Friedrich, *Man and His Government* (New York: McGraw-Hill, 1963), pp. 19–215.

6. Fred Greenstein, *Children and Politics* (New Haven, CT: Yale University Press, 1969), Ch. 4.

7. M. Kent Jennings and Richard G. Niemi, *Generations and Politics* (Princeton, NJ: Princeton University Press, 1981), p. 51.

8. Robert Hess and Judith Horney, *The Development of Political Attitudes in Children* (Garden City, NY: Doubleday, 1967).

9. Elizabeth Cook, Ted Jelen, and Clyde Wilcox, *Between Two Absolutes: Public Opinion and the Politics of Abortion* (Boulder, CO: Westview Press, 1992).

10. David Leege, Kenneth Wald, and Lyman Kellstedt, "The Public Dimension of Private Devotionalism," in David Leege and Lyman Kellstedt, eds., *Rediscovering the Religious Factor in American Politics* (Armonk, NY: Sharpe, 1993), pp. 139–156; and Alan Hertzke and John Rausch, "The Religious Vote in American Politics: Value Conflict, Continuity, and Change," in Stephen Craig, ed., *Broken Contract* (Boulder, CO: Westview Press, 1996), p. 188.

11. Warren Miller and Santa Traugott, *American National Election Studies Data Sourcebook, 1952–1986* (Cambridge, MA: Harvard University Press, 1990), pp. 316, 332.

12. For a survey of positive and negative findings see Jack Citrin and Donald Green, "The Self-Interest Motive in American Public Opinion," *Research in Micropolitics,* Vol. 3 (Greenwich, CT: JAI Press, 1993), pp. 1-28.

13. Douglas Hibbs, *The American Political Economy* (Cambridge, MA: Harvard University Press, 1987), Ch. 5.

14. David Sears and Jack Citrin, *Tax Revolt* (Cambridge, MA: Harvard University Press, 1985), Chs. 6–7.

15. David Sears and Leonie Huddy, "On the Origins of Political Disunity Among Women," in L. Tilly and p. Gurin, eds., *Women, Politics, and Change* (New York: Russell Sage, 1990), pp. 249-277.

16. Norman Nie, Jane Junn, and Kenneth Stehlik-Barry, *Education and Democratic Citizenship in America* (Chicago: University of Chicago Press, 1996).

17. Larry Bartels, "Messages Received: The Political Impact of Media Exposure," *American Political Science Review* 87 (1993): 267–285.

18. Don Van Natta, Jr., "Polling's 'Dirty Little Secret': No Response," *New York Times,* November 21, 1999, Sect. 4, pp. 1, 16.

19. John Brehm, *The Phantom Respondents* (Ann Arbor, MI: University of Michigan Press, 1993), Ch. 2.

20. Everett Ladd, "The Pollsters' Waterloo," *Wall Street Journal,* November 19, 1996.

21. "Poll Leaves Democrats with Red Faces," Reuters, January 5, 2000.

22. For a full discussion, see David Moore and Frank Newport, "Misreading the Public: The Case of the Holocaust Poll," *Public Perspective,* March/April 1994: 28–30; and Tom Smith, "Review: The Holocaust Denial Controversy," *Public Opinion Quarterly* 59 (1995): 269–295.

23. "Survey Looks at Political Insight," *Boston Globe,* February 11, 1996: 32 (citing results of a *Washington Post* survey conducted in November 1995).

24. Tom Smith, "Public Support for Public Spending, 1973–1994," *The Public Perspective* 6 (April/May 1995): 2.

25. Jon Krosnick and Matthew Barent, "Comparisons of Party Identification and Policy Preferences: The Impact of Survey Question Format," *American Journal of Political Science* 37 (1993): 941–964.

26. On these topics, see Howard Schuman and Stanley Presser, *Questions and Answers in Attitude Surveys* (New York: Harcourt, Academic Press, 1981); and the

essays in Thomas Mann and Gary Orren, eds., *Media Polls in American Politics* (Washington, DC: Brookings, 1992).

27. Tamar Lewin, "Study Points to Increase in Tolerance of Ethnicity," *New York Times,* January 8, 1992: A12.

28. For a comprehensive breakdown of federal spending, see "Where the Money Goes," *Congressional Quarterly,* December 11, 1993.

29. Anthony Downs, *An Economic Theory of Democracy* (New York: Harper & Row, 1957), Chs. 11–13.

30. Morris p. Fiorina, "Information and Rationality in Elections," in John Ferejohn and James Kuklinski, eds., *Information and Democratic Processes* (Urbana: University of Illinois Press, 1990), pp. 329-342.

31. John Krosnick, "Government Policy and Citizen Passion: A Study of Issue Publics in Contemporary America," *Political Behavior* 12 (1990): 59–92; and Peter Natchez and Irvin Bupp, "Candidates, Issues, and Voters," *Public Policy* 1 (1968): 409–437.

32. Anthony Downs, "Up and Down with Ecology—The Issue Attention Cycle," *The Public Interest* 28 (1972): 38–50.

33. Fiorina, "Information and Rationality."

34. Anthony King, "Names and places lost in the mists of time," *Daily Telegraph,* August 26, 1997, p. 4.

35. Stephen Bennett et al., "Citizens' Knowledge of Foreign Affairs, *Press/Politics* 2 (1996): 10–29.

36. "The Nature of Belief Systems in Mass Publics," in David Apter, ed., *Ideology and Discontent* (New York: Free Press, 1964), pp. 206–261.

37. There is a huge literature debating the size of the increase in ideological thinking. See *inter alia,* Norman Nie and Kristie Andersen, "Mass Belief Systems Revisited: Political Chance and Attitude Structure," *Journal of Politics* 36 (1974): 540–580; John Field and Ronald Anderson, "Ideology in the Public's Conceptualization of the 1964 Election," *Public Opinion Quarterly* 33 (1969): 380–398; and

John Sullivan, James Piereson, and George Marcus, "Ideological Constraint in the Mass Public: A Methodological Critique and Some New Findings," *American Journal of Political Science* 22 (1978): 233–249.

38. Miller and Traugott, *American National Election Studies Data Sourcebook,* p. 94.

39. *Washington Post*/Kaiser Family Foundation/Harvard University Survey Project, *Why Don't Americans Trust the Government?* (Menlo Park, CA: The Kaiser Foundation, 1996), p. 9.

40. Vernon Van Dyke, *Ideology and Political Choice* (Chatham, NJ: Chatham House Publishers, 1995), Chs. 3–5.

41. David Moore and Lydia Saad, "Budget Battle Now a Political Standoff," *Gallup Poll Monthly,* January 1996: 15–16.

42. James A. Davis, "Changeable Weather in a Cooling Climate Atop the Liberal Plateau," *Public Opinion Quarterly* 56 (1992): 261–306; and Morris p. Fiorina, "The Reagan Years: Turning to the Right or Groping Toward the Middle?" in Barry Cooper, Allan Kornberg, and William Mishler, eds., *The Resurgence of Conservatism in Anglo-American Democracies* (Durham, NC: Duke University Press, 1988), pp. 430–459.

43. "Public Expects GOP Miracles," *Times-Mirror News Release,* December 8, 1994.

44. Morris p. Fiorina, *Divided Government,* 2nd ed. (Boston: Allyn & Bacon, 1995), pp. 173–177.

45. *Ibid.*

46. Samuel Stouffer, *Communism, Conformity, and Civil Liberties* (New York: Doubleday, 1955); and James Prothro and Charles Grigg, "Fundamental Principles of Democracy: Bases of Agreement and Disagreement," *Journal of Politics* 22 (1960): 176–194.

47. For evidence that people's opinions reflect a smaller number of "core beliefs" that may conflict with each other or situational characteristics, see Stanley Feldman, "Structure and Consistency in Public Opinion: The Role of Core Beliefs and Values,"

*American Journal of Public Opinion* 32 (1988): 416–440; and Stanley Feldman and John Zaller, "A Simple Theory of the Survey Response: Answering Questions versus Revealing Preferences," *American Journal of Political Science* 36 (1992): 579–616.

48. R. Michael Alvarez and John Brehm, "American Ambivalence Toward Abortion Policy," *American Journal of Political Science* 39 (1995): 1055–1082.

49. On the effects of posing political conflicts as matters of conflicting rights, see Mary Anne Glendon, *Rights Talk: The Impoverishment of Political Discourse* (New York: Free Press, 1991).

50. Cook, Jelen, and Wilcox, *Between Two Absolutes,* Ch. 2.

51. "Abortion: Overview of a Complex Opinion," *The Public Perspective,* November/December, 1989: 19, 20.

52. *Ibid.,* 20.

53. "Abortion," *The American Enterprise,* July/August 1995: 107.

54. Dan Carney, "House GOP Embrace of Gun Curbs Not Yet Lock, Stock and Barrel, *CQ Weekly,* May 29, 1999: 1267.

55. Dan Carney, "Beyond Guns and Violence: A Battle for House Control," *CQ Weekly,* June 1999: 1426–1432.

56. Frank Newport, "Fort Worth Shootings Again Put Focus on Gun Control," Gallup News Service Poll Release, October 15, 1999.

57. Kathy Keily, "After Failed Gun Legislation, Political Finger Pointing Begins," *USA Today,* June 21, 1999: 14A.

58. ABC News/*Washington Post* poll of August 30–September 2, 1999.

59. Francis X. Clines, "In a Bitter Cultural War, an Ardent Call to Arms," *New York Times,* June 17, 1999.

60. Personal communication.

61. "A Macro Theory of Information Flow," in John Ferejohn and James Kuklinski, eds., *Information and Democratic Processes* (Urbana, IL: University of Illinois Press, 1990), pp. 345–368.

62. James Stimson, *Public Opinion in America: Moods, Cycles, and Swings* (Boulder, CO: Westview Press, 1991).

63. Benjamin Page and Robert Shapiro, *The Rational Public* (Chicago: University of Chicago Press, 1992).

64. Christopher Wlezien, "The Public as Thermostat: Dynamics of Preferences for Spending," *American Journal of Political Science* 39 (1995): 981–1000.

## CHAPTER 6

1. Steven Rosenstone and John Mark Hansen, *Mobilization, Participation, and Democracy in America* (New York: Macmillan, 1993), p. 51.

2. Benjamin Barber, *Strong Democracy: Participatory Politics for a New Age* (Berkeley and Los Angeles: University of California Press, 1984), p. xiii.

3. John Aldrich, *Why Parties?* (Chicago: University of Chicago Press, 1995), pp. 106–107.

4. Chilton Williamson, *American Suffrage from Property to Democracy: 1760–1860* (Princeton, NJ: Princeton University Press, 1960).

5. *Ibid.*, p. 277.

6. On Republican withdrawal from the South after the realignment of the 1890s, see Richard Vallely, "National Parties and Racial Disenfranchisement," in Paul Peterson, ed., Classifying by Race (Princeton, NJ: Princeton University Press, 1995), p. 188–216. On black exercise of voting rights, see J. Morgan Kousser, *The Shaping of Southern Politics* (New Haven, CT: Yale University Press, 1974).

7. Eleanor Flexner, *Century of Struggle,* rev. ed. (Cambridge, MA: Harvard University Press, 1975); and Anne Scott and Andrew Scott, *One Half the People* (Philadelphia: Lippincott, 1975).

8. "18-Year-Old Vote: Constitutional Amendment Cleared," *Congressional Quarterly Almanac* (Washington, DC: Congressional Quarterly, 1972), pp. 475–477.

9. For a comparative study of the American and Swiss suffrage movements, see Lee Ann Banaszak, *Why Movements Succeed or Fail* (Princeton, NJ: Princeton University Press, 1996).

10. "Can the Black Vote Hold Up?" *The Economist,* April 3, 1999: 24.

11. Paul Peterson, "An Immodest Proposal," *Daedalus* 121 (1992): 151–174.

12. Rosenstone and Hansen, *Mobilization, Participation, and Democracy,* Ch. 2.

13. Jeffrey Jones, "Does Bringing Out the Candidate Bring Out the Votes?" *American Politics Quarterly* 26 (1998): 406.

14. John Milholland, "The Danger Point in American Politics," *North American Review* 164 (1897).

15. Raymond Wolfinger and Steven Rosenstone, *Who Votes?* (New Haven, CT: Yale University Press, 1980), p. 101.

16. John Ferejohn and Morris Fiorina, "The Paradox of Not Voting: A Decision Theoretic Analysis," *American Political Science Review* 68 (1974): 525–535.

17. Anthony Downs, *An Economic Theory of Democracy* (New York: Harper & Row, 1957), Ch. 14.

18. Howard Rosenthal and Subrata Sen, "Electoral Participation in the French Fifth Republic," *American Political Science Review* 67(1973): 29–54.

19. Wolfinger and Rosenstone, *Who Votes?* p. 116.

20. Ruy Teixeira, *The Disappearing American Voter* (Washington, DC: Brookings, 1992), p. 10.

21. Stephen Knack, "Drivers Wanted: Motor Voter and the Election of 1996," PS: *Political Science and Politics* 32 (1999): 237–243; and Michael Martinez and David Hill, "Did Motor Voter Work? *American Politics Quarterly* 27 (1999): 296–315.

22. Martha Angle, "Low Voter Turnout Prompts Concern on Hill," *Congressional Quarterly Weekly Report,* April 2, 1988: 864; and Stephen Bennett, "The Uses and Abuses of Registration and Turnout Data," PS: *Political Science and Politics* 23 (1990): 166–171.

23. Wolfinger and Rosenstone, *Who Votes?* p. 88.

24. Mark Franklin, "Electoral Engineering and Cross-National Turnout Differences: What Role for Compulsory Voting? *British Journal of Political Science* 29 (1999): 205.

25. Richard Boyd, "Decline of U.S. Voter Turnout: Structural Explanations," *American Politics Quarterly* 9 (1981): 133–159.

26. Stephen Knack, "The Voter Participation Effects of Selecting Jurors from Registration Lists," Working Paper No. 91–10, University of Maryland, Department of Economics; and J. Eric Oliver and Raymond Wolfinger, "Jury Aversion and Voter Registration." Paper presented at the 1997 Annual Meeting of the American Political Science Association, Washington, DC.

27. Martin Wattenberg, *The Decline of American Political Parties,* 1952–19. Interestingly, the percentage of voters who reported being contacted by a party rose from 1956 to 1982 but declined thereafter. Party efforts would appear to have met with very limited success, inasmuch as turnout was falling throughout the period. See Rosenstone and Hansen, *Mobilization, Participation, and Democracy,* p. 163.

28. G. Bingham Powell, "American Voter Turnout in Comparative Perspective," American Political Science Review 80 (1986): 17–43; and Robert Jackman, "Political Institutions and Voter Turnout in the Industrial Democracies," *American Political Science Review* 81 (1987): 405–423.

29. Sidney Verba, Kay Schlozman, and Henry Brady, *Voice and Equality* (Cambridge, MA: Harvard University Press, 1995), p. 72.

30. David Nexon, "Asymmetry in the Political System: Occasional Activists in the Democratic and Republican Parties, 1956–1964," *American Political Science Review* 65 (1971): 716–730; and Warren Miller and M. Kent Jennings, *Parties in Transition* (New York: Russell Sage, 1986), Ch. 2.

31. Rosenstone and Hansen,

*Mobilization, Participation, and Democracy,* pp. 63–70. There is some conflict between their figures and those reported by Verba, Schlozman, and Brady in Voice and Equality, pp. 69–74. Part of the explanation may be that the survey items relied on by Rosenstone and Hansen generally have more specific referents (such as this year's elections), whereas the items relied on by Verba, Schlozman, and Brady ask more generally about activity in the last year or two years. Thus the Verba, Schlozman, and Brady figures may reflect the increasing number of opportunities.

32. Jack Citrin, "Comment: The Political Relevance of Trust in Government," *American Political Science Review* 68 (1974): 973–988.

33. Teixeira, *The Disappearing American Voter,* p. 49.

34. Richard Brody, "The Puzzle of Political Participation in America," in Anthony King, ed., *The New American Political System* (Washington, DC: American Enterprise Institute, 1978, pp. 287–324; and Paul Abramson and John Aldrich, "The Decline of Electoral Participation in America," *American Political Science Review* 76 (1982): 502–521.

35. Rosenstone and Hansen, *Mobilization, Participation, and Democracy,* p. 183.

36. *Ibid.,* Ch. 7, p. 175.

37. Marshall Ganz, "Motor Voter or Motivated Voter," *The American Prospect,* September-October, 1996: 46–48; and Marshall Ganz, "Voters in the Crosshairs," *The American Prospect,* Winter 1994: 100–109.

38. Warren Miller, "The Puzzle Transformed: Explaining Declining Turnout," *Political Behavior* 14 (1992): 1–43.

39. Robert Putnam, "Tuning In, Tuning Out: The Strange Disappearance of Social Capital in America," *PS: Political Science and Politics* 28 (1995): 664–683.

40. Stephen Knack, "Civic Norms, Social Sanctions, and Voter Turnout," *Rationality and Society* 4 (1992): 133–156.

41. Eric Uslaner, "Faith, Hope, and Charity: Social Capital, Trust, and Collective Action" (College Park, MD: University of Maryland, unpublished manuscript).

42. Rosenstone and Hansen, *Mobilization, Participation, and Democracy,* Ch. 7; and Teixeira, *The Disappearing American Voter,* Ch. 2.

43. Laura Stoker and M. Kent Jennings, "Life-Cycle Transitions and Political Participation: The Case of Marriage," *American Political Science Review* 89 (1995): 421–433.

44. "Politics Brief: Is There a Crisis?" *The Economist,* July 17, 1999: 50.

45. For detailed analyses of the relationship between demographic characteristics and voting see Raymond Wolfinger and Steven Rosenstone, *Who Votes?* (New Haven, CT: Yale University Press, 1980), and Rosenstone and Hansen, *Mobilization, Participation, and Democracy,* Ch. 5.

46. Verba and Nie, *Participation in America: Political Democracy and Social Equality* (New York: Harper & Row, 1972), pp. 170–171; and Wolfinger and Rosenstone, *Who Votes?* p. 90.

47. Rosenstone and Hansen, *Mobilization, Participation, and Democracy in America,* Ch. 5.

48. Katherine Tate, "Black Political Participation in the 1984 and 1988 Presidential Elections," *American Political Science Review* 85 (1991): 1159–1176.

49. On language and political participation, see Sidney Verba, Kay Schlozman, and Henry Brady, *Voice and Equality: Civic Volunteerism in American Politics* (Cambridge, MA: Harvard University Press, 1995).

50. Russell Dalton, *Citizen Politics in Western Democracies* (Chatham, NJ: Chatham House, 1988), pp. 51–52.

51. Herbert Tingsten, *Political Behavior: Studies in Election Statistics* (London: King & Son, 1937), pp. 225–226.

52. "The Democratic Distemper," *The Public Interest* 41 (1975), pp. 36–37.

53. Quoted in Seymour Martin Lipset, *Political Man* (New York: Anchor, 1963), p. 228, note 90.

54. George Will, "In Defense of Nonvoting," in George Will, ed., *The Morning After* (New York: Free Press, 1986), p. 229.

55. Stephen Bennett and David Resnick, "The Implications of Nonvoting for Democracy in the United States," *American Journal of Political Science* 34 (1990): 771–802.

56. U.S. Bureau of the Census, *Current Population Reports,* P20–485, Table B. For a general discussion see Peverill Squire, Raymond Wolfinger, and David Glass, "Residential Mobility and Voter Turnout," *American Political Science Review* 81 (1987): 45–65.

57. Teixeira, *The Disappearing American Voter,* p. 92.

58. "A Three-Party Election Won't Address Issue of Economic Injustice," *Boston Globe,* July 26, 1996, A17.

59. Political theorist Benjamin Barber refers to the former as an example of "strong democracy" and to the latter as an example of "thin democracy." See Barber, *Strong Democracy* (note 2).

CHAPTER 7

1. The following account is based on Phil Kunz, "Home Schooling Movement Gives House a Lesson," *Congressional Quarterly Weekly Report,* February 26, 1994: 479–480.

2. There is some controversy about how to measure group membership and consequently about the exact figures. For differing viewpoints, see Frank Baumgartner and Jack Walker, "Survey Research and Membership in Voluntary Associations," *American Journal of Political Science* 32 (1988): 908–928; Tom Smith, "Trends in Voluntary Group Membership: Comments on Baumgartner and Walker," *American Journal of Political Science* 34 (1990): 646–661; and Baumgartner and Walker, "Response to Smith's 'Trends in Voluntary Group Membership,'" *American Journal of Political Science* 34 (1990): 662–670.

3. Alexis de Tocqueville, *Democracy in America,* ed. J. p. Mayer (New York: HarperPerennial, 1969), p. 513.

4. Kay Schlozman and John Tierney, *Organized Interests and American Democracy* (New York: Harper & Row, 1981), p. 75.

5. Robert Wiebe, *The Search for Order, 1877–1920* (New York: Hill and Wang, 1967).

6. Kristen Luker, *Abortion and the Politics of Motherhood* (Berkeley: University of California Press, 1984), Chs. 5–6.

7. "Interest Representation: The Dominance of Institutions," *American Political Science Review* 78 (1984): 64–76.

8. Jeffrey Berry, *Lobbying for the People* (Princeton, NJ: Princeton University Press, 1977).

9. Jack Walker, *Mobilizing Interest Groups in America* (Ann Arbor: University of Michigan Press, 1991), p. 10.

10. An excellent source of basic information about groups and associations in the United States is the *Encyclopedia of Associations,* ed. Carol Schwartz and Rebecca Turner (Detroit: Gale Research, Inc., annual editions).

11. These figures represent the combined membership of the Sierra Club, Environmental Defense Fund, Friends of the Earth, the Audubon Society, the National Wildlife Federation, the Natural Resources Defense Council, and the Wilderness Society (Encyclopedia of Associations, 2000 edition).

12. Henry Brady, Sidney Verba, and Kay Schlozman, "Beyond SES: A Resource Model of Political Participation," *American Political Science Review* 89 (1995): 271–294.

13. James Q. Wilson, *Political Organizations* (New York: Basic Books, 1973), Ch. 3.

14. Mancur Olson, *The Logic of Collective Action* (Cambridge, MA: Harvard University Press, 1965).

15. R. Cornes and T. Sandler, *The Theory of Externalities, Public Goods and Club Goods* (Cambridge, England: Cambridge University Press, 1986), Ch. 6.

16. George Miller, *Railroads and the Granger Laws* (Madison: University of Wisconsin Press, 1971).

17. The law, known as the McCrary bill after its sponsor George McCrary (R-IA), died in the Senate. As the Founders intended, the House yielded to popular passion, whereas the Senate resisted.

18. Jane Mansbridge, *Why We Lost the ERA* (Chicago: University of Chicago Press, 1986).

19. Kenneth Wald, *Religion and Politics in the United States,* 2nd ed. (Washington, DC: CQ Press, 1992), Ch. 7.

20. Murray Edelman, *The Symbolic Uses of Politics* (Urbana IL: University of Illinois Press, 1964), Ch. 2.

21. The term is from Richard Wagner, "Pressure Groups and Political Entrepreneurs," *Papers in Nonmarket Decision Making* 1 (1966): 161–70. For extended discussions, see Norman Frolich, Joe Oppenheimer, and Oran Young, *Political Leadership and Collective Goods* (Princeton, NJ: Princeton University Press, 1971); and Terry Moe, *The Organization of Interests* (Chicago: University of Chicago Press, 1980), Chs. 3–4.

22. "As Green Turns to Brown," *The Economist,* March 5, 1994: 28.

23. Walker, *Mobilizing Interest Groups in America,* pp. 98–99.

24. Jack Walker, "The Origins and Maintenance of Interest Groups in America," *American Political Science Review* 77 (1983): 390–406.

25. Schlozman and Tierney, *Organized Interests and American Democracy,* Ch. 4.

26. Expenditures were $1.4 billion in 1998, the latest year for which we have figures. "Spending on Lobbying Rises," *USA Today,* November 16, 1999, 11A.

27. Carl Weiser, "Enforcement of Law Almost Non-existent," *USA Today,* November 16, 1999: 11A.

28. *American Lobbyists Directory,* ed. Robert Wilson (Detroit: Gale Research Inc., 1995). The estimate of Washington lobbyists is that of James Thurber, cited in Burdett Loomis, *The Contemporary Congress* (New York: St. Martin's, 1996), p. 35.

29. Chuck Henning, *The Wit and Wisdom of Politics* (Golden, CO: Fulcrum Publishing, 1992), p. 137.

30. For figures see Mark Petracca, ed., *The Politics of Interests* (Boulder, CO: Westview Press, 1992), pp. 14–15; and Edward Laumann, John Heinz, Robert Nelson, and Robert Salisbury, "Washington Lawyers–and Others: The Structure of Washington Representation," *Stanford Law Review* 37 (1985): 465–502.

31. Lobbyist Michael Bromberg, quoted in Eleanor Clift and Tom Brazaitis, *War Without Bloodshed: The Art of Politics* (New York: Scribner, 1996), p. 100.

32. Jackie Koszczuk, "Hitting Them Where They Live," *Congressional Quarterly Weekly Report,* October 2, 1999: 2283–2286.

33. *Pressure Politics: The Story of the Anti-Saloon League* (New York: Columbia University Press, 1928), p. 76.

34. Frank Sorauf, *Inside Campaign Finance* (New Haven, CT: Yale University Press, 1992), Ch. 4. A basic reference on PACs is *The PAC Directory* (Cambridge, MA: Ballinger, various editions).

35. Ross Baker, *The New Fat Cats: Members of Congress as Political Benefactors* (New York: Priority Press, 1989); and Eliza Carney, "PAC Men," *National Journal,* October 1, 1994: 2268–2273.

36. See Edward Epstein, "Business and Labor Under the Federal Election Campaign Act of 1971," in Michael Malbin, ed., *Parties, Interest Groups, and Campaign Finance Laws* (Washington, DC: American Enterprise Institute, 1980), pp. 107–151.

37. Thomas Ferguson and Joel Rogers, *Right Turn: The Decline of the Democrats and the Future of American Politics* (New York: Hill and Wang, 1986).

38. For a discussion, see Richard Hall and Frank Wayman, "Buying Time: Moneyed Interests and the Mobilization of Bias in Congressional Committees," *American Political Science Review* 84 (1990): 797–820.

39. Jim Drinkard, "Issue Ads Crowd Airwaves Before 2000 Election," *USA Today,* November 29, 1999, 11A.

40. R. Kenneth Godwin, *One Billion Dollars of Influence* (Chatham, NJ: Chatham House, 1988).

41. Andrew McFarland, *Common Cause: Lobbying for the People* (Chatham, NJ: Chatham House, 1984), pp. 74–81.

42. Ed Henry, "It's the '90s: Old Dogs, New Tricks," *Roll Call Monthly*, November 1997: 13.

43. For elaboration, see Hugh Graham and Ted Gurr, *The History of Violence in America* (New York: Bantam, 1969).

44. For an analysis of the expansion by the judiciary of federal programs for the handicapped and the poor, see R. Shep Melnick, *Between the Lines* (Washington, DC: Brookings, 1994).

45. Karen O'Connor and Bryan McFall, "Conservative Interest Group Litigation in the Reagan Era and Beyond," in Mark Petracca, ed., *The Politics of Interests* (Boulder, CO: Westview Press, 1992), pp. 263–281.

46. Jonathan Rauch, *Demosclerosis* (New York: Random House, 1994).

47. Philip Stern, *The Best Congress Money Can Buy* (New York: Pantheon, 1988).

48. John Heinz, Edward Laumann, Robert Nelson, and Robert Salisbury, *Representing Interests: Structure and Uncertainty in National Policy Making* (in press).

49. J. Leiper Freeman, *The Political Process*, rev. ed. (New York: Random House, 1965); Grant McConnell, *Private Power and American Democracy* (New York: Knopf, 1966); and Theodore Lowi, *The End of Liberalism* (New York: Norton, 1969).

50. David Hosansky, "House and Senate Assemble Conflicting Farm Bills," *Congressional Quarterly Weekly Report*, February 3, 1996: 298.

51. Hugh Heclo, "Issue Networks and the Executive Establishment, in Anthony King, ed., *The New American Political System* (Washington, DC: Brookings, 1978), pp. 87–124.

52. Robert Salisbury, John Heinz, Robert Nelson, and Edward Laumann, "Triangles, Networks, and Hollow Cores: The Complex Geometry of Washington Interest Representation," in Mark Petracca, ed., *The Politics of Interests* (Boulder, CO: Westview Press, 1992), pp. 130–149.

53. John Chubb, *Interest Groups and the Bureaucracy* (Stanford, CA: Stanford University Press, 1983), pp. 249–265; and Richard Harris, "Politicized Management: The Changing Face of Business in American Politics," in Richard Harris and Sidney Milkis, eds., *Remaking American Politics* (Boulder, CO: Westview Press, 1989), pp. 261–286.

54. Schlozman and Tierney, *Organized Interests and American Democracy*, pp. 314–317.

55. John Hibbing and Elizabeth Theiss-Morse, *Congress as Public Enemy* (New York: Cambridge University Press, 1995), pp. 63–65, 147.

56. Earl Latham, *The Group Basis of Politics* (New York: Cornell University Press, 1952); and David Truman, *The Governmental Process* (New York: Knopf, 1958).

57. *The Semisovereign People* (New York: Holt, 1960), pp. 34–35.

58. *Politics, Pressures, and the Tariff* (New York: Prentice-Hall, 1935).

59. "The Gerontocrats," *The Economist*, May 13, 1995: 32.

60. Mansbridge, *Why We Lost the ERA*, p. 73.

61. Peter Aranson and Peter Ordeshook, "A Prolegomenon to a Theory of the Failure of Representative Democracy," in Aranson and Ordeshook, eds., *American Re-evolution* (Tucson: University of Arizona, 1977), pp. 23–46.

CHAPTER 8

1. This short account is based on James MacGregor Burns, *The Deadlock of Democracy* (Englewood Cliffs, NJ: Prentice-Hall, 1964), Ch. 2.

2. Jackson Turner Main, *Political Parties Before the Constitution* (New York: Norton, 1973).

3. Richard Katz, "Party Government: A Rationalistic Conception," in F. Castles and R. Wildenmann, eds., *Visions and Realities of Party Government* (Berlin: deGruyter, 1986), p. 31.

4. Geoffrey Smith, "The Futures of Party Government," in F. Castles and R. Wildenmann, eds., *Visions and Realities of Party Government* (Berlin: de Gruyter, 1986), p. 206.

5. Martin Wattenberg, *The Decline of American Political Parties, 1952–1992* (Cambridge, MA: Harvard University Press, 1994).

6. *Party Government* (New York: Farrar and Rinehart, 1942), p. 1.

7. John Aldrich, *Why Parties?* (Chicago: University of Chicago Press, 1995), Ch. 2.

8. See, for example, James Campbell, *The Presidential Pulse of Congressional Elections* (Lexington: University Press of Kentucky, 1993).

9. V. O. Key, Jr., *Southern Politics* (New York: Knopf, 1949).

10. Richard Fenno, *Home Style* (Boston: Little, Brown, 1978), Ch. 3.

11. Anthony Downs, *An Economic Theory of Democracy* (New York: Harper & Row, 1957).

12. Gavin Wright, "The Political Economy of New Deal Spending: An Econometric Analysis," *Review of Economics and Statistics* 56 (1974): 30–38.

13. Morris Fiorina, *Divided Government*, 2nd ed. (Boston: Allyn & Bacon, 1996), pp. 107–110.

14. R. Michael Alvarez and Jonathan Nagler, "Economics, Issues, and the Perot Candidacy: Voter Choice in the 1992 Presidential Election," *American Journal of Political Science* 39 (1995): 714–744.

15. Austin Ranney, *Curing the Mischiefs of Faction* (Berkeley: University of California Press, 1975); and Nelson Polsby, *Consequences of Party Reform* (New York: Oxford University Press, 1983).

16. James Bryce, *The American Commonwealth*, 4th ed. (London: Macmillan, 1910), vol. 2, p. 5.

17. See, for example, William Chambers and Walter Dean Burnham, eds., *The American Party Systems: Stages of Political Development* (New York: Oxford University Press, 1975).

18. The seminal contribution was V. O. Key, Jr., "A Theory of Critical Elections," *Journal of Politics* 17 (1955): 3–18. The most influential elaborations and extensions of the idea are Walter Dean Burnham, *Critical Elections and the Mainsprings of American Politics* (New York: Norton, 1970) and James Sundquist, *Dynamics of the Party System,* rev. ed. (Washington, DC: Brookings, 1983).

19. Robert Remini, *Martin Van Buren and the Making of the Democratic Party* (New York: Columbia, 1959); and Donald Cole, *Martin Van Buren and the American Political System* (Princeton, NJ: Princeton University Press, 1984).

20. For a recent history of the period, see Paul Kleppner, *The Third Electoral System, 1853–1892: Parties, Voters, and Political Cultures* (Chapel Hill: University of North Carolina Press, 1979).

21. Charles Stewart and Barry Weingast, "Stacking the Senate, Changing the Nation: Republican Rotten Boroughs, Statehood Politics, and American Political Development," *Studies in American Political Development* 6 (1992): 223–271.

22. Michael McGerr, *The Decline of Popular Politics* (New York: Oxford University Press, 1986).

23. Harold Gosnell provides a classic study of a machine. See his *Machine Politics: Chicago Model* (Chicago: University of Chicago Press, 1937). For a more recent study, see M. C. Brown and C. N. Halaby, "Machine Politics in America, 1870–1945," *Journal of Interdisciplinary History* 17 (1987): 587–612.

24. John D. Hicks, *The Populist Revolt* (Minneapolis: University of Minnesota Press, 1931).

25. E. E. Schattschneider, "United States: The Functional Approach to Party Government," in Sigmund Neumann, ed. *Modern Political Parties* (Chicago: University of Chicago Press, 1956), pp. 194–215.

26. Richard Vallely, "National Parties and Racial Disenfranchisement," in Paul Peterson, ed., *Classifying by Race* (Princeton, NJ: Princeton University Press, 1995), pp. 188–216.

27. Alan Lichtman, *Prejudice and the Old Politics* (Chapel Hill: University of North Carolina Press, 1979).

28. Richard Hofstadter, *The Age of Reform* (New York: Vintage, 1955); Gabriel Kolko, *The Triumph of Conservatism* (New York: Free Press, 1963).

29. Joel Silbey, "Beyond Realignment and Realignment Theory," in Byron Shafer, ed., *The End of Realignment?* (Madison: University of Wisconsin Press, 1991), pp. 3–23.

30. Walter Dean Burnham believes that a realignment did indeed occur in the early 1990s. See his "Realignment Lives: The 1994 Earthquake and Its Implications," in Colin Campbell and Bert Rockman, eds., *The Clinton Presidency: First Appraisals* (Chatham, NJ: Chatham House, 1996), pp. 363–395.

31. Steven Rosenstone, Roy Behr, and Edward Lazarus, *Third Parties in America* (Princeton, NJ: Princeton University Press, 1981).

32. Maurice Duverger, *Political Parties: Their Organization and Activity in the Modern State* (New York: Wiley, 1963), Book II, Ch. 1.

33. *Ibid.* For elaboration, see Thomas Palfrey, "A Mathematical Proof of Duverger's Law," in *Models of Strategic Choice in Politics,* Peter Ordeshook, ed. (Ann Arbor: University of Michigan Press, 1989), pp. 69–91.

34. Douglas Rae, *The Political Consequences of Electoral Laws,* rev. ed. (New Haven, CT: Yale University Press, 1971), p. 98. Compare Arend Lijphart, who argues that Rae's figures exaggerate the difference; see Lijphart, "The Political Consequences of Electoral Laws, 1945–1985," *American Political Science Review* 84 (1990): 481–496.

35. *Critical Elections,* Ch. 5.

36. *Trans Action* 7 (1969): 12–22.

37. *The Party's Over: The Failure of American Politics* (New York: Harper & Row, 1971).

38. Xandra Kayden and Eddie Mahe, Jr., *The Party Goes On: The Persistence of the Two-Party System in the United States* (New York: Basic, 1985); and Larry Sabato, *The Party's Just Begun: Shaping Political Parties for America's Future* (Glenview, IL: Scott, Foresman, 1988).

39. Leon Epstein, *Political Parties in the American Mold* (Madison: University of Wisconsin Press, 1986); and Joseph Schlesinger, "The New American Party System," *American Political Science Review* 79 (1985): 1152–1169.

40. The following classification of parties as organizations, parties in the electorate, and parties in government is a standard one developed most fully in Frank Sorauf's text, *Party Politics in America* (Boston: Little, Brown, various editions).

41. Julius Turner, *Party and Constituency: Pressures on Congress* (Baltimore, MD: Johns Hopkins University Press, 1951).

42. *The Deadlock of Democracy.*

43. Writing in the 1970s, Hugh Heclo put the number at 3000. See his *A Government of Strangers* (Washington, DC: Brookings, 1977). By 1992, Thomas Weko put the number at about 3700. See *The Politicizing Presidency* (Lawrence: University of Kansas Press, 1995), p. 161.

44. Stephen Skowronek, *Building a New American State* (New York: Cambridge University Press, 1992), p. 69.

45. Stephen Frantzich, *Political Parties in the Technological Age* (New York: Longman, 1989).

46. Gordon Baker, *The Reapportionment Revolution* (New York: Random House, 1966).

47. Cornelius Cotter, James Gibson, John Bibby, and Robert Huckshorn, *Party Organizations in American Politics* (New York: Praeger, 1984).

48. *Ibid.*

49. John Coleman, "Resurgent or Just Busy? Party Organizations in Contemporary America," in John Green and Daniel Shea, eds., *The State of the Parties,* 2nd ed. (Lanham, MD: Rowman and Littlefield, 1996), pp. 312–326.

50. David Hosansky, "House Torn

on Agriculture; Senate Makes Progress," *Congressional Quarterly Weekly Report,* September 30, 1995: 2980–2984.

51. Robert Dahl, *Dilemmas of Pluralist Democracy* (New Haven, CT: Yale University Press, 1982).

CHAPTER 9

1. Quoted in Peter Braestrup, *Big Story,* abridged edition (New Haven, CT: Yale University Press, 1983), p. 134.

2. Austin Ranney, *Channels of Power: The Impact of Television on American Politics* (New York: Basic Books, 1983), p. 4.

3. David Halberstam, *The Powers That Be* (New York: Knopf, 1979), p. 514.

4. Don Oberdorfer, *Tet!* (New York: Doubleday, 1971).

5. Braestrup provides the most ambitious account, comparing, in *Big Story,* the reality of the war to the news coverage.

6. In December, the chairman of the Joint Chiefs of Staff noted the possibility of an all-or-nothing offensive such as the Battle of the Bulge launched by the Germans as they retreated during World War II. *Ibid.,* p. 54.

7. For a thoughtful treatment of the media's impact, see Braestrup, *Big Story,* pp. 505–507.

8. David Altheide, *Creating Reality: How TV News Distorts Events* (Beverly Hills, CA: Sage, 1976).

9. Lewis Chester, Godfrey Hodgson, and Bruce Page, *An American Melodrama* (New York: Viking, 1969), p. 582.

10. *Ibid.,* p. 592.

11. John Robinson, "Public Reaction to Political Protest: Chicago 1968," *Public Opinion Quarterly* 34 (1970): 1–9.

12. Frank Luther Mott, *American Journalism* (New York: Macmillan, 1950).

13. Samuel Kernell, *Going Public: New Strategies of Presidential Leadership* (Washington, DC: CQ Press, 1986). Compare Mel Laracey, "The

Presidential Newspaper: The Forgotten Way of Going Public" (manuscript, Harvard University, 1993).

14. Mott, *American Journalism,* p. 216.

15. Personal communication of Premier Radio, which manages and distributes the Limbaugh show, with research assistant Sam Abrams, March 28, 2000.

16. 1999 annual radio station survey by M Street Corporation of Nashville (**http://www.mstreet.net**).

17. Mary Ann Watson, *The Expanding Vista: American Television in the Kennedy Years* (New York: Oxford University Press, 1990), p. 76.

18. Austin Ranney, "Broadcasting, Narrowcasting, and Politics," in Anthony Kind, ed., *The New American Political System,* second version (Washington, DC: AEI Press, 1990), pp. 175–201.

19. Pew Research Center for the People and the Press (**http://www.peoplepress.org/ med98rpt.htm**). Mediamark Research Inc., "Multimedia Audiences," 1999.

20. William Mayer, "The Rise of the New Media," *Public Opinion Quarterly* 58 (1994): 124–146.

21. **www.nua.ie/surveys/how_ many_online/index.html**

22. Mark Gillespie, "'Cyber-Politics' May be More Hype Than Reality . . . So Far," Gallup Poll Release, February 25, 2000.

23. Jim Puzzanghera, "Candidates Rake in Funds on Internet, *San Jose Mercury News,* January 5, 2000.

24. Jeff Glasser, "Virtual Campaign Pays Off," *U.S. News and World Report,* March 6, 2000.

25. Rebecca Fairley Raney, "Experts Want to Dissect McCain's Internet Fundraising," *New York Times,* February 18, 2000.

26. Eve Gerber, "Six Arguments for Online Fund Raising," *Slate,* January 18, 2000; and Lindsey Arent, "Candidates Eye Check Republic," *Wired News,* January 13, 2000.

27. William Mayer, "Trends in Media Usage," *Public Opinion Quarterly* 57 (1993): 597, 610.

28. For example, Doris Graber, *Mass Media and American Politics*

(Washington, DC: CQ Press, 1993), Ch. 7.

29. Russell Neuman, Marion Just, and Ann Crigler, *Common Knowledge: News and the Construction of Political Meaning* (Chicago: University of Chicago Press, 1992); and Jeffrey Mondak, "Newspapers and Political Awareness," *American Journal of Political Science* 39 (1995): 513–527.

30. William Kornhauser, *The Politics of Mass Society* (New York: Free Press, 1959).

31. An example is the study of the 1940 presidential campaign reported in Paul Lazarsfeld, Bernard Berelson, and Hazel Gaudet, *The People's Choice* (New York: Columbia University Press, 1948).

32. Joseph Klapper, *The Effects of Mass Communication* (New York: Free Press, 1960).

33. Bernard Cohen, *The Press and Foreign Policy* (Princeton, NJ: Princeton University Press, 1963), p. 13.

34. Presentation by Steven Livingston at the John F. Kennedy School of Government, Harvard University, March 1996.

35. Robert Rotberg and Thomas Weiss, eds., *From Massacres to Genocide* (Washington, DC: Brookings, 1996).

36. M. McCombs and D. Shaw, "The Evolution of Agenda-Setting: Twenty-Five Years in the Marketplace of Ideas," *Journal of Communications* 43 (1993): 58–67.

37. Steven Livingston and Todd Eachus, "Humanitarian Crises and U.S. Foreign Policy: Somalia and the CNN Effect Reconsidered," *Political Communication* 12 (1995): 413–429.

38. Lawrence Jacobs and Robert Shapiro, *Politicians Don't Pander* (Chicago: University of Chicago Press, 2000).

39. Shanto Iyengar and Donald Kinder, *News That Matters: Television and American Opinion* (Chicago: University of Chicago Press, 1987).

40. Jon Krosnick and Laura Brannon, "The Impact of the Gulf War on the Ingredients of Presidential Evaluations," *American Political Science Review* 87 (1993): 963–975.

41. Everett Carll Ladd, "As Much About Continuity as Change: As Much About Restoration as Rejection," *The American Enterprise* (January/February 1993): 49–50; and Marc Hetherington, "The Media's Role in Forming Voters' National Economic Evaluations in 1992," *American Journal of Political Science* 40 (1996): 372–395.

42. The most extensive study of framing is by Shanto Iyengar, *Is Anyone Responsible?* (Chicago: University of Chicago Press, 1991).

43. *Public Opinion*, December/January 1985: 39.

44. Iyengar and Kinder, *News That Matters*, Chs. 6, 10.

45. Bernard Cohen, *The Press and Foreign Policy*. See also Lutz Erbring, Edie Goldenberg, and Arthur Miller, "Front-Page News and Real-World Clues: A New Look at Agenda-Setting by the Media," *American Journal of Political Science* 24 (1980): 16–49.

46. S. Robert Lichter and Stanley Rothman, "Media and Business Elites," *Public Opinion*: October/ November 1981: 43. Freedom Forum survey cited in Jill Zuckman, "Dole Says Media Overplay GOP View on Abortion," *Boston Globe*, June 25, 1996, 10.

47. William Schneider and I. A. Lewis, "Views on the News," *Public Opinion*: August/September 1985, 6–11; and "Ordinary Americans More Cynical Than Journalists: News Media Differs with Public and Leaders on Watchdog Issues" (Washington, DC: Times Mirror Center on People and the Press, May 22, 1995).

48. Maura Clancy and Michael Robinson, "The Media in Campaign '84: General Election Coverage, Part I," *Public Opinion*, December/January 1985: 49–54, 59.

49. Daniel Amundson and S. Robert Lichter, "Heeeeeeree's Politics," *Public Opinion*, July/August 1988: 46.

50. Schneider and Lewis note that in the *Los Angeles Times* study, "Views on the News," that they report on, one-quarter of the readership thought their papers were conservative, one-quarter thought liberal, one-quarter thought moderate, and one-quarter didn't know.

51. Jeff Leeds, "More Negative Coverage for Gore than Bush This Fall," *San Fransisco Chronicle*, November 1, 2000: A2.

52. Martha Moore, "Candidates Try to Reach Voters by Joking with Jay, Dueling with Dave," *USA Today*, March 1, 2000, 14A.

53. Thomas Palmer, "Reputation for Bias Seems Well Earned," *Boston Globe*, January 3, 1993, 65, 68.

54. For an example of the media's tone after the election, see Robert Woodward, *The Agenda: Inside the Clinton White House* (New York: Simon and Schuster, 1994).

55. David Mayhew, "The Return to Unified Party Control Under Clinton: How Much of a Difference in Lawmaking?" in Dryan Jones, ed., *The New American Politics* (Boulder, CO: Westview Press, 1995), pp. 111–121.

56. Harold Stanley and Richard Niemi, *Vital Statistics on American Politics*, 5th ed. (Washington, DC: CQ Press, 1995): 73.

57. Ben Bagdikian, *Double Vision* (Boston: Beacon Press, 1995), p. 48.

58. G. C. Stone and E. Grusin, "Network TV as Bad News Bearer," *Journalism Quarterly* 61 (1984), 517–523; R. H. Bohle, "Negativism as News Selection Predictor," *Journalism Quarterly* 63 (1986): 789–796; and D. E. Harrington, "Economic News on Television: The Determinants of Coverage," *Public Opinion Quarterly* 53 (1989): 17–40.

59. Larry Sabato, *Feeding Frenzy* (New York: Simon and Schuster, 1991).

60. Michael Robinson, "Public Affairs Television and the Growth of Political Malaise," *American Political Science Review* 70 (1976): 409–432. On TV making people more negative about human nature generally, see George Comstock, *The Evolution of American Television* (Newbury Park, CA: Sage, 1989), pp. 265–269.

61. A widely cited study of what constitutes news is provided by Herbert Gans, *Deciding What's News: A Case Study of CBS Evening News, NBC Nightly News, Newsweek and Time* (New York: Vintage, 1979).

62. Quoted in James Fallows, *Breaking the News* (New York: Pantheon, 1966), p. 137.

63. The following account is based on Thomas Romer and Barry Weingast, "Political Foundations of the Thrift Debacle," in Alberto Alesina and Geoffrey Carliner, eds., *Politics and Economics in the 1980s* (Chicago: University of Chicago Press, 1981), pp. 175–214.

64. Ellen Hume, "Why the Press Blew the S&L Scandal," *New York Times*, May 24, 1990, A25.

65. Mark Rom, *Public Spirit in the Thrift Tragedy* (Pittsburgh: University of Pittsburgh Press, 1996).

66. John David Rausch, Jr., "The Pathology of Politics: Government, Press, and Scandal," *Extensions*: A Publication of the Carl Albert Congressional Research and Studies Center (Norman, OK: Carl Albert Congressional Research and Studies Center, Fall 1990), pp. 11–12.

67. A Gallup survey of former Nieman Journalism Fellows found that more than three-quarters believe that traditional journalism is being replaced by tabloid journalism. See "The State of the Public Media Today" (Cambridge, MA: Nieman Foundation, April 1995).

68. Sabato, *Feeding Frenzy*.

69. Fallows, *Breaking the News*, p. 132.

70. John Kramer, vice-president for Communication, Institute of Justice, personal communication, September 9, 1999.

71. Alison Carper, "Paint-by-Numbers Journalism: How Reader Surveys and Focus Groups Subvert a Democratic Press" (Barone Center on the Press, Politics and Public Policy, Harvard University Kennedy School of Government, Discussion Paper D–19, April 1995).

72. Peter Canellos, "Perot Ad Announcement is Also-Ran Against Reruns," *Boston Globe*, September 13, 1996, A24.

73. Thomas Patterson, *Out of Order* (New York: Knopf, 1993), Ch. 2.

74. Kiku Adatto, *Picture Perfect* (New York: Basic, 1993), Ch. 25.

75. *Ibid.*

76. Pippa Norris, "Editorial," *Press/Politics* 2 (1997): 1.

77. *Washington Post,* "Parties Take Their Conventions to the Web" July 14, 2000.

78. Elihu Katz and Jacob Feldman, "The Debates in the Light of Research: A Survey of Surveys," in Sidney Kraus, ed., *The Great Debates* (Bloomington: University of Indiana Press, 1962), pp. 173–223.

79. Thomas Holbrook, "Campaigns, National Conditions, and U.S. Presidential Elections," *American Journal of Political Science* 38 (1994): 973–998.

80. Quoted in Matthew Kerbel, *Remote & Controlled* (Boulder, CO: Westview Press, 1995), p. 93.

81. Michael Robinson and Margaret Sheehan, *Over the Wire and on TV* (New York: Russell Sage, 1983).

82. S. Robert Lichter and Daniel Amundson, "Less News Is Worse News: Television News Coverage of Congress, 1972–92," in Thomas Mann and Norman Ornstein, eds., *Congress, the Press, and the Public* (Washington, DC: American Enterprise Institute, 1994), pp. 131–140.

83. Iyengar, *Is Anyone Responsible?*

84. David Broder, "The Heroism of Hard Work," *Boston Globe*, October 18, 1995, 23.

85. Lichter and Amundson, "Less News Is Worse News."

86. *Ibid.*

87. S. Robert Lichter, Linda S. Lichter, and Daniel Amundson, "Government Goes Down the Tube, Images of Government in TV Entertainment, 1955-1998," *Press/Politics* 5(2) (2000): 96–103.

88. Quoted in Fallows, *Breaking the News*, pp. 187–188.

CHAPTER 10

1. For a fuller discussion see Barbara Sinclair, "Trying to Govern Positively in a Negative Era: Clinton and the 103rd Congress," in Colin Campbell and Bert Rockman, eds., *The Clinton Presidency: First Appraisals* (Chatham, NJ: Chatham House, 1996), pp. 101–109.

2. "The Race is on—for 2004," *Slate*, August 14, 2000.

3. "Fresh Light on Primary Colors," *The Economist*, February 24, 1996: 23.

4. A good current description of the caucus system can be found in William Mayer, "Caucuses: How They Work, What Difference They Make," in William Mayer, ed., *In Pursuit of the White House* (Chatham, NJ: Chatham House, 1996).

5. On the history of the presidential primary, see James Davis, *Springboard to the White House* (New York: Crowell, 1967).

6. Nelson Polsby, *Consequences of Party Reform* (New York: Oxford University Press, 1983), Ch. 1.

7. For a participant observer's account of the post-1968 reforms, see Austin Ranney, *Curing the Mischiefs of Faction* (Berkeley: University of California Press, 1975).

8. John Kessel, *The Goldwater Coalition* (Indianapolis: Bobbs-Merrill, 1968), Ch. 3.

9. On primary dynamics see John Aldrich, *Before the Convention* (Chicago: University of Chicago Press, 1980) and Larry Bartels, *Presidential Primaries and the Dynamics of Public Choice* (Princeton, NJ: Princeton University Press, 1988).

10. Stephen Wayne, *The Road to the White House, 1996* (New York: St. Martin's, 1997), Ch. 2.

11. Jim Drinkard, "Let the Fundraising Begin–Again," *USA Today*, March 10, 2000, 14A.

12. Elizabeth Shogren, "Bush Cracks Records for Campaign Spending," *USA Today*, March 21, 2000, 13A.

13. John Haskell, *Fundamentally Flawed* (Lanham, MD: Rowman and Littlefield, 1996).

14. Pew Research Center for the People and the Press, "It's Still Too Early for the Voters," **http://www. people-press.org/june99rpt.htm**.

15. Kathy Kiely, "Wealth of Debates Keeps the Hopefuls Talking," *USA Today*, January 26, 2000, 8A.

16. Paul Simon, "The Wrong Way to Fix the Primaries," *New York Times*, January 25, 2000.

17. Larry Sabato, "Presidential Nominations: The Front-Loaded Frenzy of '96," in Larry Sabato, ed., *Toward the Millennium: The Elections of 1996* (Boston: Allyn & Bacon, 1997), pp. 37–91.

18. "A Good Fight Draws a Crowd," *New York Times*, March 12, 2000, 5.

19. On popular perceptions of Democratic and Republican presidential versus congressional candidates, see Robert Erikson, "Roll Calls, Reputations, and Representation in the U.S. Senate," *Legislative Studies Quarterly* 15 (1990): 630.

20. See John G. Geer, *Nominating Presidents* (New York: Greenwood Press, 1989), Ch. 2; and Barbara Norander, "Nomination Choices: Caucus and Primary Outcomes, 1976–1988," *American Journal of Political Science* 37 (1993): 343–364.

21. James McCann, "Presidential Nomination Activists and Political Representation: A View from the Active Minority Studies," in William Mayer, ed., *In Pursuit of the White House* (Chatham, NJ: Chatham House, 1996), pp. 72–104.

22. On presidential fund raising see Clifford Brown, Lynda Powell, and Clyde Wilcox, *Serious Money* (Cambridge, England: Cambridge University Press, 1995).

23. Thomas Patterson, *Out of Order* (New York: Vintage, 1994), p. 74.

24. "Once Again, 2 Small States Warp Political Process, *USA Today*, January 24, 2000, 18A.

25. *Ibid.*, p. 82.

26. Most research finds only small electoral impacts for the vice-presidential nominees. See Steven Rosenstone, *Forecasting Presidential Elections* (New Haven: Yale University Press, 1983), pp. 64–66 and pp. 87–88.

27. *A Heartbeat Away: Report of the Twentieth-Century Fund Task Force on the Vice-Presidency* (New York: Priority Press, 1988).

28. During the last two months of the presidential campaigns of 1976–1988, about 40 percent of the lead stories on the CBS evening news were about the election, as were 20 percent of all the stories reported. See Stephen J. Rosenstone and John Mark Hansen, *Mobilization, Participation, and Democracy in America* (New York: Macmillan, 1993), p. 178, n. 26.

29. Anthony Corrado, "Financing the 1996 Presidential General Election," in John Green, *Financing the 1996 Election* (Armonk, NY: M.E. Sharpe, 1999), pp. 84–85.

30. Thomas Patterson and Robert McClure, *The Unseeing Eye: The Myth of Television Power in National Elections* (New York: Putnam, 1976); and Stephen Ansolabehere and Shanto Iyengar, *Going Negative: How Attack Ads Shrink and Polarize the Electorate* (New York: Free Press, 1995).

31. Darrel West, *Air Wars: Television Advertising in Election Campaigns, 1952–1992* (Washington, DC: Congressional Quarterly, 1993).

32. Edwin Diamond and Stephen Bates, *The Spot,* 3rd ed. (Cambridge, MA: MIT Press, 1992).

33. William Mayer, "In Defense of Negative Campaigning," *Political Science Quarterly* 111 (1996): 437–455.

34. Craig Brians and Martin Wattenberg, "Campaign Issue Knowledge and Salience: Comparing Reception from TV Commercials, TV News, and Newspapers," *American Journal of Political Science* 40 (1996): 172–193.

35. *Ibid.* Not all scholars agree that negative ads are more effective than positive ones or that negative ads depress turnout. For a thorough airing of the issues, see the Forum in the December 1999 issue of the *American Political Science Review*.

36. David Abbott and James Levine, *Wrong Winner* (New York: Praeger, 1991).

37. For a discussion, see Nelson Polsby and Aaron Wildavsky, *Presidential Elections*, 10th ed. (Chatham, NJ: Chatham House, 2000), pp. 245–253.

38. Rhodes Cook, "Dole's Job: To Convince His Own Party," *Congressional Quarterly Weekly Report*," August 3, 1996: 9–10.

39. Although the general notion of "partisanship" has been around for centuries, the social-psychological concept of party ID was advanced in the pioneering work of Angus Campbell, Philip Converse, Warren Miller, and Donald Stokes, *The American Voter* (New York: Wiley, 1960), Chs. 6–7.

40. Morris Fiorina, *Retrospective Voting in American National Elections* (New Haven, CT: Yale University Press, 1981); and Michael MacKuen, Robert Erikson, and James Stimson, "Macropartisanship," *American Political Science Review* 83 (1989): 1125–1142.

41. Charles Franklin and John Jackson, "The Dynamics of Party Identification," *American Political Science Review* 77 (1983): 957–973.

42. Helmut Norpoth, "Under Way and Here to Stay: Party Realignment in the 1980s?" *Public Opinion Quarterly* 51 (1987): 381–387.

43. The classic demonstration appears in Chapter 8 of Campbell et al., *The American Voter*, although there is general agreement that the picture presented there is overstated. For balanced treatments of policy issues in recent campaigns, see the series of *Change and Continuity* volumes by Paul Abramson, John Aldrich, and David Rohde, published by CQ Press.

44. Benjamin Page and Richard Brody, "Policy Voting and the Electoral Process: The Vietnam War Issue," *American Political Science Review* 66 (1972): 979–995.

45. Edward Carmines and James Stimson, "The Two Faces of Issue Voting," *American Political Science Review* 74 (1980): 78–91.

46. *Ibid.* Also see R. Douglas Arnold, *The Logic of Congressional Action* (New Haven, CT: Yale University Press, 1990), Ch. 2.

47. Richard Trilling, *Party Image and Electoral Behavior* (New York: Wiley, 1976).

48. Fiorina, *Retrospective Voting.*

49. Scott Teeter, "Public Opinion in 1984," and Gerald Pomper, "The Presidential Election," both in Gerald Pomper et al., *The Election of 1984* (Chatham, NJ: Chatham House, 1985).

50. Samuel Popkin, *The Reasoning Voter* (Chicago: University of Chicago Press, 1991), pp. 60–67.

51. Donald Stokes, "Some Dynamic Elements of Contests for the Presidency," *American Political Science Review* 60 (1966): 19–28.

52. Fiorina, *Retrospective Voting*, pp. 150–153.

53. Stokes, "Some Dynamic Elements," p. 222.

54. Indeed, by some calculations, Kennedy ran worse than a "generic" Democrat for that time. See Angus Campbell, Philip Converse, Warren Miller, and Donald Stokes, "Stability and Change in 1960; A Reinstating Election," in *Elections and the Political Order* (New York: Wiley, 1966), pp. 78–95.

55. Thus an important correlate of support for Bush in 1988 was what citizens thought of *Reagan's* performance as president. See Paul Abramson, John Aldrich, and David Rohde, *Change and Continuity in the 1988 Elections* (Washington, DC: CQ Press, 1990), Ch. 7.

56. James Campbell, "When Have Presidential Campaigns Decided Election Outcomes?" Paper presented at the 1999 Annual Meeting of the American Political Science Association, Atlanta.

57. See Thomas Holbrook, *Do Campaigns Matter?* (Thousand Oaks, CA: Sage, 1996).

58. For a discussion, see Marjorie Hershey, "The Campaign and the Media," in Gerald Pomper et al., *The Election of 1988* (Chatham, NJ: Chatham House, 1989), Ch. 3.

59. See, for example, Adam Nagourney and Elizabeth Kolbert, "Missteps Doomed Dole from the Start," *New York Times*, November 8, 1996, A1.

60. Donald Kinder and Lynn Sanders, *Divided by Color* (Chicago: University of Chicago Press, 1996).

61. Paul Sniderman and Thomas Piazza, *The Scar of Race* (Cambridge, MA: Harvard University Press, 1993).

62. Paul Abramson, John Aldrich, and David Rohde, *Change and Continuity in the 1992 Elections* (Washington, DC: Congressional Quarterly, 1994); and Herbert Weisberg and David Kimball, "Attitudinal Correlates of the 1992 Presidential Vote: Party Identification and Beyond," in Herbert Weisberg, ed., *Democracy's Feast: Elections in America* (Chatham, NJ: Chatham House, 1995), pp. 72–111.

63. Everett Ladd, "The Public's Views of National Performance," *The Public Perspective*, October/November 1996: 17–20.

64. Rhodes Cook, "Race of Muted Differences Has the Nation Yawning," *Congressional Quarterly Weekly Report*, October 19, 1996: 2950.

65. Peter Canellos, "New TV Ad Mentions a GOP Unmentionable," *Boston Globe*, October 29, 1996, A23.

66. Jane Mansbridge, "Myth and Reality: The ERA and the Gender Gap in the 1980 Election," *Public Opinion Quarterly*, 49 (1985): 164–178.

67. Emily Stoper, "The Gender Gap Concealed and Revealed," *Journal of Political Science* 17 (1989): 50–62; and Tom Smith, "The Polls: Gender and Attitudes Toward Violence," *Public Opinion Quarterly* 48 (1984): 384–396.

68. For discussions, see Pamela Conover, "Feminists and the Gender Gap," *Journal of Politics* 50 (1988): 985–1010; and Elizabeth Cook and Clyde Wilcox, "Feminism and the Gender Gap–A Second Look," *Journal of Politics* 53 (1991): 1111–1122.

69. "Where the Parties Are," *The Public Perspective*, March/April 1994: 78–79. "Which Party Is Better on Which Issues?" *The Public Perspective*, June/July 1996: 65.

70. This was first noted by Herbert Weisberg, "The Demographics of a New Voting Gap: Marital Differences in American Voting Behavior," *Public Opinion Quarterly* 51 (1987): 335–343.

71. Robert Merry, "A Rule for Presidents: Go Centrist or Perish," *Congressional Quarterly Weekly Report*, October 26, 1996: 3106.

72. Michael Kinsley, as quoted by Howard Kurtz, "The Premature Post-Mortems Are Starting," *Washington Post*, online extras, October 31, 2000.

## CHAPTER 11

1. Quoted in George Hager and David Cloud, "Democrats Tie Their Fate to Clinton's Budget Bill," *Congressional Quarterly Weekly Report*, August 7, 1993: 2123.

2. Martha Angle, "Tallying Up the Thank-Yous," *Congressional Quarterly Weekly Report*, May 29, 1993: 1344.

3. Hager and Cloud, "Democrats Tie Their Fate to Clinton's Budget Bill," pp. 2127, 2125.

4. "Federalist 52," *The Federalist Papers*, Clinton Rossiter, ed. (New York: Mentor, 1961), p. 327.

5. Max Farrand, ed., *The Records of the Federal Convention of 1787* (New Haven, CT: Yale University Press, 1966), Vol. 1, p. 151.

6. Morris Fiorina, David Rohde, and Peter Wissel, "Historical Change in House Turnover," in Norman Ornstein, ed., *Congress in Change* (New York: Praeger, 1975), pp. 24–57. Nelson Polsby, "The Institutionalization of the U.S. House of Representatives," *American Political Science Review* 62 (1968): 144–168.

7. James Young, *The Washington Community, 1800–1828* (New York: Harcourt, 1966), Ch. 2.

8. The South was primarily agricultural and had fewer high-status career opportunities outside of politics. From the very beginning, southern members of Congress stayed longer than northerners. Fiorina, Rohde, and Wissel, *Historical Change in House Turnover*, pp. 34–38.

9. Robert Struble, Jr., "House Turnover and the Principle of Rotation," *Political Science Quarterly* 94 (1979–1980): 660.

10. Douglas Price, "The Congressional Career—Then and Now," in Nelson Polsby, ed., *Congressional Behavior* (New York: Random House, 1971), pp. 14–27.

11. A good overview of the variety of rules governing congressional primaries is contained in Kristin Kanthak and Rebecca Morton, "The Effects of Electoral Rules on Congressional Primaries," in Peter Galdersis and Mike Lyons, eds., *Nomination Politics and Congressional Representation* (Lanham, MD: Rowman and Littlefield, 2000).

12. "Congressional Primary Schedule," *Congressional Quarterly Weekly Report*, January 1, 2000: 16–17.

13. On the failure of incumbency to provide a complete explanation of Democratic dominance during this era, see Morris Fiorina, *Divided Government*, 2nd ed. (Boston: Allyn & Bacon, 1996), pp. 18–23.

14. Norman Ornstein, Thomas Mann, and Michael Malbin, *Vital Statistics on Congress, 1998–2000* (Washington, DC: American Enterprise Institute, 2000).

15. Robert Erikson, "Malapportion-ment, Gerrymandering and Party Fortunes in Congressional Elections," *American Political Science Review* 66 (1972): 1234–1245. Gary King and Andrew Gelman, "Systemic Consequences of Incumbency Advantage in U.S. House Elections," *American Journal of Political Science* 35 (1991): 110–138.

16. Ornstein, Mann, and Malbin, *Vital Statistics*, pp. 67–68.

17. John Ferejohn, "On the Decline of Competition in Congressional Elections," *American Political Science Review* 71 (1977): 172–174.

18. Gary Jacobson, *The Politics of Congressional Elections*, 4th ed. (New York: Longman, 1997).

19. Heinz Eulau, "Changing Views of Representation," in Heinz Eulau and John Wahlke, eds., *The Politics of Representation* (Beverly Hills, CA: Sage, 1978), pp. 31–53.

20. Morris Fiorina, *Congress–Keystone of the Washington Establishment*, 2nd ed. (New Haven, CT: Yale University Press, 1989).

21. *Ibid.*, Ch. 10. See also Bruce Cain, John Ferejohn, and Morris Fiorina, *The Personal Vote*

(Cambridge, MA: Harvard University Press, 1987), Ch. 2.

22. Walter Gellhorn, *Ombudsmen and Others: Citizens' Protectors in Nine Countries* (Cambridge, MA: Harvard University Press, 1966).

23. Richard H. Shapiro, *Frontline Management* (Washington, DC: Congressional Management Foundation, 1989), p. 94.

24. Morris Fiorina, "Congressmen and Their Constituents: 1958 and 1978," in Dennis Hale, ed., *The United States Congress: Proceedings of the Thomas p. O'Neill, Jr., Symposium* (Leominster, MA: Eusey Press, 1982), pp. 33–64.

25. Burdett Loomis, "The Congressional Office as a Small Business: New Members Set Up Shop," *Publius* 9 (1979): 35–55.

26. Ornstein, Mann, and Malbin, *Vital Statistics*, pp. 126, 130.

27. Glenn Parker, *Homeward Bound* (Pittsburgh, PA: University of Pittsburgh Press, 1986).

28. E. Scott Adler, Chariti Gent, and Cary Overmeyer, "The Home Style Homepage: Legislator Use of the World Wide Web for Constituency Contact," *Legislative Studies Quarterly* 23 (1998): 585–595.

29. Diana Owen, Richard Davis, and Vincent James Strickler, "Congress and the Internet," *Press/Politics* 4 (1999): 10–29.

30. Roger Davidson and Walter Oleszek, *Congress and Its Members*, 4th ed. (Washington, DC: CQ Press, 1994), p. 149.

31. Federal Election Commission (**www.fec.gov**).

32. Gary Jacobson, "Practical Consequences of Campaign Finance Reform: An Incumbent Protection Act?" *Public Policy* 42 (1976): 1–32.

33. Gary Jacobson, *Money in Congressional Elections* (New Haven, CT: Yale University Press, 1980).

34. Jacobson, *Politics of Congressional Elections*, p. 40.

35. Kenneth Bickers and Robert Stein, "The Electoral Dynamics of the Federal Pork Barrel," *American Journal of Political Science* 40 (1996): 1300–1326.

36. David Magleby and Kelly Patterson, "The Polls–Poll Trends: Congressional Reform," *Public Opinion Quarterly* 58 (1994): 420–421.

37. Douglas Arnold, *The Logic of Congressional Action* (New Haven, CT: Yale University Press, 1990), Ch. 2.

38. Amihai Glazer and Bernard Grofman, "Two Plus Two Equals Six: Tenure in Office of Senators and Representatives, 1953–1983," *Legislative Studies Quarterly* 12 (1987): 555–564.

39. Alan Abramowitz and Jeffrey Segal, *Senate Elections* (Ann Arbor, MI: University of Michigan Press, 1992), pp. 34–35.

40. Morris Fiorina, *Representatives, Roll Calls, and Constituencies* (Lexington, MA: D.C. Heath, 1974), pp. 90–100.

41. Joe Foote and David Weber, "Network Evening News Visibility of Congressmen and Senators," paper presented to the Association for Education in Journalism and Mass Communication, August 1984.

42. Glenn Parker, "Interpreting Candidate Awareness in U.S. Congressional Elections," *Legislative Studies Quarterly* 6 (1981): 219–233.

43. Abramowitz and Segal, *Senate Elections*, pp. 228–231. Jonathan Krasno, *Challengers, Competition, and Reelection: Comparing Senate and House Elections* (New Haven, CT: Yale University Press, 1995).

44. Joseph Schlesinger, *Ambition in Politics* (Chicago: Rand McNally, 1966).

45. These were charges leveled at Senator John Tunney of California in his losing 1976 race and at Senator Dick Clark of Iowa in his losing 1978 race.

46. David Brady and Morris Fiorina, "Ruptured Legacy: Presidential Congressional Relations in Historical Perspective," in Larry Berman, ed., *Looking Back on the Reagan Presidency* (Baltimore, MD: Johns Hopkins University Press, 1989), pp. 268–287.

47. John Ferejohn and Randall Calvert, "Presidential Coattails in Historical Perspective," *American Journal of Political Science* 28 (1984), pp. 127–146.

48. Morris Fiorina, *Divided Government*, 2nd ed. (Boston: Allyn & Bacon, 1996), p. 14.

49. *Ibid.*, pp. 135–139.

50. Janet Hook, "Freshmen in Congress Find Uses for Pork as They Seek Reelection, *Boston Globe*, July 2, 1996, 6.

51. Hook, "Freshmen in Congress . . . ."

52. Healey, "'Projects' Are His Project." Also see Jonathan Salant, "Some Republicans Turned Away from Leadership," *Congressional Quarterly Weekly Report*, December 7, 1996, 3352–3354; and Andrew Taylor, "GOP Pet Projects Give Boost to Shaky Incumbents," *Congressional Quarterly Weekly Report*, August 3, 1996, 2169–2173.

53. Karen Foerstel, "Slouching Toward Election Day, Democrats Are Anxious and Angry," *Congressional Quarterly Weekly Report*, September 12, 1998: 2383–2385.

54. David Rohde, *Parties and Leaders in the Postreform House* (Chicago: University of Chicago Press, 1991).

55. **www.commoncause.org**

56. Donna Cassate, "'Independent Groups' Ads Increasingly Steer Campaigns," *Congressional Quarterly Weekly Report*, May 2, 1998, 1114.

57. "Minorities in Congress," *Congressional Quarterly Weekly Report*, January 4, 1997, 28.

58. Carol Swain, *Black Faces, Black Interests: The Representation of African Americans in Congress* (Cambridge, MA: Harvard University Press, 1993).

59. For a thoughtful treatment of these and related issues, see Jane Mansbridge, "In Defense of Descriptive Representation," working paper, Harvard University, 1997.

60. "Americans Rate Their Society and Chart Its Values," *The Public Perspective*, February/March, 1997: 25.

61. David Lublin, "Racial Redistricting and Public Policy in the U.S. House of Representatives," unpublished manuscript.

62. Juliana Gruenwald, "Incumbents Survive Redistricting,"

*Congressional Quarterly Weekly Report,* November 9, 1996, 3229.

63. Lee Sigelman and Susan Welch, *Black Americans' Views of Racial Inequality* (Cambridge, England: Cambridge University Press, 1991).

64. Donald Kinder and Lynn Sanders, *Divided by Color* (Chicago: University of Chicago Press, 1996).

65. Former Representative Mike Espy (D-MS), who harbored gubernatorial or senatorial ambitions, openly espoused such beliefs. More recently, the relatively moderate record of Representative Harold Ford (D-TN) has been explained by reference to his interest in being Tennessee's first black governor or senator. Nancy Zuckerbrod, "Tennessee Democrat Has His Sights Set High," *USA Today,* March 27, 2000, 29A.

66. Writing about politics in New Haven, then an old-style machine city, in the 1950s, Dahl observed that African Americans were much better represented in government jobs and political offices than in the private sector. See Robert Dahl, *Who Governs* (New Haven, CT: Yale University Press, 1961), p. 294.

CHAPTER 12

1. The blow-by-blow account appears in various issues of *Congressional Quarterly Weekly Report* published in 1992. See pages 1605, 1860, 1927, 2154, 2251, 2354, 2435, 3020, 3134, and 3556.

2. Speaker Thomas Reed, as quoted in Neil McNeil, *Forge of Democracy* (New York: McKay, 1963).

3. David Mayhew, *Congress: The Electoral Connection* (New Haven, CT: Yale University Press, 1974), pp. 81–82. John Aldrich, *Why Parties?* (Chicago: University of Chicago Press, 1995).

4. Richard Fenno, *The United States Senate: A Bicameral Perspective* (Washington, DC: American Enterprise Institute, 1982).

5. "Voting Participation: House," *Congressional Quarterly Weekly Report,* January 27, 1996: 256.

6. Nelson Polsby, Miriam Gallagher, and Barry Rundquist, "The Growth of the Seniority System in the U.S. House of Representatives," *American Political Science Review* 63 (1969): 787–807.

7. For a more extensive discussion, see Charles Jones, "Joseph G. Cannon and Howard W. Smith: An Essay on the Limits of Leadership in the House of Representatives," in Nelson Polsby, ed., *Congressional Behavior* (New York: Random House, 1971), pp. 203–224.

8. Jackie Koszczuk, "For Embattled GOP Leaders, Season of Discontent," *Congressional Quarterly Weekly Report,* July 20, 1996: 2019–2023. Jackie Koszczuk, "Unpopular, Yet Still Powerful, Gingrich Faces a Critical Pass," *Congressional Quarterly Weekly Report,* September 14, 1996: 2573–2579.

9. Barbara Sinclair, *Majority Leadership in the U.S. House* (Baltimore. MD: Johns Hopkins University Press, 1983).

10. For a full discussion, see Steven S. Smith and Marcus Flathman, "Managing the Senate Floor: Complex Unanimous Consent Agreements Since the 1950s," *Legislative Studies Quarterly* 14 (1989): 349–374.

11. Lawrence Dodd and Richard Schott, *Congress and the Administrative State* (New York: Wiley, 1979), Ch. 3. For further discussion, see Kenneth Shepsle, "The Changing Textbook Congress," in John Chubb and Paul Peterston, eds., *Can the Government Govern?* (Washington, DC: Brookings, 1989).

12. "Democrats Oust Hebert, Poage; Adopt Reforms," *Congressional Quarterly Weekly Report,* January 18, 1975: 114.

13. Barbara Sinclair, *Legislators, Leaders, and Lawmaking: The U.S. House of Representatives in the Postreform Era* (Baltimore, MD: Johns Hopkins University Press, 1995).

14. David Brady, *Congressional Voting in a Partisan Era* (Lawrence: University of Kansas Press, 1973).

15. Gary Cox and Mathew McCubbins, *Legislative Leviathan* (Berkeley: University of California Press, 1993).

16. David Rohde, *Parties and Leaders in the Postreform House* (Chicago: University of Chicago Press, 1991).

17. Jim Drinkard, "Confident Candidates Share Campaign Wealth," *USA Today,* April 19, 2000, 10A.

18. Gerald Gamm and Kenneth Shepsle, "Emergence of Legislative Institutions: Standing Committees in the House and Senate, 1810–1825," *Legislative Studies Quarterly* 14(1989): 39–66. Joseph Cooper, *The Origins of the Standing Committees and the Development of the Modern House* (Houston, TX: Rice University Studies, 1970).

19. Richard Fenno, *Congressmen in Committees* (Boston: Little, Brown, 1973), p. 172.

20. Karen Foerstel, "Gingrich Flexes His Power in Picking Panel Chiefs," *Congressional Quarterly Weekly Report,* November 19, 1994: 3326.

21. Mark Ferber, "The Formation of the Democratic Study Group," in Nelson Polsby, ed., *Congressional Behavior* (New York: Random House, 1971), pp. 249–267.

22. Norman Ornstein, "Causes and Consequences of Congressional Change: Subcommittee Reforms in the House of Representatives, 1970–1973," in Norman Ornstein, ed., *Congress in Change* (New York: Praeger, 1975), pp. 88–114. Roger Davidson and Walter Oleszek, *Congress Against Itself* (Bloomington: Indiana University Press, 1977).

23. Dodd and Schott, *Congress and the Administrative State,* p. 124. Roger H. Davidson and Walter J. Oleszek, *Congress and Its Members,* 2nd ed. (Washington, DC: CQ Press, 1985), pp. 228–230.

24. Barry Weingast and William Marshall, "The Industrial Organization of Congress," *Journal of Political Economy* 91 (1988): 132–163.

25. John Ferejohn, *Pork Barrel Politics* (Stanford, CA: Stanford University Press, 1974); and R. Douglas Arnold, *Congress and the*

*Bureaucracy* (New Haven, CT: Yale University Press, 1979).

26. Keith Krehbiel, *Information and Legislative Organization* (Ann Arbor: University of Michigan Press, 1991).

27. Morris Fiorina, *Representatives, Roll Calls, and Constituencies* (Lexington, MA: D.C. Heath, 1974), Chs. 2–3; and R. Douglas Arnold, *The Logic of Congressional Action* (New Haven, CT: Yale University Press, 1990), Chs. 2–4.

28. Jeffrey Talbert, Bryan Jones, and Frank Baumgartner, "Nonlegislative Hearings and Policy Change in Congress," *American Journal of Political Science* 39 (1995): 391–392.

29. For a detailed study of how and why individual members participate at these various stages of the legislative process, see Richard Hall, *Participation in Congress* (New Haven, CT: Yale University Press, 1996).

30. Paul Light, *Forging Legislation* (New York: Norton, 1992), p. 199.

31. On the conference committee in recent years, see Stephen Van Beek, *Post-Passage Politics: Bicameral Relations in Congress* (Pittsburgh: University of Pittsburgh Press, 1995).

32. Richard Munson, *The Cardinals of Capitol Hill* (New York: Grove Press, 1993).

33. Quoted in Stephen Skowronek, *The Politics Presidents Make* (Cambridge, MA: Harvard University Press, 1993), p. 389.

34. Diana Evans, "Policy and Pork: The Use of Pork Barrel Projects to Build Policy Coalitions in the House of Representatives," *American Journal of Political Science* 38 (1994): 894–917.

35. The Model Cities case provides an older, similar example. See Douglas Arnold, *Congress and the Bureaucracy* (New Haven, CT: Yale University Press, 1979), Ch. 8.

36. Harrison Donnelly, "Reagan Opposition Threatens EDA Development Program," *Congressional Quarterly Weekly Report* 40 (1982): 2295–2296.

37. Chuck Henning, *The Wit and Wisdom of Politics* (Golden, CO: Fulcrum, 1992), p. 39.

38. For institutional comparisons, see John Hibbing and Elizabeth Theiss-Morse, *Congress as Public Enemy* (New York: Cambridge University Press, 1995), Ch. 2.

39. Kelly Patterson and David Magleby, "Trends: Public Support for Congress," *Public Opinion Quarterly* 56 (1992): 539–551.

40. Richard Fenno, "If, as Ralph Nader Says, Congress is the 'Broken Branch,' How Come We Love Our Congressmen So Much?" in Norman Ornstein, ed., *Congress in Change* (New York: Praeger, 1975), pp. 277–287.

41. Richard Fenno, *Home Style: House Members in Their Districts* (Boston: Little, Brown, 1978), p. 168.

42. Glenn Parker and Roger Davidson, "Why Do Americans Love Their Congressman So Much More Than Their Congress? *Legislative Studies Quarterly* 4 (1979): 52–61.

43. Mark Petracca, "Predisposed to Oppose: Political Scientists and Term Limitations," *Polity* 24 (1992): 657–672.

44. George F. Will, *Restoration: Congress, Term Limits, and the Recovery of Deliberative Democracy* (New York: Free Press, 1992).

CHAPTER 13

1. As quoted in Chuck Henning, *The Wit and Wisdom of Politics: Expanded Edition* (Golden, CO: Fulcrum Publishing, 1992), p. 214.

2. *Atlanta Journal and Constitution,* November 12, 1992.

3. "Gay Activists' Cash, Votes Ride on Ban Decision," *Congressional Quarterly Weekly Report,* July 10, 1993: 1815.

4. *New York Times,* January 27, 1993, 14.

5. *New York Times,* January 23, 1993, 1.

6. *New York Times,* January 27, 1993, 1.

7. *New York Times,* January 28, 1993, 1.

8. *Congressional Quarterly Weekly Report,* January 30, 1993: 229.

9. *New York Times,* July 18, 1993, Sect 4, p. E19.

10. Servicemembers Legal Defense Network, "Gay Discharge Figures at Highest Levels Since 1987" (**http://www.sldn.org/scripts/sldn.ixe?page=alert_01_23_99**), accessed 11/30/99.

11. Terry Moe, "The Politicized Presidency," in John Chubb and Paul E. Peterson, eds., *The New Direction in American Politics* (Washington, DC: Brookings, 1985).

12. Mark Peterson, *Legislating Together: The White House and Capitol Hill from Eisenhower to Reagan* (Cambridge, MA: Harvard University Press, 1990), Ch. 6; and Jon R. Bond and Richard Fleisher, *The President in the Legislative Arena* (Chicago: University of Chicago Press, 1990), Ch. 4.

13. Pietro S. Nivola, *The Politics of Energy Conservation* (Washington, DC: Brookings, 1986).

14. Peterson, *Legislating Together,* p. 157.

15. Charles O. Jones, "Campaigning to Govern: The Clinton Style," in Colin Campbell and Bert A. Rockman, eds., *The Clinton Presidency: First Appraisals* (Chatham, NJ: Chatham House, 1996), p. 16. Also, see Michael L. Mezey, *Congress, the President and Public Policy* (Boulder, CO: Westview, 1989).

16. As quoted in Henning, *Wit and Wisdom of Politics,* p. 240.

17. Bradley H. Patterson, Jr., *The Ring of Power: The White House Staff and Its Expanding Role in Government* (New York: Basic Books, 1988), p. 31.

18. Richard E. Neustadt, *Presidential Power and the Modern Presidents* (New York: Free Press, 1990), p. 29.

19. Benjamin Ginsberg and Martin Shefter, *Politics by Other Means: The Declining Importance of Elections in America* (New York: Basic Books, 1990).

20. James S. Young, *The Washington Community 1800–1828* (New York: Columbia University Press, 1966).

21. Daniel Stid, *The Statesmanship of Woodrow Wilson: Responsible Government under the Constitution* (Lawrence, KS: University Press of Kansas, 1998), Ch. 6.

22. Jeffrey Tulis, *The Rhetorical Presidency* (Princeton, NJ: Princeton University Press, 1987), p. 91.

23. Thomas Bailey, *The American Pageant* (Boston: D.C. Heath, 1956), p. 669.

24. Samuel Kernell, *Going Public* (Washington, DC: CQ Press, 1986).

25. Inaugural Address, January 20, 1961, as quoted in *Bartlett's Familiar Quotations, Revised and Enlarged* (Boston, MA: Little, Brown, 1980), 15th ed., p. 890.

26. Neustadt, *Presidential Power,* p. 274.

27. Denis G. Sullivan and Roger D. Masters, "Happy Warriors: Leaders' Facial Displays, Viewers' Emotions and Political Support," *American Journal of Political Science* 32 (1988), pp. 345–368.

28 Henning, *Wit and Wisdom of Politics,* p. 240.

29. Norman C. Thomas, Joseph A. Pika, and Richard A. Watson, *The Politics of the Presidency,* 3rd ed. (Washington, DC: CQ Press, 1993), p. 204.

30. John F. Harris, "Both Sides Frustrated as Budget Wars End," *Washington Post,* November 15, 1999, p. A1.

31. As quoted in James P. Pfiffner, *The Modern Presidency* (New York: St. Martin's, 1994), p. 114.

32. John Hart, *The Presidential Branch: From Washington to Clinton,* 2nd. ed. (Chatham, NJ: Chatham House, 1995), pp. 26–30.

33. See Matthew Dickinson, *Bitter Harvest: FDR, Presidential Power, and the Growth of the Presidential Branch* (New York: Cambridge University Press, 1997).

34. Paul Quirk, "Presidential Competence," in Michael Nelson, ed., *The Presidency and the Political System,* 4th ed. (Washington, DC: CQ Press, 1994), pp. 171–221; and John P. Burke, *The Institutional Presidency* (Baltimore, MD: Johns Hopkins University Press, 1992), pp. 40–42.

35. Colin Campbell, "Management in a Sandbox," in Colin Campbell and Bert A. Rockman, *The Clinton Presidency: First Appraisals* (Chatham, NJ: Chatham House, 1996), p. 60.

36. Charles O. Jones, "Campaigning to Govern: The Clinton Style," in Campbell and Rockman, *The Clinton Presidency,* p. 16.

37. Terry Moe, "The Politicized Presidency." Andrew Rudalevige, "The President's Program and the Politicized Presidency," paper presented at the Annual Meeting of the American Political Science Association, Atlanta, GA, September 2–5, 1999.

38. Bruce E. Altshuler, *LBJ and the Polls* (Gainesville: University of Florida Press, 1990); and Lawrence R. Jacobs, "The Recoil Effect: Public Opinion in the U.S. and Britain," *Comparative Politics* 24 (1992): 199–217.

39. *Wall Street Journal,* December 22, 1993, A4.

40. Jack Mitchell, *Executive Privilege: Two Centuries of White House Scandals* (New York: Hippocrene Books, 1992), p. 89–90.

41. John Farrell, "Embattled Security Official Quits, Calls Getting FBI Files a 'Mistake,'" *Boston Globe,* June 27, 1996, p. 12.

42. *Ibid.*

43. John W. Kingdon, *Agendas, Alternatives and Public Policies* (Boston: Little, Brown, 1981).

44. Tulis, *Rhetorical Presidency,* Ch. 3.

45. *Ibid.*

46. Harry McPherson, *A Political Education* (Boston: Little, Brown, 1972, p. 268), as quoted in Paul C. Light, *The President's Agenda: Domestic Policy Choice from Kennedy to Reagan* (Baltimore, MD: Johns Hopkins University Press, 1991), p. 13.

47. Stephen Hess, *Organizing the Presidency* (Washington, DC: Brookings, 1988), pp. 11–18.

48. Richard Brody, *Assessing the President: The Media, Elite Opinion and Public Support* (Stanford, CA: Stanford University Press, 1991), p. 40.

49. Rockman, "Leadership Style and the Clinton Presidency," in Campbell and Rockman, *The Clinton Presidency,* p. 334.

50. Ibid.

51. Walter Bagehot, *The English Constitution* (London: Fantana, 1993).

52. Stanley Elkins and Eric McKitrick, *Age of Federalism* (New York: Oxford University Press, 1993), p. 48.

53. The phrase is taken from Margery Allingham's *The Estate of the Beckoning Lady* (New York: Doubleday, 1955), p. 2.

547. Gerald F. Seis, "Soul on High: Clinton Strikes Deeper Chords," *Wall Street Journal,* December 15, 1993.

55. Lou Cannon, *President Reagan: The Role of a Lifetime* (New York: Simon & Schuster, 1991), p. 25.

56. Doris Kearns Goodwin, *No Ordinary Time: Franklin and Eleanor Roosevelt: The Home Front in World War II* (New York: Simon & Schuster, 1994).

57. Rockman, "Leadership Style and the Clinton Presidency," p. 334–336.

58. Helen Thomas, "Clinton Excited Wife Is Running," UPI, November 24, 1999.

59. Henning, *Wit and Wisdom of Politics,* p. 261.

60. Paul C. Light, *Vice Presidential Power* (Baltimore, MD: Johns Hopkins University Press, 1984), p. 258.

61. Sidney Milkis, *The President and the Parties: The Transformation of the American Party System Since the New Deal* (New York: Oxford University Press, 1993), p. 81.

62. Theodore Sorensen, as quoted in M. Miller, *Lyndon: An Oral Biography* (New York: Putnam, 1980), p. 254.

63. *New Republic,* June 6, 1983, as quoted in Light, *Vice Presidential Power,* p. 137.

64. Stephen Skowronek, *The Politics Presidents Make: Leadership from John Adams to George Bush* (Cambridge, MA: Harvard University Press, 1993), p. 250.

65. As quoted in James L. Sundquist, *The Decline and Resurgence of Congress* (Washington, DC: Brookings, 1981), p. 31.

66. *United States v. Belmont* 301 US 324 (1936); Harold Bruff and Peter Shane, *The Law of Presidential Powers: Cases and Materials* (Durham, NC: Carolina Academic Press, 1988), p. 88; and Joseph Paige, *The Law Nobody Knows: Enlargement of the Constitution–Treaties and Executive Orders.* (New York: Vantage Press, 1977), p. 63.

67. Louis Fisher, *Constitutional Conflicts Between Congress and the President,* 3rd ed., rev. (Lawrence: University of Kansas, 1991), p. 154.

68. *United States v. Nixon,* 418 US 683, 709 (1974).

69. The man who cast the decisive vote provided subject matter for John F. Kennedy's *Profiles in Courage* (New York: Harper & Row, 1964).

70. Peter Baker and Helen Dewar, "'Honor' of Presidency Invoked at Trial," *Washington Post,* January 17, 1999, A1.

71. *Washington Post*/ABC News Poll, January 28–30, 1999.

72. *Congressional Record,* February 12, 1999, p. S1568.

73. Robert J. Spitzer, "Clinton's Impeachment Will Have Few Consequences for the Presidency" *PS: Political Science and Politics* 32:3 (September 1999): 541–545.

74. Naftali Bendavid, "Independent Counsel Law to Die Without Mourners," *Chicago Tribune,* June 27, 1999.

75. David Johnston, "With Counsel Law Expiring, Attorney General Takes Reins," *New York Times,* June 30, 1999.

76. *Wall Street Journal,* December 22, 1993, A1.

77. Neustadt, *Presidential Power,* Ch. 4.

78. Henning, *Wit and Wisdom of Politics,* p. 219.

79. As quoted in Henning, *Wit and Wisdom of Politics,* p. 222.

80. The effect of time on presidential support is stressed by Paul Brace and Barbara Hinckley, "The Structure of Presidential Approval: Constraints Within and Across Presidencies," *Journal of Politics* 53 (November 1991): 993–1017 and by John Mueller, "Presidential Popularity from Truman to Johnson," *American Political Science Review,* March 1970: 18–24. For contrasting views, which stress events rather than time, see Brody, *Assessing the President;* and Samuel Kernell, "Explaining Presidential Popularity," *American Political Science Review,* June 1978: 506–522. Also see Michael MacKuen, "Political Drama, Economic Conditions, and the Dynamic of Public Popularity," *American Journal of Political Science,* May 1983: 165–192; Charles Ostrom and Dennis Simon, "Promise and Performance: A Dynamic Model of Presidential Popularity," *American Political Science Review,* June 1985: 334–358; and James Stimson, "Public Support for American Presidents," *Public Opinion Quarterly* 1976: 401–421.

81. These are averages for the Gallup polls taken throughout each year.

82. "Gallup Poll Trends: Clinton Job Approval," The Gallup Organization, **http://www.gallup. com/poll/trends/ ptjobapp.asp**, accessed December 18, 1999.

83. Samuel Kernell, *Going Public,* 2nd ed. (Washington, DC: CQ Press, 1993), Ch. 5.

84. Anthony Stephen King, *Running Scared: Why America's Politicians Campaign Too Much and Govern Too Little* (New York: Free Press, 1997).

85. "Transcript: Vice President Gore on CNN's 'Late Edition,'" March 9, 1999, **http://cnn.com/ALLPOLITICS/stories/ 1999/03/09/president.2000/transcript. gore**, accessed December 19, 1999; Frank Bruni, "Inventors of Paper Clips and Tall Tales," *New York Times,* March 13, 1999.

86. George C. Edwards III, *At the Margins: Presidential Leadership of Congress* (New Haven, CT: Yale University Press, 1989), pp. 120–124; Calvin Mouw and Michael MacKuen, "The Strategic Configuration, Political Influence, and Presidential Power in Congress" (paper prepared for the annual meeting of the Midwest Political Science Association, Chicago, 1989); and Terry Sullivan, "Headcounts, Expectations and Presidential Coalitions in Congress," *American Journal of Political Science* 32 (1988): 567–589.

87. James Barber, *The Presidential Character: Predicting Performance in the White House* (Englewood Cliffs, NJ: Prentice-Hall, 1972).

88. For criticism of Barber's analysis, see Michael Nelson, "The Psychological Presidency," in Michael Nelson, ed., *The Presidency and the Political System,* 4th ed. (Washington, DC: CQ Press, 1994), pp. 198–224; Alexander George, "Assessing Presidential Character," *World Politics* 26 (January 1974): 234–282; Jeffrey Tulis "On Presidential Character," in Jeffrey Tulis and Joseph M. Bessette, eds., *The Presidency in the Constitutional Order* (Baton Rouge: Louisiana State University Press, 1981); and Erwin C. Hargrove, "Presidential Personality and Leadership Style," in George C. Edwards III, John H. Kessel, and Bert A. Rockman, eds., *Researching the Presidency: Vital Questions, New Approaches* (Pittsburgh, PA: Pittsburgh University Press, 1993), pp. 93–98.

89. Fred Greenstein, *The Hidden-Hand Presidency: Eisenhower as Leader* (New York: Basic Books, 1982).

90. Charles O. Jones, "The Separated Presidency–Making It Work in Contemporary Politics," in Anthony King, ed., *The New American Political System,* second version (Washington, DC: American Enterprise Institute, 1990), p. 24.

91. Stephen Skowronek, *The Politics Presidents Make.*

92. Henning, *Wit and Wisdom of Politics,* p. 92.

## CHAPTER 14

1. Bill Clinton and Al Gore, *Putting People First: How We Can All Change America* (New York: Times Books, 1992).

2. *New York Times,* September 9, 1993, D20.

3. *New York Times*, September 8, 1993, B10.

4. *New York Times*, September 8, 1993, B10.

5. *Washington Post*, August 12, 1993, A6.

6. Ross E. Milloy, "Years After Davidian Cult Fire, Legal Battles Gather Force," *New York Times*, November 26, 1999.

7. *New York Times*, September 5, 1993 Sec. I, p. 39.

8. *New York Times*, September 5, 1993, Sec. I, p. 39.

9. *New York Times*, September 9, 1993, D20.

10. Committee on Government Reform and Oversight, U.S. House of Representatives, *U.S. Government Policy and Supporting Positions ("Plum Book")* (Washington, DC: U.S. Government Printing Office, 1996).

11. General Accounting Office, *Government Corporations: Profiles of Existing Government Corporations*, (GAO/GGD-96-14) (Washington, DC: General Accounting Office, 1995).

12. Martha Derthick, *Agency Under Stress: The Social Security Administration in American Government* (Washington, DC: Brookings, 1990).

13. Max Weber, *Essays in Sociology* (New York: Oxford University Press, 1958); and Max Weber, *Economy and Society* (Berkeley: University of California Press, 1978).

14. James Q. Wilson, "The Bureaucracy Problem," *The Public Interest* (Winter 1967): 3–9.

15. Michael Lipsky, *Street-Level Bureaucracy: Dilemmas of the Individual in Public Services* (New York: Russell Sage, 1980).

16. Lipsky, *Street-Level Bureaucracy*.

17. William A. Niskanen, *Bureaucracy and Representative Government* (Chicago: Aldine-Atherton, 1971), Chs. 2–4.

18. Aaron Wildavsky, *The New Politics of the Budgetary Process* (Boston: Little, Brown, 1988), pp. 84–85.

19. Graham Allison, *Essence of Decision: Explaining the Cuban Missile Crisis* (Boston: Little, Brown, 1971), Ch. 3.

20. Herbert Kaufman, *Red Tape: Its Origins, Uses and Abuses* (Washington, DC: Brookings, 1977), as reprinted in Francis E. Rourke, *Bureaucratic Power in National Policy Making*, 4th ed. (Boston: Little, Brown, 1986), p. 442.

21. Laurence J. Peter, as quoted in Chuck Henning, *The Wit and Wisdom of Politics: Expanded Edition* (Golden, CO:Fulcrum Publishing, 1992), p. 16.

22. Kaufman, *Red Tape*, p. 434.

23. Virginia Ellis, "I-10 Is Repaired–But Spans Need Retrofitting," *Los Angeles Times*, April 12, 1994, A1; "Accelerated Earthquake Repair Allows I-5 to Reopen Early," *Los Angeles Times*, May 18, 1994, B6; and Henry Chu, "Quake-Damaged Freeway Link Opens," *Los Angeles Times*, July 8, 1994, B1.

24. Lucius Wilmerding as quoted in Herman Finer, "Better Government Personnel," *Political Science Quarterly* 50, 4 (1936): 577.

25. Stanley Elkins and Eric McKitrick, *The Age of Federalism* (New York: Oxford University Press, 1993), p. 170.

26. James Young, *The Washington Community 1800–1828* (New York: Harcourt, 1966), p. 49. Ellipses deleted.

27. John Bartlett, *Familiar Quotations: Revised and Enlarged*, 15th ed., (Boston: Little, Brown, 1980), p. 455.

28. Seymour J. Mandelbaum, *Boss Tweed's New York* (New York: Wiley, 1965).

29. As quoted in Henning, *Wit and Wisdom of Politics*, p. 11.

30. A. James Reichley, *The Life of the Parties* (New York: Free Press, 1992), pp. 157–158.

31. Eugene Kennedy, *Hurrah! The Life and Times of Mayor Richard J. Daley* (New York: Viking, 1978), pp. 255, 274.

32. Robert Dahl, *Who Governs?* (New Haven, CT: Yale University Press, 1961); Raymond E. Wolfinger, *The Politics of Progress* (Englewood Cliffs, NJ: Prentice-Hall, 1974), Ch. 4; Edward Banfield and James Q. Wilson, *City Politics* (New York:

Random House, 1963); and Robert K. Merton, *Social Theory and Social Structure* (Glencoe, IL: Free Press, 1957), pp. 71–81.

33. Quoted in Reichley, *Life of the Parties*, p. 212.

34. Paul E. Peterson, *The Politics of School Reform, 1870–1940* (Chicago: University of Chicago Press, 1985), pp. 86–87.

35. Rufus p. Browning, Dale Rogers Marshall, and David H. Tabb, *Protest Is Not Enough: The Struggle of Blacks and Hispanics for Equality in Urban Politics* (Berkeley: University of California Press, 1984), Ch. 5.

36. Alben W. Barkley, vice-president of the United States, 1949–1953, as quoted in Henning, *Wit and Wisdom of Politics*, p. 17.

37. Paul Light, *Thickening Government: Federal Hierarchy and the Diffusion of Accountability* (Washington, DC: Brookings, 1995), Ch. 1.

38. G. Calvin MacKenzie, "The Presidential Appointment Process: Historical Development, Contemporary Operations, Current Issues" (background paper for the Twentieth Century Fund Panel on Presidential Appointments, March 1, 1994; p. 1).

39. David Houston, secretary of agriculture from 1913 to 1920 and secretary of the treasury from 1920 to 1921, as quoted in Richard F. Fenno Jr., *The President's Cabinet* (Cambridge, MA: Harvard University Press, 1959), p. 221.

40. Leonard White, *Introduction to the Study of Public Administration*, 4th ed. (New York: Macmillan, 1955), p. 80.

41. As quoted in G. Calvin MacKenzie, *The In- and Outers: Presidential Appointees and Transient Government in Washington* (Baltimore, MD: Johns Hopkins University Press, 1987).

42. Haynes Johnson and David Broder, *The System: The American Way of Politics at the Breaking Point* (Boston: Little Brown, 1996).

43. *Wall Street Journal*, February 9, 1994, 1.

44. Lyn Ragsdale, "Studying the Presidency: Why Presidents Need

Political Scientists," in Michael Nelson, ed., *The Presidency and the Political System*, 5th ed. (Washington, DC: CQ Press 1998), p. 50.

45. Thomas E. Cronin, *The State of the Presidency,* 2nd ed. (Boston: Little, Brown, 1980).

46. Jefferson Cohen, *The Politics of the U.S. Cabinet* (Pittsburgh, PA: University of Pittsburgh Press, 1988).

47. Martha M. Hamilton, "For Executives, Search for Business Turns to Tragedy," *Washington Post*, April 4, 1996, A26.

48. Kermit Gordon, *Reflections on Spending* (Washington, DC: Brookings, 1967), p. 15.

49. Marver H. Bernstein, *Regulating Business by Independent Commission* (Princeton, NJ: Princeton University Press, 1955); Harold Seidman, *Politics, Position and Power: The Dynamics of Federal Organization*, 2nd ed. (New York: Oxford University Press, 1975); George J. Stigler, "The Theory of Economic Regulation," *Bell Journal of Economics and Management Science* 2 (Spring 1971): 3–21; Terry Moe, "Regulatory Performance and Presidential Administration," *American Journal of Political Science* 16 (May 1982), 197–224; and B. R. Weingast and M. J. Moran, "Bureaucratic Discretion or Congressional Control? Regulatory Policymaking by the Federal Trade Commission," *Journal of Political Economy* 91, 5 (1983): 765–800; B. R. Weingast, "The Congressional-Bureaucratic System: A Principal–Agent Perspective (with Application to the SEC)," *Public Choice* 44, 1 (1984): 147–191.

50. Robyn Meredith, "Credit Unions Help Finance a Bid for Reinstatement by a Dismissed Federal Regulator," *New York Times*, July 20, 1996, 7.

51. United States Court of Appeals for the District of Columbia Circuit, November 22, 1996, No. 96–5193.

52. Herbert Kaufman, *The Administrative Behavior of Federal Bureau Chiefs,* p. 183, n. 8.

53. .Hugh Heclo, "OMB and the Presidency–the Problem of 'Neutral Competence,'" *Public Interest* 38 (Winter 1975): 80–98; and Karen Hult, "Advising the President," in George C. Edwards, John H. Kessel, and Bert A. Rockman, *Researching the Presidency: Vital Questions, New Approaches* (Pittsburgh, PA: University of Pittsburgh Press, 1992), p. 126.

54. David Stockman, *The Triumph of Politics* (New York: Harper & Row, 1986).

55. As quoted in Kaufman, *Administrative Behavior of Federal Bureau Chiefs*, pp. 169–70.

56. Johnson and Broder, *The System,* p. 116.

57. Johnson and Broder, *The System,* p. 397.

58. Derthick, *Agency Under Stress*, p. 200.

59. Frederic Ogg and p. Orman Ray, *Introduction to American Government* 10th ed. (New York: Appleton-Century-Crofts, 1951), p. 405

60. Carolyn Lochhead, "Lott Backs Drive to Block All Clinton Nominations," *San Francisco Chronicle*, June 11, 1999, A1.

61. David King, "The Nature of Congressional Committee Jurisdictions," *American Political Science Review* 88 (March 1995): 48–62.

62. Beryl A. Radin and Willis D. Hawley, *The Politics of Federal Reorganization: Creating the U.S. Department of Education* (New York: Pergamon Press, 1988).

63. James Q. Wilson, *Bureaucracy: What Government Agencies Do and Why They Do It* (New York: Basic Books, 1989), pp. 295–314; and Ezra N. Suleiman, *Politics, Power and Bureaucracy in France: The Administrative Elite* (Princeton, NJ: Princeton University Press, 1974).

64. T. J. Pempel, "The Bureaucratization of Policymaking in Postwar Japan," *American Journal of Political Science* 18 (November 1974): 64.

65. R. Shep Melnick, *Regulation and the Courts: The Case of the Clean Air Act* (Washington, DC: Brookings, 1983).

66. Dick Kirschten, "Slicing the Turf," *Government Executive*, April 1999.

67. Robert L. Park, director of the Washington office of the American Physical Society, as quoted in Graeme Browning, "Fiscal Fission," *National Journal*, June 8, 1996: 1259.

68. Graeme Browning, "Fiscal Fission," p. 1259.

69. Cindy Skrzycki, "The Regulators: Congress Isn't Taking EPA for Granted," *Washington Post*, December 31, 1999, E1.

70. Bill McAllister, "Byrd's Big Prize: Bringing Home the FBI," *Washington Post*, March 13, 1991, A1.

71. Joel Aberbach, *Keeping a Watchful Eye* (Washington, DC: Brookings, 1990), p. 38.

72. Grant McConnell, *Private Power and American Democracy* (New York: Knopf, 1966); Theodore Lowi, *The End of Liberalism,* 2nd ed. (New York: Norton, 1979); and Mark P. Petracca, ed., *The Politics of Interests: Interest Groups Transformed* (Boulder, CO: Westview, 1992).

73. Joel Aberbach, *Keeping a Watchful Eye* (Washington, DC: Brookings, 1990), pp. 162–166.

74. Graeme Browning, "Fiscal Fission," p. 1260.

75. "Public Broadcasting Develops Dialogue with House GOP," *Congressional Quarterly Weekly Report*, March 23, 1996: 791.

76. Hugh Heclo, "Issue Networks and the Executive Establishment," in Anthony King, ed., *The New American Political System* (Washington, DC: American Enterprise Institute, 1978), pp. 87–124.

77. John E. Chubb, *Interest Groups and the Bureaucracy* (Stanford, CA: Stanford University Press, 1983); John Chubb "U.S. Energy Policy: A Problem of Delegation." in John E. Chubb and Paul E. Peterson, eds., *Can the Government Govern?* (Washington, DC: Brookings, 1989); Seong-Ho Lim, "Changing Jurisdictional Boundaries in Congressional Oversight of Nuclear Energy Regulation: Impact of Public Salience" (paper presented before the annual meeting of the American Political Science Association, 1992);

and Frank R. Baumgartner and Bryan D. Jones, "Agenda Dynamics and Policy Subsystems," *Journal of Politics* 53 (November 1991): 1044–1074.

78. Paul E. Peterson, Barry G. Rabe, and Kenneth K. Wong, *When Federalism Works* (Washington, DC: Brookings, 1986), Ch. 8; John J. Harrigan, *Political Change in the Metropolis,* 2nd ed. (Boston: Little, Brown, 1981), pp. 267–268, 350–351; and Rochelle L. Stanfield, "Communities Reborn," *National Journal,* June 22, 1966: 1371.

79. Wolf, "What History Advises."

80. John DiIulio, *No Escape: The Future of American Corrections* (New York: Basic Books, 1991), pp. 19–26.

81. James A. Morone, *The Democratic Wish: Popular Participation and the Limits of American Government* (New York: Basic Books, 1990).

82. Francis Rourke, "Executive Secrecy: Change and Continuity," in Rourke, *Bureaucratic Power in National Policy Making,* pp. 536–537.

83. Jeffrey Birnbaum, Eileen Gunn, et al., "Unbelievable! The Mess at the IRS *Is* Worse Than You Think" *Fortune,* April 13, 1998.

84. Birnbaum, Gunn, et al.

85. Birnbaum, Gunn, et al.

86. Albert B. Crenshaw, "Witnesses Say IRS Agent Tried to Frame Ex-Senator," *Washington Post,* May 1, 1998, A1.

87. Albert B. Crenshaw, "IRS Overhaul Set for Passage; Measure Gives Taxpayers New Rights, Includes Capital Gains Break," *Washington Post,* June 25, 1998, A1.

88. Martha Derthick, *Agency Under Stress,* p. 87.

89. Former Bureau of the Budget Director Kermit Gordon, as quoted in Kaufman, *Administrative Behavior,* p. 443.

90. Paul J. Quirk, "Food and Drug Administration," in James Q. Wilson, *The Politics of Regulation* (New York: Basic Books, 1980), p. 199.

91. Terry Moe, "The Politics of Bureaucratic Structure," in John E. Chubb and Paul E. Peterson, *Can the Government Govern?* (Washington, DC: Brookings, 1988).

92. Brian Hassel, "Charter Schools: Designed to Fail?" (Ph.D. dissertation, John F. Kennedy School of Government, Harvard University, 1997).

93. Robert L. Kahn, Barbara A Gutek, Eugenia Barton, and Daniel Katz, "Americans Love Their Bureaucrats," *Psychology Today* (1975), as reprinted in Rourke, *Bureaucratic Power in National Policy Making,* p. 290.

94. Charles Lindblom, "The Science of 'Muddling Through,'" *Public Administration Review* XIX (Spring 1959): 79–88.

95. Herbert Kaufman, *The Forest Ranger: A Study in Administrative Behavior* (Baltimore, MD: Johns Hopkins University Press, 1960).

CHAPTER 15

1. As quoted in Chuck Henning, *The Wit and Wisdom of Politics* (Golden, CO: Fulcrum Publishing, 1992), p. 250.

2. Ruth Marcus, "Plain-Spoken Marshall Spars with Reporters," *Washington Post,* June 29, 1991, A1.

3. David Brock, *The Real Anita Hill: The Untold Story* (New York: Free Press, 1993), p. 66.

4. Paul Simon, *Advice and Consent* (Washington, DC: National Press Books, 1992), p. 89.

5. *Ibid.,* p. 93.

6. Bob Dart, "Abortion Key to Hearing Today," *Atlanta Journal and Constitution,* Sept. 11, 1991, A1.

7. Simon, *Advice and Consent,* Chs. 5–6.

8. *Ibid.,* p. 122.

9. *Ibid.,* p. 122.

10. Brock, *The Real Anita Hill,* p. 17.

11. Gerald Pomper, "The Presidential Election," in Gerald M. Pomper et al., *The Election of 1992: Reports and Interpretations* (Chatham, NJ: Chatham House, 1993), p. 138.

12. As quoted in Henning, *Wit and Wisdom,* p. 107.

13. Carl B. Swisher, *American Constitutional Development,* 2nd ed.

(Boston: Houghton Mifflin, 1954), pp. 1075–1079.

14. Simon, *Advice and Consent,* p. 275.

15. Henry J. Abraham, *Justices and Presidents: A Political History of Appointments to the Supreme Court,* 3rd ed. (New York: Oxford University Press, 1992).

16. Gloria Borger with Kenneth T. Walsh, Ted Gest, and Sharon Golden, "Going . . . Going; How the White House Booted the Nomination of Judge Robert Bork," *U.S. News and World Report,* October 12, 1987: 20.

17. Stephen L. Carter, "Looking for Law in All the Wrong Places," *Manhattan Lawyer,* September 1990: 20.

18. Twentieth Century Fund, *Judicial Roulette* (New York: Priority Press, 1988), pp. 10–11.

19. Ethan Bronner, *Battle for Justice: How the Bork Nomination Shook America* (New York: Norton, 1989), pp. 158–59.

20. Henning, *Wit and Wisdom,* p. 250.

21. Robert G. McCloskey, *The American Supreme Court* (Chicago: University of Chicago Press, 1960), p. 14.

22. *Lochner* v. *New York* 195 US 45 (1905).

23. *Beau harnais* v. *Illinois* 343 US 250 (1952).

24. *New York* v. *United States,* 488 US 1041 (1992).

25. *Dred Scott* v. *Sandford* 19. How. 393 (1857).

26. *Lochner* v. *New York* 198 US 45 (1905). Ellipses deleted from excerpt.

27. *Schechter Poultry Corp.* v. *United States* 295 US 495 (1935).

28. Congressional Research Service, Library of Congress, *The Constitution of the United States of America: Analysis and Interpretation, 1998 Supplement* (Washington, DC: Government Printing Office, 1999).

29. Excerpted with ellipses deleted. Robert A. Dahl, "Decision-making in a Democracy: The Supreme Court as a National Policy-Maker," *Journal of Public Law* 6 (Fall 1957): 293–294. See also Richard Y.

Funston, "The Supreme Court and Critical Elections," *American Political Science Review* 69 (1975): 795–811.

30. James A. Stimson, Michael B. Mackuen, and Robert S. Erikson, "Dynamic Representation," *American Political Science Review* 89 (September 1995): 555. Also see William Mishler and Reginald S. Sheehan, "The Supreme Court as a Counter-Majoritarian Institution? The Impact of Public Opinion on Supreme Court Decisions," *American Political Science Review* 87 (1993): 87–101; and Helmut Norpoth and Jeffery Segal, "Popular Influence on Supreme Court Decisions," *American Political Science Review* 88 (September 1994): 711–724.

31. John C. Jeffries, Jr., *Justice Lewis F. Powell, Jr: A Biography* (New York: Scribner, 1994), p. 248.

32. *Ibid.,* p. 323.

33. David O'Brien, "Background Paper," in Twentieth Century Fund, *Judicial Roulette* (New York: Priority Press, 1988), p. 37.

34. As quoted in Robert A. Carp and Ronald Stidham, *The Federal Courts,* 2nd ed. (Washington, DC: CQ Press, 1991), p. 97.

35. Thomas B. Edsall, "Clinton Plans Judicial Offensive; Administration Will Hit GOP Efforts to Thwart Nominees," *Washington Post,* January 16, 1998, A1.

36. C. K. Rowland, Donald Songer, and Robert Carp, "Presidential Effects on Criminal Justice Policy in the Lower Federal Courts: The Reagan Judges," *Law and Society Review* 22/1 (1988): 191–200.

37. "Leadership Speaks out on Judicial Issues," *The Third Branch: Newsletter of the Federal Courts* 29:6 (June 1997).

38. Henning, *Wit and Wisdom,* p. 108.

39. Joan Vennochi, "The White Knight Makes His Move," *Boston Globe,* May 24, 1988, 25.

40. Richard N. Smith, *Thomas E. Dewey and His Times* (New York: Simon & Schuster, 1982), Chs. 5–9.

41. As quoted in C. Herman Pritchett, *The American Constitution* (New York: McGraw-Hill, 1959), pp. 65, 215.

42. Congressional Research Service, Library of Congress, *The Constitution of the United States of America: Analysis and Interpretation, 1998 Supplement* (Washington, DC: Government Printing Office, 1999).

43. Pritchett, *American Constitution,* p. 134.

44. Herbert Jacob and Kenneth Vines, "Courts," in Virginia Gray, Herbert Jacob, and Kenneth Vines, eds., *Politics in the American States: A Comparative Analysis,* 4th ed. (Boston: Little, Brown, 1983), p. 238.

45. Jacob and Vines, "Courts," p. 239.

46. Excerpted with ellipses deleted. Milton Rakove, *Don't Make No Waves; Don't Back No Losers* (Bloomington: Indiana University Press, 1975), pp. 223–225.

47. "Process Has No Merit," *Chicago Sun Times,* January 3, 2000, 21.

48. Jamie B. W. Stecher, "Democratic and Republican Justice: Judicial Decision Making in Five State Supreme Courts," *Columbia Journal of Law and Social Problems* 13 (1977): 137–181.

49. Mark Hansen, "A Run for the Bench," *ABA Journal,* October 1998, p. 68.

50. John Paul Ryan, Allen A. Ashman, Bruce D. Sales, and Sandra Shane-Dubow, *American Trial Judges* (New York: Free Press, 1980), p. 125.

51. "Investigate, Then Prosecute; Bungled Lewis Trial: Atlanta Prosecutors, Police Rushed to Indict Before They Had All the Evidence," *Baltimore Sun,* June 14, 2000, 22A.

52. Cynthia Tucker, "My Opinion; Murder Acquittals: Running for Glory, Fulton DA Fumbles. *Atlanta Constitution,* June 14, 2000, p. 14A.

53. Henning, *Wit and Wisdom,* p. 187.

54. *In re Chapman* 16 US 661 (1897).

55. Linda Greenhouse, "Legacy of a Term," *New York Times,* July 3, 1996, A1.

56. *Parts and Electric Motors* v. *Sterling Electric* 866 F 2d 288 (1988).

57. Henning, *Wit and Wisdom,* p. 213.

58. Hart Pomerantz, as quoted in Henning, *Wit and Wisdom,* p. 250.

59. H. W. Perry, Jr., *Deciding to Decide: Agenda Setting in the United States Supreme Court* (Cambridge, MA: Harvard University Press, 1991), p. 27.

60. *Ibid.,* pp. 218–219.

61. *Ibid.,* p. 99.

62. Joan Biskupic, "The Rehnquist Court: Justices Want to Be Known as Jurists, Not Activists," *Washington Post,* January 9, 2000, B3.

63. Address of Chief Justice Vinson before the American Bar Association, September 7, 1949, as quoted in Perry, *Deciding to Decide,* p. 36.

64. Joan Biskupic and Howard Kurtz, "Police Can Be Sued for Letting Media See Raids," *Washington Post,* May 25, 1999, A8.

65. Jeffries, *Justice Lewis F. Powell, Jr.,* p. 248.

66. Bernard Schwartz, *A History of the Supreme Court* (New York: Oxford University Press, 1993), Ch. 13.

67. This was true for the period 1958–1967; with the reduction in the number of certs accepted, this percentage has undoubtedly declined. Robert Scigliano, *The Supreme Court and the Presidency* (New York: Free Press, 1971), as quoted in Rebecca M. Salokar, *The Solicitor General: The Politics of Law* (Philadelphia: Temple University Press, 1992), p. 3.

68. Scigliano, *Supreme Court and the Presidency,* p. 162.

69. Jeffrey A. Segal, "Amicus Curiae Briefs by the Solicitor General During the Warren and Burger Courts: A Research Note," *Western Political Quarterly* 41 (March 1988): 135–144.

70. Perry, *Deciding to Decide,* p. 71.

71. Schwartz, *History of the Supreme Court,* p. 372.

72. Perry, *Deciding to Decide;* Schwartz, *History of the Supreme Court,* Ch. 16.

73. Simon, *Advice and Consent,* p. 128.

74. As quoted in Henning, *Wit and Wisdom,* p. 106.

75. Jeffries, *Justice Lewis F. Powell, Jr.,* p. 247.

76. Jeffries, *Ibid.,* pp. 245–247.

77. *Harris v. Forklift* 508 US 938 (1993).

78. *Regents of the University of California v. Bakke* 438 US 265 (1978).

79. James F. Simon, *The Center Holds: The Power Struggle Inside the Rehnquist Court* (New York: Simon & Schuster, 1995), pp. 227, 229.

80. Jeffrey A. Segal and Albert D. Cover, "Ideological Values and the Votes of U.S. Supreme Court Justices," *American Political Science Review* 83 (June 1989): 557–565.

81. Henning, *Wit and Wisdom,* p. 250.

82. As quoted by Austin Ranney, "Peltason Created a New Way to Look at What Judges Do," Public Affairs Report, Institute of Governmental Studies, Vol. 36, No. 6, November 1995, p. 7.

83. Excerpted with ellipses deleted. "Federalist 2," edited, and with introduction, by Jacob E. Cooke (Middletown, CT: Wesleyan University Press, 1961), pp. 522–523.

84. Pritchett, *American Constitution,* p. 99.

85. Robert H. Birkby, "The Supreme Court and the Bible Belt: Tennessee Reaction to the 'Shempp Decision,'" *Midwest Journal of Political Science* 10 (August 1966), as reprinted in Theodore L. Becker and Malcolm M. Feeley, eds., *The Impact of Supreme Court Decisions* (New York: Oxford University Press, 1973), p. 114.

86. Steven Lee Myers, "U.S. Judge Upsets Rules to Control How Jails Are Run," *New York Times* July 24, 1996, B2.

87. Abram Chayes, "The Role of the Judge in Public Law Litigation," *Harvard Law Review* 89 (May 1976): 1281–1316.

88. Alexis de Toqueville, *Democracy in America,* ed. J. p. Mayer (New York: Harper, 1988), p. 270.

89. R. Shep Melnick, *Between the Lines* (Washington, DC: Brookings, 1994), p. 149.

90. Myron Levin and Henry Weinstein, "Big Tobacco Must Pay Damages in Florida Case," *Los Angeles Times,* April 8, 2000, A1.

91. Amy Stevens, "The Mouthpieces: Class-Action Lawyers Brawl Over Big Fees in Milli Vanilli Fraud," *Wall Street Journal,* October 24, 1991; and "Judge Approves Settlement of Some Milli Vanilli Suits," *Wall Street Journal,* March 25, 1992.

CHAPTER 16

1. Michael Decourcy Hinds, "A Campus Case: Speech or Harassment?" *New York Times,* May 15, 1993, I62. "Blacks at Penn Drop a Charge of Harassment," *New York Times,* May 25, 1993, A10.

2. Linda Greenhouse, "High Court Rejects Bid to Revive Jeffries's Suit," *New York Times,* October 3, 1995, 3.

3. Henry Steele Commager, ed., *Documents of American History,* 6th ed., (New York: Appleton-Century-Crofts, 1958), pp. 125–126. Also see Willi Paul Adams, *The First American Constitutions: Republican Ideology and the Making of the State Constitutions in the Revolutionary Era* (Chapel Hill: University of North Carolina Press, 1980).

4. Charles R. Ritcheson, "'Loyalist Influence' on British Policy Toward the United States After the American Revolution," *Eighteenth Century Studies* 7/1 (Autumn 1973): 1–17. See also Paul A. Smith, "The American Loyalists: Notes on Their Organization and Numerical Strength," *William and Mary Quarterly,* Third Series, 25/2 (April 1968): 259–277.

5. Arthur M. Schlesinger, *Prelude to Independence: The Newspaper War on Britain, 1764–1776* (New York: Alfred Knopf, 1958), pp. 297–298.

6. *Ibid.,* p. 299.

7. *Barron v. Baltimore,* 1833, as quoted in C. Herman Pritchett, *Constitutional Civil Liberties* (Englewood Cliffs, NJ: Prentice-Hall, 1984), p. 6.

8. "Federalist 2."

9. John Dalberg-Acton, 1907, as quoted in John Bartlett, *Familiar Quotations,* 15th ed. (Boston: Little, Brown, 1980), p. 616.

10. John Stuart Mill, as quoted in Bartlett, *Familiar Quotations,* p. 508.

11. Schlesinger, *Prelude to Independence,* pp. 64–65.

12. Robert G. McCloskey, *The American Supreme Court* (Chicago: University of Chicago Press, 1960), p. 224.

13. Quoted in Robert Goldstein, *Political Repression in Modern America: 1870 to the Present* (New York: Schenkman, 1978), p. 565.

14. *Schenck v. United States* 249 US 47 (1919).

15. *Stromberg v. California* 283 US 359 (1931).

16. *Near v. Minnesota* 283 US 697 (1931).

17. Goldstein, *Political Repression,* p. 262.

18. *Chaplinsky v. New Hampshire* 315 US 568 (1942).

19. As quoted in C. Herman Pritchett, *The American Constitution,* 3rd ed. (New York: McGraw-Hill, 1969), p. 375.

20. *United States v. Carolene Products Co.* 304 US 144 (1938).

21. George Anastaplo, as quoted in Goldstein, *Political Repression,* p. 532.

22. *Papish v. the Board of Curators of the University of Missouri* 410 US 667 (1973).

23. Robert Goldstein, *Saving "Old Glory": The History of the Desecration Controversy* (Boulder, CO: Westview, 1995).

24. *Texas v. Johnson* 491 US 397 (1989).

25. *Texas v. Johnson* 491 US 397 (1989).

26. *United States v. Eichman* 496 US 310, (1990).

27. *R. A. V. v. City of St. Paul, Minnesota* 112 S Ct. 2541 (1992).

28. Anthony Lewis, *Make No Law: The Sullivan Case and the First Amendment* (New York: Random House, 1992).

29. Felicity Barringer, "Appeals Court Rejects Damages Against ABC in Food Lion Case," *New York Times,* October 21, 1999, 1.

30. *Jenkins* v. *Georgia* 418 US 153 (1974).

31. Linda Greenhouse, "Court, 9 0, Upholds State Laws Prohibiting Assisted Suicide, Protects Speech on Internet," *New York Times*, June 27, 1997, A1.

32. As quoted in Charles L. Glenn, Jr., *The Myth of the Common School* (Amherst, MA: University of Massachusetts Press, 1987), p. 84.

33. Diane Ravitch, *The Great School Wars: New York City, 1805–1973* (New York: Basic Books, 1974); and Paul E. Peterson, *The Politics of School Reform, 1870–1940* (Chicago: University of Chicago Press, 1985).

34. *Meek* v. *Pittenger* 421 US 349 (1975).

35. *gel* v. *Vitale* 370 US 421 (1962); *School District of Abington Township* v. *Schempp* 374 US 273 (1963); and *Wallace* v. *Jaffree* 472 US 38 (1985).

36. Benjamin I. Page and Robert Y. Shapiro, *The Rational Public: Fifty Years of Trends in Americans' Policy Preferences* (Chicago: University of Chicago Press, 1992), p. 113.

37. *Board of Education* v. *Mergens* 496 US 226 (1990).

38. *Mitchell* v. *Helms* 98-1648 (2000).

39. *Meyer* v. *Nebraska* 262 US 399 (1923). See also *Pierce* v. *Society of Sisters* 268 US 510 (1925).

40. Pritchett, *The American Constitution,* p. 477.

41. *Ibid.,* p. 478.

42. *Wisconsin* v. *Yoder* 406 US 205 (1972).

43. Paul E. Peterson, "The New Politics of Choice," in Diane Ravitch and Maris Vinovskis, eds., *Learning from the Past* (Baltimore, MD: Johns Hopkins University Press, 1995).

44. Joan Biskupic, "Vouchers for Religious Schools Allowed" *Washington Post*, November 10, 1998, A2.

45. Publius Syrus, as quoted in John Bartlett, *Familiar Quotations*, p. 111.

46. *Olmstead* v. *United States* 277 US 438 (1927).

47. *New York Times*, November 12, 1993, 1.

48. Senator Joe Biden, as quoted in Chuck Henning, *The Wit and Wisdom of Politics: Expanded Edition* (Golden, CO: Fulcrum Publishing, 1992), p. 47.

49. New York Mayor Ed Koch, as quoted in Henning, *Wit and Wisdom of Politics,* p. 107.

50. *Mapp* v. *Ohio* 167 US 643 (1961).

51. *Washington* v. *Chrisman* 455 US 1 (1982), 182.

52. Joan Biskupic, "Police May Stop, Frisk Those Who Flee at Sight of Officer," *Washington Post*, January 13, 2000, A10.

53. *Dickerson* v. *US* 99-5525 (2000).

54. Pritchett, *Constitutional Civil Liberties,* p. 78.

55. *Sheppard* v. *Maxwell* 384 US 333 (1966).

56. *Nebraska Press Association* v. *Stuart* 427 US 539 (1976).

57. Lisa J. McIntyre, *The Public Defender: The Practice of Law in the Shadows of Repute* (Chicago: University of Chicago Press, 1987), p. 162.

58. Jonathan D. Casper, *American Criminal Justice: The Defendant's Perspective* (Englewood Cliffs, NJ: Prentice-Hall, 1972), p. 101.

59. McIntyre, *The Public Defender,* p. 41.

60. *In re Chapman* 166 US 661 (1897).

61. Casper, *American Criminal Justice;* and Jerome Skolnick, *Justice Without Trial* (New York: John Wiley, 1966).

62. *Santobello* v. *New York* (1971), as quoted in Lawrence M. Friedman, *Crime and Punishment in American History* (New York: Basic Books, 1993), p. 392.

63. Keith Bradsher: "Boy Who Killed Gets Seven Years; Judge Says Law Is Too Harsh," *New York Times,* January 14, 2000, A1.

64. Robert H. Bork, "Neutral Principles and Some First Amendment Problems," *Indiana Law Journal* 47 (1971): 8.

65. *Griswold* v. *Connecticut* 381 US 479 (1965).

66. *Ibid.*

67. *Bowers* v. *Hardwick* 106 SCt 2841 (1986).

68. Pamela Coyle, "Second State Court Overturns Sodomy Law," *New Orleans Times-Picayune*, March 18, 1999, A1; and Amy Argetsinger, "Maryland Judge's Ruling Protects Private, Consensual Sex Acts," *Washington Post*, January 20, 1999, B8.

69. "The Gallup Poll: Social and Economic Indicators–Homosexual Relations," **www.gallup.com/poll/ indicators/indhomsexual.asp**, accessed March 22, 2000.

70. *Harris* v. *McRae* 448 US 297 (1980).

71. *Webster* v. *Reproductive Health Services* 492 US 490 (1989).

72. *Planned Parenthood* v. *Casey* 112 SCt 291 (1992).

73. *Stenberg* v. *Carhart* 99-830 (3000).

CHAPTER 17

1. Amy Wallace and Diana Marcum, "Prop. 209 Foes Seize Building at UC Riverside," *Los Angeles Times*, November 12, 1996, A3.

2. Robert Pear, "The 1996 Elections: The Nation—The States; In California, Voters Bar Preferences Based on Race," *New York Times*, November 6, 1996, B7.

3. Wallace and Marcum, "Prop. 209 Foes Seize Building."

4. Bill Stall and Dan Morain, "Prop. 209 Wins, Bars Affirmative Action Initiatives," *Los Angeles Times*, November 6, 1996, A1.

5. Tanya Schevitz, "UC Berkeley Minority Applications on Rise," *San Francisco Chronicle*, January 27, 2000, A22; and "Affirmative Action in California: Passed," *The Economist*, April 8, 2000: 29.

6. Ruth Bader Ginsburg, "Employment of the Constitution to Advance the Equal Status of Men and Women," in Shlomo Slonim, ed., *The Constitutional Bases of Political and Social Change in the United States* (New York: Praeger, 1990), p. 188.

7. Philip Converse, "The Nature of Belief Systems in Mass Publics," in David E. Apter, *Ideology and*

*Discontent* (New York: Free Press, 1964), pp. 206–261.

8. John Agresto, *The Supreme Court and Constitutional Democracy* (Ithaca, NY: Cornell University Press, 1984), p. 27. Ellipses deleted.

9. John D. Hicks, *The American Nation* (Cambridge, MA: Riverside Press, 1949), p. 21.

10. Eric Foner, *A Short History of Reconstruction* (New York: Harper, 1990).

11. Richard M. Valelly, "National Parties and Racial Disfranchisement," in Paul E. Peterson, ed., *Classifying by Race* (Princeton, NJ: Princeton University Press, 1995), pp. 188–216.

12. U.S. Commission on Civil Rights, *Report of the Commission on Civil Rights* (Washington, DC: Government Printing Office, 1959), p. 32. Ellipses deleted.

13. V. O. Key, Jr., *Southern Politics* (New York: Random House, 1949).

14. J. Morgan Kousser, *The Shaping of Southern Politics: Suffrage Restriction and the Establishment of the One-Party South, 1880–1910* (New Haven, CT: Yale University Press, 1974), p. 61.

15. *Civil Rights Cases* 109 US 3 (1883).

16. *Plessy v. Ferguson* 163 US 537 (1896).

17. Edward Banfield and James Q. Wilson, *City Politics* (New York: Vintage Books, 1963); and James Q. Wilson, *Negro Politics* (New York: Free Press, 1960). For caveats, see Steven p. Erie, *Rainbow's End: Irish-Americans and the Dilemmas of Urban Machine Politics, 1840–1985* (Berkeley: University of California Press, 1990).

18. Harold Gosnell, *Negro Politicians* [1935] (Chicago: University of Chicago Press, 1967); Thomas M. Guterbock, *Machine Politics in Transition* (Chicago: University of Chicago Press, 1980); and Ira Katznelson, *Black Men, White Cities* (Chicago: University of Chicago Press, 1976).

19. *Nixon v. Herndon* 273 US 536 (1927).

20. Gerald N. Rosenberg, *The Hollow Hope: Can Courts Bring About Social Change?* (Chicago: University of Chicago Press, 1991), p. 61.

21. *Smith v. Allwright* 321 US 649 (1944).

22. *Shelley v. Kraemer* 334 US 1 (1948).

23. *Cumming v. Richmond County Board of Education* 357 US 528 (1899).

24. *Missouri ex rel. Gaines v. Canada* 305 US 337 (1938).

25. *Sweatt v. Painter* 339 US 629 (1950).

26. *Brown v. Board of Education* 347 US 483 (1954).

27. *Brown v. Board of Education* 347 US 483 (1954), note 11. The citation of six psychological and sociological studies in this note led Herbert Garfinkel to charge that the Court was making decisions on the basis of sociology, not law. "Social Science Evidence and the School Segregation Cases," *Journal of Politics* 21 (Feb. 1959): 37–59. Kenneth B. Clar, "Effect of Prejudice and Discrimination on Personality Development" (Midcentury White House Conference on Children and Youth 1950, as cited in note 11 to *Brown*).

28. *San Antonio School District v. Rodriguez* 411 US 1 (1973). Similar reasoning can be found in *Cooper v. Aaron* 358 US 1 (1958).

29. A. Leon Higgenbotham, Jr., *Shades of Freedom: Racial Politics and Presumptions of the American Legal Process* (New York: Oxford University Press, 1996).

30. A. D. Morris, *Origins of the Civil Rights Movement: Black Communities Organizing for Change* (New York: Free Press, 1984).

31. *Ibid.*, pp. 51–63.

32. Michael Lipsky, "Protest as a Political Resource," *American Political Science Review* LXII (December 1968): 1144–1158.

33. University of Georgia, Carl Vinson Institute of Government, "Historical Documents Related to Georgia," **http://www.cviog.uga.edu/ Projects/gainfo/gahisdoc.htm**, accessed April 6, 2000.

34. Rosenberg, *The Hollow Hope*, p. 50.

35. Gerald D. Jaynes and Robin M. Williams, Jr., eds., *A Common Destiny: Blacks and American Society* (Washington, DC: National Academy Press, 1989), p. 224.

36. Patricia Gurin, Shirley Hatchett, and James S. Jackson, *Hope and Independence: Blacks' Response to Electoral and Party Politics* (New York: Russell Sage, 1989), pp. 42–49.

37. Jaynes and Williams, *A Common Destiny,* p. 233.

38. Joint Center for Political and Economic Studies, *Focus* (Washington, DC: Joint Center for Political and Economic Studies 1993); and "Joint Center Releases 1998 National Count of Black Elected Officials," press release (Washington, DC: Joint Center for Political and Economic Studies), November 9, 1999.

39. William J. Grimshaw, *Bitter Fruit: Black Politics and the Chicago Machine, 1931–1991* (Chicago: University of Chicago Press, 1992).

40. Gary Orfield, *The Reconstruction of Southern Education: The Schools and the 1964 Civil Rights Act* (New York: Wiley, 1969); Gary Orfield, *Must We Bus?* (Washington, DC, Brookings, 1978); and Jennifer Hochschild, *The New American Dilemma* (New Haven, CT: Yale University Press, 1984).

41. Katherine Tate, *From Protest to Politics* (Cambridge, MA: Harvard University Press, 1993), Ch. 8.

42. *Milliken v. Bradley* I 418 US 717 (1974); 433 US 267 (1977).

43. *Regents of the University of California v. Bakke* 438 US 265 (1978).

44. "Affirmative Action in Florida; But Look Under the Other Bush," *The Economist*, March 11, 2000.

45. Jeb Bush, "Better Than Affirmative," *New York Times,* September 15, 2000, A35.

46. U.S. Bureau of the Census, *Statistical Abstract of the United States, 1999*, Table 760.

47. U.S. Bureau of the Census, *Statistical Abstract of the United States, 1999*, Table 680.

48. U.S. Bureau of the Census,

*Statistical Abstract of the United States, 1999,* Tables 99 and 133.

49. Jaynes and Williams, *A Common Destiny,* p. 313.

50. U.S. Bureau of the Census, *Statistical Abstract of the United States, 1999,* Tables 298 and 302.

51. U.S. Bureau of the Census, *Statistical Abstract of the United States, 1999,* Table 760; and Robert Pear, "Black and Hispanic Poverty Rate Falls, Reducing Overall Rate for Nation," *New York Times,* September 25, 1998, A1.

52. U.S. Census Bureau, *Statistical Abstract of the United States, 1999,* Table 13.

53. Michael Jones-Correa, *Between Two Nations: The Political Predicament of Latinos in New York City* (Ithaca, NY: Cornell University Press, 1998).

54. National Election Studies; *Newsweek* Poll conducted by Princeton Survey Research Associates. June 25–30, 1999.

55. *Lau v. Nichols* 414 US 563 (1974).

56. Bernard Grofman, Lisa Handley, and Richard G. Niemi, *Minority Representation and the Quest for Voting Equality* (New York: Cambridge University Press, 1992), pp. 16–25. Also see Thomas Weyr, *Hispanic U.S.A.: Breaking the Melting Pot* (New York: Harper, 1959); and Peter Skerry, *Mexican Americans: The Ambivalent Minority* (New York: Free Press, 1993).

57. Daron Shaw, Rodolfo O. de la Garza, and Jongho Lee, "Examining Latino Turnout in 1996: A Three State, Validated Survey Approach," *American Journal of Political Science* 44/2 (April 2000): 332–340.

58. Steven Greenhouse, "About Face; Guess Who's Embracing Immigrants Now," *New York Times,* March 5, 2000, D4.

59. U.S. Bureau of the Census, *Statistical Abstract of the United States, 1999,* Tables 18 and 57.

60. Stanley Karnow and Nancy Yoshihara, *Asian Americans in Transition* (New York: Asia Society, 1992).

61. William Schneider, "Asian Americans Will Matter More,"

*National Journal,* August 14, 1999, 2398.

62. Asian Pacific American Institute for Congressional Studies, "Statement from APA Community Organizations," n.d. **http://www.apaics.org/statement.html**, accessed April 10, 2000.

63. Angelo Ancheta, *Race, Rights, and the Asian-American Experience* (New Brunswick, NJ: Rutgers University Press, 1997).

64. Timothy Cook, "The Empirical Study of Lesbian, Gay, and Bisexual Politics: Assessing the First Wave of Research," *American Political Science Review* 93/3 (September 1999): 679.

65. Shawn Zeller, "Gay Rites: Giving to Democrats," *National Journal,* May 8, 1999: 1241.

66. Matthew Brelis, "From the Closet to the Campaign Trial; Being Gay Once Defined a Candidate. Now the Issues Do," *Boston Globe,* August 30, 1998, E1.

67. Deb Price, "Gays Need Democrats to Win 2000 Elections," *Detroit News,* November 1, 1999, A7; and Human Rights Campaign, **http://www.hrc.org,**, accessed April 11, 2000.

68. *Boy Scouts of America et al.* v. *Dale* 99 US 699 (2000).

69. Vine Deloria, Jr., "The Distinctive Status of Indian Rights," in Peter Iverson, ed., *The Plains Indians of the Twentieth Century* (Norman: University of Oklahoma Press, 1985), p. 241.

70. Deloria, *Ibid.,* pp. 237–248.

71. Deloria, *Ibid.,* p. 237.

72. Agresto, *The Supreme Court and Constitutional Democracy,* pp. 148–149.

73. Theda Skocpol, *Protecting Soldiers and Mothers: The Political Origins of Social Policy in the United States* (Cambridge, MA: Harvard University Press, 1992); and Sara Evans, *Personal Politics: The Roots of Women's Liberation in the Civil Rights Movement and the New Left* (New York: Knopf, 1979).

74. Nancy McGlen and Karen O'Conner, *Women's Rights: The Struggle for Equality in the Nineteenth and*

*Twentieth Centuries* (New York: Praeger, 1983), Ch. 9.

75. Jane J. Mansbridge, *Why We Lost the ERA* (Chicago: University of Chicago Press, 1986).

76. Ruth B. Mandel, "The Political Woman," in Sherri Matteo, ed., *American Women in the Nineties: Today's Critical Issues* (Boston: Northeastern University Press, 1993), pp. 34–65.

77. *Hoyt* v. *Florida* 368 US 57 (1961).

78. *Craig* v. *Boren* 429 US 190 (1976).

79. Ginsburg, *Employment of the Constitution,* p. 191.

80. *Rostker* v. *Goldberg* 453 US 65 (1981).

81. Mansbridge, *Why We Lost the ERA,* Ch. 7.

82. *Watson* v. *Fort Worth Bank & Trust* 487 US 997–999; *New York City Transit Authority* v. *Beazer* 440 US at 587, no 31; and *Griggs* v. *Duke Power,* 401 US at 432.

83. *Wards Cove* v. *Antonio* 490 US 642, (1989).

84. *Ibid.,* p. 661.

85. *Meritor Savings Bank* v. *Vinson* 477 US 57 (1986).

86. *Harris* v. *Forklift Systems* 510 US 77 (1993).

87. "Hillary's Class," *Frontline* (PBS television broadcast, No. 15, 1994), as cited in Karla Cooper-Boggs, "The Link Between Private and Public Single-Sex Colleges: Will Wellesley Stand or Fall with the Citadel?" *Indiana Law Review* 29 (1995), p. 137.

88. Cooper-Boggs, "The Link Between Private and Public Single-Sex Colleges," p. 135.

89. *United States* v. *Virginia* 116 SCt 2264 (1966).

90. Stephen L. Percy, *Disability, Civil Rights, and Public Policy: The Politics of Implementation* (Tuscaloosa: University of Alabama Press, 1989), p. 3.

91. Authors' 1995 estimate based on 1989 estimate provided by Percy, *Ibid.,* Ch 5.

92. Robert A. Katzman, *Institutional Disability: The Saga of Transportation Policy for the Disabled*

(Washington, DC: Brookings, 1986).

93. Frederick J. Weintraub, ed., *Public Policy and the Education of Exceptional Children* (Washington, DC: Council for Exceptional Children, 1976).

94. Paul E. Peterson, "Background Paper," in Twentieth Century Fund, *Making the Grade: Report of the Twentieth Century Fund Task Force on Federal Elementary and Secondary Education Policy* (New York: Twentieth Century Fund, 1983), Ch. 5.

95. *Southeastern Community College* v. *Davis,* 442 US 397 (1979).

96. Rufus Browning, Dale Rogers Marshall, and David H. Tabb, *Protest Is Not Enough: The Struggle of Blacks and Hispanics for Equality in Urban Politics* (Berkeley: University of California Press, 1984).


CHAPTER 18

1. John Kingdon, *Agenda, Alternatives and Public Policies* (Boston: Little, Brown, 1984); and Paul Light, *The President's Agenda* (Baltimore, MD: Johns Hopkins University Press, 1991).

2. Arthur Maass, *Congress and the Common Good* (New York: Basic Books, 1983).

3. Eugene Bardach, *The Implementation Game,* 4th ed. (Cambridge, MA: MIT Press, 1982); and Jeffrey L. Pressman and Aaron Wildavsky, *Implementation,* 3rd ed. (Berkeley: University of California Press, 1984).

4. Thomas R. Dye, *Politics, Economics and the Public: Policy Outcomes in the American States* (Chicago: Rand McNally, 1966).

5. Amy Goldstein, "Forgotten Issues; Welfare Reform's Progress Is Stalled," *Washington Post,* June 1, 2000, A1.

6. Timothy Smeeding, Michael O'Higgins, and Lee Rainwater, eds., *Poverty, Inequality and Income Distribution in Comparative Perspective*

(New York: Harvester Wheatsheaf, 1990); and Lee Rainwater and Timothy M. Smeeding, "Doing Poorly: The Real Income of American Children in a Comparative Perspective," Maxwell School of Citizenship and Public Affairs, Syracuse University, Syracuse, NY, August 1995, Working Paper No. 127.

7. Neil Howe and Richard Jackson, *Entitlements and the Aging of America* (Washington, DC: National Taxpayers Union Foundation, 1994).

8. *Ibid.,* Chart 4-27, comment.

9. Thomas A. Bailey, *The American Pageant: A History of the Republic* (Boston: D.C. Heath, 1956), p. 840. The figure is in 1999 dollars—the amount was $200 in 1930s dollars.

10. Martha Derthick, *Policymaking for Social Security* (Washington, DC: Brookings, 1979); and Theda Skocpol, *Protecting Soldiers and Mothers: The Politics of Social Provision in the United States* (Cambridge, MA: Harvard University Press, 1993).

11. R. Kent Weaver, *Automatic Government: The Politics of Indexation* (Washington, DC: Brookings, 1988).

12. Neil Howe and Richard Jackson, *1998 Chartbook: Entitlements and the Aging of America* (Washington, DC: National Taxpayers' Union Foundation, 1998), Chart 4-26.

13. *Boston Globe,* December 27, 1994, 70.

14. As quoted in Chuck Henning, *Wit and Wisdom of Politics,* expanded edition (Golden, CO: Fulcrum, 1992), p. 252.

15. As quoted in Henning, *Wit and Wisdom of Politics,* p. 95.

16. Paul Light, *Artful Work: The Politics of Social Security Reform* (New York: Random House, 1985).

17. *Budget of the United States Government, Fiscal Year 2001, Historical Tables* (Washington, DC: Office of Management and Budget, 2000), Table 16.1, p. 279.

18. *Ibid.*

19. U.S. Census Bureau, *Current Population Reports,* July 1998, pp. 20–504.

20. U.S. Census Bureau, *Current Populations Reports,* May 2000, pp. 20–523.

21. Don't Ask, Don't Vote: Young Adults in the 2000 Presidential Primary Season, *Third Millenium,* April 2000, p. 9.

22. Susan A. MacManus, with Patricia A. Turner, *Young v. Old: Generational Combat in the 21st Century* (Boulder, CO: Westview, 1996), pp. 60, 141.

23. Employment information: Susan Levine, "AARP Hopes Boom Times Are Ahead," *Washington Post,* June 2, 1998, A1; Membership and volunteer numbers: "What is AARP?" Washington, DC: AARP, **http://www.aarp. org/what_is.html**, accessed May 28, 2000; Budget figures: *AARP: 1999 Financial Statements* (Washington, DC: AARP, 2000).

24. Robert Rector, *Welfare Reform* (Washington, DC: Heritage Foundation, 1996).

25. Michael Lipsky, *Street Level Bureaucracy* (New York: Russell Sage Foundation, 1980); and Theda Skocpol, "Targeting within Universalism: Politically Viable Policies to Combat Poverty in the United States," in *The Urban Underclass,* ed. Christopher Jencks and Paul E. Peterson (Washington, DC: Brookings, 1991), pp. 411–436.

26. *Publication 596: Earned Income Tax Credit* (Washington, DC: Internal Revenue Service, 1999).

27. *2000 SSI Annual Report* (Washington, DC: Social Security Administration, 2000).

28. Percentage of monies going for services to the elderly in fiscal year 1993. Marilyn Werber Serafini, "Pinching Pennies," *National Journal* 27/37 (September 16, 1995): 2273. Also see Mark Rom, "Health and Welfare in the American States," *Politics in the American States,* 6th ed., ed. Virginia Gray and Herbert Jacob (Washington, DC: CQ Press, 1995).

29. Paul E. Peterson, "An Immodest Proposal," *Daedalus* 121 (Fall 1992): 151–174.

30. Calculated from Green Book, Table 1, 1579. Until 1995, the Green Book, issued annually since 1981, was one of the most comprehensive sources of information on U.S. social policy. U.S. House of Representatives, Committee on Ways and Means, Overview of Entitlement Programs: Background Material and Data on Programs within the Jurisdiction of the Committee on Ways and Means (otherwise known as the 1992 Green Book) (Washington, DC: U.S. Government Printing Office, 1992), Table 1, p. 1579. All subsequent references to this document in this chapter will be simply to the Green Book. They refer to the 1992 edition.

31. Green Book, Table 2, p. 1582.

32. U.S. Department of Health and Human Services, Administration for Children and Families, Office of Family Assistance, *TANF Selected Provisions of State Plans*, **http://www.acf.dhhs.gov/ programs/ofa/provis.htm**, accessed July 24, 2000.

33. Green Book, Table 12, pp. 643–645.

34. Paul E. Peterson and Mark Rom, *Welfare Magnets: A New Case for a National Standard* (Washington, DC: Brookings, 1990).

35. Green Book, Table 12, p. 1212.

36. "Social Security Penalty on Earnings Is Repealed," *Los Angeles Times*, April 8, 2000, A14.

37. Skocpol, *Protecting Soldiers and Mothers*.

38. Charles Murray, *Losing Ground: American Social Policy, 1950–1980* (New York: Basic Books, 1984).

39. Christopher Jencks, "Is the American Underclass Growing?" in *The Urban Underclass,* ed. Christopher Jencks and Paul E. Peterson (Washington, DC: Brookings, 1991), pp. 33, 88.

40. William J. Wilson, *The Truly Disadvantaged: The Inner City, the Underclass, and Public Policy* (Chicago: University of Chicago Press, 1987).

41. Christopher Jencks, "Is the American Underclass Growing?" in *The Urban Underclass,* ed. Christopher Jencks and Paul E. Peterson (Washington, DC: Brookings, 1991), p. 56.

42. Associations Unlimited (online database); The Gale Group, 2000.

43. *Public Perspective,* February/ March 1995, p. 39; *The Gallup Poll* **www.gallup. com**, Accessed July 24, 2000.

44. Eliza Newlin Carney, "Family Time," *National Journal,* 30 (July 29, 1995): 1947–1949.

45. Jeff Shear, "The Credit Card," *National Journal* 27/32 (August 12, 1995): 2056–2058; and Marilyn W. Serafini, "Turning Up the Heat," *National Journal* 27/32 (August 12, 1995): 2051–2055.

46. Steve Chabot, "Q: Should Congress Close Down the Department of Education? Yes: Give Parents and Communities More Control," *Insight on the News,* August 7, 1995, 18.

47. Paul E. Peterson, "Background Paper," in Twentieth Century Fund Task Force on Federal Elementary and Secondary Education Policy, *Making the Grade* (New York: Twentieth Century Fund, 1983).

48. "Land Ordinance of 1785," in Henry S. Commager, ed., *Documents of American History* 6th, ed. (New York: Appleton-Century-Crofts, 1958), p. 124.

49. Charles L. Glenn, Jr., The Myth of the Common School (Amherst, MA: University of Massachusetts Press, 1987); Diane Ravitch, *The Great School Wars: New York City, 1805–1973* (New York: Basic Books, 1974); David Tyack and Elizabeth Hansot, *Managers of Virtue: Public School Leadership in America, 1820–1980* (New York: Basic Books, 1982); and Paul E. Peterson, *The Politics of School Reform, 1870–1940* (Chicago: University of Chicago Press, 1985).

50. Helen F. Ladd, "Introduction," in Helen F. Ladd, ed., *Holding Schools Accountable: Performance-Based Reform in Education* (Washington, DC: Brookings, 1996), pp. 1–22.

51. National Education Association Research Division, *Salaries Paid Classroom Teachers, Principals, and Certain Others,* 1960–61, *Urban Districts 100,000 and Over in Population; ibid.,* 1970–71; Educational Research Service, *Salaries Paid Professional Personnel in Public Schools,* 1974–75; *ibid.,* 1979–80; *ibid.,* 1984–85; *ibid.,* 1989–90; National Education Association, *Estimates of School Statistics,* 1960–61, 13; *ibid.,* 1989–90, p. 19; National Center for Education Statistics, *Digest of Education Statistics,* 1988, table 57, p. 72.

52. Eric A Hanushek, "School Resources and Student Performance," in *Does Money Matter? The Effect of School Resources on Student Achievement and Adult Success,* ed. Gary Burtless (Washington, DC: Brookings, 1996), pp. 43–73.

53. The Gallup Organization. Roper Center for Public Opinion Research Database, Question ID Numbers USGALLUP. 870.Q005A; USGALLUP. 99JNE25R11E

54. Peter W. Cookson, Jr., *School Choice: The Struggle for the Soul of American Education* (New Haven, CT: Yale University Press, 1994); Carnegie Foundation for the Advancement of Teaching, School Choice (Princeton, NJ: Carnegie Foundation, 1992); Larry V. Hedges and Rob Greenwald, "Have Times Changed? The Relation Between School Resources and Student Performances," in *Does Money Matter? The Effect of School Resources on Student Achievement and Adult Success,* ed. Gary Burtless (Washington, DC: Brookings, 1996), pp. 74–92; Amy Gutmann, *Democratic Education* (Princeton, NJ: Princeton University Press, 1987); Jeffrey Henig, *Rethinking School Choice: Limits of the Market Metaphor* (Princeton, NJ: Princeton University Press, 1994).

55. *Statistical Abstract of the United States,* 1999, Table 163 and 1434.

56. U.S. Department of Education, National Center for Education Statistics, *Digest of Education Statistics*, 1999, May 2000 (NCES 2000-031), Table 419, p. 471.

57. Eric A. Hanushek, "The Economics of Schooling: Production and Efficiency in Public Schools," *Journal of Economic Literature* 24 (September 1986): 1141–1177.

58. Diane Ravitch, *National Standards in American Education: A Citizen's Guide* (Washington, DC: Brookings, 1995).

59. Position papers from **www.georgewbush.com** and **www. algore2000.com.**

60. David K. Kirkpatrick, *Choice in Schooling: A Case for Tuition Vouchers* (Chicago: Loyola University Press, 1990); Terry Moe, ed., *Private Vouchers* (Stanford, CA: Hoover Institution Press, 1995).

61. William H. Clune and John F. Witte, eds., *Choice and Control in American Education*, vols. I and II (New York: Falmer Press, 1990); and Henig, *Rethinking School Choice*.

62. Terry M. Neal, "GOP Right Accepts Bush's Move to the Middle," *Washington Post*, May 27, 2000, A01.

63. Robert Manor, "Firms Linked in Plane Crash Ignored Rules, Oxygen Generators Improperly Loaded," *St. Louis Post-Dispatch*, June 2, 1996, 11A.

64. Craig Petersen, *Business and Government*, 2nd ed. (New York: Harper & Row, 1985), p. 173.

65. *Heart of Atlanta Motel* v. *United States* 322 US 533 (1964); *United States* v. *South-Eastern Underwriters Association* 322 US 533 (1944).

66. Gregg Easterbrook, *A Moment on the Earth: The Coming Age of Environmental Optimism* (New York: Penguin, 1995), p. xv. For a more pessimistic view, see Paul R. Ehrlich and Anne H. Ehrlich, *Betrayal of Science and Reason: How Anti-Environmental Rhetoric Threatens Our Future* (Washington, DC: Island Press, 1996).

67. Murray Weidenbaum, "Government Power and Business Performance," in *The United States in the 1980s*, ed. Peter Duignan and Alvin Rabushka (Stanford, CA: Hoover Institution Press, 1990), pp. 197–220.

68. Douglas Jehl, "National Parks Will Ban Recreation Snowmobiling; A Further Curb on the Use of Public Lands," *New York Times*, April 27, 2000, A14.

69. Clair Wilcox, Public Policies Toward Business, 4th ed. (Homewood, IL: Irwin, 1971), p. 589.

70. Marc K. Landy, Marc J. Roberts, and Stephen R. Thomas, *The Environmental Protection Agency: Asking the Wrong Questions from Nixon to Clinton*, expanded edition (New York: Oxford University Press, 1994).

71. Landy, Roberts, and Thomas, *The Environmental Protection Agency*.

72. *Ibid.*, p. 290.

73. Kenneth Meier, *Regulation: Politics, Bureaucracy, and Economics* (New York: St. Martin's, 1985).

74. Lawrence L. Knutson, "'Rebirth of Our National Symbol'; Bald Eagle Soars Off Endangered List," *Boston Globe*, July 3, 1999, A3.

75. Martha Derthick and Paul Quirk, *The Politics of Deregulation* (Washington, DC: Brookings, 1985); and Mark C. Rom, *Public Spirit in the Thrift Tragedy* (Pittsburgh, PA: University of Pittsburgh Press, 1996).

76. Cited in Robert Hardaway, "Transportation Deregulation (1976–1984): Turning the Tide," *Transportation Law Journal* 14 (1985): 101–152.

77. H. Craig Petersen, *Business and Government*, 2nd ed. (New York: Harper & Row, 1985), p. 198.

78. Hardaway, "Transportation Deregulation," p. 143. Another view is given by Paul Dempsey, "The State of the Airline, Airport and Aviation Industries," *Transportation Law Journal* 129 (1992), pp. 130–200.

79. David Monk, "The Lessons of Airline Regulation and Deregulation: Will We Make the Same Mistakes in Space?" *Journal of Air Law and Commerce* 57/3 (Spring 1992): 715–753.

80. See, for example, Dennis Carlton and William Landes, "Benefits and Costs of Airline Mergers: A Case Study," *Bell Journal of Economics and Management Science* 65, 11 (1982): 65–83.


CHAPTER 19

1. United States Bureau of the Census, *Statistical Abstract of the United States, 1999*, Table 724.

2. United States Bureau of the Census, *Statistical Abstract of the United States, 1999*, Table 1430; and "Hot Jobs Market Fuels Consumer Confidence," *Los Angeles Times*, May 31, 2000, C1.

3. United States Bureau of the Census, *Statistical Abstract of the United States, 1999*, Table 1436.

4. A.W. Phillips, "The Relationship Between Unemployment and the Rate of Change of Money Wage Rates in the United Kingdom 1862–1957," *Economica* 25 (1958): 283–299.

5. Morris Fiorina, "Elections and Economics in the 1980s," in Alberto Alesina and Geoffrey Carliner, eds., *Politics and Economics in the 1980s* (Chicago: University of Chicago Press, 1991), pp. 17–38.

6. John Mueller, *Wars, Presidents, and Public Opinion* (New York: Wiley, 1973); and Douglas Hibbs, *The American Political Economy* (Cambridge, MA: Harvard University Press, 1987), Ch. 5.

7. For a summary of the relevant literature, see Fiorina, "Elections and Economics in the 1980s."

8. Morris Fiorina, *Retrospective Voting in American National Elections* (New Haven, CT: Yale University Press, 1981), pp. 164–167.

9. John Chubb, "Institutions, the Economy, and the Dynamics of State Elections," *American Political Science Review* 82 (1988), pp. 133–154; and Dennis Simon, Charles Ostrom, and Robin Marra, "The President, Referendum Voting, and Subnational Elections in the United States," *American Political Science Review* 85 (1991), pp. 1177–1192.

10. *A Citizen's Guide to the Federal Budget: Budget of the United States Government, Fiscal Year 2000* (Washington, DC: Office of Management and Budget, 1999).

11. *Ibid.*

12. Paul Peretz, *The Political Economy of Inflation in the United States* (Chicago: University of Chicago, Press, 1983), p. 42.

13. Peretz, *The Political Economy of Inflation.*

14. Bruce Oppenheimer, "The Importance of Elections in a Strong Congressional Party Era: The Effect of Unified v. Divided Government," manuscript, 1995.

15. Paul Krugman, *Peddling Prosperity* (New York: Norton, 1994), Chs. 3 and 6.

16. Louis Uchitelle, "Ideas and Trends: The Bondholders Are Winning: Why America Won't Boom," *New York Times,* June 12, 1994, D4.

17. For a general discussion, see Steven Sheffrin, *Rational Expectations* (London: Cambridge University Press, 1983).

18. *Annual Report: Budget Review* (Washington, DC: Board of Governors of the Federal Reserve System, 1999).

19. William Greider, *Secrets of the Temple: How the Federal Reserve Runs the Country* (New York: Simon & Schuster, 1987).

20. Schrage, Michael, "It's Time to Put a Transaction Tax on Credit Card Purchases," *Washington Post,* October 17, 1990, F3.

21. John Wooley, *Monetary Politics: The Federal Reserve and the Politics of Monetary Policy* (New York: Cambridge University Press, 1984).

22. Alberto Alesina, "Macroeconomics and Politics," in Stanley Fischer, ed., *NBER Macroeconomics Annual, 1988* (Cambridge, MA: MIT Press, 1988), pp. 13–52.

23. Douglas Hibbs, "The Dynamics of Political Support for American Presidents Among Occupational and Partisan Groups," *American Journal of Political Science* 26 (1982), pp. 312–332.

24. Douglas Hibbs, "The Partisan Model of Macroeconomic Cycles: More Theory and Evidence for the United States," *Economics and Politics* 6 (1994), pp. 1–23.

25. "America's Amazing Expansion," *The Economist,* February 5, 2000.

26. Edward Tufte, *Political Control of the Economy* (Princeton, NJ: Princeton University Press, 1978), Ch. 2.

27. Donald Kettl, *Leadership at the Fed* (New Haven, CT: Yale University Press, 1986).

28. "Steady Greenspan; Clinton Plays It Safe on Choice of Fed Chief," *San Diego Union-Tribune,* February 26, 1996, B4.

29. Susan Milligan, "Greenspan Nominated to Fourth Term as Fed Chairman," *Boston Globe,* January 5, 2000, C1.

30. *Budget and Economic Outlook, Fiscal Years 2000–2009* (Washington, DC: Congressional Budget Office, January 1999).

31. *Budget and Economic Outlook, Fiscal Years 2001–2010* (Washington, DC: Congressional Budget Office, January 2000).

32. Bush: "A Tax Cut with a Purpose," speech to Greater Des Moines Chamber of Commerce, December 1, 1999; and Gore: "Remarks as Prepared for Delivery at ABNY Breakfast," New York, NY, April 25, 2000.

33. David Bradford, *Untangling the Income Tax* (Cambridge, MA: Harvard University Press, 1986).

34. Calculated by authors from U.S. Bureau of the Census, *Statistical Abstract of the United States, 1999,* Tables 1434 and 1443.

35. "Governor George W. Bush: A Tax Cut with a Purpose," Fact sheet, George W. Bush for President campaign, December 1, 1999.

36. "Al Gore Calls for Middle Class Tax Cuts That Are Responsible, Fair, and Puts [sic] 'First Things First,'" press release, Al Gore 2000, July 30, 1999.

37. Figures on tax expenditures for this and the following tax preferences are drawn from the *Budget of the United States Government, Fiscal Year 2001* (Washington, DC: Office of Management and Budget, 2000), Table 32-4. College tuition tax credit figures include both the Lifetime Learning Tax Credit and the HOPE Tax Credit.

38. Howard Schuman, *Politics and the Budget,* 3rd ed. (Englewood Cliffs, NJ: Prentice Hall, 1992), p. 121.

39. The specific statistic in the text is for a family of four with median income. Reductions were similar for both higher and lower income families. C. Eugene Stuerle, *The Tax Decade* (Washington, DC: Urban Institute Press, 1992), p. 216.

40. The intellectual basis of such proposals is usually credited to Robert Hall and Alvin Rabushka, *The Flat Tax* (Stanford, CA: Hoover Institution Press, 1985).

41. "Why Tax Reform?" *The American Enterprise,* July/August 1995: 17; Murray Weidenbaum, "The Nunn-Domenici 'USA Tax' Proposal," *The American Enterprise,* July/August 1995: 67.

42. U.S. Bureau of the Census, *Statistical Abstract of the United States, 1999,* Table 1372.

43. "Judgment Day," *The Economist* (February 18, 1995): 49–51.

44. Study by the McKinsey Global Institute summarized in "How Regulation Kills New Jobs," *The Economist,* November 19, 1994: 78.

45. U.S. Bureau of the Census, *Statistical Abstract of the United States, 1999,* Tables 1432 and 1442.

46. *The Emerging Digital Economy II* (Washington DC: U.S. Department of Commerce, Economics and Statistics Administration, June 1999).

47. For a critical survey, see Krugman, *Peddling Prosperity*, Ch. 5.

## CHAPTER 20

1. Aaron Wildavsky, "The Two Presidencies [1965]," in Steven A. Shull, *The Two Presidencies: A Quarter Century Assessment* (Chicago: Nelson Hall, 1991), pp. 11–25.

2. Alexander Hamilton, *The Federalist Papers, No. 70,* (Baltimore, MD: Johns Hopkins University Press, 1981), p. 199.

3. Chuck Henning, *The Wit and Wisdom of Politics: Expanded Edition* (Golden, CO: Fulcrum, 1992), p. 56.

4. Wildavksy, "The Two Presidencies," p. 15.

5. John E. Mueller, *War, Presidents and Public Opinion* (New York: Wiley, 1973); and Gary King and Lyn Ragsdale, *The Elusive Executive: Discovering Statistical Patterns in the Presidency* (Washington, DC: CQ Press, 1988).

6. Mueller, *War, Presidents and Public Opinion.*

7. George F. Kennan, "Somalia, Through a Glass Darkly," *New York Times,* September 30, 1993, A25.

8. Jessica Mathews, "Policy vs. TV," *Washington Post,* March 8, 1994, A19.

9. John Donnelly, "U.S. General Sees Long Role in Balkans; Says NATO Needs 'At Least a Generation,'" *Boston Globe,* May 2, 2000, A1.

10. Wildavksy, "The Two Presidencies," p. 16.

11. James Baker, III, with Thomas M. DeFrank, *The Politics of Diplomacy: Revolution, War, and Peace, 1989–1992* (New York: Putnam, 1995), p. 116.

12. American Israel Public Affairs Committee, "AIPAC Ranked #2 for Second Consecutive Year in *Fortune* Magazine's 'Power 25,'" November 23, 1998 press release.

13. *Statistical Abstract,* 1996, p. 3.

14. Middle East expert William Quandt, as quoted in Steven Erlanger, "Albright May Be Facing Unfamiliar Tests," *New York Times,* December 7, 1966, 5.

15. Wildavksy, "The Two Presidencies," p. 17.

16. Barry M. Blechman, *The Politics of National Security: Congress and U.S. Defense Policy* (New York: Oxford University Press, 1990); Duane M. Oldfield and Aaron Wildavsky, "Reconsidering the Two Presidencies," in Steve A. Shull, ed., *The Two Presidencies: A Quarter Century Assessment* (Chicago: Nelson Hall, 1991), pp. 181–90; Thomas Franck and Edward Weisband, *Foreign Policy by Congress* (New York: Oxford University Press, 1979); Thomas E. Mann, ed., *A Question of Balance: The President, the Congress and Foreign Policy* (Washington, DC: Brookings, 1990); and Stephen R. Weissman, *A Culture of Deference: Congress's Failure of Leadership in Foreign Policy* (New York: Basic Books, 1955).

17. Paul E. Peterson, "The International System and Foreign Policy," in Paul E. Peterson, ed., *The President, the Congress, and the Making of Foreign Policy* (Norman, OK: Oklahoma University Press, 1994), pp. 3–22.

18. Hamilton, *Federalist 74,* ellipses deleted.

19. Speech before the House of Representatives, March 7, 1800, as quoted in *Marbury* v. *Madison* 5 US (1 Cranch) 137 (1803).

20. As quoted in Henning, *The Wit and Wisdom of Politics,* p. 240.

21. *U.S.* v. *Curtiss Wright Export Corporation* 299 US 304 (1936).

22. *Youngstown Sheet & Tube Co.* v. *Sawyer* 343 US 579 (1952).

23. Harold Hongju Koh, *The National Security Constitution: Sharing Power after the Iran–Contra Affair* (New Haven, CT: Yale University Press, 1990); Gordon Silverstein, "Judicial Expansion of Presidential Power," in Peterson, "The International System," pp. 23–48; and Gordon Silverstein, *The Imbalance of Powers: Constitutional Interpretation and the Making of American Foreign Policy* (New York: Oxford University Press, 1996).

24. Joint Resolution of Congress, H.J. RES 1145 August 7, 1964.

25. Louis Fisher and David Gray Adler, "The War Powers Resolution: Time to Say Goodbye," *Political Science Quarterly* 113/3: 1–20.

26. Bill Miller, "Hill Lawsuit on War Powers Is Dismissed," *Washington Post,* June 9, 1999, A22.

27. James L. Sundquist, *The Decline and Resurgence of Congress* (Washington, DC: Brookings, 1981), p. 93.

28. *United States* v. *Belmont* 301 US 324 (1937).

29. Ann Devroy, "Pact Reached to Dismantle Ukraine's Nuclear Force; Detailed Plan to Be Signed Friday, Clinton Announces," *Washington Post,* January 11, 1994, A1.

30. Address at Westminster College, Fulton, Missouri, March 5, 1946, as reprinted in John Bartlett, *Familiar Quotations* (Boston: Little, Brown, 1980), p. 746.

31. George F. Kennan, "The Sources of Soviet Conduct," *Foreign Affairs* 25 (July 1947), pp. 566–82.

32. George Marshall, secretary of state under Harry Truman, as quoted in Alexander De Conde, "George C. Marshall," in Norman A. Graebner, ed., *An Uncertain Tradition: American Secretaries of State in the Twentieth Century* (New York: McGraw Hill, 1961), p. 252.

33. Henning, *The Wit and Wisdom of Politics,* p. 69.

34. *Ibid.,* p. 68.

35. Norman A. Graebner, "Dean G. Acheson," in Norman A. Graebner, ed., *An Uncertain Tradition: American Secretaries of State in the Twentieth Century* (New York: McGraw Hill, 1961), p. 13.

36. Barry Rubin, *Secrets of State: The State Department and the Struggle Over U.S. Foreign Policy* (New York: Oxford University Press, 1985), p. 64.

37. Rubin, *Secrets of State,* p. 239.

38. Dan Kubiske, "The Issue of Gender," *Foreign Service Journal* 73/11 (November 1996).

39. Stephen Holmes, "What Russia Teaches Us Now; How Weak States Threaten Freedom," *The American Prospect,* July-August 1997: 30.

40. General Omar Bradley, Chair of Joint Chiefs, Testimony to the Committee on Armed Services, House of Representatives, October 19, 1949, as quoted in Bartlett, 1980, p. 824.

41. Andrew Krepinevich, quoted in Justin Brown, "How Many Weapons Is Too Many?" *The Christian Science Monitor,* November 4, 1999, 1.

42. Bradley Graham, "Senators Scold Military Chiefs, Top Officers Accused of Failing to Warn Soon Enough of Readiness Decline," *Washington Post,* September 30, 1998, A2.

43. Loch K. Johnson, *America's Secret Power: The CIA in a Democratic Society* (New York: Oxford University Press, 1989), pp. 12, 43.

44. *Ibid.,* Ch. 2.

45. Johnson, *America's Secret Power;* Rhodri Jeffreys–Johnes, *The CIA and American Democracy* (New Haven, CT: Yale University Press, 1989).

46. *Director of Central Intelligence Annual Report for the United States Intelligence Community*, (Washington, DC: Central Intelligence Agency, 2000).

47. Rubin, *Secrets of State,* p. 50.

48. Jane Perlez, "With Berger in Catbird Seat, Albright's Star Dims," *New York Times*, December 14, 1999, A14.

49. As quoted in Pastor, "Disagreeing on Latin America," p. 217.

50. *New York Times,* January 23, 1993, E 4.

51. Speech at the Constitutional Convention, as quoted in Hans J. Morgenthau, *Politics Among Nations,* 4th ed. (New York: Knopf, 1966), p. 12.

52. Speech in Philadelphia, February 22, 1861, as quoted in Morgenthau, *Politics Among Nations,* p. 35.

53. Annual Message to Congress, December 2, 1823, as quoted in Bartlett, *Familiar Quotations,* p. 408.

54. Address to Congress, asking for a declaration of war, April 2, 1917, as reprinted in Bartlett, *Familiar Quotations,* p. 682.

55. Carl B. Swisher, *American Constitutional Development,* 2nd ed. (Boston: Houghton Mifflin, 1958), pp. 992–993.

56. Address at Sioux Falls, September 8, 1919, as quoted in Bartlett, p. 682.

57. George Washington, *Farewell Address*, September 17, 1796, as quoted in Bartlett, p. 379.

58. Message to the Senate, August 19, 1914, as quoted in Bartlett, p. 682.

59. Campaign speech in Boston, October 30, 1940, as reprinted in Bartlett, p. 780.

60. "Fireside Chat to the Nation," December 29, 1940, as quoted in Bartlett, p. 780.

61. Robert Keohane, *After Hegemony: Cooperation and Discord in the World Political Economy* (Princeton, NJ: Princeton University Press, 1984).

62. Morgenthau, *Politics Among Nations;* Kenneth N. Waltz, *Theory of International Politics* (New York: McGraw Hill, 1979); John J. Mearscheimer, "Back to the Future: Instability in Europe after the Cold War," *International Security* 15/1 (Summer 1990): 5–56; and Samuel Huntington, *The Clash of Civilizations* (New York: Simon & Schuster, 1996).

63. Joel R. Paul, "The Geopolitical Constitution: Executive Expediency and Executive Agreements," *California Law Review* 86/671 (July 1998): 749–752.

64. Marcus Noland, "Learning to Love the WTO," *Foreign Affairs,* September-October 1999: 78.

65. Patrick J. Buchanan, "America First, NAFTA Never; It's Not About Free Trade—It's About Our Way of Life," *Washington Post*, November 7, 1993, C1.

66. "Reactions," *Seattle Times,* December 1, 1999, A17.

# NAME INDEX

# SUBJECT INDEX

1924 presidential, 162
1930 congressional, 231
1932 presidential, 231, 305
1936 presidential, 231, 232, 301
1948 presidential, 305, 513
1952 presidential, 232
1954 congressional, 232
1956 presidential, 232, 303
1960 presidential, 257, 304–305, 305, 517
1964 presidential, 232, 248, 305,
    518–519, 546
1968 presidential, 232, 248, 285–286
1972 presidential, 291, 305, 484
1974 congressional, 484
1976 presidential, 305, 484
1980 presidential, 305, 576
1984 presidential, 222, 264, 274, 291, 295,
    301, 303, 305
1988 presidential, 173, 184, 232, 274, 291,
    295, 304, 306
1992 presidential, 4–5, 162, 173, 235, 241,
    274, 291, 294, 295, 306, 309, 460,
    544, 567
1994 congressional, 162, 206–207, 235, 255,
    275, 282, 304, 335, 356, 357, 361,
    380–381, 391, 577
1996 congressional, 335, 337
1996 presidential, 5, 49, 134, 162, 169, 222,
    235, 241, 274, 288, 294, 295, 296, 297,
    298, 301, 305, 306, 309, 335, 549
1998 congressional, 14, 169, 335–336
2000 congressional, 336
2000 presidential, 14, 21, 122, 162, 206,
    274, 282, 283, 286, 287, 293, 294, 295,
    297, 523, 526, 531, 542, 561, 574, 607
2000 Russian presidential, 271
2004 presidential, 14, 282, 283
a century ago, 15
American democracy and, 6
American versus foreign, 7, 9
block grants and, 81
bureaucracy and, 434–437
campaign finance for, 294–296, 297
as charades, 183–184
competitiveness of, 179
congressional, 318–319, 319–321, 321–322,
    322–331, 331–334, 334–338, 338–344
constituencies in, 13
costs of, 19–21
criminal justice and, 491–493
critical, 227
death penalty and, 492
economy and, 576–578
equal protection clause and, 509
federalism and, 71
first national, 33–34
free, 12
frequency of, 9
general, 8
good government and, 25
House, 323–331
judicial appointments and, 443, 445–446
Latin Americans in, 526
local, 7, 85–86
majorities and, 23
media coverage of, 272–275
mid-term, 334–335
minorities and, 21–23
misinformed voters in, 22–23
national, 7
nomination of candidates for, 21–22
nonpartisan, 8
in parliamentary government, 352
party organizations and, 239

persons elected via, 7
political parties as simplifying, 222–223
political purposes of, 6–7
in popular and responsible democracies, 13
popular ignorance and, 139–140
presidential, 177, 178
presidential versus congressional, 334
primary, 7–8
of prime ministers, 381
realigning, 227
recall, 7
Senate, 331–334
soft money and, 241
state, 7
in states following Revolutionary War, 41–42
types of, 8
voter participation in, 21
Electoral college, 49, 57
in 1788 presidential election, 59
in the Constitution, 49–50
in presidential election strategy, 296–299
reform of, 51
Electoral incentive, 24
Electoral inversion, presidential elections
    exhibiting, 296
Electoral participation, by Americans, 175–177
Electoral system, 233
in foreign countries, 234–237
political parties as simplifying, 222–223, 225
women politicians and, 340
Electoral votes
Constitutional amendment on, 56
media coverage versus, 291
in presidential elections, 296–299
reform of, 72
Electronic media, government regulation of,
    259–260
Elementary and Secondary Education Act of
    1965, 190
Eleventh Amendment, 467
Eligibility for matching funds, 286
Eligible voting-age population, 170
Elites. See Leadership elites; Political elites;
    Washington elites
Elitist argument, pro low voter turnout, 183
"Elitist democracy," 12
E-mail, as new medium, 256–259
Emancipation Proclamation, 19, 401, 513
Embassies, 616
Emergency Banking Relief Act of 1933, 391
Emergency Conservation Work Act of 1933, 391
Emergency Planning and Community Right-to-
    Know Act, 565
Emperor, as Japanese dignified chief of state, 394
Employment, 596–597
Endangered species, laws protecting, 454–455,
    566–568
Endangered Species Act of 1973, 566–568
"End of American Party Politics, The"
    (Burnham), 238
End runs, around Office of Management and
    Budget, 427
Energy and Natural Resources Committee, of
    Senate, 359
Energy crisis, 385
English Civil War, in settlement of America, 100
English language
among immigrants, 123
Latin Americans and, 525–526
English-only instruction, 122
Enterprise zones, 348
Entertainment
politics versus, 140–141
as professional bias, 268–269

Environment. See Conservation
Environmental Protection Agency, 199
Environmental Protection Agency (EPA), 412,
    414, 424, 425, 433, 563, 566
Environment and Public Works Committee, of
    Senate, 359
E Pluribus Unum, 100
Equal Employment Opportunity Commission
    (EEOC), 426, 442, 517, 530
Equality
economic, 112, 113
individualism and, 115–116
intensity problem and, 156
Equality of condition, 116
Equality of opportunity, 116, 232
Equal protection clause, 509–515
redefining, 515–524
Equal Rights Amendment, 56
Equal Rights Amendment (ERA), 199, 310,
    529–531
interest groups against, 200, 213–214
Equal-time rule, 259
Era of good feeling, 163
Espionage, 619–620
by Chinese Americans, 527
Espionage Act of 1917, clear and present danger
    doctrine and, 480
ESPN network, 256
Establishment of religion clause
in the Constitution, 487–488, 488–489
free exercise of religion clause versus,
    489–490
Estonia, voter turnout in, 171
Ethics, of Congress, 371
Ethiopia, media coverage of famine in, 262
Ethnicity
American unity and, 109
citizenship and, 97
clear and present danger doctrine and, 480
of congressmen, 338–339
"Ethno-cultural" political conflicts, immigration
    and, 101–102, 105
Europe
American individualism from, 119
bureaucracies in, 415, 428
bureaucratic secrecy in, 434
campaign finance in, 297
corporatist systems in, 212
emergence of liberalism in, 109–110
Monroe Doctrine versus, 622
New Deal and, 231
party organizations in, 239
political parties in, 226
privacy in, 500
radio and politics in, 261–262
state religions in, 116–117
thalidomide in, 436
United States fiscal policy and, 582
in United States foreign policy, 623
voter turnout in, 172, 175
European Community, on political parties, 221
European Union, privacy and, 500
European University Institute, on political
    parties, 221
Evangelical Protestantism, 118
public opinion and, 131
in schools, 488
Executive agreements, in foreign policy, 612, 613
Executive branch
administration and, 387
the Constitution and, 47–48, 49, 54
executive privilege and, 397–398
presidential appointments to, 387–390
in Savings and Loan disaster, 268

# REFERENCE INDEX

# PHOTO CREDITS

# United States of America
## The States in Proportion to Their Electoral Votes

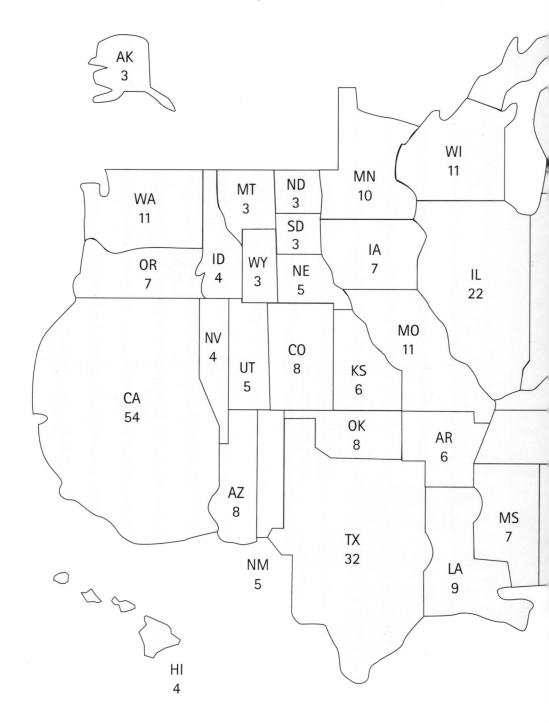